Mexico City Metro

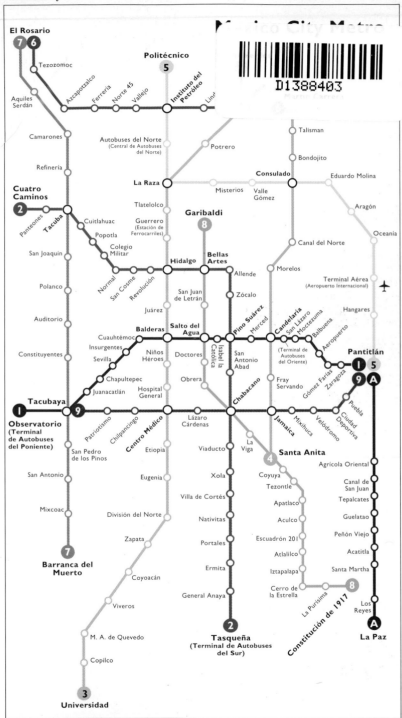

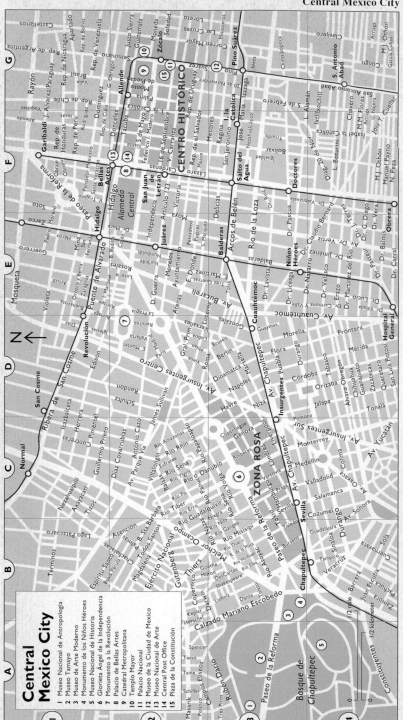

Central Mexico City

1 Museo Nacional de Antropología
2 Museo Tamayo
3 Museo de Arte Moderno
4 Monumento de los Niños Héroes
5 Museo Nacional de Historia
6 Glorieta Angel de la Independencia
7 Monumento a la Revolución
8 Palacio de Bellas Artes
9 Catedral Metropolitana
10 Templo Mayor
11 Palacio Nacional
12 Museo de la Ciudad de Mexico
13 Museo Nacional de Arte
14 Central Post Office
15 Plaza de la Constitución

CENTRO HISTÓRICO

ZONA ROSA

Bosque de Chapultepec

1/2 mile
1/2 kilometer

LET'S GO:
Mexico

"Its yearly revision by a new crop of Harvard students makes it as valuable as ever."
—*The New York Times*

"Value-packed, unbeatable, accurate, and comprehensive."
—*The Los Angeles Times*

"A world-wise traveling companion—always ready with friendly advice and helpful hints, all sprinkled with a bit of wit." —*The Philadelphia Inquirer*

"Lighthearted and sophisticated, informative and fun to read. [Let's Go] helps the novice traveler navigate like a knowledgeable old hand."
—*Atlanta Journal-Constitution*

"All the essential information you need, from making a phone call to exchanging money to contacting your embassy. [Let's Go] provides maps to help you find your way from every train station to a full range of youth hostels and hotels." —*Minneapolis Star Tribune*

"Unbeatable: good sight-seeing advice; up-to-date info on restaurants, hotels, and inns; a commitment to money-saving travel; and a wry style that brightens nearly every page." —*The Washington Post*

Let's Go researchers have to make it on their own.

"The writers seem to have experienced every rooster-packed bus and lunar-surfaced mattress about which they write." —*The New York Times*

"Retains the spirit of the student-written publication it is: candid, opinionated, resourceful, amusing info for the traveler of limited means but broad curiosity." —*Mademoiselle*

No other guidebook is as comprehensive.

"Whether you're touring the United States, Europe, Southeast Asia, or Central America, a Let's Go guide will clue you in to the cheapest, yet safe, hotels and hostels, food and transportation. Going beyond the call of duty, the guides reveal a country's latest news, cultural hints, and off-beat information that any tourist is likely to miss." —*Tulsa World*

Let's Go is completely revised each year.

"Up-to-date travel tips for touring four continents on skimpy budgets."
—*Time*

"Inimitable.... Let's Go's 24 guides are updated yearly (as opposed to the general guidebook standard of every two to three years), and in a marvelously spunky way." —*The New York Times*

Let's Go Publications

Let's Go: Alaska & The Pacific Northwest
Let's Go: Britain & Ireland
Let's Go: California
Let's Go: Central America
Let's Go: Eastern Europe
Let's Go: Ecuador & The Galápagos Islands
Let's Go: Europe
Let's Go: France
Let's Go: Germany
Let's Go: Greece & Turkey
Let's Go: India & Nepal
Let's Go: Ireland
Let's Go: Israel & Egypt
Let's Go: Italy
Let's Go: London
Let's Go: Mexico
Let's Go: New York City
Let's Go: Paris
Let's Go: Rome
Let's Go: Southeast Asia
Let's Go: Spain & Portugal
Let's Go: Switzerland & Austria
Let's Go: USA
Let's Go: Washington, D.C.

Let's Go **Map Guide:** Boston
Let's Go **Map Guide:** London
Let's Go **Map Guide:** New York City
Let's Go **Map Guide:** Paris
Let's Go **Map Guide:** San Francisco
Let's Go **Map Guide:** Washington, D.C.

LET'S GO

The Budget Guide to
Mexico
1997

Daniela Bleichmar
Editor

Siham Nurhussein
Associate Editor

St. Martin's Press ✻ New York

Maps by David Lindroth copyright © 1997, 1996, 1995, 1994, 1993, 1992, 1991, 1990, 1989, 1988 by St. Martin's Press, Inc.

Map revisions pp. 2-3, 36-37, 125, 127, 143, 157, 207, 261, 197, 315, 327, 331, 335, 367, 389, 405, 417, 427, 443, 457, 491, 499, 527 by Let's Go, Inc.

Distributed outside the USA and Canada by Macmillan.

ISBN: 0-312-14660-4

First edition
10 9 8 7 6 5 4 3 2 1

Let's Go: Mexico is written by Let's Go Publications, 67 Mt. Auburn Street, Cambridge, MA 02138, USA.

Let's Go® and the thumb logo are trademarks of Let's Go, Inc. Printed in the USA on recycled paper with biodegradable soy ink.

About Let's Go

THIRTY-SIX YEARS OF WISDOM

Back in 1960, a few students at Harvard University banded together to produce a 20-page pamphlet offering a collection of tips on budget travel in Europe. This modest, mimeographed packet, offered as an extra to passengers on student charter flights to Europe, met with instant popularity. The following year, students traveling to Europe researched the first, full-fledged edition of *Let's Go: Europe*, a pocket-sized book featuring honest, irreverent writing and a decidedly youthful outlook on the world. Throughout the 60s, our guides reflected the times; the 1969 guide to America led off by inviting travelers to "dig the scene" at San Francisco's Haight-Ashbury. During the 70s and 80s, we gradually added regional guides and expanded coverage into the Middle East and Central America. With the addition of our in-depth city guides, handy map guides, and extensive coverage of Asia, the 90s are also proving to be a time of explosive growth for Let's Go, and there's certainly no end in sight. The first editions of *Let's Go: India & Nepal* and *Let's Go: Ecuador & The Galápagos Islands* hit the shelves this year, and research for next year's series has already begun.

We've seen a lot in 37 years. *Let's Go: Europe* is now the world's bestselling international guide, translated into seven languages. And our new guides bring Let's Go's total number of titles, with their spirit of adventure and their reputation for honesty, accuracy, and editorial integrity, to 30. But some things never change: our guides are still researched, written, and produced entirely by students who know first-hand how to see the world on the cheap.

HOW WE DO IT

Each guide is completely revised and thoroughly updated every year by a well-traveled set of 200 students. Every winter, we recruit over 120 researchers and 60 editors to write the books anew. After several months of training, Researcher-Writers hit the road for seven weeks of exploration, from Anchorage to Ankara, Estonia to El Salvador, Iceland to Indonesia. Hired for their rare combination of budget travel sense, writing ability, stamina, and courage, these adventurous travelers know that train strikes, stolen luggage, food poisoning, and marriage proposals are all part of a day's work. Back at our offices, editors work from spring to fall, massaging copy written on Himalayan bus rides into witty yet informative prose. A student staff of typesetters, cartographers, publicists, and managers keeps our lively team together. In September, the collected efforts of the summer are delivered to our printer, who turns them into books in record time, so that you have the most up-to-date information available for *your* vacation. And even as you read this, work on next year's editions is well underway.

WHY WE DO IT

At Let's Go, our goal is to give you a great vacation. We don't think of budget travel as the last recourse of the destitute; we believe that it's the only way to travel. Living cheaply and simply brings you closer to the people and places you've been saving up to visit. Our books will ease your anxieties and answer your questions about the basics—so you can get off the beaten track and explore. Once you learn the ropes, we encourage you to put Let's Go away now and then to strike out on your own. As any seasoned traveler will tell you, the best discoveries are often those you make yourself. When you find something worth sharing, drop us a line. We're Let's Go Publications, 67 Mt. Auburn St., Cambridge, MA 02138, USA (e-mail: fanmail@letsgo.com).

HAPPY TRAVELS!

Contents

Acknowledgements

Muchísimas gracias to our fantastic team of RWs for doing all we had hoped for and so much more; to Allison for her support, direction, sensitivity, and overall greatness; to Liz for being Allison, and herself; to Mike and Dan for all the help with computers; to Amanda, Mark, and Jonathan for the map savvy; to Jake, Alex, Steve, Dave, and Michelle for absolutely everything; to Jen for calling it like it is; to everyone in the Domestic Room for the energy, laughter, and camaraderie; to CenAm for letting us bum off Guatemala; to the entire LG team for working like one; to all who welcomed and helped our Researchers during their travels; and to all the readers who wrote in to share their great finds.

Thanks to Siham for being a trooper and a joy to work with; to Allison (again); to Mami, Papi, Guille y Fer for their love and support; to Chad for the same, but different; to Andrea for our conversations, her understanding, and all the laughter; to Elissa and Liz for our friendship, past and future; to Eleni and Neela for chuchiness; to Alberto for sharing the complexities of life lived with a foot on each side; to Aaron for his insight and friendship; to Ale, Mariana y Mónica for (still) being there; to Mark for the postcards, the phonecalls, and everything else; to Sandra Nadaff for her support; to the people I'm forgetting for understanding. My work in this book is dedicated to the memory of Gabriel Piedrahita, a dear friend much loved and missed. —**DB**

What an intense five months it's been! Thanks to Daniela for bringing tons of wit and savvy to the book and for keeping us smiling even in 95° weather; to Allison for just being; to México for making typing and editing so addictive; to old friends back in Shao-Lin and my roomies on both ends of the coast for reminding me that there is in fact life outside of *Let's Go;* and of course to Mom, Dad, Nadia, and Safy—I'll love you till the end of the world. —**SN**

Editor	Daniela Bleichmar
Associate Editor	Siham Nurhussein
Managing Editor	Allison Crapo
Publishing Director	Michelle C. Sullivan
Production Manager	Daniel O. Williams
Associate Production Manager	Michael S. Campbell
Cartography Manager	Amanda K. Bean
Editorial Manager	John R. Brooks
Editorial Manager	Allison Crapo
Financial Manager	Stephen P. Janiak
Personnel Manager	Alexander H. Travelli
Publicity Manager	SoRelle B. Braun
Associate Publicity Manager	David Fagundes
Associate Publicity Manager	Elisabeth Mayer
Assistant Cartographer	Jonathan D. Kibera
Assistant Cartographer	Mark C. Staloff
Office Coordinator	Jennifer L. Schuberth
Director of Advertising and Sales	Amit Tiwari
Senior Sales Executives	Andrew T. Rourke
	Nicholas A. Valtz, Charles E. Varner
General Manager	Richard Olken
Assistant General Manager	Anne E. Chisholm

Maps

Color Maps

Researcher-Writers

Peter S. Cahn   *Central Mexico, Veracruz, Southern Pacific Coast*
A born Researcher-Writer, Peter put his anthropology degree to good use in Mexico, bringing great insight and originality to our coverage of one of the country's most culturally diverse regions. Peter danced the night away in Veracruz, nibbled on grasshoppers in Oaxaca, and sampled the beaches off the coast of Guerrero. More bubbly than a bottle of *manzanita*, he made friends left and right, and managed to get adopted at least once in every town. A thorough researcher and sharp observer, he crafted page after page after page of lively, beautifully handwritten copy.

Marc P. Díaz   *Northeast Mexico, Mexico City, Northern Veracruz*
Marc poured his heart and soul into the book: he researched the territory before setting off for the *frontera*, fact-checked with relish, wrote detailed descriptions and thoughtful marginalia, and showered us with more maps and brochures than we could have dreamed of. Marc's copy effortlessly weaved his personal interest in architecture, a deep concern with economics, and impressive insights into subtle nuances of Mexican life—from car culture to whistling. His enthusiasm and dedication were inspiring and contagious.

Alberto Hazan   *Baja California, Northwest Mexico*
Skimming the rim of the Copper Canyon, sweeping through the blistering heat of the Chihuahua desert, and swimming with the sharks off the coast of Baja, Alberto never lost his cool—or his smile. Al covered a vast expanse of territory and managed to retain his enthusiasm up to the very last day of a grueling itinerary. Seventeen-hour ferry ride on choppy waters? No problem. We knew we could always count on him to thoroughly check every minute fact and diligently report back with refreshing candor. Thanks for keeping us smiling all summer long.

Mateo C. Jaramillo   *Yucatán Peninsula, Chiapas, Tabasco*
Mateo just did it all. Zipping through the jungle like a mellow Indiana Jones, he somehow found the time to learn a few words of Mayan, chill with the locals in Isla Holbox, scale every single ruin along the Ruta Puuc, and phone us from the middle of nowhere to wax poetic about San Cristóbal. Hey—the man slept in his own hammock. An indefatigable researcher and a mordant writer, Mateo lived it up in Mexico, bringing incisive wit and a touch of quirky madness to our coverage of the *Sureste*. Nothing, not the killer mosquitoes, not watching a pig being butchered, not even the torrential downpours, could faze Mateo.

Lesley D. O'Connell   *Central Mexico, Aguascalientes,*
                                        Central Pacific Coast, Michoacán
Having grown up on the U.S.-Mexico border and studied Latin-America in graduate school, Lesley, our lone female Researcher, approached Mexico with confidence and determination. She effortlessly breezed through colonial towns, captured shore upon shore of rugged coastline, and delved into Michoacán with savvy and charm, while still managing to expand coverage and discover the hippest hangouts in town. She wrote Let'sgoese like a native, sent back impeccable copy, and kept mesmerizing us with her romantic prose. Only Lesley could do justice to Guanajuato.

Lider Sucre   *Guatemala*

How to Use This Book

Let's Go: Mexico is written for the adventurous budget traveler. In the hot and humid Cambridge summer of 1996, we sent five roving researchers out on a shoestring budget with your concerns in mind: how to get from place to place, find salvation in local cuisine, enjoy the evenings, and get some sleep—all in the most economical way possible. In researching and writing the book, we have tried to accommodate the diverse backgrounds and tastes of our readers. Ultimately, we have tried to produce a book deeply infused with a sense of place and to present the distinctive history, culture, and ways of life of the remarkable country of Mexico.

The first chapter of this book, **Essentials,** is chock full of information you'll want to have a look at before leaving. Turn to this chapter for information on anything and everything—booking a flight, enrolling in a language school, procuring a passport, changing money, packing, securing car insurance, and, perhaps most imporant of all, phoning home. Subsections focus on safety and security, health, women and travel, older travelers, bisexual, gay and lesbian travelers, disabled travelers, travelers with children, vegetarian and kosher travelers, minority travelers, and solo travelers. The chapter ends with **Let's Go Picks,** our very favorite places, meals, and beaches in the country. The second chapter, succinctly entitled **Mexico,** provides a brief introduction to Mexican history, culture, and character, in its wonderfully various forms. Read it before you go in order to have a better, deeper sense of what life is like there.

Coverage of Mexico begins in Mexico City; from there, coverage generally proceeds in a northwest-southeast direction, starting with Baja California and rounding out with the Yucatán peninsula and a short jaunt into Guatemala. Each city or town is sub-divided into care-packages. Introductions focus on culture and history and aim to answer a simple question: why should I go there? Introductions are followed by **Orientation,** which describes the layout of the city, and **Practical Information,** which lists essential schedules, addresses, and numbers. **Accommodations, Food, Sights,** and **Entertainment** are fairly self-explanatory. Please note that listings are subjectively given in order of preference, according to the judgment of our team.

The book ends with a series of **Appendices** meant to make your traveling life easier. An extensive **Glossary** will provide basic morsels of Spanish; it is arranged thematically, from "Accommodations" to "Romance" (and back). The **Weights and Measures** table will allow you to convert back and forth to your heart's content; the **Temperature** chart will let you know how warm it is throughout the country. Finally, a list of **Fiestas and Holidays** will tell you where it's at.

We wish you an exciting and enjoyable trip. *Ándale, pues,* and happy travels.

A NOTE TO OUR READERS

The information for this book is gathered by *Let's Go*'s researchers during the late spring and summer months. Each listing is derived from the assigned researcher's opinion based upon his or her visit at a particular time. The opinions are expressed in a candid and forthright manner. Other travelers might disagree. Those traveling at a different time may have different experiences since prices, dates, hours, and conditions are always subject to change. You are urged to check beforehand to avoid inconvenience and surprises. Travel always involves a certain degree of risk, especially in low-cost areas. When traveling, especially on a budget, always take particular care to ensure your safety.

ESSENTIALS

PLANNING YOUR TRIP

▓ Climate

The Tropic of Cancer bisects Mexico into a temperate north and tropical south, but the climate varies considerably even within these belts. For each of the geographic divisions used in this book, very general climate conditions hold true. **Northwest Mexico,** including Baja California, is the driest area of the country, but still offers a unique array of desert flora and fauna, while the **Northeast** is a bit more temperate. Known as the "The Mexican Riviera," the **West Coast** boasts warm, tropical weather. Pleasant beaches are scattered throughout the humid **Gulf Coast.** The central region north of Mexico City, known as the **Bajío,** and **South Central Mexico** both experience spring-like weather; the cooler climates of the highlands are tempered by coastal warmth, and natural beauty ranges from world-famous beaches to inland forests. Lush, green jungles obscure ruins of the ancient civilizations of the **Yucatán Peninsula;** interior jungles are hot and humid, while trade winds keep the areas along the coast cool and pleasant.

There are two seasons in Mexico: rainy and dry. The rainy season lasts from May until November (with a hurricane season in the south Aug.-Oct.). The southern half of the country averages over 250cm per year (75% of that during the rainy season), so a summer vacation is likely to be on the damp side. Expect a good two to three hours of rain every afternoon. The best time to hit the beaches is during the dry season (Nov.-May), when afternoons are sunny, evenings balmy, and nights relatively mosquito-free. The tourist season consists of the month of December, the entire summer, and Easter. If you travel to Mexico during this time, you can expect to pay higher prices at hotels and restaurants. Exhaustive statistics on climate are available in a chart at the end of the guide (see p. 561).

▓ Useful Information

GOVERNMENT AGENCIES

Embassy of Mexico, 1911 Pennsylvania Ave. NW, Washington, D.C. 20006 (tel. (202) 728-1600; fax 728-1718); in the **U.K.,** 42 Hertford St., Mayfair, London W1 (tel. (0171) 495-4024; fax 495-4035); in **Canada,** 45 O'Connor St. #1500, Ottawa, Ont. K1P 1A4 (tel. (613) 233-8988; fax 235-9123); in **Australia,** 14 Perth Ave., Yarralumla, 2600 Canberra (tel. (6) 273-3905 or 273-3947; fax 273-1190).

Consulate of Mexico, 2827 16th St. NW, Washington, D.C. 20036 (tel. (202) 736-1000) or 8 E.41st St., New York, NY 10017 (tel. (212) 545-8197, fax (212) 689-0456); in **Canada,** 199 Bay St., Commerce Court West, Toronto, Ont. M5L1E9 (tel. (416) 368-2875); in the **U.K.,** 8 Halkin St., London SW1 X7DW (tel. (0171) 235-6393); in **Australia,** 135-153 New South Head Rd., Edgecliff, Sydney 2027 NSW (tel. (2) 326-1311 or 326-1292; fax (2) 327-1110).

Mexican Government Tourism Office (Secretaría de Turismo or **SECTUR),** in the **U.S.,** 405 Park Ave. #1401, New York, NY 10022 (tel. (212) 421-6656; fax 755-7261; 24-hr. information tel. (800) 262-8900); 1801 Century Park East, #1080, Los Angeles, CA 90067 (tel. (310) 203-8191 or 203-8328; fax 203-8316); 2333 Ponce de Leon Blvd., #710, Coral Gables, FL 33134 (tel. (305) 443-9160; fax 443-1186); 70 E. Lake St. #1413, Chicago, IL 60601 (tel. (312) 606-9015; fax 606-9012); 1911 Pennsylvania Ave., Washington, D.C. 20036 (tel. (202) 728-1750; fax 728-1758); in **Can-**

Mexico

STATES

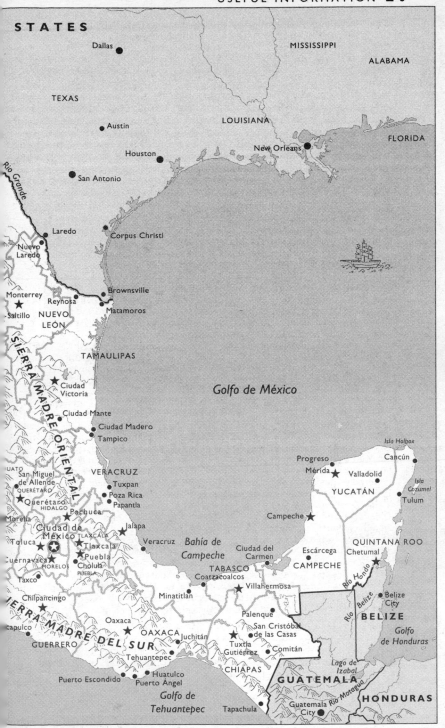

ada, 2 Bloor St. W #1801, Toronto, Ontario M4W 3E2 (tel. (416) 925-0704 or (416) 925-2753; fax 925-6061) or 1 Place Ville Marie #1526, Montreal, Quebec H3B 2B5 (tel. (514) 871-1052; fax 871-3825); in the **U.K.,** 60/61 Tragalfar Sq. 3rd. Fl., London WC2N 5DS (tel. (4471) 839-3177). Provides maps, information and tourist cards. Check your phone book for local offices. Also operates a 24-hr. hotline out of Mexico City (tel. (5) 250-01-23) for complaints, emergencies, and less urgent information.

TRAVEL ORGANIZATIONS

Council on International Educational Exchange (Council), 205 E. 42nd St., New York, NY 10017-5706 (tel. (888) COUNCIL; fax (212) 822-2699). A private, non-profit organization. Administers academic, volunteer, work, and professional programs around the world. They also offer identity cards, including the ISIC and the GO25, and a range of publications, including the magazine *Student Travels.* Call or write for more information.

Servicio Educativo de Turismo de los Estudiantes y la Juventud de México (SETEJ), Hamburgo 305, Col. Juárez, Mexico, D.F. 06600 (tel. (5) 211-07-43 or 211-66-36; fax 211-13-28). Sells ISIC and GO25 cards. Arranges group tours with Mexican students and language courses. Helps with domestic and international Provides information about hostels and budget hotels (see Hostels, p. 43).

PUBLICATIONS

Adventures in Mexico (AIM), Apdo. 31-70, Guadalajara, Jalisco, 45050 Mexico. Newsletter on retirement and travel in Mexico. Endearing approach to the country's quirks. Annual subscription (6 issues) costs US$16 or CDN$22. Personal checks accepted. Back issues, most of which are devoted to a single city or region, available for US$2.50 each, or 3 issues for US$6.

Animal and Plant Health Inspection Service, Attn.: USDA APHIS PPQ, 4700 River Road, Unit 60, Riverdale, MD 20737 (tel. (301) 734-8295). Publishes the *Traveler's Tips* pamphlet, which provides information on which plant and animal products you can safely bring home from other countries. Consult your local Blue Pages for the number of the nearest branch.

Forsyth Travel Library, P.O. Box 480800, Kansas City, MO 64148 (tel. (800) 367-7984; fax (816) 942-6969). Mail-order maps and travel guides for Mexico.

Hippocrene Books, Inc., 171 Madison Ave., New York, NY 10016 (tel. (212) 685-4371, orders (718) 454-2366; fax (718) 454-1391). Publishes travel reference books, travel guides, maps, and foreign language dictionaries. Free catalog.

John Muir Publications, P.O. Box 613, Santa Fe, NM 87504 (tel. (800) 888-7504; fax 988-1680). Publishes the *People's Guide to RV Camping in Mexico* (US$20), plus general guides to Mexico, Belize, Costa Rica, and Guatemala. Shipping fees US$4.25-6.25, depending on order size.

México Desconocido, Monte Pelvoux 110-104, Lomas de Chapultepec, Mexico, D.F. 11000 (tel. (5) 202-65-85 or 259-09-39; fax 540-17-71). Monthly travel magazines in Spanish and English describing little-known areas and customs of Mexico.

Superintendent of Documents, U.S. Government Printing Office, P.O. Box 371954, Pittsburgh, PA 15250 (tel. (202) 512-1800; fax 512-2250). Publishes *Your Trip Abroad* (US$1.25), *Health Information for International Travel* (US$14), and "Background Notes" on all countries (US$1). Postage included.

Wide World Books and Maps, 1911 N. 45th St., Seattle, WA 98103 (tel. (206) 634-3453; fax 634-0558, e-mail travelbk@nwlink.com). Wide selection of books about Mexico and hard-to-find maps of the country.

INTERNET RESOURCES

Budget travel is moving rapidly into the information age, and with the growing user-friendliness of personal computers, much of this information can be yours with just the click of a mouse. The most popular ways to access the Internet are through America On-Line (tel. (800) 827-6394) or Compuserve (tel. (800) 433-0389). The following listings are from the World Wide Web, the most exciting destination on the Internet. Start surfing!

Dr. Memory's Favorite Travel Pages (http://www.access.digex.net/ldrmemory/ cyberTtravel.html) is a great place to start surfing. Dr. Memory has links to hundreds of different web pages of interest to travelers of all kinds.

The CIA World Factbook (http://www.odci.gov/cia/publications/95fact) has tons of vital statistics on the country you want to visit. Check it out for an overview of a country's economy or an explanation of their system of government.

Shoestring Travel (http://www.stratpub.com) is a budget travel e-zine, with feature articles, links, user exchange, and accommodations information.

Foreign Language for Travelers (http://www.travelang.com) can help you brush up on your Spanish. *Te ayuda a practicar tu español.*

The Interactive Travel Guide (http://www.developnet.com/travel), formerly the Cheap Travel Page, remains useful for budget travelers.

■ Documents and Formalities

TOURIST CARDS

All persons visiting Mexico for tourism or study for up to 180 days must carry a **tourist card** (**FMT,** for *Folleto de Migración Turística*) in addition to proof of citizenship. U.S. and Canadian citizens can skip the FMT if they don't expect to travel past border towns or stay anywhere in the country for more than 72 hours. U.S. and Canadian citizens traveling to Baja California will need a card only if they plan to venture beyond Maneadero on the Pacific Coast, south of Mexicali on Rte. 5

Tourist cards, like all entry documents, are free of charge. Many people get their cards when they cross the border or when they check in at the airline ticket counter for their flight into Mexico; however, you can avoid delays by obtaining one from a Mexican embassy, consulate, or tourist office before you leave (see Useful Information, p. 1). You will have to present proof of citizenship, and if your financial condition looks suspect, officials will ask you to flash your return ticket. Travelers from outside North America must present a passport. U.S. and Canadian citizens can obtain a tourist card with an original birth certificate or naturalization papers, plus some type of photo ID (with the exception of naturalized Canadians, who must carry a passport). But be forewarned: traveling in Mexico without a passport is asking for trouble. A passport carries much more authority with local officials than does a birth certificate. Returning home by air is particularly difficult with only a birth certificate. Finally, a passport is mandatory for anyone going on to Central America.

On the FMT, you must indicate your intended destination and expected length of stay. Tourist cards are valid for 90 days and must be returned to border officials upon leaving the country. If you stay in Mexico past your 90-day limit, you will be slapped with a fine. Request a special, 180-day **multiple-entry permit** at your point of entry if you plan to leave and re-enter the country several times within a short time period. Otherwise, you must get a new FMT every time you re-enter the country, even if your old one has not expired. Try to get a card that will be valid longer than your projected stay, since obtaining an extension on a 90-day FMT is a huge hassle: you'll need a physician's authorization stating that you are too ill to travel. If you do need an extension, visit a local office of the Delegación de Servicios Migratorios several weeks before your card expires. They also take care of lost cards.

Special regulations apply if you are entering Mexico on a business trip, or if you expect to study in the country for more than six months. Contact a Mexican consulate several months before you leave home to obtain a visa or permit. Steep fines face any business travelers caught with only a tourist card. If you are planning on residing or retiring in Mexico, consult a Mexican consulate about long-term visas.

If you're breezing through Mexico *en route* to Guatemala or Belize, ask for a **transmigrant form,** which will allow you to remain in Mexico for up to 30 days. You'll need

a passport or current photo ID, a Guatemalan or Belizean visa, and proof of sufficient funds for your trip.

While in Mexico, you are required by law to carry your tourist card at all times. Make a photocopy and keep it in a separate place. Although it won't **replace** a lost or stolen tourist card, a copy should facilitate replacement. If you do lose your card, expect hours of delay and bureaucratic inconvenience while immigration verifies your record of entrance.

PASSPORTS

As a precaution in case your passport is lost or stolen, be sure *before you leave* to photocopy the page of your passport that contains your photograph and identifying information. Especially important is your passport number. Carry this photocopy in a safe place apart from your passport, perhaps with a traveling companion, and leave another copy at home. Better yet, carry a photocopy of all the pages of the passport, including all visa stamps, apart from your actual passport, and leave a duplicate copy with a relative or friend. Consulates also recommend that you carry an expired passport or an *official* copy of your birth certificate in a part of your baggage separate from other documents. These measures will help prove your citizenship and facilitate the issuing of a new passport.

If your passport is lost or stolen, immediately notify the local police and the nearest embassy or consulate of your home government. To expedite the replacement of your passport, you will need to know all the information that you had previously recorded and photocopied and to show identification and proof of citizenship. Some consulates can issue new passports within two days if you give them proof of citizenship. In an emergency, ask for immediate temporary traveling papers that will permit you to return to your home country.

United States Citizens may apply for a passport, valid for 10 years (5 years if under 18), at any one of several thousand federal or state courthouses or post offices authorized to accept passport applications, or at a U.S. Passport Agency. For more information, contact the Agency's 24-hour recorded message (tel. (202) 647-0518). Abroad, a U.S. embassy or consulate can usually issue a new passport, given proof of citizenship. Processing usually takes three to four weeks, more in spring and summer. *File your application as early as possible.* Passports are processed according to the departure date indicated on the application form. If you fail to indicate a departure date, the agency will assume you are not planning any immediate travel. Passport agencies offer rush service: if you have proof that you are departing within five working days (e.g. an airplane ticket), a passport agency will issue a passport while you wait. Your passport will be mailed to you; you may pay for express mail return of your passport. For inquiries regarding the processing of your passport write the National Passport Center, 31 Rochester Avenue, Portsmouth, NH 03801 or call (603) 334-0500.

Canada Application forms are available in English and French at all passport offices, post offices, and most travel agencies. Citizens may apply in person at any one of 28 regional passport offices across Canada. Citizens who reside in the U.S. can contact a Canadian diplomatic mission; those outside Canada and the U.S. should contact the nearest embassy or consulate. You can apply by mail by sending a completed application form with appropriate documentation and fee to Passport Office, Foreign Affairs, Ottawa, Ontario, K1A 0G3. The processing time is approximately five business days for in-person applications and three weeks for mailed ones. A passport is valid for five years and must be reissued, because it is not renewable. For additional information, call the 24-hour number (tel. (800) 567-6868 from Canada only) or consult the booklet *Bon Voyage, But...*, available free of charge from any passport office or from Info-Export (BPTE), External Affairs, Ottawa, Ontario, K1A 0G2.

ESSENTIALS

The World At a Discount

Save **20%** to **50%** on Airfare (major carriers)

Save **10%** to **50%** on Museums & Theaters

Save **10%** on AT&T Calls to the U.S.

Save up to **40%** on Train Passes

Save **15%** on Greyhound Travel

Save **10%** to **30%** on Accommodations

Worldwide Discounts in more than **90** countries

The International Student Identity Card
Your Passport to Discounts & Benefits

With the ISIC, you'll receive discounts on airfare, hotels, transportation, computer services, foreign currency exchange, phone calls, major attractions, and more. You'll also receive basic accident and sickness insurance coverage when traveling outside the U.S. and access to a 24-hour, toll-free Help Line. Call now to locate the issuing office nearest you (over 555 across the U.S.) at:

Free 40-page handbook with each card

1-888-COUNCIL (toll-free)

For an application and complete discount list, you can also visit us at **http://www.ciee.org/**

Council

CIEE: Council on International Educational Exchange

Great Britain British Dependent Territories citizens, and British Overseas citizens can obtain a full passport valid for 10 years (5 years if under 16) by applying in person or by mail to the London Passport Office or by mail to a passport office located in Liverpool, Newport, Peterborough, Glasgow, or Belfast. Applications are available at post offices. Processing usually takes four to six weeks. The London office offers same-day walk-in rush service, provided you arrive early enough.

Australia Citizens must apply for a passport in person at a local post office, a passport office, an Australian diplomatic mission overseas, or one of nine passport offices. Application fees are adjusted frequently, so call the toll-free information service for current details (tel. 13-12-32).

New Zealand Citizens can obtain an application from their local Link Centre, travel agent, or New Zealand Representative. Questions should be addressed to the New Zealand Passport Office, Documents of National Identity Division, Department of Internal Affairs, Box 10-526, Wellington (tel. (04) 474 81 00). Standard processing time is 10 working days from receipt of completed application. Overseas citizens should send the passport application to the nearest embassy, high commission, or consulate that is authorized to issue passports.

VISAS

A **visa** is an endorsement that a foreign government stamps into your passport; it allows you to stay in that country for a specified purpose and period of time. For stays up to six months, visas are not necessary for citizens of Australia, Great Britain, Canada, U.S., New Zealand and most E.U. countries. Businesspeople, missionaries, and students must obtain appropriate visas. Applications are processed by consulates in one day.

YOUTH, STUDENT, AND TEACHER IDENTIFICATION

You might consider spending your hard-earned money on an **International Student Identity Card (ISIC),** administered by the **International Student Travel Confederation (ISTC),** Store Kongensgade 40H, 1264 Copenhagen K, Denmark (tel. 33-93-93-03), and available at many student travel offices worldwide. For US$15, the ISIC card provides access to student airfares and discounts, US$3000 of accident-related coverage with no daily limit, and a toll-free Traveler's Assistance hotline whose multilingual staff can provide help in medical, legal, and financial emergencies overseas. The card is valid from September to December of the following year, and can be obtained at Council Travel, Let's Go Travel, and STA Travel in the U.S; Travel CUTS in Canada; and any of the organizations under the auspices of the International Student Travel Confederation (ISTC) around the world (see Budget Travel Agencies, p. 31). Applicants must be at least 12 years old and degree-seeking students of a secondary or post-secondary school. To obtain a card by using a credit card, please call (800) 255-1000, extension 425. For US$19, the **International Teacher Identity Card (ITIC)** offers similar but limited discounts, as well as medical insurance coverage. For more information on these cards, consult the organization's web site at http://www.istc.org.

If you are under 26, you can take advantage of the **GO 25 Card,** issued by the **Federation of International Youth Travel Organizations (FIYTO),** Bredgade 25H, DK-1260 Copenhagen K, Denmark (tel. (33) 33 96 00), and available through most of the travel organizations listed above. The GO 25 card entitles you to some price reductions in Mexico. To get the card, you must submit proof of birthdate, a passport-sized photo with your name printed on the back, and US$16.

ESSENTIALS

DRIVER'S LICENSE AND VEHICLE PERMITS

An international driver's license is not necessary for driving in Mexico; any valid driver's license is acceptable. To drive a foreign car into Mexico and beyond the Border Zone or Free Trade Zone (Baja California peninsula and Sonora), you need to obtain a **vehicle permit** when you cross the border. As of July 1996, the original and a photocopy of the following documents are needed to obtain a vehicle permit: passport, state vehicle registration certificate and vehicle title, valid driver's license, and insurance policy. If leasing a vehicle, you must provide the contract in your name (also in duplicate). A credit card issued outside Mexico will make your life much easier—simply charge the US$11 fee. Without plastic, you will need to make a cash deposit calculated according to the value of your vehicle. In exchange for all these photocopies, you'll receive two punched stickers bearing the expiration date of your permit. To extend a vehicle permit beyond its original expiration date and avoid confiscation, contact the temporary importation department of Mexican customs. Regulations change frequently; for updated information contact a consulate or from the US call (800) 446-8277.

A vehicle permit is valid only for the person to whom it was issued unless another driver is approved by the federal registry. Violation of this law can result in confiscation of the vehicle or heavy fines. Furthermore, only legitimate drivers may purchase car-ferry tickets.

Resist the temptation to abandon, sell, or give away your car in Mexico. Once you enter the country with a car, your tourist card will be marked such that you will not be allowed to collect the bond or to leave without the vehicle. Even if your car disintegrates somewhere in Mexico, you must get permission to leave without it; approval can be obtained (for a fee) at either the federal registry of automobiles in Mexico City or a local office of the treasury department.

PHOTOGRAPHY PERMITS

You need to buy a permit (25 pesos) to use a **video camera** at archaeological sites. Tripods are only allowed for commercial purposes and require more expensive permits. Nobody, not even Madonna, is allowed to use a flash. For permits, contact the Instituto Nacional de Antropología e Historia, Dirección de Asuntos Jurídicos, Córdoba No. 45, 2o piso, Col. Roma, Mexico, D.F. 06700 (tel. (5) 511-08-44).

CUSTOMS: ENTERING MEXICO

Crossing into Mexico by land can be as uneventful or as complicated as the border guards want it to be. You might be waved into the country or directed to the immigration office to procure a tourist card (FMT) if you don't have one already and a car permit if you're driving. Customs officials will then inspect luggage and stamp papers. If there is anything amiss when you reach the immigration checkpoint 22km into the interior, you'll have to turn back.

A clean, neat appearance will help upon your arrival. Don't pass out *mordidas* (bribes; literally "bites"). They may do more harm than good. Border officials may still request a tip, but they're not supposed to. Above all, do not attempt to carry drugs across the border since the German shepherds will not be amused. Indeed, don't even think of buying or using drugs in Mexico—you could spend some serious time in jail, and your embassy and consulate will be powerless to help you.

Entering Mexico by air is easier. Agents process forms and examine luggage, using the press-your-luck traffic light system, right in the airport. Electronics, such as personal computers, might make customs officers uneasy; it is a good idea to write a letter explaining that you need to take your precious laptop into the country for personal use and that it will go back home with you and have the document certified by a Mexican consulate. Because air passengers are rarely penniless, immigration officials are less strict than at the border.

CUSTOMS: LEAVING MEXICO

Crossing the border can take five minutes or five hours—the better your paperwork, the shorter your ordeal. When reentering your home country, you must declare all articles acquired abroad (even duty-free ones) and pay a duty on those which exceed customs allowance. To establish value when you return home, keep receipts for items purchased abroad. Since you pay no duty on goods brought from home, before you begin your travels record the serial numbers of any expensive items (cameras, computers, radios, etc.) you are taking on vacation and check with your country's customs office to see if it has a special form for registering them.

Most countries object to the importation of firearms, explosives, ammunition, obscene literature and films, fireworks, and lottery tickets. Do not try to take illegal drugs out of Mexico. Label prescription drugs clearly and have the prescription or a doctor's certificate ready to show the customs officer. If you have questions, call the Mexican Customs office in the U.S. at (202) 728-1669; fax (202) 728-1664.

Crossing the border (on your return) with live animals is usually prohibited. For information on wildlife products, contact TRAFFIC USA, World Wildlife Fund, 1250 24th St. NW, Washington, D.C. 20037 (tel. (202) 293-4800; fax (202) 293-9211), or the Animal and Plant Health Inspection Service (see Useful Information, p. 1).

If you are a resident alien of the United States or simply have a Latino surname you may receive a lot of hassling from immigration upon your return. You must make up your own mind as to how to react to racist harassment. Pragmatists answer as straigh-forwardly as possible any questions the border patrol might ask (they have been known to ask "who won the Civil War" and other "prove-it" puzzles).

United States Citizens returning home may bring US$400 worth of accompany-ing goods duty-free and must pay a 10% tax on the next US$1000. You must declare all purchases, so have sales slips ready. Goods are considered duty-free if they are for personal or household use (this includes gifts) and cannot include more than 100 cigars, 200 cigarettes (1 carton), and 1L of wine or liquor. You must be over 21 to bring liquor into the U.S. If you mail home personal goods of U.S. origin, you can avoid duty charges by marking the package "American goods returned." For more information, consult the brochure *Know Before You Go,* available from the U.S. Cus-toms Service, Box 7407, Washington D.C. 20044 (tel. (202) 927-6724).

Canada Citizens who remain abroad between two and six days may bring back up to CDN$200 of products except tobacco and alcohol; those traveling for at least one week may bring back up to CDN$500 worth of goods duty-free once per calendar year. Citizens of legal age (which varies by province) may bring back up to 200 ciga-rettes, 50 cigars, 400g loose tobacco, 400 tobacco sticks, 1.14L wine or alcohol, and 24 355mL cans/bottles of beer. The value of these products is included in the CDN$500. For more information, contact Canadian Customs, 2265 St. Laurent Blvd., Ottawa, Ontario K1G 4K3 (tel. (613) 993-0534).

Great Britain Citizens or visitors over 17 must declare any goods in excess of: 200 cigarettes, 100 cigarillos, 50 cigars, or 250g tobacco; 2L still table wine, 1L strong liqueurs (over 22% volume) or fortified or sparkling wine, or other liqueurs; 60mL perfume or 250mL *eau de toilette;* and UK£136 worth of all other goods including gifts and souvenirs. For more info, contact Her Majesty's Customs and Excise, Custom House, Nettleton Road, Heathrow Airport, Hounslow, Middlesex TW6 2LA (tel. (0181) 910-3744; fax 910-3765).

Ireland Citizens over 17 may bring back 200 cigarettes, 100 *cigarillos,* 50 cigars, or 250g tobacco; 1L liquor or 2L wine; 2L still wine; 50g perfume; and 250mL toilet water. Everything in excess of IR£34 above these allowances must be declared. For more information, contact The Revenue Commissioners, Dublin Castle, Dublin 1 (tel.

(01) 679 27 77; fax 671 20 21; e-mail taxes@ior.ie; www http:\\www.revenue.ie) or the Collector of Customs and Excise, The Custom House, Dublin 1.

Australia Citizens over 18 may import AUS$400 (under 18 AUS$200) of goods duty-free, in addition to the allowance of 1.125L alcohol and 250 cigarettes or 250g tobacco. For information, contact the Regional Director, Australian Customs Service, GPO Box 8, Sydney NSW 2001 (tel. (02) 213-2000; fax 213-4000).

New Zealand Citizens over 17 may bring home up to NZ$700 worth of goods duty-free if they are intended for personal use or are unsolicited gifts. The concession is 200 cigarettes (1 carton) or 250g tobacco or 50 cigars or a combination of all three not to exceed 250g and 4.5L of beer or wine and 1.125L of liquor. For more information, get the *New Zealand Customs Guide for Travelers,* New Zealand Customs, 50 Anzac Ave., Box 29, Auckland (tel. (09) 377 35 20; fax 309 29 78).

South Africa Citizens may import duty-free: 400 cigarettes, 50 cigars, 250g tobacco, 2L wine, 1L of spirits, 50mL perfume, 250mL *eau de toilette,* and other items up to a value of SAR500. You may not export or import South African bank notes in excess of SAR500. For more info, contact Commissioner for Customs and Excise, Private Bag X47, Pretoria 0001. In the U.S., contact the Embassy of South Africa, 3051 Massachusetts Ave., NW, Washington D.C. 20008 (tel. (202) 232-4400; fax 244-9417) or the South African Home Annex, 3201 New Mexico Ave. #380, NW, Washington D.C. 20016 (tel. (202) 966-1650).

■ Money Matters

All prices in this book are listed in Nuevos Pesos (N.P., "new pesos"), the official currency since January 1993—"old" pesos trimmed down of three zeros. In December 1994, the most dramatic devaluation in ten years halved the value of the peso in relation to the U.S. dollar. Since then, further devaluation and inflation have made the cost of living increasingly high for Mexican...and low for travelers with hard currency. Although the situation is almost stable, prices are likely to change. The prices given in the book were accurate in August 1996 but may have risen since. Please understand that neither *Let's Go* nor hotel owners can be responsible for changes in the economy.

US$1 = 7.56 pesos	**1 peso = US$0.13**
CDN$1 = 5.51 pesos	**1 peso= CDN$0.18**
UK£1 = 11.74 pesos	**1 peso = UK£0.09**
IR£1 = 12.20 pesos	**1 peso = IR£0.08**
AUS$1 = 5.88 pesos	**1 peso = AUS$0.17**
NZ$1 = 5.0 pesos	**1 peso = NZ$0.20**
SARand = 1.70 pesos	**1 peso = SARand$0.59**

CURRENCY AND EXCHANGE

Be sure to buy approximately US$50 worth of pesos, including the equivalent of US$1 in change, before leaving home, especially if you will arrive in the afternoon or on a weekend. This will save you time at the airport and help you avoid the predicament of having no cash after bank hours. It's sometimes very difficult to get change for large Mexican bills in rural areas. Therefore, it's wise to obtain (and hoard) change when you're in a big city. The symbol for pesos is the same as for U.S. dollars (although an "S" with *two* bars is always a dollar-sign); frequently **"N"** or **"N.P."** (for "New Pesos"), or **"M.N."** (for "*Moneda Nacional*") also stand for the peso.

Changing money in Mexico can be inconvenient. Some banks won't exchange until noon, when the daily peso quotes come out, and then stay open only until

INSTITUTO FALCON, A.C.
MEXICO
Spanish Language Program in Guanajuato

Spanish Language Instruction at all Levels:

Mexican History, Mexican Politics, Mexican Culture, Latin American Literature, Local Legends, Mexican Cuisine, Mexican Folk Dancing

● Scheduling: All Ages & Nationalities
　　　　　　　Personalized Instruction
　　　　　　　(2-5 students or one-on-one)
　　　　　　　Priority given on a First come First serve basis

● Teaching Method:　A Wide Variety of Modern Techniques

● Highlights:　Homestays with Mexican Families,
　　　　　　　Cultural Events, Sporting Events, Hikes,
　　　　　　　Classroom Field Trips, Cultural Movies,
　　　　　　　Weekly Fiestas - All taking place in the most
　　　　　　　beautiful colonial setting in Guanajuato

● Dates:　　Year-round Classes begin every Monday

● Costs:　　$925 for 4 weeks
　　　　　　Includes: Lifetime registration fee, Group
　　　　　　classes (5 sessions per day: Monday-Friday),
　　　　　　Homestay with 3 meals per day,
　　　　　　Lower prices for fewer weeks/classes

● Contact:　Registrar Jorge Barroso, Instituto Falcon, A.C.
　　　　　　Mora 158, Guanajuato, GTO., 36000 Mexico
　　　　　　Tel/Fax: (473) 2-36-94
　　　　　　Web Site: http://www.infonet.com.mx/falcon

1:30pm. You can switch U.S. dollars for pesos anywhere, but some banks refuse to deal with other foreign currencies; non-American travelers would be wise to keep some U.S. dollars on hand. Banks use the official exchange rates, but they sometimes extract a flat commission as well; therefore, the more money you change at one time, the less you will lose in the transaction (but don't exchange more than you need or you'll be stuck with *muchos* pesos when you return home). The lineup of national banks in Mexico includes **Banamex, Bancomer, Comermex,** and **Serfin.** Most banks are normally open 9am-2:30pm, weekdays only.

Casas de cambio (currency exchange booths) may offer better exchange rates than banks and are usually open as long as the stores near which they do business. In most towns, the exchange rates at hotels, restaurants, and airports are extremely unfavorable; avoid them unless it's an emergency.

TRAVELER'S CHECKS

Traveler's checks are probably the safest way to hold money; if they get lost or stolen, you will be reimbursed by the checks' issuers. Many banks and companies sell traveler's checks, usually for the face value of the checks plus a 1 to 2% commission. To avoid problems when cashing your checks, always have your passport with you (not just the number); it often means the difference between apologetic refusal and grudging acceptance. Remember that some places (especially in northern Mexico) are accustomed to the real, green dollar and will accept no substitute. Carry traveler's checks in busy towns and cities, but stick to cash, risky though it may be, when traveling through the less touristed spots.

The following toll-free numbers provide information about purchasing traveler's checks and obtaining refunds:

American Express, in the **U.S.** and **Canada,** tel. (800) 221-7282; in the **U.K.,** tel. (0800) 52 13 13; from elsewhere, call the U.S. collect (801) 964-6665 for referral to offices in individual countries. AmEx traveler's checks are easy to replace if lost or stolen. Checks can be purchased for a small fee at American Express Travel Service Offices, banks, and American Automobile Association Offices (members can buy the checks commission-free). AmEx offices cash their own checks commission-free (except where prohibited by national governments). AmEx check-holders entitled to use the offices to receive mail. Call (800) 673-3782 to find out more, or check ExpressNet on America OnLine.

Citicorp, in the **U.S.** and **Canada,** tel. (800) 645-6556; in the U.K., tel. (44) 982 40 40; elsewhere call collect (813) 623-1709. Sells Citicorp and Citicorp Visa traveler's checks in U.S. and Canadian dollars, British pounds, German marks, Swiss francs, and Japanese yen for a 1-2% commission. Checkholders are automatically enrolled for 45 days in Travel Assist Hotline (tel. (800) 250-4377, or collect (202) 296-8728) which provides check refund assistance and referrals to English-speaking doctors and lawyers. World Courier Service delivers traveler's checks anywhere in the world.

Thomas Cook MasterCard, in the **U.S., Canada,** and **Mexico,** tel. (800) 223-9920; in the **U.K.,** toll-free tel. (0800) 622 101 or collect tel. (1733) 502 995; elsewhere, call the U.S. collect (609) 987-7300. Checks available in 11 currencies. Participating banks (look for the MasterCard logo in the window) will charge a 1-2% commission. For potentially lower commissions (0-2%), try buying the checks at a **Thomas Cook** office.

Visa, in the **U.S.** and **Canada,** tel. (800) 227-6811; in the **U.K.,** tel. (0800) 89-54-92; from anywhere else in the world call collect (017) 33-31-89-49. To buy traveler's checks by mail, from the U.S. call (800) 235-7366. Any kind of Visa traveler's checks can be reported lost at the Visa number.

Each agency refunds lost or stolen traveler's checks, but expect hassles if you lose track of them. When buying checks, get a list of refund centers. To expedite the refund process, separate your check receipts and keep them in a safe place. Record check numbers as you cash them to help identify exactly which checks might be missing. As an additional precaution, leave a list of the numbers with someone at home. Even with the check numbers in hand, you will probably find that getting a refund involves hours of waiting and spools of red tape.

It's best to buy most of your checks in small denominations (US$20) to minimize your losses at times when you need cash fast and can't avoid a bad exchange rate. Don't keep all your money in the same place: split it up among pockets and bags, or better yet, use a money belt. If possible, purchase checks in U.S. dollars, since many *casas de cambio* refuse to change other currencies.

CREDIT CARDS AND CASH CARDS

Most of the banks that cash traveler's checks will make cash advances on a credit card, but be prepared to flash your passport. Major credit cards can prove invaluable in a financial emergency; **Visa** and **MasterCard** are accepted by many Mexican businesses, **American Express** and **Diners Club** to a lesser degree. Major credit cards can also work in some **automated teller machines (ATMs)**.

All major credit card companies have some form of worldwide lost card protection service, and most offer a variety of additional travel services to cardholders—make sure to inquire before you leave home. Students and other travelers who may have difficulty procuring a credit card should know that family members can sometimes obtain a joint-account card.

Cirrus now has international cash machines in 60 countries, including Mexico; call (800) 424-7787 for current ATM availability information. ATMs offer low, "wholesale" exchange rates, but Cirrus charges US$5 to withdraw outside the U.S., so it's only worthwhile if you withdraw large amounts of money. The PLUS network can also be accessed in 51 countries; call (800) 843-7587 to see if there's a machine near you. Foreign ATM machines often have keypads with numbers only. If you remember your ATM password by letters, be sure to jot down its numeric equivalent before leaving the U.S. Also, four-digit PINs are standard in most countries. If you don't have a four-digit PIN, contact your bank or credit card company so they can assign you one before you leave.

Some Mexican ATM machines have been known to withdraw money from an account without issuing any money. If you attempt to withdraw money and are turned down, write down the time, location and amount of the transaction, and check this against bank statements.

SENDING MONEY

The cheapest way to receive emergency money in Mexico is to have it sent through a large commercial bank that has associated banks within Mexico. The sender must either have an account with the bank or bring in cash or a money order, and some banks cable money only for customers. The service costs US$25-80, depending on the amount sent. Cabled money should arrive in one to three days if the sender can furnish exact information (i.e. recipient's passport number and the Mexican bank's name and address); otherwise, there will be significant delays. To pick up money, you must show some form of positive identification, such as a passport.

Western Union (tel. (800) 325-6000) offers a convenient service for cabling money. Visa or MasterCard holders can call (800) 225-5227, recite their card number, and send up to US$10,000. If the sender has no credit card, he or she must go in person to one of Western Union's offices with cash—no money orders accepted, and cashier's checks are not always accepted. The money will arrive at the central telegram office or post office of the designated city. If you are in a major city, the money should arrive within 24 hours or less. In a smaller town, it could take 48 hours. The money will arrive in pesos and will be held for 30 days. Cabling costs run up to US$50 for sending as much as US$1000.

Finally, if you are a U.S. citizen and suddenly find yourself in an extreme emergency, you can have money sent via the State Department's **Citizen Emergency Cen-**

ter (tel. (202) 647-5225; open Mon.-Fri. 8:15am-10pm, Sat. 9am-3pm; after hours and Sundays call (202) 647-4000). The quickest way to get the money (preferably less than US$500) to the State Department is to cable it through Western Union or else to drop off cash, certified check, bank draft, or money order at the center itself. It takes longer to send the money through your own bank. Once they receive it, the State Department will cable the money, for a fee of US$15, to the nearest embassy or consulate, which will then release the cash according to the sender's instructions. The money should arrive within 24 hours. If you want to, you can send a short telegraphic message along with the money. The center's address is: State Department Citizen Emergency Center, U.S. Dept. of State, 2201 C St. NW, Washington, D.C. 20520.

TIPPING

In Mexico, it can often be hard to know when to leave a tip and when to just walk away. Avoid committing a faux pas by handing a peso or two to anyone who provides you with some sort of service; this includes the bagboy at the supermarket, the shoeshiner, the old man who offers to carry your luggage half a block to your hotel, the young boys who wash your windshield at the carwash, the eager porters who greet you at the bus station, and the street savvy local who shows you the way to the tourist office. Oddly enough, cab drivers (except in Mexico City) aren't tipped since they don't run on meters. In a Mexican restaurant, waiters and waitresses are tipped based on the quality of service; good service deserves at least 10%, especially since devaluation makes meals so cheap to begin with. And never, ever leave without saying *Gracias*.

■ Safety and Security

Mexico is relatively safe, although large cities (especially Mexico City) demand extra caution. For up-to-date information on any current travel advisories on Mexico, call the U.S. State Department's Citizens Emergency Hotline at (202) 647-5225.

After dark, keep away from bus and train stations, subways, and public parks. Shun empty train compartments; many travelers avoid the theft-ridden Mexican train system altogether. When on foot, stay out of trouble by sticking to busy, well lit streets. Many isolated parks and beaches attract unsavory types as soon as night falls. Act as if you know exactly where you are going: an obviously bewildered bodybuilder is more likely to be harassed than a stern and confident 98-pound human stick figure. Ask the manager of your hotel for advice on specific areas; whenever possible, *Let's Go* warns of unsafe neighborhoods and areas, but only your eyes can tell you for sure if you've wandered into one. In small, cheap, and dark accommodations, check to make sure your door locks.

Keep your money and valuables near you at all times—under the pillow at night and in the bathroom while you shower. A **money belt** is probably the best way to carry cash; you can buy one at most camping supply stores or through the Forsyth Travel Library (see Useful Information, p. 1). The best combination of convenience and invulnerability is the nylon, zippered pouch with belt that should sit *inside* the waist of your pants or skirt. A **neck pouch** is equally safe, although less accessible. Do avoid keeping anything precious in a fanny-pack (even if it's worn on your stomach): your valuables will be highly visible and easy to steal. In city crowds and especially on public transportation, pickpockets are amazingly deft at their craft. Hold your bags tightly. *Ladrones* have been known to surgically remove valuables by slitting the underside of bags as unsuspecting travelers hold on to them. Make two photocopies of all important documents; keep one copy with you (separated from the original) and leave one with someone at home.

Driving hazards in Mexico may be different from those you are used to at home. Watch out for open manholes and irregular pavement. Be sure to learn local driving signals and avoid driving alone at night. Drive slowly, especially in the rain; some cars have only one headlight, and in some areas, loose livestock may appear unexpectedly. Avoid sleeping in your car; if your vehicle breaks down, wait for the police or the Green Angels for roadside assistance. Certain roads should be avoided altogether; for more information on driving in Mexico, see p. 39

DRINKING AND DRUGS

Drinking in Mexico is not for amateurs; bars and *cantinas* are strongholds of Mexican *machismo*. When someone calls you *amigo* and orders you a beer, bow out quickly unless you want to match him glass for glass in a challenge that could last several days. Avoid public drunkenness—it is against the law. Locals are fed up with teen-age (and older) *gringos* who cross the border for nights of debauchery.

Mexico rigorously prosecutes drug cases. Note that a minimum jail sentence awaits anyone found guilty of possessing more than a token amount of any drug, and that Mexican law does not distinguish between marijuana and other narcotics. Even if you aren't convicted, arrest and trial will be long, dangerous and unpleasant: think Cormac McCarthy's *All the Pretty Horses*. Derived from Roman and Napoleonic law, the Mexican judicial process does *not* assume that you are innocent until proven guilty but vice versa, and it is not uncommon to be detained for a year before a verdict is even reached. Foreigners and suspected drug traffickers are not released on bail. Ignorance of Mexican law is no protection whatsoever—"I didn't know it was illegal" won't get you out of jail. Furthermore, there is little your consulate can do other than inform your relatives and bring care-packages to you in jail.

Finally, don't even think about bringing drugs back into the U.S. Customs agents and their perceptive K-9s are not to be taken lightly. On the northern highways, especially along the Pacific coast, expect to be stopped repeatedly by burly, humorless troopers looking for contraband. That innocent-looking hitchhiker you were kind enough to pick up may be a drug peddler with a stash of illegal substances. If the

The best places to travel may be the best places to get hepatitis A.

You can pick up hepatitis A when traveling to high-risk areas outside of the United States. From raw shellfish or water you don't think is contaminated. Or from uncooked foods—like salad—prepared by people who don't know they're infected. At even the best places.

Symptoms of hepatitis A include jaundice, abdominal pain, fever, vomiting and diarrhea. And can cause discomfort, time away from work and memories you'd like to forget.

The U.S. Centers for Disease Control and Prevention (CDC) recommends immunization for travelers to high-risk areas. *Havrix*, available in over 45 countries, can protect you from hepatitis A. *Havrix* may cause some soreness in your arm or a slight headache.

Ask your physician about vaccination with *Havrix* at your next visit or at least 2 weeks before you travel. And have a great trip.

Please see important patient information adjacent to this ad.

Havrix®
Hepatitis A Vaccine, Inactivated

The world's first hepatitis A vaccine

For more information on how to protect yourself against hepatitis A, call

1-800-HEP-A-VAX (1-800-437-2829)

Manufactured by
SmithKline Beecham Biologicals
Rixensart, Belgium

Distributed by
SmithKline Beecham Pharmaceuticals
Philadelphia, PA 19101

Havrix is a registered trademark of SmithKline Beecham.
HA8606   © SmithKline Beecham, 1996

Hepatitis A Vaccine, Inactivated
Havrix®

See complete prescribing information in SmithKline Beecham Pharmaceuticals literature. The following is a brief summary.

INDICATIONS AND USAGE: *Havrix* is indicated for active immunization of persons ≥ 2 years of age against disease caused by hepatitis A virus (HAV).

CONTRAINDICATIONS: *Havrix* is contraindicated in people with known hypersensitivity to any component of the vaccine.

WARNINGS: Do not give additional injections to patients experiencing hypersensitivity reactions after a *Havrix* injection. (See CONTRAINDICATIONS.)

Hepatitis A has a relatively long incubation period. Hepatitis A vaccine may not prevent hepatitis A infection in those who have an unrecognized hepatitis A infection at the time of vaccination. Additionally, it may not prevent infection in those who do not achieve protective antibody titers (although the lowest titer needed to confer protection has not been determined).

PRECAUTIONS: As with any parenteral vaccine (1) keep epinephrine available for use in case of anaphylaxis or anaphylactoid reaction; (2) delay administration, if possible, in people with any febrile illness or active infection, except when the physican believes withholding vaccine entails the greater risk; (3) take all known precautions to prevent adverse reactions, including reviewing patients' history for hypersensitivity to this or similar vaccines.

Administer with caution to people with thrombocytopenia or a bleeding disorder, or people taking anticoagulants. Do not inject into a blood vessel. Use a separate, sterile needle or prefilled syringe for every patient. When giving concomitantly with other vaccines or IG, use separate needles and different injection sites.

As with any vaccine, if administered to immunosuppressed persons or persons receiving immunosuppressive therapy, the expected immune response may not be obtained.

Carcinogenesis, Mutagenesis, Impairment of Fertility: *Havrix* has not been evaluated for its carcinogenic potential, mutagenic potential or potential for impairment of fertility.

Pregnancy Category C: Animal reproduction studies have not been conducted with *Havrix*. It is also not known whether *Havrix* can cause fetal harm when administered to a pregnant woman or can affect reproduction capacity. Give *Havrix* to a pregnant woman only if clearly needed. It is not known whether *Havrix* is excreted in human milk. Because many drugs are excreted in human milk, use caution when administering *Havrix* to a nursing woman.

Havrix is well tolerated and highly immunogenic and effective in children.

Fully inform patients, parents or guardians of the benefits and risks of immunization with *Havrix*. For persons traveling to endemic or epidemic areas, consult current CDC advisories regarding specific locales. Travelers should take all necessary precautions to avoid contact with, or ingestion of, contaminated food or water. Duration of immunity following a complete vaccination schedule has not been established.

ADVERSE REACTIONS: *Havrix* has been generally well tolerated. As with all pharmaceuticals, however, it is possible that expanded commercial use of the vaccine could reveal rare adverse events.

The most frequently reported by volunteers in clinical trials was injection-site soreness (56% of adults; 21% of children); headache (14% of adults; less than 9% of children). Other solicited and unsolicited events are listed below:

Incidence 1% to 10% of Injections: Induration, redness, swelling; fatigue, fever (>37.5°C), malaise; anorexia, nausea.

Incidence <1% of Injections: Hematoma; pruritus, rash, urticaria; pharyngitis, other upper respiratory tract infections; abdominal pain, diarrhea, dysgeusia, vomiting; arthralgia, elevation of creatine phosphokinase, myalgia; lymphadenopathy; hypertonic episode, insomnia, photophobia, vertigo.

Additional safety data

Safety data were obtained from two additional sources in which large populations were vaccinated. In an outbreak setting in which 4,930 individuals were immunized with a single dose of either 720 EL.U. or 1440 EL.U. of *Havrix*, the vaccine was well-tolerated and no serious adverse events due to vaccination were reported. Overall, less than 10% of vaccinees reported solicited general adverse events following the vaccine. The most common solicited local adverse event was pain at the injection site, reported in 22.3% of subjects at 24 hours and decreasing to 2.4% by 72 hours.

In a field efficacy trial, 19,037 children received the 360 EL.U. dose of *Havrix*. The most commonly reported adverse events were injection-site pain (9.5%) and tenderness (8.1%), reported following first doses of *Havrix*. Other adverse events were infrequent and comparable to the control vaccine Engerix-B® (Hepatitis B Vaccine, Recombinant).

Postmarketing Reports: Rare voluntary reports of adverse events in people receiving *Havrix* since market introduction include the following: localized edema; anaphylaxis/anaphylactoid reactions, somnolence; syncope; jaundice, hepatitis; erythema multiforme, hyperhydrosis, angioedema; dyspnea; lymphadenopathy; convulsions, encephalopathy, dizziness, neuropathy, myelitis, paresthesia, Guillain-Barré syndrome, multiple sclerosis; congenital abnormality.

The U.S. Department of Health and Human Services has established the Vaccine Adverse Events Reporting System (VAERS) to accept reports of suspected adverse events after the administration of any vaccine, including, but not limited to, the reporting of events required by the National Childhood Vaccine Injury Act of 1986. The toll-free number for VAERS forms and information is 1-800-822-7967.

HOW SUPPLIED: 360 EL.U./0.5 mL: NDC 58160-836-01 Package of 1 single-dose vial.

720 EL.U./0.5 mL: NDC 58160-837-01 Package of 1 single-dose vial; NDC 58160-837-02 Package of 1 prefilled syringe.

1440 EL.U./mL: NDC 58160-835-01 Package of 1 single-dose vial; NDC 58160-835-02 Package of 1 prefilled syringe.

Manufactured by **SmithKline Beecham Biologicals**
Rixensart, Belgium
Distributed by **SmithKline Beecham Pharmaceuticals**
Philadelphia, PA 19101
BRS–HA:L5A

Havrix is a registered trademark of SmithKline Beecham.

police catch it in your car, the drug possession charges will extend to you, and your car may be confiscated.

For the free pamphlet *Travel Warning on Drugs Abroad*, send a self-addressed, stamped envelope to the Bureau of Consular Affairs, Public Affairs #6831, Dept. of State, Washington, D.C. 20520-4818 (tel. (202) 647-1488).

■ Health

Before you can say "pass the *jalapeños*," a long-anticipated vacation can turn into an unpleasant study of the wonders of the Mexican health care system. Local pharmacists can give shots and dispense other remedies for mild illnesses. Wherever possible, *Let's Go* lists a pharmacy open for extended hours. If not listed, you can ask a policeman or cab driver where the pharmacy is. If you have an emergency and the door is locked, knock loudly; someone is probably sleeping inside.

For minor health problems, bring along a compact first-aid kit with band-aids, aspirin or other pain killer, a thermometer, medicine for diarrhea or stomach problems, a decongestant for colds, sunscreen, and insect repellant.

Contact lens wearers should bring an adequate supply of cleaning solutions and lubricating drops from home. Mexican equivalents can be hard to find and could irritate your eyes, although almost all pharmacies will carry saline solution. If you wear glasses or contact lenses, bring along an extra prescription.

Anyone with a chronic condition requiring medication should see a doctor before leaving. Allergy sufferers should find out if their conditions are likely to be aggravated in the regions they plan to visit. Obtain a full supply of any necessary medication before your trip, since matching your prescription to a foreign equivalent is not always easy, safe, or possible. Always carry up-to-date, legible prescriptions or a statement from your doctor, especially if you use insulin, a syringe, or a narcotic.

Those with medical conditions that cannot be immediately recognized (e.g. diabetes, allergies to antibiotics, epilepsy, heart conditions) should obtain a steel **Medic Alert identification tag** (US$35 the first year, $15 annually thereafter). Contact Medic Alert Foundation International, 2323 Colorado Ave., Turlock, CA 95382, or call their 24-hour hotline at (800) 825-3785.

The **International Association for Medical Assistance to Travelers (IAMAT)** provides free brochures describing immunization requirements, various tropical diseases, climate, and sanitation, as well as a free directory of English-speaking doctors around the world who have agreed to treat members for a set fee schedule. Doctors are always on call for IAMAT members. Membership to the organization is free, but donations are welcome. Contact chapters in the **U.S.,** 417 Center St., Lewiston, NY 14092 (tel. (716) 754-4883; fax (519) 836-3412) and in **Canada,** 40 Regal Rd., Guelph, Ontario, N1K 1B5 (tel. (519) 836-0102), and 1287 St. Clair Ave. West, Toronto, Ontario M6E 1B8 (tel. (416) 652-0137; fax (519) 836-3412).

BEFORE YOU GO

Take a look at your **immunization records** before you go. Visitors to Mexico do not need to carry vaccination certificates (though anyone entering Mexico from South America or Africa may be asked to show proof of vaccination for yellow fever). No vaccinations are required for Americans entering Mexico; however, a few medical precautions can make your trip a safer one. **Typhoid fever** is common in Mexico, especially in rural areas. Transmitted through contaminated food and water and by direct contact, typhoid produces fever, headaches, fatigue, and constipation in its victims. Vaccinations are 70-90% effective and last for three years. In recent years **cholera,** caused by bacteria in contaminated food, reached epidemic stages in parts of Mexico. Cholera's symptoms are diarrhea, dehydration, vomiting, and cramps, and can be fatal if untreated. Vaccines are recommended for those planning travel to rural areas and persons with stomach problems. Gamma globulin shots are strongly recommended before traveling to these areas. **Hepatitis A** is a risk in rural parts of the country; vaccines are available in the U.S.

Malaria, transmitted by mosquitoes, is a risk in many rural regions of Mexico, particularly along the southwest coast (Oaxaca, Chiapas, Guerrero, Campeche, Quintana Roo, Sinaloa, Michoacan, Nayarit, Colima, and Tabasco). Flu-like symptoms can strike up to a year after returning home; visit a doctor if you're in doubt, since untreated malaria can cause anemia, kidney failure, coma, and death. Consult your physician before leaving about taking the recommended dosage of chloroquine. Your best protection is to wear long pants and long sleeves and to use insect repellent. Malaria transmission is most common from dusk until dawn. If you're hiking or camping, tuck long pants into socks and use a bednet at night. You may also want to bring anti-malarial tablets from home. **Dengue** is just one more reason to arm yourself against dive-bombing mosquitoes. Transmitted by blood-sucking insects, dengue produces flu-like symptoms and a rash. Recent epidemics have been reported in parts of Mexico. Unlike malaria, the mosquitoes that transmit dengue bite during the day rather than at night. No vaccine or treatment is available.

TRAVELER'S DIARRHEA (TURISTA)

One of the biggest health threats in Mexico is the water. **Traveler's diarrhea,** known in Mexico as *turista,* is the dastardly consequence of ignoring the following advice. *Turista* often lasts two or three days; symptoms include cramps, nausea, vomiting, chills, and a fever as high as 103°F (39°C). Consult a doctor if symptoms persist. To combat *turista,* forget the Pepto-Bismol and take **Lomotil,** a miracle drug sold over the counter in Mexican pharmacies. It will provide immediate relief.

To avoid *turista,* never drink unbottled water; ask for *agua purificada* in restaurants and hotels. If you must purify your own water, bring it to a rolling boil (simmering isn't enough) and let it boil for about 30 minutes, or treat it with iodine drops or tablets. Don't brush your teeth with tap water, and don't even rinse your toothbrush under the faucet. Keep your mouth closed in the shower. Many a sorry traveler has been fooled by the clever disguise of impure water—the treacherous ice-cube. Stay away from those tasty-looking salads: uncooked vegetables (including lettuce and coleslaw) are a great way to get *turista.* Other culprits are raw shellfish, unpasteurized milk, and sauces containing raw eggs. Peel fruits and vegetables before eating them, and beware of watermelon and oranges, which are often injected with impure water. Beware of food from markets or street vendors that may have been "washed" in dirty water or fried in rancid oil. Juices, peeled fruits, and exposed coconut slices are all risky. Also beware of frozen treats that may have been made with bad water. A golden rule in Mexico: **boil it, peel it, cook it—or forget it.** Otherwise, your stomach will never forgive you.

HEAT

Common sense goes a long way in preventing **heat exhaustion:** relax in hot weather, drink lots of non-alcoholic fluids, and lie down inside if you feel terribly ill or exhausted. Continuous heat stress can eventually lead to **heatstroke,** characterized by rising body temperature, severe headache, and cessation of sweating. The victim must be cooled off with wet towels and taken to a doctor immediately. Though you may not consider it a serious malady, be aware that thousands die each year due to heat related sickness.

Finally, be sure to drink plenty of liquids—much more than you're accustomed to drinking. Heat and high altitudes will dehydrate you more swiftly than you'd expect, and you can avoid many health problems if you drink enough fluid to keep your urine clear. Alcoholic beverages are dehydrating, as are coffee, strong tea, and caffeinated sodas. You'll be sweating a lot, so be sure to eat enough salty food to prevent electrolyte depletion—otherwise, you may be stricken with headaches.

Less debilitating, but still dangerous, is sunburn, which in serious cases can produce painful blistering, fever, and unsightly peeling. If you're prone to sunburn, carry sunscreen with you and apply it liberally and often—when it comes to your health, don't be cheap. If you do get sunburn (despite all the warnings!), drink even more water and non-alcoholic fluids than you normally would; it'll cool you down and help your poor, overdone skin recover faster.

WOMEN'S HEALTH

Women traveling in unsanitary conditions are vulnerable to urinary tract infections—bacterial diseases with uncomfortable symptoms like a frequent desire to urinate and a burning sensation during urination. Untreated, these infections can lead to bladder, or even kidney infections. To minimize their risk, women should drink plenty of fluids, especially juice rich in vitamin C (such as cranberry), and urinate frequently, particularly right before and after intercourse. If you exhibit symptoms, contact a doctor to get a urinalysis and at least three days of antibiotics (**Bactrim** or **Cipro** are commonly used). Doctors can also prescribe **pyridium,** a magical pill that gets rid of symptoms almost immediately, allowing you to live like a human being until the antibiotic kicks in. Women prone to vaginal yeast infections should pack a reliable brand of over-the-counter medication, as treatment may not be readily available in Mexico. Similarly, certain brands of tampons and pads are not sold overseas; if you're loyal to a particular one it may be advisable to take supplies along.

BIRTH CONTROL AND ABORTION

Reliable **contraception** may be difficult to come by when traveling. Women on the pill should bring enough to allow for possible loss, and anyone planning to use a diaphragm should stock up on contraceptive jelly. Although **condoms** are widely available in Mexico, quality is variable, so stock up before you leave.

Abortion is illegal in Mexico; you'll have to cross the border to have one performed legally and safely. The U.S. **National Abortion Federation's hotline** can direct you to organizations which provide information on abortion in other countries (tel. (800) 772-9100, Mon.-Fri. 9:30am-12:30pm, 1:30-5:30pm). Your embassy may also be able to provide a list of doctors who perform abortions. The **International Planned Parenthood Federation,** European Regional Office, Regent's College Inner Circle, Regent's Park, London NW 14NS (tel. 44 (0171) 486-0741; fax (44-0171-487-7950) is a source of general information on contraception and abortion worldwide.

AIDS AND HIV

All travelers should be concerned about **Acquired Immune Deficiency Syndrome (AIDS,** or **SIDA** in Spanish), transmitted through the exchange of body fluids with an individual who is HIV-positive. *Do not* share syringes, intravenous or tattooing needles, and *never* have vaginal, oral, or anal sex without using a latex condom, preferably one lubricated with the spermicide nonoxynol-9. Latex condoms are safer than lambskin ones, which have virus-permeable pores. Avoid oil-based lubricants like Vaseline, which destroy the integrity of the latex, rendering them useless in the prevention of HIV transmission.

The U.S. Center for Disease Control's 24-hour **AIDS Hotline** provides information on AIDS in the U.S. and can refer you to other organizations with information on Mexico (tel. (800) 342-2437; TTD (800) 243-7889, Mon.-Fri. 10am-10pm; Spanish tel. (800) 344-7332, open daily 8am-2am). Call the **U.S. State Department** for country-specific restrictions for HIV-positive travelers (tel. (202) 647-1488; fax 647-3000) or write the Bureau of Consular Affairs, #6831, U.S. Dept. of State, Washington, D.C. 20520. The **World Health Organization** provides written material on AIDS internationally (tel. (202) 861-3200 in the U.S.). Council's brochure, *Travel Safe: AIDS and International Travel,* is available at all **Council Travel** offices (p. 31). Those travelers

ESSENTIALS

Earth Girls Are Easy

What's that giant sucking sound? From Mexico to Monterrey, scientists and sci-fi fans alike have turned their heads to the sky to await the next imperialist invasion. Fresh after the summer movie blockbuster *Independence Day*, researchers at NASA have discovered potential trace residues of microbial life in an Antarctic meteorite that suggest that primitive life may have once existed on the **Red Planet**. The findings have sparked intrigue the world over about the possibility of alien life within our solar system. This may not have much to do with Mexico, but, trust us, it has a great deal of bearing for budget travelers. Look for *Let's Go Mars* to hit the bookshelves much sooner than any of us had thought.

who are HIV-positive should thoroughly check possible immigration restrictions in the country which they wish to visit.

■ Insurance

Beware of unnecessary coverage—your current policies might well extend to many travel-related accidents. **Medical insurance** (especially university policies) often cover costs incurred abroad, although **Medicare's** foreign travel coverage is valid only in Canada and Mexico. Canadians are protected by their home province's health insurance plan for up to 90 days after leaving the country; check with the provincial Ministry of Health or Health Plan Headquarters. Your **homeowners' insurance** (or your family's coverage) often covers theft during travel. Homeowners are generally covered against loss of travel documents (passport, plane ticket, railpass, etc.) for up to $500.

To supplement **ISIC's** insurance, Council offers the inexpensive Trip-Safe plan with options covering medical treatment and hospitalization, accidents, baggage loss, and charter flights missed due to illness; **Council Travel** and **STA** also offer more comprehensive and expensive policies.

ARM Coverage, Inc./Carefree Travel Insurance, 100 Garden City Plaza, P.O. Box 9366, Garden City, NY 11530 (tel. (800) 645-2424 or (516) 294-0220; fax (516) 294-0268). Offers two comprehensive packages including coverage for trip delay, accident and sickness, medical assistance, baggage loss, accidental death and dismemberment, and more. Trip cancellation or interruption may be purchased separately at a rate of US$5.50 per US$100 of coverage. 24-hr. hotline.

Travel Assistance International, by Worldwide Assistance Services, Inc., 1133 15th St., NW, Suite 400, Washington, D.C. 20005-2710 (tel. (800) 821-2828 or (202) 828-5894; fax (202) 828-5896). TAI provides its members with a 24-hr. hotline for emergencies and referrals. Their year-long frequent traveler package (starting at $226) includes medical and travel insurance, financial assistance, and help in replacing lost documents.

Travel Insured International, 52-S Oakland Ave., P.O. Box 280568, East Hartford, CT 06128-0568 (tel. (800) 243-3174; fax (203) 528-8005). Insurance against accident, baggage loss, sickness, trip cancellation or interruption, travel delay, and default. Covers emergency medical evacuation and automatic flight insurance.

■ Alternatives to Tourism

STUDY

A number of organizations publish useful resources for those wishing to study abroad in Mexico. **UNIPUB,** 4611-F Assembly Dr., Lanham, MD 20706-4391 (in U.S., tel. (800) 274-4888; in Canada, tel. (800) 233-0504) distributes UNESCO's unwieldy but fascinating book *Study Abroad* (US$25.95 plus $3 shipping). Programs are described in Spanish. **Institute of International Education Books (IIE Books),** 809 United

Nations Pl., New York, NY 10017 (tel. (212) 984-5412; fax 984-5458) publishes *Academic Year Abroad* (US$43, $4 shipping), which has information on courses, costs, and accommodations for programs in Mexico. **Council** sponsors over 40 study abroad programs throughout the world (p. 31).

If you're already fluent in Spanish, consider enrolling in the regular programs of a Mexican university. Applications to Mexican state universities are due in early spring. For information contact the Secretaría de Relaciones Exteriores, Homero 213, P.B., Colonia Chapultepec Morales, 11560, Mexico, D.F. (tel. (5) 255-09-88, ext. 2006 or 2013, ask for the *beca* office). Don't expect to receive credit at your home institution, however. The only Mexican university accredited in the U.S. is the **Universidad de las Américas,** Ex-Hacienda Santa Catarina Martír, Apartado Postal 100, Cholula, Puebla 72820 (tel. (22) 29-20-00 or 29-20-17; ask for the *decanatura de asuntos internacionales*).

Many U.S. universities offer students the opportunity to study in Mexico for a semester or a year, and some Mexican universities organize programs designed specifically for foreign students. The **Centro de Enseñanza para Extranjeros (CEPE),** part of the **Universidad Nacional Autónoma de México (UNAM),** provides semester, intensive, and summer programs in Spanish, art, history, literature, and Chicano studies. The program is open only to undergraduate and graduate foreign students. The school also has a campus in Taxco, a colonial mining town located on the road between Mexico City and Acapulco. Write to UNAM, Apdo. 70-391, Ciudad Universitaria, Delegación Coyoacán, Mexico, D.F. 04510 (tel. (5) 622-24-70; fax 616-26-72).

Cuernavaca, San Miguel de Allende, Oaxaca, Guanajuato, and Mexico City are all well known for language programs. Smaller local schools are generally cheaper, but international organizations may be better able to arrange academic credit at your home institution.

School for International Training (SIT), College Semester Abroad Admissions, Kipling Rd., P.O. Box 676, Brattleboro, VT 05302 (tel. (800) 336-1616 or (802) 258-3279; fax 258-3500). Runs semester-long programs in Mexico that include cross-cultural orientation, intensive language study, homestay, field study, and independent study projects. Semester programs US$8200-10,300, including tuition, room and board, roundtrip international airfare, and insurance. But take heart: financial aid available. Some home institutions will provide additional aid and often accept SIT transfer credits.

American Institute for Foreign Study, College Division, 102 Greenwich Avenue, Greenwich, CT 06830 (tel. (800) 727-2437, e-mail http//www.afs.org). Organizes academic year and/or summer programs in Mérida. Minority and merit scholarships available. High school programs also available; call (800) 888-2247.

American Field Service Intercultural Programs (AFS), 220 E. 42nd St., 3rd Floor, New York, NY 10017 (tel. (800) 237-4636 or (212)-AFS-INFO (876-2376); fax (212) 949-9379; http://www.afs.org/usa). AFS administers summer, semester, and year-long homestay exchange programs for high school students in many countries including Mexico.

Language Link Incorporated, P.O. Box 3006, Peoria, IL (tel. (800) 552-2051). Runs the Spanish Language Institute-Center for Latin American Studies in Cuernavaca, Morelos. Program offers beginning, intermediate, and advanced level language courses. Students live with Mexican families. To contact the Institute directly, call (73) 11-00-63.

WORK AND VOLUNTEERING

Volunteering is an excellent way to combine language study and cultural immersion with humanitarian work. There are plenty of volunteer opportunities available, and a little research will pay off in locating worthwhile and interesting positions. Paid work, on the other hand, is difficult to obtain. The Mexican government is wary of giving up precious jobs to traveling *gringos* when many of its own people are unemployed. It used to be that only 10% of the employees of foreign firms located in Mexico could have non-Mexican citizenship; now the limit depends on the sector. Hotels, for instance, are often eager to hire English-speaking personnel for prestige and the convenience of their patrons and are allowed as many legal work permits as they wish. It is no longer the case that to get a job you must have some specialized skill that cannot be found in Mexico, but attitudes are in flux, and you might still be unwelcome even as an English teacher. If you manage to secure a position with a Mexican business, your employer must get you a work permit. It is possible, but illegal, to work without a permit. You risk deportation if caught. Adventurous job-hunters can arm themselves with a battery of books; a few are published by the following organizations:

Council, 205 E. 42nd St., New York, NY 10017 (tel. (888) 268-6245; fax 822-2699). Offers 2- to 4-week environmental or community service projects in over 30 countries around the globe through its Voluntary Services Department (US$250-750 placement fee). Participants must be at least 18 years old.

Addison-Wesley, Order Department, 1 Jacob Way, Reading, MA 01867 (tel. (800) 822-6339). Publishes *International Jobs: Where They Are, How to Get Them* (US$16); also available at many bookstores.

Peterson's, P.O. Box 2123, Princeton, NJ 08543 (tel. (800) 338-3282). Their *Directory of Overseas Summer Jobs* lists 50,000 volunteer and paid openings worldwide (US$14.95, $4.75 shipping)

The following organizations may be able to arrange volunteer opportunities, paid positions, or internships in Mexico and Central America. In addition, the **American Chamber of Commerce**, Lucerna 78, Col. Juárez, 06600 Mexico, D.F. publishes *Mexico: Oportunidades de Empleo*, which lists companies accepting U.S. and Mexican students for internships. Call (011) 52-5-724-3800 to order.

American Friends Service Committee, 1501 Cherry St., Philadelphia, PA 19102-1479 (tel. (215) 241-7295). Runs volunteer work camps in Mexican villages for 18- to 26-year-olds. Work has included construction, gardening, reforestation, health and nutrition, and education. Programs run each summer from late June to mid-August (participation fee US$900). Fluency in Spanish required. Limited financial aid available. Address inquiries to the Human Resources Dept.

Global Volunteers, 375 E. Little Canada Rd., St. Paul, MN 55117 (tel. (800) 487-1074; fax (612) 482-0915). Volunteers teach English to university and highschool students in Guanajuato. Participation fee $950.

International Association for the Exchange of Students for Technical Experience (IAESTE), 10400 Little Patuxent Pkwy., #250, Columbia, MD 21044 (tel. (410) 997-3068 or 3069). Runs an internship exchange for science, architecture, engineering, agriculture, and math students who have completed at least two years at an accredited four-year institution. There is a non-refundable application fee of US$75; apply by December 10 for summer placement.

International Schools Services, Educational Staffing Program, 15 Roszel Road, P.O. Box 5910, Princeton, NJ 08543 (tel. (609) 452-0990). Coordinates the placement of teachers in schools in Mexico and Central America.

Los Niños, 287 "G" Street, Chula Vista, CA 91910 (tel. (619) 426-9110; fax 426-6664). Accepts short-term volunteers to a variety of programs to work near the U.S.-Mexico border in a combination of community projects and education programs. Participation fee is US$225 per week, US$1350 for the summer.

WorldLearning, Summer Abroad, P.O. Box 676, Brattleboro, VT 05302 (tel. (800) 345-2929 or (802) 257-7751). WorldLearning (formerly the Experiment in International Living) runs 3-5 week summer programs in Mexico and Costa Rica for high school students; program leaders are paid for all expenses. Leaders must be at least 24 years old, have lived in Mexico or Costa Rica, and speak fluent Spanish.

■ Specific Concerns

WOMEN TRAVELERS

Women who travel through Mexico are often surprised by the unwanted attention they receive. If you have two X chromosomes, and especially if you look like an *extranjera* (foreigner), you will find it difficult to remain alone except when locked in a hotel room, and even then you might want to look under the bed. Persistent men will insist on joining you; walking down the street, you will hear whistles and propositions. If you're fair-skinned, *"güera, güera"* will follow you everywhere. Offer no response or eye contact, since they will be interpreted as a come-on. Attention is often more annoying than dangerous, but in real emergencies scream for help. Don't consider yourself safe just because people in uniform are around.

Awareness of Mexican social standards can prevent unpleasant and dangerous confrontations. Wearing short shorts or halter tops (or not wearing bras) will result in extra harassment; it's best to wear knee-length shorts. Bring a lightweight long skirt to wear in churches or in conservative regions like Chiapas. Almost without exception, *cantinas* are all-male institutions; the only women who ever enter are working, either as servers or as prostitutes.

If you are traveling with a male friend, it may help to pose as a couple: it will make it easier to share rooms and will also chill the blood of horny Romeos. Wearing a "wedding ring" on the left hand might discourage unwanted attention. Northern Mexico, especially the border towns, is less congenial to women travelers. Oaxaca, Chiapas, and the Yucatán are friendlier, safer places.

Travel bookstores abound in publications catered towards solo female travelers. **Women Going Places**, a travel and resource guide emphasizing women-owned enterprises, caters to lesbians but offers advice appropriate for all women (US$14; available from Inland Book Company, 1436 W. Randolph St., Chicago, IL 60607; tel. (800) 243-0138). Other helpful resources include **Women's Travel in Your Pocket,** an annual guide for women, especially lesbians, traveling in the U.S., Canada, the Caribbean, and Mexico (US$14; available from Ferrari Guides, PO Box 37887, Phoenix, AZ 85069; tel. (602) 863-2408).

OLDER TRAVELERS

Senior travelers should bring a medical record that includes an update on conditions and prescriptions; the name, phone number, and address of a regular doctor; and a summary of their recent medical history. Find out if you have insurance that will cover costs you may incur in Mexico. And don't forget to ask about discounts: they are frequently available, though not always listed.

Elderhostel, 75 Federal St., 3rd floor, Boston, MA 02110-1941 (tel. (617) 426-7788; fax 426-8351; e-mail http//www.elderhostel.org). Programs at colleges and universities in over 50 countries focus on varied subjects and generally last one to four weeks. For members 55 or over. Spouses (of any age) welcome.

Gateway Books, 2023 Clemens Road, Oakland, CA 94602 (tel. (510) 530-0299, credit card orders (800) 669-0773; fax (510) 530-0497; e-mail at donmerwin@aol.com; http://www.hway.com/gateway/). Publishes *Adventures Abroad* (US$13), packed with general hints for longer stays or retiring abroad.

Pilot Books, 103 Cooper St., Babylon, NY 11702 (tel. (516) 422-2225). Publishes *The International Health Guide for Senior Citizens* (US$5, postage US$2) and *The Senior Citizens' Guide to Budget Travel in Europe* (US$6, postage US$2), among others. Call or write for a complete list of titles.

BISEXUAL, GAY, AND LESBIAN TRAVELERS

Mexican law does not mention homosexuality. Attitudes change throughout the country: while some states have ongoing campaigns against this "social threat," there is a gay rights movement in Mexico City and discreet homosexuality is tolerated in most areas. Public displays of gay affection might be the quickest way of getting beaten up. The **International Gay Travel Association,** Box 4974, Key West, FL 33041 (tel. (800) 448-8550; fax (305) 296-6633; e-mail IGTA@aol.com; http://www.rainbow-mall.com/igta) and the **International Lesbian and Gay Association (ILGA),** 81 rue Marché-au-Charbon, B-1000 Bruxelles, Belgium (tel./fax 32-2-502-24 71; e-mail ilga@ilga.org) are formidable sources of information. **Giovanni's Room,** 345 S. 12th St., Philadelphia, PA 19107 (tel. (215) 923-2960; fax 923-0813; e-mail gilphilp@netaxs.com) is an international feminist, lesbian, and gay bookstore with mail-order service which carries many of the publications listed here.

Damron Travel Guides, P.O. Box 422458, San Francisco, CA 94142 (tel. (800) 462-6654 or (415) 255-0404). Publishes *Damron Address Book* (US$15), *The Women's Traveller* (US$12). *Damron's Accommodations* (forthcoming), lists gay and lesbian hotels around the world (US$19).

Ferrari Guides, P.O. Box 37887, Phoenix, AZ 85069 (tel. (602) 863-2408, fax 439-3952) publishes a large number of travel guides. Write for complete catalogue.

Spartacus International Gay Guides (US$33), published by Bruno Gmunder, Postfach 110729, D-10837 Berlin, Germany (tel. (30) 615 00 30; fax (30) 615-9134). Lists bars, restaurants, hotels, and bookstores around the world catering to gays. Also lists hotlines for gays in various countries and homosexuality laws for each country. Available in bookstores and in the U.S. by mail from Giovanni's Room (listed above).

DISABLED TRAVELERS

Mexico is becoming increasingly accessible to travelers with disabilities, especially in popular resorts such as Acapulco and Cancún. Northern cities closer to the U.S. also tend to be more accessible; Saltillo might be the most wheelchair-friendly city in the entire country. Money talks—the more you are willing to spend, the less difficult it is to find accessible facilities. Most public and long-distance modes of transportation and most of the non-luxury hotels don't accommodate wheelchairs. Public bathrooms are almost all inaccessible, as are many ruins, parks, historic buildings, and museums. Still, with some advance planning, an affordable Mexican vacation is not impossible. The following organizations provide useful information and can help plan your vacation:

American Foundation for the Blind, 11 Penn Plaza, New York, NY 10011 (tel. (212) 502-7600). Provides information and services for the visually impaired. For a catalogue of products, call (800) 829-0500.

Directions Unlimited, 720 N. Bedford Rd., Bedford Hills, NY 10507 (tel. (800) 533-5343; in NY (914) 241-1700; fax 241-0243). Arranges individual and group vacations, tours, and cruises for the physically disabled.

Flying Wheels Travel Service, 143 W. Bridge St., Owatonne, MN 55060 (tel. (800) 535-6790; fax 451-1685). Arranges trips in the USA and abroad for groups and individuals in wheelchairs or with other sorts of limited mobility.

Mobility International, USA (MIUSA), P.O. Box 10767, Eugene, OR 97440 (tel. (514) 343-1284 voice and TDD; fax 343-6812). International Headquarters in Brussels, rue de Manchester 25 Brussels, Belgium, B-1070 (tel. (322) 410 6297; fax 410 6874). Contacts in 30 countries. Information on travel programs, international work camps, accommodations, access guides, and organized tours for those with physical disabilities. Offers a series of courses that teach strategies helpful for travelers with disabilities (call for details). Sells the periodically updated and expanded *A World of Options: A Guide to International Educational Exchange, Community Service, and Travel for Persons with Disabilities* (US$14, nonmembers US$16). Membership US$25 per year, newsletter US$15.

Moss Rehab Hospital Travel Information Service, (tel. (215) 456-9600, TDD (215) 456-9602)). A telephone information resource center on international travel accessibility and other travel-related concerns for those with disabilities.

Society for the Advancement of Travel for the Handicapped (SATH), 347 Fifth Ave., #610, New York, NY 10016 (tel. (212) 447-7284; fax (212) 725-8253). Publishes quarterly travel newsletter *SATH News* and information booklets (free for members, nonmembers US$13) with advice on trip planning for people with disabilities. Annual membership US$45, students and seniors US$25.

The Guided Tour Inc., Elkins Park House, Suite 114B, 7900 Old York Road, Elkins Park, PA 19027-2339 (tel. (800) 783-5841 or (215) 782-1370; fax 635-2637). Organizes travel programs for persons with developmental and physical challenges and those requiring renal dialysis. Free brochure.

Twin Peaks Press, PO Box 129, Vancouver, WA 98666-0129 (tel. (360) 694-2462, orders only MC and Visa (800) 637-2256; fax (360) 696-3210). Publishers of *Travel for the Disabled*, which provides travel tips, lists of accessible tourist attractions, and advice on other resources for disabled travelers ($20). Also publishes *Directory for Travel Agencies of the Disabled* ($20), *Wheelchair Vagabond* ($15), and *Directory of Accessible Van Rentals* ($10). Postage $3 for first book, $1.50 for each additional book.

TRAVELERS WITH CHILDREN

Children should not be deprived of the life-altering experience of a Mexican vacation; just slow your pace and plan ahead to ward off disaster. If you plan on going on walking trips, consider bringing along a papoose to carry your baby. If you rent a car, make sure the company provides a seat for younger children. Some of the following publications offer tips for adults traveling with children or distractions for the kids themselves.

Backpacking with Babies and Small Children (US$10). Published by Wilderness Press, 2440 Bancroft Way, Berkeley, CA 94704 (tel. (800) 443-7227 or (510) 843-8080; fax 548-1355).

Travel with Children by Maureen Wheeler (US$11.95, postage US$1.50). Published by Lonely Planet Publications, Embarcadero West, 155 Filbert St., #251, Oakland, CA 94607 (tel. (800) 275-8555 or (510) 893-8555, fax 893-8563; e-mail info@lonelyplanet.com; http://www.lonelyplanet.com). Also at P.O. Box 617, Hawthorn, Victoria 3122, Australia.

VEGETARIAN AND KOSHER TRAVELERS

It's not easy for vegetarians in Mexico: most meals include meat or are prepared with animal fat. Always find out if your *frijoles* were prepared using *manteca* (lard). *Let's Go* mentions vegetarian restaurants whenever we've been able to find them. For more, contact the **North American Vegetarian Society,** P.O. Box 72, Dolgeville, NY 13329 (518-568-7970). **The International Vegetarian Travel Guide** (UK£2) was last published in 1991. Order back copies from the Vegetarian Society of the UK (VSUK), Parkdale, Dunham Rd., Altringham, Cheshire WA14 4QG (tel. (61) 928 07 93).

Travelers who keep kosher should contact synagogues in larger cities for information on kosher restaurants; your own synagogue or college Hillel should have access to lists of Jewish institutions across the nation. If you are strict in your observance, consider preparing your own food on the road. **The Jewish Travel Guide** (US$12, postage US$1.75) lists synagogues, kosher restaurants, and Jewish institutions in over 80 countries. Buy it from Sepher-Hermon Press, 1265 46th St., Brooklyn, NY 11219 (tel. (718) 972-9010; $13.95, $2.50 shipping) or Ballantine-Mitchell Publishers, Newbury House 890-900, Eastern Ave., Newbury Park, Ilford, Essex, U.K. IG2 7HH (tel. (0181) 599 88 66; fax 599 09 84).

MINORITY TRAVELERS

Although culturally diverse, Mexico is largely racially homogeneous. Mexicans are *indígenas* (indians), white, or some mixture of the two. The whiter your skin the better treatment you'll get in larger cities, and the more you'll stand out in rural areas.

Practically any other ethnicity will mark you as a foreigner in Mexico, and as a result you might receive attention from curious locals, particularly in smaller communities. On most occasions this attention (stares, giggling, questions) is not meant with hostility and arises from curiosity rather than racism. Try to be understanding of the excitement produced by difference. In most cases, Mexicans react more strongly to foreignness, particularly Anglophone, than to ethnicity.

TRAVELING ALONE

Traveling alone results in greater freedom: you choose which museums to visit and which to avoid, whether to take the early bus or the midnight train. It is the perfect opportunity to write a great travel journal, in the grand tradition of Mark Twain or John Steinbeck. When you get sick of yourself, it annihilates shyness and pushes you to meet people. On the other hand, it makes you a more vulnerable target for robbery and harassment. Lone travelers need to be well organized and look confident at all times. Do not wander around back alleys looking confused, and try to regularly contact someone at home who knows your itinerary. **A Foxy Old Woman's Guide to Traveling Alone,** by Jay Ben-Lesser, encompasses practically every specific concern, offering anecdotes and tips for anyone interested in solitary adventure. Available from Crossing Press in Freedom, CA (tel. 800-777-1048, US$11). For more information, see Safety and Security (p. 17).

■ Packing

LUGGAGE

Before embarking on your dream vacation, set out everything you'll need, and then take half of that plus more money. Remember: you'll hate that Conair hair dryer when you have to trek 8km uphill on hot asphalt. One *New York Times* correspondent recommends that you "take no more than you can carry for half a mile at a dead run." This advice may be extreme (unless you expect to be pursued by *federales*), but the gist is clear. Don't forget to leave room for souvenirs and gifts.

If you will be riding a lot of buses or covering a lot of ground by foot, a **backpack** may be the best choice for toting your loot. An internal-frame model is less bulky and can't be broken as easily by baggage handlers. For hiking, external frames lift weight off the back and distribute it more evenly, allow for some ventilation, and are more pleasant to carry over uneven terrain; internal frames mold to the back better, keep a lower center of gravity, and are more comfortable for long-distance hiking on the level. If you're taking a sleeping bag, keep in mind that you can strap it onto the outside of an external frame, while you usually must allow room for bedding inside an internal frame pack. Remember that zippers and flaps make easy targets for pickpockets. Decent packs start at about US$120. A **daypack** enables you to leave your cargo in the hotel room while you go sightseeing; make sure there's enough room for a water bottle, a camera, and *Let's Go*. If you are planning on staying in a large city for an extended period of time, you may want to bring along a **shoulderbag** to conceal your identity as a budget traveler.

CLOTHING AND FOOTWEAR

Footwear is not the place to cut costs. Comfortable walking shoes or a good pair of running shoes is essential; save your sandals for short walks and evenings out. If you plan to hike or climb over pyramids and ruins, bring a pair of sturdy hiking shoes. Your feet will thank you for it.

Avoid fabrics that wrinkle easily; rolling your clothes (instead of folding) and wrapping a rubber band around them will cut down on wrinkles and save space. **Shorts**, on either sex, are not appropriate in rural areas, in churches, in the more traditional southern states, or in more cosmopolitan cities like Mexico City and Guadalajara.

Save them for the beach. Women may want to bring along a simple dress that can be worn casually or dressed up with a scarf; men can get by with a pair of khakis and white shirt. Anything in **black** is a must; you can wear it when you hit the clubs, and the stains won't show if you wear it days in a row. Pack a rain poncho if you're traveling between May and October, and bring a sweater for chilly nights if you're going to the mountains—or if you'll be spending a lot of time traveling in air-conditioned first-class buses.

MISCELLANEOUS

You can never pack enough **resealable plastic bags;** they don't take up any space, and you can use them to store wet bathing suits, safeguard your coughdrops from the roaches, or keep your shampoo from spilling all over your underwear. **Toilet paper** is often elusive; always carry some for those out-of-the way places and extra, extra cheap hotels. **Mosquito repellant** can also prove invaluable, especially if you plan on traveling in rural regions or during the rainy season. Nobody's invincible; bring along a compact first-aid kit (see Health, p. 19). Most toiletries, such as aspirin and razor blades, are available in Mexican pharmacies, but bring prescription drugs and contraceptives from home. Even when these items are available over the counter, their ingredients may differ from the same-named product in the U.S.

GETTING THERE

▓ Budget Travel Agencies

Council Travel, the travel division of Council, specializes in student and budget travel. Over 50 offices worldwide. Sells charter flight tickets, guidebooks (including *Let's Go*), ISICs, ITICs, GO 25 cards, hostel cards, and gear. **Atlanta,** Emory Village, 1561 N. Decatur Rd., GA 30307 (tel. (404) 377-9997). **Austin,** 2000 Guadalupe, TX 78705 (tel. (512) 472-4931). **Boston,** 729 Boylston St., Suite #201, MA 02116 (tel. (617) 266-1926). **Chicago,** 1153 N. Dearborn St., 2nd floor, IL 60610 (tel. (312) 951-0585). **Los Angeles,** 10904 Lindbrook Dr., CA 90024 (tel. (310) 208-3551). **Miami,** One Datran Center, 9100 S. Dadeland Blvd., FL 33156 (tel. (305) 670-9261). **Minneapolis,** 1501 University Ave. SE, MN 55414. **New York,** 205 E. 42nd St., NY 10017 (tel. (212) 661-1450). **San Diego,** 953 Garnet Ave., CA 92109 (tel. (619) 270-6301). **San Francisco,** 530 Bush St., CA 94108. **Seattle,** 4311½ University Way, WA 98105. **Washington, D.C.,** 3300 M St. NW 20007. For U.S. cities not listed, call 1-800-226-8624.For **Britain,** 28A Poland St., Oxford Circus, London WIV 3DB (tel. (0171) 437-7767). **France,** 22, rue des Pyramides, 75001 Paris (tel. (1) 44 55 55 65).

STA Travel: Over 100 offices worldwide. Call (213) 937-1150 for general information or (800) 777-0112 for travel sales. Discount airfares for travelers under 26 and full-time students under 32; sells ISICs, rail passes, accommodations, tours, and insurance. Sixteen **U.S.** offices include: **Boston,** 297 Newbury St., MA 02115 (tel. (617) 266-6014). **New York,** 10 Downing St., Ste. G, New York, NY 10003 (tel. (212) 627-3111). **San Francisco,** 51 Grant Ave., CA 94108 (tel. (415) 391-8407). **Chicago,** 429 S. Dearborn St., IL 6065. In the **U.K.,** 6 Wrights Ln., London W8 6TA (tel. (0171) 938 47 11 for North American travel). In **Australia,** 222 Faraday St., Melbourne, VIC 3053 (tel. (03) 349-6911). In **New Zealand,** 10 High St., Auckland (tel. (09)309 97 23).

Let's Go Travel, Harvard Student Agencies, 67 Mt. Auburn St., Cambridge, MA 02138 (tel. (800) 553-8746 or (617) 495-9649). Let's Go Travel offers railpasses, HI-AYH memberships, ISICs, International Teacher ID cards, GO 25 cards, guidebooks, maps, bargain flights, and a complete line of budget travel gear. All items available by mail; call or write for a catalog (or see catalog in center of this guide).

ESSENTIALS

International Student Exchange Flights (ISE), 5010 E. Shea Blvd., #A104, Scotsdale, AZ 85254 (tel. (602) 951-1216). Budget student flights to Europe and Asia, Eurail, HI-AYH memberships, ISIC cards, and travel guides. Free catalog.

Travel CUTS (Canadian Universities Travel Services, Ltd.), 187 College St., Toronto, Ontario M5T 1P7 (tel. (416) 979-2406; fax 979-8167). In **Britain,** 295-A Regent St., London W1R 7YA (tel. (0171) 637-3161). The Canadian equivalent of Council. 40 offices across Canada. Discounted European, South Pacific, and domestic flights; special student fares to all destinations with valid ISIC. Issues ISIC, FIYTO, HI hostel cards, and discount travel passes. Special fares with valid ISIC or FIYTO cards. Offers free *Student Traveller* magazine and info on Student Work Abroad Program (SWAP).

■ By Plane

A little research can pay off with discounts or cheaper flights. A travel agent is often a good source of information on scheduled flights and fares, and student travel organizations provide leads on airfare discounts (see above). If you're coming from Europe, it's cheapest to fly first to a U.S. city, then connect to Mexico City or some other Mexican airport.

Mexicana (tel. (800) 531-7921) and **Aeroméxico** (tel. (800) 237-6639) are the two major national airlines. Together, they cover most of Mexico; regional airlines also provide service in many areas. Be aware of the **departure tax** levied at Mexican international airports (US$12). These taxes are often included in the ticket price.

The availability of standby flights is declining on many airlines, but if you can find them, their advantage is flexibility. The disadvantage is that flying standby can randomize your vacation more than you would like. Call individual carriers for availability and prices. Tickets are usually sold at the airport on the day of departure.

Travelers who agree to serve as **couriers** receive a considerable discount (often 50%) on their airfare; in return, they surrender luggage space and must have a flexible itinerary. Couriers must be at least 18 years old and possess a valid passport. **Now Voyager,** 74 Varick St. #307, New York, NY 10013 (tel. (212) 431-1616) and **Halbart Express,** 147-05 176th St., Jamaica, NY 11434 (tel. (718) 656-5000), among other firms, mediate such transactions.

Discount clearing houses also offer savings on charter flights, commercial flights, tour packages, and cruises. These clubs make unsold tickets available from three weeks up to a few days before departure. Annual dues run US$25-50, but the fares offered can be extremely cheap. Places to investigate include:

Last Minute Travel Club, 1249 Boylston St., Boston, MA 02215 (tel. (800) 527-8646 or (617) 267-9800). No membership fee.

Discount Travel International, 169 W. 81st St., New York, NY 10024 (tel. (212) 362-3636; fax (212) 362-3236). No membership fee.

Moment's Notice, 425 Madison Ave., Suite 702, New York, NY 10017 (tel. (718) 234-6295). US$25 annual fee per family. World-wide service.

Travel Avenue, 10 S. Riverside Plaza, Suite 1404, Chicago, IL 60606 (tel. (800) 333-3335). For a ticketing fee of 5-12%, depending on the number of travelers and the itinerary, Travel Avenue will search for the lowest international airfare available, and then take 7% off the base price.

An even more adventurous option is to register for a flexible flight. Flying with these carriers is sort of like hitchhiking on the road: sometimes they'll take you where you want to go, sometimes they'll get you *near* your destination. Typically, travelers register with a company, specify a preferred destination, and give a two- to five-day travel window. If there isn't a flight within your window, you get a refund. Two companies offer this service:

Airhitch, 2641 Broadway, 3rd. Floor, New York, NY 10025 (tel. (212) 864-2000 or (800) 326-2009). Guarantee flight and destination for cheap. The hitch is that destinations are limited and highly variable. Cancún today, Ixtapa tomorrow.

AirTech Unlimited, 584 Broadway #1007, New York, NY 10012 (tel. (212) 219-7000; e-mail: dirtcheap@aerotech.com). Handles flexible, couriers, and confirmed or reserved flights. Flights from the U.S. to Mexico as low as US$139 each way. Days-long waits for flights could incur costs that outweigh initial savings.

■ By Bus or Train

Greyhound serves many border towns, including El Paso and Brownsville, Texas. Smaller lines serve other destinations. Buses tend not to cross the border, but at each of these stops you can pick up Mexican bus lines (among them Tres Estrellas de Oro, Estrella Blanca, and Transportes Del Norte) on the other side.

By train, you can take Amtrak to El Paso, walk across the border to Ciudad Juárez and from there use other forms of transportation to reach points within Mexico. Amtrak also serves San Diego and San Antonio, where you can catch a bus to the border towns (US$318-518 roundtrip from New York to El Paso, San Diego, or San Antonio).

■ By Car

Driving entails no bureaucratic complications within the Zona Libre (Free Zone). The Zona Libre extends from the U.S. border 22km into Mexico; it also includes all of Baja California. You will encounter checkpoints as soon as you reach the end of the Zona Libre. For more information, see Driver's License and Vehicle Permits (p. 10). On the U.S. side of the border, several **auto clubs** provide routing services and protection against breakdowns. Members of the **American Automobile Association (AAA),** 1000 AAA Drive (mail stop 100), Heathrow, Fl. 32746 (tel. (407) 444-8411) can receive free road maps and the excellent Mexico guide; members can also buy traveler's checks commission-free and are eligible for Mexican auto insurance. (AAA members needing road assistance should call (5) 588-70-55 or 588-93-55). The **Canadian Automobile Association,** 60 Commerce Valley Dr. E., Thorn Hill, Ontario L3T 7P9 (tel. (905)771-3170; fax (905) 771-3087) provides members with free maps and will highlight routes.

All non-Mexican car insurance is invalid in Mexico, no matter what your policy says. Make sure you arrange to have your car insured in Mexico if you plan to drive it there. You can buy insurance at the border from one of the many small insurance offices located next door to the Mexico immigration offices. **Sanborn's,** Home Office, 2009 South 10th St., McAllen, TX 78503 (tel. (210) 686-0711; fax 686-0732) offers Mexican and Central American insurance through each of its 21 U.S. agencies located at major border cities in California, Texas, and Arizona. Along with insurance, you get all the trimmings including road maps, newsletters, a ride board, mile-by-mile guides to all the highways in Mexico called the Travelog. Remember, in Mexico the law code is Napoleonic (guilty until proven innocent). If you do not purchase a separate Legal Aid policy, and you are involved in an accident, the police might hold you in jail until everything is sorted out and all claims are settled.

ONCE THERE

■ Embassies and Consulates

Embassies and **consulates** provide a plethora of services for citizens away from home. They can refer you to an English-speaking doctor or lawyer, help replace a lost tourist card, and wire family or friends if you need money and have no other means

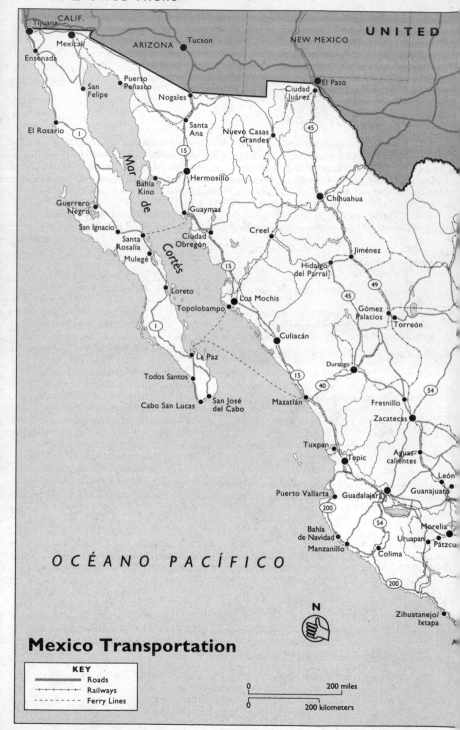

Mexico Transportation

KEY

Roads

Railways

Ferry Lines

0   200 miles

0   200 kilometers

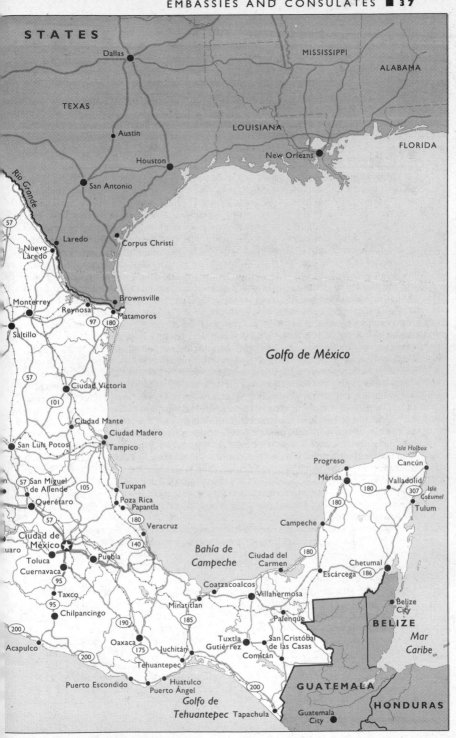

of obtaining it. They cannot, however, cash checks, act as a postal service, get you out of trouble, supply counsel, or interfere in any way with the legal process in Mexico. Once in jail, you're on your own.

The **Mexican Government Tourism Office** (Secretaría de Turismo or SECTUR) has branches in the capital city of each state and wherever else tourists gather. In Mexico City, it is located at Mariano Escobedo 726, Col. Anzures, C.P. 11590, Mexico D.F. (tel. (5) 254-8967; fax 254-4036).

■ Getting Around

BY BUS

Mexico's extensive, astoundingly cheap bus service never ceases to amaze. Travel *servicio ejecutivo* (executive service) and you'll get the royal treatment: reclining seats, sandwiches and soda, A/C, and a movie. This is the Mercedes-Benz of the Mexican bus system. Only slightly less fancy is *primera clase* (first-class). Buses are relatively comfortable and efficient; they occasionally even have videos, bathrooms and functioning air-conditioners (ask at the ticket window). *Segunda clase* (second-class) buses, which are only slightly cheaper than *primera clase,* are sometimes overcrowded, hot, and uncomfortable. To maximize your comfort, at night choose a seat on the right side of the bus (to avoid the constant glare of oncoming headlights); during the day try to get the cooler shady side of the bus. Mexicans usually refuse to open the windows when the bus is moving. A/C can be refreshing... until the icicles start forming; bring a sweater or be prepared to sniffle.

Buses are either *local* or *de paso* (passing). *Locales* originate at the station from which you leave. If few *locales* leave each day, try to buy your ticket in advance. Once you get on the bus, keep your ticket stub in case you're asked to show it later. *De paso* buses originate elsewhere and pass through your station. First-class *de pasos* sell only as many tickets as there are available seats—when the bus arrives, the driver disembarks to give this information to the ticket seller. When these tickets go on sale, forget civility, chivalry, and anything which might possibly stand between you and a ticket, or plan to spend the greater portion of your vacation in bus stations. You may end up sitting on the floor of a second-class *de paso* bus; ticket sales are based on the number of people with assigned seats who have gotten off the bus. This system does not, unfortunately, take into account the people and packages jammed into the aisle. You may find someone (or something) already in your assigned seat when you reach it; in this case, enlist the bus driver's help. Hold your ground and try to keep calm. It might come down to holding someone's heavy equipment (such as children or chickens), but if you feel the urge to give up your seat to someone who looks more in need of a rest than you, just envision how much you'll need it in ten hours. This is the time for being merciless.

If you know when boarding the bus that no seats are available, it's best to wait and board last. That way, while all other passengers without seats have to stand in the

---

Speed

When boarding your bus, try to carry on everything you may need. No matter how much you may need that security blanket or *Newsweek,* once bags have been checked, you can't retrieve anything from them—not even at rest stops. The driver is not allowed to break the inspection sticker. Buses generally make rest stops every couple of hours, and 5-10 minutes is usually allotted for bathroom and snack breaks. While feeding on potato chips or the twinkie-like Tía María processed pastry snacks, keep your eye on the bus. The drivers aren't always aware that you're intending to get back on. Many horror stories have resulted from buses leaving behind unsuspecting rest-stoppers. Verbally informing the driver of your existence and travel plans is always a good idea.

aisle, you are able to sit semi-comfortably on the step between the driver's compartment and the aisle.

Food and drinks at terminal restaurants are generally overpriced and unappetizing. Bring your own grub whenever possible. Drinking alcoholic beverages during bus rides is prohibited. Do not bring drugs or guns on board; federal law enforcement officials regularly stop buses and search riders' belongings. Keep your tourist card handy during baggage inspection.

BY CAR

Driving in Mexico is as exciting as swimming in shark-infested waters, and much more dangerous. The maximum speed on Mexican highways is 100km per hour (62mph) unless otherwise posted, but is often ignored. Be especially careful driving during the rainy season (May-Oct.), when roads are often in poor condition, potholes become craters, and landslides are common.When driving on roads near the capital, watch out for fog. A sign warning *Maneje despacio* (Drive slowly) should be taken seriously. At night, pedestrians and livestock pop up on the roadway at the darndest times. This doesn't seem to bother the locals, many of whom drive without headlights. If you can help it, don't drive at night. Whatever you do, never spend the night on the side of the road. When approaching a one-lane bridge, labeled *puente angosto* or *solo carril,* the first driver to flash headlights has the right of way. Lanes are narrow, so if a truck tries to pass your car on a two-lane road, you might need to pull off onto the gravel or graded dirt in order to give the vehicle enough room. (But be careful: the shoulder is often nonexistent or covered with vegetation.)

Roadwork is continually in progress across Mexico; you will regularly drive by construction workers making utterly incomprehensible codified signals, at which point you should slow down until you figure out what is going on. One particularly confusing signal looks like a plea for you to back up—in fact, it is a request to move forward. In general, take it easy until you master the sign language of Mexican roads.

Exercise particular caution when driving along potentially dangerous Rte. 15 in the state of Sinaloa; Rte. 2 in the vicinity of Carborca, Sonora; Rte. 57 between Matehuala and San Luis Potosí; the highway between Palomares and Tuxtepec, Oaxaca; and Rte. 40 between the city of Durango and the Pacific Coast. If possible, avoid Rte. 1 in Sinaloa. Check with local authorities or the nearest U.S. consulate to update the situation and to identify other areas of potential danger.

In Baja California, if you want to leave your car and go somewhere by public transportation for a few days, you must pay to park in an authorized lot; otherwise, the car will be towed or confiscated. The Motor Vehicle Office will tell you where to leave your car legally. To help reduce the heinous pollution in Mexico City, traffic in the metropolitan area is restricted (see p. 81).

Taxi Driver

If you've had it with riding next to unfriendly chickens on Mexican buses and don't feel up to walking to your intended destination, taxis are always a practical and fairly economical alternative, provided you know what you're getting into when you step into the vehicle. Taxi drivers can be ruthless opportunists, experts at spotting green tourists and their greenbacks—don't be taken for a ride! Be sure to ask the driver what the fare is expected to be, and act like you know the route; consulting with tourist officials or hotel staff about distance and routes beforehand is very helpful in this situation. If the meter works, require that it be used (don't trust the driver's interesting calculating methods). Some taxis offer hourly and daily rates with fares that become miraculously un"fixed" with aggressive haggling. So look smart, be wary, and as David Horowitz would say, "don't let anyone rip you off"—the chickens back on the *segunda clase* Malinalco bus would be proud.

PEMEX (Petroleos Mexicanos) sells two types of gas: Nova (regular) and Extra (unleaded). Nova (*no va* in Spanish means "doesn't go") is appropriately named, and one whiff of a Nova-burning car will make you realize why emissions controls are so important. Unless your car is old, rugged, and satisfied with low-quality leaded gas, this is not the brightest idea. Unleaded gas is now almost universally available in Mexico; you will find it throughout the Baja as well as in Guadalajara, Monterrey, Mexico City, most border towns, and all major metropolitan areas. But beware: even if you do find a silver Extra pump, it may be filled with Nova gasoline.

Both Nova and Extra are extremely cheap by all but Saudi Arabian standards. Don't get overcharged: know how much gas you'll need before you pull in and make sure the register is rung back to zero before pumping begins. PEMEX accepts cash and checks only. When checking the tires, remember that pumps in Mexico are calibrated in kilograms (1kg = 2.2 lb.).

The heat, bumpy roads, and fair-to-middling gas may well take a toll on your car. Mexican mechanics are good and charge very reasonable rates, but if they've never seen your model, reconcile yourself to a lengthy stay. Parts are available only for those models that Mexicans drive; all the various VWs are in plentiful supply, especially the Beetle (known as the *Vochito*), as are Datsun/Nissans and 1970s Detroit boat-cars. No matter what kind of car you sport, bring spare oil, spark plugs, fan belts and air, and fuel filters—these should take care of all but the biggest problems. If you break down on one of the major highways between 8am and 8pm, pull completely off the road, raise the hood, and wait for the **Ángeles Verdes** (Green Angels) to come to the rescue. Green Angels are green-and-white emergency trucks dispatched by radio, staffed by almost a thousand mechanics, and equipped for performing common repair jobs, towing, changing tires, and addressing minor medical problems. If you're near a phone, you can speed things up by calling the radio communications office at (5) 250-48-17. Your green saviors may take a while to show up, but the service (except for parts, gas, and oil) is free. Tipping is optional but polite. These guardian angels will assist you anywhere but in the *Distrito Federal*, where you can contact the **Asociación Mexicana Automovilística (AMA)** at (5) 207-44-48 or the **Asociación Nacional Automovilística (ANA)** at (5) 597-42-83, 597-49-22 or 782-35-31.

While on the road in Mexico, you'll probably be stopped at least once by agents of the Federal Public Ministry and the Federal Judicial Police for a search of your car and its contents. To avoid being detained or arrested, be as cooperative as possible. Do *not* carry drugs or firearms in your car.

BY PLANE

Flying within Mexico is more expensive than taking a bus or train, but it is considerably cheaper than comparable flights between U.S. cities. Check with Mexican airlines for special rates (see p. 33).

BY TRAIN

The Mexican railroads are all government-owned, with most lines operating under the name of **Ferrocarriles Nacionales de México** (National Railways of Mexico). The train system is not as extensive, punctual, cheap, comfortable or efficient as the bus system. Even when they are on time, trains (yes, even the "fast" ones") can take twice as long as buses to reach their destination. Other than the spectacular ride through the Copper Canyon (Los Mochis-Creel), you probably won't rely on trains unless you're nearly broke or crave a leisurely crawl through the country.

There are two types of trains in Mexico: the slow *estrella* and the unbearably slow *burro* (literally "donkey"). The *estrella* is generally about twice as fast and twice as expensive as the *burro;* reservations for the former are often made a day or two in advance. If for some reason you must travel by train (you need to in order to claim your great aunt Bertha's inheritance, for example) take the *estrella,* and make sure you get a *primera clase especial* ticket (comparable to business or ambassador class). Otherwise, it's going to be a long hard night.

BY THUMB

Let's Go urges you to use common sense if you decide to hitch, and to seriously consider all possible risks before you make that decision. The information listed below and throughout the book is not intended to recommend hitchhiking; *Let's Go* does not recommend hitchhiking as a means of transportation.

The Mexicans who pick up tourists are often friendly, offering meals, tours, or other extras, but always be careful. Women should **never** ever hitchhike alone. Hitchhikers should size up the driver and find out where they're going before geting in. Think twice if a driver opens the door quickly and offers to drive anywhere. Some bandit-ridden highways are particularly dangerous for hitchhikers (see p. 35).

Before getting in, make sure the passenger window or door opens from inside. If there are several people in the car, do not sit in the middle. Assume a quick-exit position, which rules out the back seat of a two-door car. Keep backpacks and other baggage where they are easily accessible—don't let the driver store them in the trunk. If you have trouble getting out for any reason, affecting the pose of someone about to vomit works wonders.

Every city and every road has a best and worst spot for hitchhiking. Hitchers recommend stretches near a major intersection where many cars converge or PEMEX stations. They also recommend that hitchers should be cautious when standing on the shoulders of highways, since they are not considered off-limits to drivers, and that they should bring along something to drink and some sort of protection from the sun

and rain. Furthermore, we are told that those who appear neat and travel light have a better chance of getting a ride.

■ Accommodations

HOTELS

Though hotels in Mexico include some of the world's most overpriced, the majority are shockingly affordable. Usually located within a block or two of the *zócalo*, the cheapest hotels rarely provide private bathrooms or other amenities. Slightly higher-priced hotels usually reside in the same district but are much better equipped, including rooms with private bathrooms. Before accepting any room, ask to see it, and always ask if the price includes any meals.

All hotels, ranging from luxury resorts in Cancún to dumps in Monterrey, are controlled by the government's **Secretaria de Turismo** (SECTUR). This ensures that hotels of similar quality charge similar prices; you should always ask to see an up-to-date **official tariff sheet** if you doubt the quoted price. Although hotel prices are regulated, proprietors are not prohibited from charging *less* than the official rate. If the hotel looks like it hasn't seen a customer in several days, a little bargaining may work wonders, especially if you offer to stay a number of days. For a room with one bed, request *un cuarto con una cama*. If bedding down with a fellow wayfarer, ask for one *con dos camas* (with two beds).

If the hotels listed in *Let's Go* are full or don't appeal to you, ask cab drivers or vendors in the market for a good recommendation. Hotel people in one town are often a good source for hotel leads in the next town on your itinerary. For the bare-bones budget traveler the hammock is the way to go, particularly in the coast. If you plan to travel on a shoestring, buy one. Most beach towns in Mexico are dotted with *palapas* (palm-tree huts). For a small fee, open-air restaurants double as places to hang your hat and hammock when the sun goes down. In small *yucateco* towns, locals often let travelers use hammock hooks for a pittance.

Hotels in Mexico often lock their doors at night, and small-town establishments may do so surprisingly early. A locked door doesn't necessarily mean "closed for the night," as someone usually is on duty. By arriving early in small towns or calling ahead if you can't avoid arriving late, and by checking with the hotel desk before going out for a late night on the town, you'll be able to stay out as late as you want to, and help dispel the Mexican myth of the obnoxious foreigner.

Reservations are absolutely necessary during Christmas, *Semana Santa* (Easter), and local festivals.

HOSTELS

With a few exceptions, Mexican hostels tend to be run-down and far from town. Their ban on alcohol, smoking restrictions, and limited hours (most are open from 7-9am and 5-10pm) also deter many budget travelers. Although a bit cheaper than hotels, the couple of dollars you save don't make up for the inconvenience. Therefore, **Hosteling International** cards are not as useful in Mexico as they are in other countries. You can buy one from the travel organizations listed on page 9 or, in Mexico, from the **SETEJ** (see p. 4). Most hostels will give you a bed even if you don't have a hostel card. They may, however, charge you more for it. For listings of **YMCAs** in Mexico, call or write Y's Way International, 224 E. 47th St., New York, NY 10017 (tel. (212) 308-2899, fax (212) 308-3161).

CAMPING

For the budget travel experience par excellence, try camping in Mexico. Campers accustomed to prim and proper campgrounds will be taken aback, however. Mexican national parks often exist only in theory; many are indistinguishable from the surrounding cities. Trails, campgrounds, and rangers are strictly *gringo* concepts. For information on hostel-affiliated campgrounds, write to **SETEJ** (see page 4).

Privately owned **trailer parks** are relatively common on major highways—look for signs with a picture of a trailer, or the words *parque de trailer, campamento,* or *remolques.* These places may or may not allow campers to pitch tents. Don't set up camp next to a well-traveled road, or screeching brakes and the shattering glass of your car may shake you from that peaceful slumber.

The best guide for campers is *The People's Guide to RV Camping in Mexico,* available through John Muir Publications (see p. 1). Adventurers will want to check out *Mexico's Volcanoes, A Climbing Guide* (US$14.95), which contains maps, photos, and a bilingual mountaineering glossary. Available from **Mountaineers Books,** 1001 SW Klickitat Way, Ste. 201, Seattle, WA 98134 (tel. (800) 553-4453 or (206) 223-6303; fax 223-6306; http://mbooks@mountaineers.org). **Wilderness Press** disseminates general backpacking information and publishes outdoor guides which include information on Mexico (see p. 29).

■ Keeping in Touch

MAIL

Mexican mail service is slow but (generally) dependable. It can take anywhere from one to three weeks for *correo aéreo* (airmail) to reach the U.S., and at the very least two weeks to reach Europe and other destinations. Official estimates average 40 days by boat, but in reality it will take months. Never deposit anything important in the black holes Mexicans call mailboxes; take it straight to the *oficina de correos* (post office) instead. There you can buy all the *estampillas* or *timbres* (stamps) that your *carta (letter)* needs. Anything important should be sent *registrado* (registered mail) or in duplicate. It's wise to use the Spanish abbreviations or names for countries (EU or EUA for the U.S.). Write *Por Avión* on all postcards and letters not otherwise marked, unless you don't mind it arriving sometime in the next millennium.

There is no size limitation for packages, but parcels cannot weigh more than 25kg. Regulations for mailing parcels may vary from state to state. While it is often possible to send packages from smaller towns, post offices in large cities (especially ports or trade centers such as Mérida and Acapulco) provide more reliable service. Mailing a package involves locating a box, tape, string, wrapping paper, and the correct forms to be stamped and signed by the appropriate officials. Before attempting to send anything, go to the post office and note the weight limitations, necessary documentation, addresses and hours of the customs and trade offices in the city, and whether the box should be brought open or sealed. After the contents have been inspected at the post office and at customs, you can wrap your package (usually on the post office floor). All packages are reopened and inspected by customs at the border, so closing the box with string rather than tape is recommended.

In some cases, customs and the post office are under the same roof. In others, the two lie at opposite ends of town and have conflicting schedules. In general, in order to send packages you must provide the following: tourist card data (number, duration of validity, date of issue, place of issue), list of contents including estimated value and nature of the package ("Gift" works best), address and return address. It is customary for those mailing parcels to use their home address, or at least some address in the same country as the parcel's destination, as a return address to ensure eventual delivery. In a trade office, you may need to show receipts for each item purchased in Mexico. Postal officials usually record the information from the customs form on the front of the package as well.

You can have letters sent to you in Mexico through **Lista de Correos,** a letter-holding service available at any post office. When picking up mail sent to you via *Lista de Correos,* look for the list posted, and check it carefully for any possible misspellings. If there is no list posted, ask the attendant, *"¿Está la lista de hoy?"* (Is today's list here?). If it is, give your name. Letters should be marked *Favor de retener hasta la llegada* ("Please hold until arrival"); they will be held up to 15 days. If you know people in Mexico, using their address may be better.

Mail sent to *Lista de Correos* should be addressed to a first and last name only, capitalizing and underlining the name under which the item should be filed alphabetically. Keep names as simple as possible. Because Mexicans use both the paternal and maternal *apellidos* (last names), confusion arises for foreigners with more than a simple first and last name, or in the case of mail addressed to more than one person. A letter could be filed under any misspelled permutation of the recipient's names. If possible, go through the *Lista de Correos* yourself. If not, watch the person who does and ask for the mail under both your first and your last name, just to make sure. Address letters as follows:

Beto <u>BLEICHMAR</u>
Lista de Correos
Calle 65 (street address for post office, if known)
Mérida (city), Yucatán (state)
79000 (postal code), MEXICO

Hotels where you have reserved a room will usually hold mail for you, but let them know ahead. **American Express offices** will hold mail for 30 days before returning it; just write "Client's Mail" on the envelope. You don't need to be a cardholder to receive the service as long as you purchase traveler's checks from AmEx. Call American Express customer service at (800) 528-4800 for information and ask for the free *Directory of Traveler Service Offices.*

TELEPHONES

When trying to reach Mexico from another country, patience is the key to success. Dial your country's international long-distance access number (011 from the U.S.), then 52 (Mexico's country code), then the city code (listed in this guide at the end of each city's practical information section), and then the phone number.

Once in Mexico, getting lines to foreign countries can be very difficult. Many public phones don't access international lines. Dial 09 for an English-speaking international long-distance operator. If you speak Spanish fluently and can't reach the international operator, dial 07 for the national operator, who will connect you (sometimes even a local operator can help). The term for a collect call is a *llamada por cobrar* or *llamada con cobro revertido*. Calling from hotels is usually faster.

Taxes and surcharges make it extremely expensive to call abroad from Mexico. Call collect if you can; not only is it cheaper (about half the price of direct), but you will also avoid enormous surcharges from hotels. Remember, however, that there can be a fee of one to five pesos for collect calls that are not accepted.

International calls using **LADATEL** touch-tone payphones are cheaper and involve less waiting than any of the alternatives. LADATELS accept coins or phone cards you can buy at most *papelerías* (stationers) or *abarrotes* (grocers). Without the cards, the challenge is to find enough coins of large denominations: these phones take no more than 10 coins at a time and some calls require a minimum initial deposit. When dialing, use the station-to-station prefixes. The blue push-button phones do direct dial while the orange old-fashioned ones do not. To reach an **AT&T** operator from a LADATEL phone, call 95-800-462-4240; for **MCI** call 95-800-674-7000; for **Sprint** call 95-800-877-8000.

To reach the English-speaking international operator on a plain old phone, dial 09 and wait until the operator answers (sometimes immediately, but be prepared to wait 30min. or more). For direct calls, dial 01; national operator 02; directory assistance 04; for bilingual (Spanish and English) **emergency operators 06.** To make long-distance phone calls within Mexico, dial 91 plus the telephone code and number (station to station), or 92 plus the telephone code and number (person to person). The prefixes for calling the U.S. or Canada are 95 for station to station and 96 for person to person; for all other countries the prefixes are 98 and 99, respectively.

Let's Go Picks

Best Places to Chill Isla Holbox, where all you need is a hammock (p. 532); Bahía Kino, where the living is easy (p. 178); **Barra de Potosí,** where worries drift out to sea (p. 324); **Zipolite,** where time passes really, really slowly (p. 356); and the **Gran Café de la Parroquia,** in Veracruz, where the coffee is as good as it gets (p. 429).

Best Ruins and Churches Chichén Itzá, especially during the Equinox (p. 515); **Palenque,** for the inscriptions and the dense jungle (p. 469); **Tulum,** for the ruins and the Caribbean (p. 543); the **Iglesia de San Juan Chamula,** for the mixture of Catholicism, Maya ritual, and burping (p. 462); **Xilitla,** a place where Alice would feel right at home (p. 252); and the **Iglesia de Santa Prisca,** in Taxco—it outshines the silver (p. 313).

Best Nightlife Acapulco, a decaying diva that just won't quit ; **Guanajuato** (p. 361) and **Coyoacán** (México City, p. 92), for the bohemian option; **Cancún** (p. 526) and **Tijuana** (p. 126), if that's what you're into; and **Mexico City,** duh (p. 114).

Best Beaches Laguna de Chankaaab, in **Cozumel,** with unbelievable coral and tropical fish (p. 539); **Bahía de la Concepción,** a piece of paradise pie on the Sea of Cortez (p. 150); **Puerto Escondido,** an old favorite that hasn't lost its fresh appeal (p. 357); **Zihuatanejo,** which won't let go of its small town charm (p. 320).

Hedonist's Bests Floating, weightless, in the warm transparent waters of the Caribbean; **slurping** a cold, thick *licuado de mamey* in an outdoor café in the *zócalo de Coyoacán;* breakfast of *churros con chocolate* on a cold day in mountainous San Cristóbal; sipping an iced *Negra Modelo* **beer** as you dip your toes in the cool waters of the Pacific. **Aaahhh.**

Best This-is-the-Real-Mexico Experience Riding a **second-class bus** with a million people and their chickens; **watching life go by** while sitting on the *zócalo* of a **small Maya village,** where nobody cares you're a tourist; buying fresh fruit for lunch at a local farmer's market, anywhere in Mexico.

Picks Among Picks If we weren't typing this, here's where we'd be: **Oaxaca** (p. 333), for the *zócalo,* the *chocolate caliente,* and the insane markets nearby; the **Copper Canyon** (p. 198), for its mind-numbing beauty; **Mexico City** (p. 70), for its surreal excesses; **Guanajuato** (p. 361), especially during the *Cervantino,* and, of course, **San Cristóbal de las Casas** (p. 455), for everything.

MEXICO

◼ A Brief History

PRE-COLUMBIAN SOCIETIES

The Mysterious Olmecs

Little is known about the Olmecs, the first settled peoples of Mexico. The Olmecs inhabited the cities now known as La Venta (p. 446), San Lorenzo, and Tres Zapotes (p. 441) from 1200-100 BCE, yet no skeletal remains have ever been discovered. Archaeologists didn't even recognize their existence as a distinct civilization until the early 1940s, when an archaeologist stumbled upon an immense basalt head standing several meters tall in the jungles of southern Mexico. In the years that followed, several more heads were found, all with characteristically thick eyelids, big lips, and broad noses. The Olmecs apparently lived in socially stratified communities concentrated in what is now Tabasco and southern Veracruz, though their cultural influence can be traced as far south as Costa Rica. It was among the Olmecs that the feathered serpent—a figure ubiquitous in pre-Hispanic Mexico—had its origins. The jaguar was a symbol of utmost importance in Olmec mythology; sculpted human figures often have feline forms and mouths curled into jaguar-like snarls, symbolizing the intermingling of the divine and the mortal. Among their most notable developments were a glyphic writing system and recorded dates. San Lorenzo was violently destroyed around 900 BCE, and La Venta suffered a similar fate several centuries later. While the Olmecs perished, many of their cultural achievements were transmitted to other Mesoamerican peoples, including the Maya.

The Maya Dominion and Toltec Influence

The genius of the Maya can be seen in the remains of their ancient cities—most notably Palenque, Chichén Itzá, Uxmal, and Tulum—scattered throughout the Yucatán Peninsula and modern-day Chiapas. During the first 300 years of the Mexican Classic Period (300-900 CE), the Maya became proficient in engineering, mathematics, art, architecture, calendrical calculations, and astronomy, devising a method to predict the movement of celestial bodies with startling precision. Ironically, this sophisticated society never used the wheel as anything but a children's plaything.

Around 900 CE, the Maya empire mysteriously collapsed. It seems that the Maya had farmed the land into exhaustion, causing food shortages and perhaps peasant revolts. A Maya renaissance occurred in the northern Yucatán after 1200 CE. It was strongly influenced by Teotihuacán culture, as elaborated by the Toltecs. The Maya adopted the legends of Quetzalcóatl (The Feathered Serpent, a.k.a. Kukulcán), a great Toltec king who broke away from the Toltec empire and made his way to the Yucatán with his people. The myths predicted his eventual return.

The Toltec empire dominated most of central Mexico during the Post-Classic Period (900-1540 CE) with Xochicalco, Cholula, and Tula serving as their most prominent cities. The bellicose Toltecs practiced human sacrifice and, like the Olmecs, placed the jaguar at the center of their iconography. This violent and powerful culture provided the framework for the Aztec empire.

The Aztecs: An Age of Violence

After the fall of Toltec civilization, the Aztecs, or Mexica, wandered nomadically from the end of the 12th century until 1325. Legend has it, in that year, the Aztec peoples arrived at the southwestern border of Lake Texcoco, an unappealing swamp that no other group had claimed. There, they beheld an eagle perched upon a cactus with a serpent in its talons: the vision was taken as a sign to build the legendary floating city of Tenochtitlán on this sacred site.

The Aztecs practiced a religion derived from their Toltec predecessors; they worshipped a supreme being, the aggregate force of numerous deities. The chief Aztec god was the young warrior Huitzilopochtli, the personification of the sun. According to legend, he perished red and sated every evening, only to be reborn anemic the following dawn, craving the blood of human victims. In contrast to this solar vampire, Quetzalcóatl, the god of the air, instructed the natives in the use of metals, in agriculture, and in the art of government. He was thought to have been light-skinned with dark hair and a long flowing beard.

The Aztec civilization was as bloody and hierarchical as any that followed it in Mexican history. At the height of their power, Aztec priests practiced human sacrifice on a large scale. In the yearly offering to Tezcatlipoca, the god of honor, the most attractive youth in the land was selected to live like a king for eleven months and then, stripped of his lavish accoutrements, to part with his heart at the hands of the head-priest and master of ceremonies.

Motivated by a literal need for human blood, the Aztecs built Mexico's largest *indígena* empire, and one of the larger cities in the world. About five million people inhabited a territory that stretched from the Atlantic to the Pacific and all the way to Guatemala and Nicaragua. *Chinampas* (floating gardens) enabled the Aztecs to cultivate the swamp efficiently. The beauty and architectural sophistication of the island city Tenochtitlán, connected to the mainland by a network of canals and causeways, led Western chroniclers to dub it the Venice of the New World.

CONQUEST AND COLONIZATION

The Arrival of Cortés

Suddenly, history ended and began again. When Hernán Cortés landed on the island of Cozumel in 1519 in search of slaves and gold, he turned the old world upside down. Arriving in enormous ships and wearing shiny shells of armor, Cortés and his men resembled nothing the *indígenas* had ever seen. The Spaniards carried "fire-breathing" guns, sat atop armored horses—which the *indígenas* believed to be immortal—and rode with packs of huge, vicious war-dogs. Some communities capitulated instantly, showering the Spaniards with fruit, flowers, gold, and women; other towns fought the invaders tooth and nail. But Cortés, heavily in debt and fleeing arrest by the Spanish governor of Cuba, had no choice but to press ahead. He sunk his own ships to prevent his men from turning back, cut off the feet of those who attempted mutiny, and marched on toward the great Aztec capital of Tenochtitlán with the assistance of Jerónimo de Aguilar, a Spaniard who had been shipwrecked there several years earlier and spoke the native language. As they moved westward through Tabasco, the Spaniards acquired a second interpreter, La Malinche, an Aztec princess who became Cortés's mistress and adviser, and is regarded as both the mother of *mestizo* Mexico and the primeval traitor to the nation. Along the way to the capital, Cortés recruited about 6000 warriors from the Totonacs and Tlaxcalans—enemies of the Aztecs—and massacred 6000 of the Aztecs' allies at Cholula.

The Aztec emperor Moctezuma II (1502-1520) received word of Cortés's approach, and politely sent a message to the Spaniards, discouraging them from traveling to the capital. Moctezuma, however, also grappled with rumors that Cortés was the light-skinned, bearded god Quetzalcóatl, who had sailed away after incurring the wrath of the gods, declaring that he and his descendants would one day return. Plagued by conflicting advice, Moctezuma finally welcomed the Spaniards into the city. An initial period of peaceful, if tense, relations quickly soured when Moctezuma was kidnapped by the Spanish, and Cortés was driven from the city. An incredible string of lucky coincidences let Cortés regroup quickly, and two years later, on August 13, 1521, the Aztecs, though valiantly led by their new emperor Cuauhtémoc, were soundly defeated at Tlatelolco. The empire had fallen.

The Great Death

The Spaniards' arrival triggered what may be the most devastating biological holocaust in world history. Geographically isolated for millennia, the indigenous peoples of the Americas lacked natural resistance to European diseases. Smallpox, typhoid, yellow fever, and dysentery spread ravenously through Mesoamerica. The mild childhood diseases of Europe—measles, mumps, influenza, and chicken pox—proved fatal to *indígenas*. Within 100 years of Cortés' landing, a silent viral bomb had wiped out as much as 96% of the indigenous population—about 24 million people. Smallpox was by far the biggest killer: encrusted with running sores, victims vomited dried black blood as their skin gradually sloughed off their bodies. Those who lived were sometimes left blind or hideously scarred. Entire villages disappeared from the map, and Spaniards simply moved onto the empty lands, called *tierras baldías*, or bought deserted acreage at bargain prices. Settlers quickly grabbed huge estates; by 1618, one family had acquired over 11 million acres on the northern frontier.

Land and Power

Epidemics meant, from the Spaniards' point of view, chronic labor shortages. For a time, *conquistadores* enslaved prisoners captured in battle, but due to rampant disease and maltreatment, *indígena* slavery was abolished in 1542. (Owning black slaves, however, was legal in Mexico until 1829.) Instead, royal officials gave Spanish settlers *encomiendas* (labor grants): *indígena* villages had to send a quota of workers to labor on the Spaniards' farms, and in return, the *encomendero* was supposed to educate and defend the village. In practice, *indígena* workers were overworked, abused, and segregated from their families.

Afraid that maverick *encomenderos* would challenge royal authority, the crown tried to restrict faraway *encomiendas*. But the crown had its own concerns at stake, not those of natives: regulations protecting *indígenas* were rarely enforced—"do little and do it slowly" was the motto of New Spain's first viceroy. After the Church and crown began imposing taxes on villagers, *encomenderos* had an easier time recruiting *indígena* labor: since *indígenas* needed the once-useless colonial currency to pay taxes, they were forced to work for inadequate wages in Spanish farms.

Abuses were worst where wealth was greatest—in the mines. Rich veins of silver were discovered in central Mexico in the 1540s, and mining camps proliferated overnight, fueling the growth of colonial boom towns. Miners climbed out of the shafts on ladders made of notched logs, and at night they slept on the same pieces of cloth they used to haul their loads of ore. *Indígenas* forced to work in the mines died in the pits by the thousands, felled by floods, explosions, and noxious gases.

The Church

Christianization was central to the Conquest—even Cortés took every opportunity to lecture indigenous villages on their salvation. When the Spaniards took Tenochtitlán, they razed the Aztecs' central temple and built a cathedral atop the rubble. Such bombastic tactics often backfired, and some communities, like the tenacious Lacandóns, fiercely defended their native religions.

Later missionaries were more successful; many *indígenas* were especially impressed by the arrival of the first 12 Franciscan friars, who walked barefoot all the way from Veracruz to the capital. While the Franciscans concentrated their efforts in the center of the country, the Jesuits pushed northwards and the Dominicans moved into the southern regions. Religious services and holidays were the only sanctioned days of rest for many villagers, and by the mid-1500s missionaries had won millions of converts. But Catholic ritual and belief mixed with traditional practices, creating a vibrant and often peculiar brand of religious syncretism that persists today in many rural areas.

Many clergymen tried to protect *indígenas* against exploitation, often locking horns with local *encomenderos* and crown officials. The militant Dominican Bartolomé de Las Casas, a vocal critic of the *encomienda* system, was largely responsible for early crown laws protecting *indígenas*. The Franciscan Juan de Zumárraga, Mexico's first archbishop, personified the best and worst of colonial Catholicism. Zumárraga bravely condemned corrupt judges and lobbied for *indígena* rights—yet burned native nobles at the stake on charges of heresy, and regularly boasted that he had razed 500 temples and crushed 20,000 idols.

Race and Class

When the Spanish built a new city on the ruins of Tenochtitlán, they tried to establish clear racial boundaries. Only whites could live in the city's core; *indígenas* were confined to the fringes and had to commute into the city each day, rowing through narrow canals in dugout canoes. But complete segregation was impossible, and within a few generations, a new racial group had emerged—*mestizos,* children of mixed Spanish and *indígena* parentage. African slaves, permitted to live as domestic servants in the city center, added to the genetic soup.

At the top of the heap were *peninsulares,* whites born in Spain. Just below them were *criollos,* whites born in the Americas. Many whites born in the New World bitterly resented the gulf between *peninsulares* and *criollos.* All *peninsulares* expected to be addressed as "Don" or "Doña," regardless or their actual rank. Certain professions were closed to *criollos,* and Spanish-born settlers typically refused to marry outside their class. Though indignant, *criollos* were hardly interested in leveling social barriers—they simply wanted to join the aristocracy. *Mestizos* were the great, amorphous class of colonial Mexico, outnumbering *criollos* by the end of the colonial period. Some lived in white districts, while others were absorbed into the *indígena* villages of their mothers. Still others wandered the countryside or made their living on the streets, rejected by both cultures. *Indígenas* formed the bottom rung of the socio-economic ladder, vastly outnumbering all other racial groups. Physically isolated from whites, most *indígenas* spoke no Spanish and were barred from almost all occupations. Spaniards were loath to hire them as domestic servants. Though the Spanish brought horses to the Americas, they used *indígenas* to haul all sorts of loads—even employing dark-skinned porters to carry their dogs. Clothing was restricted as a mark of race and class: an *indígena* caught wearing European garb was punished with 100 lashes and a month in jail.

INDEPENDENCE AND REFORM

The First Calls for Freedom

Enter Miguel Hidalgo y Costilla, an iconoclastic priest in the small parish of Dolores. Always rebellious, Hidalgo had been tried by the Inquisition on charges of gambling, dancing, reading forbidden books, fornicating, questioning the immaculate conception, and denouncing the king of Spain. (He was acquitted on insufficient evidence.) Hidalgo spent little time proselytizing; instead, he tried to improve parishioners' economic lot by introducing new trades and crafts to the village of Dolores. He also stockpiled guns. When Spanish officials discovered his hidden reserve, Hidalgo ran to Dolores' church and rang the bells to summon the parishioners. As stunned villagers listened, Hidalgo delivered a ringing call to arms—*El Grito de Dolores*—and verbally whipped his congregation into an instant army. *Indígena* resentment was high; the summer of 1809 had been so dry that corn withered in the fields, and shortages had sparked 400% inflation in some regions. Hidalgo's army quickly swelled, capturing several major cities before Hidalgo was killed in an ambush by Spanish troops in March 1811.

Another parish priest, José María Morelos y Pavón, rose to lead the Independence movement after Hidalgo's death. Under his command the rebels captured Mexico City, but the tide soon turned and Spanish troops took the capital once again. But history plays funny tricks: after Napoleon's troops invaded Spain and forced a liberal constitution on the king, many conservative colonists decided to cut their ties to Spain. Frightened by the spectre of a revolutionary French government, wealthy *criollos* swallowed their pride and joined the liberal Independence movement. The most famous turncoat was Agustín de Iturbide, a *criollo* loyalist who had led Spanish troops into battle against Hidalgo. In 1820, he suddenly defected, uniting forces with rebel leader Vicente Guerrero. Reassuringly conservative, Iturbide and Guerrero proclaimed Mexico an independent monarchy and endorsed the Catholic church—the compromise won wide support and by September 1821, Spain had been thoroughly defeated.

The First Empire

"He is prompt, bold, and decisive, and not scrupulous about the means he employs to obtain his ends." So wrote a U.S. visitor of Iturbide, who had promptly crowned himself emperor of Mexico. As the uneasy compromise between liberals and conservatives crumbled, Iturbide simply dissolved the legislature—setting a dangerous precedent. Anticlericalists, *indígenas,* and *criollos* of modest means rebelled against Iturbide, led by the *criollo* military commander Antonio López de Santa Anna. In 1823, Iturbide finally resigned, but his legacy of despotism endured.

Mexico was in shambles. In the fighting between 1810 and 1823, half a million people—one in 12 Mexicans—had died. War had dislocated the entire colonial economy as trade with Spain dried up. Battles had left mines flooded and fields fallow. Idle ex-soldiers roamed the country, and unemployment was rampant. The fledgling government was flat-out broke.

The Era of Santa Anna

Into the void stepped Santa Anna. Though the presidency of Mexico officially changed hands 36 times between May 1833 and August 1855, Santa Anna dominated the political scene. Initially elected on a liberal, mildly anticlerical platform, Santa Anna quickly abandoned his duties and retired to his personal estate. When his vice-president implemented promised reforms, Santa Anna led a conservative uprising and recaptured the presidency, this time as a conservative and a supporter of the church. Irony piled upon injustice, and the megalomaniac Santa Anna eventually occupied the presidency no fewer than 11 times.

As his cronies grew rich on graft and bribery, Santa Anna drained the state coffers, desperately levying taxes on gutters, dogs, and wheels to build a huge standing army. Sure enough, Mexico was soon at war again. In 1838, France attacked Veracruz, demanding reparations for property damaged during the war. The conflict was dubbed "The Pastry War" in honor of a French pastry cook whose wares had been gobbled by marauding Mexican troops. The attacking French ships were driven back to sea, but Santa Anna lost his leg in the bombardment. Four years later, Santa Anna had his severed leg removed from its grave, carried to the capital in a huge procession, and entombed in an urn atop a towering pillar as the Congress, cabinet, diplomatic corps, and army serenaded the decayed limb.

Meanwhile, the Mexican army was fighting a losing battle on its northern frontier. Angered by Mexico's abolition of slavery in 1829, and under-represented in the legislature, Texan settlers demanded independence from Mexico in 1830. Santa Anna's troops overwhelmed Texan rebels holed up in an old Franciscan monastery called the Alamo. But when the U.S. annexed Texas in 1845, Mexico found itself up against a more formidable adversary. U.S. forces closed in on Mexico City from the north and east. Young cadets, the Niños Héroes (Boy Heroes), valiantly fought off U.S. troops from their military school in Chapultepec Castle, then (according to legend) wrapped themselves in the Mexican flag and leapt off the tower when all hope was lost. Under the terms of the Treaty of Guadalupe Hidalgo, the U.S. bought Texas, New Mexico, and California for a paltry sum. Two thousand Mexicans had died in the battle for Mexico City—only to lose half the nation's territory in the war. Five years later, Santa Anna sold off in the Gadsden Purchase what today is Arizona and southern New Mexico.

Daily Life in the Mid-19th Century

"The Mexican population presents the most striking contrasts," wrote a German immigrant in Veracruz in the mid-1800s. "On one side splendour and luxury, elegant carriages, and Parisian toilette, on the other dirt and indigence." While Iturbide commissioned a French baroness to design the costumes for his lavish coronation, and Santa Anna made himself a millionaire, most Mexicans lived as they had for centuries—poor and isolated. Over one-third of the population lived in remote *indígena* villages. Though *pueblos* were largely self-governed, most villagers lived in grinding poverty. Rural *indígenas* lived in dirt-floored huts furnished mainly with grass mats, which served as tables, chairs, and beds. *Puebleros* grew their own corn, beans, squash, and chiles, with women working alongside men in the fields. In a male-dominated society, hard-working *indígena* women earned a reputation for frugality. According to a common saying, *"Donde las mujeres comen, las hormigas lloran."* (Where the women eat, the ants cry.)

Despite economic chaos, provincial capitals grew quickly during the early 19th century. The traditional Spanish pattern of these larger towns is still visible today: major streets enclosed a *zócalo* (central plaza) bordered on four sides by the town cathedral, governmental offices, and sometimes a string of stone *portales* (arcades). Inhabitants of these mid-sized towns enjoyed more amenities than residents of small *pueblos*, yet *indígenas* who relocated to larger cities to live among *mestizos* fared little better than their rural cousins. In order to fill the ranks of the army, the government forcibly conscripted urban males into the military; military scouts would ambush unsuspecting revelers outside bars and bullfights, tearing conscripts from their families and leaving them vagrant and jobless at the end of their service.

Education was a luxury enjoyed only by the *criollo* elite; only 1% of the total population was enrolled in school. There were just 1300 schools in the entire nation in 1842 and of these, only one-third were free. But even wealthy families neglected to educate their daughters. A typical case was the rich and powerful Gordoa family: one son became a senator and a college administrator, while another son was sent to study languages, drawing, and music in Europe. The daughters of the family, however, were barely literate: *"No boi hoi a verte,"* wrote one of the Gordoas to her sister (instead of *"no voy hoy a verte"*).

Juárez and Reform

Eventually, the façade of Santa Anna's regime cracked under enormous opposition. The emerging leader of the reform movement was Benito Juárez, who has become one of the more revered presidents in Mexican history. His childhood was the stuff of legend: born in a tiny Zapotec *pueblo* in Oaxaca, at age 12 Juárez walked 66km to the state capital (today known as Oaxaca de Juárez), where he apprenticed himself to a book-binder and earned a law degree. Elected governor of Oaxaca, Juárez expanded the school system while reducing state debt. Exiled to New Orleans by Santa Anna, Juárez joined other liberal politicians and journalists in whipping up opposition to Santa Anna abroad, while dissidents in Mexico raised rebel armies. In 1855, Santa Anna was forced to resign.

The new government's policies reflected the ideology of 19th-century liberalism. The reformers abolished the old *fueros*, special regulations protecting the military and church from prosecution under civil laws. Juárez pushed through a new law prohibiting any institution from owning property not directly used in its day-to-day operations. Intended to weaken the church, which owned vast rural and urban properties, the new law ended up stripping *indígenas* of their lands and livelihood, since *ejidos* (indigenous communal lands) had to be auctioned off as well.

Conservatives reacted violently, provoking the War of the Reform, Mexico's bloodiest civil war to date. The church joined the military and dispossessed *pueblos* in fighting the liberal government. Meanwhile, the liberals were aided by *mestizo* reformers and many *indígenas* who supported Juárez, Mexico's first *indígena* president. Both sides committed atrocities: conservatives shot doctors who treated liberal casualties, while liberals defaced churches and executed priests who refused to give the sacrament to their troops.

French Intervention

After the liberals finally regained the upper hand in 1861, Juárez faced a massive federal budget deficit. He declared a moratorium on payment of Mexico's foreign debts—prompting Spain, Britain, and France to attack Veracruz once again. Spain and Britain soon pulled out, but Napoleon III sent his troops inland. On May 5, 1862, outnumbered Mexican troops successfully repelled diarrhea-plagued French soldiers from the city of Puebla. Cinco de Mayo is now a huge national holiday—but the invaders captured the capital anyway a year later.

When Napoleon selected Austrian archduke Ferdinand Maximilian of Hapsburg as emperor of Mexico, he made a poor choice. Maximilian was extremely naive: he insisted that the Mexican people approve his ascension in a national plebiscite (Napoleon saw to it that Maximilian "won" overwhelmingly), then immediately hired a Spanish tutor for his wife Carlota. Maximilian and Carlota landed in Veracruz expecting a grand welcome, but *veracruzanos* refused to leave their houses. The royal couple drove through silent streets in a delicate Viennese carriage, which soon became mired in the muddy roads leading to Mexico City. Carlota cried.

"The so-called entertainments of Europe, such as evening receptions, the gossip of tea parties, etc. are quite unknown here," Maximilian wrote, "and we shall take good care not to introduce them." Weirdly idealistic, Maximilian felt a duty to shelter Mexico from the decadence of the Old World—not realizing he was the puppet of European imperialism. The new emperor was moderately liberal and anti-Catholic; instead of rescinding Juárez's anticlerical laws, Maximilian imposed forced loans on the church to shore up the collapsing treasury. Mexican conservatives were predictably infuriated; Maximilian's modest popularity evaporated. Meanwhile, liberals stockpiled weapons and hired thousands of U.S. Civil War veterans to fight against the French. Napoleon belatedly withdrew his troops in 1867, abandoning Maximilian despite Carlota's wild pleas. After Carlota went mad, Maximilian surrendered himself to Juárez, who had him promptly shot. The human toll of the war was far higher on the Mexican side: 50,000 had died fighting the French.

Struggling to Rebuild

Juárez returned to the capital in a solemn black carriage—a stark contrast to Maximilian's flimsy Viennese vehicle. Juárez's characteristically dour appearance seemed appropriate, since the Mexican economy was once again in tatters. Unemployment was rampant: to assert the executive's control over the military, Juárez had slashed the size of the Mexican army by two-thirds, so thousands of decommissioned soldiers wandered through the countryside, raiding *haciendas* and rural villages for food. *Léperos* (beggars) roamed the streets of Mexico City. Even the small middle class— merchants, bureaucrats, prosperous shopkeepers—lived in modest homes without running water. There were only enough schools for 10% of Mexican children to attend classes; of these students, just 22% were girls. When Juárez died in office in July of 1872, Mexico enjoyed peace but not prosperity.

The Porfiriato

The regime of José de la Cruz Porfirio Díaz, which lasted from 1876 to 1911, is one of the more colorful and brutal chapters in Mexican history. In the 55 years since Independence, the Mexican presidency had changed hands 75 times; now stability was vital. Díaz's official motto was "Liberty, Order, and Progress"—but for the dictator, the price of order and progress was liberty itself. Elections were rigged, dissident journalists were jailed (one more than 30 times), and Díaz's more strident critics were assassinated. The provinces were controlled by retired generals and *jefes políticos* (political bosses). When uprisings erupted, they were swiftly smothered by bands of *rurales* (rural police).

Díaz's wealthy, European-trained, *criollo* advisors believed that the nation's problems could be solved with scientific techniques. Under Díaz, Mexico was mechanized, paved, and electrified. Ironically, the regime that brought prosperity to Mexico harbored deeply anti-Mexican prejudices. The Positivist *científicos*—as Díaz's advisors were called—believed that *indígenas* were weak, immoral, and ineducable. Few of the new schools built during the Porfiriato were located in indigenous *pueblos*. When the Fifth Pan-American Congress was held in Mexico City just after the turn of the century, *indígenas* and *mestizos* were prohibited from serving foreign dignitaries; only whites could work as waiters and porters during the congress. French, not Mexican, culture was the rage among the upper classes. French furniture, food, dance, opera, and fashion were *de rigueur* among the *criollo* elite.

Díaz brought in French and British firms to build a vast infrastructure of railroads linking agricultural areas to urban factories. As a result, industry prospered and land values skyrocketed. But few poor Mexicans profited from the economic boom. Under a new law, indigenous *ejidos* could be forced to sell their public lands if they couldn't show a legal title to the plots they farmed. By the turn of the century, most villages saw their *ejidos* taken by wealthy individuals and private companies. In one case, a town was so entirely stripped of its communal lands that it no longer had space to bury its dead. Meanwhile, *científicos* made millions speculating in the volatile land market, manipulating railroad contracts to their own advantage.

Vast *haciendas* sprung up in the north, some as large as seven million acres, fed by cheap land prices. Half of Mexico's rural population worked as *peones* on such *haciendas*, and were typically paid only with coupons redeemable at the company store, where prices were artificially inflated. *Hacendados* charged *peones* for funerals, weddings, and fiestas—even for the privilege of patronizing the company store. Driven into debt, *peones* were legally bound to work on their *haciendas* until the money was repaid. The price of corn and chile more than doubled during the 19th century, and the price of beans rose by 500%—but the average daily wage for a farm worker remained stagnant, at about 35 centavos per day. Meanwhile, generals, cabinet ministers, and the president paid 700 pesos per month for membership at the Jockey Club in Mexico City, where they whiled away evenings at backtrack.

REVOLUTION

Challenges from All Sides

Unlike the war for Independence, which was ignited by *criollo* discontent, the Revolution began smoldering in the lower levels of Mexican society. In 1906, copper miners in Sonora went on strike, citing low wages and the discriminatory policies of the mine's U.S. owners. The protest was quashed when Díaz permitted U.S. mercenaries to cross the border and kill strikers in order to protect the interests of U.S. investors. But a similar strike erupted seven months later in the textile mills of Reo Blanco, fueling a growing sense of instability.

In the 1910 presidential election, Díaz faced a vocal opponent. Francisco Madero, a wealthy *hacienda* owner from Coahuila, was no social revolutionary, but his calls for liberty and democracy were enough for Díaz to throw him into jail. Escaping to the U.S., Madero orchestrated a series of grass-roots rebellions in northern states from his base in San Antonio. Meanwhile, Emiliano Zapata led the revolt against Díaz in the southern state of Morelos. Unlike Madero, Zapata believed the rebels' first priority was to restore communal lands to the indigenous *pueblos*. Traveling to remote pueblos and addressing villagers in Náhuatl when necessary, Zapata quickly raised an army of angry *indígenas*.

After Madero's troops captured Ciudad Juárez, the 81-year-old Díaz fled to Paris. But once in power, the cautious Madero hesitated to restore any land to the Zapatistas, and ordered the rebels in the south to disband. Zapata resisted the order, and the Zapatistas tangled with General Victoriano Huerta's troops. A pattern for the Revolution had been set.

The Coalition Collapses

After fending off rebellions from radical factions, Madero's government finally fell to a conservative uprising led by Huerta and Díaz's nephew. Venustiano Carranza, the governor of Coahuila, urged state governors to revolt against the federal government.

Guerrilla armies sprung up, led by Pancho Villa in Chihuahua and Álvaro Obregón in Sonora. Provisional governments proliferated; by late 1913, there were more than 25 different types of paper money in circulation. After U.S. troops bombed Veracruz in 1914, Huerta resigned.

Now Obregón seized the capital; Carranza controlled Veracruz; Villa ruled the north; Zapata held the south. When Villa's troops attacked Obregón's forces at the bloody battle of Celaya, 4000 Villistas were shredded on barbed wire entrenchments; 5000 more were wounded. As Villistas wreaked havoc on Texas border towns, Carranza's own government found itself hopelessly divided between old-style liberals and radical land reformists. The fighting in the south was the most vicious. Thousands of civilians were executed as alleged Zapatista sympathizers, and Zapata responded by blowing up a train and killing some 400 innocent passengers. In 1919, Carranza's men assassinated Zapata in an ambush, and Carranza assumed the presidency, inaugurating a period of relative calm.

One in eight Mexicans had died in the wars of 1910-1920. Civilian casualties were high, and many of those killed in battle were unwilling victims of forced conscription. Soldiers on every side took advantage of helpless villagers, stealing livestock and food, trampling crops, and torching homes. As all the rebel governments had printed their own money, the economy was in ruins. Inflation slashed the real wages of urban laborers; flooding and sabotage put miners out of work. Many Mexicans were on the brink of starvation.

Institutionalized Revolution

In 1917, Carranza gathered delegates to draft a new constitution; the document they produced still governs the Republic. Zapatistas, Villistas, and Huertistas were barred from the convention, yet delegates outlined a thoroughly radical agenda for the nation. Present was the familiar liberal anticlericalism of the 19th century; more startling were the socialistic articles of the new constitution. Private ownership of land was declared to be a privilege, not a right, and the state was supposed to redistribute lands seized from *pueblos* during the Porfiriato. Workers were guaranteed an eight-hour day, a six-day week, and a minimum wage; the right to strike was protected. But the moderate Carranza failed to implement most of the radical document, and the Revolution drifted to the right as successive presidents reversed modest gains in land reform and workers' rights.

The Constitution of 1917 codified the Revolution; the machine politics of the 1920s institutionalized it. Plutarco Elías Calles, elected president in 1924, ruled the country for a decade through a series of puppet presidents. Calles, known as the "Jefe Máximo," consolidated the government's support in the new Partido Nacional Revolucionario (PNR), which has ruled Mexico unopposed in the 65 years since.

MODERN MEXICO

A Return to Redistribution

The Great Depression hit Mexico in the gut: as the value of the peso plummeted, wages dropped by 10%, and many Mexicans began to question the direction of the Revolution. Reacting to the mood of the times, Mexico's new president, Lázaro Cárdenas, seized the reins from his PNR handlers and steered the Revolution sharply to the left. Cárdenas redistributed 49 million acres—twice as much as all his predecessors combined—to thousands of indigenous *ejidos,* where lands were farmed in common as they had been for hundreds of years before the Porfiriato. Economically, most *ejidos* were a failure, and agricultural productivity dropped drastically. But the *ejido* program won an enormous symbolic goal: no longer a peon, the rural *indígena* had regained some of the political and social autonomy that disappeared with the loss of communal lands in the late 19th century.

Industrial Capitalism and the Problem of Liberty

By drawing labor groups and agrarian reformers into the government, Cárdenas immeasurably strengthened the ruling party, now called the Partido Revolucionario Institucional (PRI). At the same time, however, land reform stalled and the government limited the right to strike. Meanwhile, WWII speeded the pace of Mexican development, accelerating the shift from socialism to industrial capitalism. But the working class didn't share proportionately in the new prosperity. Policy-makers believed that some measure of inequity was necessary in order to increase the size of the economic pie. Mexican industrialists were urged to keep costs down—and, by implication, to keep wages low. When oil workers went on strike in the early 1950s, the army was called in and dozens of union leaders were fired.

Clearly, the way to get ahead was to play by the rules. The PRI has been likened to a floating log: if you want to stay afloat, you have to grab on. Lured by the promise of cushy government jobs, union officials and peasant leaders joined the PRI's swelling political machine. Enjoying wide institutional support, the PRI has not yet lost a presidential election since its inception in 1929. But the stability of single-party rule has come at the price of liberty. Even under president Adolfo López Mateos, who between 1958 and 1964 expanded social security coverage and redoubled efforts at land reform, Mexicans were not free to speak their minds. López Mateos removed the Communist leadership of the teachers' and railroad unions and sent in the army to break a railroad-workers' strike in 1959. When the head of the PRI tried to reform the party's nomination process, he was fired by the president under pressure from state political bosses. Student unrest and worker dissatisfaction culminated in 1968 at Mexico City's Tlatelolco Plaza, where police killed an estimated 300 to 400 peaceful demonstrators and jailed another 2000 protesters just 10 days before the Olympic Games were to open (see p. 105).

Salinas: Towards Democracy

"The era of one-party rule in Mexico is over," declared PRI presidential candidate Carlos Salinas de Gortari during the tense week following the 1988 presidential elections. Salinas officially (and conveniently) received 50.4% of the vote when the final contested results were announced, but many hopefully interpreted his remarks and the election itself as a fresh start for Mexican politics.

Mexico's ruling party did not lose a single presidential, senatorial, or gubernatorial race from 1929 to 1988; in the few local elections that it did lose, the PRI often installed its own candidates anyway. Through a combination of patronage, fraud and ineffectual opposition, the party stayed in power and ran Mexico uncontested. But in the 1982 election, the murmurs of dissent were heard, and the right-of-center National Action Party (PAN) won 14% of the vote, most of it in the northern states. In 1983, when the PRI experimented with fraud-free elections, the PAN picked up three mayorships in the state of Chihuahua alone.

When Salinas began his six-year term as president on December 1, 1988, he had to confront high unemployment, a US$105 billion foreign debt, the domestic production and transport of drugs, and a skeptical nation. Salinas instituted wage and price controls to keep inflation down, then boosted his popularity with several prominent arrests of a union boss, a fraudulent businessman, and a drug trafficker.

On February 4, 1990, representatives of the Mexican government and its 450 foreign commercial creditors signed a debt reduction agreement designed to ease the U.S. banking crisis and deflect outlandishly high interest payments. This reprieve, along with Salinas's austerity program, led to growing foreign investment and steady growth (3% a year) in Mexico's gross domestic product. Unemployment, however, remains near 20%. Reduced or not, foreign debt has continued to suck capital out of the country, and a blossoming trade deficit is squeezing out small and medium businesses as foreign franchises muscle in.

The fate of these smaller firms was at the center of the controversial North American Free Trade Agreement (NAFTA). The treaty eliminated the tariffs, quotas, and subsidies that had protected Mexican industry and agriculture since the 1940s.

Smaller Mexican-owned businesses are being driven out of business by *maquiladoras,* U.S.-owned assembly and automotive-sector factories. On the other hand, freer trade means cheaper consumer goods for financially strapped Mexicans—a blessing in a nation plagued by constant inflation. Increased competition may eventually reap profits for the Mexican economy, but development is now exacting high human and environmental costs.

In 1991, PRI technocrats dismantled the *ejido* system, which ostensibly guaranteed communal land rights for rural *campesinos.* With this constitutional reform and other changes, including rapid privatization, an agrarian culture thousands of years old is being phased out to pave the way for industrialism. Traditional support systems are lost in urbanization while government safety nets are eliminated, all part of an economic streamlining backed by the U.S. and international lenders. The costs of this structural adjustment program (centered around NAFTA) have yet to be determined, but in the meantime they fall squarely on the shoulders of the lower classes, while benefits still loom on the long-term horizon.

The Zapatistas

On January 1, 1994, the day that NAFTA took effect, Maya rebels rose up and captured San Cristóbal de Las Casas, the largest city in Chiapas state. Within days, government troops had driven the rebels back into the highlands and the Lacandón rainforest, leaving about 150 dead. Months of negotiations followed, during which the government's top negotiator resigned after accusing the PRI of sabotaging his efforts. The rebels rejected the government's peace plan, and threatened to shatter the fragile cease-fire unless upcoming presidential elections were free and fair.

In an election year that was supposed to express Mexico's material progress and fledgling democracy, the rebels drew attention to the vast inequities that still exist within the Republic. Led by a mysterious masked man known only as Subcomandante Marcos, the Zapatista rebels (named after revolutionary war hero Emiliano Zapata) demanded land, food, housing, education, health care, and autonomy. Chiapas is Mexico's poorest state: four out of five homes have dirt floors without drains, the majority of land is in the hands of a few powerful bosses, and more than half of the area's inhabitants are malnourished. President Salinas de Gortari had poured more anti-poverty money into the state than any other—but to little avail. The price of coffee, the state's major crop, had dropped on the world market, and the labor market was glutted with refugees from Guatemala and El Salvador. Furthermore, *indígena* rebels clearly harbored deep resentments that no amount of PRI money could assuage. The uprising marks the latest and most strident call for *indígena* equality. "We are the product of 500 years of struggle," read a statement posted in San Cristóbal by the Zapatistas. Memories of the Conquest are still fresh in a state where, as late as the 1950s, *indígenas* were expected to step off a narrow sidewalk when a white person passed.

The Zapatistas' call for reform has split the conscience of the nation in half, bringing the often muted tension between *mestizos* and *indígenas* to the foreground. For *indígenas* and the poor, Marcos and his heroic band of Maya rebels have taken on an almost mythical identity, and even the government will cede that the mysterious Zapatista leader has charisma. Zapatismo has swept the nation, cutting across class and race lines, and every day the spirit of reform manifests itself in peaceful marches and rallies in the *zócalo.* There has been some dialogue between the Zapatistas and government representatives, and progress is slow but visible. After three seasons of deadlocked negotiations, the violence has been quelled and the military presence in the region's once heavily patrolled cities has slackened considerably. In the streets, billboards proclaim 1996 "El Año de Paz y Reconciliación en Chiapas" and the word *Chiapaz* (Peace in Chiapas) appears on the walls of tenement buildings. The dust has finally started to settle, but it's a very precarious peace, and underneath the apparent calm, the situation in Chiapas continues to smolder.

Mexico at a Crossroads

The Zapatista uprising foreshadowed turmoil to come. On March 23, 1994, the PRI presidential candidate, Luis Donaldo Colosio, was assassinated as he left a rally in Tijuana. It is a measure of Mexicans' political cynicism that many believed the PRI had killed its own candidate; the subsequent killing of the Tijuana police chief investigating the assassination simply fueled the rumors. Meanwhile, the PRI closed ranks, tapping Budget and Planning minister Ernesto Zedillo Ponce de León to replace the slain candidate, and rebuild the campaign from scratch. The PRI used to win elections by fraud, recruiting union officials and peasant leaders to twist voters' arms. Such tactics are no longer acceptable; instead, the PRI relied on more than 800,000 grass-roots organizers to comb the country door-to-door, building on an old network of patronage and pork-belly politics. Sure enough, the PRI won hands down, faring especially well among Mexico's poorer voters.

Just months into his presidency, on December 20, 1994, Zedillo confronted a precipitous drop in the peso. Spurred by the assassination of Colosio and the unsettling events in Chiapas, foreign investors had dumped US$25 billion of Mexican government peso bonds, heralding the imminent monetary devaluation. Aided by the International Monetary Fund (IMF) and the U.S. government, Mexico was salvaged from the depths of economic crisis. Still, severe economic difficulties persisted: in March 1995, interest rates skyrocketed to above 90 percent, bringing the banking system to a near collapse. The growing legions of middle-class professionals and entrepreneurs that relied on foreign dollars were left frustrated and frightened. Mexicans have laid the blame squarely on Zedillos's shoulders, citing his delay in appointing key cabinet posts and in instituting promised economic initiatives.

Though the prospect of successfully taming the economy seems distant, Zedillo has sought to pacify the anxious masses with further political reforms. Rumors of former president Salinas's frauds and of his complicity in the assassination of a 1994 presidential candidate have lowered the morale of the Mexican people. The president has committed himself to decentralizing power and exposing corruption in an attempt to restore the nation's faith in the government. Whereas the PRI used to control all state governorships, several state governors, including that of Jalisco, now belong to the opposition Partido de Acción Nacional (PAN). Zedillo has attacked corruption in other realms, arresting high-level officials—including Salinas's brother—on charges of conspiracy and murder. Mexico seems to be inching toward democracy. The PRI has loosened its grip on the media, and independent observers enjoyed unprecedented latitude in supervising the 1994 elections.

Mommie Dearest

Mexicans revere mother and motherhood only slightly less fervently than they adore Jesus. In traditional *ranchera* songs, macho singers bitterly complain of a lover's betrayal and make it all better by rushing back to their mother's arms. Mother's Day, May 10th, is a de facto national holiday—instead of going to work, the entire Mexican population celebrates mothers with songs, meals, and flowers. And, while the Eskimo might have twenty or so names for snow, Mexicans have an almost infinite number of usages and meanings for the word *madre*. Something can be *una madre* (a mother), meaning a piece of shit. Or a situation can be a *desmadre* (un-mother), a bruhaha; while *hechar desmadre* (to throw an un-mother) is equivalent to partying or having fun. *Ni madres* (not even mothers) means no way. The general *madrear* (to mother) stands for beating up, while the unequivocal *partir la madre* (to break the mother) reflects more severe damage. *Mamacita* (little mama) is a lecherous catcall. *¡Puta madre!* (whore mother!) expresses either frustration or astonishment. *¡Tu madre!* (your mother!) is an insult, but the ultimate curse, naturally, is *¡chinga tu madre!* (fuck your mother!). In contrast to these varied usages, *padre* has a single, simple meaning—cool.

The past two years have been perhaps Mexico's most tumultuous time since the Revolution—even an entrenched political machine can be shocked into change without the full-scale violence that has plagued much of the nation's history. Despite unemployment, crisis, and a political system that hasn't helped or worked for them, Mexicans go about their daily lives with characteristic patience and resignation, finding hope and pleasure in the few things that won't crumble: family, religion, and humor.

■ Culture and Character

ART AND ARCHITECTURE

The art of Mexico has always been deeply rooted in the spiritual, political, and environmental interactions of its people. Though this might easily be said of all cultures, it would be very difficult, if not impossible, to find another people whose tools, techniques, materials, and models have varied to such a remarkable degree. For instance, temples like those found at Palenque in Chiapas state attest to the mathematical aptitude of the Maya. The temples' striking symmetry and elaborate ornamentation inspire even today's seen-it done-that tourist as they must have the *indígenas* when they were first erected. Much of what archaeologists have been able to piece together about the daily life and beliefs of Mexico's ancient peoples stems mainly from the artifacts—both functional and purely decorative—they left behind. Early Mexican art, like Western art, was devoted to the sacred. The colonial period favored stilted European imitation, but the Revolution instilled a sense of nationalism and resuscitated native styles, now informed by modern themes. Art historians tend to classify works within three periods: the Indigenous (6000 BCE-1525 CE), the Colonial (1525-1810), and the Modern (1810-present). While such timeframes are helpful in organizing an extraordinary amount of artistic works, it is important to note that stylistic continuities from one period to another do exist.

Art on a Grand Scale: The Olmecs

The colossal heads found at La Venta, San Lorenzo, and Tres Zapotes, stone monuments thought to represent human-like deities, are the best-known creations of the Olmec civilization (1200-100 BCE). Incredibly, the Olmecs imported the massive basalt stones—some weighing as much as twenty tons—from other areas by floating them across waterways on highly effective rafts.

Not all Olmec artistry was this large in size. Olmecs were also fine potters and expert jade carvers; their handicrafts were esteemed and emulated later by the Maya. Tending away from idealization, many Olmec figurines take as their subjects plump children, child-men, hunchbacks, and half-man half-jaguar beings in various positions of repose, reverence, and agitation. The fluid lines of the numerous acrobat and contortionist figures that have been unearthed provide further evidence of Olmec skill as well as the value they placed on performance and entertainment. The eventual demise of the Olmec culture marked a transition from the Pre-Classic period (2000-100 BCE) to the Classic (100 BCE-900 CE), and the dawn of other powerful cultures, most notably, Teotihuacán and the Maya.

An Artistic Metropolis: Teotihuacán

Located in the Valley of Mexico about 50km northeast of Mexico City, Teotihuacán was the Americas' first metropolis, a great commercial and artistic center with over 25,000 inhabitants (see p. 119). The achievements in architecture are obvious: a number of pyramids, temples, and dwelling units, where Teotihuacanos worshipped, transacted business, slept, ate, and celebrated still stand to this day and are one of Mexico's main touristic draws. In order to maintain a harmonic balance with the heavens, pyramids were built according to specific geomantic positions in relation to the sun. The Pyramid of the Sun, for instance, aligns with the sunset point at the summer solstice. In general, the pyramids were constructed by setting down layers of clay on an earth or masonry foundation; the main structural features are the *talud* (sloping wall) and the *tablero* (entablature). This type of architectural design lend the pyramids their characteristic severity.

Temples and pyramids were both a source of civic pride and a religious necessity. The structures were ornamented in relief with images of serpents, jaguars, gods, and, though not as evident today, were also often decorated with vibrant colors. Frescoes on interior walls of buildings depict, among other subjects, paradise scenes, floral arrangements, religious rituals, and athletic events.

It says something about the Teotihuacanos' level of organization and technological savvy that they were able to "mass-produce" figurines; from clay molds, copies were made, remnants of which have been discovered throughout the region. The people of Teotihuacán even left behind statuettes with moveable appendages. Precursors of the modern-day G.I. Joe or Barbie? Archaeologists and scientists have yet to come to a definitive conclusion.

The Origins of Glamour

Heirs to the artistic and scientific achievements of the Olmecs, the Maya, undisputed representatives of Mexico's golden age, reached their cultural pinnacle in the period between 300 and 600 CE. The Maya flourished in areas of the Chiapas highlands, northern Yucatán, and Guatemala—impressive ruins can be found at Chichén Itzá, Palenque, and Uxmal. Despite the fact they had no metal tools or use of the wheel, the Maya built temples, palaces, altars, stelae (pillar-shaped monuments), calculated a 365-day calendar, and developed a mathematical system, based on the number twenty, which used zero as a value.

A brief glimpse at the characters populating Maya artifacts—in colorful frescoes, pottery decoration, and stelae—reveals their unflagging devotion to fashion and accessories. Gods and nobility (of both genders) adorn themselves with massive headdresses replete with lengthy feathers, necklaces with beads the size of eggs, and gold and copper bracelets to match the enormous bangles hanging from their ear-lobes. An unapologetic Maya get-up would give most participants of Wigstock (the annual New York City drag festival) a run for their money.

The materials of choice for Maya artisans were limestone, sandstone, and to a lesser degree, wood and jade. Using only stone tools, they modeled figurines, vessels, and architectural frieze. A masterwork in bas-relief, the Temple of Inscriptions at Palenque, in one of its scenes, documents pictorially two nobles making offerings to a king sitting on the backs of slaves. Above the figures are numerous glyphs convey-ing religious and calendrical information. Characteristic of Maya relief, contour is pre-dominate and facial features are stylized.

The Aztecs: The Sunset of Indígena Art

Founders of Tenochtitlán (modern-day Mexico City), the Aztecs built a truly remark-able city, sprawling, yet highly organized according to a rectangular grid-plan. In the central area, where important religious events such as human sacrifices were held, pyramids and temples stood majestically as symbols of technological achievement and spiritual devotion.

The clearly stratified society of Tenochtitlán produced an organized labor force that undoubtedly contributed much to the city's marketplace, a center that drew crowds of up to 30,000. From this milieu of expert craftsmanship resulted two of the Aztec's more recognizable and famous creations: the Stone of the Sun (Aztec Calen-dar), measuring nearly four meters in diameter, and Tenochtitlán's great Coatlicue sculpture, a monumental statue almost two-and-a-half meters tall representing the Goddess of the Earth. The Stone of the Sun's narrative is a tragic one: within its con-centric rings are contained the four symbols of previous suns—rain, tiger, water, and wind, the elements responsible for the destruction of earlier populations. Aztecs believed they were living in the period of the fifth sun, and expected to be obliterated by an earthquake, the symbol for which also ominously appears on the stone. But it wasn't a pernicious earthquake that irreversibly altered the Aztec culture—it was the landing of the *conquistadores* in 1521.

The Architecture of New Spain

Not surprisingly, the first examples of colonial art were created specifically to facilitate religious indoctrination. Churches were often constructed on top of Indian temples and pyramids, causing serious and irreparable damage to ancient sites. Volcanic stone, plentiful in most areas, was the main building material. In general, colonial architecture, much of it recalling Romanesque and Gothic stylistic elements, is characterized by the use of huge buttresses, arches, and crenelations (indented or embattled moldings). An architectural phenomenon that developed early on was the open chapel *(capilla abierta)*, a group of arches "enclosing" an atrium. The open chapels were a sort of architectural ideal for they could be built quickly (a good thing in the eyes of the clergy, lest the *indígenas* die heathens), and could accommodate large numbers of worshippers.

The monasteries and churches under the direction of Franciscan, Dominican, and Augustinian missionaries were built according to climactic and geographic limitations. The Franciscan style tended to be functional and economic, the Dominican ascetic and harsh, due to earthquake danger and warm weather. The Augustinian style was clearly the most free-spirited and grandiose, indulging in sumptuous decoration whenever and wherever possible. Remarkable Augustinian buildings include the Monastery of St. Augustin of Acolman near Mexico City and the Monastery of Actopán in Hidalgo state.

A Blossoming of the Baroque

The steady growth and spread of the Catholic church throughout the 17th and 18th centuries necessitated the construction of cathedrals, parochial chapels, and convents; moreover, this period produced the birth and eventual climax of the Baroque style in New Spain. By turns elegant and garish—but always luxurious—Baroque façades teem with dynamic images of angels and saints. The role of art in colonial Mexico, as in the Middle Ages and much of the Renaissance, was to produce a feeling of awe and respect in the hearts of the converted *indígenas*. The narratives set in stone were accessible to the illiterate and easily committed to memory. A look at the cathedrals of Zacatecas and Chihuahua reveals the degree of artistry Baroque ideals encouraged.

Baroque painting found its expression in the works of Alonso López de Herrera, Baltazar de Echave Orío (the elder), Baltazar de Echave Ibía, and Alonso Vázquez. In López de Herrera's the *Assumption of the Virgin,* the holy mother, surrounded by angels, hovers over an enthralled crowd while a sunburst in the background casts a luminous aura about her figure. Similarly, the *Martyrdom of San Ponciano* by de Echave Orío expresses a dramatic religious event through the use of Renaissance conventions, particularly in the figures' gestures and by their hierarchical arrangement on the canvas.

Sumptuousness, frivolity, ornamentation—it appears as though late 18th century artists and builders couldn't have too much of a good thing, and so came the Churrigueresque style, Mexican High Baroque carried to the extreme. The hallmarks of the Churrigueresque are excessively and intricately decorated *estípites* (pilasters); at times these were installed merely for looks and not support. The Church of Santa Prisca in Taxco (p. 313) is a mind-boggling example of Churrigueresque style.

20th Century Murals: The Political Aesthetic

As the Revolution reduced their land to shambles, Mexican painters developed an unapologetic national style. This success was made possible by José Vasconcelos' Ministry of Education program, which commissioned murals for public buildings and sent artists into the countryside to teach and participate in rural life.

The Mexican mural, unequivocally nationalistic in its current form, ironically dates back to the early days of the conquest when Catholic evangelists, fighting the language barrier, used allegorical murals to impart the rudiments of Christian iconography. Diego Rivera is perhaps the most renowned of the *muralistas*. His murals at the Rockefeller Center in New York City and the Palacio Nacional in Mexico City exposed his political themes—land reform, Marxism, the marginalization of *indígena* life—to a wide audience and embroiled him in international controversy. But some later Mexican artists turned against Rivera's didacticism. "Diego Rivera created a completely bureaucratic art," the Mexican abstract painter Juan Soriano once grumbled. "He made himself a propagandist of the victorious revolution...I reproach him for having completely prostituted the pictoral language, reducing it to little more than a caricature, vulgarizing it."

The others in the "Big Four" pantheon were David Alfaro Siqueiros, who brought new materials and dramatic revolutionary themes to his murals; the Cubism-influenced Rufino Tamayo, arguably the most abstract of the four; and José Clemente Orozco. The anguished, dynamic figures in a number of Siqueiros's formally innovative works appear to threaten the boundaries of the picture plane. Orozco focused on the violence and brutality of the Revolution, but was less explicitly political than his colleagues. In his work, the mythic dimension of human history and existence prevails. "Good murals are really painted bibles," Orozco said, "and the people need them as much as written bibles."

Frida Kahlo and the Woman Artist

And where are the women artists? In a culture anchored by misogyny and machismo, within an art world unabashedly biased toward the U. S. and Western Europe, it is not surprising that the art of Mexican women wasn't dealt with seriously until the latter half of this century. Among celebrated 20th-century Mexican women artists are the painters María Izquierdo (she had a lengthy relationship with Rufino Tamayo), Lilia Carrillo, and the photographer Lola Álvarez Bravo.

Due in part to her appalling talent and Hayden Herrera's landmark biography, Frida Kahlo (1907-54) surpasses all other Mexican artists—men included—in terms of current worldwide recognition. Partially paralyzed in a traumatic bus accident at the age of 18, Kahlo married Diego Rivera and was welcomed by Andre Breton into the Surrealist fold of the 1930s. Her paintings and self-portraits are icons of pain: red smudges on the frame of *Unos Cuantos Piquetitos* (A Few Small Nips) project the bed-ridden, writhing body from the canvas into the realm of the viewer. In *La Columna Rota* (The Broken Column), a weeping Kahlo appears in a desolate landscape, her body riddled with nails, a cracking Greek column enmeshed in her body where her spinal chord should be—again, the viewer is forced to confront the artist's self-obsession in its most violent and extreme manifestations. The Museo Frida Kahlo is in the house she shared with Rivera in Coyoacán, Mexico City (p. 108).

LITERATURE

Pre-Hispanic Writing: A Multi-Media Affair

As far as linguists and archaeologists have been able to tell, three languages were dominant in Mexico before the arrival of the Spanish: Náhautl, Mayan, and Cakchiquel. The earliest examples of writing are thought to be the glyphs inscribed at Monte Albán, Oaxaca, a site containing astounding reliefs dating back to 600 BCE. The Spaniards' destructive rampage, particularly in the initial years of the Conquest, and the imposition of the Spanish language resulted in the loss of valuable information relating to *indígena* language. Considered a dangerous affront to Christian teachings, Maya and Aztec codices (unbound "books" or manuscripts) were, naturally, fed to the flames, but due either to the grace of God or less than scrupulous destruction, a number of Maya codices did survive. The Dresden, Paris, and Madrid codices convey important information about divination and the Maya calendar.

The *Popol-Vuh* (Book of Advice), a pre-eminent example of Náhuatl poetry which was kept alive through oral transmission and later recorded in Latin characters, imparts moral counsel and different versions of the Maya creation myth. Along with the *Popol-Vuh,* works such as the *Libros de Chilam Balam* (Books of the Speaker of the Jaguar), transcribed into Maya in 1782, and the Annals of the Cakchiquel cover a range of topics. They are not exclusively historical works, but narrative and poetic, laden with symbolism and lofty metaphor. The *Rabinal Achi* (Knight of Achi), the story of a sacrificed warrior, is considered to be the only surviving example of pre-Hispanic drama. A production even Andrew Lloyd Webber would be proud of, the *Rabinal Achi* was originally performed with elaborate costumes and song and dance routines. The friars were not ones to let a good proselytizing tool get away, and it was no time until they adopted the methods of *indígena* ritual drama to widely disperse Christian teachings.

Colonial Literature

Like astronauts on a new planet, the Spanish were eager to send news home about the land they had conquered and the ways of life of Mexico's indigenous population. These letters home, among them Cortes's *Cartas de relación* (Letters of Relation), were mainly Crown- and Church-flattering documents detailing the exhaustive efforts being undertaken to educate and Christianize *indígenas.* Other chronicles, such as the *Nuevo Mundo y conquista* (New World and Conquest), by Francisco de Terrazas, and *Grandeza Mexicana* (Mexican Grandeur), by Bernardo de Balbuena, were rhymed in order to take the edge off the monotonous melange of factoid stew.

In the harsh and brutal society of New Spain, only religious orders enjoyed the luxury of genuine intellectual freedom. Many clergymen worked to preserve indigenous languages and texts, and a handful of universities sprung up. The Jesuits' 23 colleges were the best in the colony—until the crown expelled the Jesuits from the Americas in 1767 because of their growing influence.

Though historical texts dominated Mexico's literary output throughout much of the 16th and 17th centuries, substantial achievements in poetry were made. Sor Juana Inés de la Cruz (1648-1695) became a master lyricist known for her razor-sharp wit. A *criolla* of illegitimate birth, Sor Juana turned to the cloistered life and married God, instead of the numerous suitors she undoubtedly had—her beauty was legendary. In the Church she found a moral and physical haven where she produced her most famous works, *Respuesta a Sor Filotea* (Response to Sor Filotea) and *Hombres Necios* (Injudicious Men). Her love poems display a passionate sensibility, and many verses display a witty feminism ahead of their time:

¿Cuál es más de culpar,	Who deserves the sterner blame,
aunque cualquiera mal haga:	Though both be wrong:
la que peca por la paga	She who sins for pay,
o el que paga por pecar?	Or he who pays to sin?

Struggling for a Literary Identity

During the 18th century, the Inquisition vied with the French Enlightenment to distract Mexican writers from anything that could be described as innovative. The establishment of the *Academia de la Lengua Española* (Academy of the Spanish

---

Pulp Fiction

If one genre could be said to define Mexico's pop literary scene, it would have to be that of the *revista. Revistas* are most easily likened to American comic books directed towards an adult audience. Filled with colorful pictures, bonehead language, and shallow plot lines, the short "novels" are clearly targeted at the masses. The *revistas* cover a whole range of subject matter, including adventure, romance, politics, science fiction, humor, and religion. The romance theme is probably the most popular, and while from the cover of most *revistas* one would expect a pornographic slant, the stories tend to be relatively tame. *Revistas* have become ingrained into Mexican culture, as some series, such as *Kalimán: El hombre increíble* (since 1965), have been running for decades.

Language) in 1713 grew out of a desire to regulate Spanish where it was spoken, including colonies. An explosion of writing focusing on science occurred about this time. Studies of Mexican geography, weather, flora, and fauna swept away scientists and writers on a wave of rational and analytical thought.

The literary impetus of philosophical movements eventually gave way to political ones. The struggle toward independence, by the end of the 18th century, became the singular social fact from which many Mexican texts grew. In 1816, Jose Fernández de Lizardi, a prominent Mexican journalist, wrote the first Latin American novel: *El periquillo sarniento* (The Itching Parrot), a picaresque tale which revealed Mexican society's displeasure with the status quo. His ideological, moralizing angle on fiction has been very influential. With the Spanish-American modernists of the 19th century, poetry reached an affective level it had not achieved since Sor Juana. At the same time, Manuel Gutierrez Nájera composed the poem *De Blanco* (On Whiteness), linguistic representation at its most distilled and self-contained.

Many romantic novels of the period used historical themes to introduce sweeping indictments of the military and clergy. Novelists sought to define Mexico's national identity, glorifying strength, secularism, progress, and education. Artists were similarly didactic, producing works with such inspirational titles as *Triumph and Study Over Ignorance*. Whereas European romanticism was an aesthetic challenge to Neoclassicism, Mexican romanticism was an artistic response to the country's political and social realities. Shortly after the heyday of the romantic novel came the popular novel of manners, significant among them being *El fistol del diablo* by Manuel Payno, *Juanita Sousa* and *Antón Pérez* by Manuel Sánchez Mármol.

Literature during the Porfiriato (1876-1911) abandoned romanticism for realism, and most writers expressed little sympathy with the poor. Wrote José López Portillo y Rojas, the preeminent realist of the period, "Our workers will come out of their abject condition when they aspire to eat well, to dress decently, and to acquire the comforts of life." Others adopted a modernist style, emphasizing language and imagery, and replacing didactic social themes with psychological topics. Visual artists, by contrast, had begun to reject the creed of the *científicos*. Many favored experimental techniques and chose to depict slums, brothels, and scenes from indigenous life. Their iconoclasm foreshadowed a growing dissatisfaction with the Díaz regime.

20th Century Global Perspectives

Mexican literature in the post-Revolutionary era is marked by a frustrated desire to forge a national tradition from the vestiges of pre-colonial culture. Nobel prize winner Octavio Paz, in such works as *El laberinto de la soledad* (The Labyrinth of Solitude), draws on Marxism, romanticism and post-Modernism to explore the making and unmaking of a national archetype. Paz, like his equally famous successor Carlos Fuentes, concerns himself with myth and legend in an effort to come to terms with Spanish cultural dominance. Fuentes, one of Mexico's more celebrated authors, published his first novel, *La region más transparente*, in 1958. His latest novel, *Cristobal nonato* (Christopher Unborn), chronicles the lengthy search for a god-head who will accurately and unproblematically personify the true spirit of the Mexican people. Juan Rulfo's *Pedro Páramo*, set in rural Jalisco, blurs the line between life and death, past and present, as it relates one man's search for his father.

Since the 1960s, Mexican literature has become even more pluralistic. The wildly popular works of Gustavo Sainz and Jose Agustín, the instigators of *literatura de la onda* ("hip" literature), address universal concerns like getting laid and getting stoned. Of late, the work of female writers, such as Hollywood darling Laura Esquivel, has been well received both nationally and internationally.

POPULAR CULTURE

Music

Like most other components of its culture, Mexican music is an eclectic stew of styles and flavors borrowed from all across the continent and overseas. Mexico's traditional music is mostly regional, making for a rich and varied collage of styles and artists. Up north, one will hear groups such as Los Bukis, Bronco, and Los Tigres del Norte sing in the style aptly labeled *norteño*. One of the more popular and well-known styles of traditional Mexican music is *mariachi*, which is especially popular in Jalisco, but heard all over the country. *Mariachi* songs, commonly called *rancheras,* are usually played live, and the world-famous tradition of women being serenaded by a group of *mariachis* in traditional Mexican garb is seen as an almost obligatory supplement to a romantic evening—foreplay, if you will. Traditionally macho *rancheras* tend to deal with one or several of the following topics: being very drunk, being abandoned by a woman, being cheated on by a woman, getting drunk, leaving a woman, the fidelity of one's horse, one's gun, and wanting to get drunk. While male singers like José Alfredo Jiménez and Vicente Fernández continue to sing popular tunes in this tradition, Lupita D'Alessio provides the angry-woman response. Although she gets betrayed or left on almost every one of her songs, the culprit men often get their due.

The Mexican music scene is adorned with both Spanish and American influences. The former is apparent with young artists such as the pop group Garibaldi, whose scantily clad bods perennially grace (disgrace?) music and teen fanzines. Travelers from up north won't feel too far from home, as American music in all forms is ubiquitous both on the radio and in bars and *discotecas*. Always striving to Mexicanize imports in some way, Mexican artists will often take an American piece and make it their "own" with altered lyrics or a slightly more Latin beat. At last glance, Michael Jackson, Madonna, Aerosmith, Nirvana, The Cranberries, and Whitney Houston all mirrored the popularity they enjoy in the U.S. Cotton-candy pop is sung by such artists as Luis Miguel (sigh), Lucero, Alejandra Guzmán, and Christian Castro.

Television

Mexican television can, for the most part, be broken down into four categories: *telenovelas* (soap operas), weekly dramas, sitcoms, and imported American shows. *Telenovelas* are by far the most popular and widely aired of the bunch. Occupying a huge block of air time from noon to early evening, these hour-long shameless examples of dramaturgy tend to run for two to four months before being ousted for a fresh group of characters and convoluted conflicts. Don't be surprised if you witness Erik Estrada (yes, that's Frank "Ponch" Poncherello of CHiPs) embroiled in a Spanish-language love triangle.

The half-hour sitcoms that dominate American TV don't seem to be as popular in Mexico, though there are a few. Popular shows include *Papá Soltero, Chespirito,* and just about anything on the *Canal de las Estrellas.*

American shows are often dubbed, though they can be found in their original English forms on cable television, which is out of the financial reach of many Mexicans. As in the U.S., shows such as Melrose Place (featuring Heather Locklear's boundless treachery) and Baywatch (showcasing Pamela Anderson's truly amazing life-saving techniques) are very popular. Cartoons are imported from both the U.S. and Japan. One cannot claim to have lived fully without having watched at least one episode of *Los Simpson.*

Film

"Popular cinema is still alive and well in Mexico," wrote one disgruntled director, "mainly as sex comedies and cop dramas." The recent recession, as well as a lack of fiscal support to IMCINE, the umbrella organization that finances Mexican films, has led to an influx of subtitled Hollywood imports.

Mexico's golden age of cinema *(cine de oro)* was kicked off in the 1940s and 50s with Emilio "El Indio" Fernández's *María Candelaría* (1943), an honoree at the first Cannes Film Festival in 1946, and Luis Buñuel's *Los Olvidados* (1950), a grisly portrait of barrio life in Mexico City. The past decade has seen the rise of such luminaries as Arturo Ripstein *(La Mujer del Puerto; Reina de la Noche),* Jorge Fons *(Rojo Amancecer),* and Paul Leduc. Known for his experiments without dialogue, Leduc's *Frida* provides an unsettling look at one of Mexico's more controversial cultural icons. The one Mexican film that has enjoyed enormous cross-over success is *Como agua para chocolate* (Like Water for Chocolate), based on the best-selling Laura Esquivel novel and directed by Alfonso Arau, her now ex-husband. A family saga with a supernatural edge, some critics quibble that *Como agua para chocolate* is "a syrupy fantasy... no more about Mexico than the *The Lion King* is about Africa." The film may have well been geared towards an American audience; it has the distinction of being the highest-grossing foreign film in U.S. history.

FOOD AND DRINK

Mexican food isn't just good; it's **orgasmic.** In Laura Esquivel's *Como agua para chocolate,* Tita, the young protagonist, tastes her latest creation and finds it "voluptuously, ardently fragrant, and utterly sensual." There's no denying it; Mexican food is in a class by itself, and visitors should prepare themselves for the rich sensual experience that is Mexican dining. Although you will find a Taco Bell billboard on the border at Nogales, real Mexican food (like most foreign cuisines) bears little resemblance to its counterpart across the border.

Mexicans usually choose to have their big meal of the day—the *comida*—between 2 and 4pm. Restaurants often offer *comida corrida,* sometimes called *la comida* or *el menú,* a fixed price meal including soup, salad, tea or *agua fresca,* a *plato fuerte* (main dish), and sometimes a dessert. The main dish is often a *guisado*—a soup or stew with meat—although a *caldo* (broth-like soup) and a regular plate of meat are also common; *arroz* (rice, sometimes *con huevo,* with chopped egg), beans, and tortillas are always included; as often is dessert. Breakfasts *(desayunos)* range from the continental-style *café con leche* (thick coffee with steamed milk) and pastry to *almuerzos,* almost a full meal with eggs, steak, or other meat. Dinner *(cena)* is usually a light meal served around 8pm.

The Staples

From tacos slapped together at a roadside *taquería* to a magnificent plate full of garlic shrimp or chicken with *mole* sauce, Mexican food invariably maintains one common link: the tortilla. This most ubiquitous staple of Mexican cuisine is a flat, round, thin pancake made from either wheat flour *(harina),* or, more often, corn flour *(maíz).* You will surely develop a preference for one or the other early on, and most restaurants will let you choose which kind you want with your *antojito* or full meal.

The other two staples of Mexican food are the always cheap, always filling, and most nutritious pair—rice and beans. Rice *(arroz)* is usually standard fare; yellow Spanish or Mexican rice prepared with oil and tomato sauce is a special treat. Beans

---

The Breakfast Club

Aside from the standard *café con leche* or *pan dulce* (sweetened bread), almost any breakfast in Mexico will include eggs in some shape or form. *Huevos al gusto* (eggs any style) provides people with a choice of *jamón* (ham), *tocino* (bacon), or *machaca* (dried, shredded beef). Tortillas, *frijoles,* and sometimes rice or *papas fritas* (french fries) are served on the side. The eggs themselves are usually *revueltos* (scrambled) with the meat mixed in, but you can ask for the meat fried on the side or the eggs *estrellados* (fried) instead. Other popular styles of preparing *huevos* include *rancheros* (fried eggs served on corn tortillas and covered with a spicy red salsa), *albañil* (scrambled eggs cooked in green sauce), *a la mexicana* (scrambled with onion, tomato, and chopped green chile), *motuleños* (fried eggs served on a fried corn tortilla, topped with sauteed green peas and ham, sam i am), and *ahogados* (eggs cooked in boiling red sauce), and *borrachos* (fried eggs served with beans cooked in beer). More expensive Mexican breakfasts include omelettes with any of the above meats, seafood such as *camarones* (shrimp), or even *langosta* (lobster) and *pan francés* (french toast).

(frijoles) are soft and range from soupy to pasty *(refritos)*. These three foods will be served in various forms with just about every full plate of food you order, be it breakfast, lunch, or dinner.

Ah, Antojitos

Antojito comes from the word *antojo,* craving. Although anything could be an *antojito,* the term is often, but not always, restricted to eight categories. Tacos are small, grilled chunks of meat (sometimes chicken, fried fish, or fried shellfish) placed on an open, warm tortilla, left for you to top yourself with a row of condiments ranging from lettuce and tomato to guacamole and hot sauce. Burritos are thin, rolled flour tortillas filled with meat (often *machaca*, chicken, or beans) and a few cooked vegetables such as green peppers and onions. Occasionally you will see tex-mex-style *súper burritos* filled with everything but the kitchen sink. Burritos in general are not very common in the southern parts of Mexico. Enchiladas are corn tortillas filled with meat or chicken, topped with red or green sauce and shredded cheese, and then baked or fried. Some variations exist, such as enchiladas *suizas* (topped with sour cream) or enchiladas *de mole. Quesadillas* are filled with melted cheddar cheese. Sometimes other things are added: with ham they become *sincronizadas,* with *pastor* (gyro style) pork meat, *gringas. Tostadas* consist of a deep-fried tortilla garnished with vegetables, cheese, and almost anything else, from meat or chicken to exotic seafood like *pulpo* (octopus). *Tostadas* are the only *antojito* to which raw vegetables are always added; prudent travelers should beware of uncooked vegetables, especially lettuce, while in Mexico. A *chile relleno,* a unique and wonderful Mexican creation, consists of a large, green chile pepper stuffed with cheese (and occasionally meat), dipped in a batter, fried, and topped with red *salsa.* They are not particularly *picante* (spicy-hot)—the frying process rids the chile of most of its potency. *Tamales,* also unique, are ground-corn dough packed with meat or chicken in corn husks; they have the consistency of thick dumplings. Finally, *chimichangas* are essentially the same as burritos but deep fried to produce a rich, crunchy, artery-hardening shell.

Meats, Poultry, and Seafood

Meat platters are usually either *bistek* (derived from the little-used English term "beefsteak"), which is a standard fried cut of beef; *carne asada,* thin slices of beef fried until crispy; or a pricier cut of steak such as T-bone, filet mignon, or New York steak (English names are used). The meat can be prepared normally (it's usually served fairly well done), *empanizada* or *milanesa* (breaded or fried), or *a la mexicana* which means served charred up and topped with a Mexican red *salsa. Encebollado* means served with grilled onions. In any case, meat dishes are accompanied by *arroz, frijoles,* tortillas, and sometimes *papas fritas.*

   Pollo (chicken), if by itself or included in a platter, is either *rostizado* (spit-roasted over an open fire, "rotisserrie"-style) or *asado* (grilled), served with the same side dishes mentioned above.

   Seafood dishes include *pescado* (generic fish fillet, usually a local catch), *camarones* (shrimp), *langosta* (lobster), *calamar* (fillet of squid), and *huachinango* (the exceedingly tasty red snapper, with the name that's as fun to pronounce—wa-chee-NAAN-go—as it is to eat). Seafood is usually served either *empanizado* (breaded and fried) or *al mojo de ajo* (in garlic). *A la veracruzana* is a special preparation, native to Veracruz, in which the fish is decked out in olives, capers, and olive oil.

When You Get Thirsty

Cerveza (beer) ranks only slightly below tortillas and beans on the list of Mexican staples. It is impossible to drive through a Mexican town, anywhere, without coming across a double-digit number of Tecate (and, only slightly less so, *Corona*) billboards, painted buildings, and *agencias,* cheap beer stores, selling anywhere from one beer to several cases at a time. *Tecate* is Mexico's version of Budweiser—it's cheap and none too good. Popular pilsner beers in Mexico (listed in order of quality) are *Bohemia* (a world-famous, outstanding beer), *Pacífico, Dos Equis, Corona Extra, Carta*

Blanca, Modelo, and the unfortunate *Tecate.* Lovers of dark beer will enjoy delicious *Negra Modelo.*

Tequila is king when it comes to Mexican liquor. It is the quintessential Mexican drink, a famous version of *mezcal* (distilled from the *maguey* cactus). *Herradura, Tres Generaciones,* and *Cuervo 1800* are among the more famous, more expensive, and better brands of *tequila.* Cheap *tequila* can be bought for prices you wouldn't believe: one Hermosillo supermarket frequently advertises a liter of tequila for US80¢! Non-*tequila mezcal,* found mainly in Oaxaca, is sometimes served with the worm native to the plant—upon downing the shot, you are expected to ingest the worm. Some say it induces hallucination; however, evidence is to the contrary. If you get a chance to sample *pulque,* the fermented juice of the *maguey,* don't hesitate—it was the sacred drink of the Aztec nobility.

Fear not, there are non-alcoholic drinks in Mexico. Coca-Cola ("Coca") is perhaps even more universal in Mexico than in the U.S. Pepsi, Sprite, 7-Up, and orange sodas are also available, as expected, as are some unique Mexican *refrescos* (sodas). *Soda de fresca* (strawberry soda) is delicious; also try *soda de piña* (pineapple soda), *toronja* (grapefruit soda), *manzanita* (apple soda), and *sangría* (a non-alcoholic, carbonated version of wine with fruit juice). Soda rarely costs more than 4 pesos (US65¢), even at fancy restaurants, and usually costs between 2 and 3 pesos (US32-48¢) for a bottle or can. *Aguas frescas,* including *limonada* (lemonade), are fruit-based drinks with sugar. Don't miss delicious *aguas de horchata* (sweetened rice and cinnamon), *tamarindo* (tamarind), and *jamaica* (jamaica flower). Don't drink them, however, unless you're sure they're purified, and that includes the *hielo* (ice).

INTRODUCTION

Mexico City

"City" is not really the word for it: the 1,480 square kilometers of urban settlement that line the Valley of Mexico constitute far more than one single city. The high-efficiency bustle of the executive areas on Reforma, the impoverished neighborhoods on the northern outskirts, the commercial coagulation of the *centro,* and the wealthy southern ultra-suburbs of Coyoacán and San Ángel cohabitate under the omnipresent smog. The impromptu shantytowns that sprawl out bereft of public support are themselves as large as cities—one of them, Ciudad Netzahualcóyotl, is home to two million inhabitants.

This phoenix-like metropolis contains a plurality of cities, and no one can decide upon a single significance for any structure. The massive Templo Mayor, the main religious building of the Aztec empire that once claimed the valley as its own, stands next to the grand Catedral Metropolitana, the object of both profound reverence and bitter resentment at the economic and cultural imperialism of the colonizers. A few blocks away from the cathedral stands the Palacio de Bellas Artes, a glorious symbol of modern Mexico built by the dictator Porfirio Díaz, whose grand projects also sapped the money of a struggling nation. A kilometer to the west, the Monumento a la Revolución, originally intended by Díaz as the spectacular seat of his regime's legislature, commemorates ten years of bloody struggle to establish a more just society—a fight that had a questionable outcome.

Mexicans call this oxymoronic conglomeration **el D.F.** (DEH-effeh), short for *Distrito Federal* (Federal District), or simply *México*. The *defectuoso* (defective), as local *chilangos* teasingly call the city, is a breeding ground for staggering statistics. It is home to between 20 and 25 million people and has over 220 *colonias* (neighborhoods). Virtually the entire federal bureaucracy inhabits the D.F., including the Ministry of the Navy—2240m above sea level. The principal national collections of art, ethnography, and archaeology are also found here; the gargantuan Museo Nacional de Antropología is reason enough for a visit. The Aztec Templo Mayor still inspires awe. Spectacular mosaics and murals by Rivera, Orozco, Siqueiros, and Tamayo adorn the walls of the city.

While people from all around the country continue to arrive in hopes of finding scarce jobs, Mexico City's infamous demographic crisis becomes more difficult to ignore. As rural migrants flock to the shantytowns on the city's edge and the city expands to engulf their abandoned plots, the prospect of feeding everyone becomes increasingly unrealistic. With serious water shortages, citizens curse the topography of their metropolis: landlocked and ringed by mountains, it lets neither water in nor sewage out. The enclosed valley also traps in poisonous air pollution, perhaps the most immediate of the city's many environmental concerns.

One-quarter of Mexico's population lives in the D.F., and one-quarter of those are employed as *comerciantes,* the independent vendors who crowd the streets, struggling to survive with a patience and tenacity characteristically Mexican. The city lives loudly, quickly, and unabashedly—it has neither the space nor the desire to hide its history, culture, and manic vitality. Even art takes on this massive and external character in the immense and awesome murals that celebrate Mexican life. Here, no one buries the ruined triumphs and fiascoes of the past nor apologizes for the excesses of the present.

◾ Getting There

All roads lead to Mexico City. Buses, trains, and planes haul passengers from every town in the republic into the smoggy hyperactivity of the city's many temples of transport—the expanding Benito Juárez International Airport, four crowded bus stations, a desolate train station, and a network of freeways. Fortuitously, airports and stations in Mexico City nearly always have information booths for frazzled tourists

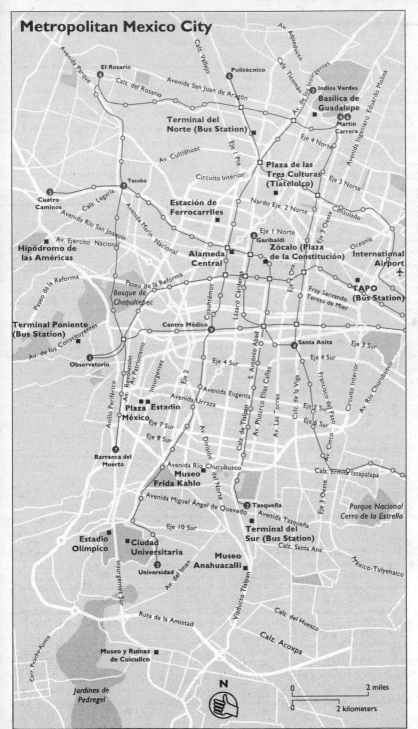

Metropolitan Mexico City

Avenida Parque

Calz. Valleio

Av. Aqueducto

Av. de los Insurgentes

El Rosario **6**

Politécnico **5**

Calz. Ticoman

Indios Verdes **3**

Calz. del Rosario

Avenida San Juan de Aragón

Basílica de
Guadalupe

4 4

Martín
Carrera

Terminal del
Norte (Bus Station)

Eje 4 Norte

Av. Cultláhuac

Eje I Pte.

Avenida Ingeniero Eduardo Molina

Circuito Interior

Plaza de las
Tres Culturas
(Tlatelolco)

Eje 3 Norte

Tacuba **7**

Estación de
Ferrocarrlles

Nardo Eje 2 Norte

Consulado

Cuatro
Caminos **2**

Calz. Legaria

Avenida Río San Joaquín

Avenida Marín Nacional

Eje 3 Oeste

Oceanía

International
Airport

Av. Ejército Nacional

Eje 1 Norte

8 Garibaldi

Hipódromo de
las Américas

Alameda
Central

Zócalo (Plaza
de la Constitución)

Eje Ote.

Paseo de la Reforma

Paseo de la Reforma

Bosque de
Chapultepec

Cuauhtémoc

Lázaro Cárdenas

Eje Ote.

TAPO
(Bus Station)

Fray Servando
Teresa de Mier

Terminal Poniente
(Bus Station)

Centro Médico **9**

Av. de los Constituyentes

Observatorio **1**

Av. Revolución

Av. Patriotismo

Insurgentes

Eje 4 Sur

S. Antonio Abad

Santa Anita **6**

Eje 4 Sur

Eje 3 Sur

Eje 2

Avenida Eugenia

Av. Plutarco Elías Calles

Av. Las Torres

Calz. de la Viga

Francisco del Paso

Circuito Interior

Av. Río Churubusco

Avenida Urraza

Plaza
México

Estadio

Eje 7 Sur

Av. División

Calz. de Tlalpan

Eje 5 Sur

Eje 6 Sur

Av. Cinco

Eje 8 Sur

Barranca del
Muerto **7**

Avenida Río Churubusco

del Norte

Museo
Frida Kahlo

Avenida Miguel Ángel de Quevedo

Tasqueña **2**

Avenida Tasqueña

Eje 3 Oeste

Parque Nacional
Cerro de la Estrella

Eje 10 Sur

Terminal del
Sur (Bus Station)

Calz. Ermita Iztapalapa

México-Tulyehaico

Estadio
Olímpico

Ciudad
Universitaria

Museo
Anahuacalli

Calz. Santa Ana

Universidad **3**

Insurgentes Sur

Av. del Imán

Viaducto Tlalpan

Calz. del Huesco

Ruta de la Amistad

Calz. Acoxpa

Carr. Picacho-Ajusco

Museo y Ruínas
de Cuicuilco

Jardines de
Pedregal

N

0   2 miles

0   2 kilometers

MEXICO CITY

equipped with quasi-English-speaking personnel, free or cheap maps, some sort of referral service to lead you into the *centro,* and heaps of advice.

BY AIR

Flying into Mexico City from abroad entails the usual customs and immigration procedures. **Tourist cards (FMTs)** are distributed on the plane and stamped at the airport. Although many border officials are lax about enforcement, the "stoplight" customs system at the airport ensures that a certain percentage of random passengers are inspected—those unlucky enough to get a red light. Be prepared to allow an agent to sift through your silky intimates.

The **Benito Juárez International Airport** (tel. 571-32-95) lies 6.5km east of the *zócalo,* the formal center of the city. Blvd. Capitán Juan Sarabio heads northeast to the airport from Blvd. Puerto Aéreo, one of the major roads circling the city. The airport is jam-packed with facilities:

Tourist Office: INFOTUR, *Sala* A and *Sala* F (tel. 762-6-63 or -73). Invaluable information and free maps of the city and the Metro. Pick up a copy of *Concierge,* an incredibly comprehensive guide to hotels, restaurants, and attractions mapped out for the various regions of the city. Open daily 8am-9pm, and often after hours.

Cultural Information: Instituto Nacional de Antropología e Historia, *Sala* A. Information about archaeological sites and museums throughout the country. Open Mon.-Sat. 8am-10pm, Sun. 8am-3pm.

Hotel Reservations: In *Sala* E. Name an area and they'll make the reservation for you. No charge, but be prepared to pay for the first night on the spot. English spoken. Open daily 7am-midnight.

Currency Exchange: Banks exchange currency and traveler's checks at branches in different *salas.* **ATMs** in *Sala* A, directly under *Sala* B, and scattered throughout *Salas* E, F, and H. *Casas de cambio* in *Salas* B, D, and E. Open 6am-10pm.

Telephones: LADATELs around the airport accept phonecards sold at nearby magazine stands. Some phones take international credit cards. Long-distance **caseta** at the end of the international concourse, past *Sala* F. Open 7am-8pm.

Telegrams: In *Sala* A. Open Mon.-Fri. 9am-8pm, Sat. 9am-noon.

Car Rental: In *Sala* E (see p. 81).

Storage Lockers: Next to the snack bar, to the left of the arrival gate in *Sala* A and in *Sala* E. Storage 18 pesos per 24hr., 20-50 pesos for larger bags.

Bookstore: In *Sala* F, on the second floor. Novels in Spanish and English. Maps available. Open Mon.-Sat. 7am-9:30pm, Sun. 8am-8pm.

Pharmacy: In *Sala* C. Open daily 6am-10pm.

Restaurants and **cafeterias** are open 24hr.

Insurance: In *Sala* B, in two locations.

Maps and Mexican Statistics: In *Sala* B. Open 7am-9pm.

Lost and Found: Bags overflow in a small room next to Aeropost in *Sala* D.

Police Office: (tel. 625-70-07). Outside the airport in front of *Sala* C. Open 24hr.

Post Office: In *Sala* A. Open Mon.-Fri. 8am-7pm, Sat. 9am-5pm.

Flight info: Call tel. 571-36-00 or 571-44-00, then specify domestic or international.

Carriers: *Sala* A: All **Aeroméxico,** baby. Has the most complete air transportation throughout the republic. *Sala* B: **Mexicana** plays a strong second fiddle. *Sala* C: Really tiny, with only **AVIACSA** and **Aeroexco.** *Sala* D: **TAESA, ALLEGRO,** and charter flights. *Sala* E: International arrivals. *Sala* F_1: **Delta, America West, Continental, Avianca,** and **Lan Chile.** *Sala* F_2: The big one! **KLM, Northwest, Copa, Lufthansa, Air France, British Airways, Lacsa, Taca, Aviateca, Malaysia, Varig, JAL, Canadian,** and **Cubana.** *Sala* F_3: **American Airlines, Iberia,** and **United Airlines.**

Domestic Flights: Flight schedules and prices change frequently. Prices are roughly the same from airline to airline. There are usually no discounts for students, but always ask about *tarifas promocionales,* which can save you up to 50%. Either of the following two airlines can take you anywhere in the country, provided there's an airport. **Aeroméxico,** Paseo de la Reforma 445 (tel. 327-40-00), close to Mississippi, and Reforma 80 (tel. 566-1078). Both open Mon.-Sat. 9am-6:15pm. At the airport, *Sala* A (tel. 762-18-18). Open daily 5am-10pm. **Mexicana,** Amberes and Reforma 312 (tel. 511-04-24), in the Zona Rosa, and Reforma 51 (tel. 592-17-71), at Lafragua. Both open Mon.-Fri. 9am-6pm. At the airport, *Sala* B (tel. 227-02-61, for reservations 325-09-90). Open daily 6am-11:30pm.

International Flights: Air Canada, Hamburgo 108, 5th floor (tel. 280-3434 or 281-4581). **Air France,** Reforma 404, 15th floor (tel. 627-6000 or -6060, at airport 571-6150). **American,** Reforma 314, 1st floor (tel. 209-1400, at airport 571-3219). **British Airways,** Reforma 10, 14th floor (tel. 628-0500, toll-free 91-800-00-657). **Canadian Airlines,** Reforma 390-1402 (tel. 208-18-83). **Continental,** Andrés Bello 45 (tel. 280-34-34, toll-free 91-800-90-050, at airport 571-3665). **United,** Hamburgo 213, ground floor (tel. 627-0222, toll-free 91-800-00-307). **Delta,** Reforma 381 (tel. 202-16-08 or 207-34-11, toll-free 91-800-90-221, at airport 571-3237). **KLM,** Paseo de las Palmas 735, 7th floor (tel. 202-4444, toll-free 91-800-90-747, at airport 571-3246). **Lufthansa,** Las Palmas 239 (tel. 230-0000, toll-free 91-800-90-600, at airport 571-2713). **Swissair,** Hamburgo 66, 3rd floor (tel. 207-2455). **Aeroméxico** and **Mexicana** fly to Central America and the U.S.

Transportation into the city is uncomplicated. Buy a *transporte terrestre* ticket from the *venta de boletos* desk in *Sala* A and *Sala* E, and present it to any of the white-and-yellow authorized taxis waiting outside. The price is set by the zone of the city you're traveling to (47 pesos to the *centro,* 20% more after-hours). Ask to see the map—just because it's an official-looking booth does not mean you won't be overcharged. Avoid unauthorized taxis: they will invariably rip you off. Call 784-48-11 or 571-36-00 (both available 24hr.) to get a taxi back to the airport from the city. For more taxi etiquette, see p. 80.

The Metro is by far the cheapest (1 peso) route to the city. The airport **subway** station, **Terminal Aérea** (Line 5), located at the junction of Capitán Juan Sarabio and Blvd. Puerto Aéreo, is only a ten-minute walk from *Sala* E. Signs will point you in the right direction (see p. 78 for the scoop on the Metro). Large bags are officially prohibited, but it's not uncommon for somebody to waltz aboard with bulky items. Provided you avoid rush hours and can maneuver through the turnstile, a typical pack should not pose much of a problem. For your own safety and the comfort of others, remove the pack from your back when you're on the subway. Also, try to ride in the less crowded first or last cars. If a train appears frighteningly jam-packed, simply let it pass; another will arrive within minutes. **If you return to the airport by Metro, do not get off at the Aeropuerto stop. The correct stop is Terminal Aérea.**

BY TRAIN

Estación Buenavista of the **Ferrocarriles Nacionales de México** (tel. 547-10-97) is located north of the **Monumento de la Revolución** at the corner of Insurgentes and Mosqueta (Eje 1 Alzate), five long blocks from the nearest Metro station, Revolución (Line 2; open daily 6am-10pm). **Taxis** leave from the parking lot on the Mosqueta side of the main building. Be sure to check the meter and the official fare chart in the cab before you pay, as abuses are par for the course.

An **information booth** (tel. 547-10-84, -97, or 91-800-90-392 for tourist info) to the left of the ticket windows does little more than dispense train schedules (information booth and the ticket windows open daily 6:30am to 9:30pm). Get train information in English from the **Departamento de Tráfico de Pasajeros,** hidden off to the right of long-distance booth #6 in the main station lobby (tel. 547-86-55; fax 547-89-72; open Mon.-Fri. 6am-10pm). The station has a **long-distance phone/fax service** (open Mon.-Sat. 8am-9:30pm, Sun. 9am-3pm) and a 24-hour **ATM. Luggage storage** is provided in the second-class area, down the walkway from the main *sala* (10 pesos per day; open daily 6:30am-9:30pm). There are also a few 24-hour restaurants.

Mexican trains tend to be **excruciatingly slow** (for more on that, see p. 41). The fastest routes—to Guadalajara (12hr.), Veracruz (14hr.), and Monterrey (17hr.)—are barely bearable. Other popular destinations from Mexico City include Ciudad Juárez

(23hr.), Oaxaca (14½hr.), and Nuevo Laredo (22hr.). There are four classes of trains: *primera especial* (first-class reserved, without bed), *dormitorio camarín* (reserved, with two separate beds per compartment), *alcoba* (reserved, with bunk bed), and *primera general* (unreserved). First-class tickets can be purchased up to a month in advance. Other than *Semana Santa,* spots are usually available up to one hour before departure. Buying second-class tickets is as unpleasant as riding second-class trains; arrive at the station five hours early to stand in the snail-paced line.

BY BUS

Mexico City's four main bus stations correspond to the points of the compass. **Central de Autobuses del Norte** (North Station) serves the Bajío, northern Veracruz, Jalisco, and most of northern Mexico; **Terminal Central de Autobuses del Sur** (South Station) launches buses to Morelos, Guerrero, and Oaxaca; **Terminal de Autobuses de Pasajeros de Oriente (TAPO)** (East Station) sends buses to Puebla, southern Veracruz, Oaxaca, Chiapas, and the Yucatán Peninsula; and the **Terminal de Autobuses del Poniente** (West Station) serves México state and Michoacán.

All stations are served by the Metro and offer an official 24-hour taxi service that charges fixed rates for a ride to any point in the city (rates set by zones) or adjacent parts of Mexico state. Buy your ticket inside to avoid a rip-off, but be wary of being charged for an extra zone—if you can find it, consult the zone map. *Peseros* (a.k.a. *colectivos*) also serve the four stations. Quality budget hotels near the bus stations (see p. 89) are rare; it's a much safer bet to head toward the city center. The following listings are by no means comprehensive; given the extensive network, it is possible to go almost anywhere at any time.

Central de Autobuses del Norte

The Central de Autobuses del Norte (tel. 587-15-52) is on Cien Metros, Metro station Autobuses del Norte (Line 5). Banamex ATM, restaurant, and luggage storage (10-20 pesos per 24hr., or 1.50 pesos per hr.) are all open around the clock. A *casa de cambio* near the main entrance offers poor rates (open Mon.-Fri. 7am-9pm, Sat.-Sun. 8am-4pm). The post office and telegram office are nearby (open Mon.-Fri. 8am-5pm, Sat. 8am-1pm). A "Hoteles Asociados" (hotel reservations service) booth is occasionally open near the main entrance (supposedly open 8am-9pm). More companies than those listed below operate out of this terminal/zoo. They are listed in the order they appear from waiting room 1 to 8.

Transportes del Norte (tel. 587-54-00). To Cd. Juárez (6 per day, 24hr., 461 pesos), Celaya (7 per day, 3½hr., 68 pesos), Matamoros (1 per day, 15hr., 261 pesos), Matehuala (2 per day, 8hr., 153 pesos), Monterrey (every hr. from 7am, 12hr., 234 pesos), Nuevo Laredo (4 per day, 15hr., 300 pesos), Reynosa (2 per day, 15hr., 263 pesos), Saltillo (2 per day, 10hr., 212 pesos), and San Luis Potosí (2 per day, 5hr., 212 pesos).

Ómnibus de México (tel. 567-67-58 or 567-72-87). To Aguascalientes (6 per day, 6½hr., 137 pesos), Cd. Valles (6 per day, 9hr., 73 pesos), Colima (3 per day, 13hr., 190 pesos), Durango (7 per day, 12hr., 228 pesos), Fresnillo (11 per day, 9hr., 174 pesos), Guadalajara (12 per day, 8hr., 164 pesos), Guanajuato (3 per day, 5hr., 93 pesos), Querétaro (every 30min., 3hr., 54 pesos), Tampico (8 per day, 9hr., 130 pesos), and Zacatecas (15 per day, 8hr., 161 pesos).

Autobuses de Oriente (ADO; tel. 587-66-88). **GL *ejecutivo*** (first-class) and **UNO** (mega-luxury, with huge leather chairs and cafeteria) service. To Jalapa (2 per day, 5½hr., 75 pesos), Oaxaca (2 per day, 6hr., 115 pesos), Papantla (5 per day, 6hr., 67 pesos), Puebla (every 30min., 2hr., 34 pesos), Tuxpan (7 per day, 5hr., 75 pesos), and Veracruz (4 per day, 9hr., 107 pesos).

Elite. To Celaya (5 per pay, 3½hr., 68 pesos), Colima (2 per day, 3hr., 190 pesos), Guadalajara (7 per day, 8hr., 164 pesos), Los Mochis (15 per day, 24hr., 436 pesos), Manzanillo (2 per day, 14hr., 198 pesos), Mazatlán (15 per day, 16hr., 314 pesos), Puerto Vallarta (4 per day, 14hr., 292 pesos), Tepic (12 per day, 12hr., 238 pesos), and Tijuana (9 per day, 42hr., 600 pesos).

Estrella Blanca (tel. 587-54-00). To Chihuahua (8:30pm, 20hr., 318 pesos), Durango (1:15am, 12hr., 196 pesos), San Luis Potosí (every hr., 5hr., 91 pesos), Torreón (8:30pm, 14hr., 223 pesos), and Zacatecas (4 per day, 9hr., 136 pesos).
Futura (587-5511). To Acapulco (7 per day, 5hr., 135 pesos), Aguascalientes (13 per day, 6½hr., 137 pesos), Cd. Juárez (4 per day, 24hr., 461 pesos), Chihuahua (4 per day, 20hr., 368 pesos), Matamoros (3 per day, 15hr., 261 pesos), Monterrey (7 per day, 12hr., 234 pesos), and Tampico (3 per day, 9hr., 130 pesos).
Frontera (587-1712). To Cd. Victoria (4 per day, 10hr., 163 pesos), Matehuala (5 per day, 8hr., 132 pesos), Monterrey (7 per day, 12hr., 201 pesos), Nuevo Laredo (6 per day, 15hr., 261 pesos), and Saltillo (3 per day, 10hr., 183 pesos).
Flecha Amarilla (tel. 587-52-00). Second-class service to Guadalajara (every hr., 9hr., 144 pesos), Guanajuato (2 per day, 5hr., 83 pesos), León (every hr., 5hr., 88 pesos), Manzanillo (3 per day, 16hr., 185 pesos), Morelia (every 40min., 5hr., 77 pesos), Querétaro (every 15min., 3½hr., 45 pesos), San Luis Potosí (9 per day, 6hr., 90 pesos), and San Miguel de Allende (every 40min., 4hr., 58 pesos).

Terminal de Autobuses de Pasajeros de Oriente (TAPO)

The TAPO (tel. 762-59-77) is on General Ignacio Zaragoza 200, adjacent to Metro station San Lázaro (Line 1). Ticket counters await in a rotunda at the end of a long, store-lined passageway. Helpful police booths are scattered throughout the station. A tourist information kiosk (supposedly open daily 10am-8pm) and taxi ticket booths are near the entrance to the Metro. The station also contains a 24-hour ATM, restaurant, pharmacy, and currency exchange services (open daily 7am-11pm).

Autobuses Unidos (AU; tel. 542-42-10, ext. 19). To Córdoba (35 per day, 5hr., 82 pesos), Oaxaca (11 per day, 9hr., 99 pesos), San Andrés Tuxtla (2 per day, 9½hr., 121 pesos), and Xalapa (18 per day, 5hr., 69 pesos).
ADO (tel. 542-71-92). First-class to Campeche (5 per day, 20hr., 309 pesos), Cancún (3 per day, 26hr., 340 pesos), Oaxaca (16 per day, 9hr., 115 pesos), Palenque (4 and 6:10pm, 14hr., 245 pesos), Tuxtla Gutiérrez (5:15 and 8pm, 15hr., 253 pesos), Veracruz (20 per day, 7hr., 107 pesos), Tulum (1 per day, 384 pesos), Mérida (5 per day, 319 pesos), Córdoba (39 per day, 5hr., 82 pesos), Villahermosa (21 per day, 14hr., 214 pesos), and Xalapa (25 per day, 5hr., 750 pesos).
Estrella Roja (tel. 522-72-00). To Puebla (every 10min. 5am-11pm, 1¾hr., 27 pesos).
Autobuses Cristóbal Colón (tel. 542-72-63). First-class to Oaxaca (8 per day, 9hr., 115 pesos), San Cristóbal de las Casas (4 per day, 17hr., 266 pesos), Tonalá (4 per day, 13hr., 207 pesos), Tuxtla Gutiérrez (5 per day, 16hr., 253 pesos), and service to Central America.
UNO (tel. 522-11-11). To Oaxaca, Puebla, Tampico, Veracruz, Villahermosa, Xalapa, and other cities. Only if you must live in the lap of luxury.

Terminal de Autobuses del Poniente

The Terminal de Autobuses del Poniente (tel. 271-00-38) is on Av. Sur 122, Metro station Observatorio (Line 1). Take a left as you exit the Metro station; a bridge leads to the terminal. Most of these are second-class routes; brace yourself for slow, indirect service. The station is built in the shape of a "V" with most important services clustered at the vertex. Round-the-clock station services include a restaurant, long distance *caseta*, and luggage storage (12 pesos for 24hr., 20 pesos for subjectively determined "larger" bags). There is also a pharmacy (open daily 6am-10pm), a post office (open Mon.-Fri. 8am-7pm, Sat. 9am-1pm), a telegram office (open Mon.-Fri. 9am-5pm, Sat. 9am-1pm), and foodstands, shops, and newspaper stands.

ETN (tel. 273-02-51). Plush first-class service to Guadalajara (4 per day, 12hr., 220 pesos), Morelia (24 per day, 4hr., 125 pesos), Toluca (26 per day, 1½hr., 22pesos), Uruapan (6 per day, 6hr., 165 pesos), and many, many more cities.
Autobuses de Occidente (tel. 271-01-06). To Guadalajara (8 per day, 12hr., 144 pesos), Manzanillo (4 per day, 16hr., 185 pesos), Morelia (every 20min., 6hr., 77 pesos), and Tuxpan (every 20min., 4hr., 53 pesos).

Estrella Roja (522-7200) straight to Puebla (every 2hr. 6am-8pm, 2hr., 34 pesos), Querétaro (every hr. 5:30am-8pm, 5hr., 45 pesos), Toluca (every 10min., 1½hr., 15 pesos), and other destinations.

Elite (368-0622) travels in style to Morelia (2 per day, 6hr., 90 pesos) and Guadalajara (1 per day, 12hr., 164 pesos).

Servicios Coordinados to León (1 per day, 8hr., 88 pesos), Morelia (10 per day, 6hr., 77 pesos), Querétaro (1 per day, 5hr., 45 pesos), and Toluca (9 per day, 1hr., 15 pesos).

Caminante offers first-class service to Toluca (every 5min., 1½hr., 16 pesos).

Terminal de Autobuses del Sur (Tasqueña)

The Tasqueña terminal (tel. 689-97-45) is on Tasqueña 1320, Metro station Tasqueña (Line 2)—exit to the right, through the market. The station has a post office (open Mon.-Sat. 8am-7pm), telegram office (open Mon.-Fri. 8am-6pm, Sat. 9am-5pm), long-distance *caseta* with fax service (open daily 7am-9:30pm), and LADATELs scattered about. There is also a mini-travel agency for hotel reservations in Mexico City, Acapulco, and Mazatlán (open Mon.-Fri. 9am-7pm, Sat. 9am-3pm), a 24-hour pharmacy, and a round-the-clock cafeteria. Luggage lockers (small 20 pesos, large 18 pesos for 24hr.) are near exit #3.

Pullman de Morelos (tel. 549-35-05). First-class to Cuautla (every 20min. 6am-11pm, 2hr., 25 pesos), Cuernavaca (every 10min. 5:30am-midnight, 1¼hr., 22 pesos), Oaxtepec (every 30min. 6am-11pm, 1¾hr., 24 pesos), and Tepotzlán (every 15min. 6:30am-8:30pm, 1½hr., 20 pesos). Serves Morelos.

Cristóbal Colón to Cuautla (every 15min., 2hr., 25 pesos), Oaxtepec (every 20min., 2hr., 24 pesos), Tepoztlán (every 30min., 1¾hr., 19 pesos), Yautepec (every hr., 2hr., 24 pesos), and some places in the Gulf Coast and Yucatán.

Estrella de Oro (tel. 549-85-20, ext. 29). First-class to Acapulco (8 per day, 7hr., 120 pesos), Chilpancingo (10 per day, 4½hr., 66 pesos), Cuernavaca (5 per day, 1½hr., 19 pesos), Iguala (6 per day, 3hr., 41pesos), Ixtapa/Zihuatanejo (5 per day, 11hr., 143 pesos), and Taxco (4 per day, 3½hr., 32 pesos).

Servicios Coordinados (tel. 689-80-00). First-class to Acapulco (every 30min. 5:15am-10pm, 1¼hr., 128 pesos) and Puebla (5 per day, 2hr., 34 pesos).

BY CAR

No other vehicular endeavor matches the experience of driving into Mexico City. Serene mountain roads slowly metamorphose into blaring, multi-lane highways. Any semblance of defensive driving dives out the window. Welcome to the city where stoplights are only suggestions.

Several major highways lead into the city and intersect with the **Circuito Interior,** the highway that rings the city, at which point they change names. Route 57, from Querétaro and Tepotzlán, becomes **Manuel Ávila Camacho** just outside the Circuito. Route 15, from Toluca, turns into **Av. Reforma** as it enters the city. Route 95, from Cuernavaca and Acapulco, becomes **Av. Insurgentes,** which plugs into the Circuito on the south side. Route 150, from Puebla and Texcoco, becomes **Ignacio Zaragoza,** which connects to the Circuito on the east side. Route 85, from Pachuca, Teotihuacán, and Texcoco, also becomes **Av. Insurgentes** in the city.

■ Orientation

As if. It's practically impossible to be oriented in a city this big, this messy, this mutant. Don't worry, though—nobody expects you to know how to get around. It's not uncommon for *taxistas* to ask a passenger if they know how to get to their destination. Note that different neighborhoods can use the same street name; the 300 Benito Juárez streets in the city attest to this tradition of redundancy. To make your daily comings and goings less frustrating, make sure you always know the *colonia* (neighborhood) to which you're going. Street numbers are often useless; ask for cross streets and landmarks instead.

Surprisingly, street names tend to be clustered logically and systematically. Streets in the Zona Rosa are named after European cities; the streets directly across Reforma are named after large rivers of the world; and the streets in Polanco are named after famous philosophers. The **Guía Roji *Ciudad de México*** (60 pesos), a comprehensive street atlas, is a valuable aid for anyone planning to stay in the city for an extended period of time. It's available at many newsstands, bookstores, Sanborn's, and at the airport. Or try the abridged **mini-Guía Roji** (15 pesos).

Mexico City sprawls outward from the Centro roughly 20km to the south, 10km to the north, 10km to the west, and 8km to the east. Year after year, the city's boundaries extend hungrily into neighboring cities. Because of the central location of most sights, few travelers venture past the Bosque de Chapultepec to the west, La Basílica de Guadalupe to the north, the *zócalo* or La Merced marketplace to the east side of the *Centro,* or San Ángel and the UNAM to the south.

The accommodations and food listings for Mexico City are divided according to the four areas of most interest to tourists. The **Centro** contains most of the historic sights and museums, extensive budget accommodations, and lively inexpensive restaurants. Metro stops Allende (closer to accommodations and Alameda) and Zócalo (literally the center of Mexico) serve the *centro* (Line 2). This area is bounded by Cárdenas to the west, Uruguay to the south, Pino Suárez to the east, and Rep. de Peru to the north. The **Alameda** contains budget accommodations and many restaurants, and it is accessible by Metro at Hidalgo (Lines 2 and 3), Bellas Artes (Lines 2 and 8), and San Juan de Letran (Line 8; closer to most food and accommodations listings). The area is bounded by Eje 1 Pte. (known as Rosales, Guerrero, and Bucareli) to the west, Arcos de Belén to the south, Cárdenas to the east, and Violeta to the north. The **Monumento a la Revolución/Buenavista** area, like the Alameda, contains many inexpensive hotels and eateries. It is bounded by Insurgentes Norte to the west, Reforma to the south and east, and Mosqueta to the north. The **Zona Rosa** (Pink Zone) is the capital's most touristy, commercial district. This neighborhood is accessible by Metro at Insurgentes (primary location) and Sevilla (both on Line 1). The Zona Rosa is bounded by Reforma to the north and west, Av. Chapultepec to the south, and Insurgentes to the east. A few of our listings for this area lie just east of Insurgentes, and a gaggle of bars and clubs spill south past Chapultepec along Insurgentes Sur.

CIRCUITO INTERIOR AND EJES VIALES

The **Circuito Interior** is a roughly rectangular artery made up of several smaller, connected highways. **Boulevard Puerto Aéreo** forms the upper east side of the box, running north from the airport. As it bends left at the northeast corner of the box and heads west, it becomes **Av. Río Consulado.** Río Consulado turns south and becomes **Calzada Melchor Ocampo.** Ocampo heads south until it intersects **Paseo de la Reforma** at Bosque de Chapultepec, after which it continues as **Av. Vasconcelos.** From Vasconcelos, two roads run to the southwest corner of the Circuito, **Av. Patriotismo** and **Av. Revolución,** either of which could be considered the Circuito at this point. They turn into **Av. Río Mixcoac,** which becomes **Av. Río Churubusco,** running east-west. Río Churubusco is the longest and sneakiest of the highways that constitute the Circuito. It continues east, turns north for a while, heads east again, then turns north once more to connect with Blvd. Puerto Aéreo south of the airport to complete the Circuito.

Aside from the large thoroughfares—Insurgentes, Reforma, and Miguel Alemán—a system of **Ejes Viales** (axis roads) conducts the majority of traffic within the Circuito. *Ejes* run one way—**except for the bus lanes, which go against traffic.** Running east-west, Eje 1 Nte. and Eje 2 Nte. are north of the *zócalo,* while Ejes 2 through 8 Sur run south of it. The numbers increase heading away from the *zócalo.* **Eje Central Lázaro Cárdenas** runs north-south and bisects the box formed by the Circuito. East of it and parallel lie Ejes 1 through 3 Ote., which veer off to the northwest; west of it are Ejes 1 through 3 Pte. Theoretically, using the Ejes together with the Circuito, you can reach any general area of the city without much delay.

CITY CENTER

Huge as Mexico City is, almost everything of interest to visitors lies within the northern half of the area circumscribed by the Circuito Interior. Moreover, many attractions are within easy reach of **Paseo de la Reforma,** the broad thoroughfare that runs southwest-northeast, or **Av. Insurgentes,** the boulevard running north-south through the city. These are the city's main arteries. The **Bosque de Chapultepec,** home to the principal museums of the city, is served by Metro stops Chapultepec (Line 1) and Auditorio (Line 7). From Chapultepec, Reforma proceeds northeast, punctuated by *glorietas* (rotaries), each with a monument in the center. Moving up Reforma from Chapultepec, the Zona Rosa is followed by Buenavista (near the Monumento a la Revolucíon), the Alameda, and the Centro.

SOUTHERN DISTRICTS

The major southern thoroughfare is **Insurgentes Sur.** Most sights to the south, including **San Ángel, Coyoacán, Ciudad Universitaria,** and the **Pyramid of Cuicuilco,** lie near or along Insurgentes. Metro Line 3 parallels Insurgentes on Cuauhtémoc and then Universidad, ending at Ciudad Universitaria (C.U.). Two other important avenues are **Av. Revolución,** which runs parallel to Insurgentes, and **Av. Miguel Ángel de Quevedo,** which runs parallel to **Francisco Sosa,** in Coyoacán. Metro Line 2 runs east of Line 3 and is closer to **Xochimilco,** one of the few southern sights not along Insurgentes.

■ Getting Around

While most neighborhoods are easily traversed by foot, public transportation is necessary to travel between different areas. While the Metro is usually the fastest, cleanest, and quickest mode of transportation, it becomes inhumanly crowded during rush hour (7:30-9:30am and 6-9pm) and doesn't reach all parts of the city. More thorough are the thousands of white-and-green mini-buses known as *peseros, micros,* or *colectivos* (1-2.50 pesos). The municipal gray buses with blue-and-green stripes (0.40 pesos) tend to be very congested. Taxis are relatively inexpensive and omnipresent. The ancient *tren ligero* (trolley) still travels some routes, mainly at the city's edge and in some suburbs.

Travelers who plan to make frequent use of the Metro and bus systems should purchase an *abono de ahorro de transporte* (26 pesos) at a subway ticket window. *Abonos* entitle the bearer to unlimited use of the Metro (the blue card) and city buses (the purple card) for 15 days following the purchase date. *Abonos* are sold at the beginning and in the middle of every month. Be sure to go early—the cards disappear faster than you can say peso devaluation.

BY METRO

The Metro never ceases to amaze—trains come quickly and regularly, the fare is insanely cheap, the crowds are enormous and bizarre, the ride is smooth, the service is extensive, and the stations are immaculate and marmoreal. Built in the late 1960s, the Metro transports five million people and travels the equivalent of 2½ trips around the earth every day. Its tracks and stations are in continual pursuit of Mexico City's ever-expanding perimeter.

Metro tickets are sold in *taquilllas* (booths) at every station. Lines can stretch for huge distances so buy in bulk. Come prepared with exact change, since the *taquillas* are often short of small denominations. The one-peso fare includes transfers. Gates operate by inserting a magnetically coded ticket. Transfer gates are marked *correspondencia* and exits are marked *salida.* Passing through the turnstiles leaves you outside the station, and means you must pay again to re-enter. While some of the connections are difficult to locate, most transfer stations have information booths to help clueless travelers. Just remember that passing through the turnstile is the *wrong* direction if getting to another line is the goal. If you have an *abono,* be sure to enter only through the blue turnstiles. If you use a yellow turnstile your ticket will be swallowed. Color-coded subway guides are available at the tourist office or at the Metro information booths.

Directions are stated in terms of the station at the end of a given line. Each of the two *andenes* (platforms) has signs indicating the terminus toward which trains are heading. For example, if you are on Line 3 between Indios Verdes and Universidad, you can go either "Dirección Indios Verdes" or "Dirección Universidad." If you realize you are headed in the wrong direction, fear not; simply get off and walk under (or sometimes over) to the other side.

For Lines 1, 2, 3, and A, the first train runs Monday through Friday at 5am, Saturday at 6am, and Sunday at 7am. For Lines 4-9, the first train runs Monday through Saturday at 6am and Sunday at 7am. For all Lines the last train runs at 1am from Sunday through Friday, and on Saturday as late as 2:30am. Try to avoid the Metro from 7:30 to 9am, 2 to 4pm (lunchbreak), and 6 to 9pm on weekdays; huge crowds attract pickpockets. Cars at either end of the train tend to be slightly less crowded, *ergo* safer and less uncomfortable.

Safety is a big concern in the Metro. As in many parts of Mexico, being single and having two X chromosomes just isn't a convenient combination while using the Metro. Lewd remarks and stares are a given, and the horrible experience of being groped is a very distinct possibility when the train is crowded or if the train stops mid-tunnel between stations. Do not be afraid to call attention to the offender. During rush hours many lines have cars reserved for women and children. If you are female, use them. They are usually located at the front of the train and designated by a partition labeled *Mujeres.* Often you will see women and children gathering on a separate part of the platform for the reserved car.

Theft is a chronic problem on the Metro. Carry bags in front of you or on your lap; simply closing the bag does little good, because thieves use razors to slit the bag open from the bottom. Subway thieves often work in pairs—one will distract you while the other pulls your wallet. Rear pockets are easy to pick, front pockets are safer; empty pockets are best. If you ride with a backpack on your back, the small pocket is likely to be violated. The safest place in a crowded car is with your back against the wall and your backpack (if you have one) in front of you. Because of overcrowding, large bags or suitcases are not allowed on the Metro. Some travelers have slipped bags past the gate, but on a crowded train, luggage will make fellow passengers uncomfortable and will attract thieves. If you are intent on making it on the Metro with that overstuffed pack, come very early or after 10:30pm, when the Metro is fairly empty and guards are more likely to look the other way.

For Metro and bus information, ask at any information booth or contact **COVITUR (Comisión de Vialidad y Transporte Urbano del D.F.),** Public Relations, Universidad 800, 14th floor (tel. 512-01-12 or 627-48-61), at the corner of Félix Cuevas just outside the Zapata Metro station (Line 3). To complain about the Metro, dial 709-11-33, ext. 5051 or 5052. Nearly all stations have guards and security offices;

Metropolitan

Some Metro stops are sights in their own right. Pino Suárez (Lines 1 and 2) houses a small Aztec building located at mid-transfer. The *Tunel de la Ciencia* (science tunnel) in the marathon transfer at La Raza (Lines 3 and 5) is an educational experience: marvel at the nifty fractals, or wear your whites and glow in the dark under a map of the constellations. The stop even has a small science museum (open Mon.-Sat. 10am-6pm). The Zócalo stop (Line 2) has scale models of the plaza as it has appeared throughout its history, the *andenes* at Copilco (Line 3) are lined with murals, and the Bellas Artes stop (Lines 2 and 8) houses Aztec statuettes. In fact, nearly every Metro transfer stop has some kind of exhibit, from elementary school drawings of the subway system to a re-creation of a London theater.

MEXICO CITY

immediately report any problems or incidents. Further, all trains have an emergency red handle, to be pulled in the event of severe harrassment or any emergency. If you lose something on the Metro, call the **Oficina de Objetos Extraviados** (tel. 709-11-33, ext. 4643), located in the Fray Servando station (Line 4). Keep hope alive, but don't hold your breath.

BY PESERO

Peseros, a.k.a. *colectivos, combis,* or *micros,* are white-and-green minibuses, often with a "Magna Sin" gasoline logo on the side. The name *pesero* comes from the time when they used to cost one old peso, equivalent to 0.01¢ today. Priced economically between cabs and buses, they cruise the streets on set routes. Though no printed information is available, destinations are either painted on or posted on the front window. There are *pesero* starting and ending bases, but no set stops. To hail a *pesero,* wave your hand or hold out as many fingers as there are people in your group. To get off, ring the bell if there's one, or simply shout loudly *¡Bajan!* (coming down). To prevent a missed stop, pay when you get on and tell the driver your destination. Drivers will typically honk (horns are often rigged to play an annoying melody) during rush hours to signal availability.

Fares vary according to distance; expect to fork over 1 to 2.50 peso for cross-city rides, 4 pesos for long-distance trips over 17km. Fares are 10% higher between 10pm and 6am. Some *peseros* run only until midnight, but the major routes—on Reforma, between Chapultepec and San Ángel, and along Insurgentes—run 24 hours. Other well traveled *pesero* routes include: Metro Hidalgo (Lines 2 and 3) to Ciudad Universitaria (via Reforma, Bucareli, and Av. Cuauhtémoc); La Villa to Chapultepec (via Reforma); Reforma to Auditorio (via Reforma and Juárez); *zócalo* to Chapultepec (via 5 de Mayo and Reforma); San Ángel to Izazaga (via 5 de Mayo and Reforma); Bolívar to Ciudad Universitaria/Coyoacán (via Bolívar in the *Centro*); and San Ángel to Metro Insurgentes (Line 1; via Av. de la Paz and Insurgentes Sur). Many depart from the Chapultepec Metro station (Line 1) to San Ángel, La Merced, and the airport. Routes are written on the windshield.

BY BUS

There is no published information about routes and schedules for the extensive bus system. Unless you stick to the major thoroughfares, you might find it difficult to navigate the city by bus. Moreover, buses are usually slower than the Metro, particularly during rush hours. Buses cost 0.50 to 2 pesos; have change ready when you board. They run daily from 5am to midnight, but are scarce after 10pm. Keep in mind that each one-way Eje has a single bus lane running in the *opposite* direction to traffic. Anywhere, flag down the bus by holding out your arm and pointing at the street in front of you. To get off the bus, press the button above the exit door at the rear of the bus. If you don't hear a buzz, bang once on the wall or bark *¡Bajan!* to let the driver know you want out.

Like the Metro, buses are crowded and seats are hot items. The popular routes along Paseo de la Reforma are notorious for robbery. Leave your valuables at the hotel; don't keep money in your pockets; put your bag in front of you, and keep your fingers crossed.

BY TAXI

Cabs constantly cruise the major avenues. Most taxis are equipped with meters; base fares typically begin at 3 pesos, and at night drivers will add 20% to the meter rate. Be certain that the meter is functioning as soon as you plop onto the cushion; meters are often conveniently *descompuesto*. If a meter is out of order, insist on setting the price before the driver goes anywhere. Another commonly used trick is for a normally functioning meter to suddenly jump into the triple digits—watch the meter at all times and immediately threaten a driver with non-payment if the price instantaneously skyrockets. Some taxis have meters that display reference numbers for the driver's price conversion table instead of prices. Ask to see it before you pay, to ensure that the price you're given matches the meter number. Carry small denominations, as drivers will often cite no change as a reason to pocket some extra pesos. Tips are unnecessary unless you are granted some sort of special service—if the cabbie helps carry your luggage or gives you a previously agreed-to tour, hand over a *propina*.

Hotel cabs and *turismo* taxis have no meters and charge up to three times more than regular taxis; the ubiquitous green VW bugs are the cheapest but must be hailed. At the airport and at all bus terminals, purchase a taxi ticket for a set fee (according to destination) at a registered booth. In the rare instance that no taxi is in sight, call **Servi-taxi** (tel. 271-2560) or **Taxi Radio Mexicana** (tel. 519-7690). VW- bug taxis should display the driver's photo, credentials, and license over the glove compartment. Taxis commonly prey on the easy tourist victim. At the airport or bus terminals, try to consult a zone map before buying your ticket and always count your change. On the street, ask a local what the fare should be and insist on paying that and no more; there'll always be a driver who will accept.

There are several *sitios* (taxi bases) in every neighborhood. *Sitios* will respond to your phone call by sending out a car to pick you up. Since their taxis don't use meters, ask the operator what the trip will cost. The great advantage of *sitio* taxis, in addition to home pick-up, is that they are much safer than anonymous cabs; the disadvantage is that they are more expensive. However, rising crime rates make the benefits outweigh the cost. Women going out at night should strongly consider using *sitio* taxis; find out phone numbers from your hotel or the tourist office.

BY CAR

You must be insane. Driving is the most complicated and least economical way to get around the city, not to mention the easiest way to get lost and lose your sanity. Mexico City's drivers are notoriously evil; they became that way in large measure because highway engineers did not think about them at all when designing city roads. Highway dividers are often absent, and stop signs are planted midstream. Is it any wonder that red lights are routinely defied? Even angels fear to tread in the D.F.: the fast and free *Ángeles Verdes* do *not* serve the Distrito Federal. If your car should break down within city boundaries, call the **Asociación Mexicana Automovilística (AMA;** tel. 207-44-48) or the **Asociación Nacional Automovilística (ANA;** tel. 597-4283), and request assistance. Wait for them beside your car, with the hood raised. If you leave your car alone, give it a good-bye kiss before you go.

Parking within the city is seldom a problem: parking lots are everywhere (4-8 pesos per hr., depending on the location and condition of the lot). Street parking is difficult to find, and vandalism is extremely common. Never leave anything valuable inside your car. Police will put an *inmobilizador* on your wheels if you park illegally; they will often tow your car. If you return to an empty space, try to locate the nearest police depot (not station) to figure out if your auto has been towed—if it's not there, it was stolen. If anything is missing from your car and you suspect that the police tampered with it, call the English-speaking LOCATEL (tel. 658-11-11).

All vehicles, even those of non-Mexican registration, must follow Mexico City's anti-smog regulations. Depending on the last digit of the license plate, cars are forbidden from driving one day a week, according to this schedule: Monday final digits: 5 or 6; Tuesday: 7 or 8; Wednesday: 3 or 4; Thursday: 1 or 2; Friday: 9 or 0. Restrictions apply from 5am to 10pm, and penalties for violations are very stiff. There are no limitations on weekends and on weekdays between 10pm and 5am.

Car rental rates are exorbitant, driving a hassle, and the entire process draining. Still interested? Then you must have a valid driver's license (from any country), a passport or tourist card, and be at least 25 years old. Some agencies will be lenient with the minimum age if you have a major credit card. Prices for rentals tend to be similar: a small VW or Nissan with free mileage, insurance and tax costs about 270-370 pesos per day, 3,300 pesos per week. Most agencies have offices at the airport and in the Zona Rosa: **Avis,** at the airport (tel. 762-3688, open 7am-11pm) and at Reforma 308 (tel. 511-2228, open 9am-6pm); **Budget,** at the airport (open Mon.-Fri. 7am-9pm, Sat. 8am-6pm) and at Hamburgo 71 (tel. 533-0450); **Dollar,** at the airport (tel. 207-38-38) and at Av. Chapultepec 322 (open daily 7am-8pm); **Hertz,** at the airport (tel. 571-3239, open 7am-11pm); **National,** Reforma 219 (tel. 566-0555); **Thrifty,** Sevilla 4 (tel. 207-75-66).

■ Safety

Like all large cities, Mexico City presents safety problems to the traveler. Misery-induced crime, corruption, authority abuse and impunity, and a lax justice system don't help a bit. This is the asphalt jungle, where people fend for themselves. In general, the downtown area, where most sights and accommodations are located, tends to be safer, although the backstreets near Buenavista and the Alameda are significantly less so. Try to avoid carrying large amounts of cash, and use a money belt or similar security device. Ignore strangers who seem even slightly suspicious, no matter how friendly their chatter or smile may seem. Speaking in Spanish makes would-be attackers far less likely to bother you. Never follow a vendor or shoeshiner out of public view. Don't wear cameras, expensive watches, or flashy jewelry if you want to be left alone. Sunglasses for men convey don't-mess-with-me *machismo;* for women they may be less advisable.

Women are, unfortunately, at higher risk of attack. Women in Mexico receive attention that you may not be used to; insistent stares, provocative smiles, whistling, cat-calling, and even extremely vulgar propositions are all part of everyday life. Light hair and skin, revealing or tight clothing, or any sign of foreignness will result in even more attention. Although horribly annoying, most such displays are harmless...provided you take good care of yourself. Stick with other people, especially at night or in isolated areas. Learn a few basic curses (see p. 558). A loud clear *¡Déjame!* (leave me alone, DEH-ha-meh) will make your intentions clear. If in trouble, don't be shy about screaming *¡Ayúdame!* (help me; ah-YOO-dah-may).

Transportation presents its own safety concerns (see Getting Around, above). Mexico City's drivers are notoriously aggressive and often ignore traffic signals. Locals warn of late-night attacks by *bandidos* posing as police officers.

The city that used to be known as *la región más transparente del aire* (the most transparent region of air) is now the most polluted in the world. The city's smoggy air may cause problems for contact-lens wearers and people with allergies. Pollution is particularly bad during the winter, due to thermic inversion; the summer rainy season does wonders in cleaning the air.

■ Practical Information

Navigating the city will be easier if you pick up a few current publications. *Concierge,* available at government tourist offices, is jam-packed with helpful tourist tips and practical information. The *Mexico City Daily Bulletin,* which includes news, information on tourist sights, and a helpful map of Mexico City, is available free at the City Tourism Office and all over the Zona Rosa. *Tiempo Libre* (Free Time), a weekly on sale at most corner newsstands, covers movies, galleries, restaurants, dances, museums, and most cultural events (comes out Thurs., 5 pesos). *The Mexico City News* (4 pesos), an English-language daily, and *La Jornada,* a top national newspaper (3 pesos), have film and theater listings. *Macho Tips,* available at newsstands along Reforma, has information on gay events in the city. *Ser Gay,* available at newsstands and many gay bars, is less widely distributed but has a more complete listing of gay nightlife options.

If you come during the summer, keep a light rain poncho or umbrella handy. The rainy season (May-Oct.) features daily, one- or two-hour-long rain storms anywhere from 4-6pm. Otherwise, sunny and moderate weather prevails year-round.

Ministry of Tourism: Presidente Masaryk 172 (tel. 250-8555, ext. 11), at Hegel in Col. Polanco. From Metro Polanco (Line 7), walk one block down Arquímedes, take a left on Masaryk, and walk 3½ blocks—the building is to your right and easy to miss. Friendly staff makes hotel reservations and offers copious amounts of brochures, information, and advice. Open Mon.-Fri. 8am-9pm (24-hr. phone lines).

Federal Tourist Office: Infotur, Amberes 54 (tel. 525-9380 or 525-9382), at Londres in the Zona Rosa. Metro: Insurgentes (Line 1). Helpful and friendly. Some officials speak English. Maps of the city and Metro upon request. Lists hotels, grouped by region and price range. Open daily 9am-8pm. The office operates information booths in *Sala* A (tel. 762-6773) at the airport, and at the TAPO and Terminal Central del Norte bus stations (daily 8am-9pm).

Department of Tourist Security: Presidente Masaryk 172 (tel. 250-0151 or 250-0493), in Col. Polanco. A very good place to start after a mishap. Responds to complaints, questions, emergencies, and reports of suspected abuses. Some English. Open 24hr. for phone calls; staffed daily 8am-8pm.

Legal Advice: Supervisión General de Servicios a la Comunidad, Florencia 20 (tel. 625-8761), in the Zona Rosa. Metro: Insurgentes (Line 1). Call the 24-hr. **hotline** (tel. 625-8664) if you are the victim of a robbery or accident and need legal advice. Some employees speak English.

LOCATEL: (tel. 658-11-11.) Officially the city's lost-and-found hotline. Call if your car (or friend) is missing. Also provides help in cases of medical emergencies and information about sports events, etc. Limited English spoken.

Tourist Card (FMT) info: Secretaría de Gobernación, Dirección General de Servicios Migratorios, Av. Chapultepec 284, 5th floor (tel. 626-7200 or 206-0506), in Col. Juárez. Metro: Insurgentes (Line 1). Come here to extend the date on your FMT or to clear up any immigration problems. Open Mon.-Fri. 8am-2pm.

Accommodations Service: Hoteles Asociados, Airport *Sala* E (tel. 571-5902 or 571-6382) and the Central de Autobuses del Norte. Up-to-date information on prices and locations of Mexico City hotels. Give 'em a price range and an area, they'll get you a reservation free of charge. For budget lodgings, be sure to ask for rock-bottom prices. English spoken.

Embassies: Will replace lost passports, issue visas, and provide legal assistance. Visa processing can take up to 24hr.; bring plenty of ID. If you find yourself in an emergency after hours, try contacting the embassy anyway—you could be in luck. **Australia,** Jaime Balmes 11, 10th floor (tel. 395-9988), between Ejército Nacional and Homero. Open Mon.-Wed. 8am-5pm, Thurs.-Fri. 8am-2pm. **Belize,** Bernardo de Galvez 215 (tel. 520-1274). Open Mon.-Fri. 9am-1:30pm. **Canada,** Schiller 529 (tel. 724-7900), behind the Museum of Anthropology. Open Mon.-Fri. 8:30am-noon for immigration concerns, 9am-2:30pm for library, and 9am-1pm and 2-5pm for general information. **Costa Rica,** Río Po 113 (tel. 525-7764, -65, -66), between Río Lerma and Río Panuco, behind the U.S. embassy. Open Mon.-Fri. 9am-4pm. **Guatemala,** 1025 Av. Explanada (tel. 540-7520). Open Mon.-Fri. 9am-1:30pm. **Honduras,** Alfonso Reyes 220 (tel. 211-5747), between Saltillo and Ometusco. Open Mon.-Fri. 10am-2pm. **New Zealand,** Homero 229, 8th floor (tel. 281-5486). Open Mon.-Fri. 9:30am-5:30pm. **Nicaragua,** Payo de Rivera 120 (tel. 540-5621), between Virreyes and Monte Atos. Open Mon.-Fri. 9:30am-3pm. **U.K.,** Río Lerma 71 (tel. 207-2149), at Cuauhtémoc. Open Mon.-Fri. 9am-2pm for visas, 9am-3pm for general info. **U.S.,** Reforma 305 (tel. 211-0042), at Glorieta Ángel de la Independencia. Open Mon.-Fri. 8:30am-12:45pm for passports and visas, Mon.-Fri. 8:30am-5:30pm for general business. In an emergency, call after hours.

Currency Exchange: *Casas de cambio* keep longer hours than banks, give better exchange rates, and typically stay open on Sat. There are many in the *centro,* along Reforma, and in the Zona Rosa. Most can change other currencies in addition to U.S. dollars. Call the **Asociación Mexicana de Casas de Cambio** (tel. 264-0884 or 264-0841) to locate the exchange bureau nearest you. In the Centro: **Casa de Cambio Euromex,** Venustiano Carranza 64, 3rd fl. (tel. 518-4199); **Casa de Cambio Tíber,** on Río Tíber and Papaloapan (722-0800), one block from the Ángel. Open Mon.-Fri. 8:30am-5pm, Sat. 8:30am-2pm. On the south side of the Alameda: **Casa de Cambio Plus,** Juárez 38 (tel. 510-8953). Open Mon.-Fri. 9am-4pm, Sat. 10am-2pm. On Reforma, near the Monumento a la Revolución/

Buenavista: **Casa de Cambio Catorce,** Reforma 51 (tel. 705-2460). All banks offer the same exchange rate and usually charge commissions. All banks exchange 9am-1:30pm, but the wait may be considerable. The nation-wide **ATM** network, **Red Cajeros Compartidos,** takes MC and Visa for cash advances, and many ATMs work with other U.S. system cards. Scores of ATMs are located along Reforma, in the Zona Rosa, in Polanco, and in the Centro. Lost or stolen cards can be reported 24hr. to 227-2777. In case of a lost **Visa** card, call 625-21-88. **Citibank,** Reforma 390 (tel. 211-3030, open 24hr.), and **Bank of America,** Reforma 116, 10th-12th floors (tel. 591-0011), can also help in an emergency.

American Express: Reforma 234 (tel. 207-7282), at Havre in the Zona Rosa. Cashes personal checks, accepts customers' mail and money wires. Travel service. Report lost credit cards to the main office at Patriotismo 635 (tel. 326-2666), lost traveler's checks to either branch. Open Mon.-Fri. 9am-6pm, Sat. 9am-1pm.

Telephones: Look for glorious **LADATELs** at the airport, bus stations, Metro stations, VIP restaurants, and on the street in the Zona Rosa or the Centro. LADATELs (also marked LADA 91, as in the national long-distance prefix) can be used for international collect and credit card calls, and also with a LADATEL card (10, 20, and 50 pesos). For those who miss the golden days of the Mexican phone system, long-distance *casetas* are at Airport *Sala* F (open daily 6am-8:30pm), the train station (open Mon.-Sat. 8am-9:30pm, Sun. 9am-3pm), or Central Camionera del Norte (open daily 8am-9pm).

Telegrams: Tacuba 8 (tel. 512-2195), at the Museo Nacional de Arte in the right wing of the building, behind the central post office. Domestic and international service. From the U.S., send through Western Union to **México Central Telégrafos.** Open Mon.-Fri. 8am-midnight, Sat. 9am-12:45pm. To send telegrams by phone, call 709-8500 domestic, 709-8625 international. Western Union service at the airport in *Sala* A (open Mon.-Fri. 8am-6pm, Sat. 9am-10pm) and at the Central Camionera del Norte.

English Bookstores: American Bookstore, Madero 25 (tel. 512-7284), in the Centro, has an extensive selection of fiction, guide books, and a matchless Latin American history and politics section. Also a branch at Insurgentes Sur 1636 (tel. 661-6608), in San Ángel. Both branches open Mon.-Sat. 10am-7pm; *centro* store also open Sun. 10am-3pm. **Pórtico de la Ciudad de México,** Central 124 (tel. 510-96-83 or 280-54-72), at Carranza. Sells English and Spanish books on Mexican history and guides to archaeological sites. Open Mon.-Sat. 10am-7pm. **La Casa de la Prensa Internacional,** Florencia 57 in the Zona Rosa, sells magazines and newspapers in Spanish, English, French, and German. Open Mon.-Sat. 8am-10pm, Sat.-Sun. 8am-4pm. Also popular is the **Librería Gandhi,** M.A. de Quevedo 128, in San Ángel. The **Museo Nacional de Antropología** has a selection of archaeological guides in English (see p. 103). *The Mexico City News* and the new *Mexico City Times* are sold at most newsstands.

English Library: Biblioteca Benjamín Franklin, Londres 16 (tel. 211-0042, ask for the library), at Berlín, 2 blocks southeast of the Cuauhtémoc monument. Books, newspapers, and periodicals. Council and Fullbright fellas on the second floor. Open Mon. and Fri. 3-7:30pm, Tues.-Thurs. 10am-3pm.

Cultural and Arts Info: Palacio Nacional de Bellas Artes (tel. 709-31-13), Juárez and Eje Central, for info and reservations for Bellas Artes events. Open Mon.-Sat. 11am-7pm, Sun. 9am-7pm. Check *Tiempo Libre* for city-wide listings.

Supermarket: Most supermarkets are far from the *centro*, at residential Metro stops. **Bodega,** Serapio Rendón 117, just south of Antonio Caso. Open Mon.-Sat. 8am-9pm, Sun. 9am-8pm. **Aurrerá,** 5 blocks north of Puente de Alvarado on Insurgentes. Open daily 9am-9pm. **Comercial Mexicana,** at Corregidora and Correo Mayor, on the side of the Palacio Nacional, in the *centro.* Open daily 8am-8pm. **Superama,** Río Sena and Balsas, in the Zona Rosa. Open daily 8am-9pm.

Laundromats: Near the Monumento a la Revolución: **Lavandería Automática,** Edison 91. Wash or dry 16 pesos per 2¼kg. Full service 34 pesos. Soap 5 pesos. Open Mon.-Sat. 10am-6pm. In the Zona Rosa: **Lavanderet,** Chapultepec 463 (tel. 514-01-06), at Toledo. Wash or dry 15 pesos. Full service 32 pesos. Open Mon.-Sat. 9am-7pm. **LavaJet,** Danubio 119 (tel. 207-3032), behind the U.S. embassy. Wash or dry 10 pesos. Full service 43 pesos. Open Mon.-Fri. 8:15am-6pm, Sat. 8:15am-5pm. Most hotels have laundry service.

Rape Crisis: Hospital de Traumatología de Balbuena, Cecilio Robelo 103 (tel. 552-1602 or 764-0339), near Calle Sur, east of Alameda. **Hospital de la Mujer** (tel. 541-4661). Also call 06 or LOCATEL.

Sexually Transmitted Disease Info: Secretaría de Salud (tel. 277-6311 or 533-7204). Open Mon.-Fri. 8am-2pm and 3:30-7pm, Sat. 9am-1pm.

AIDS Hotline: TELSIDA/CONASIDA, Florencia 8 (tel. 207-4143 or 207-4077), Col. Roma. Metro: Cuauhtémoc (Line 1). Information and help center.

Gay, Lesbian, and Bisexual Information: Colectivo Sol. Write to Apdo. 13-320 Av. México 13, D.F. 03500. Offers information on upcoming political and social events. Events publicized at gay bars and clubs and in *Tiempo Libre* and *Ser Gay*.

Red Cross: Ejército Nacional 1032 (tel. 395-1111, 557-5758 or -57), in Polanco. Open 24hr. Fastest and most efficient ambulance service. No English spoken.

Pharmacies: All **Sanborns** have well stocked pharmacies, open daily 9am-11pm. **Farmacia El Fénix,** Isabel La Católica 15 (tel. 585-04-55), at 5 de Mayo. Some English spoken. Open Mon.-Sat. 9am-10pm. **VYR,** San Jerónimo 630 (tel. 595-5983 or 595-5998), near Perisur shopping center. Open 24hr. Call; they might have a branch near you. Big supermarkets have well stocked pharmacies.

Medical Care: The **U.S. Embassy** has a list of doctors, with their specialties, addresses, telephone numbers, and languages spoken. **Dirección General de Servicios Médicos** (tel. 518-5100) has information on all city hospitals. Open Mon.-Fri. 9am-6pm. **American British Cowdray (ABC) Hospital,** Calle Sur 136 (tel. 227-5000 or 515-8359 in an emergency), at Observatorio, Col. Las Américas. Expensive but generally trustworthy and excellent. No foreign health plans valid, but major credit cards accepted. Open 24hr. **Torre Médica,** José Maria Iglesias 21 (tel. 546-2485), at Metro Revolución (Line 2), near Monumento de la Revolución.

Emergency Shelter: Casa de Protección Social (tel. 530-8536).

Police: Secretaría General de Protección y Vialidad (tel. 256-0606 or 768-8044). Dial 08 for the Policía Judicial to report assaults, robberies, crashes, abandoned vehicles, or emergencies. Be careful about abuse of authority.

Courier Services: UPS, Reforma 404 (tel. 207-6957), provides international shipping services and express mail. Open Mon.-Fri. 8am-8pm. **Federal Express,** Estocolmo 4-2 (tel. 208-6768, 208-9670, toll-free 91-800-900-11), in the Zona Rosa on Reforma across the street from the U.S. embassy. Send before 5:30pm Mon.-Fri., 1:30pm Sat. for overnight service. Open Mon.-Fri. 8am-7pm.

Central Post Office: Lázaro Cárdenas (tel. 521-7394), at Tacuba across from Bellas Artes. Open for stamps Mon.-Fri. 8am-6pm, Sat. 9am-8pm; for registered mail Mon.-Fri. 8am-5:30pm, Sat. 9am-4:30pm; for *Lista de Correos* Mon.-Fri. 8am-9pm, Sat. 9am-5pm. Postal museum upstairs. **Postal Code:** 06002.

Telephone Code: 5.

■ Accommodations

Rooms abound in the *Centro* (between Alameda and the *zócalo*) and near the Alameda Central, and are sprinkled throughout the area surrounding the Monumento a la Revolución on the Pl. de la República. Rooms priced at 60-80 pesos for one bed and 85-100 pesos for two beds should be clean, have carpeting, a TV, and a telephone with free local calls. Most budget hotels charge according to the number of beds needed and not per person; beds tend to be large enough for two people. If you don't mind, snuggling is a potential source of substantial savings.

Avoid the filthier sections of the Alameda and any area that makes you feel uncomfortable—there are plenty more from which to choose. Don't be put off by the mid-to high-priced hotels around Insurgentes Sur and Reforma, just northeast of the Zona Rosa tourist belt; they are still inexpensive by U.S. standards. In an attempt to cut down on problems with prostitution, many budget establishments have adopted "No Guests Allowed" policies. Beware of any place where the hotel itself (and not the parking lot) is marked "Hotel Garage." These rooms are frequented by businessfolk

Central Mexico City

SIGHTS

Casa de los Azulejos, **38**
Catedral Metropolitana, **46**
Centro Cultural José Martí, **26**
Glorieta Ángel de la
  Independencia, **8**
Glorieta Cristóbal Colón, **13**
Glorieta Cuauhtémoc, **12**
Lotería Nacional, **20**
Mercado de Artesanías de la

Ciudadela, **21**
Monte Nacional de Piedad, **45**
Monumento a la Revolución, **14**
Monumento de los Niños Héroes, **7**
Museo de Arte Moderno, **6**
Museo de la Alameda, **24**
Museo de la Ciudad de México, **51**
Museo Franz Mayer, **27**
Museo Nacional de Antropología, **3**
Museo Nacional de Arte, **32**

Museo Nacional de Historia,
Museo Nacional de la Estamp
Museo Siqueiros, **2**
Museo Tamayo, **4**
Palacio de Bellas Artes, **30**
Palacio Nacional, **49**
Pinacoteca Virreinal de San
  Diego, **25**
Plaza de la Constitución, **47**
Plaza de las Tres Culturas

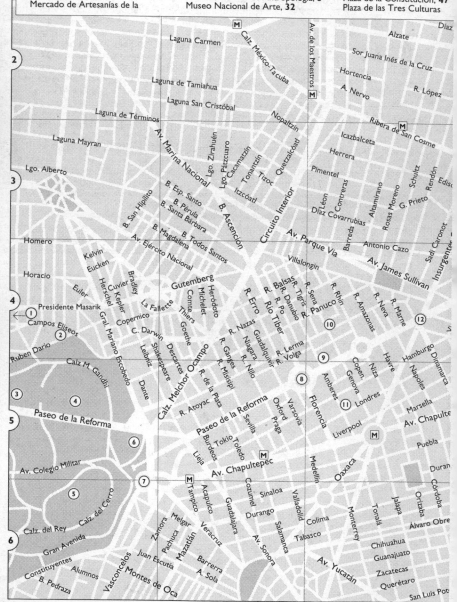

D   E   F

28 (Tlatelolco), **31**	Train Station, **18**	Hotel Florida, **35**
Plaza Garibaldi, **32**	Ministry of Tourism, **11**	Hotel Hidalgo, **29**
Suprema Corte de Justicia, **50**	U.S. Embassy, **9**	Hotel Isabel, **42**
Templo de San Francisco, **40**	U.K. Embassy, **10**	Hotel Juárez, **44**
Templo Mayor, **48**		Hotel Londres, **17**
Torre Latinoamericana, **39**	**HOTELS**	Hotel Manolo Primero, **23**
	Casa de los Amigos, **15**	Hotel Monte Carlo, **43**
SERVICES	Hotel Antillas, **33**	Hotel Oxford, **16**
Central Post Office, **37**	Hotel Atlanta, **34**	Hotel Principal, **41**
Federal Tourist Office, **1**	Hotel Conde, **22**	Hotel Yale, **19**

"working late at the office" and are designed to allow entry directly from the garage to the room. Always ask to look at a room before you accept it; this is easier to do after check-out time (between noon and 2pm). Hotels with rooms more expensive than 65 pesos per single and 75 pesos per double usually accept MC and Visa. AmEx is rarely taken, except at the more expensive Zona Rosa hotels.

For hostel information, call **Villa Deportiva Juvenil** (tel. 525-26-99), the city's lone hostel on Plaza de la Independencia, near the Zona Rosa (25 pesos per night). They can't guarantee a spot and are often full with visiting sports teams.

CENTRO

Situated between the *zócalo* and Alameda Central, this neighborhood is the historic colonial heart of Mexico City. Its hotels are reasonably priced and feel fairly safe, although the streets become relatively empty once the locals head home for the night. Nonetheless, the *centro* remains the most exciting place to stay and the best base from which to explore the traditional core of one of the world's magnificent cities. Of course, with action inevitably come noise and congestion. If you crave quieter surroundings, consider moving west to the Buenavista or Alameda areas.

Many of the hotels listed below are north of Madero and 5 de Mayo, the parallel east-west streets that connect the Alameda with the *zócalo,* and east of Lázaro Cárdenas, the north-south Eje Central that runs one block east of Alameda. Metro stations Bellas Artes (Lines 2 and 8) and Allende (Line 2) are nearby. Hotels on 5 de Mayo, Isabel la Católica, and Uruguay are better served by Metro stations *Zócalo* (Line 2) and Isabel la Católica (Line 1). Street names change north of Tacuba: Isabel la Católica becomes República de Chile, and Bolívar turns into Allende. Except for Hotel Principal, Hotel Juárez, and Hotel Congreso, hotels listed below credit cards.

Hotel Atlanta, Belisario Domínguez 31 (tel. 518-1200 and 518-1203), at Allende. The wood-paneled lobby leads to mandarin-colored rooms bedecked with imitation Mirós. Great value, with TV, phone, and refreshingly uncramped bathrooms. Singles 60 pesos. Doubles 85 pesos.

Hotel Antillas, Belisario Domínguez 34 (tel. 526-5674 through -79), between Allende and República de Chile. The colonial exterior promises a history-drenched grandeur: the dim interior does not disappoint. The eager staff and clean bathrooms make for a relaxing stay, complete with TVs, bottled water, and lounge areas. Singles 92 pesos. Doubles 120 pesos.

Hotel Monte Carlo, Uruguay 69 (tel. 521-2559), between Metro stops Isabel la Católica (Line 1) and Allende (Line 2). Relaxing lounge and top-floor skylight. Large, colorful rooms. Clean bathrooms. Singles 75 pesos. Doubles 100 pesos.

Hotel Principal, Bolívar 29 (tel. 521-1333), by the Parilla Leonesa restaurant. Friendly staff bustles about under the arched brick ceiling. Simple tan rooms have a balcony, mirror, TV, telephone, and bottled water. Singles with communal bath 45 pesos, with private bath 80 pesos. Doubles 110 pesos.

Hotel Isabel, Isabel la Católica 63 (tel. 518-1213 through -17), between El Salvador and Uruguay. Neither the large foyer nor the king-sized rooms are particularly attractive. On the up side: a bathtub, huge chest of drawers, electronic safe, TV, bottled water, and cleanliness. Singles 85 pesos. Doubles 100 pesos.

Hotel La Marina, Allende 30 (tel. 518-2445). Ample rooms decorated in bright and gaudy red, orange, and pink. King-sized beds. Singles 60 pesos. Doubles 85 pesos.

NEAR THE MONUMENTO A LA REVOLUCIÓN/ BUENAVISTA

Hotels near the Monumento a la Revolución are cheaper and quieter than their counterparts in the Centro or the Alameda. Budget travelers tend to congregate here, particularly in the hotels on Mariscal and Edison. Metro Revolución (Line 2) serves hotels south of Puente de Alvarado/Hidalgo, while Metro Guerrero (Line 3) serves those to the north, near the train station.

Casa de Los Amigos, Ignacio Mariscal 132 (tel. 705-05-21 or 705-06-46), across from Gran Hotel Texas. Metro: Revolución (Line 2). Originally the home and studio of painter José Clemente Orozco, now a Quaker-run guest house for tourists and social activists. More than a hostel, it's a world-view. Visitors must agree to respect their cooperative atmosphere in order to stay. Dynamic, youthful, international atmosphere, and reasonable requirements. Weekly cultural exchanges, ample library offerings, and an always engaging lounge. Kitchen and laundry facilities. Minimum 2-day stay, maximum 15-day. Key deposit 10 pesos. Breakfast 10 pesos. Dorm rooms 40 pesos. Private rooms 60 pesos. Doubles 80-90 pesos.

Hotel Oxford, Ignacio Mariscal 67 (tel. 566-05-00), at Alcázar, next to the small park. Metro: Revolución. Large, colorful rooms, many with great views of the park. Clean and inviting bathrooms with huge sinks in which to do laundry. TV, telephone, and bottled water included. Singles 60 pesos. Doubles 90 pesos.

Hotel America, Calle Buenavista 4 (tel. 566-9677), on the corner with Alvarado. Small, clean rooms with oversized TVs. New bathrooms. The location and prices make it a great deal. Singles 45 pesos. Doubles 70 pesos.

Hotel Yale, Mosqueta 200 (tel. 591-15-45 or 591-14-88), between Zaragoza and Guerrero, to the left as you exit the train station. Metro: Guerrero. This New Haven of a hotel has recently remodeled rooms, full-length mirrors, TVs, and (surprise) orange furniture that doesn't quite match. An endearing hotel, for those who can't get into a better place. Singles 55 pesos. Doubles 90 pesos.

ALAMEDA CENTRAL

The expansive Alameda is always throbbing with activity. But the greenery fades over the course of a few blocks, making way for dirt and danger in some of the surrounding streets. Women may feel safer in other parts of the city.

Hotel Hidalgo, Santa Veracruz 37 (tel. 521-8771 through -77), just north of the Alameda. Metro: Bellas Artes (Lines 2 and 8). Located up the 2 de Abril walkway to the left of Teatro Hidalgo. Swank renovations include elegant wood paneling, beautiful carpeting, and tasteful decorations. Queen singles and pleasant courtyard views make it well worth the price. Singles 125 pesos. Doubles 150 pesos.

Hotel Manolo Primero, Luis Moya 111 (tel. 521-7709), just north of Arcos de Belén, three blocks west of Metro Salto del Agua (Lines 1 and 8). Spacious blue hallways and cavernous lobby lead into large bathrooms with gigantic mirrors. Rooms have king-sized beds and big-screen TVs. Singles and doubles 80 pesos.

Hotel Conde, Pescaditos 15 (tel. 521-10-84), at Revillagigedo. Metro: Juárez (Line 1). Follow Artículo 123 to Revillagigedo, then take a right and walk 3 blocks. Blue-green color scheme, cute fake plants "growing" beneath the TV, and bathrooms with both toilets and bidets. Singles and doubles 80 pesos.

NEAR THE BUS STATIONS

There are few good budget accommodations in the vicinity of any of the four bus stations. For travelers just passing through who arrive at the **Central de Autobuses del Norte** (northern station), **Hotel Acuario,** Poniente 112 #100 (tel. 587-26-77), offers medium-quality rooms in a very low-quality neighborhood. Use the subway tunnel to pass under the road, walk left for two blocks, make a right onto Poniente, and go west for half a block. A strict "no guest" policy ensures a good night's sleep (singles 70 pesos; doubles 90 pesos). For a pricier but definitely more comfy option, **Hotel Brasilia,** Av. de los 100 Mts. 4823 (tel. 587-85-77), is three blocks to the left along the main thoroughfare as you exit the bus station. It's all you could possibly expect in a major U.S. chain (singles 120 pesos; doubles 160 pesos). The closest place near the **Terminal de Autobuses del Sur** (south station) is **Hotel Montreal,** Calzada de Tlalpan 2073 (tel. 689-00-11), at M. A. Quevedo. Exit the bus station to the right, follow the train tracks up three blocks, and cross the highway on the pedestrian bridge. The message is clear: rooms have mirrors galore, complimentary condoms, and the adult channel (singles 130 pesos; doubles 180 pesos). If you arrive at the **TAPO** (east station), take the Metro to the *centro,* and if you are at the **Terminal de Autobuses del**

Poniente (western station), swing over to the Tacubaya Metro stop (Lines 1, 7, and 9) for the nearest hotels.

■ Food

Culinary options fall into six basic categories: the very cheap (and very risky) vendor stalls scattered about the streets; fast, inexpensive, and generally safe *taquerías;* slightly more formal *cafeterías;* more pricey and decorous Mexican restaurants; locally popular North-Americanized eateries; and expensive international fare. In addition, U.S. fast-food chains mass-produce predictable fare for the timid palate. **VIPs** offers 60 commercialized Denny's-like eateries throughout the D.F. If you're preparing your own food, local neighborhood markets and supermarkets stock almost anything you could need. For a good time, try **La Merced** market—it's the mother of all markets. As always, avoid unpurified water, including ice, uncooked or unpeeled vegetables, and meat that is not fully cooked. For more on this, see p. 20.

Soda is sold at every corner. *Agua mineral* means mineral water, *sidral* is a great carbonated apple drink, and *refrescos* are your standard soda pops. Bottles are recycled, and patrons pay extra for the privilege of keeping them. Avoid a deposit by imitating the locals and taking your drink in a plastic bag *(bolsa)* with straw *(popote),* to go. For more information, see Food and Drink (p. 67).

CENTRO

The historic downtown area of Mexico City offers a wide selection of food at superlow prices. Slick U.S. fast-food establishments, enormous *cafeterías,* and countless small eateries offer inexpensive *comida corridas,* tacos, *tortas,* and other staples.

Café Tacuba, Tacuba 28 (tel. 518-49-50). Metro: Allende (Line 2). A bastion of serenity in the heart of downtown since 1912. A must. Mexican cuisine and murals depicting scenes of the colonial aristocracy. *Antojitos* 13-35 pesos, entrees 25-35 pesos, breakfast specials 12-30 pesos. Be patient: all dishes are made from scratch, and are well worth the wait. Open daily 8am-11:30pm.

Comedor Vegetariano, Motolinía 315, 2nd floor (tel. 512-65-75). A little hard to find, this yellow Quixote-themed restaurant serves a scrumptious fruit buffet and a filling *menú del día* (17 pesos) on its balcony tables. Open Mon.-Fri. 1-6pm.

Restaurante El Vegetariano, Filomeno Mata 13 (tel. 510-01-13), between 5 de Mayo and Madero. The sunshine-yellow decor and nature photographs are appropriate for this shiny, happy, healthy eatery. Spaghetti with mushroom sauce 18 pesos, spinach salad 25 pesos. Open Mon.-Sat. 8am-8pm.

Pastelería La Ideal, 16 de Septiembre 14, 1 block east of Cárdenas. Lovers of all that is baked and good come for the food and stay for the fun. 4 huge sections, one each for plain bread, cakes, pies, and pastries. A battalion of towering wedding cakes, some of which tower over 3m high. Open daily 7am-10pm.

Restaurant Danubio, Uruguay 3, just east of Lázaro Cárdenas. Stately seafood joint boasts its own coat-of-arms and hefty price tags. Famous artsy types have left their scribbling framed on the walls. Entrees (22-36 pesos) and specials (35-60 pesos) are big enough for two. 5-course *comida corrida* 50 pesos. Open daily 1-10pm.

Súper Soya, Tacuba 40 and several locations throughout the *centro.* A wildly colorful grocery store/café/diner/yogurt stand that has it all—for under 10 pesos. Vegetarian pizzas 5 pesos, *tacos de guisado* 4 pesos. Open daily 9am-9pm.

ZONA ROSA

The myth: only loaded tourists eat in the Zona Rosa. The reality: although the area has some of the city's more expensive restaurants, serving everything from international cuisine to traditional Mexican cooking, many eateries cater chiefly to clerks from the scores of surrounding office buildings. The Zona Rosa also has more fast-food joints than any other area of the city. If you're more interested in the Zona Rosa's slick party atmosphere than in filling your stomach, skip dinner and settle for a drawn-out evening appetizer.

Ricocina, Londres 168 (tel. 514-0648), east of Florencia. This new family-owned restaurant might be the Zona's best-kept culinary secret. Enjoy a delicious *menú del día* (15 pesos) in a soothing soft-peach environment decorated with Mexican art. Yummy *camote* (sweet potato) dessert. Open Mon.-Fri. 1-6pm.

La Luna, Oslo 11, on the narrow walkway between Niza and Copenhagen. Fresh flowers grace every table in this intimate, cozy restaurant. The 12-peso *comida corrida* includes soup, a small and a large entree, and beverage—a great budget value. Very popular; avoid the 2-3pm lunch rush. Open Mon.-Sat. 8am-10pm.

Vegetariano Yug, Varsovia 3 (tel. 525-5330), near Reforma. This sophisticated, 2-floor restaurant with lanterns and wicker furniture makes a great spinach lasagna (18 pesos). Breakfast 17-20 pesos, *antojitos* 12-20 pesos, daily specials 13-20 pesos, and a large variety of salads. Open Mon.-Sat. 1-9pm.

La Mesa de Babette, Reforma 408, east of Florencia. Elegant and fun garden atmosphere is created by potted plants, a beautiful wood interior, and colorful tablecloths with cute seashell chairs. Serves breakfast all day long, great *botanas surtidas* (assorted hors d'œuvres, 12 pesos for 1 person, 20 pesos for 2, 29 pesos for 3), entrees (18-20 pesos), and pastas (28 pesos). Great place to hear the ivories tinkled, too—the bar has live music at night. Open Mon.-Sat. 8am-midnight.

París 16 Café, Reforma 368 (tel. 511-99-11), down the hallway to the right. Jazz discreetly piped in, sharp blue tiles contrasting with the white walls, and framed pencil sketches lend the café a very cosmopolitan feel. Devour the delicious potato chips that come with the Ensalada París 16 (15 pesos) or a great deli sandwich (16-40 pesos). Delivery to surrounding area. Open daily 7:30am-5pm.

Salón de Té Auseba, Hamburgo 159-B (tel. 511-37-69), near Florencia. Comfy though slightly dated tea-room pushes calories on a quiet, upper-class clientele. A nice place to sit out a rainshower. Pastries, cakes, and pies (10-14 pesos), as well as 13 varieties of tea (6 pesos). Open Mon.-Sat. 9am-10pm, Sun. 11am-10:30pm.

ALAMEDA CENTRAL

The convivial atmosphere that permeates the Alameda carries over to the various restaurants that pepper the area. Gone is the stuffy elitism of the Zona Rosa and the frenetic pace of the *centro*. Instead, you'll find good, cheap, back-to-basics food. For something a bit different, try one of the Chinese restaurants on Dolores, two blocks west of Cárdenas and one block south of the Alameda.

Fonda Santa Anita, Humboldt 48 (tel. 518-46-09). Metro: Hidalgo (Lines 2 and 3). Go one block south to Juárez, then two blocks west to the unlabeled Humboldt; it's 2 blocks down the street. A classic restaurant that has represented Mexico in 5 World's Fairs. Serves incredible versions of old standards. Friendly service and tasty portions. Enormous *comida corrida* 20 pesos. Open Mon.-Fri. 1:30-9pm.

Salón Cantina Monteloro, Revillagigedo 52 (tel. 518-63-24), 2 blocks south of the Alameda. *Platillos típicos* (28 pesos) and big, juicy steaks (28-35 pesos) complement the vast selection at the bar. Open Mon.-Sat. 10am-midnight.

Centro Naturista de México, Dolores 10 (tel. 512-53-77), ½ block south of Juárez near the southeast corner of the park, under the big yin 'n' yang. A drab cafeteria-style vegetarian/egalitarian utopia. Don't be afraid to squeeze in at the table—there's room for all, my sister. *Comida corrida* 12-14 pesos. Open daily 12:30-6:30pm. Adjoining store open daily 11am-7pm.

NEAR THE MONUMENTO A LA REVOLUCIÓN

Without many affluent residents or big tourist draws, this area lacks the snazzy international cuisine of other areas. Instead, homey cafés, *torterías,* and *taquerías* abound. For hearty portions and low prices, this is your spot.

La Especial de París, Insurgentes Centro 117 (tel. 773-23-16). Oh God! Oh my God! Yes! Yes! This *nevería* has been scooping up ecstasy since 1921. A wide variety of 100%-natural treats, ranging from *malteadas* (milkshakes) to *frutas glacé*. It's hopeless to order a single scoop—you'll claw your way back to the front of the line for seconds. Was it as good for you as it was for me? Doubles 8 pesos, triples 11 pesos, 4 scoops 14 pesos.

La Taberna, Arriaga at Ignacio Mariscal, below street level. Next to Hotel Pennsylvania. The service is fast, the tables checkered, and the Italian *comida corrida* cheap and generous (5 courses 13-24 pesos). Open Mon.-Sat. 1-10pm.

Restaurante Samy, Ignacio Mariscal 42 (tel. 591-11-00). The tie-wielding business-class clientele is soothed by soft rock (Elton John) and even softer prices. 5-course *comida corrida* 16 pesos. Open Mon.-Fri. 8am-6pm, Sat. 9am-6pm.

Restaurante María Candelaria, Arriaga 23 (tel. 705-2597), one block north of the Monumento. Chirping birds welcome you to a rustic dining room with sleek chairs and purple tablecloths. Sky murals (*sans* pollution) ring the walls, providing a relaxing environment to tackle breakfast (12 pesos) or entrees (22-30 pesos). Open Mon.-Wed. 8am-6pm, Thurs.-Sat. 8am-10pm.

NEAR CHAPULTEPEC

The immediate vicinity of the Bosque de Chapultepec is cluttered with vendors and small restaurants offering the popular and mundane *torta*. A bit farther east, however, lie restaurants that will please even the most fickle palate. The eateries on Cozumel are within walking distance of the Sevilla Metro station (Line 1); Cozumel is just around the corner from the southern *salida*. The entrance to the park lies five long blocks west along Av. Chapultepec. A ritzier alternative might be *antojitos* in beautiful *colonia Polanco*, north of the Anthropology Museum.

Centro Macrobiótico Tao, Cozumel 76 (tel. 211-46-41), south of Colima. No steak and potatoes here. Everything is all-natural, and the adjoining store is a haven for the utterly health-conscious: diet books, spices, and breads line the walls. New Age music and floor seating. Most vegetarian entrees run 20-25 pesos. Open daily 1:30-5pm. Store open 10am-6pm.

Los Sauces, Av. Chapultepec 530, at the corner of Acapulco Roma, 1½ blocks east of the Chapultepec Metro stop (Line 1). Uniquely tiled bar/grill and walls cluttered with pictures of Mexican politicians and stars. 4-peso taco special, 12-peso house specialties—try the *alambre con queso*. Open daily 10am-10pm.

COYOACÁN

The southern suburb of Coyoacán attracts students, young couples, and literati to its restaurants. If you crave brie, cheesecake, or pesto, spend an afternoon here. Outdoor cafés and ice cream shops fill the colonial buildings that line the cobbled streets. For some great ice cream, try **Santa Clara,** at Allende and Cuauhtémoc, (9 pesos a scoop), and **La Siberia** (tel. 554-4537), on the northeast corner of Jardín Centenario (7 pesos a scoop, floats 10 pesos).

Café El Parnaso, Carrillo Puerto 2, on Jardín Centenario across from the cathedral. A celebrated and popular book and record store with an outdoor café in a prime locale on the plaza's edge. Although the food is a bit pricey, the people-watching and eavesdropping you can do here are unbeatable. Have a coffee and a mocha cake or cheesecake with strawberries (12-16 pesos). Open daily 8:30am-10:30pm.

El Morral, Allende 2 (tel. 554-02-98), one block north of Plaza Hidalgo's northeast corner. Wins points for aesthetics—beautifully tiled walls, artwork, and a glass roof, though the flashing cross almost goes over the top. A great tradition: Sunday after Sunday, Mexican families meet here for lengthy lunches. *Comida corrida* 40 pesos, pastas and *cazuelitas* hover in the teens. Open daily 7:30am-10pm.

El Jarocho (tel. 554-5418), on Allende 1 block north of Plaza Hidalgo. The aroma of freshly roasted and ground coffee and the long line will lead you to this corner stand serving some of the best java in the city. Americano, cappuccino, mocha, as well as hot chocolate, all under 4 pesos. Open daily 6am-midnight.

El Jardín del Pulpo (tel. 658-6152), on the corner of Allende and Malintzin. This outdoor seafood restaurant's shrimp and fish cocktails and *ceviches* draw enormous crowds. Cooked is always safer than raw. Open daily 10am-5:30pm.

SAN ÁNGEL

The chic restaurants and *típico* taco stands of San Ángel pack 'em in, especially on Saturdays, when crowds of well-to-do tourists and Mexicans flock to the booths of overpriced art in the Bazaar Sábado. If you want to dine in style and don't mind dropping lots of pesos, Plaza San Jacinto is the place to be.

Chucho el Roto, Madero 8 (tel. 616-2041) by the northeast corner of the Bazar del Sábado. A budget gem situated steps from the action. The *menú del día* serves up soup, rice, an entree, and dessert for 12 pesos. A bright, relaxing bargain. Entrees 17-25 pesos. Open daily 9am-5:30pm.

Restaurante Hasti Bhawan: La Casona del Elefante, Pl. San Jacinto 9 (tel. 616-22-08). Hindustani ambiance: swaying palm trees, authentic sculpture and paintings, kingly South Asian chairs, and elephant-shaped planters. Scrumptious Indo-Thai chicken 28 pesos, vegetarian platter 25 pesos. Treat yourself to a *lassi,* a thick yogurt drink (7 pesos); *pakoras* or *samosas* 7 pesos. Live jazz Thurs. 9pm-midnight, Fri.-Sat. until 1am. Open Tues.-Sat. noon-midnight, Sun. 1-6pm.

El Rincón de La Lechuza, Miguel Ángel de Quevedo 34 (tel. 661-59-11), straight down from Metro M. Á. Quevedo (Line 3), just before the Parque de la Bombilla. Joyfully crowded and decorated. Tasty tacos 10-16 pesos, *menú del día* 25 pesos. Open Mon.-Thurs. 1pm-1am, Fri.-Sat. 1pm-2am, Sun. 1pm-midnight.

■ Sights

It would be impossible to find an appetite which can't be satiated by Mexico City's incredibly diverse range of sights and attractions. While there are no beaches or intact Mayan temples here, there's a little bit of just about everything else. A well-rounded picture of Mexico City's sights will require a week at the very least.

CENTRO

The heart of Mexico City, the *centro,* is in some ways at the heart of the Republic as well. The *centro's* most impressive structures, the **Palacio Nacional** and the **Catedral Metropolitana,** lord over the national consciousness and highlight the uneasy truce that has been struck throughout the country between indigenous and European ways of life. The temples of the old Aztec capital of Tenochtitlán, the cathedral of a religion that substituted ancient beliefs, and the Palacio Nacional, from which modern state is run, all stand side by side.

The sights described in this section are divided into those east, north, and south of the *zócalo.* To reach the *zócalo* by Metro, take Line 2 to *Zócalo.* The station's entrance sits on the east side of the square, in front of the Palacio Nacional. The Catedral Metropolitana lies to the north, the Federal District offices to the south, and the Suprema Corte de Justicia (Supreme Court) to the southeast. For an intelligently annotated checklist of every sight in the *Centro,* get a copy of the *Historic Center of the City of Mexico* from the map's publisher, SAC BE, Apdo. 22-315, 14000 México, D.F. *The Official Guide to Mexico City's Historic Center* (50 pesos), available in the shops of the Museum of Anthropology, Palacio de Bellas Artes, and major English-language bookstores is another excellent and detailed source of information. The **Promoción Social del Centro Histórico,** Chile 8 (tel. 510-25-41, ext. 1499), sponsors free walking tours in English, a different one each Sunday. Call for the week's destination and meeting spot.

The *Zócalo*

Officially the **Plaza de la Constitución,** the *zócalo* is the principal square of Mexico City. Now surrounded by imposing colonial monuments, the plaza was once the nucleus of **Tenochtitlán,** the Aztec capital. Cortés's men razed the city; atop the ruins they built the power center from which they would rule New Spain. Stones from the destroyed city were used to construct Spanish churches and government buildings. To the southwest of the **Templo Mayor** (the Aztecs' principal place of worship, which they called Teocalli) was the Aztec marketplace and major square. Cortés paved this expanse with stones from the main pyramid, calling it Plaza de Armas or Plaza Real. The Plaza went up in flames during the riots of 1692; it was leveled and reorganized in 1790 in accord with Moorish design principles, which stressed the aesthetic importance of fountains. During rebuilding, two important objects were unearthed: a statue of **Coatlicue** (deity of life and death) and the **Piedra del Sol** (Stone of the Sun, the Aztec calendar). This second stone spent nearly a century leaning quietly against the cathedral's west side before the old Museo Nacional claimed it in 1885.

The square became the Plaza de la Constitución in 1812, when the representative assembly of the viceroyalty adopted the liberal Constitución de Cádiz here to protest Napoleon Bonaparte's occupation of Spain. In 1843, the dictator Santa Ana destroyed the Mercado del Parián and ordered that a monument to independence be constructed in the center of the square. Only the monument's *zócalo* (pedestal) was in place when the project was abandoned. The citizens of Mexico began to refer to the square as *el zócalo,* which has become the generic name for the central plazas which mark the Republic's cities and towns.

These days, the *zócalo* is filled with protesters, *artesanías,* street artists, and gaping tourists. Labor rallies and booming megaphones electrify the plaza. Street vendors, selling everything from hard liquor to holy water, hawk their wares along the square. Unemployed men sit by the cathedral holding crudely written paper signs describing their skills, and hoping to be approached by an employer. Just east of the Catedral Metropolitana, a group of folk dancers performs a traditional Aztec dance— and listens to Peter Gabriel during a break. The Mexican flag looms large above all the politics, commerce, culture, and chaos. To the sound of drums, young military cadets raise it every morning and lower it every afternoon at 6pm.

East of the *Zócalo*

Palacio Nacional

Aztec ruler Moctezuma II built a palace, the "New Houses," just south of the Teocalli. The Spaniards obliterated it, and in 1529 the King of Spain granted the land to Hernán Cortés, who proceeded to erect a home for himself there. Designed by architects Rodrigo de Pontecillas and Juan Rodríguez, the building was constructed by *indígena* slave laborers using stones from Moctezuma's palace. In 1562, the King of Spain bought back the house from Don Martín Cortés (illegitimate son of the conquistador) to make it the palace of the king's viceroys. The palace was destroyed during the Riot of 1692 and rebuilt a year later with stones from the original building. Subsequent modifications have given the building a Baroque character, although vestiges of ear-

---

It Could Happen To You

If you're into spectacle but running low on pesos, head for the live drawing of the **Lotería Nacional** at the National Lottery Building, an art-deco structure at Juárez and Reforma. Every Monday, Wednesday, and Friday, crowds gather at 8pm to find out if they've gotten rich quick. Uniformed boys draw the winning numbers from an immense golden ball and then shout them out robot-like, a hushed crowd hanging on their every syllable. Meanwhile, lottery officials circulate throughout the crowd, distributing free lottery paraphenalia. If you're looking for a cheap gift, snag a free set of Lotería Nacional matches and keychains.

lier styles remain. Now called the **Palacio Nacional de México** (tel. 512-20-60), the building occupies the entire east side of the *zócalo*, and is bounded by Calle de la Moneda (on the north) and Corregidora (south). Chief executive center of the Republic, the Palacio houses monumental murals and a museum in honor of Benito Juárez.

It took Diego Rivera from 1929 to 1951 to sketch and paint the **frescoes** on the Palacio's western and northern walls. *Mexico Through the Centuries,* one of his most famous works, is on the west wall of the Palacio at the top of the grand staircase. The mural is divided into eight smaller scenes, each of which depicts an event in the social history of Mexico. Each of the five arches at the top of the mural deals with the Mexican nation—from the beginning of the fight for independence in 1810 up to the start of the Mexican Revolution in 1910. Near the bottom of the mural are scenes depicting the founding of Tenochtitlán in 1325 through its fall and rule by the Spanish colonists. To the left and right of this grand central mural are two other famous works by Rivera. Covering the southern portion of the palace's western wall, *La Lucha de las Clases* (The Class Struggle) depicts Mexican *campesinos* next to workers from around the world. Opposite it on the northern wall is a work entitled *La Leyenda de Quetzalcóatl,* which illustrates the life of the legendary Toltec priest-king who conquered the Mayan people, and ruled over the Yucatán Peninsula before fleeing his kingdom. The murals on the second floor of the palace continue the dramatic history lesson. On the east wall, *El Desembarco en Veracruz* graphically depicts the injustices of the slave trade. Three murals relate the achievements of the Tarascan, Zapotec, and Totonac civilizations. Other murals depict patrio-agricultural topics: the evolution of corn, the harvesting of cacao, and the processes by which *maguey* is harvested and used in tequila production. *La Gran Tenochtitlán* is dominated by the Mercado de Tlatelolco and filled out with the Temple of Tlatelolco, the center of Tenochtitlán, and the volcanoes Popocatépetl (Smoking Mountain) and Itzaccíhuatl (Sleeping Woman). These murals remain unfinished to this day—a result of Rivera's age and pressing political agendas. Guides to the murals and postcards are sold at the base of the central staircase (20 pesos), but are sometimes unavailable. Guided tours (Mon.-Fri. 10am-4pm) are available for 50 pesos; discreetly joining a tour that has already begun is completely free.

The Palacio also contains the **Bell of Dolores,** which was brought to the capital in 1896 from Dolores Hidalgo, in Guanajuato state. It can be seen from outside, at the top of the Palacio's Baroque façade. Miguel Hidalgo rang this bell on September 16, 1810, summoning Mexicans to fight for their independence. Every year on that date it rings in memory of the occasion, and the Mexican President repeats the words once shouted by the father of independence (Palacio open daily 8am-6pm).

On the east side of the Palacio's second floor is the **Cámara de Dipuestos,** which served as a legislative chamber for a few years after the drafting of the 1857 constitution. The dark ante-chamber displays an original 1857 constitution and is graced by the stern faces of politicians who have played important roles in the history of the Republic. You'll hear these names again and again in every city in the nation; try matching the faces to street names (open Mon.-Fri. 9am-8pm).

Connected to the palace is the **Museo Nacional de las Culturas,** Moneda 13 (tel. 512-7452 or 542-0187), housed in Mexico City's former mint. The museum takes a serious look at the lives of various ethnic groups from around the world—peruse the impressive collection of utensils and masks from African countries. In the main lobby sits the enrapturing mural *Revolución* by Rufino Tamayo, which depicts the Mexican Revolution (open Tues.-Sat. 9:30am-5:45pm, Sun. 9am-3:45pm; free).

Other Sights

La Merced, Circunvalación at Anaya east of the *zócalo* (Metro: Merced, Line 1, turn left out of the subway's eastern exit), is the largest food market of its kind in the world. Sprawling over 600 square blocks, farmers from all over Mexico sell their goods here. You'll find every kind of fruit imaginable—papayas, homegrown litchi nuts, delicious salmon-colored *mameyes,* mangos, at least nine different kinds of *plátanos* (bananas), hot tamales, and two full blocks of assorted chiles. Indigenous foods such as fried turtles, steamed chicken intestines, *charales*—corn husks stuffed with shiners—and steamed crayfish abound. Die of happiness among displays of *dulces* (candies) that stretch for five blocks; each stall sells over 300 kinds.

Near the market, on the corner of Manzanares and Circunvalación, is **El Señor de la Humildad.** Only 6 by 9m, and with a seating capacity of 20 thin people, it is reputed to be the smallest church in the world. With a bright pink exterior and an interior altar inlaid with gold and silver, this symbol of humility (however small it is) provides quite a bit of bang for the buck (open daily 9am-8pm). On the corner of Calle de la Santísima and Zapata is the exquisitely ornamented **Templo de la Santísima.** Finished in 1783, the church is one of Mexico City's most important examples of the Churrigueresque style. Avoid the church after dusk; the *templo* is lit but not well-patrolled (open daily 7am-1pm and 5-8pm).

North of the Zócalo

Catedral Metropolitana

In the wake of Cortés's military triumphs, a land devoted to Quetzalcóatl, Tlaloc, and Huitzilopochtli became a stronghold of Christianity. The third cathedral built in New Spain was the **Catedral Metropolitana** (tel. 521-76-37), the massive structure on the north side of the *zócalo*. The 109m-long and 54m-wide cruciform cathedral encompasses the architectural styles of three centuries. Construction started in 1544 under the direction of architect Claudio Arciniega, who modeled the cathedral after the one in Sevilla, Spain. Though it was dedicated in the middle of the 17th century, the Catedral Metropolitana wasn't finished until 1813. In that year, Manuel Tolsá completed the great central dome, the façade, and the statues of Faith, Hope, and Charity which crown the clock tower.

The cathedral has several attached annexes. The main annex, with its door to the left of the cathedral, holds the **Altar de Perdón** (Forgiveness), a replica of a Churrigueresque altarpiece built by Jerónimo de Balbás between 1731 and 1736 and destroyed by fire in 1967. The cedar interior of the choir gallery, constructed in 1695 by Juan de Rojas, is decorated with an elegant grille of gold, silver, and bronze. Juan Correa's murals of the coronation of Mary, St. Michael's slaying of the dragon, and the triumphant entrance of Jesus into Jerusalem cover the sacristy's walls. Cristóbal de Villalpando painted the two other grand murals in this section, *La Concepción Imaculada* and *El Triunfo de la Iglesia.* Of the cathedral's many altars, one of the most magnificent is Balbás's Churrigueresque **Altar de los Reyes** (Kings), which is dedicated to those kings who were also saints. In the annex holding the Altar de Perdón, there are 14 *capillas* (chapels) dedicated to saints. Two chapels near the entrance honor Mexico's patron, the Virgin of Guadalupe.

The eastern annex holds the **Sagrario Metropolitano** (sanctuary), closed to the public (as of the summer of 1996) since its floor is heavily damaged from sinking into the ground. Primarily reserved for baptisms and confirmations, the Sagrario holds six chapels, with one main and two lateral altars. Designed by the great Churrigueresque architect Lorenzo Rodríguez, the Sagrario was built between 1749 and 1768. Since then, its façades have been copied in thousands of Mexican churches. Left of center are statues of the 12 apostles; to the right, the 12 prophets. In the center, above the door, are statues of St. John and, above him, St. Joseph. Elaborate reliefs decorate the whole façade, and the Virtues crown the structure.

Unfortunately, the splendor of the cathedral is occluded by the green erector-set support structures placed to combat the temple's sinking into the ground. Ongoing renovations mean scaffolding and partitions occasionally obscure parts of the exterior (open daily 8:30am-8pm; avoid visiting during Mass—schedule posted on the westernmost door).

Templo Mayor (Teocalli)

North of the *zócalo's* northeast corner, a pool of water laps at a brass model of the Aztec capital, Tenochtitlán. At the center of this city was a great square surrounded by walls 550m long. According to myth, the city was the first place the Aztecs could call home, arriving at this spot after wandering for hundreds of years, driven by the hummingbird god Huitzilopochtli. When Tenoch, the high-priest, spied an eagle consuming a snake while perched on a cactus, he took it as a sign that the Aztecs' wandering was over; the Templo Mayor, or Teocalli, was built on the spot where the eagle was spotted. On the corner of Seminario and República de Guatemala, and a few meters north of the brass model, Teocalli is the major excavated archaeological site in Mexico City.

On February 28, 1978, workers digging east of the cathedral struck a massive rock. They eventually unearthed an eight-ton stone on which the Aztecs had carved the dismembered figure of the moon goddess Coyolxauhqui, sister of Huitzilopochtli. The stone identified the area as the site of Teocalli, earlier believed to be buried under the Catedral Metropolitana to the southwest.

According to Aztec legend, Coatlicue, the goddess of earth and death (whose monolithic statue now sits in the Museo Nacional de Antropología) became pregnant while sweeping out the temple. Her daughter Coyolxauqui grew jealous of her and plotted with her 400 brothers to kill their mother. When they reached her, however, they discovered that Coatlicue had given birth to a full-grown Huitzilopochtli. The new-born god beheaded his sister; his brothers he turned into the planets and stars— all this with a withered foot. By any standard, Huitzilopochotli was a great Aztec warrior; after his death, he came to be associated with war and the sun in its passage across the sky. The stone that the diggers found had been part of the base of a great pyramid. At the pyramid's summit were two temples, one of which was dedicated to the almighty god Huitzilopochtli. The practice of ritually sacrificing humans to Huitzilopochtli was popularized by Moctezuma I, who ruled from 1440-1468. The Aztecs believed that Huitzilopochtli craved gallons of warm, beating human hearts. As sacrifice claimed 10,000-20,000 lives each year, the supply of local victims ran low and Moctezuma I devised the "Flower Wars"—the Aztecs demanded sacrificial victims from their neighbors, and threatened to attack if their bloody demands were not met.

When the conquistadors arrived, Teocalli measured 103m by 79.5m at its base and was 61m high. Moctezuma II led Cortés on the grand tour of the temple, proudly pointing out the caked walls and sacrificial stones. Instead of lauding the Aztecs' blood-spilling, Cortés requested that Moctezuma clear a small place in the temple for an altar to the Virgin Mary. The Emperor's refusal to do so marked the first rift in a relationship that soon deteriorated into war.

Today, the ruins are just east of the cathedral and north of the Palacio Nacional. At first, the huge site appears to be little more than the foundation of a demolished modern complex. Before making any judgments, however, have a look inside. The excavated ruins reveal five layers of pyramids, built one on top of the other as the Aztec empire grew. Signs along the paths help explain which layer belongs to which temple. Over 7000 artifacts, including sculpture, jewelry, and pottery, have been found amid the ruins. Many of the pieces have been traced to distant societies dominated by the long arm of the Aztec Empire. The extraordinary **Museo del Templo Mayor** (tel. 542-06-06), now part of the archaeological complex, houses this unique collection. This museum is a *de rigeur* stop even for visitors on a whirlwind tour of Mexico City. The exhibit is divided into eight *salas* (halls): antecedents and the settling of the Aztecs at the site of Tenochtitlán, war and sacrifice, tribute and commerce, Huitzilopochtli, Tlaloc, fauna, religion, and the fall of Tenochtitlán. The museum was designed to imitate the layout of the original temple, and is constructed so that the artifacts found in the excavation are accompanied by excerpts from the ancient Aztec texts which describe them. Highlights of this exhibit are a scale model of Tenochtitlán at the height of its power, along with the stone of Coyolxauqui and the *tzompantli* (skull rack), a platform where the freshly picked skulls of sacrificial victims were displayed to the public and the gods above. Along with the silent and decapitated ruins adjacent to it, the museum bears witness to the glories of México-Tenochtitlán and makes the arrogant pride of their *cantares mexicanos* more understandable: "Oh giver of life! Bear it in mind, oh princes. Forget it not. Who can siege Tenochtitlán? Who can disturb the foundations of the sky? With our arrows, with our shields, the city exists. México-Tenochtitlán persists! Proud of herself rises the city of México-Tenochtitlán. No one fears death in combat here. This is our glory. This is your mandate." (Museums and ruins open Tues.-Sun. 9am-5pm. Guided tours in Spanish free, in English 10 pesos per person. Admission 16 pesos, 10-peso fee to take pictures, free Sun. and for children under 13.)

South of the Zócalo

In 1691, a heavy rainfall destroyed the wheat crop, causing a famine among the working classes the following year. The viceroy, Count de Gálvez, initiated rationing, and later turned away a group of *indígenas* who asked if the supplies were running out. Panic of a famine brought about the Riot of 1692, the most violent Mexico has ever seen. Several buildings were burned, including part of the palace and much of the Casas del Cabildo, which had sheltered the city government offices and archives. These are now located in the two buildings that comprise the offices of the **Departamento del Distrito Federal** (tel. 518-11-00). The older of the buildings, located on the southwest end of the *zócalo*, was built according to the same plan as the pre-riot structure; on the exterior of this building are tiled mosaic shields that chronicle scenes from the history of Mexico. The newer building, on the southeast end of the *zócalo*, was built between 1940 and 1948, 400 years after its twin.

Suprema Corte de Justicia

The Suprema Corte de Justicia, built in 1929, stands on the corner of Pino Suárez and Corregidora, on the spot where the southern half of Moctezuma's royal palace once stood. After the palace was leveled, Spanish colonists turned the area into a garbage dump. Cortés claimed the property, had it cleared, and designated it the site of city festivities, including a maypole dance, in which men suspended by ropes swung in circles from a pole. Four rather ferocious murals by José Clemente Orozco cover the second-floor walls of the present day Supreme Court. On the west wall hangs *Riquezas Nacionales,* in which a giant tiger, representing the national conscience, defends the mineral riches of the Republic. The mural on the east wall, *El Trabajo* (Work), symbolizes Article 123 of the Mexican Constitution, which guarantees workers' rights. The two remaining murals are called *La Justicia.* The one on the north wall shows a bolt of fire taking human form; the apparition wields a huge axe, with which it threatens a group of masked evildoers. On the south wall, Justice sleeps on a pedestal, holding a sword and the law (murals can be viewed by appointment only, call 522-15-00 Mon.-Fri. 10am-2pm to schedule a visit).

Museo de la Ciudad de México

The Museo de la Ciudad de México, Pino Suárez 30 (tel. 542-04-87), at República del Salvador, three blocks south of the *zócalo*'s southeast corner, houses maps, photographs, lithographs, and murals charting the lives and achievements of the city's founders. The exhibits start on the ground floor and chronologically illustrate pre-Conquest development in the Valley of Mexico. The first exhibit showcases the geological formation of the Valley of Mexico and Lake Texcoco. Other rooms detail the rise of the Aztec Empire in the 15th and 16th centuries, with models of Tenochtitlán and diagrams of its social structure. An upstairs exhibit chronicles the evolution of "New Spain," from the 16th century to the usurpations, betrayals, and victories of 1910. The final exhibit is in the south wing of the second story; it portrays contemporary Mexico City, highlighting the construction of the Metro and showcasing a gigantic model of the Torre Latinoamericana. A photo of modern Mexico City center fills an entire wall, successfully communicating the metropolis's immensity. The museum provides a broad background for further sight-seeing and is an ideal place to begin exploring the city (open Tues.-Sun. 10am-6pm; free).

Other Sights

Across the street from the cathedral's west side on Calle Monte de Piedad is the **Nacional Monte de Piedad** (tel. 521-19-46), the national pawn shop. In pre-Hispanic times the building was part of the Palace of Axayácatl; today it houses a state-controlled flea market where dealers sell reasonably priced jewelry and astonishingly expensive gift items (market open Mon.-Fri. 10am-5pm, Sat. 10am-3pm).

Calle Corregidora, the street between the Suprema Corte and Palacio Nacional, skirts part of an ancient **canal system** that once connected the Aztec capital to the *pueblos* around Xochimilco. After the conquest of Tenochtitlán, Cortés ordered that the remains of the buildings he destroyed be dumped into the canals, and they fell into disuse. But as late as 1945, canals still connected some parts of the city. Today, both sides of the ancient canal system are paved as a pedestrian thoroughfare and the canal itself is covered by shrubs and small flower bushes.

Southwest of the *zócalo*, just west of the corner of 5 de Febrero and 16 de Septiembre, is the famous **Gran Hotel de la Ciudad de México.** Visit at midday to see the light shine through the Tiffany stained-glass ceiling with three flower-shaped central domes. Every detail is pure art nouveau; even the parakeets live in elaborate brass cages with stained glass ceilings. Directly above Restaurante El Malecón, three blocks west of the plaza at Carranza 9, is what was once considered the **skinniest apartment building in the world,** 11m high and only 3m wide.

ALAMEDA

The area around the Alameda Central is doubly blessed, filled with must-see sights and easily accessible by public transportation. Near the park are three Metro stations: **Hidalgo** (Lines 2 and 3), at the intersection of Hidalgo and Paseo de la Reforma, just one block west from the park; **Bellas Artes** (Lines 2 and 8), one block east of the park's northeast corner, between the park and Bellas Artes itself; and **San Juan de Letrán** (Line 8), one block south of the *Torre Latinoamericana*.

Alameda Central

Amid the howling sprawl that is downtown Mexico City, the Alameda is a verdant oasis of sanity and photosynthesis. But while the green Alameda can feel like an island, it is not impervious to the urban life which bustles all around it—three major thoroughfares flank the Alameda and the park is packed with mimes, young lovers, protesters, and *comerciantes* hawking their wares.

The Alameda was designed several hundred years ago by Don Luis de Velasco II, who intended it as a place for the wealthy to relax and stroll. The park takes its name from the rows of shady *álamos* (poplars) which flood it. Since it was opened to the public in this century, Mexico City has fallen in love with the park. Mexicans of all sorts enjoy the Alameda, and even in a city where real-estate values have soared and over-crowding is endemic, no one even considers paving over the park.

At the center of the Alameda's southern side is the **Monumento a Juárez,** a semi-circular marble monument constructed in 1910 to honor the revered former president on the 100th anniversary of Mexican Independence. A somber-faced Juárez sits on a central pedestal among 12 doric columns. On July 19th of each year, a civic ceremony commemorates the anniversary of Juárez's death.

Palacio de Bellas Artes

This impressive white Art Nouveau palace, located at Juárez and Eje Central, at the northeast corner of Alameda Central (tel. 512-3633), is but one result of the "capitalization" plan established during the dictatorship of Porfirio Díaz (1876-1911). Soon after construction began, the theater started to sink into the city's soft ground—it now lies 5m lower than when it was built.

Much of the museum's collection is 19th-century Mexican art; José María Velasco, Eugenio Langesio, Julio Ruelasa, and Joaquín Clausell are prominently featured. Most tourists, however, come to the palace to see the second and third floors, where the walls have been painted by the most celebrated Mexican muralists of the 20th century. On the east wall of the third floor, murals by the leftist José Clemente Orozco depict the supposed tension between natural human characteristics and industrialization. In addition to Orozco's work, the Palacio displays the frescoes of David Alfaro Siqueiros, the 20th-century Mexican muralist, Stalinist, nationalist, and would-be assassin of Leon Trotsky. Siqueiros experimented with lighting, colors, and surfaces, but he is best known as a *típico* muralist. Look for his work on the third floor of the Palacio. Like his contemporary Diego Rivera, Siqueiros favored themes of class struggle and social injustice, and like Rivera he flaunted a cavalier disregard for topical subtlety. One example of the latter is *Tormento de Cuauhtémoc*, which describes Cortés's attack on the last vestiges of the Aztec nation. Beyond the cruelty exhibited by the *conquistadores*, Siqueiros plays upon the theme of old technology encountering the new, represented by the armor of the Spanish. Another mural, *Víctimas del Fascismo*, decries the horrible outcomes of fascism throughout the world. Many of Siqueiros's paintings are layered with masonite, giving them a three-dimensional effect. A good example of this technique is *Explosión en la Ciudad*, in which the smoke from an explosion seems to stream toward the viewer. Rufino Tamayo's more abstract murals illuminate the second floor, further illustrating the incredible talent of 20th century Mexican muralists.

If you have time for only one mural, see Diego Rivera's, on the west wall of the third floor. John D. Rockefeller commissioned Rivera to paint a mural with the topic "Man at Crossroads Looking with Hope and High Vision to the Choosing of a New and Better Future" in New York City's Rockefeller Center. Rivera, however, was dismissed from the project when Rockefeller discovered Lenin's portrait in the foreground. The Mexican government allowed Rivera to duplicate the work in the Palacio. The result, *El Hombre, Controlador del Universo, 1934*, includes an unflattering portrayal of John D. Rockefeller.

On the fourth floor of the palace is the **Museo Nacional de Arquitectura** (tel. 709-3111). It exhibits early sketches and blueprints for the most architecturally distinctive buildings in the city, including the *Teatro Nacional,* the monument to the Revolution, and the Hotel Del Prado. A bookstore on the first floor of the museum sells numerous books about the history of art and Mexican artists, as well as guides to museums in Mexico City (complex open Tues.-Sun. 10am-6pm; admission 10 pesos to see the murals and art exhibits on the upper floor, free for students and teachers with ID; temporary exhibits on the first floor are generally free).

The **Ballet Folklórico de México** performs regional dances in the **Palacio de Bellas Artes** and the **Teatro Ferrocarrilero** (tel. 529-17-01), near the Revolución Metro stop. Their two companies, one resident and one traveling, are world-renowned for their choreographic and theatrical skill. Bellas Artes performances are the only way to see the crystal curtain designed by Gerardo Murelli, made up of almost one million pieces of multicolored crystal which, when illuminated from behind, represent the Valley of Mexico in twilight. The Bellas Artes ticket office sells tickets for these and other artistic performances throughout the city (open Mon.-Sun. 11am-7pm). Travel agencies snatch up lots of tickets during Christmas, *Semana Santa,* and summer; check first at Bellas Artes, then try along Reforma or in the Zona Rosa (performances Wed. 8:30pm, Sun. 9:30am and 8:30pm; tickets 120, 150, and 180 pesos, sold 3 or 4 days in advance at Bellas Artes, but usually available Mon.-Sat. 11am-3pm and 5-7pm, Sun. 9am-1pm and 4-7pm).

Museo Nacional de Arte

The **Museo Nacional de Arte,** Tacuba 8 (tel. 512-32-24), half a block east of the Palacio's north side, was built during the Porfiriato to house the Secretary of Communications. The building's architect, Silvio Conti, designed the building's façade and paid particular attention to the central staircase—its sculpted baroque handrails were crafted by artists in Florence. The design leaves the museum with an empty feel, and footsteps echo through the lonely galleries. The museum contains works from the stylistic and ideological schools of every era in Mexican history. Look for Guerra's *Monumento a José Martí,* a celebration not only of the young revolutionary's life, but also of color and space. The upper floors exhibit art ranging from Greek and biblical themes to 17th- and 18th-century historical depictions. José María Velasco's panoramic landscapes of the Valley of Mexico take up an entire *sala* and are excellent fodder for a picture. "No Flash!" three guards will simultaneously chime (open Tues.-Sun. 10am-5:30pm; admission 10 pesos, free Sun. and for students and teachers with ID, adults over 60, and children under 13).

Near Alameda Central

The **Museo Mural Diego Rivera** (formerly known as **Museo de la Alameda;** tel. 512-07-54), on Calzada Colón and Balderas, facing the small park at the west end of the Alameda, holds Diego Rivera's *Sueño de un Tarde Dominical en la Alameda Central* (Sunday Afternoon's Dream at the Alameda Central), originally commissioned by the Hotel del Prado in 1946. Rivera finished the masterpiece in 1948, but when the Hotel Del Prado proudly hung the just-finished work, a national controversy ensued over the figure of Ignacio Ramírez, who is shown holding up a pad of paper that reads "God does not exist," an excerpt from a speech he gave in 1836. The archbishop of Mexico refused to bless the hotel, and on June 4th at dawn, more than 100 angry students broke into the hotel, erased the "does not exist" fragment from the original phrase and damaged the face of the young Diego Rivera in the center of the mural. The Hotel del Prado partially collapsed during the 1985 quake, and the mural was moved to the museum, which was constructed solely to hold this piece. The key in front of the mural, a sort of *Where's Waldo?* of Mexican culture, points out the portrayal of historical figures woven into the crowd: Frida Kahlo, José Martí, and a chubby young Rivera, among others. José Guadalupe Posada's *La Calavera Catrina,* the central figure in the mural, mocks the aristocratic pretentions under the Díaz presidency (museum open daily 10am-2pm and 3-5pm; admission 7 pesos, free Sun. and for students and teachers with ID).

The **Pinacoteca Virreinal de San Diego,** Dr. Mora 7 (tel. 510-27-93), next door to Centro Cultural José Martí, was once a monastery. The building was originally constructed in the Baroque style, but Neoclassical elements were added in the 19th century. Now the monastery's rooms with high, decorated ceilings and wooden floors contain an extensive collection of Baroque and Mannerist paintings, generally with religious themes. No photos allowed (open Tues.-Sun. 9am-5pm; admission 7 pesos, free Sun. and for students with ID).

A poet, José Martí was a leader of the Cuban independence movement in the late 19th century. He dreamed of a united and free Latin America, led by Mexico, and repeatedly warned of the dangers of North American imperialism. Martí's visionary poetry figures prominently at the **Centro Cultural José Martí,** Dr. Mora 2 (tel. 521-21-15), at Hidalgo on Alameda's west end. In a small library graced by both a colossal bust of Martí and his words, *"De America soy hijo...a ella me debo"* ("Of the Americas I am a son, to her I am indebted"), the center preserves a collection of writing by Martí and other anti-interventionists. Covering three walls of the building is a rainbow-colored mural depicting Martí and the people of Latin America. A tally sheet in the corner of the mural records Spanish, British, French, and U.S. interventions in Latin America from 1800-1969; the grand total is a staggering 784 (open Mon.-Fri. 9am-9pm, Sat. 9am-2pm; free).

The second tallest building in the city, the **Torre Latinoamericana** (Latin American Tower), 181m and 42 stories high, touches the sky over the corner of Lázaro Cárdenas and Madero (the continuation of Juárez), one block east of Alameda Central's southeast corner. Its 44th-floor observatory, a good 2422m above sea level, commands a startling view of the city (top-floor observatory open daily 10am-11pm; admission 18 pesos, 14 pesos for children under 12, telescope fee 1 peso). The 38th floor holds "the highest **aquarium** in the world." While their gimmicky boast is probably correct, the place seems more like a neighborhood pet store than a real aquarium (open daily 10am-10pm; admission 12 pesos, children 10 pesos). Similar views can be had for free from the top floors of the Hotel Sevilla Palaca and Hotel María Isabel Sheraton, by the Ángel de la Independencia.

Built in 1716, **La Iglesia de San Francisco** rests in the shadow of the Torre Latinoamericana, just to the east on Madero. It was once a vast Franciscan complex that included several churches, a school, and a hospital. Two fragments of the original cloisters can be seen at Gante 5, on the east side of the church, and Lázaro Cárdenas 8, behind a vacant lot. The Franciscans were the first order to arrive in Mexico; the first 12 Franciscan friars in the country landed in Veracruz and walked barefoot to the capital—today a seven-hour bus ride. The church is open daily 7am to 8:45pm, but avoid visiting Saturday morning and afternoon and all day Sunday during mass hours (open Mon.-Fri. 9am-1pm and 5-7pm, Sat. 9am-1pm).

Across the street from San Francisco shimmers the **Casa de los Azulejos,** an early 17th-century building covered with *azulejos* (blue-and-white tiles) from Puebla. To be able to afford even a token few of these tiles was a mark of considerable status. This mansion was festooned by an insulted son who set out to prove his worth to his father. There is an Orozco mural on the staircase wall, and a great view of the building can be had from the second-floor balcony, but you have to pass through Sanborn's restaurant to view them (open daily 7:30am-10pm).

Palacio Iturbide (tel. 521-57-97), at Madero 17 between Bolívar and Gante, one and a half blocks east of Lázaro Cárdenas and near the Iglesia de San Francisco, is a grand 18th-century palace with an impressive colonnaded courtyard. The Count of San Mateo Valparaíso lived here, but in 1821 Emperor Agustín de Iturbide took over the residence. Banamex took over the building from the Emperor—a case of capitalism succeeding nationalism succeeding aristocracy. There is a gallery on the ground floor; exhibitions change every three months (open daily 9am-2pm and 4-6pm).

Just north of the Alameda is the **Museo Franz Mayer,** Hidalgo 45 (tel. 518-22-66), at Pl. de Santa Veracruz. Formerly the Hospital de San Juan de Dios, the building has been expertly restored and now houses an extensive collection of ceramics, colonial furniture, and religious paintings. The first-floor exhibit of colonial processional and ceremonial crosses is neat-o (open Tues.-Sun. 10am-5pm; admission 8 pesos, 4 pesos for students with ID, half-price Sun.; guided tours Tues.-Sat. in the early afternoon). Next door to the Franz Mayer museum in the pink building at Hidalgo 39 (tel. 521-22-24) is the **Museo Nacional de la Estampa.** Here lies the National Institute of Fine Arts's graphic arts and engraving collection, tracing the art of printmaking from pre-Hispanic seals to contemporary engravers. The highlight of the museum is the work of the acclaimed José Guadalupe Posada, Mexico's foremost engraver and printmaker. His woodcuts depict skeletons dancing, singing, and generally cavorting in ridiculous costumes—a graphic indictment of the Porfiriato's excesses (open Tues.-Sun. 10am-6pm; admission 8 pesos, free Sun.).

At the Plaza de la República under the **Monumento a la Revolución** is the **Museo Nacional de la Revolución** (tel. 546-21-15). Díaz originally planned the site as the seat of Congress, but as revolutionary fighting entered the city streets, progress was halted, and the dome was left only half-completed. It wasn't until the 1930s that the monument and space below were finally dedicated to the memory of the revolution. Today 32 flag poles representing the Mexican states line the pathway to this marmoreal dome. The entrance to the museum's subterranean exhibition is just north-

---

Far Away, So Close

One kilometer east of Chapultepec Park is the **Ángel de la Independencia.** Situated at the fourth traffic circle on the Paseo de la Reforma, the Ángel soars 50m above passing cars. Designed by Antonio Rivas Mercado, the monument is a stone column capped by a golden angel; its round-terraced base holds the remains of Hidalgo, Allende, and other national heroes. The original angel fell during an earthquake in 1957, and the head was so mangled that a new one had to be cast. Solid ever since, the Ángel stands erect as a symbol of Mexican victory, and crowds often converge here after major *fútbol* triumphs. The view at night, when the angel is embraced by the surrounding lights and skyline of the city, is magnificent.

east of the monument, in a black-stone park. Just inside the doors, a thorough chronology (in Spanish) of the revolution unfolds (museum open Tues.-Sat. 9am-5pm, Sun. 9am-3pm; free; call to arrange for a tour).

The **Museo San Carlos** (tel. 566-8522), at the corner of Puente de Alvarado and Ramos Arizpe, three blocks north of the Monumento a la Revolución, houses an old art school and an impressive collection of European painting spanning the 16th through the 19th centuries, including works by Rubens and Goya (open Tues.-Sun. 10am-6pm; admission 7 pesos, free Sun.).

BOSQUE DE CHAPULTEPEC

Literally "Forest of Grasshoppers," this is the area on the western side of the city center where the Aztecs, new and unwelcome arrivals to the Valley of Mexico, first settled. Today, this 2100-acre expanse is one of the older natural parks in the New World. With its manifold museums, hiking paths, and modern sports facilities, one could easily spend several days in the Bosque. Mexico's most famous museum, the **Museo Nacional de Antropología,** sits among the hills of the park.

Although signs warn visitors about the stiff penalties for littering (three months' salary), the park is hardly elysian. Stray garbage and scraggly patches of browned grass pepper the lawn. The area is relatively safe during the day, but women should remain alert and should avoid the more remote or isolated areas of the park. Despite these detractions, on the right sort of day the Bosque can be downright wonderful. Try to visit the Bosque on Sunday, when families flock here for cheap entertainment. Musical spectacles and open-air concerts enliven the park, and voices fill the air promoting foods and trinkets. Best of all, the zoo and most of the museums in the area are **free** on Sundays (everything open daily 5am-5pm).

All the museums listed are in Old Chapultepec, the eastern half of the park, which fans out to the west of the Zona Rosa. To reach the park, take the Metro to Auditorio (Line 7, closer to the **zoo**) or to Chapultepec (Line 1, closer to the **Niños Héroes** monument, most of the museums, and much more convenient).

Museo Nacional de Antropología

Some journey to Mexico just to consult this magnificent and massive mega-museum, located at Paseo de la Reforma and Gandhi (tel. 553-62-66). It is 4km of Mexico's finer archaeological and ethnographic treasures and the yardstick by which all other Mexican museums are measured. Constructed of volcanic rock, wood, and marble, the museum opened in 1964. Pedro Ramírez Vásquez and his team of 42 engineers and 52 architects designed and built the structure in 18 months; meanwhile, archaeologists, buyers, and 20 teams of ethnographers scrambled to enlarge the museum's collection. The huge stone image of the rain-god Tláloc greets you outside, and 23 exhibition halls await within. Poetry from ancient texts and epics graces the entrances from the main courtyard. In the center of the courtyard, a stout column covered with symbolic carvings supports a vast, water-spouting aluminum pavilion.

You would need about three days to pay homage to the entire museum, though many are afflicted with pottery overload after a few hours. As you enter on the right side of the ground floor, a general introduction to anthropology precedes a series of chronologically arranged galleries; moving from the right to the left wings of the building means advancing chronologically. These trace the histories of many central Mexican groups, from the first migrations to the Americas up to the Spanish Conquest. The Oaxacan, Mayan, Gulf Coast, Northern, and Western displays are on the left (southern) side—keep an eye out for the massive Aztec stone calendar. Upper-level rooms contain modern ethnographic displays (museum open Tues.-Sat. 8am-7pm, Sun. 10am-6pm; admission 16 pesos, free Sun.).

The museum also contains a **restaurant** (open Tues.-Sun. 9am-6pm) and a large **bookshop** that sells English guides to archaeological sites around the country, as well as histories and ethnographies of Mexico's indigenous populations. Some of these guides are not available at the sites themselves, so plan ahead.

MEXICO CITY

To reach the museum, take bus #55 or 76 southwest on Reforma and signal the driver to let you off at the second stop after entering the park. On the Metro, take Line 7 to the Auditorio station; the museum is just east down Reforma. Take the first left on Gandhi for the main entrance. For a more scenic route, take Line 1 to Chapultepec station.

At the end of the long walkway just inside the park on the east side stands the **Monumento a los Niños Héroes,** six white pillars capped with monoliths and teased by small fountains. The monument is dedicated to the young cadets of the 19th-century military academy, then at the Castillo de Chapultepec. In 1847, during the last major battle of the war with the U.S., the Niños Héroes fought the invading army of General Winfield Scott. Refusing to surrender, the last five boys and their lieutenant are said to have wrapped themselves in the Mexican flag before throwing themselves from the castle wall. To the side of the monument is the **Tree of Moctezuma,** boasting a circumference of 13 meters and reputed to have been around since the time of the Aztecs. Behind the monument, Gran Av. cuts through the park. Walk west on this street and take the second right on Gandhi. A five-minute stroll north takes you to Reforma and the museum.

Museo Tamayo and Museo de Arte Moderno

Just to the east of the Museo Nacional de Antropología is the **Museo Tamayo de Arte Contemporáneo** (tel. 286-65-19), on the corner of Reforma and Gandhi. The museum is hidden by the vegetation and therefore easy to miss: take the first right on Gandhi from the Chapultepec Metro stop (Line 1). After a five-minute walk on Gandhi, the museum lies to the left down a small, almost hidden, path through the trees. Alternatively, walk due east from the entrance of the anthropology museum down the path into the woods; Tamayo is 100m straight ahead. The Mexican government created the nine halls of the museum—remarkably reminiscent of the Smithsonian's National Gallery's East Wing—after Rufino and Olga Tamayo donated their international collection to the Mexican people. The murals of Rufino Tamayo were much criticized in the wake of the Revolution of 1910 for not being sufficiently nationalistic. Since the museum's opening in 1981, however, his reputation has been rehabilitated and he has taken his place with Rivera, Siqueiros, and Orozco among the key figures of modern Mexican art. The museum, opened in 1981, houses a large permanent collection of Tamayo's work, as well as important works by de Kooning and Surrealists Miró, Ernst, and Masson. Some of the world's premier artists regularly stage exhibitions (open Tues.-Sun. 10am-5:45pm; admission 10 pesos, free for students and teachers with ID; call to arrange guided tours).

The **Museo de Arte Moderno,** at Reforma and Gandhi (tel. 553-62-33), north of the Monumento a los Niños Héroes, houses a stellar collection of contemporary paintings by Kahlo, Siqueiros, José Luis Cuevas, Rivera, Orozco, Velasco, and other Mexican artists. The museum is linked to the Galería Fernando Camboa—a very modern assemblage of sculptures and exhibitions—by a remarkable outdoor sculpture garden with pieces by Moore, Giacometti, and others (open Tues.-Sun. 10am-6pm; admission 10 pesos, free Sun. and for students and teachers with ID).

Museo Nacional de Historia

Inside the Castillo de Chapultepec, on top of the hill behind the Monumento a los Niños Héroes, is the Museo Nacional de Historia (tel. 286-0700), which narrates the history of Mexico from before the time of the Conquest. An immense portrait of King Ferdinand and Queen Isabella of Spain greets visitors in the first *sala.* Galleries contain displays on Mexican economic and social structure during the war for independence, the Porfiriato, and the Revolution. The upper level exhibits Mexican art and dress from the viceroyalty through the 20th century. Other galleries exhibit carriages used by Maximilian (the elaborate ones) and Juárez (the basic black ones), and a Juan O'Gorman mural depicting the revolution, from the cruelties of the aristocracy to the triumph of the constitution. The walls of *sala* 13 are completely covered by Siqueiros's *Del Porfirismo a la Revolución.* To get to the top, walk up the road directly behind the Niños Héroes monument (open Tues.-Sun. 9am-5pm, tickets sold until 4pm; admission about 14 pesos, bring change, free Sun., but all 2nd-floor *salas* are closed; video 10 pesos; camera 5 pesos).

Museo del Caracol

The **Museo Galería de la Lucha del Pueblo Mexicano por su Libertad** (The Museum of the Struggle of the Mexican People for Liberty, tel. 553-62-85), is on the southern side of Chapultepec hill. Designed by Pedro Vásquez, the museum is often listed as **Galería de Historia** or even more commonly as **Museo del Caracol** (Conch) because of its spiral design. The gallery consists of 12 halls dedicated to the greatest hits of Mexican history from the early 19th to the early 20th century. A lengthy quotation at the entrance urges visiting Mexicans to live up to the legacy embodied in the museum. From the start of your downward spiral, the gist of the museum's message is clear: foreign intervention has made Mexico's fight for its liberty an uphill battle. Especially interesting are exhibitions on the executions of Hidalgo and Morelos, the flight of Benito Juárez, the execution of Maximilian, and the battles of Villa, Zapata, and Obregón. The museum's exhibitions consist of amazingly life-like mini-dioramas, scores of paintings, and various other historical artifacts. However, visitors unfamiliar with the contours of Mexican history will be bewildered by the Spanish-only explanations. The staircase leads to a beautiful round skylit hall, the sides of which form the inner wall of the spiral you have been ascending. Also inside is a copy of the Constitution of 1917 handwritten by Venustiano Carranza himself (open Tues.-Sat. 9am-4:30pm, Sun. 10am-3:30pm; admission 7 pesos, free Sun.).

Elsewhere in *Chapultepec*

Twenty-five days before his death in January, 1974, David Alfaro Siqueiros donated his house and studio to the people of Mexico. In compliance with his will, the government created the **Museo Sala de Arte Público David Alfaro Siqueiros,** Tres Picos 29 (tel. 531-33-94), at Hegel just outside the park. Walk north from the Museo Nacional de Antropología to Rubén Darío. The street Tres Picos forks off to the northwest on the left; follow it for one block. The funky little museum is on the right. Siqueiros was not only an artist, but also a revolutionary soldier, propagandist, communist, republican, Stalinist, and anti-fascist. Fifteen thousand murals, lithographs, photographs, drawings, and documents recount his fascinating life (open Mon.-Fri. 10am-2pm and 5-7pm, Sat. 10am-2pm; admission 7 pesos, students with ID 3 pesos, free Sun, call to arrange a guided tour in English or Spanish).

West of the Siqueiros museum along Rubén Darío, at the intersection with Reforma, is the **Jardín Escultórico,** a sculpture park containing realist and symbolist statues. To the south and east of the sculpture garden, at Reforma and Av. Heroico Colegio Militar, flourishes the **Jardín Botánico,** a botanical garden with a lake (open daily 9am-5pm; free). The **Lago de Chapultepec,** situated at the heart of the park, has rowboats for rent (daily 7:30am-4:30pm, 9 pesos per hr.). Or, make a bee line for **Parque Zoológico de Chapultepec,** just east of the Jardín Botánico. Though the zoo's collection is quite impressive, the humble habitats and the city's pollution might make animal lovers shed a tear (open Wed.-Sun. 9am-4:45pm; free).

TLATELOLCO

Archaeological work has shown that the city of Tlatelolco ("Mound of Sand" in Náhuatl) existed long before the great Aztec capital of Tenochtitlán. The first king of Tlatelolco, Teutléhuac, began his rule in 1375. He and his warriors distinguished themselves in battle, conquering enemy territory near Tepeyac on the outskirts of Tenochtitlán. By 1463, the Tlatelolco king, Moquíhuix, had built his city into a busy trading center coveted by the Aztec ruler, Axayácatl. Tension mounted over territorial and fishing boundaries, and soon Moquíhuix learned that the Aztecs were preparing to attack his city. Even forewarned, Moquíhuix couldn't handle the Aztec war machine, and Tlatelolco was absorbed into the huge empire. Ironically, it was here that the Aztec nation made its own last stand against Cortés.

Today, a monstrous state low-income housing project looms over the 17th-century church that stands on the grounds of Tlatelolco's ancient temple. Three cultures—ancient Aztec, colonial Spanish, and modern Mexican—have left their mark on this square, giving rise to the name **Plaza de las Tres Culturas,** at the corner of Lázaro Cárdenas and Ricardo Flores Magón, 13 blocks north of the Palacio de Bellas Artes. The plaza's history has been extremely bloody, beginning in 1521, when the last Aztec emperor Cuauhtémoc made his last stand here. With stoic optimism, a plaque in the southwest corner of the plaza asserts: "On August 13, 1521, heroically defended by Cuauhtémoc, Tlatelolco fell to Hernán Cortés. It was neither a triumph nor a defeat, but the birth of the *mestizo* city that is the México of today." More than 400 years later, the plaza was the site of the Tlatelolco Massacre of October 2, 1968. An adolescent rivalry between two secondary schools led to fighting in the streets; with the Mexico City Olympic games just a few months away, the government thought it necessary to forcefully quell all disturbances. Fueled by anger at the government's violence, the street fighting gave way to protests, which were answered with even more violence: in September the national university was occupied by soldiers. On October 2, a silent pro-peace sit-in was held at the Plaza de Las Tres Culturas. Toward the end of the day, government troops descended on the plaza, shooting and killing hundreds of protesters; prisoners were taken and tortured to death. In memory of the victims of the massacre, a simple sandstone monument was erected in the plaza and dedicated in 1993, on the 25th anniversary of the incident—before then, the government had repressed any mention of the event, going as far as removing from all national archives the newspapers for the day after the massacre. The humble monument lists the names of the dead and bitterly expresses outrage at the lack of attention paid to the horrific shootings. A small plaque on the back of the monolith explains that the present monument, already dirtied and defaced, is but a temporary construction, and that a more fitting memorial will be built when more funds are collected. At times, the plaza can feel eerie and desolate, abandoned to slow decay. Litter and vandalism mar the plaza.

In the plaza, parts of the **Pyramid of Tlatelolco** (also known as the **Templo Mayor**) and its ceremonial square remain dutifully well kept: one part of history is simply not mentioned, the other glorified. Enter from the southwest corner, in front of the Iglesia de Santiago, and walk alongside the ruins, down a steel and concrete path which overlooks the eight building stages of the main pyramid. At the time of the Conquest, the base of the pyramid extended from what is now Insurgentes to the current site of Iglesia de Santiago. The pyramid was second in importance to the great Teocalli of the Aztec capital, and its summit reached nearly as high as the modern skyscraper just to the south (the **Relaciones Exteriores** building). During the Spanish blockade of Tenochtitlán, the Aztecs heaved the freshly sacrificed bodies of Cortés's forces down the temple steps, within sight of the *conquistadors* camped to the west at Tacuba. Aztec priests would collect the leftover body parts at the foot of the steps; food was scarce during the siege and all meat was valuable. Another notable structure is the **Templo Calendárico "M,"** an M-shaped building used by the Aztecs to keep time. Near its base, scores of skeletons were discovered; a male and female pair that were found facing each other upon excavation have been dubbed "The Lovers of Tlatelolco."

On the east side of the plaza is the simple **Iglesia de Santiago,** an enormous, fortress-like church erected in 1609 to replace a structure built in 1543. Continue past the church towards the skyscraper for two blocks, right through the parking lot, to reach the **Museo de Siqueiros,** a white building housing a lone three-dimensional mural (open Tues.-Sun. 9am-5pm; free).

To get to Tlatelolco, take the Metro to the Tlatelolco stop (Line 3) and exit through the González *salida.* From the exit, turn right on González, walk three blocks east until you reach Cárdenas (Eje 2 Norte), turn right at the small park, and walk one very long block south until you see the plaza on your left. Two hundred meters farther south is a yellow pedestrian bridge that makes crossing Cárdenas feasible. This area is marginally safe during the day and should be avoided at night.

LA BASÍLICA DE GUADALUPE

According to a legend that has become central to Mexicans' religious identity, the Virgin appeared on a mountain before a poor peasant named Juan Diego, entreating him to have a church built in her honor at that site. In order to convince the Mexican bishop of his vision, Diego laid a sheet full of fresh roses cut during the cold of December in front of the bishop. Both in awe, they watched the Virgin's portrait emerge on the sheet. Our Lady of Guadalupe has since become the patron of Mexico, an icon of the nation's religious culture. Diego's mantle can be seen in **La Basílica de Guadalupe,** north of the city center. Designed by the venerated Pedro Ramírez Vásquez in the 1970s, the new Basílica is an immense, aggressively modern structure that bears an uncanny resemblance to Disney World's Space Mountain. The Basílica draws crowds of thousands daily to the Virgin's miraculous likeness; the devout and the curious alike flock around the central altar and impressive organ to catch a glimpse of Diego's holy cloak. Just outside, a huge statue of Pope John Paul II stands watch (open daily 5am-9pm). On December 12th, the Virgin's name day, pilgrims from throughout the country march on their knees up to the altar, among other surreally bizarre devout celebrations.

Next to the new Basílica is the old Basílica, built at the end of the 17th century. These days, the old Basílica houses the **Museo de la Basílica de Guadalupe,** Pl. Hidalgo 1 (tel. 577-60-22), in the Villa de Guadalupe. The colonial paintings dedicated to the virgin pale beside the intensely emotional collection of *retablos,* small paintings made by the devout to express their thanks to the Virgin of Guadalupe for coming to their assistance. A large room at the base of the staircase contains a pair of golden soccer shoes offered to the Virgin before the 1994 World Cup by the Mexican star Hugo Sánchez (museum open Tues.-Sun. 10am-6pm; admission 2 pesos).

Behind the Basílica, winding steps lead up the side of a small hill, past lush gardens, crowds of the faithful, and cascading waterfalls. A small chapel dedicated to the Virgin of Guadalupe, the **Panteón del Tepeyac,** surmounts the hill. The bronze and polished wood interior of the chapel depicts the apparitions witnessed by Juan Diego. From the steps beside the church, one can absorb a breathtaking panoramic view of the city framed by the hillsides and distant mountains. Descending the other side of the hill, past the spouting gargoyles bearing a surprising resemblance to Quetzalcóatl, statues of Juan Diego and a group of *indígenas* kneel before a gleaming Virgin doused with the spray from a rushing waterfall. On the other side of the hill, another waterfall drenches a bed of flowers. Vendors, both in and around the Basílica's grounds, hawk religious paraphernalia: holy water, holy shoes, holy t-shirts, holy jeans, and more. You'd be wise, however, to heed the signs and ignore those selling stamps and other allegedly consecrated doo-dads.

To get to the Villa de Guadalupe, take the Metro to La Villa (Line 6), go past the vendor stands, and make a right onto Calzada de Guadalupe. A small walkway between the two lanes of traffic leads directly to the Basílica. Alternatively, take the Metro to Basílica (Lines 3 and 6). Walk along Insurgentes in the direction of traffic. At Montiel, turn right, and head 500m east straight to the plaza.

COYOACÁN

The Toltecs founded Coyoacán (Place of the Coyotes in Náhuatl) between the 10th and 12th centuries. Cortés later established the seat of the colonial government here, and, after the fall of Tlatelolco, had Cuauhtémoc tortured here in the hope that he would reveal the hiding place of the legendary Aztec treasure. South of the center, Coyoacán today is the city's most attractive suburb, worth visiting for its museums or simply for a stroll in beautiful **Plaza Hidalgo** and neighboring **Jardín Centenario,** or nearby **Placita de la Conchita.** Come to Coyoacán for a respite from the hurried *centro;* the pace is slower here. Coyoacán is centered on the Pl. Hidalgo, which is bounded by the cathedral and the Casa de Cortés. The two parks are split by Calle Carrillo Puerto, which runs north-south just west of the church.

One of Coyoacán's more affecting sights is the **Museo Frida Kahlo,** Londres 247 (tel. 554-59-99), at Allende five blocks north of Pl. Hidalgo's northeast corner, in the colorful indigo and red building at the northeast corner of the intersection. Works by Rivera, Orozco, Duchamp, and Klee hang in this restored colonial house, the birthplace and home of Frida Kahlo (1907-1954), whose work has gained a lot of popularity in the U.S. Having suffered a debilitating accident as a young woman, Kahlo was confined to a wheelchair and bed for most of her life. While married to Diego Rivera, she began painting and became a celebrated artist. Her chronic health problems, together with her devotion to an adulterous husband (she, by the way, was also quite adulterous), inspired the shockingly morbid subject matter of her works (open Tues.-Sun. 10am–6pm; admission 10 pesos, students and teachers with ID 5 pesos).

Near Plaza Hidalgo's northeast corner is a bronze statue of Miguel Hidalgo. The **Casa de Cortés** (tel. 544-78-22), a one-story, reddish structure at the north end of the plaza, was originally Cortés's administrative building; now it houses the municipal government. Inside are murals by local artist Diego Rosales, a student of Diego Rivera's, showing scenes from the Conquest (open Mon.-Fri. 9am-2pm).

South of the plaza, beyond the Hidalgo statue, is the 16th-century **Parroquia de San Juan Bautista,** bordered by Pl. Hidalgo on the north and Jardín Centenario on the west. The church interior is elaborately decorated with gold and bronze. Enter south of the church's main door (open Tues.-Sat. 5:30am-8:30pm, Mon. 5:30am-7:30pm). A few blocks southeast of Pl. Hidalgo, facing the Placita de la Conchita and marked by the gardened plaza at the end of Higuera, is the **Casa Colorada,** Higuera 57, which Cortés built for Malinche, his Aztec lover. When Cortés's wife arrived from Spain, she stayed here briefly with her husband, but soon disappeared without a trace. It is believed that Cortés murdered his spouse because of his passion for Malinche, although he later gave her away as loot to one of his *conquistador* cronies. On the street running east from the northeast corner of Plaza Hidalgo is the **Museo Nacional de Culturas Populares,** Hidalgo 289 (tel. 658-12-65). Temporary exhibitions on the history of popular culture in Mexico are the mainstay here (museum open Tues.Thurs. 10am-6pm, Fri.-Sun. 10am-8pm; free).

After Leon Trotsky was expelled from the U.S.S.R. by Stalin in 1927, he wandered in exile until Mexico's President Lázaro Cárdenas granted him political asylum at the suggestion of Trotsky's friend, muralist Diego Rivera. Trotsky arrived in 1937 with his wife and settled into the house that's now the **Museo y Casa de León Trotsky,** Viena 45 (tel. 658-87-32), seven blocks north of Pl. Hidalgo's northeast corner up Allende, then three blocks east on Viena to the corner of Morelos. The entrance is around back at Río Churubusco 410. Bullet holes riddle the walls—relics of an attack on Trotsky's life led by the Stalinist muralist David Alfaro Siqueiros on May 24, 1940. Trotsky survived that attack, only to be stabbed in the skull with an ice pick three months later. The museum displays many of the couple's belongings (open Tues.-Sun. 10am-5pm; admission 10 pesos, students with ID 5 pesos, free Sun.).

The **Convento de Nuestra Señora de Los Ángeles de Churubusco,** 20 de Agosto and General Anaya, was built in 1524 over the ruins of a pyramid dedicated to the Aztec war god Huitzilopochtli. The present structure was built in 1668. Inside, an old garden grows, its walls scratched with indecipherable inscriptions (open Mon.-Fri. 7am-10pm, Sat. noon-2pm and 6-8:30pm, Sun. 8am-2pm and 5:30-8pm). Mexico has been invaded more than 100 times, most often by the U.S. Inside the Convento de Churubusco is a museum dedicated to the history of the invasions, the **Museo Nacional de Las Intervenciones** (tel. 604-0699). The museum's halls cover four eras, from the late 18th century to 1917. A few halls are also dedicated to exhibitions on North American expansionism and cruelty to *indígenas,* U.S. slavery and its significance for Mexico, and European imperialism (museum open Tues.-Sun. 9am-6pm; admission 14 pesos, free Sun. and for students and teachers with ID). To get to the convent and museum from Coyoacán, walk four blocks down Hidalgo and then follow Anaya as it branches left, four blocks farther to the convent grounds. Far easier is to take the Metro, get off at General Anaya (line 2), and walk two blocks west on 20 de Agosto.

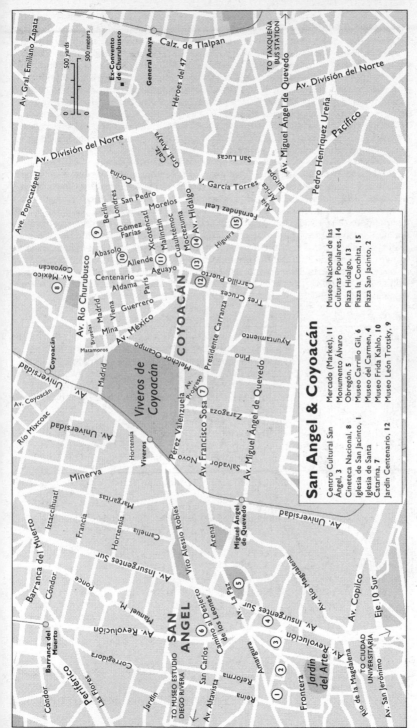

MEXICO CITY

San Angel & Coyoacán

Centro Cultural San Ángel, 3
Cineteca Nacional, 8
Iglesia de San Jacinto, 1
Iglesia de Santa Catarina, 7
Jardín Centenario, 12
Mercado (Market), 11
Monumento Álvaro Obregón, 5
Museo Carrillo Gil, 6
Museo del Carmen, 4
Museo Frida Kahlo, 10
Museo León Trotsky, 9
Museo Nacional de las Culturas Populares, 14
Plaza Hidalgo, 13
Plaza la Conchita, 15
Plaza San Jacinto, 2

Frida

Depending on whom you talk to, many residents of Coyoacán would say their most cherished product was *la heroína del dolor* (the heroine of pain), the artist Frida Kahlo. Famously self-obsessed, famously morbid, and famously shocking, Kahlo's work, in recent years, has been riding a wave of unprecedented popularity and critical success. *Self-Portrait with Monkey and Parrot* (1942) recently sold for 3.2 million dollars. The Frida files are burdened once again with the recent publishing of a facsimile of the diary Kahlo kept in the last ten years of her life. The colorful, idiosyncratic journal, filled with frantic drawings and cryptic phrases, may well add to the ever-growing Kahlo mythology rather than shed a clarifying light on the artist's life and body of work.

The **Museo Anahuacalli** (tel. 677-29-84), on Calle Museo, was designed by Diego Rivera with Aztec and Mayan architectural motifs. It houses the artist's huge collection of pre-Hispanic art. Built atop a hill, Anahuacalli commands one of the best views in Mexico, comparable to those of the Torre Latinoamericana and Castillo de Chapultepec (open Tues.-Sun. 10am-2pm and 3-6pm). To reach the museum from Pl. Hidalgo or Churubusco, take a *pesero* 5km going south on Av. División del Nte. and get off at Calle Museo. You might want to ask the driver to point out the stop as it is not visible immediately. Turn right onto Museo and soon you'll reach the place

To reach Coyoacán from downtown, take the Metro directly to the Coyoacán station (Line 3). *Pesero* "Coyoacán" (every 20min., 1 peso) at the station stops within two blocks of Pl. Hidalgo. Taxis cost about 6 pesos. It's also a pleasant walk.

SAN ÁNGEL

South of Mexico City near Coyoacán is the wealthy, suburban community of San Ángel. Dotted with churches and exquisite colonial homes, San Ángel is a great place for a stroll. To reach the area, 10km south of the Centro along Insurgentes, take the Metro to the M.A. Quevedo station (Line 3). Head west on Quevedo (away from the big *Santo Domingo* bakery) for three blocks; when it forks take a left onto Av. La Paz, and continue along the wonderfully verdant **Parque de la Bombilla.** One block later you'll arrive at the intersection with Insurgentes. The centerpiece of this lovely park is the shaft-like concrete **Monumento al General Álvaro Obregón.** Obregón was one of the revolutionary leaders who united against Huerta, the usurper who executed President Madero and seized power in 1913. In 1920, Obregón became the first president of the post-revolutionary era. Reliefs on the four sides of the monument represent peace, agriculture, industry, and the people in arms. The inscription on the far wall of the chamber reads, "I die blessing the revolution." In the main hall of the monument is a shiny green statue of the one-armed Obregón and a plaque that reads "in place of your sacrifice." The lower-level contains a small jail cell which houses a wooden replica of Obregón's arm (open daily 7am-4:30pm; free).

Cross the big Insurgentes intersection, and walk up La Paz one block until you come to the intersection with Av. Revolución. One block to the south (left) are the three tiled domes of **Iglesia del Carmen,** Revolución at Monasterio. Designed and built between 1615 and 1626 by Fray Andrés de San Miguel of the Carmelite order, the church and adjacent ex-convent are decorated with tiles and paintings. An outstanding statue of Christ the Nazarene is located in the Capilla del Señor Contreras (open daily 7am-1pm and 4:30-9pm). The ex-convent has been converted into the **Museo del Carmen** (tel. 616-28-16). The museum displays colonial art, tons of crucifixes, and portraits of various saints and nuns. Also exhibited are typical convent rooms—look out for the flat wooden bed and oh-so-comfy log pillow. Most tourists come to see the mummies; located in an underground crypt, the grotesque cadavers were originally disturbed in 1916 when the Zapatistas arrived in search of treasure (open Tues.-Sun. 10am-5pm; admission 14 pesos, free Sun.).

The Plaza del Carmen is across the street from the church. The large yellow building on its southern side is the **Centro Cultural,** which hosts changing art exhibitions.

One block up Av. La Paz, now called Frontera, is the **Plaza de San Jacinto,** at San Francisco and Benito Juárez. Every Saturday, the plaza fills up with ritzy shoppers scoping pricey arts and crafts at the **Bazaar Sábado.** Although many pieces are beyond the budget travelers' economic grasp, there are plenty of bargains and shady places to relax. On the north side of the plaza is the **Casa de Risco,** Plaza San Jacinto 15 (tel. 550-92-86), a well preserved 17th-century house holding an important collection of 14th- through 18th-century European art. The whitewashed inner courtyard contains an exquisitely tiled fountain made out of pieces of bowls and plates (called *riscos*) that were collected from around the world. Also look out for *Crisol de las Razas,* a painted colonial chart that lists racial combinations with names like *lobo* (wolf) and *salto atrás* (a step backwards; open Tues.-Sun. 10am-5pm; free). One block farther up Juárez lies the beautiful **Iglesia de San Jacinto,** a 16th-century church with an ancient orange façade, beautifully carved wooden doors, and a peaceful courtyard. This neighborhood, the oldest in San Ángel, contains some swank modern mansions as well (church open daily 8am-8pm).

Three blocks north on Revolución from the intersection with La Paz, to the right if coming from the Parque de la Bombilla, is the **Museo Carrillo Gil,** Revolución 1608 (tel. 550-6289), a modern building housing the contemporary art collection of the late Carillo Gil. The small museum contains paintings by Siqueiros as well as a whole floor of Orozcos and some works by the young Rivera. Siqueiros's famous *Caín en los Estados Unidos* is on the third floor (open Tues.-Sun. 10am-6pm; admission 7 pesos, students with ID 3 pesos, free Sun.).

CIUDAD UNIVERSITARIA

The **Universidad Nacional Autónoma de México** (National Autonomous University of Mexico), or **UNAM,** is the country's largest public university, boasting an enrollment of over 300,000. Immediately after the new colonial regime was established, the religious orders that arrived in Mexico built elementary and secondary schools to indoctrinate new converts and to educate young men who had come over from Spain. After petitioning the king of Spain, the first university was established in 1553 in the building at the corner of Moneda and Seminario, just off the *zócalo.* As the university grew, classes were moved to the building that now houses the Monte de Piedad, on the west side of the *zócalo,* and then to a building at the east end of the Pl. del Volador, where the Suprema Corte now stands. **Ciudad Universitaria (C.U.)** was completed on 1954. The area, 7.3 million square meters, boasts 26km of paved roads, 430,000 square meters of greenery, and 4 million planted trees. The university is not residential. Today's ultramodern buildings belie UNAM's status as one of the three oldest universities in the Americas.

Despite the rock-bottom tuition, the university is still able to support an amazingly varied collection of student groups, activities, and social and cultural events. Films, shows, and club meetings abound. You name it, it's here—from a Tae Kwon Do club, to a film about young gay Mexicans, to tribal dances that explore Mexico's indigenous heritage. *Tiempo Libre* magazine and the leaflets **Cartelera** and **Los Universitarios** provide comprehensive schedules; hundreds of other events are posted on bulletin boards in the **Centro Cultural Universitario (C.C.U.).** This pleasant, modern complex houses the **Teatro Juan Ruiz de Alarcón** (tel. 662-7166), **Sala Netzahualcóyotl** (tel. 622-7021) and several other concert halls, and two movie theatres, **Salas José Revueltas** and **Julio Bracho** (tel. 665-2850). A student ID gets you 50% off already cheap prices. The C.C.U. can be reached through the UNAM shuttles leaving the Universidad Metro station (Line 3), or by taking a bus down Insurgentes and getting off at the yellow pedestrian crossing two stops south of the Olympic stadium.

The **Espacio Escultórico** is a sculpture park just west of the Biblioteca y Hemeroteca Nacional, just outside of C.C.U. Out of a huge lava bed and surrounding cave formations rises a pan-chromatic collection of metal, cement, and wood Herculean sculptures constructed in the early 1980s. The artists wanted to revive, through modern techniques, the architectural traditions of pre-Hispanic ceremonial centers. The

Espacio Escultórico should only be visited during the day; its secluded location make it dangerous after nightfall.

From the center of the university, take bus #17 or #130 ("San Fernando") from the stadium and get off at the first designated stop (at the yellow pedestrian overpass). Across the esplanade from the library is **MUCA (Museo Universitario Contemporáneo de Arte;** tel. 622-0304). It holds powerful exhibitions of mid-century modern art. The museum is usually dedicated to a single artist, so it provides a comprehensive examination of his/her work (open Mon.-Fri. 11am-6pm, Sat. 11am-2pm; admission 6 pesos, students and teacher with ID 3 pesos; for 5 pesos, guided tours for groups of five or more can be arranged—call 622-04-05).

Hop on the yellow and blue UNAM shuttle to get to the heart of the UNAM campus. The **Estadio Olímpico 1968** is located on the west side of Insurgentes Sur, just past the entrance to Ciudad Universitaria. The stadium was built in the 1950s, designed to resemble a volcano with a huge crater—an appropriate motif since lava coats the ground on which it is built. The impressive mosaic that covers the stadium was made by the indefatigable Rivera using large colored rocks; it depicts a man and a woman holding two torches, symbolic of the 1968 Olympics held in the stadium. Unfortunately, the gates to the stadium are usually locked.

Although the university's architecture is impressive, most visitors come to see the mosaic murals that cover its larger buildings. From the stadium, cross Insurgentes (a pedestrian tunnel under the thoroughfare leads to the main part of campus), and continue east (straight ahead). West of the Jardín Central's southern half, the university's administrative building is distinguished by a 3-D Siqueiros mosaic on the south wall, which shows students studying at desks supported by society. One of the world's larger mosaics, the work of Juan O'Gorman, wraps around the university library, a nearly windowless box next to the rectory tower. A pre-Hispanic eagle and Aztec warriors peer out from the side facing the philosophy department. The side facing the esplanade shows the Spaniards' first encounter with the natives; the opposite side depicts a huge atom and its whirling components. Farther east is the expansive Jardín Central; this vast, tree-lined quadrangle is popular with students looking to relax or start a pick-up game of *fútbol*. All of the murals were being renovated the summer of 1996, and the O'Gorman may still be under partial scaffolding.

A beautiful and pleasantly secluded attraction is the Jardín Botánico, a stop on the free UNAM shuttle leaving from the Metro station (Line 3). From the endless and extremely unique species of cacti to the shady arboretum to the tropical plants pavilion, the Jardín is a welcome change from the city's urban sprawl, and it offers a peak into the Valley of Mexico as it was hundreds of years ago. The trails of red volcanic sediment, which wander past the lagoons and glens, and a helpful map at the entrance provide just enough guidance (open Mon.-Fri. 9am-4:30pm; free).

To get to Ciudad Universitaria, take the Metro to Universidad (Line 3) and exit to *salidas* D and E. Free shuttle service, though limited and irregular after classes end, is available to all campus areas. From Metro Universidad, take Line #1 to both the stadium and esplanade/museum areas (about 5 stops). Many *peseros* will be waiting just below the station, but follow the students past the vendors to the free buses. The free university buses run along the circular streets around the main campus. For transportation along Insurgentes Sur, the *peseros* (1 peso) are generally the best option. The university can also be reached by taking the Metro to Copilco (Line 3). Take the first left as you exit the station and walk two blocks, crossing Av. Copilco. Turn right at

---

Higher Learning

Part of UNAM's mandate is fulfilling Mexico's constitutional guarantee of universal education to all citizens. In 1992, students' strikes shut down the university in defense of this right, in response to proposals to raise tuition from a virtually nonexistent 0.20 pesos to 20 pesos per anum. These days, classes still cost less than US$5 per semester for nationals and roughly US$10 for foreign students.

the dead end and then left to reach the edge of campus, the Paseo de las Facultades. A right on this main street will lead eventually to the junction with Insurgentes near the Estadio Olímpico.

Near Ciudad Universitaria

Near the end of the pre-Classic Period, the tiny volcano **Xitle** erupted, leaving eight square kilometers covered with several meters of hardened lava. The lava flow preserved one of the first pyramids constructed in the Valley of Mexico and formed what is now the **Cuicuilco Archaeological Zone** (tel. 553-22-63) on the southeast corner of the intersection of Insurgentes Sur and Anillo Periférico. Take bus #130 ("San Fernando Huipulco," 1 peso) to the entrance on the west side of Insurgentes Sur, south of the Periférico. The **Pyramid of Cuicuilco,** which means "Place of the Many-Colored Jasper," was built between 600 and 200 BCE by the early inhabitants of the Valley of Mexico, about when ceremonial centers first began to spring up in Mesoamerica and priests gained extraordinary powers. Measuring 125m across at its base and 20m in height, Cuicuilco consists of five layers, with an altar to the god of fire at its summit. The lava rock around the base has been removed, allowing visitors to walk along it and up to the altar. From here, on less smoggy days, you can see Xitle to the south and Popocatépetl to the east (zone open daily 9am-4pm; free). Next to the pyramid is a museum with exhibitions on volcanology, the geology and ecology of the area, and the eruption of Xitle (open Tues.-Sun. 9am-4pm; free).)

XOCHIMILCO

Multicolored *chalupa* boats crowd the maze of fairly filthy canals, ferrying passengers past a floating market offering food, flowers, and music. The market is especially popular on Sundays, when hordes of city dwellers and tourists pack the hand-poled *chalupas.* They lounge and listen to the water-borne *mariachis,* celebrating Mexico City's aquatic past as they munch tacos from the floating taco bars which tie up pirate-style to the passenger boats. Delicate orchids and bubbly beer are also on sale.

The keyword for almost anything you do in Xochimilco is bargaining. From the markets to the boats, this is the only way to get around in this overly-popular tourist spot. Be aware that if you come earlier, you'll find a much emptier Xochimilco, with far fewer boats and much higher prices. For a private boat for six people, expect to pay about 50 pesos per hour; consult the official diagram for prices, as boat owners will try to charge eight or 10 times as much. If confronted with inflation, wait for more people to arrive and begin bargaining. On weekend afternoons, *colectivo* boats are cheaper and more fun than the private boats (3 pesos). The standardized rates price *mariachis* at 30 pesos per song.

To get to Xochimilco, take the Metro to Tasqueña (Line 2) and then use the *tren ligero* (trolley, 1 peso; follow the *correspondencia* signs inside the station) in the *Embarcadero* direction and get off at that stop. The boats are three blocks east of the station—exit to your left. *Peseros* below the station will also take you there; ask to be let off at *las canoas* (the canoes). To reach the central marketplace, walk south down Embarcadero, turn right onto Violeta, and then left onto Nuevo León. The market is just beyond the **Iglesia de San Bernandino de Cera.**

■ Shopping

While most Mexican cities have a single central market, Mexico City has one specializing on every retail good. These markets are relatively cheap. Each *colonia* has its own market, but the major marketplaces are all in the center of town. Shopping throughout the *centro* and the Alameda proceeds thematically: there is a wedding-dress street, a lighting fixtures street, a lingerie street, a windowpanes street, a power tools street, a military paraphernalia street, and so on.

La Merced, Circunvalación at Anaya, east of the *zócalo.* Metro: Merced (Line 1). A huge selection of fresh produce, grown all over the country, at rock bottom prices. Locals claim that La Merced moves as much money daily as the entire city of Monterrey. Open daily 8am-7pm (see p. 99).

Sonora, Teresa de Mier and Cabaña, 2 blocks south of Merced. Specializes in witchcraft, medicinal teas and spices, figurines, and ceremonial images. Search no further for lucky cows' feet, shrunken heads, eagle claws, aphrodisiacs, black salt (for nosy neighbors), talismans to ward off the evil eye, poison antidotes, powdered skull (for the domination of one's enemies), amber, patchouli incense, energy pills, courage powder, bath oil (for success in business), black candle figurines, and dead butterflies, among other things. Open daily 8am-7pm.

Mercado de La Ciudadela, just north of Metro Balderas (Lines 1 and 3). An incredible array of *artesanías,* crafts and traditional clothing, at some of the lower prices in the city. Bargaining is often unnecessary. Open daily 8am-7pm.

La Lagunilla, Comonfort at Rayón, east of the intersection of Lázaro Cárdenas and Reforma. Two large yellow buildings on either side of the street. Although famous for the antiques and old books sold here on Sun., the market has metamorphosed into a daily vending site for practical goods. Open daily 8am-7pm.

Bazaar del Sábado, Pl. San Jacinto 11, in San Ángel. Open on Sat. only, as the name suggests. High quality folk crafts: dolls, paintings, rugs, papier-mâché, jewelry, and much more. A great place to browse, but bring lots of cash if you plan to buy. Slightly cheaper bazaar in the plaza just outside. Open Sat. 10am-7pm.

FONART. Patriotismo 691; Juárez 89 (Centro); Insurgentes 1630 Sur; Londres 136 (Zona Rosa); Av. de La Paz 37 (San Ángel); Manuel Izaguirre 10 (Cd. Satélite); and other locations. A national project to protect and market traditional crafts. Sells *artesanías* from all over the country: giant tapestries, Oaxacan rugs, silver jewelry, pottery, and colorful embroidery. Open Mon.-Sat. 10am-7pm.

Tepito, between Metro stops Revolución and San Cosme (Line 2), accessible by "Tepito" *pesero* along Reforma. The "Thieves Market," Tepito is the national clearinghouse for gray-market imports from the U.S. and South Asia. Neat-o police raids daily. Watch your wallet—better yet, don't bring it. Open daily 9am-9pm.

San Juan, Pl. El Buen Tono, 4 blocks south of Alameda Central, 2 blocks west of Lázaro Cárdenas. Bounded by Ayuntamiento, Aranda, Pugibet, and Dolores. Follow the painted footprints indoors. Targeting tourists, sells an incredible variety of baskets, furniture, blankets, traditional clothing, keychains, T-shirts, dolls, *sombreros,* and wall hangings. Open Mon.-Sat. 9am-7pm, Sun. 9am-4pm.

Buenavista, Aldama 187 (tel. 529-12-54), at Degollado, in Col. Guerrero. Geared almost exclusively to the tourist, sells a somewhat overpriced but wide selection of stuffed bulls' heads, obsidian blades, and videos about traditional Mexico. Open Mon.-Sat. 9am-6pm, Sun. 9am-2pm.

■ Entertainment

Fear not the humdrum discos that dominate the nightlife in small towns throughout the country—you're in the largest and most populated city in the world. The chameleon that is entertainment in the nation's capital can turn any color you choose. Be it the Ballet Folklórico at Bellas Artes, an old film at an art cinema, a bullfight, or blues in a smoke-filled bar, the city has something for everyone.

At many large nightclubs, dates of the opposite sex are sometimes prerequisites for admission. Cover charges range from 15 to 80 pesos, but women are sometimes admitted free. A very steep cover charge may mean open bar; be sure to ask. Places with no cover often have minimum consumption requirements and high drink prices. Covers magically drop during the week when business is scarce, especially for *norteamericanos* with reputedly hearty appetites and deep pockets. If prices are not listed, be sure to ask before ordering, lest you be charged exorbitant *gringo* prices. Be aware that *bebidas nacionales* (Mexican-made drinks, from Kahlúa to *sangría*) are considerably cheaper than imported ones. Watch out for ice-cubes—unpurified water in disguise. *Cantinas,* bars with dimly lit interiors, no windows, or swinging doors reminiscent of Wild West saloons, are often not safe for women.

The Zona Rosa and the strip along Insurgentes Sur offer the most variety for your entertainment peso. Tourists and Mexicans alike flood the streets in the evenings, often dressed to the hilt and set to have a good time. Bars and discos clog the streets, each attempting to outdo the others in flashiness and decibel output. Although the Alameda and other areas also have some places to dance, discos in more run-down parts of town can get seedy. Women venturing out alone should be aware that they will most likely be approached by men offering drinks, dances, and their firstborn.

Different areas of the city boast different entertainment specialties. As a general rule, the best *discotecas* are found along Insurgentes Sur, and a few spill over into the Zona Rosa. Rock clubs abound in the Zona Rosa, and a few exist around the Alameda. *Mariachi* bands teem in Garibaldi Plaza, while *merengue* and *salsa* clubs cluster near the *zócalo* and in San Ángel and Coyoacán. Jazz bands, some *salsa* and traditional Mexican music, and generally lighter fare appealing to an older crowd can also be found in the city's southern suburbs.

For safety, the Zona Rosa offers the best lighting and least lonely streets, which are a problem in other areas. Taxis run all night and are the safest way of getting from bar to disco to breakfast to hotel. Try to avoid going out at night alone; as always, the bigger the group, the safer you'll be.

ZONA ROSA

Bars

The Zona Rosa is a bar-hopper's dream come true. While taverns in this area are generally upscale and expensive, high price tags often mean live performers and tasty *botanas* (appetizers). Zona Rosa bars cater to all ages and tastes, from teenybopper to elderly intellectual. Many feature live music or beamed-in video entertainment. Women will probably feel safer in this area, but men still aggressively try to pick up anything with two X chromosomes. Catch a ride home in a *pesero* running all night along Reforma or Insurgentes Sur (1-1.50 pesos). Or better, yet take a cab.

Harry's Bar and Grill, Liverpool 155 (tel. 208-62-98), enter half a block north of Liverpool on Amberes. An international thirtysomething crowd carouses and chats amid the dull din of a piped-in soccer match. Walls are cluttered with beer bottles and menus from bars and *cantinas* all over the Republic. Beers a hefty 12-15 pesos. Mini *botanas* 17-30 pesos. Open Mon.-Sat. 1pm-midnight.

Bar Osiris, Niza 22 (tel. 525-66-84). Suffers from mid-week attendance problems, but on weekends, it turns into a hard-rock party pit. Live bands perform after 8pm. Cover Fri.-Sat. 15 pesos. 6 beers 50 pesos. Open Wed.-Sun. 7pm-3am.

Yarda's Bar, Niza 39 (tel. 514-57-22). The packed dance floor shakes rhythmically with the pumping bass and techno tunes. The 30-peso pitchers of beer and the 16-peso mixed drinks make this young, ultra-suave crowd get down. Cover Fri.-Sat. 30 pesos. Open Mon.-Sat. 4pm-3am.

Xcess, Niza 39 (tel. 525-5317). A more mellow techno beat and fog machine compete with a mirrored video bar serving 6-peso ¼-*yardas* of beer (about ¼ liter). Open Thurs. (no cover) 2pm-2:30am, Fri.-Sat. (cover 30 pesos) 2pm-3am.

El Chato, Londres 117 (tel. 533-28-54), with a stained glass doorway. Only for those with a penchant for kitsch. No glitz, no booming beat, but the somewhat older crowd likes it that way. Occasionally visited by *trovas* from the Yucatán, when a 30-peso cover charge take effect. Beer 12 pesos. Don't miss the informal jazz-piano bar with Sinatra sound-alikes. Open Mon.-Sat. 1pm-1am.

Discos

The Zona Rosa has some of the Republic's flashier discos and higher cover charges—on weekend nights, the Zona can seem like the epicenter of the entire universe. Club-hopping, however, is becoming more difficult, as many discos are moving over to the high cover charge and open bar system. Long lines are sure signs that a disco has become the joint *du jour*. Inside, expect anything from a sweaty, throbbing mass of humanity to a slightly more reserved jacket-and-tie crowd enjoying the U.S. pop/rock fare. Sidewalk recruiters will likely try to lure in groups, especially those with high female to male ratios; hold out and you just might be offered a deal. If you can't find something to your liking here, head east to Insurgentes Sur, and then south along the thoroughfare—you'll run across the whole gamut of clubs.

Rock Stock Bar & Disco, Reforma 260 (tel. 533-09-06), at Niza. Clubs come and go, but *el estok* remains packed and fun year after year. Single men might have difficulty getting in, but looking foreign usually helps. Follow the street signs through the rotating darkroom-style doors and upstairs into a huge open attic room in which railings, scaffolding, and metal cages are doused in fluorescent paint. Lively action, with everything from rave to underground rhythms. Open bar. Thurs. cover 80 pesos for men, free for women. Fri-Sat. cover 120 pesos for men, 80 pesos for women. Open Thurs. 8pm-1am, Fri.-Sat. 8am-3am.

Casa Rasta, Florencia 38. They be jammin' to a wide range of music—the emphasis, not surprisingly, is on reggae. Rugged Mexican crowd and island decor make it an intense dance experience. Open Wed.-Sun. 9pm-3am.

Celebration, Florencia 56 (tel. 541-6415). Rigged with speakers heard 'round the world. Modern dance rock accompanies a stylish set and varied theme nights—you just might wind up boogeying next to masked horror aficionados. Scattered tables provide an oasis from the active dance action. Cover includes *barra nacional* (open bar, national brands). Cover 90 pesos. Open daily 7pm-3am.

Papa's Disco, Londres 142 (tel. 207-77-02). For the true dancing machine. Come prepared to shed a few pounds while experiencing a Latin grind mixed in with hard rock, pop, and techno. Wed.-Thurs. and Sun. cover 60 pesos for men, free for women. Fri.-Sat. cover 90 pesos for men, 40 pesos for women after 10pm. Cover includes open bar for Mexican drinks. Open Wed.-Sun. 8pm-3am.

CENTRO

Many of the bars here are popular among the desk-job jet-set, and some have as long and distinguished a history as the buildings that lord over them. Explore, but bear in mind that by midnight the Centro's streets are completely deserted and potentially dangerous. One word: taxi. While the following bars spill over into the Alameda area, they are distinguished by their clientele and atmosphere.

El Bar Mata, Filomeno Mata at 5 de Mayo (tel. 518-02-37). Packs in a youthful crowd ready to party. Sophisticated design with mood lighting and hip architecture. Equals nearly everything the Zona Rosa has to offer mid-week, although on non-band nights (no cover) the clientele noticeably thins out. Live bands Wed. and Sun. Cover 30 pesos. Open daily 6pm-2am.

La Ópera, 5 de Mayo 10 (tel. 518-02-37), just west of Filomeno Mata. A restaurant and bar with baroque ceilings, mirrored walls, a grandfather clock, and dark wood booths filled with chattering couples. While relatively low-key today, showdowns, secret government conferences, even alliances were made and lost within these walls. Drinks 12-19 pesos. Open daily 1pm-midnight.

Bar de los Azulejos, Casa de los Azulejos on Madero 14 (tel. 518-66-76), 2nd floor. Small bar tucked away in a corner of Sanborn's. Spiral staircase, leather chairs, and dimmed lights lend a touch of class. Mixed drinks 12-18 pesos. 50% off domestic drinks Mon.-Thurs. 4-6pm and Fri.-Sun. 6-8pm. Open daily 7am-11pm.

Bar León, Brasil 5 (tel. 510-30-93), just west of the Templo Mayor and cathedral. Appealing to a slightly older crowd, León offers nightly performances by *merengue* or *salsa* bands. Dark atmosphere invokes the Mexico of yesteryear. In business for 45 years. Bacardi rum 17 pesos, beer 12 pesos. Open Wed.-Sat. 4pm-1am.

ALAMEDA CENTRAL

While bars and discos near the Alameda can't compare in luster to those in the Zona Rosa, prices are refreshingly low. Unfortunately, surrounding neighborhoods may be dangerous, especially late at night. Taxis are somewhat sparse in this area, so ask for the phone number of a nearby *sitio*.

Especially popular is the **Hostería del Bohemio,** Hidalgo 107 (tel. 512-83-28), just west of Reforma. Leave the Hidalgo Metro stop (Lines 2 and 3) from the Av. Hidalgo/ Calle de Héroes exit and turn left. This romantic café is saturated with music, singing, and poetry in the evenings. Seating is on the outdoor terraces of both levels and all four sides of a lush, two-tiered courtyard with a burbling central fountain. The slice-of-a-tree tables and chairs are lit by old-fashioned lanterns, making it the perfect spot for intimate conversations. Guitars strum in the background. Coffees, cakes, and ice creams run high at 15 pesos each (no cover; open daily 5-11pm).

GARIBALDI PLAZA

Garibaldi Plaza hosts some of Mexico City's gaudiest and seediest nightlife. On weekend nights, roving *mariachis* compete for pesos with *ranchero* groups, who will play your favorite tune for 25-40 pesos. Tourists, locals, prostitutes, musicians, vendors, and the entire rainbow of human fruit flavors mingle here, many reeling from the copious amounts of liquor they've just downed. Big nightclubs, each with their own *mariachi*, do their best to lure the crowds. Though they advertise no cover, per-drink prices are staggeringly high. Beware of pickpockets and purse-snatchers; it's best to leave your credit card, wallet, and purse at home.

Possibly one of the most peculiar attractions of the plaza is **Pulquería Familiar,** Honduras 4, on the northwest corner of the plaza. It claims to be the only *pulque* (fermented cactus juice) bar where women are admitted—provided they're accompanied by a male. Taste the precolonial alternative to beer. Have a glass of *blanco* (the pure stuff, 1.50 pesos) to get a feel for it; then move onto the fruity flavorings to actually enjoy the experience. Flavored liters of *pulque* run 8 pesos—mango comes closest to duplicating a nice tropical mixed drink (open daily 4pm-2am).

The plaza is at the intersection of Lázaro Cárdenas and República de Honduras, north of Reforma. Take the Metro to Bellas Artes (Lines 2 and 8) and walk three blocks north along Cárdenas; Garibaldi is the plaza on your right. The Garibaldi stop on Metro Line 8 takes you three blocks north of the plaza. Exit to your left from the stop and walk south. The best time to visit Garibaldi is from 8pm-2am on weekends, but it's also the least safe then. Prostitutes turn tricks here, and the neighboring streets and *cantinas* can be dangerous. Women should take particular caution.

COYOACÁN AND SAN ÁNGEL

While generally very safe sections of town, these two southern suburbs fall just outside many of Mexico City's public transportation axes. The Metro serves both until midnight, after which a taxi is the best option.

El Hijo del Cuervo, north side of the Jardín Centenario, in Coyoacán. A motley crue of joe-chugging, people-watching, liquor-downing folks crowd here weekend nights. Tourists and locals both enjoy the occasional live rock and Latin music.

El Arcano, División de Norte 2713 (tel. 689-82-73), near the San Andrés park in Coyoacán. A live jazz/rock combo brightens the dark interior. The cover depends on the group. No cover Mon.-Wed. Open daily 8:30pm-1am.

GAY BARS AND DISCOS

Mexico City offers the full range of social and cultural activities for gays and lesbians. Pick up a copy of *Ser Gay,* a free pamphlet available at Butterfly (see below) that details gay entertainment and art events in the city and provides a complete listing of all the gay bars in town, and many throughout the country.

Butterfly, Izazaga 9, near Metro Salto del Agua (Lines 1 and 8), ½ block east of Lázaro Cárdenas, just south of the cathedral. The biggest, brashest gay night spot in town. The dance floor is a crowded tangle of humanity. Video screens and a superb lighting system. Male revue late on weekend nights. Tues.-Thurs. no cover, Fri.-Sat. cover 35 pesos with 2 drinks. Gay events throughout the city are advertised from here. Open Tues.-Sun. 7pm-3:30am.

El Taller, Florencia 37-A (tel. 533-49-84), in the Zona Rosa. Underground; watch carefully or you'll miss the entrance. Well known hangout for blue-collar gay men. Wed. and Sun. attract a twentyish crowd; private barroom attracts an older crowd. Male revue Wed. at midnight. Sun.-Tues. and Thurs. 20-peso cover includes 1 drink. Wed. and Fri.-Sun. cover 35 pesos. Open Tues.-Sun. 9pm-3am.

Famoso 42, Cuba 42 (tel. 355-75-59), between Allende and República de Chile in the *centro.* Couples cuddle in the dark corners or slow-dance to mellow musical fare: Mexican *merengue,* but mostly American top-40 ballads. Pauses in the music bring strippers, videos, and calls for drinks. Open Tues.-Sun. 4pm-dawn.

GATS, Oaxaca 85 (tel. 208-3464), in Colonia Roma. Women of all ages enjoy nightly shows and live music. Open Tues.-Sun. 6pm-3am.

■ Sports

Whether consumed by bullfighting, soccer, jai alai, or horse racing, Mexican fans share an almost religious devotion to *deportes.* If sweaty discos and cavernous museums have you craving a change of pace, follow the crowds to an athletic event and prepare yourself for a rowdy good time.

Plaza México, Insurgentes Sur (tel. 563-39-59). Accessible by the Metro station San Antonio (Line 7), Mexico's principal bullring, sitting 50,000 fans. Bullfights begin Sun. at 4pm. Professionals fight only Dec.-April; *novilladas* (young *toreros* and bulls) during the off-season. Tickets are 15-80 pesos, depending on proximity to the ring and whether they fall on the *sombra* (shady) or *sol* (sunny) side. If you're going cheap, try to bring sunglasses, a hat, and a pair of binoculars.

Aztec Stadium, Calz. de Tlalpan 3465 (tel. 677-71-98). Take a *pesero* or *tren ligero* (trolley) directly from the Tasqueña Metro station (Line 2). How big is it? Really big. The Azteca is the greatest of many Mexican stadiums where professional soccer is played, and one of the larger in the world. Read the sports pages of any newspaper for information on games. The season runs Oct.-July.

Frontón México (tel. 543-32-40), Pl. de la República, 3 blocks south of the Revolución Metro station (Line 2), facing the north side of the monument. Watch and bet on jai alai. Officially dressy—men are supposed to wear coats and ties, women dresses or skirts—but a decent shirt and jeans is the unspoken standard for admission. Games Tues.-Thurs. and Sat. starting at 9pm, Sun. at 7pm. Box office opens at 6:30pm. Admission 25 pesos. Betting (optional) starts at 1 peso.

Hipódromo de las Américas, Av. Ávila Camacho. Take an "Hipódromo" *pesero* west along Reforma, or bus #17 from Metro Tacuba (Lines 2 and 7). The horsetrack is on the outskirts of the city. Races Thurs. and Sat.-Sun. at 2:15pm. Admission free unless you sit in the upper level, where purchase of food is obligatory.

True Lies

In a Republic where elections are all too often rigged, perhaps it's no surprise that **Lucha Libre** (fake, fixed wrestling) is so popular. Watch men of immense proportions pin each other to mats throughout the city. The strict honor system imposes steep penalties on losers: *máscaras* (masked fighters) have to reveal their faces, *caballeros* (long-haired fighters) shear their locks. For information on the wheres and the whens, consult the sports section of *Tiempo Libre.* Expect to pay 12-24 pesos for the privilege of screaming and swearing at the wrestlers along with hundreds of screaming and swearing Mexican families.

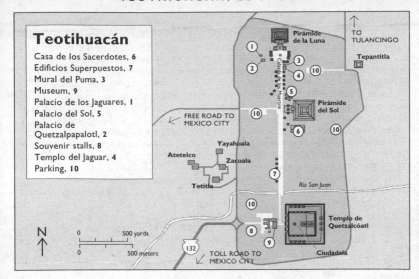

Teotihuacán

Casa de los Sacerdotes, 6
Edificios Superpuestos, 7
Mural del Puma, 3
Museum, 9
Palacio de los Jaguares, 1
Palacio del Sol, 5
Palacio de
Quetzalpapalotl, 2
Souvenir stalls, 8
Templo del Jaguar, 4
Parking, 10

MEXICO CITY

NEAR MEXICO CITY

■ Teotihuacán, Edo. de México

For about 1000 years, a consummately organized, theocratic society thrived in the Valley of Mexico, then disappeared as mysteriously as it had arisen. The cultural and commercial center of this society was Teotihuacán, founded in 200 BCE. An important holy city, Teotihuacán drew hundreds of pilgrims and became something of a market town in order to accommodate their needs. Its influence on architecture and art was so great that many of the styles that developed here can be found in the legacies of civilizations as far south as Guatemala.

Scholars speculate that the city eventually collapsed under its own weight, that it grew so unwieldy that it could no longer produce enough food to keep its inhabitants well fed. At its heyday between 150 and 250 AD, Teotihuacán covered nearly 22.5 square kilometers and accommodated a population of nearly 200,000. Overcrowding resulted in construction superimposed on older buildings during the twilight of the city. To make matters worse, importing food was complicated by the fact that the Teotihuacanos never discovered the wheel.

By 850 CE, only a trickle of people were left in the enormous urban complex. When the Aztecs founded Tenochtitlán in 1325, Teotihuacán, 50km northeast of their capital, lay in ruins. The Aztecs adopted the area as ceremonial grounds and believed its huge structures had been built by giants who inhabited the world during the era of the first sun. Believing that those buried in this hallowed place had become gods, the Aztecs called the area Teotihuacán, meaning "Place of the Gods."

The ruined city's latest incarnation is the most-visited archaeological site in the Republic. The archaeological zone, more commonly referred to as **Las Pirámides**, covers a vast area. The ceremonial center, a 13-square-kilometer expanse, was built along a 2km stretch now called **Calle de los Muertos** (Road of the Dead) for the countless human skeletons that were discovered alongside it. The road leads from the Pyramid of the Moon to the Temple of Quetzalcóatl. Since the Teotihuacanos planned their community around the four cardinal points, Calle de los Muertos runs in what is almost a perfectly straight north-south line. The main structure, the **Pirámide del Sol** (Pyramid of the Sun), is on the east side and is squared with the point on the horizon where the sun sets at the summer solstice. On the north end of Calle de los Muertos are the **Plaza** and **Pirámide de la Luna** (Pyramid of the Moon). The **Palacio de Quetzalcóatl** stands on the east side of the southern end.

The best way to explore the ruins is from south to north, starting your visit on the west side of the Calle de los Muertos, just south of the Pyramid of the Sun, at the **Museo de Sitio.** Barely two years old, this beautifully designed museum's marble tiling and design imitate the forms and colors of the site's ancient cultures. Displays compare the size of the ancient city with various present-day cities, illustrate the architecture and technology of the pyramids, describe the social, religious, and economic organization of the society, and exhibit *indígena* art. However, the museum's *coup de grace* is an enormous floor model of Teotihuacán at the height of its glory. All the pieces in the museum are replicas. The originals are at the Museo Nacional de Antropología in Mexico City.

To the south of the museum is the expansive **Ciudadela,** where priests and government officials once lived. At the center of the Ciudadela is the **Templo de Quetzalcóatl,** once a giant walled-in stadium sheltering a group of ancient temples. Its four flanking platforms served as grounds for priestly ceremonies and dances. The central plaza houses an altar upon which the centennial sacrifice of the "New Fire" was celebrated. Although the temple has lately suffered tremendous wind and rain erosion, on the east side of the pyramid you can still see the fierce heads of Tláloc, the rain god, and the serpent Quetzalcóatl, as well as traces of the red paint that originally decorated them.

Continuing north along the Calle de los Muertos, you will cross what was once the San Juan river. On the west side of the street are the remains of two temples, known as the **Edificios Superpuestos,** that were built in two phases, 200-400 and 400-750 CE, atop older, partially demolished temples.

Farther to the north and east is the **Pirámide del Sol,** the most massive single structure in the ceremonial area. Second in size only to the pyramid at Cholula, its base measures 222m by 225m—dimensions comparable to those of Cheops in Egypt. The pyramid rises 63m, but the grand temple that once crowned its summit is missing. The miniature temple that now stands atop the pyramid once served Tonacatecutli, the sun god. During the summer solstice, the sun falls vertically over the center of the pyramid, thereby bringing the temple that once existed on top in direct contact with its object of worship. The grueling climb to the top of the pyramid pays off with a superb view of the entire site and surrounding valley (don't worry—a rope rail runs the length of the pyramid, and the platforms of the multitiered pyramid make convenient rest stops).

Between the Pyramid of the Sun and the Pyramid of the Moon on the west side of the street is the **Palacio de Quetzalpapalotl** (Palace of the *Quetzal* Butterfly). This columned structure was the residence of nobles who staked out an area next to the ceremonial space and far from the residential complexes of the common folk; bird motifs and geometric patterns adorn the columns. The inner patio is one of the most beautiful sights of the ancient city; the colored frescoes and bird glyphs have survived years of decay and retain much of their original, intricate detail.

Behind the first palace is the **Palacio de los Jaguares** (Palace of the Jaguars). Although this palace is entirely restored, complete with fluorescent lights and plastic handrails, some of the original frescoes remain, adorned with red, green, yellow, and white symbols representing birds, corn, and water.

At the northern end of the Calle de los Muertos is the stunning **Pirámide de la Luna** (Pyramid of the Moon). Although it appears to be as tall as the Pyramid of the Sun, it is in fact much shorter, but built on higher ground. Two somewhat different stages of construction are noticeable in the structure, and the tall steps of the lower section makes the climb more difficult than at the Pyramid of the Sun. A sculpture of **Chalchiutlicue,** a water goddess, was found here during excavations. The view from the summit down the Calle de los Muertos hints at the magnitude of Teotihuacán.

If you still have the energy, there are two other areas that you can visit. Both are unmarked, off Calle de los Muertos on the outskirts of the excavated site. On the northeast side of the Pyramid of the Sun near entrance #4 is the **Palacio de Tepanti-tla,** which has some of the best-preserved frescoes on the site. You can still make out priests with elaborate headdresses and representations of Tláloc. The lower part of the mural displays the Teotihuacano ideal of paradise.

On the southwest border of the site are **Atetelco, Yayahuala, Zacuala,** and **Teti-tla.** While each of these structures was once a palace, these days they can seem more like a crumbling maze. Vestiges of eagle and jaguar frescoes can still be found.

There are five entrances to the site. Buses drop visitors off by *Puerta* 1, the main entrance, surrounded by souvenir stalls. *Puerta* 5, the easternmost entrance, is by the Pirámide del Sol. Free guided tours for groups of 5 or more can be arranged at the administration building by *Puerta* 1 (southwest corner). The museum and souvenir stalls sell guidebooks for about 30 pesos. Expect to spend about 30 minutes at the museum and another three to four hours exploring the ruins. Be sure to bring plenty of water, a hat, and sunglasses. Rapacious vendors descend upon the slew of interna-tional tourists offering water, as well as obsidian, hats, silver, and *"piezas originales"* (original pieces). A firm *"¡No, gracias!"* will sometimes help keep vendors away; if it doesn't suffice, try to avoid eye contact. (Site open daily 8am-5pm. Admission 16 pesos, kids under 13 free. Free parking. To contact the Teotihuacán offices, dial 6-01-88 or 6-00-52; from Mexico City add the prefix 91-595.)

Getting There: Direct bus service from Mexico City to the pyramids is available from **Autobuses Teotihuacán** (every 15min. 5am-6pm, 1hr., 9.50 pesos), located in the Terminal de Autobuses del Norte at *Sala* 8 (tel. 567-14-94). The same bus line runs from Tepexpan, should you come from Texcoco or Chiconcuac. The last bus back from the pyramids to Mexico City leaves the main entrance at 6pm. A few kilo-meters before reaching Teotihuacán, the bus passes just to the right of the town of Acolmán, founded shortly after the Conquest by Franciscans. The majestic lines of the ex-monastery of Acolmán rise to the sky, breaking the monotony of the corn fields. If you want to stop at the ex-monastery on your way back to Mexico City, take the "Indios Verdes" bus from the main entrance and get off at Acolmán.

■ Yet More Fun

For those itching to escape the smog and bustle of Mexico City, the following cities also make delightfully convenient daytrips.

DAYTRIPS

Cuautla, Morelos

Sure, this town has seen more action than Madonna. The real draw, however, is not the history but the nearby *balnearios* (spas), especially Oaxtepec. Waterslides, natu-ral springs, and sulphur baths make for a refreshing daytrip. Mudmask, anyone? (Distance: 70km. See p. 396.)

Cuernavaca, Morelos

The quintessential weekend get-away for thousands of *chilangos* (inhabitants of Mex-ico City) and English-speaking, Spanish-studying, *Let's Go*-toting youngsters. (Distance: 85km. See p. 387.)

Malinalco, Edo. de México

Malinalco's **Templo de la Iniciación** (Temple of the Initiation), one out of the four monolithic pyramids in the world, was the sacred place where Aztec young men went through the rituals that officially transformed an Aztec youth into a *guerrero tigre* or *guerrero águila* (tiger or eagle warrior). (Distance: 133km. See p. 386.)

Popocatépetl and Ixtaccíhuatl Volcanoes

Veiled in Aztec mythology, the snow-capped **Popocatépetl** (Smoking Mountain) and **Ixtaccíhuatl** (Sleeping Woman) volcanoes overlook the state of Morelos and nearby

Puebla. Both peaks can be climbed to a small degree on well marked tourist trails, or to the very peaks in organized tour groups. They're most easily accessible from Cuautla, Morelos. (Distance: 60km. See p. 397.)

Tepotzotlán, Edo. de México

On the highway from Mexico City to Tula and Querétaro (57D), Tepotzotlán offers a glimpse of small-town life, and its church and monastery house exquisite examples of religious art. The beautiful *zócalo* and religious museum can be comfortably enjoyed in four hours. (Distance: 36km. See p. 386.)

Tepoztlán, Morelos

Surrounded by towering cliffs, this quiet *pueblo* occupies one of Morelo's more scenic sites. The cobbled *indígena* village preserves a colonial feel amid growing modernization, and many indigenous people still speak Náhuatl. On Sundays, the *zócalo* comes alive with vibrant market activity. (Distance: 70km. See p. 395.)

Toluca, Edo. de México

The capital city of the Estado de México has a beautiful botanical garden and stained glass mural, the **Cosmovitral.** (Distance: 67km. See p. 383.)

Tula, Hidalgo

The archaeological site at Tula houses the ruins of what was the main city of the Toltec civilization. Particularly interesting are the famous **Atlantes,** massive stone statues almost 10 meters tall. It is 80km away from Mexico City. (Distance: 65km. See p. 381.)

Xochicalco, Morelos

Ceremonial center, fortress, and trading post rolled into one, Xochicalco (Náhuatl for Place of the Flowers) is the most impressive archaeological site in the state, worth the trip if only for the awesome vistas. (Distance: 120km. See p. 394.)

Near Mexico City

Baja California

The peninsula of Baja California is cradled by the warm, tranquil Sea of Cortés on the east and the cold, raging Pacific Ocean on the west. Baja claims one of the most spectacular and diverse landscapes in the world—barren desert mountains jut at breathtaking angles high into Baja's traditionally cloudless sky, whose color is contested only by the idyllic blue-green waters in the sea below. The paradisiacal beaches of the Bahía de Concepción are watched over by many of the thousands of species of cacti that thrive on Baja's otherwise barren hillsides.

Until relatively recently, Baja was an unknown frontier of sorts; the only way to reach its rugged desert terrain was by plane or boat. With the completion of the Transpeninsular Highway (Rte. 1) in 1973, and the addition of better toll roads and ferry service, Baja has become a popular vacation spot among Californians, Arizonans, Mexicans, and others. Vacationers range in type from hardy campers setting out to tame the wild deserts of central Baja to the ubiquitous wealthy Americans who prefer a day on the beach, an evening when they can drown their inhibitions in many a *cerveza* and *margarita,* and a night of posh resort life, all without the inconvenience of changing their dead presidents into Mexican pesos.

Large resort hotels and condominium complexes are sprouting to house the human torrents, but they have a ways to go before filling Baja California. The heavily-Americanized Los Cabos on the southern tip are beautiful, but have close to as little integrity as Tijuana, the wasteland at the northern extreme. But much of Baja's middle section—from glorious Mulegé and Loreto to the oasis town of San Ignacio and thousands of undisturbed beaches along both coasts—is still pristine. The central mountains and desert beaches, down to the beautiful port city of La Paz, beckon a visit to this still-mysterious peninsula.

■ Getting Around

BY LAND

Driving through Baja is far from easy. The road was not designed for high-speed driving; often you'll be safely cruising along at 60mph and suddenly careen into a hidden, poorly banked, rutted curve that can only be taken at 30mph. Still, a car (especially if it's 4WD) is the only way to get close to the more beautiful and secluded areas of Baja, opening up an entire world of hiking and camping opportunities. The ride through Baja is probably one of the more beautiful in Mexico. During the journey, you will see vast deserts filled with cacti, gigantic mountains with ominous peaks, and stupendous cliffs that will make you hold on to your seat. If you need roadside assistance, the Ángeles Verdes (Green Angels) pass along Rte. 1 twice per day. Unleaded gas may be in short supply along this highway, so don't pass a PEMEX station without filling your tank. All of Baja is in the *Zona Libre* (Free Zone), so strict vehicle permits are not required. If you will be driving in Baja for more than 72 hours, you only need to get a free permit at the border by showing the vehicle's title and proof of registration. The **AAA Guide to Baja** is absolutely essential if you're traveling by car. Pick one up (US$4, free for members) at any AAA office in Southern California. It includes important auto information as well as valuable, detailed descriptions of off-road jaunts along all highways. (For more information on driving in Mexico, see p. 39.)

If you plan to navigate the peninsula by bus, be forewarned that almost all *camiones* between Ensenada and La Paz are *de paso.* This means you have to leave at inconvenient times, fight to procure a ticket, and then probably stand the whole way. A much better idea is to buy a reserved seat in Tijuana, Ensenada, La Paz, or Los Cabos, and traverse the peninsula in one shot while seated. Unfortunately, you'll miss the fantastic Mulegé-Loreto beaches (for more info on buses, see p. 38).

Baja California Norte

San Diego

Tijuana

Rosarito

Tecate

CALIFORNIA

La Rumorosa

Mexicali

UNITED STATES

MEX 2

Ensenada

Punta Banda
La Bufadora

Parque
Nacional
Constitución
de 1857

Yuma

ARIZONA

Santo Tomas

MEX 5

Lázaro
Cárdenas

SIERRA SAN PEDRO MARTIR

Punta Colonet

Parque
Nacional
del Gran
Desierto del
Pinacate

San José

Colonia Vicente
Guerrero

Observatorio
San Pedro

San Felipe

San Quintín

Misión de
San Pedro Martir

Puerto
Peñasco

El Rosario

Puertecitos

MAR DE CORTÉS
(SEA OF CORTES)

M E X I C O

Santa Catarina

MEX 1

OCÉANO
PACÍFICO

Isla Ángel
de la Guarda

SONORA

Isla
Cedros

Punta Prieta

Puerto
de la
Libertad

Bahía Sebastián
Vizcaíno

Los Ángeles
Rosarito

Isla
Tiburón

N

Bahía de
Tortugas

Guerrero
Negro

El Arco

0   50 miles

Bahía de
Asunción

MEX 1

BAJA CALIFORNIA SUR

TO GUAYMAS ↓

0   50 kilometers

BAJA CALIFORNIA

Anyway you cut it, Baja's beaches and other points of interest off the main highway are often inaccessible via public transportation. Some swear by hitching—PEMEX stations are thick with rides (for more info on hitchhiking, see p. 42). *Let's Go* does not recommend hitchhiking; it is unpredictable and potentially hazardous.

BY SEA

Ferry service was instituted in the mid-1960s as a means of supplying Baja with food and supplies, not as a way for tourists to get from here to there—passenger vehicles may take up only the ferry space left over by the top-priority commercial vehicles. There are three different ferry routes: Santa Rosalía to Guaymas (8hr.), La Paz to Topolobampo/Los Mochis (9hr.), and La Paz to Mazatlán (17hr.). The La Paz to Topolobampo/Los Mochis route provides direct access to the train from Los Mochis through the Barrancas del Cobre (Copper Canyon).

Ferry tickets are generally expensive, even for *turista*-class berths, which cram two travelers into a cabin outfitted with a sink; bathrooms and showers are down the hall. It's extremely difficult to find tickets for *turista* and *cabina* class, and snagging an *especial* berth (a real hotel room) is as likely as stumbling upon a snowball in the central Baja desert—there are only two such suites on each ferry. This leaves the bottom-of-the-line *salón* ticket, which entitles you to a bus-style seat in a large, smelly room with few communal baths. If, as is likely, you find yourself traveling *salón*-class at night, ditch your seat early on and stake out a spot on the floor, or outside on the deck—simply spread out your sleeping bag and snooze. A small room is available to store your belongings, but once they're secured there is no way of retrieving any items, so make sure you take what you'll need during the trip. A doctor or nurse is always on board in the (rare) event that someone gets seasick. For those who plan to take their car aboard a ferry, it's a good idea to make reservations a month in advance; consult a travel agent or contact the ferry office directly. For further ferry information, contact the State Tourist Department (tel. 2-11-99 or 2-79-75; fax 2-77-22).

BAJA CALIFORNIA NORTE

■ Tijuana

Tijuana is exactly how its thirty million yearly *gringo* visitors would have it. The city comes complete with English-speaking, patronizing club promoters; Mexican artisans selling fluorescent *sombreros* and day-glo souvenirs; and attractions covering every decadent way of blowing money, from a glitzy jai alai palace to dark, dingy strip joints, from Las Vegas-style hotels to wet, throbbing dance clubs. This has been U.S. citizens' number one cheap party spot ever since Prohibition brought a "drought" to the 1920s. Now it's hard to say whether it's the city's skanky charm, its cheap booze, or its sprawling, unapologetic hedonism that attracts tourists like flies.

ORIENTATION

From San Diego to Tijuana, take the red **Mexicoach** bus (tel. 81-84-54 or 800-628-3745) from its terminal at the border (every 30min. until 9pm, US$1). It passes Plaza Pueblo Amigo on the Mexican side and eventually drops you off beside the Frontón Palacio on Revolución between Calles 7 and 8. An easier way might be to grab a **trolley** to San Ysidro, at Kettner and Broadway, in downtown San Diego (US$1.75), and to walk across the border. Transfers from airport buses are also available.

Driving across the border may seem appealing at first, but the hassles of obtaining Mexican insurance, parking, and the mobs of cars clogging the auto port of entry make this a bad idea for a daytrip. If you get into an accident and you don't have insurance, your car may be confiscated (for more info on driving into Mexico, see p. 10). It's a much better idea to leave your car in a lot on the U.S. side and join the throngs

BAJA CALIFORNIA

UNITED STATES
MEXICO

Manuel Contreras
Carretera Aeropuerto
TO AIRPORT
Avenida Defensores de Baja California
José María Velasco
Aguaje de la Tuna
Rodríguez
José Clemente Orozco
Río Tijuana
Luis Moya
Avenida Padre Kino
ZONA RÍO
Domínguez
Paseo
Tijuana
Avenida
Avenida
Av. Independencia
Avenida Oriente
Avenida Poniente
Av. Cuauhtémoc
Luis Cabrera
Antonio Caño
Blvd. Sánchez Taboada
Av. Río Zuchiate
Av. Río Colorado
Av. Río Bravo
Blvd. Agua Caliente
Av. 16 de Sep.
Paseo de los Héroes
Castellanos
Leona Vicario
Javier Mina
Camino Nuevo
Unión
Rosales
Quintana Roo
Cjón. Quintana Roo
Pío Rico
Cjón. Ocampo
Ocampo
Galeana
Hidalgo
Madero
Zaragoza
Negrete
Sarabia
P. E. Calles
Brasil
Colombia
España
Blvd. Agua Caliente
Blvd. de los Fundadores
Benito Juárez
Carrillo Puerto
Díaz Mirón
Emiliano Zapata
Flores Magón
Hotel La Posada
Hotel San Jorge
Revolución
Constitución
Calle II
Calle 8
Calle 9
Calle 10
Huitzilao
Cjón. B.C.
Hotel El Jalisciense
Artículo 123
Hotel Perla de Occidente
Niños Héroes
Martínez
Mutualismo
Calle 7
Michoacán
Baja California
Coahuila
5 de Mayo
Calle 5
Calle 6
Gonzáles Ortega
Parque Teniente Guerrero
Cristóbal Colón
Arias Bernal
Lucrecia Toris
Josefa Ortiz
Calle 1
Calle 2
Calle 3
Calle 4
Michoacán
Carranza
Av. Internacional
Río Tijuana

N

Tijuana

of people walking across the border for the day. Parking rates start at US$3 per day and increase as you move closer to Mexico. Bring proper ID to re-enter the U.S. While a driver's license or other photo ID is acceptable, a passport will ensure the speediest passage. Leave fruits, vegetables, and firearms behind (see p. 11).

If you arrive at the central **bus station,** avoid the cab drivers' high rates (60 pesos to downtown) and head for the public bus (every 5min. 5am-10pm, 30min., 2 pesos). When you exit the terminal, turn left, walk to the end of the building, and hop on a bus marked "Centro Línea." It will let you off on Calle 3 and Constitución. Other *avenidas* run parallel to **Constitución,** notably **Niños Héroes** and **Martínez** to the west and **Revolución** (the main tourist drag), **Madero, Negrete,** and **Ocampo** to the east. *Calles* run east-west; *avenidas* run north-south.

PRACTICAL INFORMATION

Tourist Office: (tel. 88-05-55), Revolución at Calle 1. English-speaking staff doles out maps and advice. Open Mon.-Sat. 9am-7pm, Sun. 10am-5pm. A booth on Revolución between Calles 3 and 4 has maps and may be less crowded. **State Attorney for the Protection of the Tourist:** Same address as tourist office. Don't hesitate to call—the answering machine operates after hours.

Customs Office: (tel. 83-13-90), at the border. Open Mon.-Fri. 8am-3pm.

Consulates: U.S., Tapachula Sur 96 (tel. 81-74-00), in Col. Hipódromo, adjacent to the Agua Caliente racetrack southeast of town. In an emergency, call 619-585-2000 in the U.S. After hours, leave a message on the answering machine and they'll respond shortly. Open Mon.-Fri. 8am-4:30pm. **Canada,** German Gedovius 10411 (tel. 84-04-61), in the Zona del Río. Open Mon.-Fri. 9am-1pm.

Currency Exchange: Banks along Constitución exchange currency at the same rate. **Banamex** (tel. 88-00-21, -22, or 85-82-06), Constitución at Calle 4. Open for exchange Mon.-Fri. 9am-5pm. *Casas de cambio* all over town offer better rates, but do not exchange traveler's checks.

Telephones: Tijuana's streets are paved with **LADATELs.** There is a reasonably priced *caseta* at Motel Díaz (see below), and at Hotel San Jorge, Calle 1 at Constitución, which also has a **fax** machine. Open daily 7:30am-9:30pm.

Telegrams: (tel. 84-79-02; fax 84-77-50), to the right of the post office, in the same building. Open Mon.-Fri. 8am-7pm, Sat.-Sun. 8am-1pm.

Buses: (tel. 21-29-83 or -84). To reach the bus station from downtown, board the blue-and-white buses marked "Buena Vista" or "Camionera" on Niños Héroes between Calles 3 and 4 (2 pesos), or jump in a brown-and-white communal cab on Madero between Calles 2 and 3 (3 pesos). The cheapest carrier is **Transportes Norte de Sonora** (tel. 21-29-48), which serves Ensenada (6 and 10:30am, and 2pm, 1½hr., 25 pesos), Guadalajara (every 30min., 36hr., 404 pesos), Guaymas (every hr., 15hr., 199 pesos), and Hermosillo (every 30min., 12hr., 244 pesos). **Autotransportes de Baja California** (tel. 21-29-82 to -87, ext. 2408) runs to La Paz (8am, noon, 6, and 9pm, 24hr., 297 pesos), Loreto (8am, noon, 6, and 9pm, 18hr., 228 pesos), Mexicali (every 30min., 3hr., 45 pesos), San Felipe (8:30am, 11:30am, noon, and 4pm, 5hr., 98 pesos; try to go through Ensenada, not Mexicali), and Santa Rosalía (8am, noon, 6, and 9pm, 15hr., 179 pesos). **Greyhound** (tel. 21-29-82, ext. 2618) runs to Los Angeles (every hr. 7am-4pm, 3hr., US$18), and connects there to other locations. **Communal cabs** are all over town; some go to Rosarito (30min., 5 pesos).

Car Rental: Dollar, Blvd. Sánchez Taboada 10521 (tel. 81-84-84), in front of the VW dealership. Starting at 248 pesos per day, including insurance and 200km free mileage. Minimum age to rent a car is 25; license and credit card are a must. Open Mon.-Fri. 9am-6pm, Sat. 9am-2pm. **Avis** (tel. 86-15-07). **Hertz** (tel. 83-20-80).

Car Insurance: If you'll be driving in Mexico, spend US$5 per day in San Ysidro to get insurance. There are several drive-through insurance vendors just before the border at Sycamore and Primero who distribute a free booklet with maps and travel tips (see p. 124).

Library: In Parque Teniente Guerrero. Small collection of English books. Open Mon.-Fri. 8am-8pm, Sat. 8am-1pm.

Supermarket: Calimax (tel. 88-08-94), Calle 2 at Constitución. Open 24hr.
Red Cross: (tel. 21-77-87, emergency 132), Calle Alfonso Gamboa at E. Silvestre.
Pharmacy: Farmacia Vida (tel. 85-14-01), Calle 3 at Revolución. Some English spoken. Open 24hr. **Discount Pharmacy,** Av. Revolución 615 (tel. 88-31-31).
Hospital: Centenario 10851 (tel. 84-09-22), in the Zona del Río.
Emergency: Dial 134.
Police: (tel. 38-51-60), Constitución at Calle 8.
Post Office: (tel. 84-79-50), Negrete at Calle 11. Open Mon.-Fri. 8am-7pm, Sat.-Sun. 9am-1pm. **Postal Code:** 22000.
Telephone Code: 66.

ACCOMMODATIONS

Tijuana's budget hotels cluster on Calle 1 between Revolución and Mutualismo. The area is teeming with people during the day and is relatively safe. Come nightfall, however, the neighborhood becomes something of a red-light district, especially on Calle 1 between Revolución and Constitución. Women should be extra cautious when walking in this area at night; to return to your hotel, head down Calles 2 or 3.

Hotel El Jalisciense, Calle 1 #1715 (tel. 85-34-91), between Niños Héroes and Martínez. A great deal. Clean, smallish rooms with high, resilient beds and private baths. Singles and doubles 80 pesos, each additional person 10 pesos.
Hotel Perla de Occidente, Mutualismo 758 (tel. 85-13-58), between Calles 1 and 2. A healthy hike from the bedlam of the city center. Large, soft beds, roomy bathrooms, and fans available upon request. Ah, life is sweet. Singles are a steal at 60 pesos. Spacious doubles 140 pesos.
Hotel San Jorge, Constitución 506 (tel. 85-85-40), between Calles 1 and 2. A large, mirrored lobby leads up to rooms with clean private baths; soft beds tend to cave in. Singles 99 pesos. Doubles 110 pesos. Each additional person 20 pesos.
Hotel La Posada, Calle 1 #1956 (tel. 85-54-33), at Revolución. Just seconds away from all the action. Spacious rooms have fans, comfy beds, and small, clean bathrooms. Singles 50 pesos, with bath 100 pesos. Doubles 140 pesos.

FOOD

Cheap *típico* restaurants line Constitución and the streets leading from glitzy Revolución to Constitución. Even cheaper are the mom-and-pop mini-restaurants. For your stomach's sake, avoid the ubiquitous taco stands. Tourist-oriented restaurants and *gringo* fast-food chains (think KFC) crowd Revolución, usually with slightly higher prices than their American counterparts. Pay in pesos, even if the menu quotes prices in dollars.

Los Panchos Taco Shop (tel. 85-72-77), Revolución at Calle 3. Orange plastic booths are packed with hungry locals munching on cheap Mexican faves. Ultrafresh tortillas. New York steak taco US$1, bean burritos US$2. Open Sun.-Thurs. 8am-midnight, Fri.-Sat. 8am-2am.
El Pipirín Antojitos, Constitución 630 (tel. 88-16-02), between Calles 2 and 3. Load up your tacos with a counterful of condiments. *Flautas gigantes* 12 pesos, *super quesadilla* with meat and cheese 18 pesos. Open daily 8am-10pm.
Hotel Nelson Restaurant (tel. 85-77-50), Revolución at Calle 1, under the Hotel Nelson. Good, cheap food served in a clean, fan-cooled, coffee-shop atmosphere. *Gringo* breakfast of 2 eggs, hot cakes, and ham for 15 pesos; 3 enchiladas are 18 pesos. Open daily 8am-11pm.
Tía Juana Tilly's (tel. 85-60-24), Revolución at Calle 7, in the shadow of the jai alai palace. Black and white photos tell the story of this legendary joint's early days. Live music and dance floor. Mexican plate (taco, burrito, and enchilada) US$6. Open Sun.-Thurs. 11am-11pm, Fri.-Sat. 11am-5am.

BAJA CALIFORNIA

SIGHTS

Fun in Tijuana has long revolved around clubs and money and their concomitant vices—shopping, drinking, and gambling. Of late, numerous diversions outside the conventional bar scene have cropped up. Try people-watching while strolling down **Revolución;** you'll see plenty of surprising and revolting sights, like tourists having their pictures taken with donkeys painted as zebras and wearing gaudy *sombreros.* When you get tired, relax in the beautiful and shady **Parque Teniente Guerrero,** Calle 3 and 5 de Mayo. It's one of the safer, more pleasant parts of town, and only a few blocks from Revolución. The **cathedral,** with its massive chandelier, is nearby at Niños Héroes and Calle 2. The **Morelos State Park,** Blvd. de los Insurgentes 26000 (tel. 25-24-70), features an exotic bird exhibition and picnic area (open Tues.-Sun. 9am-5pm; admission 4 pesos, children 1.50 pesos). To get there, board the green-and-white bus on Calle 5 and Constitución.

The family-owned **L.A. Cetto Winery,** Cañón Johnson 8151 (tel. 85-37-43), just off Constitución at Calle 10, squeezes its specialty from grapes grown in the Valle de Guadalupe, northeast of Ensenada. Tours are available; just don't try to remove a bottle from the storeroom—one American woman recently did so, causing a wine avalanche that broke and spilled thirty cases of bottles (tours Tues.-Sun. every 20min. 8:30am-6:30pm; US$1, with wine-tasting US$2, with wine tasting and souvenir goblet US$3; reservations recommended an hour before the tour).

Walk off your wine buzz with a visit to one of Tijuana's museums. The **Museo de Cera** (tel. 88-24-78), on Calle 1 between Revolución and Madero, is home to a motley crew of wax figures, including such strange bedfellows as Miguel Hidalgo, Dracula, Mikhail Gorbachev (complete with birthmark), Benito Juárez, and Tom Cruise (open Mon.-Fri. 10am-7pm, Sat. 10am-8pm; admission US$1 or 7 pesos, kids under 6 free). The nearby **Mexitlán** (tel. 38-41-01), Calle 2 and Ocampo, showcases a vast field of over 200 intricate miniatures depicting famous historical, religious, and cultural monuments. Absorb Mayan architecture, Mexico City's Paseo de la Reforma, and Teotihuacán without having to consult a single bus schedule. Mexican folk art is also sold (open Wed.-Fri. 10am-6pm, Sat.-Sun. 9am-9pm; admission US$3.25).

SPORTS

Jai alai is played in the majestic **Frontón Palacio** (tel. 85-78-33), Revolución at Calle 7 (open Mon.-Tues. noon-8pm, Wed.-Sat. 8pm-midnight). Two to four players take to the three-sided court at once, using arm-baskets to catch and throw a Brazilian ball of rubber and yarn encased in goatskin. The ball travels at speeds reaching 180mph; jai-alai is reputedly the world's fastest game. After each point, the winning one- or two-player team stays on the court, while the losing team rotates out in king-of-the-hill style. The first team to score seven points wins; after the first rotation through the entire 8-team lineup, rallies are worth two points, not one. If you can, try to catch a doubles match—the points are longer and require more finesse. Players are treated like horses, with betting and odds. All employees are bilingual, and the gambling is carried out in greenbacks. (Admission US$3-15; free-admission coupons are often distributed outside).

Tijuana has two bullrings. **El Toreo de Tijuana** (tel. 86-12-19), downtown to the east of Agua Caliente and Cuauhtémoc, hosts *corridas* (bullfights) on chosen Sundays at 4:30pm from early May to July. The more modern **Plaza Monumental** (tel. 80-18-08), northwest of the city near Las Playas de Tijuana (follow Calle 2 west), employs famous *matadores* and hosts fights from August to mid-September. Tickets to both rings are sold at the gate and sometimes at the tourist booth on Revolución, between Calles 3 and 4 (tel. 85-22-10; admission 40-140 pesos in the sun, 50-190 pesos in the shade). To get to the Plaza Monumental, catch a blue-and-white bus on Calle 3, between Constitución and Niños Héroes.

ENTERTAINMENT

If bullfighting turns your stomach, head for the **Tijuana Centro Cultural,** on Paseo de los Héroes at Mina (tel. 84-11-11, ext. 301; open daily 8am-9pm); it houses the **Space Theater,** an auditorium with a giant 180° screen that shows American Omni-Max movies dubbed in Spanish (showtimes Mon.-Fri. every hr. 3-9pm, Sat.-Sun. every hr. 11am-9pm; admission 16 pesos, children 8 pesos; center open daily 11am-9pm; free). A performance center **(Sala de Espectáculos)** and open-air theater **(Caracol al Aire Libre)** host visiting cultural attractions, including the **Ballet Folklórico.** The **Sala de Video** screens free documentaries, and the **Ciclo de Cine Extranjero** shows foreign films (Wed.-Fri. 6 and 8pm, Sat.-Sun. 4, 6, and 8pm; 9 pesos). Pick up a monthly calendar at the information office in the *centro.*

All of this is just swell, but if you've come to party, brace yourself for a raucous good time. Strolling down Revolución after dusk, you'll be bombarded by thumping music and abrasive club promoters hawking two-for-one margaritas. All Tijuana clubs check IDs (18-plus), with varying criteria for what's acceptable. Many places also routinely body-search patrons for firearms.

Iguanas-Ranas, (tel. 88-38-85), Revolución at Calle 3. Lively on weeknights; packed on weekends. A younger crowd drinks and raises hell on the dance floor amid the pervasive clown motif. For a break, head to the tables on the outdoor terrace. Beer US$2, margaritas two for US$4. Open daily 10am-4pm.

People's Sports N' Rock Member's Club (tel. 85-45-72), Revolución and Calle 2. Every night, sweaty masses of half-naked collegiates wriggle and writhe on the striped dance floor, as a more mellow crowd looks on, margaritas (US$3) in hand. Neon bikes, golf clubs, and roller skates hang menacingly from the ceilings. Cover Fri.-Sat. after 10pm US$2. Open Sun.-Thurs. 9am-5am, Fri.-Sat. 9am-6am.

Caves (tel. 88-06-09), Revolución and Calle 5. Flintstonian entrance leads to a dark but airy bar and disco with orange decor, stalactites, and black lights. Beer US$1.50 weekdays, US$2 weeknights. Margaritas 2 for US$3.50. No cover. Open Sun.-Thurs. 11am-2am, Fri.-Sat. 11am-6am.

Tilly's 5th Avenue (tel. 85-90-15), Revolución and Calle 5. The tiny wooden dance floor in the center of this upscale, balloon-filled restaurant/bar resembles a boxing ring. Side tables are illuminated by lovely stained-glass lamps. Packed on weekends. Beer US$1, margaritas 2 for US$3.50. Wed. night is "Student Night"—all drinks are US$1. Open Mon.-Thurs. 10:30am-2am, Fri.-Sun. 10:30am-5am.

■ Rosarito

Once a playground for the rich and famous, Rosarito has expanded at breakneck speed to accommodate the throngs of sunseekers who flood its hotels, restaurants, shops, and beaches. A favorite destination for tourists and semi-permanent U.S. expatriates, Rosarito is a virtual *gringo* colony—English is ubiquitous and prices are quoted in dollars. On weekends, the sands and surf overflow with people, volleyball games, and horses; finding a place for your towel may be a struggle.

Orientation and Practical Information Rosarito lies about 27km south of Tijuana. Virtually everything in town is on the main street, **Boulevard Juárez.** Street numbers are non-sequential. Almost everything listed below is near the purple Ortega's Restaurant in Oceana Plaza.

To get to Rosarito from Tijuana, grab a yellow-and-white *taxi de ruta* (30min., 5 pesos) that leaves from Madero, between Calles 5 and 6. To return to Tijuana, flag down a *taxi de ruta* along Juárez or at its starting point in front of the Rosarito Beach Hotel. Getting to Ensenada is more of an adventure. Take a blue-and-white striped cab marked "Primo Tapia" from Festival Plaza, north of the Rosarito Beach Hotel, to the toll booth *(caseta de cobro)* on Rte. 1 (3 pesos). There you can catch a bus to Ensenada (every 30min. until about 9pm, 18 pesos).

BAJA CALIFORNIA

The **tourist office** (tel. 2-02-00), on Juárez at Centro Comercio Villa Floreta, has tons of brochures. Some English is cautiously spoken (open Mon.-Fri. 9am-7pm, Sat.-Sun. 10am-5pm). **Banamex** (tel. 2-15-56/-57/-58 or 2-24-48/-49) is on Juárez at Ortiz, (open for exchange Mon.-Fri. 9am-5pm). On weekends, you'll have to go to a *casa de cambio*, which charges a commission. **LADATELs** are scattered throughout town; there's one in front of Hotel Brisas del Mar at Juárez and Acacias, another in front of Banamex, and yet another in front of the Hotel Quinta del Mar, on north Juárez. The well-stocked **Comercial Mexicana Supermarket** (tel. 2-09-34) is at the north end of Juárez before Quinta del Mar (open daily 8am-10pm). **Lavamática Moderna** is on Juárez at Acacias (wash and dry 10 pesos; open Mon.-Sat. 8am-8pm, Sun. 8am-6pm). The **Red Cross** (tel. 132) is on Juárez and Ortiz just north of the tourist office. **Farmacia Hidalgo** (tel. 2-05-57) is on Juárez at Acacias (open Mon.-Sat. 8am-10pm, Sun. 8am-9pm). The **IMSS Hospital** (tel. 2-10-21) is on Juárez and Acacias behind the post office (open 24hr.). In an **emergency,** dial 134. The **police** (tel. 2-11-10) are located next to the tourist office. The **post office** (tel. 2-13-55) is across from Oceana Plaza (open Mon.-Fri. 8am-5pm, Sat. 9am-1pm). **Postal Code:** 72100. **Telephone Code:** 661.

Accommodations Budget hotels in Rosarito are either inconvenient or cramped, with the exception of the outstanding **Hotel Palmas Quintero** (tel. 2-13-49), on Lázaro Cárdenas near the Hotel Quinta del Mar, three blocks inland from north Juárez. A friendly staff and dog welcome tourists to giant rooms with double beds and clean, private baths with hot water. Chill on the patio under the palm trees (singles US$15 or 110 pesos). **Rosarito Beach Rental Cabins** (tel. 2-09-68), on Lázaro Cárdenas two blocks toward the water, are so cheap that most cabins are already occupied by permanent residents. You get what you pay for—each bug-sized cabin contains bunk beds, a toilet, and a sink. Disney-castle spires make the cabins hard to miss (erratically open 8am-2pm and 4-7pm; singles US$7, with shower US$10; doubles US$12, with shower US$15; key deposit US$5).

Food Fresh produce and seafood abound in the restaurants that line Juárez. For an economical seafood dinner, head to **Vince's Restaurant** (tel. 2-12-53), on Juárez next to Motel Villanueva. Enjoy a feast of soup, salad, rice, potatoes, tortillas, and an entree—*filete especial* (fillet of Halibut, 28 pesos), jumbo shrimp (40 pesos), or a veritable seafood extravaganza of fish, shrimp, octopus, and lobster (46 pesos). The casual atmosphere is enhanced by plastic plates and vacationers in swimwear (open daily 8am-10pm). **Tacos Sonora,** on Juárez 306, serves fresh fish tacos and *quesadillas* (7 pesos; open daily 7am-until the last customer leaves). Sit down to a staggeringly cheap breakfast at **Ortega's Ocean Plaza,** Juárez 200 (tel. 2-00-22), in a gaudy purple building. Prick your appetite with a cactus omelette (US$2), or catch the all-you-can-eat Mexican buffet (open Sun.-Thurs. 8am-10pm, Fri.-Sat. 8am-11pm).

Sights and Entertainment People don't come to Rosarito to change the world; they come to swim, dance, and drink. **Rosarito Beach** boasts soft sand and gently rolling surf. Once the sun goes down, travelers live the dream at **Papas and Beer,** Calle de Coronales 400 (tel. 2-04-44), one block north of the Rosarito Beach Hotel and two blocks toward the sea. The open-air dance floor, bar, and sandy volleyball courts are packed with revelers on the weekends. Beer is 15 pesos, mixed drinks 17-25 pesos (cover US$5-10 on Saturdays and holidays; open daily 11am-3am). Don't forget the ID; they take carding very seriously.

■ Mexicali

The highly industrialized capital of Baja California Norte, Mexicali (pop. 1,000,000) nudges the state's border with both the U.S. and the Mexican mainland. A rich and fertile valley cradles the city; nourished by soil deposits from the Colorado River and artificially irrigated by water from the nearby Morelos Dam, it is one of the most important agricultural regions in the Republic. Lured by the prospect of farming productive land, thousands of Chinese immigrants came to Mexicali around the turn of the century. By 1918, when further immigration was prohibited, the city had 10,000 Chinese residents in Mexicali and only 700 Mexicans. The immigrants had to face formidable linguistic and cultural barriers; discrimination and even violence were not uncommon. In one gruesome incident, over 100 Chinese laborers were murdered in the mountains 170 km south of town; to this day, the mountains bear the name "El Chinero" in memory of the event. Time diluted the locals' hatred and tensions have virtually disappeared. In today's Mexicali, Chinese food is wildly popular, and a Chinese influenced dialect has emerged in the city center. Of late, several U.S. firms have relocated to Mexicali to take advantage of low labor costs; the 11 industrial plants which now ring the city have fueled a recent growth spurt.

ORIENTATION

Though far from the ordinary route between the U.S. and Mexico, Mexicali can still serve as a starting point for travelers heading south. The city lies on the California border 189km inland from Tijuana, with Calexico and the Imperial Valley immediately to the north. Because of its valley location, Mexicali experiences chilly winters and mega-hot summers.

Mexicali is perhaps one of the most difficult cities in Mexico to navigate. Run directly to the tourist office and pick up a deluxe **map,** or grab a basic one at the border. Mexicali is plagued with streets that zigzag haphazardly and street numbers slightly less patterned than the digits of π. The main boulevard leading away from the border is **López Mateos,** which heads southeast, cutting through the downtown area. Both north-south *calles* and east-west *avenidas* intersect Mateos, causing even more confusion. **Cristóbal Colón, Madero, Reforma, Obregón, Lerdo,** and **Zaragoza** (in that order, from the border) run east-west. From west to east, **Altamirano, Morelos, México,** and streets **A-L** run north-south, starting from where Mateos meets the border (a gigantic green canopy marks the spot). Don't try to make sense of the border area (particularly the intersection of Morelos and Obregón) from a map; guesswork and a few well directed questions might be your best bet.

To reach the border from the bus station, take the local bus marked "Centro" (every 10min., 5am-11pm, 2 pesos) from outside the bus terminal, just across the footbridge. Ride past the Vicente Guerrero monument and the enormous new mall; get off at López Mateos and walk down until the border crossing.

PRACTICAL INFORMATION

Tourist Office: Comité de Turismo y Convenciones (tel. 57-23-76, fax 52-58-77), a white building at Mateos and Compresora facing the Vicente Guerrero monument and park, 3 km from the border. Open Mon.-Fri. 8am-6pm. English spoken. Get a city map right across the border in the *Comandancia* building. **Tourist cards** are available at the Federal Immigration office at the border.

Currency Exchange: Exchange currency at any *casa de cambio* along Madero, or try **Banamex** (tel. 54-28-00 or 54-29-29), at Altamirano and Lerdo, where traveler's checks are accepted. Open Mon.-Fri. 9am-5pm.

Telephones: LATADELs are all over the city; one is in the post office, another is on Madero between Alta and Azulea, and a swarm are outside the white "Comandancia de la Policía Fiscal Federal" building right across the border. There is a *caseta* at the **Farmacia de Dios** (see listing below). Local calls 1 peso, long-distance within Mexico 3 pesos per min., calls to U.S. 5.50 pesos and up per min.

Telegrams: (tel.53-99-19, 57-10-86, or 66-82-53), in the same building as the post office. **Fax service** available to the U.S. (10 pesos per page) and Mexico (7 pesos per page). Open Mon.-Fri. 8am-4pm, Sat. 8am-1pm.

Buses: (tel. 57-24-10, 57-24-15, 57-24-22, or 57-24-55), near the intersection of Mateos and Independencia, about 4km south of the border. A blue-and-white bus will take you to the station from the border (2 pesos). **Transportes Norte de Sonora** (tel. 57-24-10) sends buses to Guadalajara (every hr., 33hr., 440 pesos), Guaymas (every hr., 11hr., 179 pesos), Hermosillo (every hr., 9hr., 144 pesos), Los Mochis (every hr., 17hr., 265 pesos), Mazatlán (every hr., 24hr., 353 pesos), Tepic (every hr., 30hr., 402 pesos), and Tijuana (*de paso*, 3hr., 52 pesos). **Caballero Azteca** and **Elite** (tel. 56-01-10) send buses to most of the above locations at higher prices, plus Chihuahua (10:25am and 3pm, 17hr., 291 pesos), Juárez (3:30pm, 14-16hr., 188 pesos), and Nogales (11:35pm, 9hr., 140 pesos). **Autotransportes de Baja California** (tel. 57-24-20, ext. 2229) sends buses to Ensenada (4 per day, 14hr., 66 pesos), La Paz (5:30pm, 27½hr., 343 pesos), Puerto Peñasco (9am, 2pm, and 8pm, 5hr., 60 pesos), San Felipe (5 per day, 8am-8pm, 2½hr., 45 pesos), and a roller-coaster ride to Tijuana (every hr., 3½hr., 52 pesos). **Transportes del Pacífico** (tel. 57-24-61) offers *de paso* service to most of the above locations for slightly higher fares than Norte de Sonora, as well as second-class buses for around 15% less that take 2-6 hours longer. Service to Tijuana (*primera clase* 50 pesos, *segunda clase* 45 pesos), Guaymas (440 pesos, 388 pesos), and more. **Golden State** (53-61-69) sends buses to Californian cities, including Los Angeles (8am, 2:30pm, and 10pm, 4½hr., US$26), Palm Springs (8am, 2:30pm, and 10pm, 2½hr., US$18), and Pomona (8am, 2:30pm, and 10pm, 4hr., US$26).

Trains: (tel. 57-24-20), at Independencia and Mateos, near the bus station. To get there, turn off Mateos opposite Denny's onto Ferrocarrileros. Take the first right and it's on the right. Service to Guadalajara (*estrella* 36hr., 296 pesos; *burro* 72hr., 165 pesos), Mazatlán (*estrella* 24hr., 215 pesos; *burro* 30hr., 120 pesos), and other destinations. The estrella departs at 9am daily; make reservations 1-2 days in advance (tickets on sale 7-9am). The *burro* departs at 9am daily; tickets are only sold on the day of departure (4:30-8:30pm).

Red Cross: (tel. 132), at Quinte Durango, Colonia Pueblo Nuevo. Very little English spoken. Open 24hr.

Pharmacy: Farmacia de Dios (tel. 54-15-18), at López Mateos and Morelos. With a name like this, how can you go wrong? Some English spoken. Features a telephone *caseta*. Open Mon.-Fri. 8am-1:30am, Sat. 8-11:30pm, Sun. 8am-6pm.

Hospital: IMSS Centro de Salud (tel. 53-56-16), Lerdo at Calle F, has an English-speaking staff. Otherwise, try the **Hospital Civil** (tel. 54-11-23 or 54-11-30).

Police: (tel. 134, 54-21-32, or 52-91-98), at Calle Sur and Mateos. English spoken.

Post Office: Madero 491 (tel. 52-25-08), at Morelos. Open Mon.-Fri. 8am-3pm, Sat. 9am-1pm. **Postal Code:** 21000.

Telephone Code: 65.

ACCOMMODATIONS

Budget hotels crowd the noisy bar strip on Altamirano between Reforma and Lerdo and line Morelos south of Mateos. Hotels on Madero close to Mateos will dig deeper into your wallet but are cleaner.

Hotel México, Av. Lerdo 476 (tel. 54-06-69), at Morelos. Excellent value. Newly remodeled, this hotel offers rooms as clean and pink as a bouncing baby boy. Rooms boast A/C and color TV and overlook a central patio. Bathrooms are small but clean. The office doubles as a grocery store. Check-out 1pm. Singles 80 pesos. Doubles 140 pesos.

Hotel Imperial, Madero 222 (tel. 53-63-33, 53-61-16, or 53-67-90), at Azulea. Rock-hard beds. Minty-fresh rooms are stocked with desks, squeaky fans, A/C, and color TVs. Private baths with narrow showers. Key deposit 5 pesos. Check-out noon. *Agua purificada*. Singles 110 pesos. Doubles 135 pesos.

FOOD

With Mexicali's large Chinese-Mexican population, you can count on finding tasty chow mein around every corner.

Restaurant Buendía, Altamirano 263 (tel. 52-69-25). Despite sharing a name with the illustrious family of Gabriel García Márquez's epic, Buendía specializes in Chinese cuisine—but chefs are always happy to whip up some *antojitos*. Try a heaping plate of beef with broccoli, fried rice, egg roll, and fried chicken (18 pesos). Three burritos are 18 pesos. Vegetarians can delight in a veggie combo for only 20 pesos. Open daily 7am-9pm.

Tortas El Chavo, Reforma 414 at Altamirano, off Mateos, three blocks from the border. A fast-food joint with plastic booths; mirrored walls reflect the green-and-yellow "furniture." *Tortas,* any style, are 11 pesos; *tacos de machaca* (tacos filled with strips of beef) go for a mere 3.50 pesos. Open daily 8:30am-8pm.

Café Yin Tun, Morelos 379, has A/C and Christmas colors all year long—red tablecloths, fake green plants. Chinese specials 12-18 pesos. The ubiquitous beef with broccoli and breaded shrimp 18 pesos each. Special plates with more exotic seafood offerings are 35 pesos. Open daily 9am-midnight.

SIGHTS

Mexicali's **park, forest, lake,** and **zoo** (tel. 55-28-33) are located in the southwestern part of town, on Alvarado between San Marcos and Lázaro Cárdenas. Wink at the birds in the aviary, pedal a paddleboat on the lake, or admire lions and tigers from the train that circles the park and nature reserve. The grounds contain carousels, bumper cars, a pool, and a science museum (open Tues.-Sat. 9am-5pm, Sun. 9am-5pm; admission 3 pesos, children 2 pesos). To reach the park area, board a black-and-white *colectivo* marked "Calle 3" downtown. If you've got wheels, drive south on Azulea over the Río Nuevo. The road becomes Uxmal south of the river; turn left on Independencia, then right on Victoria. The city's **Parque Vicente Guerrero** (tel. 54-55-63), across from the mall and busier sections of the main street, has jungle gyms, as well as picnic spots and party space rentals (open daily 9am-9pm).

ENTERTAINMENT

Bullfights are staged regularly in the fall at the **Plaza de Toros Calafia** (tel. 56-11-96), on Calafia at Independencia in the *centro;* take a 10-minute ride on the blue-and-white bus from the centro to the plaza (2 pesos). Wild and crazy rodeos rampage in the winter and spring at **Lienzo Charro del Cetys,** Cetys and Ordente. Check with the tourist office for schedules. Good, clean fun awaits at **Mundo Divertido,** an amusement park at Mateos 850 (tel. 52-56-75), across from Parque Vincente Guerrero (open Mon.-Fri. noon-9pm, Sat.-Sun. 11am-10pm). To get to the park, board a blue-and-white bus marked "Centro Cívico" departing from Madero and Altamirano (every 10min., 5am-11pm, 1.50 pesos). **Cinema Gigante,** Juárez 21 (tel. 66-07-48), at Montejano in the **Centro Comercial Gigante** mall, screens American films (15 pesos). The mall is also outfitted with an arcade and dozens of stores.

▓ Ensenada

The secret is out—beachless Ensenada is fast becoming a weekend hot spot. The masses of Californians that arrive every Friday evening have *gringo*-ized the town to an incredible degree; everyone speaks some English, and store clerks resort to calculators if you try to buy something with pesos. Still, Ensenada is less brash than its insatiable cousin to the north, the infamous TJ. Cooled by sea breezes, Ensenada is quite pleasant—particularly during the week, when fewer tourist-consumers populate the city—and the center of town is even somewhat endearing.

The ride from Tijuana to Ensenada offers continuous views of the Pacific, and its last twenty minutes are breathtaking if you take the Ensenada *cuota* (toll road)—the buses do. There are three toll gates along the way, each charging US$1.61. Don't begrudge the money, though; you'll enjoy a smashing view of the ocean, large sand dunes, stark cliffs, and broad mesas—if busing it, be sure to grab a seat on the right-hand side. If you're coming by car, you may want to drive during the day—there are no streetlights. Be sure to drive in the right lane; the left is for passing only. Some great rest spots can be found along the road to absorb the view, or to hike down and walk along the lonely cliffs.

Orientation Ensenada is 108km south of Tijuana on Rte 1. Buses from Tijuana arrive at the main terminal, at Calle 11 and Riveroll. Turn right as you come out of the station, walk 10 blocks, and you'll be at **Mateos** (also called **Primera**), the main tourist drag. **Juárez** (Calle 5) runs parallel to Mateos, while from north to south, Avenidas Ryerson, Moctezuma, Obregón, Ruiz, Gastelum, Miramar, Riveroll, Alvarado, Blancarte, and Castillo are perpendicular to it above the *arroyo,* a grassy trench crossed by small bridges; below the *arroyo,* Avenidas Espinoza, Floresta, Guadalupe, Hidalgo, Iturbide, and (later) Balboa also run perpendicular to Mateos. **Blvd. Costero** traces the shoreline, parallel to (and west of) Mateos. Streets are numbered, avenues are named; together they form a grid. *Calles* run northwest-southeast, while most *avenidas* run northeast-southwest (Juárez and Mateos are exceptions). After sundown, avoid the area near the shoreline and the regions bounded by Avenidas Miramar and Macheros, and Mateos and Cuarta. Always keep in mind while orienting yourself that the large residential Chapultepec Hills lie to the north, and the water to the west.

Practical Information The **tourist office,** Blvd. Costero 540 (tel. 8-24-11 or 800-310-968; fax 8-85-88), at Gastelum, has maps and pamphlets in English (open Mon.-Fri. 9am-7pm, Sat.-Sun. 10am-3pm). The **Chamber of Commerce,** Mateos 693, 2nd floor (tel. 8-37-70, 8-23-22, or 4-09-96), at Macheros, is closer to the center of town and provides brochures and city maps (open Mon.-Fri. 8:30am-2pm and 4-6:30pm). **Banks** cluster along Juárez at Av. Ruiz. **Bancomer** (tel. 8-11-08), on Juárez at Av. Ruiz, exchanges dollars and traveler's checks (open Mon.-Fri. 9am-12:30pm). **ATMs** are along Juárez in the bank district, including one at **BanOro,** Juárez and Gastelum. **LADATEL** phones line Juárez and Mateos. **Telegrams** (tel. 7-05-45) can be sent from Av. Floresta at Calle Tercera (open Mon.-Fri. 8am-6pm, Sat. 8am-2pm).

Transportes Norte de Sonora (tel. 8-67-70) sends buses to Guaymas (5 per day 7:30am-midnight, 16hr., 223 pesos) and Los Mochis (20hr., 296-344 pesos). **Autotransportes de Baja California** (tel. 8-66-80) runs to Guerrero Negro (6 per day 10am-11pm, 10hr., 115 pesos), La Paz (6 per day, 22hr., 263 pesos), Loreto (6 per day, 16hr., 200 pesos), Mexicali (5 per day, 4hr., 63-73 pesos), San Felipe (8am and 6pm, 3hr., 63 pesos), Santa Rosalía (6 per day 10am-11pm, 13hr., 150 pesos), Tijuana (every hr., 1½hr., 20-25 pesos). **Transportes Aragón** (tel. 4-07-17), on Riveroll between Octava and Novena, runs to Tijuana (every hr. 6am-9pm, 20 pesos). 50% discount for students and seniors. Local *urbano* buses (tel. 8-25-94) leave from Juárez and Sexta, and from Segunda and Macheros (every 8-15min., 2.50 pesos).

Viajes Las Dunas, Costero 1001 at Alvarado (tel. 8-82-28), next to the Costa del Mar, has the best prices in town for car rental (open daily 8am-2pm and 4-6pm). **Luggage storage** is available at the main bus terminal (4 pesos for the first 5hr., 0.50 pesos each additional hr.). **Supermarket Calimax** (tel. 8-33-97), Gastelum at Calle 4, has just about everything (open daily 6am-2am). A laundromat, **Lavandería Lavadero** (tel. 8-27-37) is on Obregón between Sexta and Séptima, across from Parque Revolución (open Mon.-Sat. 8am-7pm, Sun. 8am-2pm). The **Red Cross** (tel. 4-45-85, emergency 132) is on Blvd. de Jesús Clark at Flores. **Farmacia del Sol** (tel. 6-37-75) is at Cortés and Reforma, in the Limón shopping center (open 24hr.). The **Hospital General** (tel. 6-78-00 or 6-44-44) is on the Transpeninsular Highway at the 111km mark (open 24hr.). In an **emergency,** dial 134. **Police** (tel. 6-24-21) are at Calle 9 at Espinoza. The **post office** (tel. 6-10-88) is on Mateos at Espinoza (open Mon.-Fri. 8am-7pm, Sat. 9am-1pm). **Postal Code:** 22830. **Telephone Code:** 617.

Accommodations Budget hotels line Mateos between Espinoza and Riveroll and at Miramar. Most rooms are a 25-minute hike from the beaches and 10 minutes from the popular clubs. Although many owners quote prices in greenbacks, they also accept pesos. **Motel Pancho,** on Alvarado at Calle 2 (tel. 8-23-44), one block off Mateos, has big rooms and clean baths with tiny showers. Friendly and helpful staff will direct you to neighborhood bars (singles and doubles 80 pesos). **Hotel Rosita** (tel. 8-16-25), on Gastelum between Calles 3 and 4, has dark, small rooms with flies. But the bathrooms are clean, the showers work, and the toilets flush (1 bed 30 pesos, with bath 40 pesos; 2 beds 50 pesos, with bath 60 pesos; each additional person 10 pesos; sextuple with no bath 80 pesos). The beach between Tijuana and Ensenada is lined with RV parks. One close to Ensenada is **Ramona RV Park** (tel. 4-60-45), on km104 of the Transpeninsular Highway (US$9 for full hookup).

Food The cheaper restaurants in town line Juárez and Espinoza; eateries on Mateos and near the water jack up their prices. Fresh fruit stands abound, but the best bargains are at the supermarkets on Gastelum. The friendly atmosphere at **Cafetería Monique Colonial** (tel. 6-40-41), Calle 9 and Espinoza, makes it a local favorite. Diners sit in anxious anticipation of their breaded steak with salad and fries (25 pesos). No alcoholic drinks are served (open Mon.-Sat. 6am-10pm, Sun. 6am-5pm). Vegetarians will find gastronomic bliss at **Señor Salud** (tel. 6-44-15), Calle 9 at Espinoza, in the small shopping center next to Cafetería Monique. This cozy joint is famous for its *comida corrida* (15 pesos), veggie burgers (9 pesos), and *licuados* (14 pesos; open Mon.-Sat. 8am-7pm). Chefs at **Las Parrillas** (tel. 6-17-28), Espinoza at Calle 6, grill up fresh meat cutlets on the flaming pit as customers make like Pavlov's dog. Squeeze onto a counter stool in the diner-like atmosphere and scarf down burritos (18 pesos) and *súper hamburguesas* with veggies, avocadoes, and chili (13 pesos; open daily 7:30am-11pm).

Sights Seeing Ensenada requires more than a quick cruise down Mateos. For a view of the entire city, climb the **Chapultepec Hills.** The steep road to the top begins at the foot of Calle 2; expect a 10-15-minute hike. Less taxing is a stroll down **Blvd. Costero,** where herds of curio shops make for hours of mindless shopping.

The mild, dry climate of Northern Baja's Pacific coast has made it Mexico's prime grape-growing area. **Bodegas de Santo Tomás,** Miramar 666 (tel. 8-25-09), though cursed with a diabolic number, has produced wine since 1888 (thank God not 1666). Today, they distill over 500,000 cases of wine every year, including rosé and cham-

BAJA CALIFORNIA

Just Put Your Lips Together and Blow

Mexicans have transformed the simple act of whistling into a language unto its own. Stepping off a curb too soon, trying to parallel park, wearing that tank top on a hot day—all these might receive a whistle carefully selected from a copious vocabulary. There is the **attention-getting, taxi-hailing, traffic-stopping** whistle: a simple burst of sound, sometimes presented in a two tone combination, which can be your only hope of slowing down the second-class bus you're chasing. There is the pulsating, directional, **you-can-back-up-another-meter-ooops** whistle, frequently used for parallel parking, which sounds much like the high pitched sounds of a Mack truck backing up. Then there is, of course, the **my-my-don't-you-look-tasty** wolf whistle, which certainly possesses the richest repertoire of permutations, from a long, drawn out exhale to a sharp, quick, breathy whisper. You'll certainly get your share, regardless of what you wear, if you have two X chromosomes. More welcome is the **just-screwing-around-with-you** whistle, which varies according to the imagination, range, and ability of the whistler. The delight in sitting on a stoop and messing with passersby's minds may initially not be apparent to the tired traveler. After a short time in Mexico, however, you, too, will want to indulge in meaningless melodic menagerie in the dark hostel hallway or on the crowded *pesero*. Sure, it's a complicated language, but it sure is easier to pronounce than Spanish. Even Lauren Bacall would be impressed.

pagne. Tours include complimentary wine tasting and an assortment of breads and cheeses (11am, 1, and 3pm; US$2).

The **Instituto Nacional de Antropología e Historia,** Ryerson 99 (tel. 8-25-31), at Virgilio Uribe, is the oldest building in town. Artifacts from all over Baja include a charming photograph of two elderly Cucapa men standing next to their shared young wife, whom they acquired during a robbery in a nearby town (open Tues.-Sun. 8am-3pm; free). A healthy 15-minute walk from Mateos is the **Museo de Ciencias,** Obregón 1463 (tel. 8-71-92; fax 8-63-35), at Catorce. Housed in an old wooden boat, the museum displays photographs of and information about the endangered species of Baja (open Mon.-Fri. 9am-5pm, Sat.-Sun. noon-5pm; admission 5 pesos).

Contemplate great men in the well manicured **Plaza Civil,** on Costero between Riveroll and Alvarado. The larger-than-life golden busts of Venustiano Carranza, Miguel Hidalgo, and Benito Juárez seem to be grimacing. The nearby gardens of the **Centro Cívico, Social, y Cultural de Ensenada** (tel. 6-43-10 or 6-42-33) are one block from Costero. High, flapping flags, each symbolizing a Latin American country, sprout from flowerbeds.

Entertainment Most of the popular hangouts along Mateos are members of the hybrid species known as the restaurant/bar/disco. Food and drink are served only until 8pm or so, when the eateries metamorphose into full-fledged dance club monsters. On weekends, almost every place is packed with festive-feeling *gringos*.

Better known than Ensenada itself is **Hussong's Cantina** (tel. 8-32-10), on Ruiz between Mateos and Calle 2; now 102 years old, it's the prototypical Mexican watering hole. Gulp down beer (7-9 pesos) or a margarita (12 pesos) at the long, shiny bar (open daily 10am-1am). When you tire of the continuous stream of *mariachis,* cross the street to **Papas and Beer** (tel. 4-01-45), a high-tech music emporium popular with a young crowd that swigs large margaritas (20 pesos) and spends horse-choking wads of cash. Escape the congestion and decor by stepping onto the terrace, where hockey-rink-like plexiglass boards prevent carousers from cross-checking each other off the balcony to the street below. Thursday night is theme night (birthday night, pajama night, etc.) and Sunday is ladies night; women get drunk for free, and men aren't let in until 10pm (cover US$3-5; open Wed., Sat. 10am-3am, other days noon-3am).

If you don't drink and don't like to party, join the gyrating mass of teens whirling and bopping to late-80s pop hits at **Roller Ensenada** (tel. 6-11-59), a roller rink on Mateos at Iturbide (open Tues.-Sun. 2-10pm, Fri.-Sun. noon-10pm; admission 7 pesos per hr.). If you just want to zone out in front of a big screen, **Cinema Gemelos** (tel. 6-36-16/-13), on Balboa and Mateos at the southern end of town, screens subtitled U.S. features (shows 4-10pm; admission 15 pesos).

■ Near Ensenada

Ensenada is an excellent base from which to explore Baja's natural wonders. Unfortunately, to reach most of them, you'll need some wheels—preferably a 4WD or all-terrain vehicle. Cars can be rented in Ensenada (see p. 135).

BEACHES

Good sand to accompany your swim in the idyllic Bahía de Todos Santos can only be found outside of the city. To the north, **Playa San Miguel,** with its rocky coastlines and large waves, is great for surfers, but might not be ideal for others. To get there, drive north up Calle 10 until the toll gate; turn left at the sign marked "Playa San Miguel." Buses also run to this beach—catch a bus marked "San Miguel" departing from Gastelum and Costero (2.50 pesos). Buses back must be flagged down.

Somewhat less attractive beaches lie 8km south of Ensenada off the Transpeninsular Highway. Probably the nicest beach on the peninsula is **Playa Estero,** dominated by the Estero Beach Resort, which is so Americanized that finding a single Mexican anywhere on the beach could be an impossible task. Volleyball courts fill the beach's clean, but hard and unforgiving sand. The **Estero Beach Museum** (tel. 6-62-35) displays Mexican folk art (open Wed.-Mon. 9am-6pm; free). To get to Estero, take a right at the "Estero Beach" sign on Rte. 1 heading south. Parking costs US$5 at the resort. Alternatively, catch a bus marked "Aeropuerto," "Zorrillo," "Maneadero," or "Chapultepec" from Pl. Cívica. **Playa El Faro** (tel. 7-46-30; fax 7-46-20) is similarly rife with volleyball courts and Americans, but has slightly better sand, and offers the opportunity to camp on the beach (camp space, parking, and bathroom privileges US$7 for four people; full RV hookup US$12; rooms with bath US$30 for two people). Another nearby beach is **Playa Santa María.**

Heading onto the Punta Banda peninsula, you'll find lonelier beaches along the stretch known as **Baja Beach.** Horses are available for rent, and you can swim anywhere along the clean, soft-white sand, in front of a quiet scattering of Americans in semi-permanent RV parks. The rolling hills and marshes provide a pleasant backdrop. To get to Baja Beach, take a right onto the smaller peninsula which juts off the Punta Banda en route to La Bufadora. Look for a "Horses for Rent" and "Aguacaliente" sign. You can also take a bus to La Bufadora (see below) and ask the driver to let you off there, but don't count on a ride back. Some people hitch a ride; *Let's Go* does not recommend hitchhiking as a safe means of travel. Farther south you'll find passable beaches. **San Quintín,** two hours south of town on the Transpeninsular Highway, is popular for its cool climate, lack of tourists, and the large clam population at **Molino Viejo** (6km south of the city of San Quintín). **Rosario,** another modest beach town, is 58km south of San Quintín on the highway.

HIKING

The area's most beautiful spots remain essentially undiscovered by most tourists. Breathtaking hikes around the mountains of the Punta Banda peninsula approaching La Bufadora can be completed on well kept trails of a National Park quality. Take in spectacular views of cliffs, the mountainside, and blue sea floating off into oblivion as you circle the peaks. Bring a snack, as there are some good spots to stop and picnic. And don't forget a bathing suit—when you reach the bottom, you can relieve your sweaty body with a dip amid the rocks in the chilly Pacific.

The best spot to enter the trails is **Cerro de la Punta,** on the road to La Bufadora near the end of the Punta Banda Peninsula. Turn right up a long driveway at the "Cerro de la Punta" sign (parking 10 pesos). You'll see a small clearing and a large house on the cliffs; here, you can hike up among the cacti to the top of the mountains for views of the surrounding area or down beautiful trails on the oceanside.

Other stops earlier along the road to La Bufadora are equally scenic, and a few are near unique cave-like rock enclosures created when the mountain was blasted to build the road. The bus to La Bufadora (see below) will drop you off anywhere along this road, including Cerro de la Punta, but if you can't hitch you may be waiting quite a while for the bus back. **Punta Banda** itself is a pleasant little town with a grocery market, post office (open Mon.-Fri. 8am-2pm), and restaurant all around a small plaza just after the exit onto Baja Beach, which juts back towards the mainland. A good place to camp or park an RV in Punta Banda is **Villarino** (tel. 3-20-45 or 6-42-46; fax 3-20-44), adjacent to the plaza, which has modern shower and bathroom facilities and full hookups (US$5 per person per night).

Hiking options farther outside of Ensenada include the **Parque Nacional Constitución de 1857** to the east; follow Rte. 3 to Ojos Negros and depart from there for the mountains. Be forewarned that you'll need an all-terrain vehicle or pick-up truck to make the trek. If you don't have such resources, tours are available from **Ecotur** (tel. 6-44-15; fax 4-67-78). The owner, Francisco Detrell, works for the tourist office and leads tours in Ensenada and other parts of Baja. Expeditions include surfing and whale-watching trips. Amateurs, don't fret—he'll provide most of the equipment.

BAJA CALIFORNIA

LA BUFADORA

La Bufadora, the largest geyser on the Pacific coast, is 30km south of Ensenada. On a good day, the "Blowhole" shoots water 40m into the air out of a water-carved cave. Unfortunately, the droves of visitors, cheesy curio shops, and food vendors have made the area rather unpleasant. Yet despite the tourists and litter, the geyser is interesting enough to make a trip. To get to La Bufadora, drive south on the Transpeninsular Highway (take a right onto the highway off López Mateos at the southern end of town), head straight past exits for the airport, military base, and Playa Estero, and take a right after about 20 minutes at the sign marked "La Bufadora." Continue on that road until its end, where the geyser will be heavily advertised (parking US$1 or 7 pesos). Alternatively, you can take a yellow *microbús* to Maneadero (2.50 pesos), and a connecting bus to La Bufadora (2 pesos).

■ San Felipe

San Felipe may put on Mexican airs, but it's a tourist-oriented beach town at heart. Christened by San Felipe de Jesús in 1721, San Felipe remained essentially isolated until the 19th century, when a U.S. firm began harvesting tons of seafood from the deserted shores of Bahía San Felipe. In the 1950s, northern snowbirds claimed the area as a regular hangout, bringing with them handfuls of greenbacks and a new industry—tourism. San Felipe offers a stellar selection of seafood and a beautiful stretch of beach teased by the warm, shallow waters of the Gulf. Although more than 200 *gringo* RV parks now line the coast of the greater San Felipe area, the town still attracts many Mexicans and has managed to retain its charm.

Orientation and Practical Information San Felipe is 198 km south of Mexicali at the end of sizzling-hot Rte. 5. The town is also accessible via a paved road from Ensenada—if coming from Tijuana, the later makes for a more pleasant ride. A dirt and gravel road connects San Felipe to points farther south. **Los arcos** (a tall arched structure) is immediately recognizable when entering the village; **Chetumal** is the street continuing straight from the arches toward the sea. Hotels and restaurants cluster on **Mar de Cortés,** one block from the beach. **Malecón,** lined with seafood stands, is right on the beach. All cross-streets named "Mar" run parallel to the beach; from south to north, **Manzanillo, Topolobampo, Ensenada, Chetumal,** and **Acapulco** run perpendicular. To get downtown from the **bus station,** walk north on Mar Caribe to Manzanillo and turn right toward the water.

The **tourist office,** Mar de Cortés 300 (tel. 7-11-55), at Manzanillo, has English-speaking staffers. Ask for Sr. Manuel González; he's a great help (open Mon.-Fri. 8am-7pm, Sat. 9am-3pm, Sun. 10am-1pm). **Bancomer** (tel. and fax 7-10-51), Mar de Cortés Nte. at Acapulco, near Rockodile Bar, exchanges currency from 8am-2pm and has a 24-hr. **ATM. Farmacia San Angelín** (tel. 7-10-43), Chetumal at Mar de Cortés, has *casetas* for **long-distance calls** (calls US$1 plus credit card charges). **Telegrams** (tel. 7-11-12) can be sent from the yellow office on Mar Bermejo between Puerto Peñasco and Zihuatanejo (open Mon.-Fri. 8am-2pm).

Catch **buses** at the terminal (tel. 7-15-16) on Mar Caribe, a 15-minute walk from the center of action. **Autotransportes de Baja California** runs buses to Ensenada (8am and 6pm, 3½hr., 64 pesos), Mexicali (6am, noon, and 4pm, 2½hr., 41 pesos), and "Plus" service to Mexicali (7:30am and 8pm, 2½hr., 45 pesos), and Tijuana (4 per day, 5hr., 95 pesos). Ticket sales daily 5:30am-10:30pm. **Luggage storage** at the bus station (5 pesos). The **Red Cross** (tel. 7-15-44), at Mar Bermejo and Peñasco, has English-speaking staffers (open 24hr.). **Farmacia San José,** Pto. Mazatlán 523 (tel. 7-13-87), is open 24 hours. The **Centro de Salud** (tel. 7-15-21) is on Chetumal near the fire and police station. English spoken (open 24hr.). In an **emergency,** dial 134. The **police** (tel. 7-13-50 and 7-10-21) are on Mar Blanco Sur just south of Chetumal. The **post office** (tel. 7-13-30) is on Mar Blanco between Ensenada and Chetumal, five blocks inland from Cortés (open Mon.-Fri. 8am-3pm, Sat. 9am-1pm). **Postal Code:** 21850. **Telephone Code:** 657.

Accommodations There are two kinds of accommodations in San Felipe: those with walls and A/C, and those without. Travelers who prefer the former will end up paying *mucho dinero* for mediocre rooms. A cheaper option is to rent a room in a private residence; check with the tourist office for a list. **Carmelita** (tel. 7-18-31), across from the Chapala Motel, is one of the private residences renting out rooms with A/C and private bath. Four rooms are available, housing single people or "married" couples only (US$25 per room). Crammed between curio shops and administered from the liquor store next door, **Motel El Pescador** (tel. 7-11-83 or 7-10-44), on Mar de Cortés at Chetumal, offers spacious and nicely furnished rooms right on the beach with A/C, color TV, and private baths. It is a real bargain (at least by San Felipe standards). Check-out time is noon. Singles 150 pesos. Doubles 180 pesos). **Chapala Motel,** on Mar de Cortés and Ensenada (tel. 7-12-40), has clean baths, A/C, and TVs. Ask for a room with a kitchen, then chill your head in the fridge. Check-out time is 2pm. Singles 245 pesos. Doubles 280 pesos.

As any Californian with an RV can tell you, San Felipe is renowned for its trailer parks, which are remarkably safe. The most famous is **Ruben's** (tel. 7-14-42), toward the end of Av. Golfo de California in Playa Norte. To reach Ruben's, turn left from Chetumal onto Mar de Cortés; it's a short drive up. Individual beachfront parking spaces are topped with two-story, open-air bungalows. Each spot easily accommodates carloads of folks with sleeping bags; RVs can hook up to electricity, hot water, and sewer connections (office open daily 7am-7pm; US$20 per vehicle, up to three people, US$2 each extra person). Smack dab in the middle of town on Mar de Cortés, **Campo San Felipe** (tel. 7-10-12) lures campers with a fabulous beachfront location. A thatched roof shelters each fully loaded trailer spot. (Trailer hookup US$12-17 depending on location. US$2 per extra person, children under 6 free. Hookups US$1 extra. Tent space US$10.)

Food Mar de Cortés is crammed with restaurants advertising air-conditioned relief. Just one block over along the Malecón, *ostionerías* and fish *taquerías* serve up fresh seafood under shady thatched roofs for fewer clams. Shrimp tacos are 7 pesos, full shrimp dinners 35-45 pesos. **Los Gemelos** (tel. 7-10-63), on Mar de Cortés at Acapulco, near Bancomer, and its identical neighbor with seating on the beach, **Restaurant El Club** (tel. 7-11-75), feature beef, chicken, and shrimp enchiladas (18 pesos) and Veracruz-style fish (25 pesos) on pristine white tablecloths below hanging plastic turtles. The *camarones al mojo de ajo* (garlic shrimp; 45 pesos) is one of the world's most perfect meals. Ice-cold *agua purificada* available free. Placemats feature octopi playing tennis—really (open daily 7am-11pm).

Sights and Entertainment People come to San Felipe to swim in the warm, tranquil, and invitingly blue Gulf waters. The beach in town follows along the Malecón and gets crowded on weekends. **Jet-skis** can be rented for around US$35 per hour. Try the beaches farther south for scuba and snorkeling—the water's clearer. A booth that rents jet-skis and beach buggies is located right next to Motel El Pescador (US$20 per hr., open 8am-6pm). **Banana boats** wait along the beach in front of Bar Miramar, ready to take you for a 20-minute spin (9am-6pm, 20 pesos per person, min. 5 people).

Many local fishermen will gladly take vacationers on fishing excursions near **Isla San Felipe** and the recently planted artificial reefs; fishing is generally poor when it's windy. Wooden, motor-powered boats launch at around 6 or 6:30am for a half-day (until 1pm) of fishing and seal-watching near the rocks of the Isla (about US$30 per person, US$25 with 4 or more). One company that organizes such trips is **Alex Sport Fishing** (tel. 7-10-52). **Enchanted Island Excursions** (tel. 7-14-31) offers longer boat tours to the islands, some lasting up to three days or more.

BAJA CALIFORNIA

The whole Bahía is generally clean, safe, and appealing; beaches outside of town are more isolated, but might require a long walk or a drive. Every beach is accompanied by a commercialized RV trailer park, but, as always, beaches are free—you only need to pay if you're parking. **Playa Punta Bunda,** 3km south of town (follow Camino del Sur), **Playa del Sol, Playa Jalisco,** and **Playa de los Amigos** all come recommended by locals. The only means of getting there is by taxi (20 pesos).

Take time to visit the **Altar de la Virgen de Guadalupe,** a shrine to the virgin at the top of the *cerritos* (hills) near the lighthouse. After a scorching hike, you'll be rewarded with a spectacular view of San Felipe and the blue bay. Don't try to drive up unless you've got a 4-wheel-drive vehicle—the loose sand won't be amusing. Sixty-four kilometers south of San Felipe is the **Valle de los Gigantes National Park.** With cacti up to 15m tall, the park was the original home of the giant cactus which represented Mexico at the 1992 World's Fair in Seville, Spain. Fossil hunters will be elated to find a vast array of petrified sea life.

Seasoned veterans nurse drinks at **Bar Miramar,** Mar de Cortés 315 (tel. 7-11-92). The oldest bar in San Felipe may look like a *cantina* from the 60s, but the patrons come for company, not glitz. Push a few cues over green felt on the pool tables out front. (Beer US$1.25, margaritas US$1.75. Happy hour Mon.-Thurs. 3-7pm. Open daily 10am-2am.) Younger folks usually head a few doors down to the high-profile, high-priced **Rockodile** (tel. 7-12-19), on the Malecón at Acapulco. Check out the volleyball court, pool table, and outdoor terrace. The decor looks like an attempt to combine Keith Haring with cave paintings. Beer is US$2, margaritas a pricey US$4 (half-price happy hour Sun.-Fri. 11am-7pm; open daily 11am-2am).

BAJA CALIFORNIA SUR

■ Guerrero Negro

Twenty degrees cooler than the bleak Desierto de Vizcaíno to the southeast, Guerrero Negro (pop. 10,000), though dusty and painfully industrial, might earn a soft spot in the hearts of heat-weary northbound travelers. Be prepared for lots of wind and gray. Guerrero Negro resembles a beach town without the beach; its sandy roads and salty breeze dupe travelers into thinking that ocean waters are nearby. Situated about halfway between Tijuana and La Paz, Guerrero Negro is the place to spend a cool night if you'd like to break up the killer 25-hour trans-Baja bus trip.

In Guerrero Negro, salt is God, king, and country. So saline is Guerrero Negro that even breathing deeply of the town's air can send the hypochondriac's blood pressure soaring. The town was founded 58 years ago when a North American company began extracting and exporting salt from the Laguna Ojo de Liebre. The salt plant is now the world's largest, dominating the town's economy and attracting job-seekers from throughout the region.

Orientation Guerrero Negro sprawls along 3km of the Transpeninsular Highway. Its two main roads, the highway and **Avenida Baja California,** are home to basically all of the town's industrial and commercial centers; poor residential areas, filled with grim-looking shacks, lie one block off these roads to either side. The highway runs from the bus station at the south end to the riverbed and salt plant at the north end of town, where it turns. Av. Baja California continues into Guerrero Negro, veering to the left at the park and church. Yellow minivans run up and down the Transpeninsular Highway (every 15min. 7am-10pm, 4 pesos).

Practical Information Change money at **Banamex** (tel. 7-05-55 to -57), on Av. Baja California, just in front of the plant (open Mon.-Fri. 8:30am-1pm). Travelers heading south should change currency here, as the 24-hour **ATM** is the last of its kind

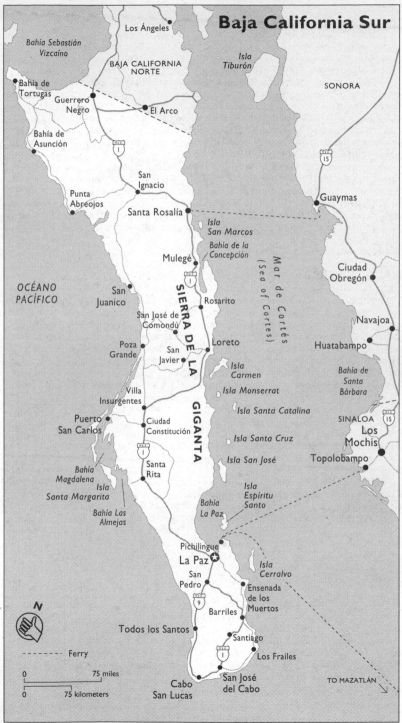

Baja California Sur

Los Ángeles

Bahía Sebastián Vizcaíno

BAJA CALIFORNIA NORTE

Isla Tiburón

SONORA

Bahía de Tortugas

Guerrero Negro

El Arco

Bahía de Asunción

Punta Abreojos

San Ignacio

Guaymas

Santa Rosalía

Isla San Marcos

Bahía de la Concepción

Mulegé

Ciudad Obregón

OCÉANO PACÍFICO

San Juanico

M a r   d e   C o r t é s   (Sea of Cortés)

SIERRA DE LA GIGANTA

Rosarito

San José de Comondú

Navajoa

Poza Grande

Loreto

San Javier

Huatabampo

Isla Carmen

Isla Monserrat

Bahía de Santa Bárbara

Villa Insurgentes

Isla Santa Catalina

SINALOA

Puerto San Carlos

Ciudad Constitución

Isla Santa Cruz

Los Mochis

Isla San José

Topolobampo

Santa Rita

Bahía Magdalena

Isla Santa Margarita

Bahía Las Almejas

Isla Espíritu Santo

Bahía La Paz

Pichilingue

La Paz

Isla Cerralvo

San Pedro

Ensenada de los Muertos

N

Barriles

Todos los Santos

Santiago

Los Frailes

------ Ferry

0   75 miles

0   75 kilometers

Cabo San Lucas

San José del Cabo

TO MAZATLÁN

BAJA CALIFORNIA

until you reach La Paz. **Telephones** are in Farmacia San Martín (tel. 7-09-11 or 7-11-11), on the Transpeninsular Highway, 100m north of the clinic (open Mon.-Sat. 8am-10pm, Sun. 9am-4pm). International collect calls or calling card calls are free at the wall phone in the lobby of Motel Brisa Salina, on the highway across from the Union 76 ball (the one farther from the bus station).

The **ABC Autotransportes de Baja California** terminal (tel. 7-06-11) is one of the first buildings from the highway on the access road. ABC sends buses north (5 per day) to Ensenada (10hr., 94 pesos), Lázaro Cárdenas (7hr., 80 pesos), Punta Prieta (4hr., 30 pesos), El Rosario (6hr., 65 pesos), Rosarito (2hr., 20 pesos), San Quintín (7hr., 80 pesos), and Tijuana (11hr., 114 pesos); and south to La Paz (5 per day, 11hr., 155 pesos), Mulegé (4 per day, 4hr., 56 pesos), Santa Rosalía (4 per day, 3hr., 46 pesos), and points in between.

Supermarket CaliMex (tel. 7-04-34) is on the highway at Adolfo Ruiz (open daily 9am-8pm). An **IMSS Hospital and Clinic** (tel. 7-04-33) is on the highway at Blvd. M. Zaragoza, half a kilometer north of the water tower. The **police** (tel. 7-02-22) are in the Delegación Municipal, a few hundred meters before the salt plant. The **post office** (tel. 7-03-44) is off Av. Baja California, two blocks past the church (open Mon.-Fri. 8am-3pm). **Postal Code:** 23940. **Telephone Code:** 115.

Accommodations The cheapest place in town, **Motel Gámez** (tel. 7-03-70), is on the Transpeninsular Highway between the IMSS Clinic and the salt plant. Each of the small, newly painted yellow rooms has a private bath (some lacking sinks) and its own quirks (singles 35 pesos; doubles 45 pesos). **Motel Las Dunas** (tel. 7-00-55 and -57), on the highway below the water tank, a short walk north from the bus station, is an excellent deal. Immaculate rooms with large showers are as worthy as those at more expensive spots. Lukewarm *agua purificada* is available free, and the extremely courteous staff helps in every way possible (singles 50 pesos; doubles 55 pesos; triples 60 pesos; key deposit 10 pesos). No one sleeps better than the guests at **Motel Brisa Salina,** across from the Union 76 ball (the one farther from the bus station). The double mattresses are so thick and high that ladders would be helpful. Most rooms are furnished with an entire entertainment system: color TV and a radio. All rooms sport wooden bureaus and chairs and face a narrow, neatly trimmed, flowery courtyard (singles 60 pesos; doubles 70 pesos, with two beds 80 pesos; each additional person 5 pesos).

Food Many aspects of Guerrero Negro are a little hard to swallow, and the city's food is no exception. If you're looking for food after 9pm, particularly during the low season, bless you. The local specialty is lobster caught in the *laguna*. La Palapa (tel. 7-16-48) is on the highway across from the PEMEX station closer to the bus station. The dining room is decorated with model boats, shells, photographs of marine life, and plastic fish caught in nets. Have a clam cocktail (18 pesos) as you await your octopus (20 pesos). A large platter of french toast goes for 12 pesos (open daily 8am-9pm). In the shadow of the water tower on the right side of the highway (coming from the bus station), **El Figón de Sal** (tel. 7-16-87) offers reasonably priced food in a small, grocery store-like dining room (*comida corrida* 17 pesos). Locals rave about **Cocina Económica Lety,** next to the Union 76 ball (the one closer to the bus station). Chicken enchiladas for 18 pesos (open 7am-10pm).

Sights and Entertainment Excitement comes to town between late December and early March with the thousands of gray whales who make the annual swim from the Bering Sea to reproduce in the waters offshore. During the rest of the year, more excitement might be found staring at a blank wall. If you time your visit correctly, you can commune with hundreds of whales in the **Parque Natural de las Ballenas Grises,** on the **Laguna Ojo de Liebre,** formerly a deep-water port facility of the salt company. In the early morning, whales swim right up to the docks; during the rest of the day, ascend a tall observation tower for a look. No public transportation is available to the park. To get there, head south on Rte. 1 toward Santa Rosalía for 8-15km. A sign points out the 30km dirt road to the *laguna*. Staffers at the park sometimes lead whale-watching tours in early January and February.

The **Bahía de los Angeles** is populated by dolphins, blue and gray whales, sea lions, and many species of birds. From January to March, **Servicios Turísticos Mario** (tel. 7-07-88), on the highway near the PEMEX closer to the bus station, offers tours to the Bahía (min. 10 people) and of indigenous cave paintings in the Sierra de San Francisco. Most cave painting excursions, however, leave from San Ignacio (see p. 145). On a four-hour tour of the *laguna*, you'll visit the **Dunas de Soledad,** 10km of pearly white dunes whose configuration changes daily due to the movement of the tides. The dunes get their name from the first residents of the area, a solitary Sinaloa couple who settled here after a three-month overland trek. An archaeological site known for its unique and impressive rock paintings, **Mesa del Carmen,** lies 68km southwest of Guerrero Negro. While it can only be reached by car, guides can be arranged in El Arco, a small town ten kilometers southwest of Guerrero Negro. For more information, contact Jorge Serrano (tel. 617-8-25-31) in Ensenada.

■ San Ignacio

More than any other stop on the arid Baja Peninsula, San Ignacio (pop. 2,000), seems like a tropical oasis. From a distance, the town appears to be a cruel illusion, a mirage of the mind—leafy date palms, flowering bushes, and broad swaths of green appear magically in the middle of the blistering desert. Chin up—you're not dreaming. The area around San Ignacio is blessed with the most plentiful underground freshwater supply in all Baja California Sur; of late, they've been dammed up to form a murky lake used for swimming and irrigating local orchards.

Though hot during summer days, San Ignacio earns points for more than just its terrain. Locals are extremely amiable, and the town is relatively undisturbed by *gringos* for most of the year. San Ignacio's intimate atmosphere, beautiful nighttime starscapes, and historic mission overlooking the *zócalo* are but a few of the reasons why the pleasure-seekers who set eyes on the town never want to leave and eventually end up settling down. San Ignacio is also a prime point of departure for both cave painting and whale-watching tours.

Orientation and Practical Information A winding road canopied by swaying date palms leads from the Transpeninsular Highway to the *zócalo*. Within 10 minutes of pulling into town, you'll know tiny San Ignacio better than your hometown. Life revolves around the *zócalo*, which is delineated by **Juan Bautista Luyando** and the mission to the north, **Morelos** to the south, **Juárez** to the east, and **Hidalgo** to the west. Locals are more than happy to give directions.

There's no official tourist office in town; but to hear friendly, informative chatter about San Ignacio, visit the elderly man who owns the mini-mart next to Restaurant Chatita on Hidalgo (tel. 4-01-50, -60, and -90; open Mon.-Sat. 7am-7pm, Sun. 7am-1pm); he also leads tours to the cave paintings and whale expeditions. A lone **public phone** stands in the north side of the *zócalo;* you can place calls and send **faxes** at a pricier *caseta*, Hidalgo 24 (tel. 4-02-50; open Mon.-Fri. 8am-1pm and 3-6pm). **Telegrams** can be sent and received at **Telecomm** (tel. 4-01-55), on Juárez facing the *zócalo* (open Mon.-Fri. 8am-2pm).

Buses pick up passengers at the sheltered bench 2km from San Ignacio on the Transpeninsular highway. *De paso* buses leave at 7pm for Tijuana (stopping at Ensenada, Guerrero Negro, and Rosario) and at 10am and 6pm for La Paz (stopping at Santa Rosalía, Mulegé, and Loreto). **Nuevos Almacenos** (tel. 4-01-22), a good-sized **grocery store,** is on the corner of Juárez and Juan Bautista Luyando, facing the *zócalo* (open Mon.-Sat. 8am-noon and 2-7pm, Sun. 8am-noon). The **pharmacy, Boticas Ceseña** (tel. 4-00-76, after hours 4-00-75), is unmarked at Madero 24A, parallel to and east of Juárez and Hidalgo (open daily 8:30am-1pm and 3-7pm). To reach the **Centro de**

Salud, walk five minutes away from the highway down Hidalgo, which turns into Ocampo. Turn right on Independencia, a tiny dirt road; it's the large white building on the right-hand side (open daily 8am-3pm). If you have a medical **emergency** after hours, call Fischer Lucero (tel. 4-01-90), the local doctor. Contact the health center or the police in an emergency only. The **police** (tel. 4-03-77) are in the Delegación Municipal on Ocampo and Zaragoza (open daily 8am-3pm). The **post office** is in the gray stone building on Juárez next to the *zócalo* (open Mon.-Fri. 8am-3pm). **Postal Code:** 23930. **Telephone Code:** 115.

Accommodations San Ignacio has few accommodations, and they don't come cheap. The family living in **Restaurant Chalita,** Hidalgo 9 (tel. 4-00-82), rents bedrooms that ooze with local culture. The small, clean rooms have fans and black-and-white TVs (singles 75 pesos). **Hotel Posada** (tel. 4-03-13), on Ocampo and Independencia, a three-minute walk down Ciprés from Hidalgo, has remarkably clean rooms with standing fans and private baths (singles and doubles 140 pesos). **El Padrino RV Park** (tel. 4-00-89) is 500m from the *zócalo* on the road connecting San Ignacio to the highway. Full trailer hookup (US$10, without electricity US$7) comes with a complimentary margarita from the pleasant Flojo's Restaurant/Bar. Motorcycles cost US$3 to park. El Padrino also offers four brand spankin' new rooms with private baths (singles 70 pesos or US$10; doubles 140 pesos or US$20).

Food Most people chow down in the *zócalo.* As in other fishing towns along the Baja coasts, seafood dishes receive top billing on restaurant menus. Eat outdoors under the wonderfully starry sky at **Restaurant-Bar Rene's** (tel. 4-02-56), just outside the *zócalo* off Hidalgo. Wash down the delectable *calamar empanizado* (breaded squid, 25 pesos) with a beer (5 pesos). If you'd rather eat under a roof, head into their round thatched hut and stare out at the small adjoining pond (open daily 7am-10pm). **Restaurant Chalita,** Hidalgo 9 (tel. 4-00-82), is housed in an old-fashioned Mexican kitchen. Sit on random furniture, listen to the caged birds sing, and find salvation in a warm plate of *pescado al mojo de ajo* (23 pesos), enchiladas (14 pesos), or *chiles rellenos* (18 pesos; open daily 7:30am-10pm). **Flojo's Restaurant/Bar** (tel. 4-00-89) is part of El Padrino RV Park (see above) and a five-minute walk from town. Even you will become *flojo* (slack) when you overstuff yourself with three chicken burritos with rice and beans (21 pesos) or breaded Italian meat (30 pesos). Lean back, watch the stars shine between the reeds of the enormous *palapa,* and listen to the crickets chirp (open daily 7am-10:30pm).

Sights The main tourist draw to San Ignacio are the **painted caves,** 75km away in the Sierra de San Francisco. Five hundred paintings, probably more than 10,000-years old, reside within a 12-square-kilometer area. Oscar Fischer of Hotel Posada and his son, Dagoberto, offer various tours to the caves (tel. 4-03-13 or 4-01-56). US$20 (during the tourist season) gets you a nine-hour trip to one cave and two petroglyphic zones. It leaves at around 8am and makes as many stops in between as requested. A two-day tour will take you to the impressive **La Pintada,** and the minor **El Ratón** caves. For US$60, you'll get transportation, a guide, and a mule. If you're planning to sleep comfortably during the trip, you'll need a tent and an additional mule (US$10) to carry it. Some adventurous travelers make the trip from cave to cave on foot (about eight kilometers each way), saving all mule costs but leaving their bodies worn, to say the least. US$80 plus tent and mule costs gets you the grandest tour of all: a three-day, eight-cave extravaganza that will show you all the indigenous paintings you probably ever wanted to see and leave all but the most resilient travelers battle-worn. For the two- and three-day trip, it is recommended that you call at least two weeks in advance so that the Fischers can arrange the excursion and clear it with the Mexican bureaucracy. The managers also run trips to the Laguna San Ignacio to spy on **gray whales.** They leave before 7am and cost US$45 per person. Note that prices for all tours (caves and whales) assume groups of six or more; smaller parties can expect to pay

CMI
Centro Mexicano Internacional

CENTRO MEXICANO INTERNACIONAL
14542 Brookhollow, Suite 279
San Antonio, Texas 78232

Please send my 1997 Eurail catalog

LET'S GO
T R A V E L
67 Mt. Auburn Street
Cambridge, MA 02138
USA

more. Tours of the painted caves and whale-watching expeditions are also led by the owner of **Flojos Restaurant/Bar** and **El Padrino RV Park** and his son (tel. 4-00-89).

A colonial colossus towering over wild, leafy vegetation, the **Mission of San Ignacio**, on the northern side of the *zócalo*, was founded in 1728 by Jesuit missionary Juan Bautista. The construction of the mission proved a logistic nightmare; wood had to be hauled in from the Guadalupe mission in the Sierras, furniture was brought from Mulegé after a scorching four-day mule ride through the unpaved desert, and the paintings were carried by boat from the mainland. The mission is a beautiful achievement, well worth the difficulties—magnificent on the outside, cool inside, and heavenly at night, when illuminated by outdoor spotlights. Inside, look up to see a a flying gold angel seemingly suspended in the dome. A particularly striking outside view of the mission poking above palms and huts in the evening can be seen from halfway between the *zócalo* and Hotel Posada, on the small path. The newly opened **Mission Museum** (tel. 4-02-22), on Loyando, 30m west of the mission, tells the story of the nearby cave paintings and even has its own huge faux-cave painting (open Mon.-Sat. 8am-8pm; free).

■ Santa Rosalía

Not only is Santa Rosalía a convenient transportation hub for buses and ferries, it is also heir to a rich and colorful history. After an enormously rich copper ore was discovered here in 1868, the French-owned, Rothschild-financed El Boleo company embarked on a mining venture of staggering proportions. The town was settled on the sides of the mountain in an orderly fashion according to rank, so that the wealthier, higher-ranking officials literally lived higher up. Their old homes crown the two cliffs that sandwich central Santa Rosalía. The town's church, Iglesia Santa Bárbara, was designed by Gustave Eiffel. Today, mountains of abandoned machinery and railroad cars bristle with rust, returning their metals to the ground. If you're planning to visit Santa Rosalía, keep in mind that the town is unbearably hot and humid in the summer. The Gulf breezes don't cool it nearly enough; temperatures of 90°F and high humidity will drench you with sweat.

Orientation and Practical Information To get from the **ferry** to **Obregón,** Santa Rosalía's main strip, turn right as you leave the ferry compound; Obregón is the second left. **Banamex** (tel. 2-00-10 or 2-09-84), on Obregón, changes traveler's checks and provides relief from the blistering heat with ice-cold A/C. Find some excuse to go in (open Mon.-Fri. 8:30am-1pm). **LADATELs** pepper the town; find some in front of the church and the Palacio Municipal. **Farmacia Central** (see listing below) has a long distance *caseta*.

Most **buses** depart from the **ABC station** (tel. 2-01-50), across the street from the ferry office. Buses travel north to San Ignacio (1hr., 18 pesos), Guerrero Negro (3½hr., 46 pesos), Punta Prieta (7hr., 67 pesos), El Rosario (9hr., 105 pesos), San Quintín (9½hr., 114 pesos), Col. Guerrero (10hr., 118 pesos), Ensenada (13½hr., 155 pesos), Tijuana (15hr., 179 pesos), and Mexicali (18½hr., 224 pesos). Heading south, all buses go to La Paz (9:30, 11am, 8, 9:30, and 11pm, 7hr., 97 pesos) via Mulegé (1hr., 14 pesos), Loreto (3hr., 35 pesos), Ej. Insurgentes (4hr., 56 pesos), and Ciudad Constitución (4½hr., 60 pesos). The **ABC Autotransportes bus office** is on Constitución, six blocks inland from the highway; from here, one bus heads south at 11am daily. From Santa Rosalía, you can catch the **ferry** connecting Baja to Guaymas on the mainland (Sun. and Wed. 8am, 7hr., *salón* 95 pesos, *turista* 189 pesos). The boat leaves from the modern, blue-and-green **Sematur** office (tel. 2-00-13) on Rte. 1 (the Transpeninsular Highway), just south of town. To reach the docks, catch a bus from the **ABC Autotransportes** station, about 200m south of the ferry. Those with cars must purchase their spot in advance and show a tourist card, registration, and proof of their Mexican insurance (cars up to 5m long 754 pesos; motorcycles 111 pesos; office open Mon., Wed., Thurs., Sat. 8am-3pm, Tues., Fri. 8am-1pm and 3-6pm).

Departure days and times, prices, and office hours are in constant flux, so be sure to call the office or talk to a travel agent to confirm the schedule. For more information on ferries, see p. 126.

Farmacia Central (tel. 2-20-70; fax 2-22-70), Av. Obregón at Plaza, is owned by English-speaking Dr. Chang Tam (open Mon.-Sat. 9am-10pm, Sun. 9am-1pm and 7-10pm). The **Centro de Salud** (tel. 2-13-37 or -36) is at Juan Michel Costeau. Send letters home from the **post office** on Constitución, between Calles 2 and Altamirano (open Mon.-Fri. 8am-3pm). **Postal Code:** 23920. **Telephone Code:** 115.

Accommodations and Food If you're going to stay in sweltering Santa Rosalía, consider popping the few extra pesos for A/C. The budget standout is **Hotel Olvera,** Calle Plaza 14 (tel. 2-00-57 or -67), about three blocks from the shore on Constitución. From the bus station, take a left and walk along the water towards town until you come to the old train engine in front of the town's two main streets—follow Constitución, the left one, and it's on your right, at the bridge. Enjoy spacious bathrooms, large double beds with patriotic American bedspreads, and free lukewarm *agua purificada.* Rooms come with color TV and hot water (singles 70 pesos, with A/C 90 pesos; doubles 90 pesos, with A/C 110 pesos). **R.V. Park Las Palmas,** 3.5km south of town, has thirty-two lots with full hookups, a laundromat, and a restaurant (US$10 for two people, UD$2 per additional person).

Sit outside under the fans at **Terco's Pollito** (tel. 2-00-75), on Obregón, horizontally across from the Hotel Olvera, and enjoy their *combinación mexicana* (*tamales, chimichanga, chile relleno, frijoles,* rice, and tortillas, 25 pesos; open daily 7:30am-11:30pm). **El Boleo Bakery,** Obregón at Calle 4 (tel. 2-03-10), known for its architecture, deserves a visit for its excellent baked goods as well. Otherwordly french bread (1.50 pesos), *pan dulce* (1.50 pesos), and donuts (2 pesos) thrill customers (open Mon.-Sat. 9:30am-7:30pm).

Sights The wooden houses, general stores, and saloons along Santa Rosalía's streets recall the town's mining-boom days. Startling specimens of 19th-century French architecture include the long and many-windowed **Palacio Municipal,** the **Hotel Francés,** and **El Boleo Bakery.** The most serendipitous of artifacts is the prefabricated white cast-iron **Iglesia Santa Bárbara,** at Obregón and Calle 1. Designed by Gustave Eiffel (of Tower fame) for a mission in Africa, the church was never picked up by the company that had commissioned it. French mining *concessionaires* spotted the iron church at the 1889 Exhibition Universale de Paris and decided Santa Rosalía couldn't do without it. Observers either love it or hate it; its outside panels look like they fell off an industrial washing machine. Those travelers looking for fun in the sun and abundant water sports would do better to make tracks south for the heavenly beaches in Bahía de la Concepción.

■ Mulegé

Located 136km north of Loreto and 300km south of dreary Guerrero Negro on the Baja peninsula, Mulegé (pop. 4400) is a pleasant, charming town in its own right, but

---

I Scream, You Scream

In Mexico, there's no escaping the *chicharrón* (pork rind), and in some towns the popular snack has become...an ice cream flavor! On sweltering hot days, vendors push long carts loaded with rows of metal casks and scoop out ice cold salvation in a crazy variety of flavors—*elote* (corn meal), *cerveza* (beer), *aguacate* (avocado), and tequila. Hand a vendor five pesos and he'll cram a mammoth portion into a cone or plastic cup. Mexican ice cream is known to harbor more than a few nasty amoebas, so verify the product's hygienic integrity before placing that spoon in your mouth. Then tuck a napkin into your shirt front, close your eyes, and lick away.

for tourists it serves mainly as a base from which to explore the marvelous beaches of nearby Bahía de la Concepción.

Orientation and Practical Information Soon after bearing left off the Transpeninsular Highway, the road into Mulegé forks. To the left is **Moctezuma;** to the right is **Martínez.** Both are soon crossed by **Zaragoza;** take a right onto Zaragoza to get to the *zócalo,* which is one block away. **Madero** heads east from the *zócalo* (away from the highway) and, after following the Mulegé River for about 3km, hits the water at the town beach, **Playa de Mulegé.**

The **Hotel Las Casitas,** Madero 50 (tel. 3-00-19), serves as an unofficial **tourist office,** with plenty of information on beaches, camping, and fishing. Ask for Javier to get to the real nitty-gritty. English-speaking **Kerry "El Vikingo" Otterstrom** has written and published a 180-page book on Mulegé and can tell you all there is to know about the town. He is a bartender at El Candil Restaurant (see below) and can always be found there, unless he is out leading a tour. **Minisúper Padilla** (tel./fax 3-01-90), on Zaragoza at Martínez, one block north of plaza, has two **phones** for international calls. An unreliable public phone is located in the plaza.

The **bus station** is simply a sheltered blue bench at the turnoff to Mulegé from Rte. 1. All buses are *de paso,* a phrase which might roughly be translated as "inevitably arrives late and full." Northbound buses stop by daily at 4:30pm and go to Santa Rosalía (1hr., 10 pesos), San Ignacio (2hr., 21 pesos), Rosarito (6hr., 87 pesos), Punta Prieta (8hr., 86 pesos), Santa Inés (9hr., 108 pesos), El Rosario (10hr., 199 pesos), San Quintín (10½hr., 136 pesos), Lázaro Cárdenas (11hr., 133 pesos), San Vicente (13hr., 166 pesos), Ensenada (14½hr., 174 pesos), Tijuana (16hr., 199 pesos), Tecate (17hr., 211 pesos), and Mexicali (19½hr., 244 pesos). Southbound buses stop by at 9:30 and 11:30am and go to Loreto (2hr., 28 pesos), Insurgentes (3hr., 52 pesos), Ciudad Constitución (3½hr., 59 pesos), and La Paz (6hr., 99 pesos).

Lavamática Claudia (tel. 3-00-57) is next to the Hotel Terrazas (16 pesos per load; open Mon.-Sat. 8am-6pm). The **Red Cross** (tel. 3-02-58 and 3-03-80, after-hours 3-01-39; CB channel 14) is on Madero, 200m east of the plaza. **Farmacia Moderna** (tel. 3-00-42) is on Madero, on the plaza (open daily 8am-1pm and 4-10pm). **Centro de Salud B (ISSTE),** Madero 28 (tel. 3-02-98), treats medical emergencies (open 8am-2:30pm). The **post office** (tel. 3-02-05) is on Martínez across from the PEMEX station (open Mon.-Fri. 8am-3pm). **Postal Code:** 23900. **Telephone Code:** 685.

Accommodations Economical hotels crowd the center of town, but they're far from the beaches. While haggling can bring room prices down, those with sleeping bags often find the best deals on the shore. **Hotel Terrazas** (tel. 3-00-09) is on Zaragoza at Cananea, two blocks north of the plaza. From the bus stop, bear left off the highway, take a right at Mulegé's initial fork, and take a left on Zaragoza. It's two blocks uphill on the right. Well kept rooms have a homey feel and free *agua purificada* (doubles 100 pesos, with A/C 120 pesos; prices negotiable). **Casa de Huéspedes Manuelita** (tel. 3-01-75), on Moctezuma next to Los Equipales, around the corner from Zaragoza, has relatively clean rooms with soft beds, table fans, and private showers. One or two friendly cockroaches have been spotted from time to time. Campers who simply need to use the bathroom and shower pay 10 pesos (singles 40 pesos; doubles 60 pesos; all prices negotiable). **Casa de Huéspedes Canett** (tel. 3-02-72), on Madero east of the *zócalo,* offers beds you can sleep on and private showers that work—not much more—but the rooms aren't filthy and you can't go wrong for the price (singles 25 pesos; doubles 50 pesos). **Orchard RV Park** and **María Isabel RV Park,** both just south of town and accessible from the Transpeninsular Highway, are near a fresh-water oasis lagoon, on Madero about 1km toward the beach (about US$15 per night; space for tents about US$6).

Food Restaurant **La Almeja,** at the end of Morelos near the lighthouse, about 3km from the center of town, is right on the beach. It offers outstanding seafood, including a tasty and filling *sopa de siete mares* (seven seas soup, which includes just about every creature that ever swam in water, 25 pesos). *Piña colada* made with fresh pineapple and coconut costs only 12 pesos. Purified water and ice are available (open daily 8am-11pm). **El Candil Restaurant,** north of the plaza on Zaragoza near Martínez, serves an enormous Mexican combination platter with rice, beans, *chiles rellenos,* and tacos (32 pesos) and an excellent fish fillet (25 pesos; open Mon.-Sat. 7am-10pm). **Los Equipales Restaurante Bar** (tel. 3-03-30) is on Moctezuma half a block from the Hotel Terrazas. Sit by the windows and let the breeze cool you down from the sweltering heat while you enjoy the tasty beef and chicken burritos (20 pesos) or a clam cocktail (20 pesos; open daily 7am-10pm, or until last customer leaves).

At night, most *norteamericanos* in the area meet, drink, and dance at the bar of **Hotel Las Casitas** (tel. 3-00-19) on Madero (Mexican *fiesta* and buffet on Fri.; reservations required; 42 pesos). The last watering holes to close are **El Candil** and the bar at **Hotel Vieja Hacienda,** on the plaza.

Sights and Sand Mulegé's lovely **mission** sits on a hill to the west. Walk down Zaragoza away from the *zócalo,* go under the bridge, and turn right on the shaded lane. The mission is not a museum; mass is still held every Sunday. For a great view of the whole town, river, and palms, climb the steps to the top of the hill.

Over seven hundred 14,000-year-old pre-Hispanic cave paintings are located at **La Trinidad** and the **Cuevas de San Borjita.** Kerry Otterstrom of El Candil Restaurant leads trips to La Trinidad that include hiking and swimming 200m in a narrow canyon (US$35 per person). The trip to San Borjita has a milder hike, no swimming, and more spectacular caves (US$50 per person). Longer trips can be arranged (up to 7 days, US$50 per person per day including hotel, food, and drink). The guide speaks English, Spanish, German, and French. Other tours available from **Salvador Castro Tours,** at Hotel Las Casitas (tel. 3-00-19).

Two beaches lie only 3km from the center of town. **El Faro** is at the end of Madero, which becomes a dirt road long before you reach the beach. Alternatively, reach the **public beach** by following the Mulegé River to the Sea of Cortés, where it drains. For a more isolated beach, walk to the PEMEX station about 4km south on the highway, continue about 20m south, and take the dirt road leading off to the left until you reach a lonely beach with sand dunes and desert hills overlooking somewhat rocky sand. Locals consider this area to be quite safe. Watch out for jellyfish, especially in June and July. Be warned, though—these beaches can't hold a candle to those 18km south, in Bahía de la Concepción.

Mulegé Divers, Madero 45 (tel. 3-00-59), down the street from Hotel Las Casitas, rents scuba equipment, leads boat excursions into Bahía de la Concepción, and sells Mulegé T-shirts (open Mon.-Sat. 9am-1pm and 3-6pm). If you already know how to scuba dive, try the five-hour trip (US$40, minimum 2 people); otherwise, an instruction course helps you get your feet wet (US$70). They also organize five-hour long snorkeling excursions (US$25 including equipment, minimum 2 people) and rent snorkeling gear (US$10). All excursions leave at 8am. Make reservations at least one day in advance. The best snorkeling is at nearby **Islas Pitahaya, San Ramón, Liebre, Blanca, Coyote,** and **Guapa.**

▓ Bahía de la Concepción

Heaven on earth may just be the 48-kilometer arc of rocky outcrops, shimmering beaches, and bright blue sea known as the Bahía de la Concepción. Forget the beaches of the northern peninsula; Bahía de la Concepción, beginning 16km south of Mulegé, is where it's at. The coves and waters look more perfect than those inhabited by Neverland's mermaids, grown sport fishers and shell collectors weep at the variety and sheer size of the specimens caught here, and divers fall under the spell of underwater sights. What are *you* waiting for?

Playa Punta Arena, 16km south of Mulegé, is far enough from the road that the roar of the waves drowns out the noise from muffler-less trucks. From the highway, travel 2km down a rocky dirt road. Bear right at all forks in the road. A dozen palm-frond *palapas* line the beach with sand-flush toilets in back (*cabañas* or parking 20 pesos). The waters near the shore are great for clam fishing, but swimming may be hazardous due to manta rays. If you walk down the dirt road to Playa Punta Arena but take a left instead of a right at the second fork, you'll end up at **Playa San Pedro** and **Los Naranjos RV Park,** where payments for your space may be made with freshly caught fish.

Playa Santispac, the most popular beach on the Bahía, is connected to Playa Punta Arena by a dirt path that winds through mountains for 1km. During the winter, Santispac is the liveliest beach on the bay; in the summer, however, the sands are nearly deserted. **Las Palapas Trailer Park** rents *palapas* and tent space (both 35 pesos per night; use of bathrooms and showers 5 pesos). At **Ana's Restaurant,** guests enjoy fried fish (23 pesos) and shrimp omelettes (26 pesos) while marveling at the exotic shells on sale to the right of the counter (open daily 7am-10pm). The restaurant doubles as a bakery and sells cakes and huge loaves of bread (10 pesos; open daily 7am-8pm). **Kayak Concepción Bay** (tel. 3-04-09; fax 3-01-90), in front of Ana's, rents kayaks (US$25-45), mask-snorkel-fin sets (US$5 per day), wet suits (US$6 per day), and VHF radios (US$8 per day; prices drop for longer rentals; open daily 8am-6pm). They also organize day-long tours which start at Playa Santispac at 8am and involve kayaking and snorkeling; with nightfall comes a clam cookout (US$39 per person, including food and drink; four people minimum). If you're swimming during the spring months, watch out for mating sting rays; throughout the summer, manta rays are a threat. In case of a sting, locals recommend treating the affected area with hot, salty water. The **hot springs** on the south end of Playa Santispac provide the perfect source. Check out these warm, bubbly waters even if you haven't been nipped by an underwater creature.

Playa La Posada, which looks essentially like a minuscule village, is covered by permanent homes, but large *palapas* house temporary visitors (US$10 with electricity, US$7 without, both include access to bathrooms). Two distant rocky islands and an overgrown islet are popular destinations for jet-skiers. **Playa Escondida** (Hidden Beach) is at the end of a 500m dirt path winding through the valley between two hills; look for a white sign with black letters at the southern end of Playa Concepción. True to its name, the short, facility-less Escondida is nicely hidden from all civilization. **Playa Los Cocos** is identified by its white garbage cans adorned with palm trees. A dozen *cabañas* where you can spend the night free of charge line the shallow beach. A grove of trees and shrubs separates the strip from the highway. At **Playa El Burro,** you can rent a *palapa* next to hordes of RVs for 20 pesos per day.

Next is **Playa El Coyote,** with *palapas* and **Estrella del Mar,** a restaurant serving meat enchiladas (12 pesos) and fried chicken (22 pesos; open Oct.-April daily 8am-8pm). The better sands and *palapas* are down on the southern end. Fifteen kilometers farther down the road is the exquisite (and even less populated) **Playa Resquesón.** Even farther south, two more spots—**La Ramada** and **Santa Bárbara**—are currently undergoing development, and *palapas* have been built in these otherwise virgin beaches. Another nearly deserted stretch of sand is the last beach before the highway climbs into the mountains separating Mulegé from Loreto. All of these beaches are marked from the main highway.

The beaches are fantastic after dark, but only come at night if you plan to stay—it's impossible to hitch back, no buses run, and even stepping onto the curvy highway is dangerous due to oncoming cars. A final note for all beaches: don't expect to find cold water or even remotely cold *anything.* Ice is rare, so unless you relish the idea of downing a hot Coke in the pounding sun, bring a cooler with some drinks.

Getting There: Many nomadic travelers hitch (known in Americanized Spanish as *"pedir* ride") from Mulegé to the beaches, catching one of the RVs or produce trucks barreling down the Transpeninsular Highway towards the bay. Those who hitch are most successful getting rides right across the island from the bus stop, and tell the driver exactly where they are heading—"Playa Santispac" usually works well. Hitching back to Mulegé is even easier, since many people leaving the beach are heading back into town. But *Let's Go* does not recommend hitchhiking. Instead, try checking at the bus station for the next *de paso* bus south (9:30 and 11:30am). Wait to pay the fare until the bus arrives, and don't get on until the driver assures you that he plans to stop at one of the beaches. But don't count on a bus to take you back; bus service to the beaches is infrequent, and drivers may not stop along the busy highway. Beach-hoppers might also consider renting a car for the day, as access to and from the beaches farther south is limited.

■ Loreto

Founded by Jesuit missionaries in 1697, Loreto (pop. 10,000) was the first capital of the Californias and a link in a chain of missions along the west coast of Baja. The town, however, was wiped out by a freakish combination of hurricanes and earthquakes in 1829. Recent construction has belatedly restored the **Misión de Nuestra Señora de Loreto** to its former beauty. Sandwiched in between the calm blue waters of the Sea of Cortés and golden mountains, Loreto remains a simple town with a long, tranquil *malecón* shaded by rows of palm trees. Most of the few visitors are middle-aged *norteamericanos* who come to fish.

Orientation and Practical Information The principal street in Loreto is **Salvatierra,** which connects the Carretera Transpeninsular to the Gulf. When Salvatierra becomes a pedestrian walkway, **Hidalgo** roughly becomes its continuation. **Independencia** intersects Salvatierra just as it turns into Hidalgo, and **Francisco I. Madero** intersects Hidalgo closer to the water. Away from the gulf, **Allende, León,** and **Ayuntamiento** cross Salvatierra before Independencia. **Malecón,** which leads north to the beach and outlines the entire width of the city at the coast, runs perpendicular to Hidalgo where Hidalgo ends. **Juárez** runs parallel to, and north of, Salvatierra and Hidalgo. The **zócalo** is at Hidalgo and Madero. To get to the center of town from the **bus station,** walk down Salvatierra in the direction of the distant cathedral (10min.) or indulge in a taxi (10 pesos).

The Palacio Municipal, on Madero between Salvatierra and Comercio facing the *zócalo,* houses the air-conditioned **tourist info center** (tel. 5-04-11). English is spoken (open Mon.-Fri. 8:30am-3pm and 6-8pm). An informal tourist info center (tel. 5-02-59) is located on Salvatierra between Independencia and Ayuntamiento in a small jewelry shop. **Bancomer** (tel. 5-00-14 or 5-09-10), on Madero across from the *zócalo,* exchanges dollars (open Mon.-Fri. 8:30am-noon). International **collect** and **credit card calls** can be made on Salvatierra at Independencia across from the supermarket (tel. 5-06-97; open daily 8am-9pm) and at the *nevería* across from Supermarket El Pescador (open Mon.-Sat. 8am-9pm, Sun. 9am-1pm and 4-8pm). The **telegram office** (tel. 5-03-87) is next to the post office (open Mon.-Fri. 8am-2pm).

Águila buses stop by the terminal (tel. 5-07-67) on Salvatierra near Allende, just off the highway, about 2km from Madero. Northbound buses leave at 2, 3, 5, 9 and 11pm and 1am; southbound buses go to La Paz (8am, 2pm, 3pm, 11pm, midnight, and 1am, 5hr., 70 pesos). **Thrifty** (tel. 5-08-15) rents cars for US$50 per day including insurance, tax, and mileage. Stock up for the day at **Supermarket El Pescador** (tel. 5-00-60), on Salvatierra and Independencia (open daily 7:30am-10:30pm). Watch clothes spin at **Lavandería El Remojón,** on Salvatierra and Independencia (tel. 5-02-59; up to 4kg 15 pesos; open Mon.-Sat. 8am-8pm, Sun. 8am-2pm). The **Red Cross** is on Salvatierra and Juárez (tel. 5-11-11; open daily 9am-1pm and 3-8:30pm). **Farmacia Misión,** Salvatierra 66 (tel. 5-03-41), is between Ayuntamiento and Independencia (open daily 8am-10pm). The **Centro de Salud** (tel. 5-00-39) is on Salvatierra, 1km from the bus terminal (open 24hr.). The **IMSS** can be reached at 5-62-70. **Medical emergency numbers** are 5-03-97, 5-09-06, and 5-00-62. The **post office** is on Salvatierra and Deportiva (tel. 5-06-47), near the bus station, behind the Red Cross (open Mon.-Fri. 8am-3pm). **Postal Code:** 23880. **Telephone Code:** 113.

Accommodations The most economical hotel in town is **Hotel San Martín** (tel. 5-04-42), two blocks north of the *zócalo*, on Juárez near the water. Rooms have small baths, fans, and warm water, but the mattresses are rather wimpy (singles and doubles 50 pesos; triples 60 pesos). **Motel Salvatierra** (tel. 5-00-21), close to the bus station on Salvatierra and Ocampo, has clean, air-conditioned rooms that are a bit small (singles 70 pesos, 80 pesos with cable TV; doubles 90 pesos, 100 pesos with cable TV). **El Moro RV Park,** Robles 8 (tel. 3-05-42), though not on the water, allows you to hook up a trailer (US$10), crash in your car (US$8), or just camp out (US$4). Showers are a two-dollar luxury. If no one is there, you can park on the honor system—leave your payment under the door (office open 7am-8pm).

Food Decent, cheap meals are served in establishments up and down Salvatierra, and a number of restaurants cluster conveniently near the bus terminal. **Café Olé,** Madero 14 (tel. 5-04-96), south of the *zócalo*, offers tasty meals and good-sized side portions. Order at the counter, then check the bulletin board for information about events in town. Fresh fish fillet with fries and refried beans costs 28 pesos, a jumbo burrito 18 pesos, and a rich sundae 12 pesos. Vegetarians will delight in their cheese-stuffed *chile relleno* (19 pesos; open Mon.-Sat. 7am-10pm, Sun. 7am-2pm). **Restaurante Bar La Fuente,** Salvatierra at Independencia, serves inexpensive Mexican platters as well as delicious seafood. Enjoy the *chimichangas* (20 pesos) or *chiles rellenos* (25 pesos). The combination cocktail, which includes shrimps, scallops, clams, and octopus, goes for 38 pesos (open daily 7am-11pm). The popular **Restaurant-Bar La Palapa,** on Hidalgo between Madero and López Mateos, fills the bellies of hungry diners with enormous Mexican combination platters (enchiladas or *quesadillas*, rice, and beans for 23 pesos; open Mon.-Sat. 1-10pm).

Sights With shaded benches along the water and the sidewalk, the *malecón* is a popular place for an evening stroll. The **Museo de las Misiones** (tel. 5-04-41), next to the reconstructed mission, one block west of the plaza, recounts the complete history of the European conquest of Baja California. Here you can also receive information on other missions scattered throughout the peninsula (open Mon.-Fri. 10am-5pm; admission 10 pesos).

If you're angling for a fresh seafood meal, rent a fishing boat and a guide (US$100 for 1 or 2 people, US$110 for 3 people; both 7hr.), or go at it alone with some fishing equipment (US$5 per day) from **Alfredo's** (tel. 5-01-32). **Arturo's Sports Fishing Fleet** (tel. 5-04-09), on Hidalgo half a block from the beach, offers five-hour snorkeling trips (US$75, minimum 3 people; equipment US$90 extra). Try approaching these companies or others for a trip to **Isla Coronado,** where wide, sandy beaches and herds of sea lions await. **Isla Carmen,** another popular destination, contains an eerie ghost town and abandoned salt mines. North of Loreto, the road passes the beautiful **Bahía de la Concepción**—with its incredible expanses of coves, blue-green water, and barren, cacti-dotted mountains jutting into the cloudless sky—on its way to Mulegé. South of Loreto, the road winds away from the coast into rugged mountains and the **Planicie Magdalena,** an intensively irrigated and cultivated plain. The striking white stripes on the first hillside beyond town are formed by millions of clams, conch, oyster, and scallop shells—refuse left by the region's Paleolithic inhabitants. Some caves on the hillside, inhabited as recently as 300 years ago, contain shells and polished stone.

■ Ciudad Constitución

You've never really seen the tumbleweed roll through town until you've visited Ciudad Constitución (pop. 32,000). The dustiest town in Baja California, Ciudad Constitución has the feel of an old frontier settlement—the landscape is dry and parched, and water is scarce. The only thing scarcer than water is tourism; most travelers use the town as a mere stopover en route to points farther south.

Orientation and Practical Information Ciudad Constitución is a two-hour ride from Loreto and a 45-minute ride from Puerto San Carlos. To reach the town center from the **bus station,** walk half a block, turn right, then walk another six blocks. The main street is **A. Olachea.** There is no tourist office, but information can be obtained by calling **Radio XEUVSD** (tel. 2-11-22). Staff speaks English (open Mon.-Sat. 9am-1pm and 3-7pm). **Hotel Conchita** (tel. 2-36-63) has the cheapest rates for long distance **phone calls** (open 24hr.). The **bus terminal** (tel. 2-03-76), on Pino Suárez and Juárez, runs **Autotransportes Águila** buses to La Paz (every hr., 2½hr., 38 pesos), Puerto San Carlos (10:30am and 5:30pm, 45min., 9 pesos), and Tijuana (12:30pm, 19hr., 262 pesos). The **Red Cross** (tel. 2-11-11) is on Degollado and Independencia. **Farmacia Beryben** (tel 2-02-62), on Hidalgo at Juárez, will provide you with drugs (open daily 9am-1pm and 3-9pm). The **hospital** (tel. 2-01-04) is on Ignacio Allende and Lerdo de Tejada (open 24hr.). The **Centro de Salud** (tel. 2-20-22) is on Niños Héroes and Lorenza Rieda de Tapia. The **police** (tel. 2-31-04) are on Olachea, in front of the Monumento Agustino Olachea. The **post office** (tel. 2-05-84) is on Ermenejildo Galeana, between A. Olachea and Lerdo de Tejada (open Mon.-Fri. 8am-3pm, Sat. 8am-1pm). **Postal Code:** 23600. **Telephone Code:** 113.

Accommodations and Food Budget accommodations abound. **Hotel Conchita** (tel. 2-36-63), Blvd. A. Olachea at Hidalgo, provides clean and nicely furnished rooms with private baths. TVs get bigger and better as the room price increases (singles 70 pesos, with A/C 90 pesos; doubles 110 pesos; triples 130 pesos). A great deal is **Casa de Huéspedes El Arbolito** (tel. 2-04-31), on Zaragoza and Zapata. Immaculate rooms more than make up for the tiny bathrooms (singles 40 pesos; doubles 50 pesos; triples 60 pesos; key deposit 5 pesos).

Most eateries are on or around A. Olachea. **Restaurant Bar Calafia,** Nicolás Bravo 161 (tel. 2-07-33), at Olachea, serves Mexican and Chinese platters in an intimate setting. Mexican platters cost 12-15 pesos, delicious fried rice with chicken and ham goes for 25 pesos (open daily 7am-10:30pm). **Ricos Tacos** (tel. 2-10-75), on the corner of Olachea and Hidalgo, serves six different types of tacos (4 pesos) and tasty *quesadillas* (4 pesos; open 24hr.).

Entertainment If you're thirsting for a cold *cerveza* and some quality nightlife, head to **Viva Baja,** Hidalgo at Cervantes del Río, six blocks from Olachea. Live bands rock the house Thursday through Saturday. Beers are 10 pesos, mixed drinks start at 15 pesos (no cover; open Tues.-Wed. 1pm-1am, Thurs.-Sat. 1pm-4am). Another hot spot is **Barra de los Comudeños,** on Cervantes del Río at Hidalgo. If you don't feel like dancing or boozing (beer 8 pesos, occasional 2-for-1 deals), grab a mike and take part in one of the karaoke contests (open Fri.-Sat. 9pm-3am).

■ Puerto San Carlos

The stunningly beautiful Puerto San Carlos (pop. 6000), 45 minutes west of Constitución, is one of the last untouched natural wonders of Baja California. Sheltered from Pacific winds by a fragmentary crescent of islands, San Carlos is perched on the edge of Bahía Magdalena on the west side of the Baja Peninsula. Each year, an estimated 18,000 gray whales migrate from the Bering Sea southward through the Pacific to Bahías Magdalena and Almejas. Whale mating season lasts from mid-January to mid-March (sometimes as late as April), and during this period the love-struck creatures wow crowds of locals with aquatic acrobatics. In a peculiar maneuver called "spy hopping," a huge hormonal whale will pop its head out of the water, fix an enormous eye on whatever strikes its fancy, and remain transfixed for minutes on end, staring hypnotically like a submarine periscope. Surprisingly, few travelers have discovered Puerto San Carlos, and locals observe *extranjeros* with the same bemused fascination with which tourists view whales.

Orientation and Practical Information To get to San Carlos, take a transfer bus from Ciudad Constitución (10:30am and 5:30pm, 45min., 9 pesos). Most services are on San Carlos's two main streets, **La Paz** and **Morelos,** which are perpendicular to each other.

The **tourist office** (tel. 6-02-53) is on La Paz, next to the IMSS Hospital. The extremely helpful English-speaking staff also leads whale-watching tours (open 24hr.). The pink **information booth** at the edge of town near the PEMEX station provides maps of the bay and islands. **Phone** friends back home at the unmarked **Papelería Chokes** (tel. 6-00-62), at Morelos and La Paz (open Mon.-Sat. 8am-1pm and 3-7pm). **Autotransportes Águila buses** leave from the small white terminal on La Paz and Morelos for Cabo San Lucas (1:45pm, 7hr., 80 pesos), Constitución (11am and 2pm, 45min., 10 pesos), and La Paz (7:30am and 1:45pm, 3½hr., 45 pesos). The **Red Cross** is on La Paz and Acapulco across from the church. **Farmacia Jazmin** (tel. 6-00-56) is on La Paz and México, facing the church (open Mon.-Sat. 9:30am-12:30pm and 4-6pm). The **IMSS Hospital** (tel. 6-02-11) is also on La Paz. The **Centro de Salud** is on La Paz in front of Hotel Alcatraz. The **police** are in the same building as the Red Cross. The **post office** is on La Paz near México (open Mon.-Fri. 8am-3pm). **Postal Code:** 23740. **Telephone Code:** 113.

Accommodations and Food Finding rooms in San Carlos is easy; head for the area around Morelos and La Paz. From the bus station, turn right on La Paz, then left on Madero to reach **Motel Las Brisas** (tel. 6-01-52/-59), on Madero between La Paz and Veracruz. Basic, clean rooms with large fans surround a stark courtyard. If you're here when the whales aren't, console yourself by studying the fading courtyard mural dedicated to these gentle giants (all rooms 80 pesos). **Hotel El Palmar** (tel. 6-00-35), Acapulco at Vallarta, lets you watch your modern color TV while lounging amid an endless variety of flowery bedspreads and curtains. Mattresses hardly cushion the hard bed-frames (singles 80 pesos; doubles 100 pesos). A **trailer park** at Playa la Curva outside of town offers full hookups for US$10.

Dining in San Carlos is homey—literally. A string of combination restaurant-living rooms along La Paz and Morelos allows you to meet locals, their kids, and pets while you enjoy delicacies from the sea. Chances are the fish on your plate was alive the last time you brushed you teeth. **El Patio Restaurant-Bar** (tel. 6-00-17; fax 6-00-86), in front of Hotel Alcatraz on La Paz, welcomes you into white plastic Corona chairs under open skies. Enjoy an oyster cocktail (40 pesos) or chicken with *mole* (20 pesos) while you watch the palm trees sway (open daily 7am-10pm).

Sights The islands and bays surrounding Puerto San Carlos teem with lifeforms. The tiny **Islote de Patos** (Duck Islet) in the middle of Bahía Magdalena is home to numerous species of birds, including pelicans and white-necks. The gangly creatures crowd every inch of the beach, standing idly like expectant guests at a failed cocktail party. The sheer number of birds (and their malodorous excrement) make landing here difficult; it's best just to cruise by. Feisty Pacific waves at **Cabo San Lázaro** and **Point Hughes,** both on the western tip of **Isla Magdalena,** will keep even veteran surfers on their toes. Reed huts scattered along the beach offer protection from the oppressive midday sun. Fifteen species of clams and starfish inhabit the waters of these immaculate beaches. Farther south, the island narrows to less than 50m in width, tapering off into perfectly white sand tufted with occasional bits of foliage, unusual flowers, and cacti. An enormous colony of sea lions (*lobos marinos)* lives near the island's southern tip. The tourist office (tel. 6-02-53) leads tours to the islands (US$30 per hour; maximum 6 people). A cheaper way to explore the island is to make an ad-hoc deal with one of the fishermen departing from Playa La Curva in front of the PEMEX station. Unless you plan to camp out on the islands, make definite pick-up plans before you disembark.

■ La Paz

The eclectic and beautiful capital of Baja Sur, La Paz (pop. 175,000) is at once a major port city and home to ten tranquil beaches along the Sea of Cortés. This is where real live Mexicans vacation, leaving the honky-tonk Cabos to Americans. La Paz's earlier days were spent as a quiet fishing village, frequently molested by pirates for the irides-cent white spheres concealed in the oysters off its coast; John Steinbeck's *The Pearl* depicted the town as a tiny, unworldly treasure chest glittering with semi-precious orbs. La Paz's hour of reckoning came in the 1940s, when the oysters sickened and died, wiping out the town's pearl industry. Within two decades, however, restless tourists and developers were scouring the country in search of prime real estate, and soon after the institution of the Baja ferries and the completion of the Transpeninsu-lar Highway in the 1960s, La Paz was rediscovered.

ORIENTATION

La Paz overlooks the **Bahía de la Paz** on Baja's east coast, 222km north of Cabo San Lucas and 1496km southeast of Tijuana, on the Transpeninsular Highway (Rte. 1). Activity centers around the area delineated by **Constitución, Ocampo, Serdán,** and the shore. The **municipal bus system** in La Paz serves the city sporadically (approxi-mately every 30min. 6am-10pm, 1.50 pesos). Flag buses down anywhere, or wait by the stop at Degollado, next to the market. From the station, try to convince your driver to drop you off in the *centro*.

CROSSING THE GULF

Ferries are the best way to get from La Paz to the mainland. Tickets can be bought at the **Sematur Company** office (tel. 5-46-66), 5 de Mayo and Prieto (open Mon.-Fri. 8am-1pm and 4-6pm, Sat.-Sun. 8am-1pm). Ferries go to Mazatlán (Sun.-Fri. at 3pm, 17hr., *salón* 142 pesos, *turista* 284 pesos, cars up to 5m long 1074 pesos, motorcycles 169 pesos) and Topolobampo (daily at 11am except for "cargo only" days—call for precise info, 8hr., *salón* 95 pesos, cars up to 5m long 656 pesos, motorcycles 82 pesos). You cannot buy tickets from the office at the dock (open daily 8am-8pm).

In order to secure a ticket, be sure to get to the Sematur main office early, ideally right after it opens. Acquiring a *salón* ticket should be no problem on the day of departure, but for other classes, call one day ahead to make reservations. During hol-idays, competition for ferry tickets is fierce. A travel agency might be the most trou-ble-free way to make reservations—it costs the same and allows you to pick up the tickets at the agency instead of having to wait in the long lines at the ferry office. Agencies include **Operadora de Mar de Cortés** (tel. 5-22-77; fax 5-85-99), in the CCC complex on Bravo and Ortega, a 15-minute walk from the center, and **Cabo San Lucas** (tel. 3-37-17; fax 3-37-07), at Hidalgo and Madero. Tickets can be picked up from 4 to 6pm the day before departure.

In order to get a vehicle on the ferry you will need (at the very least) proof of Mex-ican insurance (or a major credit card with the car owner's name on it), car registra-tion, permission for the importation of a car into Mexico, and a tourist card. Oh, and three photocopies of each. You can get a permit at **Banjercito** (tel. 2-11-16), at the ferry stop in Pichilingue, or through **AAA** in the U.S. (for more info on bringing your car into Mexico, see p. 10). Regardless of whether you have a car or not, you will need to obtain a **tourist card (FMT)** if you entered Mexico via Baja and are mainland-bound; get one from **Servicios Migratorios** (see p. 157). Clear all of the paperwork before purchasing the ticket; otherwise, Sematur will deny you a spot whether or not you hold reservations. For more information on ferries, see p. 126.

While the ferry dock in Pichilingue is a hike (17km) from the center of town, you needn't fret. **Autotransportes Águila** buses run between the dock and the down-

N

TO BEACHES

0 ———— 500 yards
0 ———— 500 meters

Bahía
de La Paz

La Paz
Cathedral, 7
Immigration Office, 10
Hotel La Purísima, 5
Hotel Posada San Miguel, 4
Hotel Yeneka, 3
Museo Antropológico, 9
Museo de las Californias, 11
Pensión California, 1
Plaza Constitución, 6
Post Office, 8
Sematur Ferries Office, 2

Álvaro Obregón
Elisario Domínguez
Francisco Madero
Revolución de 1910
Guillermo Prieto
Aquiles Serdán
Ignacio Ramírez
Ignacio Altamirano
Valentín Gómez Farías
Héroes de la Independencia
Lic. Verdad
J. O. de Domínguez
Conde de Revillagigedo
Félix Ortega
Isabel La Católica
Melitón Albáñez
México

Morelos
Hidalgo
Constitución

5 de Mayo

Independencia
Reforma

16 de Septiembre
Degollado
Ocampo
Bravo

Rosales
Allende
Juárez
Pineda
Márquez de León
Legaspy
Encinas
Navarro
5 de Febrero
Cuauhtémoc
Sonora
Sínaloa
Nayarit
Oaxaca
Jalisco

Abasolo
Topete

INSET AREA

Salvatierra
Bahía de La Paz
Victoria
Morelos
Revolución de 1910
A. Serdán
G. Prieto
I. Ramírez
I. Altamirano
V. Gómez Farías
B. Domínguez
F. Madero
Hidalgo
Constitución
5 de Mayo
Independencia
Reforma
16 de Septiembre
Degollado
Ocampo
Águila en Malecón Station
La Paz
Bañuelos
Artesanos Arreola
Enlaces Terrestres Station

BAJA CALIFORNIA

town terminal on Obregón, between Independencia and 5 de Mayo (9am and 11-4pm, approximately on the hr., 7 pesos). When you get off the ferry, hurry to catch the 9am bus to the *centro;* otherwise you'll have to wait for two hours. A taxi from dock to downtown, or vice versa, will set you back a good 40 pesos.

PRACTICAL INFORMATION

Tourist Office: (tel. 2-59-39), Obregón at 16 de Septiembre, in a pavilion on the water. Excellent city maps and information about Baja Sur, especially Los Cabos. English-speaking staff. Open Mon.-Fri. 8am-8pm.

Immigration Office: Servicios Migratorios, Obregón 2140 (tel. 5-34-93; fax 2-04-29). You must stop here to obtain a tourist card if you entered Mexico via Baja and are mainland-bound. Open Mon.-Fri. 8am-3pm. After hours, head to their outpost in the airport outside of town (tel. 2-18-29). Open daily 8am-10pm.

Currency Exchange: Bancomer (tel. 5-42-48), on 16 de Septiembre, ½ block from the waterfront. Other banks scattered in the downtown area. All open for exchange Mon.-Fri. 8:30am-2pm. The exception is **BITAL** (Banco Internacional; tel. 2-22-89), 5 de Mayo at Revolución, where you will be greeted by talking doors and a 24-hr. **ATM.** Open for exchange Mon.-Fri. 8am-6:30pm, Sat. 9am-2pm.

American Express: Esquerro 1670 (tel. 2-83-00, toll-free 91-800-00-1552; fax 5-52-72), at La Paz. Open Mon.-Fri. 9am-2pm and 4-6pm, Sat. 9am-2pm.

Telephones: Sexy **LADATELs,** as well as older payphones, pepper the downtown area and *zócalo.* **Librería Contempo,** Arreola 25A (tel. 2-78-75), at Obregón, has a *caseta.* Open Mon.-Fri. 10am-9pm, Sun. 10am-5pm.

Telegrams: (tel. 2-67-07; fax 5-08-09), upstairs from the post office. Open Mon.-Fri. 8am-6pm, Sat. 8-11am.

Airport: West of La Paz, accessible only by 35-peso taxis. Served by **Aeroméxico** (tel. 4-62-88), at Álvaro Obregón and Hidalgo, and **Aerocalifornia** (tel. 4-62-88).

Buses: There are three stations. The **main station** is on Jalisco and Independencia, about 25 blocks southeast of downtown. Two municipal buses, "Central Camionera" and "Urbano," service the terminal; catch them near the public market at Degollado and Revolución. Taxis cost 10 pesos. **Águila** and **ABC** (tel. 2-42-70) provide service to points north, including Ensenada (10am, 4, 8, and 10pm, 19½hr., 299 pesos), Loreto (8 per day 9am-10pm, 5hr., 69 pesos), Mexicali (4pm, 24½hr., 377 pesos), Mulegé (8 per day 9am-10pm, 7hr., 91 pesos), Santa Rosalía (8 per day 9am-10pm, 8hr., 107 pesos), San Ignacio (5 per day 10am-10pm, 9hr., 141 pesos), and Tijuana (10am, 4, 8, and 10pm, 21hr., 327 pesos). The new **Enlaces Terrestres station** (tel. 3-31-80), Degollado and Serdán, is more convenient for heading south. Buses run to Cabo San Lucas (7 per day 6:30am-7pm, 3hr., 35 pesos), San José del Cabo (7 per day 6:30am-7pm, 3½hr., 42 pesos), and Todos Santos (9 per day 7am-8pm, 2hr., 17 pesos). Finally, the **Águila Malecón station** (tel. 2-78-98), Independencia at Obregón, is the best way of getting to nearby beaches. Buses run to Playas Palmira, El Coramuel, El Carmancito, Tesoro, and Pichilingue (every hr. 8am-6pm except 10am, up to 30min., 3-6 pesos) and to Playas Balandras and Tecolote (weekends only, every hr. 8am-6pm, 45min., 8 pesos). The last bus back to La Paz leaves Tecolote at 6:45pm and Pichilingue at 6:30pm on weekdays, 7pm on weekends.

Laundromat: Lavandería Yoli (tel. 2-10-01), 5 de Mayo at Rubio, across the street from the stadium. Wash and dry 19 pesos. Open Mon.-Sat. 7am-9pm, Sun. 8am-3pm.

Red Cross: Reforma 1091 (tel. 2-11-11), between Isabel la Católica and Félix Ortega. Open 24hr.

Pharmacy: Farmacia Bravo (tel. 2-69-33), next to the hospital, is open 24hr.

Hospital: Salvatierra (tel. 2-14-96 or -97), Bravo at Verdad, between Domínguez and the Oncological Institute.

Police: (tel. 2-07-81), Colima at México. Open 24hr.

Post Office: (tel. 2-03-88 or 5-23-58), Revolución at Constitución. Open Mon.-Fri. 8am-6pm, Sat. 9am-1pm. **Postal Code:** 23001.

Telephone Code: 112.

ACCOMMODATIONS

The city is full of inexpensive establishments bound to satisfy even the most finicky travelers. The cluttered artistic look, however, seems to be making a resurgence in the budget hotels of La Paz. A student of Mexican folk art could skip the Museo Antropológico and tour the lobbies of these hotels instead.

CREA Youth Hostel (tel. 2-46-15), in Forjatero youth center, near the Technical University and at the 3km mark on the Transpeninsular Highway. The hostel offers small, clean rooms with bunk beds, bathrooms, and A/C, as well as a huge swimming pool, volleyball court, and a small eatery (open daily 7am-11pm). The only drawback is that it is terribly far from the center of town, approximately a 12-peso taxi ride (all rooms 30 pesos per person, 10% discount with HI card).

Pensión California Casa de Huéspedes (tel. 2-28-96), Degollado at Madero. Bungalow rooms have concrete floors and beds on concrete slabs, but you have to admire the plastic turtle sculpture, sea shells, and dysfunctional washing machine. Prices include private baths and use of the communal kitchen and TV. If you're lucky, you might get a room that has a huge tree trunk running through the bathroom shower. Bring your own blanket. Padlocks on the doors provide security. Singles 45 pesos. Doubles 60 pesos. **Hostería del Convento** (tel. 2-35-08), across the street, belongs to the same owner and offers an identical setup.

Hotel Yeneka, Madero 1520 (tel. 5-46-88), between 16 de Septiembre and Indepen
dencia. Potentially the most unique hotel in all of Baja. It doubles as a museum of
eccentric items: a 1916 model-T Ford, a pet hawk, and a live monkey who lives in
the trees. Each Tarzan-hut room has been remodeled in matching twig furniture
and painted fully with rainbow colors. All rooms come with fans, and the lucky few
with small balconies. Singles 95 pesos. Doubles 135 pesos.

Hotel Posada San Miguel, B. Domínguez 151 (tel. 2-18-02), just off 16 de Septiembre. Fountained courtyards, tiled arches, and wrought-iron scroll-work on windows and railings. Cubical rooms with sinks and large, comfortable beds. Singles
55 pesos. Doubles 75 pesos. Triples 95 pesos.

Hotel La Purísima, 16 de Septiembre 408 (tel. 2-34-44), between Revolución and
Serdan. Small, white rooms with A/C. Singles 100 pesos. Doubles 130 pesos.

FOOD

On the waterfront you'll find decor, menus, and prices geared toward peso-spewing
tourists. Move inland a few blocks and watch the prices plunge downwards. Seafood
meals are generally fresh. The **public market,** at Degollado and Revolución, offers a
cheap selection of fruits, veggies, and fresh fish.

Restaurante El Quinto Sol (tel. 2-16-92), B. Domínguez at Independencia. One of
the few vegetarian joints in Baja. Menu includes sausage *à la* soybean, as well as an
assortment of juices. Yogurt smoothie with fruit 15 pesos, vegetarian steak 21
pesos, tasty pastries 2 pesos. Open Mon.-Sat. 7:30am-9:30pm.

Restaurant Palapa Adriana (tel. 2-83-29), on the beach off Obregón at Constitución, offers patrons a stunningly beautiful view of the water 5 short meters away.
Seafood soup 25 pesos, *huachinango* (red snapper) 35 pesos, *pollo con mole* 25
pesos, *pulpo al ajo* 30 pesos. Sea breeze gratis. Open daily 10am-10pm.

Yeneka Restaurant Bar, Madero 1520 (tel. 5-46-88), adjacent to the eponymous
hotel. Features paintings by the owner, his mother, and his eight-year-old son. Like
the art, the food is home-style. Continental breakfast 10 pesos, Mexican plates 18
pesos, delicious fish fillet 28 pesos. Open daily 7am-11pm.

SAND AND SIGHTS

Instead of stretching curving expanses of wave-washed sand, the beaches of La Paz
snuggle into small coves sandwiched between cactus-studded hills and calm, transparent water. To be sure, this is prime windsurfing territory. But be careful—La Paz
lifeguards make appearances only on weekends and on popular beaches.

The best beach near La Paz is **Playa Tecolote** (Owl Beach), 25km northeast of
town. A quiet extension of the Sea of Cortés laps against this gorgeous stretch of
gleaming white sand, backed up by tall, craggy mountains. Even though there are no
bathrooms, Tecolote is terrific for **camping.** On Tecolote, jet skis, banana boats, and
boats to the nearby **Isla Espíritu Santo** are available. You may not be able to reach
Playa Tecolote without a car on weekdays; **Autotransportes Águila** buses get you
there from the mini-station on Obregón and Independencia (daily during spring
break and July-Aug., weekends only during low season, 8 pesos). Plenty of other
beaches are easily accessible by taking the "Pichilingue" bus up the coast (5 pesos).
Be forewarned that neither of these buses runs back to La Paz after 6:30 or 7pm. The
"Pichilingue" bus goes as far as the ferry dock, at which point you need to walk 2km
farther on the paved road to **Playa de Pichilingue.** This beach is a favorite among the
teen set, who splash in the shallow waters and ride in the paddle boats (10 pesos per
hr.). Along the same bus route lies **Playa El Coromuel,** near La Concha Hotel, where
visitors and locals congregate on weekends. All three beaches are a hefty hike or a
short ride away. Bear in mind that the farther you venture from La Paz, the better and
more secluded the beaches get.

The aquatic fun in La Paz doesn't stop at the shoreline. **Baja Diving and Service,**
Obregón 1665 (tel. 2-18-26; fax 2-86-44), just north of B. Domínguez, organizes daily

scuba and snorkeling trips to nearby reefs, wrecks, and islands, where you can mingle with hammer heads, manta rays, giant turtles, and other exotica (scuba trips US$77 per day without equipment, US$15 extra for equipment, snorkeling US$40 per day; trips include lunch and drinks). Equipment is also rented (snorkeling US$8, scuba about US$45). Trips leave at 7:45am and return between 3 and 5pm. **Viajes Palmira** (tel. 2-40-70), on Obregón between Rosales and Allende, in front of Hotel Los Arcos, may offers cheaper rates (snorkeling equipment US$10, scuba US$40). Trips depart at 8am and return at 4pm, and include equipment, lunch, and drinks (snorkeling US$40, scuba US$85).

■ Todos Santos

Todos Santos is paradise for the frugal surfer/painter set. Eighty kilometers north of Cabo San Lucas and 80km southwest of La Paz, Todos Santos is one of the few towns on the southern Baja coast which oozes culture, is easily accessible by bus, offers budget accommodations, and is largely unmutilated by resort development.

Founded in 1723 by Jesuit missionaries, Todos Santos was a major producer of sugar cane until 1950, when a crippling drought struck the region. The large brick chimneys scattered throughout town are all that remain of its sugar past. Todos Santos's newest incarnation is as a haven for artsy *gringos* drawn by the town's serenity and cultural sophistication—John Steinbeck used to hang his hat here, and the fine arts center was the first of its kind on the Baja Peninsula. More recently, such Hollywood luminaries as Jack Nicholson and Drew Barrymore have spent time in Todos Santos. Home to a considerable U.S. expat community, the town's somewhat Americanized charm is apparent in the myriad gourmet shops, a culturally and ecologically concerned populace, and a small community of intellectuals.

Orientation Todos Santos's two main streets, running parallel and east-west, are **Colegio Militar** and **Benito Juárez**. Juárez is just north of Militar; north of and parallel to Juárez run **Centenario** and **Legaspi**. South of Militar and parallel runs **Rangel**. From east to west, **Ocampo, Obregón, Topete, Hidalgo, Márquez de León, Morelos, Zaragoza,** and (three blocks farther west, at the end of town) **Degollado** run north-south. Activity centers around the area between **Legaspi, Militar, Morelos, and Topete;** León crosses Militar and Juárez at the church and main plaza. You may be dropped off near Degollado and Juárez, as this is where the **Transpeninsular Highway** (from La Paz) turns to head toward Los Cabos.

Practical Information Todos Santos has no tourist office, but the American-owned **El Tecolote Libros**, on Juárez and Hidalgo, sells English-language newspapers and maps (which include hand-drawn directions to nature spots outside town). Buy a book while you're there (14 pesos), or swap the one you're carrying (as long as it's not *Let's Go: Mexico '97;* open Mon.-Sat. 9am-5pm). To exchange currency, head for the *casa de cambio,* half a block from El Tecolote (open daily 9am-6pm). Make long-distance calls from the **public phone** in front of the Delegación Municipal, or at the *caseta* on the corner of Juárez and Hidalgo, adjacent to El Tecolote Libros (open Mon.-Sat. 8am-5pm). **Telegrams** (tel./fax 5-03-60) at the Delegación Municipal on Centenario and Hidalgo (open Mon.-Fri. 8am-2pm).

Buses stop at **Pilar's taco stand** (tel. 5-01-70), on the corner of Zaragoza and Colegio Militar. *De paso* buses run to Cabo San Lucas (8 per day, 1½hr., 17 pesos), San José del Cabo (8 per day, 2hr., 22 pesos), and La Paz (8 per day, 1hr., 17 pesos). Meet your recommended daily nutritional allowances at **Mercado Guluarte** (tel. 5-00-06), on Morelos between Colegio Militar and Juárez (open Mon.-Sat. 7:30am-9pm, Sun. 7:30am-2pm). The friendly, American-run **Perico Azul,** Centenario and Topete, is both a farmer's market and a boutique (open daily 9am-6pm). Other markets are on Degollado and Juárez. The **laundromat** (tel. 5-03-41) on Pedrajo, three blocks west of Degollado, lets you take care of your dirty laundry for 18 pesos, including soap. Full service is 25 pesos (open Mon.-Sat. 8am-3pm). **Farmacia Todos Santos** (tel. 5-00-30), on Juárez between Morelos and Zaragoza, is run out of a disheveled house but provides 24-hour service. In case of an **emergency,** call the hospital (tel. 5-00-95), on Juárez and Degollado (open 24hr.). The **police** are in the Delegación Municipal complex on Legaspi between León and Hidalgo. The **post office** (tel. 5-03-30) is on Colegio Militar and León (open Mon.-Fri. 8am-1pm and 3-5pm). **Postal Code:** 23300. **Telephone Code:** 114.

Accommodations The town has four main hotels; two are in the center of town and the other two are a 15-minute jaunt away. Falling asleep in Todos Santos should not pose a problem—the town is oppressively silent—but swarms of tiny mosquitoes can be annoying. The **Hotel Miramar** (tel. 5-03-41), on Pedrajo at Mutualismo, offers an excellent value in an otherwise overpriced town. From the center, head to the west end of town and turn south onto Degollado. Walk five minutes down Degollado, past PEMEX and a supermarket, until you see a sign for "Hotel Miramar." Take the following right, and it's four blocks down on your left. Clean, centrally cooled rooms, large tiled bathrooms, a pleasant courtyard and pool, and *agua purificada* will reward you at the end of your hike (singles 50 pesos; doubles 75 pesos; triples 100 pesos). **Departamentos Gabi** (tel. 5-00-06), at Juárez and Morelos, is run out of a grocery store in the Mercado Guluarte (see above). The pool is well suited to those who enjoy bathing in full view of the street, but the adjacent outdoor *palapa* is shady and has an ice-cold *agua purificada* dispenser. Clean rooms have color TVs (singles 80 pesos; doubles 100 pesos; triples 120 pesos).

Two RV parks are hidden along the coast, south of town. To reach the closer one, **San Pedrito Trailer Park,** turn right off the Transpeninsular Highway, 6km south of town—you've missed the turnoff if you pass a beer store. Pass through an arch that straddles the road, drive 3km, bear left at a fork in the road, and you're there. For reservations, call *señor* Efre Mungía (tel. 5-00-25). To get to **Los Ceritos Trailer Park,** turn right 10km south of town at a blue-and-white sign that reads "RV Park." Past a fence and the old highway to Los Cabos, 2.6km down the dirt road, you'll hit the park. A bar, pool, restaurant, TV, and awesome surfing beaches await.

Food Budget eats aren't hard to find in Todos Santos. Several *loncherías* line **Colegio Militar** near the bus station, offering triple tacos and the like for nine pesos. Locals love **Carnitas y Chicharrones,** on Degollado near Colegio Militar, where they enjoy excellent meat tacos made with some of the best beef in the country (5 pesos). **Shut Up Frank's** (tel. 5-01-46), on Degollado near Juárez, has what might be the best burgers in Baja, and they're only 20-25 pesos with fries. Wash yours down with an irresistible Snapple (10 pesos; open daily 10am-10pm). Restaurant-bar **Las Fuentes,** at

---

A League of Their Own

If you're feeling energetic at night, you might want to take in a **baseball game** at the local stadium, off Degollado to the south. Follow the light towers—any local will show you the way. Admission is only 5 pesos, though a cold Tecate's another 5 pesos. Root, root, root for the home team—Los Tiburones (the Sharks)—while analyzing the odder aspects of Mexican League professional baseball: you'll see an all-sand playing field, umpires in bright blue pants, base runners without batting helmets, players trading gloves between batters, lots of submarine-ball pitchers, some players on the same team in different uniforms, and huge crowds dancing between innings to popular dance music. Oh, and if, by chance, you catch a ball, don't even think about keeping it as a souvenir—you will first be swarmed by tiny kids paid by commission for every ball (and crushed beer can) they recover, and eventually you'll even be bothered by the police! Games are at 7pm some weeknights and 1 or 2pm on weekends (pretty soon there will also be a basketball league in Picaderos, 9km south of town).

Colegio Militar and Degollado (tel. 5-02-57), one block left of the bus station, has pleasant fountains and good food: English-Spanish menu offers fried *huachinango* (red snapper) with rice and salad for 35 pesos and breakfast for about 22 pesos (open daily 7am-9pm).

Sights The **Casa de la Cultura** is a long brick building on Topete and Legaspi. Head two blocks down Legaspi away from the cathedral, then bear left on Topete; the Casa is on the left, halfway down the hill. The Casa is filled with a melange of photos, sculptures, and religious figures from the colonial period. Don't miss the three amazing murals depicting slavery, industrialization, and "mind and muscle," done in 1933 by third- and fourth-grade students (open daily 8am-8pm; free). Todos Santos's new pride and joy (among art fans, at least) is the **Todos Santos Gallery** (tel. 5-00-40), on Legaspi and Topete, opened in 1995 by the prominent artist Michael Cope. The gallery has plenty of contemporary Mexican paintings by Cope and others (open Mon. and Wed.-Sat. 9am-5pm). Cutting-edge bronze and clay sculptures, off-the-wall wallclocks, and ornate mirrors are on parade at the **Santa Fe Art Gallery,** Centario 4 between Hidalgo and Márquez de León (open Wed.-Mon. 9:30am-5pm). **Casa Franco Gallery,** Juárez at Morelos (tel./fax 5-03-56), directly behind the Santa Fe gallery, has furniture, bowls, and pipes from Guadalajara, Todos Santos, and Puebla (open Mon.-Sat. 9am-5pm). The white-washed, colonial-style **Teatro Manuel Márquez de León,** facing the *zócalo* on Legaspi, between Hidalgo and Márquez de León, hosts many cinematic and thespian endeavors.

If you overdose on art, don't forget that Todos Santos is surrounded by some of the world's most unspoiled (and unexplored) beaches. **La Posa,** only 2km from town, is perfect for that romantic stroll or uplifting solitary walk. Unfortunately, vicious undercurrents and powerful waves make this beach unequivocally unsuitable for swimming. To get there, go up Juárez and turn left on Topete. Follow the road as it winds across the valley and comes to a white building that says "Do not pass." If you pass that, you're on the beach. Most other beaches are accessible via the Transpeninsular Highway south of town. These sights are isolated, and therefore both attractive and hazardous. Bring a friend, and plan to return before nightfall. To reach **Punta Lobos,** the stomping ground of the local sea lion population and a beach popular with locals, turn left onto Degollado as you walk away from the town center. Roughly six blocks later, the city limits end. To catch a spectacular aerial view of the sea, turn right 1.5km south on the highway at the first possible fork in the road. Follow the main dirt path east for 2.5km; the path will bear left past an old fish plant and up a hill, which falls precipitously to the seashore.

A beautiful lake atop a mountain, **Sierra de la Laguna,** is accessible only by car (it's a 90-minute drive). One kilometer down the highway past the Punta Lobos turnoff, turn left at the fenced-off cattle ranch. A 45-minute drive brings you to Rancho La Burera, which serves as the trailhead for the *laguna.* Be social and make friends in town. Invite them to show you the way. To reach the appropriately named **Playa de las Palmas,** travel another 4.6km from the Laguna down the highway, and turn right when you see the white buildings on the left. Travel another 2.6km and you'll be bowled over by palm trees; just past these is the beach. The serene and deserted beach here is excellent for swimming.

■ Los Cabos

The towns of **Cabo San Lucas** and **San José del Cabo** comprise the southwestern part of the Los Cabos district (pop. 60,000), which includes much of the coastline of Baja California's southern end. Readily accessible via air and water, Los Cabos (The Capes) is much more developed than the majority of the peninsula. Visitors are drawn to the cape by the stretch of beach leading from San José del Cabo to Cabo San Lucas, where luxury hotels form a glittering strip between the desert and the ocean, and sunbathing, sightseeing, gift-buying, sport-fishing, jet-skiing *norteamericanos* congregate by the thousands.

■ Cabo San Lucas

Perched on the southern tip of Baja, Cabo San Lucas is an eminent representative of the heavily Americanized resort industry of Mexico. Though small (pop. 4000), the town has surpassed such classic resorts as Acapulco in popularity among honeymooners due to its peaceful waters and ultra-modern pleasure domes. A favorite vacation destination among families looking for an easy, pampered escape from stress, Cabo San Lucas is particularly accommodating to those who desire neither a peek into real Mexican culture nor a word of Spanish, and don't want to deal with that hassle of changing their dollars into pesos—or of even learning what a peso is. Prices at most restaurants are high, even by U.S. standards. And smooth-talking timeshare pushers roam Cabo's streets, looking for the day's prey—an American with a credit card who, with a free dinner and some convincing words, might just feel impulsive enough to buy a US$15,000 piece of the pie in a glitzy ocean-view suite.

Despite its influx of dollar-rich, culture-poor tourists, Cabo San Lucas—the first of the two *cabos* on the *vía corta* bus route from La Paz—does have some appeal to the budget traveler, mostly due to its beaches and rock formations: **El Arco** is the famous arch rock that marks the very tip of the Californias. Until recently a peaceful fishing village, Cabo San Lucas's economic boom is fast becoming a sad lesson in the effects of unbridled growth. Dolphins and whales, once a common sight close to the coast, have all but disappeared from the area. City officials have now begun to enforce stricter pollution laws, but their efforts may be too little too late.

Cabo San Lucas has yet to develop extensive facilities for budget travelers. If you don't plan to spend lots of money, stay in town only for the day, camp on the beach, or simply treat the town as a big supermarket—buy your sunscreen and make tracks for cheaper San José del Cabo.

Orientation **Lázaro Cárdenas** is the main street in Cabo San Lucas. It runs roughly southeast-northwest, diagonally through the town's grid of streets. **Paseo de la Marina** forks off Cárdenas where the resort zone begins, continues south, and winds around the marina. From west to east, north-south streets (all branching off Cárdenas) include **Ocampo, Zaragoza, Morelos, Vicario,** and **Mendoza.** Farther west, **Cabo San Lucas, Hidalgo, Matamoros,** and **Abasolo** cross Cárdenas and continue south into the resort zone, eventually meeting Marina. From north to south, the following streets are perpendicular to those above: **Obregón, Revolución, 20 de Noviembre, Libertad, 16 de Septiembre, Niños Héroes, Constitución,** and **5 de Mayo.** South of Cárdenas, **Madero, Zapata,** and **J. Domínguez** run east-west in the resort area. Continuing south on Marina, one will pass the posh resorts, and eventually arrive at the beach, **Playa de Médano.** Restaurants and bars—and a high density of English-speaking Mexicans—are concentrated on Cárdenas between Morelos and the mountains on the western edge of town.

To get to the center of the action from the bus station, walk on Zaragoza for two blocks toward the water to Cárdenas. The grid-like pattern of the city makes it difficult to get lost. You might be dropped off at a remote bus station; from there, cross the street and walk across the sandy little park in front of the yellow complex; continue to the next street, and stand across the street from the bus stop to catch a local yellow bus to the center (every 15min., 30min., 3 pesos).

Practical Information Maps are dispensed by time-share hawkers all over the center of town. The "Marina Fiesta" salespeople have the best of the lot. To exchange money, try **Banca Serfín** (tel. 3-09-90 or -91), at Cárdenas and Zaragoza (open Mon.-Fri. 8:30am-1:30pm). It also has a friendly **ATM** that's fluent in English. Otherwise try

Bancomer (tel. 3-19-50), across the street (open 8:30am-1pm), as will the *casa de cambio* on Cárdenas at Zaragoza (tel. 3-19-50). Most hotels and restaurants will gladly exchange dollars at lower rates. There are **LADATELs** all over town, including on Cárdenas and Ocampo, and a long-distance *caseta* (tel. 3-00-25; fax 3-00-19) at Cárdenas and Hidalgo (open daily 8am-10pm).

ABC Autotransportes and **Águila buses** (tel. 3-04-00) are located at Zaragoza and 16 de Septiembre. The two most common destinations are San José del Cabo (every 30min. 7am-10pm, 30min., 8 pesos) and La Paz (6 per day, 3hr., 35 pesos) via Todos Santos (1½hr., 17 pesos). One bus per day leaving at 4:30pm heads north, stopping at La Paz (3hr., 35 pesos), Cd. Constitución (6hr., 42 pesos), Loreto (8½hr., 69 pesos), Mulegé (10½hr., 91 pesos), Santa Rosalía (11½hr., 107 pesos), San Ignacio (12½hr., 141 pesos), Vizcaíno (13½hr., 153 pesos), Guerrero Negro (14½hr., 260 pesos), El Rosario (18hr., 369 pesos), San Quintín (19hr., 255 pesos), Ensenada (23hr., 337 pesos), and Tijuana (26½hr., 369 pesos). **Avis Rent-a-Car** (tel. 3-46-07) is at Plaza Los Mariachis, across from the Giggling Marlin. A VW Sedan, including insurance and unlimited mileage, costs US$38 per day (open daily 8:30am-6pm).

The **English-language bookstore** (tel. 3-31-71), at Marina and Cárdenas in the Plaza Bonita Mall, has U.S. magazines, popular novels, and *USA Today* (open daily 9am-9pm). Get your groceries from **Supermercado Plaza** (tel. 3-14-50), at Zaragoza and Cárdenas (open daily 7am-11pm). **Farmacia Aramburo** (tel. 3-14-89) is next door to the supermarket, at Plaza Aramburo (open 7:30am-11pm). The **Red Cross** (tel. 3-33-00) is on Delegación, on the outskirts of town towards San José del Cabo, 200m from the gas station. The **hospital** (tel. 3-01-02) is on Zaragoza. In an **emergency,** dial the **police** (tel. 3-49-77). **Telephone Code: 114.**

Accommodations and Food Multi-million-dollar resorts with every service imaginable dominate San Lucas's coast line; *ergo,* simple, cheap beds are seriously lacking. During the winter high season make reservations early and be prepared to shell out more *dinero* than you would during the slower summer months. The only legitimate budget accommodation remaining may be the **Hotel Casa Blanca,** on Revolución and Vicario (tel. 3-02-60). Slightly less luxurious than its namesake, the hotel provides clean, simple, cement rooms with fans and functional private bathrooms (singles 100 pesos; doubles 120 pesos). To get to the **CREA Youth Hostel (HI;** tel. 3-01-48) from Cárdenas, walk ten minutes down Morelos to Av. de la Juventud, and then turn right and hike five minutes to the Instituto Sur Californiano building. The street is not well lit; lone travelers would be wise to check in before twilight or stay in town. They have the cheapest beds in town, but not much company—you may well have the entire place to yourself. Bring your own pillow (dorm bunk with communal bath 30 pesos; singles with private bath 40 pesos; bunk doubles with bath 60 pesos; camping 20 pesos).

Restaurant-bars along the water gang up on tourists; the cheap spots line Morelos, a safe distance from the million-dollar yachts. King of *taquerías,* the **Asadero 3 Hermanos,** Morelos at 20 de Noviembre, serves up scrumptious, cheap, and safe tacos and *quesadillas* (5-6 pesos; open daily 9am-4am). Growling stomachs gravitate toward the enormous rotating chickens at **El Pollo de Oro** (tel. 3-03-10), Cárdenas at Morelos. Half a chicken goes for 22 pesos, quarter-bird 13 pesos (open daily 6am-11pm). The brand-new **Boca del Río,** Cárdenas at Morelos, will quell your voracious appetite. The exquisite fish filets (35 pesos) come with salad, tortillas, and rice. All cocktails cost 20 pesos (open daily noon-11pm).

Sights and Entertainment All major activity in Cabo San Lucas revolves around the pristine waters that surround the coast. **Playa del Médano,** one of the better beaches in the area, stretches east along the bay around the corner from the marina. Escape the blazing sun in one of the beach's many restaurants or *palapas.* The waters of the Playa de Médano are alive with parasailers and motorboats full of lobster-red, beer-guzzling vacationers. **Cabo Aguadeportes** (tel. 3-20-60), in front of the Hotel Hacienda, rents out water equipment (open 9am-5pm), as does **JT Watersports** (tel. 6-68-96), adjacent to Hotel Plaza Las Glorias (snorkeling gear US$10 per day, wave runners US$35 per 30min.; open 9am-6pm).

The famous **Arch Rock** (El Arco) of Cabo San Lucas rises only a short boat ride from the marina. To get there, walk through the Plaza Las Glorias hotel or the big Mexican crafts market farther down Paseo Marina to the docks. Eager, English-speaking boat captains will be happy to take you on a 45-minute glass-bottom boat ride to El Arco and back (US$6). On the way, you may be treated to an inordinate number of tasteless or corny jokes. Other than the picturesque Arch and the sea lions that visit it, the only thing you'll see are the summer dwellings of Sly Stallone, Michael Jackson, Madonna, Van Halen, and others—those with weak stomachs can turn the other way. The boat also stops at **La Playa del Amor** (yes, that's the Beach of Looove) right near El Arco and allows you to get out and head back later on a different boat for no additional charge. This beach, perennially mobbed, is the only one with access to both the rough, deep blue Pacific and the light, tranquil Sea of Cortés. Swimming is good on the gulf side, but beware of the Pacific's currents; two unlucky swimmers died recently after being dragged out to sea on this side. Another beautiful and secluded beach where you shouldn't swim is **Playa del Divorcio** (Divorce Beach). To get there, hop on a yellow bus (1.50 pesos) or walk out on Marina and turn right across from the Mexican crafts market. Slip out to the beach between massive condo complexes right after you pass the Terra Sol Hotel.

Snorkeling is popular on La Playa del Amor and around the rocks between the marina and the beach, where tropical fish abound. Bring your own gear or dish out those dollars for rented equipment from one of the many vendors that populate the marina area (see above). The best snorkeling beach is said to be **Playa Santa María,** between Cabo San Lucas and San José del Cabo.

The eight-peso bus ride to San José del Cabo provides access to more beaches along the way. Choose your spot carefully in order to avoid the crowds. **El Chileno,** halfway between the two towns, offers phenomenal opportunities for swimming as well as snorkeling in one of the only live coral reefs in the world, but **Tulé** boasts nicer surf. Just ask around to find names and descriptions of other good sites, and ask the driver to leave you at the beach of your choice. Beaches closer to (and in) San José, past El Chileno, are generally unswimmable due to the surf.

At night, you too can join rich Americans in the nightly ritual of alcohol-induced gastrointestinal reversal. Typical Cabo San Lucas bar decor is in the same booze-can-punish vein—off-the-wall signs like "Sorry, We're Open" and "Wrong Way—Do Not Exit" vie for space with assorted driver's licenses. Begin (or end) your single-minded quest for inebriation at **Squid Roe,** Cárdenas at Zaragoza (tel. 3-06-55 or 3-12-69), by far the hottest spot in town (beer 15 pesos, national mixed drinks 16 pesos). Dancing—on any and all surfaces—10pm-3am (open daily noon-3am). A louder, middle-aged crowd hangs at the expensive **Giggling Marlin,** Marina at Matamoros (tel. 3-11-

---

The Player

Timeshare vendors disguised as "tourist officials" roam the streets of Cabo San Lucas. If you want to take advantage of what they have to offer for free, you must be 25 years old (or tell them you're 25—they'll believe you) and possess a major credit card. If you have both, and a free afternoon, it's quite possible to go on the Arco boat ride for free and order anything you want at an expensive restaurant in exchange for an hour and a half of "listening," ears closed but eyes open, mouth pleasantly grinning, and head nodding to the English-speaking con man's pitch. He will try to convince you to dump US$15,000 into his hands in exchange for yearly time at an exclusive, American-oriented resort in Cabo. Don't admit until after dinner that you're not prepared to spend $15,000 (unless you want a struggle). Other lures include a free car rental for a day and a free day at a resort.

82), quaffing a full mug or a tall *yarda* while hanging upside-down like the day's big catch. Beers start at 10 pesos, national drinks are 12 pesos (half-price beer and margaritas during happy hours daily 2-7pm; open daily 7am-1am).

■ San José del Cabo

San José del Cabo remains relatively untouristed and peacefully Mexican, a haven from the Resortville that dominates the rest of the cape. While the town may be larger and more populated than its sister city, San José is strikingly more tranquil and collected, lacking the boisterous tourist merriment of San Lucas. In fact, "Los Cabos," when said colloquially, often refers only to Cabo San Lucas and the surrounding beaches and resort, and does not include quieter less commercial San José. Unlike its neighbor, San José has retained a proportion of its historical and cultural points of interest.

Orientation The **Transpeninsular Highway** on the west and **Avenida Mijares** on the east, both running north-south, connect the town with San José's broad sweep of beautiful beach 2km away. From north to south, cross-streets, running east-west between the above two include **Obregón, Zaragoza, Doblado, Castro, Coronado, González,** and much farther south along the resort-laden beach, **Paseo San José.** Between the two main north-south streets, **Green, Degollado, Guerrero, Morelos,** and **Hidalgo** run parallel from west to east. The conspicuous cathedral and *zócalo* are on Zaragoza near Hidalgo. To get to town from the Águila/ABC bus station, walk up González and turn right on the highway. Walk three blocks, turn right on Zaragoza, and follow it to the cathedral, a good 10 minutes away.

Practical Information The **tourist center** (tel. 2-29-60, ext. 150) is in the beige building next to the *zócalo,* on Zaragoza and Mijares (open Mon.-Fri. 8am-3pm). Change money at **Bancomer,** on Zaragoza and Morelos (tel. 2-00-30 or -40; open for exchange 8:30am-noon). **ATMs** can be found in many banks, including **Banco Unión** (tel. 3-34-34), near the *zócalo.* You can also take advantage of that bank's wonderfully clean, air-conditioned bathroom. There are **LADATELs** all over town; **free local calls** can be made from the booth outside the tourist office. Make long-distance calls from the *caseta* beside the cathedral, Hidalgo 9 (tel. 2-04-53; fax 2-00-14), between Zaragoza and Obregon (open daily 8am-10pm).

San José del Cabo is such a whirring, buzzing metropolis that it needs two bus stations. **Águila** and **ABC Autotransportes** launch **buses** from the station on Mijares at González (tel. 2-11-00) to La Paz (every hr. 6am-7pm, 3hr., 42 pesos), Cabo San Lucas (every 30min., 30min., 8 pesos), and Todos Santos (8 per day, 1½hr., 25 pesos). The **Frailes/Delfines terminal** is on Doblado and Privera (tel. 2-19-06), a five-minute walk from the *centro* and about 10 minutes from Mijares. Hop on a **Frailes** "Unión de Transporte Urbano" yellow-and-blue school bus anywhere along the Transpeninsular Highway; they run to Cabo San Lucas (every 30min. 5:30am-7:10pm, 25min., 8 pesos). **Dollar Rent-A-Car** (tel. 2-01-00; at the airport 2-06-71), across from the supermarket (see below), will set you on the road for US$49 per day plus US$11 per day insurance and free mileage. You need a credit card and at least twenty-five candles on your last birthday cake. To corral a **taxi,** call 2-04-01. Buy groceries at the **Supermercado Aramburo** on Zaragoza and Guerrero (tel. 2-01-88 or 2-00-48; open daily 7am-9pm). **Farmacia La Moderna** (tel. 2-00-50) is on Zaragoza and Degollado (open daily 8am-9pm). The ever-ready **Red Cross** (tel. 2-03-16 or -61) is on Mijares next to the post office. The **hospital** (tel. 2-37-13 or 2-38-13) is on Retorno Atunero, in Col. Clamizal; the **Centro de Salud** is at Manuel Doblado 39 (tel. 2-02-41). For **police,** call 2-03-61. The **post office** is on Mijares and González (tel. 2-09-11), several blocks toward the beach on the right-hand side (open Mon.-Fri. 8am-6pm, Sat. 9am-1pm). **Postal Code:** 23400. **Telephone Code:** 114.

Accommodations and Food As prices rise with the approach of the mega-resorts, rooms in the center of town look less and less appealing: imagine waking up US$16-40 poorer, then having to face a scorching 25-minute walk to the beach. Many **random rooms** are for rent for about 30 pesos per day; look for signs, especially on Obregón. Otherwise, you can enjoy multi-colored bedspreads and ancient paint jobs at **Hotel Ceci,** Zaragoza 22 (tel. 2-00-51), a block and a half up from Mijares. Spanking clean, cold rooms put guests in a positive mood, ready to appreciate the pastel curtains and matching lampshades (singles 60 pesos, with A/C 77 pesos; doubles with A/C 77 pesos). **Hotel/Youth Hostel San José Inn** (tel./fax 2-24-62), on Obregón and Guerrero, has relatively clean and spacious pink rooms with fans, thick mattresses, and warm water. The hotel offers mail service, bike rentals, and long-distance phone calls (singles 50 pesos; spacious doubles with TV 80 pesos; suites with five beds 35 pesos per person). **Trailer Park Brisa del Mar,** just off the highway to San Lucas when it reaches the coast, provides beach campers, communal bathrooms, and a bar with TV (full hookup US$6 plus tax; US$5 for tent).

Budget restaurants in San José del Cabo are being pushed out by real estate offices and fancy tourist eateries, leaving few options between taco stands and filet mignon. A healthy suspicion of anglophone restaurants will save you money: if the menus are printed in flawless English, the food is probably more expensive than it ought to be. Good, moderately priced meals hide near the Frailes bus terminal and along Zaragoza, between the cathedral and the banks. The best deal in town might be found at the **Mercado Municipal** restaurant building, near the ABC bus station. Among the eight small eateries in the market is **Dalia,** on your right as you enter. Tasty meat or fish main dishes plus a large *refresco* cost only 20 pesos (open daily 7:30am-5pm). **Restaurante Vista al Mar** (tel. 2-06-32), on Castro and Doblado, offers homecooked meals and an authentic ambiance absent elsewhere in town. Locals sit on the airy covered porch and heartily devour economical food prepared by the family, such as enchiladas (15 pesos) and *pollo frito* with chile, beans, and rice (20 pesos; open daily 8am-5pm). The food at **Cafetería Rosy,** on Zaragoza and Green, will leave you riveted. Seafood dishes like *sopa de camarones* (shrimp soup, 27 pesos), *pescado en mantequilla* or *al mojo de ajo* (fish in butter or garlic sauce, 30 pesos), and *pollo a la naranja* (chicken in orange sauce, 18 pesos) are tasty and hearty (open Oct.-May daily 8am-10pm; June-Sept. daily 8am-6pm).

Sights and Entertainment The most popular beach in town (for surfing, if not swimming) is **Costa Azul,** on Palmilla Pt., 1km south of the Brisa del Mar trailer park. To get there, take a bus headed for San Lucas (every 30min.) and ask the driver to drop you off at Costa Azul; or take a bus from Valerio González (3 pesos). A 15-minute walk down Mijares will lead you to good beaches much closer to town. The newer luxury hotels mar the sand at some spots, but there's plenty of natural, clean coastline in the stretches between the artificial structures. If you want to swim, try either the **Playa Palmilla,** 3km toward Cabo San Lucas from Costa Azul, or **Playa Santa Mónica,** a prime spot for snorkeling. Some people hitch along that road; *Let's Go* does not recommend hitchhiking as a safe means of travel.

Folks at the **Killer Hook Surf Shop (tel. 2-24-30),** on Hidalgo between Doblado and Zaragoza, are friendlier than the name suggests. They rent snorkel gear (US$8), fishing poles (US$10), and surfboards (US$15); they also repair surfboards and provide tips (open Mon.-Sat. 9am-8pm). **Trader Dick's** (tel. 2-28-28), next to La Jolla Resort, rents sand buggies (US$35 for 1½hr.).

If you can find time between trips to the beach, stop by **Los Cabos Centro Cultural,** on Mijares. Feast your eyes on reproductions of wall paintings, regional antiques, and an original Pericúe home. Guided tours are available (open Mon.-Fri. 8am-3pm). At night, **Eclipse** (tel. 2-16-94), on Mijares one block down from Doblado, pumps out rock tunes (beer 15 pesos, national drinks start at 10 pesos; open Tues.-

Sun. 9pm-3am). The real nighttime action, however, is in Cabo San Lucas, a piggy-bank-shattering 90-peso taxi ride away.

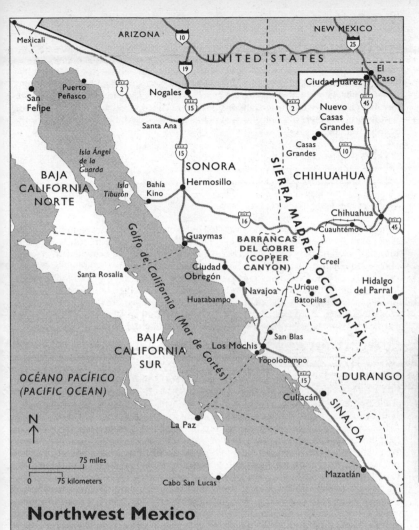

Northwest Mexico

The first taste of life south of the border for many *gringos* consists of nights of debauchery, rounds of tequila shots, gaudy felt sombreros, and blistering heat. But things calm down considerably as you venture farther south. The grime and frenetic madness of Tijuana and Ciudad Juárez, Mexico's baddest border towns, give way to bustling markets, colonial mansions, iconoclastic museums, and a surreal landscape. In some parts, things slow to a virtual standstill—you can hear the flies buzz and the wind whistle through the desert. Though swaggering *vaqueros* clad in tight jeans are almost obsolete, you may want to bring along a pair of cowboy boots and a wide-brimmed *sombrero*—the rugged terrain requires a lot of stamina and the *noroeste* sun is merciless.

The Sierra Madre Occidental rips through the heart of Northwest Mexico. To the east of the mountains, the parched desert landscape gives towns like **Chihuahua** a dusty Old West feel. Sandstorms and cacti enhance the mood. Along the coast, a melange of commercial ports, quiet fishing villages, and sprawling beaches overlook the warm waters of the Sea of Cortés. The most stunning sight in the *noroeste* are the **Barrancas de Cobre (Copper Canyon),** a series of deep gorges and unusual rock formations brimming with tropical vegetation. The caves in the area are home to the reclusive Tarahumara Indians.

SONORA

■ Nogales

Pushed up against the border and straddled by two steep hills bearing tin houses and block-long Corona signs, Nogales can seem like the archetypal border town—cheap curio shops, off-track betting, and cheesy bars. The streets are crowded with street vendors expectantly waiting for pocketbook-happy Americans to dip below the border for a day and purchase tiny rag dolls as proof of having set foot in a foreign land. However, the cultural syncretism and fast-paced bustle which animate life in other border towns are notably absent here and Nogales remains more or less unalloyed by *gringo* influences. Born out of the 1848 Mexican-American War as something of an unarmed fortress, Nogales has remained distinctively Mexican.

ORIENTATION AND PRACTICAL INFORMATION

If you plan to venture beyond Nogales, obtain a **tourist card** at the border. It's much simpler and cheaper to get the card here than farther south. When you cross the border—which, incidentally, has a huge Taco Bell billboard (they really did "make a run for the border")—through the new arched crossing complex, turn right into the first building you encounter; it's the immigration and tourist office (see p. 10).

The **bus terminal** and **train station** are directly across from each other on Carretera Internacional, 4.5km from town. A taxi from the bus station to the center of town will cost an exorbitant 25 pesos; instead cross the street and walk north to the end of the block, where you can board one of the white buses (1.50 pesos) marked "Parque Industrial" or "Villa Sonora." Downtown Nogales is the last stop. Relatively small Nogales makes for easy navigating. If you're crossing the border by foot, you'll be on **Pesqueira;** by car, you'll drive in on **Juárez.** From east to west, **Pesqueira, Juárez** (which becomes **López Mateos** several blocks south), **Morelos, Obregón** (the main tourist drag), **Ingenieros,** and **Hidalgo** run parallel to each other and perpendicular to the border. **Internacional** runs parallel to the tall picket fence that marks the border. Proceeding south, away from the border, **Campillo, Ochoa, Pierson, Aguirre, Vázquez, Díaz,** and **González** all run parallel.

Tourist Office: (tel. 2-06-66), to the left of the border from the Mexican side, in the Edificio Puerta de México, room #1. The friendly, English-speaking staff is best at directing visitors to curio shops or bars, but they will also hand out a crude map of the downtown area and various other brochures. Open Mon.-Sat. 8am-3pm.

Currency Exchange: Banks line Obregón near the border. **Banamex** has two central locations: one at Obregón and Ochoa (tel. 2-34-34; fax 2-34-88) resembles the control tower of the Starship *Enterprise* (open Mon.-Fri. 9am-3pm); another at Obregón and Uchón (tel. 2-34-81; fax 2-38-20) could pass for the *Enterprise*'s docking station (open Mon.-Fri. 9am-3pm). Both exchange dollars and traveler's checks and feature two 24-hr. **ATMs.**

Telephones: Downtown Nogales has a high concentration of **LADATELs**. Look for them at Obregón and Campillo, Obregón and Flores Guerra, and at the border in front of the tourist office. The *caseta* in the bus terminal (tel. 3-50-81, fax 3-50-82) offers overpriced international calls and fax service (open 24hr.). **Puesta del Sol,** Campillo 115 (tel. 2-00-16; fax 2-17-14), at Obregón, has a *caseta* where you can make international calls and a fax service (5 pesos per page; local calls 3 pesos for 3 min; open daily 8am-9pm).

Telegrams: Campillo 68 (tel. 2-00-81 or 2-15-51), next door to the post office. Open Mon.-Fri. 8am-6pm, Sat. 9am-noon.

Buses: Tres Estrellas de Oro (tel. 3-16-03) sends its crew to Chihuahua (12hr.), Mexicali (10hr.), Tecate (11hr.), and Tijuana (12hr.). **Autotransportes Caballero Azteca** (tel. 3-02-33) goes to Ciudad Juárez (9:30pm, 10hr., 116 pesos). **Transportes Norte de Sonora** (tel. 3-16-03) runs to Hermosillo (8:30am-6:30pm every 2hr., 3½hr., 46 pesos), Los Mochis (7:30am-11:30pm, 11hr., 141 pesos), Mazatlán (7:30am-11:30pm every 2hr., 16hr., 288 pesos), Guadalajara (7:30am-11:30pm every 2hr., 26hr., 356 pesos), and Mexico City (11:30am, 1:30pm and 9:30pm, 32hr., 430 pesos). **Transportes del Pacífico** (tel. 3-16-06) sends buses to Guaymas (8:30am-6:30pm every 2hr., 6hr., 70 pesos), Puerto Vallarta (26hr., 350 pesos), Querétaro (32hr., 440 pesos) and Tepic (22hr., 200 pesos); call for schedules. **Pitic** (tel. 4-59-99) runs to Guadalajara, Hermosillo, Los Mochis, Mexico City, and Monterrey. **Greyhound** buses (tel. in Tuscon: (95) 602-287-5628) leave for Tucson (every hour, 7am-7pm and 9pm, US$6.50) from their station ½ block from the U.S. side of the border.

Trains: (tel. 3-10-91). Two southward-bound trains depart daily; the slow *burro* (literally "donkey") leaves at 7am and the faster *estrella* leaves at 3:30pm, though times do change. Destinations include Mazatlán (90 pesos *burro*, 162 pesos *estrella*) and Guadalajara (136 and 243 pesos respectively). Tickets sold 6-7am and 8am-3:30pm. Reservations for the *estrella* can be made by phone.

Luggage Storage: Available 6am-10pm at the bus terminal, one peso per hr.

Market: VH Supermarket, Obregón 375 (tel. 2-41-24), between Ramos and Rodríguez, 10min. from Av. Juárez. Open Mon.-Sat. 8am-10pm, Sun. 8am-8pm.

Laundromat: Nuevas Lavanderas de Nogales, Ingenieros 332 (tel. 3-15-75), between Gonzáles and Díaz, partially obscured by a large white awning. Wash 4 pesos; 30-min. dry 9 pesos. Open Mon.-Sat. 7am-7pm, Sun. 7am-2pm.

Red Cross: (tel. 3-58-00), on Plutarco Elías and Providencia. Open 24hr.

Pharmacy: Farmacia San Xavier, Campillo 73 (tel. 2-55-03), between Juárez and Morelos (open 24hr.). **Farmacia San Andrés** (tel. 2-02-36), behind the tourist office (open daily 8am-8pm).

Medical Assistance: Seguro Social, Escobedo 756 (tel. 3-59-85), at Obregón and Roccoedo (take the "Parque Industrial" bus). English spoken. Open 24hr. Some English is spoken at the **Hospital Básico,** Dr. Francisco Arriola 1277 (tel. 3-07-94 or 3-08-59). Open 24hr.

Police: (tel. 2-01-16 or 2-01-14), at González and Leal. English-speakers on hand in the afternoon. Open 24hr. **Highway Patrol:** tel. 4-18-30.

Post Office: Juárez 52 (tel. 2-12-47), at Campillo. **Postal Code:** 84000.

Telephone Code: 631.

ACCOMMODATIONS AND FOOD

As in most of northern Mexico, rates in Nogales are steep. Fortunately, a string of budget hotels lines the block behind the tourist office on Av. Juárez and Obregón. The **Hotel San Carlos,** Juárez 22 (tel. 2-06-27, 2-13-46, or 2-14-09), features a refreshing oasis—an ever-replenished, ice-cold purified water dispenser in the lobby. Large, clean rooms have A/C, color TVs with U.S. cable, massage-showers, and phones. Ask for a renovated room. Check-out 1pm. Singles 111 pesos. Doubles 132 pesos. **Hotel Olga,** Juárez 17 (tel. 2-35-60), across from the San Carlos, offers basic, fairly clean rooms. Outdoor bathrooms are bearable. Singles 70 pesos, with bath 100 pesos; doubles 80 pesos, with bath 120 pesos).

Overpriced restaurants cluster around the *centro*. Ditch the tourist traps and head to **La Posada Restaurant,** Pierson 116 (tel. 2-04-39), off Obregón where you can mingle with the town's *petite-bourgeoisie*. Painted tiles and curious objects adorn the walls, while *burritos de machaca* (dried beef, 8 pesos), steak *milanesa* (30 pesos), and *chimichanga* (10 pesos) grace the tables. Open daily 7:45am-10pm.

SIGHTS AND ENTERTAINMENT

Most of the curio and craft shops line Obregón. You may get good deals if you bargain and know something about quality. In fact, vendors *expect* shoppers to haggle. Often, low prices can be had by pretending to walk away uninterested, but keep in mind that these salespeople barely make enough to feed their children. Before buying, ask turquoise vendors to put the rocks to "the lighter test." Plastic or synthetic material will quickly melt under a flame. Likewise, when buying silver look for a ".925" stamp on the piece; if it's not there, the goods are bad.

At night, the usual bands of *gringos* patronize the bars on Obregón. **Coco Loco,** Obregón 69, is a good place for a little drinking and dancing. Drinks start at 11 pesos (open Wed.-Sun. 1pm-2am, 20-peso cover on Fri.-Sat. includes a beer). Other places to booze and boogie on the same street include **Sr. Amigo, El Piladros, Epidaurus** and **Pancho Villa Bar.** Not in the mood to get intoxicated? Head for the **movie theater** (tel. 2-50-02), on Obregón between F. Guerra and Torres, which shows first- and second-run films daily, 3:30-9:30pm. Top off your evening with some ice-cream from **La Michoacana**, on the corner of Obregón and Aguirre (open daily 7am-7pm).

■ Puerto Peñasco

The town with the English sobriquet—Rocky Point—caters more to American resortmongers than to budget travelers; always ask for prices in pesos instead of in dollars, even if the seller is reluctant. Just 105km off the border and about three hours from Tucson, Puerto Peñasco, like northern Baja, attracts a fair share of weekenders. Despite the throngs of *gringos*, somewhat tranquil beaches and clean streets make this dusty port still worth a trip. Once a launching pad for shrimp boats, Puerto Peñasco dried up when overfishing decimated the shrimp population of the Sea of Cortés. Economically widowed, the town now courts investors with a dowry of tax breaks and other incentives. Fifty kilometers north on the road to Sonoita lies the **El Pinacate** volcanic area.

Orientation To reach the *centro* from the bus station, take a left past PEMEX and walk nine blocks down Puerto Peñasco's main road, **Blvd. Juárez;** continue south on Juárez past the **Dársena**—the port area—and eventually to **Malecón,** Peñasco's old section, on the western edge of town. **Playa Hermosa** (Beautiful Beach) lies to the northwest; **Playa Miramar** to the south. Town activity centers around two intersections: **Fremont** and **Juárez** and **Constitución** and **Juárez.** Numbered *calles* run east-west and start with 1 at **Playa Miramar** (southernmost); boulevards run north-south.

Practical Information Puerto Peñasco's **tourist office** (tel. 3-35-55) is on N. Bravo CP, Calle 18, off Blvd. Juárez and next to a travel agency. Little English is spoken (open 9am to mid-afternoon). **Bancomer** (tel. 3-24-30), on Juárez and Estrella, next to the plaza, exchanges currency and traveler's checks (open Mon.-Fri. 8:30am-2pm). **LADATELs** are not easy to find; there's one in front of the Hotel Paraíso, and another at Constitución and Simon Morva. *Casetas* are located at the Jim Bur Plaza, in Cheiky's Pizza Restaurant (tel. 3-36-27; local calls 2 pesos for 3min., calls to U.S. 7.50 pesos per min.; open daily 8am-11pm). The **telegram and fax office** (tel. 3-27-82) is in the same building (open Mon.-Fri. 8am-6pm, Sat. 9am-noon).

Buses (tel. 3-20-19) depart from Juárez and Calle 24. **Transportes Norte de Sonora** and **Autotransportes de Baja California** collectively go to Guaymas (9:30am, noon, and midnight, 9hr., 122 pesos), Hermosillo (9:30am, noon, and midnight, 7hr., 100 pesos), Mexicali (8:30am, 5pm, and 1am, 4hr., 70 pesos), and Tijuana (8:30am and 1am, 8hr., 110 pesos). **Trains** (tel. 3-26-10) leave from the station off Constitución, two blocks north of the intersection with Juárez, right behind the Hotel Paraíso del Desierto. *Estrella* trains leave at 1:40pm for Mazatlán (18hr., 181 pesos) with numerous stops along the way; *burro* trains start the crawl towards Mazatlán at 3am (21 hr., 101 pesos).

Get your supplies from **Supermercado del Pueblo** (tel. 3-23-48) on Constitución and Juárez, half a block from Hotel Paraíso del Desierto (open 8am-10pm), also try **Supermarket Jim Bur** (tel. 3-25-61), at the Jim Bur Plaza on Juárez (open Mon.-Sat. 8am-9pm, Sun. 9am-5pm). At **Lavamática Peñasco** (tel. 3-22-63), on Constitución at Morúa across from Hotel Paraíso del Desierto, a wash costs six pesos; a dry costs five (open Mon.-Sat. 8am-7pm). The **Red Cross,** on Fremont at Chiapas (tel. 3-22-66), is open 24hr. Little English is spoken. **Farmacia Botica Lux,** Merchero Campo 146, off Blvd. Juárez, two blocks from the walking bridge, will meet your need for drugs (open daily 8am-midnight). **Hospital Municipal** (tel. 3-21-10) is at Morúa and Barreras one block east of Juárez; little English is spoken (open 24hr.). **Police** (tel. 3-26-26) wait at Fremont and Juárez but speak little English (open 24hr.) The **post office** (tel. 3-23-50) is at Chiapas, two blocks east of Juárez on Fremont (open Mon.-Fri. 8am-7pm). **Postal Code:** 83550. **Telephone Code:** 638.

Accommodations and Food Budget rooms in Puerto Peñasco are a rare commodity, since cheap accommodations are being torn down left and right to clear space for expensive resorts, condos, and time-shares. One of the last remaining quasi-budget hotels is the **Motel Playa Azul** (tel. 3-62-96), Calle 13 and Pino Suárez. It offers nicely furnished rooms with ancient TVs that receive a single channel, generous A/C, and yes, private bathrooms with hot water. Bargain with the manager. Singles 140-175 pesos. Doubles 210-245 pesos. Otherwise, **Playa Miramar RV Park** (tel. and fax 3-25-87; in the U.S. call 602-994-4475 for reservations), on (go figure) Playa Miramar, rents scenic spots year-round with cable TV, full hookup, and hot water. Washers, dryers, and showers available. Check-out time is noon. (90 pesos per day for 1 or 2 people, 15 pesos per day each additional person, 540 pesos per week, beachfront spaces slightly higher; key deposit 35 pesos).

Most beachside restaurants cater to *gringos,* with their (high) prices quoted in U.S. dollars; insist on paying in good ol' *moneda nacional.* As always, *taquerías* are the spot for budget grub; find some at Juárez between Constitución and Calle 24, near the bus station. For just 23 pesos **Asadero Sinaloa** (tel. 3-40-76), Juárez and Calle 24 across from the bus station, rewards customers with five pieces of chicken. Chicken tacos (3.50 pesos) make for more dainty dining. Indoor seating is completely insect-free! Open daily 10am-10pm. **Asadero Sonora** (tel. 3-29-24), on Constitución in front of the train station, serves up toothsome handmade tortillas and grilled steak tacos (5 pesos; open daily 9am-4:30am).

Sights and Entertainment Puerto Peñasco's clean and rarely crowded beaches are blessed with clear, warm waters. Shallow tide pools cradle clams, small fish, and colorful shells. **Sandy Beach** and **Playa Hermosa** are the best choices for swimming; both have curio shops, restaurants, and hotels galore. The beaches around **Rocky Point** and **Playa Miramar,** at the southern end of town, are less crowded, but also rockier, and rougher. Playa Miramar also brims with RV parks and condominiums. For the intellectual beach bum, the **Intercultural Center for the Study of Deserts and Oceans (CEDO)** at Playa Las Conchas, 9km from town (taxi 30 pesos), gives free tours of its wet lab and museum Tuesdays at 2pm and Saturdays at 4pm. Open Mon.-Sat. 9am-5pm, Sun. 10am-2pm.

To get to Playa Hermosa, turn left on Calle 13 when heading south on Juárez; the beach is straight ahead five or six blocks down. To reach Playa Miramar, head south on Juárez and turn left onto Campeche near the Benito Juárez monument. Continue uphill on the unpaved road for three blocks; Playa Miramar will be on your left. To reach Playa Las Conchas, head south on Juárez, turn left on Fremont near the Plaza del Camaronero, take a right onto Camino a las Conchas, and follow the rock-slab road for three or four kilometers. To reach Sandy Beach, head north on Encinas or Juárez until the intersection with Camino a Bahía Choya. Take a left and follow the road; turn left on the road labeled "To Sandy Beach."

■ Near Puerto Peñasco: El Pinacate

Forty-eight kilometers north of Puerto Peñasco on Rte. 8 to Sonora is the **El Pinacate** volcanic preserve, one of the largest and most spectacular biospheres in the world. Encompassing over four million acres, and including the upper reaches of the Sea of Cortés, the biosphere was created in June 1992 to limit volcanic rock excavation and protect endangered species. Pockmarked by over 600 craters and 400 cinder cones, the Pinacate lava fields form 30,000-year-old islands in a vast sea of sand. From inside the park, the only thing visible for kilometers around are fields of igneous rock and the monochromatic moonscape punctuated by purple, white, and red wildflowers. The people of the Tohono O'odham nation have lived in this region for tens of thousands of years, crossing the desert on foot from Arizona to bathe in the waters they consider to be sacred and healing, and extracting fresh water from *saguaro* cacti.

Ecoturismo Peñasco and **Ajo Stage Lines** (tel. 3-32-09 or 3-21-75) lead tours into the area; ask at the tourist office for details or talk to Peggy at **CEDO** (see page 173 above). Prices: $50 per person (1-2 people), $40 per person (3-4 people), $35 per person (5 or more people). The vast, isolated, climatically harsh region makes a guide necessary. If you do decide to tough it out alone, four-wheel-drive, high-clearance vehicles with partially deflated tires are a must. Bring tons of water, a shovel, a spare tire, and firewood. Camping is permitted, but don't leave anything behind and don't remove any souvenirs. The ideal time to visit is November to March, when temperatures range from approximately 60 to 90°F, as opposed to summer months, when temperatures can exceed 116°F.

■ Hermosillo

The capital of Sonora, Hermosillo (pop. 700,000) is an expansive metropolis and a center for commerce and education. Beautiful cathedrals, government palaces, modern restaurants, and stylish open-air malls stand side-by-side with garbage-ridden sidewalks and a prominent red-light district. Looming large above all are Hermosillo's radio-tower-covered mountains.

If you get an early start and the buses run on time, you can breeze from Tucson to the beaches of Guaymas or Mazatlán in a single day, skipping the lonelier parts of Sonora entirely. But a layover in lively Hermosillo (its name comes from the Spanish word *hermoso*, "beautiful") can become a pleasant surprise; entertainment ranges from water parks and roller rinks to rousing clubs and bars.

ORIENTATION

Hermosillo lies 271km south of the border on Rte. 15, the main north-south highway connecting the western U.S. and central Mexico. **Buses** depart from the main terminal on Blvd. Encinas, 2km east of the city center. To get from the bus station to the center of town, cross the street and catch a bus marked "Circuito Norte-Mendoza" or "Centro" (1.50 pesos, every 10 minutes 5am-10:30pm). Taxis will ask 20 pesos for a trip to *el centro;* pay no more than 10 and don't jump in until you agree on a price. To get back to the bus station from town, wait for a bus at Elías Calles and Matamoros, across from Óptica Morfín.

At the junction of **Blvds. Luis Encinas** (also known as Transversal) and **Rosales,** the **Hermosillo Flash** (an electronic bulletin board displaying daily news) helps the mapless to orient themselves. Most of the activity lies inside the square area bordered by **Rosales** on the west, **Juárez** on the east, **Serdán** on the south, and **Encinas** on the north. The *zócalo* is bounded by **Colosio, Sonora, Guerrero,** and **Garmendia.** From west to east, the principal north-south streets are **Rosales, Pino Suárez, Yañez, García Morales, Garmendia, Guerrero, Matamoros, Juárez,** and **González.** From north to south, the east-west streets are **Encinas, Niños Héroes, Oaxaca, Sonora, Colosio, Dr. Noriega, Morelia, Monterrey, Plutarco Elías Calles,** and **Serdán.** Maps can be bought at one of the many local *papelerías* (16 pesos); better ones are distributed free at the tourist office. If you get lost, remember that the antenna capped mountain is always to the south.

PRACTICAL INFORMATION

Tourist Office: (tel. 17-29-64; fax 17-00-60), on the 3rd floor of the **Centro de Gobierno de Sonora,** Blvd. Paseo Canal and Comonfort. Walk south on Rosales over the canal, turn right, then walk one block west. Señor Eugenio Puebla provides excellent assistance and dishes out great maps. Open Mon.-Fri. 8am-3pm.

Currency Exchange: Banks line Encinas and Serdán. **Bancomer** (tel. 17-36-81), Serdán and Yañez, cashes traveler's checks. Open Mon.-Fri. 8am-2pm. **Banamex** (tel. 14-76-15), Serdán and Matamoros, is closer to the center. Open Mon.-Fri. 8:30am-4:30pm. You'll see 24-hr. **ATMs** at both.

American Express: Hermex Travel (tel. 17-17-18), Rosales at Monterrey. Open Mon.-Fri. 8:30am-1pm and 3-6:30pm, Sat. 9am-1pm.

Telephones: LADATELs in the *zócalo,* in front of the post office, at Serdán and Guerrero, and at Morelia 90 between Guerrero and Garmendia. *Casetas* can be found at nearly every pharmacy and...hair salon? Look for the blue *"teléfono público"* signs along the sidewalk. **Farmacia Margarita** (tel. 13-17-73), Morelia and Guerrero, has *casetas* for long-distance calls. Open daily 8am-midnight.

Telegrams: (tel. 12-03-56; fax 13-19-24), in the same building as the post office. Also telex and fax service. Open Mon.-Fri. 8am-7pm, Sat.-Sun. 9am-12:30pm.

Airport: 10km west of town on Transversal toward Bahía Kino (tel. 61-00-08). Get there with the help of a small red bus called *taxi colectivo;* it departs from the bus or train station (2 pesos). **Aeroméxico** (tel. 16-82-59) to Guadalajara (9am and noon, 2hr., 1388 pesos), Mexico City (9am, 3:30pm, and 8pm, 2½hr., 1166 pesos), Tijuana (11:30am and 12:30pm, 1hr., 946 pesos), and other destinations. **Mexicana** (tel. 61-01-12 or 17-11-03) to Mexico City (8am, 2½-4hr., 1166 pesos), and more.

Buses: All service out of Hermosillo is *de paso;* during holidays and weekends you'll need to lace up your boxing gloves in order to win a seat. Buses to Tijuana and Mexico City fill up early, so buy tickets at least a day in advance. The cheapest carrier is **Transportes del Pacífico** (tel. 17-05-80). To Guadalajara (*primera clase* every hour, 22hr., 303 pesos; or *segunda clase* 24hr., 303 pesos), Los Mochis (every hour, 7hr., 90 pesos; or 7hr., 80 pesos), Mazatlán (every hr., 13hr., 200 pesos; or 14hr., 190 pesos), Mexicali (every hour, 9hr., 140 pesos; or 9hr., 120 pesos), Mexico City (every hour, 30hr., 500 pesos; or 32hr., 430 pesos), Nogales (3 per day, 4hr., 60 pesos; or 4hr., 50 pesos), Tijuana (every hour, 12hr., 179 pesos; or 12hr., 150 pesos), and Guaymas (every hour, 1½hr., 20 pesos), among other destinations. **Transportes Norte de Sonora** (tel. 13-40-50) to most of the above, plus sunny, tourist-ridden Acapulco (10 per day, 35hr., 450 pesos).

Trains: Estación Pitíc (tel. 15-35-77), north of the city on Rte. 15. Take the bus marked "Anapolas" to get to the train station. Northbound *estrella* (fast) to Nogales and Mexicali leaves at 7:50am, and the *burro* (slow) at 11am. Southbound *estrella* to Los Mochis and Guadalajara leaves at 7:45pm, and the *burro* at noon. Reservations are needed for the *estrella* in advance.

Luggage Storage: At the bus station. 1-2.50 pesos per hr. Open Mon.-Fri. 7am-7pm, Sat.-Sun. 8am-6pm.

Supermarket: Ley Centro (tel. 17-32-94), Juárez at Morelia. The size of two U.S. football fields, with public toilets and hundreds of young clerks decked out in blue hats. Takes U.S. dollars at a good exchange rate. Open daily 6:30am-10pm.

Red Cross: (tel. 14-07-69), at Encina and 14 de Abril. Open 24hr. (Barely) English-speaking staff—no Florence Nightingale here—on hand daily 9am-5pm.

Pharmacy: Farmacia Margarita (tel. 13-15-90)**,** Morelia at Guerrero. Open 24hr.

Hospital: (tel. 13-25-56), Transversal at Reyes. Open 24hr. English spoken.

Emergency: 06. **Ambulance:** 76-75-27.

Police: (tel. 18-55-64), Periférico Nte. and Noreste. Little English spoken. Open 24hr. **Transit Police:** 16-08-77.

Post Office: (tel. 12-00-11), at Serdán and Rosales. Open Mon.-Fri. 8am-7pm, Sat.-Sun. 8am-noon. **Postal Code:** 83000.

Telephone Code: 62.

ACCOMMODATIONS

Hermosillo offers many budget hotels, allowing those who must watch every peso they spend to sleep comfortably and safely. Air-conditioning is costly but indispensable, especially in the blistering summer heat. For those scraping the very bottom of the barrel, five *casas de huéspedes* line Sonora, two blocks west of the park; two more are on Guerrero near Sonora. Prices here are very inexpensive, but the area, which also includes nicer hotels like the Montecarlo, is the city's red light district. Lone female travelers should be especially careful and might consider avoiding the area entirely.

Casa de Huéspedes del Viajero, Sufragio Efectivo 90, between Pino Suárez and Yañez. Walk south on Rosales until you begin to pass the tall hill (Cerro de la Campana) to your left. Turn left onto S. Efectivo before reaching the canal. Unbelievably large rooms in an 84-year-old building. Adobe construction and fans keep the rooms cool. Aging outdoor bathroom. Lock your bags, since there's not always someone at the entrance. Check-out noon. Singles 40 pesos, doubles 70 pesos.

Hotel Washington, D.C., Dr. Noriega 68 Pte. (tel. 13-11-83), between Matamoros and Guerrero. Friendly management. Good-sized rooms with erratic hot water, A/C, and clean bathrooms. You're set for a good night's sleep with the solid security and comfortable beds, but you might be serenaded by street music. LADATEL in the lobby. Check-out 1pm. Singles 70 pesos. Each additional person 10 pesos.

Hotel Niza, Plutarco Elías Calles 66 (tel. 17-20-28), between Guerrero and Garmendia. A grandiose Art Deco hotel of the bloated past. The pink atrium is graced with murals and a gigantic globe. Rooms branching off this centerpiece have A/C, color TV, and comfy beds. Singles 95 pesos. Doubles 160 pesos.

FOOD

For a cheap and quick refuel, head for the taco and *torta* places around Serdán and Guerrero, where *taquitos* and *quesadillas* cost 4-5 pesos and *comida corrida* around 12 pesos. Alternatively, try the counters lining the entrances to the public market at Matamoros, Guerrero, and Monterrey. Although busy and smelly, some are sufficiently sanitary. Choose wisely: look out for flies and dirty pans and tabletops. Most offer tacos for a paltry sum, but *Let's Go* and your mother do not recommend eating foods containing uncooked vegetables in these establishments! Stick to enchiladas, burritos, and the like, also wonderfully cheap at about 3 pesos.

Restaurant Jung, Niños Héroes 75 (tel. 13-28-81), at Encinas. A new-age vegetarian restaurant a mere six blocks from the center of town? Why, yes indeed. The *comida corrida* comes with wheat rolls, soup, fruit juice, an entree, plus *frijoles con queso,* whole-grain rice, and dessert (30 pesos). The adjoining herbal medicine, Eastern philosophy, and pseudo-psychology store is worth a peek, if only for the *agua purificada* it sells. Open Mon.-Sat. 8am-8pm. Visa, MC accepted.

Restaurant Chapala, Guerrero between Sonora and Oaxaca. Mexican golden oldies blare from the juke box while throngs of middle-aged men drown their sorrow with the help of a few Tecates. Chicken, fish, or meat dishes come fried to crispy perfection and served with french fries, *frijoles,* tortillas, and salsa (15 pesos). Aside from the tipsy men, you might as well be in your Mexican aunt's house—if you're Mexican and you have an aunt, that is. Open daily 7am-10pm.

Restaurant "My Friend" (tel. 13-10-44), Plutarco Elías Calles and Yañez. Make *amigos* as you savor cheap and yummy *huevos al gusto* (12 pesos), *quesadillas* (6 pesos), or a platter of 3 *tacos de cabeza y barbacoa* (12 pesos). Open Mon.-Sat. 7am-7pm, Sun. 8am-1pm.

SIGHTS

Cuartel Catorce (tel. 13-13-79 for Sec. de Educación, ext. 23), on Guerrero and Colosio, is a rough structure with formidable walls of brown brick. Built in 1908, it was used for 80 years as a military installation and is now home to the Secretary of Culture and Education of Hermosillo. The colonnaded inner courtyard is an oasis; the room in the back of the courtyard, now an office, was once home to the army's cavalry (open Mon.-Fri. 8am-3pm). The nearby **Museo Regional de Historia,** on Encinas and Rosales at the University of Sonora, contains exhibits on pre-Hispanic and colonial history (open Mon.-Fri. 9am-1pm and 4pm-6pm, Sat. 9am-1pm; free).

On the other side of Rosales rise the tall steeples of the architecturally eclectic **Catedral de la Asunción,** on Tehuantepec and Comonfort (tel. 12-05-01; office and gift shop open Mon.-Sat. 9am-1pm and 4-7pm). Fugitives from the blistering sun can find refuge near the cathedral in the refreshingly shady **Plaza Zaragoza,** where looming trees surround an open-air bandstand. Other shady parks dot the streets near the plaza, making this one of the more peaceful areas of Hermosillo, and a welcome change from the dusty, filth-ridden streets of the *centro.* For the kids, a **playground,** complete with basketball courts, dwells on the corner of Pino Suárez and P. Elías Calles.

Across the street from the Plaza Zaragoza is the majestic, grey-and-white **Palacio de Gobierno.** The Palacio, from where the state of Sonora is governed, should not be confused with the pink brick **Palacio Municipal** nearby, where city government functions are carried out. Both are worth investigating for their architecture. The Palacio de Gobierno contains four murals surrounding its beautiful, tree-laden inner courtyard, where statues immortalize Sonoran patriots and senators. Two of the murals, the 1984 Azteche abstract work on the lower level and the 1982 Estrada above the stairs, portray *indígenas* battling Spaniards; the mural hidden behind the stairs depicts *indígena* slavery, and the main upstairs mural recounts the ancient *indígena* legend of the five suns and the evolution of humanity. Those in need of a bit more levity can head to **Multicinemas** (tel. 14-09-70) at Transversal and Reforma to absorb American movies with Spanish subtitles (a 5-min. bus ride from the center of town; open daily 3pm-9pm; free).

■ Near Hermosillo

CENTRO ECOLÓGICO DE SONORA

Hermosillo's **Centro Ecológico de Sonora** (tel. 50-12-25), 3km south of downtown off Vildosola, is more than just your token neighborhood zoo: it boasts an impressive array of animal life, a mini-aquarium (complete with outdoor sea lions), and hundreds of plant species from Sonora and elsewhere. Founded in 1985, the Centro is also home to groundbreaking biological research.

Among the animal exhibits, the Mexican grey wolf, bearded camels, and energetic monkeys stand out. The most spectacular feature of the Centro Ecológico, however, is its incredible collection of cacti; over 340 species are labeled and displayed throughout the animal exhibits or just outside the main pavilion. Keep your eyes peeled for the rare and beautiful *cina* and *biznaga,* from which fruit and candy are made, and the *maguey bacanova,* the fanned-out, spiked cactus which is the source of all those *tequilas* you've been downing.

The Centro is an excellent place for children; they delight in the clowns and Disney-esque flicks shown every Saturday and Sunday in the air-conditioned movie theater (noon-6pm; free). The enthusiastic and knowledgeable staff is happy to answer any questions about the Centro and its flora and fauna. Cafeterias and *agua purificada* can be found throughout the park (open Wed.-Sun. 8am-6pm; admission 7 pesos, children 5 pesos).

Getting There: To get to the Centro Ecológico, catch the orange-and-green striped bus marked "Luis Orci" from the corner of Guerrero and Dr. Noriega (20min., 1.50 pesos).

■ Bahía Kino

A pair of beach towns on the beautiful Sea of Cortés (or Golfo de California) comprise Bahía Kino, a 20-km stretch of glistening sand, blue water, and radiant sun. **Kino Viejo,** a dusty, quiet fishing village, lies 4km down the road from **Kino Nuevo,** an Americanized strip of posh, secluded homes and condos. This is a place to kick back with your favorite books, paints and easel, or fishing poles. Kino (as the towns are collectively known by locals) is an ideal destination for a daytrip to the beach from Hermosillo. The soothing breezes and vast expanses of sand make the hot, rickety ride from the city worthwhile.

Orientation Bahía Kino is located 120km west of Hermosillo. **Buses** in Hermosillo leave from the old **Transportes Norte de Sonora** station on Sonora between Revolución and González, near the *zócalo* (10 per day, 5:40am-5:30pm, 2hr., 15 pesos one way). It's best to get an early start on a daytrip to Kino—try to catch an early morning bus from Hermosillo and sleep (if you can) during the ride. Missing the 5:30pm bus back to Hermosillo means spending the night in Kino.

To get from one Kino to the other, flag down the bus (every hour, 1.50 pesos) on Nuevo's main (and only) road, **Av. Mar de Cortés,** or on **Blvd. Kino** in Kino Viejo. If you choose to walk (4km), be sure to keep plenty of water or other hydrants on hand. It is also quite possible to hitchhike between the two towns, though *Let's Go* does not recommend it. As always, use your common sense.

Practical Information **Long-distance phones** are available at the clothing shop at Kino and Tampico. Local calls 1 peso per min.; long-distance calls in Mexico 4 pesos per min.; calls to the U.S. 9 pesos per min. Open daily 9am-7pm.) **Public bathrooms** are on the beach in Kino Nuevo; in Kino Viejo, some downright pleasant potties are available at the **Centro de Salud,** at Tampico and Kino. Bring your own toilet paper. Near the post office and the police is the **Red Cross,** at Kino and Manzanillo, which has no phone but can be contacted via the Hermosillo **emergency** number (dial 06). Both **Dr. Jorge Grijalba** (tel. 2-03-07) and **Dr. José Luís** (tel. 2-03-95) speak English. In any type of emergency, your best bet might be to look for the American-run **Centro Deportivo** or for an American or Canadian license plate and knock on their door; the friendly expatriate community takes good care of foreign visitors. The **police** (tel. 2-00-67) are available at Kino and Cruz, in Kino Nuevo; or call 2-00-32 in Kino Viejo. Next to the police in Nuevo is the **post office** (open Mon.-Fri. 8am-3pm). **Telephone code:** 624.

Accommodations and Food Options for the budget traveler are limited to renting a spot in Kino Viejo to pitch your tent or park your RV; nearby Hermosillo provides more choices. If you miss the bus, **Islandia Marina,** Guaymas and Puerto Peñasco (tel. 2-00-81), just off Blvd. Kino and right on the beach, charges 50 pesos per day for a spot. It also rents cabins (130 pesos for four people, 25 pesos for each additional person). It is run by two Arizona women who own a purified water plant—you'll never be short on that precious commodity. In Kino Nuevo, **Hotel Saro,** 5735 Mar de Cortés (tel. 2-00-07), is the cheapest you will find at a stratospheric 210 pesos for a single with A/C and private bath. The more adventurous traveler can easily camp for free under one of the many *palapas* (thatched umbrella structures) on the Kino Nuevo beach. Locals claim the area is fairly safe.

A decent budget meal can be found in Kino Viejo. Try **Dorita** (tel. 2-03-49), Av. Eusebio Kino and Sabina Cruz, for relatively inexpensive breakfasts (15-18 pesos), *platillos mexicanos* (18 pesos), or *carne asada* (25 pesos). Fill up on purified water there—it's free (open daily 7am-8pm). For a ritzier dining experience, try the **Marlin Restaurant and Bar** (tel. 2-01-11), Puerto Peñasco and Guaymas, where you can gorge yourself on fish dishes (30-35 pesos) or slabs o' meat (30-60 pesos; open Tues.-Sat. 1-10pm; Visa, MC accepted). For those prices, you might as well try Kino Nuevo's restaurant **La Palapa** (tel. 2-02-10), Mar de Cortés and Wellington. It boasts a round, air-conditioned dining room and several outdoor decks overlooking the sea. Savor fish fillets (25-30 pesos) or *ceviche* (20 pesos). Open daily 8am-10pm).

Sand and Sights The beaches of Kino are peacefully deserted early in the week, but as the weekend approaches, so do the masses. Americans with homes in Kino tend to populate the beaches only during the winter, making for some long, lonely stretches of sand during the summer months. Beaches in Kino (as in all Mexico) are public by law, so you can plop down right in front of anyone's RV spot or faux-villa, and they can't do a damn thing about it. Yay! In general, the beaches are better in Kino Nuevo.

In Kino Nuevo, aquatic equipment can be rented from **Diversiones Marinas** (tel. 2-02-34; pedal boats 30 pesos per hr., rowboats and canoes 15-40 pesos per hr.). Another option is to ask at **Hotel La Posada,** on Av. Mar de Cortés towards Kino Viejo, just before Kino Nuevo's main strip begins, for the names of people renting out scuba/snorkeling gear.

■ Guaymas

Looking out over the Sea of Cortés, Guaymas is the principal port in Sonora and the proud home of an active shrimping fleet and busy seafood-processing plants. The area was originally inhabited by the Guaymas and Yaqui tribes, whose lives were turned upside down when the mission of San José was established in 1701 near the present-day city. A Spanish settlement followed in 1769, and the invasion continues to this day, as waves of suntanned *norteamericanos* drop by to take a break from the resort life of nearby San Carlos.

Guaymas itself is no resort town. Although its port area offers a pleasant view of the sea and nearby mountains and its charming cathedral and companion park serve as a haven for weary travelers, Guaymas suffers from an acute lack of convenient beaches. Nevertheless, it's a nice place to rest on the trip south to the more alluring resorts at Mazatlán, San Blas, and Puerto Vallarta: its cool ocean breezes, cleanliness, and civility give it a decided advantage over Hermosillo.

ORIENTATION

Guaymas is 407 km south of Nogales on Rte. 15. Municipal buses (1.50 pesos) run up and down its main strip, **Av. Serdán.** There you can also catch buses marked "Miramar" (1.50 pesos) and "San Carlos" (3 pesos) to reach the beaches north of the city; both buses run frequently 6am-8pm. Some daredevils also try thumbing as they wait for the bus at the junction of Serdán and the highway, but *Let's Go* does not recommend hitchhiking. The center of the city lies around the crossings of Calles in the low 20s and Serdán, and buses arrive right in the thick of things at Calle 14, right off (surprise) Serdán. Women should not walk alone more than two blocks south of Serdán after dark. The waterfront begins around Calle 23 and Serdán; coming up to the water, the cool ocean breeze will immediately provide relief from the heat.

Northbound vehicles, including buses, are often stopped by narcotics police. Have your identification ready and let them search whatever they want; it's better not to assert the right to privacy when dealing with humorless armed *federales*.

PRACTICAL INFORMATION

Tourist Office: Unfortunately, there is currently no tourist office in Guaymas. You're on your own, kiddo.

Currency Exchange: Banks are located along Serdán. **Banamex,** Serdán at Calle 20 (tel. 2-00-72), exchanges traveler's checks and greenbacks, and has two 24-hr. **ATMs** that accept Visa, MC, Cirrus, and Plus. Open Mon.-Fri. 8:30am-2:30pm.

Telephones: LADATELs are scattered all along Serdán. Two quieter locations are on Calle 19 Nte. at Av. 17 Pte. and in front of the Hotel Rubi. **Santa Martha Pañalera,** Serdán 80 (tel. 4-03-54; fax 4-05-40) at Calle 19, has booths for long- distance collect calls (7 pesos per min. to the U.S., 4 pesos per min. within Mexico; Sun. and after 8pm, 5.50 pesos to U.S., 2.50 pesos within Mexico). Open Mon.-Sat. 8am-9:30pm, Sun. 8:30am-3pm. Another option is the long-distance **Computel** *caseta* at the Tres Estrellas de Oro station (tel. and fax 2-95-18). Open daily 6am-10pm.

Telegrams: (tel. 2-02-92), next to the post office. Open Mon.-Fri. 8am-7pm, Sat. 9am-noon.

Airport: To reach it, catch a bus marked "San José" or "Itson" along Serdán (1.50 pesos). **Aeroméxico** (tel. 2-01-23), Serdán at Calle 15, has daily flights to La Paz (3:45pm, 50min., 659 pesos one way), Mexico City (3:45pm, 4½hr., 1247 pesos one way), Tucson (12:15pm, 55min., 816 pesos one way).

Buses: The town's three bus terminals are on opposite sides of the street at Calle 14 and Rodríguez. **Transportes Norte de Sonora** (tel. 2-12-71) goes to Acapulco (3pm, 50hr., 528 pesos), Ciudad Juárez (2:30pm, 13hr., 200 pesos), Culiacán (every hr., 9hr., 91 pesos), Guadalajara (every hr., 23hr., 328 pesos), Hermosillo (every hr., 1¾hr., 26 pesos), Los Mochis (every hr., 6hr., 57 pesos), Mazatlán (every hr., 12hr., 175 pesos), Mexicali (every hr., 12hr., 154 pesos), Mexico City (every 2hr., 31hr., 484 pesos), Nogales (every hr., 10hr., 168 pesos), Obregón (every hr., 1¾hr., 20 pesos), Puerto Peñasco (11:00am, 9hr., 122 pesos), San Luis (every hr., 6hr., 142 pesos), Tepic (every hr., 18hr., 231 pesos), and Tijuana (every hr., 15hr., 231 pesos). **Transportes del Pacífico** (tel. 4-05-76 or 2-30-19) offers fares to most of the above destinations for about 10% more, while their second-class service runs 3-5% less. **Transportes del Norte, Chihuahuenses,** and **Futura** offer similar prices and times. **Transportes Corral Baldomero,** across the street, offers service to Navojoa (every hr., 7:45am-10:45pm, 4hr., 30 pesos) and Nogales (4 per day, 5½hr., 51 pesos)

Trains: The old train station and current office (tel. 2-00-70 or 2-49-80) are located on Serdán at Calle 30. Open Mon.-Fri. 8am-noon and 2-5pm for information or reservations. Trains actually arrive and depart from **Empalme** (tel. 3-10-65 or 3-06-16), 10km south on the International Highway. To get there from anywhere along Serdán take the municipal bus marked "Empalme" to the end of the route, then transfer to the bus marked "Estación." Tickets sold 1hr. before the train arrives. The faster *estrella* train leaves at 11:45pm; the slow *burro* leaves at 12:30pm. To Mazatlán (12hr., 104 pesos or 17hr., 54 pesos), Tepic (15hr., 148 pesos or 21¼hr., 82 pesos), and Guadalajara (21hr., 185 pesos or 28hr., 113 pesos).

Ferry Terminal: (tel. 2-23-24), on Serdán about 1km past Electricidad. The boat steams to Santa Rosalía Tues. and Fri. at 11am (arriving at 6pm); tickets may be bought on the day of departure from 6-8am or on Mon., Wed., or Thurs. from 8am-2pm (*salón* 95 pesos, *turista* 189 pesos). To get to the terminal, hop on an bus heading away from the Carretera Internacional and get off at the "Transbordador" sign, on your right. For more information, see By Sea (p. 126).

Luggage Storage: Lockers are available at the **Tres Estrellas de Oro** bus terminal. 10 pesos first 8hr., 4 pesos every extra hr. Open 24hr.

Market: VH Supermarket (tel. 4-17-08), on Serdán between Calles 19 and 20. You can't miss it. Open Mon.-Sat. 7am-9pm, Sun. 7am-8pm.

Red Cross: (tel. 2-55-55), at the northern limit of Guaymas, at the 1980km mark on the Carretera Internacional. No English spoken. Open 24hr.

Pharmacy: Farmacia Sonora (tel. 4-24-00), Serdán at Calle 15. Open 24hr.

Hospital: Hospital Municipal (tel. 4-21-38), on Calle 12 between Av. 6 and 7. Some English spoken. Open 24hr.

Police: (tel. 4-01-04), stationed on Calle 11 at Av. 9, near the Villa School. Some English spoken. Open 24hr.

Post Office: (tel. 2-07-57), on Av. 10 between Calle 19 and 20. Open Mon.-Fri. 8am-7pm, Sat. 8am-noon. **Postal Code:** 85400.

Telephone Code: 622.

ACCOMMODATIONS

Accommodations in Guaymas cluster around Av. Serdán, where tourists will find a bevy of inexpensive hotels. Budget travelers rest assured; comfortable, well kept accommodations are as ubiquitous as the seafood.

Casa de Huéspedes Lupita, Calle 15 #125 (tel 2-84-09), two blocks south of Serdán across from the *cárcel* (jail). A mammoth "house" with 30 rooms and 12 communal baths, every last corner glowingly clean. Fans in every room provide much needed ventilation; an ice-cold *agua purificada* dispenser awaits downstairs at the office. Towel deposit 10 pesos. Singles 35 pesos, with bath 45 pesos, with A/C 65 pesos. Doubles 45 pesos, with bath 55 pesos, with A/C 85 pesos.

Hotel Rubi, (tel. 4-01-69), Serdán at Calle 29. Look for the "H...EL" sign. Friendly management shows guests to large rooms equipped with black-and-white cable TV and A/C. *Agua purificada.* Check-out 1pm. Singles (with 2 beds) 80 pesos. Doubles 90 pesos. Triples 110 pesos. Quads 130 pesos.

Hotel Impala, Calle 21 #40 (tel. 4-09-22, fax 2-65-00), one block south of Serdán. The hotel reveals its antiquity through the black-and-white photos of Guaymas's past gracing the walls. Rooms are renovated to modern glory with matching polyester bedspreads and curtains, A/C, and TV. Singles 95 pesos. Doubles 110 pesos. Triples 130 pesos. Quads 150 pesos.

FOOD

Seafood is *the* Guaymas specialty. Local favorites include frog legs *(ancas de rana)*, turtle steaks *(cahuna)*, and oysters *(ostiones)* in a garlic/chile sauce. Unfortunately, if you want to sample these local delicacies, you're going to have to pay a fair sum for them. Otherwise, the **Mercado Municipal,** on Calle 20, one block from Serdán, sells fresh produce; hot dog and taco vendors line Serdán.

S. E. Pizza Buffet, (tel. 2-24-46), Serdán at Calle 20. Satisfy your deprived appetites with their all-you-can-eat buffet of pizza, spaghetti, and salad...if you-can-eat-all that! (16 pesos). Open daily 11am-11pm.

Las 1000 Tortas, Serdán 188 (tel. 4-30-61), between Calles 17 and 18. The *torta* rules at this family-run joint (9-11 pesos each). Three types of delicious *comida corrida* (18.50 pesos) are prepared daily and served noon-4pm. Energetic customers sit upright in orthopedic wooden chairs, while tired neighbors slouch in brown vinyl booths; everyone munches on enchiladas and *gorditas* (18 pesos). Tasty *burritos de machaca con frijoles* (18 pesos). Open daily 7am-11pm.

Los Barcos (tel.2-76-50 or 2-75-00), Malecón at Calle 22. Gaze at the sea and nearby mountain peaks as you savor a seafood meal that won't bust your budget. Try a platter of *chimichangas de camarón, pescado, pulpo,* or *jaiba* (32 pesos), or the *machacas* (42 pesos). Open daily.

SIGHTS AND ENTERTAINMENT

Guaymas's **beaches** are located to the north in **San Carlos** and **Miramar;** both are accessible by bus (15min.). In San Carlos, the beach gets better past the end of the bus route near Club Med and Howard Johnson's. The nicer (but smaller) beaches in Miramar are back along the bus route in front of the fancy villas. The beaches are safe, although campers should take special precautions. Overall, camping in this area is not advisable here; if you absolutely must, opt for San Carlos over Miramar.

Take a stroll in the **Plaza de los Tres Presidentes,** on Calle 23 at Serdán, in front of the **Palacio Municipal,** a classic Colonial-style structure built in 1899. The blue bay waters, the towering green-and-white **Catedral de San Fernando,** and three bronze statues of (rather obscure) Mexican presidents complete the scene. The best place to spend a quiet afternoon, however, is the small park directly in front of the cathedral; benches and many a shade-providing tree make for a prime nap area. **Cine de Guaymas** (tel. 2-14-00), Av. 11 at Calle 20 two blocks off Serdán, shows U.S. films with Spanish subtitles daily from 3:40-11pm (admission 12 pesos). For the best view in town—of Guaymas, the mountains, the port, and the bay—seek out the shady bench just off Serdán towards the water, between Calles 25 and 26. Feel the soothing sea breeze and smile. It's a beautiful world. Sniffle. (Kleenex, please.)

NORTHWEST MEXICO

CHIHUAHUA

■ El Paso, Texas

With its arid climate and disparate architectural landscape, modern El Paso (pop. 650,000) is part oversized strip mall, part Mexican mission town—a city caught between two states, two countries, and two languages. The largest of the U.S. border towns, El Paso grew up in the 17th century as a stop-over on an important east-west wagon route that trailed the Río Grande through "the pass" (*el paso*) between the Rockies and the Sierra Madres. As Spain extended its reach into the New World, El Paso became a center for missionary activity; some old missions can still be seen today. More recently, the city has been dominated by Fort Bliss, the largest air defense base in the West, and the Biggs Army Airfield.

The city's San Jacinto Square, buzzing with pedestrians, is a pleasant place to while away the time. After dark, El Paso is a lonely city: most activity leaves the relatively tame center of town and heads to the UTEP (University of Texas at El Paso) area or south of the border—to El Paso's raucous sister city, Ciudad Juárez.

ORIENTATION

Before leaving the airport, pick up maps and information from the visitors center at the bottom of the escalators descending from arrival gates. To get to the city from the airport, take Sun Metro bus #33. The stop is located on a traffic island outside the air terminal building, across from the Delta ticket window (Mon.-Fri. every 30min., 6:27am-8:57pm; Sat. every 30min., 7:57am-8:57pm; Sun. every hr., 8:12am-7:12pm. 40min. to downtown. 85¢, students and children 6-13 40¢, seniors 20¢; exact change only). Get off when the bus arrives at San Jacinto Plaza and you'll find yourself right in the thick of it, near most hotels and restaurants.

When the bus stops running late at night, the only way to get to the city is to take a taxi (approximately US$20-25). Alternative approaches include I-10 (west/east) and U.S. 54 (north/south). El Paso is divided into east and west by **Santa Fe Ave.** and into north and south by **San Antonio Ave.** Tourists should be wary of the streets between San Antonio and the border late at night.

CROSSING THE BORDER

To reach the border from El Paso, take the north-south bus (every 10min., weekdays 6:30am-9pm, Sat. 8am-9pm, Sun. 9am-7pm, 30min., 25¢) to the **Santa Fe Bridge,** its last stop before turning around. Do not confuse the inexpensive bus with the costly trolley. Two pedestrian and motor roads cross the Río Grande: **El Paso Ave.,** an over-crowded one-way street, and **Santa Fe Ave.,** a parallel road lined with Western-wear stores, clothing shops, and decent restaurants. Entry to Mexico is 25¢ and the return trip costs a whopping 30¢. Capitalist pigs.

If entering Mexico by foot, walk to the right side of the Santa Fe Bridge and pay the quarter to cross. Daytrippers, including foreign travelers with a multi-entry visa, should be prepared to flash their documents of citizenship in order to pass in and out of Mexico. You might even get your bag searched by a guard if you have a tendency to break off the short end of the wishbone, but normally you won't even have to show ID. After stepping off the bridge, head left to the near back corner of the large grey building on your left—in the air-conditioned Juárez tourist office friendly, English-speaking employees await with maps and information.

To enter the United States, cross over the Santa Fe Bridge by the large *"Feliz Viaje"* sign. Be ready to deal with U.S. border guards and show a valid visa or proof of citizenship. You may be searched or asked to answer a few questions proving that you are who you say you are. Once in El Paso, wait at the stop on the right-hand sidewalk just across from the bridge for the north south bus, which runs until 9pm to San Jacinto Plaza. For more information, see Customs: Entering Mexico (p. 10).

PRACTICAL INFORMATION

Tourist Office: 1 Civic Center Plaza (tel. 544-0062), a small round building next to the Chamber of Commerce at the intersection of Santa Fe St. and San Francisco St. Easily identifiable by the thin, water-filled moat that surrounds it. Well-stocked with brochures; sells **El Paso-Juárez Trolley Co.** tickets for day-long tours across the border leaving on the hour from the Convention Center. (Tickets US$10 adults, US$8 children 6-12, free for kids under 5. Trolleys run 9am-4pm; there is also a 5pm trolley Wed.-Sat. during the summer. Call 544-0062 for reservations, 544-0061 for recorded information.)

Mexican Consulate: 910 E. San Antonio St. (tel. 533-4082), on the corner of San Antonio St. and Virginia St. Dispenses **tourist cards.** Open Mon.-Fri. 9am-4:30pm.

Currency Exchange: Valuta, 301 E. Paisano (tel. 544-1152). Conveniently near the border. Open 24hr. **Traveler's Checks: Bank of the West,** 500 N. Mesa St. (tel. 532-1000), on the corner of Main St. and Mesa St. Open Mon.-Thurs. 9am-4pm, Fri. 9am-5pm.

AmEx Office: 3100 N. Mesa St. (tel. 532-8900). Open Mon.-Fri. 8am-5pm.

Airport: Northeast of the city center; to reach it take bus #33 from San Jacinto Square or any other central location. Daily flights to locations in Mexico, the U.S., and elsewhere on a host of carriers, most with connections at Dallas/Ft. Worth.

Buses: Greyhound, 200 W. San Antonio (tel. 532-2365 or 1-800-231-2222), across from the Civic Center between Santa Fe St. and Chihuahua St. Daily service to and from New York (7 per day, 48hr., US$109), Los Angeles (10-15 per day, 16hr., US$35), Dallas, Phoenix, and other U.S. cities. **Storage lockers** US$2 for up to 6 hr., US$4 for 6-24hr. Open 24hr.

Trains: Amtrak, 700 San Francisco St. (tel. 545-2247). Open Mon., Wed., and Sat. 11am-6:30pm, Tues., Thurs., and Sun. 9am-5pm.

Public Transportation: Sun Metro (tel. 533-3333) departing from San Jacinto Plaza, at the corner of Main St. and Oregon St. Adults 85¢, students and children 40¢, seniors 20¢.

Car Rental: Alamo (774-9855), **Avis** (779-2700), **Budget** (778-5287), **Dollar** (778-5445), **Hertz** (772-4255), **Thrifty** (778-9236) and more, all at the airport.

Hospital: Providence Memorial Hospital, 2001 N. Oregon (tel. 577-6011). Open 24hr. Immunizations are not required to enter Mexico, but are recommended. Get your shots, by appointment and on Wed. only, at **El Paso City County Health District,** 222 S. Campbell St. (tel. 543-3560). When approaching the Mexican border, turn left on Paisano St. and walk three blocks.

Post Office: 219 E. Mills (tel. 532-2652). Open Mon.-Fri. 9am-5pm, Sat. 8am-noon. **Postal code:** 79901.

Telephone Code: 915. To call Cd. Juárez, dial 011-52-16, then the local number.

ACCOMMODATIONS

El Paso offers more options for the frugal traveler than Juárez; stay north of the border if you can. Budget hotels all cluster around the center of town, near Main St. and San Jacinto Square.

Gardner Hotel/Hostel (HI-AYH), 311 E. Franklin (tel. 532-3661). From the airport, take bus #33 to San Jacinto Park, walk one block north to Franklin, turn right, and head east 1½ blocks. The Gardner is two blocks up Mesa St. from San Jacinto Park. Inexpensive, clean rooms in the heart of downtown. Reception open 24hr. Locker rental 75¢, 50¢ for 4 or more days. Amiable management is extremely vigilant of security concerns. **Hotel:** All rooms have color TV with cable (including HBO) and a phone. Check-out 1pm. Singles without bath US$25-$30, with bath US$40. Doubles US$45. **Hostel:** Small, 4-person dorm rooms and shared bathrooms. Beautiful, spacious kitchen, common room with pool table and cable TV, and couches for lounging and socializing in the basement. Check-out 10am. HI members US$14, non-members US$17. Linen $2 extra.

Gateway Hotel, 104 S. Stanton St. (tel. 532-2611; fax 533-8100), at the corner of S. Stanton and San Antonio Ave. An excellent choice—a stone's throw from San Jacinto Square and a favorite stop for middle-class Mexicans. Clean and spacious rooms, large beds and closets, and thoroughly clean bathrooms, some with bathtubs. A/C upstairs; diner downstairs. Reservations accepted up to five days in advance, except during festivals and holidays. Check-out 4pm. Parking US$1.50 for 24hr. Singles US$21, with TV US$28. Doubles US$33, with TV US$35.

Budget Lodge Motel, 1301 N. Mesa (tel. 533-6821), a 10-min. walk from San Jacinto Square, 6 blocks from UTEP, 4 blocks from the hospital, and 2 blocks from the Catholic Church. Ample rooms are remarkably clean and have warm, strong running water, A/C, and cable TV. Small café, conveniently located on the first floor, serves breakfast and lunch at reasonable rates. And there is a swimming pool! Singles US$27. Doubles US$32-41, including tax.

FOOD

El Paso is a hybrid species with North American and Mexican ancestors. Well known *gringo* chains coexist with small mom-and-pop restaurants; and burritos are the undisputed local specialty. Attention vegetarians: bean burritos and *chiles rellenos* are tasty meatless options, but beware of animal lard.

The Tap Bar and Restaurant, 408 E. San Antonio St. (tel. 546-9049), near Stanton. Not dirt cheap, but reasonably priced for the U.S. Popular with Gardner Hostel-dwellers, and one of the only places open after 7pm, outlasting even McDonald's. Excellent breakfast *huevos rancheros* US$4. The Mexican Plate #1 (tacos, *chiles rellenos,* enchilada, rice, beans, and nachos for US$5.50) reminds you of what lies across the border. Other entrees US$1.50-$7.50. Big-screen TV, live *trio* every Thurs. 7-9pm, *mariachis* every Sat. 10:30-11:30pm. Full bar with endless varieties of beer. Open Mon.-Sat. 7am-2am, Sun. noon-2am.

Sojourn's Coffeehouse, 127 Pioneer Plaza (tel. 532-2817), above the San Francisco Grill. The only coffeehouse in downtown El Paso, Sojourn's boasts an outstanding selection of coffees, veggie fare, salads, and a small but delicious choice of sandwiches (US$4.95-6.50). Interesting decoration (Balinese) and crowd; pick up a calendar of special events to catch an open-mike poetry reading, listen to some eclectic gypsy music, or have your palm read. Open Mon.-Fri. 7:30am, Sat.-Sun. 10am; open late Wed.-Sat.

Big Bun, 500 N. Stanton (tel. 533-3926). Inexpensive tacos, burritos (US$1-2), hefty burgers (99¢), and sandwiches ($1.70-3). Soda refills 25¢, free for iced tea. Open Mon.-Fri. 7:30am-7pm, Sat. 7:30am-6pm.

Ben's Restaurant/Rinconcito Café, 605 S. Mesa (tel. 544-2236), serves outrageously cheap—and tasty—burritos (US$1-1.89). Otherwise, try out the generous *comida corrida* (US$3.52). Free delivery downtown. Open daily 8am-5pm.

SIGHTS AND ENTERTAINMENT

The majority of visitors to El Paso are either stopping off on the long drive through the desert or heading south to Ciudad Juárez and beyond. For a whirlwind tour of the city and its southern neighbor, hop aboard the Border Jumper Trolleys that depart every hour from El Paso (see Practical Information: Tourist Office, page 183).

Historic **San Jacinto Plaza** swarms daily with activity; street musicians play music that evokes El Paso's roots (*conquistadores* and cavalry). South of the square, on **El Paso Street,** hundreds of locals hurry along the thoroughfare and dash into stores in search of new bargains. To take in a complete picture of the Río Grande Valley, head northeast of downtown to Rim Rd. (which becomes Scenic Drive) to **Murchinson Park,** at the base of the mountains. The park offers a commanding view of El Paso, Juárez, and the Sierra Madres. The **Cielo Vista Mall** boasts a variety of shops, as well as a movie theater, **Cinema 6** (take Sun Metro bus #63 from San Jacinto Plaza).

For nightlife, try **The Basement,** 127 Pioneer Plaza (tel. 532-7674). The gay hotspot is downtown at **The Old Plantation,** 219 S. Ochoa (tel. 533-6055), a dance club/bar (open Thurs.-Sun. 8pm-2am). For a wilder time, many people head to Juárez, with rowdiness, no minimum drinking age, and ubiquitous nightlife.

During the spring and summer, the **El Paso Diablos** (tel. 755-2000), pride of the fabled Texas League, play the best minor-league baseball around. (Games April-May Mon.-Sun. 6:30pm; June-Aug. Mon.-Sat. 7pm, Sun. 6:30pm. Call to confirm. Tickets $4 general, $6 box seats). To reach Cohen Stadium (9700 Gateway North), take Sun Metro bus #42 from San Jacinto Plaza as far north as it goes and walk the rest of the way. Ask the driver for directions.

Strategic timing can make your visit to El Paso more entertaining. The town hosts the **Southwestern Livestock Show & Rodeo** (tel. 532-1401) in February and the **World's Finals Rodeo** (tel. 545-1188) in November. Fear not: El Paso's celebrations transcend its country-western roots. Another festival is the **Sun Bowl Parade** at **UTEP,** which also offers historical campus tours (tel. 747-5000).

■ Ciudad Juárez

Although Ciudad Juárez is separated from El Paso only by the narrow Río Grande, one truly steps into another dimension upon entering Mexico. Visitors are immediately bombarded by commotion on all sides and treated to a feast of bright paint and neon. Near the border, the city is hectic, loud, and cheap; bands of carousing gringos infiltrate the area in search of cheap booze and cheaper thrills. The farther one proceeds towards the ritzy ProNaf area, the calmer, pricier, and more Americanized the establishments become. Fleeing in the face of the American advance, Mexican culture can be found in the city's cathedral square and Parque Chamizal, a pleasant respite from the industrial production centers and poor residential areas that dot most of the cityscape. For more information on entering and leaving México, see p. 10 and p. 11.

ORIENTATION

Most of Old Juárez (the area immediately adjoining the Santa Fe and Stanton bridges) can be covered on foot. Street numbers start in the 600s near the two border bridges and descend to zero at **16 de Septiembre,** where **Av. Juárez** (the main street) ends. Both **Lerdo** and **Francisco Villa** run parallel to Juárez. To reach the ProNaf center, take public bus "Ruta 8-A" (1.50 pesos) on Malecón between the *Departamento de Población* and *Secretaría de Turismo* across the street from the bus shelter. Most city buses leave from the intersection of **Insurgentes** and Francisco Villa or thereabouts; ask the driver whether that bus will take you where you want to go. Taxis are always available downtown, but fees are steep; negotiate before getting in. During the daytime, Juárez is relatively safe for the alert traveler. As darkness increases, however, so does the ratio of drunk to sober people wandering the streets. Women should not walk alone or in dark places; everyone should avoid the area more than two blocks west of Av. Juárez.

PRACTICAL INFORMATION

Tourist Office: Coordinación de Turismo (tel. 29-33-00), Malecón and Francisco Villa, in the gray *Unidad Administrativa Municipal* building to the right of the Santa Fe bridge, looking at it from the Juárez side. You must first cross a pedestrian bridge. Few helpful brochures, but it has an amiable English-speaking staff. Open Mon.-Fri. 8:30am-2pm, Sat. 9am-1pm.

U.S. Consulate: López Mateos Nte. 924 (tel. 13-40-48 or 13-40-50). From Av. Juárez, turn left on Malecón and right on López Mateos, then walk for a good 15-20min. In an emergency, call the El Paso tourist office: 95- (915) 544-0062.

Currency Exchange: Banks congregate near the bus station, on Juárez St., and on 16 de Septiembre. Most are open Mon.-Fri. 9am-1:30pm. Traveler's checks cashed by **Comisiones San Luis** (tel. 14-20-33), on the corner of 16 de Septiembre and Juárez. Open Mon.-Thurs. 9am-9pm, Fri.-Sat. 9am-9:15pm, Sun. 9am-6:15pm. Also try **Chequerama,** (tel. 12-35-99) at Unión and Juárez. Open Mon.-Sat. 10am-6pm.

Telephones: LADATEL phones are scattered throughout the city. Look for them on Juárez near 16 de Septiembre. Or try **Secrefax** (tel. 15-15-10 or 15-20-49; fax 15-16-11), on Av. Juárez near the Santa Fe bridge, partially obscured under a white awning. Long-distance service within Mexico (5.50 pesos per min.) and to the U.S. (9 pesos per min.). Calls to El Paso 4 pesos per min. Also provides **fax** service and national and international UPS shipping (60 pesos). Open 24hr.

Airport: (tel. 33-09-34) about 17 km out on Rte. 45 (Carretera Panorámica). Catch the crowded "Ruta 4" bus and get off at the San Lorenzo Church; then board the "Ruta Aeropuerto" (1.50 pesos). **Aeroméxico** (tel. 16-66-21) flies to Chihuahua, Mexico City, and Monterrey.

Buses: Central Camionera, Blvd. Oscar Flores 4010 (tel. 10-72-97 or 10-74-04), north of the ProNaf center and next to the Río Grande mall. To get there, take the **Chihuahuenses** bus from the El Paso terminal to Juárez (US$5) or cram into the "Ruta 1A" at Av. Insurgentes and Francisco Villa (1.50 pesos). Station open 24hr. Services include so-so eateries and an overpriced *caseta*. **Chihuahuenses** (tel. 29-22-01 or 29-22-06), **Ominbus de México** (tel. 10-74-04), **Estrella Blanca,** and others offer service to Chihuahua (every ½hr., 5hr., 84 pesos), Guadalajara (8:30am and 9pm, 24hr., 358 pesos), Hermosillo (noon, 6pm, and 11pm, 10hr., 165 pesos), Mazatlán (12:30pm, 24hr., 289 pesos), Mexico City (7 per day, 26hr., 419 pesos), Nogales (5pm, 8hr., 116 pesos), and more. **Greyhound** serves the U.S., including Dallas (US$59), El Paso (every hr., 50min., US$5), Los Angeles (US$35), San Antonio (US$79), and others.

Trains: (tel. 12-31-88), Av. Eje Vial Juan Gabriel at Insurgentes. Walk down Lerdo until it ends and take Juan Gabriel. Service to Chihuahua and Mexico City.

Supermarket: Smart, López Mateos and Carretera Casas Grandes, a 10/15-min. ride from Av. Juárez. The **Mercado,** at Guerrero and López Mateos, sells groceries, clothes, furniture, and much, much more.

Laundromat: Lavasolas (tel. 12-54-61), Tlaxcala and 5 de Mayo. Twelve other locations in town. Washers 8.50 pesos (large), 7.40 pesos (small); dryers 8 pesos. Open Mon.-Sat. 9am-9pm, Sun. 8am-5pm.

Red Cross: (tel. 16-58-06), in the ProNaf Center next to the OK Corral. English spoken. Open 24hr.

Pharmacy: El Félix Super Farmacia (tel. 12-08-24), 16 de Septiembre and Noche Triste across from the cathedral. Turn right from Juárez. Open daily 8am-10pm.

Hospital: Hospital Latinoamericano: 250 N. López Mateos (tel. 16-14-67 or 16-14-15). English spoken. Open 24hr.

Emergency: Tel. 06.

Police: (tel. 15-15-51), Oro and 16 de Septiembre. **Transit Police:** Tel. 12-31-97 or 14-17-04. English spoken at both.

Post Office: Lerdo at Ignacio Peña. Open Mon.-Fri. 8am-5pm, Sat.-Sun. 9am-1pm. **Postal Code:** 32000.

Telephone Code: 16.

ACCOMMODATIONS

In Juárez, a typical cheap hotel meets only minimal standards and charges some of the highest "budget" rates in Mexico. Inexpensive lodging can be found along the main strip, Avenida Juárez; pricier places are located in ProNaf, around López Matelos and Avenida de las Américas.

Hotel del Río, Juárez 488 (tel. 12-37-76), is well worth the climb up the stairs. Large, clean rooms with comfortably thick beds, A/C, and color TVs. Friendly and informative staff. Room service and parking available. Singles, doubles, or tightly-squeezed triples 140 pesos.

Santa Fé (tel. 14-02-70, 14-03-82, or 14-09-41, fax 12-56-27), Lerdo Nte. 675 at Tlaxcala. Nicely furnished rooms with clean bathrooms are cooled by A/C. Color TVs in every room. Singles 155 pesos. Doubles, some with balcony, 175 pesos.

Plaza Continental, S. Lerdo 112 (tel. 15-00-84, 15-03-18, or 15-02-59). Located in the center of town, but less expensive than one might think. Spacious rooms with

TVs and small but clean bathrooms, central A/C, (free) *agua purificada* dispenser in the hall. Singles 132 pesos. Doubles 165 pesos. Triples 176 pesos.

FOOD

Eateries vary from clean, air-conditioned restaurants catering to tourists to roadside shacks with picnic tables and TVs blasting *telenovelas* (soap operas) in Spanish. Weak-stomached travelers should avoid shacks. The quest for food that will not cause a bacteriological mutiny in *gringo* bellies is long; the prudent will beat a path to Av. Juárez and Lerdo or to the ProNaf center. In general, *mariscos* (shellfish) are overpriced and less than fresh.

Cafetería El Coyote Inválido, Juárez 615(tel. 14-27-27), at Colón. We're still wandering about the name. A bustling, clean, American-style diner with heavenly A/C. Hamburgers 14.50 pesos, burritos 10.50 pesos, and an array of Mexican plates 15-30 pesos. Open 24hr.

Hotel Santa Fé Restaurante, (tel. 14-02-70), at the Hotel Santa Fe. Roll from here to there on the wheeled chairs, but don't expect too many dining companions to share the fun. Sample the enchiladas *de pollo* or club sandwiches (17 pesos) and wash 'em down with a beer (8 pesos). Open daily 7am-11pm.

Restaurant/Bar Juárez de Noche, Juárez 222 Nte. (tel. 15-20-02). Let the tunes of the *grupo norteño* lead you to their taco platter, which comes with salad, french fries, beans, and more (20 pesos). Irrigate it all with a nice cold beer (7 pesos).

SIGHTS AND ENTERTAINMENT

The **Aduana Fronteriza** (tel. 12-47-07) stands in *el centro*, where Juárez and 16 de Septiembre cross. Built in 1889 as a trading outpost and later used for customs, it now houses the **Museo Histórico de la Ex-Aduana,** which chronicles the region's history during the Mexican Revolution. Peeking inside the antique wagons is not frowned upon (museum open Tues.-Sun. 10am-6pm; free). The **Museo de Arte e Historia** (tel. 16-74-14), at the ProNaf center, exhibits Mexican art of the past and present (open Tues.-Sun. 11am-6pm; admission 1.50 pesos, students free). Also at the ProNaf center, the **Centro Artesanal** sells handmade goods at sky-high prices; it'd be crazy not to haggle here. The "Ruta 8" bus will take you from *el centro* to ProNaf for 1.50 pesos; a taxi charges 20 times as much. Your call.

The deforested **Parque Chamizal,** near the Córdova Bridge, is a good place to escape the noise of the city, if not the heat, and enjoy a picnic. The **Museo Arqueológico** (tel. 11-10-48 or 13-69-83), Av. Pellicer in Parque Chamizal, houses plastic facsimiles of pre-Hispanic sculptures as well as trilobite fossils, rocks, and bones (open Tues.-Sun. 11am-3pm, Sat.-Sun. 10am-6pm). The **Misión de Nuestra Señora de Guadalupe** (tel. 15-55-02), on 16 de Septiembre and Mariscal, is the oldest building on both sides of the border for kilometers roundabout. It features antique paintings and altars.

The *toro* and the *matador* battle in traditional bullfights on occasional evenings during the summer at the **Plaza Monumental de Toros** (tel. 13-16-56 or 13-11-82), Paseo Triunfo de la República and López Mateos. General admission seating starting at 25 pesos, 50 pesos in the shade. Children 12 and under are free. Call for dates and times. The **Lienzo Charro** (tel. 27-05-55), on Av. Charro off República, also hosts bullfights and a *charreada* (rodeo) on Sunday afternoons during the summer. At the western edge of town, the **Juárez Racetrack** (Galgódromo, tel. 25-53-94) rises from Vicente Guerrero. Dogs run Wednesday to Sunday at 7:30pm. Sunday matinees during the summer at 2:30pm. Horse racing can be seen only on closed circuit TV.

Juárez has so many bars that counting them could make you dizzy even before you start drinking. Many establishments are unsavory, and even some of the better ones can become dangerous; stick to the glutted strip along Av. Juárez or stay in the ProNaf area. On weekends, *gringos* swarm to Juárez in a 48-hour quest for fun, fights, fiestas, and inexpensive dental work. **Mr. Fog Bar,** Juárez Nte. 140 (tel. 14-29-48), is quite popular. A cartoon crocodile adorns the mirrored walls of this dark and reddish drinking establishment. Dance floor in back (beer 7 pesos, liquor 8 pesos; open Sun.-Thurs. 11am-2am, Fri.-Sat. 11am-3am). **Palacio Coin,** Juárez 130 (tel. 15-55-68), is another popular hangout. A diverse group comes to enjoy live bands, playing Fri.-Sun. night. (beer 5 pesos; open daily noon-4am).

■ Nuevo Casas Grandes

A three-and-a-half-hour ride through the expansive Chihuahuan Desert separates Juárez from its southern neighbor, Nuevo Casas Grandes. If you snag a window seat, a panorama of sparse shrubs, distant but awe-inspiring Sierra Madres, and the occasional *vaquero* steering his herd of cows will rush by. Eight kilometers southwest of Nuevo Casas Grandes, the ruins of Paquimé (pah-kee-MEH) are the remains of what was once the most important city in pre-Hispanic northern Mexico.

Orientation and Practical Information From the **Estrella Blanca** bus station on Obregón and 16 de Septiembre, walk one block down 16 de Septiembre to reach **Constitución,** the town's main drag. The center of town is where it intersects **Domínguez.** Taxis loiter on 16 de Septiembre at Constitución and on Minerva at Obregón. Everything listed below lies within the nine-block downtown area.

The **tourist office** is at Juárez Nte. 605, in the lobby of Motel Piñón (open 9am-1pm and 4-6pm). Change money at **Casa de Cambio California,** Constitución 207 (tel. 4-32-32; open Mon.-Fri. 9am-2pm and 3:30-7pm, Sat. 9am-2pm and 3:30-6pm). **Bancomer** (tel. 4-03-90), 16 de Septiembre at Constitución, has a 24-hour **ATM. LADATELs** cluster around the central square. **Estrella Blanca** and **Caballero Azteca** (tel. 4-07-80) **buses** run to Chihuahua (11 per day 6:30am-3:30pm, 5hr., 59 pesos), Cuauhtémoc (3 per day, 6½hr., 61 pesos), and Cd. Juárez (12 per day 6:30am-2:30am, 3½hr., 50 pesos). **Chihuahuenses** (tel. 4-14-75) run all the way to Hermosillo (6:30pm and midnight, 8hr., first-class 154 pesos, second-class 137 pesos), Monterrey (5, 11am, and 4pm, 16hr., 245 pesos), and Tijuana (3am, 2, 4, and 11pm, 16hr., first-class 293 pesos, second-class 257 pesos). Next door, **Ómnibus de México** (tel. 4-05-02) sends buses to Chihuahua (*vía corta* 7 per day 5am-10:30pm, 5hr., 59 pesos; *vía larga* 7 per day 4:30am-8pm, 8hr., 85 pesos). Stock up at **Hiperama** (tel. 9-21-04), Juárez at Minerva (open daily 9am-9pm). **Farmacia Benavides** (tel. 4-55-55) is on Obregón at 5 de Mayo (open daily 8am-10pm). Try the **Red Cross** (tel. 4-20-20) on Carranza at Constitución (open 24hr.). In an **emergency,** dial 06. The police await at Blanco and Madero, on the outskirts of town. The **post office** (tel. 4-20-16) is at 16 de Septiembre and Madero (open Mon.-Fri. 8am-6pm, Sat. 8am-1pm). **Postal Code:** 31700. **Telephone Code:** 169.

Accommodations and Food Accommodations with modern conveniences cluster on Constitución and on Juárez between 5 de Mayo and Jesus Urueta. **Motel Piñón,** Juárez Nte. 605 (tel. 4-06-55; fax 4-17-05), at 5 de Mayo next to the Dodge/Chrysler dealership. Guests sit cozily among the wooden carvings in the bar, discussing the pottery pieces that they have seen in the motel's own museum, and reliving the sensation of diving into the blue waters of the outdoor pool. Clean, carpeted rooms have cable TV and colorful bathrooms with strong hot water (singles 150 pesos; doubles 170 pesos; ask for a discount). At the **Hotel Juárez,** Obregón 110 (tel. 4-02-33), a block from the bus station, you can talk and talk and talk to the friendly, English-speaking owner, Mario. Show him your book and he'll mark down a point for us on his *Let's Go* vs. *Berkeley* scorecard. Mostly clean rooms are small and not incredibly well ventilated, but have ample lighting, a bed, and a passable shower (singles 45 pesos; doubles 55-65 pesos; ask for a discount).

The low tourist count means that the food is cheap and the nightlife soporific. **Restaurante Constantino** (tel. 4-10-05), Juárez at Minerva, accompanies its enchiladas *de pollo* with fresh bread, chips, and salsa (23 pesos). The *comida corrida* is only 20 pesos (open daily 7:30am-midnight). The clean and icily air-conditioned **Dinno's Pizza** (tel. 4-02-40), Minerva and Constitución, has jalapeño, cherry, pineapple, and coconut pizzas (small 26 pesos, medium 32, large 39; open daily 8am-11:30pm). Sit down in the simple, time-worn **Café de La Esquina** (tel 4-39-59), 5 de Mayo at Obregón, and watch some serious dominoes. *Bistec à la mexicana* is yours for 22 pesos, *huevos al gusto* for 12 pesos (open daily 7am-midnight). The few bars in town do not welcome women.

SIGHTS

The pre-Conquest city of **Paquimé (a.k.a. Casas Grandes)**, 8km southwest of Nuevo Casas Grandes, lay hidden underground for 600 years. Its architecture suggests that it grew out of two different cultures: its many-storied *pueblos* resemble those in the southwestern U.S., but other structures show the influence of central and southern Mexico. Between 1000 and 1200 CE, Paquimé was the most important agricultural and trading center in northern Mexico. The inhabitants kept parrots and turkeys in adobe pens and built indoor aqueducts and hidden cisterns to supply the *pueblos* in times of siege. They earned their livelihoods by farming and by trading sea shells brought from the Pacific coast. First exhumed in the early 1970s, Paquimé is now an archaeological zone administered by the Mexican government. Unfortunately, once it had been exposed for archaeologists and tourists, its high mud walls began to crumble. Visitors should avoid eroding the thin walls.

There are three principal maze-like mounds of ruins in Paquimé that form a striking scene with the dusty mountains and ice-blue sky as the backdrop. It's easy to tell the parts that have been restored (the darker, more solid walls) from the original (cracked-looking) walls, which are located primarily in the mound to the far right. Among the ruins lie a partially excavated **market** as well as a **ball court.** The short and narrow T-shaped doors allowed inhabitants to defend themselves by pummeling unwanted visitors as they lowered their heads to enter. Look for the **House of the Macaws,** the **House of Skulls,** and the **Cross Monument,** which points to the four cardinal directions. The **museum** (tel. 2-40-37) adjacent to the site is a terrific architectural achievement. Designed to blend in with the ruins and to have a low impact on the environment, the museum displays artifacts that have been found at Casas Grandes, with an emphasis on the many pieces of polychrome pottery. Southwestern U.S. history and natural history are foci of the "Sala de las Culturas," which features a large-scale model of Mesa Verde. A cafeteria, central patio with fountains, A/V room, gift shop, and a path directly out to the ruins round out the circular stone, handicapped-accessible structure (museum and site open roughly 10am-5pm; admission 10 pesos, free Sun.).

On summer afternoons, the dry and shadeless ruins can become a blazing inferno, as temperatures near or exceed 100°F. Be sure to bring sun protection, a broad-brimmed hat (cheap *sombreros* are available in town), and, most importantly, a gigantic bottle of water to quench your thirst. Some information on the site may be obtained at **Pueblo Viejo,** a store in the town square at Independencia and Juárez, or at the Motel Piñon, back in Nuevo Casas Grandes. As always, be wary: wandering the area alone is not a wise idea.

Getting There: From Casas Grandes, take the light yellow **municipal bus** at the corner of Constitución and 16 de Septiembre (1 per hr., 10min., 1.50 pesos). Get off by the main plaza, cross the street, and continue straight down a dirt road for ten minutes. Follow the path as it turns right, then turn left at the next intersection. You have now arrived. Almost any **taxi** driver will take you to the site and walk around with you for about 60 pesos per hour.

NORTHWEST MEXICO

■ Chihuahua

The capital of the Republic's largest state, Chihuahua (pop. 800,000) is the vibrant, historically rich mecca of Northern Mexico. Exposed to the sandstorms of Mexico's vast northern desert, the city may seem like little more than a far-flung outpost of the civilization to the south. This seclusion convinced Pancho Villa to establish the head-quarters of his revolutionary División del Norte here. During the conflict, his band of cowboys, bandits, and vagabonds staged attacks against the Porfiriato, streaming down from Chihuahua and assaulting social inequities. Quinta Luz, Villa's sprawling colonial home, shines as the city's major attraction.

The peoples who converge on Chihuahua and the surrounding area are as diverse as the land itself. Mennonites came here in flocks in the 1920s, attracted by the boun-tiful pastures. Today, they maintain their seclusion in the town of Cuauhtémoc and in other agricultural communities nearby. Equally secluded but quite different, the *indí-gena* Tarahumara people live isolated in the nearby Sierra Madres, venturing into the city only on market day to sell handmade crafts.

ORIENTATION

¡Ay! Chihuahua sprawls in every direction. Skewered by Rte. 45 (the Pan American Highway), the city serves as an important transportation hub for northern Mexico. Trains arrive at the **Estación Central de los FFNN,** just north of downtown. Trains headed for Los Mochis and Creel via the Barrancas del Cobre leave from the **Chihua-hua al Pacífico** station, south of the city center off Ocampo, two blocks from 20 de Noviembre. To shorten the 20-minute walk to *el centro,* hop on one of the public buses (1.50 pesos) that run up and down Ocampo to Libertad; alternatively, snag a cab (about 15 pesos), but set the price before you step in. From the bus station, a municipal bus (1.50 pesos) will take you to the cathedral.

Libertad is a pedestrian-only shopping arcade between **Independencia** and **Guer-rero.** Two other main streets, **Victoria** and **Juárez,** run parallel to Libertad. **Av. Ocampo** crosses Juárez one block past the cathedral. Starting with Calle 2 at Av. Inde-pendencia, parallel streets *(calles)* have ascending even numbers to the south and odd numbers to the north. *Avenidas* running north-south are named. Don't let Chi-huahua's sheer size intimidate you; while the city is large, most sights are within walk-ing distance from the cathedral. Budget hotels and restaurants cluster on the streets behind the cathedral. With the exception of Av. Victoria, which perpetually cele-brates victory with the flashing lights of bars and discos, the streets in Chihuahua are poorly illuminated. Women should avoid walking alone after dark.

PRACTICAL INFORMATION

Tourist Office: (tel. 10-10-77; fax 16-00-32), in the Palacio del Gobierno, across from the Plaza Hidalgo. Wonderfully helpful, English-speaking staff. Indispensable maps and brochures. Open Mon.-Fri. 9am-7pm, Sat. 9am-1pm, Sun. 10am-2pm.

Currency Exchange: BanPaís (tel. 16-16-59), on Victoria one block from the cathe-dral. No exchange fee for traveler's checks. Open Mon.-Fri. 9am-1:30pm. **Hotel San Francisco** (tel. 16-75-50), across the street, has 24-hr. exchange. **ATMs** near the lobbies of all the tall banks downtown near the *zócalo.*

American Express: Vicente Guerrero 1207 (tel. 15-58-58), past Allende, where Guerrero curves to become Bolívar. Open Mon.-Fri. 9am-6pm, Sat. 9am-noon.

Telephones: Silver **LADATELs** gleam in the sun all over the *zócalo.* Long distance service available in expensive hotels and the plaza, in front of the cathedral.

Telegrams: Opposite the post office, in the Palacio Federal (tel. 10-47-83). Open Mon.-Fri. 9am-7pm, Sat. 9am-4pm, Sun. 9am-noon.

Airport: (tel. 20-51-04), 14km from town. **Aerolitoral,** Victoria 106 (tel. 20-83-30). **Aeroméxico,** Victoria 106 (tel. 20-09-18). **Aerovías de México,** Victoria 116 (tel. 35-17-97). **Transportes Aéreos Ejecutivos,** Coronado 421 (tel. 20-03-76). All open Mon.-Fri. 9am-6:30pm. "Aeropuerto" buses get you there from Ocampo. Buses heading downtown wait outside of the baggage area.

Buses: The main station (tel. 20-22-86) is a 20-min. ride on the "Central Camionera" bus from Ocampo and Victoria. **Ómnibus de México** (tel. 20-15-80) sends its luxurious fleet to Aguascalientes (5:30, 7, and 10:30pm, 14hr., 240 pesos), Casas Grandes (7 per day 7:30am-6:30pm, 5hr., 59 pesos), Durango (11:30am, 6, 8:30, and 11pm, 9hr., 148 pesos), Guadalajara (2:40am, 2:30, 7, and 9pm, 17hr., 300 pesos), Matamoros (2:40am and 9:30pm, 18hr., 283 pesos), Mexico City (*local* 4:30 and 9:30pm, 22hr.; direct 4:30, 9, and 10pm, 18hr., 272 pesos), Monterrey (6, 9:30, and 11pm, 12hr., 199 pesos), Querétaro (5 per day, 18hr., 314 pesos), Saltillo (2:40am, 6:30, and 9:30pm, 18hr., 181 pesos), and San Luis Potosí (6 per day 4:50am-9pm, 254 pesos). **Transportes Caballero Azteca** (tel. 29-02-42) sends buses to Hermosillo (2, 7:30, and 10pm, 14hr., 217 pesos), Nogales (8am, 12, and 9pm, 12hr., 180 pesos), Tijuana (8, 11am, 6:30, and 10pm, 22hr., 367 pesos), and Zacatecas (14 per day 6am-11pm, 12hr., 209 pesos). **Transportes Chihuahuenses** (tel. 29-02-42) sends buses daily to Cd. Juárez (every hr. until 9pm, 5hr., 92 pesos), Mazatlán (11:15am and 5:45pm, 18hr., 224 pesos). **Turismos Rápidos Cuauhtémoc-Anáhuac** (tel. 10-44-33) has service to Cuauhtémoc (every 30min. 7am-8pm, 1½hr., 20 pesos). **Estrella Blanca** has a slightly older fleet of buses that chugs to nearly all of the above cities for lower prices but requires more travel time.

Trains: FFCC Chihuahua al Pacífico (tel. 15-77-56; fax 10-90-59), the southern station near Quinta Luz. Walk south on Ocampo, turn right at 20 de Noviembre and left on Calle 24, at the end of the enormous prison. It's two blocks down. *Primera* trains leave at 7am for Creel (4½hr., 110 pesos) and Los Mochis (14hr., 243 pesos). *Segunda* trains leave at 8am for Creel (24 pesos) and Los Mochis (52 pesos). Tickets purchased on the train are 25% more expensive. Children travel at half-price. Tickets sold Mon.-Fri. 9am-2pm, Sat. 9am-10am. Only cash accepted. Two stopovers are permitted at an extra cost of 15%. The northern station, **FFCC Nacionales de México,** is on Av. Tecnológico.

Car Rental: Hertz, Av. Revolución 514 (tel. 16-64-73), at José Nari Santos. VW Beetle with insurance and free mileage, 198 pesos per day.

Supermarket: El Fénix, Libertad 505 (tel. 10-26-21). Open daily 9am-9pm.

Red Cross: Calle 24 and Revolución (tel. 11-22-11). Open 24hr.

Pharmacy: Farmacia Mendoza, Calle Aldama 1901 (tel. 16-44-14), at Calle 19. Away from the cathedral past Plaza de Hidalgo. Open 24hr.

Hospital: Hospital General, Revolución and Colón (tel. 16-69-12 or -32), in Colonia Centro. **Clínica del Centro,** Ojinaga 816 (tel. 16-58-18 or -85).

Police: (tel. 13-30-98), Av. Homero across from the Ford plant, at the exit to Juárez.

Post Office: (tel. 37-12-00). In the Palacio Federal on Libertad, between Guerrero and Carranza. Open Mon.-Fri. 8am-7pm, Sat. 9am-1pm. **Postal Code:** 31000.

Telephone Code: 14.

ACCOMMODATIONS

Hotels in Chihuahua are like the city itself—charm shines through the grit. Economical hotels lie between Victoria and Juárez in the area behind the cathedral.

Hotel del Pacífico, Aldama 1911 (tel. 10-59-13), at Calle 21, a few blocks from the Palacio de Gobierno. A great bargain. Although the lobby is dark and musty, the clean rooms have A/C, large bathrooms, and decent foam mattresses with cement bases. Restaurant. Parking available. Singles 50 pesos. Doubles 60 pesos. Triples 70 pesos. Add 5 pesos for TV.

Hotel Apolo (tel. 16-11-00 or -01; fax 16-11-02), Juárez at Carranza, in the center. A step up in price—and amenities. Dark but majestic lobby with sculptures, chandeliers, and paintings. All the clean and bright rooms have A/C and nice tiled bathrooms; those on the 3rd and 4th floors come with color TVs. Cafeteria, bar, and parking. Singles 100 pesos. Doubles 110 pesos. Discounts for large groups.

Hotel San Juan, Victoria 823 (tel. 10-00-35 and -36), one block down Victoria from the cathedral, on your right. Ravenous, he could wait no longer. After dropping his bags on the weathered wooden floor of his room and stopping in the small, clean bathroom, Don Juan took a cursory glance at the comfortable bed, made a call on the ancient phone, and rushed out through the courtyard, heading for the cheesy bar from which he could hear the strains of live *mariachi* music. Central A/C. Singles 32 pesos. Doubles 42 pesos. Add 10 pesos for color TV.

Nuevo Hotel Reforma, Victoria 809 (tel. 10-68-48; fax 16-08-35). Unique and charming architecture. The bug-free rooms have fans, flabby beds, and clean tile bathrooms. Singles 42 pesos. Doubles 45 pesos. Add 8 pesos for TV.

FOOD

Eateries in Chihuahua are not geared toward tourists. Some of the best meals can be found in small *cantinas,* where bands serenade drunken (and often rowdy) men.

Rostería Los Pollos (tel. 10-59-77), Aldama near Allende. Cafeteria-style dining at its best and brightest. Plastic booths, mirrored walls, A/C, and a pleasant atmosphere spice up your excellent *pollo en mole* with rice and tortillas (12 pesos). To finish it off, have some sweet *arroz con leche* (5 pesos). Open 9am-8pm.

Dino's Pizza, Manuel Doblado 301 (tel. 16-57-07), across from the Santa Regina. International crowd. Quaint decor and delectable pizza (4 different sizes: 23, 30, 38, and 44 pesos). The special (pizza, spaghetti, and salad) serves 5-6 people (69 pesos). Open 8:30am-midnight.

Mi Café (tel. 10-12-38), Victoria at Calle 10, across from Hotel San Juan. Put on your sunglasses to enter this bright, 50s-style diner with melon-colored vinyl booths and an orange-and-white checkered ceiling. A 22-peso order of chicken comes with bread, soup, rice, potatoes, and dessert—a huge meal. *Comida corrida* 19 pesos. Breakfast platter 18 pesos. Open daily 9am-midnight.

El Delfín del Norte (tel. 16-98-99), Juárez 301 at Calle 3. Funky shell lamps illuminate fillet of fish *a la italiana* (in oyster sauce, 22 pesos), *pulpo en su tinta* (octopus in its ink), and *calamares* (squid, 30 pesos). Open daily noon-midnight.

Restaurant-Bar Degá (tel. 16-77-70), at Hotel San Francisco, near the *zócalo.* Offers a rare (if pricey) chance at a vegetarian meal. The *plato vegetariano* (33 pesos) includes vegetarian soup, a soy steak, avocado, and white rice; the *ceviche vegetariano* (18 pesos) has mushrooms and olive oil. Fresh carrot, papaya, or grapefruit juice 10 pesos. Open 7am-10:30pm.

SIGHTS AND ENTERTAINMENT

The stately and regal 19th-century **Palacio de Gobierno** stands in the center of Chihuahua on Aldama. Inside, Aarón Piña Moratell's beautiful murals tell the story of Chihuahua. Look for a nude Emiliano Zapata. A few blocks from the palace, on Victoria and Calle 2, is the giant **cathedral**. While construction began in 1725, the church was actually finished more than a century later in 1826. The stone façade displays unique and creative talent from the Baroque period.

The area southwest of the *zócalo* offers an excellent leafy retreat from downtown. At **Quinta Luz,** also called **Museo de la Revolución** (Pancho Villa's house; tel. 16-29-58), visitors can relive the turbulence of the revolution by looking through an extensive collection of documents and photographs, paintings of Señor Villa, the bullet-ridden Dodge in which he was assassinated, his household furnishings, and his vast collection of rifles and machine guns (still enough to outfit a small army). To reach Quinta Luz, hike 1.5km south on Ocampo, turn left on 20 de Noviembre, and go two blocks to Calle 10 and Méndez. Turn right, and Villa's house is two blocks down (open daily 9am-1pm and 3-7pm; admission 5 pesos).

On the way to the Villa household is another, equally worthy museum: the **Quinta Gameros Centro Cultural Universitario,** also called the **Museo Regional de Chihuahua** (tel. 10-54-74). This amazing architectural feat, on the corner of Calle 4 and Paseo Bolívar, is one of the more stunning mansions in Mexico. The aristocrat who had it built, mining engineer Don Manuel Gameros, never lived in it—the Revolution drove him to El Paso, Texas. The house was seized by revolutionaries and at one point served as Pancho Villa's barracks. Some astounding art nouveau furniture and rooms now wow observers; look for the 3m-high toilet and the beautiful mahogany dining room woodwork. Upstairs, local painters exhibit their works (open Tues.-Sun. 10am-2pm and 4-7pm; admission 7 pesos, children 3.50 pesos).

Back in *el centro,* the basement of the cathedral hides the **Museo de Arte Sacro** (tel. 10-38-77), Libertad and Calle 2. Pastoral religious paintings from the 18th century mingle with photos and portraits from the Pope's most recent visit to Chihuahua (open Mon.-Fri. 10am-2pm and 4-6pm; admission 5 pesos, students and children 3 pesos). For those craving more secular pleasures, the recently opened **Museo de Arte Contemporáneo** (tel. 29-33-00, ext. 3700), at Carranza and Aldama across from the Palacio del Gobierno, has a formidable collection of modern art. Sebastián's geometrical sculptures and Diego Rivera's sketch of a two-headed man/beast are among the highlights (open Tues.-Sun. 10am-8pm; admission 5 pesos, students and teachers 3 pesos; free Wed.).

At night, catch a flick at **Cinepolis** (tel. 17-52-22), Vallarta at Zaragoza. Its fourteen screens show movies 3 to 9:30pm (10 pesos, Wed. half-price). To get there, hop on a "Cerro de la Cruz" bus in front of the Héroes de la Revolución building, in the *centro* (every 8min. until 9:30pm, 15min., 1.50 pesos). If the buses have stopped running, you'll have to take a 15-peso cab back. Afterwards, you can discuss the film at one of the many cafés in the center of town. **Café Calicanto,** Aldama 411 (tel. 10-44-52), serves snacks and a wide selection of coffees and beers. There is live music on weekends (open Sun.-Thurs. 4pm-midnight, Fri.-Sat. 5pm-3am). Nightclubs tend to be far away from the center, but taxis will get you there. **Quinto Sofía,** in front of Lerdo Park, brings out a twentysomething crowd to listen to live Spanish rock (beers 9 pesos; cover 10 pesos after 10:30pm). A somewhat older crowd flocks to **Old Town,** Juárez 3331 (tel. 10-32-71), between Colón and Calle 39. On weekends, there is a wild 20-minute rodeo show at midnight and country music after that (cover Fri.-Sat. 25 pesos; open Thurs. 9pm-1am, Fri.-Sat. 9pm-2:30am).

■ Cuauhtémoc Mennonite Colony

Among the masses of Mexican businesspeople, street vendors, and families around Cuauhtémoc's *zócalo,* a blond-haired, blue-eyed Caucasian in overalls or a long black dress will occasionally amble by—hardly a typical sight in Northwest Mexico. But not surprising in Cuauhtémoc, home to 40,000-60,000 Mennonites (out of a total population of 300,000). The Mennonites are a pacifist religious group founded in the 16th century in lower Germany. After being expelled from virtually every country in Europe due to their refusal to serve in their military and their steadfast determination to educate their children privately, a large number of Mennonites settled in the agricultural fields just outside Cuauhtémoc. The hard-working, almost compulsively clean group of Mennonites that now inhabits the area is renowned for the cheese that they produce. Most Mennonites speak Low German, an archaic 17th-century dialect that even those fluent in High (modern) German would not understand. Although many Cuauhtémoc Mennonites have abandoned some of the stricter restrictions, such as the prohibition to use electricity, traditional dress is still standard: wide-brimmed, white hats and long, flowered dresses for women, tall hats and overalls for men.

Orientation and Practical Information Cuauhtémoc lies midway between Creel and Chihuahua, a two- to three-hour bus ride from each. The highway into Cuauhtémoc from Chihuahua continues past the city and into the **Mennonite area,** organized in small communities called *campos.* Each *campo* has a number and is laid out in an orderly manner, with a main street, several farms, a creamery, a church, and a school. *Campos* are organized by number: on the left, numbers start at one and go up; on the right they start in the mid-20s and count down, and after a certain point, the field numbers switch to the 100s. The center of Cuauhtémoc is at the beginning of the parallel numbered streets: Melgar (Calle 1), Calle 2, and Calle 3. The cross-streets Morelos and Allende delineate the *zócalo* with Melgar and Calle 2.

Banca Serfín, (tel. 2-63-33), Melgar at Allende, has an **ATM** (open Mon.-Sat. 9am-1:30pm). **LADATEL phones** surround the *zócalo* and dot the downtown area. Call friends back home at **Servicio Técnico García,** Allende at Calle 9 (open Mon.-Sat. 9am-1pm and 3-7pm). The **Estrella Blanca bus station** (tel. 2-10-18), Allende at Calle 9, runs buses to Basaseachi (8am, 12:30, and 4:30pm, 5hr., 47 pesos), Casas Grandes (9:30pm, midnight, and 6am, 5hr., 61 pesos), Chihuahua (every 30min., 1½hr., 20 pesos), Creel (every 2hr. 7:30am-7:30pm, 3½hr., 33 pesos), Hermosillo (8am, 12hr., 152 pesos), and Cd. Juárez (9:30am, noon, and 6pm, 9hr., 100 pesos). The **Centro Comercial,** Allende and Calle 3, across from the *zócalo,* is a big-time **supermarket** (open Mon.-Fri. 9am-8pm, Sat.-Sun. 9am-9pm). **Farmacia Cuauhtémoc** (tel. 2-08-77) is on Allende between Calles 7 and 9 (open Mon.-Sat. 9am-9pm, Sun. 10am-2pm). The **police** can be reached at 2-45-99. The **post office** (tel. 2-03-14) is on Calle 4 and Guerrero (open Mon.-Fri. 8am-6pm, Sun. 9am-1pm).

Accommodations The best place to stay in Cuauhtémoc, hands down, is the **Motel Gasthaus,** the only Mennonite hotel, smack in the middle of the Mennonite area on the km13 marker. The place sparkles with an otherworldly cleanliness; you'll see your reflection in the spotless floors and immaculate walls. The rooms smell of roses, the beds are comfortable, and the bathrooms absolutely irreproachable (singles 70-75 pesos; doubles 84 pesos; huge suites with kitchen US$20-25). If you must stay in the city, there are a only few options. The **Hotel Gran Visión,** on Allende between Calles 7 and 9, across from the bus station, offers tidy, smallish rooms with A/C, TV, and phones (singles 60 pesos; doubles 70 pesos).

Food If you're here to sample Mennonite culture, you might as well get out of the dirty city and into the ultra-clean kitchen of a Mennonite restaurant. Most have sinks with hand soap *outside* the bathroom because they're used so much. A few restaurants line the main highway through the *campos*—try the **Travelers Restaurant** (tel. 2-64-70), between *Campo* 3-B and *Campo* 19. Traditional Mennonite foods are very rich and very tasty: the *empanadas de requesón* (dough filled with Mennonite cottage cheese, pierogi-like, and covered with cream sauce, 16 pesos) and *fideos con crema* (noodles with ham or sausage, also drowned in cream sauce, 15 pesos) are not exceptions. Eat here more than twice, however, and your cholesterol count may hit quadruple digits (open daily 9am-9pm). In the city, **El Den,** Allende at Calle 2 (tel. 2-38-43) has cafeteria-style service that includes *comida corrida* (23 pesos) and an excellent vegetarian platter (15 pesos; open daily 7am-10:30pm).

Sights and Entertainment There are a handful of ways to explore the Mennonite communities of Cuauhtémoc. **Public buses** head into the area (every hr., 20min., 6 pesos), letting passengers off anywhere along the way. Hitchhiking is extremely easy on and off the main highway, but as usual not recommended by *Let's Go.* The owner of **Motel Gasthaus** will pick up four people from the city for roughly 30 pesos and start a tour from there. He will also take a few people around in his car or pickup for about 50 pesos per person for the entire day, less for shorter excursions. Tours typically include a look inside an authentic Mennonite home, a tour of a cheese factory and a machinery plant, and a meal (at your expense) at a Mennonite restaurant, though the actual sights covered on a tour are up to you. The Mennonite father-and-son team **Cumbres Friesen** also offers half-day tours (US$15 per person).

If you want to check out the Mennonite colony on your own, you'll need a car to get from place to place. To see a Mennonite cheese factory in action, take a left at the 2-B/22 sign and follow the road heading down into the village. After passing a school and church (only open Sun.) on your left, take a right into the **Quesería América,** one of the 20-25 cheese factories in the 80 or so Mennonite villages in the area. Keep your eyes open for the old-fashioned timecards and the four vats in which the cheese is processed: the first one you see is actually the last stage in the process, in which a cottage-cheese-like mixture is pressed, salted, and allowed to sit for 12 hours. Cool off in the refrigeration rooms, where milk-cartoning machines and cheese waiting to be shipped are kept. You'll encounter some stares and friendly offers to buy cheese or sweets in the lobby. The workers tend to be very shy, and some don't speak Spanish (never mind English!). Make sure you visit in the morning, when the cheese is actually made.

To see a genuine **Mennonite household,** take a left at the "Hotel La Estancia" sign at *Campo* 6A. Follow the road about 2km, then take a right down another road a little ways. You'll see a white house with a blue stripe around the bottom, surrounded by a white picket fence and tall trees; it's home to the **familia Guenther.** The friendly, Spanish-speaking family will show you their huge but stark kitchen with its jam-filled pantry, their living room, and their special guest room with a valuable wooden chair. Big families are standard among the Mennonites, and the Guenthers are no exception: Mrs. Guenther's 12 children all live nearby. After taking you on a tour of the house, Mrs. Guenther will offer her traditional Mennonite knitted crafts for sale. Outside, scope out the horizon for the **radio tower,** through which Mennonites communicated before they succumbed to that modern luxury, telephones. Before, they all had walkie-talkies. 10-4 *familia* Guenther.

■ Creel

High amid the peaks of the Sierra Madres and lodged among pine forests, log cabins, and rolling hills and valleys, the small village of Creel (pop. 5,000, altitude 2340m) welcomes travelers with natural beauty, human warmth, and refreshing, mountain-pine air. The village in many ways resembles a frontier town of the late 1800s: smoke billows from the chimneys of the humble but picturesque huts to counter the chilly climate; the train rumbles through the middle of town at least twice a day; and horses, pigs, and cows are as common to Creel's streets as the rugged, cowboy-hat-wearing villagers to whom they sometimes belong. As you make your way up to Creel from the south, the sweltering Chihuahuan desert gives way to a land of spectacular gorges, looming peaks, and cool nights.

Creel is perhaps most popular as a base from which to explore the stunning Copper Canyon. Although tourism to the town has increased of late, it hasn't damaged the unique ambience of the town nor substantially altered the lives of the Tarahumara Indians, 50,000 of whom live in the Sierra Tarahumara mountains surrounding the town. Of Mexico's many *indígena* groups, the Tarahumara have best warded off modern Mexican culture, living in isolated caves and wooden houses and resisting all efforts to settle them in villages. Well adapted to their rugged environment, the Tarahumara construct plows from the limbs of oak trees and are skilled in the preparation of 200 species of edible plants. They are famous for their non-stop long-distance sacred footraces, which last up to 72 hours. Tarahumara pine-needle baskets, blankets, figurines, and violins are sold throughout town.

While many Tarahumara come to Creel to sell their crafts or pick up supplies, they greatly value their seclusion and tend to shy away from contact with tourists. If you pass Tarahumara cave dwellings, look at the caves from the road, but don't take their obvious accessibility as an invitation to approach more closely or to walk in and have a look-see, and refrain from taking photographs. The countryside around Creel is also home to a number of other *indígena* groups, including the Pima in the northwest, the Northern Tepehuan to the south, and the Guarojio to the west.

ORIENTATION AND PRACTICAL INFORMATION

The **train station** is located just northwest of the *zócalo,* and the **bus station** is right across the tracks and farther north. To reach the *zócalo,* walk one block along the tracks in the direction of Los Mochis and turn left. The main street, **Mateos,** runs parallel to the trains on the opposite side of the *zócalo.* Street numbers go up to the right and down to the left as you turn onto Mateos from the tracks. **Chapultepec,** farther north, runs parallel to Mateos and up to the tracks.

Tourist Information: Artesanías Misión (tel. 6-01-50), on the north side of the *zócalo*. Not an official tourist office, but the best source of information on Creel and the surrounding area. Sells books about the Tarahumara, crafts, and maps (12-35 pesos). The mission supports the Tarahumara's cultural development, and the local hospital receives store profits. English spoken. Open Mon.-Sat. 9:30am-1pm and 3-6pm, Sun. 9:30am-1pm.

Currency Exchange: Banca Serfín (tel. 6-02-50), next door to the Misión. Dollars exchanged 10am-1pm. Open Mon.-Fri. 9am-1:30pm.

Telephones: No **LADATELs** in town, but black coin-operated phones all around; there's one at **Restaurante Todo Rico (All-Rich),** López Mateos 37 (tel. 6-02-05), at Chapultepec. Long-distance service also available at the **Papelería de Todo,** Mateos 30 (tel. 6-01-22 or 6-02-22; fax 6-02-12). Open daily 9am-8pm.

Telegrams: In the same building as the post office. Open Mon.-Fri. 9am-4pm.

Buses: Estrella Blanca (tel. 6-00-73), in a small white-and-green building across the tracks from the *zócalo*. To Chihuahua (7 per day, 5hr., 66 pesos) via Bolonya (45min., 6 pesos), San Juanito (1½hr., 13 pesos), La Junta (2hr., 31 pesos), and Cuauhtémoc (3hr., 40 pesos). From the Restaurant Herradero at Mateos 39, **canyon buses** (tel. 6-02-79 or -30) leave for Batopilas (Tues., Thurs., and Sat. 7:15am, 8hr., 60 pesos; return-trip leaves Batopilas at 4am).

Trains: Av. Tarahumara 57 (tel. 6-00-15), right in town on the tracks—you can't miss it. Trains leave daily for Chihuahua (first 3:15pm, 6hr., 110 pesos; second 5pm, 7hr., 23 pesos) and Los Mochis (first 12:25pm, 9hr., 133 pesos; second 2pm, 10hr., 28 pesos). Ride out to the Divisadero station at Barrancas del Cobre on the Los Mochis bound train (first 12:25pm, 1½hr., 37 pesos; second 2pm, 1½hr., 5 pesos). Tickets go on sale at 11:30am for the first-class train to Los Mochis and a half-hour before departure time for other trains. Some trains might be "full," in which case you should scramble on quickly and aggressively when the train arrives and purchase a ticket on board. Never count on a train leaving on schedule or even leaving at all (station open Mon.-Fri. 10am-4pm, Sat. 10am-2pm).

Bicycle Rental: Expediciones Umarike, López Mateos 9, next to Casa de Huéspedes Margarita. Rents bikes (65 pesos per day, ½ day 40 pesos, 12 pesos per hr.), helmet and gloves (15 pesos); sells road and trail maps (12 pesos).

Market: Albarrotes Pérez, on Mateos next to Cabañas Bertis. Fruit, vegetables, and a large selection of water. Open daily 9am-9pm.

Laundromat: Lavandería Veno, Francisco Villa 112 (tel. 6-01-39). Across the tracks from the police, near the bus station. 15 pesos per load for wash and dry. Bring your load by 6pm if you want same-day service. Open daily 9am-8pm.

Pharmacy: Farmacia Rodríguez, Mateos 43 (tel. 6-00-52). Open Mon.-Sat. 9am-2pm and 3:30-9pm, Sun. 10am-1pm.

Medical Services: Clínica Santa Teresita (tel. 6-01-05), on Calle Parroquia at the end of the street, two blocks from Mateos. Little English spoken. Open Mon.-Fri. 10am-1pm and 3-5pm, Sat. 10am-1pm. Open for emergencies 24hr.

Police: (tel. 6-00-81), in the Presidencia Seccional, on the south side of the *zócalo*.

Post Office: (tel. 6-02-58), in the Presidencia Seccional, on the south side of the *zócalo*. Open Mon.-Fri. 9am-4pm. **Postal Code:** 33200.

Telephone Code: 145.

ACCOMMODATIONS AND CAMPING

Due to Creel's flourishing popularity, the number of hotels has multiplied and competition for tourists' pesos has become intense. Prices are often negotiable during low season, and budget rooms are never hard to find.

Margarita's Casa de Huéspedes, Mateos 11 (tel. 6-00-45), across from the *zócalo*. An international backpacker's mecca. You'll have no trouble finding it—a young emissary meets every train and bus to lead you to the house, where you mingle with Margarita's family, friends, and guests, who come from every corner of the globe. Make it clear that you want to go to the *casa*, not the hotel. Freshly renovated rooms are spacious and beautifully furnished with floor tiles and pine furniture. To top it all off, prices include two home-cooked meals. English-speaking staff. Tours offered (see Sights and Entertainment below). Singles 100 pesos. Doubles 120 pesos. Bed in shared rooms 20-30 pesos. A spot on the floor costs just 10 pesos. Prices are negotiable, and you may be able to work for room and board.

Cabañas Bertis, López Mateos 31 (tel. 6-00-86). Log cabin feel with paneled walls, thick wool blankets, and a fireplace or wood stove in each abode. A/C and heater. Tours offered. Singles 50 pesos. Doubles 120 pesos. Triples 150 pesos.

Pensión Creel, Mateos 61 (tel. 6-00-71; fax 6-02-00). Walk down Mateos away from the *zócalo*. Budget rooms available in the *hacienda*, farther from downtown near the trails and woods. Boasts a fully equipped kitchen, a large common room with a roaring fireplace and magazine shelf, and shared bathrooms. Complimentary bus service transports you to the *hacienda*, though it is within walking distance. Prices range from 45 pesos (if you have your own sleeping bag) to 90 pesos (with continental breakfast). French and English spoken.

Hotel Korachi (tel. 6-02-07), across the tracks from the train station. A wanna-be hunting lodge. Clean bedrooms with dark, wood-paneled walls with comfy beds, and wood and gas heaters in the bathroom. Singles 50 pesos. Doubles 80 pesos. Strange but clean *cabañas* with animal skins on the walls sit under shady trees and include private bath and wood supply. Singles 80 pesos. Doubles 100 pesos.

For those who'd rather immerse themselves in nature, the campground and lodges around Lago Arareko are the way to go. The campground (10 pesos per night per head) is on the northwestern shore, on a hill overlooking the lake. The site sports 31 barbecue and fire pits, 12 latrines, hot showers, and picnic areas. The **Segorachi Cabin** fits 16, contains a living room, kitchen, fireplace, and grill; guests are pampered with a laundry service and a complimentary boat for use on the lake. The **Batosarachi Lodge,** on the southeast corner of this vast body of water, houses up to 50 in the three Tarahumara-style cabins (each has bunk beds, a common room, heaters, and hot water). At both lakes, guests can cook their own meals or let themselves be served. The lake is 8km from town, or a 5-minute drive.

FOOD

There are several inexpensive restaurants in town with friendly atmospheres and good, home-cooked fare. Picnicking spots lie on the quiet hillsides outside town.

La Cabaña, Mateos 36 (tel. 6-00-68), south of the *zócalo*. You can almost hear the birds chirping and the sap dripping as you recline in one of the pinewood stalls. Take in the stuffed game, the landscape drawings, and a 25-peso platter of seafood. Big burritos 5 pesos. Open daily 8am-10pm.

Jorge's, Francisco Villa at Cristo Rey, south of the bus station. If thinking about the 80s leaves you hollow, don't fret; this is one place where you'll never have to ask "Where's the beef?" The super burgers (13 pesos) and enchiladas (16 pesos) practically burst at the seams with sizzling meat. Open daily 8am-11pm.

Restaurante Todo Rico (All-Rich), López Mateos 37 (tel. 6-02-05), at Chapultepec. Lip-smacking good food served up in a bright, clean, and friendly atmosphere. *Comida corrida* is a mere 12 pesos. Try the *caldo de oso* (fish, not bear soup) for 20 pesos, or the tuna salad (15 pesos). Open daily 7:30am-11:30pm.

Restaurante Veronica, Mateos 34. This simple joint's a local favorite. Enjoy *carne asada con papas* (roasted meat with potatoes) for 20 pesos, or the *comida corrida* for 12 pesos. Open daily 7:30am-11pm.

SIGHTS AND ENTERTAINMENT

The **Casa de las Artesanías del Estado de Chihuahua** is on Avenida Ferrocaril 178 (tel. 6-00-80), in the old railroad station. There, local and Tarahumara arts, crafts, and a random assortment of historical relics are on display. But what steals the show is the mummy in the back room, which some Tarahumara claim as a relative and upon which local schoolchildren periodically sprinkle flowers (open Tues.-Sat. 9am-1pm and 3-7pm, Sun. 9am-1pm).

At night, a local *cantina* with a touch of class is **Laylo's Lounge and Bar,** inside **El Caballo Bayo** restaurant and hotel, López Mateos 25 (tel. 6-01-36). Its male-dominated crowd is classic *cantina,* but the shiny wood paneling and nice decor outdo most watering holes. A pitch-black entryway lies between you and the inside—you must knock on the door to get inside. This place is very popular with Margarita's guests (open daily 2pm-1am). Many local hotels, including the **Motel Parador** and the **Hotel Margarita's,** keep their guests entertained with night-time diversions at the bar, including *mariachis.* Parador rocks with live music and many all-too-willing dance partners—it is the job of the *animador* to get the women up and dancing with the male patrons. While most establishments in Creel close before 9pm, a few are open late, and the town usually has a few tourists roaming the streets or strumming guitars until near midnight. On Saturday nights, the **Casino de Creel** in front of the plaza offers outdoor and indoor dances, to which both locals and tourists are welcome (men 15 pesos, women 10 pesos; festivities run from 8pm-1am).

Creel's real draw, of course, is the canyon and surrounding countryside, and you'll need either a car, a tour guide, or a brave heart to get there. Read on.

■ Barrancas del Cobre (Copper Canyon)

Covering an area four times the size of Arizona's Grand Canyon, the **Barrancas del Cobre** are one of the more spectacular sights in all of Mexico. Comprised of five interlocking canyons in an area more generally known as the **Sierra Tarahumara,** the Barrancas hibernate under drifts of snow during the winter months and explode with color during the rainy season (July-Sept.) when the canyon's plants are in full bloom. The Copper Canyon is criss-crossed by the tracks of the **Chihuahua-Pacífico Railroad;** trains careen along canyon walls at death-defying angles, plunge into tunnels (there are 96 of them), and briefly skim the rim of the *barrancas.* The railroad stretches from Chihuahua to Los Mochis, crossing the Continental Divide three times and soaring to a height of 2240m. Passengers peering from train windows can glimpse a breathtaking series of landscapes—cactus-covered plateaus, mountains overgrown with cedars, unusual rock formations, snow-covered summits, blue skies, and canyon floors teeming with tropical vegetation.

Perhaps the most amazing thing about the expansive and magnificent Barrancas is what a well kept secret they are. Few foreigners, even those familiar with Mexico, have ever heard of the Copper Canyon, and fewer still could place it. This bodes well for your visit: unlike the Grand Canyon, you certainly won't have to elbow your way through a crowd to look over the edge; on the contrary, you'll feel like the only person in this land hidden deep within the Sierra Madres.

Two types of trains make the daily journey between Los Mochis and Chihuahua. The first-class train is for tourists: clean, air-conditioned, equipped with bathrooms, and blessed with large, comfortable seats. The second-class train screeches along the same tracks carrying both passengers and livestock; it's a much slower, sweatier ride. Trains go from Los Mochis to Chihuahua (first-class 6am, 248 pesos; second-class 7am, 65 pesos) and vice-versa (first-class 7am; second-class 8am). Creel is the most noteworthy stop on the trip, and makes a good base from which to explore the canyon (first-class Chihuahua to Creel 6hr., 110 pesos; Los Mochis to Creel 9hr., 132 pesos; second-class 13hr.). The serious mountain scenery lies between Creel and Río Fuerte, so if you take the second-class train, you'll zoom by some great views in the dark. For more expansive natural spectacles, grab a seat on the **left side** of the train heading towards Los Mochis, and the **right side** if you're on the way to Chihuahua. For more information, see Creel (p. 195).

At the **Divisadero station,** the jagged mountain edges overlap to create a maze of gorges and rocks at the rim of the Barrancas del Cobre. Eight hours out of Los Mochis

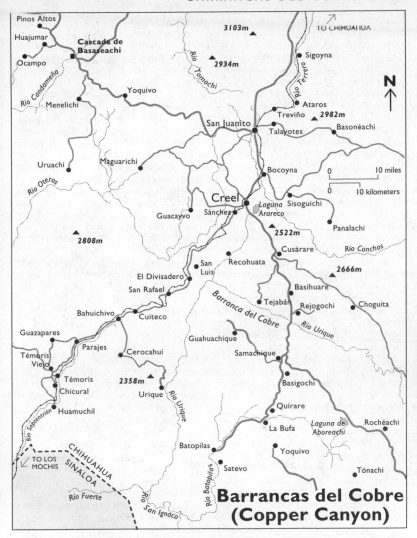

Barrancas del Cobre (Copper Canyon)

on the first-class, the train stops here for 15 minutes of sightseeing. Everyone on board scrambles out, sprints to the brink, gapes, and sprints back. On the second-class, it's less formal. Ask the conductor when the train is going to leave, and be back early. During this stop, you will also have a chance to buy crafts directly from the Tarahumara Indians who live in the area.

THE ROAD SOUTH TO BATOPILAS

Heading south from Creel, a road winds through the more scenic parts of the Copper Canyon. Buses rumble past nail-biting hairpin turns, balancing in one lane on the edges of steep cliffs that will make your heart pound both from excitement at the view and nervousness as you put your life in the hands of a stranger at the wheel. The road has been called North America's most spectacular by many, but, unpaved most

NORTHWEST MEXICO

of the way, it is also one of the continent's most treacherous. The first 75-km section of the road just south of Creel is happily two-laned and paved.

On the right side heading south, still-inhabited **Tarahumara caves** are within view of the road. On tours, it's possible to go in and visit the homes for a small donation. Beds and other furniture, woodstoves with chimneys, and kerosene lamps adorn the insides of many of the dismal, stone-walled caves.

Four kilometers down the road from Creel (and a left on a dirt road) lies the humble **San Ignacio Mission,** constructed in 1744 and still in use today—services are conducted in Rarámuri, the native language of the Tarahumara (Sun. 11am). The stone mission is dedicated to Saint Ignatius Loyola, the community's patron saint, and can easily be combined in a day trip with the **Valle de los Hongos** (Valley of the Mushroom, a.k.a. Valley of the Frogs or Ducks). The valley contains immense, oddly shaped stones formed by the San Ignacio River (admission 10 pesos). To reach the valley and mission by foot, walk down Mateos past the Motel Parador. When the road forks, take the smaller branch to the left, beside the cemetery. A kilometer or so out of town you will pass through the gates of the Tarahumara's *ejidos* (communal lands), containing the caves in which they live. After the cultivated fields, the valley is to the right and the mission at the bottom of the hill. On the way you will pass through small dells and plains surrounded by rocky cliffs, pines, and oak trees characteristic of the Tarahumara highlands.

Travelers can also hike to **Laguna Arareko,** an enormous lake 3km long and eight acres in area. Just bear right when the road forks past Mateos and follow the path 7km southeast. The water here is cold and contains dangerous weeds below the surface, so swimming is discouraged. From the small station next to the lake you can rent paddle boats (20 pesos). Nearby is **Recohuata Hot Springs;** a tour guide will take you for a one-and-a-half-hour ride and then send you on a 600m hike down into the canyon (around 60 pesos). The **Valle de las Monjas** (Valley of the Nuns), 9km away, makes for a great daytrip on horseback.

Twenty-two kilometers from Creel down the road to Batopilas is the town of **Cusárare,** which features its very own 18th-century Jesuit mission. Check out the mission's Tarahumara interior, with crude wood floors and indigenous designs. There are no pews—people sit on the floor when it's used on Sundays. A boarding house for children and a small Tarahumara craft museum are nearby, but the most popular attraction in the town's vicinity is the **Cusárare Falls,** a 3km hike uphill through a pine forest. While you can't swim in the falls, the view is spectacular.

Another 20km beyond Cusárare on the road to Batopilas, **Basíhuare** is an old overnight stop once frequented by silver carriers en route to Batopilas. Excellent views of the canyon can be had here. Twenty kilometers past Basíhuare is the crossing of the highest point of the **Río Urique.** Later, the road weaves around the narrowing canyon, offering spectacular vistas as it crawls up the **Cerro de 7 Pisos** (Seven-floor Hill), so named for the seven distinct layers that lead up along the rocky inner walls of the canyon on the most frightening stretch of this incredible one-lane path. The seven steps can best be seen from **La Bufa,** 60km from Basíhuare and past the fork, a scenic lookout that has the most magnificent view of all. If you have good vision, you can make out the tiny thread that is the Río Urique far, far below and the yellow wooden bridge that runs across it. If you're driving, pull off onto the shoulder, and try not to look down. Get out and gape. Then gape some more. If you go left at the fork, you'll come to **Norogachi,** a Tarahumara mission center at the river with beautiful (but touristy) *Semana Santa* services, and **Guachochi,** a rocky, frontier-like village with both colonial and Tarahumara influences.

The right fork will take you to the more impressive town of **Batopilas.** On the way you'll pass the bridge that spans the Urique; you can get out and walk down into the bushes for a smashing view of the waterfall down below. Keep your eyes peeled for **Tescalama trees,** which have yellow flowers and grow out of the sides of sheer rock. The last quarter of the ride to Batopilas also has plenty of **piedra cobriza** (copper rock), which gives the canyon its copper tint.

Getting There: Margarita's and **Cabañas Bertis** in Creel (see p. 196) offer trips that cover Cusárare (mission and falls), Lake Arareko, a Tarahumara cave, and the **Elephant Rock.** It's a four-hour trip and runs about 60 pesos per person for at least four people. Bertis also runs trips to San Ignacio Mission, Lake Arareko, Valley of the Mushrooms, and the Elephant Rock (2hr., 35 pesos per person). Tours that go as far as La Bufa run 100 pesos per person from Margarita's, 90 pesos from Cabañas Bertis (min. 6 people). It's a ten-hour roundtrip. On any trip—guided or not—remember to bring plenty of water and food, adequate footwear, and a sun hat. If you're averse to walking, you can arrange to navigate on bikes, horses, or even donkeys for a few extra pesos. **Pensión Creel,** Mateos 61 (tel. 6-00-71; fax 6-02-00), **Hotel Nuevo, Chihuahua Tours** (tel. 6-02-24), Mateos at Flores, and **Sartidora del Pacífico,** across from the Cabañas Bertis, all run similar tours to popular sites. **Motel Parador,** Mateos 44 (tel. 6-00-75; fax 6-00-85), offers somewhat more expensive tours.

BATOPILAS AND SATEVO

Batopilas is a tiny town nestled in the depths of the canyon along the Río Urique, a rough 35km from La Bufa and a thrilling but scary 140km (6hr. by van, 8hr. by bus) from Creel. Batopilas was a silver-mining boom town founded in 1708. Its rich silver supply lasted until the late 1800s, which is why such a secluded place was the second city in all Mexico to receive electricity. Today, electricity runs only 6 to 9am and 8pm to midnight, a symbol of how little remains of Batopilas's glory days.

Everything in Batopilas centers around the old, stone plaza. The best place to stay in town is the **Hotel Mary,** Juárez 15, next to the church near the plaza. Large, rustic adobe rooms with ceiling fans are naturally cool (40 pesos per person, with private bath 50 pesos). The nearby **Hotel Batopilas** offers dark, spacious rooms that could be cleaner (singles 25 pesos, with bath 30 pesos; doubles 40 pesos). The Hotel Mary's restaurant, **Quinto Patio,** is the only eatery in town that's reliably open. Enchiladas with fresh cheese (15 pesos), an order of tacos (16 pesos), and *bistek* (20 pesos) are on the menu, but you're limited to whatever happens to be in the fridge at the time (open daily 7am-10pm).

The magnificent **haciendas** in ruins along the river are poignant reminders of the excesses of the owners in the silver-mining days of Batopilas. The brown, castle-like **Hacienda Shepard** belonged to an American, and its ruins now stand in contrast to the green of the surrounding trees and canyon. Look for the *tescalama* tree growing sideways out of the brown wall of the hacienda. Hikes from Batopilas leave daily for the **Porfirio Díaz** mine in town and the more interesting **Peñasquito,** an hour hike up a steep hill; for **Cerro Colorado,** a section of the old Camino Real to Chihuahua during the mining boom, a 12-hour hike; and for the lost mission of **Satevo** (see below). The best source of information about departing tours is the **Riverside Lodge,** in town diagonally across from the plaza on the bench side (not the basketball-court side). A restored hacienda, the lodge is now a very fancy package-tour inn—check out the incredibly luxurious piano room. The historical photos on the walls may be the most interesting exhibits. Check out an 1899 shot of Pancho Villa at age 22, a photo of gold bars stacked to the ceiling, and another of the day when the river ran as high as the hotel wall.

The most fascinating excursion from Batopilas is to **Satevo,** a minuscule town with a spooky and beautiful mission. It's a 40-minute drive (you'll need 4WD or, better yet, pixie dust) or a two-hour walk. In the middle of a fertile valley straddled by the towering canyon rises a lonesome, round mission shrouded in mystery. Why was it built here of all places? When was it built? (The 15th or 16th century are the best guesses, but no one knows.) And finally, how did the Tarahumara, barely able to find shelter for themselves, gather up the energy, spirit, and desire to build such a thing? In any case, it's a sight to behold, especially at sunset, when the rays play off the red bricks of the roundhouse-like construction, combining with the clouds and valley to create a heavenly scene. In order to take a peek inside the mission, you'll have to tip the family living next door; they have the key. The inside of the mission is even eerier, with ancient tombs below and darkness above.

Getting There: A few places offer excursions to Batopilas. **Sergio Rascón** of **Cabañas Bertis** (p. 197) will take a van-load of people to the town for 800 pesos; he's very reliable and a cautious driver—a necessity for such a trip. **Margarita's** (p. 196) does not organize formal trips to Batopilas, but if enough people are interested, a guide will travel with a group (min. 9-10 people) for 110 pesos per person.

BASASEACHI FALLS NATIONAL PARK

With water cascading from a height of 246m, the **Basaseachi Falls** are one of the world's most spectacular waterfalls. Basaseachi (Tarahumaran for place of the cascade or place of the coyotes) is the highest waterfall in Mexico and the fourth highest in North America. Few waterfalls are blessed with such gorgeous surroundings. This is the sight most associated with the region, and a not-to-be-missed excursion from Creel and the Chihuahua-Pacífico Railroad. From the village, a 30-minute hike down leads to the "window"—the best view of the falls. The three-hour hike down to the base of the falls is picturesque and fascinating, but also steep and difficult.

Getting There: Trips to the village of Basaseachi run 120 pesos per person (min. 6). It's a 127-km trip on unpaved roads or 210 less scenic kilometers on paved roads. **Margarita's** (p. 196) runs the trip for only 100 pesos per person.

SOUTH OF CREEL TO URIQUE

It's a 154km jaunt from Creel to Urique. Along the way, partly on the Chihuahua-Pacífico railroad, are Divisadero, Bahuichivo, and Cerocahui. **Divisadero** is a train stop 51km south of Creel on the Chihuahua-Pacíficio railroad. It can also be reached by road from Creel. **Margarita's** (p. 196) charges 60 pesos per person for an excursion. Aside from claiming an amazing vista of the canyon (perhaps the fullest view of the Barrancas anywhere), Divisadero is also home to **La Piedra Volada,** a large, precariously balanced stone. It is technically possible (though quite difficult) to attempt a full-day hike between Cusárare and Divisadero, but an experienced guide is a must. A far more manageable and popular hike from Divisadero (which might force you to stay at the pricey hotel, as camping is not recommended) is down into the canyon—you can go as far as you want. A four-hour, 4km roundtrip hike leads to the Tarahumara village **Bacajipare,** while the 27km descent to the bottom of the canyon from Divisadero takes eight hours each way. Guides for hire hang around the hotel, and they'll take you down to the Río Urique, to Bacajipare, or elsewhere.

Bahuichivo, in a clearing in the forest, is another stop on the railroad, 97km south of Creel. A frontier-like town, it is often used as a departure point for spots deeper in the canyon or Cerocahui and Urique, farther south. The beautiful mountain village of **Cerocahui** (pop. 600, elevation 1,525m) is 17km southeast of Bahuichivo. You can grab a white "Transportes Cañón Urique" van, which also goes to Urique, right at the Bahuichivo train station. The main attraction is the **Jesuit Mission,** founded in 1681 by the priest Juan María de Salvatierra. **Sangre de Cristo** (gold and silver mines), the **Gallego Mountain** (38km away), the **Misión Churo,** and the **Yeparavo waterfall** (4km south) are among the possible excursions from Cerocahui.

The village of **Urique** sits in the **Barranca de Urique,** the deepest of the canyons. Overlooking the river of the same name, it affords spectacular views of the canyon. Even the most indifferent of backpackers will find themselves gaping at the stunning scenery. Accommodations in Urique are fairly cheap; options include the immaculate **Hotel Canyon** (70 pesos per person) and the **campgrounds** (12 pesos per person). Travelers can also spend the night in Bahuichivo at **Hotel Cola de Caballo** (60 pesos per night). **Restaurant Jardín,** in the center, is a local pick.

Getting There: To get to Urique from Creel, take the Los Mochis-bound morning train (9am), and get off at Bahuichivo (3½hr.). From there, take a bus to Urique (about 4hr.). If you arrive in Bahuichivo on the second-class train, there will be a van, instead of a bus, waiting to take you to Urique.

SINALOA

■ Los Mochis

The nucleus of an extremely fertile region of crops, Los Mochis (often just called "Mochis") is an important stop on a cross-country voyage, linked to the Baja peninsula (by a ferry departing from Topolobampo) and the Barrancas del Cobre (by rail). Most travelers, repulsed by the city's congested, dirty streets, smoggy air, and cultural void, use Mochis as little more than a departure point, although the surrounding agricultural area is stunning.

Orientation The city is laid out in a simple grid. Activity centers around **Obregón** and **Hidalgo** and the perpendicular **Zaragoza, Prieta,** and **Leyva.** Past Obregón, **Castro, Ordoñez, 16 de Septiembre,** and **5 de Mayo** run parallel; on the other side, past Hidalgo, lie **Independencia, Juárez, Morelos, Madero, Bravo, Carranza,** and **Serdán.** Perpendicularly, **Flores** runs after Leyva while **Allende, Degollado,** and **Constitución** run after Zaragoza on the other side.

Practical Information Set office hours are the butt of town jokes. The **tourist office** (tel./fax 2-23-83), on Cuauhtémoc and Allende, is on the left upon entering the Unidad Administrativa del Gobierno del Estado de Sinaloa. Walk down Calle Leyva two blocks past Blvd. Castro, turn left on Cuauhtémoc, and walk for three more blocks. The office is on the far right corner (open daily 9am-1pm and 4pm-6pm). Or try the **Cámara Nacional de Comercio, Servicios y Turismo** (tel. 2-04-77 or 2-08-97; fax 2-31-73), on Prieto and Cuauhtémoc, on the second floor. Ask for Lic. Francisco López Miranda for friendly help. The **Tourist Security** number is 91-800-90-392. **Bancomer,** Leyva at Juárez (tel. 8-08-49 or 5-78-08) has four **ATMs** (open Mon.-Fri. 9am-2pm). **LADATEL**s are scattered throughout downtown; when making local calls within the city, dial "1" before the number you are trying to reach.

The **ferry** to La Paz leaves from Topolobampo at 9am every day except Sunday (*salón*-class tickets 95 pesos per person; 656 per car; 82 pesos per motorcycle). Buy tickets at the **Sematur** office on Rendón 519 (tel. 2-01-41; fax 2-00-35; open Mon.-Fri. 8am-1pm and 3-7pm, Sun. 9am-1pm; hours erratic). Tickets must be purchased one day in advance (before 11am) at the Sematur office or on the day of departure on the ferry at Topolobampo. To get to the office, walk nine blocks from Juárez on Flores, then turn left on Rendón. In the mornings, a **bus** runs to Topolobampo every 20 minutes starting at 6am (5 pesos); the bus leaves from a small side street between Hidalgo and Obregón near the Hotel Santa Anita. It can also be flagged down on Cuauhtémoc between Prieta and Zaragoza.

The **Chihuahua al Pacífico train** (tel. 2-08-47) runs back and forth from Los Mochis to Chihuahua, passing through the Copper Canyon. At the Divisadero stop, just south of Creel, tourists are allowed to get off the train and gape for fifteen minutes. Unfortunately, the train is horribly unreliable; frequent problems, including **derailments** and **avalanches,** make your plans to leave Los Mochis about as secure as a savings and loan investment. The first-class train passes through at 6am (210 pesos to Creel; 248 pesos to Chihuahua); be in the station by 4:30am or earlier to get in the snail-paced ticket line. If the train looks like it's about to leave and you're still in line, you may want to ditch the line and push your way onto the train; what can the conductors do but sell you a ticket if you're already on? The train arrives in Creel around 4pm. A second-class train, even less reliable, supposedly leaves at 7am and arrives in Creel after dark, depriving you of the spectacular canyon views. A better alternative to waiting in the ticket line is buying your ticket beforehand from a travel agency; try **Paotam,** Rendón 517 (tel. 2-23-83), inside Hotel El Dorado, or **Viajes Conelva,** Leyva 357 Nte. (tel. 8-51-90; open until 7pm). No extra charge is added, and you'll have much more peace of mind come sunrise. After dark, the train-bound become the captives of cagy taxi drivers (25 pesos to downtown). This desperate situation tempts otherwise scrupulous travelers to bluff their way onto the free bus to and from the Hotel Santa Anita. To catch a public bus from the station back to town during the daylight hours (every 15min., 3pesos), just walk away from the station down the road about 100m. If you miss the train and must get to Chihuahua or Creel, the most appealing option (which is sort of like saying the coolest spot in hell) is to grab a bus to Hermosillo (8hr.) and then catch the overnight Hermosillo-Chihuahua bus (8pm, 14hr., 217 pesos). From Chihuahua, buses run regularly to Creel (5hr., 66 pesos).

Tres Estrellas de Oro (tel. 2-17-97), **Norte de Sonora** (tel. 2-04-11), and **Elite** (tel. 8-49-67) **buses** operate out of the modern terminal at the corner of Juárez and Degollado. **Transportes Norte de Sonora** (tel. 5-11-36), usually the cheapest carrier, runs buses to Guyamas (5hr., 70 pesos), Mazatlán (every hr. 5am-5pm, 5½hr., 128 pesos), Mexicali (18hr., 292 pesos), Mexico City (6 and 9 pm, 24hr., 436 pesos) via Culiacán (3hr., 50 pesos), and Tijuana (4pm, 7pm, and 8:15pm, 22hr., 349 pesos) via Hermosillo (7hr., 99 pesos). **Transportes del Pacífico** (tel. 2-03-47), on Morelos between Leyva and Zaragoza, sends *de paso* buses south to Mazatlán and north through Guaymas, Hermosillo, and Mexicali to Tijuana. These buses are relatively cheap, but often packed by the time they reach Los Mochis. Seats are easier to obtain on the slower *local* buses to Guadalajara, Tijuana, and Mazatlán (approximately 3 per day). Buses to El Fuerte and other destinations leave from Zaragoza, between Ordoñez and Cuauhtémoc. **Norte de Sinaloa** (tel. 8-03-31) sends a large fleet of rickety green buses to Culiacán (3½hr., 36 pesos), Guasave (every 30min., 1hr., 12 pesos), Guamuchil (2hr., 18 pesos). For **taxis,** call 2-02-83.

For fresh fish, fruit, and vegetables, check out the **market** on Obregón between Leyva and Zaragoza; on weekends it bustles with activity. Los Mochis's hippest threads get washed and dried at **Lavamatic,** Allende 218 just before Juárez (20 pesos; open Mon.-Sat. 7am-7pm, Sun. 7am-1pm). The **Red Cross,** at Tenochtitlán and Prieto (tel. 5-08-08 or 2-61-17), one block off Castro, has 24-hour ambulance service. **Farmacia Karla,** Obregón at Degollado (tel. 8-18-14 or -15), is open 24 hours. Hit the **Hospital Fátima,** Blvd. Jiquilpán Pte. 639 (tel. 2-12-33), to check out the local medical scene. No English is spoken. The **Centro de Salud** can be reached at 2-09-13. In case of **emergency**, call 06. The **police** are at Degollado at Cuauhtémoc in the Presidencia Municipal (tel. 2-00-33). No English is spoken. The **post office** is at Ordoñez 226 (tel. 2-08-23), two blocks off Castro, between Prieta and Zaragoza (open Mon.-Fri. 8am-7pm). **Postal Code:** 81200. **Telephone Code:** 681.

Accommodations   Budget hotels of variable quality are sprinkled throughout the downtown area demarcated by Castro, Juárez, Leyva, and Constitución. Mention that you're a tourist when negotiating a price at a hotel—Los Mochis's crusade to enhance tourism includes offering tourists lower prices at hotels. Arachnaphobes beware: crawling spiders are as ubiquitous as street noise. **Hotel Montecarlo,** Flores 322 Sur (tel. 2-18-18), a gracefully aging blue building at the corner of Independencia, has large rooms surrounding a quiet, palatial indoor courtyard. Central A/C, fans, and cable TV make life much easier. Take a room downstairs if you can—they're much cooler (singles 85 pesos, for two people 92 pesos; doubles 115 pesos). At **Hotel Hidalgo,** Hidalgo 260 Pte. (tel. 2-34-56), between Prieta and Zaragoza, ceiling fans and chilly colors (deep blue furniture and baby blue walls) cool the small rooms. If there's a soccer game on the tube, the lobby becomes a local hang-out (singles 60 pesos, with A/C 70 pesos; doubles 90 pesos; each additional person 10 pesos). **Hotel Beltrán** (tel. 12-07-10), Hidalgo and Zaragoza, is the budget equivalent of a five-star hotel. Immaculate rooms come with A/C, telephones, and cable TV. Don't complain about the hard bed—it's good for your back (singles 90 pesos; doubles 130 pesos).

Food The crowning virtue of this farming region is the **public market** between Prieto and Leyva along Castro, where prices are low and quality is high. The *taquerías* and *loncherías* in the market dish out cheap, home-brewed enigmas, many of which pack quite a wallop. Except for the *cantinas* (which women should avoid) and the corner *taquerías,* just about everything in town shuts down at 9pm; alcohol evaporates at 11pm. **El Farallón** (tel. 2-14-28 or 2-12-73) at Obregón and Flores, is the first restaurant in the city to serve shellfish, and was also famous for its sea turtles before they were outlawed. Ornate fishing nets and stately wooden fish decorate the walls. Spectacularly good flounder and sea bass (33 pesos), California sushi (25 pesos), and frog legs (35 pesos) flop onto your plate in huge portions. Cool, air-conditioned air mimics an ocean breeze (open 8am-10pm). At **El Taquito** (tel. 2-81-19), on Leyva between Hidalgo and Independencia, pitch-black windows provide shade from the offending sun, and cold A/C dries your sweaty skin and prevents the vinyl booths from sticking to the undersides of your thighs. Waiters in red jackets serve up enchiladas *suizas* (25 pesos), hamburgers and fries (17 pesos), and cheese-filled shrimp wrapped in bacon (38 pesos). Offers group discounts (open 24hr.).

Sights and Entertainment Los Mochis boasts a few modest amusements, but if you can, head to Topolobampo. One of Los Mochis's founders, the sugar baron Benjamin Johnston, assembled the extraordinary collection of trees and plants standing in **Sinaloa Park,** on Prolongación and Castro. Hundreds of species inhabit this outdoor forest-museum, where *indígena* performers strut their stuff every Sunday beginning at 11am. Bark-watchers should check out the stump at the entrance to the park; a harem of wild animals and the insignia of the state of Sinaloa have been gouged into its roughened surface. The **Museo Regional del Valle del Fuerte** (tel. 2-46-92), Pte. Municipal at Castro, was once the home of another early settler and now houses his guns and personal diary. Photographs documenting the growth and development of Northern Mexico are also on display (open Tues.-Sun. 9am-1pm and 4-7:30pm; admission 5 pesos). Across the street is the **Plaza Solidaridad,** which hosts performances every Sunday at 6pm. For a schedule of upcoming festivals and musical events at the Pl. Solidaridad and the nearby **Plazuela 27 de Septiembre,** consult the **Secretaria de Cultura y Acción Social** (tel. 5-04-05, ext. 38 or 39), in front of the tourist office. Adjoining the Plaza Solidaridad is the **Santuario del Sagrado Corazón de Jesús,** Los Mochis's oldest church, which was built after Johnston's wife donated the land to the people. Many locals find it ironic that she was not even Catholic. The **Cinema 70** is on Blvd. de la Plaza. If you spend the night in Mochis, head to the **Rodeo Bar,** on Obregón and Constitución, where you can down a few beers and take the mechanical horse for a ride (open 9pm-3am).

On the Waterfront

Topolobampo is a decent place to spend the day, especially if you're stuck in lifeless Los Mochis and willing to dish out the cash for an excursion—just about the only worthwhile activity there. When Albert Owen set out to forge his socialist utopia, he certainly didn't envision today's Topolobampo, a small fishing village helped along by the tourists who swim with the dolphins in the port's warm waters. From the bus station, hang a left and follow the street to the shore, where boats and taxis run trips to the outlying attractions. For 70 pesos, a boat will usher you to **Playa El Maviri,** a fairly well developed beach. Perhaps more interesting is **El Farallón,** a distant island where sea lions and pelicans run (er, swim and fly) free, and a hill juts out to the waters. While there are no beaches on the island, snorkeling and swimming are still possible. A full-day boat trip makes a wallet-shrinking 500 pesos roundtrip for 5-6 people. Other destinations include the **Cerro de los Patos,** an area rife with ducks; the **Copus,** a large beach with fine sand; and the **Isla Verde,** a shallow lagoon.

■ Mazatlán

Mazatlán (pop. 315,000) means "place of the deer" in Nahuatl. A less appropriate name can hardly be imagined, since there is nothing even remotely pastoral or rumi- nant about this city. The only wildlife present—genus *Gringusmaximus,* species *norteamericanus*—roams the beaches in large herds.

Mazatlán is truly a city divided. The old city is traditionally Mexican, with a *zócalo,* busy streets, and bustling markets that lend it a genuine charm. Nearby on the shore is the **Olas Altas** (Tall Waves) neighborhood, with a peaceful beach, pleasant streets, and grand old hotels that evoke Mazatlán's glory days. Eight kilometers or so up the Avenida del Mar, however, lies another city entirely—the **Zona Dorada** (Golden Zone), home to high-rise hotels, dollar-dishing Americans, and patronizingly friendly tourism agents. While Olas Altas is pleasant and the old city has its redeeming quali- ties, the Zona Dorada's Disney-castle clubs, pleasure palaces, time-share condos, and overpriced gift shops might depress some. But the honeymooners, Californians, and families that come to swim and surf on the pristine beaches of the Zona Dorada would argue otherwise.

ORIENTATION

Built on a rocky spur jutting southwest into the Pacific, Old Mazatlán's downtown area lies north of the *zócalo.* The main street running east-west is **Ángel Flores,** the southern boundary of the *zócalo.* Farther south, the *malecón* follows the shore line. It starts as **Olas Altas** on the south end near Old Mazatlán, then runs to the Zona Dorada 8km north, serving as the Zona Dorada's one main street; there it is called **Avenida del Mar.** In between the two areas, to the south of the fisherman's statue and north of Olas Altas, it is called **Paseo Clausen;** and to the far north, past Valen- tino's in the Zona Dorada, it's known as **Sábalo.**

Mazatlán's **bus station** is three blocks behind the Sands Hotel and about 2km north of Old Mazatlán, in Olas Altas. The area around the bus station, with several reason- ably priced hotels and restaurants, along with a good beach and the vital "Sábalo" bus line nearby, makes a convenient home base. You can catch the downtown-bound "Insurgentes" bus at the stand one block off the beach across from the chicken barbe- cuer. From the **train station,** on the far eastern edge of Mazatlán, the yellow "Insur- gentes" or the green, beat-up "Cerritos-Juárez" buses will take you downtown. From the **airport,** 18km south of the city, the "Central Camionera" bus makes the trip; the only way to get back from downtown is a 70-peso cab ride. It's a grueling 20-minute walk from the *centro* to the **ferry** docks; the blue "Playa Sur" school bus (1.50 pesos) makes the trip, and for 10 pesos so will a taxi.

Mazatlán's efficient **bus system** makes getting around the city a breeze. At some point, all municipal buses pass the public market on Juárez, three blocks north of the *zócalo.* The most useful bus line is the **"Sábalo-Centro."** Serviced by smaller, white, air-conditioned express buses, this line runs from the downtown market to Olas Altas and to Playa Sábalo in the Zona Dorada. The **"Cerritos-Juárez"** bus continues up to Playa Bruja at Puerta Carritos. The **"Insurgentes"** route services the bus and train sta- tions, and **"Playa Sur"** goes to the ferry dock, lighthouse, and Olas Altas (every 15min. 5am-midnight, 1.50 pesos). Feel free to wave down a bus at any point on its route—no official stops exist. For late-night disco hopping, you'll have to take a cab or a *pulmonía* (pneumonia), an open vehicle which resembles a golf cart that putters along blasting raucous music. Always set the price before you commit yourself to a ride; standard fare between Old Mazatlán and the Golden Zone is 10 pesos. If you want to save the fare, it'll take you over an hour to walk the long path between the two sections.

N

Ave. del Mar

México
16 de Septiembre
Bolívar
Quijano
Zúñiga

Miramar
Gastelum
Flores
Nájera

Paseo Claussen

Zaragoza

Guillermo Nelson
5 de Mayo
Domínguez
Arribo

Carrasco
Rosales/Cárdenas
Tampico
Zúñiga

Villa/Iturbide
Zaragoza
Morelos
Hidalgo
Germán Evers

Cerro
de la Nevería
(Ice Box Hill)

Hospital

Estrada
Ocampo
Canizales
21 de Marzo

Juárez
Serdán
Azueta

Estrada
Ocampo
Serrano

Leandro Valle

**High Divers
of Mazatlán**

Domínguez

Plaza
Revolución

Escobedo
Constitución

Canizales
21 de Marzo

Ángel Flores

Constitución
Guerrero

Olas Altas/Claussen

Venus
Osuna Rojo
Niños Héroes

Carnaval

Roosevelt

Carvajal

Galeana

Avenida Miguel Alemán

Barragán

**Old
Mazatlán**

Av. Camarón Sábalo

*Estero del
Sábalo*

(i)

**EL CID
RESORT**

**ZONA
DORADA**

Av. Lomas de Mazatlán

Bugambilia

Av. de la Marina

Laguna Sábalo

Av. Loaiza

Calz. Rafael Buelna

*Laguna del
Camarón*

*Isla de los
Lobos*

*Isla de los
Venados*

Av. Insurgentes

Mazatlán

Hotel Belmar, **2**
Hotel Cabinas, **7**
Hotel Club Playa Mar, **6**
Hotel Emperador, **8**
Hotel del Río, **3**
Hotel La Siesta, **1**
Hotel San Fernando, **5**
Market, **4**

Av. del Mar

(6)

(7)

Universidad

Bus Station

N

0 ___ 2 miles

0 ___ 2 kilometers

Bahía de Puerto Viejo

Tamazula
Beltrán
San Lorenzo
Fuerte
Baluarte
Pánuco
Pánico
Gavitas
Plaxtla

Carretera Internacional

Av. Benemérito de las Américas

*Estero
del
Infiernillo*

**OLD
MAZATLÁN
(See Detail Map)**

*Bahía de
Olas Altas*

Zaragoza

Olas Altas

Carnaval

16 de Sept.
5 de Mayo
Juárez
Serdán

G. Nájera

Carrasco
Pesqueira

Paseo Claussen

A. Flores
Azueta
Constitución

Villa/Iturbide
Germán Evers

Red Cross

Av. Miguel Alemán

Serdán

Potrero del Llano

Calz. Gabriel Leyva Solano

Av. Emilio Barragán

Canal de Navegación

Mazatlán

PRACTICAL INFORMATION

Tourist Office: (tel. 16-51-62, -65; fax 16-51-66, -67), Av. Camarón Sábalo and Tiburón, in the Golden Zone, on the fourth floor of the gray Banrural building. Helpful staff doles out much-needed Mazatlán maps. Much English spoken. Open Mon.-Fri. 8:30am-2pm and 5-7:30pm. **Tourist Assistance:** tel. 91-800-90-392.

Tourist Police: (tel. 14-84-44), at Gabriel Ruíz and Santa Mónica.

Consulates: U.S., Loaiza at Bugambilia (tel. 16-58-89), in front of Hotel Playa Mazatlán. Open daily 10:30am-1pm. **Canada,** (tel. 13-73-20), Loaiza at Bugambilia in Hotel Playa Mazatlán. Open daily 9am-1pm.

Currency Exchange: Most banks open for exchange Mon.-Fri. 8:30-11am. *Casas de cambio* are open all day in the northern section of the downtown area.

American Express: (tel. 13-04-66; fax 16-59-08), in the Centro Comercial Plaza Balboa on Camarón Sábalo. Open Mon.-Fri. 9am-6pm, Sat. 9am-1pm.

Telephones: Stainless-steel **LADATELs,** throughout the city, are best for international calls. *Caseta* at Serdán 1512 (tel. 85-39-11; fax 85-01-08).

Telegrams: (tel. 81-22-20), in the same building as the post office. Open Mon.-Fri. 8am-7pm, Sat.-Sun. 8-11am.

Airport: Rafael Buelna International Airport, 18km south of the city. **Aeroméxico,** Sábalo 310-A (tel. 14-11-11 or 91-800-36-202). **Mexicana** (tel./fax 82-77-22), B. Domínguez and Av. del Mar. **Delta** (tel. 82-41-55 or 82-13-49; fax 82-13-56). **Alaska Airlines** (tel. 95-800-426-0333: fax 85-27-30). **AeroCalifornia,** El Cid Resort (tel. 13-20-42/-18). Call for schedules and fares.

Buses: Chihuahuenses, Elite, and del Norte are nicer; Estrella Blanca and del Pacífico are a step down. **Transportes del Pacífico** (tel. 81-51-56) runs buses to Guaymas (every hr., 11hr., 220 pesos), Hermosillo (every hr., 12hr., 250 pesos), Los Mochis (every hr., 6hr., 120 pesos), Mexico City (every hr., 17hr., 314 pesos) via Guadalajara (7hr., 140 pesos) and Querétaro (15hr., 250 pesos), Tepic (every hr., 4hr., 70 pesos) via Rosario (1hr., 15 pesos), and Tijuana (every hr., 26hr., 440 pesos) via Nogales (18hr., 317 pesos) and Mexicali (24hr., 380 pesos). **Elite** and **Transpacífico** (tel. 81-38-00) are slightly cheaper but run less frequently. **Chihuahuenses, Transportes del Norte,** and **Estrella Blanca** (all tel. 81-53-81), run to Durango (7 per day, 7hr., 83 pesos), Guadalajara (6 per day, 8hr., 140 pesos), Mexico City (6 per day, 18hr., 314 pesos), Monterrey (every hr., 18hr., 263 pesos), Nogales (9:15pm, 20hr., 316 pesos), and Tijuana (1:45 and 2:45pm, 26hr., 430 pesos).

Trains: (tel. 84-67-10), in Colonia Esperanza on the eastern edge of town. One train leaves daily for Guadalajara (13½hr., 46-84 pesos), Hermosillo (16hr., 71-178 pesos), and Nogales (18hr., 93-167 pesos).

Ferry: Sematur (tel. 81-70-20 or -21), office at the end of Carnaval, south of Ángel Flores and *el centro*. Tickets are sold only on the day of departure. Arrive at the office at least 2hr. early to procure a spot, as capacity is limited to 40 people. Open Sun.-Fri. 8am-3pm, Sat. 9am-1pm. You can purchase tickets in advance at a local travel agency. During the high season (Dec., Jul.-Aug.) make reservations at least 2 weeks ahead. Travels every day except Thurs. and Sat. to La Paz, Baja California (3pm, 17hr., *salón* 142 pesos, *turista* 284 pesos, children 2-11, half-price).

Car Rental: Hertz, Sábalo 314 (tel. 13-60-60, airport office 85-05-48; fax 13-49-55). Starting at 300 pesos per day. Must be 21 years old.

Laundromat: Lavamor, G. Najera 435 (tel. 80-77-79), at Betancourt. Wash 5 pesos, 10min. dry 5 pesos. If they do it for you, it's 20 pesos per load.

Red Cross: Zaragoza and Corona (tel. 85-14-51).

Pharmacy: Farmacia Union, Domínguez and Constitución 28 Sur (tel. 81-32-31), one block from Plazuela Machado. Open Mon.-Sat. 8am-9pm, Sun. 9am-3pm.

Hospital: Clínica Siglo 21, Domínguez 2301 (tel. 85-54-18), at Morelos, near Zaragoza park. English spoken.

Emergency: tel. 06.

Police: (tel. 83-45-10), on Rafael Quelna in Colonia Juárez.

Post Office: (tel. 81-21-21), Juárez at Ángel Flores across from the *zócalo*. Open Mon.-Fri. 8am-7pm, Sat. 9am-1pm. **Postal Code:** 82000.

Telephone Code: 64.

ACCOMMODATIONS AND CAMPING

High-quality cheap rooms do exist; simply avoid the Golden Zone, where rates are exorbitant even at the shabbier joints. Budget hotels cluster in three areas: in Old Mazatlán along the three avenues east of the main square (Juárez, Serdán, and Azueta), around the bus station, and on the pleasant waterfront area along Olas Altas, west of the center of Old Mazatlán. Large groups can even find cheap beds on Sábalo, near the beaches. Look and ye shall find.

The busiest seasons in Mazatlán are Christmas and the month following *Semana Santa*—check in early. At other times, prices are negotiable, especially for extended stays. Summer nights in Mazatlán are typically hot and humid; always inspect your room's ventilation system before paying. There's a trailer park, **La Posta** (tel. 83-53-10), on Av. Rafael Buelna (full hook-up and tent space 70 pesos).

Olas Altas

Back in the 1950s, long before wily developers began constructing multi-million-dollar pleasure pits along the north shore, the focal point of Mazatlán's fledgling resort scene was Olas Altas, a winding, shore-hugging stretch southwest of town dotted with regal colonial-style hotels. Although the majority of tourists now opt to stay in the flashy hotels to the north, Olas Altas remains a welcome oasis from the grime and noise of downtown or the frosted hair of the Golden Zone.

Hotel Belmar, Olas Altas 166 (tel. 85-11-11). A resort of yesteryear, the Belmar boasts hazy marble floors, dark wood paneling, and arches lined with colorful tiles. Cool, spotless rooms have monstrous bathrooms. Match other guests ping for pong at the table tennis table, take a dip in the pool, or crawl into an antique rocker with an English book in hand (they have a small collection). Singles with A/C and TV 60 pesos, with ocean view (no A/C) 70 pesos. Doubles with A/C and TV 70 pesos, with ocean view (no A/C) 80 pesos.

Hotel La Siesta, Olas Altas Sur 11 (tel. 81-26-40 or 81-23-34, toll-free 91-800-69-770; fax 13-74-76). A jungly central courtyard spills over into huge immaculate rooms. Slackers afflicted with *ennui* can toy with the A/C, TV (10 extra pesos per night), or phone, or just lounge on the balcony overlooking the sea. Singles 100 pesos. Doubles 130pesos. Ask for a room with a view.

Old Mazatlán

This is the noisier part of town ("downtown"), and the hotels here are farther from the beach—therefore rooms are on the cheap side. This area, especially the cathedral square, is well trafficked after sundown, mainly by old men watching passers-by, and for that reason somewhat safer than other parts of town.

Hotel del Río, Juárez 144 or 2410 (tel. 82-46-54), at Alejandro Quijano, a few blocks from the shore. Stretch out on a pink wooden bed while a fan revolves hypnotically above your head. Singles 40 pesos. Doubles 60 pesos.

Hotel San Fernando, 21 de Marzo 126 (tel. 81-59-80), between Azueta and Serdán. Look forward to the tall ceilings and soft beds. Flamingoed bedspreads provide a touch of kitsch. Unfortunately, some walls are rotting, and the A/C leaks out of the holes in the windows, but still keeps the room cool. A good deal. Singles 40 pesos. Doubles 50 pesos.

Near the Bus Station

Hotels in this area are close to sandy beaches and the ritzy Golden Zone, and some rooms boast ocean views. Be forewarned: prices here are steep.

Hotel Emperador (tel. 82-67-24), on Río Panuco, across from the bus terminal. Four-story (not 4-star) hotel offers small, tiled rooms with clean bathrooms and firm beds on grim concrete slabs. 50 pesos for 1 person, 60 pesos for 2; with A/C 70 pesos for 1, 80 pesos for 2; 10 pesos for each additional person.

Hotel Cabínas, Av. del Mar 123 (tel. 81-57-52), also on the *malecón*. Run-down rooms adorned with paintings of clowns and Mexican dancers. Apartment suites for up to 6 guests with kitchen and ocean view rented on a weekly basis (190 pesos for 6 people, 130 for 2 per night). This joint is very popular with Mexicans—reservations are recommended. Singles 65 pesos, doubles 75 pesos.

Hotel Económico, Palos Prietos and Espinoza. As cheap as it gets. All of the sunny yellow rooms have fans, mirrors, and tiny bathrooms. Singles and doubles 30 pesos, with TV 50 pesos, with TV and A/C 60 pesos.

FOOD

Mazatlán's restaurants serve up everything from *comida corrida* to charbroiled T-bone steak, a *gringo* favorite. Of course, most menus are glutted with "Mexican classics"—spicy guacamole, crisp nachos dripping with cheese, and *jalapeños*. Many eateries here are relatively cheap, although prices escalate as you get sucked toward the Golden Zone. Enjoy your meal with *Pacífico* beer, the pride of Mazatlán.

Olas Altas

Restaurant Fonda Santa Clara, Olas Altas 66 (tel. 81-64-51), near Hotel Belmar. Sit outside on the low wooden chairs. Sip the local *Cerveza Pacífico*. Slip into a zen-like trance while listening to the rhythmically crashing waves. Exquisite lite meals include spaghetti (18 pesos), chef's salad (14 pesos), and *camarones mexicanos* (mexican shrimp, 24 pesos). On Sundays, you can sample the house specialty, *paella* (Spanish yellow rice with seafood, chicken, *chorizo*, and vegetables) for 30 pesos. Open daily 7am-11pm.

Old Mazatlán

The busy **public market,** between Juárez and Serdán, three blocks north of the *zócalo*, serves the cheaper meals in the area. If you need a headless pig, this is the place. Quality meals such as jumbo shrimp, *antojito* platters, and steak can be had for staggeringly cheap prices. *Comida corrida* runs a bargain-basement 5 pesos. Snacking opportunities exist outside in the *loncherías* and taco stands.

Café Pacífico, Constitución 501 (tel. 81-39-72), across from the Plazuela Machado. This famous pub is a relic, with all the charm of grand Old Mazatlán: good food and drink, a dark, artsy atmosphere, chummy service, and damn good music. A large-screen TV with ESPN and a pool table add to the fun. Let the cool tunes and A/C pump you up as you snack on chicken wings (25 pesos), tuna salad (15 pesos), or the platter of assorted cheeses (18 pesos). Open daily 10am-midnight.

Restaurante Vegetariano (tel. 82-61-43), Domínguez and 21 de Marzo. Phenomenal veggie cuisine at unbeatable prices. Enjoy the enormous *comida corrida*, which includes a salad, a special cream, a hearty main course, bread, juice, and dessert, all for only 20 pesos. Open daily 12:30-4:30pm.

Panamá Restaurant and Pastelería (tel. 85-18-53), Juárez and Canizales. A restaurant/bakery specializing in Mexican platters and sandwiches. Don't miss the *picaditas panamá* (corn patties with mushrooms and cheese, seasoned with chopped onion and green pepper, 18 pesos). Open daily 7am-10pm.

North of the Golden Zone

As you move north, prices soar and *norteamericano* culinary influence becomes more pronounced. Look no farther if you crave Caesar salads and *gringo* company.

El Mambo Lonchería, Espinoza Ferrusquilla 204 (tel. 85-04-73), across from the bus station. Mexican pottery, hanging seashells, eclectic art, a macaw, and a parrot that speaks more Spanish than most of the guests. Tasty, large, and cheap_meals. Shrimp *al mojo de ajo* (in garlic) 25 pesos. Open Mon.-Sat. 7am-7pm.

Restaurant Roca Mar (tel. 81-60-08), Av. del Mar at Isla de Los Lobos, in the Zona Dorada. Like most of its neighbors along the beach, this joint offers a full bar and a traffic-obscured view of the crashing waves. Prices tainted by tourism. Shrimp cocktail 25 pesos. Grilled fish 33 pesos. Open daily noon-1am.

SAND AND SIGHTS

Mazatlán's greatest asset is its 16km of beach. Just north of Old Mazatlán and along Av. del Mar sprawls **Playa Norte.** The *playa* is a decent stretch of sand if you don't mind small waves and the stares of local *machos* who play soccer here. Solo women should consider doing their swimming farther north. As you hone in on the Golden Zone, the beach gets cleaner, the waves larger, and Playa Norte eases into **Playa Las Gaviotas.** Just past Punta Sábalo, in the lee of the islands, basks **Playa Sábalo,** whose great waves and golden sand are enjoyed to the point of abuse by crowds of *norteamericanos.* Most area beaches are patrolled by lifeguards, who use a color-coded flag system to inform bathers of local conditions. Air-conditioned "Sábalo-Centro" buses pass by all of these beaches.

As Playa Sábalo recedes to the north, crowds thin rapidly and you can frolic on the glorious beaches all by yourself. Take the yellow "Sábalo" bus to the last stop and walk left; you'll soon reach nearly deserted **Playa Bruja,** with tons of beautiful sand and one- to two- meter waves all to yourself. Swim at your own risk: there are no life-guards. Camping is permitted, but be cautious after dark and camp in groups whenever possible. Solo women should avoid Playa Bruja, as assaults have been reported.

Yate Fiesta harbor cruises (no alcohol, lots of music) depart daily at 11am for a three-hour tour of Mazatlán by sea. Tickets (60 pesos, 30 pesos for children 5-10) are sold at the yacht office (tel. 85-22-37/-38; fax 85-04-15). To get there, take the "Playa Sur" bus to the end of the first dock, near the lighthouse. For a 360° view of Mazatlán, the sea, and the surrounding hills, climb to the top of **El Faro,** the second-tallest light-house in the world. The hike (about 30min.) is almost unbearable in the summer; avoid the heat by ascending in the early morning or late evening.

The **Acuario Mazatlán,** Av. de los Deportes 111 (tel. 81-78-15 or -16), keeps pira-nhas and other feisty fish (up to 250 breeds in all) in a slew of cloudy tanks. The aquarium, the largest in Latin America, also hosts performing sea lions and birds, and sports displays on fishing. The pet pigeons in the aviary are less interesting than the hooded orioles, bar-vented wren, and social flycatchers in the surrounding trees. The Acuario is one block back from the beach and north of the Sands Hotel; the turn-off is marked by a shimmering blue sign (open daily 9:30am-6:30pm; admission 25 pesos, children 3-13, 16 pesos).

Mazatlán's **tower divers** don't quite match the exploits of the cliff divers in Acap-ulco, but their acrobatic plunges are nevertheless extraordinarily dangerous. Perfor-mances take place daily from 10-11am and 4:30-5:30pm, weather and tides permitting, 50m from the **Monumento Mujer Mazutleca.** The best viewing angles are just south of the towers; on days when the water is too rough for diving, climb the tower to watch the waves break below. Walk to the waterfront on Zaragoza and head south to get to the towers. Be forewarned that the divers will not perform unless they can pull in a sufficient number of "tips" beforehand.

William Blake saw the universe in a grain of sand and eternity in an hour. You too may get bored at the beach. In this case, don't abandon Mazatlán—just hop on one of the boats to **Isla de la Piedra** (p. 212), where locals go to escape the crowds. Boats leave from the wharf on Av. del Puerto at Gutiérrez Najera. Buses to the wharf depart from near the public market (1.50 pesos). To walk there, take 21 de Marzo from the cathedral past Serdán to the water, then turn left on Av. del Puerto (3 pesos round-trip). **Islas Venados** (Deer Island) is a relatively deserted scrap of land with fine div-ing; catamaran boats leave for the island from the Agua Sports Center in the **El Cid Resort** (tel. 13-33-33, ext. 341) in the Golden Zone (10am, noon, and 2pm, 60 pesos). Waterpark mania has hit Mazatlán with the new **Mazagua** (tel. 88-00-41), located north of the Golden Zone near Puerta Cerritos. Go bonkers in the wave pool or shoot down slippery slides (open daily 10am-6pm; 35 pesos, children under 4 free). To get there, take a "Cerritos Juárez" bus (1.50 pesos).

ENTERTAINMENT

Hordes of *norteamericano* high schoolers ditch the prom and hit Mazatlán yearly to twist, shout, and drink. Supply rises to meet demand, and more than a dozen discos and bars clamor for *gringo* greenbacks. Inside, only the occasional Mexican rock tune will remind you you're in a foreign country. Most of the hot clubs are in the area known as **Fiesta Land,** in the Golden Zone. If you address bartenders or bouncers in Spanish, they'll smile, pat you on the head, and answer in near-perfect English, never forgetting to address you as *amigo*.

Bora-Bora (tel. 86-49-49), on Paseo del Mar at the southern end of the Golden Zone, next to the beach. Probably the hottest spot in town, Bora-Bora is always jam-packed with touring teenagers clad in neon (or nothing at all) and dancing on the bars. Those so inclined may dance in cages. Clubbers in search of more wholesome activities can head for the volleyball court and swimming pool. Drinks start at 14 pesos. Thursday is Ladies' Night. Cover Fri.-Sun. 14 pesos, including open bar. Open daily 9pm-4am.

Valentino's, in the same building as Bora-Bora, caters to an older, more upscale crowd. Dancing and drinks continue to pack 'em in. Open daily 8am-4am.

Pepe Toro, Av. de las Garzas 18. Caters to gay men. The dance floor starts hoppin' after 11pm. Open daily 7am-2am.

El Toro Bravo, Av. del Mar 550 (tel. 85-05-95). Watch twentysomething would-be cowpokes drink their bladders full of beer (12 pesos) and then attempt to ride the bucking saddle—guess where that beer goes next. Wednesday is Ladies' Night. Cover Thurs.-Sun. 15 pesos. Open daily 9pm-4am.

■ Near Mazatlán: Isla de la Piedra

Just a five-minute boat ride from the mainland, the idyllic Isla de la Piedra consists of 10km of glistening sand, crashing waves, and an assortment of marine life that would make the folks at Sea World gnash their teeth with envy. Unfortunately, money-hungry investors have been eyeing the island, and it's pristine stretches of sand could soon become cluttered with luxury hotels, *gringo*-oriented eateries, and a monstrous golf course.

Orientation and Practical Information Isla de la Piedra is just a hop, skip, and a boat ride away from the mainland. Take a green **"Independencia" bus** (2 pesos) to the **Embajadero de la Isla de la Piedra.** From there, take a **boat** (every 10min., 5min., 3 pesos) to the island; a **taxi** will be waiting for you at the dock. Ask the driver to take you to Carmelita's (6 pesos), the island's focal point.

Obtain **tourist information** at **Carmelita's,** whose owner (bearing the same name) knows the island inside-out. The island's one **telephone** (tel. 85-44-50) is located across from the dock (open daily 7am-1pm and 3-9pm). Adjacent to the phones is **Farmacia de la Piedra,** which also offers medical assistance (open daily 7am-1pm and 3-9pm).

Accommodations and Food The island is perfect for a daytrip or to camp out. **Carmelita's,** a few meters from the shore, offers space for tents, sturdy trees for hammock slinging, and use of bathroom and grill free of charge. *Gratis.* 0 pesos. If you can't camp out, she also offers clean rooms with the basics: electricity and private bathrooms with running water (60 pesos for 1-3 persons). **Lety's,** adjacent to Carmelita's, offers similar lodging, although the trees are less sturdy. Spacious rooms boast modern bathrooms, desks, lighting, 2 beds, and a sofa-bed (60 pesos for 1-3 people). There's nothing nicer than camping out on a secluded beach and gazing at the stars, but be careful and don't stray too far from the center.

Seafood rules on the island. **Carmelita's** serves shrimp platters and fish fillets, both with *frijoles,* tortillas, salad, and rice (22 pesos; open 9am-6pm). If you're tired of seafood, head to **Lety's** for a quarter chicken (20 pesos) or *quesadillas* (16 pesos; open 9am-7pm). Listen to the cool tunes and watch folks play volleyball by the shore at **Restaurant Estebin,** a two-minute walk from Carmelita's. Same ole' grub: fish fillets (20 pesos), and chicken (18 pesos; open daily 9am-7pm).

Sights The main attraction is, of course, the beautiful **beaches.** Wriggle your toes in the cool sand, duck the waves, or bask in the radiant sun. Swimming is prime in the area across from Restaurant Estebin. If you're into water sports, Carmelita's is the place to go. Huge selection of **banana boats** (25 pesos), **waverunners** (200 pesos per 30min.), **snorkeling gear** (20 pesos per hr.), and **horseback riding** (40-60 pesos). Letry's also rents **boogie boards** (10 pesos per hr.).

Northeast Mexico

With an assortment of border towns, former colonial settlements, old mining hotspots, and congested urban centers, Northeast Mexico encompasses a land of remarkable contrasts. The destiny—not to mention the size—of much of the *noreste* has been shaped by its location. Once caught in the middle of the 19th century Mexican-American conflicts, **Tamaulipas's** and **Nuevo León's** border cities are now heir to the cultural legacy of two distinct lifestyles. Many towns have the feel of an old country-western movie, with dust storms, arid landscapes, and blistering hot climate that makes a high-noon showdown completely understandable.

Farther south, the *gringo* influence is much less palpable. Straddling the border with Veracruz, hot, humid **Tampico** is molded not by the *frontera,* but by the gulf waters—fishermen make the daily trip out to sea and the smell of salt pervades the air. The lifeblood of **Zacatecas** and **San Luis Potosí** once flowed through veins of silver. Former mining towns, they've now grown into important industrial centers without sacrificing their colonial charm. The ranches and churches loom above all the skyscrapers of monstrous **Monterrey,** the region's economic powerhouse and a soulless symphony in grey. **Saltillo** provides a colonial oasis for frazzled urbanites, while **Aguascalientes** offers tranquility and oodles of small town charm. The Northeast offers Mexico in a microcosm—extreme poverty, decaying and new-found grandeur, and a proud, if complex, heritage.

■ Brownsville, Texas

The site of the first battle of the Mexican-American War and the last battle of the Civil War, Brownsville (pop. 135,000) has grown to peacefully embrace its bicultural nature. Lanky men sporting cowboy hats and leather boots and the slew of late-model American cars only thinly veil the pervasive Mexican influence. From the omnipresent Spanish chatter to the spicy culinary influence, Mexico exerts a powerful cultural influence over Brownsville that is far greater than the NAFTA-induced trade (for information on crossing the border, see p. 10 and p. 11).

ORIENTATION

Most points of interest lie northwest of the **International Blvd.** which traverses the city before turning into the **International Bridge** that leads into Mexico. Numbered streets run parallel to International Blvd., starting at **Palm Blvd.** Having studied American history will prove beneficial, as perpendicular streets are named after American presidents, starting with Georgie **Washington** and tapering off before the Great Depression. **Elizabeth St.** is the city's main commercial thoroughfare and precedes the presidential streets near the border. Tourists flock to the old city near the border and the suburban hotel strip in the northwestern part of town. At night, the area around the border is rather desolate; women and solo travelers should be careful in this part of town and probably avoid it altogether. Also avoid **Southmost Rd.,** perpendicular to and east of International Blvd.; there have been rumors of drive-by shootings and gang activity in this area.

Local buses, which travel long routes to all areas of Brownsville, run from 6am-7pm and cost 75¢ (50¢ students and seniors); all buses leave on the hour or the half-hour from City Hall on E. Washington St., between E. 11th and E. 12th. Ask for

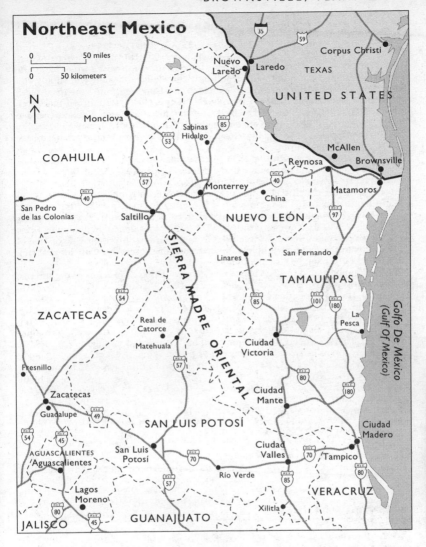

Northeast Mexico

0 — 50 miles
0 — 50 kilometers

N ↑

schedules inside the building or call 548-6050 for route and schedule information. Be prepared to practice that Spanish.

PRACTICAL INFORMATION

Tourist Office: Chamber of Commerce, 1600 E. Elizabeth (tel. 542-4341), downtown near the border. Loads of practical advice, plus the invaluable *Guide to*

Brownsville. Valuable maps and brochures. Open Mon.-Fri. 8am-5pm. **Brownsville Convention and Visitors Bureau,** 802 Farm Rd. (tel. (800) 626-2639 or 546-3721), at Central Blvd., adjacent to the Sunset Mall on Expressway 77, near Motel 6, a 15-min. bus ride from downtown. From City Hall take the "Jefferson Central" or *"Los Ébanos"* bus and get off near the highway across from the pyramid-shaped tan building. Friendly and knowledgeable staff will supply you with tons of maps and brochures. Open Mon.-Sat. 8am-5pm, Sun. 9am-4pm.

Currency Exchange: Express Money Exchange, 801 International Blvd. (tel. 548-0303), exchanges traveler's checks. Open daily 10am-6pm. *Casas de cambio* line International Blvd.; rates are nearly identical and better than banks'.

American Express: 2390 Central Road. Traveler's checks and travel arrangements. Open Mon.-Fri. 8am-5pm.

Telegrams: Western Union, 2814 International Blvd. (tel. 542-8695). Send or receive telegrams, messages, and money orders. Open daily 7:30am-8pm.

Airports: Brownsville and South Padre International Airport, at 700 S. Minnesota (tel. 542-4373). Taxis to downtown US$9. Currently offers 8 flights a day to and from Houston. Less convenient is **Valley International Airport** (tel. 430-8600), in Harlingen, Texas, 42km northwest of Brownsville. Taxis to Brownsville run US$40-45. The bus charges US$24 for the lonesome cowpoke plus $12 a head for company. Some get free rides from the airport to Brownsville on one of the vans to the expensive hotels. Both airports are served by **Continental** (tel. (800) 231-0856 and 541-2200 locally).

Buses: Greyhound, 1134 E. Charles St. (tel. 546-7171), 2 blocks from the International Bridge. To Dallas (6 per day, 13hr., US$49), Houston (5 per day, 9hr., US$22), Laredo (1 per day, 6hr., US$25), and San Antonio (6 per day, 7hr., US$31). Schedules do change; call ahead. Reservations can be made 1 day in advance. **Luggage storage** US$1 per day. **Valley Transit Company,** 1305 E. Adams (tel. 546-2264), at 13th St. **Lockers** available for 75¢ per day. To Laredo (7:15am, 6hr., US$17), McAllen (every hr. 1:15pm-5:15pm, 7:15pm and midnight, 2hr., US$9), and many towns in Texas and Mexico.

Market: H.E.B. Store #1, 924 E. Elizabeth (tel. 542-4191), across the street from the post office. Open daily 7am-9pm.

Laundromat: Holiday Laundry (tel. 542-9002), Elizabeth and West 6th. About 1.5km northwest of the Int'l Bridge. Self-service wash US$1 per load, 50¢ per dry.

Pharmacy: Walgreen's, 770 W Elizabeth St. (tel. 546-3701). Open 9:30am-10pm.

Hospital: Brownsville Medical Center, 1040 West Jefferson (tel. 544-1400), on the corner with Central Blvd.

Emergency: 911.

Police: 600 E. Jackson (tel. 548-7000).

Post Office: Elizabeth St. and E. 10th., in the beautiful Greek Revival/brick masonry courthouse building. Open Mon.-Fri. 7am-9pm.

Telephone Area Code: 210

ACCOMMODATIONS

Lacking the standardized appearance and cheap floral prints of most American motels, lodging in Brownsville gently prepares the southbound traveler for the hotel life that is to come. Brownsville prices, however, are certainly American. Expect to pay US$30-40 for a single in the downtown area; most national chains await several blocks east for slightly more. Although more convenient, the downtown area is more dangerous at night than the distant area along the North Expressway.

Cameron Motor Hotel, 912 E. Washington (tel. 542-3551). Take refuge from the interminable heat in the cool lobby/lounge. Rooms come with bath, cable TV (65 channels!), A/C, and telephones—enough equipment to drown out the noise from the cars passing on the street below. Singles US$32. Doubles US$45.

Motel 6, 2255 North Expressway (tel. (800) 466-8356 and 546-4699; fax 546-8982), off U.S. 77 and 802. The enticing advantages of a national chain (cable TV, pool, free shampoo) might be worth the jaunt kilometers away from the heart and soul of Brownsville. Downtown accessible by "Jefferson Central" or *"Los Ébanos"* bus. Reservations suggested during March due to college Spring Breakers. Singles US$29, US$6 second person, US$3 each additional person.

Plaza Square Motel, 2255 Central Blvd. (tel. 546-5104), conveniently located across the street form the AmEx office and on the bus route 7.5km from downtown. Offers the usual amenities (pool, cable TV) amid quirky decor. Inviting restaurant and lounge. Singles US$28. Doubles US$30. Each additional person US$5.

FOOD

Catering primarily to local residents, Brownsville restaurants serve up a colorless combination of simple Mexican dishes and bland American fare. Downtown, cafés open and close early following an American meal schedule; all offer similar menus of burgers and burritos.

Lucio's Café, 1041 E. Washington (tel. 542-0907). Warmly lit, clean and relaxing, the air at Lucio's is filled with conversation and the sounds of Mexican hits from the jukebox. House specialties include the *caldo de res* (beef soup, US$2.75) and *menudo* (beef tripe soup, US$3.75). Specializes in Mexican cuisine, but the fulmen will please everyone's palate. Ice-cold A/C. Open 24hr.

Rutledge's Restaurant, 1126 E. Washington, located in a narrow (read: 1.5 short meters) alleyway between two buildings. Next to Zepeda hardware. Locals claim everyone has eaten at this burger-lover's mecca. Unique atmosphere and a wide selection of hearty food for under US$2 keep the crowds coming.

Artichoke Deli, 108 E. Elizabeth St. (tel. 544-7636), a 10-min. walk from downtown. Eclectic furnishings and walls adorned with colorful pop-art liven up this haven for salsa-weary border warriors. Fresh salads and sandwiches go for about US$5. Best for lunch. Open Mon.-Thurs., Sat. 11am-4pm, Fri.11am-midnight.

SIGHTS

It may look like a humdrum run-down border town, but Brownsville is home to one of the top zoos in the nation for rare and endangered species, as well as several museums honoring the city's role in American history. The **Gladys Porter Zoo,** 500 Ringold St. (tel. 546-7187), off E. 6th St., offers a 31-acre tropical sanctuary where most animals live in open quarters surrounded only by waterways. The collection includes lowland gorillas, Sumatran orangutans, and white rhinos (open daily 9am-8pm, tickets sold only until 5:30pm; admission US$5.75, children US$2.75).

For a dose of Brownsville history, visit the **Stillman House Museum,** 1305 E. Washington St. (tel. 542-3929). Renovations have restored this brick Greek Revival structure, the home of Brownsville's founder, to its 1850s splendor. The real trip is Concepción "Kino" Camarillo, the museum's caretaker for 51 years; his stories and insightful bicultural perspectives are a delight (open Mon.-Fri. 10am-noon and 2-5pm, Sun. 3-5pm, admission US$2, children US50¢). Housed in the old Southern Pacific Railroad Depot, the **Historic Brownsville Museum,** 641 E. Madison (tel. 548-1313), emphasizes the military legacy of the region (open Mon.-Sat. 10am-4:30pm, Sun. 2-5pm; admission US$2, children under 16 US50¢).

TAMAULIPAS

▓ Matamoros

Texans joke that the narrow dusty roads of Matamoros were designed less for cars and trucks than for carts and horses. Brownsville's sister city to the south isn't the most charming of towns—it's a bit filthy and provincial—but still manages to reel in visitors. Graced with the surname "Unconquerable and Heroic Town" after its residents quelled a separatist attack following the end of the Mexican-American War, present-day Matamoros (pop. 350,000) still defends itself from the hordes of *gringo* invaders that descend on the town every spring break and summer.

ORIENTATION

Matamoros lies 38km west of the Gulf Coast on the Río Bravo. Route 2, which follows the course of the river northwest to Reynosa (100km) and Nuevo Laredo (350km), also passes through the center of Matamoros. If walking (beware of overwhelming mid-day heat) or traveling by car from Brownsville, you must cross the **International Bridge,** located at the northernmost part of Matamoros. Upon arrival in Mexico, you will pass the customs and tourist offices on your right. To reach the center of town from the border area, take one of the yellow mini-buses labeled *"Centro."* To reach the bus station, take one labeled *"Central"* (1 peso). Taxi drivers will try to charge exorbitant rates to the market area, but those who are persistent should be able to whittle them down to 10-15 pesos. If you're returning to the border, catch a mini-bus marked *"Puente"* (0.80 pesos).

From the border crossing, the city extends out in a V-shape following the bend in the Río Bravo; the left (eastern) arm of the V is defined by **Calle 1,** which runs parallel to the river and leads directly to the **Central de Autobuses,** 2km down in the southeast corner of the city. As the city opens up to the right (west), the numbered streets increase. **Álvaro Obregón** forms the other wing of the V, also running parallel with the river and the railroad tracks. It becomes **Calle Hidalgo** after **Calle 7.**

The region located directly by the border, where numbered streets intersect flower streets **(Lilas, Gladiolas),** is filled with beautiful homes. Adjacent to the west is the **Zona Rosa,** offering the biggest tourist boutiques and fanciest hotels. Heading south farther away from the border, the *centro* emerges along **Calle Sexta,** the main street packed with banks, hotels, and restaurants.

The two best options for crossing the border are by foot or in a private car (bring along all documentation). Due to prohibitive increases in insurance rates, few buses and taxis have crossed the border since 1989. A 100m-long bridge joins Matamoros and Brownsville. Pedestrians pay 25¢ or 1 peso to leave either country. Crossing by foot is as easy as dropping in a quarter and pushing through a turnstile. Autos pay US$1, but be sure you've checked your insurance before you cross—most U.S. insurance is null and void in Mexico. Pamphlets detailing rules and regulations for entering the country are available at the immigration office at the border or at most tourist centers. (For more information on crossing the border, see p. 10 and p. 11).

PRACTICAL INFORMATION

Tourist Office: Get your Matamoros maps from the Brownsville Chamber of Commerce, only two blocks from the border. Enterprising local cab drivers have established two shack-like **Información Turismo** stands: one next to the immigration office and another across from the Gran Hotel Residencial, where Obregón turns into Hidalgo; maps and other essentials are rarely available. No set hours—just pray they're open. The **Hotel Plaza Matamoros** and **Hotel Roma,** on Calle 9 between Bravo and Matamoros, distribute fantastic city maps.

U.S. Consulate: Calle 1 232 (tel. 6-72-70 or 6-72-72), at Azaleas. Open Mon.-Tues. and Thurs.-Fri. 8am for visa interviews and 1-4pm for social security, passport, and citizenship concerns. Guards can admit American citizens with emergencies.

Currency Exchange: Banks line Calle 6 and the Plaza Hidalgo and are open for exchange 9am-1:30pm. *Casas de cambio* dot the centro, particularly along Calle 5 and 6, but the best exchange rates await in the bus station or from friendly **ATMs** like the one at **Bancomer** (tel. 13-90-00), at Matamoros and Calle 6, or the one at **Red Banorte,** on the corner of Calle 6 and Morelos.

Telephones: There are **LADATELs** located inside the bus station, along Abasolo between Calle 7 and 8, and in Plaza Hidalgo. **Computel,** on Calle 5 between Gonzalez and Morelos, offers phone and fax service. Open Mon.-Sat. 8am-10pm.

Telegrams: Next to the post office in the bus station. Open Mon.-Fri. 9am-1pm.

Airport: On Rte. 101, the highway to Ciudad Victoria, 5km south of town. **Aeroméxico** (tel. 13-07-02), on the corner of Calle 7 and Matamoros, offers service to (7am and 6pm, 2hr., 555 pesos) and from (7am, 4 and 7pm, 2hr., 555 pesos) Mexico City. Open Mon.-Fri. 9am-6pm, Sat. 9am-noon.

Buses: Central de Autobuses, Canales at Aguiles, off Calle 1. Any *pesera* (minibus) marked *"Central"* will pass the station; ask the driver to stop. Luggage storage available next to the currency exchange booth, 1 peso per hour. **Ómnibus de México** (tel. 13-76-93) to Guadalajara (5 per day), Chihuahua (2 per day), Monterrey, Saltillo, Reynosa, and Río Bravo (on the hr., 12 per day). **ADO** (tel. 12-01-81) to Tampico (2 per day, 8hr., 100 pesos), Tuxpan (1 per day, 160 pesos), and Veracruz with numerous stops in between (2 per day, 300 pesos). **Noreste** (tel. 13-27-68) offers the cheapest and most frequent buses to Monterrey (16 per day, 4hr., 77 pesos), and also travels to Reynosa (14 per day, 2hr., 22 pesos). **Autobuses del Norte** (tel. 12-27-77), to Mexico City (1 *ejecutivo* per day, 290 pesos; 4 *primera* per day, 220 pesos), Saltillo (6 per day, 90 pesos), and San Luis Potosí (3 per day, 150 pesos).

Trains: Ferrocarriles Nacionales de México (tel. 6-67-06), on Hidalgo between Calles 9 and 10. Slow daily service to Reynosa and Monterrey beginning at 9:20am. If you can't take the faster, more reliable bus, buy a ticket ahead of time and arrive early for boarding.

Market: Gigante, across from the bus station. Mexico's take on Walmart: supermarket, general store, pharmacy, and cafeteria all in one. Open daily 8am-10pm.

Laundromat: Iturbide 748 #202 (tel. 13-76-93), 1 block south of Hidalgo by Calle 7. Self-service wash and dry 5 pesos each. Open daily 7am-10pm.

Pharmacy: Farmacia Aristos del Golfo, on Calle 1 between González and Morelos. Joined to the hospital. Cordial pharmacists speak limited English. Open 24hr.

Red Cross: (tel. 2-00-44), Caballero at García. English spoken. Open 24hr. For emergency medical aid also try the **clínica** along Canales, 3 blocks from the Central de Autobuses toward the center of the city along Calles 4 and 5. Open 24hr.

Police: (tel. 2-03-22 or 6-07-00). Some English spoken. Open 24hr.

Post Office: In the bus station. Open Mon.-Fri. 8am-2:30pm. **Postal Code:** 87361.

Telephone Code: 891.

ACCOMMODATIONS

The stop, shop, and go attitude of many visitors to Matamoros is painfully apparent in the underdeveloped hotel trade. Although prices are entirely reasonable, expect the basics—and little more. The cheapest hotels, among them **Hotel Majestic** (Abasolo 89, tel. 3-36-80) and **Hotel Colonial** (Matamoros 601, tel. 16-64-18), cluster in the *centro*. Spend a little extra and receive a far more pleasant, comfortable, and relaxing experience. The market area, where most of the budget accommodations are located, quickly loses the crowds after nightfall—be careful, be very careful.

Hotel México, Abasolo 87 (tel. 2-08-56), on the pedestrian mall between Calles 8 and 9. The bargain-basement of budget accommodations. Yellow walls and bare rooms emphasize the importance of basics—running water and soft mattresses. Beware the noisy street-side rooms. Singles 30 pesos. Doubles 60 pesos.

Hotel Nieto, Calle 10 #1508 (tel. 13-46-60), a block north of the Juárez Market. Do you miss Grandma? You're sure to find her late-50s furniture in this garishly decorated yet lovable hotel. A/C, pool, restaurant/bar, and huge parking lot make it worth the few extra pesos. Singles 132 pesos. Doubles 152 pesos.

Hotel Sexta Avenida (tel. 16-66-66 and 16-66-96), on Calle 6 between Zaragoza and Terán. Location, location, location! Agreeable, modern accommodations between the *centro* and the bus station (a 10-min. walk will get you to either). Singles 132 pesos. Doubles 152 pesos.

FOOD

Caught between the two extremes of *gringo*-friendly restaurants and more local eateries, a safe bet in Matamoros is to follow the crowd at meal time. Several great smaller cafés are hidden between Calle 6 and Calle 9.

Cafetería Las Vigas (tel. 13-99-05), Calle 8, between Morelos and González 104. Tastefully renovated, and blushing with colonial charm, Las Vigas is a true labor of love in *gringo*-gagged Matamoros. Huge omelettes (15 pesos), and music that'll lower the highest of stress levels. Breakfast specials 8-10 pesos.

Café y Restaurant Frontera (tel. 3-24-40), Calle 6 between N. Bravo and Matamoros. Locals stop by to marvel at the optical-illusion floor while digging into Mexican specialties for 10-15 pesos. Breakfast a bit less, larger meat and seafood entrees a bit more. Look for the heart-shaped sign. Open daily 7am-10pm.

Cafetería 1916, Calle 6 191 (tel. 3-07-27), between Matamoros and Abasolo. Try *sincronizadas 1916* (flour tortilla with ham, chicken, and avocado) for 12.50 pesos or any of the beef dishes (16-20 pesos). Their desserts are rumored to be "better than sex." You make the call. Open daily 10am-10pm.

SIGHTS AND ENTERTAINMENT

Brash vendors pounce upon any sign of interest, so look both wary and weary. The old market, or **Pasaje Juárez,** has entrances on both Matamoros and Bravo between Calles 8 and 9. Bright *piñatas* and rows of glittering jewelry brighten the dim interior of **Mercado Juárez,** the new market on Abasolo between Calles 9 and 10. Like its older cousin, the market overflows with souvenirs. The vendors in Pasaje Juárez are more eager to please and can be talked into a decent deal. Avoid succumbing to temptation, though—markets farther south offer higher quality and lower prices.

For a cultured alternative to discos, stop by the **Teatro de la Reforma** (tel. 12-51-21), on Calle 6 between González and Abasolo. Renovated in 1992, the theater shows everything from classical drama to contemporary Mexican theater. Ticket prices for most shows are 20-30 pesos. Call for tickets and schedules. After the show, tourists in need of some pampering and tender loving care can sink into the ventilated, out-of-this-dirty-hot-world-if-only-for-a-few-short-hours atmosphere of **Las Dos Repúblicas** (tel. 6-68-94), on Calle 9, between Matamoros and Abasolo. 18-oz. frozen Margaritas US$6; *piña de la casa* arrives in a real pineapple. You keep the pineapple, they keep US$7 (open daily 8am-8pm).

■ Reynosa

Despite its growth from a 1749 Spanish colony to its present size of over 600,000, the small-town atmosphere and quiet charm have yet to leave Reynosa. The surroundings recall old Zorro movies and convey a celebration of Spanish and Mexican culture tempered only slightly by economic hardship. There isn't a whole lot to see or do in Reynosa, but the wide, clean streets and delightful plaza make it a pleasant place to just mill about before venturing further south. (For information on crossing the border, see p. 10 and p. 11.)

ORIENTATION

Reynosa is 150km from Monterrey and 645km from Mexico City; it can be reached from McAllen, Texas by taking 23rd St. 12km south into Hidalgo and then over the International Bridge. From Mexico, Route 2 from Matamoros and Route 40 from Monterrey both lead straight into town. The city forms a square with the **International Bridge** border crossing forming the northeast corner. **Central de Autobuses** is located on Colón and Rubio at the southeast corner of town; the **train station** is on Hidalgo, at the southern tip of town. The city rises to the central plaza which is bordered by the church and Hidalgo marketplace. *Peseros* run in nearly all directions for about 1 peso; taxis will try to overcharge so haggle.

Hidalgo is the chief north-south thoroughfare. Perpendicular to it from north to south are Allende, Zaragoza, Morelos, Matamoros, Guerrero, Méndez, and Colón. **Morelos** is the main east-west drag, and perpendicular to it are Victoria, Díaz, Hidalgo, Juárez, Chapa, Canales, Mina, and Rubio.

PRACTICAL INFORMATION

Tourist Office: Cámara de Comercio, on Chapa and Allende, provides a very accurate, detailed map of the city. Open Mon.-Fri. 9am-4:30pm. The **Casa de la Cultura de Reynosa** (tel. 22-13-08), next door, is also extremely helpful.

Currency Exchange: *Casas de cambio* are scattered all along Hidalgo and the plaza area, but most will not accept traveler's checks; the **Centro de Cambios "Reynosa"** Matamoros 505 (tel. 22-90-60), is one of the few that will. **Erika Viajes,** Ávila Camacho 1325, a decent trek from the plaza, provides most **American Express** services, including traveler's checks. **Banco Mercantil del Norte,** on the south end of the plaza, offers 24-hr. **ATMs.**

Telephones: LADATELs are scattered throughout the plaza and Hidalgo market. **Fax de Reynosa** is on Hidalgo, on the east edge of the plaza. Open 8am-10pm.

Buses: On Colón in the southwest corner of town. Taxis linger in front of the bus station to take you to the *centro*, and are not supposed to charge you more than the rate posted on the sign out front (15 pesos). **ADO** offers primarily evening service with routes to Tampico (2 per day, 114 pesos), Veracruz (2 per day, 262 pesos), and Villahermosa (1 per day, 358 pesos). **Futurama** offers *ejecutivo* and *primera clase* service to Monterrey (4 per day, 3hr., 69 and 53 pesos), Mexico City (3 per day, 15hr., 310 and 239 pesos), and Guadalajara (2 per day, 18hr., 301 and 232 pesos). **Ómnibus de México** offers service to Monterrey (10 per day, 4hr., 53 pesos), Saltillo (9 per day, 6hr., 67 pesos), and Chihuahua (2 per day, 234 pesos). **Noreste** offers the most extensive service; it will take you to San Luis Potosí (7 per day, 145 pesos), Matamoros (25 per day, 2 hr., 21 pesos), Monterrey (30 per day, 4hr., 53 pesos), or many other destinations.

Trains: Station located in a filthy, decrepit part of town; to reach it follow Hidalgo south from the main plaza for 6 blocks. Unreliable, slow service to Matamoros (2:45pm, 2½hr., 8pesos) and Monterrey (11:40am, 4½hr., 20 pesos).

Market: Gigante, across from the bus station on Colón. Open daily 8am-10pm.

Laundromat: Peña Villarreal Antonio, Victoria Pte. 220 (tel. 22-42-34). Open Mon.-Sat. 8am-9pm.

Red Cross: (tel. 22-13-14), on Boulevard Morelos, just south of town off Chapa.

Pharmacy: Centro Médico, Rubio 531 (tel. 22-30-75) between Méndez and Madero, 3 blocks west of the bus stop next to all the *hospitales*. Open 24hr.

Hospital: Hospital San Vicente (tel. 22-50-93), on Zaragoza 3 blocks west of the plaza; **Hospital Santander** (tel. 22-96-22), 1 block north of the bus station.

Emergency: tel. 06.

Police: tel. 22-00-88 or 22-07-90.

Post Office: On the corner of Díaz and Colón by the train station. Open Mon.-Fri. 8am-8pm, Sat. 9am-1pm. **Postal Code:** 88630

Telephone Code: 89

ACCOMMODATIONS

The many hotels around the plaza and *Zona Rosa* are pricey. Look for the cheapest hotels around south Díaz and Hidalgo streets near the train station. Though boisterous and congested during the day, this area becomes desolate, and even a little scary, at night. Be very, very careful.

Hotel Avenida, Zaragoza 885 Ote. (tel. 22-05-92). The best of both worlds—central patio with lush flora and chirping birds is traditionally Mexican, but carpeted floors and deodorized bathrooms make this bargain very reminiscent of a U.S. chain. With its proximity to the main plaza and an A/C-TV combo, you just can't beat their prices. Singles 100 pesos. Doubles 150 pesos.

Hotel San Miguel (tel. 22-75-27), just 2 blocks from the bus station. Amenities galore: clean, colorful bathrooms, cable TV, and A/C (make sure it works in your room). Singles 80 pesos. Doubles 120 pesos.

FOOD

Café Paris, Hidalgo 815 (tel. 22-55-35). Elaborately woven seat cushions and modern decor set the stage for a fine dining experience. Breakfast tortillas and enchiladas 8-10 pesos, most meats 17-20 pesos. Order a *café con leche* to savor the tasty java and watch them pour the milk from a height of over a meter to make it froth. Great selection of breads. Open daily 7am-10pm.

Café Sánchez (tel. 22-16-65), on Hidalgo off the southwest corner of the plaza. Despite the classy paintings by Diego Rivera and the picture of Alameda Park, it's the food that really makes Café Sánchez shine. The feast begins with complementary sliced carrots and peppers dipped in vinegar and ends when the pastry/dessert cart rolls along. Wonderful Mexican dishes 20 pesos. Open daily 7am-10pm.

Café Veracruz, Hidalgo 510 (tel. 22-12-68). Hidden behind brash vendors in the Hidalgo marketplace, Café Veracruz offers dark atmosphere, blue neon lights, and a wide selection of seafood platters (9-20 pesos). Open daily 10am-10pm.

SIGHTS AND ENTERTAINMENT

There's nothing like the main plaza at nightfall, where couples, young and old, tend to congregate. The **Hidalgo marketplace** may not offer any substantial deals, but it is a great spot for people-watching. Also near the plaza is the **Casa de la Cultura de Reynosa,** which houses art exhibits and music recitals. For a sampling of Reynosa's history, visit the **Museo Histórico de Reynosa,** Ortega at Allende, which exhibits furniture, archaeological pieces, and photographs of the region (open Mon.-Fri. 9am-2pm and 4-8pm). For an abridged history, check out the beautiful storefront mural on the corner of Zaragoza one block east of Canales, just a few blocks south of the border crossing. It was funded by Bacardí (their billboard forms the last scene of the mural). Doesn't it just make you want to sip an historic rum and coke?

The bars and clubs scattered about the *Zona Rosa* tend to be very popular hangouts for Mexican and American youths. Locals recommend **Bonzai** on Zaragoza three blocks from the border, as well as **Pepe's, Concha,** and **Refrides,** but they warn that most other clubs have had serious barroom brawl problems. For the truly adventurous, a **patinadero** (roller-skating rink) is on Allende and Chapa (tel. 28-15-42; open Mon.-Fri. 12:30-9pm, Sat.-Sun. 10am-10pm).

■ Laredo, Texas

Laredo lacks the sordid, desperate feel of most border towns; everyone's happy to be there, and who can complain in such a verdant, laid-back border paradise? The chipper, nice-doin'-business-with-ya attitude of the town's residents make it a pleasant gateway into Mexico. For information on crossing the border, see p. 10 and p. 11.

ORIENTATION

Laredo's downtown centers around **International Bridge #1,** which becomes **Convent St.** on the U.S. side and runs north. Seven blocks north of the border on Convent is **Jarvis Plaza,** surrounded by all the main government buildings and delimited by **Matamoros** and **Farragut.** The other main thoroughfare is **San Bernardo,** which originates near the border and runs north past some of Laredo's finest historical buildings (the Laredo Civic Center and Chamber of Commerce), as well as numerous motels and restaurants. One block to the east lies **I-35,** the eastern boundary for most travelers; the **Missouri-Pacific Railroad** forms the western boundary. East-west streets are named after American and Mexican military and political figures.

Getting around town is easy thanks to **El Metro city buses,** which run every half hour Monday-Sunday 6am-9pm from Matamoros and Farragut streets on Jarvis Plaza (US60¢, children US25¢). Get schedules from their office, in the Laredo Intermodal Transit Center on the south side of the Plaza (scheduled to be completed in January 1997, tel. 795-22-80).

PRACTICAL INFORMATION

Tourist Office: Chamber of Commerce, 2310 San Bernardo (tel. (800) 292-21-22 or 722-9895), north of the border. Cordial staff offers colorful, informative, and easy-to-read maps and brochures directing you to a plethora of sights and eateries in the downtown area. Open Mon.-Sat. 8:30am-5pm.

Currency exchange: *Casas de cambio* all along Convent, a few sprinkled throughout the downtown. **Laredo National Bank,** 600 San Bernardo, is proud owner of a 24-hr. **ATM.** The building, originally the Plaza Hotel, is worth a visit.

Telegrams: Western Union, 711 Salinas (tel./fax 722-08-50), by Jarvis Plaza. Postal boxes, fax, copies, FedEx, UPS, and pool cues available. Also located in the bus station and every HEB supermarket.

Airport: (tel. 722-49-33), northeast of town on Maher. **American Eagle** (tel. (800) 433-73-00 and 722-8686) flies to and from Dallas (4 per day, 2hr.); **Continental Express** (tel. (800) 525-02-08 and 723-34-02) covers Houston (6 per day, 1½hr.); and **Taesa** (800) 328-23-72 and 725-84-14) goes to Mexico City (daily, 2hr.).

Buses: Station on San Bernardo and Matamoros. **Greyhound** affiliated service to cities throughout the U.S., as well as daily buses to San Luis Potosí (4 per day), León and Aguascalientes (1 per day), Querétaro (2 per day), and Monterrey (7 per day). However, traveling south from Nuevo Laredo is much cheaper and provides more options in terms of destinations and schedules. **Luggage lockers** (US$2 first 6hr., US$1 per 30min.).

Trains: Missouri Pacific Railroad, just west of Jarvis Plaza. Service to Nuevo Laredo, but it's much quicker and cheaper to just take a bus or to walk across.

Market: HEB, downtown 2 blocks from the courthouse. Open daily 8am-9pm.

Laundromat: Sunshine Laundromat, 2900 San Bernardo north of the Chamber of Commerce. Do it yourself (US75¢ wash, US$1 dry, detergent available), or get same-day full service (US$5 small load, US$6.50 large load). Open daily 8am-8pm.

Pharmacy: J&A Pharmacy, 201 West Del Mar Blvd. (tel. 717-38-39), far north of town. Open Mon.-Fri. 9am-8pm, Sat. 9am-4pm.

Hospital: Mercy Regional Medical Center, 1515 Logan Ave. (tel. 718-62-22).

Police: 1300 Matamoros (tel. 723-36-43), in the beautiful Greek Revival building facing Jarvis Plaza.

Post Office: 1300 Matamoros St. (tel. 723-36-43), near the Greyhound bus station. Open Mon.-Fri. 8am-5pm, Sat. 8am-noon. **Zip Code:** 78040.

Telephone code: 210.

ACCOMMODATIONS

Nice hotels in Nuevo Laredo are cheaper than the most inexpensive Laredo lodgings. Nevertheless, those who value American motel amenities (drinkable tap water or national-chain status) will find an ample selection along San Bernardo, north of the Chamber of Commerce. All lodgings are accessible by the #2 El Metro city bus.

Mayan Motor Inn, 3219 San Bernardo (tel. 722-81-81). The charming wooden furnishings, pig-leather trappings, bathtubs, A/C, TVs, parking, lobby with coffee bar, and ceremonial recreational pool would no doubt make Chac, Mayan god of water, proud. Singles US$28. Doubles US$35.

Hamilton Hotel, 815 Salinas (tel. 723-64-21), downtown facing Jarvis Plaza. An intriguing option for longer term guests, this old downtown hotel offers rooms with cable TV, bath, and A/C all for a weekly fee of US$100 (minimum stay), 2 weeks US$190, 1 month US$275 and US$50 deposit. Rates negotiable.

FOOD

Head downtown for a copious culinary selection with a strong emphasis on tex-mex cuisine (who knew?). Salsa-phobes can find salvation in seafood restaurants or Chinese buffets. Fast-food joints and yummy *taquerías* line San Bernardo.

Tacolare, 1206 San Bernardo (tel. 727-81-00), just north of the railroad tracks. Small storefront disguises a large and inviting restaurant with charming tiled decor and central kitchen area. Watch tacos being brought into the world (great selection, all under US$5). Open 11am-10pm.

La Finca Café, 503 San Bernardo. A tiny well kept local secret. Mexican music and a decidedly white-tailed deer decor create a south of the border ambience. *Antojitos* (enchiladas, *chiles rellenos, mole*) are US$3.75. On Fridays, you too can try *fritada cabrito* (fried kid goat) for US$5. Open daily noon-8pm.

SIGHTS AND ENTERTAINMENT

The **Civic Center,** on San Bernardo about 1km north of the border, is the place to catch traveling performances or the **Laredo Philarmonic Orchestra** (tel. 727-88-86). Concerts take place at 8pm during the October-May season. Drop in at the **Webb County Historical Heritage Foundation** to peruse Laredo's extensive archives; it's in Market Hall, 1005 Zaragoza St. (tel. 727-34-80) and open Monday through Friday 8:30am-5pm. Every February, Laredo turns into one big party for **Washington's Birthday Celebration,** which includes a parade—led by the town princess dressed as Pocahontas—and the Martha Washington Ball. For something a bit less exotic, try **Yerbería de San Judas,** on 711 Salinas (tel. 725-83-36), a witchcraft store selling herbs and religious charms.

■ Nuevo Laredo

Nuevo Laredo pulses with commerce from small souvenir shops to the enormous tractor trailers passing through with NAFTA-spurred trade. Originally a non-missionary, non-military *frontera* outpost, the city served as a ranching center in the 18th and 19th centuries. In the late 1800s, the city assumed its role as the commercial gateway to Mexico with the Missouri-Pacific railway connection. This pivotal role was further solidified with the arrival of the Pan-American Highway in 1935. Today, pesos and dollars pour through Nuevo Laredo at a dizzying pace, leaving its residents to snatch the crumbs that fall through the cracks.

International Bridge #1 is the main way for pedestrians to go into Mexico; simply plunk down the US35¢. (For information on crossing the border, see p. 10 and p. 11.)

ORIENTATION

Travelers stick to the *centro*. **Avenida Guerrero** emerges from **International Bridge #1** as the main thoroughfare running south from the border. Three plazas along Guerrero define the downtown, with small, inviting **Plaza Juárez** just two blocks from the border; large, central **Plaza Hidalgo** adjoining the **Palacio Federal** in the heart of the city; and **Plaza México** with its endearing fountain farthest south. The train station forms the extreme western boundary of downtown, and the bus station lies to the far south of town.

PRACTICAL INFORMATION

Tourist Office: Delegación Turismo (tel. 12-01-04), at the Nuevo Laredo tip of the bridge before Mexican customs. Useful, though slightly unwieldy map; extensive supply of brochures in both Spanish and English.

Currency exchange: As usual, *casas de cambio* (especially the one at the border) offer the best exchange rates. Major banks line Guerrero near Plaza Hidalgo. **Banamex**, on Canales and Guerrero, has a 24-hr. **ATM.**

Telephones: LADATELs are to be found throughout the downtown border area, particularly near Plaza Hidalgo and Plaza Juárez.

Telegrams: Western Union, on Valle on the east side of the Palacio Federal. Open Mon.-Fri. 9am-8pm. **Fax** 9am-7pm. *Giros* (money wire) Mon.-Fri. 8am-6pm, Sat.-Sun. 9am-noon.

Airport: (tel. 14-07-05), at the extreme southwest of the city, off Rte. 2. Purchase Aeroméxico tickets at **Viajes Furesa,** Guerrero 830 (tel. 12-96-68) for the 11:50am flight to Mexico City (via Guadalajara) or for the 6pm direct flight.

Buses: Station is at Refugio Romo 3800, southwest of the city and quite a trek from the *centro*. To get to the border take any blue-and-white or green-and-white bus marked *"Puente."* To get to the station from the border take the bus marked *"Central."* 24-hr. **luggage storage** 18 pesos. **Ómnibus de México** goes to Aguascalientes (5 per day, 186 pesos), Guanajuato (4 per day, 217 pesos), Jalapa (190 pesos), Saltillo (4½hr., 76 pesos), Zacatecas (5 per day, 9hr., 158 pesos), Monterrey (4 per day, 3hr., 44 pesos). **Noreste** travels to Matamoros (3 per day) and Reynosa (6 per day, 3½hr.). **Turistar** can take you to Acapulco (420 pesos), Morelia (267 pesos), Mexico City (*ejecutivo* 356 pesos; *primera clase* 273 pesos), Querétaro (289 pesos or 223 pesos). **Futura** travels to Guadalajara (*ejecutivo* 310 pesos; *primera clase* 223 pesos), León (282 pesos or 217 pesos), and San Luis Potosí (258 pesos or 178 pesos). **Transportes del Norte** goes to Ciudad Victoria (7 per day, 7hr., 134 pesos), Ciudad Valles (178 pesos), Monterrey (every 30min., 3hr., 58 pesos), and Tampico (1 per day, 12hr., 174 pesos).

Trains: Station on López de Lara near Gutiérrez, in the west end of town. The big event is one train per day, leaving for Monterrey at 6:55am (*primera clase* 37 pesos, *segunda clase* 21 pesos).

Market: Gigante, Reforma 4243, on the southern extension of Guerrero.

Pharmacy: Farmacia Calderón, on Guerrero west of Plaza Hidalgo. Open 24hr.

Hospital: ISSTE, on Victoria and Reynosa to the east of Plaza Juárez by the border.

Red Cross: (tel. 12-09-89), on Independencia and Méndez, east of Plaza Hidalgo.

Emergency: 06.

Police: (tel. 12-30-25), in the Palacio Federal, on the west side facing Plaza Hidalgo.

Post office: In the Palacio Federal, on the north-east corner of Dr. Mier and Camargo. Open Mon.-Fri. 9am-6pm, Sat. 9am-12:30pm.

Telephone code: 87.

ACCOMMODATIONS

Budget hotels abound in the *centro*. Both the low prices and the bare-bones quality serve as strong introductions (or lingering reminders) of the realities of life south of the border.

Motel Don Antonio, González 2435 (tel. 12-18-76), on the southeast corner of Plaza Hidalgo. Awake to the pleasant chirping of songbirds or to the cock-a-doodle-doo of the owner's rooster smack in the center of town. Imaginative decoration includes red carpets, red velvet chairs, and red Chinese-print bed covers. TV and central A/C. Arrive early to snag a room. Singles 70 pesos. Doubles 80 pesos.

Motel Las Vegas, Arteaga 3017 (tel. 12-20-30), just a couple blocks west of Guerrero and 4 blocks south of Plaza Hidalgo. Recently renovated, spacious rooms now boast folkloric wooden furniture, immaculate bathrooms, and central A/C. Stellar value. Singles 50 pesos. Doubles 60 pesos.

Gran Hotel Rendón (tel. 12-05-32), González and Juárez, 2 blocks west of Plaza Hidalgo. A sanctum of serenity. The inviting, screened atrium glows in a bath of perpetual light, which illuminates the warm orange tiling and the soothing central fountain. Rooms have fans, A/C, TVs, and modern, clean bathrooms. Singles 124 pesos. Doubles 134 pesos.

FOOD

Home to the often imitated, never duplicated *fajita,* Nuevo Laredo's culinary fortes are meat and seafood. *Cabrito,* the roasted goat kid found throughout the northeast, and *fajitas,* often sold by the kilo, are well worth the extra money. The good stuff is south of Herrera, around Guerrero 1700.

Playa Azul (tel. 14-55-35, ext. 735), around Guerrero 2000. Great place to kick back and relax as you enjoy your *ceviche* and *telenovelas* (soap operas). Homey dining room decorated with tasteful *campesino* furniture and a selection of seafood specialties (15-30 pesos) that will blow your mind. Open daily 8am-9pm.
Tortas y Tacos, Guerrero 2220. No surprises here; just plain ol' sandwiches (10-15 pesos) and a wide variety of tacos. Substantial *menús* 22-40 pesos.

SIGHTS AND ENTERTAINMENT

What's a commercial center without a **market?** The largest (and most expensive) ones are concentrated around Guerrero near the border. Since an ample selection of sturdy wooden furniture, pottery, and practical goods exists, this just may be the place for travelers departing from Mexico to load up on souvenirs. Better prices and generally higher quality goods can be found farther south.

Those in search of cultural titillation can head to the **theater** on Victoria and Reynosa, near the border. Strolling up and down Guerrero can be relaxing in the evenings when the three plazas fill with people gaily chatting and whiling away the time; the fountain on Nacatez and Guerrero is a favorite resting spot. Two **movie theaters,** one on the southwest corner of Plaza Hidalgo and the other on Madero and Guerrero, offer American films with Spanish subtitles for only 12 pesos. If all the sightseeing has left you thirsty, head to **Señor Frogs,** the self-proclaimed "Home of the Mother Margarita," just blocks south of the border. More "mature" jazz and rock lounges can be found farther south along Guererro.

Blood Simple

Inspiring more T-shirt designs than Barney and drawing more blood than Dracula, the winged, fanged creature known as **Chupacabras** has become the monster of the moment. A local club passes out flyers for a "Chupacabras dance." In the newspaper's editorial cartoons, the figure appears with the head of ex-President Carlos Salinas and the message "The Only Known Picture of the Chupacabras." No one has ever seen the creature; it is known only by its victims—domesticated animals left dead, their blood sucked dry. Literally, "Chupacabras" means "it sucks goats," but goats are not its only prey; there have been rumors of human victims with the tell-tale fang marks. Some say it's a giant bat; others claim it's an invisible monster from the movie *Predator,* which was filmed in Mexico. There may be more than one Chupacabras, but all do their killing at night. Many Mexicans fear this amorphous monster while others attribute its existence to shifty politicians who are fomenting rumors to divert attention from economic problems. Whatever the case, attacks are on the rise and spreading.

▨ Tampico

While many travelers see Tampico (pop. 270,000) as little more than a pit stop in the race south, the city has had a remarkable history. Founded in the 16th century on the ruins of an Aztec village, Tampico was destroyed by pirates in 1623. Exactly 200 years later, Santa Ana ordered the city re-settled, citing its strategic location and excellent natural harbor. By the turn of the century, Tampico had become one of the two or three most important oil ports in the world.

If you've seen Humphrey Bogart in *The Treasure of the Sierra Madre,* you might think of contemporary Tampico as the dirty, unfriendly oil town that every *gringo* is itching to skip. However, amenities have cropped up to make a brief stay tolerable for those heading south, and the Plaza de Armas, with its vibrant greenery and live concerts, provides refuge from the refuse-ridden streets. For an alternative escape, a nearby beach, **Playa Miramar,** is accessible by either the "Playa" or "Escollera" bus (1.50 pesos from López de Lara and Madero).

Orientation and Practical Information The town centers around the **Plaza de Armas** and the **Plaza de la Libertad.** To the north of the Plaza de Armas is **Calle Carranza,** to the east is **Olmos,** and to the south is **Díaz Mirón.** To get to the city center from the bus stop, take a yellow taxi (20 pesos), minibus (1.50 pesos), or *colectivo* (1.50 pesos, 3 pesos with luggage).

The **tourist office,** 20 de Noviembre 218 Nte., one block west and two blocks north of Pl. de Armas, has got the goods—maps and tourist guides to the city (open Mon.-Fri. 8am-7pm, 2hr. break in the late afternoon). The **U.S. Consulate,** Ejército Mexicano 503, Suite 203 (tel. 13-22-17), is in the northern *colonia* Guadalupe (open Mon.-Fri. 10am-1pm). Exchange currency at **Central de Divisa,** Hidalgo 215 Sur (tel. 12-90-00; open Mon.-Fri. 9am-6pm, Sat. 9am-1:30pm). **Banamex,** on Madero between Aduana and López de Lara, has a 24-hr. **ATM.** No **LADATELs,** but collect calls can be placed from **pay phones** in the plaza. The **police** (tel. 12-10-32 or 12-11-57) are at Tamaulipas at Sor Juana de la Cruz. The **post office,** Madero 309 Ote. (tel. 12-19-27), is at the intersection with Juárez on Pl. de la Libertad (open Mon.-Fri. 8am-7pm, Sat. 9am-1pm). **Postal Code:** 89000.**Telephone Code:** 12.

The **bus station,** on Zapotal, north of the city, has adjoining first- and second-class terminals. **Ómnibus de México** (tel. 13-45-47) serves Ciudad Valles (4 per day, 2hr., 30 pesos), Guadalajara (1 per day, 12hr., 168pesos), Guanajuato (1 per day, 10hr., 124 pesos), Monterrey (1 per day, 8hr., 116 pesos), Querétaro (2 per day, 9hr., 124 pesos), Saltillo (1 per day, 10hr., 125 pesos), Tuxpan (4 per day, 3hr., 51 pesos). **ADO** (tel. 13-41-88) serves Jalapa (2 per day, 9hr., 120 pesos), Matamoros (3 per day, 8hr., 112 pesos), Puebla (3 per day, 9½hr., 119 pesos), Tuxpan (18 per day, 3hr., 51 pesos), and Veracruz (12 per day, 9hr., 120 pesos). **Futura** (tel. 13-46-55) serves Mexico City (1 per day, 9hr., 122 pesos).

The **Sixpack,** Díaz Mirón 405 Ote. (tel. 12-24-15), three blocks east of the southeast corner of the Plaza de Armas, is a **market** which sells more than just beer (open daily 9am-10pm). If you need a **pharmacy,** try **Benavides,** Carranza 102 Pte. (tel. 19-25-25), on the corner of Olmos at the northeast edge of the Plaza de Armas (open Mon.-Sat. 8am-11pm, Sun. 8am-10pm). The **Red Cross** (tel. 12-13-33 or 12-19-46) offers 24-hour ambulance service. English-speaking doctors can be found at the **Hospital General de Tampico,** Ejército Nacional 1403 (tel. 15-22-20 or 13-20-35), near the bus station. In an **emergency,** dial 06. The **police** (tel. 12-10-32 or 12-11-57) are at Tamaulipas at Sor Juana de la Cruz. The **post office,** Madero 309 Ote. (tel. 12-19-27), is at the intersection with Juárez on Pl. de la Libertad (open Mon.-Fri. 8am-7pm, Sat. 9am-1pm). **Postal Code:** 89000.**Telephone Code:** 12.

Accommodations and Food Quality budget hotels are rare in Tampico, but for those willing to pay 120-160 pesos, many of the larger hotels provide excellent rooms. In the downtown area, there is **Hotel Capri,** Juárez 202 Nte. (tel. 12-26-80), between Calles Altamirano and Obregón. Clean, no-frills rooms with fans and free coffee are pleasant, except for the missing toilet seat and noise from the street below (singles and doubles 40 pesos). An equally simple option near the bus station is **Hotel Allende,** Allende 122 (tel. 13-82-57). Exit the bus station to the right, take the first right, and walk uphill half a block (singles 41 pesos; doubles 45 pesos).

Seafood is the standard fare in Tampico. **Café Mundo** (tel. 14-18-31), López de Lara y Díaz Mirón, three blocks east of Pl. de Armas, teems with locals. The menu is varied; most entrees come with beans, fresh bread, and coffee (18-21 pesos). *Torta de milanesa con queso amarillo* with french fries goes for 10 pesos; *orejita con papas rancheras* only 12 pesos (open 24 hr.). At **Cafetería Emir,** Olmos Sur 107 (tel. 12-51-39), you can catch up on the latest *telenovela* while downing a hearty meal from the *menús económicos* (12-16 pesos; open daily 6am-midnight).

NUEVO LEÓN

■ Monterrey

An architecturally avant–garde edifice towering over an aging historic site. Elderly peasants begging at the gates of an impeccable public transit system. Imposing modern buildings that try to measure up against the indomitable heights of the Sierra Madres. This is Monterrey—focused and formidable, smoggy and frenetic, the juxtaposition of wealthy yuppies and a horribly impoverished underclass desperately scrambling for a piece of the city's rapidly expanding economic pie.

Monterrey's battle-cry is progress at all costs. Since its modest beginnings in the late 16th century, the city has known all too well that to slow down is to perish; this conviction is evident in the energized, quick-paced lives led by the 4 million *regiomontanos* who inhabit this industrial base. Whether peddling watches along a commercial thoroughfare or striding, suit-clad, toward a new office in the *Zona Rosa*, citizens of Mexico's third-largest city are keenly aware of the power progress wields and are willing to accept the cultural and historical erosion it exacts.

ORIENTATION

As the largest city in northern Mexico, Monterrey serves as an important transportation hub. The bus and train stations are in the northern part of town, 3km north of the *centro*. All buses in and out of the city pass through Monterrey's huge **Central de Autobuses** at Colón and Villagrán. To reach the city center from the **bus station,** take any bus going south on Pino Suárez, the thoroughfare to the left as you exit the station (#18 lets you off at the central Gran Plaza), or walk two blocks east to the gray subway station at Cuauhtémoc and Colón, and take the **metro** (Line 2, 2 pesos) to Padre Mier or Zaragoza. The **train station** is at Calzada Victoria, six blocks west of the bus station; to get to the bus station from here, walk straight ahead on Victoria for two blocks, turn right on Bernardo Reyes, and then left on Colón.

Downtown, **Avenida Constitución** runs east-west along the Río Catarina, a 10-km long dry riverbed that has been converted into a series of athletic fields. From west to east, the largest streets running north-south across Constitución are **Gonzalitos, Pino Suárez, Cuauhtémoc, Benito Juárez, Zaragoza** and **Zuazúa.** From north to south, streets running east-west and parallel to Constitución are **Washington, 5 de Mayo, 15 de Mayo, Matamoros, Padre Mier, Hidalgo,** and **Ocampo.** The *Zona Rosa* is bounded by Padre Mier to the north, Zaragoza to the east, Ocampo to the south, and Juárez to the west.

Local buses run from 6am to midnight and cost 1.60-1.70 pesos. There are bus stops on nearly every block along Av. Benito Juárez. Buses usually head in only one

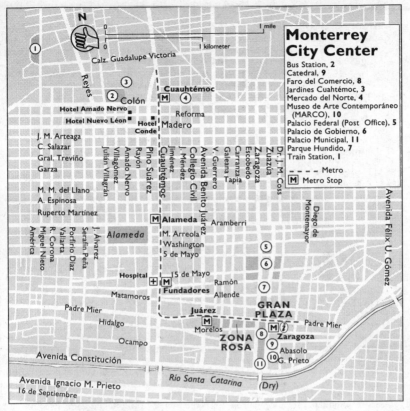

Monterrey City Center

Bus Station, 2
Catedral, 9
Faro del Comercio, 8
Jardines Cuauhtémoc, 3
Mercado del Norte, 4
Museo de Arte Contemporáneo (MARCO), 10
Palacio Federal (Post Office), 5
Palacio de Gobierno, 6
Palacio Municipal, 11
Parque Hundido, 7
Train Station, 1

- - - - Metro
Ⓜ Metro Stop

direction on any given street except for Constitución and Juárez. Buses run from the bus station to the Gran Plaza (#18 or #42), to points along Padre Mier and Hidalgo (#15), and to points on the perimeter of the downtown area (# 69). To get from the budget hotel area to the city center, take the #1 Central or #17 Pío X bus, both of which run the lengths of Pino Suárez and Cuauhtémoc. For more detailed route information, ask locals or the helpful folks at the tourist office.

Although currently under-utilized by the bus-dependent locals, Monterrey's stellar and ever-expanding **subway** system is one of the world's newest and finest, providing cheap first-class service to the *Zona Rosa* as well as many points along Av. Colón and Av. Simón Bolívar (tickets 2 pesos, 3 for 7 pesos, 4 for 9 pesos).

PRACTICAL INFORMATION

Tourist Office: Oficina de Turismo, Padre Mier and Dr. Coss (tel. 345-08-70 or 345-09-02; toll-free (800) 235-2438 from the U.S., 91-800-83-222 in Mexico). Getting here can be confusing since the blue *Infotur* signs point to the office's previous location; these should be changed by January 1997. To get to the current location from the *Zona Rosa,* walk under the Gran Plaza on Padre Mier; the office is in front of *Los Palmares* seafood restaurant. Well worth any hassle finding it. The staff is extraordinarily helpful, guiding tourists with abundant maps and brochures in both English and Spanish. Open Tues.-Sun. 10am-5pm.

Consulates: U.S., Constitución Pte. 411 (tel. 345-21-20), downtown. Open Mon.-Fri. 8am-1pm for passports and citizen's concerns; 1-5pm for visas. For emergencies after hours, U.S. citizens should dial 344-52-61. **U.K.,** Priv. Tamazunchale 104 (tel. 378-25-65). Open Mon.-Fri. 8am-5pm.

Currency Exchange: Banks dot Madero near the budget hotels and flood the *Zona Rosa,* lining Padre Mier in particular, but many refuse to cash traveler's checks. All have 24-hr. **ATMs.** Most open Mon.-Fri. 9am-1:30pm. **Mexdollar Internacional,** 1136 Nte. Pino Suárez (tel. 374-43-11), right by the bus station and Cuauhtémoc subway stop, offers 24-hr. currency exchange at a great rate and without service charge. **Casa de Cambio Trebol** (tel. 342-21-40), Padre Mier Pte., across from the Banco Internacional, changes traveler's checks. Open Mon.-Fri. 9am-6pm, Sat. 9am-1pm; traveler's checks 9am-2pm only.

American Express: Padre Mier Pte. 1424 (tel. 343-09-10), about 1.5km west of the *centro.* Take the #4 bus on Padre Mier from the *Zona Rosa.* Your best bet for changing AmEx checks. Open Mon.-Fri. 9am-1pm and 3-6pm, Sat. 9am-1pm.

Telephones: Most **LADATELs** are clustered in the *Zona Rosa;* long distance and fax service in the bus station between *Salas* 2 and 3, daily 7am-11pm.

Airport: Taxis charge 60 pesos for the 4km trip to the center, *colectivos* 40 pesos. Haggling for a lower price may work. **Aeroméxico,** Cuauhtémoc 812 Sur (tel. 343-55-60), at Padre Mier, and **Mexicana,** Hidalgo 922 Pte. (tel. 340-55-11), run flights to Mexico City, Guadalajara, and various other destinations. Offices open Mon.-Fri. 9am-7pm, Sat. 9am-1pm; make reservations at least 2-3 days in advance, more for weekend travel.

Buses: Colón at Villagrán to Amado Nervo. 24-hr. pharmacy and emergency medical unit. **Luggage storage:** Bag check 1.50 pesos per hour; 24hr. lockers 18 pesos. **Ómnibus de México** to Aguascalientes (2 per day, 8hr., 125 pesos), Chihuahua (3 per day, 12hr., 181 pesos), Guadalajara (4 per day, 11hr., 179 pesos), Mexico City (2 per day, 12hr., 213 pesos), Querétaro (every hr., 10hr., 161 pesos), Zacatecas (3 per day, 6hr., 97 pesos), and more. **Noreste** goes to Laredo, Texas (*primera clase* 4 per day, 3hr., 58 pesos, *regular* 44 pesos), Mazatlán (3 per day, 18 hr., 208 pesos), Puebla (11pm, 273 pesos), Saltillo (hourly, 1¼hr., 19 pesos), San Miguel de Allende (1 per day, 9½hr., 157 pesos), and more. Similar service provided by **Estrella Blanca** (tel. 318-37-47), **Frontera** (tel. 375-09-87), **Líneas Americanas,** and luxurious **Futura** and **Turistar.**

Trains: Región Noreste, Calzada Victoria (tel. 375-46-04). Sometimes cheaper, but always much, much slower than buses. To Matamoros (14 pesos), Mexico City (130 pesos), and Tampico (49 pesos).

Market: Gigante, on Colón, across from the bus station, offers a wide selection of clothes, food items, *panadería*, and adjoining pharmacy. Open Mon. and Wed.-Sat. 9am-10pm, Tues. 9am-9pm. **Mercado del Norte,** also known as La Pulga, is an endless maze of vendor stalls covering Reforma, the street just south of Colón; enter on Colón, two blocks east of the bus station. Everything from cologne to car tires. Haggle. Open from morning to dusk.

Pharmacy: In the bus station or **Benavides,** Pino Suárez at 15 de Mayo. 24hr.

Medical Emergencies and Assistance: Red Cross (tel. 342-12-12 or 375-12-12), at Alfonso Reyes and Henry. Open 24hr. **Cruz Verde,** at Ciudad Madero and Ciudad Victorio (tel. 371-50-50 or 371-52-59). English spoken. Open 24hr. Or try the hospital at subway stop "Hospital."

Emergency: Dial 06.

Police: Arista and Washington, 3rd floor (tel. 340-77-77) for missing persons. To report theft or loss, contact the station at the corner of Carranza and Roberto Martínez (tel. 345-11-11 or 345-30-46). Little to no English spoken.

Post Office: Zaragoza at Washington (tel. 342-40-03), inside the Palacio Federal; or on the 2nd floor of the bus station near *Sala* 3. Both open Mon.-Fri. 8am-7pm, Sat. 9am-1pm. **Postal Code:** 64000.

Telephone Code: 8.

ACCOMMODATIONS

Hotels conveniently located near the *Zona Rosa* inflate their rates to exploit tourists; budget accommodations, catering more to local businessmen, are sprinkled throughout the underdeveloped area near the bus stations. Many rooms are full by early afternoon. Unfortunately, bugs are an ever-present reality in congested Monterrey; if you prefer to sleep alone, ask the management to spray your room. Take precautions when walking in this area at night; the streets become deserted by 10pm.

Hotel Amado Nervo, Amado Nervo 1110 Nte. (tel. 375-46-32). Well furnished rooms with full-length mirrors and giant-sized showers that spew out a steady stream of blissfully hot water. Ask for a room with a view. Management is helpful in combatting insects. Singles 63 pesos. Doubles 89 pesos.

Hotel Nuevo León, Amado Nervo 1007 (tel. 374-19-00). Sure, you'll wake up to the sound of blaring horns and other street noise, but who can complain with such soft beds, warm water, and wonderful, doting staff? Hallway phone available for use by patrons. Singles 60 pesos. Doubles 80 pesos.

Hotel Conde, Reforma Pte. 419 (tel. 375-71-59 and 372-18-79), a gray building concealed by the labyrinthine *Mercado del Norte*. From the bus station, take the Colón walkway 1 block south onto Reforma, then head east. Inviting, quiet rooms with rotary phones and color TVs are marred only slightly by the insect population. Singles 80 pesos. Doubles 92 pesos. A/C 10 more pesos.

FOOD

Barbecued meats, especially *cabrito* (goat kid), are a specialty of northern Mexico; other popular dishes include *agujas* (collar bone), *frijoles a la charra* (beans cooked with pork skin, coriander, tomato, peppers, and onions), *machacado con huevos* (scrambled eggs mixed with dried, shredded beef), hot tamales, and for dessert, *piloncillo con nuez* (hardened brown sugar candy with pecans) or heavenly *glorias* (candy balls of goat's milk and nuts).

Las Monjitas (The Little Nuns), Escobedo 903 (tel. 344-67-13) and 2 other less steamy locations in the *Zona Rosa*. This dark, abbey-like restaurant with servers dressed as nuns is entirely at home in devout Mexico. For a big dinner, tackle Platillo Juan Pablo II—God knows it's good. Enchiladas and *quesadillas* run about 14 pesos; most varieties of *flautas* 13 pesos. Amen. Open daily 8am-11pm.

La Puntada, Hidalgo 123 Ote. (tel. 340-69-85), east of Juárez in the *Zona Rosa*. Designed for the Monterrey businessperson on lunch break, the service is fast and friendly, the atmosphere relaxing, and the conversation stimulating. Jabber away between mouthfuls of ultra-fresh tacos, tortillas, and *hamburguesas*. Breakfast 10 pesos, enchiladas 14 pesos, tacos 10-15 pesos. Open daily 7am-10pm.

El Cabrito, Padre Mier 276B Pte. (tel. 345-12-30), off Cuauhtémoc west of the *Zona Rosa*. Don't let the goat carcasses hanging in the window scare you away; this is *the* place to sample some of the Northeast's best cuisine. *Cabecitas* (head stew) is only 12 pesos, but *cabrito* (goat kid) and some of their finer carnivorous cuts run into the 40-peso range. Have fun, kids. Open daily 8am-10pm.

SIGHTS AND ENTERTAINMENT

Monterrey's expansive and incongruous **Gran Plaza** screams overkill. Revered architectural relics, forced to compete with looming concrete structures, seem decrepit and out-of-place surrounding the enormous, raised central plaza. Slate-grey monoliths coldly peer down at the sprawling civic center in a manner reminiscent of Orwell's *1984*. The Gran Plaza is bounded by Washington on the north, Constitución on the south, Zaragoza on the west, and Zuazúa on the east. At its northern extreme stands the **Palacio Federal,** which serves as the post office and is nearly hidden from sight by a ring of trees and an unkempt courtyard. Immediately to the south is the state capital building, the **Palacio de Gobierno,** a magnificent colonial structure graced by a columned front and a beautiful central courtyard. Outside sprawls the **Esplanada de los Héroes,** a plaza graced with the statues of four famous Mexicans (Miguel Hidalgo stands at the northwest corner, Benito Juárez at the northeast, Morelos at the southwest, and Escobedo at the southeast). Soothing fountains mark the southern end of the plaza.

Just off the northeast corner of the Gran Plaza, the **Museo de Historia Mexicana,** at Dr. Coss 445 Sur (tel. 345-98-98), mimics the ridges of the Saddle Mountain in the background. This geometric sandstone structure differs greatly from the gray edifices lining the plaza; its pyramidal form is an evocative reminder of Mexico's ancient past. Inside, two twisted staircases wind their way up to a second floor permanent collection that includes state of the art audio-visual resources, intriguing artifacts, and informative exhibitions. And it's all free.

South of the Esplanada is **Parque Hundido** (Sunken Park), a cool and verdant garden paradise for young lovebirds. A wall of water overlooks the park, and a monument to youth turns its back to the greenery, tactfully averting its eyes from the mature goings-on. Rising on both sides of the Parque Hundido and providing a harsh contrast to the park's natural overgrowth are three modern buildings: the colossal **Congreso de Estado,** in which politicians cut deals, the **Palacio de Justicia,** where the blindfolded goddess carefully weighs both sides of local cases, and the **Teatro de la Ciudad,** which offers experimental theater most nights of the week (tickets and performance information available at the box office).

Farther along the Gran Plaza lies the **Fuente de La Vida** (Fountain of Life) which douses an immense statue of Neptune surrounded by cavorting nymphs and naiads. Under the potent Monterrey sun, the figures shine with blinding brilliance. The most striking construction, however, is the bright orange **Faro del Comercio** (Commerce Lighthouse) topped with a laser beacon that circles the skies at night. The lighthouse serves a purely symbolic purpose, a testament to the economic ambitions of Monterrey's leaders. The laser doesn't begin to pulse until after 10pm, when hundreds pack the plaza in search of some late-night fun. Just across Zuazúa from the Faro de Comercio is the resplendent, pale yellow **Catedral de Monterrey.** The **Palacio Municipal** and the surrounding gardens round out the southern tip of the Gran Plaza. The sunken central area of the "people's house" plays host to various concert events. Brassy Latin dance tunes kick off the Sunday morning revelry, when the city's older citizens cha-cha, salsa, and foxtrot until the sun goes down. Evenings are reserved for **Monterrey Joven,** performances geared towards a younger audience, with dancing to *tejano* and *mariachi* music.

To the east lies the stylistically innovative and cutting-edge **Museo de Arte Contemporáneo (MARCO)** (tel. 342-48-20), where changing exhibitions display the works of prominent avant-garde painters, photographers, and other artists. An immense bronze dove guards the entrance (open Tues. and Thurs.-Sat. 11am-7pm, Wed. and Sun. 11am-9pm; admission 10 pesos, students with ID 5 pesos, free Wed).

The **Obispado** (tel. 346-04-04), former palace of the bishop of Monterrey, is now a state museum displaying murals, paintings, and old weapons from the colonial era. The real draw is the spectacular view of the city (open Tues.-Sat. 10am-6pm, Sun. 10am-5pm; admission 10 pesos). Take bus #4 from Washington, and ask the driver to point out the stop.

The Cuauhtémoc Company, for over a century the major producer of beer in Monterrey, has converted one of its old factories into the **Jardines Cuauhtémoc,** one block south of the General Anaya subway stop on Line 2. The gardens are densely covered with trees and dotted with benches and tables. Inside the old factory, the **Hall of Fame** (tel. 328-57-46) commemorates Mexico's baseball legends (open Tues.-Sun. 10am-6pm). The **Museo Deportivo,** part of the Hall of Fame, celebrates *charreadas* (rodeos), boxing, soccer, and bullfighting. The ivy-covered brick complex also contains a shrine to beer; located just to the north of the gate that leads into the gardens, the **Museo de la Cervecería** (tel. 375-22-00) foams over with beer culture artifacts, including mugs from various countries. The **Museo de Monterrey** (tel. 328-60-60) adds a dash of culture to the gardens with its tribute to leading Mexican artists and displays of modern artistic works (open Tues.-Sun. 11am-8pm, Wed.

10am-8pm; all museums are free, but an appointment must be made to see the brewery or the beer museum; complimentary beer samples).

Also worth a visit are the **Grutas de García** (Caves of García), 45km northwest of the city and accessible by car or bus. Once there, take the cable car railway in order to avoid the steep 700m uphill climb. Ticket for use of the cable car is included in the price of admission (open daily 9:30am-5:30pm, tickets 26 pesos, children 16 pesos). The Grutas are a network of natural chambers; the dozens of sedimentary layers in their walls reveal that 50 or 60 million years ago the caves lay on the ocean floor. The easiest way to get to the Grutas is on a Grayline 3-hour tour leaving from the Hotel Monterrey at 2:10pm (55 pesos). Make reservations by calling 331-22-11. A cheaper alternative, but one limited to Sundays, is to take a **Transportes Monterrey-Saltillo** bus from the bus station.

COAHUILA

■ Saltillo

After an exhilarating trek through the rugged Sierra Madre, Saltillo (pop. 700,000) materializes as the soothing colonial town of yesteryear. Unlike its booming neighbor, Saltillo retains the relaxing small-town feel that Monterrey has forsaken in its single-minded quest for economic prosperity. Few structures rise more than a few stories high, and buses travel at less than breakneck speed. Saltillo's quiet charm and dry climate make it a refuge of sorts for harried *regiomontanos* and a pleasant destination for those en route to Mexico City and other tourist meccas.

ORIENTATION

Nestled in a valley between the jagged Sierra Madre mountains, Saltillo lies 87km southwest of Monterrey, along desolate Highway 40. Frequent buses plod to and from Monterrey, Guadalajara, San Luis Potosí, and Mexico City.

The **bus station** is located about 3km southwest of the city center on Blvd. Echeverría Sur. To get to the *centro,* exit the terminal, cross the pedestrian overpass and catch minibus #10 from the small street perpendicular to the boulevard, on the side of Restaurant Jaslo. Make sure to ask if it's heading toward the *centro.* All buses cost 1.50 pesos and run daily 6:30am-11pm. Catch a return bus (#9) at the corner of Aldama and Hidalgo, a block down the street from the cathedral, in front of the entrance to the furniture store. The **train station** is much closer to the city center (about 1km) but still a hike if you are laden with luggage.

Most sights of interest are located in the center of Saltillo, in or around the two main plazas. The *centro's* streets form a slightly distorted grid not quite aligned with the four cardinal directions. The quiet **Plaza de Armas** is home to the cathedral and is bordered by **Juárez** to the south (or right, facing the cathedral) and **Hidalgo** to the east (between the Plaza and cathedral). Walk one block to the west, past the **Palacio de Gobierno,** and one block north to arrive at **Plaza Acuña,** bordered on its west (far side) by the narrow **Padre Flores** and on the east by **Allende.**

PRACTICAL INFORMATION

Tourist Office: Secretaría de Fomento Económico, Blvd. Luis Echeverría 1560 (tel. 15-17-14), on the 11th floor of the *über*-modern glass Edificio Torre Saltillo (not to be confused with the mushroom-shaped La Torre Hotel), on Saltillo's circular perimeter road. Accessible by buses 2B (to catch it, walk several blocks north on Allende to Cárdenas) and 2A (continue walking north to Coss). Worth the trek to obtain helpful maps and brochures. Open Mon.-Fri. 9am-5pm. **Tourist Hotline:** tel. 91-800-84-220 or 16-92-21, for questions or emergencies.

Currency Exchange: *Casas de cambio* offer the best rates. Closest to the city center is **Casa de Cambio Coin,** Acuña 167 (tel. 14-12-96), across the street from Hotel San Jorge. It changes traveler's checks at decent rates. Open Mon.-Fri. 9am-1:30pm and 3:30-6pm, Sat. 9am-1pm. The **banks** which line Victoria, west of the Plaza de Armas behind the Palacio de Gobierno, exchange dollars. Most are open 9am-1:30pm. **Banamex,** at Allende and Ocampo, behind the Palacio de Gobierno, has a 24-hr. **ATM.**

Telephones: LADATELs are few and far between. Collect and direct dial calls can be made from pay phones in the post office. Long distance calls paid for directly can be made from **Café Victoria,** Padre Flores 221. **Fax** available. Open daily 7am-10pm. There are long distance lines in the bus station as well.

Telegrams: Telecomm, next door to the post office on Victoria. Open Mon.-Fri. 9am-5pm, Sat. 9am-noon. Office in bus station open Mon.-Fri. 9am-3pm.

Airport: Aeropuerto Plan de Guadalupe, off Highway 40, northeast of the city center. The *"Saltillo Ramos Arizpe"* bus from the bus station or along Acuña in the center can let you off nearby (until 10:30pm, 1 peso). A taxi from the *centro* will charge 40 pesos for the trip. **Mexicana** offers daily flights to Mexico City (785 pesos). Tickets can be purchased at the travel agency in the Hotel Saade on Aldama (tel. 12-91-20). Make reservations a day or two in advance.

Buses: Central de Autobuses, Echeverría Sur and Garza, accessible by minibus #9. **Transportes del Norte** (tel. 17-09-02), to Guadalajara (5 per day, 10hr., 161 pesos), Mazatlán (3 per day, 16hr., 189 pesos), Mexico City (5 per day, 10hr., 193 pesos), San Luis Potosí (4 per day, 5hr., 96 pesos), and Zacatecas (4 per day, 5hr., 78 pesos). **Ómnibus de México** (tel. 17-03-15) to Aguascalientes (7 per day, 6hr., 108 pesos), Matamoros (13 per day, 7hr., 95 pesos), and Reynosa (13 per day, 5hr., 67 pesos). **Autobuses El Águila** (tel. 17-01-83) to Hermosillo (8:15pm, 25hr., 296 pesos), and Uruapan (6:45pm, 13hr., 184 pesos).

Trains: (tel. 14-95-84), on E. Carranza past the Alameda. Daily to Mexico City (10pm, 12hr., first-class 145 pesos, second-class 102 pesos).

Market: De Las Fuentes, Treviño 328 (tel. 12-85-54), between Allende and Acuña, across Blvd. Echeverría Sur. Open Mon.-Fri. 9am-8pm, Sat. 9am-9pm, Sun. 9am-3pm. **Soriana,** at Blvd. Francisco Coss (tel. 12-30-13). Open Mon.-Sat. 9am-8pm, Sun. 9am-3pm. Both are small grocery stores. **Mercado Juárez** on Allende adjoining Plaza Acuña, holds small produce stands and souvenir shops.

Laundry: Laundrymatic, Mutualismo Pte. 310 at Allende, at the end of the gravel road just south of the tourist office. Self- and full-service wash and dry. Open Mon.-Sat. 9am-1pm and 3:30-7:30pm.

Red Cross: Cárdenas and Rayón (tel. 14-33-33), northeast of the city center. Open 24-hr. No English spoken.

Pharmacy: in the bus station or **Farmacia Madero,** on Murguía and Madero near the hospital. Open 24hr.

Hospital: Hospital Universitario, Madero 1291 (tel. 12-30-00). Open 24hr. No English spoken.

Emergency: 06.

Ángeles Verdes (Green Angels): (tel. 12-40-50). A staff of English-speaking mechanics provide car repair assistance.

Police: Treviño and Echeverría Ote. (tel. 15-55-61 and 15-51-62).

Post Office: Victoria 453 (tel. 12-20-90), after Urdiñola. Open Mon.-Fri. 9am-5pm, Sat. 9am-1pm. Other branches in the bus station and near the tourist office. Both open Mon.-Fri. 8am-3pm. **Postal Code:** 25000.

Telephone Code: 84

ACCOMMODATIONS

Blvd. Luis Echeverría, which runs along the bus station, teems with places to rest your head. Although most of the hotels clustered in this area offer livable and inexpensive rooms, downtown establishments with similar rates are more comfortable and closer to Saltillo's major attractions. Tourists tend to flock to the *centro,* while the Echeverría clientele consists largely of Mexican businesspeople

Hotel Saade, Aldama Pte. 397 (tel. 12-91-20 or 12-91-21), 1 block west of Pl. Acuña. Earth tones dominate the clean, well-furnished, and quiet rooms in this modern hotel. Solid location places you in the heart of it all. Rooftop restaurant offers a stunning panorama of the city and the Sierra. *Agua purificada* and hot water. Singles 100 pesos. Doubles 120 pesos. TV 10 pesos extra.

Hotel Urdiñola, Victoria 207 (tel. 14-09-40), behind the Palacio del Gobierno. Very swank, with an exquisite marble staircase, beautiful stained-glass window, and charming courtyard. Rooms are well furnished with a matching set of mahogany furniture; bathrooms are adorned with beautiful tiles. This elegant retreat is also equipped with *agua purificada,* cable TVs, and phones; unfortunately, such grandeur is reflected in the prices. Singles 127 pesos. Doubles 150 pesos.

Hotel Premier (tel. 12-10-50), at the corner of Allende and Múzquiz. Bright, spacious rooms and an attractive lobby with murals depicting the town's history are the perfect recipe for a pleasant stay. Rooms come with cable TV, fans, and bottled water. Singles 115 pesos. Doubles 126 pesos.

Hotel Central, Echeverría 231 Ote. (tel. 17-00-04). Shiny yellow hallways open onto decidedly less kitschy rooms. Monotonous brown lacquered walls could put you to sleep. Singles 50 pesos. Doubles 70 pesos. TV 10 pesos extra.

FOOD

Like the residents of every other Northern Mexican city, *saltillenses* claim that their *cabrito* and *carne asada* outstrip the other towns' dishes; you be the judge. Be sure to sample delicious *pan de pulque* (bread made with tequila-like fermented cactus juice), which is a Saltillo specialty. Restaurants on Allende and Carranza cater more to the tourist masses, while the cafés on smaller streets remain local picks.

Café and Restaurant Arcasa, Victoria 215 (tel. 12-64-24). Family-run café with a touch of class. Breakfast 10 pesos. *Antojitos* 14-17 pesos. Delicious *palomitas de machacado* 17 pesos. Open daily 7am-midnight.

Restaurant Principal, Allende Nte. 702 (tel. 15-00-15), 7 blocks north of the Palacio de Gobierno. A tinkling fountain sets the mood in this cheerful joint. This is where the caged birds sing. Copious buffet options include vegetarian dishes (29-45 pesos). Their *cabecito* (19 pesos) will leave you with that invigorating after-the-hunt feel. Open daily 8am-9pm.

Señor Torta, on the corner of Hidalgo and Arizpe, 3 blocks up the hill on Hidalgo. *Señora* prepares a wide range of delicious *tortas* and Mexican specialties (7-18 pesos). *Señor* provides delightful service. Open daily 11am-8pm.

SIGHTS

Weary travelers rest assured; Saltillo does not lend itself to frenetic sightseeing. The town boasts a handful of worthwhile sights, beautiful architecture, and festive atmosphere. Saltillo's streets burst with artistry and cultural pride from July 18 to August 3 during **Feria de Saltillo.**

The **Plaza de Armas,** Saltillo's main square, is a refreshing change from the crowded and noisy *zócalos* of larger Mexican cities; the paved plaza contains neither trees nor benches, though four statuesque torch-bearing (that is, lightbulb-bearing) females guard a central fountain. Standing on the east side of the plaza, the late-18th-century Churrigueresque **cathedral** boasts an intricately wrought gray stone façade and equally elaborate interior.

On the south side of the plaza is the **Cavie Museum,** which houses changing exhibits of regional literature and art (open Tues.-Sun. 9am-7pm; free). Knock on the door of the adjoining IEBA *(Instituto Estatal de Bellas Artes)* if the museum is closed during normal hours. Watch Mexican history unfold before your very eyes through murals housed in the **Palacio de Gobierno** (tel. 14-37-00), on the west side of the plaza (open Mon.-Sat. 10am-6pm, Sun. 11am-6pm; free).

Budding ornithologists might investigate the newly opened **Museo de las Aves** (tel. 14-01-67), home to members of most species of birds native to the Americas, including several that are rare or nearly extinct. You, too, can learn about bird migration patterns, songs, and the mechanics of flight. Take either Allende or Hidalgo uphill from the Plaza de Armas; the museum is housed in the large, canary yellow building in front of the parking lot (open Tues.-Sat. 10am-6pm, Sun. 11am-7pm; admission 5 pesos, children 2 pesos; free Wed).

Plaza Acuña, two blocks northwest of the Plaza de Armas, bustles with activity. Almost romantic in a hyperactive sort of way, the plaza is a great place to people-watch or browse through the stalls that offer souvenir items, including hats, rugs, ukuleles, and colorful *sarapes.* Vendors spill out of the **Mercado Juárez,** in the northwest corner of the plaza, while *marimbas* resonate and guitar players and accordionists rove through the crowds (open daily 8:30am-8pm).

Once you've had enough of the plaza scene, try relaxing (or napping) in the **Alameda,** just west of the city center (follow Victoria west from Plaza de Armas), or the **San Francisco Park and Church,** south of Plaza de Armas at Juárez and Cepeda. The refreshingly green Alameda holds a wondrous series of fountains and aquatic gardens on the south end and an enormous playground on the north end; during the cooler hours of the day, these paths are navigated by herds of joggers.

Perched on a hill overlooking the city, **Plaza México** (or **El Mirador**), offers a smashing view of the whole area and the unconquerable mountains beyond. Take Miguel Hidalgo uphill for a kilometer, turn left on General Cepeda (unmarked, but the 900 block of Hidalgo just after the Centro Deportivo Ojo de Agua), and follow it for another 20-50m, turning onto the winding Gustavo Espinoza and up to the small plaza with benches and old street lamps. Just west of El Mirador stands the **Iglesia del Ojo de Agua,** a sparkling white church set up off the ground. Within the church is the spring which gave Saltillo its name. When Spaniards first saw the water spurt out of the ground here, they called the spot *saltillo,* or "little jump."

ZACATECAS

■ Zacatecas

A charming city is the last thing a traveler expects to find in the prickly desert of Central Mexico—yet out of nowhere rises Zacatecas. The arid surroundings augment the colonial beauty of this town, perched between, on, and over mineral-laden hills. The lifeblood of Zacatecas once flowed through veins of silver. A silver trinket, given to early Spanish colonists by an indigenous Cascane in the mid-1500s, triggered the mining bonanza that was the city's *raison d'être.* In the 200 years following the Conquest, the hills surrounding Zacatecas were stripped of 6000 tons of silver. As far as mining towns go, Zacatecas was unusually fortunate: the arts flourished under the patronage of affluent silver barons, and the rows of grand colonial mansions downtown testify to an era of lavish consumption.

The tumultuous history of modern Mexico has left its thumbprint on Zacatecas; in 1914 Francisco "Pancho" Villa's revolutionary forces triumphed here in a day-long battle with Carranza's troops. As revolution atrophied into institution and the mines ran dry, Zacatecas emerged as a hub of sophistication with architectural, artistic, and natural treasures, as well as a delightful dearth of tourism.

ORIENTATION AND PRACTICAL INFORMATION

Zacatecas is 347km north of Guadalajara, 135km south of Aguascalientes, and 832km south of Chihuahua. All buses arrive and depart from the **central bus terminal** on the outskirts of town. City buses (1 peso; Ruta 8 to the *centro*) and taxis (10 pesos to the *centro*) wait outside.

Zacatecas has no identifiable city center. Activity revolves around two streets, **Juárez** and **Hidalgo** (**González Ortega** southwest of Juárez). Use the Juárez-Hidalgo intersection, which falls one block northwest of **Plaza Independencia,** as your point of orientation. Many of the city's colonial monuments are on or near Hidalgo. Zacatecas can get chilly, so sweaters and jackets come in handy.

Tourist Office: Infotur, Hidalgo 629 (tel. 4-03-93), at Callejón del Santero across from the cathedral. Young, helpful staff distributes useful maps and lists of museum schedules. A touch screen video tells you about the city, hotels, and restaurants. No English spoken. Open Mon.-Sat. 9am-8pm, Sun. 9am-7pm. For more in-depth information about the city and state, visit the tremendously informative **Dirección de Turismo,** Explanada del Ferrocarril (tel. 4-03-93; fax 2-93-29), near the train station. **TIPS,** a Spanish-language weekly listing cultural events and tour-ist services, is available during high season in hotels and at various newsstands.

Guided Tours: Asociación de Guías Turistas, Calle del Ángel 202 (tel. 4-18-17 or 2-85-09), behind the cathedral. Guided tours of the city (90 pesos, including admis-sion to museums and transportation. Open Mon.-Sun. 10am-8pm.

Currency Exchange: Banamex, Hidalgo 132 (tel. 2-59-20). **ATM.** Open Mon.-Fri. 9am-3pm. **Banco Internacional (BITAL),** Hidalgo 107 (tel. 2-61-09 or 2-61-10), at Juárez. Open for exchange Mon.-Fri. 8am-7pm, Sat. 9am-2pm. **Cordisa Casa de Cambio,** González Ortega 142 (tel. 2-55-04), one block from Juárez, has great rates and changes traveler's checks and money orders. Open daily 9am-7pm.

Telephones: LADATELs throughout the city. Callejón de Cuevas 113 (tel. 2-68-10), off Hidalgo across from Banamex. International collect calls in a big empty room soon to be filled with comfy chairs and steamy hot coffee. Open Mon.-Fri. 9am-8pm, Sat.-Sun. 9am-2pm and 5-8pm.

Telegrams and Fax: Hidalgo at Juárez (tel. 2-00-60; fax 2-17-96). Open Mon.-Fri. 8am-6pm, Sat. 9am-noon.

Airport: (tel. 498/5-08-63 or 5-81-99). Accessible by *combis* (tel. 2-59-46) from the Mexicana office (leave 1¼hr. before flight, 20min., 25 pesos). **Mexicana,** Hidalgo 406 (tel. 2-32-48). Open Mon.-Fri. 9am-7pm. **Taesa,** Hidalgo 306 (tel. 2-00-50 or 2-02-12). Open Mon.-Fri. 9am-7pm, Sat. 10am-6pm.

Buses: Central de Autobuses (tel. 2-06-84), Lomas de la Isabélica at Tránsito Pesado. From the *centro,* take the "Camionera Central" or Ruta 8 bus from González Ortega (one block from Juárez). **Estrella Blanca** (tel. 2-00-07) to Maza-tlán (2:30pm, 12hr., 145 pesos), Mexico City (1:30 and 10:05pm, 8hr., 136 pesos), and Tijuana (2:30pm, 36hr., 494 pesos). **Transportes Chihuahuenses** (tel. 2-00-42) to Ciudad Juárez (9 per day 12:15am-3:45pm, 16hr., 304 pesos) and Guadala-jara (8 per day 12:10am-2:30pm, 6hr., 90 pesos). **Ómnibus de México** (tel. 2-54-95) to Mexico City (10 per day 1am-10:50pm, 8hr., 161 pesos) via San Luis Potosí (3hr., 42 pesos) and Querétaro (5½hr., 104 pesos).

Trains: Estación de Ferrocarriles (tel. 2-12-04). Within walking distance of down-town and accessible by the Ruta 8 bus. From Juárez, follow González Ortega until you see the train cars. To Mexico City (first-class 8:10pm, 13hr., 97 pesos; second-class 4:45am, 13hr., 56 pesos). Night tickets sold daily 7-9pm.

Car Rental: Budget, Mateos 104 (tel. 2-94-58). Deals start at 300 pesos per day including insurance, taxes, and 200km daily. Must be 25 years of age with valid credit card and driver's license. Open Mon.-Fri. 9am-3pm and 5-8pm, Sat. 9am-2pm.

Luggage Storage: at the bus station, 1-3hr. 3 pesos, 3-6hr. 6 pesos, 6-12hr. 9 pesos, 12-24hr. 12 pesos. Open daily 7am-10pm.

Laundromat: Lavandería del Indio Triste, Juan de Tolosa 826, an extension of Hidalgo, about 3 long blocks past the cathedral. 5.50 pesos per kilo; same day service if dropped off before 5pm. Open Mon.-Sat. 9am-3pm and 4-9pm.

Red Cross: Calzada de la Cruz Roja 100 (tel. 2-30-05), off Héroes de Chapultepec near the exit to Fresnillo. English spoken. Open 24hr.

Pharmacy: Farmacia Issstezac, Callejón de las Campanas 103 (tel. 4-37-25, ext. 19), on the right side of the cathedral. Open 24hr.

Hospital: Hospital General, García Salinas 707 (tel. 3-30-04). Open 24hr. Dr. José Cruz de la Torre González speaks English (tel. 4-07-03).

Emergency: Dial 06.

Police: Héroes de Chapultepec 1000 (tel. 2-05-07 or 2-43-79). No English spoken.

Post Office: Allende 111 (tel. 2-01-96), off Hidalgo. Open Mon.-Fri. 8am-7pm, Sat. 9am-1pm. **Postal code:** 98000.

Telephone Code: 492.

ACCOMMODATIONS

The less expensive hotels in Zacatecas tend to be dingy, and middle-range accommodations are hard to come by. Unless you're willing to pay over 90 pesos for a single, hotels farther away from the *centro* are your best option.

CREA Youth Hostel (HI), Parque La Encantada (tel. 2-02-23, ext. 7), southwest of the city. Take the Ruta 8 bus (0.80 pesos) from Pl. Independencia or the bus station, and get off at the sign for La Encantada. Walk down Calle 5 Señores; turn left on Calle Ancha and walk up the hill until you see the grounds of the youth camp, veering right around the red building. The sherbet green hostel is behind the pool to the left. Equipped with a soccer field and courts for basketball, volleyball, and racquetball. Small, sterile quads. Single-sex floors. Clean communal bathroom. 13 pesos per person. Breakfast 10 pesos. Lunch and dinner 25 pesos each. Open daily 7am-11pm. **CREA Youth Hostel II (HI)** (tel. 2-93-77), Av. de los Deportes, just before the soccer stadium, is another option but is pretty far out of town (take the Ruta 11 bus) and not as well maintained. 15 pesos per person. Breakfast 9 pesos. Lunch and dinner 11 pesos each. Open daily 7am-11pm.

Hotel El Parque, González Ortega 302 (tel. 2-04-79), near the aqueduct. A tad out of the way, but in a nice area 3 blocks from Juárez just past the beautiful Parque Enrique Estrada. Vanilla decor. Clean rooms are sort of dark, though the TVs brighten things up. Singles 48 pesos. Doubles 58 pesos.

Fonda de Villareal, Plazuela de Zamora 303 (tel. 2-12-00). Within 1 block of the Jardín Independencia opposite Juárez. Central location, friendly management, and low prices are its only virtues. Lots of traffic and loitering outside at night. Singles 30 pesos. Doubles 35 pesos, with two beds 40 pesos.

Hotel María Conchita, Av. López Mateos 401 (tel. 2-14-94 or 2-14-96), 3 blocks south of the Jardín Independencia. Looks like it was designed by Mike Brady. Comfortable rooms have TVs and phones. Singles 53 pesos. Doubles 65 pesos.

FOOD

The sophistication of Zacatecas seeps out of its museums and mansions and into its restaurants—the city boasts a network of gourmet cafés. Coffee aside, however, budget meals in Zacatecas often fail to impress. Indulge your sweet tooth with a chunk of sugary-sweet *dulce con leche, camote,* or *cocada,* on sale near the Alameda on Juárez or Torreón (1 peso). Taco and *gordita* (a fat tortilla stuffed with beans or tongue) stands are scattered along Hidalgo and Juárez.

El Tragadero, Av. Juárez 132 (tel. 2-43-32), just after the intersection with Hidalgo. The open kitchen and light decor keep this family-run joint nice and cozy. Yummy vegetarian platter 18 pesos. Enchiladas 14 pesos. Open daily 8am-10pm.

La Terraza (tel. 2-32-70), next to the cathedral. A lovely outdoor café. The menu is limited and servings are small, but it's still a great place to stop for coffee and a snack. Burgers 7 pesos. Ice cream 6 pesos. Open daily 10am-9:30pm.

El Jacalito, Av. Juárez 18 (tel. 2-07-71), near the Jardín Independencia. Belying its name (The Little Shack), there will always be a table waiting for you in this spacious white-walled restaurant. Popular with locals. Hot cakes breakfast combo 18 pesos. Enchiladas 16 pesos.

SIGHTS

The 18th-century **cathedral,** on Hidalgo four blocks northeast of Juárez, combines three architectural styles. The northern façade is Churrigueresque, the southern façade is European Baroque, and the western façade—a richly carved celebration of the Eucharist—is among the country's most lavish examples of Mexican Baroque. Surprisingly, the interior of the church is not as arresting (open daily 6am-1pm and 4-9pm). Next to the cathedral, the **Palacio de Gobierno** is notable for the mural which surrounds its interior stairwell. Painted in 1970 by Antonio Pintor Rodríguez, the work traces the history of Zacatecas from the pre-Hispanic era until the present. Much of the mural devotes itself to the mugs of Zacatecas's historical players (open Mon.-Fri. 8am-8pm).

Across Hidalgo and up the steep Callejón de Veyna is the **Templo de Santo Domingo.** Built by the Jesuits in 1746, the church contains eight impressive Baroque altars of gilded wood and an elaborate 18th-century German pipe organ (open daily 7am-1pm and 3:30-9pm; quiet, respectful visitors are welcome during services). Next door, in a building whose past incarnations include a monastery and a jail, is the **Museo de Pedro Coronel** (tel. 2-80-21). Housing the tomb, sculptures, and paintings of the Zacatecan artist Pedro Coronel, the museum houses one of the best modern art collections in Latin America. Works by Picasso, Braque, Chagall, and Miró jostle for space. Mesoamerican and African masks, as well as Japanese, Chinese, and Tibetan pieces break the Eurocentric spell (open Fri.-Wed. 10am-2pm and 4-7pm, Sun. 10am-5pm, admission 10 pesos, students and seniors 5 pesos, children under 10 free).

The dramatic **Ex-Convento de San Francisco,** an attraction in itself, houses the **Museo Rafael Coronel** (tel. 2-81-16). To reach the museum from the cathedral, follow Hidalgo, bearing left at the first fork and right at the second. The museum is renowned for its fabulous collection of masks from around the world. (Open Mon.-Tues. and Thurs.-Sat. 10am-2pm and 4-7pm, Sun. 10am-5pm. Admission 10 pesos, students, teachers, and seniors half-price, kids free. Ex-convent open same hours, free.) Southeast of the downtown area, 39 pink stone arches mark the end of Zacatecas's famous colonial aqueduct, **El Cubo.** Beside the aqueduct, the verdant **Parque Estrada** with winding stone pathways borders the former governor's mansion, now the **Museo de Francisco Goitia,** Enrique Estrada 102 (tel. 2-02-11; open Tues.-Sat. 10am-1pm and 5-8pm, Sun. 10am-5pm; admission 10 pesos, seniors and kids 12 and under free).

The **Cerro de la Bufa,** named for its resemblance to a Spanish wineskin, peers down from the city's highest crag. Adjacent to the Cerro is the **Museo de la Toma de Zacatecas** (tel. 2-80-66). Erected to commemorate Pancho Villa's decisive victory over federal troops in the summer of 1914, the museum lays claim to a fascinating array of revolutionary memorabilia, including photographs, cannons, and small arms (open Tues.-Sun. 10am-5pm; admission 5 pesos, students, seniors, and teachers half-price, kids under 11 free). The museum is flanked on one side by the 18th-century **Capilla del Patrocinio,** whose gracefully sculpted façade and cloistered courtyards are carved from deep-red stone. Nearby shops sell arts, crafts, and loads of geodes. A short but steep walk up the hill leads to the ornate Moorish **Mausoleo de los Hombres Ilustres de Zacatecas,** worth the hike if only for the view of the city it affords (open daily 10am-6pm). There's an even better vista from the **Meteorological Observatory** behind the museum. Public buses run to La Bufa only on Sundays and religious holidays (take Ruta 9 from the Plaza de Armas), and taxis suck up 16 pesos. The most appealing way to make the trip is by **teleférico** (suspended cable car; tel. 2-56-94), which runs between the peak of El Grillo and La Bufa every 10 minutes. Follow García Rojas northwest to its end to the cable car stop (open daily 10am-6pm; 5 pesos each way).

The **Mina de Edén** (tel. 2-30-02) was one of the region's most productive silver mines until about 30 years ago, when continual flooding made mineral extraction futile. You may enter the mine from either the top or the side. The top entrance is 100m to the right as you leave the *teleférico*. From there, walk into the mountain, take the elevator down, and begin the tour. Otherwise, follow Juárez northwest along the **Alameda,** a tree and fountain filled park lined by some of Zacatecas's grandest colonial mansions. Continue along Torreón until it ends, and then turn right and walk one block, veering to the left. From there, a mini-locomotive whisks tourists into the mountain. A one-hour guided tour (in Spanish) of the cool subterranean tunnels ensues. Tour groups cross rope bridges and learn about the haunting myths of the mine (open daily 11am-6:30pm; admission 12 pesos).

ENTERTAINMENT

Zacatecas's nightlife kicks off on Thursday and Friday nights, when the university students slam the books shut and head to the bars and discos. Not surprisingly, the tourist favorite is **El Malacate** (tel. 2-30-02), a rare opportunity to boogie in an old mine shaft. Solid rock walls are tastefully decorated with helmets, shovels, and plush green sectionals, and partiers quaff expensive drinks and dance to a mix of the latest U.S. top-40 hits and Latin rhythms (cover 30 pesos, beer 8 pesos, mixed drinks 16 pesos; open Thurs.-Sat. 9pm-2:30am). Revelers can also be found jamming to rock music just next to the *teleférico* station at **El Elefante Blanco** (tel. 2-71-04). The club offers a stunning view of the city at night, in addition to pool tables, foosball, and a happenin' dance floor (cover 30 pesos; open Fri.-Sat. 9pm-2:30am; taxi to either club 8 pesos). For some great tunes, beer, and karaoke during the week, visit **Mi Canto,** Juárez 421 (tel. 2-19-12). The framed album covers and blue neon lighting give the place lots of pizzazz (open Mon.-Sat. 7:30pm-1am).

If you're feeling a bit more mellow, the **Video Club de la Biblioteca Mauricio Magdaleno,** Jardín Independencia 1 (tel. 2-59-29), is the place to be. It shows movies from just about every country and in just about every genre, including cartoons! (free screenings Mon.-Fri. 11:30am and 5:30pm; look for the movie schedule in *TIPS* or inquire at the library). Also check out **Nova Cinema,** Constituyentes 300 (tel. 2-54-04), for the latest in Mexican and American films. On Thursdays and Sundays at 7pm, take advantage of the free performance by the **Banda del Estado** in the Plazuela Goitia, next to the cathedral.

The Miracle Worker

Just before daybreak, an elderly woman from Zacatecas begins a 60km pilgrimage on foot to the sanctuary in Plateros. Beads of sweat roll down her leathery skin and the blistering heat leaves her feet chafed. In her hands, she carries roses for her saviour. The thorns prick her fingers, but she just licks the blood away and smiles in spite of herself. Today is the happiest day of her life. After ten years of paralysis and acute pain, she is miraculously cured. The object of her gratitude is not the town doctor, but a young boy: the **Santo Niño de Atocha.** The image of the baby Jesus in the **Sanctuary of Plateros** is one of the more venerated in Mexico. Since the 1800s, throngs of devotees from around the world have been visiting the Santo Niño to ask for favors and express their gratitude for everything from surviving a plane crash to winning the lottery. Word has it that the pilgrims who visit the sanctuary don't actually find the Niño resting there—he's too busy performing miracles.

The yearly cultural highlight is **Zacatecas en la Cultura,** a festival during **semana santa** in which concerts, expos, and different artistic activities are held throughout the city in the elegant **Teatro Calderón,** on Hidalgo, near the cathedral, and throughout the city. From about September 5-22, the city celebrates the **Feria Nacional de Zacatecas** with musical and theatrical events, bullfights, agricultural and crafts shows, and sporting events.

The **Museo de Arte Virreinal,** also known as the **Museo Regional de Guadalupe** (tel. 3-20-89), is in the splendid village of Guadalupe, 7km east of Zacatecas on the highway to Mexico City. Highlights include the first series on the Virgin of Guadalupe, painted by the 18th-century artist Miguel Cabrera, and a 1621 Gutenberg volume on mining (open Tues.-Sun. 10am-4:30pm; admission 14 pesos, free Sun. and for students and teachers with ID, seniors, and children under 14). The collection of antique vehicles housed next door in the **Anexo al Convento de Guadalupe** (tel. 3-20-89) is also worth a peek (open Tues.-Sun. 10am-4:30pm; free). To get there, catch a Ruta 13 bus to Guadalupe (every 15min., 1 peso) at the corner of Salazar and López Mateos, right outside the Centro Comercial car-park.

AGUASCALIENTES

■ Aguascalientes

Aguascalientes (Hot Waters) presents the average visitor with just enough diversions to deserve a stopover. The pride and joy of the city is the eagerly anticipated **Feria de San Marcos,** three weeks of festivities from the second half of April through the first week of May. Aside from its yearly extravaganza, Aguascalientes offers a small range of attractions, including the regal looking Plaza de la Patria, a few pleasant gardens, beautiful churches with interesting stories attached, and museums to commemorate its relatively undistinguished history.

Orientation Aguascalientes is 168km west of San Luis Potosí, 128km south of Zacatecas, and 252km northeast of Guadalajara. **Av. Circunvalación** encircles the city, while **Av. López Mateos** cuts through town east to west. The **bus station** is on Av. Convención, a few blocks west from Av. José María Chávez. All city buses are green and white; "Centro" buses (1 peso) run from outside the bus station to the Mercado Morelos, two blocks north of the **Plaza de la Patria.** To return to the station, "Central Camionera" buses traverse the length of **Rivero y Gutiérrez** (parallel to and one block north of Madero). The drivers of Aguas are one of the city's miracles—due to a recent (and strictly enforced) city ordinance, everyone here wears a seatbelt. Those strapped-in *taxistas* charge about eight pesos from the bus terminal to the center of town. From the Plaza de la Patria, most sights are either on **Montoro** (the street that runs east from the southeast corner of the plaza) or on **Carranza,** which begins to the west of the plaza, behind the basilica. When you plan your day in Aguas, keep in mind that the city absolutely dies during *siesta* hours (2-5pm).

Practical Information The **tourist office** (tel. 15-11-55 or 16-03-47) is on the first floor of the Palacio de Gobierno, the first door to the right of the main entrance. The helpful staff hands out a so-so map (open Mon.-Fri. 9am-3pm and 5-7pm, Sat. 9am-2pm). **Bancomer,** 5 de Mayo 112 (tel. 17-19-00), a block from the Plaza de la Patria, has shorter lines and a slightly better rate than the competition (open for exchange Mon.-Fri. 8:30am-2:30pm and 4-6pm, Sat. 10am-2pm). **Casa de Cambio Cedinsa,** Hospitalidad 104B (tel. 18-27-84), next to the post office, also has good rates (open Mon.-Fri. 9am-7pm, Sat. 9am-2pm). **LADATELs** are along the Plaza de la Patria; there is a *caseta* at the **Tabaquería Plaza,** Colón 102 (tel. 17-31-78 or 17-20-45; open daily 9am-9:30pm). **Telecomm** (tel. 16-14-27 or 16-12-52), Galeana at Nieto, behind the Basílica, provides **telegram and fax service** (open Mon.-Fri. 8am-6pm, Sat. 9am-1pm).

The **bus station,** on Av. Circunvalación, is served by **Ómnibus de México, Estrella Blanca, Flecha Amarilla, Rojo de los Altos,** and a slew of smaller companies. **Estrella Blanca** (tel. 78-20-54) has decent fares and frequent service to every destination imaginable, including Guadalajara (every hr. 6am-noon and 2-8pm, 2¾hr., 59 pesos), Matamoros (8pm, 13hr., 198 pesos), Monterrey (6 per day 5am-11pm, 10hr., 109 pesos), and Nuevo Laredo (5 per day 5-10pm, 12hr., 186 pesos). **Flecha Amarilla** (tel. 78-26-61) runs to Guanajuato (12:10 and 8:30pm, 3½hr., 35 pesos), Mexico City (6 per day 2am-10pm, 6hr., 100 pesos), and Morelia (9 per day 12:30am-8pm, 6hr., 66 pesos). **Primera Plus** (tel. 78-26-61) serves Manzanillo (9:30pm, 8hr., 139 pesos), Puerto Vallarta (10:30pm, 8hr., 148 pesos), and Querétaro (5 per day 9am-11:30pm, 4½hr., 80 pesos). **Rojo de los Altos** (tel. 78-20-54) sends most of its buses to Zacatecas (every 30min. 6am-8:30pm, 2½hr., 24 pesos). **Ómnibus de México** (tel. 78-27-70) runs to Acapulco (11:30pm, 10hr., 253 pesos) and Cuernavaca (11:30pm, 7½hr., 147 pesos). **Luggage Storage** is available at the bus station (1.50 pesos per hr.). The **train station** (tel. 15-38-58 or 15-22-55) is on 28 de agosto off Héroes de Nacozari, north of Madero.

Wash your clothes at **Súper Lavandería,** 224 Carranza (tel. 15-61-88), two blocks before the *jardín* (open Mon.-Fri. 10am-2pm and 4-8pm, Sat. 10am-6pm). The **Red Cross** (tel. 15-20-55) is at Enrique González Medina. **Farmacia Sánchez,** Madero 213 (tel. 15-35-50), sells drugs one block from the plaza (open 24hr., doors close at midnight, but don't hesitate to knock). **Hospital Hidalgo** is at Galeana 465 (tel. 17-19-30 or 17-17-30; open 24hr.). In an **emergency,** dial 06. The **police** (tel. 12-01-70) are at the corner of Libertad and Gómez Orozco. The **post office** resides at Hospitalidad 108 (tel. 15-21-18), one block east of the plaza on Madero, then left on Morelos and right on Hospitalidad (open Mon.-Fri. 8am-7pm, Sat. 9am-5pm). **Postal Code:** 20000. **Telephone Code:** 49.

Accommodations

Budget accommodations in Aguascalientes lack the charm of colonial architecture and the sharpness of modern hotels. Stay in the *centro* rather than near the bus station; it's an infinitely nicer part of town. During the Feria de San Marcos (mid-April to early May), reservations are a must. The somewhat pricey **Hotel Señorial,** Colón 104 (tel. 15-16-30), is right on the Plaza de la Patria. It provides all the amenities—TV, phone, desk, fan, carpet, and purified water—but the furniture is ancient and rooms are cramped (singles 65 pesos; doubles 85 pesos). **Hotel Rosales,** Guadalupe Victoria 104 (tel. 15-21-65), across from the cathedral, offers ancient, somewhat eery rooms, but the management keeps them clean (singles 50 pesos; doubles 60 pesos). The **Hotel Continental** awaits at Brasil 610 (tel. 78-28-29), at Guatemala, bordering the left side of the bus station as you exit. It's in a noisy and dirty part of town, but may be convenient for the one-night-stay traveler. All rooms come with ceiling fans and little TVs. The aging bathrooms gush hot water (singles 50 pesos; doubles 60 pesos).

Food

Walk a block or two away from the plaza to find some mighty fine dining establishments. Rose walls and wood paneling give flair to **Mitla,** Madero 220 (tel. 16-36-79), a block north of Montoro near the plaza. Sandwiches average 12 pesos, enchiladas 17 pesos (open daily 7:30am-11:30pm). **La Maceta,** Madero 427, a sweet mom and pop restaurant with happy toned blue, yellow, purple, and green walls, serves up cheap and tasty breakfast combos (12 pesos) and *comida corridas* (12 pesos; open daily 8am-8pm). **Cocina Mexicana Doña Petra** is waiting for you at J. Pani 133 (tel. 18-30-01), on the Expo Plaza two blocks left of the Jardín de San Marcos. If colors made noise, this place would be deafening! Treat your palate to tasty tacos (2 pesos) and *tortas* (4 pesos) served up under bright piñatas and paper flowers (open daily 1pm-1am). Vegetarians can get their fiber fix at **Restaurant Vegetariano,** Madero 409 (tel. 18-30-01), four blocks from the Plaza (soy burgers 8 pesos, *comida corrida* 15 pesos; open Mon.-Sat. 8am-7pm).

Sights and Entertainment The **Feria de San Marcos** (mid-April to early May) constitutes the soul of Aguascalientes. Most of the Feria's events, which include everything from cockfights and bullfights to milking contests, take place in the **Jardín de San Marcos,** a 5-10-minute walk on Carranza from the **Plaza de la Patria.** The area around the Jardín was originally an Indian *pueblo,* but around the year 1600, *indígena* labor erected the **Templo Evangelista San Marcos** at the site. The church is most notable for housing José de Alsivar's *La Adoración de los Reyes Católicos* (open daily 7am-2pm and 4-9pm). Walk two blocks to the left as you face the *templo* to reach the **Expo Plaza,** filled with shops and restaurants. If you can't stomach a real bullfight in the adjacent **Plaza de Toros,** just watch the little gold matador and shiny black bull exit the clock of Fiesta America (just behind the statue of the horseman and running bulls) and do their passes at noon, 3, 5, 7, and 9pm.

The **Museo de Guadalupe Posada** (tel. 15-45-56), on León next to the Templo del Encino, four blocks south of López Mateos, displays turn of the century political cartoons and provides interesting insights into Mexico's morbid humor. The museum holds 220 original works by Mexico's most famous printmaker; almost all are skeletal figures caricaturing dictator Porfirio Díaz. The most famous image is that of *la Catrina,* a society lady-*calavera* wearing an outlandish hat; Diego Rivera used her figure in his *Sueño de Una Tarde Dominical en la Alameda,* now on display in Mexico City (see p. 101). The museum also shows 100 works by Posada's mentor, Manuel Manilla, and contemporary art from around the world (open Tues.-Sun. 10am-6pm; admission 3 pesos, students 1.50 pesos, children under 12 free).

The soft grays and rose-colored Solomonic baroque façade of the **Basílica de la Asunción de las Aguascalientes** make it the most remarkable structure on the Plaza. Look out for the sculptures of church patrons San Gregorio, San Jerónimo, and San Agustín. The cathedral's interior is graced with high ceilings, gold trimmings, and ornate icons, as well as paintings by José de Alcíbar, Andrés López, and Miguel Cabrera (open daily 7am-2pm and 4-9pm). Another beautiful church is the **Templo de San Antonio,** on Pedro Parga and Zaragoza; from the plaza walk three blocks down Madero, then three blocks left on Zaragoza. Every inch of the interior is painstakingly decorated with a collage of soft blues, pinks, and gold leafing. The mix of patterns on the murals, frescoes, oil paintings, and delicate stained glass windows match the mix of architectural styles of the exterior, built by a local self-taught architect (open daily 7am-2pm and 4-9pm).

The **Instituto Cultural de Aguascalientes,** popularly known as the **Casa de la Cultura,** Carranza 101 (tel. 15-34-73), hosts temporary sculpture, painting, and photography exhibits (open Mon.-Fri. 10am-2pm and 5-8pm, Sat.-Sun. 10am-9pm; free). Kiosks in the courtyard just drip with listings for cultural events; you can also check the Casa's monthly bulletin or call 16-62-70. The **Centro Cultural Los Arquitos** (tel. 17-00-96), on the Alameda at Héroes de Nacozari, served as public bathrooms from 1821 until 1973. After a magnificent restoration process, in 1994 the building became a beautiful cultural center with a bookshop, a video room that shows children's movies (Fri. 5pm), and a small museum (open Mon.-Fri. 9am-1pm and 3-8pm, Sat. 9am-1pm and 3-6pm, Sun. 9am-2pm; center open daily 10am-2pm and 4-8pm).

During the week, boys can play pool (12 pesos per hr.) and dominoes (6 pesos per hr.) at **Casa Verde,** Montoro 107 (tel. 15-33-32). Men drop their jaws and the earth stops rotating when the lone female arrives (open daily 10:30am-11pm). On weekends, shake your caboose at **Disco El Cabús** (tel.73-00-06), Blvd. Zacatecas at Campestre, in the Hotel Las Trojes (cover Thurs.-Fri. 20 pesos, Sat. 30 pesos; open Thurs.-Fri. 9pm-3am; no shorts). The dimly lit and booming **Meneos,** on the Centro Comercial El Dorado, is also popular. Beer is 10 pesos, mixed drinks about 14 pesos (cover 30 pesos; open Fri.-Sat. 9pm-3am).

SAN LUIS POTOSÍ

■ San Luis Potosí

Though founded in 1583 as a Franciscan mission, San Lus Potosí forgot its religious calling when somebody discovered silver in the mountains around town. In 1592, the town of royal fortune was given a royal name—San Luis, after King Louis IX of France. As the earth coughed up more and more shiny metal, miners optimistically tacked on yet another title—"Potosí," the name of a prosperous Bolivian mining town. Mining soon vaulted San Luis Potosí to the center of Mexico's export-based economy. Precious silver bought political clout, and the city eventually became the power-center of northern Mexico, including present-day Texas and Louisiana.

While San Luis Potosí may have lost its political pull, the city has grown comfortably over the past 400 hundred years. Today, San Luis (pop. 800,000) retains much of its colonial charm. Bands, magicians, and women blowing soap bubbles gather in the town plazas at dusk to entertain the assembled crowds of young and old. In a graceful bargain with modernity, automobile traffic along the cobblestone streets has been shunted away from the central plaza, creating a truly peaceful preserve of land in the middle of a vibrant city.

ORIENTATION

San Luis Potosí is at the center of a triangle formed by Mexico's three largest cities—Monterrey, Guadalajara, and Mexico City. Five main highways (Rte. 57, 85, 70, 49, and 80) snake their way into the city. To get downtown from the **bus station,** catch an "Alameda" or "Centro" bus (daily 5:30am-10:30pm, 1.30 pesos) and hop off at **Parque Alameda,** the first big stretch of green. A **taxi** costs 15 pesos.

San Luis's main drag is **Avenida Carranza,** which runs east-west and passes the north side of the **Plaza de Armas,** the city's historic center. East of the plaza, Carranza is called **Los Bravos. Madero** runs parallel to Carranza one block south, touching the Plaza de Armas's south side. East of the plaza, Madero goes by **Othón.** The **Plaza del Carmen** is two blocks east of the plaza on Madero. A block farther east lies the Alameda, where the bus from the station drops off visitors. The **train station** is on Othón opposite the Alameda. **Zaragoza** forms the east side of Pl. de Armas; north of the plaza it goes by **Hidalgo.** On the west side of the plaza is **Cinco de Mayo,** known as **Allende** farther north. **Aldama** is one block west of 5 de Mayo.

PRACTICAL INFORMATION

Tourist Office: Calle Obregón 520 (tel. 12-30-68), one block west of Pl. de los Fundadores. Open Mon.-Fri. 8am-8pm, Sat. 8am-3pm. There is a **tourist center** on the first floor of the Palacio Municipal, on the northeast corner of Pl. de Armas.

Consulate: U.S., Mariel 103 (tel. 12-15-28); take the "Morales" bus. Open Mon.-Fri. 8:30am-1:30pm, but sometimes available in the afternoons. The police and the tourist office have consulate employees' home numbers in case of emergency.

Currency Exchange: Casa de Cambio, Morelos 400 (tel. 12-66-06). Better rates than the banks. Open Mon.-Fri. 9am-2pm and 4:30-8pm. Many banks around Pl. de Armas open Mon.-Fri. 9am-1:30pm, including **Banamex,** at Allende and Obregón, one block east of Pl. de Armas, which has a 24-hr. **ATM.**

American Express: Grandes Viajes, Carranza 1077 (tel. 17-60-04).

Telephones: No **LADATELs. Computel,** Carranza 360, opposite the Hotel Panorama. International collect calls and public **fax.** Open Mon.-Sat. 7:30am-9pm.

Telegrams: Escobedo 200 (tel. 12-33-18), at the south end of the Plaza del Carmen, up the stairs to your right. Open Mon.-Fri. 9am-5pm, Sat. 9am-1pm.

Airport: (tcl. 2-22-29). Tickets can be purchased at **2001 Viajes,** Obregón 604 (tel 2-29-53). Flights to Mexico City and Monterrey. Open Mon.-Fri. 9am-6pm.

Buses: Central de Autobuses (tel. 12-74-11), 2 blocks south of the chaotic convergence of highways that wrap around the Glorieta Benito Juárez, 4km east of the city center along Av. Universidad. **Luggage** can be stored with the bus companies—negotiate a deal. **Estrella Blanca** (tel. 18-30-49) goes to Aguascalientes (6 per day, 2hr., 32 pesos), Chihuahua (2 per day, 14hr., 231 pesos), Cuernavaca (2 per day, 8hr., 109 pesos), Monterrey (every hr., 7hr., 86 pesos), Querétaro (4 per day, 2½hr., 37 pesos), Saltillo (every hr., 5hr., 75 pesos), and Zacatecas (7 per day, 3hr., 35 pesos). **Ómnibus de México** (tel. 12-75-16) to Guadalajara (1 per day, 5hr., 82 pesos), Matehuala (1 per day, 3hr., 41 pesos), Monterrey (3 per day, 7hr., 106 pesos), Reynosa (1 per day, 10hr., 130 pesos), and Saltillo (2 per day, 5½hr., 89 pesos). **Transportes Tamaulipas** and **Noreste** (tel. 18-29-15) jointly trek to Matehuala (6 per day, 2½hr., 41 pesos), Monterrey (8 per day, 7hr., 101 pesos), and Reynosa via Linares or Monterrey (9 per day, 7hr., 145 pesos). **Del Norte** (tel. 16-55-43) goes to Acapulco (2 per day, 10hr., 206 pesos), Cuernavaca (every hr., 8hr., 95 pesos), and Mexico City (every hr., 5hr., 95 pesos).

Trains: Station on Othón near the north side of the Alameda. To Mexico City (10am, 6hr., 38 pesos), Monterrey (2 per day, 8hr., 39 pesos), and more.

Car Rental: Hertz, Obregón 670 (tel. 12-95-00). Small Nissan 175 pesos per dayplus 80 pesos for insurance. Must be 25. Open Mon.-Fri. 9am-5pm, Sat. 9am-noon.

Laundromat: Lavandería La Burbuja Azul, Carranza 1093. Open Mon.-Sat. 8am-8pm, Sun. 9am-2pm.

Red Cross: (tel. 15-33-22 or 15-36-35), Juárez at Díaz Gutiérrez.

Pharmacy: Botica Mexicana, Othón 180 (tel. 12-38-80), by the cathedral. Open 24hr. Yessssir, this drugstore is always open.

Hospital: Carranza 2395 (tel. 13-03-43 or 13-43-95), several km west of *el centro*.

Emergency: 06.

Police: (tel. 12-28-04 or 12-54-76), in the Palacio Municipal.

Post Office: Morelos 235 (tel. 2-27-40), between Salazar and Insurgentes, 1 block east and 4 blocks north of the Plaza de Armas. Open Mon.-Fri. 9am-5pm, Sat. 9am-1pm. **Postal Code:** 78000.

Telephone Code: 48.

ACCOMMODATIONS

Some good accommodations can be found near the bus station; for those who don't mind staying in this noisy part of town, a viable option is the youth hostel. Hotels closer to *el centro* typically boast commodious *cuartos* for reasonable prices.

Villa Juvenil San Luis Potosí CREA Youth Hostel (HI), (tel. 55-73-60), near the Glorieta Benito Juárez as you exit the bus station. Walk straight ahead one block—those are the sports fields for the hostel. Smallish, 4-person rooms are clean, with new bunks and mattresses. Sports complex with basketball courts, soccer fields, and track. Curfew 11pm. 20 pesos per person, 10% discount with HI card. Breakfast 9 pesos, lunch and dinner 13 pesos each. Make reservations.

Hotel de Gante, 5 de Mayo 140 (tel. 12-14-93), half a block south of the Pl. de Arma. Enormous rooms have well equipped bathrooms and a marvelous view of the plaza. The lounges on each floor provide space to hang out and chug the free bottled water. Singles 85 pesos. Doubles 95 pesos.

Hotel Plaza, Jardín Hidalgo 22 (tel. 12-46-31), on the south side of the Pl. de Armas. The rooms show signs of wear, but how can you complain when the beds are so soft, the fans so soothing, and the view from the balcony so beautiful? Ask for a room facing the plaza. Singles 65 pesos. Doubles 70 pesos.

Hotel Progreso, Aldama 415 (tel. 12-03-66), 1 block west and a ½ block south of the Plaza's southwest corner. Formerly a monastery. Big comfy rooms are a bit dark, but the central location, the building's many quirks, and the price, all make it worth it. Singles 67 pesos. Doubles 72 pesos. Triples 77 pesos. Quads 82 pesos.

FOOD

Many touristy restaurants lie on Carranza or one block north on Arista. While prices are jacked up along this strip, so is originality and the chance for a nice atmosphere. Both *tacos potosinos* and enchiladas *potosinas* are stuffed with cheese and vegetables, then fried. *Nopalitos* are tender pieces of cactus (spines removed) cooked in a salty sauce of garlic, onion, and tomato. *Chongos coronados* (curdled milk in sweet maple water) is a popular dessert.

La Corriente, Carranza 700 (tel. 12-93-04). A stunning series of dining rooms, each with a unique variation of colonial decor, surrounds a central fountain and a Babylonian glass ceiling dripping with hanging plants. The house special, *chamorro pibil* (pig leg cooked in a banana leaf) accompanies the *comida corrida* (20 pesos). Sample the *afrodisíacos* (12 pesos) for a sexy fruit juice concoction (*Let's Go* does not recommend libidinal carelessness). Open daily 8am-midnight.

Restaurante-Cafetería Posada del Virrey, Jardín Hidalgo 3 (tel. 12-70-55), on the north side of the Plaza de Armas. A popular plaza restaurant with an unbeatable 18-peso *menú del día*. Breakfast buffet 15-20 pesos. Open daily 8am-11pm.

Yu Ne Nisa, Arista 360 (tel. 14-36-31). A Yucatec celebration of vegetarianism. Bright eating area is decorated with plants and matching green chairs. Veggie burgers are just 15 pesos, and that *quesadilla* you've been craving is a rock-bottom 10 pesos. Large variety of fruit juices and yogurt concoctions. Open Mon.-Sat. 9am-7pm.

SIGHTS

Dubbed the "City of Plazas", San Luis Potosí has three main town squares. The most central of these is the **Plaza de Armas** (also known as **Jardín Hidalgo),** replete with trees and relaxing *potosinos*. At the beginning of the 17th century, residents watched bullfights from the balconies of the surrounding buildings. Since 1848, a red sandstone gazebo bearing the names of famous Mexican musicians has graced the plaza; on Thursday and Sunday evenings, it hosts a local band that attracts a romantically inclined older crowd.

The west side of the Plaza de Armas is marked by the Neoclassical façade of the **Palacio del Gobierno.** Constructed in 1798 and briefly occupied by the exiled national government in 1863, the structure was renovated in 1950 and continues to serve as San Luis Potosí's administrative seat. On the second floor, in the **Sala Juárez,** is a diorama of the dramatic meeting between Juárez and Princess Salm-Salm, the wife of one of Maximilian's advisors. Legend has it that the princess begged Juárez for Maximilian's life on the eve of his execution. Plastic figures of the unmoved Juárez and the beautiful princess Salm-Salm are positioned in front of the table where Juárez signed Maximilian's sentence. As you enter the palace, go upstairs and turn left at the top of the staircase—the *Sala* Juárez is the first room on your left. Ask the guard to unlock the door (open Mon.-Fri. 9am-2:30pm; free).

Opposite the Palacio de Gobierno stands the **cathedral,** with two bell towers that toll a different melody every 15 minutes. Both magnificent and ominous, the cathedral was completed in 1710, but in 1855, when San Luis became a diocese, the building was "upgraded." Miners are said to have donated gold and silver to beautify the interior, and marble statues of the apostles (small copies of those at the Basilica of San Juan de Letrán in Rome) were placed in the niches between the Solomonic columns of the Baroque façade. Paintings can be admired in the sacristy (cathedral open daily 8am-7pm; tourists should avoid visiting on Sundays or during mass).

The **Palacio Municipal,** on the northeast corner of the plaza, was rebuilt after local citizens torched the original structure to protest Carlos III's expulsion of the Jesuits from Spanish America. A traditional red-stone courtyard leads to a painted stairwell and simple mosaic steps in pseudo-Pompeiian style. *Sala* Cabildo, on the second floor, features ceilings elaborately painted by Italian artist Erulo Eroli. One block west of the southwest corner of the Pl. de Armas is the **Antigua Caja Real** (Old Royal Treasury/Monetary Repository), the city's only existing secular baroque building. The small sculpture which accents the corner of the façade is La Purísima.

East of the Plaza de Armas on Othón is the modest **Casa Othón,** home of the illustrious *poeta potosino* Manuel José Othón (1858-1906). The yellow walls of this museum contain manuscripts, memorabilia, and a furniture collection from the Othón household. Check out the bathtub (open Tues.-Fri. 10am-2pm and 4-6pm, Sat.-Sun. 10am-2pm; 1 peso donation recommended).

Nicolás Fernando de Torres, a rich *sevillano* of the early 18th century, made his fortune in San Luis Potosí. After his death, his estate was used to found a church and a convent of the ascetic Carmelite order. Today, only the **Iglesia de Carmen** remains on the northeast corner of the plaza of the same name. Many *potosinos* claim the church is the most beautiful religious building in the city; it features hanging chandeliers, golden altars, and a huge mural of the crucifixion. Affixed to its façade are statues of San Eliseo, San Elías, and, at the very top, the Madonna (open daily 7:30am-1:30pm and 4-9pm; avoid visiting during mass).

The pink sandstone **Museo Nacional de la Máscara,** Villerías 2 (tel. 12-30-25), in the Palacio Federal, half a block south of Pl. del Carmen along Villerías, displays hundreds of masks from every Mexican region. Be sure to see the ceremonial masks used in colonial and pre-Hispanic times during pagan religious celebrations (open Tues.-Fri. 10am-2pm and 4-6pm, Sat.-Sun. 10am-2pm; 1 peso).

Two blocks south and one block west of the Plaza de Armas's southwest corner is the **Plaza de San Francisco.** The plaza is distinguished by its bronze fountain, quaint cobblestone streets, and red sandstone buildings. Elderly *potosinos* often congregate here, carrying grandkids and tossing crumbs to the pigeons. Soon after the city's founding, construction began on the **Iglesia de San Francisco,** on the west side of the plaza. Less ornate than its nearby counterparts, the orange stucco façade boasts a Sevillian clock (1785) and statues of St. Francis. Inside, the doorway to the Salón de Profundis depicts St. Frailón washing the sacred cuts of St. Francis. Each morning, Franciscans chanted the *De Profundis* in the salon, which is dominated by a magnificent Churrigueresque fountain (open daily 8am-7pm).

The **Museo Regional Potosino,** Galeana 450 (tel. 12-51-85), along the street on San Francisco's southern side, occupies the grounds of the former Franciscan convent. The government seized the land in 1950 and converted part of it into a museum. On the museum's second floor is the marvelous **Capilla a la Virgen de Aranzazu.** A shepherd found the altar's image of the Virgin in a prickly thicket, hence the name (*aranzazu* means "from within the thorns"). The *ex-votos* along the walls are a tradition among Mexico's faithful; each depicts a miracle that a parishioner has experienced. They are often painted anonymously and hung in the church near an image of the Virgin. The first floor exhibits artifacts from all of Mexico, including an exhibition of pre-Hispanic artifacts (open Tues.-Sat. 10am-1pm and 3pm-6pm; free). Three blocks east along Manuel Othón from the Plaza de Armas is the expansive **Alameda Juan Sarabia.** During the day you can admire its trees, benches, statues, and artificial ponds; avoid the Alameda at night.

The *Zona Rosa,* the area along Carranza west of the *centro,* teems with trendy restaurants and clubs. Here, the swank **Jardín de Tequis** is a great place to relax and listen to the trickle of four beautiful fountains. The Zona Rosa is accessible via the "Morales" bus. More impressive is **Parque Tangamanga,** with three lakes for paddle-boating and fishing, a baseball field, electric cars, a jogging path, and grounds for driving and biking. The open-air **Teatro de la Ciudad** hosts frequent cultural and artistic events. To get to the park, catch a "Perimetral" bus (0.80 pesos) on Constitución across from the Alameda. Get off at the Monumento a la Revolución and walk south for three blocks (open Tues.-Sun. 9am-6pm; free).

ENTERTAINMENT AND SEASONAL EVENTS

Taxis are nearly impossible to catch on Saturday nights, so if you plan on hitting the clubs, leave early. Chic *potosinos* flock to **Arusha,** Muñoz 195 (tel. 17-42-30), the best club in town. To understand the kitschy grandeur of the club's decor—it consists of a gigantic elephant head (fake), some stuffed animals (real), and a light system to create that jungle mood—you need to know that Arusha is a city in Tanzania. Now, party on. The music ranges from techno to top-40 to *tejano*. Don't come in shorts, sneakers, or sandals, or the fashion police at the door will turn you away (drinks 12-20 pesos; cover 35 pesos; open Thurs.-Sat. 9pm-3am). A little closer to the *centro* is **Huff!,** Carranza 1145 (tel. 13-65-53). Drawing a 25+ crowd, this hip disco has no cover (open daily). At **Staff,** Carranza 423, near the *centro,* a younger crowd grooves to Latin and dance music (cover 20 pesos).

The last two weeks of August mark the **Fiesta Nacional Potosina.** Concerts, bullfights, fireworks, and a parade guarantee that a swell time will be had by all.

■ Matehuala

The indigenous founders of Matehuala (pop. 75,000) must have anticipated the trickle of backpackers who traverse this central Mexican crossroads: the town's name derives from a Huachichil phrase meaning "don't come." Founded in 1590 as a mining colony meant to take advantage of the mineral deposits in the nearby mountains, today Matehuala promotes itself through its proximity to the remnants of this mining legacy at Real de Catorce. While its list of attractions may be sparse, Matehuala promises a relaxing stay; unlike many other Mexican cities, the city has slid into the modern age with grace.

ORIENTATION

Matehuala is 261km from Saltillo and 191km from San Luis Potosí. The **Central de Autobuses** is located on Calle 5 de Mayo, just south of the city and near the large, red **Arco de Bienvenida. Cinco de Mayo** runs north-south through the center of town. From the station, a *pesera* labeled "Centro" will take you to the downtown area for 1.30 pesos—ask the driver to let you off near the cathedral, or easier still, get off at Hidalgo, next to the Chalita market. Taxis charge 8 pesos for the trip.

Constantly forking or changing names, the streets of Matehuala are terribly confusing even for longtime residents. Try to procure a map at the tourist office on Highway 57, or better yet, at the Monterrey or San Luis Potosí tourist offices. **Miguel Hidalgo** runs north-south through most of the city; **Benito Juárez** runs parallel to it, one block west. Most points of interest lie somewhere on or between these streets.

PRACTICAL INFORMATION

Tourist Information: Cámara de Comercio, Morelos 427, one block east of Hidalgo. Low on maps, but high on knowledge. Open Mon.-Fri. 8am-1:30pm and 4-7:30pm, Sat. 8am-1pm. Small-scale **tourist office** (tel. 2-12-81), next to the Padregal Motel on Highway 57, north of the city. Open Mon.-Fri. 10am-4pm.

Currency Exchange: Casa de Cambio San Luis Divisa (tel. 2-31-46), at Colón and Hidalgo, north of Hotel Matehuala. They also cash traveler's checks. Open 9am-8pm. **Banca Serfín** (tel. 2-12-82), at Reyes and Hidalgo, has a 24-hr. **ATM.**

Telephones: No **LADATELs** in town. Long distance service at **Domi's,** Morelos 701, off Plaza de Armas. Open daily 7am-2pm.

Telegrams: Telecomm, Madero 119A (tel. 2-00-08). Also houses a **Western Union** office. Open Mon.-Fri. 9am-7pm.

Buses: Central de Autobuses, on 5 de Mayo south of the downtown area. Consolidated service of **Transportes del Norte, Frontera, Estrella Blanca** (tel. 2-01-50), and **El Águila** (tel. 2-28-60) to Mexico City (5 per day, 8hr., first-class 139 pesos, second class 118 pesos), Monterrey (7 per day, 4-5hr., 67 pesos), Nuevo Laredo (every hr. 3pm-6am, 9-10hr., 136 pesos), Querétaro (2 per day, 6hr., 83 pesos), Saltillo (5 per day, 3hr., 48 pesos), and San Luis Potosí (every hr., 2½hr., 39 pesos). **Noreste** (tel. 2-09-97) serves Monterrey (7 per day, 4hr., 67 pesos) and Reynosa (3 per day, 6hr., 106 pesos). **Tamaulipas** (tel. 2-27-71) to Monterrey via Saltillo (17 per day, 67 pesos), Real de Catorce (5 per day, 13 pesos), Reynosa (3 per day, 7hr., 106 pesos), and San Luis Potosí (7 per day, 35 pesos).

Market: Chalita, Hidalgo between Constitución and Madero. Open Mon.-Fri. 9am-2pm and 3:30-8:30pm, Sat. 10am-2pm. The indoor market next to the Templo de la Imaculada Concepción sells crafts and produce. Open daily 9am-6pm.

Laundromat: Lavandería Acuario, Betancourt and Madero (tel. 2-70-88). Self-service wash or dry 3kg for 9 pesos. Open daily 8:30am-2pm and 4-8pm.

Red Cross: (tel. 2-07-26), Ignacio and Ramírez and Betancourt.

Pharmacy: Farmacia Rex (tel. 2-02-49), Madero at Morelos. Open 8am-10pm.

Emergency: 06. Dial it.

Police: tel. 2-06-47.

Post Office: (tel. 2-00-73), Leandro Valle and Negrete. Open Mon.-Fri. 8am-3pm, Sat. 9am-1pm. **Postal Code:** 78700.

Telephone Code: 488

ACCOMMODATIONS

Budget accommodations dot the *centro*. The *casas de huéspedes* on **Calle Bocanegra** are the cheapest options (singles 15 pesos; doubles 30 pesos).

Hotel Blanca Estela, Morelos 426 (tel. 2-23-00), next to the video store. Fans cool small, super clean, colorful rooms with TVs. Beautiful wooden furnishings lend a luxurious feel to the rooms. Singles 65 pesos. Doubles 75 pesos.

Hotel Matehuala, Bustamante 134 (tel. 2-06-80), just north of the Plaza de Armas. High-ceilinged, well furnished rooms overlook a gargantuan central courtyard. Singles 60 pesos. Doubles 70 pesos.

Hotel María Esther, Madero 111 (tel. 2-07-14). White-washed exterior encloses rooms with an outdoor balcony, a slightly beat-up couch, comfy beds, and big, bright bathrooms. Singles 52 pesos. Doubles 65 pesos.

FOOD

Restaurant Fontella, Morelos 612 (tel. 2-02-93). Colorful hanging lamps illuminate a tranquil, flora-filled dining area, while the murals of the city evoke a sense of yesteryear. *Comida corrida* offers copious servings of fresh vegetable soup, rice, chicken or steak, and dessert for 18 pesos. Open daily 7:30am-2am.

La Cava, Callejón del Arte 1 (tel. 2-28-88), just east of Hotel Matehuala. The elegant dining room provides a pleasant escape from the merciless sun. Traditional Mexican fare and an array of healthy sandwiches for around 15 pesos. Huge steaks 32 pesos. Smooth cocktails. Open daily 7:30am-10:30pm.

Restaurant y Mariscos Santa Fe, Morelos 709 (tel. 2-07-53), on the east side of the Plaza de Armas. Endless options include *pollo empanizado* (15 pesos), *bistek ranchero* (15 pesos), and seafood (under 20 pesos). Open daily 7am-midnight.

SIGHTS

Standing solemnly at the center of Matehuala between Calles Juárez and Hidalgo is the as-yet-incomplete **Templo de la Inmaculada Concepción,** a copy of Saint Joseph's cathedral in Lyon, France. Construction began in 1905, but poor funding has slowed progress on the project. (Sigh. Maybe someday.) The large clock and seemingly impenetrable gray exterior of this Gothic-style edifice belie a beautiful interior flooded with light. Another cathedral, the **Templo del Santo Niño,** stands four blocks west on Constitución and is currently closed for renovations.

Just in front of the main cathedral is the **Plaza Juárez,** now permanently occupied by vendor stalls and small, makeshift cafés. Sprawling out onto adjoining streets, the bazaar is collectively known as **Mercado Arista.** Leather and ceramic goods as well as the usual slew of cheap plastic toys and trinkets figure prominently here.

Two large parks stand at the northeast and southeast corners of the downtown area. Approximately three blocks east of Hidalgo, between Bocanegra and Alta-mirano, is the soothing and peaceful **Parque Vicente Guerrero** (also called the Parque del Pueblo). Vicente Guerrero's counterpart is the more lively **Parque Álvaro Obregón,** just south of Insurgentes. With basketball courts and benches aplenty, Álvaro Obregón draws entire families in the early evening hours.

■ Real de Catorce

Only a stretch of pavement separates the cobblestone streets of Real de Catorce from ultra-modern Matehuala, but the two towns seem light-years away. Once a thriving mining town with 30,000 inhabitants, Real de Catorce now looms mysteriously on the side of a mountain, a veritable ghost town. The town sprung up in a glittery flash in 1772, when veins of silver and gold were uncovered in a remote part of the Sierra Madre. Visitors must journey through the arid moonscape terrain to reach the sun-bleached hills that are a lingering reminder of Real de Catorce's mining heyday. Men and women still traverse the city's clumsily constructed streets, pulling their horses and donkeys behind them, in the meditative calm of a little town left behind by time.

Orientation and Practical Information Tourists from all over Mexico travel to Real de Catorce to investigate this dusty anachronism of a town and to explore hallucinogens. *Let's Go* does not recommend illegal drug use. Self-appointed guides, offering **tourist information** and **peyote,** can be found in the back streets of the city. Most services (i.e., the civil registry, police station, and municipal government) run out of the **Presidencia Municipal,** just by the Plaza Principal. The **post office** is on Calle Constitución (open Mon.-Fri. 9am-1pm and 3-6pm). The town's single **telephone** (tel. 2-37-33) will put you in touch with the hotels.

Accommodations and Food Real de Catorce has a conspicuous lack of decent budget accommodations and an unusual abundance of Italian restaurants. The best option may be **Quinta La Puesta Del Sol,** a variation of a bed and breakfast across from the Capilla de Guadalupe (rooms with TV and bathroom 135 pesos; doubles 160 pesos). **El Real,** Morelos 20, has colorful, spic-and-span rooms with candlelight and mosaics. Some rooms boast skylights and fireplaces, and the roof terrace offers a smashing view (90-150 pesos). Italian dishes (15-20 pesos) are the forte of the hotel's restaurant. **Hotel Providencia,** Lanzagorta 29, is cheaper, but the rooms are barebones (singles 50 pesos; doubles 100 pesos). The **Eucalipto Restaurant** on Calle Lerdo offers reasonably priced *comida italiana.*

Sights Calle Lanzagorta runs past most major sights. The **Templo de la Purísima Concepción** is down the road on the right; ascend the white walkway to reach the entrance. Inside, the floor seems to be composed of rectangular blocks of wood; the blocks are actually doors to subterranean **tombs,** each of which contains several bodies. The **cathedral** resembles a brightly colored fabergé egg, with pastel decor and plastic figurines. It houses a lifelike image of St. Francis, whose miracles have created a devoted following; on October 4, the saint's feast day, the town attracts a flock of pious visitors hoping to pray at the cathedral. A side room is filled with thousands of letters as testament to Saint Francis's ability to work miracles. Across from the cathedral along Lanzagorta is the **Museo Parroquial,** which exhibits relics from the town's past (open Thurs.-Sun., 10am-4pm). Uphill on the right, after the cathedral (a steep climb) is the **Plaza Principal,** where today only a crumbling fountain remains. Next to the plaza is the **Casa de Moneda,** formerly a mint, whose third floor houses a photography exhibit of Real de Catorce. Enter the museum by the plaza (open daily 10am-4pm; free).

Turning right immediately after the Jardín, continue two blocks uphill, then head one painfully uphill block to the left. There the terraced steps of the **Palenque de Gallos** (cock-fight ring) replicate the layout of a classical Athenian theater (ask someone in the Casa de Moneda to unlock it for you). The cliff known as **El Voladero** offers breathtaking views of the surrounding mountains and valleys. To reach it, walk uphill on Calle Constitución. At the top of Calle Zaragoza stands the stark white **Capilla de Guadalupe** (also called the Panteón), which overlooks a cemetery tightly paved with the graves of local saints. For a **guided horseback tour** of the region, contact expert trail masters at Hotel El Real.

Getting There: Autobuses Tamaulipas (tel. 2-08-40) runs buses from Matehuala to Real de Catorce (every 2hr. 6am-6pm, 1½hr., 18 pesos roundtrip); always arrive 15-30 minutes early. Taking the last bus means spending the night at Real de Catorce. Buses leave from a station at Guerrero and Méndez, near *el centro.* Finding the station is quite tricky; ask a local to point you in the right direction. The ride is guaranteed to whiten the knuckles of the timid traveler: the bus rambles along a cobblestone road and a winding path chiseled into the mountainside.

■ Ciudad Valles

With wide, clean sidewalks, sprawling parks, and chipper locals, Ciudad Valles (pop. 300,000) has a certain Main Street, U.S.A. feel. A major crossroads between the *noreste* and central Mexico, Valles isn't chock full of sights, but its small town charm makes it a pleasant place to rest en route to more exotic destinations.

Orientation and Practical Information Ciudad Valles's main thoroughfare is **Calle Hidalgo.** Most accommodations and points of interest lie between **Jardín Hidalgo** and **Glorieta Hidalgo.** Terrific maps of the town can be purchased for five pesos at the **Cámara de Comercio,** Carranza Sur 55 (tel. 2-01-44 or 2-45-11), a half block south of Hidalgo, or at a hotel. **Banamex** (tel. 2-11-17), on the corner of Hidalgo and Madero, has a 24-hour **ATM. LADATELs** are scattered throughout town. Many hotels offer international long distance service. **Western Union,** Hidalgo 234 (tel. 91-800-5), in the **Elektra** appliance store, offers **telegram** service. The **Central de Autobuses,** on the outskirts of town, is accessible by bus from Calle Hidalgo (1.50 pesos) or taxi (15 pesos). **Oriente** bypasses Asia to serve Guadalajara (3 per day, 10-12hr., 119-130 pesos), Matamoros (10 per day, 8hr., 103 pesos), Querétaro (1 per day, 8hr., 96 pesos), San Luis Potosí (every hr., 5hr., 53-64 pesos), Tampico (every hr., 2½-3hr., 30-33 pesos), and Xilitla (5 per day, 2½hr., 13 pesos). **Frontera** runs buses to Monterrey (2 per day, 8hr., 116 pesos) and Nuevo Laredo (2 per day, 11hr., 160 pesos). **Estrella Blanca, Ómnibus de México, Línea Azul,** and **Transportes del Norte** offer similar service. The **market** is at the corner of Díaz and Hidalgo. The **Red Cross** (tel. 2-00-56) is behind city hall on Morelos. **Farmacia Plaza,** Hidalgo 113 (tel. 2-04-80), is open 24 hours. In case of an **emergency,** dial 91-800-90-392. The **police** can be reached at tel. 12-10-32. The **post office** is on Juárez 520 (open Mon.-Fri. 8am–7pm, Sat. 9am-noon). **Telephone code:** 138.

Accommodations and Food Several hotels dot the *centro.* **Hotel Piña,** Juárez 210 (tel. 2-01-83), offers clean (if somewhat dated) rooms with private bath. Some have A/C and TVs (66-104 pesos; discounts for longer stays; adjoining restaurant open daily 7:30am-midnight). Another great deal is **Hotel Rex,** Hidalgo 418 (tel. 1-04-11), with spacious, elegant rooms and clean new bathrooms. Kick back in the shady lounge or balcony (singles 84 pesos, with TV 94 pesos; doubles 105 pesos, with TV 125 pesos). There are few restaurants in town, but *loncherías* are ubiquitous. **La**

Bella Napoli (tel. 2-33-84), adjoining Hotel Piña, offers pizzas (16-52 pesos), pasta, sandwiches, and *antojitos* (open daily 7:30am-midnight).

■ Near Ciudad Valles: Xilitla

A serpentine road winds through the rocky *huasteca* highlands to the tiny hamlet of Xilitla, two hours from and 1000m above Ciudad Valles. Xilitla's main attraction is the **Enchanted Garden of Edward James (a.k.a. Jardín Encantado or Casa del Inglés).** The bastard son of King Edward VIII, James rubbed elbows with a number of avant-garde artists from Luis Buñuel and Salvador Dalí to Aldous Huxley and Pablo Picasso. One prophetic night, when a cloud of butterflies blackened the sky, the bearded messiah decided to bring his surrealist dreams to fruition. The wacky Englishman created a slew of concrete, steel, and stone structures in often wild colors and even wilder forms throughout the jungle. Probably the only non-Indian ruins in Mexico, James' melange of bridges, arches, and artistic relics, recall Alice in Wonderland or Disney World on acid, with winding staircases that lead to nowhere, a library without books, and other touches of madness. To reach the Jardín, take a taxi from Xilitla, or, if you're truly adventuresome, walk down the two-lane road that skirts the edge of the cliff, turning left onto the gravelly dirt road just past the bridge; then walk 4km, staying to the left (admission 5 pesos; open daily 9am-5pm).

Tourist information can be acquired at the **Cámara de Comercio** or **La Canasta** bookstore, both in Ciudad Valles. Exchange currency at **Compra y Venta Dólares,** Escobedo 204, on the second floor, half a block east of the Plaza Principal. The **Cruz Roja** (tel. 5-02-47) is on the road descending Xilitla. **Farmacia San Augustín** (tel. 5-00-11) is on Hidalgo, at the northwest corner of the Plaza Principal (open daily 8:30am-9pm). The Palacio Municipal, on the plaza, houses the **police** and rudimentary tourist information. Behind the Palacio on Calle Zaragoza (south side of the plaza) is the **post office,** located on the second floor (open Mon.-Fri. 9am-4pm). The **postal code** is 79902. **Casa María,** farther west on Hidalgo, near the market, offers clean rooms with bathrooms and hot water (singles 50 pesos; doubles 85 pesos).

Getting There: Oriente runs buses to Xilitla (5 per day, 2½hr., 13 pesos) from the Central de Autobuses in **Ciudad Valles.**

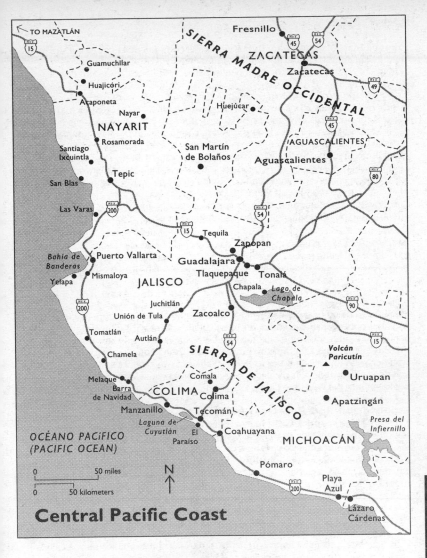

Central Pacific Coast

Stretching from the quiet fishing villages near San Blas to the glossy resort of Manzanillo, the Central Pacific Coast boasts kilometer after kilometer of smooth sand tickled by the ebb and flow of the tide. A Pacific breeze keeps the desert climate at relatively mild temperatures, and the sun never fails to illuminate the azure skies.

A state with diverse terrain, **Nayarit** is marked by volcanic highlands, tropical jungles, and a network of lakes and rivers. This verdant and fertile region grows the lion's share of the nation's marijuana and served as the setting for *Journey to Ixtlán*, Carlos Castañeda's renowned book describing experiences with hallucinogens in a small town between Tepic and Guadalajara. Hallucinogen use has long been part of

Cora and Huichol *indígena* traditions and is still common practice among shamans in their incantations. *Let's Go* does not recommend illegal drug use.

South of Nayarit lies **Jalisco,** the most touristed state along the Central Pacific Coast. Much of the world's popular image of Mexico could be stamped "Hecho en Jalisco"—the *jarabe tapatío* (hat dance), *mariachis, charros,* and tequila all appeared first in this state. However, the province remained isolated from the rest of Mexico for hundreds of years, possessing neither silver nor gold, jewels nor water, fertile land nor agricultural climate. It wasn't until the 1920s, when railroad tracks extended to Guadalajara, that this mountainous town (elevation 1552m) began to grow into a metropolis; today, it is the second largest city in the country.

Tiny **Colima** boasts yet more beaches and some small pleasant towns where tourists can escape the resort scene and rest in the shady *zócalo.* The state is also home to Manzanillo, the workhorse of Mexico's Pacific coast. The port has not paused once in 700 years of commerce with Asia to wipe its sweaty brow, and only recently has it attempted to polish its image for the benefit of visitors.

NAYARIT

■ San Blas

San Blas is a blend of shoe-worn buildings and crumbling relics from its glory days as a central port in Spain's colonial empire. Today, this tiny fishing village feeds off its ecological wealth: awesome beaches, over 300 species of birds (just listen as you exit the bus station), and the nearby jungle attract *norteamericano* expatriates, bird-watchers, and tourists en route to Puerto Vallarta. Also a mecca for surfers, San Blas's *zócalo* is a cool-dude sort of place; skate-rats, surfers, and video game junkies swagger about into the wee hours.

Orientation and Practical Information San Blas is 69km northeast of Tepic by Rte. 15 and 54. **Calle Juárez,** San Blas's main drag, runs parallel to the bus station on the south side of the *zócalo.* **Batallón** runs perpendicular to Juárez from the *zócalo's* center and leads to the closest beach, **Playa Borrego.**

The **Comunidad Cultural Huichol,** Juárez 28 West (tel. 5-00-01), across from Restaurant McDonald, functions as tourist office and Huichol crafts store. It can arrange trips to La Tovara (see p. 256) and hikes to some of Nayarit's more beautiful waterfalls (office open Mon.-Fri., May-Oct. 9am-noon and maybe 7-9pm, Nov.-April, 9-11am and 6-10pm). Rates aren't that great at **Banamex** (tel. 5-00-30), on Juárez east of the *zócalo* (open Mon.-Fri. 8:30-11am). They're just as bad at the *casa de cambio,* Mercado 32 (tel. 5-02-68), with another entrance on Juárez across from the bank (open Mon.-Sat. 8am-2pm and 4-8pm, Sun. 8am-2pm). Make long-distance **phone** calls from the *caseta de larga distancia* at Juárez 3 (tel. 5-06-10 or -11; fax 5-06-65; open daily 8am-10pm). The **telegram and fax** office is at Sonora 56 (tel. 5-01-15; open Mon.-Fri. 8am-2pm).

Transportes Norte de Sonora (tel. 5-00-43) **buses** run to Guadalajara (9am, 5hr., 75 pesos), Tepic (every hr. 6am-7pm, 1¾hr., 17 pesos), Santiago Ixcuintla (8:45, 11am, 1, and 4:30pm, 1¾hr., 15 pesos), Mazatlán (5pm, 5hr., 66 pesos), and Puerto Vallarta (7 and 10am, 3hr., 45 pesos). **Farmacia Económica** is at Batallón 49 (tel./fax 5-01-11; open daily 8am-2pm and 4-9pm). The **Centro de Salud** (tel. 5-02-32) is on Batallón and Campeche, five blocks south of the *zócalo.* No English is spoken (open 24hr.). Another medical center, the **Clínica IMSS,** Batallón 10 (tel. 5-02-27), is two blocks towards the *zócalo* from the Centro de Salud (open for consultation Mon.-Fri. 8am-5pm; at other times enter on Canalizo). The **police** (tel. 5-00-28) are on Sinaloa opposite the bus station; it's the last door in the Palacio Municipal as you walk away from the *zócalo* (open 24hr.). The **post office** (tel. 5-02-95) is at Sonora and Echeverría, one block north and one block east of the northeast corner of the *zócalo* (open Mon.-Fri. 8am-1pm and 3-5pm, Sat. 8am-noon). **Postal Code:** 63740. **Telephone Code:** 328.

Accommodations and Food Finding a place to sleep in San Blas isn't difficult during the off-season, but autumn storms bring mile-long waves and bed-seeking surfers. In September and October make reservations. The blood-sucking mosquitoes near the water make camping a no-no and rooms inland the best choice. Both **Casa María,** Batallón 108 (tel. 5-06-32), and **Hotel Morelos,** across the street and owned by the same family, rent simple, white concrete rooms set around grassy, if slightly overgrown courtyards. Some of the rooms lack private baths, but the communal ones are clean. They rent bikes (25 pesos per day) and provide purified water, postal service, washing machine, and a communal kitchen (singles 40 pesos, with bath 50 pesos; doubles with bath 70 pesos; add 15 pesos during high season). **El Bucanero,** Juárez 75 (tel. 5-01-01), is reminiscent of a creaky pirate ship. It offers large, dim rooms with high ceilings, clean bathrooms, a swimming pool, and a huge fading crocodile in the lobby. Hot water and fans make things comfy (singles 77 pesos, in high season 98 pesos; doubles 100 pesos, in high season 130 pesos; prices vary). **Los Cocos** (tel. 5-00-55), on Batallón just before the Playa Borrego, is a trailer park with bathrooms, electricity, and a 24-hour guard (two people 60 pesos). Larger parties should scout **Bungalows Puesta del Sol** (tel. 5-00-66), on Paredes at Campeche, two blocks from Playa Borrego. Remodeled four-person bungalows have teal and white tiles, spacious kitchens, color TV and A/C (150 pesos per unit). To get there, turn right (facing the beach) on the street by Hotel Marino.

Restaurant **McDonald,** Juárez 36, opposite the tourist office, is just as popular with locals and travelers as the real Mickey D's. The little flowering plants give the place an odd, shimmering feel—imagine painting a black and white movie light blue (*comida corrida* 15 pesos, *plato de frutas* 9 pesos; open daily 7am-10pm). **La Familia,** Batallón 18 (tel. 5-02-58), is a family joint, right down to the tablecloths, TV, and conversation-starting wall-mounted shark's teeth, sea bottles, and indigenous drums. Chicken costs 20 pesos, and fresh fish 24 pesos (open daily 8am-10pm, in low season usually won't open until noon). **La Isla** (tel. 5-04-07), on Mercado and Paredes, lives up to its name—every space, crack, and crevice is covered with shells. The food will knock you out (fried fish 24 pesos; open daily 8am-10pm).

Sand and Sights San Blas, known for its perfectly symmetric waves and safe sandy bottom, has churned out many a surfing champ. To rent surfing equipment or take lessons, drop by **La Tumba de Yako,** Batallón 219 (tel. 5-04-62), run by Juan García, president of San Blas's surfing club and technical director of Mexico's surf team. Also known as "Juan Bananas" (as in banana bread), he also runs a vegetarian shop during high season.

San Blas's main attraction is the smooth water, packed sand, and long waves of **Playa Las Islitas.** During the stormy months of September and October, surfers flock to San Blas in hopes of catching the famous yearly mile-long wave which carries them from Las Islitas all the way to Playa Matanchén. To reach Las Islitas, take a bus from the bus station (every hr. 7am-5pm, 3pesos; returning every hr. 7:30am-4:30pm). There is another bus, leaving from the corner of Sinaloa at Paredes in front of the green trim building (5:20am and every 2hr. 8:20am-2:30pm, 15min., 3 pesos; returning every 2hr. 7:50am-3:50pm). Don't settle for the first few stretches of sand that greet you—prettier coves and seclusion await farther along the shore.

At the southern end of Batallón, **Playa Borrego** is easily accessible from town and offers a relaxing, though somewhat bland, view of the coast. Borrego's sand is gray and its mosquitoes ravenous. Quiet and pretty **Playa del Rey,** off the coast of Borrego, has somewhat stronger currents. A *lancha* will take you there from the pier at the west end of Juárez (roundtrip about 5 pesos; boats run daily about 7am-7pm).

Locals hype La Tovara—not the beaches—as San Blas's can't-miss attraction. While the winding jungle boat ride to **La Tovara** springs can be expensive, seeing a live crocodile just might make it worthwhile. Guides navigate the shallow, swampy waters, pointing out rare and interesting birds and the stilted huts left over from the set of the film *Cabeza de Vaca.* The path clears to reveal hordes of turtles and huge fish. Trips can be arranged through the tourist office or directly with a boat owner; find them at the small docking area on Juárez's eastern end. Trips last about four hours and can be made any day between 7am and 4pm, but it's best to journey to La Tovara early in the morning, when the water is still calm and the birds undisturbed by the *lanchas.* Expect to pay 130 pesos for a group of four, depending on the tour.

The short hike to the top of **La Contaduría,** the hill near town, affords a beautiful view of the city and coast. The splintering stone fortress that protected the city impresses from above, while an 18th-century church stands farther downhill. To get there, head east on Juárez as if leaving town. Just before the bridge and the sign that reads "Cape Victoria 7," turn right onto the dirt road behind the houses and restaurants; veer right off that road onto the stone path that winds uphill .

After hours in San Blas, there's not much to do except down a few at the local watering hole. **Mike's CantaBar,** above Restaurant McDonald, rarely gets wild or crazy, but it's an interesting place to pass the evening. Mike no longer performs vintage rock, but he sings live salsa in what looks like an antique airport lounge (no cover; open daily 6pm-1am, live music Thurs.-Sun. starting around 10pm).

■ Near San Blas: El Custodio de las Tortugas

El Custodio de las Tortugas (The Guardian of the Turtles, tel. (329) 2-29-54, toll-free 1-800-891-3670) is an eco-resort in the tiny village of **Platanitos,** an hour and a half south of San Blas and two hours north of Puerto Vallarta. Its villa, perched 9m on a precipice, overlooks 20km of virgin beach and the longest stretch of turtle camp in Nayarit. Between July and August, owners Min and Mona, in collaboration with the Mexican government and several ecological organizations, collect turtle eggs, protecting them from thieves and predators. The elegant two bedroom, two bath villa has TV, A/C, and huge breezy terraces for whale watching and sunset worshipping. It's best enjoyed as a group (villa rental US$200 per person per week, min. 4 people; US$100 per person per weekend; or US$25 per night to help out and bunk in the turtle camp; some meals and kayak trips to the lagoon included). Don't miss going into town to try local specialty *pescado sarandeado* (mesquite-grilled fish, 40 pesos per kilo—enough to feed 3-4 people).

Children of the Corn

The Huichol Indians of Nayarit, Jalisco, Zacatecas, and Durango are believed to be the oldest native group in Mexico, and 5000-year-old petroglyphs attributed to them have been discovered along Mexico's west-central coastal area. The Huichol are deeply religious people; their rituals are based on the songs of the shamans. Their main song goes something like this: "If you have been made of *eeko* (corn), and you the *heekoori* (peyote, "the cactus that is the real core of the corn"), you become a *maye* (jaguar), that hunts your *maxra* (deer), that is your own spirit, and listen to the song of the *tamatx kauyumari* (oldest and biggest deer), who gives you the power...to heal, sing, and dance." For centuries, the Huichol have created unique crafts depicting scenes from their mythology. They are also known for yarn paintings, a craft more common in cities, where the material is readily available. But the more than 15,000 Huichol who still live in rural mountain regions are easily taken advantage of by agencies that purchase their work for a paltry sum and sell it for fifty times the price the artisan was paid. Furthermore, Huichol artists are often coerced into reproducing identical designs and figures, a practice in conflict with traditional Huichol beliefs. The **Comunidad Cultural Huichol** of San Blas, a three-year-old non-profit organization, provides a non-exploitative forum of expression for Huichol artists.

Getting There: Transportes Norte de Sonora gets you there from San Blas (tel. 5-00-43) or Puerto Vallarta (tel. 2-66-66; noon, 2:30 and 3pm, 2hr., 30 pesos). Ask the bus driver to let you off at Platanitos, then walk down the road and up the hill.

■ Tepic

Tepic is 169km north of Puerto Vallarta, 228km northwest of Guadalajara, and 295km south of Mazatlán. State capital and an important crossroads for the entire region, hard-working Tepic (pop. 450,000) fits its name well—it comes from the Náhuatl words *tetl* (rock) and *pic* (hard). Aside from a few historical sites and La Loma Park, there is little of touristic interest here. At best, the city can be used as a transportation hub and a base for exploring nearby towns.

Orientation and Practical Information As you leave the bus station, *el centro* is down the highway **(Insurgentes)** to the left; cross the street and catch one of the yellow buses (daily 6am-9pm, 1 peso). **Avenida México,** running north-south six blocks west of the bus station, is downtown Tepic's main drag. Addresses on Av. México change from Norte to Sur about four blocks north of **Insurgentes,** the largest east-west street. The yellow minivan *combis* (daily 6am-9pm, 1 peso; 9pm-midnight, 2 pesos) run back and forth along Av. México and Insurgentes. At its northern terminus, the many-fountained **Plaza Principal** (officially the **Centro Histórico**) is incessantly active, dominated on one end by the cathedral and on the other by the **Palacio Municipal.** Six blocks to the south, **Plaza Constituyente** is shockingly desolate. Most tourist services lie on or near Av. México.

Información Turística, Av. México Nte. 178-A (tel. 12-19-05), left of the cathedral, hands out handy little maps and brochures (open daily 9am-2pm and 3-8pm). **Banks** (most open Mon.-Fri. 8am-1:30pm) and *casas de cambio* (commonly open Mon.-Sat. 9am-2pm and 4-7pm) clutter México Nte. Both **Banamex** and **Bancomer,** on Av. México Nte., a few blocks south of the plaza, have **ATMs.** There are card-operated **LADATELs** in the bus station and along Av. México, as well as two **computel** booths in the bus station. For telegrams and faxes, try **Telecomm,** on Av. México Nte. 50 (tel. 12-96-55; open Mon.-Fri. 8am-6pm, Sat. 8am-noon).

Buses leave Tepic from the newer long-distance station (the smaller one downtown, three blocks north of the plaza on Victoria, only serves local destinations). To get to the new station, take a 15-1 or "Mololoa Llanitos" bus from the corner of México Sur and Hidalgo. Only partial listings are provided. **Norte de Sonora** (tel. 3-23-15) runs to Culiacán (every hr., 8hr., 125 pesos), Guadalajara (every hr., 4hr., 65 pesos), Mazatlán (every hr., 5hr., 64 pesos), Santiago Ixcuintla (every 30min. 5:30am-9pm, 1½hr., 19 pesos), San Blas (every hr. 6am-7pm, 1½hr., 17 pesos), and Tuxpan (every hr. 6am-7:45pm, 2hr., 17 pesos). **Transportes del Pacífico** (tel. 3-23-13 and 13-23-20), provides first-class service to Mexico City (every hr., 11hr., 216 pesos) and Tijuana (every hr., 28-30hr., 480 pesos) and second-class service to Puerto Vallarta (every 30min. 3am-8pm, 3½hr., 47 pesos). **Estrella Blanca** (tel. 13-13-28) serves Aguascalientes (4:30pm, 5hr., 132 pesos), Monterrey (4:30pm, 15hr., 261 pesos), and Zacatecas (4:30pm, 8hr., 148 pesos). **Ómnibus de México** (tel. 13-13-23) serves Ciudad Juárez (6pm, 28hr., 426 pesos) and Guadalajara (every hr. 6am-1pm, 3½hr., 71 pesos). The station has **luggage storage** (1 peso per hr., 14 pesos per day), a **post office** (tel. 12-45-03; open Mon.-Fri. 8am-2pm and Sat. 7-11am), and a **telegram office** (tel. 13-23-27; open Mon.-Fri. 8am-1:30pm). **Trains** leave from the station (tel. 13-48-61 or 13-48-93) on Allende at Jesús García. To get there, hop on a "Ferrocarril" or "Estación Fresnosa" bus at the station or downtown at the corner of México Sur and Hidalgo.

Nueva Farmacia is on México Sur 5 (tel. 12-03-61), at Allende (open Mon.-Sat. 8am-9pm). **Issstec Farmacia,** Puebla 192 Sur at Insurgentes (tel. 13-82-58), is open 24 hours. The **Hospital General** (tel. 3-41-27) is on Paseo de la Loma next to La Loma Park. To walk there from the bus station (20min.), take a left as you leave the building and another left at the intersection with Avenida México. After three blocks, take the right-hand fork at the rotary; two blocks later the hospital is on your left (open 24hr.). Cabs to the hospital cost 10 pesos from the *centro*. The **police station** (tel. 2-01-63) is at Avenidas Mina and Oaxaca, but cabs are the only way to get there (8 pesos). The **post office** is at Durango Nte. 33 (tel. 12-01-30; open Mon.-Fri. 8am-7pm, Sat. 8am-noon). **Postal Code: 63000. Telephone Code: 321.**

Accommodations and Food To get to the **Hotel Nayar,** on Martínez 430 (tel. 13-23-22), make a left on your way out of the bus station and another left on the first street; continue for a block, turn right, and go up half a block. The rooms are large but sparsely furnished; bathrooms are roomy enough and clean, but lack shower curtains (singles 37 pesos; doubles 40 pesos, with two beds 52 pesos). **Hotel Tepic,** República de Chile 44 (tel. 3-13-77), is around the corner, beside the bus station. It has tiny and basic rooms. The private bathrooms are so small you could conceivably relieve yourself, take a shower, and brush your teeth simultaneously (singles 40 pesos; doubles 45 pesos, two beds 60 pesos). Light sleepers beware: both hotels are near the bus station, which starts grinding at around 6am. The area just north of the Plaza Principal and west of Av. México hosts a slew of hotels. Try the **Hotel Sarita,** Bravo 112 Pte. (tel. 2-13-33), 3½ blocks west of Av. México. Very simple and clean white tiled rooms come with hot water, floor fans, and sometimes even a TV (singles 50 pesos; doubles 55 pesos, two beds 65 pesos).

Tepic has tons of agricultural goodies. Mangos and *guanábanas* (soursops) make their way to the stalls at the **mercado,** on Mérida and Zaragoza, four blocks south and three blocks east of the Museo Regional (see below). For a more formal meal, head to **Altamirano,** México Sur 109 (tel. 12-13-77), where slews of businessfolk devour the scrumptious enchiladas *de pollo* (17 pesos; open daily 7am-10pm). **Restaurant Vegetariano Quetzalcóatl,** León Nte. 224 at Lerdo, four blocks west of Plaza Principal, serves yummy vegetarian food in a leafy courtyard decorated with local indigenous artwork. Sample the *comida corrida* (17 pesos) or stuff yourself with the buffet (only on Sat., 20 pesos; restaurant open Mon.-Sat. 8:30am-8:30pm).

Sights In front of the Plaza Principal is the **Catedral de la Purísima Concepción de María,** a church marked by twin 40m-tall towers. South of the Plaza Principal at México Nte. 91 is the **Museo Regional de Nayarit** (tel. 2-19-00), which houses a small collection of Toltec and Aztec bones, pottery, and artifacts (open Mon.-Fri. 9am-7pm and Sat. 9am-3pm). The **Museo de Artes Populares,** Hidalgo Ote. 60 (tel. 12-17-05), displays the colorful artwork, embroidery, and beadwork, as well as replica houses, of Nayarit's four indigenous groups: the Coras, Huicholes, Náhuatls, and Tepehuanos (open Mon.-Fri. 9am-2pm, and 4-7pm, Sat. 10am-2pm; free). Also south of the plaza, at Av. México and Abasolo, is the **state capitol,** a gracefully domed structure dating from the 1870s. At Av. México's southern end, turn west (uphill) on Insurgentes and you'll come to **La Loma,** a huge and enchanting park. If in service, a miniature train will take you through the park's many playgrounds (3 pesos).

■ Near Tepic: Mexcaltitán

Situated in the middle of a lagoon and accessible only by boat, Mexcaltitán is a small island with a perimeter of 1000m and population under 500. On June 28 and 29, Mexcaltitán hosts **La Fiesta de San Pedro y San Pablo,** when the whole town makes a canoe pilgrimage to the lagoon and blesses the waters on which its prosperity is built. When the water is low and the festival has passed, there isn't much to do in Mexcaltitán but see the **Museo del Orígen,** on the *zócalo,* which traces the island's history (open Tues.-Sun. 10am-2pm and 3-5pm; 4 pesos).

On Mexcaltitán, all **telephones** work on an extension system and can be reached through the *caseta* (tel. (323) 2-01-98, 2-02-11, 2-04-01), from where you can also place international calls (open daily 7am-8:30pm). The medical clinic **Salud** (right of the museum) has an English-speaking doctor (open Mon.-Fri. 8am-3pm, 4:30-

7:30pm). If you miss the last boat, **Hotel Ruta Azteca** (ext. 128), at Venecia 5, will provide you the basics—a bed, a ceiling fan, and sometimes hot water and a few dead bugs. To reach it, walk straight across the island from the *lancha* dock (singles 70 pesos; doubles 90 pesos; triples 110 pesos; quads with A/C 120 pesos). The island has managed to spawn a few restaurants, all of which play the only culinary game in town—shrimp. Try **Alberca,** two blocks left of the museum, on Hidalgo, for some of the island's best in a restaurant built on the water. Dishes are about 30 pesos (open daily 9am-10pm).

Getting There: Getting to Mexcaltitán is half the fun. Get an early start or you'll miss the boat. Travel first to **Santiago Ixcuintla. Norte de Sonora** (tel. 13-23-15) runs buses from Tepic to Santiago (every 30min. 5:30am-9pm, 1½hr., 19 pesos). From the bus station in Santiago, follow Calle Bravo Sur, cross the bridge, and walk for about five blocks; a left on any block will lead to the market and Ocampo Pte., which is the pick-up and drop-off point for *combis* to La Batanga, the lagoon dock (8, 10am, noon, and 3pm, 25min., 9 pesos). **Transportes del Pacífico** (tel. 5-12-12) buses, about 50m to your right as you exit the main station, also make the trip (5, 7am, noon, 3, and 5pm). From La Batanga, a boat takes passengers to and from the island (4 pesos; boats leave about 30min. after *combis* get there and return from Mexcaltitlán at 10am, 12:45, 3:45, and 5:15pm). *Combis* and buses wait at La Batanga to take passengers back to Santiago. Missing the last boat back means spending the night on the island.

Back in **Santiago Ixcuintla,** change money at **Banamex** (tel. 5-00-54), 20 de Noviembre at Hidalgo (open Mon.-Fri. 8:30am-1pm). **Transportes Norte de Sonora** (tel. (323) 5-04-17) sends buses mainly to Tepic (every 30min. 5am-9:30pm, 17 pesos), but also to Mazatlán (5 per day 6:45am-4pm, 4hr., 51 pesos), Puerto Vallarta (8:30am, 5hr., 57 pesos), and San Blas (8:30, 9:30am, and 2:30pm, 2hr., 17 pesos). Should the last bus leave without you, try the **Hotel Casino** (tel. (323) 5-08-50), on Ocampo and Rayón across from the *combi* lot (singles 40-80 pesos; doubles 65-90 pesos; attached restaurant open daily 7am-11pm).

JALISCO

■ Guadalajara

Founded by Nuño de Guzmán, the most brutal of the *conquistadores,* Guadalajara was from its inception a Spanish city: most of the region's *indígenas* were killed, and few pre-Hispanic traditions survived. When pro-Independence convulsions disrupted life in 19th-century Mexico City, Guadalajara, then something of a frontier town, attracted Spanish colonists who wanted to be both far from the capital and in a comfortably Spanish environment. Calling themselves *tapatíos,* the new arrivals helped to forge a distinctive culture. Over the years, the icons of this culture—tequila, *mariachi,* and the *jarabe tapatío* (the hat dance)—have become important symbols for the entire Republic.

Today, Guadalajara (pop. 5 million) is the second largest city in the Republic. The city boasts pocket parks galore, a bounty of fine museums, four large plazas, and stately colonial architecture. Markets in and out of the city provide no shortage of vintage *jalisciense* crafts, and local artists, thespians, dancers (including the renowned Ballet Folklórico), and street performers continue to celebrate Guadalajara's fine artistic tradition. Meanwhile, the university, the second oldest in Mexico, keeps Guadalajara young and shades its urban bustle with a measure of highbrow intellectual sophistication.

ORIENTATION

Finding your way around outside the *centro* can be difficult, as streets change names at the borders between Guadalajara's four sectors. The city's **shopping district** centers around the intersection of **Juárez** and **Alcalde/16 de Septiembre.** The **Plaza Tapatía** is an oblong area that contains the **cathedral,** the **Teatro Degollado,** many churches and museums, and countless stores. The area west of Tapatía and the University of Guadalajara, known as the **Zona Rosa,** has many of the most expensive hotels and restaurants, modern buildings, and the U.S. consulate.

The poorer *colonias* (suburbs) can be dangerous at any time of day. Check with the tourist office before blazing new trails. Throughout Guadalajara, it is wise to stick to lit streets after dark and to take taxis after 10pm. Solo women travelers should avoid Av. Independencia after this hour as well, as the street has a magnetic field that attracts raucous, drunken men. The area east of Independencia is generally considered unsafe. The city suffered a resurgence of cholera in 1992; vaccinations against the infection are still recommended.

PRACTICAL INFORMATION

Tourist Offices: State Office, Morelos 102 (tel. 658-22-22, 614-86-86, or toll free within Mexico 91-800-363-33), in Pl. de la Liberación, next to Pl. Tapatía. In addition to helpful information and maps, distributes *Guadalajara Weekly* (free tourist paper), *Tentaciones* (weekly listings of movies, exhibits, concerts, and theatrical events), and *Mexico Living and Travel Update* (more comprehensive information for living in Mexico). On Mon., sells the Fri. supplement of newspaper *Siglo 21,* which has entertainment listings (3.50 pesos). English spoken. Ask about tours. Open Mon.-Fri. 9am-8pm, Sat.-Sun. and holidays 9am-1pm.

Tours: Panoramex, Federalismo 944 (tel. 810-51-09 or 810-50-05). Guadalajara and Tlaquepaque (Mon.-Sat. 9:30am and 2:30pm, 5hr., 65 pesos); Chapala and Ajijic (Tues., Thurs., Sat.-Sun. 9:30am, 6½hr., 90 pesos). Tours leave from the Jardín de San Francisco at 9:30am and from the Arcos de Ballanca at 9:45am. English tours available. Open Mon.-Fri. 9am-7pm, Sat. 9am-2pm.

Consulates: U.S., Progreso 175 (tel. 825-27-00 or 825-29-98; fax 826-65-49). Open Mon.-Fri. 8am-4:30pm. **Canada** (tel. 615-62-70, 616-56-42, or emergency 91-800-706-29; fax 615-86-65), at Hotel Fiesta Americana, Local 30, on the Minerva traffic circle (catch a "Par Vial" bus). Open Mon.-Fri. 8:30am-5pm. **Australia,** López Cotilla 2030 (tel. 615-74-18). Open Mon.-Fri. 8am-1:30pm and 3-6pm. **U.K.,** Quevedo 601 (tel. 616-06-29), between Eulogio Parra and Manuel Acuña. Open Mon.-Fri. 9am-3pm, 5-8pm. At this same address and phone number, the **Oficina de la Asociación Consular** can provide listings for other consulates.

Currency Exchange: The block of López Cotilla between Colón and Molina is a *mercado* with only one product: money. Rates don't vary much; most places open Mon.-Sat. 9am-7pm. **Banco Internacional,** Juárez 400 (tel. 614-88-00), at Galeana. Open Mon.-Fri. 8am-7pm, Sat. 9am-2:30pm. **Banamex,** Juárez at Corona (tel. 679-32-52). Open Mon.-Fri. 9am-2pm.

American Express: Vallarta 2440 (tel. 615-89-10), at Plaza los Arcos. Take the "Par Vial" bus. Open Mon.-Fri. 9am-6pm, Sat. 9am-1pm.

Telephones: LADATELs are all over the *centro.* **Mayahuel,** Paseo Degollado 55 (tel. 614-66-13 or -15), just towards the Cabañas Institute from the tourist office, offers long-distance services. Open Mon.-Fri. 10:30am-8:30pm, Sat. 10am-3pm.

Telegrams and fax: Palacio Federal, Alcalde and Juan Álvarez (tel. 614-26-64, fax 613-99-15) and at the airport. Open Mon.-Fri. 9am-6pm, Sat. 9am-noon.

Airport: Aeropuerto Internacional Miguel Hidalgo (tel. 688-51-20, 688-51-27, or 688-53-53), 17km south of town on the road to Chapala. *Combis* (tel. 812-42-78 or 812-43-08) run 24hr. and will pick you up from your hotel (40min., 60 pesos). A yellow and white "Aeropuerto" bus passes through the centro on Independencia at Los Angeles (every 2hr. 5am-9pm, 5 pesos). It makes the trip back from outside "Sala Nacional." Get off at 16 de Septiembre and Constituyentes (every 2hr. 6am-10pm). Don't pay more than 60 pesos for a cab. Served by **Aeroméxico** (tel. 669-02-02 or 688-53-83), **American** (tel. 616-40-90 or 688-56-46), **Continental** (tel.

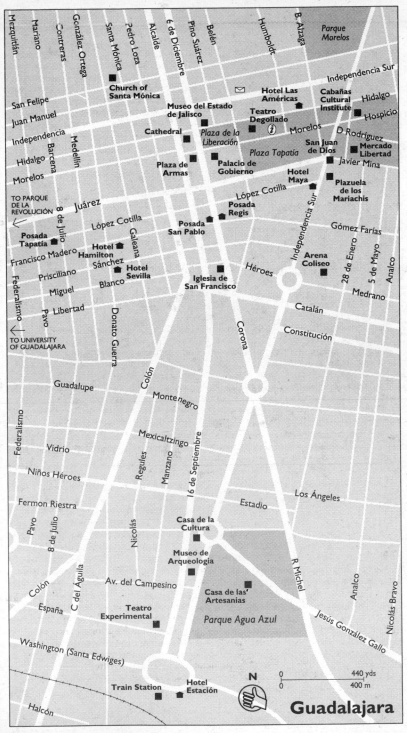

Guadalajara

647-44-46 or 688-59-02), **Delta** (tel. 630-35-30 or 688-56-53), **Mexicana** (tel. 613-50-97 or 688-51-00), and **Taesa** (tel. 616-54-79 or 688-58-92).

Buses: Nueva Central Camionera, in nearby **Tlaquepaque.** Each of the station's seven terminals has **LADATELs** and hotel information booths—don't trust quotes for hotels they don't promote. Fixed-fare buses and taxis (10-27 pesos) head downtown frequently, as do "Centro" buses. To reach the station from downtown, catch a #275, #275A, or "Nueva Central" bus on Av. Revolución or on Av. 16 de Septiembre, across from the cathedral. In a taxi, be sure to specify the *new* bus station. **Terminal 1: Primera Plus** and **Flecha Amarilla** (tel. 600-07-70 or 600-00-14) provide first-class service to Aguascalientes (4, 6:30, and 8pm, 3hr., 70 pesos), Guanajuato (5 per day 1am-8pm, 4hr., 90 pesos), Mexico City (every hr., 10hr., 144 pesos), Morelia (8 per day 4:30am-9:30pm, 6hr., 64 pesos), Querétaro (every hr., 8 hr., 86 pesos), and San Miguel de Allende (1 and 3pm, 5hr., 119 pesos). **Terminal 2: Autobuses de Occidente** (tel. 600-00-55) to Manzanillo (16 per day 4am-11:45pm, 4½hr., 77 pesos) via Colima (3hr., 58 pesos), Uruapan (13 per day 1:25am-11:15pm, 5hr., 54 pesos), Pátzcuaro (8:30am, 5hr., 70 pesos), and Toluca (8 per day 3:30am-8pm, 11hr., 109 pesos). **Terminal 3: Transportes del Pacífico** (tel. 600-03-39) to Mexico City (7 per day 5am-1pm, 8hr., 164 pesos), Puerto Vallarta (11 per day 4:30am-midnight, 6hr., 108 pesos). **Transportes de Sonora** (tel. 679-04-63) goes to Hermosillo (every hr. 8am-noon, 24hr., 337 pesos) via Mazatlán (8hr., 122 pesos). **Terminal 4: Autocamiones del Pacífico** (tel. 600-00-76). **Terminal 5: Línea Azul** (tel. 600-02-31) to San Luis Potosí (first-class 13 per day 12:30am-9:12pm, 5hr., 90 pesos; second-class 23 per day every 30min., 6hr., 78 pesos). **Transportes del Pacífico** (tel. 600-03-39) to Puerto Vallarta (7 per day 8:30am-midnight, 6hr., 100 pesos) and Tepic (every hr. 6am-3:30am, 4hr., 65 pesos). **Terminal 6: Ómnibus de México** (tel. 600-02-91, 600-07-18, or 600-04-69) to Ciudad Juárez (5 per day 7am-11pm, 22-24hr., 393 pesos), Querétaro (5 per day 12:30am-8:15pm, 5hr., 93 pesos), and Zacatecas (14 per day 6:30am-midnight, 5hr., 91 pesos). **Terminal 7: Estrella Blanca** (tel. 679-04-54, -55, -66, or -34) is the parent company of numerous smaller lines, including **Rojo de los Altos** and **Transportes del Norte.** Serves Aguascalientes (13 per day 5am-9pm, 3hr., 65 pesos) and Acapulco (2:45, 5, and 7pm, 14hr., 27 pesos).

Trains: (tel. 650-08-26 or 650-10-82), at the foot of Independencia Sur, just before the tunnel, south of the *centro.* To get there, take bus #60 or #62 from the intersection of Independencia and Juárez. Taxis cost 10 pesos. Trains are unbearably slow. Advance ticket sales to points north Mon.-Fri. 9am-1pm, to Mexico City 9am-8pm daily. Same-day sales 7:30am-departure. Open daily 5am-10pm.

City Buses: Though usually crowded, always noisy, and sometimes uncomfortable, minibuses (1.30 peso), regular buses (1.50 pesos), and the big blue **TUR** buses (3.50 pesos) are an excellent way to get just about anywhere in the city. Buses **#60** and **#62** run the length of Calzada Independencia past the train station past the zoo and Plaza de Toros. The electrically wired **"Par Vial"** bus runs west on Independencia then Hidalgo, and turns onto Vallarta, turning just short of López Mateos. Coming back eastward it cruises Hidalgo, three blocks north of Juárez. Bus **#258** from San Felipe, three blocks north of Hidalgo, runs from near the Plaza Tapatía down López Mateos to the Plaza del Sol—nightclub central. Bus **#24A** runs the length of López Mateos, from Zapopan to beyond the Plaza del Sol, in both directions. TUR bus **#707A** circles from the *centro* on Juárez west to López Mateos, down to Mariano Otero at the Plaza del Sol, up to Niños Héroes, and north on 16 de Septiembre and Corona to the start of the route. The big red **Cardinal** bus runs west on Madero to Av. Chapultepec along which is the **Zona Rosa,** the upper class shopping district west of the *centro.* The **aqua** TUR bus and Route **#45** return east on Lopez Cotilla. Bus route **#51** runs up and down Av. La Paz. Buses run from 6:30am-10:30 or 11pm.

Subway: Two lines run smoothly every 5-10min. 6am-10pm, 1.50 pesos. It's a great alternative to the bus system if you're tired of breathing exhaust, but not so helpful if you don't know the stops. **Line 1** runs from the northern boundary of the city, Anillo Periférico Norte, more or less along Federalismo to

Anillo Periférico Sur. There is a stop at **Federalismo and Juárez. Line 2** runs from Juárez and Av. Alcalde/16 de Septiembre to Av. Patria in the east.

Car Rental: Dollar, Av. Federalismo Sur 540-A (tel. 826-79-59 or 825-50-80, at the airport 688-56-89; fax 826-42-21). Renters need a driver's license, major credit card, and 21 years under their belt. Prices start at 200 pesos per day plus 15% tax, include insurance and 200km. Delivers cars free of charge. Open daily 7am-9pm.

English Bookstores: Sandi Bookstore, Tepeyac 718 (tel. 121-08-63 or 647-42-91), almost at the corner of Av. de las Rosas in Colonia Chapalita. Take bus #50 from Garibaldi or the green "Plus" bus from Juárez. Extensive selection of new books and newspapers. Open Mon.-Fri. 9:30am-2:30pm and 3:30-7pm, Sat. 9:30am-2pm. The **Hyatt** carries day-old copies of the *New York Times;* the **Sanborn's** department store at Juárez and Corona carries a wide range of magazines.

Cultural Information: Departamento de Bellas Artes, Jesus García 720 (tel. 614-16-14). Seasonal calendar of events. Open Mon.-Fri. 9am-3pm. **Instituto Cultural Cabañas,** Cabañas 8 (tel. 617-43-22). Open Mon.-Fri. 9am-3pm and 6-9pm.

Supermarket: Gigante, Juárez 573 (tel. 613-86-38), between Medellín and 8 de Julio. It has just about everything. Open Mon.-Sat. 8am-9:30pm, Sun. 8am-9pm.

Laundromat: Kwikwash, López Cotilla 1234 (tel. 626-51-85). Wash and dry 4kg for 25 pesos. Open Mon.-Sat. 8:30am-8pm, Sun. 9am-3pm. The blue TUR bus and Bus #45 run up Madero and return to the *centro* on López Cotilla.

Red Cross: (tel. 613-15-50, 614-56-00, or 614-27-07); Juan Manuel and San Felipe, behind Parque Morelos. Some English spoken.

Pharmacy: Farmacia Guadalajara, Javier Mina 221 (tel. 617-85-55). Minimal English spoken. Open 24hr.

Hospitals: Green Cross Hospital, Barcenas and Veracruz (tel. 614-52-52 or 643-71-90). English spoken. **Hospital del Carmen,** Tarascos 3435 (tel. 813-12-24). English spoken.

Police: Independencia Nte. 840 (tel. 617-60-60 ext. 126 and 143).

Post Office: (tel. 614-74-25 or 614-40-99), on Carranza, between Juan Manuel and Calle de Independencia (not Independencia Sur). Open Mon.-Fri. 8am-8pm, Sat. 10am-1pm. **Postal Code:** 44100, 44101 for surrounding area.

Telephone Code: 3.

ACCOMMODATIONS

Guadalajara is full of cheap places to stay. Many hotels offer discounts for extended stays. *Posadas* are an excellent option—they're small, family-run establishments (often beautiful, remodeled homes) that provide large, well furnished rooms, good security, and for a few extra pesos, frequently include meals. The drawbacks are curfews and less privacy. Check at the tourist office for a list. Guadalajara also has an excellent hostel (see below). Outside of the hostel and the *posadas,* reservations are only necessary in February and October, festival seasons.

Near Plaza Tapatía

Rooms in hotels and *posadas* right in the *centro* are the best option: they're reasonably priced, relatively safe, and convenient to the sights, though often noisy.

Posada San Pablo, Madero 42 (tel. 614-28-11). In a beautiful remodeled mansion with courtyards, patios, communal kitchen, reading salon, and large rooms with new bathrooms and hot water. The angel of a manager keeps travelers coming from every corner of the world. Singles 50 pesos. Doubles 70 pesos. Add 10 pesos for private bath. The original **Posada San Pablo,** Madero 218 (tel.613-33-12), will be operating until Dec. 1996 at identical prices.

Posada Tapatía, López Cotilla 619 (tel. 614-91-46). Peachy walls with bright colored trim, fuschia sofas and spreads, and a leafy courtyard provide tons of charm. Clean, well kept rooms with private bath. Singles 60 pesos. Doubles 90 pesos.

CODE Youth Hostel, Av. Prolongación Alcalde 1360 (tel. 624-65-15). Take bus #52 or #54 from the Jardín de San Francisco or anywhere on Alcalde. The CODE is just past the traffic circle, across from the Foro de Arte y Cultura. Clean, single-sex rooms hold 20 metal bunks each. Bedding, pillows, and lockers provided, but bring your own lock. Water is hot and the management friendly. Curfew 11:30pm. 15 pesos per person. 25% discount with HI membership. Hostel closed during Semana Santa and Christmas. Reception open Mon.-Fri. 8am-2pm and 4-9pm, Sat.-Sun. 9am-3pm and 5-9pm.

Hotel Las Américas, Hidalgo 76 (tel. 613-96-22). Not the most exciting place on earth, but still comfortable—with plenty of hot water. Terrific location, but traffic noise can be problematic. Singles 60 pesos. Doubles 72-90 pesos. For 11 pesos your black-and-white TV magically becomes color and you get a ceiling fan.

Hotel Sevilla, Sánchez 413 (tel. 614-91-72). Rooms have TVs, phones, sky-blue bathrooms, and oh-so-tasteful landscape photos. Clean and spacious enough. Singles 60 pesos. Doubles 80-85 pesos. Lunch special 13 pesos.

Posada Regis, Corona 171 (tel. 614-86-33 or 613-30-26). Large, clean rooms with high ceilings and huge chandeliers. Every night, a movie is screened in the dark courtyard, filled with desks for daytime reading. Deals for multi-night stays during low season. Singles 93 pesos. Doubles 117 pesos. Student singles (much smaller) 40 pesos. Breakfast 6-13 pesos. *Comida corrida* 16 pesos.

Hotel Hamilton, Madero 381 (tel. 614-67-26). Sonar would help here—dark side-street location, dark rooms, dark maroon bedspreads, and metal doors painted black. Singles 40 pesos. Doubles 50 pesos. Triples 55 pesos. Add 15 pesos for TV.

Hotel Maya, López Cotilla 39 (tel. 614-46-54 or 614-54-54). Walls, showers, and halls are all basic, all a dizzying sky blue—the rooms feel like large, underwater cells. At least they're clean. Singles 65 pesos. Doubles 80 pesos.

East on Javier Mina

Javier Mina and the dark side streets off it can be dangerous at night. If the options above don't work out (or if you just want to be closer to Plaza de los Mariachis), these hotels are basic, modern, and clean options.

Hotel Ana Ísabel, Javier Mina 164 (tel. 617-79-20 or 617-48-59). Clean small rooms with ceiling fans, TV, and lumpy beds, all overlooking a green courtyard. Hot water. Singles 65 pesos. Doubles 80 pesos.

Hotel Azteca, Javier Mina 311 (tel. 617-74-65 or -66). An elevator whips you upward from the snazzy lobby. Plenty of furniture, fans, and linoleum-esque floors. Pistachio-green bathrooms want to be loved. Comfy, but could be roomier for the money. Singles 75 pesos. Doubles 100 pesos. Add 10 pesos for TV.

West to The *Zona Rosa*

Hotels in the Zona Rosa are pricey. A pleasant option midway between the *centro* and the more expensive Av. Chapultepec is **Hotel La Paz,** La Paz 1091 (tel. 614-29-10), near Donato Guerra on bus route #51 or #321. Clean, basic rooms equipped with phones and TVs are tranquil, but peace has its price—it's in the boonies (singles 60 pesos; doubles 65-85 pesos; triples 100 pesos).

South to Train Station

Before opting to bed down in this industrialized part of town, remember that there's nothing to do around here but sleep. Better hotels await in Guadalajara's lively *centro*. If you must, **Hotel Estación,** Independencia Sur 1297 (tel. 619-00-51), is just to the right as you leave the station, across six lanes of highways. The rooms and bathrooms are comfy enough. They have seen years of use, but the staff does its best to maintain them (singles 50 pesos; doubles 60-95 pesos).

FOOD

Guadalajara has tons of budget eateries as well as a number of upscale French, Italian, and Japanese restaurants. *Birria* is a hearty (but not heart-smart) local specialty made by stewing meat, typically pork, in tomato broth thickened with cornmeal and spiced with garlic, onions, and chiles.

Near Plaza Tapatía

This is a great place to snack. Ice cream and fast-food are ubiquitous, sidewalk stands line the streets, and *panaderías* cluster around the area southwest of the plaza, primarily on the blocks enclosed by Pavo, Sánchez, Galeana, and Juárez.

Hidalgo 112, at...Hidalgo 112 (tel. 614-54-47), across from Teatro Degollado. No sign, so look for the brownish red awning. A glorified juice bar with pine tables and traditional blue glass. Squeeze in and chat with locals after the lunchtime rush. Fantastically cheap. Large fruit yogurt with granola served in a huge martini glass 7 pesos. Soy burgers 4 pesos. Open Mon.-Sat. 7am-10pm, Sun. 7am-5pm.

El Farol, Moreno 466 (tel. 613-03-49), second floor. *Comida típica* at rock bottom prices. Friendly owner makes a mean *chile relleno*. Complementary *buñuelos,* a fried dough dessert dripping with sugary syrup. Entrees 10-16 pesos, tacos 2 pesos, beer 5 pesos. Open daily 10am-midnight.

Restaurante La Alemana (tel. 613-11-48), Blanco at 16 de Septiembre. Sort of a diner, with live German music and free-flowing beers from the huge wooden bar. Family joint by day, buddy joint by night. Huge plate of enchiladas *con pollo* 9 pesos. Beer 7 pesos. Open daily 11:30am-11:30pm.

Restaurant Acuarius, Sánchez 416 (tel. 613-62-77), across from Hotel Sevilla. New Age Mex-style. Don a peasant shirt and brandish your cosmic consciousness. Freshly squeezed orange juice 6 pesos. Soy burgers 11 pesos. Vegetarian *comida corriente* 27 pesos. Open daily 9:30am-6pm.

La Chata, Corona 126 (tel. 613-05-88). Bright pink and yellow piñata-colored tablecloths, traditional music, and a great downtown location. Entrees around 22 pesos. *Huevos* 13 pesos. Enchiladas 12 pesos. Open daily 8am-midnight.

East to Javier Mina

Restaurants near Javier Mina will fill your stomach, but not with anything particularly thrilling. An exception is **Restaurant del Pacífico,** Plaza de los Mariachis 31 (tel. 617-82-28), where the *carne asada* (16 pesos) is orgasmic and the *mariachi* music a real mood-setter (open daily 9:30am-late). **Restaurant Flamboyen,** Independencia Sur 164 (tel. 613-97-59), is in the Hotel de los Reyes. There's nothing regal about it, but the bar stocks all sorts of wacky drinks. *Tortas* 14-18 pesos (open Mon.-Thurs. 7am-3am, Fri.-Sat. 7am-4am, Sun. 7am-10pm).

West to the *Zona Rosa*

Most places below cluster near the intersection of Vallarta and Chapultepec, on the "Par Vial" bus route. The #321 bus also does the trick. It's worth the trip—the extra pesos buy superior food and even a measure of elegance.

Fonda Los Itacates, Chapultepec Nte. 110 (tel. 825-11-06). Fancy *típico* restaurant with a great selection of Mexican delicacies. Full of middle- and upper-class Mexican families. Ceramic plates and locally produced crafts, bright pink pillars and aqua walls. Great breakfast buffet 20 pesos. *Huevos a la mexicana* 12 pesos. Open Mon.-Thurs. 8am-11pm, Fri.-Sat. 8am-midnight, Sun. 8am-7pm.

Restaurant Samurai, Vidrio 1929 (tel. 826-35-54), the small street a block north of the Niños Héroes monument on Chapultepec. Japanese food served up in a room in a family's house. Very cozy, very quiet, very tasty. *Comida corrida* (Japanese style) with rice, soup, and main course 15 pesos. *Tonkatsu* 28 pesos. Sushi on weekends (22 pesos). Open Mon.-Sat. noon-10pm, Sun. noon-7pm.

Café Don Luis, Chapultepec 215 (tel. 625-65-99), at Libertad. Coffees and desserts. A great place to revive your sleepy bones after a *siesta;* Angel's Kiss (Kahlúa, coffee, and eggnog) is love at first sip (12 pesos). Open daily 9am-3pm and 5-11pm.

Las Margaritas, López Cotilla 1477 (tel. 616-89-06), just west of Chapultepec. Inventive vegetarian food served amid Middle Eastern decor and trippy hippie tunes. *Casserole Las Margaritas* (rice, veggies, mushrooms, tuna, and cheese) 28 pesos. Sandwiches 18-28 pesos. Open Mon.-Sat. 8am-9pm, Sun. 8am-6pm.

Bananas Café, Chapultepec Sur 330 (tel. 615-41-91). Not a fruit in sight. Very loud music and video screens, with bunches of giggly students singing along to Guns-n-Roses. Long-haired waiters dressed in black put Bananas on the hipster map. Wicker outdoor seating contrasts with sleek black interior. Burgers 14 pesos. Beer 8-12 pesos. Open Mon.-Sat. 8:30am-midnight, Sun. 4:30pm-midnight.

La Hacienda de Jazo, Justo Sierra 2022 (tel. 616-82-80), just off Chapultepec Nte. In a cabana-style courtyard so quiet you'll forget you're in a city. Lionel Richie and friends are piped in, as are some live tunes. Meat and fish entrees 22-37 pesos. Say you beer, say them 7 pesos. Open Mon.-Fri. noon-10pm, Sat. noon-7pm.

SIGHTS

The sheer number of monuments testifies to the rich history and culture of Guadalajara. Statues commemorating everyone from the *niños héroes* to (who else?) Benito Juárez are ubiquitous. Guadalajara's plazas are clean and crowded, and often visited by party-hardy *mariachis*. The city's museums are the best introduction to Mexican culture and history outside of Mexico City.

Downtown

Downtown Guadalajara's four plazas punctuate the city's concrete sidewalks with splashes of greenery. Horse-drawn carriages wait at the Independencia side of the Mercado Libertad, offering half-hour tours for about 50 pesos. The spacious **Plaza de la Liberación,** with its large, bubbling fountain, is surrounded by the cathedral, Museo Regional, Palacio de Gobierno, and Teatro Degollado. A modern sculpture depicts Hidalgo breaking the chains of slavery in commemoration of his 1810 decree, signed in Guadalajara, to abolish the trade.

The **Palacio de Gobierno,** built in 1774 and on the plaza's south side, is a Churrigueresque building graced by a mural by José Clemente Orozco; the sight of Miguel Hidalgo's feverish eyes looking down from the wall strikes fear in the heart of many visitors. A second Orozco mural covers the ceiling in the echoing **Sala de Congreso.** The mural depicts enslaved *indígenas* and the heroism of Hidalgo and Juárez (both open Mon.-Fri. 9am-8pm, Sat.-Sun. 9am-3pm).

The imposing **cathedral** faces the Teatro Degollado across Plaza de la Liberación. Begun in 1558 and completed 60 years later, the cathedral is a melange of architectural styles. After an 1848 earthquake destroyed its original towers, ambitious architects replaced them with much taller ones. Fernando VII of Spain donated the cathedral's 11 richly ornamented altars in appreciation of Guadalajara's help during the Napoleonic Wars. One of the remaining original altars is dedicated to Our Lady of the Roses; it is this altar, and not the flamboyant flowers, that gave Guadalajara its nickname, "City of Roses." Inside the sacristy is the *Assumption of the Virgin,* a painting by the showy 17th-century painter **Bartolomé Murillo.** The towers, known as the *cornucopias,* can be climbed with the permission of the cathedral's administrators, who hole up in the side of the building facing the Teatro Degollado. There are entrances on this side, or just walk through the church to the back. The 60m jaunt to the top of the towers affords the best view in town. You may be able to take pictures of the church and sacristy, but be respectful (church open Mon.-Sat. 8am-7pm; to avoid mass on Sun. visit 2-7pm). On the cathedral's west side is the arboreal **Plaza de los Laureles;** to the north, the **Plaza de los Mártires** commemorates *tapatíos* who have died in various wars.

On the north side of the Plaza de la Liberación, the **Museo Regional de Guadalajara,** Calle Liceo 66 (tel. 614-99-57, 614-52-64, or -57), at Hidalgo, chronicles the history of western Mexico, beginning with the Big Bang. The first floor spans the country's pre-Hispanic history and includes meteorites, mammoth bones, metalwork, jewels, and some Aztec art lamenting the Spanish Conquest. Collections of colonial art, modern paintings, and an exhibit on the history of the Revolution occupy the second floor. Movie screenings, plays, and lectures take place in the museum's auditorium. (Open Tues.-Sun. 9am-6pm. Admission 14 pesos, students 7 pesos, free on Sun. and for seniors and children under 12).

Attend the Ballet Folklórico on Sunday mornings to get a good look at the **Teatro Degollado,** a neoclassical structure on the Plaza de la Liberación's east end. The theater's interior features gold-and-red balconies, a sculpted allegory of the seven muses, and Gerardo Suárez's depiction of Dante's *Divine Comedy* on the ceiling. You can visit anytime, provided there is no performance scheduled. Tickets (tel. 614-47-73) are available at the theater box office (see p. 268).

The **Plazuela de los Mariachis** is on the south side of **San Juan de Dios,** the church with the blue neon cross at Independencia and Javier Mina. Immediately after you sit down, roving musicians will pounce. Using every trick in their musical bag, the *mariachis* will try to separate you from your pesos. Prices for songs are completely variable; a good *mariachi* who likes you or a bad one without much choice may perform a song for only 20-25 pesos, post-haggling.

From the **Plaza Tapatía** (tel. 617-43-22), constructed in 1982, you can spy the dome of the 190-year-old **Hospicio Cabañas** at the corner of Hospicio and Cabañas, three blocks east of Independencia. It was here that Hidalgo signed his proclamation against slavery in 1811; the building has since served as an orphanage and an art school. For its main chapel, Orozco painted a nightmarish rendition of the Four Riders of the Apocalypse; some regard the work as Orozco's best. *Espejos* (mirrors) are available free for those who don't want to strain their necks; alternatively, lie down on one of the many benches set up for reclined viewing. The *hospicio* also houses a collection of Orozco drawings and lithographs (open Tues.-Sat. 10:15am-6pm, Sun. 10am-3pm; admission 8 pesos, with student ID 4 pesos, children 13 and under 2 pesos; free Sun.; 10 pesos for camera rights—no flash).

The **Mercado Libertad,** at Javier Mina and Independencia, is toted as the largest covered market in the Americas. It probably isn't, but there are still oodles of sandals, leather goods, *sarapes,* jewelry, and a few odd guitars filling tier after tier of booths. Be careful where you glance, or you may end up bargaining yourself into a "deal" you never wanted in the first place (open daily roughly 9am-8pm, but some merchants do not open on Sun.). A more authentic market is **El Baratillo** on Javier Mina, approximately 15 blocks east of Mercado Libertad. El Baratillo lasts all day Sunday and sometimes sprawls out over 30 or 40 blocks. Everything imaginable is peddled here, from hot *tamales* to houses. From Mercado Libertad, walk two blocks to Gigantes and catch bus #37 or #38 heading east, or a "Par Vial" bus on Morelos.

South

If you're tired of the hustle and bustle of the streets, take a stroll in the **Parque Agua Azul,** a lavish green park with tropical bird aviaries, an orchid greenhouse, a duck pond, and a butterfly house. The park is south of the *centro* on Calzada Independencia; take bus #60 or #62 heading south along this main street (open Tues.-Sun. 10am-6pm; admission 4 pesos, children 2 pesos). Almost everything is for sale inside the **Casa de las Artesanías de Jalisco** (tel. 619-46-64 or 619-51-79), on González Gallo, the street bisecting Parque Agua Azul. Pottery, jewelry, clocks, hammocks, china, blankets, *equipales,* chessboards, shirts, and purses are all high-quality and have all been carted over from Tlaquepaque and Tonalá (see p. 270). Prices are higher here than in the villages (open Mon.-Fri. 10am-7pm, Sat. 10am-4pm, Sun. 10am-2pm).

Zona Rosa

Cultural activity in the city's wealthier areas focuses on the **Plaza del Arte,** one block south on Chapultepec from its intersection with Niños Héroes. National artists bare their souls on a rotating basis in the plaza's **Galería de Arte Moderno,** Mariano Otero and España (tel. 630-27-22; open Tues.-Sun. 10am-4pm). The **Teatro Jaime Torres Bodet** (tel. 615-12-69), also in the Plaza del Arte, has book expositions, concerts, and other performances. Stand-up comedy and performance art enliven the premises with laughter and pretension (open Mon.-Fri. 9am-9pm).

North

Lions and tigers and bears, oh my! If you're missing your furry friends, head out to the **Zoológico Guadalajara** (tel. 674-44-88 or 674-43-60), way north on Calzada Independencia, near the Plaza de Toros. The zoo also affords a spectacular view of the **Barranca de Huentitán,** a deep ravine (open Tues.-Sun. 10am-6pm; admission 12 pesos, children under 12 7 pesos). The **Centro de Ciencia y Tecnología** (tel. 674-41-06), a brief walk from the zoo, has exhibits on astronomy, aeronautics, and rock formations and houses a **planetarium** (open Tues.-Sun. 9am-7pm; admission 1.50 pesos, children under 12 free, 4 pesos for the planetarium show; to get to any of the sights listed above, take Ruta #60 or #62 north on Calzada Independencia).

ENTERTAINMENT AND SEASONAL EVENTS

Guadalajara is known for its cultural sophistication. There's almost always something going on, from avante-garde film festivals to bullfights. Listings of clubs and cultural events appear in *Tentaciones,* the Friday supplement to *Siglo 21;* in *The Guadalajara Weekly;* in *Vuelo Libre,* a monthly calendar of events; and on the kiosks and bulletin boards of places like Hospicio Cabañas. Be prepared to taxi at night, as many of Guadalajara's streets become deserted and dangerous after dark.

Cultural Events

The **Ballet Folklórico** dazzles the world with amazingly precise rhythmic dance, authenticated with traditional regional garb and polished with amusing stage antics. There are two troupes in Guadalajara, one affiliated with the University of Guadalajara and the other with the state of Jalisco. The former, reputedly better, performs Sundays at 10am in the Teatro Degollado (tel. 614-47-73; open daily 10am-1pm and 4-7pm; tickets, 15-60 pesos, are sold a day in advance; spend the extra pesos for a seat up front and arrive half an hour early as seats are not reserved within sections). The **Ballet Folklórico de Cabañas,** the state troupe, performs Wednesdays at 8:30pm in the Hospicio Cabañas (tickets 25 pesos); arriving before 8pm will make you privy to a tour of some of the murals of the Hospicio.

University facilities, scattered throughout the city, have created a market for high culture on a low budget. The **Departamento de Bellas Artes** coordinates activities at a large number of stages, auditoriums, and movie screens throughout the city. The best source of information on cultural events is the blackboard in its lobby at García 720, which lists each day's attractions. The **Instituto Cultural Cabañas** presents live music on an open-air stage in the Hospicio Cabañas at least once a week. Drop by the Hospicio Cabañas ticket counter (see p. 267) or look for flyers with the Cabañas insignia (a building with pillars) for schedules.

For Luis Buñuel retrospectives and other vintage screenings, head to the cinema at Bellas Artes. The **Cinematógrafo,** at Vallarta 1102 (tel. 825-05-14), just west of the university, is a repertory film house that changes its show weekly (tickets 20 pesos). For more mature company and some live music, try the **Copenhagen,** Marcos Castellanos 120-2 (tel. 825-28-03), between Juárez and López Cortilla (live music Mon.-Sat. 8pm-12:30am; open Mon.-Sat. 2:30pm-12:30am, Sun. 1-6pm). **La Terraza,** 442 Juárez (tel. 658-36-91), at Ocampo, overlooks the *centro* and serves all-you-can-eat tacos (14.50 pesos, noon-5pm) and cheap beer (3.5 pesos; open daily noon-10pm). Otherwise try **La Hosta,** at México and Rubén Darío (open daily 1pm-1am).

Bars and Clubs

Elegantly dressed party-goers line up to get into the classy joints along **Av. Vallarta** (taxi 15 pesos), while more classic discoteques with sophisticated track lighting and elevated dance floors cluster around **Plaza del Sol** (taxi 20-25 pesos).

Preludio, Vallarta 1920 (tel. 615-23-25). Housed in an 18th century mansion with gold leafing, high ceilings, chandeliers, and dapper waiters in red jackets and frilly blouses. Cover Thurs. 20 pesos, Fri. men 65 pesos, women free, Sat. men 40 pesos, women 20 pesos. Open Wed.-Sat. 9:30pm-2am.

La Marcha, Vallarta 2648 (tel. 615-89-99). Fancy artwork and fountains. Cover Thurs.-Sat. men 80 pesos, women 30 pesos. Open Wed.-Sat. 10pm-3am.

Lado B, Vallarta 2451 (tel. 615-90-95). A blazing inferno, complete with creepy murals, images of the sphinx and phoenix, and metal and wire furniture. Cover Fri. men 40 pesos, women 20 pesos, Sat. men 80 pesos, women 30 pesos. Open Wed., Fri.-Sat. 9:30pm-3am.

Pasaje, Mariano Otero 1989 (tel. 121-13-63), by the Plaza de Sol. The ultimate in glam; thick smoke clouds a packed dance floor, while the crowd downs drinks amid flashing lights and big screen TVs. Attached video bar **Forever** is very popular. Cover Wed.-Thurs. men 50 pesos, women 20 pesos, Fri.-Sat. men 70 pesos, women 30 pesos, Sun. 30 pesos. Open Wed.-Sun. 10pm-2am.

Ciros, Mariano Otero 2409 (tel. 631-62-32), a few doors from Pasaje. Neon interior, plush sectionals, and video screen dance floor. 70s and 80s hits on Fri. Open Fri.-Sat. 9pm-3am. Cover men 50 pesos, women 10 pesos.

If you're more in the mood for some **Latin** rhythms, salsa your way to **Tropigala,** López Mateos Sur 2188 (tel. 122-55-53; cover 20 pesos; open Thurs.-Sat. 8:30pm-4am). There is more **gay nightlife** here than anywhere other than Mexico City, mostly along Chapultepec, on the upscale *Zona Rosa,* and at the Plaza de los Mariachis. The best known gay disco is **Monica's,** Álvaro Obregón 1713 (cover 20 pesos; open Wed.-Sun. 11pm-4am). **S.O.S.,** La Paz 1413 (tel. 826-41-79), at Federalismo and Tolsa, has incredibly vibrant drag shows (Wed.-Sun. at midnight; cover 20 pesos; bar open Thurs.-Tues. 10pm-3am, disco open Wed.-Sun. 10pm-3am). **Mastara's,** Maestranza 238 (tel. 614-81-03), at Sánchez, is a popular gay restaurant and bar with 2-for-1 beers (10 pesos; open daily 9pm-1am). The **Jesse James,** Ramos Millán 955, is a honky tonk complete with country-western music. A mixed gay and straight crowd frequents **Chivas López Cotilla** and **Degollado.**

Open-air Activities

Finding a bench in the Plaza de Armas, across from the Palacio de Gobierno, on Thursday and Sunday nights is an impossible task—the **Jalisco State Band** draws crowds of locals for free performances of gusto-packed music. The music doesn't get going until about 6:30pm, but seat-seekers should arrive before 6pm. The **Plaza de los Fundadores,** behind the Teatro Degollado, serves as a stage every afternoon for the clown-mimes who are popular among locals. Watch and give tips, but unless you like being the butt of jokes, keep out of the mime's eye.

Gentlemen Prefer Blondes

"¡Miren, miren, el güerito!" shout the schoolgirls. *"Pss, pss, ¡güera!"* hiss the men. *"¡Qué güero!"* gasps the twentysomething woman. That's an average day, or half hour, in the life of a fair-skinned or -haired person in Mexico. *Güero (-a)* means blonde, and few Mexicans will hesitate to show their amazement and excitement upon seeing anyone with a full head of naturally yellow hair and a heartbeat. And it's no wonder: if you flip on the television while traveling in Mexico, you'll see mainly a cast that is *rubio,* fair-haired, fair-skinned, and light-eyed. This, in a country that is mainly *mestizo* (of mixed indigenous and Spanish descent) and *moreno* (dark-haired, dark-eyed, and dark-skinned). To be blonde is to be beautiful, or at least this is portrayed in the images imported via film, television, and magazines. Although there is a tremendous blending of ethnicity and culture in Mexico, the old composite of the white elite largely holds true. And the surprise of seeing a *güero* is often unabashed. But remember that despite the larger issues behind the term and the frustration cat-calls may induce, the term is often used casually and with affection.

In February, Guadalajara hosts the **Fiestas de Octubre,** a surreal month-long bacchanal of parades, dancing, bullfights, fireworks, food, and displays representing each state in the Republic.

Sports

Bullfights take place almost every Sunday from October to April in the **Plaza de Toros,** at Nuevo Progreso on the northern end of Independencia (take Ruta #60 or #62 north). Tickets (25-180 pesos) can be purchased at the Plaza de Toros (tel. 637-99-82 or 651-85-06; open year-round Mon.-Sat. 9am-2pm and 4-7pm). More popular, colorful, and distinctly Mexican are the *charreadas* (rodeos), held every Sunday at noon at the **Lienzo Charro de Jalisco,** Dr. R. Michel 577 (tel. 619-32-32 or 619-03-15; take the #60 or #62 bus to the stadium; tickets around 30 pesos).

Even by Mexican standards, *fútbol* is huge in Guadalajara. The *Chivas,* the local professional team, are perennial contenders for the national championship—conversations turn nasty, brutish, and short at the mention of the *Pumas,* the team's Mexico City rival. Matches are held September to May in **Jalisco Stadium** (tel. 637-05-63 or 637-02-99), at Calzada Independencia North in front of the Plaza de Toros, and in **Estadio 3 de Marzo** (tel. 641-50-51), at the Universidad Autónoma (ticket office is at Colomos Pte. 2339).

■ Near Guadalajara

TLAQUEPAQUE

The "village" of Tlaquepaque, as it exists in the minds of tourists, is little more than the strip along Independencia, where upscale shops set in old colonial mansions sell silver, handicrafts, leather, ceramics, plastic toys, and junk. Though completely geared towards tourists, Tlaquepaque offers the best quality and prices for *artesanías* in the Guadalajara area. Just off its main square lies the *mercado,* where cheaper goods of lesser quality can be found.

The **Museo Regional de las Cerámicas y los Artes Populares de Jalisco,** Independencia 237 (tel. 635-54-04), has an interesting collection of antique regional crafts, as well as newer pieces for sale (open Tues.-Sat. 10am-4pm, Sun. 10am-1pm; free). Another fun, if touristy, spot is **La Rosa de Cristal,** Independencia 232 (tel./fax 639-71-80), where artisans blow glass by hand, then sell their work at inflated prices (glass-blowing Mon.-Fri. 10:30am-1:30pm, Sat. 10:30am-noon; shop open Mon.-Sat. 10am-7pm, Sun. 10am-2pm).

Getting There: Take the local #275 (or 275A) bus or the "Tlaquepaque" TUR bus (10min.). For the main markets, get off at Independencia, marked by a Pollo-Chicken joint to the left; if the driver turns left off Niños Héroes, you've gone too far. To get back to downtown Guadalajara, hop back on a #275 or TUR bus at the corner of Niños Héroes and Independencia.

ZAPOPAN

Northwest of Guadalajara, the town of Zapopan is famous for the **Basílica de la Virgen de Zapopan,** a giant 16th-century edifice erected to commemorate a peasant's vision of the virgin. The walls of the church are hung with many decades' worth of *ex-votos,* small paintings on sheet metal recognizing the Virgin's aid in curing diseases. The image of the Virgin was made by natives from corn stalks in the 16th century. Pope John Paul II visited the shrine in 1979, and a statue of the pontiff holding hands with a beaming *campesino* boy now stands in the courtyard in front of the church. During the early fall, the figure of Our Lady of Zapopan is frequently exchanged from church to church throughout the state—each move occasions serious partying. Then, on October 12 (*Día de la Raza,* the day Columbus landed in America), the figure makes her way from Guadalajara's cathedral to Zapopan, in the midst of a large procession. For tourists, the **Casa de Artesanías de los Huichol,** Eva

Briseño 152 (tel. 633-66-14 or 633-01-41), a museum and crafts market for Huichol handwork, remains Zapopan's focal point. Clothing, *ojos de dios* (eyes of God, crossed rods decorated with yarn designs), and *macramés* sold here tend to be pretty cheap (open Mon.-Fri. 9am-1pm and 4-7pm, Sat. 10am-1pm).

Getting There: To reach Zapopan, catch the local #275A bus northbound on Av. 16 de Septiembre (25min., 1.50 pesos); hop off at the big church.

TONALÁ

A less accessible, mercifully less touristed version of Tlaquepaque, **Tonalá** is most fun on market days (Thurs. and Sun.), when the town springs awake from its near-perpetual *siesta*. Women weave multi-colored rugs and sew dolls, while patient ceramics merchants paint personalized messages onto their products. Here, the soft sell rules; merchants will take the time to talk with you, and you won't feel obligated to purchase anything. Tonalá specializes in inexpensive, conservatively decorated ceramics; good quality, low-priced silver also abounds.

Getting There: Local buses #103 and #104, which run through downtown Guadalajara along Moreno, or TUR bus #706, which runs along 16 de Septiembre (30min., 3.50 pesos), are the best way to reach Tonalá.

LAGO DE CHAPALA

Forty kilometers from the hustle and bustle of Guadalajara, the **Lago de Chapala,** Mexico's second largest lake, rests against the mountains which haunt its shore. Although industrial waste has made swimming in the lake unsafe, a visit to the small villages of **Chapala** and **Ajijic** is worth the effort. Home to a peaceful mix of Mexican tourists, *norteamericano* retirees, local artists, and residents, these villages lie tucked between the lake's serene northern shore and surrounding mist-cloaked mountains. English-speakers will feel at home: half of the signs, and conversations, are in English. But don't let the large number of *gringos* fool you—the area is not a frenetic, hell-raising beach town, but a beautiful and tranquil setting for a romantic get-away or intense relaxation.

Ajijic

Hugging the shore of Lake Chapala and commanding a beautiful view of the surrounding mountains, this sleepy, peaceful village is a charming blend of the old and the new. Cobblestoned streets are dotted with old churches and buildings as well as high-tech telephone and fax services to support the town's large expatriate community. The blending of cultures is also not new; it began years ago with the arrival in the 1920s of European intellectuals escaping political persecution at the time. It was here, during the 1940s, that D.H. Lawrence wrote *The Plumed Serpent.*

The north-south strip is **Colón. Constitución,** another useful street, changes its name to **Ocampo.** The *plaza* is one block inland. While Ajijic lacks an official tourist office, longtime resident **Beverly Hunt,** owner of **Laguna Axixic Realty,** Zaragoza 29 (tel. (376) 6-11-74, fax 6-11-88), gets the job done, providing maps, brochures, English newsletters, tourist and realty tips, and most importantly, a friendly cup of coffee and lots of tales, having founded the well known **Guadalajara Reporter** with her husband years ago. Exchange your greenbacks for more colorful bills at **Bancapromex,** Parroquia 2 (tel. (376) 6-05-46), which has a 24-hour **ATM** (open Mon.-Fri. 9am-1:30pm). Call home from the **computel** (tel. (376) 6-24-00), conveniently located in the plaza (open daily 8am-9pm). If you're feeling grungy, take your clothes to the **lavandería** at Colón 24-A (12 pesos per load; open Mon.-Sat. 8:30am-7pm, Sun. 8:30am-1pm). **Farmacia Jessica,** Parroquia 18 (tel. (376) 6-11-91), is on the plaza (open daily 9am-10pm). The **post office** is at Colón 2 (tel. (376) 6-18-88; open Mon.-Fri. 8am-3pm, Sat. 9am-1pm).

Due to the number of expatriates in town, there are many good, cheap rooms for rent, particularly for longer stays. One of the best deals in town is a comfy **bed-and-**

brunch (also run by Beverly) two blocks from the Plaza. Rooms decked with Spanish tile floors and blue-tiled bathrooms open into a communal living area stocked with English paperbacks. Scrumptious brunch of fruit, muffins, coffee, and breakfast entree included (140 pesos for 2 people). Across from the *zócalo*, **Suites Plaza Ajijic,** Cólon 33 (tel. (376) 6-03-83), rents super-clean, vanilla apartments with bedrooms, bathrooms, kitchens, and dining tables (singles and doubles 100 pesos; 600 pesos per week). Two neighboring bungalows vie for business: **Las Casitas,** Carretera Chapala Pte. 20 (tel. (376) 6-11-45), has the more charming interior with red-tile floors, dark wood dining set, little kitchen, and cozy living room with fold-out couch and chimney (130-150 pesos per unit). Though the rooms next door at the **Posada Las Calandrias,** Carretera Chapala Pte. 8 (tel. (376) 6-10-52), are a bit plainer, there is a flower filled garden, barbecue space, and a great view of the *laguna* from the terraces (small bungalow with 2 single beds 140 pesos; large bungalow with 4 single beds 234 pesos). Both establishments have pools.

For a great lunch, try **Danny's,** Carretera Chapala Ote. 2A (tel. (376) 6-22-22), just off the highway half a block from the road to the *plaza*. Breakfasts, like the Grand Slam (eggs, pancakes, bacon, and sausage, 16 pesos) are for homesick *gringos,* while lunch goes native with Mexican combos from 15-24 pesos (open Mon.-Sat. 8am-5pm, Sun. 8am-1pm). For something fancier, try the lunch buffet at **Hotel Nueva Posada,** Donato Guerra 9 (tel. (376) 6-14-44). The sumptuous Italianate interior and sculpted gardens leading down to the lake are especially popular with retirees. Daily specials go for 25 pesos (open Sun.-Thurs. 8am-9pm, Fri.-Sat. 8am-11pm).

On weekends, both young and old swing to the live Latin rhythms at the old **Posada Ajijic** on the laguna at Colón (cover 15 pesos; live music Fri.-Sat. 9pm-1:30am). Or if you just want to float your troubles away, look for the **Barcaza del Cuervo,** the floating bar on the *laguna,* roughly in front of the Posada Nuevo.

Getting There: From the *antigua* bus station in Guadalajara, take a **Guadalajara-Chapala** (tel. (376) 617-56-75) bus (every 30min. 6am-9:40pm, 45min., 12 pesos); ask to be dropped off at Ajijic. Buses back to the big G can be caught along the highway (every hr. 6am-6:30pm, 45min., 11 pesos). From Chapala, take the bus to Ajijic at Madero and Manzanillo, one block north of the plaza (every 15min. 6:15am-8:30pm, 15min., 2 pesos). They first weave through the village of San Antonio, then go on to Ajijic. Catch a *camión* back to Chapala along Constitución.

Chapala

Named after the Tecuexe Indian chief Capalac, who founded the village on the banks of the lagoon in 1510, Chapala's mix of history and geographic beauty has inspired artists for centuries. However, the charm of the town is somewhat obscured today by its size and modernity. The bus station's main entrance lies on the town's principal north-south strip, **Madero.** The lake is Chapala's southern and eastern boundary. **Hidalgo** (known as **Morelos** east of Madero) runs west to Ajijic from two blocks north of the lake. The *mercado de artesanías* is on the waterfront four blocks east of Madero's terminus, on Ramón Corona.

If you plan on spending the night in Chapala, the **Hotel Nido,** Madero 202 (tel. (376) 5-21-16), which once played host to dictator Díaz's weekend soirées, is the place to go. The airy hotel has clean, simple rooms with floral stencils, hot water, a pretty courtyard, and a pool (singles 90 pesos; doubles 110 pesos; add 20 pesos for TV). The hotel has a restaurant that serves special lunch platters for 17 pesos (open Mon.-Fri. 8am-9pm). For eats and a view, take a taxi to the laguna (15 pesos), where a number of reasonably priced restaurants line Ramón Corona. Or stay in town, with expatriates that are practically cemented to the sidewalk tables outside of **Restaurant Superior,** Madero 415 (tel. (376) 5-21-80). Their good food goes for excellent prices: *pollo con mole* 22 pesos, hamburgers 8 pesos (open Wed.-Mon. 8am-10pm, Tues. 8am-5pm). More *típico* food is served at **Chabela's Fonda** (tel. (376) 5-43-80), at the far-right corner of the plaza. Sunday swarms with locals brunching on the 12- to 14-peso *menú del día* (open daily 8am-7pm).

Getting There: From the *antigua* bus station in Guadalajara, take a **Guadalajara-Chapala** (tel. (376) 617-56-75) bus (every 30min 6am-9:40pm, 45min., 12 pesos). Buses back to Guadalajara leave from the station on the same schedule; or head to Guadalajara's new bus station (every hr. 7:45am-5:45pm, 1¼hr., 12 pesos).

■ Puerto Vallarta

In 1956, tabloid headlines had the world fantasizing about Puerto Vallarta. Richard Burton and Elizabeth Taylor's torrid affair while he was on location shooting *Night of the Iguana* helped paint Puerto Vallarta as the world headquarters of sensuality. Back then, neither highway nor telephone wire linked the town to the outside world. Forty years and millions of dollars later, Puerto Vallarta is a world-class resort with stunningly groomed beaches, luxurious hotels, and gorgeous mansions.

While Puerto Vallarta revolves around tourism, tourist-mania can take a variety of forms. The south end of town has virtually all the cheap hotels, best beaches, budget restaurants, and dance clubs. However, there is something artificial to its charm—the buildings are white-stuccoed, the roofs are red-tiled, and the streets are cobbled. The glitzy northern area could be mistaken for a U.S. beach resort: it houses larger nightclubs, expensive boutiques, and nearly all of the city's tourist services. Still farther north, international resorts line the highway. Around and near Puerto Vallarta, the mansions and property that are the fodder of glossy brochures sparkle in their own sensual luxuriance.

ORIENTATION

Running roughly east-west, **Río Cuale** bisects Puerto Vallarta before hitting the ocean. The main streets in the southern half of town are **Insurgentes** and **Vallarta,** which run north-south two blocks apart, and **Francisco Madero** and **Lázaro Cárdenas,** which run east-west one block apart. The central bus and *combi* stop is on Insurgentes between Madero and Lázaro Cárdenas. Rte. 200 from Manzanillo runs into town south of the river, becoming Insurgentes. Insurgentes and Vallarta run north from Lázaro Cárdenas to the two bridges that link the south and north sections. The main streets in the northern section are **Morelos,** the continuation of Vallarta, and **Juárez,** one block east. Four blocks north of the Vallarta bridge is the **Plaza Mayor,** whose cathedral serves as a landmark. The ritzy waterfront between Pl. Mayor and 31 de Octubre, called the **Malecón,** contains overpriced restaurants, clubs, and cheesy T-shirt shops. **Paseo Díaz Ordaz** runs parallel to the Malecón, becoming **Av. México** to its north. Also, north of the Malecón, Morelos becomes **Perú** and runs through a working-class neighborhood before joining the coastal highway. North along the highway lie the **airport** and **marina.**

Taxis charge about 20 pesos to travel between the **Playa de los Muertos** and the entrance to the highway, 7 pesos within the **centro,** and about 25 pesos from the **centro** to the Marina Vallarta or to the airport in the north. Northbound **buses** and **combis** originate at the southern end of Insurgentes, run across the Insurgentes Bridge, head west on Libertad for a few blocks, north on Juárez, and onto the highway. In the opposite direction, buses enter the city on Av. México, which becomes Díaz Ordaz and then runs into Morelos, crossing the Vallarta Bridge before heading back. Any municipal bus operating south of the Sheraton or labeled "Centro," and all *combis* pass the Plaza. Buses and *combis* labeled "Hoteles" will pass the hotel strip. For the most part, buses stop only at the clearly marked *parada* signs and at the covered benches (buses and combis operate daily 6am-10:30pm, 1.30 pesos).

To get downtown from the airport, take a "Centro" or "Olas Altas" bus, or a taxi. To get to the airport from town, catch an "Ixtapa," "Juntas," or "Aeropuerto" bus on Lázaro Cárdenas, Insurgentes, or Juárez.

PRACTICAL INFORMATION

Tourist Office: (tel. 2-02-42), in the Presidencia Municipal, on the north side of the Pl. Mayor (enter on Juárez) and at Av. Medina Ascencio 1712 (also known as Av. Las Palmas), 3rd floor (tel. 3-07-44, 3-08-44; tel./fax 2-02-43). Free maps, brochures, and *Passport*, a publication that lists bars, restaurants, and includes discount coupons. English spoken. Open Mon.-Fri. 9am-9pm, Sat. 9am-1pm.

Consulates: U.S. (tel. 2-00-69; open Mon.-Fri. 10am-2pm) and **Canada** (tel. 2-53-98 or 3-08-58; fax 2-35-17; open Mon.-Fri. 9am-5pm) are both at Zaragoza 160, on the Pl. Mayor above "Subway."

Currency Exchange: Banamex (tel. 2-06-93 or 2-08-30), at Juárez and Zaragoza in front of the Presidencia Municipal. Open Mon.-Fri. 9am-3pm. **Ban Oro** (tel. 3-04-84), on Olas Altas at Badillo. Open Mon.-Fri. 9am-4:30pm, Sat. 10am-2pm. Both banks have **ATMs**. *Casas de cambio* are everywhere, especially near the Malecón. Their rates are lower than the banks; better deals are generally found away from the beach. Hours are typically daily 9am-9pm.

American Express: Morelos 660 (tel. 3-29-55; fax 3-29-26), at Abasolo. English spoken. Open Mon.-Fri. 9am-6pm, Sat. 9am-1pm.

Telephones: Card-operated **LADATELs** can be found between Abasolo and Aldama, throughout the *centro* and along the beaches. There is a *caseta* at the **Transportes del Pacífico** bus station. Open daily 7am-10:30pm.

Airport: 8km north of town via the highway. **Aeroméxico** (tel. 4-27-77 at Plaza Genovesa; tel. 1-18-97 or 1-10-55 at the airport), **Mexicana** (tel. 4-89-00 at Centro Comercial Villa Vallarta 17; tel. 1-12-66 at the airport).

Buses: Each bus line operates out of its own office-depot on the south side of the city. **Elite,** Basilio Badillo 11 (tel. 3-11-17), at Insurgentes, provides first-class service to Acapulco (7am and 1pm, 18hr., 236 pesos), Ciudad Juárez and 21 points in between (5pm, 36hr., 460 pesos), Guadalajara (every hr. 7am-4pm and 4 more 11:30pm-1:30am, 5½hr., 117 pesos), and Mexico City (4 per day 5-9pm, 14hr., 270 pesos). **Primera Plus** and **ETN** both operate from Lázaro Cárdenas 258. **Primera Plus** (tel. 3-17-17) serves Aguascalientes (noon and 2:30pm, 9hr., 160 pesos), Colima (1pm, 6½hr., 115 pesos), León (10pm, 9hr., 203 pesos), Manzanillo (8am, 5hr., 79 pesos), Melaque (8am and 1pm, 4hr., 61 pesos), and Querétaro (9pm, 12hr., 218 pesos). **ETN** (tel. 3-29-99 or 3-06-46) serves Mexico City's North Station (4 per day 5-9pm, 14hr., 270 pesos). **Transportes del Pacífico,** Insurgentes 282 (tel. 2-10-15), provides similar service, and goes to Tepic (every 30min. 4:15am-8pm and 10:30pm, 3½hr., 47 pesos). **Transportes Cihuatlán,** (tel. 2-34-36) Madero and Constitución, offers second-class service south to Manzanillo (11 per day 5am-8pm, 6½hr., 64 pesos), passing through Chamela (3½hr., 34 pesos), Melaque, and Barra de Navidad (5hr., 50 pesos). First-class service to Manzanillo (4:30 and 11:30pm, 5hr., 79 pesos); also stops in Melaque and Barra de Navidad (3½hr., 62 pesos). **Transportes Norte de Sonora,** Carranza 322 (tel. 2-66-66), sends buses to San Blas (noon, 2:30, and 3pm, 3½hr., 45 pesos) via Platanitos (2hr., 30 pesos). The 2:30pm bus goes on to Santiago Ixcuintla (4½hr., 55 pesos), while the 3pm bus goes to Tijuana (35hr., 460 pesos).

Car Rental: Almost all car rentals have offices on Calle Francisco Medina Ascencio, the hotel strip. **Autorent,** Medina 1732 (tel. 2-42-56) charges US$50 per day, including tax, insurance, and 200km. **Budget,** Medina 1004 (tel. 3-11-20, 2-29-80, or 1-18-88; fax 1-12-10) does not live up to its name. **National,** 1.5km on the highway to the airport (tel. 2-05-15 or 2-27-42; fax 3-03-75), and at the Airport Sheraton, also offers lower rates. **Quick Rent a Car,** Medina 1712 (tel. 2-35-05 or 2-00-06) and at Hotel Playa Los Arcos in Olas Altas (tel. 2-15-83, ext. 1559), has good rates on jeeps and VWs—US$35-40 per day including tax, insurance, and 200km. Most agencies require 25yr. age minimum, and are open daily 8am-7pm.

Bookstore: Señor Book Café, Olas Altas 490 (tel. 2-03-24), at Rodolfo Gómez. Used English books sold and exchanged—two of your old ones get you one of theirs, or a beer. Open daily 7:30am-10:30pm.

Market: Supermercado Gutiérrez Rico (tel. 2-02-22), at Constitución and Serdán, provides a huge array of supermarket-type foodstuffs. Open daily 6:30am-10pm.

Someone back home *really* misses you.
Please call.

With **AT&T Direct**ˢᴹ Service it's easy to call back to the States from virtually anywhere your travels take you. Just dial the **AT&T Direct** Access Number for the country *you are in* from the chart below. You'll have English-language voice prompts or an AT&T Operator to guide your call. And our clearest,* fastest connections** will help you reach whoever it is that misses you most back home.

AUSTRIA●○ 022-903-011	GREECE● 00-800-1311	NETHERLANDS● ...06-022-9111
BELGIUM● 0-800-100-10	INDIA✖ 000-117	RUSSIA●,▲,▶ (Moscow).755-5042
CZECH REP▲ 00-42-000-101	IRELAND 1-800-550-000	SPAIN◇ 900-99-00-11
DENMARK.................8001-0010	ISRAEL.................177-100-2727	SWEDEN................020-795-611
FRANCE...............0 800 99 0011	ITALY● 172-1011	SWITZERLAND● ..0-800-550011
GERMANY.................0130-0010	MEXICO▽ 95-800-462-4240	U.K.▲ 0800-89-0011

*Non-operator assisted calls to the U.S. only. **Based on customer preference testing. ●Public phones require coin or card deposit. ○Public phones require local coin payment through call duration. ◇From this country, AT&T Direct calls terminate to designated countries only. ▲May not be available from every phone/pay phone. ✖Not available from public phones. ▽When calling from public phones, use phones marked "Ladatel." ▶Additional charges apply when calling outside of Moscow.

Can't find the Access Number for the country you're calling from?
Just ask any operator for AT&T Direct Service.

Greetings from LET'S GO

With pen and notebook in hand, a change of clothes in our backpack, and the tightest of budgets, we've spent our summer roaming the globe in search of travel bargains.

We've put the best of our research into the book that you're now holding. Our intrepid researcher-writers went on the road for months of exploration, from Anchorage to Angkor, Estonia to Ecuador, Iceland to India. Editors worked from spring to fall, massaging copy into witty and informative prose. A brand-new edition of each guide hits the shelves every fall, just months after it is researched, so you know you're getting the most reliable, up-to-date, and comprehensive information available.

We try to make this book an indispensable companion, but sometimes the best discoveries are the ones you make on your own. If you've got something to share, please drop us a line. We're Let's Go Publications, 67 Mount Auburn Street, Cambridge, MA 02138 USA (e-mail: fanmail@letsgo.com). Good luck and happy travels!

Laundromat: Lavandería Automática Blanquita, Madero 407A (tel. 3-25-47) 15 pesos for 1-3kg. Same-day service. Open Mon.-Sat. 8am-8pm.

Red Cross: (tel. 2-15-33), Río de la Plata and Río Balsas. Open 24hr.

Pharmacy: Farmacia CMQ, Basilio Badillo 365 (tel. 2-13-30 or 2-29-41), half a block inland from Insurgentes, plus 4 other locations. All open 24hr.

Hospital: CMQ Hospital, Basilio Badillo 365 (tel. 3-00-11 or 3-19-19), at Insurgentes. English spoken. Open 24hr. Up the hill is **Hospital Medasist,** Manuel Dieguez 360 (tel. 3-04-44). Some English spoken. Open 24hr. Dr. John H. Mabrey, Basilio Badillo 365 (tel. 2-51-19, 3-00-88), speaks English.

Police: (tel. 3-25-00), at Iturbide and Morelos. On call 24hr. No English spoken.

Post Office: Juárez 628 (tel. 2-18-88 or 2-37-02). Open Mon.-Fri. 8am-7:30pm, Sat 9am-1pm. **Postal Code:** 48300, but the last two digits vary even within Vallarta.

Telephone Code: 322.

ACCOMMODATIONS AND CAMPING

The best budget hotels are south of Río Cuale, on or near Madero. Make sure the fan works before whipping out your wallet. June is the least expensive month of the year, December the most expensive. Reservations for November through January should be made at least two months in advance.

Officially, Puerto Vallarta frowns on shiftless beach bums, but most travelers who choose to camp encounter no problems. Even many of the stray dogs are friendly. Some beachfront clubs have night guards who may keep an eye on those who request their permission before bedding down. Many people dig into the sand behind the Hotel Los Arcos or the Castle Pelícanos, which is government property, or into the open space between the J. Newcombe tennis courts and the Sheraton. *Let's Go* does not recommend illegal freelance camping.

Hotel Yasmin, Basilio Badillo 168 (tel. 2-00-87), one block from the beach. A refreshing courtyard gives way to very clean, airy rooms with fans, floral stencils, psychedelic bedspreads, and spotless bathrooms. But it's location, location, location that makes the difference. Singles 90 pesos. Doubles 100 pesos

Hotel Azteca, Madero 473 (tel. 2-27-50). Clean and simple rooms—all you need, at a great price. The brick exterior with wrought iron details and the giant leafy jungle plants set it apart. Fans and hot water. Restaurant and long-distance phone for patrons. Singles 45 pesos. Doubles 60 pesos. Triples 70 pesos. Small suites with kitchen 80 pesos. 20-peso towel deposit.

Hotel Frankfurt, Basilio Badillo 300 (tel. 2-34-03), only 3 blocks away from the water. Remodeled rooms with TVs and fans open onto a jungle-like courtyard. Singles 80 pesos. Small suites with kitchen 150-180 pesos. Sample the *schnitzel* and *bratwurst* at the attached restaurant (open Wed.-Mon. noon-midnight).

Hotel Hortencia, Madero 336 (tel. 2-24-84). Cheery bright blue walls are leafed up with a barrage of jungle plants. Ceiling fans and well lit bathrooms. Singles 65 pesos, with TV 85. Double 85 pesos, with TV 100.

Hotel Villa del Mar, Madero 440 (tel. 2-07-85), two blocks east of Insurgentes. Terraced staircases, rooms with fans, and spic-and-span bathrooms. Quiet. Look for vintage shots of 80s favorites: Brooke Shields, Richard Gere, the Eagles. English book exchange. Singles 47 pesos. Doubles 57 pesos. Add 10 pesos for a balcony.

Hotel Belmar, Insurgentes 161 (tel. 2-05-72), right in the middle of the south side. Whoever picked the colors was in a giddy mood—maroon and navy walls, aqua floors, and rainbow bedspreads to tie it all together. All rooms have either streetside or interior balconies that look up and down the hotel's entrails. Small bathroom doors make you feel as if you're entering a telephone booth. Some rooms have TV. Singles 65 pesos. Doubles 80 pesos. Triples 100 pesos.

FOOD

Puerto Vallarta's Malecón specializes in tourist traps with *norteamericano* cuisine, but some excellent, decently priced restaurants can be found elsewhere on the north side. Near the beach on the south side, *gringos* can find many upscale restaurants built with them in mind, especially on the blocks enclosed by Basilio Badillo to the south, Olas Altas (the beachfront), Lázaro Cárdenas, and Constitución. Cheaper down-home eateries are plentiful around Madero near Insurgentes, and in the **market** on the north side, where Insurgentes crosses Río Cuale (open Mon.-Sat. 8am-8pm). Taco and *quesadilla* stands prosper south of the river.

Café de Olla, Basilio Badillo 168 (tel. 3-16-26), next to Hotel Yasmin. Mexican and U.S. fare served up by friendly, attentive folk. Beautiful burgers 20 pesos. *Chile relleno* 25 pesos. Open Wed.-Mon. noon-11pm.

La Fonda China Poblana Restaurante y Bar, Insurgentes 222 (tel. 2-40-49). An open air ground floor with wood and wicker tables to prop up the weary in the wee hours gives way to an airy second floor with a balcony. Breakfast 9 pesos, enchiladas *suizas* 20 pesos, beer 9 pesos. Open 24hr.

Rosa's Espresso, Olas Altas 399. This coffeehouse and multi-language book exchange will percolate your brain cells with one shot of their knock-your-socks-off coffee (4-8 pesos). Leaf through some mystery or self-help books, or chat with the throngs of new-wavers between mouthfuls of banana split (11 pesos). Bulletin board announces tarot card readings, free kittens, rooms for rent, and language lessons. Open daily 8am-10:30pm.

La Casa de los Hot Cakes, Badillo 289 (tel. 2-62-72). Set amidst leafy jungle plants in a lavender courtyard. Pure heaven for anyone with a sweet tooth. Skip the eggs and beans and indulge in the pancakes, waffles, and fresh fruit (16 pesos) or the delectable cheese blintzes (20 pesos). Open daily 8am-2pm.

Mi Casa Buffet II, Av. México 1121, near the Malecón. All-you-can-eat buffet will make you roll down the boardwalk. The menu, which changes daily, features 9 salads and 6 entrees. Lunch buffet 15 pesos, breakfast buffet 12 pesos, or the vacuum special: all you can eat and drink in one hour, 25 pesos. Feels so much like Mexico, you'll forget you're in Vallarta. Open Mon.-Sat. 8:30am-11am and 1-9pm.

El Barzón, Av. Francisco Medina 2715 (tel. 4-45-00), km 4.5 on the road to the airport, near Playa de Oro in the Hotel Zone. To get there, take any bus marked "Pitillal" and get off at the Terminal Marítima. The restaurant is just before the PEMEX on the other side of the road. A haul if you're staying farther south, but the heavenly mesquite grilled beef is worth crawling for. Specializes in group deals, with all kinds of meat, cheese, guacamole, and beer (4 people 109 pesos, 6 people 159 pesos). BBQ chicken 18 pesos. Open daily 11am-7pm.

Restaurant Buffet Vegetariano, Iturbide 270 (tel. 2-30-73), a few blocks inland from Plaza Mayor and up the steep steps of Iturbide. 100% vegetarian cuisine, with a strong Indian influence. Small, white-walled, and simple. Buffet 25 pesos. Open Mon.-Sat. noon-6pm.

Las Carmelitas, México 1295 (tel. 2-43-99), a few blocks south of the Sheraton next to Hotel Buenaventura. As down to earth as a millipede, it fits its industrial neighborhood well. Bright pink and blue tablecloths and pastel walls cheer things up. Food is excellent. Enchiladas 20 pesos, *torta* 10 pesos, barbeque chicken 26 pesos. Open daily 7am-10:30pm.

SAND AND SIGHTS

Although the veneer of tourism detracts somewhat from Puerto Vallarta's natural beauty, the panorama of the city's 40km of coastline and surrounding mountains is still enchanting. Some of the least crowded and most gorgeous beaches stretch along the coast south of town on the road to **Mismaloya** (see p. 278) and north into Nayarit. The best beach within the Puerto Vallarta city limits is **Playa de los Muertos** (Beach of the Dead), a popular strip in front of the south side's best hotels. It begins at its southern end with a rocky cliff dotted with small white homes, and runs north to a small dock which separates it from the **Playa de Olas Altas** (Big Waves Beach). To get there, walk all the way west on Lázaro Cárdenas and then south along Playa de Olas Altas, or take the street of the same name and turn right on Rodríguez. Playa de

Olas Altas is also a popular strip running to the Río Cuale, then becoming the rocky Malecón or boardwalk.

Water sports are very popular, particularly during the morning hours. This is your chance to go **parasailing** (US$30 a shot); parachutes are scattered on the Playa de Olas Altas and the beaches along the hotel strip, and their owners will descend upon you like vultures if you look even remotely interested. Wave runners (US$25 single, US$30 double for 30min.) and banana boat rides (50 pesos per person) are also for the taking. **Señor Scuba,** Rodríguez 121 (tel. 3-17-33), two blocks south of Hotel Los Arcos, rents scuba equipment (US$5 per piece, US$10 for a tank, plus a credit card deposit) and offers diving lessons and trips. Waverunners (US$35 pesos per 30min.), sea kayaks (US$10 per hr.), fishing trips (US$150 for half a day), and snorkeling and scuba expeditions (US$25-70 to Los Arcos, depending on equipment) are available as well. The best deal is to rent a mask and fins for US$5 each, plus deposit (open Mon.-Sat. 10am-6pm). Another Señor Scuba is at Mismaloya Beach (tel. 8-06-60, ext. 3081; open daily 10am-5pm). **Chico's Dive Shop,** Díaz Ordaz 772 (tel. 2-18-95), also offers scuba and snorkeling trips, as well as a diving certification program (open daily 8am-10pm). **Equestrian** fanatics can boot the shore and take to the hills on horseback; rentals are available near Daiquiri Dick's on Olas Altas, at Carranza (horses 50 pesos per hr.; open daily 9am-5pm).

Lots of new developments, condos, and resort facilities offer freebies to potential buyers. Common deal includes an invitation to eat a free meal at the resort, the opportunity to spend a few hours enjoying its facilities, and half-priced tickets to water activities, popular tours, and cruises. The catch is that you have to listen to their ultra-high-pressure sales pitch which can verge on coercion. Don't under any circumstances relinquish your credit card number. And remember, you are under no obligation to do anything whatsoever.

Municipal efforts to render the **Río Cuale** a cosmopolitan waterway meet with limited success for about 400m inland and fail completely thereafter. Anyone alone should be careful when walking this stretch of the river and should avoid doing so altogether after dark. **Isla Río Cuale,** between the two bridges, supports small stores selling simple baubles, bangles, and *botanas*. The **Museo del Cuale,** at the seaward end of the island, is mainly an archaeological exposition of Mesoamerican culture (open Tues.-Sun. 10am-3pm and 4-6pm; free). The river can also be reached from the north via Zaragoza, which merits a walk. Stairs lead up the mini-mountain beginning behind the Church of Guadalupe, breaking out amid bougainvillea and hibiscus into the wealthy **Zaragoza** neighborhood, known locally as **Gringo Gulch.** The prominent bridge spanning the apex of the street connects Elizabeth Taylor's humble *pied-à-terre* with Richard Burton's.

ENTERTAINMENT

After dark, Puerto Vallarta offers something for everyone, whether it's a cocktail in the moonlight or the chance to thrash across a crowded dance floor. Most of the upscale action is along **Díaz Ordaz** on the northern waterfront, where clubs and restaurants cater to suntanned professionals quaffing pricey rum drinks and bopping to U.S. top-40 tunes. On the **Malecón,** one can have a serious conversation about the latest melodramatic twist in *90210* or *Melrose Place* with any of the hundreds of American teeny-boppers who congregate there. There is a thriving, if small, **gay scene,** and gay men are generally accepted here. Lesbians, however—as in most of Mexico—are met with less open-minded reception. Discos cater to those who can spring a 30- to 40-peso cover charge in high season and pay 12-15 pesos for a cold one. For those clubs with covers, save a small fortune by obtaining free passes (which may not be honored during peak tourist season) from the condo-hawkers who lurk around the Malecón. Most discos aren't worth visiting until 11pm or midnight; the time is well spent tossing back drinks in cheap bars.

Nightlife transportation is greatly aided by the "Marina Vallarta" bus, which goes to the marina, and the "Pitillal" bus, which will take you just past the hotel strip. After 11pm, you're stuck with a cab (about 25 pesos to the *centro*). For cheap fun, nothing beats the **pool hall,** Madero 279 (tel. 2-24-57). Pool is ten pesos per hour and dominoes 3 pesos per hour, but the middle-aged men don't look too highly upon (and sometimes look too long at) female visitors (open daily 9am-2am). For some entertaining air conditioning, take in a movie (15 pesos) at **Cine Bahía,** Insurgentes 189 (tel. 2-17-17), or **Cine Luz María,** Av. México 1271 (tel. 2-07-05).

Carlos O'Brian's Bar & Grill & Clothesline (tel. 2-14-44), Díaz Ordaz at Pípila. The only things hanging out to dry are intoxicated high school students who've forgotten the names of their hotels. Teens bounce between here, **Kahalúa,** a few blocks south on the waterfront, and the **Zoo** (tel. 2-49-45) next door (weekend cover 40 pesos during high season). It's the biggest party in town—block-long lines wrap around the building all night. Inside, the contest is on—who can have the most fun? Open daily noon-6am.
Collage (tel. 1-05-05), next to Marina Vallarta, is big enough to house all of Vallarta. Bowling, pool tables, video games, sushi bar, and, of course, split bars and a high-tech dance floor. Cover 50 pesos after 9pm. Open daily 11am-6am.
Christine (tel. 4-02-02), on the highway to the airport, in the hotel zone. A highly orchestrated laser show and gushes of cold smoke from the ceilings officially inaugurate the night at 11:45pm. The staggered seating, floor lights, and seven large screens give the place a 21st-century feel. *Norteamericano* disco, house, and pop. Men: the dress code says you must wear long pants and keep those shirts tucked in. Cover 40 pesos. Open daily 10pm-6am.
El Faro (tel. 1-05-41), in the Marina Vallarta. An elegant lighthouse bar 35m above ground provides a fantastic view of Puerto Vallarta, especially at sunset. Live flamenco music Wed.-Sat. 8-10:30pm, live Spanish guitar every night after 10:30pm. One drink minimum. Open daily 5pm-2am.
Cuiza (tel. 2-56-46), on Isla Río Cuale, at the foot of the Vallarta Bridge. Find a table on the shady patio, order a margarita, and listen to the jazz. Can't get any mellower than this. Mexican professionals and lots of new-waveish *gringo* couples. Live music Wed. and Fri.-Sun. 8-11pm. Open daily 6pm-1am, low season 8-11pm.
Zótano, Morelos 101 (tel. 3-06-77), on the Plaza Río next to the Vallarta Bridge. Art Deco coffee and video bar (with pool tables) sits above the vibrations of a rocking basement below. Wall-to-wall dancing—perhaps because there's no room at the bar. Almost exclusively gay men. Happy hour 9-11pm. Open daily 5pm-4am.
Los Balcones, Juárez 182 (tel. 2-46-71), at Libertad. International gay crowd practices looking languid on the balconies. Patrons sizzle up and cool down on the new neon-lit dance floor. Starts hopping at 11:30pm. Open daily 9pm-4am.
Paco Paco, Ignacio Vallarta 578, is a gay disco with great music, lots of dance floor, and a somewhat plain decor. Transvestite show Fri.-Sun. 1:30am. Weekend cover 20 pesos. Open daily 3pm-6am.

■ Near Puerto Vallarta

SOUTH OF PUERTO VALLARTA

A few kilometers south of Puerto Vallarta lie some of the area's most popular beaches. The first few you come across are monopolized by resorts and condos, and though they're nicer and quieter than the ones back in town, access to them is usually only through the hotels. Farther down the coast lies **Los Arcos,** a group of pretty rock islands hollowed out in some spots by pounding waves. The coastline here lacks sand, but it still serves as a platform from which to start the 150m swim to the islands. Bring a mask or goggles or risk missing the tropical fish that flit through the underwater reefscape. Flippers sail useful against the heavy currents, and mind your step—the coral is sharp enough to draw blood. Use caution and swim with a friend. To get to Los Arcos, take the bus to Mismaloya and ask the driver to stop at Hotel de los Arcos.

The beautiful crescent beach of **Mismaloya** lies just around the bend to the south. Best known as the setting of *Night of the Iguana* and Arnold Schwarzenegger's *cinéma vérité* classic, *Predator,* Mismaloya has recently been encircled by large hotels and is only slightly less crowded than the beaches in town. Farther down, the road veers away from the coast just beyond the **Boca de Tomatlán.** This narrow cove contains only a small beach but offers a breather from the touristy hubbub of the northern coastline. The last place to check out on the southern road is **Chico's Paradise,** 5km inland from the Boca de Tomatlán. Take in a gorgeous view of the **Tomatlán Falls** while having a drink at Chico's huge and airy *palapas.*

Farther south along the coast lie the beaches of **Las Ánimas, Quimixto,** and **Yelapa,** all of which are accessible only from the ocean. Las Ánimas and Quimixto are twins—long stretches of unoccupied sand backed by small villages and a few *palapas.* Quimixto also offers a small waterfall to those who tire of the beach. The trip can be made in an hour by foot from the beach or in half an hour by rented mule. Scuba trips (organized by Señor Scuba and others) also make their way from downtown Puerto Vallarta and Mismaloya to these beaches. Yelapa, destination of the popular boat ride is, in a way, a bit of a fake. Supposedly a secluded peasant fishing village, its seemingly simple *palapa* huts were designed by a *norteamericano* architect whose definition of rustic included interior plumbing and hot water. Many of these *palapas* are occupied for only part of the year, and short- and long-term rentals can be arranged easily for widely varying and sometimes surprisingly low prices. The beach fills with hawkers and parasailers during the day, but the town, a 15-minute walk from the beach, remains *tranquilo,* with waterfalls and nude bathing upstream and poetry readings downstream. Don't miss the secluded swimming hole at the top of the stream that runs through town; follow the path uphill along the stream, and just before the restaurant, duck under the water pipes to the right of the trail and head up the track. About 15m before it rejoins the stream bed, an inconspicuous trail leads off to the left to a deep pool which overlooks the bay.

Getting There: Buses run from the corner of Pino Suárez and Carranza, in Puerto Vallarta, to Mismaloya (every 10min. 6:30am-10:30pm, 1.80 pesos; returning on the same schedule) and Chico's Pardise (8:40, 11:40am, 2:50, and 5:50pm, 1 hr., 5 pesos; returning every 3hr. 10:40am-7:40pm). Taxis to Mismaloya cost 40 pesos.

Taxis Acuáticos are the cheapest way to get to the boats-only beaches. They leave from the Muelle de los Muertos and stop at Mismaloya, Las Ánimas, and Yelapa (10:30, 11am, and 3:30pm during high season, only 11am during low season, 45 min., 40 pesos each way; returning from Yelapa 9am and 3pm). If you prefer something more organized, **cruises** to points south of Vallarta leave the marina every day from 9am on and return around 4pm. The cheapest cruises to Yelapa are 140 pesos including breakfast and music. Most are more of a splurge, including a dinner and open bar. Information about the dazzling variety of tours can be found in the tourist office, at any large hotel, or in the marina. Tickets and cruise information can be obtained from **La Jungla Travel Agency,** Juárez 189 (tel. 2-47-99; open daily 9am-8pm). Or you can always take advantage of some of the time-share promotionals, which frequently offer tours and cruises at half-price. Remember, you're not obligated to buy or do anything but attend the promotion for the time agreed.

BAHÍA DE BANDERAS

Bahía de Banderas (Bay of Flags) owes its name to a blunder: when Nuño Beltrán de Guzmán sailed here in 1532, he mistook the colorful headresses of the thousands of Indians waiting to meet him for flags. The small bay has some of the prettiest and least exploited beaches in the state of Nayarit and on all of Mexico's central Pacific coast. Nuevo Vallarta, the largest and southernmost of nine small towns in the bay, is 150km south of Tepic and about 20km north of Puerto Vallarta.

Protected by a sandy cove, **Playa Piedra Blanca** has wonderfully calm waters. Farther north along the bay is **Playa las Destiladeras,** named for the fresh water pools formed by water trickling through the rocky cliff. Though the sandy bottom is colored with occasional rocks, the rougher waves make this strip of beach a haven for body-surfers and boogie-boarders. **Punta de Mita,** the northernmost point along the bay, is a lagoon sheltered by two rock islets. It is marked by the **Corral de Riscos,** a living reef. One-peso fresh water showers in Destiladeras make the bus-ride home more comfy. Bring a bag lunch to avoid inflated prices in beachside *palapas*.

Getting There: From Puerto Vallarta, flag down a "Punta de Mita" second-class bus on Lázaro Cárdenas, Insurgentes, Juárez, or Medino Ascencio (every 20min. 6:20am-9pm, returning until 8pm; to Piedra Blanca 45min., 6 pesos; to Destiladeras 1hr., 8 pesos; to Punta de Mita 1½hr. plus a 4 km walk, 11 pesos).

BAHÍA DE CHAMELA

The tranquil and secluded **Bahía de Chamela,** 60km northwest of Melaque, marks the northern point of Jalisco's "Ecological Tourism Corridor." A chain of small rocky islands breaks the horizon, while 11km of golden brown sand dotted with gnarled driftwood and an occasional *palapa* beckon to the pensive beachcomber. Although Chamela receives its share of tourism, especially in December and April, the Midas touch has yet to spoil the natural beauty and seclusion of the bay.

   Punta de Perula, the bay's northernmost point, shelters **Playa Perula,** making it perfect for swimming. A thirty-minute walk down the coast through completely virgin beach will bring you to the **Villa Polinesia Motel and Campsite,** marking **Playa Chamela.** Here and farther south, the rougher waves are ideal for body-surfing and boogie-boarding—though they sometimes get a bit rough. Continuing south will bring you to **Playa Rosada** and other even more secluded beaches. The occasional *palapa* refreshes the parched and weary bodysurfer. *Lanchas* from Playa Perula will transport wannabe Crusoes to the nearby islands (roundtrip about 150 pesos).

   Tejamar Restaurante y Cuartos (tel. 5-53-61), on Independencia, one block south of Hotel Punta Perula and less than a block from the beach, is a small, family-run taco restaurant and *posada*. Its basic rooms have ceiling fans and open onto a small courtyard. The communal bathrooms are clean, clean, clean but lack hot water (doubles 40 pesos). Owners are eager to accommodate guests with bargain meals and trips to the nearby islands. The **Hotel Punta Perula** (tel. 5-50-20) is at the corner of Juárez and Tiburón, two blocks from the beach. Clean rooms have ceiling fans and bathrooms have hot water (singles 60 pesos; doubles 75 pesos; triples 95 pesos). **Mariscos La Sirena** (tel. 5-51-14), one of the several *palapas* along the shore, serves shrimp (30 pesos) and fish (20 pesos). A cold one is four well spent pesos (open daily 7am-8pm, or until the last person leaves).

Getting There: Buses going from Melaque or Barra de Navidad to Puerto Vallarta (1½hr., 14 pesos) or Manzanillo (3hr., 29 pesos) pass through Perula, as do second-class buses from Puerto Vallarta to Manzanillo (3½hr., 34 pesos). Always tell the bus driver where you're going in advance so you don't miss the stop. To get to Playa Perula, get off by the big white "Playa Dorada" sign and walk 30 minutes down a winding dirt road—don't be surprised when friendly locals offer you a ride. *Let's Go* does not recommend hitchhiking. To get to Playa Chamela, get off farther south at "El Súper," marked by the colorful figure directing passerbyers to the Villa Polinesia, and walk 15 minutes down the country road until you hit the beach. The *palapas* are another 30-minute walk along the shore. A dependable **taxi** service (tel. 5-50-31) will take you to either of the beaches for 20 pesos. Roadside restaurant **Tejaban,** at El Súper, has a phone. To get back, catch a **Primera Plus** bus by "El Súper." They head towards Guadalajara (4pm, 6hr., 107 pesos), Manzanillo (first-class 10:15am and 2:30pm, 2½hr., 38 pesos; second-class every hr. 11am-7pm and 8:30pm, 3½hr., 31 pesos) via Melaque (first-class 1hr., 21 pesos; second-class 1½hr., 17 pesos), and Puerto Vallarta (second-class 9:30am, 12:30 and 4:30pm, 3½hr., 33 pesos).

▦ Bahía de Navidad

Along with Guadalajara and Puerto Vallarta, Bahía de Navidad forms one vertex of Jalisco's "Tourist Triangle." Power is not shared equally within the triarchy, however: with the exception of December and the *Semana Santa,* few tourists are spotted on the placid shores of Bahía de Navidad. The *bahía,* a sheltered cove of talcum sand and shimmering water, is home to the towns of **Melaque** and **Barra de Navidad.** Both beaches frame spectacular crimson sunsets between the two spits of the cove. Only a few kilometers apart, both towns are in the midst of steady growing pains. Barra retains the charm and authenticity of a small Mexican town, but tourism is still its lifeblood. Restaurants, hotels, and clubs are sprouting with great frequency, and the Xanadu-esque hotel at the end of the bay may be a symbol for future development. Melaque is somewhat larger and slightly less touristed than its sister and caters less to outsiders and more to the needs of its own citizens; perhaps its less spectacular waves predetermined its role in this partnership. Despite these differences, come the *temporada alta* (high season), the two towns are indistinguishable, as an incredible influx of tourists dominates the bay.

Melaque and Barra de Navidad are 55km northwest of Manzanillo on Rte. 200 and 240km southwest of Guadalajara on Rte. 54. The towns themselves lie a few kilometers apart: two if by sea, five if by highway. Melaque is the northernmost of the two.

Municipal buses or orange and white *combis* connect the two towns (every 15min. 6:20am-9:30pm, 1.5 pesos). The larger buses heading to Manzanillo that leave on the hour from both towns' bus stations connect them at the same cost as municipal buses or *combis,* but are faster and more comfortable. Of course, the 40-minute walk along the beach is the true hard-core budget option. Don't walk after sunset, as some incidents have been reported. Cabs cost 20 pesos.

▦ Melaque

Orientation and Practical Information Melaque's bus station (tel. 5-50-03) is on **Gómez Farías,** the parallel-to-the-beach main drag. From the bus station, turn left on Gómez Farías and walk two blocks to reach **López Mateos.** Another left turn takes you to the plaza, a few blocks inland. López Mateos and **Hidalgo** are the main cross streets towards the ocean.

The folks at **Agencia Fénix** (tel. 7-11-88), facing the bus station, offer tourist info (open daily 9am-1pm and 4-8pm). There is no bank in Melaque. Cihuatlán, 20 minutes away, has two: **Banamex,** Av. Alvaro Obregón 58 (tel. 5-23-38 or 5-20-48), and **Bancomer** (tel. 5-22-38 or 5-23-23), across the street (both open Mon.-Fri. 9am-3:30pm). Both have **ATMs.** In Melque, a *casa de cambio* (tel. 5-53-43) across from the bus station past the pharmacy and inside the **centro comercial** changes dollars at a poor rate, but there's no commission and, well, it's the only option (open Mon.-Sat. 9am-2pm and 4-7pm, Sun. 9am-2pm). For access to **telephones,** visit **Jimmy's Lonchería y Caseta,** Gomez Farías 34, next to the bus station (tel. 5-63-10; fax 5-54-52; open Mon.-Sat. 8:30am-9pm, Sun. 8:30am-3pm; open until 10pm daily during high season). The public telephones by the bus station will let you make long-distance collect calls.

Autocamiones Cihuatlán (tel. 5-50-03) sends **buses** to Guadalajara (first-class 7 per day 9am-1:15am, 5hr., 87 pesos; second-class 14 per day 4am-12:30am, 6½hr., 70 pesos), Manzanillo (second-class every hr., 1½hr., 14 pesos), and Puerto Vallarta (first-class 9:15am and 1:30pm, 3½hr., 61 pesos; second-class 12 per day, 3am-11:30pm, 6hr., 50 pesos) via Chamela (1½hr., 14 pesos). A few doors down, **Primera Plus,** Gomez Farías 34 (tel. 5-61-10), has first-class service to Guadalajara (8am, 3:15 and 6:15pm, 5hr., 87 pesos), Manzanillo (11:30am, 2 and 7:15pm, 1hr., 16 pesos), Puerto Vallarta (1:15 and 4am, 4hr., 61 pesos) and second-class service to Guadalajara (7 per day 5am-8:30pm, 6½hr., 70 pesos), Manzanillo (11 per day 2am-10:30pm, 1½hr., 14 pesos), and Puerto Vallarta (6 per day 8am-12:30am, 5hr., 49 pesos) via Chamela (1½hr., 15 pesos).

Tidy those whities at the **Lavandería Industrial Hotelera** at Gómez Farías 26, next to the bus station (7 pesos per kg; open Mon.-Sat. 9am-6pm). The **Red Cross** (tel. 5-23-00) is 15km away in Cihuatlán, accessible by buses which leave from the plaza (every 15min., 4 pesos) or by taxi (40 pesos). **Súper Farmacia Plaza,** López Mateos 48 (tel. 5-51-67), is south of the plaza (open Mon.-Sat. 8am-3pm and 5-9:30pm, Sun. 8am-2pm). The **hospital** (often called **Centro de Salud**), on Cordiano Guzmán, between Corona and G. Farías, is open 24 hours for emergencies (consultations Mon.-Fri. 9am-2pm and 5-8pm). **Clínica de Urgencias,** Carranza 22 (tel. 5-61-44), two blocks from the bus station, also provides emergency service. Dr. Marco Tiscarreño López speaks English. The **police** (tel. 5-50-80) are on López Mateos 52, north of the plaza. The **post office,** José Clemente Orozco 13 (tel. 5-52-30), is two blocks left of the plaza as you face the beach and a block and a half towards the beach on Orozco, in the green building on your left (open Mon.-Fri. 8am-3pm, Sat. 8am-noon). **Postal Code:** 48980. **Telephone Code:** 335.

Accommodations and Camping Melaque is larger than Barra de Navidad and has more hotels; most budget accommodations are inland, near the *centro.* A bargain occasionally lurks among the beachside bungalows. All rates rise during the high season. Check with expatriates to locate good deals. **Hotel Hidalgo,** Hidalgo 7 (tel. 5-50-45), halfway between the plaza and the beach, is a friendly family affair. The small, clean rooms have spotless but microscopic bathrooms (singles 35 pesos; doubles 50 pesos; triples 89 pesos; quads 119 pesos). Large and well scrubbed **Bungalows Villamar,** Hidalgo 1 (tel. 5-50-05), just off the beach, have two bedrooms, each with two double beds, lots of furniture, and a fully equipped kitchen. Decks provide spectacular views of the ocean. Call in advance to reserve during high season (one person 75 pesos; 2 people 120 pesos; 3 people 150 pesos; 4 people 180 pesos; up to 8 people per bungalow). **Posada Clemen's,** Gómez Farías 70 (tel. 5-54-04), around the corner from Bungalows Villamar, offers cozy rooms and a flowery courtyard (1 person 40 pesos; add 20 pesos per additional person; high season rates increase by 20 pesos). **Playa Trailer Park** (tel. 5-50-65), at Gómez Farías and López Mateos, affords a great ocean-front view. Its 45 lots have electricity, water, and sewer hook-ups (2-person trailer spot or camping site 55 pesos). There are public bathrooms (1 peso) and showers (6 pesos). Reservations are recommended. Many people park trailers or pitch tents at the far western end of Melaque, between the sandy beach and rock formations—not the safest option, even when the place is packed during high season.

Food During the summer, restaurants ship in shrimp from the north, but come high season, local fishing boats catch everything that is served on the waterfront. Lobster is trapped here illegally; aid the persecuted crustacean's cause by ordering oysters. More authentic (and less expensive) Mexican places can be found near the central plaza. Cheaper still are the sidewalk food stands that materialize after the sun sets and the nameless, dirt-floored eateries in the *mercado* and near the bus station.

A trip to Melaque wouldn't be complete without a visit to **Los Pelícanos,** at the end of the row of *palapas* on the beach, 200m beyond the huge pink Hotel Casa Grande. The proprietor, New Yorker "Phil" García, considers herself the fairy godmother of the road-weary *gringo* and is a fixture of the local expatriate scene. Her wise and weathered husband, Trinidad, is a charmer and a domino fiend. Enjoy breakfast (around 12 pesos), burger and fries (18 pesos), fish filet (35 pesos) and a gorgeous view of the bay (open daily 7am-11pm; off-season daily 10am-8pm). **La Flor Morena,** Juárez 21, facing the plaza, welcomes locals and expats alike with great, filling Mexican food at unbelievably low prices. Feast on vegetarian dishes, *tostadas* (2-4 pesos), or scrumptious tacos (2 pesos each; open Tues.-Sun. 6-11pm). **César y Charly,** Gómez Faías 27-A, midway down the beach, serves spaghetti with cream (15 pesos), breaded steak (24 pesos), and an orgasmic flaming banana (8 pesos; open daily 7am-

10pm). **Juguería Maria Luisa,** Corona 1 (tel. 5-61-15), has every imaginable type of fruit juice (4 pesos; open daily 7am-midnight.)

Sights and Entertainment Waves get smaller and the beach more crowded toward the western end of Melaque's sandy strip. Rent **jet-skis** at the Restaurant Moyo (tel. 7-11-04), on the far west end of the beach (160 pesos per 30min., available daily 9am-7pm). For the thrill of a lifetime, ride a banana boat (15 pesos).

Although few people come to Melaque for the nightlife, few refuse when it's thrust upon them. **Disco Tango,** (tel. 5-54-72, -75) where Gómez Farías runs into Vallarta, monopolizes the action and is the after-hours oasis of Melaque's under-30 (but over-18, mind you) tourist crowd (cover 15-20 pesos; open daily 10pm-3am during high season, Wed.-Sun. low season). For something a bit more mellow and smoky, you can always twirl cues with the middle-aged men at **Billiard San Patricio,** Melaque's pool hall, on Orozco and Juárez, up the street from the post office about three blocks from the plaza (pool and *carambola* 8 pesos per hr., dominoes 2 pesos per hr.; open daily 11am-11pm). And, of course, there's always Barra.

■ Barra de Navidad

Orientation and Practical Information Barra de Navidad is a narrow peninsula flanked on its eastern shore by a sleeping laguna; the restless ocean tugs at her western shore. **Veracruz,** the main street, runs southeasterly, angling off at its end. There it meets **Legazpi,** another main street, which runs roughly north-south hugging the beach. Barra de Navidad's bus stop is at Veracruz 226, on the corner of Nayarit. Turn left on Veracruz from the bus station to get to *el centro.* The **tourist office** is at Veracruz 81 (tel. 5-51-00; tel./fax 5-64-00; open Mon.-Sat. 9am-8pm). The friendly Texans at **Crazy Cactus** (tel. 5-60-99), next to the church on Jalisco between Legazpi and Veracruz, can help you out with insider's advice. Barra has no bank, but a **casa de cambio,** Veracruz 212-C (tel. 5-61-77), exchanges dollars at a poor rate (open Mon.-Sat. 9am-2pm and 4-6:30pm). **Telephones** are available at the *caseta* next to Hotel Pacífico on Legazpi. Public phones are on Veracruz next to the police station. The **telegram office** (tel. 5-52-62) is at Veracruz 96, on the corner by the plaza (open Mon.-Fri. 9am-2:30pm).

Buses depart from **Primera Plus,** Veracruz 228 (tel. 5-52-65), to Guadalajara (first-class 5 per day 10am-midnight, 5hr., 88 pesos; second-class 12 per day 3:45am-10:20pm, 6½hr., 71 pesos) and Puerto Vallarta (9am and 1pm, 3½hr., 62 pesos). **ETN,** Veracruz 204, sells tickets for buses departing from Manzanillo. **Autocamiones Cihuatlán,** Veracruz 269 (tel. 5-61-11), serves Guadalajara (first-class 7:45am, 3 and 6pm, 5½hr., 88 pesos; second-class 5 per day 8:15am-5:15pm, 6½hr., 71 pesos) and Manzanillo (first-class 11:45am, 2:30 and 7:30pm, 1hr., 17 pesos; second-class 9 per day 8:45am-10:15pm, 1½hr., 14 pesos). **Lavandería Jardín,** Jalisco 71, just left on Veracruz before Morelos, will wash and dry 3kg for 16 pesos (open Mon.-Fri. 9am-2pm and 4-5pm, Sat. 9am-2pm). **Farmacia Marcela** is on Veracruz 69 (tel. 5-54-31; open daily 9am-2pm and 4-10:30pm). The **Centro de Salud** (tel. 5-62-20), on Puerto de la Navidad, is down Veracruz and out of town. Make a right just after the signs for El Márquez, just before Veracruz becomes a highway; the Centro is the second building on the right, with the red and white gate. 24-hour emergency service. **Police** wait 'round-the-clock at Veracruz 179 (tel. 5-53-99).The **post office,** Guanajuato 100, is one and a half blocks inland from the plaza, behind the market (open Mon.-Fri. 8am-3pm, Sat. 9am-1pm). **Postal Code:** 48987. **Telephone Code:** 335.

Accommodations and Camping Budget accommodations in Barra are available only to the keen-eyed (or *Let's Go*-armed) traveler. Most hotels are on or near the water and cater to the well heeled tourist. However, persistent and frugal groups can find bargains in doubles, triples, and quads. Of course, all prices are subject to hikes during the *temporada alta.* Reasonable accommodations are sometimes available in private residences—ask around and look for signs in restaurants. It's no longer possible to camp in Barra de Navidad; you're better off trying Melaque. The red and white brick **Posada Pacífico,** Mazatlán 136 (tel. 5-53-59), features breezy white rooms, a pleasant courtyard, and killer fans (singles 50 pesos, 65 in winter; doubles 80 pesos, 90 in winter). It also has four newly constructed, spacious bungalows (85 pesos, 105 in winter.) **Casa de Huéspedes Caribe,** Veracruz 69 (tel. 5-50-88), at Sonora, has a family feel. Wooden doors lead to rooms with cool blue walls, cute beds, spotless red floors, and fans. Communal bathrooms lack hot water (25 pesos per person, discounts for longer stays). **Bungalows Karelia,** on Legazpi, on the beach next to the Hotel Bogavante, are a good deal for three or more people. Airy but worn suites house a refrigerator, table, chairs, stove, fan, and kitchen utensils (suites for 2 people 150 pesos; for 3, 170 pesos; for 4, 190 pesos).

Food For delicious, inexpensive Mexican food in a pleasant atmosphere, try **Restaurant Paty,** Jalisco 52, at Veracruz. Grilled *pollo* is 15 pesos. Small *pozole* goes for 8 pesos, large for 10 (open daily 8am-11pm). The beachside tables at **Restaurant Pacífico,** Legazpi 206 (tel. 5-59-10), offer a stunning vista. The breakfast special is a bargain (11 pesos) and the shrimp *brocheta* mighty tasty (24 pesos; open daily 8am-10pm). **Los Arcos,** Mazatlán 163 (tel. 5-58-76), across from the Posada Pacífico, has some of the best Mexican food in town. *Huevos al gusto,* juice, and coffee go for 12 pesos (open daily 9am-9pm).

Sights and Entertainment **Crazy Cactus,** at the corner of Jalisco and Veracruz (tel. 5-60-99), rents out snorkeling equipment and boogie boards (12 pesos per hr., 60 pesos per day), surfboards (20 pesos per hr., 100 pesos per day), and bikes (80 pesos per day). It also organizes bilingual day trips to secluded **Tenacatita** bay, where you can snorkel along a coral reef (boat trip, seafood, drinks, and all the gear cost 350 pesos per person). Serious fishers will want to call **Z Pesca,** Legazpi 213 (tel. 5-64-64, fax 5-64-65), for rod, reel, and tackle (100 pesos per day) or a day-long deep-sea fishing expedition (800 pesos per day; open daily 9am-9pm).

The short trip across the lagoon to the village of **Colimilla** is pleasant; a *lancha* will deposit up to eight passengers at the far end of the lagoon or amid Colimilla's palms, pigs, cows, and open-air restaurants (50 pesos). Deserted **Playa de los Cocos,** 1km away, has larger breakers than those in Barra. If you don't want to swim back, remember to set a time to be picked up. Up to eight people can tour the lagoon behind Barra for 80 pesos. For 120 pesos per hour, up to four people can zoom off in a fully equipped *lancha* for tuna or marlin fishing. Operators have formed a cooperative, so prices are fixed. Their office and docks lie at the very end of Veracruz (open daily 7am-7pm).

Bibliophiles should not miss **Beer Bob's Book Exchange,** Mazatlán 61, a few blocks to the right as you face the Posada Pacífico. It's purely a book *exchange*—no cash involved. And what a collection! In the back room sits Bob and company, watching TV, playing cards, or engaging in "some serious beer drinking." This is Barra's

---

Jesus Christ Superstar

A source of pride for Barra is the **Iglesia de San Antonio,** on the corner of Jalisco and Veracruz, four blocks south of the bus station. The church is a modern structure famous for its miraculous icon, *El Cristo del Ciclón* (Christ of the Hurricane). Its arms, instead of extending to form the traditional crucifix, are bent and, though still attached to the body, droop earthward as if in a shrug. Local lore has it that when Hurricane Lilly furiously struck the bay on September 10, 1971, a young girl burst into the church begging the icon for help, causing Christ's arms to detach from the crucifix in order to hold the hurricane back and save the town from destruction. The church is open daily 7am-9:30pm; masses are held daily at 8am, noon, and 8pm.

expat core, a welcome spot for travelers to stop by and pick up a good read (open when the door's open, usually Mon.-Fri. 1-4pm).

Everyone out past midnight parties at **El Galeón Disco**, Morelos 24 (tel. 5-50-18), in Hotel Sand's. Quaff a beer for 5 pesos or a mixed drink for 10 (cover 10 pesos; open Fri.-Sat. 9pm-3am, daily during high season). Things get pretty hot amid the potted plants next door at **Casablanca** (tel. 5-05-40), especially on Fridays and Saturdays (cover Fri.-Sat. 10 pesos; open high season 10pm-late). Those who prefer singing to dancing may want to mellow out at the **Terraza Bar Jardín**, Jalisco 71 (tel. 5-65-31), a local roof garden and karaoke bar. Somebody will sing "New York, New York" all night if you won't. Beer goes for 5 pesos (happy hour 6-9pm; open 6pm-2am.) A number of two-for-one happy hours along Legazpi make the **giddy trip towards inebriation** that much cheaper.

COLIMA

■ Manzanillo

Manzanillo is home of the state's finest beaches, but you'd never know it from the dynamic, sweaty *centro* and the throngs of ships hugging the shore. Most tourists avoid central Manzanillo altogether and head to the glossy resorts on the city's two bays of golden-brown sand north and west of town. Thanks to a fortuitous combination of currents and latitude, Manzanillo is cooler in the summer than Puerto Vallarta and Acapulco. Reasonably priced hotels all lie in the midst of the loud and brazen port action—those seeking only sand and surf would do better to retreat to some secluded village, such as Cuyutlán or Barra de Navidad, where there is no metropolis between the hotels and the Pacific. But for those excited by the prospect of beautiful beaches *and* a real city, Manzanillo will certainly deliver.

ORIENTATION

Manzanillo lies 98km west of Colima and 355km south of Guadalajara. The **Jardín Obregón,** Manzanillo's *zócalo,* is the most useful orientation point in town. It faces north onto the harbor, but boxcars often obstruct the glorious view of oil tankers (sigh). **Morelos** runs east-west along the north (waterfront) edge of the plaza; **Balvido Dávalos,** becoming **Juárez,** runs along the south. **Avenida México,** Manzanillo's main street, runs south from the plaza; most hotels and services are nearby. The "Centro" bus runs from the station to the corner of 21 de Marzo and Hidalgo (1.50 pesos). From the corner, a right turn on Allende and another on México will take you to the *zócalo.* A taxi from the bus station to the center of town costs five pesos. White and blue "Miramar" buses provide the main transportation to Manzanillo's beaches and the main strip **Costera Miguel de la Madrid;** they run along México, around the Plaza, and turn on Morelos heading for the boulevard (about every 15min. 5am-11pm, price varies by destination).

PRACTICAL INFORMATION

Tourist Office: Blvd. Costera Miguel de la Madrid 4960 (tel. 3-22-64/-77), two blocks past Fiesta Mexicana. Catch a "Miramar" bus (3.50 pesos) and tell the driver where you're headed. Open Mon.-Fri. 8:30am-3pm and 6-8pm.

Currency Exchange: Banco Internacional, México 99 (tel. 2-21-50), at 10 de Mayo, has slightly better rates and longer hours than most banks. Open Mon.-Fri. 8am-7pm, Sat. 9am-2:30pm. **ATM** across the street at **Banamex.**

Telephones: Computel, México 302 (tel. 2-47-52), and on Morelos, a ½ block east of the *zócalo,* next to Banca Serfín. Open daily 7am-10pm.

Telegrams: Telecomm (tel. 2-30-30), in the Palacio Municipal, to the left of the stairs as you enter. Open Mon.-Fri. 8am-10pm, Sat. 9am-1pm.

Airport: (tel. 4-15-55), in Playa de Oro, on the highway between Barra de Navidad and Manzanillo. **Mexicana** (tel. 3-23-23). **Aeromar** (tel. 3-01-51). **Aerocalifornia** (tel. 4-14-14). **Viajes Vamos,** Carrillo Puerto 107 (tel. 2-17-11), one block west of México and three blocks south of the *zócalo*, can facilitate ticket purchase. Open Mon.-Fri. 9am-2pm and 4-7pm, Sat. 9am-2pm. Taxis cost 120 pesos. *Colectivos* (42 pesos) take passengers to the airport 2hr. before take-off (9am-1:30pm and 5-7pm daily, 45min.); call the airport to make arrangements.

Buses: On Hidalgo, on the outskirts of town between Laguna Cuyutlán and the ocean. Taxis to the *centro* 5 pesos. **Autobuses de Occidente** (tel. 2-01-23) serves Mexico City (2:45, 5:45, 11:45am, and 7:30pm, 16hr., 85 pesos). **Autobuses de Jalisco** (tel. 2-01-23) provides first-class service to Colima (10 per day, 1¼hr., 19 pesos), Guadalajara (10 per day 1am-11:30pm, 4¼hr., 77 pesos), Morelia (10:45pm, 8hr., 121 pesos), and Uruapan (8:15pm, 8hr., 96 pesos). **Autocamiones Cihuatlán** (tel. 2-05-15) provides second-class service to Guadalajara (12 per day, 8hr., 84 pesos) and Puerto Vallarta (10 per day 4:30am-10pm, 6hr., 64 pesos), stopping at Melaque and Barra de Navidad (1½hr., 14 pesos). **Autotransportes del Sur de Jalisco** (tel. 2-10-03) serves Colima (5 per day 1:15-7:40pm, 1½hr., 18 pesos). **Primera Plus** (tel. 2-02-10) provides first-class service to Puerto Vallarta (midnight, 5hr., 79 pesos) and Querétaro (8am, 8hr., 185 pesos). **Transportes Costalegre** (tel. 2-02-10) runs buses to Melaque and Barra de Navidad (11 per day 6:30am-7pm, 1¼hr., 14 pesos). **Elite** (tel. 2-01-35) provides cushy service to Acapulco (noon and 5pm, 12hr., 167 pesos) and Tijuana (10am and 9pm, 36hr., 568 pesos) passing through Tepic (7hr., 118 pesos), Mazatlán (11hr., 190 pesos), and Hermosillo (25hr., 447 pesos).

Trains: (tel. 2-19-92), on Niños Héroes near Morelos. Office open daily 8am-2pm.

Laundromat: Lavi-Matic, Hidalgo 1 (tel. 2-08-44), all the way down México across the small plaza. Open Mon.-Sat. 8am-7pm.

Red Cross: Juárez 190 (tel. 2-59-83), one block from the Plaza. Open 24hr.

Pharmacy: Farmacia Manzanillo, Juárez 10 (tel. 2-01-85 or 3-24-11), on the south side of the *zócalo*. English spoken. Open daily 9am-midnight. **Farmacia Continental** (tel. 3-02-86), at Playa Miramar, across from Restaurante Juanitos. Dr. Joseph Cadet speaks English. Open Mon.-Sat. 10am-2pm and 5-9pm.

Hospital: tel. 2-00-29 or 2-19-03, Calle Hospital, Colonia San Pedrito. Open 24hr.

Police: (tel. 2-10-02/-04), on Juárez, inside the Palacio Municipal, facing the Jardín.

Post Office: Calle Miguel Galindo 3D (tel. 2-00-22). Open Mon.-Fri. 8am-7pm, Sat. 9am-1pm. **Postal Code:** 28200.

Telephone Code: 333.

ACCOMMODATIONS

Hotels near the *zócalo* are in a safer area than those near the bus station. **Camping** on Playa Miramar is feasible during Semana Santa and in December, when bathroom facilities are available and security is heightened.

Hotel Flamingo, Madero 72 (tel. 2-10-37), 1 block south of the *zócalo*. Old Spanish style rooms with stucco walls and heavy wooden furniture. Dimly lit rooms are perfect for a siesta, although the place could use more ventilation. Clean bathrooms. Singles 40-50 pesos. Doubles 60-80 pesos. Triples 70-100 pesos.

Hotel Emperador, Dávalos 69 (tel. 2-23-74), 1 block west of the plaza. Rooms with ceiling fan and rustic wooden furniture aren't exactly fit for an emperor, but they do the trick for beachbums. Singles 40 pesos. Doubles 50-60 pesos.

Hotel Miramar, Juárez 122 (tel. 2-10-08). Groovy winding staircases lead up to large, worn rooms that appear to have been untouched since the birth of rock-and-roll. Vast, checkered balconies offer a view of the *zócalo* or the port. Singles 40 pesos. Doubles 60 pesos. Triples 75 pesos.

Casa de Huéspedes Petrita, Allende 20 (tel. 2-01-87), 4 blocks down México, and a quick left on Allende. Beige and white lobby leads to tiny but clean rooms with fans (some lack windows). Try to snag the triple with the squeaky-clean bathroom. Otherwise, work those hamstrings—clean communal bathrooms lack toilet seats. Singles 25 pesos. Doubles 30 pesos. Triples 40-50 pesos.

FOOD

Since tourists mostly put up closer to the beach, food at the market and in restaurants downtown is simple, local, and cheap.

Restaurant Emperador, Dávalos 69 (tel. 2-23-74), below the eponymous hotel. The blank walls, white tablecloths, and fluorescent lights aren't nearly as pleasing to the eye as the food is to the palate. Great *comida corrida:* a gargantuan dinner of vegetable soup, filet-of-fish, and steamed vegetables, including rice, tortillas, and *agua fresca,* for a mere 12 pesos. Open daily 7am-11pm.

Restaurante Chantilly (tel. 2-01-94), on the plaza at Juárez and Moreno. Crowds of newspaper-reading professionals, flocks of families, and stragglers off the *zócalo* munch on Mexican staples in a diner-like setting. Enchiladas 14 pesos. Mango *agua fresca* (5 pesos) is as good as it gets. Open Sun.-Fri. 7am-10pm.

Los Naranjos, México 366. Look hard: the white and blue café is hard to spot. When it rains, time stands still here; so do the flies and fans. Locals come here in droves to chow down on tasty entrees served with a mountain of tortillas, rice, beans, and a glass of juice (14 pesos). Open daily 7am-7pm.

Nevería La Michoacana, Av. Mexico 51 (tel. 2-22-73), on the Jardín. One lick and you'll be in heaven. Less cream and sharper flavors than most ice cream parlors (4.50 pesos per cone). Open daily 9am-11pm.

SIGHTS

Manzanillo's beaches stretch from west to east along two bays, **Bahía de Manzanillo** and **Bahía de Santiago,** formed by the Santiago and Juluapan Peninsulas. The Bahía de Manzanillo has more expensive hotels and cleaner golden sand. Unfortunately, its beach slopes steeply, creating a strong and sometimes dangerous undertow. The beaches at Bahía Santiago, though twice as far from the *centro* and bordered by a noisy highway, are better protected by the Juluapan peninsula, providing a panoramic vista of the rugged terrain and more tranquil surf. The bay is perfect for swimming and water sports and is very popular with sun worshippers.

The closest good beach on Bahía Manzanillo, **Playa Las Brisas,** has a few secluded spots but is for the most part crowded with luxurious hotels and bungalows. To get to Las Brisas from downtown Manzanillo, take a taxi (18 pesos) or the "Las Brisas" bus (2.50 pesos). Catch the bus on México or on the highway going toward the airport and Barra de Navidad. Alternatively, catch the "Miramar" bus and ask the driver to let you off at the *crucero* (crossroads), then turn left to populated shores or stake out a private piece of beach right at the junction.

The "Miramar" bus continues west of Peninsula Santiago, gear-grinding toward other excellent beaches on Bahía Santiago. Because this part of the bay is not used for shipping, the water is cleaner than at Las Brisas. Beyond **Olas Altas,** a beach popular with experienced surfers but infamous for its powerful waves and dangerous undertow, is **Miramar Beach,** a stretch of golden beach with solid waves adequate for **boogie-boarding** or **body-surfing.** Get off where the footbridge crosses the highway. This is the most crowded section of the beach, but it boasts top-notch beachfront restaurants from which you can rent body boards and surfboards (5-10 pesos per hr.). Crowds thin out 20m to the east or west.

The calmer waters of the *palapa*-lined **Playa la Boquita,** the westernmost point on the Juluapan Peninsula, make this a popular spot for children and water sports. Two-seater **wave runners** (US$32 for 30min.) or **banana boats** (10 pesos per person) can slip you around the bay. **Windsurfing** (60 pesos per hr.), **parasailing** (100 pesos per hr.), and **kayaks** (60 pesos per hr.) are also available. **Snorkeling** gear (60 pesos) is rented out at the last *palapa* on the shore (tel. 6-57-02; open daily 10am-5pm). If you're not much of a deep sea enthusiast, Blas at **Hotel Palma Real** (tel. 5-00-00) rents **horses** (70 pesos per hr.). To get to Playa La Boquita, take a "Miramar" bus to Club Santiago (3.50 pesos, 40min.). Walk through the white arches along the cobble-stoned and palm-lined street, which becomes a dirt road; you'll hit the road after 25 minutes. Also oozing tranquility is **Playa Audiencia,** a small but magnificent cove with calm waters, light brown sand, a few small boats, and a gorgeous rocky vista. To reach the *playa,* take a "Las Hadas" bus from Niños Héroes or anywhere on Miramar Highway to the Sierra Radison (3.50 pesos), then follow the path to the beach. The bus ride back to town offers a spectacular view of the peninsula.

ENTERTAINMENT

Manzanillo doesn't sleep when the sun sets. After frolicking in the sun and splashing in the sea, locals and tourists alike show off their **tans** and **cool threads** at **Vog** (tel. 3-19-92 or 4-16-60), Av. Miguel de la Madrid, in the hotel strip. At 11:30pm, sophisticated track lighting rhythmically sprays beams across Flintstone-like stone walls (cover 30 pesos; open Thurs.-Sat. 10pm-4am, daily during high season). Next door at the **Bar de Félix** (tel. 3-18-75), an older crowd reclines in plush red chairs while the packed dance floor pulsates to a melange of disco and Latin rhythms (2-drink or 35-peso minimum Fri.-Sat. during high season; open Tues.-Sun. 9pm-4am). "Miramar" buses run down the hotel strip. Taxis back to the *centro* cost 25 pesos.

■ Near Manzanillo

PARAÍSO

Paraíso may soon be destroyed by the gods for its hubris, but for now it outclasses its unsightly sister city, nearby **Armería.** A well paved road connects the two towns, cutting through 7km of banana and coconut plantations before it dead-ends at the lava-black sands that surround Paraíso's few hotels and thatched, beachfront restaurants. A shoreline strewn with an endless row of lawn chairs and umbrellas backs the emerald green surf. Paraíso is a popular destination among Mexicans for daytrips and weekend vacations; during the high season and on Sundays, the beachfront has a true family atmosphere, and the town's single dirt road is often crammed with buses and cars blaring music. But on a lazy summer weekday, the beach is almost deserted, and a few lucky swimmers have the waters all to themselves.

Just before the main road becomes the beach, you'll see Paraíso's only other street, the dirt road **Av. de la Juventud** (extravagantly called **Calle Adán y Eva** by locals) which runs along the back of the beachfront restaurants. The first building on the beach to your left is **Hotel Equipales** (call the town's *caseta* at tel. 4-60-24 or -26), where you'll find funky green walls adorned with red silk roses and a view of the shore. Clean rooms boast ceiling fans but no frills, and the cramped bathrooms lack hot water (singles 40 pesos; doubles 60 pesos). Farther to the left lies **Hotel Paraíso** (tel. 8-10-09), a cut above Equipales. Spacious beachfront rooms have yellow-tiled floors, ceiling fans, and spotless showers; the pool is crammed with kids (singles and doubles 125 pesos). At the opposite end of the strip lies **Posada Valencia** (call the town *caseta* at tel. 4-60-24 or -26), where the beds are waist-high, the rooms clean, and the bathroom tiles scrubbed spotless. Alas, the plain cement floors put a damper on it all (singles and doubles 40 pesos).

There are countless alternatives to spending the night in a hotel. Paraíso's extensive beach makes a soft pillow for campers, and the Hotel Paraíso provides showers (5 pesos) and free access to bathrooms. Hotel Equipales also offers bathroom (1 peso) and shower (3 pesos) use. Some *enramada* owners may let you hang your hammock under their thatched roofs. During the high season (especially Dec. and April), rooms may be available in private houses; ask around.

Restaurants run the slim gamut from rustic *enramadas* to cement-floored *comedores*. Not surprisingly, locally caught seafood dominates menus. **Restaurant Paraíso,** in the Hotel Paraíso, is as popular as the hotel pool. Uniformed waiters provide snazzy service, and string quartets and *mariachis* sometimes pop in in the afternoon. Tasty shrimp dishes cost 28 pesos (open daily 8am-6pm). The restaurants at Hotel Equipales and Posada Valencia also offer pleasant atmospheres and reasonable prices. Long-distance **phone** calls can be made across the street from the bus stop in the *tienda rural* (tel. 4-60-24 or 26; open Mon.-Sat. 9am-9pm, Sun. 9am-6pm). And remember to bring plenty of cash—there's no credit in Paradise.

Getting There: Autobuses Nuevos Horizonte y Rojos (tel. 2-39-00) runs buses from Manzanillo to Armería (every 15min. 4:20am-10:30pm, 45min., 9.50 pesos). Get off at the blue "Paraíso" sign and cross the highway. Buses to Paraíso leave from the corner by Restaurante La Frontera, where the remains of the paved road meet Adán y Eva (every 45min. 6am-7:30pm, 15min., 2.50 pesos). Buses return from Paraíso to Armería on the same schedule and depart from the same spot.

CUYUTLÁN

With its lush vegetation and mysterious lagoon, **Cuyutlán** (pop. 1650) offers a budding Thoreauvian hungry for solitude and tranquility just that. A generous stretch of black sand beach pounded by wild waves invites a stroll along the shore. In the off season, shut-up buildings and silent streets give the place a ghost-town feel, and the huge golden head of Benito Juárez is often the only face visible amid the palm trees of Cuyutlán's green and white *zócalo*. Summer weekends are slightly busier, but it is only during the high tourist season (Dec.-May) that Cuyutlán truly comes to life. If you have to choose between Paraíso and Cuyutlán, the latter offers tourists a better beach, better hotels, and a greater variety of food.

Orientation and Practical Information The road from Armería, 15km from Cuyutlán, runs parallel to the coast and becomes **Yavaros** as it enters town. It intersects **Hidalgo,** which runs along the east side of the town square; a left at this intersection takes you to the beach. **Veracruz,** Cuyutlán's other mighty boulevard, runs parallel to and three blocks from Yavaros, one block off the beach.

Most of Cuyutlán's municipal services are within one block of the *zócalo*. The bilingual owners of the **Hotel Fenix** will **change money** if they have the cash. Bring an adequate supply of *pesos* just in case. The only **telephone** is at Hidalgo 47 (tel. 6-40-00), one block inland from the *zócalo*. **Farmacia del Carmen** is at Yavaros 6, facing the plaza (open daily 9am-2pm and 4-7pm). For those who fall sick, the blue and white **Centro de Salud** (tel. 6-42-10) is one block west of the *zócalo* on Yavaros at Madero (open 24hr. for emergencies, Mon.-Fri. 9am-2pm and 4-7pm for consultation; no English). The **police** reside at Hidalgo 144 (tel. 6-40-14, ext. 113), one block south of the *zócalo*. **Telephone code:** 332.

Accommodations and Food Waves lap at the doorsteps of most nearby budget hotels. Most are well maintained and very affordable. During high season (mainly Dec. and Semana Santa), expect rates to skyrocket to 100-120 pesos per person, with meals included to help justify the price. Make reservations a month in advance during this time. Almost all the food in Cuyutlán is served up in the hotel restaurants. Seafood is the obvious specialty. Most restaurants are on Yavaros. **Hotel Morelos,** Hidalgo 185, at Veracruz, offers plush rooms with carved wooden furniture. Tiled floors, festive colors, and what seems like all the flowers in Cuyutlán give the place pizzazz (30 pesos per person). The rooms at **Hotel Fénix** (tel. 6-40-82), Hidalgo 201 at Veracruz, may be taller than they are wide, but there's a fan in each one, and the bathrooms are tidy. The friendly English-speaking owners run a popular bar that serves as the town watering hole (30-35 pesos per person; open during high season only). The **Hotel San Rafael,** Veracruz 46 (tel. 6-40-15), dishes out old Spanish charm with white stucco walls, wooden-shuttered windows, leafy greens, and ocean views (singles 50 pesos; doubles 100 pesos; high season 100 pesos per person). There's a **disco** next door.

Cabañitas del Ejido Cuyutlán, a 10-minute walk east along the beach (or along Veracruz past the Hotel San Rafael), offers campsites and cabañas with electricity and access to extremely rustic showers and toilets. But you can't beat the price, and the super-friendly caretaker Rafles will treat you right (10 pesos for 24hr.). Unofficial camping sites lie 200m from Cuyutlán's hotels, in a private patch of black sand. Some travelers string up a hammock in one of the *palapas* near the hotels. For five pesos, campers and daytrippers can use the toilets and showers at Hotel Fenix (or buy a drink at the bar).

Sights Cuyutlán's biggest claim to fame is the **green wave,** a phenomenon that occurs regularly in April or May. Quirky currents and phosphorescent marine life combine to produce 10m swells that glow an unearthly green. The town itself reaches high tide during the **Festival de la Virgen de Guadalupe** (the first twelve days of December), when twice a day—at 6am and 6pm—men, women, and children clad in *traje de indios* walk 5km to the town's blue church. The celebrations peak on the twelfth day, when *mariachis* accompany the procession and the marchers sing *las mañanitas* in tribute to the Virgin. Don't let the hare beat you to the **turtle camp,** 4km east of town, next to the coastal lagoon beach. The camp is a symphony in green, housing a melange of reptiles and amphibians that includes turtles, iguanas, and crocodiles (admission 5 pesos; taxi to the camp 20 pesos).

Getting There Buses to Cuyutlán leave Armería from the corner of Restaurante La Frontera (every 30min. 7am-8pm, 20min., 3 pesos). Buses depart from Cuyutlán on the same schedule (sometimes a bit early) from the plaza. There is no public transportation between Paraíso and Cuyutlán.

■ Colima

With 160,000 residents, the capital of Colima state can hardly be called a *pueblo,* but it does manage to maintain a certain small-town benevolence and informality: the streets and parks are magnificently groomed, the civic-minded inhabitants are remarkably friendly, and on Sundays, slews of stores close up shop as families head off to church. Blessed with cool mountain air and a string of little museums and theaters, under-touristed Colima provides relief from the well trodden coastal route and proves a great place to shake the sand from your shoes.

ORIENTATION

A string of plazas runs east to west across downtown Colima. The arcaded **Plaza Principal,** flanked by the cathedral and the Palacio de Gobierno on the east side, is the business center of town. Just past the cathedral and *palacio* is the smaller, quieter **Jardín Quintero,** marked by the large fountain in its center. Three blocks farther east on **Madero** (which runs along the north side of the plaza) is the large, lush **Jardín Núñez,** the other significant reference point in town. Many tourist services are on **Hidalgo,** which runs parallel to Madero one block to the south. The main **bus station** is 2km out of town, but mini-buses zip by incessantly (6am-8:30pm, 1.50 pesos). **Taxis** charge 4 pesos within the *centro,* 6 pesos to the outskirts.

PRACTICAL INFORMATION

Tourist Office: Portal Hidalgo 20 (tel. 2-43-60 or tel./fax 2-83-60), on the west side of Pl. Principal, across the *zócalo* from the Palacio de Gobierno. Extremely helpful staff speaks English. Open Mon.-Fri. 8:30am-3pm and 5:30-9pm, Sat. 9am-1pm.
Currency Exchange: Banamex, Hidalgo 90 (tel. 2-01-03), 1 block east of Pl. Principal. **ATM.** Open Mon.-Fri. 9am-3pm. **Majapara Casa de Cambio,** Morelos 200 (tel. 4-89-98; fax 4-89-66), corner of Juárez at Jardín Núñez, has slightly better rates. Open Mon.-Fri. 9am-2pm and 4:30-7pm, Sat. 9am-2pm.
Telephones: LADATELS abound in the plazas. **Computel,** Morelos 234 (tel. 4-59-05), on the south side of Jardín Núñez. Open daily 7am-10pm.

Telegrams and Fax: Madero 243 (tel. 2-60-69), next to the post office. Open Mon.-Fri. 8am-6pm, Sat. 9am-noon.

Buses: La Línea (tel. 4-81-79) runs buses to Guadalajara (10 per day 1am-11pm, 3hr., 58 pesos) and Lázaro Cárdenas (12:10, 3:20, and 9:30am, 6hr., 70-81 pesos). **Autotransportes del Sur de Jalisco** (tel. 2-03-16) runs second-class buses to Manzanillo (7 per day 6am-12:45pm, 2hr., 18 pesos) via Armería (1¼hr., 10 pesos). **ETN** (tel. 2-58-99; fax 4-10-60) has first-class service to the Guadalajara airport (3am and 9:30am, 3hr., 90 pesos). **Ómnibus de México** (tel. 4-71-90) goes to Aguascalientes (3pm, 6½hr., 122 pesos), Guadalajara (5 per day 8:15am-6:50pm, 3hr., 58 pesos), Mexico City (5 per day 7:45pm-midnight, 10hr., 186 pesos), and Monterrey (6:50pm, 15hr., 247 pesos). **Primera Plus** (tel. 4-80-67) runs first-class buses to Aguascalientes (12:30pm, 6hr., 128 pesos), Guadalajara (10 per day 5am-5:30pm, 3hr., 65 pesos), Manzanillo (9 per day 1:50am-11:30pm, 1½hr., 22 pesos), and Querétaro (9:30pm, 8hr., 161 pesos). **Autobuses de Occidente** (tel. 4-81-79) sends second-class buses to Mexico City (5, 8am, 2 and 10pm, 11hr., 165 pesos) via Morelia (8hr., 86 pesos), and to Uruapan (11am, 7hr., 70 pesos). **Flecha Amarilla** (tel. 2-11-35) provides second-class service to Manzanillo (5 per day, 1¾hr., 18 pesos), Morelia (6pm, 8hr., 86 pesos), and Querétaro (4 per day 9:30am-8:30pm, 10hr., 136 pesos). **Elite** (tel. 2-84-99) goes to Tijuana (5pm, 36hr., 557 pesos) via Tepic (7hr., 131 pesos), Mazatlán (12hr., 202 pesos), and Hermosillo (27hr., 458 pesos).

Trains: (tel. 2-92-50), Av. Colón by Parque Hidalgo, at the southern edge of town. The #6 and 7 buses go to the station. Second-class service to Guadalajara (1:30pm, 7hr., 19 pesos) and Manzanillo (3am, 2hr., 8 pesos). Offices open daily 8am-3pm.

Luggage Storage: At the bus station. 2 pesos per bag for 6hr., 0.50 pesos each additional hour. Open daily 6am-10pm. 24-hr. restaurant can assist after hours.

Laundromat: LavaTec, Rey Colimán 4. Open Mon.-Sat. 8:30am-8:30pm.

Red Cross: (tel. 2-14-51 or 2-22-42), Aldama at Obregón. Open 24hr.

Pharmacy: Sangre de Cristo (tel. 4-74-74), Obregón at Madero. Open 24hr.

Hospitals: Hospital Civil (tel. 2-02-27 or 2-09-11), San Fernando at Ignacio Zandoval. **Centro de Salud** (tel. 2-00-64 or 2-32-38), Juárez at 20 de Noviembre. Dr. Armando López speaks English. Open Mon.-Fri. 7am-2:30pm, Sat. 7am-1:30pm.

Emergency: dial 06.

Police: (tel. 4-59-44), Juárez at 20 de Noviembre.

Post Office: Madero 247 (tel. 2-00-53), on the northeast corner of the Jardín Núñez. Open Mon.-Fri. 8am-7pm, Sat. 8am-noon. **Postal Code:** 28000.

Telephone Code: 331.

ACCOMMODATIONS

A smattering of inexpensive hotels line Jardín Núñez and outlying streets, while higher-priced hotels cluster around the university. Expect most fellow lodgers to be natives. Purified water is often not available.

Casa de Huéspedes, Morelos 265 (tel. 2-34-67), off the southeast corner of Jardín Núñez. A friendly family-run *posada* with breezy rooms and billions of blooming plants. Singles 30 pesos, with bath 35. Doubles 50 pesos, with bath 55.

Hotel La Merced, Hidalgo 188 or Juárez 82 (tel. 2-69-69). The entrance is on the west side of Jardín Nuñez—wind through the walkway and parking lot. A colorful motel-esque establishment with an outdoorsy feel. Well furnished rooms sport ceiling fans and private baths. Singles with double bed 60 pesos. Doubles with both a single and a double bed 75 pesos. Triples 90 pesos. Quads 105 pesos.

Hotel San Lorenzo, Calle Cuauhtémoc 149 (tel. 2-20-00). From Pl. Principal walk west 2 blocks to Calle Cuauhtémoc, then left 3 blocks. Tiled stairs, silk flowers, and a snazzy lobby seem an oasis in this dingy neighborhood. Baby blue and white walls enclose spotless rooms with private bathrooms, hot water, floor fans, and June Cleaver curtains. Singles 45 pesos. Doubles 60 pesos. Triples 70 pesos.

FOOD

Most restaurants in Colima serve up the traditional *pozole blanco,* but others tread the cutting edge, affecting a modern air. Huge *equipales* (Colima's traditional bamboo chairs) scoop hungry Euro-types into cafés serving wine and cheese. A few pleasant establishments cluster around the Plaza Principal, but a jaunt down any of the plaza's sidestreets will lead to more authentic, less expensive eateries.

Samadhi, Medina 125 (tel. 3-24-98), 2½ blocks north of Jardín Núñez. Walk down Juárez (the western border of the Jardín); Samadhi is next to the red and white church. Enter the leafy courtyard enclosed by soft yellow, orange, and pink walls for some delicious vegetarian cuisine. Breakfast *Samadhi* (orange or carrot juice, fruit plate with yogurt, cereal, granola, and honey) goes for 17 pesos. Enchiladas *rojas* 12 pesos. Open Fri.-Wed. 8am-10pm, Thurs. 8am-5pm.

Comedor Familiar El Trébol, 16 de Septiembre #50 (tel. 2-29-00), at Degollado on the Pl. Principal. Family joint packed with kids laughing and stuffing their faces. Checkered tablecloths, shamrock covered lime green walls, and a colorful fresco of Colima's volcanoes make this a festive place. *Comida corrida* 12 pesos, breakfast 8 pesos, beer 5 pesos. Open Sun.-Fri. 8am-11pm.

Los Naranjos, Barreda 34 (tel. 2-00-29), almost a block north of Madero, just behind the Plaza Principal. *Periódico*-perusing middle-aged men sip coffee amid mellow lilac and beige walls. Glass vases and wicker chairs add some flair. *Pollo Los Naranjos* 23 pesos. *Antojitos* 6-18 pesos. Open daily 8am-11:30pm.

Cenaduría Morelos, Morelos 299 (tel. 2-93-32), at Domínguez, 1 block off the southeast corner of Jardín Nuñez. As *sabroso* as it gets. Locals stream in and stare at the funky optical illusion tile floor. Enjoy the lettuce and diced turnip that comes with the *pozole, tostadas, sopes,* sweet enchiladas, and *taquitos* (entrees 9 pesos), but watch the hot sauce! Open Tues.-Sat. 5-11pm, Sun. 5pm-1:30am.

SIGHTS

In Colima's **Plaza Principal,** the gazebo and fountains of the **Jardín Libertad** lure bureaucrats on their lunch break to the garden's ornate white wrought-iron benches. The double arcade around the plaza encompasses the **Museo Regional de Historia de Colima.** On the east side of the plaza, much of the state government is housed in the **Palacio de Gobierno,** an inviting beige and white building with a breezy courtyard and a four-wall mural, completed in 1954 by Jorge Chávez Carrillo in honor of the bicentennial of Hidalgo's birth. The intricate mural moves counterclockwise through Mexico's tumultuous history, beginning with a powerful depiction of the Spanish conquest and ending at the Mexican Revolution with Pancho Villa's infamous bravado. Adjoining Colima's municipal complex is the colonial **Santa Iglesia Cathedral,** a pawn in the battle between humanity and nature—or, depending on your perspective, between Catholicism and the ghost of indigenous religions. The Spanish first built a church on this spot in 1527, but an earthquake destroyed the original wood and palm structure; fire consumed its replacement. Undeterred, the Spanish built another church. The cathedral's Neoclassical interior sparkles with gilt paint, chandeliers, and polished marble. In the pulpit designed by Othón Bustos rests a statue of San Felipe de Jesús, the city's patron saint (open 6am-2pm and 4-8:30pm).

A block south of the tourist office, on the west side of Plaza Principal, stands **Teatro Hidalgo,** completed in 1883. Unmarred by the passage of time, the theater's four tiers of side-seating barely touch the high ceiling, and its swooping red curtains lend the stage a 19th-century ambience. Occasional performances enliven the majestic interior beyond those large wooden doors; inquire at the tourist office.

Colima's **Museo de Las Culturas de Occidente** (tel. 2-31-55), on Calle Calzada Galván, is an excellent museum devoted to local pre-Hispanic art. Rarely seen outside the state, the Colima ceramic figurines on display here are among the most playful and captivating artifacts in Mexico. The figurines possess exaggerated, disproportionate bodies, showing the importance of symbolism in the indigenous cultures. The museum provides an excellent narrative of the artifacts' importance for indigenous life (open Tues.-Sun. 7am-9pm). The **Casa de la Cultura** (also tel. 2-31-55), the university's cultural center, shows diverse exhibitions and is the best source of information on cultural events in Colima (open daily 8am-9pm). To get to the museum, take the yellow "Ruta #3 Sur" bus on Av. Rey Colimán at Jardín Núñez and get off at Casa de la Cultura, the university's arts center.

Colima's newest museum, the **Museo de Historia,** Portal Morelos 1 (tel. 2-92-28), is at 16 de Septiembre and Reforma on the south side of the Pl. Principal, next to the bookstore. Facing a lovely courtyard, the museum houses a small collection of pre-Hispanic ceramics. In the same courtyard, the university runs a gallery featuring an eclectic art collection unearthed from the *"tumbas de tiro,"* a burial custom emphasized by pre-Hispanic indigenous groups in Colima (both open Tues.-Sat. 9am-6pm, Sun. 5-8pm; free). Also sponsored by the institution is Colima's **Museo Universitario de Culturas Populares** (tel. 2-68-69), at Barreda and Gallardo, which boasts a collection of traditional dresses and masks, figurines recovered from nearby tombs, and descriptions of the pre-Aztec western coast. A gift shop sells handmade reproductions of local ceramics (museum open Mon.-Sat. 9am-2pm and 4-7pm; free). Getting there is an easy 15-minute walk north on 27 de Septiembre from the Plaza Principal. Alternatively, catch the #7 bus on Gabino Barreda between Zaragoza and Guerrero, and take it to the corner of Barreda and Gallardo.

The **Parque Regional Metropolitano** (tel. 4-16-76), four blocks south of the Pl. Principal on Degollado, offers nature-lovers an afternoon stroll along a human-made duck pond, home to two absurdly large pelicans who pester young children for fish. A miniature **zoo** houses not-so-lucky monkeys, crocodiles, and lions in confining cages. Children, oblivious to the crocodile's tears, feed the deer ice cream cones through wire fences and frolic in the pool, zooming down the **waterslide.** (Zoo open daily 6am-7:30pm; pool and waterslide open Wed.-Sun. 10am-4:30pm. Admission to zoo 1 peso, to the pool 4 pesos, waterslide and boat rides 5 pesos per hr., children 3 pesos.)

Erupting volcanoes aren't the only goings-on shaking things up in Colima. **Cheers** (tel. 4-47-00), on Zaragoza, the landmark disco in town, greets you with copper ornaments on Alice in Wonderland colored walls and rainbow-colored seats (cover 20 pesos; open Fri.-Sat. 10pm-3am). For some sappy tunes that'll make you cry in your beer, visit the Casa de la Cultura's café, **Dalí.** Prints by you-know-who drip from the walls under dim, smoky lights. The food isn't exactly cheap, but it's worth it just to drink *cervezas* or smoke cigars with the conflicted intellectuals. Weekend nights between 9 and 11pm, a **sensitive Mexican man** stands on the café's small platform wailing love songs, a guitar cradled in his arms. *Muy romántico* (open Mon.-Fri. 8am-midnight, Sat.-Sun. 4pm-midnight). Other hot spots include **Bariloche,** Av. Rey de Colimán 440 (tel. 4-55-00), with huge screen videos, 2 pool tables, and a funky motif (30 pesos minimum intake; open Wed.-Sat. 8pm-1am) and **Atrium,** Sevilla de Río 174 (tel. 3-04-77), which sports hockey and pool tables and peppy music (open daily noon-2am).

■ Near Colima

VOLCANOES

In Náhuatl, Colima means "place where the old god is dominant." The old god is **El Volcán de Fuego** (3820m), 25km from Colima city. Recorded eruptions date back to the pre-Conquest era, and lava was visible from the capital once again on June 24, 1994, when El Fuego reasserted its status as an active volcano. The tourist office assures visitors that the volcano is not a threat to the city. **El Nevado de Colima** (4240m) stands taller than its neighbor but is dormant and not much fun at parties. The **Joya Cabin,** near the summit, lacks all amenities except a roof. The park is only open sporadically; if you're planning a trip to the top, call the **police** ahead of time (tel. 2-18-01). As always, be cautious. The ascent should not be attempted by solo travelers or by those with little hiking experience.

Getting There: Guadalajara-bound *locales* (from the new bus station) pass through the town of **Atenquique,** 57km away. From here a 27km unimproved dirt road runs to the summit of El Fuego. The trip is only recommended for four-wheel-drive vehicles, though logging trucks based at the factory in Atenquique make trips up the road to spots near the summit. You can get to El Nevado by car or by bus. Flecha Amarilla (tel. 2-11-35) runs buses from Colima to **Guzmán,** 83km away (5 per day 7am-5:30pm, 1¾hr., 24 pesos). Buses from Guzmán limp up to Joya, where you can make your epic assault on the summit.

LAGUNAS CARRIZALILLO AND LA MARÍA

If you don't mind insects, frogs, and huge lizards, and just want to bask in peace, make a daytrip to **Laguna Carrizalillo,** 27km north of Colima. Larger, closer to the volcanoes, and more visited is **Laguna La María,** whose calm, green waters surrounded by a dense wall of plant life attract flocks of ornithologists in search of tiny yellow Singing Wilsons. If birds aren't your thing, try fishing at the shore or from a rented *lancha* (about 25 pesos per hour). Two pesos buys access to either lagoon for a day. **Avitesa Agencia de Viajes,** Andador Constitución 43 (tel. 2-19-84), bordering Pl. Principal, can also make arrangements for *cabañas* (150-180 pesos; open daily 9am-8pm).

Getting There: Los Rojos buses (tel. 3-60-85) destined for "San Antonio" or "Zapotitlán" leave the suburban bus station and chug up and down the mountain road to La María (7am, 1:20, 2:30, and 5pm, 1½hr., 6.50 pesos; buses return at 6:30am, 1:30, 3, and 4pm). Those who survive the painfully bumpy ride are rewarded with a magnificent view of the mountains just before the bus reaches the tiny crossroads that leads to the lagoon. To get to the entrance from here, follow the wooden sign that says "La María" (a 15-min. hike). The bus back leaves from the same crossroads on the opposite side of the street.

COMALA

South of the lagoons and just 9km north of Colima is the picturesque town of **Comala,** known as "El Pueblo Blanco de América" (The White Town of America). Originally, all the façades in town were white, with red-tiled roofs, huge porches, and windows filled with flowers. Today, Comala's small town feel persists in the *zócalo,* which is surrounded by cobblestone streets and dotted with white benches, fountains, and orange trees. The south side of the *zócalo* is lined by lively restaurants in which *mariachis* perform and waiters supply patrons with a steady stream of free *botanas* (Mexican appetizers) to whet the appetite for *ponche* (warm rum and fruit punch), one of the region's vertigo-inducing traditional drinks.

Comala's main claim to fame is its colony of *indígena* artisans who craft wooden furniture, leather goods, clocks, and bamboo baskets in accord with the dictates of pre-Hispanic traditions. The **Cooperativa Artesenal Pueblo Blanco,** a small *tianguis* (market), stands just outside Comala's *centro,* about 200m past the strip of restaurants on Progreso. It's a 15- to 20-minute walk from the *zócalo* (open Mon.-Fri. 8am-3pm, Sat. 9am-2pm).

To the east of the *zócalo* lies the **Iglesia San Miguel del Espíritu Santo,** whose unfinished bare-bricked rear gives it character. Watch your head as you enter, for perched above is a sinister flock of pigeons. Once inside, you are met not by ornate stained-glass windows but by a sky blue ceiling. The nave of the church is occupied by still more birds, chirping a deafening cacophony. On the other side of the *zócalo* are the city offices, where a four-wall mural commemorates Comala's 130 years as a city and celebrates the "richness of its soil." Unfortunately, the birds who have control of the church have also settled across the way, and have graciously added their own artistic expression to the mural. For more information, contact Ignacio Zamora,

Director of Education, Culture, and Tourism, next door in the municipal building (tel. 5-50-22; available Mon.-Fri. 8:30am-12:30pm and 6:30-8:30pm).

Getting There: Los Rojos sends buses to Comala from Colima's suburban bus station (every 15min. 6am-10pm, 30min., 2 pesos).

Southern Pacific Coast

Because many of the region's indigenous Purépecha subsisted by the rod and the net, the Aztecs dubbed the lands surrounding Lake Pátzcuaro **Michoacán** (Country of Fishermen). The distinctive language the Purépecha spoke (a variant of which is still widely spoken) and the terraced agricultural plots they built have convinced scholars that they were not originally indigenous to the area but in fact immigrants from what is today Peru. Purépecha hegemony lasted from around 800 CE, when they first settled Michoacán, until the Spanish arrived in 1522. Since the colonial period, Michoacán has become an agricultural juggernaut, parlaying mild weather, abundant rains, and red, fertile soil into huge corn harvests. Of late, the forest-covered mountain ranges which surround Michoacán have attracted wildlife enthusiasts, and pretty beaches and inexpensive handicrafts have attracted tourists.

Guerrero is a state that has been blessed by fortune. During the colonial period, the rich mining town of Taxco kept not only the state but much of the New Spain swimming in silver. More recently, the state's precious commodities have not come from high upon the rocky Sierra de Guerrero but rather from the rugged shores just past it, on the Pacific coast. In the 1950s, Acapulco came out as the darling of the international resort scene; twenty-odd years later, wallflower Ixtapa and even quieter Zihuatanejo have almost managed to take their older sister's role. Today, most of the glitter has subsided, and Guerrero's beautiful colonial towns and Pacific beaches are almost as popular with budget travelers as those of the two states between which it is sandwiched.

Oaxaca, one of Mexico's economically poorer but culturally richer states, is fractured into a crazy quilt by the rugged heights of the Sierra Madre del Sur. Despite its intimidating terrain, the land has inspired a violent possessiveness in the many people—Zapotecs, Mixtecs, Aztecs, and Spaniards—who have fought each other over the area. More than 200 indigenous tribes have occupied the valley over the past two millennia. Over one million *oaxaqueños* still speak an *indígena* language as a mother tongue, and more than one-fifth of the state's population speaks no Spanish whatsoever. This language barrier, and the cultural gap which it symbolizes and exacerbates, has long caused tensions between the Oaxacan government and its indigenous population. Many *oaxaqueños*, disillusioned by the wrenching harshness of their lives, look favorably on the Zapatista revolt in neighboring Chiapas.

MICHOACÁN DE OCAMPO

◼ Uruapan

Surrounded by red soil, lush rolling hills, and rows upon rows of avocado trees, Uruapan (pronounced ur-WA-pan, pop. 300,000) sits amid a checkerboard of farmland. Farmers and their families come to Uruapan to sell their produce and to buy bags of fried plantains, wristwatches, and other necessities of modern life. Uruapan is no mere market town, though: thick traffic, smoggy air, and a Kentucky Fried Chicken indicate the city's development into a commercial center. Tourists come to the Uruapan in droves to explore the nearby waterfall, national park, and Paricutín Volcano.

Orientation Uruapan lies 120km west of Morelia and 320km southeast of Guadalajara. Everything in town is within easy walking distance of the *zócalo,* known as **Jardín de los Mártires** on its west side and **Jardín Morelos** on its east end. The statue in the center faces south, looking down **Cupatitzio. Emiliano Carranza** runs into the southwest corner of the square from the west, and **Obregón** is its continuation on the eastern side of the plaza. Don't let all the "Carranzas" fool you—**Venustiano**

Michoacán de Ocampo

Carranza runs into the *zócalo's* north side, and **Manuel Ocaranza** runs one block west of Cupatitzio into the plaza's south side. **Ocampo** runs along its western edge. To reach the center from the **bus station** on Benito Juárez in the northeast corner of town, hail a taxi (8 pesos) or hop aboard an "El Centro" bus (6am-9pm, 1.50 pesos).

Practical Information The **tourist office,** Ocampo 64 (tel. 3-61-72), on the basement level of the Hotel Plaza, provides a good map (open Mon.-Sat. 9am-2pm and 4-7pm, Sun. 9am-2pm). Good exchange rates and an **ATM** await at **Banca Serfín,** Cupatitzio 17 (tel. 3-54-11; open Mon.-Fri. 9am-2pm) and **Bancomer,** Carranza 7 (tel. 3-65-22; open Mon.-Fri. 8:30am-1:30pm, Sat. 10am-2pm). **LADATELs** line the plaza. Otherwise, make long-distance phone calls from **Computel,** Ocampo 3 (tel./fax 4-54-82), on the plaza (open daily 7am-10pm).

Buses leave from Benito Juárez, in the northeastern part of town, from the corner of Obregón and 5 de Febrero. To reach the station from the *zócalo*, take either the "Central Camionera" or "Central" bus (1.50 pesos). A cab to the station costs 8 pesos. **Elite** (tel. 3-44-50/-67) runs cushy first-class service to Mazatlán (5 and 7:30pm, 204 pesos), Mexico City (11:30pm, 6hr., 127 pesos), Monterrey (noon, 1, and 6:30pm, 15hr., 272 pesos), and San Luis Potosí (noon, 1, and 6:30pm, 8hr., 136 pesos). **Flecha Amarilla** (tel. 4-39-82) runs second-class buses to Aguascalientes (5:20, 7:40am, and 1pm, 8½hr., 99 pesos), Guadalajara (5 per day, 5hr., 72 pesos), Mexico City (7:30am, 7, and 10pm, 10hr., 113 pesos), Morelia (10 per day, 2hr., 31 pesos), Querétaro (5 per day, 6hr., 68 pesos), and San Luis Potosí (4pm and midnight, 9hr., 110 pesos). **La Línea** (tel. 3-18-71) is a good bet for Guadalajara (16 per day, 4½-6½hr., 59-72 pesos).

Transportes del Pacífico (tel. 7-03-73) goes to Tijuana (4 and 7pm, 36hr., 458 pesos) via Guadalajara (5hr., 69 pesos), Hermosillo (24hr., 393 pesos), and Nogales (27hr., 450 pesos). **ETN** (tel. 4-78-99) and **Primera Plus** (tel. 4-39-82) offer similar service. The station offers **luggage storage** (1.50 pesos per 3hr., 3 pesos per day; open daily 7am-midnight). The **train station** (tel. 4-09-81) is on Lázaro Cárdenas in the eastern part of town, and is accessible by the "Zapata" or "Zapata Revolución" buses.

A laundromat, **Autoservicio de Lavandería,** is on Emiliano Carranza 47 (tel. 3-26-69), at García, four blocks west of the *zócalo* (open Mon.-Sat. 9am-2pm and 4-8pm). Pharmacies rotate 24-hour shifts; call the Red Cross to find out which is on duty. **Farmacia Fénix,** Carranza 1 (tel. 4-16-40), is at Ocampo (open daily 8am-9pm). The **Red Cross,** Del Lago 1 (tel. 4-03-00), is a block down from the **Hospital Civil** on Calzada Fray Juan de San Miguel 6 (tel. 3-80-93), seven blocks west of the northern edge of the *zócalo* (both open 24hr.). The **police** (tel. 3-27-33) are at Eucaliptos and Naranjo. The **post office,** on Reforma 13 (tel. 3-56-30), is three blocks south of the *zócalo* on Cupatitzio and left one block (open Mon.-Fri. 8am-7pm, Sat 9am-1pm). **Postal Code: 60000. Telephone Code: 452.**

Accommodations Uruapan's cheaper hotels tend to be sleazy, with tattered bedspreads, filthy bathrooms, and a fraternity of jumbo *cucarachas* hosting 24-hour parties. Even worse, many of these inexpensive joints let rooms by the hour. Unless you're into prostitution, stay away from establishments oozing from the eastern edge of the *zócalo.* The best bargain in town is **Hotel Los Tres Caballeros,** Constitución 50 (tel. 4-71-70). Go north up Portal Santo Degollado, the eastern border of the *zócalo,* into the market for about two blocks; the hotel is on the right. Red tile floors and stone stairways give the place old world charm. Rooms are clean and loaded with furniture (singles 40 pesos; doubles 50 pesos). The posh **Hotel Regis,** Portal Carillo 12 (tel. 3-58-44 or 3-59-66), on the south side of the *zócalo,* offers spotless rooms, each with a TV, phone, and fan. Caged birds and sherbert-green walls covered with murals liven up the joint (singles 90 pesos; doubles 120 pesos; triples 135 pesos; quads 150 pesos; prices increase during high season). **Hotel Villa de Flores,** Carranza 15 (tel. 4-28-00), a block and a half from the *zócalo,* is reminiscent of an old Spanish hacienda with white stucco walls, tiled floors, black pillars, and iron lanterns. The hotel boasts massive, breezy rooms, tiled bathrooms overlooking a beautiful flower-filled courtyard, and a restaurant (singles 85 pesos; doubles 110 pesos; triples 120 pesos; quads 135 pesos).

Food Vendors at the **market** (half a block north of the *zócalo* on Constitución) and around the *zócalo* sell fresh fruit and delicious one-peso hotcakes for breakfast. Nearby **Mercado de Antojitos,** between Constitución and Pátzcuaro y Quiroga, is an outdoor square where you can sample Michoacán specialties for a pittance. Don't miss the green chile *tamales* (2 pesos; open daily 7am-11pm). Hotel restaurants are the most common option for a sit-down meal, and cafés specializing in coffees and desserts unleash their aromas up and down Carranza. Follow your nose to the **Café Tradicional de Uruapan,** Carranza 5-B, where locals sit sipping their *café* so slowly that they might lose a race with a Mexican train. Dining here is like sitting inside a cigar box—the café's entire surface area is covered in richly stained wood, from the wood bannisters to the checkered ceilings and floors. Specialties are breakfast, snacks, and coffee. *Huevos rancheros* 11 pesos, *capuchino* 6.50 pesos (open daily 8:30am-10pm). The delightful **Comedor Vegetariano,** Aldama 14 at Morelos, a block south and a block east of the *zócalo,* serves cheap and delicious *tortas* (4 pesos), fruit and yogurt (7 pesos), and juices (4 pesos; open daily 8am-8pm).

Sights and Entertainment If you don't have time to catch the natural wonders surrounding Uruapan, the **Parque Nacional Barranca del Cupatitzio** (tel. 4-01-97), at the western end of Independencia, fringes the town with a bit of jungle, a gurgling river, and frothy waterfalls. Endless, dense green bush is split by the Río Cupatitzio and cool, shaded cobblestone walkways. The park makes for an excellent afternoon walk or picnic (open daily 8am-6pm; admission 2 pesos, children 1 peso). Uruapan's other big attraction is the **Museo Regional de Arte Popular** (tel. 4-34-34), on the *zócalo,* which displays Michoacán crafts (open Tues.-Sun. 9:30am-1:30pm and 3:30-6pm; free).

At night, Uruapan comes out to play. **La Scala Disco,** Madrid 12 (tel. 4-26-09), in Colonia Huerta del Cupatitzio, is a bit outside of town on the road to Tzaráracua and an 8-peso cab ride from the center of town. Local youths dance to U.S. Top-40 mixed with Mexican dance music (cover Tues.-Thurs. 10 pesos, Fri. 15 pesos, Sat. 20 pesos; open Tues.-Fri. 9pm-2am). Nearer the *zócalo* is **La Kashba,** Ocampo 64 (tel. 3-37-00), in the Hotel Plaza, where a post-collegiate crowd dances to live salsa and rock music. Comedy shows begin at 11pm (cover 15-30 pesos; open Tues.-Sun. 9:30pm-4am). For a more low-key evening, saunter over to **Club 1910,** Cupatitzio 5 (tel. 3-20-25), less than a block from the *zócalo,* for some pool (11 pesos per hour) or dominoes (6 pesos per hour; open daily 10am-11pm).

∎ Near Uruapan

PARICUTÍN VOLCANO

A visit to the beautiful, black, and still-active Paricutín Volcano makes a great daytrip from Uruapan. In 1943, the volcano began erupting. By the time it quit spewing lava eight years later, there was little dust left to settle—the land had been coated in a thick and hardening layer of porous lava. Along the way, entire towns had been consumed and a 700m dark-side-of-the-moon sort of mountain had sprung up. In one area, the lava covered the entire village of San Juan except for the church steeple, which now sticks out of a field of cold, black stone. At the Angahuan Centro Turístico (tel. 452-03-83), you can rent horses and a guide to ascend the volcano (75 pesos). Before you do, however, reconcile yourself to some serious haggling and some serious saddle sores—wooden saddles are the rule here. Allow at least four or five hours for a guided trip or for a journey into the valley to see the steeple. Decathlon contenders may consider the six- to eight-hour walking tours (30-40 pesos).

Getting There: Paraíso Galeana buses (tel. 4-00-90) headed for Los Reyes run to Paricutín and nearby Angahuán (every 30min. 5am-7:45pm, 40min., 6 pesos).

SAN JUAN NUEVO PARANGARICUTIRO

Ten kilometers west of Uruapan is the new **San Juan,** formed after the burial of the old village with the eruption of the Paricutín Volcano in 1934. Many devotees come to the village to see the **Lord of Miracles,** an image of Christ dating back to the late 16th century. The image is revered for answering countless prayers and miracles. When the volcano erupted, San Juan's 2000 inhabitants abandoned the village and began a three day, 33km pilgrimage carrying their beloved Lord of Miracles. A beautiful rose brick **sanctuary** with blue and yellow tile *capillas* was eventually built to

---

Heart of Darkness

At Uruapan's Parque Nacional Barranca del Cupatitzio, young children will give you a tour of **La Rodilla del Diablo** (The Devil's Knee) for a small fee. Legend has it that the river at one time dried up, leaving the surrounding lands stark and bare. The village prayed in silent desperation, left without food or water. One day, the friar Juan de San Miguel led a procession to the river's parched mouth, carrying an image of the Virgin. The friar halted the procession to sprinkle some holy water on the Virgin's image and on the rocks at the river's mouth. Suddenly, Satan appeared, saw the Virgin, and with a tumultuous shaking of the earth, retreated into the rocks, resuming the flow of water. One rock still bears the imprint of the knee of the *Príncipe de las Tinieblas* (Prince of Darkness).

house the image. The interior's white and pale green walls and vaulted ceilings are adorned with gold leafing, delicate stained glass windows, and sparkling chandeliers. A colorful mural depicts the eruption of the Paricutín volcano. Ask Eloise at the information booth out front for a tour (open daily 6am-8pm; to avoid mass visit Mon.-Sat. 1-5:30pm and 6:30-8pm, Sun. 6:30-8pm). The **Museo del Volcán,** Av. 20 de Noviembre, around the corner from the sanctuary, exhibits photos depicting the volcano's eruption, as well as before and after shots of the village (open Mon.-Sat. 9:15am-7pm, Sun. 9:15-6:30pm; free).

Getting There: Take a **Galeana** (tel. 4-00-90) bus to San Juan Nuevo (every 10min. 5am-9:30pm, 30min., 3.50 pesos).

TZARÁRACUA AND TZARARECUITA

The waterfalls at **Tzaráracua** (sah-RA-ra-kwa), 10km from Uruapan, cascade 20m into a series of small pools, surrounded by dense lush vegetation. The first waterfall, Tzaráracua, is about 1km from the small parking lot—walk or ride a horse through steep, tree-lined paths (guides and horses await tourists at the lot). Expect to pay 25 pesos for a roundtrip to the first waterfall. You can also hoof it to the waterfall on foot—the path descends a flight of cobbled stairs and culminates at the base of the falls after about 20 minutes. Look but don't swim; there's a dangerous undercurrent. A worker will take you over the water in a suspended boxcar (2 pesos).

Tzararecuita, a privately owned waterfall with two smaller pollution-free pools that are perfect for swimming, is another 1.5km beyond the large pool. Rumor has it that the owner doesn't mind visitors to the falls and that skinny-dipping is popular. Watch out for peepers and keep an eye on your clothes. The aid of a guide is necessary to find the falls. Guides don't charge a set fee but expect a generous tip.

Getting There: "Tzaráracua" buses leave from the south side of the *zócalo* at the corner of Emiliano Carranza and Cupatitzio (every hr. 8am-5pm, 2.50 pesos). During the week the schedule is so imprecise that you could be stuck there all day; Sundays are a bit more reliable. Taxis cost about 20 pesos.

PARACHO

Thirty kilometers north of Uruapan, **Paracho** gives aspiring *guitarristas* a chance to strum their hearts out and unleash the *mariachi* within. Carefully crafted six-strings pack just about every store. Fantastic bargains are available for all varieties of guitar. In the first week of August the town holds an internationally renowned **guitar festival.** Musicians and craftspeople partake in a **musical orgy** that includes classical concerts, fireworks, dancing, and guitar-strumming competitions.

Getting There: Hop on a **Galeana** (tel. 4-00-90) bus bound for Zamora via Paracho (every 15min. 4am-8:30pm, 45min., 7 pesos) from the Central Camionera.

▓ Pátzcuaro

Michoacán's earthy jewel, Pátzcuaro (pop. 70,000) is slowly becoming a travelers' favorite. Set high in the mountaintops, the city is surrounded by land that bends and lilts, rolling up and over hills and extending to the shores of Lake Pátzcuaro. The city center is nearly as striking as the surrounding landscape—the tolling of the bells resonates through charming cobblestone streets and white stucco colonial style buildings. But Pátzcuaro is best known for its crafts. In order to further economic development, the Spanish bishop Vasco de Quiroga encouraged residents of each Purépecha village around the lake to specialize in a different craft. Today the plazas overflow with stacks of locally produced woolen sweaters, meticulously carved wooden toys, and decorative masks.

ORIENTATION

Pátzcuaro lies 56km southwest of Morelia and 62km northeast of Uruapan. To reach the *centro* from the **bus station,** catch a *combi* (7am-9:30pm, 1.50 pesos) or city bus (6:30am-10pm, 1.20 pesos) from the lot to the right as you leave the station. A taxi costs 10 pesos. The city consists of two distinct areas: the downtown, perched on a hill, and a residential part of town 2.5km to the north, fronting the lake. Downtown centers around Pátzcuaro's two main squares. The smaller **Plaza Bocanegra** is all bustle and thick crowds; it is bordered by **Padre Lloreda** to the north, **Dr. Bendito Mendoza** to the west, and **Iturbide** to the east. One block south on Dr. Benito Mendoza is the larger **Plaza Quiroga,** an elegant and quiet plaza with a fountain and well shaded, rosebush-lined paths. Streets form a rough grid, changing names at each plaza. Addresses on the plazas are not given with the street name, but rather with the name of the *portal* (arcade). For example, at Plaza Quiroga, Benito Mendoza, which borders the plaza's western side, becomes **Portal Hidalgo.** Summers in Pátzcuaro can be wet and cool, so bring along some raingear and a light sweater.

PRACTICAL INFORMATION

Tourist Office: Delegación Regional de Turismo, Ibarra 2, Int. 4 (tel. 2-12-14), at Benito Mendoza, just past the northwest corner of Plaza Quiroga. It's in the medical building; the office is the 3rd door on the right in the courtyard. Helpful staff hands out a good map. Some English spoken. Open Mon.-Sat. 9am-3pm and 4-7pm, Sun. 9am-2pm. A smaller **information booth** is on Pl. Bocanegra, next to the library. No English spoken. Open Mon.-Sat. 10am-2pm and 4-6pm.

Currency Exchange: Banca Serfín, Portal Morelos 54, on the north side of Plaza Quiroga, has an **ATM** (open for exchange Mon.-Fri. 9am-2pm). **Sociedad Cambiaria Pátzcuaro,** Benito Mendoza 7 (tel. 2-02-40), also changes dollars. Open Mon.-Fri. 9am-4:30pm, Sat.-Sun. 10am-2pm.

Telephones: No **LADATELs** in town. **Computel,** (tel./fax 2-27-56), Padre Llorona, on Pl. Bocanegra. The *caseta* in the Posada de la Rosa has better rates and doesn't charge a fee for collect calls to the U.S.

Telegrams: Telecomm, Títere 15-A (tel. 2-18-00 or 2-12-25; fax 2-00-10), near the library. Open Mon.-Fri. 8am-6pm, Sat. 9am-noon.

Buses: Off Circunvalación, south of town. **Herradura de Plata** (tel. 2-10-45) runs to Mexico City (first-class 7 per day 9:15am-12:30am, 5hr., 105 pesos; second-class 8 per day 7:35am-11pm, 7hr., 85 pesos). **Galeana** (tel. 2-08-08) goes to Lázaro Cárdenas (every 2hr. 8am-7pm, 7hr., 70 pesos), Morelia (every 15min., 1hr., 10 pesos), Santa Clara del Cobre (every 30min., 25min., 3 pesos), and Uruapan (every 10min., 1hr., 15 pesos). **Primera Plus** (tel. 2-01-70) serves Guadalajara (11:30pm, 5hr., 70 pesos), Mexico City (8, 11:30am, and 1:45pm, 7hr., 105 pesos), Querétaro (4 per day noon-11:15pm, 7hr., 53 pesos), and San Luis Potosí (6:20am and 7pm, 8hr., 16 pesos). **Autobuses de Occidente** (tel. 2-00-92) sends buses to Guadalajara (noon, 5hr., 70 pesos). **Elite** (tel. 2-14-60) goes to Nuevo Laredo (1 and 7:45pm, 16hr., 330 pesos) via Monterrey (12hr., 259 pesos).

Trains: (tel. 2-08-03), at the bottom of Av. de las Américas, near the lakefront.

Luggage Storage: At the bus station. 3 pesos per 1½hr., 6 pesos per day.

Public Library: On Pl. Bocanegra in the Ex-Templo de San Agustín. Small selection of English books. Open Mon.-Fri. 9am-7pm.

Laundromat: Lavandería Automática, Terán 14 (tel. 2-39-39), two blocks west of Plaza Quiroga. Open Mon.-Sat. 9am-2pm and 4-8pm.

Pharmacy: Principal, Benito Mendoza 1. Open daily 9am-10pm. **Farmacia del Carmen** (tel. 2-26-52), at the corner of Romero and Navarrete. Open 24hr. Doors open daily 8am-10pm, after hours knock at the window on Navarrete.

Hospital: Romero 10 (tel. 2-02-85), next to the San Juan de Dios church.

Emergency: Cuerpo de Rescate, Calle Benito Juárez 88 (tel. 2-10-91), near the Santuario. Some doctors speak English. Open 24hr.

Police: (tel. 2-00-04), corner of Ibarra and Tangara, four blocks from Pl. Quiroga.

Post Office: Obregón 13 (tel. 2-01-28), half a block north of Plaza Bocanegra. Open Mon.-Fri. 8am-7pm, Sat. 9am-1pm. **Postal Code:** 61600.
Telephone Code: 434.

ACCOMMODATIONS

Pátzcuaro is home to just enough hotels to accommodate its small tourist industry. Rooms tend to be adequately kept and well priced. Expect to lodge with large numbers of Mexican, European, and some American travelers.

Hotel Valmen, Lloreda 34 (tel. 2-11-61), one block east of Plaza Bocanegra. Popular with international travelers. A great deal if you don't mind a mushy bed. Vibrant Aztec tile and squawking birds fill the lime-green courtyards. Well lit rooms, some with balconies. Plumbing is a bit erratic. Strict lock-out 10pm. Reserve 2 weeks in advance. 35 pesos per person.

Posada de la Salud, Serrato 9 (tel. 2-00-58), three blocks east of either plaza, half a block past the basilica. Beautiful courtyard draped in tropical scarlet flowers, gorgeous carved furniture, cloud-soft mattresses, and clean bathrooms. Rooms can be cold and damp during the rainy season. Singles 45 pesos. Doubles 80 pesos.

Posada de la Rosa, Portal Juárez 29 (tel. 2-08-11), on the west side of Pl. Bocanegra. Red tiles and lots of sunlight. Simple, musty rooms have a lone lightbulb hanging from the ceiling. Ask for a room overlooking the plaza. Singles and doubles 40 pesos, with bath 50 pesos.

FOOD

Pescado blanco is the most popular dish in Pátzcuaro. *Charales* (smelts), served in the restaurants along the lakefront and on Janitzio, are fried, sardine-like fish which are eaten whole and by the fistful. *Caldos de pescado* (fish broths) bubble in large clay vats outside open-air restaurants on Janitzio; loaded with fish, shrimp, crab, or squid, these spicy soups are a meal in themselves. Most of the restaurants by the docks close at 7pm. More formal restaurants ring Plaza Quiroga, while the cheaper, more casual joints cluster around Plaza Bocanegra and the market.

El Buho, Tejerías 8 (tel. 2-14-39), two blocks east of Pl. Bocanegra. Pottery, wood chairs, little flowers on each table, and splashes of Chaplin and Marilyn Monroe on the walls. A down-to-earth sort of place, popular with both backpackers and young locals. Burritos 12 pesos. Small pizza 25 pesos. Open daily 8am-10pm during the summer, December, and *Semana Santa.* Otherwise open daily 5-10pm.

Dany's Restaurant Cafetería, Dr. Mendoza 30, between Pl. Quiroga and Pl. Bocanegra. Filled with ferns, plaid tablecloths, masks, oil paintings, and half of Pátzcuaro. Live organ music keeps 'em hoppin'. 3 *quesadillas* with beans 15 pesos. Breakfast combos 19 pesos. Open daily 8am-10pm.

Restaurant El Patio, Plaza Quiroga 19 (tel. 2-04-84), on the south side of the plaza. Pricey, but the food is good and the ambience pleasant. The sophisticated decor blends still-lifes, empty wine bottles, and pillars of rough stone. Breakfasts 12-22 pesos. Fish 25-40 pesos. *Comida corrida* 25 pesos. Open daily 8am-10pm.

Restaurant Posada la Basílica, Arciga 6 (tel. 2-11-08), in front of the basilica. A flowery courtyard leads to an elegant room with tiled floors, colorful tablecloths, and windows overlooking the town and nearby lakes. Steak *a la Mexicana* 17 pesos. Open Wed.-Mon. 8am-4pm.

SIGHTS

Pátzcuaro's unique handcrafts—hairy Tócuaro masks, elegant Sierran dinnerware, and thick wool textiles—are sold in Plaza Bocanegra's **market** and in the small shops along the passage next to Biblioteca Gertrudis Bocanegra. Bargaining is easier in the market or when you buy more than one item, but don't expect much of a discount on the stunningly handsome wool articles. The thick sweaters, brilliantly colored *saltillos* and *ruanas* (stylized ponchos), rainbow-colored *sarapes*, and dark shawls are Pátzcuaro's specialty. Most shops are open daily 8am to 8pm.

Down the street from the basilica, on Lerín near Navarette, is the **Casa de Artesanías** (a.k.a. La Casa de los Once Patios, so named for the 18th century building's eleven patios). Originally a convent for Dominican nuns, the complex now houses craft shops, a small gallery of modern Mexican art, and a mural depicting Vasco de Quiroga's accomplishments. The *casa* sells cotton textiles and superb musical instruments (guitars, flutes, and *güiros*) at decent prices (guitars 150-700 pesos; open daily roughly 10am-2pm and 4-7pm). The **Museo Regional de Artes Populares** (tel. 2-10-29), one block south of the basilica at the corner of Lerín and Alcanterillas, is housed within old fort-like walls, stone floors, and a flower-filled arcaded courtyard. It displays pottery, copperware, and textiles, as well as an arresting collection of *maque* and *laca* ceramics (open Tues.-Sat. 9am-8pm, Sun. 9am-3pm; admission 7 pesos, free on Sun. and for children under 13).

When the Spanish bishop Vasco de Quiroga came to Pátzcuaro, he initiated not only social change but bold architectural projects as well. Quiroga conceived the **Basílica de Nuestra Señora de la Salud,** at Lerín and Serrato, as a colossal structure with five naves arranged like the fingers of an extended hand. Each finger was to represent one of Michoacán's cultures and races, with the hand's palm as the central altar representing the Catholic religion. Today the basilica features a grandiose Romanesque altar. Intricate frescoed arabesques cross the high, concave ceiling of the church, forming impressive vaults. An enormous glass booth with gilded Corinthian columns and a dome protects the statue of the *Virgen de la Salud;* when Vasco de Quiroga asked Tarascan artisans to design an image of the Virgin in 1546, they complied by shaping her out of *tatzingue* paste made from corn cobs and orchid honey, a typical 16th-century statue-making technique. Native groups had used this method to create idols of their own gods before the Conquest and continued the practice to mold the images of the Virgin and saints. The resulting statue is durable and incredibly light, weighing only 5 kilograms (open daily 8am-8pm).

Statues of Pátzcuaro's two most honored citizens stand vigil over the town's principal plazas. The ceremonious, banner-bearing Vasco de Quiroga inhabits **Plaza Quiroga,** a vast and well forested space which seems more like a humble city zoo than a *zócalo*. The massive, bare-breasted Gertrudis Bocanegra looks out from the center of **Plaza Gertrudis Bocanegra.** A martyr for Mexican independence, Bocanegra was executed by a Spanish squadron in the Plaza Quiroga in October of 1817. Locals claim that bullet holes still mark the ash tree to which she was tied.

Biblioteca Gertrudis Bocanegra, on the plaza of the same name, occupies the former site of an Augustine convent. The library's multicolored mural, *La Historia de Michoacán,* by Juan O' Gorman, illustrates the history of the Purépecha civilization from pre-Hispanic times to the 1910 Revolution (open Mon.-Fri. 9am-7pm). When the adjacent **Teatro Caltzontzín,** once part of the Augustinian convent, became a theater in 1936, an as-yet-unfulfilled prophecy was uttered: one Holy Thursday, the theater will crumble as punishment for the sin of projecting movies in a sacred place. Catch a Mexican or U.S. film...if you dare (admission 5 pesos).

Three kilometers east of the city, at the end of Av. Benigno Serrato, is **El Humilladero** (Place of Humiliation), where the cowardly king Tangaxhuán II surrendered his crown and his daughters to Cristóbal de Olid and his Spanish troops. Two peculiar features distinguish this chapel: on its altar stands a rare monolithic cross, undoubtedly older than the date inscribed on its base (1553); and on the chapel's façade are images of gods which represent the sun and the moon. To reach it, take a *combi* marked "Panteón" or "El Cristo" (1.50 pesos).

ENTERTAINMENT AND SEASONAL EVENTS

Aside from chilling in restaurants, there isn't much to do in Pátzcuaro at night. The off-beat **El Viejo Gaucho,** Iturbe 10 (tel. 2-03-68), a colorful Argentinian bar and restaurant with mask and painting exhibitions, features live Andean music, dramatic readings, and an open mike. Burgers (12-15 pesos), thick-crusted pizzas (20-35 pesos), and delicious *empanadas* (5 pesos each) entertain the tastebuds (cover 10 pesos per person; open Tues.-Sun. 5pm-2am). A young crowd hangs out and listens to tunes at **El Rincón Video Café,** on Quiroga just east of Plaza Quiroga's northeast corner (open Tues.-Sun. 5-11pm). At **Charanda's N,** Plaza Vasco de Quiroga 61B, an eclectic crowd gathers amid white walls decorated with fanciful etchings and salamanders. Live music stirs things up on weekends (cover weekends 8-11pm; open Tues.-Sun. noon-1am).

Pátzcuaro hosts several fantastic fiestas during the year. Soon after Christmas celebrations come to a close, the town is electrified by **pastorelas,** celebrated on January 6 to commemorate the Adoration of the Magi, and on January 17 to honor St. Anthony of Abad, the patron saint of animals. On both occasions, citizens dress their domestic animals in bizarre costumes, ribbons, and floral crowns. A few months later, Pátzcuaro's *Semana Santa* attracts devotees from all over the Republic. On Thursday, all the churches in town are visited to accompany the Nazareth, and on the night of Good Friday, the **Procesión de Imágenes de Cristo** is held, during which images of a crucified Christ are carried around town. The faithful flock from all over the state on Saturday for Pátzcuaro's **Procesión del Silencio,** celebrated everywhere else the day before. On this day, a crowd marches around town mourning Jesus's death in silence. Pátzcuaro and the surrounding regions party down with religious fervor on Sunday. Along with *Semana Santa,* the most important celebration of the year is **Noche de Muertos** (Nov. 1-2), which holds special importance for the Tarascans. Candle-clad fishing boats row out to Janitzio on the first night, heralding the start of a two-night vigil in the graveyard. The first night commemorates lost children; the second remembers deceased adults.

■ Near Pátzcuaro

AROUND LAGO DE PÁTZCUARO

The tiny island of **Janitzio,** inhabited exclusively by Tarascan *indígenas* who speak the Purépecha dialect, subsists on its tourist trade. There are basically two directions in Janitzio—up and down. The town's steep main street is lined with stores selling woolen goods, hand-carved wooden chess sets, masks, and assorted knick-knacks. Between the shops, the bulk of which are quite pricey, numerous restaurants offer *pescado blanco* and *charales.* A low hill towers over the island; atop it is a statue of Morelos so big it can be seen clearly from Pátzcuaro. Inside the statue, a mural traces the principal events in Morelos's life and the struggle for independence that he led. Morelos may not hold the world in the palm of his hand, but you can certainly see the world from his sleeve. Endless steps lead you to this fantastic lookout point. There are two paths to the monument—one steep, and one steeper (which is more direct); both are to your left as you leave the market.

Getting There: First, hop on a "Lago" *combi* or bus at the corner of Portal Regules and Portal Juárez, at Plaza Bocanegra in Pátzcuaro (1.50 pesos). At the docks, buy a ferry ticket (ferries leave whenever they're full, about every 10min. 8am-7pm on weekends and every 20min. during the week, 40min., 16 pesos roundtrip). Find out when the last boat leaves the island for Pátzcuaro, as Janitzio does not accommodate the stranded.

TZINTZUNTZÁN

The most exciting thing about **Tzintzuntzán** (Place of the Hummingbirds) is saying the name—it is believed to be the phonetic sound of the many **hummingbirds** that flit through the sky. Tzintzuntzán was the last great city of the Tarascan empire. Before his death in the middle of the 15th century, the Purépecha lord Tariácori divided his empire among his three sons. When the empire was reunited some years later, Tzintzuntzán was chosen as its capital. Today, its claims to fame are the delicate, multi-colored **ceramics** displayed on tables along Calle Principal.

The **Yácatas,** a peculiar pre-Hispanic temple, sits on a hill just outside the city on the road to Pátzcuaro. To reach the entrance, walk up the street in front of the market and convent. It's a bit of a hike—follow the road all the way around the hill until you reach the small museum/ticket booth. The bases of the structures, all that remain today, are standard rectangular pyramids. The missing parts of the *yácatas,* however, are what made them unique; each was originally crowned with an unusual elliptical pyramid constructed of shingles and volcanic rock. The pyramids are situated along the long edge of an artificial terrace. Each building represents a bird. At the edge of the hill overlooking the lake is a sacrificial block from which victims were hurled; the bones of thousands of victims lie at the base. The **museum** at the entrance includes some Mesoamerican pottery, jewelry, and a narrative of Tarascan history (site open daily 9am-6pm; admission 10 pesos, free Sun.). Also of interest is the 16th-century Franciscan **convent** closer to town. The olive shrubs that now smother the extensive, tree-filled atrium were originally planted under Vasco de Quiroga's instructions over 450 years ago (open daily 10am-8pm).

Getting There: Tzintzuntzán is perched on the northeastern edge of the Lago de Pátzcuaro, about 15km from Pátzcuaro on the road to Quiroga and Morelia. Second-class **Galeana** (tel. 2-08-08) buses leave the Pátzcuaro bus station for Tzintzuntzán (every 15min. 6am-8:30pm, 30min., 3.50 pesos) en route to Quiroga.

SANTA CLARA DEL COBRE

Santa Clara del Cobre, 16km south of Pátzcuaro, truly shines when it comes to crafting copper. Long ago, rich copper mines filled the area, but they were hidden from the Spanish during the Conquest, never to be found again. The townspeople's passion for copperwork is unrivaled. When electricity was brought to the town, blackouts occurred when the artisans hammered the wires into pots and pans. Nearly every store in town sells unique decorative copper plates, pans, bowls, and bells. Prices here are only slightly better than elsewhere in Mexico, but Santa Clara is unbeatable for quality and variety. For a quick look at some highly imaginative pieces, step into the **Museo del Cobre,** near the plaza. Santa Clara celebrates the **Feria del Cobre** in early August. Like Quiroga, there is little to see in Santa Clara beyond *artesanías;* budget only a couple of hours for a trip here from Pátzcuaro.

Getting There: Take a **Galeana** bus (every 30min. 7am-8pm, 20min., 4-5 pesos).

LAGO DE ZIRAHUÉN

If you're into camping, the **Lago de Zirahuén** (Where Smoke Rose) makes for a fun trip from Pátzcuaro. Smaller than Lake Pátzcuaro, Zirahuén is bordered by green farmland and gently sloping hills unobstructed by marshes and islands. On weekends, the lakefront fills with locals in search of a *tranquilo* place to relax. To **camp,** hike up one of the ridges that border the lake and set up in any one of the spots overlooking the water; if the land is privately owned (usually fenced off), you may have to pay a few pesos. A choice spot is the sizeable piece of lakefront on the west (left, as you face the lake) end of town. The strip, about 15m wide, is covered by grass cut short by grazing horses and is near a *colonia,* a poor community of little wooden houses. The *cabañas,* a five-minute walk to the right along the dirt road bordering the lake, allow campers to use the bathrooms for one peso. Be forewarned: heavy afternoon rains during June and July can turn summer camping into a soggy experience. For those not inclined towards camping, the only other lodging options are the beautiful but pricey lakefront *cabañas* (tel. 431-227-01/05; fax 15-04-91; 2 people 230 pesos; 4 people 345 pesos; prices increase during high season).

After roughing it in the great outdoors, head to the *lancha* dock for a silky smooth one-hour ride around the lake (15 pesos in a collective boat; 120 pesos for a private ride, up to 10 people), then sit down at one of informal lakefront restaurants, where a stack of tortillas, rice, salad, and fresh white fish will run you a mere 10 pesos.

Getting There: From Pátzcuaro, catch one of the Zirahuén-bound cabs from Obregón and Industrial, past the post office, a block north of Plaza Bocanegra (about every 20min. 8am-6pm, 7 pesos). Cabs returning to Pátzcuaro leave a block inland from the church at "La Posta," by the "Marilu" sign (about 7 pesos).

■ Morelia

The capital of Michoacán, Morelia (pop. 500,000) drifts in and out of the 20th century like a busy, dizzy honeybee caught between two equally scrumptious hunks of *pan dulce*. Vendors hawk extension cords and Chicago Bulls caps in the crowded *centro;* nearby stand incongruous relics of Morelia's colonial magnificence—rose-colored stone arcades and grand, white-washed houses. Swollen with bureaucrats and students, the city sometimes feels like an over-sized flea market glutted with *norteamericano* mass-culture. However, its bustling, eminently habitable spirit and sophisticated air charm visitors without drawing crowds of tourists.

ORIENTATION

The streets in Morelia form a large grid, so navigating the city is relatively uncomplicated. Most sights are within walking distance of the *zócalo* and the adjacent cathedral on **Av. Madero,** Morelia's main thoroughfare. North-south streets change name at Madero, while east-west street change name every other block.

Getting downtown from the **bus station** requires a 10-minute walk. Walk to the left (east) as you exit the building, take the first right onto Valentín Gómez Farías, walk three blocks, then make a left on Av. Madero—the *zócalo* is three blocks ahead. A taxi to the *centro* costs eight to 10 pesos.

Buses and *combis* serve the city (daily 6am-10pm, 1.30 pesos). Most routes can be picked up on Nigromante and Galeana, one block west of the *zócalo* and on Allende, south of the *zócalo*. Taxis cluster in front of the bus station. It is not a good idea to walk around after 10pm, especially on streets parallel to Madero.

PRACTICAL INFORMATION

Tourist Offices: State Tourist Office, Nigromante 79 (tel. 17-23-71), at Madero Pte., 2 blocks west of the *zócalo*. Friendly staff distributes maps and a monthly list of cultural events. Free city tours with 1 week's notice. Open daily 9am-3pm.
Currency Exchange: Banks cluster on Av. Madero. **Bancomer,** Madero Ote. 21 (tel. 12-29-90). Excellent rates. Open Mon.-Fri. 8:30am-1:30pm. **BITAL,** Madero Ote. 24 (tel 13-98-00). Open Mon-Fri. 8am-7pm, Sat. 9am-2:30pm.
Telephones: Credit card-operated **LADATELs** are at Pino Suárez and Serdán, 1 block east of the *zócalo*. 24-hr. long-distance *caseta* in the bus station, but no collect calls. **Computel,** Portal Galeana 157 (tel./fax 13-62-56), on the *zócalo*. **Fax** service. Open daily 7am-10pm.
Telegrams: Av. Madero Ote. 371 (tel. 12-06-45), in the Palacio Federal next to the post office. Open Mon.-Fri. 8am-6pm, Sat. 9am-noon.
Airport: Aeropuerto Francisco J. Múgica (tel. 13-67-80), on the Carretera Morelia-Cinapécuaro at marker km27. **Mexicana,** Pirinda 435 (tel. 24-38-28, -08, -18). Open Mon.-Fri. 9am-6:30pm. **Taesa,** Av. Acueducto 60 (tel. 17-09-81). Open Mon.-Fri. 9am-2pm and 4-7pm, Sat. 9am-1pm. **Aeromar** (tel. 12-85-45 and 13-05-55). All have offices at the airport. Taxi (tel. 12-22-21) to the airport 70 pesos.
Buses: Leave from the station (tel. 13-55-89), on Ruiz at V. Gómez Farías. **Herradura de Plata** (tel. 12-29-88) to Mexico City (first-class 13 per day 12:30am-11pm, 4¼hr., 85 pesos; *plus* every 45min. midnight-11:30pm, 4hr., 95 pesos). **Flecha Amarilla** (tel. 13-55-89) goes to Colima (8am and noon, 6½hr., 86 pesos), Guanajuato (6 per day 6:10am-4:10pm, 4hr., 41pesos), Querétaro (14 per day 12:30am-11:30pm, 4hr., 37 pesos), and San Luis Potosí (8 per day 3:50am-8:30pm, 6hr., 80

pesos). **Ruta Paraíso/Galeana** (tel. 12-55-05) goes to Pátzcuaro (every 10min. 6am-9pm, 1hr., 14 pesos), Lázaro Cárdenas (every hr. 6:40am-7:50pm, 8hr., 87 pesos), and Uruapan (every 20min. 6am-9pm, 2¼hr., 31 pesos). **Elite** (tel. 12-24-62) provides first-class service to Acapulco (5 per day 7am-2:30am, 12hr., 186 pesos), Nuevo Laredo (3, 6, and 9:30pm, 16hr., 316 pesos) via Monterrey (13hr., 244 pesos), Reynosa (5pm, 16hr., 269 pesos) via San Luis Potosí (6hr., 100 pesos), and Tijuana (1, 4:40, 9, and 11:45pm, 40hr., 591 pesos) via Mazatlán (16hr., 216 pesos). **Transportes Fronteras** (tel. 12-24-62) serves Cd. Juárez (10:30am, 24hr., 423 pesos) via Zacatecas (9hr., 125 pesos). **Primera Plus** (tel. 13-55-89) runs first-class buses to Aguascalientes (5 per day 2:30am-3:05pm, 6hr., 94 pesos) and San Luis Potosí (8 per day 12:15am-11:20pm, 6hr., 99 pesos). **Servicios Coordinados** (tel. 13-55-89) serves Guadalajara (7 per day 1am-6pm, 5hr., 76 pesos) and Querétaro (12 per day 5:20am-7:20pm, 3½hr., 42 pesos). **Autobuses de Occidente** (tel. 12-06-00) serves Manzanillo (5 per day 6:55am-1am, 10hr., 109 pesos) and Mexico City (every 20min. 5am-5pm, 6hr., 77 pesos). **ETN** (tel. 13-74-40) has executive service to Mexico City (24 per day 2am-midnight, 4¼hr., 125 pesos).

Trains: (tel. 16-39-65), on Av. del Periodismo.

Laundromat: Lavandería Cuautla, Cuautla 152 (tel. 12-48-06), south of Madero. 15 pesos per 3kg. Open Mon.-Fri. 9am-2pm and 4-8pm, Sat. 9am-1:30pm.

Red Cross: Ventura 27 (tel. 14-51-51 or 14-50-25), next to Parque Cuauhtémoc. Some English spoken. Open 24hr.

Pharmacy: Farmacia Fénix, Allende 69 (tel. 12-84-92), behind the *zócalo.* Open Mon.-Sat. 9am-9pm, Sun. 9am-8:30pm. Red Cross has a **24-hr. pharmacy** (tel. 14-51-51, ext. 18).

Hospital: Hospital General Dr. Miguel Silva (tel. 12-22-16), Isidro Huarte and F. de Mogil. No English spoken. Open 24hr.

Emergency: Dial 06.

Police: (tel. 13-74-37 and 26-33-33), on 20 de Noviembre, 1 block northwest of the Fuente de las Tarascas at the end of the aqueduct. No English spoken. Open 24hr.

Post Office: Av. Madero Ote. 369 (tel. 12-05-17), in the Palacio Federal, 5 blocks east of the cathedral. Open Mon.-Fri. 8am-7pm. **Postal Code:** 58000.

Telephone Code: 43.

ACCOMMODATIONS

Most budget hotels lie south of Madero and just west of the cathedral. The only time you may have trouble finding a room is during *Semana Santa,* although there is a slight influx of summer school students during July and August.

IMJUDE Villa Juvenil Youth Hostel, Chiapas 180 (tel. 13-31-77), at Oaxaca. A 20-min. walk from the *zócalo.* Walk west on Madero Pte., turn left on Cuautla, walk for 6 blocks, then turn right on Oaxaca and continue for 4 blocks to Chiapas. Very happening for a Mexican youth hostel. Exceptionally well maintained dormitories, bathrooms, and red-tiled lobby. Sports facilities and pool. 25 pesos per person. 20-peso linen deposit. Breakfast 10 pesos, lunch and dinner 13 pesos. Curfew 11pm. Open daily 7am-11pm.

Mansión Posada Don Vasco, Vasco de Quiroga 232 (tel. 12-14-84), 2 blocks east and 1½ blocks south of the cathedral. Cheery guests and friendly atmosphere. Rooms come with cable TV, telephones, wood furniture, and purified water. Basic rooms 50 pesos for 1 person, 60 pesos for 2. Posh rooms 78 pesos for 1 person, 92 pesos for 2, 106 pesos for 3, 121 pesos for 4. Reserve 2 weeks ahead.

Hotel Mintzicuri, Vasco de Quiroga 227 (tel. 12-06-64), across from the Posada Don Vasco. Wrought iron railings overflowing with flowers enclose cozy, wood-paneled rooms equipped with phones, cable TV, and hot water. Singles 78 pesos. Doubles 92 pesos. Triples 106 pesos. Quads 121 pesos.

Hotel Colonial, 20 de Noviembre 15 (tel. 12-18-97). Cozy courtyard glows a deep yellow. Friendly staff. Rooms boast high ceilings, large windows, and private baths. Singles 40 pesos. Doubles 50-80 pesos. Triples 90 pesos. Quads 100 pesos. Add 10 pesos for TV.

Posada de Villa, Padre Lloreda 176 (tel. 12-72-90), 3 blocks south of the Museo de las Artesanías. Huge rooms with soft beds, light wood paneling, and funky green tile. Bathrooms are a bit trodden, but very clean, scrubbed down by the manager. Pastel rooms with kitchen and dining table available for long-term rent. Regular singles 64 pesos. Doubles 80 pesos, with two beds 96 pesos. Swank rooms 700 pesos per month for 1 person, 1200 pesos for 2.

FOOD

Finding good, cheap food is a breeze in Morelia—almost every thoroughfare has at least one family-run restaurant that dishes out inexpensive *comida corrida* (usually around 9 pesos). Restaurants on the *zócalo* tend to be more pricey but are great place for breakfast, since other eateries tend to open late and close early.

Restaurante-Bar La Huacana, Aldama 116 (tel. 12-53-12), at Obeso. A gargantuan oil painting forms the backdrop for the large cafeteria-style dining area. Stone walls provide great acoustics for the *mariachis* who play Mon.-Fri. 3-5pm. *Comida corrida* 15 pesos. Enchiladas 15 pesos. Open Mon.-Sat. 9am-8pm.

Restaurante Vegetariano Aquarias, Hidalgo 75, at the end of the walkway south of the *zócalo.* Set in a blue-tiled courtyard littered with plants, bikes, and a random assortment of junk. Locals scarf down yummy vegetarian food as they listen to Mexican tunes. Breakfast combos 12 pesos. Open daily 8:30am-5:30pm.

Hindú Vegetariano Govina, Morelos Sur 39 (tel. 13-38-86). Don't expect any reposeful poses of Shiva or battle scenes between the Pandavas and the Kauravas—just good vegetarian food. You'll grow roots waiting for service, but the food is worth it. *Comida corrida* 15 pesos. Open Mon.-Sat. 10am-5pm.

Súper Pozole, Antonio Anzate 302-B, just off Quiroga. Bright pink and purple trimmed walls enclose cafeteria-style rooms. Cheap grub and late hours. Enchiladas or *tamales* 10 pesos. Open Tue-Sun. 6:30-10:30pm.

SIGHTS

In 1986, for its 100th birthday, the **Museo Michoacano,** Allende 305 (tel. 12-04-07), one block west of the *zócalo* at Abasolo, got a great big facelift. The museum was spiffed up, and exhibitions were divided into five categories: ecology, archaeology, the colonial period, the struggle for freedom, and independent Mexico. The most notable object on display is a huge, anonymous painting completed in 1738, *La Procesión del Traslado de las Monjas de una Universidad a su Convento Nuevo* (The Procession of the Nuns from the University to Their New Convent). Comments penned by Diego Rivera call the painting ground-breaking and note that it was produced in an era when religious themes dominated Mexican art. As if to underscore Rivera's point, a number of ecclesiastical paintings hang nearby, including works by Miguel Cabrera and a trio of 19th-century *indígena* artists—Manuel Ocaraza, Félix Parra, and Jesús Torres. Near the stairway, a mural by Alfredo Zalce portrays those who have shaped Mexico's history and skewers those who blindly admire U.S. mass culture (open Tues.-Sat. 9am-7pm, Sun. 9am-2pm; admission 14 pesos, free for students, teachers, children, seniors, and on Sun.).

Overlooking the *zócalo,* the massive **cathedral** has a stunning interior, graced by vaulted ceilings, chandeliers, tapestries, and beautiful stained glass windows. The church's oldest treasure is the *Señor de la Sacristía,* an image of Christ that was sculpted by *indígenas* out of dry corn cobs and orchid nectar; in the 16th century, Felipe II of Spain donated a gold crown to top off the masterpiece. In the 19th century, a bishop tipped the careful balance that had existed between Neoclassical and Baroque elements by removing the elaborate Baroque filigree from the altarpieces and frescoes and renovating the church's interior in the conservative Doric Neoclassical style (open daily 7am-9pm; free).

The former residence of José María Morelos, the parish priest who led the Independence movement after Hidalgo's death, is now the **Museo de Morelos,** Morelos Sur 323 (tel. 13-26-51), one block east and two blocks south of the cathedral. The museum displays Morelos' religious vestments, military ornaments, and uniform, as well as other mementos of the surge for independence (open Mon.-Sun. 9am-7pm; admission 10 pesos, free for students, children, seniors, and on Sun.). More of a civic building than a museum, the **Casa Natal de Morelos** (Birthplace of Morelos; tel. 12-27-93) is on Corregidora 113, at García Obeso, one block south of the cathedral. Glass cases preserve Morelos' wartime cartography, communiqués, and letters. Also notable are murals by Alfredo Zalce and a shady courtyard watched over by the martyr's bust (open Mon.-Sat. 9am-7pm; free).

The **Casa de Cultura,** Morelos Nte. 485 (tel. 12-41-51), is housed in the **Monasterio de los Carmelitas Descalzos,** four blocks north of Madero. A gathering place for artists, musicians, and backpackers, the *casa* houses a bookstore, art galleries, a theater, and a lovely café. Dance, voice, theater, guitar, piano, and sculpture classes are offered, and concerts, book presentations, art festivals, and literature workshops are held here (20-30 pesos). The on-premises **Museo de la Máscara** exhibits a small collection of masks from all over the Republic. (Center and museum open Mon.-Fri. 9am-3pm and 4-8pm, Sat.-Sun. and holidays 10am-6pm. Free. Café open Mon.-Fri. 10am-3pm and 5-9pm, Sat. 10am-3pm. For information on cultural events, call tel. 13-12-15 or 13-13-20, ext. 233.)

The **Casa de las Artesanías** (tel. 12-12-48), Humbolt at Fray Juan de San Miguel, is a huge craft museum and retail store, selling colorful macramé *huipiles,* straw airplanes, pottery, carved wood furniture, and guitars (open Mon.-Sat. 10am-8pm, Sun. 10am-6pm; free). Better prices await in Pátzcuaro.

ENTERTAINMENT

Listings of events can be found at the Casa de Cultura and at the tourist office. Bright lights, musical celebrations, and thespian allure draw crowds to the **Teatro Morelos** (tel.14-62-02), on Av. Camelina at Calzada Ventura Puente, and the **Conservatorio de las Rosas** (tel. 12-74-06), at the corner of Guillermo Prieto and Santiago Tapia. The **Casa Natal de Morelos** shows artsy films and holds cultural events on Fridays at 7pm (films screened last Tues.-Thurs. of every month, noon and 7pm; admission 1 peso). **Multicinema Morelia** (tel. 12-12-88), at Santiago Tapia and Bernal Jiménez, behind the Palacio Clavijero, features Hollywood's latest (open daily 3-10pm; 10 pesos). If you find heavenly bodies more fascinating than scantily clad ones, head for the **Planetario** (tel. 14-24-65), in the Centro de Convenciones at Calzada Ventura Puenta and Ticateme (shows Tues.-Sat. 7pm, Sun. 6:30pm; 10 pesos). To get there, take the "Ruta Rojo #3" *combi* from Av. Allende/Valladolid.

La Casona del Teatro, Aquiles Serdán 35 (tel. 17-33-53), one block north of Madero, hosts comedies in Spanish (shows Tues.-Sat. 8:30pm, Sun. 7:30pm; 20 pesos, 50% discount for students). The coffee shop/theater is popular with students and bohemian types who play chess and drink coffee (5 pesos) until showtime. A similar hangout is the bookstore and café **La Librería,** Calzada Fray Antonio de San Miguel 324 (tel. 12-02-87), which sometimes has films and music.

University students flock to **Dalí's,** Av. Campestre 100 (tel. 15-55-14; beer 10 pesos; cover 25 pesos; open Mon.-Sat. 9pm-2am, Sun. 4pm-2am). Another popular hangout is **Siglo 18** (tel. 24-07-47), Blvd. García León and Turismo, where the only requirement is that you buy 20 pesos worth of drinks (open Thurs.-Sun. 9pm-2am). Down the street, local teens and a handful of *gringo* students celebrate birthdays with ice cold Coronas at **Carlos 'n Charlie's,** Av. Carmelinas 3340 (tel. 24-37-39), near the Hotel Calinda (open daily 1pm-2am). Also popular but a tad more sedate is **Canta Bar,** Lázaro Cárdenas 2225 (tel. 15-53-54). Domestic drinks run about five pesos (cover 10 pesos; open Thurs.-Sun. 9pm-2am). **Bola Suriana,** on Bartolomeo de las Casas, a few blocks east of the Museo de Artesanías, anchors the local Latin music scene, while **Freedom,** Av. Campestre 374 (tel. 15-66-61), draws a younger crowd (open daily 1pm-2am).

■ Lázaro Cárdenas

Named after *michoacano* President Lázaro Cárdenas, whose progressive socialist measures included nationalizing oil in 1938, the city of Lázaro Cárdenas (pop. 135,000) is the most active port in Michoacán. It also houses the largest steel factory in Latin America. As if that weren't reason enough to stop by, the city's size, services, and location make it a strategic departure point or pit stop on an exploration of Michoacán's 260km of deserted, rugged, beautiful coast.

Orientation Lázaro Cárdenas lies near the border of Michoacán and Guerrero states, 382km southwest of Morelia and 122km northwest of Ixtapa. Most services lie on the town's principal thoroughfare, **Av. Lázaro Cárdenas,** usually near its intersection with **Corregidora.** The main *zócalo,* **Plaza de la Reforma,** is three blocks east of the intersection, on Guillermo Prieto. *Combis* and buses run up and down Av. Lázaro Cárdenas and are the best way of traveling to nearby beaches.

Practical Information Get the maps and info needed to attack the coast from the **Delegación Regional de Turismo,** Nicolás Bravo 475 (tel. 2-15-47; fax 2-40-36), one block east of Av. Lázaro Cárdenas and two blocks north of Corregidora, in the big white Hotel Casa Blanca (open Mon.-Sat. 9am-3pm and 5-7pm). **Banamex** (tel. 2-20-18) and **BITAL** (tel. 2-26-23), on Av. Lázaro Cárdenas, exchange currency and have **ATMs** (both open Mon.-Sat. 9am-2:30pm). *Casa de cambio* **Multivisas Las Truchas,** Av. Lázaro Cárdenas 1750 (tel. 2-44-37), provides equivalent rates (open Mon.-Sat. 9:30am-2pm and 4:30-7pm). Long-distance international **phone calls** can be made from **Caseta Goretti,** Corregidora 79 (tel. 7-31-55; open daily 7am-1am). Send **telegrams** and **faxes** from **Telecomm** (tel. 2-23-37), Nicolás Bravo at Vicente Guerrero, next to the post office (open Mon.-Fri. 8am-6pm, Sat. 9am-noon). The **airport** (tel. 7-17-18 or 2-19-20), named after you-know-whom, hosts carriers **Aerosudpacífico** (tel. 7-11-77 or -78), **Transporte Aeromar** (tel. 7-10-84 or -85), and **Aerolínea Cuahonte** (tel. 2-36-35).
  Buses run out of independent stations on or close to the main drag. **Sur de Jalisco, Autobuses de Occidente,** and **La Línea Plus,** Av. Lázaro Cárdenas 1791 (tel. 7-18-50), provide second-class service to Colima (10:30am, 6hr., 72 pesos), Guadalajara (*plus* 6:45 and 8:45pm, 9hr., 152 pesos; first-class 10:40pm, 10hr., 133 pesos), Mexico City (4 per day 3-11pm, 13hr., 143 pesos) via Uruapan (6hr., 56 pesos) and Morelia (8hr., 87 pesos), and Manzanillo (2:30 and 5:30pm, 7hr., 71 pesos). **Estrella de Oro,** Corregidora 318 (tel. 2-02-75), travels to Acapulco (first-class 6, 10am, and 9pm, 5½hr., 71 pesos; second-class every hr. 4:50am-4:50pm, 6½hr., 52 pesos) and Mexico City (first-class 8pm, 10hr., 180 pesos; second-class 6, 10am, and 9 pm, 10hr., 175 pesos). **Autotransportes del Sur Cuauhtémoc** and **Estrella Blanca,** Francisco Villa 65 (tel. 2-11-71), four blocks west of Corregidora, sends first-class buses to Tijuana (4:30am and 2:30pm, 48hr., 620 pesos), stopping at Mazatlán (20hr., 272 pesos) and points along the way. **Autotransportes Galeana,** Av. Lázaro Cárdenas 1810 (tel. 2-02-62), provides second-class service to Morelia (13 per day 2am-7pm, 8hr., 87 pesos) via Uruapan (6hr., 56 pesos) and Pátzcuaro (7hr., 70 pesos). From the same station, **Rutas de Transportación Colectiva** sends second-class buses to Caleta de Campos (every hr. 5am-8:10pm, 1½hr., 18 pesos) and coastal points along the way.
  Wash your dirty laundry at **Lavandería Olimpia,** Av. Francisco J. Mújica 49 (tel. 2-46-00; open Mon.-Sat. 9am-2pm and 4-8pm). The **Red Cross,** at Aldama 327 (tel. 2-05-75), is there for you day or night. **Farmacia AS** resides at Av. Lázaro Cárdenas 1742 (tel. 7-24-08; open daily 9am-2pm and 4-9pm). Pharmacies alternate 24-hour service; call the Red Cross to find out who's on duty. The **Hospital General** is on Av. Lázaro Cárdenas (tel. 2-08-21). The **police** (tel. 2-18-55) await at the Palacio Municipal, on Av. Lázaro Cárdenas at Av. Río Balsas. Send those postcards home from the **post office,** at Nicolás Bravo 1307 (tel. 2-05-47; open Mon.-Fri. 8am-7pm, Sat. 9am-1pm). **Telephone Code:** 753.

Accommodations and Food After a long bus ride, treat yourself to the cushy beds, clean bathrooms, and hot water of **Hotel Delfín,** Av. Lázaro Cárdenas 1633 (tel. 2-03-73), at Javier Mina (singles 50 pesos, with A/C 70 pesos; doubles 60 pesos, with A/C 80 pesos; triples and quads 120 pesos). Fill up that stomach at **El Chile Verde,** Francisco I. Madero 66 (tel. 2-10-85), across from Av. Lázaro Cárdenas. The casual open air café serves spicy enchiladas *verdes* (11 pesos) and *comida corrida* (13 pesos; open daily 7am-10pm). For a taste of the sea and rowdy *mariachi* music, visit **Mariscos el Güero,** Ignacio Zaragoza 179 (tel. 2-01-78), near the plaza. Shrimp any style goes for 40 pesos (live music 4-6pm.; open daily 11am-11pm).

■ Michoacán Coast

Like a temperamental lover, Michoacán's coastline offers solace and tranquility one moment, then suddenly erupts into foaming turbulent surf, ripping and throbbing around jagged rocks. Route 200, the solitary coastal highway, twists up, down, and around Michoacán's angry terrain. Hills are pushed up, piling and thrusting against each other; rocks are defaced by crashing white waves spraying against blue skies. Lush tropical vegetation lends a loving touch of green to this primal scene, making the state's 260km of virgin beaches wildly beautiful.

Michoacán's coast is to be treated with cautious respect. Powerful waves make its beaches better suited for surfing than swimming, and the currents are strong even in the areas recommended for swimming. Since there are no lifeguards, exercise great caution. Route 200 tends to be deserted and dangerous at night; we recommend you travel during the day only.

PLAYA AZUL

Playa Azul (pop. 5000), a small *pueblo* and nascent beach resort 26km west of Lázaro Cárdenas, is renowned for its long stretch of soft golden sand and its majestic rose-golden sunsets. Here, the sea is temptress—the tide rises high onto the shore, tracing the base of a line of *palapa* restaurants, then quickly recedes under crashing waves, good for surfing and boogie-boarding. Swimmers shouldn't stray too deep, as this open stretch of sea has a strong undercurrent.

Orientation and Practical Information Far from being a polished tourist town, Playa Azul is typically *michoacano.* Unmarked dirt roads are the main thoroughfares, lined with thatched roof houses, open-air markets, and the occasional pig. The village is so small that street names are seldom used (or known) by locals. The *malecón* borders the beach; it is called **Aquiles Serdán** to the west of the plaza and **Emiliano Zapata** to the east. The other streets bordering the plaza are **Montes de Oca,** to the west, and **Filomena Mata,** to the east. **Av. Lázaro Cárdenas** runs into Playa Azul from the highway, runs perpendicular to the beach, and intersects **Carranza, Madero,** and **Independencia,** the three main streets parallel to the beach.

Though Playa Azul doesn't have a bank or *casa de cambio,* it does offer most other services. For long-distance **phone calls,** visit the town's *caseta* (tel. 6-01-22, -23, or -24), on Independencia (open Mon.-Sat. 8am-9pm, Sun. 8am-1pm). The **market** is on Flores Magón, two blocks east of the plaza. Dr. Isidoro Veas Castro runs the **Centro de Salud,** next door to the post office (open 24hr.). The **police** (tel. 2-18-55) reside across from the PEMEX station. **Farmacia Eva Carmen,** Av. Lázaro Cárdenas at Madero, satisfies your drug needs (open daily 8am-9:30pm). The **post office** is on Madero at Montes de Oca, just behind Hotel María Teresa (open Mon.-Fri. 8am-3pm). **Telephone Code:** 753.

Accommodations and Food Bucolic Playa Azul offers several budget hotels from which to choose. All are a hop, skip, and a jump to the beach, and reasonably priced. Reservations are recommended in August, December, and during *Semana Santa.* **Hotel Costa de Oro,** on Madero three blocks away from Lázaro Cárdenas, is one of the cheaper options. White stucco walls and an elegant scalloped bannister lead to clean, comfortable rooms with basic wood furniture but no hot water (small room, for 2-3 people, 50 pesos; large room, for 4 people, 60 pesos). **Hotel Delfín** (tel. 6-00-07), on Venustiano Carranza one block from Lázaro Cárdenas, is closer to the beach. The airy white hotel offers a sparkling blue pool, a leafy red-tiled courtyard, and clean rooms (singles 60 pesos; doubles 90 pesos; triples 120 pesos). **Bungalows de la Curva** (tel. 6-00-58 or 2-28-55), on Carranza at Lázaro Cárdenas, is a good deal for groups. Clean but worn bungalows have kitchenettes, basic furniture, and hot water (small, for 3 people, 100 pesos; large, for 4 people, 150 pesos). The pool is only open during the high season.

Palapa restaurants are so close to the shore that the waves will come up and tickle your toes. The bubbly owner of **Coco's Pizza** will make you feel right at home. The *camarones a la diabla* (shrimp with *chile*, 25 pesos) are a spicy taste of heaven. Cool off with a beer (4 pesos; open daily 8am-7pm). Inland, **Restaurante Familiar Mitita**, on Flores Magón at Madero, is a cozy family-run restaurant with heavy carved wooden chairs and fishnets on the walls. The *comida corrida* costs 15 pesos, while breakfast combos go for 12 pesos (open daily 7am-11pm).

Getting There: From Lázaro Cárdenas, take a "Playa Azul" *combi* on Av. Lázaro Cárdenas (every 5min. 5am-9pm, 30min., 5 pesos).

CALETA DE CAMPOS

A tiny fishing village 47km west of Playa Azul, Caleta de Campos stretches along a sandy beige cove lined with palms. The combination of green twisted terrain and brilliant blue surf massaging the shore is truly beautiful. A dirt path climbs along the hills to the village above, offering a spectacular view of the coast. Because the water is somewhat sheltered, the surf is calmer than at Playa Azul, though the rolling waves still make for good boogie boarding and body surfing.

Orientation and Practical Information Caleta de Campos has one paved main street, Melchor Ocampo, universally known as **Av. Principal.** There are few private telephones in town; almost everybody just uses the *caseta* on the right hand side of Av. Principal (tel. 6-01-92 or -93). Farther up the road is **Farmacia Morelia,** which will sometimes change dollars (open daily 7:30am-9pm). To get to the **Centro de Salud,** turn right on the side street before the paved road runs left and walk three blocks (open 24hr.). The **police, post office** (open Mon.-Fri. 8am-3pm), and **bus stop** are all on Av. Principal. **Telephone Code:** 753.

Accommodations and Food Caleta's hotels are exceptionally nice and affordable. The new **Hotel los Arcos** (tel. (755) 7-55-83), next to the church as Av. Principal turns left, has very clean rooms with tiled floors and bathrooms, fans, and hot water. The rooms are perched on a bluff, providing a fantastic view of the coast (singles 50 pesos; doubles and triples 70 pesos; quads 100 pesos). **Hotel Yuritzi,** off Av. Principal one block after the church to the left, is a landmark in Caleta. Its clean and cozy rooms have hot water (singles 52 pesos; doubles 70 pesos; triples 85 pesos; quads 95 pesos). To get to the beach from the hotels, walk to the end of Av. Principal. Pass the church and the Lonchería Bahía, on your right, and follow the dirt road as it bends to the right. The beach lies at the bottom of the hill. The entire walk takes about 10 minutes.

Across the street from Hotel Yuritzi is one of Caleta's only restaurants, **Lonchería Bahía.** The classy and laid-back café serves hamburgers (8 pesos), *tortas* (6-10 pesos), and fruit drinks (5 pesos; open daily 8am-10pm). Also popular is **Enramada Omar,** the third *palapa* restaurant on the sandy cove. It specializes in seafood and serves shrimp any style for 25 pesos (open daily 7am-9pm).

Getting There: From Lázaro Cárdenas, **Rutas de Transportación Colectiva** (tel. 2-02-62) buses run from the Galeana bus station to Caleta (every hr. 5:40am-8:10pm, 1½hr., 18 pesos). You can also board a "Caleta" *combi* anywhere along Av. Lázaro

Cárdenas (every 30min. 5:20-8pm, 1½hr., 16 pesos). To return to Lázaro Cárdenas from Caleta, pick up a bus or *combi* at the stop near the end of Av. Principal (5am-7:30pm). From Playa Azul, take a "La Mira" *combi* (every 10min., 5min., 2.50 pesos). Get off at La Mira and take a green-and-white *combi* to Caleta at the rotary across from Autotransportes Galeana (every 30min. 5:45am-8:40pm, 1 hr., 14 pesos). You'll also need to stop by La Mira on your way back to Lázaro Cárdenas.

Near Playa Azul and Caleta de Campos

Beautiful beaches cover the 43km of coast stretching from Playa Azul to Caleta de Campos. **Las Peñas,** 13km west of Playa Azul, is a beach that is better appreciated from the shore: its surf is terribly turbulent and its waters are infested with sharks. **El Bejuco,** only 2km farther west, has a sandy cove with tamer waves and fewer rocks. Another 12km west, you'll find **Chuquiapan,** a long stretch of sandy beach with reasonable waves and a shore studded with tall green palms. **La Soledad,** enclosed by rocky formations 4km farther west, is more secluded and cozy, lying at the base of a hill covered with dense vegetation. Its grey sands are strewn with rocks and driftwood. As usual in Michoacán's Pacific coast, rough waters don't make for safe swimming. Mexcalhuacán, 2km west, offers a fantastic view from a bluff overlooking a rocky coast. Caleta de Campos comes 7km later. Nexpa, a sandy beach with powerful waves, is a surfer's heaven 5km west of Caleta. *Palapa* restaurants, known as *enramadas,* line most of the beaches. To be safe, bring bottled water and a snack.

   Getting There: Buses and *combis* running from Lázaro Cárdenas to Caleta de Campos pass by each of the beaches listed above, except Nexpa (every 30min. 5am-7:30pm; Las Peñas 30min., 6 pesos; Chuquiapan 40min., 8 pesos; La Soledad 45min., 9 pesos). The beaches are a five- to 10-minute walk from the highway. To return to Playa Azul or Caleta, you'll have to wave a towel and flag down a *combi*—be sure to confirm when the last one is expected. To get to Nexpa, take a white *combi* from the bus depot at the beginning of Av. Principal, in Caleta de Campos, Nexpa (every 40min. 7am-7pm, 10min., 3 pesos).

GUERRERO

▓ Taxco

From the stunning Church of Santa Prisca to the glinting wares of silver shops, Taxco (pop. 100,000) is meant to be seen and savored from all angles. The tangled web of streets leads pedestrians to unexpected vistas of the surrounding hillsides, while students sit in the *zócalo* staring at the VW bugs that come careening down the narrow cobblestone roads. Beneath all the swarming confusion and old-fashioned beauty are the veins of silver which have shaped Taxco's history. When silver was discovered here in 1534, Taxco became the continent's first mining town, luring fortune seekers and artisans alike. Today, tourists buzz through the labyrinthine streets, drawn like bees to the sweet honey of countless jewelry shops.

ORIENTATION

Taxco lies 185km southwest of Mexico City. The city consists of a maze of twisting streets leading up a hill to the *zócalo,* **Plaza Borda,** and the town's centerpiece, the **Catedral de Santa Prisca.** The main artery is **Av. J.F. Kennedy (Av. de los Plateros).** From Mexico City, visitors enter Taxco on J.F. Kennedy through white arches. The road winds past the **Flecha Roja** bus station and continues to the **Estrella de Oro** bus station before heading out of the city for Acapulco.

   To reach the town center from the Flecha Roja bus station, walk uphill on J.F. Kennedy and turn left on **Juan Ruiz de Alarcón,** which feeds into the *zócalo.* From the Estrella de Oro station, cross the street and walk up the steep hill known as **Pilita.** When you reach the **Plazuela San Juan,** with a small fountain and a Bancomer, veer left and you will come out facing Santa Prisca. Keep in mind that the streets are narrow and uncomfortably steep. A *"zócalo"* *combi* will take to the center for one peso. Taxis charge six pesos.

PRACTICAL INFORMATION

Tourist Office: Info Booth, J.F. Kennedy 1 (tel. 2-07-98). Take a "Garita" *combi* from the *zócalo.* Open daily 9am-7pm. **Subsecretaría de Fomento Turístico** (tel. 2-22-74), at the entrance to town. "Los Arcos" *combis* end their route in front of the office. The most helpful map is in the program for *Semana Santa en Taxco.* Open daily 9am-7pm. **Procuraduría del Turista** (tel. 2-22-64 or 2-66-16) offers assistance in emergencies. Open Mon.-Fri. 9am-7pm.

Telephones: LADATELs throughout town. **Farmacia Guadalupana,** Hidalgo 18 (tel. 2-03-95), near Pl. San Juan. Long-distance *caseta.* Open daily 8:30am-10pm.

Telegrams: Alarcón 2 (tel. 2-48-85), by the *zócalo.* **Fax.** Open Mon.-Fri. 9am-3pm.

Currency Exchange: Confía (tel. 2-45-10), on the *zócalo.* Has an **ATM.** Open Mon.-Fri. 9am-2:30pm.

Buses: Estrella de Oro, Kennedy 126 (tel. 2-06-48), at the southern end of town. From the *zócalo,* head downhill and hang a right on Kennedy. To Acapulco (5 per day, 2hr., 32-37 pesos), Cuernavaca (9am and 4pm, 1½hr., 16 pesos), and Mexico City (5 per day, 3hr., 32-37 pesos). **Flecha Roja,** Kennedy 104 (tel. 2-01-31), downhill from the cathedral. To Cuernavaca (7 per day 6am-6pm, 1½hr., 19 pesos) and Mexico City (12 per day 5am-8pm, 3hr., 32 pesos).

Market: Mercado Tetitlán. Take the street to the right of Santa Prisca, then descend the stairs to the right. At the bottom level are several *fondas* for meals.

Red Cross: (tel. 2-32-32), J.F. Kennedy, near the tourist info *caseta* (booth).

Pharmacy: Farmacia Guadalupana, Hidalgo 8 (tel. 2-03-45). Open daily 8:30am-10pm.

Hospital: IMSS, Kennedy 114 (tel. 2-03-36). 24-hr. emergency service.

Police: (tel. 2-00-07). Always on duty.

Post Office: Kennedy 124 (tel. 2-05-01), near the Estrella de Oro station. Open Mon.-Fri. 8am-7pm, Sat. 9am-1pm. **Postal Code:** 40200.

Telephone Code: 762.

ACCOMMODATIONS

Budget lodgings in Taxco are classy and conveniently located near the *zócalo.* Make advance reservations during local holidays.

Posada de Los Castillo, Alarcón 7 (tel. 2-13-96). Facing Santa Prisca, take the street to the left and turn right. As exquisite as the pricey silver shop downstairs. All the furniture, from the doors to the headboards, is carved in reassuring earth tones. Firm beds with fluffy pillows and first rate bathrooms. Singles 90 pesos. Doubles 120 pesos. Triples 160 pesos.

Hotel Los Arcos, Alarcón 12 (tel. 2-18-36), across the street from Posada de Los Castillo. With the black iron fixtures and cavernous rooms around a central courtyard, the hotel feels like a medieval manor. Tiled bathrooms come complete with purified water and bottle opener. Singles 90 pesos. Doubles 125 pesos.

Hotel Casa Grande, Pl. de San Juan 7 (tel. 2-11-08), on the small plaza down Cuauhtémoc from the *zócalo.* Worn rooms receive haphazard housecleaning. Hot water 24hr. Singles 60 pesos. Doubles 80 pesos. Triples 100 pesos. Quads 120 pesos.

Casa de Huéspedes Arellano, Pajaritos 23 (tel. 2-02-15). From the *zócalo,* walk down the street to the right of the cathedral and descend the stairs; the hotel will be about 3 levels down. Box-like rooms pale next to the live birds and potted plants that enliven the terrace. Try to land a room with a private bath—or share it with up to 7 people. Singles 40 pesos. Doubles 70 pesos. Triples 100 pesos.

FOOD

The narrow cobblestone streets of Taxco lack the push-cart vendors and sidewalk cafés that are so common in other Mexican cities. *Taquerías* and *torterías* are virtu-

Guerrero

ally extinct around Plaza Borda, but as you descend into the swarming market areas, their numbers increase.

Restaurante Santa Fé, Hidalgo 2 (tel. 2-11-70), down from Pl. San Juan. Locals flock here for filling Mexican food. Sit at the wooden tables to enjoy delicious *tortas* (6 pesos), tacos (12 pesos), and enchiladas (14 pesos). Open daily 8am-11pm.

El Rincón del Abuelo, Callejón del Nogal 1 (tel. 2-30-77), at Cuauhtémoc, before Pl. San Juan. The name (Grandpa's Corner) belies the sleek hipness of the café. *Gringos* come in droves for the dance music and healthy entrees. *Tortas* run 8-9 pesos, hamburgers 14-20 pesos, and *comida corrida* 20 pesos. Sit upstairs for more private chats above the din of rock music. Open daily 10am-midnight.

La Concha Nostra, Pl. de San Juan 7 (tel. 2-79-44), in the Hotel Casa Grande. A Bohemian hangout with a stage, communal guitars, and live music some Saturday nights. Slacker service to match the ambience. While you're waiting for your hotcakes (12 pesos), *quesadillas* (12 pesos), lasagna (22 pesos), or pizza (9-42 pesos), watch the city's language students blow smoke rings through their noses and scribble angst-ridden prose in their notebooks. Open daily 8am-midnight.

Bora Bora Pizza, Delicias 4 (tel. 2-17-21), on the unmarked street that slopes up to the right from Cuauhtémoc, just off the *zócalo*. Fishing nets and basket lamps dangle from the ceiling. Dimly lit with low tables and stools. Pizzas start at 17 pesos, spaghetti at 20 pesos. Open daily 8pm-midnight.

SIGHTS

Over 300 shops cater to the busloads of tourists who are drawn to Taxco by the glint of silver. For an example of original silver craft, visit **Emilia Castillo** at Posada de los Castillo (see p. 314). Like many Taxco families with traditions in silverwork, the Castillo family keeps its workshop (right on top of their store) open for tourists to visit. Skills are passed down through the generations—the work of the youngest Castillo, Alejandra, figures prominently (open Mon.-Fri. 9am-7pm, Sat. 9am-6pm, Sun. 10am-3pm, but the workshop is often closed). If you're dipping so deep into your pockets that you can feel your knees, head for **El Mercado de Artesanías,** off Veracruz just behind Santa Prisca. Merchants sell silver and peddle pomegranates and painted ashtrays. The market is open daily from 10am to 6pm but is most crowded during *siesta*, when confused *gringos* hit Taxco's version of a mall instead of sleeping. At the **Pineda** silver store to the left of Santa Prisca, winners of the **Feria Nacio-**

nal de la Plata contest are on display. You'll also see a photo of the famous Guillermo Spratling and get to ogle some expensive merchandise.

Even more impressive than the silver trinkets that shine from every shop window is the *zócalo's* **Catedral de Santa Prisca,** with its beautiful baroque façade of pink stone. Among the designs and figures on the façade, the standouts are the Churriguer-esque *interestípite*—decorative inverted columns with a Corinthian flourish at the bottom. Inside the church, a canvas by renowned 18th-century Mexican artist Miguel Cabrera depicts the martyrdom of Santa Prisca, who was tortured and killed by Roman guards in the first century for defending Christians (open daily 6am-8pm).

To the left of the church is **Casa Borda,** a stately 18th century building that was the home of José de la Borda; his family's coat of arms can still be seen beside the entrance. Enter through the bookstore on the *zócalo.* The interior gardens and several floors have been turned into the **Instituto Guerrerense de Cultura** (tel. 2-66-17). In addition to a library and dance studio, the center has ample gallery space for rotating exhibitions and photographs of Taxco's *Semana Santa* celebrations (galleries open daily 10am-3pm and 5-7:30pm).

The **Casa Humboldt,** Alarcón 6 (tel. 2-55-01), down the street past the Hotel Los Arcos, is one of the older colonial homes in town. With its unusual bas-reliefs in Moorish *mudéjar* style, the *casa* served as the temporary home of South American explorer Alexander von Humboldt, whose bust still overlooks the interior. The beautifully restored house now houses the collection of the **Museo de Arte Virreinal.** Exhibitions provide a detailed look at 18th-century Catholic rituals and dress (open Tues.-Sat. 10am-5pm, Sun. 9am-3pm; admission 10 pesos).

The **Museo de Arqueología Guillermo Spratling,** Delgado 1 (tel. 2-16-60), down the street to the right of Santa Prisca, displays pre-Conquest art, mostly from cultures along Mexico's west coast. William Spratling, the *norteamericano* who taught locals the art of silver-smithing, donated his ceramics and figurines to the museum (open Tues.-Sat. 10am-5pm, Sun. 9am-3pm; admission 10 pesos, free for students and teachers with ID).

The **Ex-Convento de San Bernandino,** in the Plaza del Convento, was built in 1592 as a Franciscan monastery. Destroyed by a fire two centuries later, the building was reconstructed in Neoclassical style in 1823. The struggle for independence officially ended when the Plan of Iguala was signed within the walls of this ex-convent in 1821. Now a school convenes under its roof. To get to the ex-convent, follow Juárez past the city offices (open daily 10am-5pm; free).

One of the more striking views of the city and the surrounding hills is from the **Church of Guadalupe.** The neoclassical church becomes the center of festivities during the celebration of the Virgin in December. From the *zócalo,* take Ojeda, the street to the right of Cuauhtémoc, to Guadalupe, and veer right until you reach the plaza in

---

The Shining

Although unscrupulous sellers and cheating craftspeople occasionally pass off *alpaca* (fool's silver) or *plateados* (silver-plated metals) as the real McCoy, buying silver in Taxco is usually a sure thing. Larger pieces, such as necklaces and bracelets, are consistently striking. Many proprietors speak English and accept U.S. currency, but if you stick with Spanish and talk in pesos while bargaining, you don't risk being charged tourist prices. In general, the farther one walks from the Plaza Borda, the cheaper the sterling products become. Bargain at stores with silver workshops by faking out the clerk and heading straight for the artisan. Most shops have two prices: *menudeo* (retail) and *mayoreo* (wholesale), the latter for those profit-oriented people who load their bags with silver in Taxco to resell at lofty prices back home. Remember that only the official ".925" stamp on the object's side guarantees that your shiny new charm is indeed silver; inspect merchandise carefully before purchasing anything.

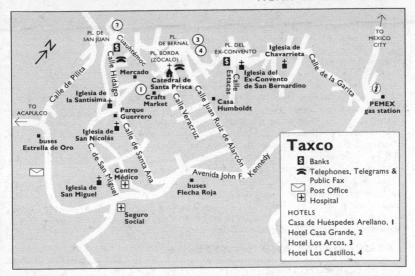

Taxco

- $ Banks
- ☎ Telephones, Telegrams & Public Fax
- ✉ Post Office
- ✚ Hospital

HOTELS
Casa de Huéspedes Arellano, 1
Hotel Casa Grande, 2
Hotel Los Arcos, 3
Hotel Los Castillos, 4

front of the church. For a more sweeping vista, you can take a **teleférico,** or **cable car,** to Hotel Monte Taxco. Take a "Los Arcos" *combi* to the white arches at the entrance of the city (1.50 pesos). Before passing through the arches, turn left up a hill and bear right into the parking lot for the cable cars. The ride is exhilarating, with waterfalls on one side and the city on the other (20 pesos roundtrip, free for hotel guests). **Góndolas** (tel. 2-14-68) run until 7pm.

ENTERTAINMENT AND SEASONAL EVENTS

Taxco's crowded streets somehow accommodate a tsunami of tourists during its two major festivals. The **Feria Nacional de la Plata,** a national contest designed to encourage silver artisanship, takes place the first week of December. *Semana Santa* festivities are even more popular in Taxco. On Good Friday, hooded *penitentes* carry logs made out of cactus trunks on their shoulders or subject themselves to flagellation in order to expiate their sins and those of the town. During the annual **Día del Jumil,** Taxco residents make a pilgrimage to the *Huizteco* hill, where they collect insects known as *jumil* to eat them live or add them, along with chiles, to salsa. The 1.5-cm long brown insects contain more protein per gram than beef.

After silver shops close, most of Taxco gathers at the **Plaza Borda** in front of the illuminated façade of Santa Prisca. Those still up for dancing after a day of hiking up and down Taxco's relentless hills will have to wait until the weekend. **Windows,** in the Hotel Monte Taxco (tel. 2-13-00), has the area's hottest dancing (cover 15 pesos; open Fri.-Sun. 10pm-late). Two other discos, **2001** and **Tequilas Disco,** are on the Carretera Nacional and J.F. Kennedy, respectively. Expect American dance tunes and a 10 peso cover. **Cine Alarcón,** near Plaza de San Juan, shows American and "adult-interest" movies.

■ Near Taxco

GRUTAS DE CACAHUAMILPA

While the scenery around Taxco has an awe-inspiring rugged grandeur, it is the beauty of an extensive network of caves that compels tourists to forget about silver shopping and venture out of the city limits. According to lore, the **Grutas de Cacahuamilpa** were once a hideaway for runaway *indígenas*. Twenty huge *salones* (halls) are filled with stalactites, stalagmites, and rock formations in curious shapes, sizes, and colors. The columns and ceilings—some as high as 85m—are the work of the subterranean stream that developed into the Río San Jerónimo. Explorers hoping to traverse the caves have not always had great success—the makeshift grave of an English spelunker is the highlight of any tour of the *grutas.*

Tours leave on the hour from the visitor's center and afford little opportunity for traipsing about on your own. After dishing out a bit of history, the guide directs the crowd's attention to rock formations which, he claims, bear remarkable likenesses to Santa Claus, Dante, and—who else?—the Virgin of Guadalupe. Since many of the figures require an impeccable vocabulary and religious background, knowledge of Spanish and a good imagination help. The two-hour tour also requires a great deal of stamina. Some of the guides speak English, but only for a good-sized group of *gringos* (Fri.-Sun.). Beware of the slick pavement; shoes with good traction are helpful (caves open daily 10am-5pm; admission 15 pesos, children 10 pesos).

Getting There: "Grutas" *combis* leave from Taxco's Flecha Roja bus station, dropping passengers off at the parking lot for the caves (7 pesos). Flecha Roja buses also make the trip (every hr. 10am-4pm, 45min., 7 pesos), but will drop you off at an intersection a short jaunt from the caves. To get to the parking lot at the caves, take a right, then another right after the curve.

LAS GRANADAS AND IXCATEOPAN

Twenty-six kilometers away from Taxco, the ecological reserve of **Las Granadas** provides an Edenic respite from both Volkswagen-clogged streets and silver pushers. In addition to the flora and fauna, there are stunning natural waterfalls. There is no admission charge and no set hours.

Forty-two kilometers from Taxco, the town of Ixcateopan is known for both its beauty and its history. The marble and stone streets supply the former, while the **Museo de la Resistencia Indígena** provides information on the latter. The remains of Cuauhtémoc, the last Aztec emperor, are said to be kept here in the **Templo de Santa María de la Asunción.**

Getting There: *Combis* leave Taxco from in front of the Seguro Social, on J.F. Kennedy. To get to Las Granadas, head to the town of Acuitlapan, 20km from Taxco (every 30min. until 7pm, 40min., 6 pesos). There you can get transportation to the reserve. To get to Ixcateopan, just take the eponymous vehicle (every 30min. 6am-9pm, 1¼hr., 9 pesos).

■ Chilpancingo

Home to the Universidad Autónoma de Guerrero, Chilpancingo is a consummate college town: students rush through its streets with backpacks and books in hand, cheap entertainment and food establishments are the norm, and the *zócalo* feels something like a campus quad with its modern architecture and abstract sculptures. Those who aren't students are probably affiliated with the state government, which has its capital here. Other than books and bureaucracy, not much goes on here. The city shows travelers a glimpse of an untouristed Guerrero that is light years away from the silver of Taxco or the sands of Acapulco.

Orientation and Practical Information Chilpancingo is 130km north of Acapulco and 270km south of Mexico City. Streets run in straight lines, forming easy-to-follow blocks. **Av. Juárez** runs along one side of the *zócalo,* which is bounded by **Madero** on one side and **Colón** on the other. Parallel to Juárez, behind the cathedral, is **Abasolo.** The two **bus stations** are across the street from each other on **21 de Marzo.** To reach the *centro* from the bus stations, walk two blocks down 21 de Marzo until you see the market, and make a right on **Insurgentes.** From here it's a 20-minute walk or a short bus or *combi* ride (1 peso) to downtown.

Limited **tourist information** is available from **Sedentel** (tel. 2-14-51), the telephone office to the right of the ticket counters at the Estrella Blanca bus station (open daily

7am-10pm). For currency exchange, head to **Bancomer** (tel. 2-25-75), in the *zócalo,* or to **Banamex,** next door (both open Mon.-Sat. 9am-1:30pm). The latter has an **ATM. LADATELs** line the *zócalo.*

Estrella de Oro buses (tel. 2-21-30 and 2-48-14), go to Acapulco (6 per day 8:30am-11:30pm, 1½hr., 32 pesos; *deluxe* 7 per day 9:30am-7pm, 36 pesos), Cuernavaca (3:30 and 7pm, 2½hr., 42 pesos; *deluxe* 6 per day 6am-7pm, 56 pesos), Mexico City (5 per day 5am-7pm, 3½hr., 66 pesos; *deluxe* 6 per day 6:15am-12:30am, 81 pesos), Taxco (9, 11am, 1:30, and 6:30pm, 2½hr., 37 pesos), and Zihuatanejo (5:30pm, 7hr., 73 pesos). **Estrella Blanca,** 21 de Marzo (tel. 2-06-34 and 2-06-41) and several smaller lines have similar routes.

Buy fresh produce at **Mercado Baltazar R. Leyva Mancilla,** Insurgentes at 21 de Marzo, near the bus station (open daily 6am-8pm). **Farmacia Nueva Alameda** (tel. 2-70-13), Catalán at Zapata, is between Guerrero and Juárez, on the side of the park closest to the *zócalo* (open 24hr.). **Hospital General** (tel. 2-20-21) is on the Guerrero side of the park (open 24hr.). The **Red Cross** (tel. 2-65-61), Juárez at Apresa near the park, has a 24-hour ambulance service. To reach the state **police,** dial 2-20-68. The **post office** is at Hidalgo 9 (tel. 2-22-75), one and a half blocks up from the left side of the cathedral (open Mon.-Fri. 8am-7pm, Sat. 9am-1pm). **Postal Code:** 39000. **Telephone Code:** 747.

Accommodations and Food Without the demand to support it, the budget hotel industry in Chilpancingo is not well developed. **Hotel María Isabel,** Madero 1 (tel. 2-48-80), is decent. Walk one block from the *zócalo* and make a left on Abasolo; the hotel is a block farther down. Rooms upstairs are larger and brighter than those downstairs, which almost makes up for their utter lack of charm. All bathrooms have hot water and noise, courtesy of the bar next door (singles 60 pesos, with TV 90 pesos; doubles 75 pesos, with TV 100 pesos). Rightfully less expensive is **Hotel Chilpancingo,** Alemán 8 (tel. 2-24-46), on a pedestrian street between Colón and the *zócalo.* Cramped cement rooms are lit by dangling lightbulbs. The extra pesos for a private bathroom are well spent (singles 25 pesos, with bath 40 pesos; doubles 35 pesos, with bath 60 pesos).

Cheap food is easy to find in the streets around the *zócalo.* Even an upscale, consciously hip place like **Taco Rock,** Colón 5 (tel. 2-34-91), on the *zócalo,* is affordable. Despite the name, the restaurant makes sandwiches (12 pesos), hamburgers (11-17 pesos), and pizza (28-38 pesos; open daily 9am-10pm). **Restaurant Cuauhtémoc,** Alemán 14 (tel. 2-32-23), near the *zócalo,* tends to get crowded at *comida* time—maybe it's the *mariachis* who stop in on occasion, maybe it's the *telenovelas* on TV (*comida corrida* 12 pesos; open Mon.-Sat. 7am-10pm).

Sights and Entertainment The most important **fair** of the year runs from December 18 to January 10 in honor of Christmas and New Year's. Festivities include a bullfight, games, and the sale of artisanry. At other times, Chilpancingo's main tourist attraction is the **Museo Regional de Guerrero,** in the Instituto Guerrerense de la Cultura, an old government building to the right of the cathedral. Though the beautiful and historic building may be more interesting than the museum itself, it's still worthwhile to peek into the courtyard and take a look at the murals depicting the history of Guerrero. Some ancient items unearthed nearby are positioned sporadically around the courtyard (open Tues.-Sat. 11am-6pm; free).

Lovers of all things *folklórico* may want to take a look at **La Casa de las Artesanías,** a short ride from the *zócalo* via the "Jacarandas" *combi.* Their name says it all: *artesanías* of all shapes, sizes, and prices can be found and bought here (open Mon.-Fri. 9am-9pm). For a larger selection at cheaper prices, catch a bus to the town of **Chilapa** (53km. east), which sponsors a large crafts market on Sundays.

If the sights are on the paltry side, never fear: what Chilpancingo lacks in museums, it makes up for in bars. A good place to start your search for other forms of not-so-intelligent nightlife is the **Casino del Estudiante,** Guerrero at Madero, just off the *zócalo.* Basically, it's a student hangout that houses bulletin boards with current listings to complement some very popular ping-pong tables. *Antojitos* are just 7 pesos (open daily 9am-10pm). The **movie theater** is also near the *zócalo,* on Bravo off Juárez. To dance, you'll have to catch a taxi. **Disco Gamba,** Blvd. Guerrero, way out by the highway, has a lively mix of rock and salsa music (cover 10-20 pesos; open Thurs.-Sun. 9pm-late).

■ Zihuatanejo and Ixtapa

Six kilometers and a million light years separate the small towns of **Zihuatanejo** and **Ixtapa.** Both thrive on tourism, offering the requisite stretches of sand, the whole range of watersports, and the sunset-framing restaurants. However, while Ixtapa has been meticulously constructed to please moneyed foreign visitors, Zihuatanejo hasn't shaken the grip of the net that marks it as a fishing town. In downtown Zihuatanejo, there are actually budget hotels, all a few steps from excellent beaches. Ixtapa, on the other hand, has no downtown, no budget accommodations, and a surfeit of fancy restaurants. The tourist brochures aren't kidding when they promise two vacations in one.

As a budget traveler, you're likely to spend one and a half of those vacations in Zihuatanejo. Ironically enough, the original plan designed the nascent resort paradise around Zihuatanejo Bay; complications with land rights forced development farther north to Ixtapa. A visit only to peaceful Zihuatanejo would be satisfying, yet the sanitized, glitzy Ixtapa, with its air-conditioned comfort and sophisticated nightlife, adds just the right amount of decadence. Together, Ixtapa/Zihuatanejo provide the complete escape that Mexico's other Pacific beaches hamper with pollution or lack of services.

ORIENTATION

Buses arrive in Zihuatanejo. The **Estrella Blanca** lies outside the *centro* and is connected to downtown by buses heading to the left as you leave the station (1 peso) or taxis (10 pesos). **Estrella de Oro** is on the edge of town on **Paseo del Palmar.** To reach the *centro,* turn right from the station and walk until you reach a rotary with a Japanese-looking temple. Turn right on **Paseo de la Boquita,** which runs into the center of town. Resort goers usually arrive at the **International Airport,** 15km outside of town. Taxis to Zihuatanejo charge 50 pesos.

As seen from the bay, downtown Zihuatanejo extends from the *muelle* (pier) on the left to the canal on the right. **Paseo del Pescador** runs along the waterfront. Seven blocks separate that walkway from **Av. Morelos,** which runs parallel to the water and marks the edge of the town. The two boundary streets perpendicular to the water are **5 de Mayo,** by the pier, and **Benito Juárez,** by the canal. Ixtapa's main road, **Blvd. Ixtapa,** parades past a phalanx of huge luxury hotels towards the water on the left, and overpriced stores to the right. Buses shuttling between the two cities leave Zihuatanejo from the intersection of Juárez and Morelos, across from the yellow Elektra store, and leave Ixtapa from various stops on the boulevard (every 15min. 6am-7pm, 15-25min., 2 pesos from any stop). Cab fare between the two towns runs about 15 to 20 pesos by day, 25 pesos at night.

If an address listed below is not on Blvd. Ixtapa, it is in Zihuatanejo.

PRACTICAL INFORMATION

Tourist Office: Info booth (tel. 4-20-01), on Juan N. Álvarez, to the left of the small town square. Maps and basic information. Some English spoken. Open Mon.-Fri. 9am-3pm and 6pm-8pm, Sat. 9am-2pm. **SEFOTUR** (tel. 3-19-67), on Blvd. Ixtapa, across from Hotel Presidente. Comprehensive *Guía Turística Urbana* to beaches and services. Some English spoken. Open daily 9am-8pm.
Currency Exchange: Banco Mexicano (tel. 4-51-60), Los Mangos at Juárez. **Banca Serfín,** Juárez (tel. 4-47-80), has an **ATM.** Both open Mon.-Fri. 9am-1:30pm.

Money Exchange (tel. 4-35-22 or 4-36-22), on Galeana. From the beach, walk one block on Cuauhtémoc, take a right on Bravo, and make the first left onto Galeana. Worse rates than the banks, but no commission. Open daily 8am-9pm.

Telephones: LADATELs at the Estrella Blanca bus station and on streets downtown. Or try **Servicio Telefónico** (tel. 4-28-10), P. Ascencio at Galeana. Open Mon.-Sat. 8:30am-10pm, Sun. 8am-noon and 6-10pm.

Telegrams: Edificio Telecomm (tel. 4-21-63), just one door over from the post office. Open Mon.-Fri. 9am-1pm and 3-5pm, Sat. 9am-noon.

Airport: (tel. 4-20-70). **Aeroméxico,** Álvarez 34 (tel. 4-20-18), at 5 de Mayo, one block from the water. Open Mon.-Sat. 9am-6:30pm. **Mexicana** (tel. 4-22-06), Guerrero at Bravoa. Open Mon.-Sat. 9am-6:45pm, Sun. 9am-2pm and 3-5:45pm.

Buses: Estrella de Oro, Paseo Palmar 54 (tel. 4-21-75), sends its crew to Acapulco (every hr. 7am-5pm except 11am and 2pm, 4½hr., 35 pesos), Cuernavaca (8am, noon, and 11pm, 10hr., 113 pesos), and Mexico City (*ordinario* 8am, noon, 8, and 11pm, 12hr., 143 pesos; *plus* 10pm, 9hr., 180 pesos; *deluxe* 9:15pm, 9hr., 255 pesos). **Estrella Blanca** (tel. 4-34-77) goes to Chilpancingo (4:20, 5am, and midnight, 5½hr., 75 pesos), Huatulco (7:45pm, 13hr., 146 pesos), and Puerto Escondido (7:45pm, 11½hr., 123 pesos).

Car Rental: Hertz, Bravo 9 (tel. 4-22-55). Small VW 200 pesos per day with unlimited mileage. Insurance 80 pesos. Open daily 8am-2pm and 4-8pm.

Bookstore: Byblos, Galeana 211 (tel. 4-38-11). English magazines, paperback novels, and the handy *Owen's English Language Guide to Ixtapa and Zihuatanejo* (written by a member of Cousteau's team). Open daily 9am-10pm.

Market: The **mercado** on Benito Juárez, 4 blocks from the water, sells fresh produce and has several small countertop eateries.

Laundromat: Súper Clean, Catalina González 11 (tel. 4-23-47), between Cuauhtémoc and Guerrero. 21 pesos per 3 kg. Open Mon.-Sat. 8am-8pm.

Red Cross: (tel. 4-20-09), on Av. de las Huertas as you leave Zihuatanejo. 24-hr. emergency and ambulance service.

Pharmacy: Farmacia Principal (tel. 4-42-17), Cuauhtémoc at Ejido, 3 blocks from the water. English spoken. Open Mon.-Sat. 8am-9:30pm.

Medical Services: Centro de Salud (tel. 4-20-88), Paseo de la Boquita at Paseo del Palmar. Open for consultations Mon.-Sat. 8am-3pm. **Dr. Rogelio Grayel** (tel. 4-79-00 or 7-04-52) speaks English and makes house calls for 100 pesos.

Police: In the Palacio Municipal (tel. 4-20-40 or 4-23-66) in Zihuatanejo.

Post Office: (tel. 4-21-92), off Paseo del Palmar. Walking away from the beach, turn right on Morelos, walk a block past the blue wall, then turn right. Open Mon.-Fri. 8am-6pm. **Postal code:** 40880.

Telephone code: 753.

ACCOMMODATIONS AND CAMPING

Zihuatanejo has plenty of budget accommodations within a few blocks of the Playa Municipal. Prices rise substantially during the high season (Dec.-March). If you visit at an off-time, with a large group, or plan to stay several days, you will have excellent leverage for negotiating a discount. The tourist office discourages unofficial camping, possibly because they believe *gringos* can't do without the amenities of a five-star hotel, but also for safety reasons. If you insist on pitching a tent, Playa Barra de Potosí (see p. 324) and Playa Quieta, near Club Med in Ixtapa, are the most sensible places to camp. For info on the countless *casas* and *departmentos* for long-term rent, call Mahara Heard-White at RelMax Realty (tel. 7-09-19). During the summers, you can also contact Leigh Roth (tel. 4-37-55).

Casa Elvira, Juan N. Álvarez 8 (tel. 4-26-61), 1 block from the Playa Municipal. The first guest house in Zihuatanejo remains a bargain. Excellent location. Rooms are clean, if unspectacular, with portable fans, cold water, and small bathrooms. The treat is outside—an inviting courtyard filled with family members and close proximity to the beach. 30 pesos per person, high season 40 pesos.

Hotel Casa Bravo, Bravo 11 (tel. 4-25-48), near the intersection with Juárez. Lots of bang for the buck. Large rooms have TVs and hot water. Singles 50 pesos. Doubles 80 pesos. Triples 120 pesos. Quads 150 pesos.

Posada Citlali, Vicente Guerrero 3 (tel. 4-20-43), near Blvd. Álvarez. Vines dangle lazily in the central courtyard; wooden rockers on the terrace encourage you to do the same. All rooms have overhead fans and hot water. Bathrooms are in impressive condition. Singles 80 pesos. Doubles 100 pesos. High season 20 pesos more.

Hotel Amueblados Valle, Vicente Guerrero 14 (tel. 4-20-84). Eight fully equipped apartments that would make any grad student jealous. Large kitchens, ceiling fans, balconies, hot water, and daily towel service. One bedroom (2-4 people) 130 pesos. Two bedrooms (4-6 people) 200-250 pesos. Monthly rates available.

Las Gatas Beach Club (tel. 4-83-07), at the end of Playa Las Gatas. Five secluded bungalows with screens, mosquito nets, private bathrooms with cold water, and hammocks. Some have kitchens; all benefit from the volleyball net and the serenity of being close to nature. Up to three people 225 pesos per night. Minimum stay 2 nights. Substantial savings for stays over two weeks.

Villas San Sebastián (tel. 4-82-78), the blue and pink chalets uphill at Playa La Ropa, next to the Villa del Sol. Five exquisite units with unobstructed ocean views, even from the showers. Full kitchens with all the trimmings, terraces, colorful bedrooms, and luxurious bathrooms. The kind of bungalow they give away on game shows. Up to 5 people U.S.$95 per day, but the owner will give students a 50% discount! Does life get any better than this?

FOOD

Like the neighboring hotels, restaurants in Ixtapa are pricey. However, they are spotlessly clean and make Italian food that actually tastes Italian. The meal can be a reasonable splurge, especially if you eat at a café before they switch to the main menu (around 2pm). For consistent budget eats, restaurants in Zihuatanejo serve fish that were swimming in the bay this morning. The farther you get from the beach, the cheaper and more authentic the restaurant.

Los Braseros, Ejido 21 (tel. 4-48-58). The *platos combinados* provide massive amounts of stir-fried meat and vegetables with hot tortillas on the side (25 pesos). Sample some *ballena* (whale) for 21 pesos or the delicious "TutiFruti" (crepes topped with fruit salad and yogurt). Open daily 4pm-1am.

La Sirena Gorda (The Fat Mermaid), Paseo del Pescador 20A (tel. 4-26-87), next to the pier. Start your morning off with a stack of hotcakes (13-15 peso) or eggs (15-18 pesos); dine on seafood tacos (18-35 pesos) when the sun goes down. Open Thurs.-Tues. 7:30am-10:30pm.

The Deli, Cuauhtémoc 12 (tel. 4-38-50). With a mission to keep the *gringos* happy, the restaurant prides itself on purified everything, vintage music, and uncommonly clean bathrooms. The familiar food will also please foreigners: honey mustard chicken sandwich 20 pesos. Open Mon.-Sat. 8am-11pm.

Ruben's Hamburgers, Adelita 1 (tel. 4-46-17), on Playa Madera. Follow the Paseo del Pescador to the canal, turn left and cross the bridge. Walk straight down the street for 2 blocks—it's on the right, up the stairs. The original of an expanding chain. Loud and fun, with booming jukebox and rolls of paper towels dangling overhead. Self-service, literally: you get your drinks from the freezer and add up your own check. Delicious char-broiled hamburgers (16 pesos) and sour cream-stuffed baked potatoes (10 pesos). Open daily 6pm-midnight.

Figaro's Restaurante (tel. 3-14-52), Plaza Ixpamar off Blvd. Ixtapa, in the mall. Italian *comida del día* a multi-course bargain at 16 pesos. Individual pizzas start at 17 pesos. *Quesadillas* 16 pesos. Open daily 8:30am-11pm.

SAND AND SIGHTS

Neither Zihuatanejo's self-conscious charm nor Ixtapa's resorts could ever eclipse the area's natural beauty. In Zihuatanejo, four stretches of sand line the water. They are, clockwise from the municipal pier, Playa Principal, Playa La Madera, Playa la Ropa, and Playa Las Gatas. Ixtapa overlooks the unbroken stretch of Playa del Palmar on the Bahía del Palmar, but the prettiest beaches lie beyond Laguna de Ixtapa: Playa Quieta, Playa Linda, and, at the bay's west edge, Isla Ixtapa.

Zihuatanejo

Downtown Zihuatanejo's beach, **Playa Municipal,** in front of the Paseo del Pescador, is more suited to seashell stores and fishing boats than swimmers. The attractions here are the basketball court, the pier, and the hauls of fish the boats unload onto the dock. The beach ends at a canal that empties into the bay. Get your feet wet crossing over the rocks to **Playa Madera.** Its name refers to the local hardwoods that used to be exported from the shore, but the fine sand and gentle waves bear no trace of the lumberyard past. Good for bodysurfing, the shallow beach hosts a number of restaurants and bungalows.

Zihuatanejo's two best beaches cannot be reached by walking along the bay's shores. Protected from the rough Pacific by the shape of the bay, **Playa La Ropa's** crescent of sumptuous white sand attracts tourists from the hotels on the surrounding cliffs. Because La Ropa is nearly 1-km long, it never feels too crowded. Taxis are the easiest way to reach La Ropa (10 pesos). The 30-minute walk can be unshaded at points and close to traffic at others. Follow Paseo de la Boquita along the canal to the bridge, cross over and turn left, passing Playa Madera. The road curves to the right and passes Hotel Casa Que Canta. Follow the stone road down to the left to the beach. At the opposite end of the beach you can reward yourself with a meal at one of the waterfront seafood restaurants.

According to local lore, Tarascan King Calzontzin ordered the construction of the barrier reef in **Playa Las Gatas** as protection from the sharks that give the beach its name. Since then, coral and an abundance of marine life have taken over the stone barricade. The calm, transparent waters welcome snorkelers (equipment can be rented for 30 pesos per day). Escape the shops and restaurant tables by taking a path behind the last restaurant to the **Garrobo Lighthouse,** which offers a panoramic view. Since it's well hidden, ask any of the waiters for specific directions to *"el faro."* To reach Las Gatas, take a *lancha* from the pier in downtown Zihuatanejo (boats leave every 15min. 9am-4pm, last boat leaves Las Gatas 6pm, 10min., roundtrip 15 pesos). It is possible, but not easy, to walk to Las Gatas from La Ropa.

Ixtapa

Guarded by a row of hotels, **Playa del Palmar** is a people-watching, wave-hopping, massage-receiving paradise. Not only is it one of the more attractive beaches around, it is perhaps the most active. Without the protection of a bay, the beach is pummeled by sizeable waves, attracting parasailers, scuba divers, and jet skiers. All along the sand next to the swimming pools, people play volleyball, soccer, and jog (swimmers should obey the lifeguards and red-yellow-green flags). The beach can be reached from public access paths in its two extremes, near the Sheraton hotel or near Carlos n' Charlie's. Otherwise, clutch your *Let's Go* confidently, wear your swimsuit proudly, and walk right through the hotel lobbies.

To the northwest of Ixtapa are less crowded and more stylish **Playa Cuatas, Playa Quieta,** and **Playa Linda.** To drive here from Ixtapa, follow the boulevard northwest beyond most of the hotels and turn right at the sign for Playa Linda. If you're driving from Zihuatanejo, the access road from Rte. 200 is more convenient; go past the exit for Ixtapa in the direction of Puerto Vallarta and take the next left, marked Playa Linda. The road skirts **Laguna de Ixtapa** and hits the beach farther northwest. A taxi to Playa Linda or Playa Quieta costs about 15 pesos from Ixtapa or 40 pesos from Zihuatanejo. Crystal clear water and bodysurfing waves await at Playa Cuatas, across the street from the tennis courts at Club Med on Playa Linda. Both Playa Linda and Playa Quieta are known for their tranquil waters and calm swimming conditions. At Playa Linda it is possible to rent horses that ride all the way to the Ixtapa River. Bring a lunch; services here are limited.

Some claim that of all the area's beaches, the most picturesque are those on **Isla Ixtapa,** about 2km offshore from Playa Quieta. Activity picks up in a few shoreside restaurants by day, but the island's 10 acres remain uninhabited at night. The main beach is **Playa Cuachalalate,** frequented by fishermen and vacationers eager to waterski. **Playa Varadero** is a small beach with calm waters and *palapa*-covered restaurants. On the ocean side of the island, **Playa Coral** is the least visited beach of the three. It has no services and is not that great for swimming, but the coral makes for excellent scuba diving. To get there, take a boat from the pier at Zihuatanejo (boats leave at noon, return 5pm, 1hr., 40 pesos). A cheaper alternative is to take a *microbús* from Ixtapa to the pier at Playa Quieta (2 pesos) and catch a *lancha* from there (every 15min. 9am-5pm, roundtrip 15 pesos).

ENTERTAINMENT

The beaches of Ixtapa and Zihuatanejo may be similar, but by nightfall the contrast between the cities becomes clear. Ixtapa supports a varied collection of dance clubs and dress-up restaurants, all of them on Blvd. Ixtapa. The premier place for dancing is **Christine** (tel. 3-03-33), in the Hotel Krystal. With its tiered seats, hanging vines, and light show, it is as artificially beautiful as Ixtapa itself (cover 40 pesos; open daily 10pm-6am). A restaurant by day, **Los Mandriles,** in the commercial center, becomes a nightclub around 11pm (cover 30 pesos for men, 15 pesos for women). **Carlos n' Charlie's,** at the end of the Playa Palmar next to Hotel Posada Road, attracts a large crowd to its bar and beachfront dancing (cover 30 pesos for men, 15 pesos for women; open daily 4pm-3am). **Señor Frog's** (tel. 3-06-92) is a restaurant until midnight; at that point, American dancers climb on the tables and the party begins.

Choices for nightlife in Zihuatanejo are slim. There is a disco, **Rocka Rock,** at 5 de Mayo, but it lacks pizzazz and attendance. Look for the green building facing the Mercado de Artesanías (cover 15 pesos; open Thurs.-Sun. 11pm-late). If you're in Zihuatanejo at night, dancing is probably not on your mind. Dinner at **Morro Viejo,** inside the **Hotel Puerto Mío,** Playa del Almacén 5 (tel. 4-27-48), may be expensive, but drinks are reasonable and the view of the sunset priceless. From the pier, cross the rickety wooden bridge over the estuary, then turn left. The road ends at the hotel; the restaurant is to the right.

■ Costa Grande

The Guerrero coast north of Acapulco is often called the Costa Grande to distinguish it from its smaller counterpart (Costa Chica) to the south. Trade with Asia centuries ago explains the Polynesian features of some of the area's inhabitants—silk wasn't the only thing exchanged here. Of specific interest are Barra de Potosí, 20km southeast of Zihuatanejo, and Papanoa, another 60km farther along Rte. 200.

BARRA DE POTOSÍ

For the *gringo* whose head is spinning from ruins, cathedrals, and souvenirs, there is no better tonic than a spell at the seemingly infinite stretch of sand known as **Playa Barra de Potosí.** Life here just couldn't get any more *tranquila.* Tourists bask in the sun, their words rolling lazily off their tongues and their thoughts drifting effortlessly out to sea. *Camionetas* putter along the single sandy road, bouncing the inhabitants back and forth to their secluded homes. Now and then, someone stirs for a bit of fishing. The owners of the 12 or so open-air *enramadas* (informal *palapa* restaurants), just past the strip that constitutes "town," are proud of Playa Potosí's laid-back friendliness—and its reasonable prices.

Visitors to Barra de Potosí are expected to sleep in the hammocks that adorn each *enramada.* The owners don't care if you sack out in their hammocks forever—as long as you buy a meal from them every now and then. *Baños,* too, are free of charge. The owners will let you leave your pack in the *enramadas* for as long as you like.

The *enramadas* farthest from the lagoon avoid flooding and tend to be the most magical in Barra de Potosí. Flex your travel-savvy and sleep on the diagonal, so as to support your back. The mosquitoes are also free, so bring plenty of repellent.

Those still unskilled in the art of hammock-snoozing can indulge themselves at **Hotel Barra de Potosí** (tel. 4-82-90, 4-82-91, or 4-34-45), an unfinished resort hotel that has nevertheless opened its doors for business. From the *enramadas*, walk away from the lagoon; you'll immediately see its name on the sidewalk. Rooms in the completed portion of the hotel include a view of the beach, TV, ceiling fan, washing machine, and kitchen. Not all rooms have the same amenities, but all have access to the beachside swimming pool and restaurant (4-person rooms with water view and kitchen 200 pesos, without kitchen 150 pesos, without either 100 pesos).

In keeping with the casual spirit, restaurants do not have set menus; rather, they ask you what type of seafood you'd like to eat (expect to spend 15-20 pesos per person). **Enramada Bacanora,** the third restaurant from the right as you face the water, offers the friendliest atmosphere and cheapest prices (open daily 7am-6pm).

If you simply *must* exert yourself while in Barra de Potosí (something the locals may not understand), your only option is to hike up the dirt road to the lighthouse that sits atop **Cerro Guamiule** (2000m), the peak near the restaurants that guards the southern entrance to the bay. After a half-hour walk, you will be rewarded with a view of the bay and its 20km of beaches. After gaping, walk north along the shore of Playa Potosí, the southernmost beach on the bay, to the aptly named **Playa Blanca** (3km). You will pass **Playa Coacoyul** (8km), **Playa Riscaliyo** (19km), and pebbly **Playa Manzanillo** (24km) before reaching another lighthouse (26km), which overlooks the northern edge of the bay. All beaches are free of tourists in the summer months but fill up with a few hundred Mexican visitors during Christmas.

Getting There: From Zihuatanejo, "Petatlán" buses for Potosí leave from a station outside Restaurante La Jaiba on Las Palmas, off Juárez (every 15min. 6am-9pm, 30min., 3 pesos). Ask to be let off at Achotes, an unmarked intersection. A pick-up truck will be waiting (or will be arriving soon) on the side road to pick up passengers and make the bumpy trip to the *enramadas* (30min., 4 pesos). Trucks return to the intersection from the same spot (every 30min. until 5pm); the bus to Zihuatanejo leaves from the other side of the highway. Expat Robert Edmiston (tel. 4-22-43) will drive groups of two or more to the beach of their choice (US$25 roundtrip).

■ Acapulco

Once upon a time, Acapulco was the stunningly beautiful playground of the rich and famous. It was where Hollywood legends celebrated their silver-screen successes and where scores of passengers on "The Love Boat" bought straw *sombreros* for their new-found TV loves. But time passes and fairy tales fade: Acapulco's glamour went out just about the time that Gopher hung up his cruise ship whites and got himself elected to the U.S. Congress. Today, Acapulco is a slim, glitzy hangnail of a resort. Vendors crowd the streets and cling to slow-moving or indecisive visitors and restaurant owners attempt to suck in the older *norteamericanos*, Europeans, and Mexicans who still think of Acapulco as "the city that never sleeps." Indeed, perhaps the best time to visit the city is at night, when darkness shrouds the grime and allows the glitter of the street lamps to evoke Acapulco's fairy tale past.

ORIENTATION

Acapulco Bay lies 400km south of Mexico City and 239km southeast of Ixtapa Zihuatanejo. Route 200 feeds into **La Costera (Avenida Costera Miguel Alemán),** the main drag. The traditional downtown area, with the *zócalo* and the cathedral, is in the western part of town (to the left as seen from the water). **Acapulco Dorado,** full of fast food chains, malls, and luxury hotels, stretches from **Parque Papagayo** to the naval base. The ultra-chic resorts on **Acapulco Diamante,** farther east towards the airport, wipe out any dirty trace of Mexico that would disturb the paying guests. Most budget accommodations and restaurants lie between the *zócalo* and **La Quebrada,** the famous cliff-diving spot. In southwest Acapulco, a peninsula with **Playas Caleta** and **Caletilla** juts out into the bay.

"Hornos" or "Cici" buses run from Caleta along the Costera all the way to the naval base (1.80 pesos for old orange and white buses, 2.50 for air-conditioned buses). "Cine Río-La Base" buses go from the *zócalo* to the base down Av. Cuauhtémoc. To get from the **Estrella de Oro** bus station to the *zócalo* (a 40-min. walk), cross the street and flag down any bus heading southwest (1.80 pesos). A "*zócalo*" bus (1.80 pesos) will do the trick from the **Estrella Blanca** station. A **taxi** from the *zócalo* to the bus station costs 10 pesos, to the airport 50 pesos.

PRACTICAL INFORMATION

Tourist Offices: SEFOTUR, Costera 187 (tel. 86-91-64), on Playa Hornos across from Banamex. Open Mon.-Fri. 9am-2pm and 4-7pm, Sat. 10am-2pm. In an **emergency,** contact the **Procuraduría del Turista,** Costera 4455 (tel. 84-45-83), in the Centro Internacional in front of CICI waterpark. Open daily 9am-9pm.
Tourist police: (tel. 85-04-90). Officers clad in white wander around the *zócalo.*
Travel Agency: M&M Tours, Costera 26-A L-2 (tel. 84-89-60), on Playa Condesa between McDonald's and the Fiesta Americana. Open daily 8am-10pm.
Consulates: U.S., Costera 187 (tel. 85-72-07 or 85-66-00), in Hotel Club del Sol. Open Mon.-Fri. 10am-2pm. **Canada** (tel. 85-66-21), next to the U.S. Consulate. Open daily 10am-2pm. **U.K., Australia,** and **New Zealand** (tel. 84-16-50 or 84-66-05), in the Hotel Las Brisas. Open Mon.-Fri. 9am-2pm and 4-7pm. **Casa Consular** (tel. 84-70-50, ext. 116 or 117), in the Centro Internacional Acapulco, provides information on other consulates. Open Mon.-Fri. 9am-2pm and 4-7pm.
Currency Exchange: Banks on the Costera have decent rates. All open Mon.-Fri. 9am-3pm. *Casas de cambio* are ubiquitous, and often open until 8pm.
American Express, Costera 1628 (tel. 69-11-00 to -24; fax 69-11-88), on the bottom floor of the shopping center. Open Mon.-Sat. 10am-7pm.
Telephones: LADATELs line the Costera. **Caseta Carranza,** Carranza 9, is two blocks from the *zócalo* towards the strip. Open daily 8am-10pm.
Telegrams: (tel. 82-26-21; fax 83-84-82), on the Costera next to the post office. Open for telegrams and money orders Mon.-Fri. 8am-7pm, Sat. 9am-noon.
Airport: (tel. 84-03-03), on Rte. 200, 26km south of the city. **Aerocaribe** (tel. 84-23-42). **Aeroméxico** (tel. 85-16-25). **American** (tel. 66-92-33). **Continental** (tel. 60-90-63). **Delta** (tel. 84-14-28). **Mexicana** (tel. 84-68-90). **Taesa** (tel. 86-56-00).
Buses: Estrella de Oro (tel. 85-87-05), on Cuauhtémoc. To Cuernavaca (10:30am, 3:40, 5:30, and 8pm, 4hr., 100 pesos), Mexico City (11 per day 6:45am-12:30am, 5hr., 128-180 pesos), Taxco (7, 9am, and 4:30pm, 4hr., 73 pesos), and Zihuatanejo (10:50am and 3pm, 3hr., 43 pesos). **Estrella Blanca,** Av. Ejido 47 (tel. 69-20-29). To Chilpancingo (every 30min. 3:40am-10pm, 2hr., 30 pesos), Cuernavaca (11:20am, 3, 8, and 11:50pm, 5hr., 85 pesos), Mexico City (9 per day 1:20am-11:16pm, 5hr., 135 pesos), Puebla (12:15, 2:15, and 11pm, 7hr., 121 pesos), and Querétaro (5 per day 8-10hr., 162-182 pesos).
Car Rental: Hertz, Costera 1945 (tel. 85-68-89), past La Gran Plaza on the left. Small VW with insurance 285 pesos per day. Open daily 8am-7pm.
Bookstore: Sanborn's, Costera 209, two blocks from the *zócalo* towards the hotel zone. Great selection of English paperbacks. Open daily 7:30am-11pm.
Markets: Mercado, Av. Constituyentes at Hurtado. Open daily 6am-9pm. **Supermarket Comercial Mexicana,** near the tourist office. Open daily 8am-8pm.
Laundromat: Lavadín (tel. 82-28-90), on José Iglesias, one block left of the cathedral. Same day and delivery service. Open Mon.-Sat. 8am-8pm.
Red Cross: (tel. 85-41-00), on Ruiz Cortínez, north of the *zócalo.* Take a "Hospital" bus. 24-hr. emergency service. No English spoken. **Sociedad de Asistencia Médica Turística** (tel. 85-58-00 or 85-59-59) has a 24-hr. doctor. English spoken.
Pharmacy: Faber Farmacia, Azueta 6, two blocks left of the cathedral. Open 24hr. **ISSTE Farmacias,** Quebrada 1 (tel. 82-34-77), directly behind the cathedral on the *zócalo.* The storefront faces Independencia. Open daily 8am-8pm.

Acapulco

Estrella Blanca buses, 13
Estrella de Oro Buses, 14
Casa de Huéspedes Anita, 9
Casa de Huéspedes La
   Mamá Hélène, 10
Catedral de Nuestra Sra.
   de Solidad, 11
CICI Waterpark, 17
La Diana, 15
Fuerte de San Diego, 12
Hotel Angelita, 5
Hotel Asturias, 4
Hotel Misión, 8
Hotel Torre Eiffel, 3
Jovito's, 16
Mágico Mundo Marino, 1
Muséo del Arqueologia, 21
Palacio Municipal, 6
Plaza de Toros Caletilla, 2

Hospital: IMSS, Ruiz Cortínez 128 (tel. 86-36-08), north of the *zócalo* along Madero. Take a "Hospital" bus. 24-hr. emergency service.

Police: LOCATEL (tel. 81-11-00 or -64), next door to the SEFOTUR office. Locates lost people and vehicles. Contacts police or ambulance. Open 24hr.

Post Office: Costera 215 (tel. 82-20-83), on the ground floor of the Palacio Federal. Open Mon.-Fri. 8am-7pm, Sat. 9am-1pm. **Postal Code:** 39300.

Telephone Code: 74.

ACCOMMODATIONS

Sleeping on the beaches of Acapulco Bay is unsafe. Fortunately, budget accommodations are easier to find here than anywhere else on Mexico's Pacific coast. Acapulco is a haggler's dream: be certain to inquire about discounts before paying for a room. However, during *Semana Santa* rooms are nearly double the off-season prices, and

it's hard to find lodgings without a previous reservation. The first three hotels listed are near the *zócalo*. The last four are near *la Quebrada;* to get there, take Hidalgo and follow it to the right as it forks uphill.

Hotel Misión, Prof. J. Felipe Valle 12 (tel. 82-36-43), two blocks left of the *zócalo*. The guests chatting over breakfast (9-15 pesos) in the courtyard and the lazy cats sprawled out on the stairway give this place a homey feel. All rooms have ceiling fans and private baths; some have desks and sofas. 70 pesos per person.

Casa de Huéspedes Anita, Teniente José Azueta 12 (tel. 82-50-46), at La Paz, 3 blocks from the *zócalo*. All rooms have fans, private bathrooms, and hot water if you ask for it the day before. 30 pesos per person, up to 5 people per room.

Casa de Huéspedes Mama Hélène, Benito Juárez 12 (tel. 82-23-96; fax 83-86-97). French owner holds court over a posse of ping-pong-playing, coffee-drinking, chain-smoking Euro backpackers. Haphazard collection of English novels. Flowery rooms with fans but no hot water. Singles 60 pesos. Doubles 100 pesos.

Hotel Angelita, Quebrada 37 (tel. 83-57-34). Fans keep the rooms cool, hot water makes the bathrooms special. 30 pesos per person, up to 5 people per room.

La Torre Eiffel, Inalámbrica 110 (tel. 82-16-83). At the top of La Quebrada, turn left and walk up a very steep hill. All rooms have hot water, fans, and TVs. Shady terrace offer a clear view of the ocean. Swimming pool. 40-50 pesos per person.

Hotel Asturias, Quebrada 45 (tel. 83-65-48), near Hotel Angelita. All rooms have fans, 24hr.-hot water, and at least 2 beds. Guests enjoy attentive staff and a swimming pool. Singles 50 pesos. Doubles 80 pesos. Each additional person 40 pesos.

FOOD

Acapulco's restaurants are a godsend for Americans homesick for fast-food *gringo* cuisine. The many chic restaurants between Playa Condesa and the base cater mainly to tourists who apparently don't fret about money. If you insist on eating on the Costera, try **El Fogón,** across from the Continental Plaza (sandwiches 10 pesos; open 24hr.) or **Jovito's** (tel. 84-84-33), across from the Fiesta Americana at Playa Condesa (*tacos de mariscos* 23 pesos; open daily 1pm-midnight). As usual, *típico* spots serve cheaper meals; try the hundreds of *fondas* (food stands) throughout the city or the Mercado Central.

100% Natural, Costera 248 (tel. 85-13-12, ext. 100), at the corner of Sebastián Vizcaíno, across from the tourist office. Several other branches line the Costera. Health food restaurant serving hearty sandwiches with sprouts and lettuce (20-24 pesos), fruit salad (19-22 pesos), and chilly, smooth *licuados* (13.50 pesos). Open daily 8am-midnight. Other branches open 24hr.

The Fat Farm/La Granja del Pingui, Juárez 10, next door to Mama Hélène. Vegetable soup (7 pesos) is a specialty. Watch TV as you enjoy your poultry and meat (14-23 pesos) or fish (14–24 pesos) entree. Open daily 10am-10pm.

Mariscos Nacho's (tel. 82-28-91), Azueta and Juárez, one block from the Costera. An open air *marisquería* serving seafood with rice (20 pesos) and delicious *camarones al mojo de ajo* (garlic shrimp, 35 pesos). Open daily 8am-11pm.

Tepoznieves, in the corner of the *zócalo* near the Costera. Branches throughout the city. Ice cream in every flavor imaginable, from rose petal to burnt milk, including all-time favorites like strawberry and rum raisin. Small *nieve* 6 pesos, medium 8 pesos. Open daily 9:30am-10:30pm.

SAND AND SIGHTS

Península de las Playas

At **La Quebrada,** speedo-clad daredevil **clavadistas** (divers) perform death-defying dives that make Olympians look like wusses (shows at 12:45, 7:30, 8:30, 9:30, and 10:30pm). Each performance includes at least two 25-meter and one 35-meter dives. Though most spectators congregate at the bottom level, closest to the cliff, the view is better from the levels to the immediate right of the ticket booth. La Quebrada is a

15-minute walk from the *zócalo*, following the road that starts to the left of the cathedral's entrance. Continue until it ends at the parking lot of the hotel.

At the westernmost tip of Acapulco Bay, on the seaward side of the peninsula, lie **Playas Caleta** and **Caletilla.** Their gently rolling waves are ideal for swimming and attract hundreds of local families. The narrow causeway that separates the two beaches leads to the island occupied by **Mágico Mundo Marino** (tel. 83-11-93), a waterpark with slides and pools (sea lion show 1 and 4pm; open daily 9am-7pm; admission 20 pesos, children under 12, 15 pesos).

The **Plaza de Toros Caletilla,** Acapulco's main bullring, sits beyond the abandoned yellow jai alai auditoriums 200m west of Caletilla beach. *Corridas* take place from Sundays at 5pm, December until Easter week, when the best-known *matadores* appear. Buy tickets at the Centro Kennedy box office (tel. 85-85-40), Costera at Álvaro Saavedra, or at the bull ring after 4:30pm on the day of the fight.

From the Tourist Office to Parque Papagayo

The stretch of sand along the Costera, away from Old Acapulco, is blessed with few highrises and smaller crowds than the beaches at Caleta or farther down the bay. Playas **Tamarindos, Hornos,** and **Hornitos,** between Las Hamacas Hotel and the Radisson, are called the "afternoon beaches." This is where the fishermen bring in their catches. The waves are moderate; the sand great for beach sports.

Mexican families who seek an alternative to the beach come to **Parque Papagayo,** which sprawls from Costera to Av. Cuauhtémoc. Entering on Costera by the Gigante supermarket, you'll find a **skating rink** (admission 10 pesos, 6 pesos to rent regular skates, 8 pesos for rollerblades; open daily noon-midnight). The rest of the park has shaded paths for bikes and walkers. There's an aviary in the center, surrounded by an artificial lake where you can rent paddleboats (10 pesos). Kids will find a wading pool, exotic birds from Australia, and a zillion shady spots for hide and seek (tel. 85-71-77; open Mon.-Fri. 6am-7pm, Sat.-Sun. 6am-8pm).

From La Diana to the Naval Base

A trip to **Playa Condesa,** at the center of the bay, is always exhilarating. Exercise caution: the waves are strong, and the sea floor drops without warning. The poor swimming conditions don't bother the throngs of sun worshippers who alternately lounge under their blue umbrellas and treat the beach as a runway for their minimal clothing fashion shows. Farther down the bay, between the golf course and naval base, is **Playa Icacos.** As you move towards the base, the waves become gentler.

CICI (tel. 84-80-33), Costera at Cristóbal Colón, is a state-owned **waterpark.** Let artificial waves toss and hurl you headfirst down the long, winding water slides, then rush to watch trained dolphins perform (shows at 12:30, 2:30, and 5pm; open daily 10am-6pm; admission 40 pesos, children under 11, 34 pesos). To reach the park, follow Costera until you see the walls painted with bright blue waves and larger-than-life dolphins, or simply take a "CICI" or "Base" bus (1.80 pesos).

Puerto Marqués

Lacking the pre-packaged polish of the strip only a few kilometers away, the beach town of **Puerto Marqués** encompasses an unremarkable ribbon of sand lined wall-to-wall with restaurants so close to the water that the bay's waves lap at diners' feet. The bus ride to this bay is the real attraction, thanks to a magnificent vista from the top of the hill before descending into town. Take a "Puerto Marqués" bus across the street from La Diana or by Comercial Mexicana supermarket at Playa Hornitos, on the beach side of the street (about every 30min. 5:30am-9pm, 45min., 1.80 pesos). As the bus rambles along, the Bahía de Puerto Marqués and the pounding surf of **Playa Revolcadero** come into full view. Beautiful **Playa Pichilingue,** a small, often deserted patch of sand on the Bay, is inaccessible by land.

ENTERTAINMENT

In Acapulco, every night is Saturday night. Most clubs pulsate with activity from 11pm to 5am and charge 80- or 90-peso covers, which usually include open bar. It's always easier, and cheaper, for women to get in. The newest sensation is **Palladium** (tel. 81-03-00), at Escénica Las Brisas, which draws in crowds with a dazzling laser show. **Andrómedas,** on the Costera near both the Hard Rock Café and Planet Hollywood, features a giant fish tank, dance space for 2000 people, and a whopping 250-peso cover for men (50 pesos for women). Alternatives to the hi-tech, exclusive discos include **Disco Beach** (tel. 84-70-64), on Condesa Beach, an open air club where the dancing often spills over onto the sand, and **Nina's,** Costera 2909 (tel. 84-24-00), on the beach side near CICI, with live tropical music. Unlike most places in Mexico, Acapulco has a visible gay and lesbian nightlife. **Gallery,** de los Deportes 11 (tel. 84-34-97), one block inland from the Calinda Quality Inn, is popular for its famous female impersonators (shows 11pm and 1am; cover 50 pesos; dancing begins daily at 10pm). The **Open House Bar,** Plaza Condesa M. Alemán at Piedra Picuda Puerta 4 (tel. 84-72-85), is another hotspot (no cover; open daily 8pm-4am).

Non-dancers flock to **Plaza Bahía,** a large shopping mall on Costera, past La Gran Plaza on the water side, to satisfy the urge to acquire, speed around a mini race course at **Go-Karts** (tel. 86-71-47), on the third floor (15 pesos for 5min., 25 pesos for 10min; open daily 10am-1am), or bowl at the **Boliche** (tel. 85-09-70), on the fourth floor (100 pesos per hr., shoes 7 pesos; open daily 11am-2am).

■ Near Acapulco: Pie de la Cuesta

Pie de la Cuesta is known for its truly magnificent sunsets—the lazy sun lingers beautifully over the Pacific horizon just before dropping out of view. A single-lane highway runs through Acapulco's hills to Pie de la Cuesta, ending at the narrow road that separates the Pacific from the placid waters of **Laguna de Coyuca,** and the hustle and bustle of Acapulco from the serenity of a small beach community.

At Playa Pie de la Cuesta, pleasure-seekers can choose between salt and fresh water. Since the Pacific's rough waves preclude swimming, many head to the lagoon instead, the site of the area's best **waterskiing.** Several ski clubs line the lagoon (ski rental about 200 pesos per hr., 30 pesos for a lesson). Rest and relaxation is all too often interrupted, unfortunately, by aggressive *lancha* agents. Their tours of the lagoon include visits to the area where the exploding helicopter scene from *Rambo* was filmed (about 30 pesos per person in a *colectivo* boat). *Lancha* agents notwithstanding, the serenity of Pie de la Cuesta is worth at least a daytrip. The air is cleaner here, the water bluer, the surf stronger, the beach less crowded, and the scenery more stunning than in Acapulco. **Villa Nirvana** (tel. 60-16-31), a blue and white building a few blocks from the bus stop, carves out its own utopia complete with restaurant, swimming pool, and rooms with fans and private baths (60 pesos per person; high season 120 pesos). Beyond the pharmacy towards the base is **Acapulco Trailer Park** (tel. 60-00-10), with campgrounds, trailer hook-up sites, bathrooms, and ocean views (40 pesos per night).

Getting There: Buses leave from the Costera, across from the post office in Acapulco. Buses marked "Pie de la Cuesta Playa" go directly to the road along the beach; those labeled "Pie de la Cuesta Centro" stop on a parallel street in a small market place (40min, 1.80 pesos). From there, turn left down a dirt road; you should be able to see the shimmering ocean in the distance. At the end of the road, turn right and you're headed towards the base. A *combi* will take you as far as **La Barra,** the enchanted spot where the water from the lagoon flows into the ocean (2 pesos). To return to Acapulco, go back to the market and hail a bus going to the right.

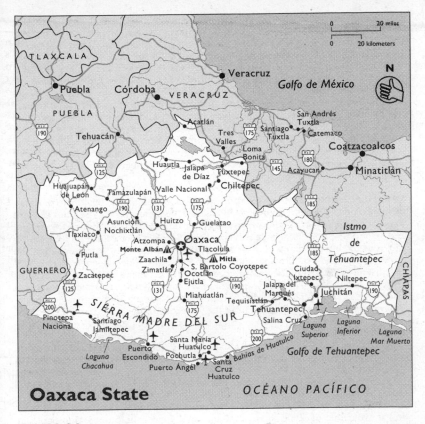

Oaxaca State

OAXACA

■ Tuxtepec

After years of neglect by Oaxaca's highland capital, Tuxtepec is now booming—and the signs of growth are everywhere, from the massive Corona brewery on the city's edge to the dozens of new storefronts that lie in its shadow. In the past two decades, the city's population has skyrocketed from 20,000 to about 110,000. Boom and beauty rarely go hand in hand, and this is no exception: busy and hard-working Tuxtepec is a far cry from the sleepy colonial towns that lure tourists to the state. Nevertheless, it's a decent place to pass a night en route from the Gulf to Oaxaca.

Orientation Tuxtepec is on the northern frontier of Oaxaca state, 222km from the state capital and 165km south of Veracruz. The Papaloapan River forms a U-shaped bend here, running along one edge of the city. The two main plazas—**Parque Juárez,** the *zócalo* proper, located at one end of the *centro,* and **Parque Hidalgo,** at the opposite side of downtown—are connected by **Av. Independencia,** where many of the restaurants, hotels, and banks cluster. The two bus stations form the base of a "T" shape with Independencia and the river as the top line. From the **ADO** station at Ortiz and Primero de Mayo, exit the waiting area and turn right around the corner. Walk straight for one block and turn right on **Blvd. A. Camacho,** the wide thoroughfare, continue past the statue on **Matamoros,** which makes up the long, vertical part of the "T." The **AU** and **Cuenca** station is on the right side of Matamoros as you head towards the river. Exiting from that station, turn right and follow Matamoros for 3½ blocks until it dead-ends at Independencia. Taxis will take you for 8 pesos.

Walking down Matamoros from the bus stations, the cross streets will be, in order, **Carranza, Libertad, 5 de Mayo, 20 de Noviembre,** and then **Independencia.** To reach the *zócalo,* turn left on Libertad, and follow it up to **Allende,** which constitutes one side of the *zócalo.* To get to **Parque Hidalgo,** turn right on Libertad. Buses are not plentiful in Tuxtepec, but the whole commercial district can be walked in 20 minutes. Be aware that **Calle Benito Juárez,** a block from the *zócalo,* is different from **Blvd. Benito Juárez,** near Parque Hidalgo. Street names are usually labeled on building walls at the intersections. Street numbers are also clearly marked, but often with more than one number. Addresses below follow the numbers displayed on blue and white placards with the city seal on them.

Practical Information Tuxtepec has no tourist office, but the offices of **Ayuntamiento** on the second floor of the **Palacio Municipal** (tel. 5-15-66) and **Cultura Popular** on the first can answer queries or give directions (open Mon.-Fri. 9am-2pm and 5-8pm). The only full-service **travel agent** is **Sotelo Viajes,** Morelos 118 (tel. 5-26-65), near the intersection with 5 de Mayo, six blocks towards Matamoros from the *zócalo* (open Mon.-Fri. 9am-2pm and 4-6pm). **Banamex,** Independencia 36 (tel. 5-23-28), just off the corner of the *zócalo,* accepts both cash and traveler's checks and has an **ATM** (open Mon.-Fri. 9am-3pm). There are **long-distance telephone** *casetas* at Calle Juárez 17, just off Independencia (open Mon.-Sat. 8am-9:30pm, Sun. 8am-3pm). **Telegrams** and **faxes** can be sent from the **Telecomm** office, Av. Carranza 875 (tel. 5-05-01), four blocks from Independencia between Aldama and Morelos (open Mon.-Fri. 8am-6pm, Sat. 9am-noon).

ADO buses (tel. 5-04-73) travel to Mexico City (9 per day, 8hr., 115 pesos), Oaxaca (7:30am, 10:30pm, midnight, 6hr., 46 pesos), Puebla (5 per day, 6hr., 84 pesos), Tuxtla Gutiérrez (1am, 9hr., 133 pesos), Veracruz (12 per day, 3hr., 38 pesos), Xalapa (5am, 5hr., 59 pesos), and other destinations. **AU** (tel. 5-04-73), on Matamoros, and **Cuenca** (tel. 5-02-37), in the same station, offer similar service.

The **markets** are on Independencia between Juárez and Arteaga, near the *zócalo,* and at the corner of 20 de Noviembre and Blvd. Juárez (both open Mon.-Sat. 7am-8pm, Sun. 7am-2pm). There is a **supermarket, Súperperchín,** on Independencia 314 (tel. 5-04-35), near the *zócalo* (open Mon.-Sat. 8am-9pm, Sun. 8am-3pm). Take dirty laundry to **Tintorería Iris,** Independencia 363, at Morales (open daily 8am-8pm). **Farmacia Albatros,** 20 de Noviembre 996 (tel. 5-25-82), at the intersection with Aldama, is open 24 hours. The **Red Cross,** Madero 110 (tel. 5-00-57), one block west of Blvd. Benito Juárez, and **Hospital IMSS** (tel. 5-04-27), Blvd. Juárez and Reforma, are open 24 hours. No English is spoken. The **police** (tel. 5-31-66) are available 24 hours in the Palacio Municipal. In case of **emergency,** call the **Policía Preventiva** (tel. 5-15-45) anytime. The **post office** is at the corner of Independencia and Hidalgo (open Mon.-Fri. 8am-7pm). **Postal code:** 68300. **Telephone Code:** 287.

Accommodations Tuxtepec has several inexpensive hotels. Particularly well located is **Hotel Posada Guadalupana,** Independencia 584 (tel. 5-11-95), between Matamoros and Aldama. From the second-class bus station, follow Matamoros until it hits Independencia, then turn left; the hotel will be on the left side of the block. The rocking chairs around the patio provide an escape from the bustle of Independencia. Older rooms are clean but lack hot water and are beginning to show their age; newer rooms are spacious, with cable TV and well equipped bathrooms. All rooms have fans; no credit cards accepted (old singles 30 pesos, new ones 60 pesos; old doubles 40 pesos; new ones 70 pesos). Unlike the breezy sitting room with a TV, the bedrooms at **Hotel La Misión,** Hidalgo 409 (tel. 5-23-81), are spartan and rather somber. From Matamoros, turn left on Carranza and walk five blocks to Hidalgo towards the *zócalo;* the hotel is on the left side. Hot water all day, fans in the rooms, but no credit cards (singles 35 pesos; doubles 40 pesos; triples 45 pesos).

Food Tuxtepec is a solidly working- and middle-class city, so there are lots of affordable restaurants along Independencia. For super-cheap eats, head to the **market** on Independencia and Calle Juárez and the stalls along Matamoros. Enjoy juice squeezed fresh from the cornucopia for 6 pesos at **Cocina Económica La Flor de Café,** Independencia 35, near the *zócalo. Tortas* are 5 pesos; a *comida corrida* (10 pesos) is served quicker than you can chew it (open daily 7am-7pm). At **Los Caporales,** on the second floor of Independencia 560 (tel. 5-44-05), next to Hotel Posada Guadalupana, silk flowers and faux marble tabletops provide a refreshing break from the town's ubiquitous plastic Corona chairs and tables (*comida corrida* 15 pesos; open daily 8am-10pm).

Sights and Entertainment When it comes to tourist attractions, Tuxtepec comes up empty-handed. The city serves mainly as a base for daytrips to the surrounding area. When you return to Tuxtepec at night, dusty and tired, you can keep yourself amused at the **Centro Recreativo "Alf,"** 20 de Noviembre 1364 (tel. 5-40-09), near Parque Hidalgo. No alien life forms spotted, but you can shoot pool with the locals (3 pesos per ½hr.), rattle the foosball table, or catch some table hockey. The center serves snacks, pizza, and *refrescos;* the premises are alcohol-free (open daily 11am-midnight). **Cinema Plus,** 20 de Noviembre 1364, and **Cinema Tuxtepec,** Blvd. Camacho 945 (tel. 5-01-76), on the way to the ADO station from the city center, show English-language movies (7 and 8 pesos respectively).

In the evening, locals gather in the squares and on the few terraces along Independencia that offer views of the river. If you would rather find crowds than escape them, you might head to one of the two discos in town. **Fettiche** (tel. 5-23-39) is at Av. 2 and Calle 3, west of the ADO station (open Thurs.-Sat. 9pm-3am), while **Chichos** is on Blvd. Juárez (cover charge 15-20 pesos; open Thurs.-Sat. 9pm-3am and Sun. 6-11pm). **Bars** line Independencia, and abound in the area bounded by Blvd. A Camacho and Calle de la Felicidad, a few blocks from the ADO station. For more wholesome diversions, Tuxtepec sponsors an annual exposition for 12 days at the end of April and beginning of May with fireworks, music, dances, and cattle. Day of the Dead at the beginning of November is celebrated with up to 15 altars in the *zócalo* and a display of indigenous crafts and cooking. The city ends the year with rides and revelry from December 20 to January 6.

■ Near Tuxtepec

The area around Tuxtepec is renowned for its scenic beauty; unfortunately, most of it is not easily accessible by bus. The sites along the road to Oaxaca are perhaps the easiest to reach; they are served by an AU bus en route to **Valle Nacional,** a small tobacco-growing town 58km from Tuxtepec, where Porfirio Díaz once built a work camp for his political enemies. On the way there, the bus passes through **Chiltepec,** a town famous among gastronomes for its renditions of regional cuisine, and crosses a small suspension bridge on its way to **Jacatepec.** Another bus passes through **San Lucas Ojitlán** and **Jalapa de Díaz,** 42km and 70km from Tuxtepec, respectively. Ojitlán is notable for its *artesanías,* while Jalapa is known for its brightly colored *huipiles.* Other destinations are accessible by *colectivo* from the Mercado Flores Magón, on 20 de Noviembre between Riva Palacio and Blvd. Juárez, two blocks west of Parque Hidalgo. Consult the folks at the office for *cultura popular* about musical events and crafts in nearby towns.

▓ Oaxaca de Juárez

The ascent to the city of Oaxaca (pop. 700,000) winds through stomach-churning mountain roads. The sharp turns, however, are the only thing about Oaxaca that doesn't welcome tourists. The city itself offers wonderful colonial architecture, well placed green spaces, and cobblestone pedestrian streets. Oaxaca doesn't just beckon to foreigners—it sucks them in. One month stays at a language school turn into whole summers of immersion, and those who do leave make plans to return to sip rich Oaxacan hot chocolate in the *zócalo* as soon as they can. The many foreigners that have come to Oaxaca over the years to study Spanish, shop for wooden animals, or tour archaeological sites have left their mark—English appears on signs and menus and is often spoken, vegetarian meals and long-distance telephones are easy to find, and some places even offer temporary e-mail accounts.

Though Oaxaca strives to accommodate visitors, it resists the dilution of its culture and history. The state's 16 indigenous groups make it the most cultural diverse in Mexico. Many *oaxaqueños* still speak indigenous languages like Mixtec and Zapotec, wear traditional clothes, and venture into the city only on Saturdays for market day. Benito Juárez, Mexico's only *indígena* president, was a Oaxacan Zapotec, and the city's most visible monuments are dedicated to him. With a future that looks increasingly touristy, the city must struggle to maintain its authenticity and allure. Though the path ahead may be windy, the view will always be spectacular.

ORIENTATION

Oaxaca de Juárez rests in the Oaxaca Valley, between the towering Sierra Madre del Sur and the Puebla-Oaxaca range, 523km southeast of Mexico City, 435km south of Veracruz, and 526km west of Tuxtla Gutiérrez. Principal access to Oaxaca from the north and east is via Rte. 190.

While most of Oaxaca's streets form a grid, many change names as they swing by the *zócalo*. The large English-language maps posted around the *zócalo*, at the bus stations, and in the lobbies of fancy hotels clearly mark all sights. There are two main squares in the center of the historic district. The *zócalo*, or **Plaza de la Constitución,** is formed by the side of the cathedral and the arches of the **Palacio de Gobierno** opposite it. The main entrance to the cathedral faces the **Plaza Alameda de León,** bounded by the post office on the opposite side. The street that runs between the two squares is **Av. Hidalgo,** one of the few streets that does not change names. The street that runs behind the cathedral and the *zócalo* begins as **Bustamante** below the *zócalo*, turns into **Valdivieso** behind the cathedral, and ends up as the **Andador Turístico (Av. Macedonio Alcalá),** a museum-lined pedestrian walkway, past the Plaza Alameda.

Oaxaca's downtown is circumscribed by a busy peripheral expressway, called the **Periférico** in the south but known by other names as it loops above the Church of Santo Domingo. Avenida Hidalgo divides *el centro* into two principal areas: the bud-

---

The Pick-up Artist

The main plaza in Oaxaca, with its live music and numerous cafés, draws out crowds of locals and foreigners every night. "*Zócalo* Boys," as everyone calls them, are an integral part of the culture that has developed around this international mix of people. These playful men tend to come from wealthy Oaxacan families and have artistic and intellectual leanings; they are well dressed and often speak English. And they spend their nights at the cafés, striking up conversations with foreign women sitting at nearby tables. Part of their attraction to their pasttime is approaching a woman to have the kind of flirtatious, carefree, frank conversation that would not always be possible within the norms of machismo. Another part of the fascination for the enounter, undoubtedly, is the physical intrigue of their conversational partners. Casual conversations easily turn into lunch or movie dates. *Zócalo* boys are not confined to the *zócalo;* many frequent the salsa bar *Candela,* where they charm foreign women with their moves. One is so renowned for his rhythm that he offers dance lessons—*por supuesto,* only to women.

Oaxaca

Casa Arnel, 1
Hotel Chayo, 10
Hotel Lupita, 8
Hotel Mesón del Ángel, 2
Hotel Pasaje, 9
Hotel Pombo, 7
Hotel Reforma, 3
Iglesia de Santo Domingo, 6
Palacio Municipal
(Tourist Office), 4
Tourist Office, 10
Youth Hostel El Pasador, 5

NOTE: Streets generally change their names at ZOCALO

SOUTHERN PACIFIC COAST

get district lies south of Hidalgo, while expensive hotels and restaurants cluster around the *zócalo* north of and on Hidalgo. Most of Oaxaca's sights are snuggled between lavish private residences in the neighborhood north of Hidalgo. The main street that runs to the left of the entrance to the cathedral is **Av. Independencia.** Banks, long distance phones, and newsstands cluster around the two blocks between Independencia and **Trujano/Guerrero,** which runs along the *zócalo.*

The **first-class bus station** is on **Calzada Niños Héroes de Chapultepec,** 11 blocks from the *zócalo* past the Andador Turístico. To reach the *zócalo* from the bus station, cross the street and catch a bus marked "Centro," (1.20 pesos). The bus turns left on Juárez. If you get off at Hidalgo, the *zócalo* will be three blocks to your right. To make the 20-minute walk from the station, head left on Chapultepec for six blocks to Alcalá and turn left, then walk 12 blocks to the main plaza. From the **AU station,** take the *colectivo* marked "Centro," which will eventually head down Independencia. Ask to be let off at García Vigil, which will put you at the end of the Plaza Alameda away from the *zócalo;* the main square is one block towards the cathedral. If you care to make the 2km walk from the station (not recommended after dark), take a left coming out of the door, walk to the stoplight, take a right onto Madero, and follow it to the **train station.** A 25-minute walk stretches ahead of you: turn right as if coming out of the station, walk five long blocks, then turn left onto Independencia, which will lead you to the *zócalo.* You can also catch the *colectivo* marked "Centro" at the train station. From the **second-class bus station,** exit the terminal, and cross the street to take a bus or taxi to the *centro.* Or, you could walk to the left, cross the busy Periférico at the stoplight, follow it for a block, turn on Trujano and follow it east for eight long blocks until you hit the *zócalo.* **Taxis** charge 10 pesos from any of these stations. It's a good idea to take taxis when crossing town late at night, but be aware that cabbies charge extra from 11pm to 5am.

PRACTICAL INFORMATION

Tourist Offices: SEDETUR provides brochures, maps, assistance in finding hotel rooms, information on fairs, and details on the surrounding villages. English spoken. Main office at 5 de Mayo 200 (tel. 6-48-28), at the corner of Morelos. Smaller office at Independencia 607 (tel. 6-01-23), inside the Palacio Municipal. Both open daily 9am-8pm. **CEPROTUR,** Alcalá 407 (tel./fax 6-72-80), on the Andador Turístico at Allende, and in the Plaza Santo Domingo, provides assistance to tourists. Open daily 9am-9pm. **Info booth** at the airport (tel. 1-50-40).

Consulates: In an emergency, **CEPROTUR** (above) will get consular assistance. **U.S.,** Alcalá 201 #204 (tel. 4-30-54). Hidden under an arched doorway. Open Mon.-Fri. 9am-2pm. **Canada,** Dr. Liceaga 119 #8 (tel. 3-37-77; fax 5-21-47). Open Mon.-Fri. 9am-2pm. **Germany** and **U.K.,** Hidalgo 817 #5 (tel. 3-08-65 and 6-72-80). Open Mon.-Fri. 9am-8pm.

Currency Exchange: Banamex, Hidalgo 821 (tel. 6-59-00), one block from the *zócalo,* has an **ATM** (open Mon.-Fri. 9am-11:30am). **Banco Serfin,** Independencia 705, to the left of the cathedral's entrance also has an ATM (open Mon.-Fri. 9am-2pm). **Cash Express,** Alcalá 201, exchanges money at more flexible hours. Open Mon.-Sat. 8am-8pm. **Western Union,** inside the Elektra Store at 210 Cristóbal Colón, two blocks from the *zócalo,* will wire money in minutes.

Telephones: LADATELs are in front of the post office, at La Iglesia de Santo Domingo, and at the ADO station. *Casetas* available at **Computel,** Hidalgo 204 (tel. 4-80-84). Discount rates after 7pm. Open daily 7am-10pm.

Telegrams: Independencia at 20 de Noviembre (tel. 6-49-02), around the corner from the post office. Open for telegrams Mon.-Fri. 8am-6pm, Sat. 9am-noon. Open for money orders Mon.-Fri. 9am-6pm, Sat. 9am-noon.

American Express: Valdivieso 2 (tel. 4-62-45 or 6-27-00). Open Mon.-Fri. 9am-2pm and 4-6pm, Sat. 9am-1pm. It also houses a travel agency that sells plane tickets and first-class bus tickets to Mexico City and Puebla. English spoken. Office open Mon.-Fri. 9am-2pm and 4-7pm, Sat. 9am-2pm for travel services.

Airport: Aeropuerto Juárez, on Rte. 175, 8km south of the city. **Airport Information:** tel. 1-50-36. **Mexicana** (tel. 4-12-48), Independencia at Fiallo. **Aeroméxico,** Hidalgo 513 (tel. 6-37-65, airport 1-50-44). **Aero Caribe** (tel. 6-02-29). **Taxis** 40 pesos. **Transportes Aeropuerto** (tel. 4-43-50), next to the post office on the Plaza Alameda, will pick you up at your hotel (*colectivo* 10 pesos, *especial* 39 pesos). Arrange a day in advance. Office open Mon.-Sat. 9am-2pm and 5-8pm.

Buses: Only partial listings are given; it is possible to go almost anywhere in the Republic at any time. **First-class station,** Niños Héroes de Chapultepec 1036. From this station, **ADO** (tel. 5-17-03) runs to Mexico City (19 per day 1am-midnight, 9hr., 115 pesos), Palenque (5pm, 115 pesos), Puebla (6 per day, 7hr., 93 pesos), Tuxtepec (3pm and 11:30pm, 6hr., 47 pesos), and Veracruz (8:30am, 8:30pm, 9hr., 120 pesos). **Cristóbal Colón** (tel. 5-12-14) goes to Puerto Escondido (9:30am and 10:30pm, 9hr., 109 pesos), San Cristóbal (7:30pm, 12hr., 124 pesos), Tehuantepec (9 per day, 5hr., 51 pesos), and Tuxtla Gutierrez (7:30pm, 10:15pm, 11hr., 111 pesos); **Autobuses Cuenca del Paloapan** (tel. 5-09-03) offers similar service. The **UNO** bus to Mexico City is the next best thing to a corporate jet (6 per day 12:15am-midnight, 9hr., 178 pesos). Tickets for ADO and Cristóbal Colón are also available at 208 Noviembre 204. Open Mon.-Sat. 9am-2pm and 4-7pm, Sun. 9am-3pm. **Travel to Oaxacan beaches is cheaper and faster by second-class bus.** The **second-class station** is just past the Central de Abastos (big market), across the Periférico from the western end of Trujano. Small regional bus lines, many without signs or ticket windows, provide frequent service to every small town near Oaxaca, usually for under 3 pesos. **Estrella del Valle** (tel. 4-57-00 or 6-54-29) runs to Puerto Escondido (8 per day 7am-11pm, 8hr., 49 pesos). The **Hotel Mesón del Ángel,** Mina 518, between Mier y Terán and Díaz Ordaz, serves as a **bus stop** for **Autotransportes Turísticos** (tel. 6-53-27 or 4-31-61). Buses to Monte Albán (peak season every 30min. 8am-3:30pm, off season 5 per day, 30min., roundtrip 10 pesos).

Trains: Ferrocarriles Nacionales de México, Calzada Madero (tel. 6-26-76). In a stone building set back from the road on the western end of Madero. Tickets sold 6-11am and 3:30-7pm. Arrive early and make reservations in advance if possible.

Car Rental: Budget, 5 de Mayo 305 (tel. 6-44-45). Must be over 21, with license and credit card. Small VWs 289- 330 pesos per day, depending on the season. Free mileage. Open daily 8am-1pm and 4pm-7pm.

Bike Rental: Bicicletas Bravo, M. Bravo 214, two blocks from the Andador Turístico, rents mountain bikes (15 pesos per hr., 50 pesos per day, 250 pesos per week, 600 pesos per month, including gear). Passport needed for a deposit. Cool English-speaking owner provides maps of trails to villages the tourist office doesn't even know exist and sponsors group tours—midnight full moon run to Monte Albán, anyone? Open Mon.-Sat. 8:30am-7:30pm, Sun. by appointment.

Laundromat: Súper Lavandería Hidalgo, J.P. García 200 (tel. 4-11-81), two blocks from the *zócalo.* Open Mon.-Sat. 8am-8pm.

Bookstore: Librería Universitaria, Guerrero 104 (tel. 6-42-43), off the corner of the *zócalo.* Small selection of English-language used paperbacks (10 pesos) and books on Mexico. Open Mon.-Sat. 9:30am-2pm and 4-8pm. **Códice,** Alcalá 403 (tel. 6-03-39), on the Andador Turístico. Books about Mexico and Oaxaca in Italian, French, Japanese, German, English, and Spanish. Open daily 9am-9pm.

Libraries: Biblioteca Circulante, Alcalá 305. A haven for displaced Americans, complete with bulletin board and 4th of July party. Everything from the New Yorker to Sports Illustrated. Open Mon.-Fri. 10am-1pm and 4-7pm, Sat. 10am-1pm. **Biblioteca Pública,** Alcalá 200 (tel. 6-47-14). Some English-language books on Oaxaca. Open Mon.-Fri. 9am-8:30pm. **Instituto Welte Para Estudios Oaxaqueños,** 5 de Mayo 412 (tel. 6-54-17). Large collection of English-language books and journals on Oaxacan history and anthropology. Open Mon.-Fri. 9:30am-1:30pm, Tues. and Thurs. also open 5-7pm, Wed. also open 4-7pm.

Internet: Antequera Red, H. Colegio Militar 1009-4 (tel. 3-05-58; http://antequera.antequera.com/Oaxaca/). Follow Calz. Niños Heroes de Chapultepec past the ADO station, turn left on H. Colegio Militar. Monthly and hourly e-mail and web access. Open Mon.-Fri. 9am-2pm and 4-8pm, Sat. 11am-6pm.

Cultural Center: Instituto Oaxaqueño de las Culturas (tel. 6-24-83), Calz. Madero at Av. Técnica. Hosts plays, dance performances, and concerts. Check the monthly *Guía Cultura* for listings (5 pesos). **Casa de la Cultura,** González Ortega 403 (tel. 6-24-83) at Colón. Poetry readings and art galleries. Open Mon.-Fri. 8am-8pm, Sat. 8am-2pm.

Women's Center: La Casa de La Mujer, Constitución 301 (tel. 4-69-27). Counseling, medical advocacy, and a library specializing in women's issues. Sponsors movies and discussion groups. Volunteer help welcomed. English spoken. Open Mon.-Fri. 9am-2pm and 5-8pm.

Markets: Mercado Benito Juárez, at the corner of 20 de Noviembre and Aldama two blocks from the *zócalo* away from the cathedral, sells crafts, produce, flowers, and clothing. Its annex, **Mercado 20 de Noviembre,** on the next block away from the *zócalo,* has gastronomic goodies. Both open daily 6am-9pm. Saturday is the big day at **Central de Abastos,** at the end of Trujano across from the second-class bus station, but vendors offer up every type of product—including live animals—every day. Beware of pickpockets.

Red Cross: Armenta y López 700 (tel. 6-44-55 or 6-48-09), between Pardo and Burgoa. Ambulance service. English spoken. Open 24hr.

Pharmacies: Farmacia El Fénix, Flores Magón 104 (tel. 6-60-11), next to the *zócalo* on the way to the market. Open daily 8am-9pm. **Farmacia Héroes de Chapultepec** (tel. 3-35-24), half a block east of 1st-class bus station. Open 24hr.

Hospitals: Hospital Civil, Porfirio Díaz 400 (tel. 5-31-81), 1.5km out of town, offers free medical service. **IMSS,** Chapultepec 621 (tel. 5-20-33). **Sanatorio Reforma,** Reforma 613 (tel. 4-62-77). Both open 24hr. English spoken.

Police: Aldama 108 (tel. 6-27-26), south of the *zócalo* between Miguel Cabrera and Bustamante. Some English spoken. Open 24hr. For an emergency, dial 06.

Post Office: (tel. 6-26-71), in the Pl. Alameda de León. Open Mon.-Fri. 8am-8pm, Sat. 9am-1pm. **Postal Code:** 68000.

Telephone Code: 29.

ACCOMMODATIONS AND CAMPING

As Oaxaca attracts more *norteamericanos,* some old budget standbys have upgraded their rooms in an attempt to attract more upscale tourists. But bargains still await the penny-pinching soul, especially in the busy blocks south of the *zócalo,* which are within easy walking distance of the second-class bus station and all major sights and services. Reservations are a must on *fiesta* weekends, especially during the *Guelaguetza* in July.

Outside the downtown area are a number of trailer parks. The **Trailer Park Oaxaca,** Violetas 900 (tel. 5-27-96), is near the *Zona Militar* in the northeast part of town. To get there, take the "Colonia Reforma" bus from the stop on García just north of Hidalgo. The **Trailer Park San Francisco,** Madero 705, in the northwest part of town, is accessible on the "Santa Rosa" bus from the same García stop.

For longer stays, many families rent rooms, advertising at the Biblioteca Circulante or the tourist offices. **Departmentos del Cuento,** Quintana Roo 107 (tel. 4-22-88), off Berriozabal past the Santo Domingo Church, rents six one- or two-person rooms with kitchen and bath (1300 pesos per month, utilities included).

Near the First-Class Bus Station

This area is a residential neighborhood not far from the *zócalo* and the sights. **Parque Juárez** and the nearby movie theater lend a very laid-back feel to life here.

Casa Arnel, Aldama 404 (tel. 5-28-56), in the Colonia Jalatlaco, a 20-min. walk from the *zócalo.* Take a right coming out of the bus station, walk two blocks, and turn right on Aldama; it's seven blocks down, across from a stone colonial church. From the *zócalo,* walk north on the *Andador Turístico,* make a right on Constitución, and follow it for 6 blocks. Turn left on Calz. de la República, and right several blocks later at the church. Spotless, homey rooms open onto a quiet jungle-like courtyard, complete with parrots and laundry facilities. Large English-language library and tourist information. An international backpacking crowd chats over breakfast. Curfew 11pm. Singles 35 pesos, 70 pesos with bath. Doubles 90 pesos with bath. Discounts for longer stays.

North of the Zócalo

The northern part of town is more prosperous, residential, tranquil, and attracts more tourists than the southern. Hotels here offer desirable locations.

Hotel Reforma, Reforma 102 (tel. 6-09-39), four blocks past the left side of the cathedral. Kick back on the rustic, hand-carved wood furniture and pretend you're on a *hacienda;* the view from the rooftop table allows you to take in the city. Rooms are usually full; reservations help. Singles 60 pesos. Doubles 70 pesos.

Las Bugambilias, Reforma 402 (tel. 6-11-65). The friendly Cabrera family rents six rooms in their spacious home, complete with double beds and flawlessly clean bathrooms you could bathe a whole family in. Amalia also gives massages and mineral baths and the adjoining café prepares its delicious oatmeal chocolate chip cookies in the kitchen for a dose of aromatherapy. Home-cooked breakfast included. 84 pesos per person, up to two people per room.

Hotel Pombo, Morelos 601 (tel. 6-26-73), between Vigil and Díaz, one block from the Plaza Alameda. The superb location compensates for the small, musty rooms. Five rooms have no bathroom. Singles 30 pesos, 50 pesos with bath. Doubles 40 pesos, 60 pesos with bath. Can accommodate quads.

South of the Zócalo

South of the *zócalo,* you'll find a legion of budget hotels; often four or five share the same block, particularly along **Díaz Ordaz.** Because of their proximity to the market and second-class bus terminal, many of these hotels front noisy, dirty streets; ask for a room in the back. Be very cautious when walking in this area at night.

Youth Hostel El Pasador, Fiallo 305 (tel. 6-12-87). Walk two blocks on Guerrero then turn right. The hostel is on the left; ring the bell for an attendant. Three bunk beds are grouped together and separated by bamboo from the other sex. Bedding and laundry facilities provided. Though there are three bathrooms, the communal atmosphere fosters tooth brushing on the patio or in the group kitchen. 30 pesos per person per night, half-day 15 pesos. Somewhat private two-person cabana 60 pesos. Key deposit 10 pesos. No curfew, but quiet time after 11pm.

Hotel Pasaje, Mina 302 (tel. 6-42-13), three blocks south of the *zócalo.* Well-scrubbed rooms open onto a plant-filled courtyard. Rooms near the street are assaulted with traffic noise, but you can smell the chocolate from the nearby sweet shops. Singles 50 pesos. Doubles 70 pesos, with two beds 80 pesos.

Hotel Chayo, 20 de Noviembre 508 (tel. 6-41-12), one block past the market. Despite diligent cleaning, remodeled rooms still look plain. Suites available. Every room has at least two beds. Singles or doubles 72 pesos. Triples 83 pesos.

Hotel Lupita, Díaz Ordaz 314 (tel. 6-57-33). Off Trujano, three blocks from the *zócalo.* Don't confuse this aqua green hotel with its neighbor, the more expensive Hotel Fortín. Known for rockbottom prices rather than their comfort. Often full. Singles without bath 35 pesos. Doubles 40 pesos, with bath 60 pesos.

FOOD

With food to please every palate, Oaxaca is a city to grow fat in. Even in heavily touristed areas, fresh, well prepared meals at bargain prices await the jaded traveler. Oaxaca has 7 versions of *mole,* a delicious sauce made of a myriad of ingredients including *chiles* and chocolate. Many restaurants also serve up *tlayudas,* large, crisp tortillas topped with just about everything. *Botanas oaxaqueñas* also make an appearance on menus throughout the city; they are plates full of regional goodies including *chile, quesillo* (boiled string cheese), *chorizo* (sausage), and *guacamole.*

Sunny Oaxaca summers were made for *nieves,* sorbet-like treats. For the best frozen confections, head to the area in front of the Iglesia de la Soledad, 3 blocks past the post office on Independencia. You'll have several umbrella-covered stands to pick from and even more flavors. Two of the most typical flavors are *leche quemada* (burnt milk) and *cajeta* (caramel). Also a must is Oaxaca's spicy cinnamon hot chocolate. The cafés in the *zócalo* offer great views at fairly high prices, but if you order something less expensive (breakfast, coffee, or drinks), you'll get to sit and watch Oaxaca for hours on end.

The **markets** (see p. 332) offer *chapulines* (dried crickets) and spiced *jícama* (a beet-shaped fruit), as well as the usual inexpensive fare. On **20 de Noviembre,** you'll find row after row of eateries. Avoid the ones with fancy lights and signs. Look for **Angelita's,** whose proprietor is used to serving foreigners and won't change her prices for them. At the adjacent Benito Juárez market, **Aqua Casilda** produces famous flavored waters (4 pesos) and fresh juices (4.50 pesos).

Flor de Loto, Morelos 509 (tel. 4-39-44), between Díaz and Tinoco y Palacios. Vegetarian and regional specialties tempt the diner in a clean, comfortable setting. *Tortas* (6-8 pesos), tacos (16 pesos), and a filling *comida corrida* (20 pesos) make the flower smell even sweeter. Open daily 10am-10pm.

Antojitos Regionales Los Arnos, Alcalá 301, on the *andador* at the corner of Matamoros. Every night, the family that lives in this hedonist haven opens up their courtyard to share dinner with whomever is savvy enough to know about it. No menus, and you can watch the food being prepared. At 6 pesos, the *tamales de mole* is the most expensive item served. Open daily 8am-11pm.

Restaurant Quickly, Alcalá 100 (tel. 4-7-76), on the *andador,* just steps from the cathedral. The atmosphere and central location attract scores of diners. Extensive menu includes breakfast (6-9 pesos), sandwiches (9 pesos), *comida corrida* (12 pesos; 14 pesos for vegetarian), and a buffet (19 pesos). Open Mon.-Fri. 8am-10:30pm, Sat.-Sun. 2-10:30pm.

Cafeteria Santa Anita, Calz. Niños Héroes de Chapultepec 801, down the street from the ADO station at the intersection with Juárez. Far removed from the tourist territory, but convenient for a quick bite before a bus trip. From 2-5pm, they serve a delicious, multi-course *comida corrida* for 15 pesos. Giant *tortas* cost 12 pesos; paternal staff gives advice for free. Open Mon.-Sat. 8am-9pm.

La Soledad, Mina 212 (tel. 4-22-02), behind the 20 de Noviembre market. A chocaholic's fantasy: eight deliciously decadent types of hot chocolate (4-5 pesos), and— for the die-hard cocoa fiend—chocolate *tamales* (3 pesos). Breakfast too (7 pesos). Open Mon.-Sat. 7am-8:30pm, Sun. 7am-2pm.

Restoran Café Alex, Díaz Ordaz 218 (tel. 4-07-15). An extensive menu that runs the gamut of Mexican cuisine, with English explanations for the uninitiated. Garden seating available. Breakfasts (12.50-15 pesos), *comida corrida* (15 pesos), and vegetarian specialties (17 pesos) are a cut above the grittier storefront fare in the neighborhood. Open Mon.-Sat. 7am-9pm, Sun. 7am-noon.

La Tropical, Mina 400 (tel. 6-67-52), at J.P. Garcia. A juice bar serving exotic concoctions to complement the orange-and-green decor. A great place to watch Oaxaca pass by while sipping a banana or strawberry *licuado* (6 pesos). Medicinal concoctions 7 pesos. Open Mon.-Sat. 8am-8pm, Sun. 9:30am-4pm.

Classic Cafés

La Olla Café, Reforma 402 (tel. 6-66-68), in front of Las Bugambilias B&B. English-language magazines, rotating art exhibits, and fresh food made with lots of tender loving care keep customers coming back. *Comida corrida,* topped with home-made cake, 20 pesos. Open daily 8am-10pm.

La Casa de Don Porfirio, Porfirio Díaz 208 (tel. 6-37-72), between Morelos and Matamoros. Skip the expensive sandwiches (26 pesos) and opt for the bagels (10-15 pesos) and soy burgers (18 pesos), both quite a find in Mexico. Open Mon.-Sat. 11am-11pm, Sun. 3-11pm.

Coffee Beans, 5 de Mayo 400, one block from Santo Domingo. Shiny, brassy, lively, slightly overpriced, but still worth it. Drinks (10 pesos), *empanadas* (12 pesos), and chewy brownies and savory pies (15 pesos). Open daily 9am-10pm.

Café Mestizo, Pino Suárez 508 (tel. 5-56-45), near Parque Juárez. Everything still gleams at this pleasing new café—especially the fine grub. Sample some hot flaky pie (6 pesos) and chase it down with an aromatic cup o'joe (3 pesos). The owner also rents rooms in her house, right behind the café. Open Mon.-Sat. 8am-8pm.

SIGHTS

Oaxaca has a multitude of museums, churches, and historical venues that merit a visit. Luckily for the weary traveler, the major sites are all located within walking distance on the pedestrian-only *Andador Turístico*. Don't leave without seeing the **Museo Regional de Oaxaca,** the **Iglesia de Santo Domingo,** and the **Museo de Arte Contemporáneo de Oaxaca (MACO).**

The Zócalo

The **Catedral de Oaxaca** and the **Palacio de Gobierno** (not to be confused with the Palacio Municipal, which contains the tourist office) sit on opposite sides of the *zócalo*. Originally constructed in 1535, the cathedral was damaged and finally destroyed by a series of earthquakes. In the 18th century it was rebuilt with *oaxaqueño* green-brown stone and ornamented in filigree. The ornate bishop's seat, in the central altar, provides a structural focus (open daily 7am-8pm).

Inside the **Palacio de Gobierno,** through the set of arches that don't shelter cafés, a mural by Arturo García Bustos presents an informative historical collage. On the left wall, scenes of pre-hispanic life with maize cultivation, weaving, and temples give way to the political and religious figures that dominate the other panels. The center panel celebrates *oaxaqueño* Benito Juárez, his wife Margarita Masa, and one of his oft-repeated phrases, *"El respeto al derecho ajeno es la paz."* ("Respect for the rights of others is peace.") On the wall to the right as you ascend the staircase is a portrait of Sor Juana Inés de la Cruz, the 17th century poet, nun, theologian, and astronomer. Considered Mexico's first feminist, she impersonated a man for several years in order to attend the university in Mexico City and penned a diatribe against misogynists called *Hombres Necios* (Foolish Men; palace open 24hr.).

Along the Andador Turístico

To the left of the Cathedral, a cobbled pedestrian street leads to museums, restaurants, and stores. After a block down the *andador* (also known as **Alcalá**), you'll come to the **Museo de Arte Contemporáneo de Oaxaca (MACO),** Alcalá 202 (tel. 4-71-10), on the right. This beautifully constructed colonial building is known as the Casa de Cortés, although historians insist that it is not in fact Cortés's estate. The museum features both rotating and permanent exhibitions by contemporary *oaxaqueños* like Rufino Tamayo, and shows free movies on its large-screen TV. The bookstore carries a large number of artbooks and magazines plus English guidebooks to the region (open Wed.-Mon. 10:30am-8pm, free).

Following the walkway for three more blocks, the imposing **Iglesia de Santo Domingo** looms on the right. The church is the tallest building in Oaxaca, and its Baroque interior has some of the most stunning interior decoration of any church in the Republic. Waves of gilded stucco dance elegant arabesques around arches, across ceiling vaults, and above altars and chapels. Construction on the church began in 1575, the structure was consecrated in 1611, and improvements and artistic work continued after that. Built 2m thick as protection against earthquakes, the walls served the convent well when it saw service as military barracks for both sides during the reform wars and the Revolution (open daily 7am-1pm and 4-8pm).

The ex-convent next door was converted in 1972 into the city's prestigious **Museo Regional de Oaxaca** (tel. 6-29-91). After walking through the metal detector, begin your visit with a chronology of the cultures that inhabited and continue to populate the state of Oaxaca. The archaeology lesson starts in the corner diagonal from the entrance. As evidenced by a 10,000-year-old clovis point found in the area, the state has been occupied since the beginning of human habitation in the Americas. Towns formed around 1400BCE, followed by a distinct culture characterized by gray pottery, a ritual calendar, and social stratification; by 500BCE small Mixteca and Zapotec cities had developed. Proceed upstairs and to the right to see mannequins sporting traditional clothes from 16 Oaxacan indigenous groups; the costumes are markers of ethnic and community identity. Back downstairs, on the right before exiting, marvel at the sumptuous treasure found in Tomb 7 of Monte Albán; the exquisite pieces of gold, turquoise, bone, and obsidian testify to the sophistication of New World cultures (open Tues.-Fri. 10am-6pm, Sat.-Sun. 10am-5pm; admission 14 pesos; free Sun. and holidays).

Across the street, the small **Instituto de Artes Gráficas (AGO),** Alcalá 507 (tel. 6-69-80), displays prints and graphic art from around the world. Exhibitions change every three months. The museum also houses a café and an amazing art library containing many English-language volumes (open Wed.-Mon. 9am-8pm; free).

Near the Andador Turístico

The renowned **Museo de Arte Prehispánico de México Rufino Tamayo,** Morelos 503 (tel. 6-47-50), between Díaz and Tinoco y Palacios, shows off the *oaxaqueño* artist's personal collection of pre-Hispanic objects. The figurines, ceramics and masks that Tamayo collected were selected for their aesthetic value as well as for anthropological interest. Pieces are arranged in roughly chronological order rather than by culture (open Mon., Wed.-Sat. 10am-2pm and 4-7pm, Sun. 10am-3pm; admission 12 pesos).

The **Teatro Macedonio Alcalá,** on 5 de Mayo at Independencia, two blocks behind the cathedral, is one of the most beautiful buildings in Oaxaca and an example of the art and architecture fostered by dictator Porfirio Díaz. Díaz's regime (1876-1911) had a taste for French art and intellectual formulas. Oaxaca, Díaz's birthplace, remained close to the dictator's heart. His support was instrumental in the theater's construction. On the ceiling, scantily clad Muses float above the giant candelabra (occasionally open for shows Mon.-Sat. 8pm, Sun. 6pm).

A minor but absorbing attraction is the funky museum of religious art at the **Basílica of Our Lady of Solitude,** Independencia 107 (tel. 6-75-66), three and a half blocks behind the post office. It houses an astonishing array of objects sent from around the world as gifts to the Virgin, who is said to have appeared here in 1620. Packed cabinets overflow with everything from model ships to shell-and-pasta figurines to wedding bouquets (open Mon.-Sat. 10am-2pm and 4-6pm, Sun. 11am-2pm; admission 1 peso).

ENTERTAINMENT AND SEASONAL EVENTS

Keeping track of Oaxaca's cultural and music events requires some effort. The *Guía Cultural,* distributed at the MACO and tourist offices (5 pesos), lists monthly activi-

Local Hero

Five blocks north of the post office is the **Casa de Benito Juárez,** García Vigil 609 (tel. 6-18-60), once home to Mexico's famous ex-president. Although Juárez came from humble beginnings, the house hardly looks like the spot where a poor, 19th-century Zapotec *campesino* grew up. Benito's sister left the Juárez home in Guelatao to come to Oaxaca as the domestic servant of the wealthy Masa family who actually owned the house. The Masas were *paisanos* from Spain and good friends with the equally wealthy Salanueva family. The Salanuevas took interest in young Benito, adopted him and brought him to Oaxaca. His subsequent education and upbringing qualified him to marry the Masas's daughter, Margarita, and to pursue a career in law and reform-minded politics. The house—living room, bedrooms, kitchen, well, and "bookbinding/weaving shop"—is a replica of a 19th-century upper-middle-class *oaxaqueño* home (open Tues.-Sat. 10am-6pm, Sun. 10am-5pm; admission 5 pesos, free Sun.).

ties, many of them free. The *Oaxaca Times*, published monthly in English, is a free guide to the city available at many hotels and tourist offices. During the summer, the streets fill with free music: Sundays at 12:20pm the Oaxacan Orchestra plays in the Plaza Alameda; Mondays and Saturdays *marimba* performers hammer away after 7pm in the *zócalo* kiosk; Tuesdays and Thursdays the state band stages concerts—same place, same time.

Discos and **bars** are packed—and dripping with sweat—on weekend nights. The swingers at **Candela**, Allende 211 (tel. 4-12-54), could teach the cast of *Dirty Dancing* a lesson or two. Things get specially hot and saucy on weekend nights after 10pm, when the live salsa begins (cover 20 pesos; open Tues.-Sat. 2pm-1:30am). **Tequila Rock,** Calz. Porfirio Díaz 102 (tel. 5-15-00), by the ADO station, is the club of the moment. Around 11pm, the staff performs a short dance that eases the awkwardness of being the first one on the floor. Sweaty dance tunes soon take over (cover Fri.-Sat. 35 pesos; open Wed.-Sat. 9pm-3am). Farther down the street, **María Sabina** threatens to steal the spotlight. Though not the center of action, **Eclipse,** Porfirio Díaz 219 (tel. 6-42-36), at the corner of Matamoros, is convenient. Young crowd boogies under plastic-and-pipe palm trees and groovy mood lighting (cover Fri.-Sat. 35 pesos; open Thurs.-Sat. 10:30pm-3am).

Watch a film at MACO and La Casa de la Mujer, or simply catch a recent flick in English with Spanish subtitles (12 pesos) at **Ariel 2000** (tel. 6-52-41), corner of Juárez and Berriozabal on Parque Juárez. **Sala Versalles,** M. Ocampo 105 (tel. 6-23-35), three blocks behind the cathedral, host live shows as well as movies.

On the two Mondays following July 16, representatives from every part of Oaxaca state converge on a hill overlooking the city for the **Guelaguetza.** The event grew out of an indigenous tradition of making offerings on the **Cerro del Fortín** (The Hill with the Beautiful View); the days of dancing in the theater on the hill are called *los lunes del cerro* (Hill Mondays). "Guelaguetza" refers to the Zapotec custom of reciprocal gift-giving. During the two public gatherings, groups from the seven regions of Oaxaca give the audience a taste of their heritage through dance, music, and dazzling costumes. In between the two spectacles, food and handicraft exhibitions, art shows, and concerts take place. Tickets cost up to 250 pesos; a handful of free seats are snatched hours before the show begins. A better alternative is to walk on Independencia past the post office and turn right on Crespo; at the top of the hill on the left are the stairs leading up Cerro del Fortín to the auditorium, a panoramic view of the city, and the **planetarium** (tel. 6-69-84; 6 pesos; open Tues.-Sun. 6-7pm). If you miss the Guelaguetza, sample dances are performed year-round at the Hotel Camino Real and Hotel Monte Albán for a hefty fee.

The night of December 23, Oaxacans celebrate the unique **Noche de los Rábanos** (Night of the Radishes). Masterpieces of historic or biblical themes expressed with radishes fill the *zócalo,* where judges determine the best. Hundreds of people admire the artistic creations and eat sweet *buñuelos.* Upon finishing the treat, you're supposed to make a wish and throw the ceramic plate down on the ground; if the plate smashes into pieces, your wish will come true. We promise.

■ Near Oaxaca

The villages surrounding Oaxaca are known both for their ancient Zapotec and Mixtec ruins and for their production of artisanry. As everyone from museums of folk art to the Nature Company took interest in the imaginative handicrafts made in these villages, many residents left farming work to devote themselves full-time to craft production. Villages often specialize in specific products: **Arrazola** and **San Martín Tilcajate** make wooden animals, **San Bartolo Coyotepec** black clay pottery, **Atzompa** green clay pottery, **Ocotlán** natural clay pottery, **Teotitlán del Valle** wool *sarapes,* and **Villa Díaz Ordaz** and **Santo Tomás Jalietza** textiles and weavings. All these villages can be reached by *colectivo* from the *Central de Autobuses;* or, for that adrenaline rush, rent a bike and transport yourself (see p. 337).

The tourist office in Oaxaca (SECTUR, tel. 6-01-23 or 6-48-28) rents out **Yú'ù** (guest house in Zapotec) in the communities of Abasolo, Papalutla, Teotitlán del Valle, Benito Juárez, Tlacolula, Quialana, Tlapazola, Sta. Ana del Valle, and Hierve el Agua. Accommodations include four beds, kitchen, and clean bedding; proceedings benefit the community (cabin 100 pesos, one person 30 pesos, students 20 pesos, campers in the garden 10 pesos). Or try one of the *paseos culturales,* which introduce visitors to the traditional medicinal, agricultural, and artistic practices of fifteen villages in the area. Contact **Museos Comunitarios de Oaxaca,** Tinoco y Palacios 311, *interior* (room) 16, for more information.

ATZOMPA, ARRAZOLA, CUILAPAN, AND ZAACHILA

A culture and lifestyle different from the sophistication of Oaxaca de Juárez emerges in these small towns, all of which lie near Rte. 131. **Atzompa** is where that magnificent blend of clay and sprouts, the **Chia Pet,** was invented. Pottery, the town's specialty, can be had here at better prices than in the city. Atzompa's *Casa de Artesanías* is a publicly funded forum that brings together the work of the town's specialized artisans. Selection is good at the *Casa,* but bartering is easier with the artisans themselves.

Arrazola is the hometown of Manuel Jiménez, one of Mexico's most famous artisans. Jiménez is the originator of *alebrijes,* the brightly colored figurines of demons that rank among Mexico's most sought-after handicrafts. While success has made his pieces simply unaffordable for most—think US$150 and upwards—his workshop is worth a visit. Cheaper versions of Jiménez work, as well as wooden animals, are sold everywhere in town. What the copies lack in grace and originality they make up for in intricacy and elaborate painting. Particularly interesting are Miguel Santiago Soriano's curvaceous iguanas and Maximiliano Morales Santiago's haughty lions.

Cuilapan de Guerrero has an isolated but lovely 17th-century Dominican monastery, once the home of one of the most powerful and wealthy religious orders in Mexico. Never finished, the ruined monastery's crumbling stone arcades frame the fields of the surrounding valley and the sinews of the hills that embrace it (gates open daily 10am-6pm; admission to grounds free, 7 pesos to interior).

Zaachila, the last political capital of the Zapotecs before they fell to the Spanish in 1521, hosts a fascinating market each Thursday. Drop your pesos on preserved bananas, and squealing pigs. The middle of town is dominated by the fuchsia and yellow cathedral. Behind the church, a street heads uphill to an archaeological site that has been only partially uncovered. Until 1962, locals prohibited excavations to prevent outsiders from dissecting their Zapotec heritage. Little has since been explored, but two Mixtec tombs with well-preserved architecture and jewelry have been uncovered. The treasure of gold, turquoise, jade, and bone artifacts has been spirited away to museums in Oaxaca and Mexico City, but the tombs—the only decorated ones in Oaxaca—are easily accessible (open daily 8am-6pm).

Getting There: Take a *colectivo* leaving from the parking lot on the side of the Central de Abastos in Oaxaca; destinations are labeled on the windshields (2.50 pesos, 10min. to Cuilapán, 15min. to Aztompa, Arrazola, or Zaachila). It's easy to hop from one town to the next; take a *colectivo* back to the main road and flag down another that's headed for your next destination. All four towns are ideally accessible in the course of a day, though your best bet is to start out in Arrazola or Atzompa and to head back to Oaxaca Cuilapan or Zaachila.

SAN BARTOLO COYOTEPEC AND POINTS SOUTH

San Bartolo Coyotepec, 12km south of Oaxaca on Rte. 175, is the source of the ink-black pottery that populates souvenir shops throughout the state. Fine pieces are available here at fairly low prices. Valente Nieto, son of the creator of the craft, Doña Rosa, gives demonstrations for visitors. If you didn't pick up quite enough brightly colored animals in Arrazola, head to **San Martín Tilajete,** 21km south of Oaxaca and about 1km off the main road. Four kilometers farther south, **Santo Tomás Jalietza** specializes in weaving on back-strap looms. The town also boasts a 17th-century church dedicated to its patron saint. In **Ocotlán de Morelos,** 33km out of the city, leather goods, wrap-type traditional clothing, and herbal remedies can be had for a song. Swashbuckle your way through Mexico with one of the swords produced here. Market day is Friday; most of the action takes place between 10am and 5pm.

Getting There: Take one of the *colectivos* leaving from the end of the Central de Abastos opposite the second-class bus station (about 6 pesos). Estrella del Valle buses leave from their terminal on González Ortega for Ocotlán (every 8min. 5:45am-9:30pm, 30min., 2.50 pesos) and will make stops at other villages.

GUELATAO

The *pueblito* of **Guelatao,** 57km north of Oaxaca, became a national monument on March 21, 1967 (the centenary of the victory of Mexican forces over the French occupation) when the government ordered the construction of a civic plaza, a museum, statues, and a mausoleum to honor Benito Juárez, Guelatao's native son. Guelatao now seems less a living town than a memorial park, adrift in the Cuenca del Papaloapan mountain range. Should you catch it between national holidays, political campaigns, and TV docu-drama filmings, you will find Guelatao empty and peaceful. The tiny **Museo Benito Juárez** delineates Juárez's life. The museum balcony commands a view of Guelatao's rugged landscape.

Getting There: To get from Oaxaca to Guelatao, take a Benito Juárez bus, the line farthest to the right as you enter the second-class terminal. Get an early start for this trip; the 2½ hour ride is rough (11 pesos). The crowded bus back to Oaxaca passes about every two hours.

OAXACA TO THE PACIFIC

Depending on which bus you take, seven to nine arduous but beautiful hours separate Oaxaca from the beaches of the Pacific coast. Second-class **Estrella del Valle** buses running from Oaxaca to Pochutla also stop in **Ocotlán** and **Miahuatlán,** two hours by bus from Oaxaca, in a region renowned for its *mezcal.* Market day (Mon.) brings textiles of all types and *huaraches* (sandals) made out of strips of car tires (steel-belted radials are best). **Buses** from Miahuatlán head south to Pochutla roughly every half-hour from 6am-8pm.

If you're heading for the coast, chances are you'll touch base in **Pochutla,** an important transportation hub. Currency can be exchanged at **Inverlat** or **Bancomer,** on Lázaro Cárdenas farther down from the bus station (open Mon.-Fri. 9am-2pm). From the station on the left side of Lázaro Cárdenas just as you enter the city, **Cristóbal Cólon** (tel. 4-02-74) sends first-class buses to Huatulco (9:45am, 4:30, 7:15, and 9pm, 1hr., 10 pesos), Mexico City (4:30pm, 15hr., 200 pesos), Oaxaca (10pm, 8hr., 94 pesos), and Tehuantepec (9:45am, 4:30, 7:15, and 9pm, 4½hr., 43 pesos). Across the street, under the yellow "Posada San José" sign, **Estrella Del Valle** (tel. 4-01-38) runs buses to Mexico City (6 and 7pm, 12hr., 138 pesos), Oaxaca (5 per day, 6hr., 48 pesos; *ordinario* 16 per day 5am-11:15hr, 8hr., 38 pesos), and Puerto Escondido (every hr. 5am-9pm, 1hr., 10 pesos). A *microbús* leaves from the driveway next to the Estrella del Valle station for Puerto Angel (every 20min. 6am-8pm, 20min., 2 pesos), then Zipolite (30min., 3 pesos), and finally Mazunte (40min., 4 pesos). **Estrella Blanca** (tel. 4-03-80), on Lázaro Cárdenas a block down from Cristóbal Colón, goes to Acapulco (semi-direct 6 per day 6:15am-10pm, 8hr., 91 pesos; *ordinario* every 2hr. 7:15am-1:15pm, 9hr., 79 pesos), Huatulco (11 per day 8am-9:50pm, 1hr., 7 pesos), and Mexico City (7pm, 13hr., 170 pesos).

If the wait for your bus will be a long one, you can spend a pleasant night in the **Hotel Posada San José,** down the alleyway next to the Estrella del Valle station (tel. 4-01-53). Rooms are well kept and have generously sized bathrooms with hot water.

A swimming pool and a pet monkey named Pancho provide the entertainment (singles 40-80 pesos; doubles 50-95 pesos).

OAXACA TO MITLA

The road from Oaxaca east to Mitla, the Pan-American Highway (Rte. 190), cuts through a valley full of artisanal towns, *mezcal* distilleries, and archaeological sites. **Santa María El Tule,** just 14km outside the city, houses one of Mexico's great roadside attractions: the **Tule Tree.** The 2000-year-old and 40-meter-tall tree has an astounding perimeter of 52m—the largest girth of any tree on earth. Ask the bus to driver to drop you off at El Tule; then ask for *"el árbol."* The **Dainzú** ruins, 22km from Oaxaca, just off the road branching to **Macuilxochitl,** date from Monte Albán's final pre-Hispanic epoch. A series of magnificently carved figures at the base of the tallest pyramidal monument represent ballplayers in poses similar to the "dancers" at Monte Albán (see p. 347). Two humans and two jaguars, gods of the sport, supervise the contest. Up the hill from the pyramid, another game scene is hewn in the living rock (open daily 10am-6pm).

The walls of the church in nearby **San Jerónimo Tlacochahuaya,** 23km from Oaxaca, illustrate Zapotec decorative techniques as applied to Catholic motifs. It was built at the end of the 16th century by Dominicans seeking to escape from worldly temptations (open daily 7am-noon). **Teotitlán del Valle,** 28km from Oaxaca, is the oldest community in the state. The source of extremely beautiful woolen *sarapes,* Teotitlán's 200 to 300 families earn their livelihood largely by spinning and weaving. Many allow tourists to visit their workshops and witness the process of natural-dye coloring and weaving. **Tlacolula de Matamoros,** 33km from Oaxaca, hosts a lively market every Sunday morning—the specialty is the potent liquor *mezcal.* The market is officially open until 6pm, but activity starts to wind down at around 2pm.

Yagul, 36km from Oaxaca, was a Zapotec city inhabited from 700BCE-1521CE (guess what happened then). Less impressive archaeologically than Mitla, rarely visited Yagul is perhaps more striking aesthetically. The city is built into the skirts of a hill overlooking a spectacular mountain-ringed valley. Most of the more famous buildings and tombs are in the **Acrópolis,** the area closest to the parking lot about 2km north of the highway. The restored ballcourt is the largest of its kind in the Oaxaca valley; the **Court of the Triple Tomb** is on its left. Carved with an image that is probably a jaguar, the tomb is in—you guessed it—three sections. Stone faces cover the largest portion. Beyond the ballcourt rises the **Council Hall;** behind lies the **Palace of the Six Patios,** believed to have been the home of the city's ruler. Heading back to the parking lot, take the trail that climbs uphill to the rocky outcropping to catch a spectacular view of the cactus-covered hills. Look for the small stone bridge; it's behind the tomb on your right as you climb the hill (open daily 8am-5:30pm; admission 7 pesos, free Sun.)

Beyond Mitla, **Hierve el Agua** (The Water Boils), 57km from Oaxaca, takes its name from two springs of carbonated water that look like...boiling water. The waters are not actually hot and make for refreshing baths.

Getting There: All destinations listed above are accessible via a Mitla-bound bus, which leaves the second-class station in Oaxaca (daily every 15min. 8am-8pm, 2.50 pesos to Mitla). Ask the driver to let you off where you want to go. Most people visit these sites on daytrips, but the tourist office at Oaxaca can arrange for overnight stays in Teotitlán del Valle, Tlacolula, or Hierve el Agua (see p. 344).

■ Mitla

Tucked away in a mostly Zapotec-speaking village, the archaeological site at Mitla, 44km east of Oaxaca, is smaller and less popular with tourists than the immense Monte Albán. Mitla was built in 800CE by the Zapotecs; it was later appropriated by the Mistecs and eventually became the largest and most important of the late Mixtec cities. When the Spaniards arrived in the valley, Mitla was the only ceremonial center of the Mesoamerican Classical period still in use. Ironically, the Catholic archbishop of Oaxaca built his home to echo the horizontal lines of the Zapotec priest's residence in Mitla, thus paying architectural tribute to an ancient indigenous religion virtually exterminated by Catholicism.

Walking about 2km from the bus stop and then through the village, you'll happen onto the doorstep of the Catholic church and the official entrance to the archaeological zone. The ticket booth is on the far side of the red-domed church. To the left of it, behind the church, are the three patios known as the **Group of the Church.** One of them has been almost completely buried by the church, and only a few of the original palace walls remain visible. The central patio is on the other side of the church; here and in the surrounding rooms you can still see pieces of Mixtec decorative paintings glowing red against the stone, supposedly telling Mitla's history.

More impressive ruins are across the road in the fenced-in area enclosing the **Group of the Columns.** Beyond the entrance are two patios joined at one corner On the first one lie the tombs of the pyramids, forming a cross. For years Spaniards thought this proved that the Mixtecs somehow knew the story of Jesus. On the second patio, two temples have tombs that are open to visitors. The tomb in the east temple has large stones covered with mosaic patterns. The roof of the tomb in the north temple rests on a single huge column known as the **Column of Life.** Pilgrims travel here each year to embrace the column; in exchange for the hug, the column tells them how much longer they will live. Explanatory signs throughout this area are in English (site open daily 8am-5pm; admission 10 pesos, free Sun).

On the central plaza back in town, the unexciting **Frissell Museum** contains thousands of figurines from Mitla and other Mixtec sites, all arranged around a courtyard. Some descriptions are in English (open daily 9am-5pm; admission 10 pesos).

If you must stay in Mitla, try the **Hotel Zapoteca,** 5 de Febrero 12 (tel. 8-00-26), on the way from the bus stop to the ruins. The stucco-walled rooms are big, the bathrooms clean enough. Rooms upstairs are a bit nicer. The hotel's restaurant is not expensive (singles 45 pesos; doubles 60 pesos).

Getting There: Take a bus from Oaxaca's second-class terminal (every 15min. 8am-8pm, 45min., 2.50 pesos). The last Oaxaca-bound bus leaves Mitla at 8pm. **Autotransportes Turísticos Aragal** offers 4-hour trips that leave from Oaxaca and visit Mitla, Yagul, and the Tule Tree (10am and 2pm, 25 pesos). Reservations (required) can be made at the **Hotel Trébol** (tel. 6-38-66), Las Casas at Flores Magón, across from the Benito Juárez market.

■ Monte Albán

Monte Albán, one of the most important and spectacular pre-Hispanic ruins in Mexico, sits regally atop a green mountain 10km from Oaxaca. The monolithic, geometrically precise stone structures that constituted the ceremonial center of the city are the culmination of Zapotec efforts to engineer a world that fused the religious, political, and social realms. As Monte Albán grew to become the major Zapotec capital, daily life was carefully constructed to harmonize with the supernatural elements. Architecture adhered to the orientation of the four cardinal points and the proportions of the 260-day ritual calendar. Residences were organized in families of five to ten people in four-sided houses with open central courtyards. To emphasize the congruence between the household and the tripartite cosmos, families buried their ancestors underneath their house to correspond to the level of the underworld. Excavations of burials in Monte Albán have yielded not only dazzling artifacts, but also valuable information on social stratification.

Monte Albán flourished during the Classic Period (300-750 CE), when it shared the spotlight with Teotihuacán and Tikal as a major cultural and ceremonial center of Mesoamerica. This was the greatest of Zapotec capitals—maize was cultivated, water was supplied through complex drainage systems, and the city engaged in extensive exchange networks in Mesoamerica, especially with Teotihuacán (see p. 119). Teotihuacán's influence is visible in the murals painted and pottery made in Monte Albán. Artists used representations of divinities to legitimate the kings' power, and many stones share the theme of defeated enemies being sacrificed.

Archaeologists have divided the history of the site into five periods. Objects from **Monte Albán I,** dating from about 500 BCE, generally show the influence of the oldest civilization in Mesoamerica, the Olmecs. By the end of Monte Albán I, the city was the largest and most important community in Southern Mesoamerica. During the period known as **Monte Albán II** (100 BCE-300 CE) the Zapotecs consolidated their empire and expanded their commercial trading routes. It was an era of wild cultural cross-pollination: the Maya borrowed the calendar and writing system already in use at Monte Albán, while the Zapotecs borrowed from the Maya their steep staircased pyramids and *juego de pelota,* a ball game played on a special court. Flourishing simultaneously with Teotihuacán, Monte Albán reached its apogee during the period known as **Monte Albán III** (300-750 CE). Almost all of the extant buildings and tombs as well as several urns and murals of *colanijes* (richly adorned priests) come from this period. Burial arrangements of variable luxuriousness and size show the social division of the period: priests, clerks, and laborers lived apart, died apart, and were buried in very different tombs. For reasons that remain unknown, Monte Albán shriveled up and died around 750 CE. Construction ceased, and control of the Zapotec empire shifted from Monte Albán to other cities such as Zaachila, Yagul, and later Mitla. Explanations for the abandonment of the city include drought, overexploitation of resources, or inability of the leaders to maintain stability. In the midst of this disastrous period, known as **Monte Albán IV** (750-1000 CE), the Mixtec people invaded from the northwest and took over many of the Zapotec cities. During **Monte Albán V,** from 1000 CE to the arrival of the Spaniards, the city functioned as both a fortress and a sacred necropolis. The members of the Mixtec nobility were buried in the tombs left by the Zapotecs, together with elaborate treasures that possibly venerated Monte Albán as a place of origin. When the most noteworthy, **Tomb 7,** was discovered in 1932 by Dr. Alfonso Caso, the treasure found within more than quadrupled the number of previously identified gold Mixtec objects.

As you enter the **Central Plaza,** the most prominent building to the right is the **Northern Platform.** Bear left as you enter the site, and walk along the edge of the Central Plaza; the first structure on the left is the ball court. Originally smothered in stucco, the steps of the court were not spectators' stands, but rather part of the playing area. After passing a series of related substructures, you'll reach two pyramids which dominate the center and southern end of this side of the plaza. The inclined walls were originally flat and covered with stucco like the ball court and frescoes.

Building P, the first of the two pyramids, fascinates archaeologists because of an inner stairway feeding into a tunnel to the central structures. The tunnel apparently allowed priests to pass into the central temples unseen by the public. The second pyramid, the **Palace,** was once a wealthy Zapotec residence; it is graced by a patio-courtyard and a garden in which a cruciform grave was discovered.

Outside the palace are the four central monuments of the plaza. **Buildings G, H,** and **I** together constitute what was likely the principal altar of Monte Albán. Directly to the east, between the central Building H and Building P, is the small, sunken **Adoratorio,** where archaeologists dug up an intricate jade bat mask. This is Monte Albán's oldest structure, dating from Monte Albán II. A sacred icon and the most famous piece from this period, the mask contains 25 pieces of polished, forest-green jade with slivers of white conch shell forming the teeth and eyes of the bat. In 1994, the mask was stolen from the Museo Nacional de Antropología in Mexico City.

The fourth of the central structures, **Building J** is formed in the bizarre shape of an arrowhead on a platform and contains a labyrinth of tunnels and passageways. Unlike any other ancient edifice in Mexico, it is asymmetrical and built at an angle to the other structures around the plaza. Its broad, carved slabs suggest that the building is one of the oldest on the site. Many of the glyphs depict an upside-down head below a stylized hill; the glyphs are thought to represent a place and a name. Archaeologists speculate that this image indicates a conquest, the head representing the defeated tribe and the name identifying the region conquered.

Behind Building J stands the highest structure at Monte Albán: the **Southern Pyramid.** On both sides of the staircase on the plaza level are a number of stelae carved with rain gods and tigers. The stela on the pyramid's right side contains a precise date, but archaeologists lack the point of reference needed to coordinate this date with the modern calendar. The neighboring stela is believed to depict the king of Monte Albán. If you climb only one pyramid in Mexico, make it this one: the top affords a commanding view of the ruins, the valley, and the mountains beyond.

Along the border of the Central Plaza, to the left as you descend the pyramid, are the foundations of **Building M,** followed by the **Platform of the Dancers** at the foot of Building L. The low platforms in front of Building M were apparently designed to make the plaza, which was built around inconveniently located rock formations, more symmetrical. In front of Building M and to the left as you face it are the haunting reliefs known as the **Dancers.** Among the most interesting examples of pre-Hispanic sculpture, the reliefs date from the 5th century BCE, and are nearly identical to contemporary Olmec sculptures along the Gulf Coast. Many of the dancers show evidence of genital mutilation. There is much speculation whether these men were commoners or of high status. Beyond the Platform of the Dancers, the **Northern Platform,** which is almost as large as the Central Plaza itself, dominates the entire site. Steps rise to meet a sunken patio. **Building B,** to the left as you face north on top of the steps, is believed to be a Mixtec-influenced addition to the site.

The path exiting the site passes the gift shop and cafeteria on the way to **Tomb 104.** Duck underground, look above the entrance, and gaze at the urn. It is covered with a motif which interweaves images of the maize god and rain god. Near the parking lot is the entrance to **Tomb 7,** where the spectacular cache of Mixtec ornaments mentioned above was found.

The **museum** at the site's entrance was recently remodeled; it offers a chronological survey of Monte Albán's history and displays sculpted stones from the site's earlier periods. Unfortunately, the truly spectacular artifacts from the site have been hauled off to museums in Oaxaca and Mexico City (site open daily 8am-5pm; admission 14 pesos, 25 if you want to use a camcorder, free Sun. and holidays).

Getting There: Buses to Monte Albán leave from the Hotel Mesón del Ángel, Mina 518, between Mier y Terán and Díaz Ordaz in Oaxaca. Monte Albán is only 10km from Oaxaca, but the ride through mountainous terrain takes 30 minutes. The normal procedure is to buy a roundtrip ticket, with the return fixed two hours after arrival at the site (about the right amount of time for a full perusal); if you want to stay longer you can pay an extra five pesos to come back on one of the later buses. During high season, buses from the hotel leave daily every hour between 8:30am and 5:30pm; during low season, buses leave five times per day during the week and six times per day on Sunday (10 pesos roundtrip). To avoid the tourist hordes, leave early. Travel agencies around the *zócalo* in Oaxaca arrange special excursions to the ruins, some with English-speaking guides. Expect to pay around US$30 per person. TV and A/C 95 pesos).

■ Tehuantepec

East of Oaxaca de Juárez, the North American continent narrows to a slender strip of land just 215km wide, known as the Isthmus of Tehuantepec. Inhabitants of the region preserve a unique Zapotec tradition most visible in Tehuantepec (pop. 60,000), the oldest of the isthmus's principal cities. Tehuantepec is a matriarchal society; the birth of a daughter is cause for celebration, and men turn their wages over to their wives, who control family finances. This family structure is most apparent during the frequent *fiestas* that punctuate rural life. Women dance together, clothed in embroidered silk *huipiles* (blouses) and long, billowing *enaguas* (skirts). But liberation is limited even in Tehuantepec: while women enjoy a uniquely privileged social and economic status, they still can't ask men to dance.

Orientation and Practical Information From the bus station, walk to the street at the end of the lot and turn left. When a bridge becomes visible on the right, turn left at Restaurant Mariscos Angel. That street will become **5 de Mayo** and lead to the front steps of the **Palacio Municipal.** Taxis will take you there for 2 pesos; walking takes 20 minutes. Facing the two-story Palacio with its shattered clockface, **Juárez** is on your left, and **Juana C. Romero** runs along the right side. Behind you is the *zócalo;* the street on the opposite end of the *zócalo* is **22 de Marzo.**

For tourist information, visit the **Casa de la Cultura,** Callejón Rey Cosijopi (tel. 5-01-14; open Mon.-Fri. 9am-2pm and 5-8pm, Sat. 9am-2pm). **Banca Serfin** (tel. 5-09-16), on 22 de Marzo to the left of the post office, exchanges U.S. dollars and traveler's checks; they also have an **ATM** (open Mon.-Fri. 9am-2pm). There are no **LADATELs** in this town, but you can make long-distance phone calls from the Hotel Donaji (7:30am-11pm). The **telegraph** office is next door to the post office (open for telegrams and **faxes** Mon.-Fri. 8am-6pm, Sat. 9am-noon).

From the **bus station** on the highway, **Cristóbal Colón** and **ADO** (tel. 501-08 and 5-09-33) travel to Mexico City (7:30 and 9:15pm, 11hr., 186 pesos; deluxe 8:30pm, 10hr., 215 pesos), Oaxaca (7 per day 5:30am-12:35am, 4hr., 51 pesos), Puebla (8:45 and 9:15pm, 10hr., 178 pesos), and San Cristóbal (8:20am, 1pm, and midnight, 7hr., 77 pesos). A bus goes to Huatulco (12:10, 2, 6am, and 2pm, 3½hr., 34 pesos), Pochutla (5hr., 43 pesos), and Puerto Escondido (6hr., 58 pesos); another leaves for Juchitán (every 30min., 30min., 6.5 pesos) and Salina Cruz (4 pesos).

The **market** is on the right side of the *zócalo* as you face the Palacio. The **Red Cross** (tel. 5-02-15) is on the highway to Salina Cruz, past the bridge (ambulance service 24hr.). **Farmacia del Rosario** (tel. 5-01-18) is on Romero at the corner of Ocampo, behind the Palacio (open daily 8am-10:30pm). The **Centro de Salud** (tel. 5-01-80) is on Guerrero. Facing the post office, take Hidalgo and turn right when it splits; the center is on the right before the Casa de la Cultura (open 24hr.). The **police** (tel. 5-00-01) are in the back of the Palacio Municipal, next to the volleyball courts. The **post office** is on 22 de Marzo, facing the *zócalo* and the Palacio (open Mon.-Fri. 8am-7pm, Sat. 8am-noon). **Postal Code:** 70760. **Telephone Code:** 971.

Accommodations and Food Tehuantepec has a few small but clean hotels and *casas de huéspedes,* all within a few blocks of the *zócalo.* **Casa de Huéspedes el Istmo,** Hidalgo 31 (tel. 5-00-19), has shady and spacious rooms with fans. Some have their very own baths, others share a communal one, and none have hot water (20 pesos per person). **Hotel Oasis,** Melchor Ocampo 8 (tel. 5-00-08), on the right behind the Palacio, offers fans, faded tile floors, bathrooms with hot water, and a restaurant in the lobby (singles 60 pesos, with A/C 85 pesos; doubles 75-85 pesos, with A/C 125 pesos; triples 85 pesos).

Tehuantepec doesn't have many cheap restaurants, but paying extra ensures cleanliness and proper sanitation. **Café Colonial,** Romero 66 (tel. 5-01-15), to·the right of the Palacio, serves breakfast (12-15 pesos), *antojitos* (20 pesos), and *comida corrida* (20 pesos; open daily 8am-7pm). **Restaurante y Mariscos Ángel** (tel. 1-37-89), on 5 de Mayo between the market and the highway, feeds you lobsters (starting at 80 pesos), fish fillet (25-35 pesos), or, for land-lovers, chicken (25-30 pesos; open daily 7am-midnight). To reach the chic **Scarú,** Leona Vicario 4 (tel. 5-06-46), take Juárez until it ends at a park at the Hotel Donaji. Make a left and walk one and a half blocks; it's uphill and to the left. A good example of 18th-century Tehuantepec architecture, the building has a back patio with columns rising to meet colonial tile. Inside, the prices match the elegant ambience (shrimp 50 pesos, fish fillets 30-40 pesos, and chicken 25-30 pesos), but the large portions and live marimba music (Fri.-Sun.) make it worthwhile (open daily 8am-11pm).

Sights and Entertainment Tehuantepec's real attractions are its *fiestas*. Each of the town's 14 *barrios* hosts an annual week-long celebration beginning on the eve of their patron saint's feast day. Since feast days are concentrated in the summer, *fiestas* tend to blend into an undifferentiated season of revelry. The festivities begin on May 1, with the *barrio* of Santa Cruz Tagolaba's, and continue through the second Sunday in October, when the *barrio* of Jaliso begins its celebration. There is a hiatus during most of July. Of all the festivals, the most colorful and spectacular are those of **Sandonga** (beginning May 28), **Santa María** (Aug. 14-20), and **Laborío** (Sept. 6-10). When it's *fiesta*-time, Tehuantepec explodes with dances, parades, fireworks, and special masses. Daytime festivities are relatively safe, but after dark, things can get dicey; don't go out alone and look out for inebriated bullies trying to provoke fights. Brush up on your dance steps, keep a good hangover cure up your sleeve, and remember: women run the show

The oldest building in town is the old Dominican **monastery,** now the **Casa de la Cultura,** down a short alley off Guerrero, next to the Centro de Salud. The monastery was commissioned by Cosijopi, the last of the Zapotec kings, who converted to Christianity and quickly handed over the reins of the city when the Spanish arrived at his doorstep. Today, the 16th-century structure's colonial frescoes vie for attention with modern paintings (open Mon.-Fri. 9am-2pm and 5-8pm, Sat. 9am-2pm).

■ Bahías de Huatulco

With its wide, palm-lined streets, shiny new electric lights, and sprawling resorts, Huatulco is a paradise for those who like their vacations packaged, planned, and posh. If everything looks new here, that's because it is: Mexican government officials settled on the area as a prime candidate for resort development in the 1980s, and began building from the bottom up. As a result, the entire city feels something like a seaside country club; even the *zócalo* smacks of freshly poured concrete and professional landscaping. Most visitors are moneyed Mexicans and *norteamericanos* drawn to Huatulco's reputation as "the new Cancún." Huatulco's nine breathtakingly beautiful bays are still relatively untouched, filled with sapphire-blue waters and lined with lush vegetation. But the days of Huatulco's virginal splendor are numbered—by 2018, every bay will be accessible by land, and the area will welcome two million visitors a year.

ORIENTATION

Huatulco is 750km from Mexico City and 950km from Acapulco. The small downtown area, **La Crucecita,** is in the middle of the string of nine bays. It houses the bus stations and most budget accommodations. The *zócalo,* four blocks from the bus stations on **Gardenia,** is bordered by **Bugambilias** on the other side. **Carrizal,** one more block away from the *zócalo,* leads to the bays. **Santa Cruz,** the bay closest to downtown, is also the most developed of the lot. Hotels and an *artesanías* market clutter its main road, **Blvd. Santa Cruz.** From there, the bays of **Chahué, Tangolunda,** and **Conejos** lie to the south. Tangolunda is also known as the **zona hotelera** because it houses the Western hemisphere's largest Club Med and several other luxury lodgings. Its main road is **Blvd. Benito Juárez.** From Santa Cruz, the bays to the north are **El Órgano, Maguey, Cacaclutla, Chachacual,** and **San Augustín.**

PRACTICAL INFORMATION

Tourist Office: Módulo de Información, Guamuchil 210 (tel. 7-13-09), on the side of the *zócalo* opposite the church. Open daily 9am-8:30pm. **Asociación de Hoteles y Moteles** (tel. 7-08-48), Blvd. Santa Cruz at Monte Albán, in Santa Cruz. Open Mon.-Fri. 9am-2pm and 4-6pm, Sat. 10am-1pm.

Currency Exchange: Bancomer (tel. 7-00-03), Blvd. Santa Cruz at Pochutla, exchanges cash and traveler's checks. Open Mon.-Fri. 9am-1:30pm. **Banamex** (tel.

7-03-22), next door, houses a 24-hr. **ATM.** Open Mon.-Fri. 9am-1:30pm. Large hotels also exchange money at slightly less favorable rates.

Telephones: LADATELs all along Carrizal, Blvd. Santa Cruz, and Blvd. Benito Juárez. *Caseta* at the **Telefónica** (tel. 7-03-14), Bugambilias at Flamboyan. Open Mon.-Sat. 7:30am-9:30pm, Sun. 8am-1pm and 4-9pm.

Telegrams: Telecomm, (tel. 7-08-85) next to the post office. Open Mon.-Fri. 8am-6pm, Sat. 9am-noon.

Airport: (tel. 1-03-10), 19km from Santa Cruz. Taxis charge 70 pesos for the 25-min. trip; *microbuses* get you within a 10-min. walk from the terminal for 5 pesos. **Aerocaribe** (tel. 7-12-20). **Mexicana** (tel. 7-02-43). **Bahías Plus Travel Agency** (tel. 7-08-11), Carrizal between Guamuchil and Guanacas, sells plane tickets (open Mon.-Fri. 9am-2pm and 4-8pm).

Buses: Cristóbal Colón (tel. 7-02-61), Gardenia at the corner of Ocotillo, has first-class service to Mexico City (5:30pm, 12½hr., 192 pesos), Oaxaca (*deluxe* 10pm, 7hr., 100 pesos; *ordinario* 11pm, 7hr., 85 pesos), Puebla (5:30pm, 11hr., 167 pesos), Puerto Escondido (6 per day 5am-6pm, 2hr., 24 pesos), San Cristóbal (10:45am, 7:05, and 11:30pm, 10hr., 111 pesos), and Tuxtla Gutiérrez (10:45am, 7:05, and 11:30pm, 9hr., 94 pesos). **Estrella Blanca** (tel. 7-01-03), on Gardenia and Palma Real, sends buses to Acapulco (10 per day 5:30am-7pm, 9hr., first-class 100 pesos, *ordinario* 86 pesos), Mexico City (6pm, 13½hr., 180 pesos), Pochutla (10 per day 5:30am-9pm, 1hr., 7 pesos), and Puerto Escondido (10 per day 5:30am-9pm, 2hr., 20 pesos). **Estrella del Valle** (tel. 7-01-93), on Jasmín at the corner of Sabali, provides service to Oaxaca (direct 10:15pm, 6½hr., 57 pesos; *ordinario* 8:30 and 12:30pm, 8hr., 45 pesos).

Car Rental: Budget (tel. 7-00-10), Ocotillo at Jazmín, one block from Cristóbal Colón station. Small cars 350-450 pesos per day, including mileage and insurance. Ask about special promotions. Open Mon.-Fri. 9am-1pm and 4-9pm.

Market: 3 de Mayo, on Guamuchil off the *zócalo*.

Laundromat: La Estrella (tel. 7-05-85), Carrizal at Flamboyan, across from Hotel Busanvi. 3kg for 21 pesos. Open Mon.-Sat. 8am-9pm.

Red Cross: (tel. 7-11-88), on Carrizal across from Gran Hotel Huatulco. Open 24hr.

Pharmacy: Farmacia Aries (tel. 7-00-48), Guamuchil at Carrizal, past the market. Open Mon.-Sat. 8am-9pm.

Hospital: IMSS (tel. 7-02-64), on Blvd. Chahué past the government building. 24-hr. service. No English spoken.

Emergency: The police provide English-speaking interpreters and assistance.

Police: Blvd. Chahué 100, (tel. 7-02-10), in the pink government building 1½ blocks from the tourist office. Open 24hr.

Post Office: Blvd. Chahué 100 (tel. 7-05-51), in the pink government building. Open Mon.-Fri. 9am-1pm and 3-6pm, Sat. 9am-1pm. **Postal Code:** 70989.

Telephone Code: 958.

ACCOMMODATIONS AND CAMPING

Camping is a way to escape Huatulco's high-priced hotel scene, but is allowed only on Chahué, Cacaluta, and Conejos. The other bays are off-limits because they lack security and are hard to get to, being accessible only by boat. Under no circumstances should you try to camp on Santa Cruz or Tangolunda; hotel security will not be kind. If camping isn't your thing, be prepared for slim pickings. All affordable rooms are located in La Crucecita, and tend to be overpriced even though they're somewhat removed from the ocean. Hot water is rare, but usually not too necessary. Rates rise by about 50% during the high season (July-Nov.); the listings below show low-high season ranges.

Hotel Posada San Agustín (tel. 7-03-68), on Macuil, at the corner of Carriza. From the bus station on Gardenia, walk 1 block to the left, turn left on Macuil, and walk for 2 blocks. In the midst of Huatulco's budding glitz, this family-run hotel remains frills-free. Clean bathrooms have no hot water. Singles or one-bed doubles 50-60 pesos. Two-bed doubles 80-90.

Hotel Benimar, Bugambilias 1404 (tel. 7-04-47), at Pochote, three blocks from the bus station on Gardenia. Overwhelmingly yellow rooms come with ceiling fans and full bathrooms that have hot water—if you tell the management to turn it on. Singles 70-100 pesos. Doubles 80-100 pesos. Triples 90-150 pesos.

Hotel Busanvi, Carrizal 601 (tel. 7-00-56), off Guamuchil. Room sizes vary, but all have a ceiling fan, balcony, and a bathroom without hot water. Singles 90-140 pesos, with A/C 100-190 pesos. Doubles 110-200 pesos, with A/C 120-220 pesos.

FOOD

Huatulco's cuisine runs the financial spectrum from pricey French food to cheap *típico* kitchens. As a general rule, the closer the restaurant is to the *zócalo,* the more expensive it will be. Carrizal is lined with small places that offer cheap food.

Restaurant-Bar Gina, Guarumbo 201 at Carrizal, one block from the *zócalo*. Standard *típico* fare served on standard plastic tables. Refreshingly free of pretension and resort-goers. Fish soup or *comida corrida* 12 pesos. Open daily 7am-9pm.

Oasis Café (tel. 7-00-18), Bugambilias at Flamboyan, at the *zócalo*. This is where the contestants in the Miss Huatulco beauty pageant come to dine. They get fed Oaxacan specialties (22-35 pesos), seafood (24-35 pesos), and sushi (45-75 pesos). Open daily 7am-midnight; Japanese food served 2-11pm only.

Restaurant-Bar La Tropicana (tel. 7-06-61), Guanacastle at Gardenia, across from Hotel Flamboyant. The cheapest option on the *zócalo,* serving breakfasts (10-22 pesos), *tortas* (12 pesos), *antojitos* (14-15 pesos), and fish (22 pesos). Open 24hr.

SAND, SUN, AND ENTERTAINMENT

Until the planners manage to finish paving the roads, Huatulco's nine bays and 36 beaches, spread across 35km, pose a transportation challenge. None of the bays can be seen from any of the others, and some are accessible only by boat. Santa Cruz, Tangolunda, and Chahué can all be reached by the blue and white *microbús* that leaves from Carrizal, near the Hotel Busanvi (2 pesos). A taxi will take you to a beach at Santa Cruz, Chahué, Tangolunda, Conejos, Maguey, or San Agustín and retrieve you at a pre-set time for 40 pesos.

To get from the *zócalo* to **Santa Cruz,** walk on Guamuchil two blocks past the market and turn right on the road behind the pink government building. As you descend, the sparkling water comes into view. Turn right on Blvd. Santa Cruz and then left on Mitla; the sands of **Playa Principal** are only a few meters away. A taxi can take you to **Playa Entrega,** also in Santa Cruz, which has a coral reef for snorkelers, a cave for explorers, and minimal waves for swimmers.

The next bay over, **Chahué,** contains the beaches of **Esperanza** and **Tejón,** ideal for suntanners. **Conejos** features calm and transparent water suited for scuba diving, fishing, and swimming. **Maguey** has 400m of waterfront perfect for snorkeling or boatriding. The calm waves of **El Órgano** beckon to watersport novices. **Cacaluta** is known for its lush plant life and cooling breeze. **Tangolunda** has five beaches, but is proudest of its 18-hole golf course and five-star accommodations. **San Agustín** is the most distant and widest bay. There are no hotels here yet—just outdoor *palapas*.

The tourist office near the *zócalo* organizes a variety of excursions, all with bilingual guides. Make reservations a day in advance (tel. 7-13-09) to take a yacht to see **El Bufadero,** the geyser between Santa Cruz and El Órgano (135 pesos), ride three and a half hours on horseback (250 pesos), or go on a 15-minute hot air balloon ride (Wed. nights, 75 pesos). They also rent snorkeling equipment (35 pesos per day) and arrange scuba diving trips (90-200 pesos). **Bicirent** (tel. 7-06-71), on Gardenia next to the Estrella Blanca bus terminal, rents mountain bikes (15 pesos per hr., 60 pesos per day) and can suggest routes to explore.

Huatulco's night scene is just getting off the ground, leaving travelers with few options after the sun has set. Most large hotels have their own bars, but the only full-fledged disco is **Magic Circus** (tel. 7-00-17), on Blvd. Santa Cruz next to the Hotel Marlin (cover Thurs.-Sun. 50 pesos; open bar Thurs.; open Wed.-Sun. 10pm-late). Closer to downtown, **Magic Tropic** (tel. 7-0-7-02), upstairs on Gardenia 311, pulsates to live salsa and merengue (Wed., Fri. 2-for-1 beers; cover Wed.-Sat. 15 pesos, Sun. 10 pesos; open Wed.-Sun. 8pm-late). Buses stop running at 8pm, so a taxi from La Crucecita (7-10 pesos) will be necessary both ways.

■ Puerto Ángel

With no bank or newsstand and only a fledgling post office, Puerto Ángel's turquoise shores are a natural haven for urban escapists. The town is popular with Mexican families, Europeans, and those who want to disrobe at Zipolite without having to endure its primitive facilities. Puerto Ángel has fairly advanced accommodations and tourist services, but is by no means a built-up resort town. Hotels and restaurants intermingle with homes and businesses, and nightlife is almost non-existent. Still, the food is good, the cove beautiful, and the living tranquil.

ORIENTATION

Puerto Ángel is 240km south of Oaxaca de Juárez and 68km east of Puerto Escondido. **Taxis** link between Puerto Ángel with nearby towns (*colectivo* about 2 pesos, *especial* 10 pesos).

The road from Pochutla becomes Puerto Ángel's main drag at the edge of town; **Avenida Principal** descends a hill, then wraps around Playa Puerto Ángel, becoming **Blvd. Virgilio Uribe.** The main road crosses a small creek (really a glorified puddle) next to the naval base and forks at a sign for Hotel Ángel del Mar. The right-hand road rambles farther down the coast to Zipolite, while the left-hand road heads for Playa Panteón. The only significant side street climbs the hill near the entrance to town by Hotel Soraya. It starts out as **Vasconcelos,** then curves to the left, becomes **Teniente Azuela,** and arrives back at Uribe in front of the naval station.

PRACTICAL INFORMATION

Services in Puerto Ángel are less than minimal; most must be begged, borrowed, or imported from nearby Pochutla. There is a **long-distance *caseta*** at Vasconcelos 3 (tel. 4-03-98), around the corner from Hotel Soraya (open daily 7am-10pm).**Telegrams** can be sent from the **Telecomm** office, next door to the post office (open Mon.-Fri. 9am-2pm). The *microbús* goes to Pochutla (every 20min. 6am-8pm, 2 pesos), returns to town, and leaves again for Zipolite (2 pesos) and Mazunte (3 pesos). Hop aboard anywhere along Uribe. **Farmacia Villa Florencia** is attached to the restaurant of the same name, on the main street (open daily 8:30am-9pm). Limited **medical services** are available at the **Centro de Salud,** at the top of Vasconcelos to the left on a dirt path (open 24hr. for emergencies, Mon.-Sat. 8am-2pm and 4-8pm for consultation). The nearest **hospital** (tel. 4-02-16) is between Puerto Ángel and Pochutla. The **Agency of Public Ministry,** next to the base, will contact police in an **emergency.** The **post office** is on the main street, at the beginning of town (open Mon.-Fri. 9am-2pm). **Postal Code: 70902. Telephone Code: 958.**

ACCOMMODATIONS

Puerto Ángel's cheap, attractive hotels and *casas de huéspedes* make the town a good base for daytrips to the sultry sands of Zipolite. Budget lodgings dot the hills on the inland side of the main road that runs behind the two beaches. Hammock spaces and ceiling fans are available in all of the hotels listed, but hot water is not.

Casa de Huéspedes Gundi y Tomás (tel. 4-31-02), on Iturbide just before the bridge and across from the naval base. Stone-and-brick terraces rambling uphill overlook the beach. Nets or screens render each room mosquito-proof. Communal bathrooms sparkle. Laundry equipment and a small restaurant. English, German,

Spanish, and some French spoken. Singles 50 pesos. Doubles 60 pesos, with bathroom 70 pesos. 10 pesos extra from July-Sept. Hammocks 15 pesos.

Pensión Puesta del Sol (tel. 4-30-96), past the naval base but before the road forks. Attractive common spaces. Older rooms with cement floors can be unbearably hot during the day; all come with fans and screens. Breakfasts available for a price. Singles without bathroom 50 pesos. Doubles without bathroom 65-75 pesos, with bathroom 85-100 pesos.

Posada Rincón Sabroso (tel. 4-30-95), on the high hill at the entrance to town. Forget the beaches: just lie on the hammock in front of your room looking out over the cove. Two beds in every room. Water 7-11am and 5-10pm only. Singles 70 pesos, high season 100 pesos. Doubles 80 pesos, high season 120 pesos. Each additional person 20 pesos.

FOOD

Seafood is the specialty of nearly every restaurant, though menus make some concessions for vegetarians—think grilled cheese sandwiches. Prices at the beachfront *palapas* aren't always in the budget range, but their tranquility is priceless.

Restaurant Villa Florencia, in town on the landward side of Iturbide, before the naval station (tel. 4-30-44). This large, casual Italian restaurant serves both seafood and pasta (spaghetti 10-22 pesos, tortellini 30 pesos, pizzas 20-35 pesos). They also serve breakfast (5-10 pesos). Restaurant and bar open daily 7am-11pm.

Restaurant El Capy (tel. 4-30-02), on the right side of the dirt road that descends to Playa Panteón. Climb upstairs for fresh under-the-water fare, including fish fillets (23-28 pesos) and shrimp (28 pesos). Open daily 8am-9:30pm.

Restaurant Cordelia's (tel. 4-31-69), on Playa Panteón under a large *palapa*. A suntanned foreign crowd samples palatable yet uninspired seafood and Mexican dishes. Lobster 40 pesos, fish fillets 26 pesos. Open daily 7am-10pm.

SAND

Of Puerto Ángel's two beaches, the smaller **Playa Panteón,** on the far side of town, is the worthier. The water here is calm and warm, and the coves great for exploring. You can reach it via a cement walkway that begins right past the naval base or by car, driving uphill towards Zipolite and then turning left down a dirt road. Many of the restaurants on the beach rent equipment. **Luis y Vicente "Amigos del Mar"** (tel. 431-

---

Peel it, Slice it, Suck it, Dice it

Mangos may be one of Mexico's more delicious offerings, but the fruit's sumptuous flavor is often passed over by foreigners who can't figure out how to eat the damn thing. There are many types of mangos, but the two most popular are the *paraíso*, which is the larger of the two and red and green, and the yellow *manila*.

You can tell a lot about people from how they eat their mango. Some seem to find an acute enjoyment from sucking the fruit, turning it into almost an erotic art, while more prim folks can't stand the messiness involved. The easiest way to eat a mango is to pluck an end with your fingernail or fork, peel it like a banana, and suck away. But for hygiene's sake, consider a fancier option: cut along both sides of the seed, leaving yourself with two pieces and a seed with some fruit around the edges. Next, peel the skin around the seed and chomp away. Then take your two bowl-shaped pieces and cut down into the fruit, creating a grid in the pulp. Turn the skin inside-out and scrape your pieces onto a plate. Diced mango! Alternatively, cut the fruit into strips, shove them into your mouth, and use your teeth to scrape off the pulp. Mangos are sometimes sold on a stick, and one can eat the fruit like ice cream by turning and sucking—be sure to lean over as you eat. And the one vital rule of mango-eating: never, ever wear a white shirt.

16) rents snorkel gear (15 pesos per hr., 45 pesos per day) and arranges boat trips (up to five people, 150 pesos per hr.; open daily 7am-11pm).

Away from the polluted waters of Playa Puerto Ángel and the restaurant-studded shores of Playa Panteón is **Playa Estacahuites** (pronounced "a Stack o Wheaties"). To get there, walk on the main road towards Pochutla and ascend the hill just past the post office until you find a yellow Corona sign. The three small bays have somewhat rocky sand and gentle water for swimming.

■ Zipolite

The road to paradise is newly paved. Zipolite, once a remote hippie beach, can now be easily reached by *colectivo* from Pochutla or Puerto Ángel. The word *zipolite* means "place of the dead"—it refers to those who have lost their lives in the unforgiving surf. Of course, cynics would note that for every person who has lost her life in the waves, ten have lost their former lives to Zipolite's hypnotizing combination of wind, water, and marijuana. Come here to stroll naked down the long beach, check in with the international vagabond set, and generally partake of the fringe atmosphere. Do it soon, though—where paved roads go, clothes soon follow.

Orientation and Practical Information Zipolite lies just 4km west of Puerto Ángel; microbuses run back and forth between the two (every 20min., 2 pesos). Zipolite consists of one long stretch of beach. Get off the bus before it curves right in front of a thick grove of palm trees. Cross the street and walk towards the shining sea. If you need information, ask someone who's naked—the ones without tan lines have been here the longest. There is a **pharmacy** and a small **general store** on the road near the entrance from Puerto Ángel. **Palapa Katy,** in Zipolite about in the middle of the beach, sells bottled water for 5 pesos. You're better off buying supplies and munchies in Puerto Ángel or in Pochutla.

Accommodations and Food *Palapas* rent hammocks and the space to swing in (10 pesos a night). **Shambhala,** at the very far end of the beach across some rocks and up the stairs, is an international haven with a corresponding world peace theme. Rooms have mosquito netting and lights, and common bathrooms have water all day long (singles 30 pesos; doubles 50 pesos). All the food cooked in its café is health-conscious and purified. Unlike the other establishments it literally looks down on, Shambhala is **drug- and alcohol-free. San Cristóbal,** a cluster of *palapas* before the rocks that lead to Shambhala, has two floors of nicer-than-average wood and cement *cabañas* with lights and fans. Common bathrooms are conveniently located and clean (one or two people 40 pesos, with bathroom 60 pesos).

For fish and seafood, the *palapas* are ready and waiting (most open 8am-10pm and charge 20-30 pesos for their most expensive item). **Nuevo Sol** offers delicious pizzas prepared by the Italian owner. **3 de Diciembre,** 100m off the beach, offers vegetarian dishes and sweet desserts. **Lo Cósmico,** the last *palapa* before Shambhala, makes crepes that are out of this world.

Sand and Sights The only sight in Zipolite are the other sunbathers, none of whom is doing absolutely anything. Waves break cataclysmically offshore, slamming the carefree souls who frolic naked in the surf. The waves come in from two directions, creating a series of channels that suck unsuspecting swimmers out to sea. Though ferocious, these channels are not very wide. If you find yourself being pulled away from shore, do not attempt to swim directly towards the beach; rather, swim parallel to the beach until you're clear of the seaward current.

Zipolite is unfortunately plagued by theft, so keep an eye on everything or leave it locked up. A final warning: scorpions frequent Zipolite, so either give your cut-offs a good shake before jumping into them or blend in by going about your business in the buff. If you *must* get out and do something, catch a bus to Mazunte. Its **Museo de la**

Tortuga holds nine of the eleven turtle species in the world, and all six of the fresh-water varieties. Don't begrudge the admission price; your pesos go toward conservation (open Tues.-Sat. 10am-4:30pm, Sun. 10am-12:30pm; admission 10 pesos, children and students with ID 5 pesos).

■ Puerto Escondido

Less than two decades ago, Puerto Escondido (pop. 20,000) was a quiet fishing village where only a handful of scantily clad *extranjeros* used to gleefully romp, wheedling overnight lodging from local families. Today droves of stocky surfers ride the waves of Playa Zicatela as sun-worshippers from the world over look on. Hotels now outnumber hippies, nudity is uncommon, and excellent food, exotic drink, and kitsch trinkets compete for pedestrians' pesos. Although Puerto Escondido is no longer a remote outpost, it still entices mostly rugged-minded vacationers in search of a peaceful time. Time just doesn't seem to pass in Puerto.

ORIENTATION

Like any self-respecting seaside village, Puerto Escondido has its very own airport. It's also connected to the rest of the world by land. Routes 175 (paved) and 131 (mostly unpaved) wind treacherously through the Sierra Madres toward the coast, while an expertly paved coastal road, Rte. 200, twists through ramshackle fishing towns and coastal forests on its way to Acapulco.

Puerto Escondido is built on a hill. The **Carretera Costera** (Rte. 200) cuts across the hill, bisecting it into an uptown of well marked, perpendicular residential streets and a touristy downtown maze of paths leading to the beach. At *el crucero,* Rte. 131 from Oaxaca crosses Rte. 200 and becomes **Pérez Gasga,** which twists downhill and turns into the **Adoquín,** a pedestrian walkway leading to the beach. The **bus station** is near *el crucero.* From and to the airport, 3km away on Rte. 200, *colectivos* charge 15 pesos. Taxis can be found by the tourist information booth and along the Carretera Costera; they are the safer way of getting around after nightfall.

PRACTICAL INFORMATION

Tourist Office: Módulo de Información Turística (tel. 2-01-75), a palm-shaded information booth with its back to the beach just before the beginning of the pedestrian walkway. Advice and counsel given with good humor and the wisdom of an insider (unpredictably open Mon.-Fri.9am-2pm and 5-8pm, Sat. 9am-2pm).

Currency Exchange: Banamex (tel. 2-03-52), Pérez Gasga on the corner of the Adoquín. Exchanges travelers' checks and has an **ATM.** Open Mon.-Fri. 9am-noon. **Bancomer** (tel. 2-04-11), 1 Nte. at 2 Pte. near the bus station, also exchanges cash. Open Mon.-Fri. 8:30am-3pm. **Money Exchange** (tel. 2-05-92), on the Adoquín across from Farmacia Cortés, has bad rates but convenient hours. Open Mon.- Sat. 10am-3pm and 6-9pm.

Telephones: LADATELs line the beach side of the Adoquín. **Farmacia Cortés** sells 50-peso phone cards.

Telegrams: (tel. 2-09-57), next to the post office. Open Mon.-Fri. 8am-6pm.

Airport: (tel. 2-04-91). **AeroMorelos** (tel. 2-06-53). **Aerovega** (tel. 2-01-51).**Turismo Rodimar de Viajes,** Pérez Gasga 905B (tel. 2-07-34), on the Adoquín, sells **Mexicana** plane tickets and organizes daytrips. Open daily 7:30am-10pm.

Bus Stations: Cristóbal Colón (tel. 2-10-73), Calle 1 Nte. 207, two blocks uphill from *el crucero* and to the right. To Huatulco (6 per day 8:45am-9pm, 2hr., 24 pesos), San Cristóbal (8:45am, 5, and 9:30pm, 12hr., 134 pesos), and Tuxtla Gutiérrez (8:45am, 5, and 9:30pm, 10hr., 117 pesos). **Estrella Blanca** (tel. 2-04-27), just steps uphill from *el crucero,* goes to Acapulco (semi-direct 7 per day 7:30am-11:30pm, 7hr., 78 pesos; *ordinario* every hr. 4am-3pm, 8½hr., 66 pesos), Huatulco and Pochutla (6 per day 5am-9pm, 30min., 13-20 pesos), Mexico City (8pm, 12hr., 165 pesos), and Zihuatanejo (8:30pm, 11hr., 123 pesos). **Oaxaca-Istmo** (tel. 2-03-92), behind Estrella Blanca, travels to Pochutla and Salina Cruz (6, 8:30, 11:30am, and 1pm, 30min.; 10-39 pesos). **Estrella del Valle** (tel. 2-00-50), Hidalgo at 3 Ote., three blocks down, goes to Oaxaca (direct 8:15am and 10:15pm, 6½hr., 57 pesos; *ordinario* 6 per day 7:30am-10pm, 8½hr., 49 pesos).

Car Rental: Budget (tel. 2-03-12) has an office in Hotel Posada Real in Bacocho, 3km west of *el crucero* on Rte. 200. Small cars 370 pesos per day, including insurance and unlimited mileage. Open daily 9am-2pm and 4-8pm.

Market: Mercado Benito Juárez, 8 Nte. at 3 Pte., one block past the post office all the way up Av. Oaxaca. Open daily 7am-6pm, but most lively Wed. and Sat. **Raya Sol** (tel. 2-02-87) is a small grocery store on Pérez Gasga, near the beginning of the pedestrian mall. Open daily 8am-11pm.

Laundromat: Lavamática del Centro, Pérez Gasga 405, uphill from the pedestrian walkway on the right. Cheap. Open Mon.-Sat. 8am-8pm, Sun. 8am-5pm.

Red Cross: (tel. 2-01-46), Pérez Gasga across from Hotel Nayar. Open 24hr.

Pharmacy: Farmacia Cortés (tel. 2-01-12), on the *adoquín.* Open daily 7:30am-11:30pm.

Hospital: IMSS (tel. 2-01-42), 5 de Febrero at Calle 7 Nte. Open 24hr. **Centro de Salud,** Pérez Gasga 409 (tel. 2-00-46), below and across from the Hotel Virginia. A small medical clinic open 24hr. for emergencies. No English spoken.

Police: (tel. 2-01-11 or 2-01-55), on the Agencia Municipal on the Carretera Costera, shortly past *el crucero* on the way to the airport. No English spoken. The tourist booth will probably be more helpful—if it's open.

Post Office: (tel. 2-09-59), Calle 7 Nte. at Av. Oaxaca, uphill from *el crucero* past the bus station. Open Mon.-Fri. 8am-7pm, Sat. 9am-1pm. **Postal Code:** 71980.

Telephone Code: 958.

ACCOMMODATIONS

The beach is not safe for camping, but a multitude of hotels cater to budget travelers, particularly during the off-season. During *Semana Santa,* Christmas, July, and August, reservations are an absolute must, and the least expensive places are the rented rooms, trailer parks, and *cabañas* along the beach—you'll feel like you're on Gilligan's Island, but without the coconut radio. In a pinch, **Farmacia Cortés** has listings of rooms and suites for rent. The first three listings are on the hill; the last two lie much closer to the beach. Price ranges reflect seasonal variation.

Hotel Mayflower, Andador Libertad (tel. 2-03-67). From the bus stations, cross *el crucero,* then take a left down a steep hill. The road will end, but stairs will descend on the right to the hotel entrance. Every guest receives a complimentary margarita in the upstairs bar where young international beachgoers dust off the sand and read back issues of *Newsweek* and *Glamour.* The hospitable, multilingual owner keeps rooms immaculate. Singles 79-99 pesos. Doubles 99-120 pesos. Across the street, **Plymouth Rock** has dorm rooms with communal bathrooms, mosquito nets, fans, and a kitchen. 25 pesos per person.

Casa de Huéspedes Naxhiely, Pérez Gasga 301. At *el crucero,* cross and follow Pérez Gasga to the aqua-blue hotel on the left. A bit removed from the beach action. Provides cold water, sheets, and large plain rooms. Singles 23-130 pesos. Doubles 46-150 pesos.

Hotel San Juan, Felipe Merklin 503 (tel. 2-03-36; fax 2-06-12), right at *el crucero.* Enter from the road downhill and to the left. When the construction is through, this hotel will boast a pool and brand spankin' new suites with A/C. Until then, the screened-in rooms with 24-hr. hot water and sweeping views of the beach are reason enough to withstand all the hammering. Singles 60-80 pesos. Doubles 70-100 pesos. Color TV 20 pesos extra.

Casas de Playa Acali (tel. 2-02-78 or 2-07-54), at the beginning of Zicatela Beach just past the rocks. Wooden cabins have fans, mosquito netting, private bathrooms with 24-hr. hot water, a jug of purified water on the porch, and a swimming pool. If that's not enough, cross the road to the ocean. Singles 80-100 pesos. Doubles 100-120 pesos. Bungalows with full kitchen 200 pesos.

Restaurant y Cuartos Liza, on Playa Marinero, past Carmen's Café and Hotel Flor de María. Among the safer of beach accommodations. Four rooms with fans, screens on the windows, and private bathrooms with hot water. Attached restaurant. Singles 60-102 pesos. Doubles 102-140 pesos.

FOOD

The restaurants on Pérez Gasga know their clientele: the ubiquitous "we accept dollars" signs should say it all. The pizza, pasta, and apple pie for sale on the pedestrian walkway have just about usurped the more *típico* Oaxacan fare; you'll have to hike uphill to enjoy *mole* with the locals.

Banana's (tel. 2-00-05), the last restaurant on the beach side of Pérez Gasga, at the end of the pedestrian mall. Catering to the cable TV set, this popular hangout has a program for every meal. Enjoy your breakfast (8-11 pesos) with CNN Headline News, and your mid-day crepes (21 pesos) while listening to MTV. Every night at 8pm, they show the obscure Italian movie "Puerto Escondido," perfect with pizza (29-42 pesos). Happy hour 6-9pm. Open daily 7:30am-12:30am.

La Gota de Vida (tel. 2-09-93), on Pérez Gasga, a few stores uphill from the tourist booth. This vegetarian haven makes its own bread, pasta, yogurt, and tempeh, sterilizes all its vegetables, and prepares the most heavenly fruit *licuados* (11 pesos), tofu *tortas* (11-12 pesos), and salads (14-17 pesos). Open daily 8am-10pm.

Carmen's Café (tel. 2-08-60), on Playa Marinero, across from Hotel Flor de María. Follow the sign left up the alley, then turn right after crossing the bridge. One taste of the chocolate croissant (5 pesos) and you'll stop complaining about the *gringo* invasion of the beach. Fresh bread makes the peanut butter and banana sandwich (8 pesos) even more delicious. Extravagant fruit and yogurt salad with Carmen's own granola 13 pesos. Open Mon.-Sat. 7am-6pm, Sun. 7am-midnight. A second branch on Playa Zicatela is open daily 6am-9pm.

SAND AND SIGHTS

Beach, beach, and more beach. Past Banana's, you'll encounter fishing boats; the stretch of sand from there to the rocks is **Playa Marinero,** great for swimming or sunbathing. Stepping over the rocks will take you to **Playa Zicatela,** one of the world's best surfing beaches. Those dudes bobbing up and down in the water waiting to ride the next killer wave all have at least five years of experience. Watching them is exhilarating, but under no circumstances should you swim at Zicatela—you risk a fate worse than wiping out. Past Carmen's on the road facing the beach, **Acuario** (tel. 2-10-26) rents **snorkel** (10-15 pesos) and **scuba** gear (beginning at US$35 for a day's excursion). A few smaller beaches, suitable for snorkeling, lie on the other side of Playa Principal. The distance is short enough to walk, but you can also take a taxi (15 pesos) or a boat. From the tourist booth, walk to the right towards the lighthouse. A staircase will take you over the waves before climbing uphill to a road and a vista point. Follow the road and take the first left; stairs lead to **Playa Manzanillo.** On the other side of a rocky barrier is **Puerto Angelito.** Both tranquil beaches make for good swimming or languid lounging in the shaded hammocks or chairs (10 pesos per day). Even farther removed from civilization is beautiful **Playa Carrizalillo,** accessible by boat or taxi from Puerto Angelito.

ENTERTAINMENT

When the sun goes down, sun worshippers turn into bar crawlers, making their way to the many pubs along the strip. In the early evening, every restaurant and bar has a happy hour, which oddly enough lasts for three or four hours. Two-for-one drinks are the reason that everyone's happy. In addition to drinks and TV, **Banana's** offers pool and foosball (20 pesos per hour). Around 10pm, the music starts. **Discoteque Bacocho,** in the Bacocho residential district, is the only full-fledged dance club, meaning you have to shower and throw something nice over your swimsuit. Taxis will take you there for 15 pesos (cover 20 pesos; open Sat.-Sun. 10pm-3am). More informal places line the pedestrian walkway. **El Tubo,** on the Playa Principal, plays reggae, salsa, and rock. The bacchanalian crowd spills out onto the beach by night's end (no cover; open daily 10pm-6am). **El Son y La Rumba** and **Babalú,** both near the tourist booth, are hotspots with live music.

Central Mexico

The states of **Guanajuato** and **Querétaro** form a vast, bowl-shaped plateau of fertile soil, rolling farms, and verdant hillsides that. Since the 16th century, its silver-rich underground has brought the region prosperity and steered the course of its history. In the 18th century, the city of Guanajuato began to supply most of Mexico's minting silver and the area became one of the wealthier and more influential in the country. Guanajuato became the commercial and banking center of this thriving region, trading manufactured goods for crops from the nearby agricultural towns of Salamanca, Irapuato, León, San Miguel, and Celaya. A flourishing economy eventually brought the region both a measure of sophistication and an expat population, drawn to the region's vibrant social life and distinguished history.

Although the first part of Mexico to bear the colonial mark of Hernán Cortés was Veracruz, the Conquest did not really pick up steam until his group ventured inland to **Puebla** and **Tlaxcala,** where many local tribes joined the entourage. Mexico's older churches, some built only months after the Spaniards' arrival, mark Cortés's trail through these states. But a glimpse into one of the region's 16th-century temples, where images from *indígena* mythology mingle with Catholic icons, shows that missionaries and *conquistadores* failed to fully subjugate indigenous peoples.

Contrary to popular conception, the **Estado de México** has more to offer than easy access to the thickly populated Mexico City. In the area outside of Mexico City's smog cloud, green plains creep up snowy mountains and swollen towns continue to grow, pushing against their natural barriers. The state is speckled with stellar archaeological sites, solemn convents, and vestiges of the colonial era. Forests seem to stretch forever, and the small towns and villages within appear untouched by modernity. Small town life is alive and well here—come to get a look at Mexico sans tourists or the glimmering attractions that draw them.

After Emperor Maximilian built his summer home in Cuernavaca, thousands of Mexicans played follow-the-(unelected) leader and **Morelos** became a prime vacation spot. Once again, the state enjoyed the same interest that first brought the Olmecs from the Gulf Coast to settle the city of Tamoanchan nearly 3000 years earlier. These days, Mexicans and foreigners alike march to Morelos to take advantage of Cuernavaca's "eternal spring," Cuautla's bathing areas, Xochicalco's underground observatory, and Tepoztlán's striking landscape. Unlike the overpopulated Federal District, parts of Morelos remain undeveloped, with plentiful tree-covered vistas and unspoiled streams. Morelos is just a short jaunt from the D.F.; you can easily spend a day in Cuernavaca, Cuautla, or Tepoztlán and return to the capital in the evening.

GUANAJUATO

■ Guanajuato

Guanajuato is simply beautiful. During the ride into the city, the highway winds through lush mountains split at the base by winding streams, passing rows of *nopales* (prickly-pear cacti) that blend surreally into the landscape. The hills continue into a city where the legacy of colonial days lives on in architectural and cultural forms. Serpentine slate streets overflow with monuments deifying the silver barons that made Guanajuato one of the richer colonial mining towns in America, while *callejones* (stone alleyways) sneak through Spanish archways and courtyards, leading to the city's myriad museums, theaters, and cathedrals. Though the town's boom days are over, tourists continue to visit from all over the world, while Guanajuato's university students and musicians drive an animated and youthful social life.

ORIENTATION

Guanajuato lies 380km northwest of Mexico City. Navigating the city's tangled maze of streets and *callejones* can be a teeth-gnashing experience. The **Plaza de la Paz,** the **Basílica,** and the **Jardín Unión** mark the center of town. **Av. Juárez** climbs eastward past the *mercado* and Plaza de la Paz. Just past the basilica, the street is called **Luis Obregón;** past Teatro Juárez, the schizophrenic street becomes **Av. Sopeña.** Roughly following the path of Juárez/Sopeña, the **Subterránea** is an underground avenue built beneath the former bed of the river, which now flows in an adjacent concrete channel. When you become lost (and you will), remember that the tunnel is always downhill from you.

Guanajuato's **bus station** is 3km west of town; from there, the "El Centro" bus takes you to the heart of the city, while the "Mercado" bus takes you to the market. Buses cross the city running westward above ground and eastward underground (daily 6am-10:30pm, 1.40 pesos). A taxi from the bus station to the *centro* will cost 10 pesos. Taxis within the city cost five to eight pesos.

PRACTICAL INFORMATION

Tourist Office: Subsecretaría de Turismo, Plaza de la Paz 14 (tel. 2-15-74, 2-76-22, 2-19-82, or 2-82-75; fax 2-42-51), on your right as you pass the front of the *basílica* going uphill. English-speaking staff answers reams of questions with the help of a touch-screen video. Deluxe map is a must. Open Mon.-Fri. 8:30am-7:30pm, Sat.-Sun. 10am-2pm.

Currency Exchange: Banks line Juárez and Plaza de la Paz. **BITAC (Banco Internacional),** Plaza de la Paz 59 (tel. 2-01-87, 2-63-54, 2-25-07, or 2-00-18) has the best hours. Open Mon.-Fri. 8am-7pm, Sat. 9am-2:30pm. Across from the post office, **Cronos InterDivisas,** Plaza de la Compañía 2 (tel. 12-79-94), one of the many *casas de cambio,* has the best rates. Open Mon.-Sat. 9am-5pm.

Telephones: Lonchería y Caseta de Larga Distancia Pípila, Constancia 9 (tel. 2-00-75), behind the Templo de San Diego. Open Mon.-Fri. 10am-10pm, Sat.-Sun. 11am-9:45pm. **Computel,** Ayuntamiento 20 (tel. 2-06-48; fax 2-06-00), one block from the post office. A bit expensive. Open Mon.-Sat. 8am-9pm, Sun. 10am-6pm.

Telegrams: Sopeña 1 (tel. 2-04-29; 2-69-91), to your immediate left facing Teatro Juárez. **Fax** service too. Open Mon.-Fri. 8am-6pm, Sat. 9am-noon.

Buses: Central de Autobuses, west of the *centro.* Take the "Central de Autobuses" bus from Plaza de la Paz to the station (1.40 pesos). **Flecha Amarilla** (tel. 3-13-33) goes to Aguascalientes (5 per day 5:40am-6:10pm, 3hr., 37 pesos), Dolores Hidalgo (every 20min. 6am-10:20pm, 1½hr., 12 pesos), Mexico City (11:20am and 1:20pm, 5hr., 73 pesos), Morelia (5 per day 7:50am-3pm, 4hr., 37 pesos), Querétaro (5 per day 6:40am-4:50pm, 3hr., 29 pesos), San Luis Potosí (7:20am, 1, and 7pm, 3hr., 46 pesos), and San Miguel de Allende (8 per day 6:45am-6pm, 2hr., 18 pesos). **Servicios Coordinados** (tel. 3-13-33) runs first-class buses to Aguascalientes (6:30am, 1:05, and 5:20pm, 3hr., 40 pesos) and Irapuato (4 per day 7:10am-6:40pm, 45min., 10 pesos). **Primera Plus** (tel. 3-13-33/-42) goes to Colima (7am, 7hr., 132 pesos), Guadalajara (7 per day 8am-11:30pm, 4½hr., 82 pesos), Manzanillo (7am, 8hr., 157 pesos), and Puerto Vallarta (9:45pm, 8hr., 184 pesos). **Expresso Futura** (tel. 3-13-44) serves Acapulco (9pm, 9hr., 205 pesos) and Durango (2, 4, and 9:30pm, 7½hr., 122 pesos). **Ómnibus de México** (tel. 3-13-56) serves Zacatecas (9pm, 5hr., 67 pesos). **ETN** (tel. 3-15-79 or 3-02-89) provides luxury service to Guadalajara (8am, 12:30, and 5:30pm, 4½hr., 100 pesos) and Mexico City (5 per day 1am-6:30pm, 4½hr., 120 pesos).

Laundromat: Lavandería Automática, Manuel Doblado 28 (tel. 2-67-18). Self- and full-service. Open Mon.-Sat. 9am-2pm and 4-8pm.

Red Cross: (tel. 2-04-87), on Juárez, two blocks beyond the *mercado.* English spoken by Drs. Sánchez, Martínez, and Aguilar. 24-hr. emergency service.

Pharmacy: Farmacia La Perla de Guanajuato, Juárez 146 (tel. 2-11-75), near the Jardín Reforma. No English spoken. Open daily 9am-9pm.

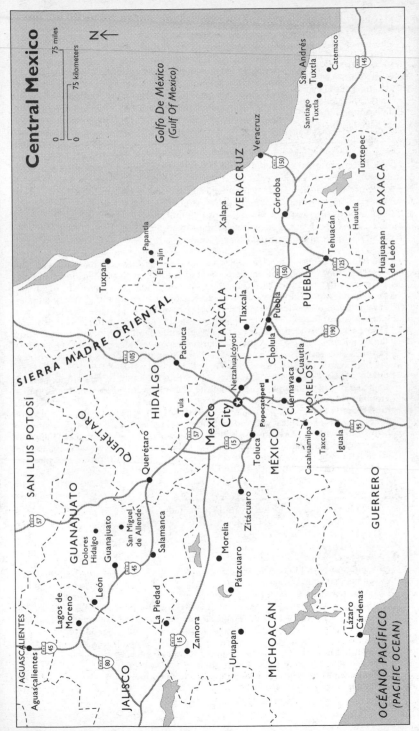

Central Mexico

N←

75 miles
0
75 kilometers
0

Golfo De México
(Gulf Of Mexico)

OCÉANO PACÍFICO
(PACIFIC OCEAN)

SIERRA MADRE ORIENTAL

SAN LUIS POTOSÍ

QUERÉTARO

HIDALGO

TLAXCALA

VERACRUZ

PUEBLA

OAXACA

GUANAJUATO

MÉXICO

MORELOS

GUERRERO

MICHOACÁN

JALISCO

AGUASCALIENTES

Mexico City

Aguascalientes
Lagos de Moreno
León
Dolores Hidalgo
Guanajuato
San Miguel de Allende
Salamanca
La Piedad
Zamora
Uruapan
Morelia
Pátzcuaro
Zitácuaro
Querétaro
Tula
Toluca
Pachuca
Netzahualcóyotl
Popocatépetl
Cacahuamilpa
Taxco
Iguala
Cuernavaca
Cuautla
Cholula
Puebla
Tlaxcala
Xalapa
Veracruz
Córdoba
Tehuacán
Huajuapan de León
Huautla
Tuxtepec
Santiago Tuxtla
San Andrés Tuxtla
Catemaco
Papantla
El Tajín
Tuxpan
Lázaro Cárdenas

57
105
57
15
95
150
150
125
190
145
45
80
15

Hospital: (tel. 3-15-73/-76/-77), behind the bus station. Dr. Arturo Acosta Arredondo (tel. 2-04-35 or emergency 2-53-56) speaks English. Open for consultation Mon.-Fri. 1-3pm and 6-9pm, Sat. 1-3pm.

Emergency: 06.

Police: Alhóndiga 8 (tel. 2-02-66 or 2-27-17), one block from Juárez. Open 24hr.

Post Office: Ayuntamiento 25 (tel. 2-03-85), across from the Templo de la Compañía. Follow Truco, the street running behind the *basílica,* for one block and turn left. Open Mon.-Fri. 8am-7pm, Sat. 9am-1pm. **Postal Code:** 36000.

Telephone Code: 473.

ACCOMMODATIONS

The quiet, pretty neighborhood around the *basílica* is home to some inexpensive hotels, often occupied by young people from every corner of the globe; Guanajuato frequently plays two-day getaway for students at language institutes in San Miguel de Allende or Mexico City. More economic lodgings cluster near the *mercado* and the Alhóndiga. Those visiting Guanajuato on weekends, during the Festival Cervantino in October, or during Semana Santa in April should make hotel reservations way in advance and expect prices to double. The tourist office keeps a list of families who rent out rooms during the festival.

Casa Kloster, Alonso 32 (tel. 2-00-88). Leaving the *basílica,* pass the garden of Plaza de la Paz, turn left on Callejón de las Estrella, and follow it to Alonso. A Garden of Eden right in the center of town. Rooms overlook an open courtyard filled with flowers and birds. Communal baths sparkle. Friendly guests and management. Reservations are recommended. 40 pesos per person.

Hotel Central, Juárez 111 (tel. 2-00-80), across the street from the Posada San Francisco, 1 block from the market. Lots of greenery and pink paint. Rooms sport desks, mirrors, and hot water. Attached restaurant. Singles 50 pesos. Doubles 70 pesos. Quads 130 pesos. Prices jump to 125, 150, and 210 pesos, respectively, during high season. Add 10 pesos for TV.

Posada Del Carmen, Juárez 111-A (tel. 2-93-30). Adjacent to Hotel Central, with virtually identical rooms, but without all the charms or amenities. Singles 50 pesos. Doubles 60 pesos.

Hotel Posada San Francisco, Juárez 178 (tel. 2-24-67), at Plaza Gavira. The big pink hotel next to the market (be prepared for street noise). Clean, carpeted bedrooms with shiny white bathrooms. All rooms come with TV, but if you feel lonely you can watch in the 2nd-floor lounge, with a suit of armor to keep you company (he won't talk, hog the remote, or steal your nachos). Singles 90 pesos. Doubles 100 pesos. High season rates approximately 110 and 125 pesos.

FOOD

Inexpensive restaurants cluster around Guanajuato's plazas and near the *basílica.* Prices rise near the Jardín Unión, as does the *gringos*-per-square-inch ratio. The Mercado Hidalgo has many fruit and taco stands.

Truco No. 7, Truco 7 (tel. 2-83-74), the first left beyond the *basílica.* Artsy, funky and immensely popular with both local and foreign students. International pop music and the smell of *carne asada* (17 pesos) fill the air. Cappuccino 5 pesos. Open daily 8:30am-11:30pm.

Cafetería y Restaurante Pinguis (tel. 2-14-14), on the Jardín Unión. Look for the burnt orange awning across from Posada Santa Fe. Great location and rockbottom prices. Bulletin board advertises local cultural events while Diego Rivera and Frida Kahlo look on. Clientele is a bizarre combination of students, *señores* sipping coffee over the newspaper, and whoever wanders in off the Jardín. *Menú del día* 15 pesos. *Huevos* 8 pesos. Juices 2.50-3 pesos. Open daily 8am-10pm.

Rincón de San Fernando, Plaza de San Fernando 43, lodged in the far right corner of the Plaza. From the *basílica,* walk down Juárez and turn right just before the *mercado.* Regal blue peacocks perch atop doorways, and lions stare vacantly at the animated crowd. The food is tasty and prepared with lots of tender loving care. *Comida corrida* 14 pesos, *chilaquiles* 8 pesos, juice 3.50 pesos. Open Mon.-Sat. 8am-6pm.

Jardín Yogurt, Juan Valle 4 (tel. 2-80-11), 2 blocks down Juárez from the *basílica,* turning right after Bancomer. The peaceful green and white tiled courtyard is as refreshing as the fruit they serve. *Huevos al gusto* 7 pesos, yogurt 8 pesos, vegetarian *comida corrida* 15 pesos. Open Mon.-Fri. 9:30am-6pm.

SIGHTS

The elegant baroque exterior of the **Basílica de Nuestra Señora de Guanajuato** rises above the Plaza de la Paz. Inside, dozens of candelabra illuminate the Doric interior, including fine ornamental frescoes and paintings of the Madonna by Miguel Cabrera. The wooden image of the city's protector, Nuestra Señora de Guanajuato, rests on a pure silver base and is believed to be the oldest piece of Christian art in Mexico (open daily 7am-8pm).

Next to the university and one block north of the *basílica* is the more interesting Jesuit **Templo de la Compañía.** Completed in 1765, the temple was shut down just two years later when the Jesuits were expelled from Spanish America. The ornate stone exterior is one of the more striking in the region and still has four of the original five Churrigueresque façades. Soft light streams in from the delicate cupola, catching on the gold brocade and brightening the gray and rose stone interior. The ex-sacristy in the back of the church holds an art exhibit containing some of the church's original collection. At the end of the exhibit is a spooky *relicario,* a wooden shelf enveloped in gold leaf, holding a collection of human bones. (Church open daily 7:30am-9:30pm. Exhibit open daily 11am-2pm and 5-6pm. Five-peso donation requested to support the restoration process.)

The **Jardín Unión,** in the heart of the city and one block east of the *basílica,* is the town's social center. This triangular plaza boasts enough shops, cafés, and guitar-strumming locals to tame the wild beast of tourism. The **Teatro Juárez** (tel. 2-01-83) faces one corner of Jardín Unión. Built in 1903 for dictator Porfirio Díaz, the theater has an unabashedly gaudy Romanesque façade—try 12 columns, 12 lampposts, eight statues, and two bronze lions. The auditorium betrays its Moorish design: half-circles, arabesques, and endlessly weaving frescoed flowers in green, red, yellow, and brown make the interior seem like a gigantic Persian rug. In addition to housing government offices, the Teatro Juárez still hosts plays and the main events of the Festival Cervantino. (Open Tues.-Sun. 9am-1:45pm and 5-7pm, except on days of performances. Admission 4 pesos.)

Another self-aggrandizing Porfirian edifice is the **Palacio Legislativo de la Paz,** the state capitol, across from the Posada de la Condesa near the *basílica.* Christened by Díaz in 1900, the building is an adaptation of the Greek Parthenon. Italian marble, wall and floor mosaics, and a decorative zinc ceiling ornament the interior (open Mon.-Fri. 10am-5pm; free).

In addition to beautiful colonial architecture, Guanajuato is home to a number of unique museums. The **Museo Iconográfico del Quijote,** Manuel Doblado 1 (tel. 2-67-21), east of the Jardín Unión, is the newest museum in town. Housed in a gorgeous colonial mansion, its ten large galleries contain over 600 works of art inspired by Cervantes's anti-hero Don Quijote, including paintings, sculptures, stained-glass windows, candlesticks, and clocks. Artists such as Dalí, Picasso, Daumier, Ocampo, and Coronel have all interpreted Quijote; so have scores of lesser-knowns, as you'll soon see (open Tues.-Sat. 10am-6:30pm, Sun. 10am-2:30pm; free).

A string of museums line Pocitos, stretching westward from the University. The **Museo del Pueblo de Guanajuato,** Pocitos 7 (tel. 2-29-90), next to the university, was inaugurated in 1979. Rotating exhibits dominate the first and third levels: Jazzmoart's vibrant post-modern splatter painting captures the movement and sound of jazz, while Andrade experiments with multi-dimensional acrylics. In stark contrast, the second floor features a permanent exhibit of 18th- and 19th-century Mexican paintings (open Tues.-Sat. 10am-2pm and 4-7pm, Sun. 10am-3pm; admission 5 pesos, children 10 and under free).

The **Museo y Casa de Diego Rivera,** Pocitos 47 (tel. 2-11-97), chronicles the life of Guanajuato's most famous native son. Arranged chronologically, the works reveal the influence of Parisian friends Picasso and Modigliani, who encouraged Rivera's move from landscapes to Cubist sketches and elongated nudes. By 1920, however, the bright colors and simple tones of Rivera's Maya-influenced style asserted themselves. Don't miss the outstanding watercolor illustrations for the *Popol Vuh* (the sacred book of the Maya), which imitate Mayan iconography. Note also Rivera's sketch for a section of the mural commissioned in 1933 by New York's Rockefeller Center—the mural was destroyed after a portrait of Lenin was discovered in it. This sketch, which portrays a woman enslaved by a machine with the head of Adolf Hitler, was not incorporated into the final composition. The museum also includes a photo-mural reproduction of Rivera's *Sueños de Una Tarde Dominicial en la Alameda,* a brightly colored piece composed of 75 representations. Exhibitions rotate every month or so (open Tues.-Sat. 10am-1:15pm and 4-6:30pm, Sun. 10am-2:30pm; admission 5 pesos, free for adults over 70 and children under 10).

The **Museo de la Alhóndiga de Granaditas** (tel. 2-11-12), on Calarza at the west end of Pocitos, is fairly conventional. Constructed as a granary between 1797 and 1809, this building witnessed some of the more crucial and bloody battles of the fight for Mexican independence. Today, the Alhóndiga is an ethnographic, archaeological, and historical museum. A chamber on the first floor charts the course of Mexican nationhood. Other exhibits display the work of *indígena* artisans of the Bajío region—check out the masks, firecrackers, engraved machetes, tapestries, and candy horse skeletons designed for consumption on *El Día de los Muertos* (Day of the Dead). Another gallery shows Romualdo García's photographs of Mexicans on the eve of the 1910 Revolution. While the hall, which contains huge busts of the heroes of 1910, is nothing short of stunning, the museum's finest exhibition traces the social history of Guanajuato from the Conquest through the Revolution.

For many who visit, the museum's more impressive pieces are the three murals gracing the building's stairwells. The works are often mistaken for those of José Clemente Orozco, Diego Rivera, or David Alfaro Siqueiros; the actual painter, José Chávez Morado, was a contemporary of all three. *Abolición de Esclavitud* (1955), the earliest of the three murals, follows Mexico's history from the Conquest, when Indians were oppressed slaves, to the Revolution, by which time native groups had regained some

---

The Color Purple

Museums in Guanajuato explore the historical, the artistic, the monumental, and the macabre. A museum of the latter variety is the **Museo de las Momias** (tel. 2-06-39), next to the city cemetery west of town. The minerals and salty water of Guanajuato's soil naturally mummified the 108 corpses now on display in the museum. A guide points out the purplish, inflated body of a drowning victim; a woman buried alive, frozen in her attempt to scratch her way out of the coffin; two fashionable Frenchmen; a man who died by hanging; and another who was stabbed. Some buried babies still wear the colorful attire of saints to ensure divine intercession on their ride to heaven. The museum's oldest mummy has been around for 130 years, while its youngest has been on display for 10. The mummies are the most popular sight in Guanajuato, drawing a larger crowd than the less ghastly museums downtown. At the exit, vendors hawk candy figurines of the more memorable mummies, some wearing little sombreros. To get to the museum, catch a "Momias" bus (1.40 pesos) in front of the Cine or Mercado. (Open daily 9am-6pm. Admission 15 pesos, students and children 5-11 years old 9 pesos, adults over 60 and children under 5 free. Camera permit 6 pesos; video camera 15 pesos.)

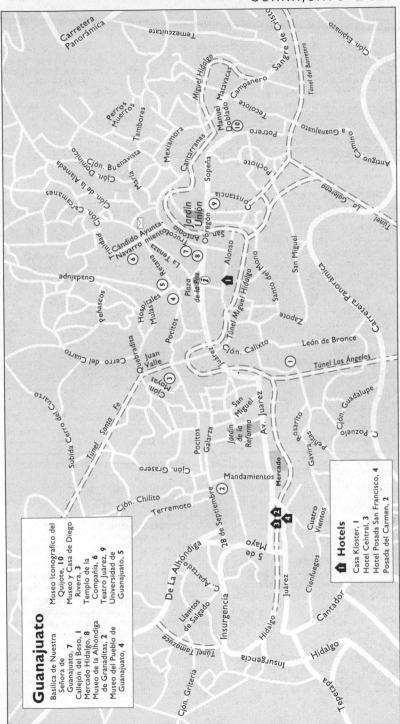

Guanajuato

Basílica de Nuestra
Señora de
Guanajuato, **7**
Callejón del Beso, **1**
Mercado Hidalgo, **8**
Museo de la Alhóndiga
de Granaditas, **2**
Museo del Pueblo de
Guanajuato, **4**

Museo Iconografico del
Quijote, **10**
Museo y Casa de Diego
Rivera, **3**
Templo de la
Compañía, **6**
Teatro Juárez, **9**
Universidad de
Guanajuato, **5**

↑ Hotels
Casa Kloster, **1**
Hotel Central, **3**
Hotel Posada San Francisco, **4**
Posada del Carmen, **2**

measure of power (open Tues.-Sat. 10am-2pm and 4-6pm, Sun. 10am-2pm; doors close 30min. before closing time; admission 13 pesos, free for students, seniors, children under 11, and on Sun.; camera permit 5 pesos).

Looking down on the Jardín from the nearby hill is the **Monumento al Pípila,** which commemorates the miner who torched the Alhóndiga's front door. The titanic Pípila looks most impressive at night, when he is illuminated by spotlights. While the view of Pípila from below is striking, the monument itself affords a magnificent panoramic vista of the city. To reach the statue, follow Sopeña to the east and take the steep Callejón del Calvario to your right (a 10-min. climb), or hop a bus marked "Pípila" from Plaza de la Paz.

The most famous alley in the city, the **Callejón del Beso** (Alley of the Kiss), is off Juárez, about two blocks down from the *basílica,* just as Juárez curves right towards the market. Local lore has it that two lovers who lived on opposite sides of the alley were kept apart by their families but could still kiss each other from their balconies. At some points the alley is an amazing 68cm wide. Another block farther down Juárez is the **Mercado Hidalgo.** Constructed in 1910, the *mercado's* entrance is a monumental Neoclassical arch. While Guanajuato's famed ceramic mugs have declined in quality, woolen items are still cheap and the wide variety of *sombreros* will satisfy even the most discerning of heads (most stalls open daily 9am-9pm).

Perhaps the most beautiful of Guanajuato's many natural attractions is the **Ex-Hacienda de San Gabriel de Barrera** (tel. 2-06-19). Seventeen glorious gardens, each laid out in a different style, cover about three acres. Cobbled paths, well groomed flora, and whistling birds make the gardens a stroller's dream. The *ex-hacienda* itself, a 16th-century structure, abuts the gardens; its rooms contain furniture, silverware, and paintings from the era in which it was built. To get there, hop on a bus marked "Puentesía" across from the *mercado* (1.40 pesos), and tell the driver you're headed to San Gabriel de la Barrera (open daily 9am-6pm; free).

About 20km from Guanajuato, on top of a mountain 2850m above sea level, is the **Monumento a Cristo Rey,** completed in 1956. The mountain, called the **Cerro del Cubilete,** is considered the geographical center of Mexico. The dark bronze statue of Jesus which lords over it is 16m tall and weighs more than 80 tons. Although the statue is striking, you may spend more time observing the surrounding landscape; long stretches of blue hills are visible from the summit. Take the "Cristo Rey" bus from the bus station (8 per day 6am-4pm, 1hr., 6 pesos).

ENTERTAINMENT AND SEASONAL EVENTS

Each year, Guanajuato explodes during the **Festival Internacional Cervantino** for two or three weeks in late October. The city invites repertory groups from all over the world to make merry with the *estudiantinas* (strolling student minstrels). Institutionalized in 1973, the festival got its start in 1954 as a production of the university's theater. The festivities take place mostly at local theaters, but Guanajuato's many museums and churches are also transformed into stages for the events. Dramatic productions are always sold out. Tickets are sold by Ticketmaster one month in advance. The Office of the Festival Internacional Cervantino (tel. 2-57-96; fax 2-67-75) can provide more information.

From June 22 to 26, Guanajuato celebrates the **Feria de San Juan,** at the Presa de la Olla, with cultural events, fireworks, and sports. Shorter celebrations occur on **Día de la Cueva** (July 31), when residents walk to a cave's entrance to honor San Ignacio de Loyola, first patron saint of Guanajuato and founder of the Compañía de Jesús. After the worshippers hold mass, they party. December religious celebrations include the famous *posadas,* which re-create Mary and Joseph's search for budget accommodations in Bethlehem without their trusty *Let's Go: Israel and Egypt.*

The rest of the year, theater, dance, and music are performed; check the tourist office for information, or consult posters around town. On Thursday and Sunday nights in the Jardín Unión, the state band performs three melodies of deceased *gua-*

najuatense, beginning at around 7pm. *Callejonadas,* sing-alongs with the student minstrels down Guanajuato's winding alleys, are organized on Friday and Saturday nights at 8:30pm, departing from the Teatro Juárez. These strolls are free for guests of sponsoring hotels, but sponsorship is rarely checked, and they're often open to the public. Student groups present films almost every day of the week. Call the **Teatro Principal** (tel. 2-15-26), the **Teatro Cervantes** (tel. 2-11-69), or the **Teatro Juárez** (tel. 2-01-83) for specifics (tickets about 10 pesos).

The core of Guanajuato's nightlife rests in the bar/café scene. Discos do exist, but they come to life only on weekends. The bars and cafés in the immediate vicinity of the Jardín Unión are friendly and comfortable, even for single women. If things slow down on the Jardín, it's because they're picking up at the **Guanajuato Grill,** Alonso 20 (tel. 2-11-57). Neon palm trees, posters of sports heroes and scantily clad men and women, a nightly DJ with bass-booming speakers, and a *zócalo*-style gazebo in the center of the bar have the grill bursting at the seams with thirsty students when school's in session. The bouncers can be selective, and they generally discriminate against men. Beer costs 8 pesos (no cover; open Mon.-Sat 7pm-late). For the more mellow and artsy crowd, there's late night salsa and Latin rhythms at **Damas de las Camelias,** Sopeña 32. Decorated by Juan Ibañez, a student of the Spanish director Luis Buñuel, the bar's walls display cave-style paintings and pictures backed by tin foil (open Fri.-Sat. 6pm-6am, Sun.-Thurs. 6pm-late). Just when you thought a bar couldn't get any mellower, **Chez Santos,** Juan Valle 19, shows up at the door. Located off Juárez just before turning up into Plaza de la Paz, the bar is set in a former horse stable—its high stone walls and large wooden beams across the ceiling make you want to whinny. The dark, romantic lighting calls for candlelight. There is none, so it's a bit hard to see, which explains its reputation as a romantic rendezvous. The most offbeat club in town is **El Rincón del Beso,** Alonso 21-A (tel. 2-59-12), east of Casa Kloster. Cozy candle-lit rooms divided by winding stairs and thick Spanish walls host nightly sing-alongs. The riotous poetry interpretations attract large crowds (beer 9 pesos; no cover; open daily 6:30pm-3am, but things start to pick up around 11pm).

▓ San Miguel de Allende

Founded by a Franciscan friar in 1542, San Miguel soon became an important stop on the route that connected the Zacatecas silver mines with Mexico City. San Miguel's moment in the spotlight came on September 16, 1810, when Hidalgo, the priest of nearby Dolores, led his rebel army into the city. Convinced by patriot Ignacio Allende of the righteousness of the pro-independence movement, San Miguel became a staunch opponent of Spanish rule. In 1826, the infant republic recognized Allende's role in the drive for independence by adding his name to San Miguel's.

Today's San Miguel is home to a large number of foreign students and expatriates. Fortunately, they see the city as far more than a Florida-like vacationland; in fact, many Americans come here with the desire to assimilate inconspicuously. Bilingual children are already entering adulthood, the product of two cultures, and few have trouble participating in both—witness the American and Mexican fathers and sons who take part in Sunday afternoon basketball games at Parque Juárez or the young blonde child discussing a Disney flick in fluent Spanish with his Mexican peer. Most locals are well disposed to *gringos* and are eager to practice English or help out with their Spanish.

Renowned for its artisanry and academics, San Miguel is also blessed with a mild climate. The town is almost never oppressively hot, thanks to its high altitude; and the average annual temperature is 18°C. Unlike other colonial towns of similar elevations, San Miguel is also a very green city, with plenty of trees, flowers, and hills. Beware the ides of June and July, when cold afternoon drizzle or drenching day-long downpours can turn the cobblestoned streets into gushing streams.

ORIENTATION

San Miguel is 94km southeast of Guanajuato and 428km northwest of Mexico City. To get from the **bus station** to the center (known as the **Jardín Allende** or **Plaza de Allende**), take a "Centro" bus to the corner of **Colegio** and **Mesones**, near the statue of Allende on horsetop (1.40 pesos). Walk two blocks down Mesones, then left one block on **Reloj** to the Plaza Allende. Or take a taxi (8 pesos). The **train station** lies 1km west of the bus station on the same road and bus route.

Most attractions are within walking distance of the Jardín, and the streets form a near-grid. **San Francisco, Reloj, Correo,** and **Hidalgo** border the Jardín. West of the Jardín, San Francisco becomes **Canal** and Correo becomes **Umarán.** Streets that run east-west south of the Jardín change their names every few blocks.

PRACTICAL INFORMATION

Tourist Office: Delegación Regional de Turismo (tel./fax 2-17-47), on the Pl. de Allende, to your left facing the Parroquia. Knowledgeable and helpful staff speaks English and distributes tiny maps that are a little skimpy for such a tourist mecca. Open Mon.-Fri. 10am-3pm and 5-7pm, Sat. 10am-5pm, Sun. 10am-2pm. *Atención,* the weekly U.S. expatriate newspaper, is a super-fabulous source of information.

Consular Representatives: U.S., Macías 72 (tel. 2-23-57, in emergencies 2-00-68 or 2-00-99; fax 2-15-88), opposite Bellas Artes. Open Mon., Wed. 9am-1pm and 4-7pm, Tues., Thurs. 4-7pm, or by appointment. **Canada,** Mesones 38 #15 (tel. 2-30-28, emergencies 91-800-7-06-29; fax 2-68-56). Open Mon.-Fri. 10am-2pm. For other countries, contact the **Delegación Regional,** Plaza Real del Conde (tel. 2-25-42 or 2-28-35). Open Mon.-Fri. 9am-3pm.

Currency Exchange: Helados Holanda, Juárez 1 (tel. 2-05-67), on the corner of Juárez and San Francisco. Here's the scoop: this ice cream shop is also a *casa de cambio* and gives the best rate in town. Grab a cone while you wait. Open daily Mon.-Sun. 8am-9pm; changes money Mon.-Fri. 10:30am-3:30pm, Sat.-Sun. 10:30am-2pm. Otherwise, **Deal,** Correo 15, San Francisco 4, and Juárez 27 (tel. 2-29-32, 2-17-06), has good rates. Open Mon.-Fri. 9am-6pm, Sat. 9am-2pm. **Banamex,** on the west side of the Jardín, has a 24-hr. **ATM.**

American Express: Hidalgo 1 (tel. 2-18-56). Full financial and travel services. Open Mon.-Fri. 9am-2pm and 4-6:30pm, Sat. 10am-2pm.

Telephones: LADATELs throughout town. **La Esquinita** (tel. 2-36-21 or 2-39-39), Correos at Recreo. No charge for international collect calls. Open daily 10am-2:30pm and 5-10pm. **Nortesur,** Portal de Allende 4, 2nd floor (tel./fax 2-68-78), on the Jardín, offers long distance phone, fax, e-mail, and messenger service. Student discounts. Open Mon.-Fri. 9:30am-3pm and 4-7pm, Sat. 10am-1pm.

Telegrams: Correo 16-B (tel. 2-32-15; fax 2-00-81), adjacent to the post office. Open Mon.-Fri. 9am-1pm and 3-5pm, Sat. 9am-noon.

Buses: (tel. 2-22-06), on Calzada de la Estación, 1km west of the center. Catch a "Central Estación" bus on Colegio at Mesones near the Plaza Cívica. **Herradura de Plata** (tel. 2-07-25) goes to Mexico City (*plus* 3 per day 6am-12:30pm, 3½hr., 70 pesos; second-class every 30min. 5am-7:40pm, 4hr., 53 pesos) and Querétaro (every 30min. 5am-7:40pm, 1hr., 13 pesos). **Flecha Amarilla** (tel. 2-00-84) to Dolores Hidalgo (every 20min. 6am-10pm, 45min., 6.50 pesos), Guanajuato (9 per day 6:45am-5pm, 1½hr., 18 pesos), and San Luis Potosí (6 per day 7:30am-6:40pm, 4hr., 380 pesos). **Primera Plus** (tel. 2-00-84) buses (7:40am, 9:15am, and 5:30pm) stop at Guanajuato (1½hr., 22 pesos), León (2½hr., 40 pesos), and Guadalajara (6hr., 108 pesos).

Trains: Ferrocarriles Nacionales de México (tel. 2-00-07), 2km west of town. Accessible by the "Central Estación" bus. To Mexico City (1pm, 6hr., first-class 45 pesos, second-class 25 pesos) and Nuevo Laredo (2:35pm, 17hr., first-class 130 pesos, second-class 75 pesos) via San Luis Potosí, Saltillo, and Monterrey.

Car Rental: Gama Rent-a-Car, Hidalgo 3 #1 (tel. 2-08-15). Prices start at 365 pesos per day, including insurance and free mileage. Special weekly rates. Drivers must

San Miguel de Allende

➕ Hospital
✉ Post Office
ⓘ Tourist Office

Bus Station, 1
Casa de Huéspedes, 11
Iglesia de la Concepción, 3
Iglesia de San Francisco, 9
Iglesia del Tercer Orden, 8
Jardín Allende, 5

Museo Histórico de San Miguel de Allende, 4
La Parroquia (Parish Church), 6
Santa Casa de Loreto, 12
Templo del Oratorio de San Felipe Neri, 13
ACCOMODATIONS
Hotel Parador San Sebastián, 10
Hotel Posada de Allende, 7
San Miguel International Hostel, 2

be 24 years of age with a license, a major credit card, and another form of ID. Open Mon.-Fri. 9am-2pm and 4-7pm, Sat. 9am-2pm.

English Bookstore: El Colibrí, Sollano 30 (tel. 2-07-51). Superb (but expensive) selection of paperback fiction. Open Mon.-Sat. 10am-2pm and 4-7pm.

Public Library: Insurgentes 25 (tel. 2-02-93), next to La Española. An important feature of expatriate social life. Great courtyard in which to read, kick back, or chat. Free language exchange. Sells old paperbacks for 1-3 pesos. Open Mon.-Fri. 10am-2pm and 4-7pm, Sat. 10am-2pm.

Laundromat: Lavamágico, Pila Seca 5 (tel. 2-08-99). Will pick up (9:30am-2pm) a dirty 4kg load and return it cleaned for 20 pesos. Open Mon.-Sat. 8am-8pm.

Red Cross: (tel. 2-16-16), 1 km on the Carretera Celaya. 24-hr. emergency service.

Pharmacy: Farmacia Allende, San Francisco 3 (tel. 2-00-74), near the Jardín. Open daily 9am-9pm. Call police to find out which pharmacy is on call 24hr.

Hospital: Hospital de la Fe, Libramiento a Dolores 43 (tel. 2-23-29 or -30, emergency 2-25-45; fax 2-29-00), near the bus station. Open for consultation Mon.-Fri. 10am-2pm and 4-8pm, Sat. 10am-2pm; 24hr. for emergencies. English spoken.

Police: (tel. 2-00-22), in the Presidencia Municipal. On call 24hr.

Post Office: Appropriately at Correos 16 (tel. 2-00-89), one block east of the Jardín. Open Mon.-Fri. 8am-7pm, Sat. 9am-1pm. **Postal Code:** 37700.

Telephone Code: 415.

ACCOMMODATIONS

Despite the large number of students who visit the town, San Miguel has few budget accommodations. Many hotels on the Plaza Principal provide continental breakfast and TV to justify their costliness. For short stays during the busy summer months, you may want to make a reservation several days in advance. In the winter, reservations a few months in advance may be necessary. If you're planning an extended stay, check for notices of rooms for rent on the bulletin board at the Instituto Allende, Ancha de San Antonio 20 (2-01-90), southwest of the Jardín, and in popular *norteamericano* cafés and hotels.

The San Miguel International Hostel, Organos 34 (tel. 2-06-74). You'll come for a day and stay for a month. A communal effort: Michael, the manager, hires help on a work-for-food basis; guests are expected to perform morning chores. Everybody joins in the courtyard conversations. Well stocked with English books, a sitting room, and a piano. Free kitchen use. Spanish language lessons (60 pesos per hr., but cost can be split). Washing machine (10 pesos per load, including soap). Clean single-sex dorm rooms for 4-10 people (35 pesos per person, 30 pesos with HI or ISIC membership, continental breakfast included). Also, two private double rooms (70 pesos, 75 pesos with bath). Reservations not accepted.

Casa de Huéspedes, Mesones 27 (tel. 2-13-78). Serene, flower-filled courtyard complete with ivy-covered arches, wooden lounge chairs, and back issues of the *New Yorker*. Wonderfully friendly staff. Immaculate rooms, some with kitchens. Singles 60 pesos. Doubles 100 pesos. Month-long stays: singles and doubles 1500 pesos. Reserve well in advance.

Hotel Parador San Sebastián, Mesones 7, about 2 blocks east of Plaza Allende. Vibrant bouganvillia spill over arched stone walls enclosing the sunny courtyard. Beautiful Spanish architecture. Basic rooms with heavy wood furniture and nice tiled bathrooms. 50 pesos per person, add 25 pesos for fireplace and 30 pesos for kitchen. No reservations accepted.

Hotel Posada de Allende, Cuna de Allende 10 (tel. 2-06-98), around the corner from the Parroquia. Terrific location. A *posada típica*. Aging and intimate, but the 4 rooms are clean and spacious. Singles 60 pesos. Doubles 85-95 pesos.

FOOD

The sweet aroma of international cuisine wafts through the cobbled streets of San Miguel, and fine restaurants grace almost every corner. Unfortunately, their prices can be as *norteamericano* as their clientele. For cheap eats, try the walkway on the east side of the **Jardín,** the tiny **square** on Insurgentes between Macías and Hidalgo, and the streets around the **mercado** on Colegio.

La Grotta, Cuadrante 5 (tel. 2-41-19), at Allende, one block behind the Parroquia. A cozy and artsy place a few feet below street level. Hugely popular. Pastas around 27 pesos, small pizza 32 pesos. Open daily 1-11pm.

El Ten-ten-pie, Allende 1 (tel. 2-71-89), on the corner with Cuadrante. A new-wave, old-world, politically correct restaurant: they recycle, play chess, and challenge their clientele to political debates. Ceramic tiles, Goya prints, and the work of local artisans on display. A mix of retired expats and locals jives to the tunes (they'll make you a tape) and enjoys the *comida corrida* (24 pesos), *tortas* (7 pesos), and tacos (3 pesos). Open daily noon-midnight.

El Tomate, Mesones 60 (tel. 2-03-25). You say "tomato," we say come to this cute vegetarian café. Great salad (18 pesos), spinach burger (15 pesos), and vegetarian *comida corrida* (25 pesos). Open Wed.-Sat. and Mon. 9am-9pm, Sun. 9am-6pm.

Las Palomas, Correo 9. A taco stand you can trust, at prices you can afford. In the afternoons, the counters are occupied by local teens flirting and gossiping as they munch on tacos (1.70 pesos) and *gorditas* (3 pesos). Open daily 9am-9pm.

SIGHTS

The best way to experience San Miguel is on your own two feet. During high season, groups gather in front of the church in the Jardín for 90-minute tours of the city (Tues. and Fri. 9am, 50 pesos—but the money goes to charity, so cough it up). The public library gives 2-hour guided **home and garden walking tours** of the city in English (Sun. noon, 75 pesos; get there 30min. early). San Miguel boasts some beautiful orchid-filled courtyards, but some say the tours are something of a real estate pitch. **Centro de Crecimiento,** Zamaro Ríos 6 (tel. 03-18), organizes trips to San Miguel's surroundings (Sat. 10:30am, 70 pesos). The 64-hectare **Jardín Botánico,** on the outskirts of town, offers spectacular views of the area and includes a small lake and extensive cactus life (open sunrise to sunset; admission 7 pesos, under 10 free). Inquiries about the gardens should be directed to **Cante,** a non-profit organization on Mesones 71 (tel. 2-29-90; fax 2-40-15). The ride to the garden offers a view of some of the more beautiful homes in San Miguel (taxi 10 pesos). Reverberating with the calls of tropical birds, the **Parque Juárez,** three blocks south of the Jardín, is the greenest park in San Miguel. Die-hard cagers can often join a pick-up basketball game involving both *gringos* and locals. Some of the most elegant houses in San Miguel surround the park. If you haven't had enough of the outdoors, head to the hot springs at **La Gruta** or **El Cortijo** (accessible through the Dolores Hidalgo bus).

Almost every street in town has an interesting shop or café, magnificent churches, and artisans' shops. **La Parroquia** (tel. 2-41-97 or 2-05-44), next to the Jardín, is one of the most distinctive churches in central Mexico. Its neo-Gothic façade and tower were designed by the *indígena* mason Zeferino Gutiérrez, who is said to have learned the style from postcards of French cathedrals. The pointed arches and flute-like towers pull the eyes upward; inside, the beautiful ceilings are graced by medieval-style banners, glittering chandeliers, and gold trim. At the front is a tremendous four-piece, gold-leaf altar (open daily 5:30am-9:30pm; avoid masses Mon.-Fri. 6-8am, 12-1pm, and 7-9pm, Sat. 6-8am, 11am-1:30pm, and all day Sun).

At the corner of Canal and Macías, one block west of the Jardín, stands the enormous **Iglesia de la Concepción** (tel. 2-01-48). Graced by the representation of the Immaculate Conception which crowns its two-story dome, the church was finished in 1891. Pairs of Corinthian columns adorn the church's lower level, and its interior features polychrome sculptures of St. Joseph and the Immaculate Conception. The rather heavy interior, with dark brick arches, red Spanish tile, and somewhat plain windows doesn't match the grandeur of the exterior (open daily 7am-7pm; avoid mass Mon.-Fri. 7:30am and 7pm, Sun. 9:30am, 11:30am, and 7pm).

Founded in 1712, the **Templo del Oratorio de San Felipe Neri** (tel. 2-05-21) lies at the corner of Insurgentes and Loreto, two blocks east of the library. Rebuilt many times, the church is an amalgamation of styles—its interior is mainly Neoclassical while its engraved Baroque façade shows *indígena* influences. The interior is incredibly ornate with pale pink walls, gold inlay, sparkling chandeliers, and a beautiful pink and mauve toned dome. The alta holds a figure of Christ in red robes standing upon red carpets, and surrounded by gold-leaf and marble pillars; it looks like a giant wedding cake (open daily 6:30am-12:30pm and 6:30-8:30pm). On the west side of the church, the towers and the dome belong to the **Santa Casa de Loreto,** a reproduction of the building of the same name in Italy (enter on the right side of the altar in San Felipe Neri). The floors and the lower wall friezes are covered with glazed tiles from China, Spain, and faraway Puebla (open by appointment Mon.-Fri. 4:30-7:30pm, Sat.-Sun. 7:30am-6:30pm).

One block east of the Jardín at Juárez and San Francisco, the **Iglesia de San Francisco** includes a dark red Neoclassical tower attributed to the architect Tresguerras. Finished in 1799, the church's Churrigueresque façade is decorated with the images of many saints. Several small paintings in the interior are so enveloped in darkness that you'd have to be a bat to appreciate them (open Tues. 7am-1:30pm and 5:30-8:45pm, Thurs. 10:30am-8:45pm). To the left as you face San Francisco is the **Iglesia**

del Tercer Orden, one of the oldest and most decayed churches in San Miguel. Constructed by Franciscans between 1606 and 1638, its main façade contains an image of St. Francis and symbols of the order (open daily 7am-1:30pm and 5:30-8:45pm).

The **Museo Histórico de San Miguel de Allende** (tel. 2-24-99), on the corner of Umarán and Cuna de Allende, just west of La Parroquia, resides in Allende's former home. The eclectic exhibits include tributes to Allende, seemingly unrelated exhibits on astronomy and paleobiology, and enough charts to put you to sleep (open Tues.-Sun. 10am-4pm; free).

ENTERTAINMENT AND SEASONAL EVENTS

Both **Bellas Artes** and **Instituto Allende** have bulletin boards crammed with information on upcoming concerts, theatrical productions, and lectures by both locals and *gringos.* The magazine ***Atención*** (4 pesos) lists cultural events.

There are as many clubs in San Miguel as there are churches. Did you think all these students came here to learn? The entire town usually flocks to **Mama Mía,** Umarán 8 (tel. 2-20-63), just off the Jardín—probably because the place is so damn big. A bouney younger crowd moves to the beat of live music (*salsa* Thurs.-Sun., rock Mon.-Wed; cover 10 pesos; open daily 9:30pm-3am). On the left as you enter is **Leonardo's** videobar, with cool Da Vinci etchings on the wall (open daily 7pm-late), and directly in front of the entrance is a cabana-like bar (open daily 9am-late). But there's more! The new terrace offers a great view of the city (open Fri.-Sat. 6pm-1am). Another popular joint for loud, live, and hoppin' rock is **Pancho and Lefty's,** Mesones 99 (tel. 2-19-58). The sawdust, wagon wheels, and cacti will make you thirsty for a beer (12 pesos; no cover Wed., 20 pesos Fri.-Sat.; open Wed., Fri.-Sat. 10pm-3am). **Coco,** Macías 85 (tel. 2-26-43), is a bit more tranquil. Live music of all types, including Mexican folkloric, Andean music, and rock, every night with no cover—but no dance floor either, so you're forced to sit, eat, listen, and love it (open 8am-about 2:30am, kitchen closes at 1am). The party doesn't start at **El Ring,** Hidalgo 25 (tel. 2-19-98 or 2-67-89), until around 2:30am, when indefatigable elite members of San Miguel's club-hopping brigade begin to trickle in from other spots. The place rocks with the latest dance hits from the U.S. and Latin America (cover Fri. 20 pesos, Sat. 40 pesos; Fri. two-for-one beers; no shorts or sandals for males). If you're not up for a club, there are cantinas all around town that you can stumble into—and out of, with beer costing only 4 pesos.

San Miguel is reputed to have more *fiestas* than any other town in Mexico. Besides national and religious holidays, San Miguel celebrates the birthday of Ignacio Allende on **January 21,** the Fiesta de la Candelaria on **February 2** (marking the start of spring and the birthday of El Padre de Miguel), and the festival of San Miguel's guardian saint from **September 14** to **October 3.** Mass is held on September 29, and the following Saturday a celebration begins with the singing of *Las Mañanitas* at 4am. On that day, bulls run free through the center of the city; seek cover behind a concrete barrier. The **International Chamber Music Festival** is held in late July or early August at **Bellas Artes,** Macías 75 (tel./fax 2-02-89; tickets start at 60 pesos and are sold beginning in July).

■ Near San Miguel

DOLORES HIDALGO

Mexico's "Cradle of Independence" has never eclipsed its label. The small town of Dolores Hidalgo has little more to offer than a thriving ceramics industry and an amazing story. On Sunday, September 16, 1810, Don Miguel Hidalgo y Costilla, the town's priest, learned that the pro-independence conspiracy to which he belonged had been discovered by the government. He decided to take decisive action, and at 5am woke the entire town by tolling the parish church bell. The town's residents tumbled out of bed and gathered at the church; Hidalgo delivered a ringing speech proclaiming Mexico's independence from Spain—the *Grito de Dolores.* Then, calling his flock to arms, Hidalgo rallied an army to march on to Mexico City. Thus, the priest signed his own death warrant and paved the way for an independent Mexico.

Orientation and Practical Information Dolores Hidalgo sits 50km northeast of Guanajanato and 42km north of San Miguel de Allende. To get downtown from the bus station, walk straight out the door and take a left on **Hidalgo.** Three blocks down the street are the **Jardín,** the tourist office, **Plaza Principal,** and the **Parroquia. Río Batan** runs east-west through the city; streets are arranged in a grid parallel and perpendicular to the river. A map is useful since streets have different names on opposite sides of the plaza (there is a well labeled map in the plaza). The town's points of interest all lie within three blocks of the center.

Get that map from the **tourist office** (tel/fax 2-11-64) on the Plaza Principal, facing the Parroquia (open Mon.-Fri. 10am-3pm and sometimes 5-7pm, Sat.-Sun. 10am-4pm). **Casa de Cambio Cordisa,** Jalisco 12 (tel. 2-13-35), at the corner with Puebla, has similar rates and better hours than the bank on the Plaza Principal (open daily 8am-7pm). There is a coin-operated **LADATEL** in the Presidencia Municipal, and a *caseta* in the **Restaurante Plaza** (tel. 2-01-52), on the south side of the plaza (open daily 9am-9pm). **Flecha Amarilla buses** (tel. 2-06-39) leave from the station on Hidalgo at Chiapas and go to Guanajuato (every 20min. 5:20am-7pm, every 30min. 7:30-9:15pm, 1½hr., 12 pesos) and San Miguel de Allende (every 20min. 5am-8pm and 9, 10, and 11:30pm, 40min., 8 pesos).

Find **public toilets** in the narrow arcade around the corner from the tourist office (0.50 pesos). **Farmacia Libertad** is on Hidalgo 9 (tel. 2-09-37), one block from the plaza (open daily 9am-9pm); call the police to find out which pharmacy is on call 24 hours. English is spokent at the **Hospital Ignacio Allende,** Hidalgo 12 (tel. 2-00-13), one block from the plaza (open 24hr.). The **police** (tel. 2-00-21) are in the Cárcel Municipal on San Luis Potosí, one block north of the Plaza Principal. The **post office** is on Puebla 22 (tel. 2-08-07), at Jalisco, one block from the Plaza Principal (open Mon.-Fri. 9am-4pm, Sat. 9am-noon). **Postal Code:** 37800. **Telephone Code:** 418.

Accommodations Given the low demand for overnight lodging, rooms in Dolores Hidalgo are scarce and surprisingly expensive. Expect prices to rise around 50% and rooms to fill up September 8-17, when Dolores is overrun by Independence Day celebrants. Reservations a month in advance are advisable. **Posada Hidalgo,** Hidalgo 15 (tel. 2-04-77), a block and a half south of the Jardín, has comfortable beds, stone tiles, hot water, and a spotless living space (singles 65-70 pesos; doubles 75-90 pesos). **Hotel Posada Cocomacán,** Plaza Principal 5 (tel. 2-00-18), on the Jardín, has rooms with wood furniture, tiled walls, and clean bathrooms overlooking a sunny courtyard (singles 70 pesos; doubles 85 pesos). **Posada Dolores** is on Yucatán 8 (tel. 2-06-42), a block west of the Plaza Principal. The clean, stark, pastel rooms are full of international travelers (singles 25 pesos, with bath 30 pesos; doubles 30 and 50 pesos).

Food Around the Jardín, most restaurants are reasonably priced, and those that aren't betray themselves by their touristy clientele. **Eduardo's Pizza,** Veracruz 5 (tel. 2-21-24), on Plaza Veracruz, one block east and one block south of the Jardín, has good pizza and really groovy decor that includes empty boxes of Honey Smacks, vinyl records, and cigarette cartons (pizzas 14-30 pesos, beer 3.50 pesos; open daily noon-11pm). **Restaurante Provincia,** Plaza Principal 8-B (tel. 2-22-44), on the plaza, serves cheap, basic fare (*comida corrida* 12 pesos, enchiladas 11 pesos; open Wed.-Mon. 8am-11pm). Or try the restaurants on the **Mercado Hidalgo,** a block west of Plaza Principal (most places open daily 7am-5pm).

Sights and Entertainment Most of Dolores's sights lie within four blocks of the bus station. The beautiful **Parroquia de Nuestra Señora de los Dolores,** where the *Grito* was sounded, still stands in the Plaza Principal, though the original bell now graces Mexico City's Palacio de Gobierno. Constructed between 1712 and 1778, the church, with its intricate façade and towers of pink stone, is the most awe-inspiring structure in town. Mexican presidents return here on the anniversary of Hidalgo's proclamation and repeat his words (open daily 6am-2pm and 4-9pm).

The **Museo Casa Hidalgo,** at Morelos and Hidalgo, one block from the Plaza Principal, is another nifty stop. The museum was Hidalgo's home from 1804 until 1810. The rooms remain as they were in 1810, and many of Hidalgo's belongings are on display. Documents and works of art relating to the independence movement fill rooms off a central courtyard. These include a fabulous Metepec **Tree of Life,** with Hidalgo at its center. The Metepec are famous for this type of art; the tree is made with brightly painted pottery, and figures of the Independence movement decorate the branches on this particular piece (open Tues.-Sat. 10am-6pm, Sun. and holidays 10am-5pm; admission 14 pesos; free Sun. and holidays, and for teachers and students with ID, kids under 12, and seniors). The **Museo de la Independencia,** Zacatecas 6, lies less than one block northwest of the Parroquia. To your right as you enter is a display honoring Dolores Hidalgo's favorite musical son, José Alfredo Jiménez (1926-1973). The display includes one gold and two platinum records; some of his *sarapes* and awards; a photograph of an elaborate altar built for him in the wonderful country of Colombia; and his birth certificate. The museum's other exhibits focus on life under Spanish rule, the fight for Independence, and the life and works of the town's other idol, Miguel Hidalgo (open Fri.-Wed. 10am-5pm; admission 5 pesos, free for students, seniors, and children under 12).

POZOS

Pozos, 25km northeast of San Miguel de Allende, is a lonely ghost town just waking up after a long slumber. Pozos was once a thriving mining town; the Jesuits worked the mines until their expulsion in 1767, at which point an American company took over. The town's abandoned adobe homes and once booming mines are now cloaked in an eery silence. Daytrippers from San Miguel come to Pozos to visit the mines, ramble through the town's myriad shops and chapels, and stake out new hiking trails. But the most dazzling thing about Pozos is the surrounding landscape: the color contrast of the empty, blue sky, the golden sand, and the prickly green cacti.

Getting There: Though Pozos is a mere 25km from San Miguel de Allende, it takes a good two to three hours to reach the town, as you have to first travel to Dolores Hidalgo, change buses in San Luis de La Paz, then take a local bus to Pozos. **Flecha Amarilla** (tel. 2-00-84) runs buses from San Miguel to Dolores Hidalgo (every 20min. 6am-10pm, 45min., 8 pesos), and from Dolores Hidalgo (tel. 418-2-06-39) to San Luis de La Paz (every 20min. 6am-10pm, 1hr., 11 pesos). From San Luis de La Paz, buses run to Pozos (every 20min., 20min., 5 pesos).

Truth or Dare

While textbook feminism often discusses the virgin/whore dichotomy, Mexican women live it every day. There are two kinds of women, Mexican men will explain: the ones you sleep with, and the ones you marry. These exemplary roles were established early on. The Virgin of Guadalupe, Mexico's very own national virgin, purportedly appeared before *indígena* Juan Diego in 1531. Since then, this icon of chastity and virtue has become the object of a cult so passionate that it almost dwarfs Christ's. Every December 12, on the Virgin's name day, thousands of devout Christians make a pilgrimage on their bare knees to her basilica in Mexico City. On the flip side of the coin is La Malinche, the *indígena* woman who became Hernán Cortés's mistress, confidant, and interpreter. Changing her native name, Malintzin, to the Spanish Marina, she aided her lover in a brutal conquest of her own people. Later betrayed and abandoned by her lover, La Malinche's story remains a cautionary tale on the dangers women risk by giving themselves to men.

QUERÉTARO

■ Querétaro

Situated between Mexico City and Guadalajara on the busiest stretch of highway in the Republic, Querétaro lies at the crossroads of Mexico's geography and history. With centuries-old brick streets and *andares* (pedestrian walkways), lantern lit squares, 18th-century aqueducts, and beautiful colonial architecture, Querétaro is one of the more historically rich cities in Mexico. It was here that Emperor Maximilian, abandoned by Louis Napoleon and captured by Juárez's troops, ascended Cerro de las Campanas (Hill of the Bells) and uttered his famous last words: "Mexicans, I am going to die for a just cause: the liberty and the independence of Mexico." In the subsequent 50 years, Mexico was wracked by violence. Perhaps hoping to inaugurate the peaceful era Maximilian had prematurely proclaimed, the victorious Carranza drafted the new constitution in Querétaro. While Mexico gave up much here—the Treaty of Guadalupe Hidalgo, which compelled the Republic to cede its northern territories to the U.S., was signed in Querétaro—the city proudly brandishes the marks of its history. Museums and monuments surrounded by beautifully landscaped gardens and plazas tell the tale of the city and its contribution to Mexico's history.

ORIENTATION

Querétaro's streets form a grid, and nearly all important sites are within walking distance of the **Jardín Zenea.** The Jardín is bounded by **16 de Septiembre** (north), **Madero** (south), **Corregidora** (east), and **Juárez** (west). The **bus station,** whose modernity puts most international airports to shame, is on the very south side of town. To reach downtown, walk out of the station and cross the street to the terminal marked "C." Walk to the right side of the building (a green "Paradero de Microbuses" sign points the way), where you can catch a "Centro" bus (2 pesos). A cab to the *centro* costs 12 pesos.

PRACTICAL INFORMATION

Tourist Office: State Tourist Office, Pasteur Nte. 4 (tel. 12-14-12, 12-09-07, or 12-12-87). From the Jardín, take 5 de Mayo; the office is to your left at the end of the Plaza de Armas. Friendly English-speaking staff hands out helpful maps and lists of local cultural events. City tours in English or Spanish. Open daily 9am-9pm.

Currency Exchange: Bancomer, Juárez 15 (tel. 12-06-77). Open Mon.-Fri. 8:30am-1:30pm. A good alternative is **Cambios La Posada,** Allende Nte. 2, next to the telegram office. Open Mon.-Fri. 9am-5pm, Sat.-Sun. 9am-2pm.

Telephones: Blue international **LADATELs** are everywhere, but most are coin operated. A *caseta* is at 5 de Mayo 33 (tel. 24-19-89,-79,-67). Open Mon.-Sat. 9:30am-2pm and 4:30-9pm.

Telegrams: Allende Nte. 4 (tel. 12-01-63), one block west of the Jardín. **Fax** service, too. Open Mon.-Fri. 8am-6pm, Sat.-Sun. 9am-noon.

Buses: Station accessible via the "Ruta 25" on Allende and Zaragoza, "Ruta 8" on Ocampo and Constituyentes, and "Ruta 72" on Universidad—all are labeled "Central" (6am-10pm, 2 pesos). First-class service in Accesos 1 and 2. **Primera Plus** (tel. 11-40-01) serves Aguascalientes (6 per day, 4½hr., 80 pesos), Guadalajara (5 per day 12:15am-8pm, 5½hr., 84 pesos), Mexico City (every 20min. 4:30am-9pm, 2¾hr., 52 pesos), and Morelia (5 per day 4:30am-5:30pm, 3hr., 42 pesos). **Ómnibus de México** (tel. 29-00-29) serves Acapulco (midnight, 8hr., 183 pesos). **Del Norte** (tel. 29-00-22) serves Nuevo Laredo (4 per day 3-8pm, 13hr., 223 pesos), and Ciudad Juárez (8 per day 2:15am-10:30pm, 23hr., 370 pesos). **ETN** (tel. 29-00-17/-19) offers more luxurious service to Guadalajara (5 per day, 5hr., 125 pesos), San Miguel de Allende (12:15 and 7pm, 1hr., 20 pesos), Mexico City (every 30min., 70 pesos), and Puerto Vallarta (8:30pm, 10hr., 260 pesos). Second-class service in

Accesos 3 and 4. **Estrella Blanca** (tel. 29-02-02) has buses every hr. 6:15am-8:15pm to San Juan del Río (1hr., 7 pesos). **Oriente** (tel. 29-02-58) serves Guadalajara (every 30min. 5am-4pm, 5hr., 78 pesos) and Reynosa (7 and 7:30pm, 20hr., 161 pesos). **Flecha Amarilla** (tel. 11-40-01) runs to Dolores Hidalgo (every 40min., 1¾hr., 19 pesos), Guadalajara (about every 30min. 5:30am-11:15pm, 6-7hr., 78 pesos), Guanajuato (6 per day, 3hr., 29 pesos), Irapuato (every hr. 5am-9:10pm, 2hr., 20 pesos), Manzanillo (4 per day 1:30am-7:20pm, 12hr., 140 pesos), Mexico City (every 10min. 5am-9pm, 2¾hr., 41 pesos), Morelia (every 30min., 4hr., 34 pesos), San Luis Potosí (every hr. 6:15am-8:15pm, 3½hr., 39 pesos), Toluca (4:20, 10:35, and 11:45am, 3hr., 35 pesos), and Uruapan (12:45, 5:35am, and 1:05pm). **Herradura de Plata** (tel. 29-02-45) sends buses to San Felipe (every 40min. 6am-10pm, 3hr., 28 pesos), San Juan del Río (every 40min. 5am-8pm, 45min., 7 pesos), and San Miguel de Allende (every 20min. 6am-9pm, 1hr., 11 pesos).

Trains: (tel. 12-17-03), on Héroes de Nacozari, north of Av. Universidad. From the Jardín, walk five long blocks up Juárez to Av. Universidad, cross the bridge onto Invierno, and continue 2 blocks, turning left onto Héroes de Nacozari; the station is the blue building up one block to your right (about 20-25min.). "Ruta 8" and "Ruta 13" buses run up Ocampo and make the trip for 2 pesos. Service to Guadalajara, Cd. Juárez, Mexico City, Monterrey, and Nuevo Laredo.

Laundromat: Lavandería Veronica, Av. Hidalgo 153 (tel. 16-61-68). Open Mon.-Fri. 9am-2:30pm and 4:30-8pm, Sat. 9am-3pm.

Red Cross: (tel. 29-06-65 or 29-05-45), at Balaustradas and Circuito Estadio, near the Estadio Corregidora.

Pharmacy: Farmacia Guadalupe, Madero 32 (tel. 14-10-15), a block from the Jardín. Open daily 8am-10pm. **Súper Farmacia Querétaro,** Av. Constituyentes Pte. 17 (tel. 12-44-23), 5 blocks south of the Jardín. Open 24hr.

Hospitals: Hospital Seguro Social, (tel. 16-17-57), Zaragoza at 5 de Febrero. **Hospital General,** 5 de Febrero 101 (tel. 16-00-39 or 16-20-36).

Emergency: LOCATEL (tel. 14-33-11 or 14-28-89). Will find lost people and some missing items. Also provides emergency information and numbers.

Police: (tel. 20-86-63 or 20-85-43), Pie de la Cuesta in Colonia Desarrollo San Pablo.

Post Office: Arteaga Pte. 5 (tel. 12-01-12), between Juárez and Allende, two blocks south of the Jardín. Open Mon.-Fri. 8am-7pm, Sat. 9am-1pm. **Postal Code:** 76000. **Telephone Code:** 42.

ACCOMMODATIONS

Despite a small-scale tourist industry, good and inexpensive accommodations are not difficult to find in Querétaro's *centro*.

Hotel Hidalgo, Madero Pte. 11 (tel. 12-00-81), 1 block west of the Jardín, near Juárez and Madero. Centrally located. Spanish colonial architecture and ivy-covered courtyard complement the surrounding historical sites. Rooms with terraces are the breeziest and have TVs. Small bathrooms. Popular with families, international travelers, and expats. English-speaking management. Singles 50 pesos. Doubles 60 pesos. The attached restaurant is inexpensive and tasty.

Hotel del Márquez, Juárez Nte. 104 (tel. 12-04-14 or 12-05-54), 4 long blocks north of the Jardín. Stained glass windows and *azulejos* brighten up the dark wooded lobby. Tiled staircase leads to rooms with tiled bathrooms, hot water, color TVs, and telephones. Singles 60 pesos. Doubles 75 pesos.

CREA Youth Hostel, (tel. 23-11-20), on Av. Ejército Republicano, just off Av. Independencia. From the Jardín, walk one block south on Corregidora, then walk left on Independencia for 8 blocks, just past the Convento de Santa Cruz. Single-sex dorms with 8 bunks per room. Bedrooms and bathrooms are pretty clean, but the hot water can be temperamental. Playing field and athletic complex. 20 pesos per person, 25% discount with HI. 20-peso bedding deposit. No meals provided. Open daily 7am-10:30pm, but call if you're locked out.

FOOD

Inexpensive restaurants face the Jardín Zenea, pricier *loncherías* and outdoor cafés rim the nearby Plaza Corregidora, and taco, *torta,* and other fast-food stands line 5 de Mayo. Many restaurants stop serving their *menú del día* at 5 or 6pm.

Café del Fondo, Av. Pino Suárez 9 (tel. 12-09-76), at Juárez, 1 block south of the Jardín. Existentialists and avid chess-players match their wits and fill their bellies at this local hangout. Yellow walls display the work of local artists. Great assortment of coffee. Light fare includes *tortas* and sandwiches (5 pesos). *Pollo frito* 8 pesos. Breakfasts 8-12 pesos. Open daily 7:30am-10pm.

Restaurante de la Rosa (tel. 24-37-22), Juárez at Peralta, across from the Teatro. Tasty Mexican cuisine served by the swellest, sweetest women in town. Red wooden chairs, plaid tablecloths, and brick floors give the place a rustic feel. Food gets rave reviews from locals and tourists alike. Breakfast specials 11-14 pesos, *menú del día* 14 pesos. Open Mon.-Sat. 8:30am-8pm, Sun. 9am-midnight.

Restaurante Manolo's, Madero 6 (tel. 14-05-40), on the south side of the Jardín. *Muy tranquilo.* Old world meets the new: wrought iron gates, Spanish tile, and carved wooden tables overlooking...a shoe store?! Shut up and eat your paella (30 pesos). *Menú del día* (23 pesos) served 2-6pm. Open daily 8am-9pm.

Ibis Natura Vegetana, Juárez Nte. 47 (tel. 14-22-12), a half block north of the Jardín. A long, narrow restaurant in a health-food store set up soda-fountain style, complete with natural wood finishings, a wooden counter, reflecting stainless-steel ceiling, and damn good food. Yogurt 6 pesos. Soyburger 8 pesos. Hearty *menú del día* 19 pesos. Open daily 8am-9:30pm.

SIGHTS

The most intriguing sight in Querétaro is the **Convento de la Santa Cruz** (tel. 12-02-35), south of the Jardín. Follow Corregidora to Independencia and turn left. After walking a few blocks, you'll reach the convent; it occupies a plaza dedicated to the founders of the city. Nearly everything inside Santa Cruz is original—the clay pipes and water-catching system date from the city's aqueduct days. Maximilian devotees can make a pilgrimage to the room in which the emperor spent his last minutes; it has been left exactly as it was on the day of his execution. In one courtyard, trees grow thorns in the form of crucifixes. According to legend, the thorns began growing into crosses after a friar stuck his cane in the ground near the trees. It is said that these are the only trees of their kind in the world; attempts to plant seedlings elsewhere have supposedly failed. The tree is of the *mimosas* family, and is known simply as the *Árbol de la Cruz* (Tree of the Cross; open with 20-min. guided tours Mon.-Sat. 9am-2pm and 4-6pm, Sun. 9am-4:30pm; donation expected).

Northeast of the Alameda, along Calzada de los Arcos, at the end of Independencia, the **Acueducto** rises above the city. Stretching for 1280m and reaching a height of 23m, the aqueduct dominates the valley in which it lies. Now an emblem of the city, the aqueduct, with its 74 arches of pink quarry stone, was constructed between 1726 and 1738 as a gift to a perpetually parched community from the Marqués de Villas del Águila. Up 5 de Mayo to the east of the Jardín is the **Plaza de la Independencia (Plaza de Armas),** a monument to the aforementioned *marqués.* Stone dogs hang around his statue, drooling respectfully into a fountain. The plaza is bordered by old square-rimmed trees and beautiful colonial buildings, including the **Casa de la Corregidora,** home of Doña Josefa Ortíz de Domínguez, heroine of the Independence movement. The *casa* is now the seat of the state's government, so only the courtyard may be viewed (open Mon.-Fri. 9am-3pm and 6-9pm, Sat. 8am-9:30pm). Built from 1675 to 1680, the colorful **Templo de la Congregación** (tel. 12-03-39), one block north of the Casa de la Corregidora, at Pasteur and 16 de Septiembre, has two white towers and a central dome. The church's frescoes and stained glass are splendid, and the pipe organ is one of the more elaborate in Mexico. The image of *La Guadalupana* is by

Miguel Cabrera (open daily 7am-9pm; avoid mass Mon.-Fri. at 8, 10am, and 8pm, and much more often Sat. and Sun.).

The newly remodeled **Teatro de la República** stands at Ángela Peralta and Juárez (tel. 12-03-39). Many historic events have transpired here: in 1867, the final decision on Emperor Maximilian's fate; in 1917, the drafting of the constitution; and in 1929, the founding of the Partido Nacional de la Revolución (PNR), the precursor of today's ruling Partido Revolucionario Institucional (PRI). Inside, viewers can see the **Sala de Constituyentes,** where the constitution was drafted (both open Tues.-Sun. 10am-2pm and 5-8pm; free). The **Museo Regional** is housed in the **Ex-Convento de San Francisco** (tel. 12-20-31; fax 12-20-36), at Corregidora and Madero, east of the Jardín Zenea. Exhibitions include various artifacts culled from the dustbin of history, such as the table upon which the 1848 Treaty of Guadalupe Hidalgo was signed with the U.S. While exhibitions of contemporary art and craftwork greet you at the entrance, the entire upstairs area is devoted to colonial-era religious paintings and artifacts relating to Querétaro's military and political history. (Tours Tues.-Fri. noon, Sat.-Sun. 11am and 2pm. Open Tues.-Sat. 10am-5pm, Sun. 9am-4pm. Admission 14 pesos, free for students and teachers with ID, seniors, kids under 13, and on Sun.)

Overshadowing the Museo Regional is the newer **Museo de Arte de Querétaro,** Allende 14 (tel. 12-23-57), to the left of the Jardín, between Madero and Pino Suárez. The original edifice, an 18th-century Augustinian monastery, was rebuilt in 1889. An exhibition on local architecture supplements the bounty of Baroque paintings. European canvases, 19th- and 20th-century Mexican art, and the work of the 20th-century *queretareano* Abelardo Ávila round out the formidable collection (open Tues.-Sun. 11am-7pm; admission 10 pesos, free for students with ID, seniors, children under 12, and on Tues.).

The **Cerro de las Campanas** (Hill of the Bells), named for the peculiar sound its rocks make when they collide, is where Emperor Maximilian first established his military headquarters, then later surrendered his sword to General Escobedo in 1867. To reach the monument, walk a few blocks north of the Jardín Zenea on Corregidora and turn left onto General Escobedo. Proceed on Escobedo until the street ends at Tecnológico, then take a right and you will come to the monument (about a 30-min. walk). To the left of the Cerro de las Campanas and up a low hill, Maximilian's family built a small chapel over the ground where the emperor and two of his generals were shot. Three small white memorials inside designate the places where each took his last breath. Up the stairs to the left of the chapel stands a large stone sculpture of Benito Juárez, the man responsible for Maximilian's execution (open Tues.-Sun. 7am-6pm; 1 peso).

For lazing around, nothing beats the shady trees of the **Alameda Hidalgo,** three blocks down Corregidora. The Alameda, which was built in 1790, includes a duck pond, green lawns, tree-lined paths, a skating rink good enough for star skater Paul Frey, two soda fountains, and a monument honoring Hidalgo.

ENTERTAINMENT AND SEASONAL EVENTS

Local entertainment, like most everything else in Querétaro, revolves around the Jardín Zenea. Open-air brass band concerts are given in the gazebo Sunday evenings from 6-8pm, and myriad jugglers, *mariachis,* and magicians perform there less regularly. Balloons in bunches big enough to fly you to Chicago are sold around the *jardín,* enlivening the already festive plaza. *Mariachi* goes strong in the Jardín de los Platitos, where Juárez meets Av. Universidad north of the *zócalo.* Things start to heat up at about 11pm on Fridays and Saturdays.

Call the **Academia de Bellas Artes** (tel. 12-05-70), Juárez Sur at Independencia, to find out what the students of the Universidad Autónoma de Querétaro have in store for the public. If you're lucky, you might catch a ballet recital, piano concert, theatrical event, or even a folk dance presentation. But call early; performances usually begin at 5pm. Also, find out what kind of theatrical or musical performance is taking place at **Corral de Comedias,** Carranza 39 (tel. 12-01-65 or 12-07-65).

More fun than monster trucks, **Querétaro 2000** (tel. 20-68-10 or -13), on Boulevard Bernardo Quintana, is a huge stretch of parks and facilities, including a pool, football field, basketball court, gym, cafeteria, restaurant, amusement park, library, a Hall of Fame, an open theater, and an area for camping (open daily 7am-9pm).

Querétaro's students spend their pesos at a number of discos. The local twenty-something crowd does its thing at **JBJ,** Blvd. Bernardo Quintana 109 (tel. 13-72-13 or 13-01-48). Booming rhythms and a merciless strobelite will pull you onto the dance floor (open Thurs.-Sat. 9pm-2am, live music Wed.-Sat. 7pm-3am). Next to the disco is the **JBJ Bar,** which has karaoke and pool tables. Another happening spot is the disco **Van Gogh,** at Prolongación Pasteur Sur 285 (tel. 12-65-75). More convenient to the *centro* but less popular is **Tiffani's,** at Zaragoza Pte. 67 (tel. 16-65-70; cover 15 pesos, free Thurs.; open Thurs.-Sat. 9pm-3am). Many establishments open their doors only on weekends.

The annual **Feria de Querétaro** usually takes place during the second week of December. The **Feria de Santa Ana,** complete with bulls running through congested streets, takes place July 26. *Let's Go* does not recommend bull-running, as it can be dangerous to spectators. Feisty bovines sometimes run out of control and have been known to injure passers-by. Try to observe the bulls from the safety of a balcony.

■ Near Querétaro: Tequisquiapan

Situated on a high plateau 68km southeast of Querétaro, Tequisquiapan (pop. 40,000) is a small town with a down home country feel. Narrow brick streets weave in and out of flower-filled plazas, and white stucco houses are draped in vibrant bou-ganvillea. The town is known for its sunny climate, thermal springs, and cool fresh water pools. Equestrians can go horseback riding while hunters and gatherers peruse the wicker baskets and other arts and crafts typical to the region.

Mainly an idyllic spot to while away the time, Tesquisquiapan has only a handful of sights. **La Parroquia de Santa María de la Asunción** is a Neoclassic temple with a pink quarry façade, split-level columns, and a two-body tower trimmed in white brick. Also of interest is the **Museo de la Constitución de 1917,** housed in the Relox Hotel, which contains furniture and paintings from early 1900, including a portrait of Don Venustiano Carranza. A **cross** of pink quarry stands at the corner of Cuauhtémoc and 5 de Febrero, incorporating a melange of Biblical imagery, from nails and a crown of thorns to Jesus' countenance. A good time to visit Tequisquiapan is during the famous **Feria Nacional del Queso y El Vino** (Wine and Cheese Festival), celebrated for two weeks in June or July. The fair is marked by musical and cultural festivities, bullfights, and horse shows. **Tequisquiapan Tours,** Callejón 20 de Noviembre 2A (tel. 427-3-13-62/-02), gives tours of the area and can provide additional information.

Getting There: Flecha Azul runs buses from Querétaro to Tequisquiapan (every hr. 7am-7pm, 1½hr., 8 pesos).

HIDALGO

■ Tula

Once an important Toltec City, the archaeological site at Tula lures daytrippers from both Mexico City (80km) and Pachuca (75km). Other than the ruins, Tula's quiet *zócalo,* bustling market, and ubiquitous taco stands hardly distinguish it from other Mexican towns.

Orientation and Practical Information Downtown Tula consists of a few commercial streets surrounding a central *zócalo.* To reach the *zócalo* from the **bus station,** turn right down Xicoténcatl and then left at Ocampo. Follow the signs to the centro, turn left down Zaragoza, and then right on Hidalgo. To get to Tula from Mexico City, take an **AVM** bus from the Central de Autobuses del Norte.

There is no tourist office in town. Currency can be exchanged at **Banamex,** Leandro Valle 102 (tel. 2-39-03), down Juárez from the *zócalo* (open Mon.-Fri. 9am-3pm). It also has an **ATM. Teléfonos de Mexico,** Av. 5 de Mayo 3 (tel. 2-00-41), near Mina, provides long-distance phone service (open Mon.-Sat. 8am-10pm, Sun. 8am-3pm), as does the *caseta* at the bus station (open daily 9am-9pm). Buses run out of the **AVM** terminal (tel. 2-02-25 or -64), on Xicoténcatl, to Celaya (9 per day, 3½hr., 47 pesos), Irapuato (7 per day, 5hr., 60 pesos), León (7 per day, 6hr., 72 pesos), Mexico City (every 20min. 6am-8pm, 2hr., 15 pesos), Pachuca (every 15min. 4:30am-7:30pm, 2hr., 15 pesos), and Querétaro (9 per day, 2hr., 38 pesos). For a cab, call **Taxi Sitio Tula** (tel. 2-00-39). The **IMSS Clínic** (tel. 2-10-46), Ocampo at Xicoténcatl, in the large brown building, is open for emergencies around the clock. There is a **pharmacy** in the same building (open Mon.-Fri. 8am-7:30pm, Sat. 8am-9pm). The **police** are at 5 de Mayo 408 (tel. 2-01-85). The **post office** is hidden on Av. Ferrocarril. From the top of Av. 5 de Mayo, head downhill on Av. Vicente Guerrero, along the train tracks, and continue straight ahead (open Mon.-Sat. 9am-3pm). **Postal Code:** 42800. **Telephone Code:** 773.

Accommodations and Food Because Tula is a small town and most people come just to see the ruins, budget rooms don't come easy. The best deal in town is the **Auto Hotel Cuéllar,** 5 de Mayo 23 (tel. 91-800-2-04-42). A smattering of wooden furniture and occasional patches of homey carpeting hug the rosy walls and tiled floors. Bathrooms feature showers with sliding glass doors (singles 55-65 pesos; doubles 85 pesos). **Restaurante Casa Blanca,** Hidalgo 114 (tel. 2-22-74), at Hidalgo, serves up a cheap five-course *comida corrida* (15 pesos). More typical is **Restaurante El Ranchito** (tel. 2-02-03), on Zaragoza half a block before Hidalgo. A *comida corrida* with *postre* and *refresco* goes for only 15 pesos (open daily 6am-midnight).

The Ruins Once the Toltecs' greatest city, Tula was reputedly founded during the ninth century by the legendary Ce Acatl Topitzin (a.k.a Quetzalcóatl). Ce Acatl Topitzin is the most venerated king in *indígena* history and mythology. After many years at Tula, the story goes, he abandoned the city in 884 CE and led many of his followers to the Gulf coast. The departure was due to strife with neighbors who did not agree with his peaceful ways and who rejected the god for whom he was named. In the years following Quetzalcóatl's departure, several kings expanded Tula into the center of the mighty Toltec empire. Hundreds of years later, the Aztec Emperor Moctezuma brought about his own downfall when he welcomed the recently arrived Cortés because he believe the *conquistador* was the same light-skinned Quetzalcóatl who had fled to the east so many years before.

The Toltecs, whose name means "builders" in Náhuatl, relied on irrigation for their agricultural success and modeled their architecture after the style of Teotihuacán. During the 200-year-long Toltec heyday, the kingdom abandoned its once pacific stance for the violence and viciousness for which it is now notorious. When crop failures and droughts weakened the Toltec capital in 1165 CE, the Chichimecs lashed out at the Toltecs and destroyed Tula. The ruins of the city are architecturally mediocre, partly because of poor maintenance and partly because the Toltecs experienced internal instability—at one point Quetzalcóatl urged the Toltecs to evacuate the city, prompting some residents to bury their belongings and move to the region called Tlapallan. Tula was eventually absorbed by the Aztec empire, and, to this day, Aztec ceramics and pottery can be found scattered among the ruins.

From the entrance area, a dirt path zigzags through two sets of vendor stalls before arriving at the main plaza. The first structure you see to your right (north) as you reach the main plaza is **Ballcourt #1,** just north of the large Edificio de los Atlantes. This court, nearly 60m long, once held a depiction of a ball player in ritual dress, which is now located in the archaeological sponge that is the Museo Nacional de Antropología in Mexico City.

To the left (south) is the monumental **Edificio de los Atlantes,** also called the **Edificio de Tlahuizcalpantecuhtli** (try to say that in one breath!), likely the ceremonial worship building. Along its northern side and currently covered by a tin roof is the **Coatepantli,** which depicts jaguars and serpents in procession, as well as a deity in headdress and heart-devouring eagles. Reliefs of serpents feasting on live humans adorn the adjacent wall. Standing atop the pyramid are the Atlantes, figures of carved warriors; close inspection of the Atlantes (each a whopping 9.6m tall) reveals traces of red pigment, the only remnants of the many colors the statues once wore. Each statue is actually composed of several sections of stone, carefully designed to resemble the battle garb of the ancient *guerreros.* In their left hand each carries an *atlatl* (dart thrower), while the right hand holds a sheaf of arrows. A butterfly-shaped breastplate covers each figure's front; a wide, knotted belt protects the lower regions of their anatomy. Strapped to their backs is a huge solar disk.

Immediately west of the Edifico de los Atlantes is the **Palacio Quemado** (Burnt Palace). It is thought to have been an administrative center in ancient Tula or perhaps the city market. A *chac-mool,* or messenger to the gods, was originally found in the central patio; now the black figure with a gaping mouth reclines near the steps to the Edifico de los Atlantes, under the awning. Like many other indigenous cultures, the Toltecs built their largest buildings on the eastern boundary of the plaza to witness the sunrise and to maintain socio-political control by inspiring awe. Tula's **Templo Principal** once towered over the others. On the east side of the expansive green plaza, this building may have served as living quarters for the high priests or rulers of the city. Not fully excavated and overgrown with weeds, it's not possible to climb the Templo Principal from the front, but you can scramble up a steep rocky path in its southeast corner. On the west side of the plaza lies a second ballcourt. The level side closest to the plaza served as an altar where pre-game rites were likely held. Adjoining the ballcourt on the interior of the plaza is **El Tzompantli,** a small platform built by the Aztecs. Tzompantli means "place of skulls" and was used to display the victims of sacrifice.

The only other excavated structure of interest in the area is **El Corral,** 1.5km north of the main plaza. El Corral's distinctive, rounded shape leads archaeologists to believe that it was dedicated to the god of the wind. A dirt path from the northern border of the main plaza leads north to the wind god's shrine. The unimpressive **Museo Jorge R. Acosta,** at the entrance to the ruins, focuses on Toltec religion, crafts, recreation, and socioeconomic hierarchy. Inside is a copy of the *chac-mool,* as well as a history of the different groups that occupied the site and some of their remains. The museum sells a small written guidebook (20 pesos). The museum complex also includes a cafeteria, bathrooms, and an information desk where you can request a free guided tour and brochures (site open daily 9:30am-4:30pm; admission 14 pesos, free for kids under 13 and on Sun. and holidays; museum free with admission). **Taxis** will take you from Tula's main plaza to the site (10 pesos). Taxis aren't available at the site itself for the return, but *peseros* pass frequently on the highway (1.50 pesos).

ESTADO DE MÉXICO

▓ Toluca

Capital of the Estado de México since 1846, Toluca lives in the shadow of Mexico City. As weak decentralization progresses, Toluca reaps the benefits of its growing industrial, governmental, and cultural prominence. Unfortunately, together with increasing business come ecological and developmental problems: overcrowding and traffic congestion are among the most prominent. Long one of Mexico's larger indigenous population centers, Toluca is losing some of its traditional cultural moorings in the wake of Super Wal-Marts and superhighways.

Nevertheless, the *centro* is one of Mexico's best preserved, with an elegant cathedral, eclectic shopping area, fine museums, and brilliant botanical garden encased in the glimmering Cosmovitral—all things that make the hour-long trip from Mexico City well worth the ride.

ORIENTATION AND PRACTICAL INFORMATION

Toluca is connected to Mexico City by the highway Paseo Tollocan. The *zócalo*, cathedral, and Portales shopping market constitute the *centro*, and are bounded by **Av. Hidalgo** on the south, **Lerdo de Tejada** on the north, **Juárez** on the east, and **Bravo** on the west. The **Alameda** lies three blocks west of the *centro* on Av. Hidalgo. The amazing stained glass **Cosmovitral** is one block east of the *centro* on Lerdo de Tejada. Numerous *peseros* link the bus terminal to the heart of the city.

Tourist Office: State Tourist Office, Urawa 100, Room #110 (tel. 14-78-30 or 14-79-17), in the orange municipal government building behind the Clínica IMSS and Wal-Mart. Extremely helpful.

Telephones: LADATELs are liberally scattered throughout the *centro* and bus station areas. A *caseta* in the bus station is open daily 7am-10pm.

Telegrams: Telecomm, in the bus station. Public **fax.** Open Mon.-Fri. 9am-3pm.

Buses: Terminal Toluca is tucked between Paseo Tollocan and Isidro Fabela, southeast of the *centro*. Tons of *peseros* run to the *centro* from the terminal, and return trips can be picked up on the south side of the *zócalo*. **Estrella del Noreste** has constant service to Santiago (4 pesos) and Cholula (3 pesos). **Flecha Roja** (tel. 277-30-24) serves Mexico City (every 10min., 1hr., 15 pesos), La Marquesa (every 10min., 30min., 6.50 pesos), and Querétaro (every 2hr., 3hr., 39 pesos). **Naucalpan** goes straight to Mexico City's Metro stop Toreo (Line 2, every 5min., 1½hr., 15 pesos).

Trains: Av. de la Independencia at Electrificación, a 20min. walk east of the *zócalo*.

Market: Mercado 16 de Septiembre, Manuel Gómez Pedraza between Ignacio Rayón and Sor Juana Inés de la Cruz, two blocks north of the Cosmovitral. Supplies and produce. Open daily 8am-6pm. **Super Wal-Mart.** So large it's impossible to miss it. A warehouse-like nirvana with 53 check-out lanes and everything under the hazy sun.

Red Cross: (tel. 17-25-40), on Jesús Carranza, one block south of Paseo Tollocan and one block west of Paseo Colón, southwest of the *centro*. Open 24hr.

Hospital: Clínica Hidalgo (tel. 17-07-33 or 14-91-11), on Av. Hidalgo at Humboldt, 4 blocks east of Juárez, will patch you up or medicate you, as necessary. Open 24hr. **Hospital Civil Adolfo López Mateos,** on M. Matamoros at Paseo Tollocan. Follow M. Galeana south of the *centro*. Open 24hr.

Police: In the **Palacio Municipal** (tel. 14-93-51), on Av. de la Independencia between Juárez and N. Bravo.

Emergencies: dial 06, or call **LOCATEL** (tel. 12-11-21).

Post Office: On Av. Hidalgo, just east of Sor Juana Inés de la Cruz, 2 blocks east of Juárez. Open Mon.-Fri. 8am-7pm, Sat. 9am-1pm. **Postal Code:** 50150.

Telephone code: 72.

ACCOMMODATIONS

Though far from stellar, accommodations are cheap and surround the *centro*. Avoid the noise and filth of rooms near the bus station.

Hotel San Carlos, Madero 210 (tel. 4-94-22), on the south side of Portales market in the *centro*. Central location. Peach rooms come equipped with phone, TV, and comfortable bathrooms. Singles 45 pesos. Doubles 70 pesos.

Hotel Maya, Hidalgo 413 (tel. 14-43-42), a couple of blocks west of the *centro*. Small and homey. Quirky homespun quilts, peach paint job, and clean floor bathrooms are welcome touches. Pretty plants adorn the central courtyard. Singles 27 pesos. Doubles 43 pesos.

FOOD

Restaurants and cheap stalls clutter the storefronts of the Portales. *Chorizo* (sausage), the local specialty, makes an appearance in everything from *queso fundido* (melted cheese) to *tortas*. Also popular are traditional candies like *palanquetas* (peanut brittle), candied fruits, and *dulces de leche* (burnt milk candy).

Restaurante Biarritz, Nigromante 200 (tel 14-57-57), at 5 de Febrero, just west of the *centro*. Pretty taupe tablecloths and handsome colonial furniture set a calm atmosphere in which to enjoy breakfast (10-15 pesos) or a generous *menú del día* (20 pesos). Entrees hover around 20 pesos. Open daily 7am-8pm.

Jarra's Grill (tel. 14-84-38), on Independencia near 16 de Septiembre, east of the *zócalo*. Pictures of Ye Olde Toluca hang in this clean, modern second floor restaurant. Enjoy the *menú del día* (18 pesos), *antojitos* (18-25 pesos), and entrees (about 35 pesos). Huge bar selection. Open daily 1pm-midnight.

SIGHTS

The bulk of Toluca's offerings are found in the *centro*. The **Cosmovitral** and **Jardín Botánico** are housed in a building dating back to the turn of the century, located one block east of the northeast corner of the *zócalo*. The Cosmovitral, a stained glass mural, occupies 3000 square meters and is made of half a millon pieces of glass. It depicts the universe converging into the vitality of humans. Its beauty eclipses that of the many plants and pools of the Jardín. A small plaque and friendship lantern commemorate Toluca's sister city, Saitama, in Japan (open daily 9am-5pm; admission 5 pesos, children 2 pesos).

Toluca is Mexico's museum black hole. The city's cultural centerpiece is the **Centro Cultural Mexiquense**, on the outskirts of town but accessible by the bus that stops at Independencia and Juárez, in the *centro*. The complex houses three museums. The **Museo de Culturas Populares** is a restored hacienda with a large collection of folk art and colorful, traditional Mexican crafts. The **Museo de Antropología e Historia** offers a large and informative collection of pre-Hispanic to modern Mexican artifacts and exhibits. The **Museo de Arte Moderno** provides an eclectic potpourri of modern art. (All museums open Tues.-Sun. 10am-6pm. Admission 5 pesos, free Wed. and Sun. Purchase tickets at the kiosk in the parking lot.)

The **Instituto Mexiquense de Cultura** sponsors five other museums in the *centro*. The **Museo José María Velasco** and the **Museo Felipe S. Gutiérrez** are housed in adjoining restored colonial structures off the northwest corner of the *zócalo*. They house ample collections of their namesakes' art, as well as works by other Mexican artists. The **Museo de la Acuarela,** two blocks west of the *portales,* displays all the watercolors you could possibly want to see. The **Museo de Numismática,** another half block west on Hidalgo, is ripe with coins galore. The **Museo de la Estampa,** on the south end of the Alameda, exhibits etchings, engravings, and graphic arts from all over the globe (all museums open Tues.-Sun. 10am-6pm; free).

Dirty Dancing

Manic line-dancers indulge their fancies at the **Museo de la Macarena,** a small shack in a dark alley. It accepts five guests at a time into its confines, then blares the eponymous song for seven straight hours until the visitors unwittingly become zombie-practitioners of the ritualistic dance (open 24hr.; admission free and usually unexpected).

■ Tepotzotlán

On the highway from Mexico City to Tula and Querétaro, the town of Tepotzotlán makes an easy daytrip from Mexico City. For those itching to escape the smog and bustle of the city, Tepotzotlán offers a glimpse of small-town life, and its church and monastery house exquisite examples of religious art. The beautiful *zócalo* and religious museum can be comfortably enjoyed in four hours.

In the 16th century, Jesuits established a convent in Tepotzotlán where *indígenas* could study language, art, theology, and mathematics. Martín Maldonado, an *indígena* convert, donated the land to the missionaries in 1582. Construction of the buildings continued until the end of the following century, and the huge bell in the tower was added in 1762. To the rear of the lavishly ornate Churrigueresque **Iglesia de San Francisco Javier** is the **Capilla de la Virgen de Loreto.** Behind it, the astounding **Camarín de la Virgen** (altar room) is fitted with a mirror so that visitors can see the decorations on the dome that crowns it. The golden shimmer in this octagonal room gloriously captures the godliness of this Baroque era.

After the expulsion of the Jesuits in 1767, the church and buildings became a reform school for priests. Early in this century, they were returned to the Jesuits, and in 1964, the whole complex of buildings became the **Museo del Virreinato** (tel. 207-91-37). This large, beautiful museum contains a mind-boggling amount of treasures from the colonial period. Exhibitions chronicle pre-Hispanic culture, colonial expansion, and missionary activities in the republic. Jesuit imagery dominates the monastery's halls—St. Ignatius stares out from every other altar, and St. Francis Xavier is only slightly less ubiquitous. Gregorian chants echo throughout the halls, fitting the mood perfectly.

The **Iglesia de San Francisco Javier** is a Churrigueresque masterpiece. Laden with gold, the craftsmanship is among the most intricate and well preserved in all of Mexico. Clerical vestments, the murals lining the inner courtyard, and the faded frescoes further enhance this divine religious collection. Look out for *El Crucifijo*, a 17th-century sculpture of Christ on the cross carved from a single piece of wood. Don't miss the concealed entrance to the upper floor near the exit. The hall contains paintings of priests and nuns, a map of Mexico City from 1793, and a balcony with a great view of the surrounding area. The monastery's orchard is criss-crossed by cobblestone paths (museum complex open Tues.-Fri. 10am-5pm, Sat.-Sun. 10am-6pm; admission 14 pesos, free for seniors, students, children, and on Sun.).

The plaza outside the church is packed with eateries and a few hotels. Your best bet is **Hotel Posada San José,** Plaza Virreynal 13 (tel. 876-08-35), nearly hidden right beside the Restaurant-Bar Pepe. The walls are bare brick, but the floors are carpeted and the bathrooms are tiled (singles 60 pesos; doubles 85 pesos). For cheap eats, head to **Restaurante Los Pericos,** Plaza Virreynal 7A (tel. 876-23-72), on the far side of the plaza. Dining under the shaded balcony is perfect for people-watching (open daily 8am-10pm).

Getting There: To get to Tepotzotlán from Mexico City, take the Metro to Cuatro Caminos (Line 2), then the yellow or blue bus from *salida* H (buses leave about every 20min. 6am-10:30pm, 4 pesos). To get back, catch a bus on Juárez across the street from the Hotel Posada San José to any of a number of Metro stations.

■ Malinalco

Malinalco's Aztec ruins are one of four monolithic pyramids in the world—the other three are in India, Jordan, and Egypt. On the bus ride to the ruins, *campesinos,* loaded down with the straw baskets and woolens they plan to sell in Mexico City, chew tobacco, spit on the steel floor, and chat about crops and harvests in Spanish and Náhuatl. Though Malinalco has no tourist office, the **Casa de Cultura de Malinalco,** on one corner of the *zócalo,* can help you find the ruins and just about anything else you might need (open Mon.-Sat. 9am-2pm and 4-7pm, Sun. 10am-1pm). Most important buildings in Malinalco are situated around the *zócalo* and bear their identification (i.e. *farmacia, cantina, hotel*) in the same multi-colored inscriptions. In the *zócalo*, vendors display everything from sandals to fried fish.

In front of the plaza, the town's massive church, the **Parroquia del Salvador Divino,** inspires awe. Built in the 16th century by Augustinian monks, the church boasts frescoes that depict the stations of the cross, and a spine-chilling room in which at least a dozen Christ figures suffer all sorts of torments. The outside, however, masks its former glory with dark, decaying, soot-covered walls (open daily 9am-6pm; free).

Malinalco became the sacred ground for the rituals that officially transformed an Aztec youth into a *guerrero tigre* or *guerrero águila* (tiger or eagle warrior). Because of the importance of these rituals and the ground they were performed on, Malinalco was terraced and completely fortified from the outside. On the open circular stone platform—the first structure on the right as you enter—prisoners were bound to a pole with only arms left free and made to wrestle the recently initiated warriors. If the over-matched prisoner won consecutive bouts with two *águila* and two *tigre* warriors, he was matched against a left-hander. If the prisoner defeated the lefty, he was granted freedom. Defeat, on the other hand, had macabre consequences; the small rectangular basin in front of the entryway to the pyramid was used to hold the prisoner's blood after his ritual sacrifice. Behind the pyramid, the bodies of the sacrificed were burned to ashes on the oval bed of rock.

The **Templo de la Iniciación** (Temple of the Initiation) for eagle and tiger warriors is a massive monolithic structure. All of its statues, rooms, and façades were carved from one giant slab of stone, and it was originally painted a brilliant crimson. Two stone jaguars guard the Temple's steep steps. To the right of the entrance to the inner chamber, the broken figure of an eagle warrior sits on the head of the feathered serpent Quetzalcóatl. The frame of the chamber entrance is fashioned into the fanged, open-mouthed head of a serpent. Inside the circular chamber, three supine eagles and a jaguar are carved on the floor. In the hole behind the first eagle, the beating hearts of the sacrificed awaited the initiates who would devour them.

To the right of the Templo de la Iniciación stand the remains of a **temascal,** an ancient predecessor to the sauna. Behind the *temascal,* you can still make out the small cells in which the elderly *sacerdotes* most likely used to live. Walking to the end of the platform and looking down, you'll see the ruins of the prisoners' cells situated about 15m below the whole complex. The remaining wall bases suggest very narrow and painful punishment chambers. To get to the ruins from the *zócalo,* follow the blue pyramid signs along Guerrero and go straight. Take a left on Milgar, a right at the next blue arrow, and another right at the blue sign that appears to lead visitors into someone's driveway (open Tues.-Sun. 10am-4:30pm; admission 14 pesos, free for students with ID and on Sun.).

Getting There: Malinalco is easily accessible from Cuernavaca, Mexico City, or Toluca. To get there, take a bus to Chalma. Once there, hail a taxi to Malinalco (20min., 20 pesos, 5 pesos if shared).

MORELOS

■ Cuernavaca

The quintessential colonial city and the capital of Morelos, Cuernavaca (pop. 300,000) lies about 70km south of Mexico City. With an average annual temperature of 20°C (68°F), Cuernavaca (a.k.a. City of Eternal Spring) has long attracted visitors: Emperor Maximilian, Cortés, Gabriel García Márquez, and Muhammad Ali have all kicked back in the mansions of Cuernavaca's exclusive *colonias*. Lately, the city's center of gravity has tilted away from the famous and toward the rich—Cuernavaca has become a weekend and holiday playground for wealthy Mexico City residents fleeing big-city hassles. Over the last few years, Cuernavaca has also become crammed with *norteamericanos*. Some study at the city's numerous language schools, others are drawn by the capital's reputation for captivating visitors.

Though it is dirty and crowded at times, Cuernavaca's city center lacks the utter poverty that characterizes most other Mexican towns. With a cost of living second only to Cancún's, the serpentine streets are instead filled with Mexican teenagers cruising in their fathers' Fords, upper-class families on their weekend getaways, and the inevitable rush of the under-21 U.S. crowd headed for area bars. The plaza and *centro*, though pleasant to visit, are far from authentically Mexican.

ORIENTATION

Route 95 from Mexico City intersects many of Cuernavaca's main avenues. To get to the city center, exit onto **Domingo Diez** if coming from Mexico City, or **Emiliano Zapata,** which splits into northbound **José María Morelos** and the southbound **Avenida Obregón.** Morelos serves as the principal access road, running straight through the center of town. **Benito Juárez** is the main north-south thoroughfare east of the *zócalo*. Near the *centro*, Domingo Diez merges with **Cuauhtémoc** off the México-Acapulco expressway to become **Plan de Ayala,** which turns east to become the principal east-west axis in town. Ayala later rejoins the expressway.

Two plazas together make up Cuernavaca's *zócalo*. **Plaza de la Constitución,** the main square, is a few blocks east of Morelos via Hidalgo, at the intersection of Guerrero, Salazar, Juárez, and Hidalgo. Diagonally opposite the *zócalo's* northwest corner is the smaller **Jardín Juárez.** Several blocks east of the *zócalo* is the market area, municipal bus center, and gathering place for locals. Cuernavaca's streets are jumbled—expect irregularities and unexpected turns, especially near the plaza. Even and odd numbers usually stay on different sides of the street but, because of two different numbering systems, buildings opposite each other may have addresses several hundred numbers apart.

To reach the *centro* from the **Flecha Roja bus station,** take a right at the exit and head south on Morelos. Turn left onto Rayón, Hidalgo, or any nearby cross-street. If you arrive via **Pullman de Morelos,** head straight uphill on Netzahualcóyotl to Hidalgo; most major sights can be accessed from there. Those arriving via **Estrella de Oro** should cross the street and flag down any northbound minibus on Morelos (1.70 pesos)—they all run past the center of town.

Frequent local buses (1.70-2.50 peso), called *rutas,* run up and down Morelos; the *colonia* the bus is heading for is painted on the windshield. Taxis will go anywhere in the city for 7-10 pesos. Set prices before hopping in.

PRACTICAL INFORMATION

Tourist Offices: State Office, Morelos Sur 802 (tel. 14-39-20), a 15-min. walk south from Hidalgo and Morelos. These *Let's Go* aficionados will dole out lots of helpful information, including brochures and maps for Cuernavaca and the entire state of Morelos. The informal white **info booth** on the north side of the cathedral has brochures covering the entire country.

Currency Exchange: Banca Serfín (tel. 14-08-88), at the northwest corner of Jardín Juárez. **ATM.** Currency exchange daily 9am-1:30pm. **Casa de Cambio Gesta,** Morrow 9 (tel. 14-01-95 or 18-37-50), at Comonfort. Open Mon.-Fri. 9am-2pm and 4-6pm, Sat. 9am-1pm. **Casa de Cambio Divisas de Cuernavaca,** Morrow 12A (tel. 12-85-68 or 18-35-62), also has offices at Guerrero 208 and in the Plaza Los Arcos, in the northern part of town. Open Mon.-Fri. 9am-5pm.

American Express: Marín Agencia de Viajes (tel. 14-22-66), in Las Plazas Shopping mall on the *zócalo*. Holds mail, provides travel services, and will exchange currency when pesos are available. Open Mon.-Fri. 9am-2pm and 4-6pm, Sat. 10am-2pm.

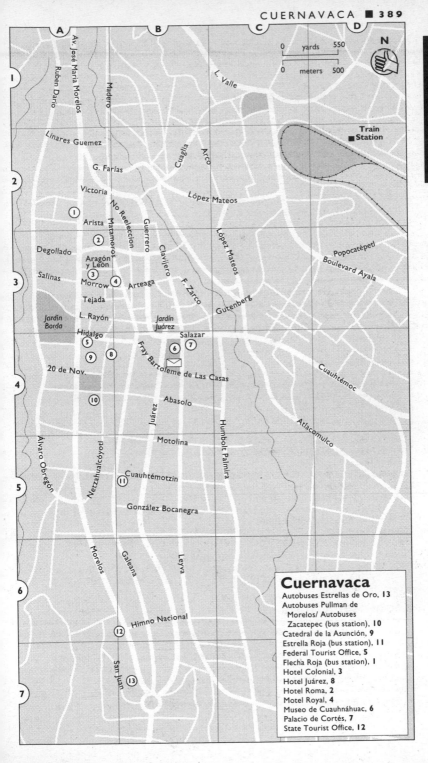

Cuernavaca

Autobuses Estrellas de Oro, 13
Autobuses Pullman de
   Morelos/ Autobuses
   Zacatepec (bus station), 10
Catedral de la Asunción, 9
Estrella Roja (bus station), 11
Federal Tourist Office, 5
Flecha Roja (bus station), 1
Hotel Colonial, 3
Hotel Juárez, 8
Hotel Roma, 2
Motel Royal, 4
Museo de Cuauhnáhuac, 6
Palacio de Cortés, 7
State Tourist Office, 12

Telephones: LADATELs are easy to find around the *zócalo,* along Morelos Sur, and in the bus stations. For a good old-fashioned *caseta,* there's **Telcom,** Salazar 8, on the eastern edge of the *zócalo.* Open Mon.-Fri. 8am-8pm, Sat. 9am-1pm.

Telegrams: Telecomm (tel. 18-05-67), to the right of the post office. Public **fax** service. Open for telegrams Mon.-Fri. 8am-7pm, Sat. 9am-1pm.

Buses: Flecha Roja, Morelos 503 (tel. 12-81-90), 4 blocks north of Jardín Borda. First-class service to Acapulco (7 per day, 5hr., 85 pesos), Grutas de Cacahuamilpa (every 40min. 6am-6pm, 1hr., 9 pesos), Mexico City (every 30min. 5:30am-9pm, 1¼hr., 22 pesos), Taxco (12 per day, 1½hr., 19 pesos), and northern cities including Guadalajara (6 and 10pm, 9hr., 186 pesos). The **Tres Estrellas del Centro** desk in the same building offers local service to Chalma (2 per day, 1¼hr., 16 pesos), Santa Marta (2 per day, 1hr., 9 pesos), Santiago (2 per day, 1hr., 14 pesos), and Toluca (every 30min., 6am-9pm, 17 pesos). The station has 24-hr. **luggage storage** (5 pesos for the first 5hr., 1 peso per hr. after) and long-distance phones. Open daily 6:30am-10pm. **México-Zacatepec (LASSER)/Pullman de Morelos,** Netzahualcóyotl 106 (tel. 14-36-50), at Abasolo, two blocks south of the *zócalo.* To Mexico City (every 30min., 1hr., 22 pesos), Zacatepec (every hr. 9am-6pm, 7.50 pesos), and small cities throughout Morelos. **Estrella de Oro** (tel. 12-30-55), on Morelos Sur at Las Palmas Circle, 10 blocks south of the intersection of Reforma and Hidalgo. First-class service to Acapulco (4 per day, 3½hr., 85 pesos), Chilpancingo (8:15pm, 2hr., 42 pesos), Iguala (1 per day, 1½hr., 20 pesos), Ixtapa/Zihuatanejo (2 per day, 8hr., 119 pesos), Mexico City (5 per day, 1¼hr., 19 pesos), and Taxco (2 per day, 1½hr., 17 pesos). **Estrella Roja,** Galeana 401 at Cuahtemotzin, 7 blocks south of the *zócalo.* First-class service to Cuautla (every 15min. 6:15am-10pm, 1hr., 9 pesos) and Puebla (every hr. 5am-7pm, 3hr., 28 pesos). Second-class **Estrella Roja** and **Ometochtli,** on López Mateos at the south end of the Mercado. Buses load in the parking lot across the highway and run to Tepotzlán (45min., 5 pesos).

Trains: Leandro Valle 33 (tel. 12-80-44). Useless.

Markets: Superama (tel. 12-81-20), at Morelos, just behind Helados Holanda north of the cathedral. Open Mon.-Sat. 7am-10pm, Sun. 7am-9pm. The market om Blvd. Alfonso López Mateos sells excellent produce. Head east on Degollado, up the pedestrian bridge, and past the vendor stands.

Laundromat: Nueva Tintorería Francesa, Juárez 2 (tel. 12-91-71), next to the Palacio de Cortés. 8 pesos per kg. Open Mon.-Fri. 9am-7:30pm, Sat. 9am-2:30pm.

Red Cross: (tel. 15-05-51 or 15-35-55), Ixtaccíhuatl at Río Panuco.

Pharmacy: Farmacia Maya, Morelos 710 (tel. 12-81-68), just north of the Flecha Roja bus station. Open 24hr.

Medical Assistance: Centro Quirúrgico, Juárez 507-B (tel. 14-23-38). A pricey doctor for every ailment. Free help at **IMSS** (tel. 15-50-00).

Hospital: Hospital Civil, Morelos 197 (tel. 14-17-44 or 18-83-17), directly across the street from the cathedral. 24-hr. emergency treatment free, except for the cost of supplies. Long lines at all hours.

Emergency: 06.

Police: Emiliano Zapata 802 (tel. 17-11-15, 12-00-36, or 17-10-00). Take Morelos north until it becomes Zapata; it's a bit farther up on the left.

Post Office: Plaza de la Constitución 3 (tel. 12-43-79), on the southwest corner of the *zócalo.* Open Mon.-Fri. 8am-7pm, Sat. 9am-1pm. **Postal Code:** 62000.

Telephone Code: 73.

ACCOMMODATIONS

Cuernavaca has become a chic upper-class getaway, so rooms are chronically over-priced. The cloud has a silver lining, though—even the barest of hotels are often outfitted with a swimming pool or lush courtyard. Although there are some extremely inexpensive *casas de huéspedes* along Aragón y León, you'd do best to pass them up—at night, many of the guests have customers of their own.

For an extended stay, it's possible to lodge with a local family through one of the city's Spanish-language schools. Students choose from a list of families willing to provide room, board, and language practice. **Cuauhnahuac,** Morelos Sur 1414 (tel. 12-36-73), is especially willing to lend their family list to backpacking visitors who wish to spend time with *cuernavaquenses*. Sharing a room with a student costs US$16 per day for room and board; for a private single, you pay US$30. Contact José Camacho at Cuauhnahuac. Also try the bilingual language school, **Experiencia,** Leyva 1130 (tel. 12-65-79), in Colonia Las Palmas.

Hotel Colonial, Aragón y León 104 (tel. 18-64-14), uphill and west of Matamoros. Pretty orange colonial home with a relaxing central courtyard and hospitable staff. Green-and-brown rooms enlivened by tiled floors and spotless bathrooms. Singles 60 pesos. Doubles 70 pesos, with two beds 80 pesos. Add 15 pesos for TV.

Hotel Juárez, Netzahualcóyotl 117 (tel. 14-02-19), half a block south of Hidalgo. Rooms are large and clean, and the sleepy atmosphere, wooden furniture, and cool pool beckon to the weary traveler. Some rooms are bright and airy, but others offer only slits for windows. Singles 65 pesos. Doubles 85 pesos.

Los Canarios, Morelos 713 (tel. 13-00-00). Well past its prime, this motor lodge groans with groovy fifties decor and furnishings. Comfy, colorful rooms provide the basics, and two swimming pools and a restaurant complement your stay. Proprietor is often willing to offer discounts. Singles 60 pesos. Doubles 110 pesos.

Hotel Papagayo, Motolinía 13 (tel. 14-17-11), by Morelos, 5 blocks south of the cathedral. A budget resort. Geared towards bilingual clientele, with clean, well furnished rooms, a pool with diving platforms, ping pong, and restaurant service. Breakfast (8am-10am) included. Singles 95 pesos. Doubles 155 pesos.

FOOD

Overflowing with tourists, Cuernavaca has more than its share of budget eateries. For your main meal, take advantage of one of the excellent restaurants around the plaza. Head up the side streets (try Aragón y León) or the larger thoroughfares Galeana and Juárez for lighter, less expensive fare. In the market, a *comida corrida* costs about 12 pesos *con refresco*. Along Guerrero, north of the plaza, street vendors sell mangos, *piñas* (pineapples), and *elotes* (corn on the cob). The health drinks sold at the Eiffel Kiosk in the Jardín Juárez include everything from the standard fruit and milk *licuados* to a spinach concoction not even Popeye could love (4-12 pesos).

Marco Polo Pizzería, Hidalgo 26 (tel. 12-34-84), on the 2nd floor. Named for the ultimate traveler, this pizzeria offers a view of the cathedral and surrounding mountains from the balcony. Candles add atmosphere to complement the delicious puffy pizzas (starting at 17 pesos). Open daily 1-10:30pm.

Restaurante Los Arcos, Jardín de Los Héroes 4 (tel. 12-44-86), on the south side of the *zócalo*. Flanked by lush plants and a bubbling fountain, nice, mosaic-inlaid outdoor tables are ideal spots from which to watch the day slip-slide away. Musicians of all abilities serenade the clientele. Breakfast specials 15-20 pesos. *Comida corrida* 17 pesos. Open daily 7:30am-midnight.

Gin Gen, Rayón 106 (tel. 18-60-46), 2½ blocks west of the Jardín Borda. Chinese fans and figurines adorn the walls. From 1-5pm, the super-filling *guisados del día* provide soup, rice, 2 entrees, and dessert for only 25 pesos. Great tofu and vegetarian options, too. Dine-in or carry-out. Open daily 1-10pm.

Helados Virginia Cuernavaca, Hidalgo 22 (tel. 12-97-42), just east of Marco Polo Pizzería. Ordinary appearance; extraordinary ice-cream flavors, including *arroz* (rice), *elote* (corn on the cob), and *jícama*, for 5 pesos. Open daily 8am-9pm. Another branch farther south at Juárez 300.

SIGHTS

Cuernavaca's popularity has little to do with scintillating sights. The **Plaza de la Constitución** extends east from the Palacio de Gobierno and is home to the machine that is the Morelos state bureaucracy. The heart and soul of the city, the tree-shaded plaza glows with fiery red *flamboyanes* (royal poinciana) and is speckled with cafés and wrought-iron benches. Food vendors and *mariachis* engage in a Darwinian struggle for pesos. A kiosk designed by Gustave Eiffel and commissioned by Cuernavaca's Viennese community stands in the **Jardín Juárez,** at the northwest corner of the Pl. de la Constitución, north of the Palacio de Gobierno. Thursdays and Sundays at 6pm, a local band commandeers the kiosk and belts out polkas, classical music, and *rancheras* (Mexican country music). The kiosk houses a fruit drink stand, and a long list describes the health benefits of each ingredient.

At the southeastern corner of the Pl. de la Constitución, east of Benito Juárez, the **Palacio de Cortés** stand as a stately reminder of the city's grim history—Cortés set Cuernavaca on fire in 1521, then built this two-story fortress from the remains of local buildings, situating the fortress atop a sacred pyramid. Completed in 1524 (when Cortés left to destroy Honduras), the building functioned as a prison in the 18th century and as the Palacio de Gobierno during the dictatorship of Porfirio Díaz.

A grant from the former British ambassador to Mexico (none other than Charles Lindbergh's father-in-law) transformed the Palacio de Cortés into the **Museo Cuauhnahuac.** On the first floor of the museum, archaeological and anthropological exhibits deal with pre-Hispanic cultures. Timelines highlight the histories of the Toltec, Olmec, Mayan, and Aztec peoples; illustrated parchments document the Xochimilca, Chalcha, Telcaneca, and Tlahuica cultures. Perhaps one of the more interesting displays is the collection of indigenous drawings and depictions of the Spanish arrival, in which valiant eagle and tiger warriors in full regalia battle the invaders. Second-floor exhibits on the Conquest and Mexican history include the first public clock ever to toll in Mesoamerica and some original clothing and furnishings from the palace. An Asian influence is visible in the early furniture and decorations, as Spain had invaded the Philippines in 1565 and maintained a steady trade with the islands throughout Mexico's colonial period. One of Diego Rivera's greatest works is on the western balcony of the second floor of the palace. The mural, commissioned by then-U.S. ambassador to Mexico Dwight D. Morrow as a gift to the people of Cuernavaca, depicts Mexico's history from the Conquest until the Revolution of 1910, proceeding chronologically from right to left. (Museum open Tues.-Sun. 10am-5pm. Admission 14 pesos; free Sun. and for students with ID.)

Black soot has darkened the tall walls and towers of the **Catedral de la Asunción,** three blocks down Hidalgo from the *zócalo,* at Morelos. Construction on the three temples of the cathedral began in 1525, making this one of the earlier churches in the Americas. Removal of the aisle altars 20 years ago revealed some fabulous Japanese frescoes depicting the persecution and martyrdom of Christian missionaries in Sokori, Japan. Historians speculate that these frescoes were painted in the early 17th century by a converted Japanese artist who had settled in Cuernavaca. The simple altar is highly unusual—seven baskets holding candles hang, seemingly suspended, within a faceless box (open daily 7am-7pm).

Site of glamorous soirées during the French occupation of Mexico, the **Jardín Borda** (tel. 12-00-86) is now a Sunday gathering spot for young couples and families on picnics. The stone entrance is on Morelos, across from the cathedral. In 1783, the priest Manuel de la Borda built a garden of magnificent pools and fountains next to the ostentatious residence of his relative, José de la Borda. The Jardín Borda's grandeur quickly gained fame and, in 1864, Emperor Maximilian and his wife Carlota established a summer residence there. Today it takes a vivid imagination to recognize the park's faded splendor amid the sometimes non-functional fountains and cracked sidewalks. However, the modern additions to the garden—an art collection near the entrance, a small theater where weekly cultural events are held, and a museum inside Maximilian's old summer home—are welcome replacements for its past elitism. Unlike the fountains and sidewalks, the mango trees, tropical ferns, ornamental plants, and giant palm trees have flourished through the years. Patchwork rowboats are available for rent (5 pesos per 30min.; park open Tues.-Sun. 10am-5:30pm; admission 5 pesos, students and teachers 2 pesos, free Wed.).

The **Pyramid of Teopanzolco** squats on a glistening green lawn at the center of a public park near the southern end of Teopanzolco, southeast of the market on Guerrero. As is frequently the case in Mexico, the pyramid actually consists of two pyramids, one within the other. The first stairway leads to a ledge, at the bottom of which a second stairway, belonging to the second pyramid, begins. Like other pre-Hispanic peoples, the Tlahuica increased the size of their monuments by encasing outdated ones in new construction. A chilling partial staircase suggests that the new pyramid was unfinished when Cortés arrived. To get to the site from the marketplace or along Morelos, take a taxi (10 pesos) or hop on local bus #10 and ask the driver to let you off at the *pirámide*. If you're in the mood to break in those walking shoes, head north along Morelos (the cathedral will be on your left), turn right on Pericón, and go right on Río Balsas to Teopanzolco (open daily 10am-5pm; admission 10 pesos).

ENTERTAINMENT AND SEASONAL EVENTS

Cuernavaca's popularity as a vacation spot fuels a fairly glitzy nightlife, and the city's *norteamericano* expatriates, now over 20,000 strong, lend a north-of-the-border feel to many festivities. Bars in Cuernavaca are modern and highly commercialized, and several have live nightly entertainment. Around the *zócalo*, many of the clubs cater to tourists; some have no cover charge but expect patrons to buy drinks.

Discos are typically open from 8pm to 4am on Friday and Saturday. To deter the fistfights and *broncas* (brawls) that used to plague Cuernavaca's clubs, some now admit only male-female couples and require reservations; most, however, do not enforce these business-diminishing rules. The more popular discos in town are not on the *zócalo* but down neighboring side streets. Many lie just out of walking distance (especially at night) and are best reached by *rutas* or a taxi after 11pm. Students from local language schools get free passes and avoid cover charges.

Barba Azul, Prado 10 (tel. 13-19-76). Popular with the early 20s, hard-hitting-techno crowd. Drinks 12-15 pesos. Cover 40 pesos. Open Fri.-Sat. 10am-5am.

Kaova, Av. Morelos Sur 302 (tel. 18-43-81), 3 blocks south of the cathedral. Rock-dance hybrid. Collegiate crowd,, with a large Mexican contingent. Small dance pit and lots of tables to people watch. National drinks 18 pesos. Fri.-Sat. cover 30 pesos after 10pm. Open Wed.-Sat. 9pm-3:30am.

Samanna, Domingo Diez 1522 (tel. 13-47-27). A twenty- and thirtysomething crowd packs it in to flaunt their dancing prowess, shaking their booties to a live *salsa* and tropical mix. Fri.-Sat. cover 40 pesos. Open Wed.-Sat. 8pm-4pm.

Ta'izz, Chapultepec 50 (tel. 15-40-60). U.S. top-40 favorites, fog machines, and light shows seduce the younger crowd. Cover 40 pesos. Open Fri.-Sat. 9pm-4am.

Shadée, at the end of Gutenberg, east of the *zócalo*. Bar during the week, dance club on weekends. Young gay crowd works up a sweat and sings along in tentative accents nurtured at nearby language schools. Drinks 15 pesos. Cover Thurs.-Sat. 35 pesos. Open Mon.-Sat. 9pm-4am.

Harry's Grill, Gutenberg 93 (tel. 12-76-39), beside the Las Plazas mall, north of the *zócalo*. U.S. top-40 dance hits, old telephone booths, airplane propellers, and *norteamericano* license plates. The pick-up scene here is no less than frantic, providing lively, loud entertainment. The slogan: "A Sunny Place for Shady People." Free *botanas*. Beer 14 pesos. Open daily 1pm-midnight.

Cuernavaca's movie houses charge 8-12 pesos per flick. Downtown, **Cinema Las Plazas** (tel. 14-07-93), across from the Jardín Juárez, screens imports and high-quality Mexican films. The colonial **Cine Alameda,** Matamoros 1 (tel. 12-10-50), one block north of the *zócalo,* shows popular titles on its ultra-wide screen. **Teatro Morelos,** on Morelos, about a block and a half north of Jardín Borda, shows excellent Mexican films (10 pesos, with student ID 5 pesos).

On Saturday and Sunday, the **market** in the Jardín Juárez specializes in silver jewelry; don't be afraid to bargain. The **Feria de la Primavera** (Festival of Spring) brings with it parades and costumes for 10 days a year at the vernal equinox (March 21-22).

■ Near Cuernavaca

XOCHICALCO

Ceremonial center, fortress, and trading post rolled into one, **Xochicalco** (Place of the Flowers) is the most impressive archaeological site in the state of Morelos, worth the trip if only for the awesome vistas. Built in the 7th century during the Toltec Classic period, Xochicalco suffered periodic invasions by the Olmecs, Maya, Zapotecs, and Mixtecs. Archaeologists speculate that the site may even be the mythical city of **Tamoanchan,** the place where wise men came to begin the cult of the new god Quetzalcóatl, as well as to synchronize civil and religious calendars. By the time of the Conquest, the city had become a tributary of Tenochtitlán.

On the road right before the ruins, a stunning modern sight appears; the speckled green **Museo del Sitio de Xochicalco** mimics the forms of the ruins, as well as the lush flora which engulfs the nearby hillsides. Inaugurated in April 1996, the museum's beautiful marble tiling and wall frescoes complement the site, and a gorgeous pyramidal motif is carried throughout the museum's skylights, tiling, and structure. Comprehensive exhibits on the site and invaluable brochures on the ruins (5 pesos) make the musem a useful stop before climbing on to the site itself (open Tues.-Sun. 10am-5pm; admission 14 pesos, free for children, students, and on Sun.).

From the museum, a rocky path leads to the ruins. The ruins are best explored in a generally circular manner, starting at the elevated plaza up to the left of the first patch of greenery. On the right side of the first plain, the **Pirámide de las Estelas** (Structure A) and the **Gran Pirámide** (Structure E) just south of it nearly dwarf the three smaller structures on the left. The Gran Pirámide forms the northern boundary of the **Plaza Central,** which can be reached by continuing straight (south) and taking the small slope down to the left. This area was most likely a trading center for the local and regional populations—many ancient roads converge here. Twin pyramids on the east and the west sides of the plaza, labeled **Structure C** and **Structure D,** were used in the worship of the sun, one oriented towards the sunrise, the other towards the sunset. At the center of the Plaza is a carved obelisk that bears two hieroglyphs related to the god Quetzalcóatl. The obelisk's shadow plotted the trajectory of the sun between the pyramids.

The southwest corner of this plaza offers a great overhead view of the **Juego de Pelota** (Ballcourt) below. To reach it, walk down the stone steps between Structures C and D. Straight ahead and off to the left lie unexcavated remnants of this sprawling city. Continue down the narrow rocky path directly to the right for the ballcourt. A statue found here bears a remarkable likeness to another found in Copán, Honduras, a possible indication of Xochicalco's commercial scope. Continuing west is the **Palacio,** a building with many of its rooms still intact. Because of its proximity to other ceremonial areas, the palace may have been the living quarters of a group of high priests. Farther ahead is the small **Building A** and a large hill which holds the unexcavated **La Malinche,** another group of living quarters and a ceremonial area. From atop this hill, a row of 21 altars connecting the ballcourt to La Malinche are visible. While only small pedestals remain, at one time these altars were used to mark the 260 days of the ceremonial calendar.

After heading back up the hill to the central plaza, make your way to the base of the **Gran Pirámide** (Structure E). Atop this pyramid rest the remains of an even more ancient structure. Follow the path down to the left (west) and over to the stairway/porticos section. This area was used to limit access to the main part of the city, in case of invasion or revolution. The design simply did not work well enough; Xochicalco eventually fell prey to a revolution.

Past the portico and up two sets of impressive stairways rebuilt in 1994 is the **Plaza Ceremonial,** which served as the main ceremonial center of the city. As you enter, the top of the Pirámide de las Estelas is accessible and holds a small temple inside, enclosing a huge pit in the center that was the burial site for high priests and a place for ritual offerings. In the center of the plaza is the renowned **Pirámide de la Serpiente Emplumada** (Pyramid of the Plumed Serpet). Sloppily reconstructed in 1910, it bears carved reliefs of Quetzalcóatl, the great feathered serpent who was a god-hero to the Toltecs. Xochicalco's commercial partnership with southern cultures is reflected in the embrace Quetzalcóatl bestows upon a priest in an elaborate Mayan headdress.

On the rear (west) end of the plaza is the tremendous **Montículo 2,** the highest area of the site, and supposedly where the rulers of Xochicalco lived. The eastern side was intended for daily activities, while the west end was exclusively ceremonial. Exit the Plaza Ceremonial on the north side and head west down the slope to the **Hall of the Polichrome Altar,** where a colored altar rests beneath an authentic reconstruction of the roofing used by the Toltecs. Farther down is a cistern used for water storage, a sauna used for pre-game initiation rites, and **Teotlachtli,** the northern ballcourt. Here, two massive rings of rock are attached in the middle, unlike most ballcourts in Mesoamerica, which have only one ring. Teams competed for the privilege of being sacrificed atop the Pyramid of Quetzalcóatl; the players' strong hearts were believed to feed the sun. Nearby, the foundations remain of the **Calmecac,** the palace in which Toltec and Aztec priests underwent training and initiation.

Continue west along the weed-ridden path, around the back of the base of Montículo 2 until you reach a large stone amalgamation. A small opening in the corner (with steps leading up) allows access to the stuccoed interior of the underground **Observatorio,** where ancient astronomers followed the cosmos. On summer solstices, Aztec sages and stargazers peered through a shaft in the ceiling to trace the path of the sun; by so doing, they hoped to verify and adjust the Aztec calendar. A guide gives periodic presentations as soon as a good-sized group has assembled. (Observatory open 11am-2pm. Site open Tues.-Sun. 9am-5pm. Admission 14 pesos, free Sun. and for students with ID.)

Getting There: From Cuernavaca, **Flecha Roja** runs buses directly to Xochicalco (6 pesos). Alternatively, snag a bus to Miacatlán from the **Autos Pullman** station at Abasolo and Netzahualcóyotl, one block south of the cathedral (6 pesos). Ask the driver to drop you off at the *crucero* de Xochicalco. **Taxis** wait at the *crucero* and, for seven pesos, will take you to the site. Otherwise, the uphill walk to the site (4km) will take you about an hour. Buses rarely stop at the *crucero* on their way back to Cuernavaca; instead, hail a nearby taxi and ask to go to the *caseta* (2 pesos), a nearby bus stop. Buses go back every 30 minutes or so. Taxis usually sit at the site entrance, but it may be a good idea to ask a driver to pick you up at a specified time.

TEPOZTLÁN

In northern Morelos, the quiet *pueblo* of Tepoztlán occupies one of the state's more scenic and impenetrable sites—towering cliffs form a natural fortress that allows entrance only from the south. Proceeding along Rte. 95-D toward Tepoztlán, keep your eyes peeled for **Popocatépetl** and **Ixtaccíhuatl,** two massive volcanoes which surge from the ground. The cobbled *indígena* village preserves a colonial feel amid growing modernization such as pool maintenance and satellite television stores, and many indigenous people still speak Náhuatl. On Sundays, the *zócalo* comes alive with vibrant market activity. During the rest of the week, however, the town is much quieter. Wobbling on a peak 360m above the village are the archaeological sites for which the town is famous. The thin air may leave you breathless and thirsty, so prepare accordingly.

The valley of Tepoztlán is charged with ages of myth, legend, and magic. It is thought that the god-hero of the Toltecs, Quetzalcóatl, was born here about 1200 years ago. Celebrations still take place every September 8, when the *pulque* flows and the dance floor fills in honor of Tepozécatl. *Los chinelos*—colorfully attired folk dancers—may invite you to join their traditional dance, *el salto*.

Travelers also come to visit the **Pirámide del Tepozteco,** perched on the northern ridge of the cliffs that rise above one end of town, about 3km above the valley.

Some say the pyramid was a Tlahuica observatory and defense post for the valley, while others swear it served as an Aztec sacrificial temple. The 10m-tall structure has a porch inscribed with barely discernible Tlahuica glyphs. To reach the pyramid, follow Av. 5 de Mayo north out of town (passing the *zócalo* on your right) until you reach its end. The hour-long climb is steep and strenuous, but is made bearable by the cooling shade of trees. If you intend to climb, be sure you are equipped with appropriate footwear, water, and spirit; many halfhearted attempts at climbing end in disappointment (open erratically Tues.-Sun. 10am-4:30pm; admission 10 pesos, free Sun. and for children under 13).

The **Museo de Arte Prehispánico,** at the rear of Capilla Asunción, holds a collection donated to the city by the poet Carlos Pellicer. The impressive display includes pottery pieces and clay figures of Olmec, Zapotec, Mayan, Totonac, and Aztec origin, as well as many objects from Teotihuacán (open Tues.-Sun. 10am-6pm; admission 3 pesos, students and teachers with ID 1.50 pesos).

Because of its natural beauty, vernal climate, and proximity to Mexico City, the area around Tepoztlán attracts an ever-growing population of wealthy *norteamericanos.* Unfortunately, these foreigners have started to drag the entire town upscale and Tepoztlán completely lacks moderately priced accommodations. **Casa Iccemanyan,** Calle de Olvido 26 (tel. 5-08-99 or 5-00-96), the first cross street after the Pullman de Morelos station, all the way down the hill, offers six bungalows for extended stays and gives travelers studying at neighboring language schools a chance to practice their skills with a Mexican family. Well maintained and decorated rooms come with clean bathrooms and lots of privacy. Beautiful pool, lawn, and Tepoztleco vistas are a plus (singles US$25; doubles US$46; rates include three meals and are negotiable).

Getting There: From Cuernavaca, **Ometochtli** buses leave from the market (5 pesos direct in the purple-and-green buses, 3.50 pesos by *pesero*). If you arrive at the Ometochtli depot, follow the main road; it will curve to become Av. 5 de Mayo. From Mexico City, take a **Pullman de Morelos** bus from the Tasqueña terminal (every 30min., 20 pesos). In Tepoztlán, buses arrive and depart from the *zócalo,* close to the market, or from the bus depot just outside town.

■ Cuautla

Known until 1869 as Ciudad Morelos, in recognition of José María Morelos' contributions to the War for Independence, Cuautla is truly the powder keg of Mexican history. The town was Emiliano Zapata's stronghold during the Mexican Revolution, and both heroes are immortalized in two of the town's three main plazas. Today, Cuautla survives primarily on the memories of its proud past, and only in small part on the tourism brought by historical relics and the many *balnearios* (hot water springs) that dot the area.

Orientation Cuautla is in the central part of eastern Morelos, about 42km east of Cuernavaca. Everything except the far-flung spas lies within a six-block radius of the *centro.* The center consists of three large plazas running in a straight line, each two blocks from the next. The southernmost plaza with the Zapata statue is the **Jardín Revolución del Sur.** Two blocks north is the *zócalo,* or **Plaza de Santo Domingo.** Two blocks farther are the **Plaza de San Diego** and the **Alameda.** The main drag connecting the plazas is **Galeana.** Note that it changes names nearly ten times; it is known as Guerrero near the Jardín del Sur and as Obregón, 19 de Febrero, Hidalgo, and Independencia farther north.

To get to the *zócalo* from the Estrella Roja station, exit to the left on Vázquez and make a right onto 2 de Mayo. Continue for two blocks and you'll run right into the southeast corner of the *zócalo.* From the Cristóbal Colón station, take a right on 2 de Mayo and walk three blocks before running into the plaza. *Rutas* (minibuses) heading to nearby cities and the *balnearios* usually gather in the Jardín del Sur and just northeast of the Alameda area. The main routes are along Obregón and Reforma.

Practical Information A small **tourist desk** is located on the ground floor of the Convento de San Diego, across from the Alameda. For **tourist help,** dial 91-800-90-392. **Cambio de Divisas Alameda,** Plaza Fuerte de Galeana 84 (tel. 2-53-53), just north of the Alameda, offers one of the best rates. **Banamex,** Galeana 33 (tel. 2-01-06), by the *cine,* has an **ATM. LADATELs** dot the *zócalo* area.

Cuautla has two main **bus stations,** both of which are best reached from Cuernavaca (via Estrella Roja) or Mexico City's Tasqueña station. The large **Cristóbal Colón** station (tel. 2-62-77), on 2 de Mayo at Reforma, serves Amecameca (every 20min. 9am-6pm, 6 pesos), Mexico City (every 15min. 6:30am-9pm, 1½hr., 25 pesos), Oaxaca (11:30pm, 8hr., 74 pesos), Tepoztlán (every 30min., 5 pesos), and Tlalmanalco (every 20min. 9am-6pm, 7.50 pesos). **Estrella Roja,** on Costeño at Vázquez, serves Cuernavaca (every 10min. 5am-8pm, 1½hr., 10 pesos), Mexico City (every 20min. 5am-6pm, 2hr., 23 pesos) via Oaxtepec (ask to be let off, 20min., 5 pesos), and Puebla (2 per day, 2hr., 17 pesos). **Farmacia Afil,** 2 de Mayo 13 (tel. 2-76-31), is just east of the *zócalo.* Medical consultations also available (open daily 9am-9pm). The **Red Cross** is at Calleja de Retirada 53 (tel. 2-21-95; open 24hr.). A nearby **hospital** is the **Sanitorio Aguilar Sánchez,** Constituyentes 180 (tel. 2-09-00). In an **emergency,** dial 06. The **police** (tel. 3-10-50 or 2-00-26) await at the Palacio Municipal on the *zócalo.* The **post office,** Ramírez Ferrera 4 (tel. 2-01-10), is open Mon.-Sat. 8am-7pm. **Postal Code:** 62740. **Telephone Code:** 735.

Accommodations and Food Cuautla's hotels offer clean, well-kept rooms for low prices to a largely Mexican clientele. Some places fill up and charge more on weekends, so try to book reservations during the week. At the **Hotel Jardines de Cuautla,** 2 de Mayo 94 (tel. 2-00-88), you'll find a relaxing yellow courtyard and a cute garden. Two small pools enable weary travelers to cool off. The bathrooms are clean and the beds somewhat soft (singles 60 pesos; doubles 90 pesos). **Hotel España,** 2 de Mayo 22 (tel. 2-21-86), is just east of the *zócalo.* The beautiful ivy-covered courtyard centers around somewhat small but well furnished rooms. Bathrooms sparkle, but hold off on those afternoon showers—there's limited hot water (singles 60-70 pesos; doubles 90-115 pesos).

Small eateries dot Galeana and the three plazas. **Tony & Tony's Pizzas,** on the southwest corner of the *zócalo,* can whip up some mean pasta dishes. Try the *spaghetti napolitano* for 13 pesos. **El Rincón del Abuelo** (tel. 2-04-86), with two locations in the *zócalo* and curious Scotch plaid tablecloths, serves up simple, tasty Mexican fare (breakfast 12–15 pesos, sandwiches 10 pesos; open daily 8am-10pm).

Sights and Entertainment Most visitors come to Cuautla not for the history but to catch some sun and soak in the springs of the nearby *balnearios* (spas). The **Centro Vacacional Oaxtepec** (tel. 6-01-01) is a *balneario* of Disneyesque proportions, well within a budget traveler's reach. Inside are over 20 giant pools with water

---

Twin Peaks

Overlooking Morelos and Puebla are two snow-capped volcanoes, **Popocatépetl** (5452m) and **Ixtaccíhuatl** (5282m), respectively the second- and third-largest peaks in the country. These magnificent mountains, which are open to both experienced climbers and less audacious backpackers, are shrouded in indigenous mythology. Legend has it that the warrior Popocatépetl (Smoking Mountain in Náhuatl) loved Ixtaccíhuatl (Sleeping Woman), the emperor's daughter. Once, when the warrior went off to battle, Ixtaccíhuatl heard erroneously that he had been killed; she subsequently died of lovesickness and grief. When Popo (as he was known to friends) learned of his lover's death, he built the two great mountains. On the northern one he placed her body, and on the southern one he stood vigil with a torch. Locals pay their respects to the supine, death-pale Ixtaccíhuatl on the mountain's snowy summit.

slides and palm trees, a lake for boating and fishing, and courts for nearly every sport. Connecting it all is a free shuttle service and a sky-tram *(teleférico)*. Under a huge geodesic dome-complex are the sulfur springs that give Oaxtepec its name. Restaurants and equipment rental facilities abound (resort open daily 8am-6pm; admission 20 pesos, seniors and children 10 pesos). To get there, catch a Oaxtepec *ruta* from the marketplace or Plaza del Sur (2.50 pesos) in Cuautla. *Rutas* returning to Cuautla pass by the main road in front of the resort.

Two *balnearios* within the city limits are worth mentioning. **Agua Hedionda** (Stinking Water; tel. 2-00-44) boasts five sulfur pools with natural water temperature of 32°C (90°F). As the name suggests, the sulfur here is strong—it may be a good idea to show up with a stuffy nose. Rumor has it that these waters can heal ulcers (open Fri.-Wed. 7am-6pm; admission 14 pesos, children 9 pesos). **El Almeal** (tel. 2-17-51), on Virginia Hernández, is more of a pool than a spring. However, it does offer campgrounds and sports facilities galore (admission 16 pesos, kids 8 pesos). *Rutas* run from the *centro* to each of the spas; catch one at the marketplace or along the Plaza de la Revolución del Sur.

Vestiges of Cuautla's revolutionary history are scattered throughout the *centro*. The **Jardín Revolución del Sur** holds both Emiliano Zapata's body and numerous monuments to his memory. Commanding center stage is a massive statue of Zapata on his legendary horse, with a hand on the shoulder of a peasant who looks up at him with admiration and gratitude. It was in Cuautla that Zapata drafted the Plan de Ayala, his program for the return of land from the landholders to the rightful hands of the peasants whose families, according to ancient documents, had originally owned it. Two blocks north is the **Plaza del Santo Domingo,** which serves as the town's *zócalo*. The **Iglesia de Santo Domingo,** on the east side of the plaza, was built in 1652 and served as a stronghold during the War for Independence. The southwest corner nearly hides the **Casa de Morelos,** an inconspicuous red building where General Morelos once stayed when organizing the struggle for freedom in the south. The museum inside is poorly kept but does hold several interesting revolutionary relics (open Tues.-Sun. 10am-3pm). Farther north is the **Plaza de San Diego,** named for the nearby **Iglesia** and **Convento de San Diego.** The War for Independence and José María Morelos are the objects of veneration. The convent on the west side doubles as a museum, housing flags and weapons from both wars (open Tues.-Sun. 9am-5pm; free). Inside, the **Casa de la Cultura** hosts a weekly speaking series and provides limited tourist information. Outside, in front of the movie theater, a small statue of Morelos honors the 1812 battle in the Alameda.

■ Near Cuautla

POPOCATÉPETL AND IXTACCÍHUATL

Veiled in Aztec mythology, the snow-capped **Popocatépetl** (Smoking Mountain) and **Ixtaccíhuatl** (Sleeping Woman) overlook the state of Morelos and nearby Puebla. Both peaks can be climbed to a small degree on well marked tourist trails; tourist organizations offer group trips to the very tops of the peaks. To get to Popocatépetl, take a bus to Amecameca (every 15min., 1½hr., 6 pesos) from Cuautla's Cristóbal Colón bus station. In Amecameca, minibus drivers will charge you a hefty sum for the trip to Tlamacas, a small village at the base of the mountain, although the minibuses from Amecameca generally do not operate on weekends. From here, another *pesero* runs to the beginning of the trail. The small **Tlamacas Lodge** provides dorm-style housing and somewhat pricey meals in its cafeteria. The lodge organizes assaults on the mountains and rents equipment at about 120 pesos per person. To reach Ixtaccíhuatl, take a bus to Tlalmanalco (every 20min., 2hr., 7.50 pesos) from Cuautla's Cristóbal Colón bus station. From here, a *pesero* runs to San Rafael, which rests at the base of Ixtaccíhuatl. Alternatively, join one of the trips that leaves from the Tlamacas Lodge.

Before beginning your climb, register at the **Club Socorro Alpino** (Alpine Assistance Club) and inform them of your expected return date. Realize that both mountains can be very dangerous and that it is unwise to climb alone or without proper equipment. Travelers have lost their lives due to inclement weather, so inquire about the current conditions before making plans, and always bring both warm clothes and raingear.

TLAXCALA

■ Tlaxcala

It's hard to believe that Tlaxcala (pop. 600,000) was not designed by Disney architects. Like its theme park counterpart, downtown Tlaxcala draws in visitors with reassuring aesthetics and meticulously planned structures. No building on the *zócalo* exceeds two stories, and many come with cornices or curlicues at the corners. Taken together, the buildings create a symphony in shades of deep orange and red that harmonizes with the well manicured green of the main plaza. Trickling fountains add to the mirthful music.

The people of Tlaxcala have a long history of welcoming foreigners. After being colonized by the Aztecs, the people of the Tlaxcalan Federation willingly allied themselves with Cortés and demonstrated such fierce loyalty in battle that they were recognized by Charles V. Today, *tlaxcalteños* limit their violent urges to the raising of bulls for fights throughout Mexico. Frequent regional fairs showcase artisans who weave *sarapes* or prepare dishes of maize. The city is also a useful base for visiting the archaeological sites of **Cacaxtla** and **Xochitécatl,** but the allure of cafés along the *zócalo* and safe, tree-lined streets are reason enough for weekenders to seek refuge in Tlaxcala from the congestion of the D.F. or Puebla.

ORIENTATION

Most services can be found in and around **Plaza de la Constitución,** the *zócalo,* and **Plaza Xicoténcatl,** diagonally adjacent to it. You'll know you're there when you see the blue-and-white tiled dome of the orange **Parroquia de San José.** To get there from the bus station, exit through the glass doors to a swarm of idling *colectivos* waiting. Those facing to the right go to the downtown area, then to the market, and finally to the hotel district on the northern edge of the city (1.50 pesos). To return to the bus station from the city center, take a "Central" *colectivo* from the market at 20 de Noviembre and Alonso Escalona, or flag it down behind San José at 20 de Noviembre and 1 de Mayo.

Facing the back of the church, the street behind you is **20 de Noviembre;** the street on the left is **Lardizábal.** Going around the church to the right will bring the entrance to the *zócalo* into view. The **Palacio de Gobierno** takes up the whole north side of the *zócalo* and will be on your left. At the end of the Palacio del Gobierno, at the corner of the *zócalo,* **Av. Benito Juárez** peels off to the left. After four blocks, Juárez veers right and becomes **Av. Guillermo Valle.** Several hotels are on the northern edge of town, where Guillermo Valle angles to the right and becomes **Blvd. Revolución.** To get there, catch a "Santa Ana" *colectivo* at 20 de Noviembre, three blocks from the *zócalo,* behind San José (1.50 pesos); walking time from the *zócalo* is about 40 minutes.

PRACTICAL INFORMATION

Tourist Office: Av. Benito Juárez 18 (tel. 2-00-27), at the intersection with Lardizábal. The *colectivo* from the bus station will drop you off on 20 de Nov. behind San José. A goldmine of information from a friendly, English-speaking staff.

Saturdays and Sundays they sponsor organized tours of the most popular sites (15 pesos). Open Mon.-Fri. 9am-7pm, Sat.-Sun. and holidays 10am-6pm.

Currency Exchange: Banamex, Plaza Xicoténcatl 8 (tel. 2-31-44) and **Banca Serfín,** Av. Independencia 4 (tel. 2-08-42), both in Plaza Xicoténcatl, have 24-hr. **ATMs.** Open Mon.-Fri. 9am-2pm. Nearby **Centro de Cambio Tlaxcala** (tel. 2-90-85), Av. Independencia at the corner of Calle Guerrero, buys or sells dollars in cash, money order, or travelers' checks. Open Mon.-Fri. 9am-4pm.

Telephones: LADATELs under the arches along the *zócalo*. Coin-operated phones in front of and behind **Parroquia de San José,** northwest of the *zócalo*.

Telegram: Telecomm, Porfirio Díaz 6 (tel. 2-00-47), behind the post office.

Buses: From the **Central Camionera, Autotransportes Tlaxcala** (tel. 2-02-17) runs to Mexico City (every 30min. 6am-8:30pm, 2hr., 32 pesos) and to Veracruz, stopping in Xalapa (10:30am and 3:30pm, 6hr., 44 pesos). **Autotransportes México-Texcoco** has similar first-class service to Mexico City. **Flecha Azul** buses run to Puebla (every 5min. 5:45am-10pm, 45min., 5 pesos).

Bookstore: Tendajón de Tlaxcala, Portal Hidalgo 6 (tel. 2-00-14 ext. 24), in the *zócalo*, sells some books in English. Open Tues.-Sun. 11am-8pm.

Cultural Center: Palacio de la Cultura, Av. Benito Juárez 62 (tel. 2-39-69), four blocks from the *zócalo* at the corner of Av. Justo Sierra. Announces and sometimes stages cultural events all over Tlaxcala. Open daily 9am-7pm.

Markets: The entire street of **Alonso Escalona** teems with *mercado* activity. From San José, cross to Lira y Ortega and walk three blocks keeping the church behind you. The vendors spill outside onto Sánchez Piedras (open daily 8am-8pm). **Gigante** is a behemoth of a supermarket on Blvd. Guillermo Valle, in the shopping center on the corner of Arévalo Vera. Open daily 8am-8pm.

Laundromat: Lavandería de Autoservicio Acuario, Lira y Ortega 3 (tel. 1-62-04). Go north from the *zócalo*, make an immediate left on Lardizábal, then take the first right on Lira y Ortega. Self-service 14 pesos, full service 15 pesos, one-hr. service with home delivery 30 pesos. Open Mon.-Sat. 9:30am-7:30pm.

Red Cross: Allende Nte. 48 (tel. 2-09-20). Go two blocks behind San José to Av. Ignacio Allende, then turn left and continue 1½ blocks past Muñoz Camargo. 24-hr. walk-in emergency service. No English spoken.

Pharmacies: Farmacia Ocotlán (tel. 2-04-50), Av. Juárez on the corner of Guridi y Alcocer. Open 24hr.

Hospital: Hospital General, Jardín de la Corregidora 1 (tel. 2-00-30, 2-03-57, 2-35-55), 4½ blocks from the *zócalo* down Av. Muñoz Camargo past the post office. English spoken. Open 24hr. **IMSS** (tel. 2-34-00 and 2-34-22), Blvd. Guillermo Valle, across the street from the stadium. Take Av. Juárez from the *zócalo* until it turns into Blvd. G. Valle; the hospital is right after the Nestlé factory. Open 24hr.

Police: (tel. 2-10-79, 2-07-35), on Av. Lardizábal one block past the tourist office, at the corner with Calle Xicoténcatl. Open daily 24hr.

Post Office: Plaza de la Constitución 20 (tel. 2-00-04), on the corner with Av. Muñoz Camargo. Open Mon.-Fri. 8am-8pm, Sat. 9am-1pm. **Postal Code:** 90000.

Telephone Code: 246.

ACCOMMODATIONS

There are few good budget accommodations in Tlaxcala. Establishments are either downtown, near most sights and services, or in the hotel district on the northern edge of the city accessible via the "Santa Ana" *colectivo*.

Hotel Mansión Xicoténcatl, Av. Juárez 15 (tel. 2-19-00). Diagonally across from the tourist office, this hotel lives up to its billing as a "mansion." With uncoordinated carpets, bedspreads, paint, and tiles, the ample rooms produce a cacophony of colors that nonetheless wrap the guest in the security of a crazy quilt. Singles with two beds 55 pesos. Doubles 65 pesos.

Posada Mary, Xicoténcatl 19. From the tourist office, head away from the church on Lardizábal and take the first left; it's a ½ block away on the right. Their eight small, moderately clean rooms are undergoing a slow but needed renovation. A restaurant is connected to the hotel. Ring bell persistently if locked. Private baths with hot water. Singles 40 pesos. Doubles 55 pesos.

Hotel Plaza Tlaxcala, Blvd. Revolución 6 (tel. 2-78-52). Take the "Santa Ana" *colectivo* from the bus station or market (1.50 pesos). Recently renovated rooms in a pleasant 3-story hotel with a small garden and play area. Private bath with hot water, wall-to-wall carpeting, and cable TV. Singles 80 pesos. Doubles 90 pesos.

FOOD

Regional specialties include *pollo en xoma* (chicken stuffed with fruits and other meats), *barbacoa en mixiote* (meat cooked in *maguey* leaves), and *pulque,* an alcoholic drink made from the *maguey* plant. You can either drink *pulque* straight, eat it with your chicken, or try *pulque verde,* a drink made with honeywater, *yerba buena* (spearmint), and lemon juice. The touristy restaurants on the *zócalo* are cheaper on weekday afternoons, when they cater to the lunch crowd rather than to tourists. Beware of *"comida típica"*—it is often a pricey journey into culinary mediocrity. There are good, inexpensive places along Av. Juárez, including the **market** on 20 de Noviembre at Alonso Escalona.

El 5° Sol (tel. 2-49-28), on Av. Juárez diagonally across from the tourist office. A popular vegetarian joint full of tempting fruits to match the orange walls outside. Scrumptious breakfasts bring sunshine to the table in the form of freshly-squeezed orange juice, yogurt, eggs, and coffee (14-18 pesos). Cheese or soybeef *tortas* 5-7 pesos; specialty cure-all juices 6 pesos. Open Mon.-Sat. 8am-8pm.

Los Portales Restaurant-Bar, Plaza Constitución 8 (tel. 2-54-19), on the side of the *zócalo* under the arches. Dapper waiters serve food *al fresco. Antojitos* 8-14 pesos, spaghetti 15-17 pesos, sandwiches 10-16 pesos, but the main attraction is the Parisian-café ambience. Open Mon.-Fri. 7am-11pm, Sat.-Sun. 24hr.

Mesón del Beso (tel. 2-30-82), Av. Guerrero on the corner of Av. Porfirio Díaz. Take Av. Independencia; at the bullring turn right onto Av. Guerrero. Fewer kisses than tacos, the sole item on the menu. The friendly chef prepares them with every imaginable filling for 12 pesos. Open daily 11am-11pm.

SIGHTS

On the north side of the *zócalo*, the 16th-century **Palacio de Gobierno** houses murals that illustrate the rich history of the city and the country with the vivid colors of Van Gogh and the controlled chaos of *Where's Waldo* (open daily 8am-8pm). On the northwest corner of the *zócalo* stands the **Palacio de la Justicia,** which was originally built in the 16th century as the Capilla Real de Indias to honor the Tlaxcaltecas who had served as Cortés's allies in the conquest of the Aztecs. Just beyond the northwest corner of the *zócalo* stands the 17th-century Baroque **Parroquia de San José.** While its interior is unremarkable, its peach-orange exterior and *mudéjar*-tiled dome gracefully punctuate the Tlaxcala sky. Cutting back along the *zócalo* under the arches and exiting its corner, you come to the **Plaza Xicoténcatl.** On weekends, the plaza is sometimes inhabited by musicians or a small fair.

At the opposite corner of the *zócalo,* a cobblestone way leads about 200m up a small hill to the cathedral, the **Ex-Convento Franciscano de la Asunción,** one of the most beautiful structures in 16th century New Spain. *Mudéjar* woodwork and gilded eight-pointed stars accent the dark wooden rafters of the choir loft and ceiling. In the chapel at the end of the nave and on the right stands the stone baptismal font purportedly used to baptize the leaders of the Tlaxcalan federation when they allied themselves with Cortés. Next door to the church is the **Museo Regional de Tlaxcala** (tel. 2-02-62), which studies pre-Hispanic and colonial cultures (open Tues.-Sun. 10am-5pm; admission 7 pesos, free Sun. and holidays).

The Ex-Convento shares the colonial limelight with the **Basílica de la Virgen de Ocotlán,** one of the masterpieces of the late Baroque Mexican style known as Churrigueresque. To get there, take an "Ocotlán" *colectivo* (1.50 pesos). It stops right in front of the church, where it waits to go back into town. To hike there, take a right on Av. Benito Juárez, head one block past the tourist office, and hang another right on Guridi y Alcocer. When the road forks, follow it up the hill to the left. The road climbs to the small **Capilla del Pocito de Agua Santa,** where it becomes a cobblestone street with a staircase alongside; the stairs lead directly to the square of the church. There, you'll be blinded by the brilliant white stucco façade, populated by figures of militant archangels and capped by a conch shell in stucco along its upper edge. The maritime theme is repeated in the interior, where golden conch shells top the pilasters and another giant shell frames the end of the nave. Its lines lead the eye up to the presbyter, which explodes in Churrigueresque splendor. The Virgin's *camarín* is a single piece that took 25 years to make. She allegedly appeared on this site in 1541, and is now the patroness of Tlaxcala.

On the other side of town is the **Museo de Artes y Tradiciones Populares** (tel. and fax 2-23-37), where craftspersons from around the region demonstrate how they ply their trades. The exhibits include a working indigenous steam bath (not for use by visitors), a loom, a demonstration of how *pulque* is made, and an exhibit of traditional carnival masks with eyes that blink. Many of these items can be bought at substantially inflated prices from the adjoining gift shop or from the artists themselves. To get there, go west on Lardizábal until it ends at Blvd. Mariano Sánchez, about four blocks from the tourist office. The museum is across the street on the left (open Tues.-Sun. 10am-6pm; admission 6 pesos, students 4 pesos).

For more indigenous beauty without the tourist packaging, the **Jardín Botánico de Tizatlán** (tel. 2-65-46) delivers Mexican plants in an other-wordly setting. From the hotel district on Blvd. Revolución, turn left at Camino Real before the brick bridge passes over the road. No bikes, balls, radios, or beer are allowed in this pastoral paradise. The rocky paths meander across a stagnant creek to reveal a tucked-away greenhouse (open daily 6am-11pm; free).

ENTERTAINMENT

The influx of tourists has made Tlaxcala quite a nightspot—at least on weekends. **Royal Adler's Disco** at the Hotel Jeroc, Blvd. Revolución 4 (tel. 2-14-99), plays current hits (cover 30 pesos; open Wed.-Sat. 9pm-3am). Other places to dance are **Armando's,** at Blvd. Independencia 60 (tel. 2-49-88; cover 20 pesos, 15 pesos drink minimum; open Thurs.-Sat. 9pm-3am). **Budweiser,** Av. Mariano Sánchez 44 (tel. 2-62-07), is two blocks from San José, parallel to Av. 20 de Noviembre (cover 20 pesos, open Thurs.-Sat. 9pm-3am). On weekdays, finding entertainment becomes a more difficult task, since much of the city shuts down by 10:30pm. Check the tourist office for concerts. **Cinevas** (tel. 2-35-44), at Guillermo Valle 113, and **Cinema Tlaxcala,** on the south side of the *zócalo* across the street from the post office (tel. 2-19-62), show first-run American movies (10 pesos). It's fairly safe to walk the streets at night in Tlaxcala. If you do feel uncomfortable walking downtown after dark, hail one of the cabs lined up in front of San José church.

■ Near Tlaxcala

CACAXTLA AND XOCHITÉCATL

The best preserved and best presented of the archaeological sites in the state are the hilltop ruins of **Cacaxtla,** 19km southwest of Tlaxcala. The culture that once dominated the southwest corner of Tlaxcala State and most of the Puebla Valley built and expanded the city between 600 and 750 CE. Cacaxtla was abandoned by 1000 CE, and its inhabitants were finally driven from the area by Toltec-Chichimec invaders in 1168. The approach to the site is marked by the walls and moats that protected the Olmec-Xicalancan inhabitants from their enemies. Excavation began at Cacaxtla in 1975, and the area is now reconstructed as the ceremonial center it once was.

Two discoveries distinguish this site from others. One is a **latticework window** on the west side, opposite from the entrance. The window is the only one of its kind in any of Mexico's archaeological sites. It was produced by surrounding a latticework of twigs and branches with mud and stucco. Cacaxtla's other chief attraction is a series of murals scattered about the site, considered some of the best preserved pre-Hispanic paintings in Mesoamerica. The largest of them, the **Battle Mural,** depicts a historical-mythological battle in which an army dressed in jaguar skins crushes the skulls of an army dressed as birds. It is believed to form part of the culture's foundational mythology.

Beyond the entrance on the right is a museum that showcases some of the ceramics and fertility figures unearthed here. From the small museum, the dirt path leads towards the pyramid. Just past a small secondary pyramid is the staircase that goes up to the site by way of the **Gran Basamento,** the thick platform upon which the center was built. Once upstairs, visitors move clockwise around the excavations of ceremonial courtyards, temples, tombs, and what appears to have been a palace. Underneath the ruins, archaeologists have found the remains of two hundred children, sacrificed during the final stages of construction.

From the Battle Mural, the official circuit takes you to an area whose bland name, **Building A,** belies its beauty. Five of the site's murals stand together, united by color and imagery into a symbolic unit. The leftmost mural depicts the god Quetzalcóatl and a human figure in jaguar skins, while the rightmost one shows a bird-man surrounded by symbols of rain god Tlaloc. Guides are available for 30 pesos per person, with reduced rates for large groups, but few speak English (open Tues.-Sun. 10am-4:30pm; admission 14 pesos; videocamera 25 pesos; free Sun.).

A ticket also offers admission to **Xochitécatl,** the pyramid on the adjacent hill. This site is not as well understood or labeled as Cacaxtla. No *colectivo* makes the 4km trip from one site to the other. Would-be Indiana Joneses must walk down the curvy road from Cacaxtla to San Martín where they can take a "San Martín" bus (1.50 pesos), get off at the intersection with San Rafael, and walk about 200m to the entrance of the site.

Getting There: From Tlaxcala, *colectivos* labeled "Texoloc-Tlaxcala" and buses marked "Nativitas" leave from the bus plaza on 20 de Noviembre next to the market or along 20 de Noviembre behind San José. Ask whether the bus goes to Cacaxtla. Some go to the town San Miguel del Milagro (San Miguelito) at the base of the site; others travel past the main entrance (40min., 4.50 pesos). If dropped off in the town, walk up the windy road, following the signs to the entrance. To return to Tlaxcala, walk downhill from the ticket booth and turn right to go down to San Martín. *Colectivos* going right go to Xochitécatl; across the street "Tlaxcala" *colectivos* return to the bus plaza next to the market (4.50 pesos).

PUEBLA

■ Puebla

The angels in Puebla de los Ángeles came from a dream that Don Julian Garcés, the Bishop of Tlaxcala, once had. In the vision, he saw angels descend from the sky, plant stakes, and stretch cords for the streets of a new city. While hiking the next day, the Bishop recognized the land of his dreams and immediately erected the altar from which Fray Toribiode Benavente delivered Mexico's first Catholic mass in 1531. The city's religious life grew to accommodate a plethora of churches, which now serve as both architectural attractions and urban sanctuaries.

As the city grows to nearly two million inhabitants, Poblanos are careful not to lose their identity. Besides the trademark churches, the city has an exquisite culinary tradition that includes delicious *dulces* (candies) and *mole poblano,* a thick, dark sauce made with chocolate and chiles among many, many ingredients and typically served over chicken, turkey, or enchiladas. While the angels may choke on the exhaust fumes and balk at the Kentucky Fried Chicken, they still smile down on amorous couples in the *zócalo*, foreign students exercising their new-found language skills at the discos, and citizens seeking redress from the state bureaucracy.

ORIENTATION

Puebla, capital of the state of the same name, is connected through an extensive highway network to Mexico City (125km northwest along Rte. 150), Oaxaca (Rtes. 190, 125, or 131), Tlaxcala (Rte. 119), Veracruz (Rte. 150), and countless other cities. All **bus** companies operate out of the CAPU (Central de Autobuses Puebla) on Blvd. Norte and Tlaxcala, in the northwest corner of the city.

The *avenidas* and *calles* of Puebla form a near-perfect grid, with the northwest corner of the *zócalo* in the center. Everything changes names at that point: the main north-south street is called **5 de Mayo** north of it and **16 de Septiembre** south of it; the main east-west drag is **Avenida Reforma** to the west, and **Avenida Máximo Ávila Camacho** to the east. *Avenidas* run east-west and are designated either *Poniente* (*Pte.*, west) or *Oriente* (*Ote.*, east), depending on where they lie with respect to that intersection. Similarly, *calles* run north-south and are labeled *Norte* or *Sur* with respect to the critical point. Numerical addresses correspond to the order of the block away from the city center. For example, 4 Ote. 212 is located on the second block of the street, in the section bounded by Calle 2 Norte and Calle 4 Norte. On the following block away from the center, addresses will be in the 400s.

Official yellow **taxis** labeled *taxis controlados* will take you to the *zócalo* from the bus station for 12 pesos, 14 pesos at night. If traveling with an independent *taxista*, set a price before getting in and don't be shy about haggling. Cabs from the train station to the *zócalo* run about 8 pesos. **Municipal buses** and *micros* or *combis,* white Volkswagen vans that operate like buses, cost 1.50 pesos. Anything labeled "Centro" should take you close to the *zócalo*. On Calle 9 Nte.-Sur you can catch buses marked "CAPU" to the bus station, or marked *"Estación Nueva Popular"* to the train station.

PRACTICAL INFORMATION

Tourist Offices: State Office, Av. 5 Ote. 3 (tel. 46-12-85 or 46-20-44), facing the cathedral's southern side, one block from the *zócalo*. Follow the blue signs with a white question mark to enjoy free maps, a monthly guide to cultural events in Puebla, and an interactive bilingual video guide to cities all over Mexico. Open Mon.-Sat. 9am-8:30pm, Sun. 9am-2pm. There is also a booth at the bus station.

Currency Exchange: Banks line Av. Reforma and Av. 16 de Septiembre around the *centro*. **Bital,** Reforma 126 (tel. 46-40-44) is blessed with a 24-hr. ATM. *Casas de cambio* offer slightly better rates and cluster in the Zona Esmeralda along Av. Juárez further away from the *zócalo*. Try **Casa de Cambio Puebla,** Av. 29 Sur. 316-A (tel. 48-01-99), at Juárez. Open Mon.-Fri. 9am-6pm.

American Express: Díaz Ordaz 6A Sur #2914, Suite 301 (tel. 40-30-18, 40-33-08, or 40-32-85), in the Plaza Dorada. Best bet for cashing and replacing AmEx checks; holds client mail for 10 days. Open Mon.-Fri. 9am-6pm.

Telephones: LADATELs are easy to find along 5 de Mayo and around the *zócalo*.

Telegrams: Telecomm, 16 de Septiembre 504 (tel. 32-17-79), just south of the post office. Open Mon.-Fri. 9am-9pm, Sat. 9am-5pm; for **money orders** Mon.-Fri. 9am-5:30pm, Sat. 9am-noon.

Airport: (tel. 32-00-32), in Huejotzingo, 22km away. Regional airlines fly to Acapulco, Cancún, Guadalajara, León, Mexico City, Monterrey, Oaxaca, and Tijuana.

Buses: CAPU (Central de Autobuses Puebla; tel. 49-72-11), at the crossroads of Blvd. Norte and Tlaxcala, in the northwest corner of the city. **ADO** (tel. 30-40-00), first-class to Cancún (11:45am, 24hr., 350 pesos), Jalapa (every 2 hr. 6:45am-9:15pm, 3hr., 40 pesos), Mérida (9:05pm, 22hr., 296 pesos), Mexico City (Tues.-Thurs. every 10 min., Fri.-Mon. every 5 min. 5am-mindnight, 2hr., 27 pesos), Oaxaca (5 per day, 8hr., 88 pesos), Veracruz (7 per day, 4½hr., 72 pesos), and many

Puebla

Puebla

Hotel Imperial, 1
Hotel Teresita, 2
Hotel Victoria, 3
Restaurant El Vegetariano, 4

N

TO FORTS

Red
Cross ✛ Oriente

Av. 20 Oriente
Av. 18 Oriente
Av. 16 Oriente
Av. 16 Oriente
Av. 12 Oriente
Av. 8 Oriente
Av. 4 Oriente
Av. 2 Oriente

Mercado el Alto Garibaldi

Templo de San Francisco

Blvd. Héroes del 5 de Mayo

Av. 5 Oriente

Av. 7 Oriente

Calle 6 Norte

Teatro Principal

Av. 6 Oriente
Museo de Alfeñique

Mercado el Parián

Av. 2 Oriente

Av. Maximino Avila Camacho

Av. 3 Oriente

Av. 5 Oriente

Calle 4 Norte

Av. 16 Oriente
Av. 14 Oriente
Av. 12 Oriente
Av. 10 Oriente
Av. 8 Oriente
Casa de Aquiles Serdán
Av. 4 Oriente

Iglesia de la Compañía

Casa de Cultura and Biblioteca Palafoxiana

Museo Amparo

Calle 2 Sur

Zócalo

Catedral

Av. 9 Oriente

Exconvento de Santa Mónica

Av. 18 Ote.

5 de Mayo

Iglesia de Santo Domingo

La Casa de los Muñecos

16 de Septiembre

Calle 3 Norte

La Cocina de Santa Rosa

Av. 10 Poniente
Av. 8 Poniente

Mercado Victoria

Museo Bello

Calle 3 Sur

Calle 5 Norte

Calle 5 Sur

Av. 12 Poniente

Av. 6 Poniente

Calle 7 Norte

TO TRAIN STATION

TO CAPU (Bus Station)

Av. 16 Poniente
Av. 14 Poniente
Av. 12 Poniente

Calle 9 Norte

Av. Reforma

Av. 3 Poniente
Av. 5 Poniente
Hospital ✛
Av. 7 Poniente
Av. 9 Poniente

Calle 11 Norte

Av. 4 Poniente
Av. 2 Poniente

Calle 11 Sur

Paseo Bravo

TO AIRPORT

other destinations. **Cristóbal Colón** (tel. 49-75-68),to Huatulco (9:45pm, 13hr., 203 pesos), Puerto Escondido (9:45pm, 14hr., 225 pesos), and Tehuantepec (9:45pm, 14½hr., 171 pesos). **Estrella Roja** (tel. 49-70-99), first-class to Mexico City (every 20min. 5am-9pm, 2hr., 32 pesos). **Estrella Blanca** (tel. 40-76-96), first-class to Acapulco (5 per day, 7hr., 150 pesos); Chilpancingo (10:30am and 12:30pm, 6hr., 111 pesos), and Taxco (8am, 5hr., 60 pesos). **Estrella de Oro** (tel. 46-14-62), to Cuernavaca (every hr. 6am-8pm, 3¼hr., 28 pesos). **Flecha Azul** (tel. 49-73-55) to Tlaxcala (every 10min. 4:40am-10pm, 45min., 5 pesos).

Trains: Estación La Unión, more commonly known as **Estación Nueva** (tel. 20-16-64 for ticket information, 20-02-79 for general information), Av. 70 Pte. and Calle 9 Nte. Just about the only tolerable route is to Oaxaca (second-class 6am and midnight, 22 pesos; first-class midnight, 40 pesos; both take 12-13hr.).

Markets: Mercados along 5 de Mayo, one block north of the *zócalo,* and along Av. 10 Poniente. If you seek A/C and order, head for **Gigante,** at 4 Nte. and Blvd. Héroes del 5 de Mayo, to the north of the Templo de San Francisco. Open daily 9am-9pm. Also try **Comercial Mexicana,** Calle 5 Sur and Av. 19 Pte., by the large pelican sign. Open daily 8am-10pm.

English Bookstore: Sanborn's, Av. 2 Ote. 6 (tel. 42-39-61). Newsmagazines and novels of the check-out stand variety. Open daily 7am-1am.

Laundromat: Lavandería Roly, Calle 7 Nte. 404 (tel. 32-93-07). Full service 7 pesos per kg. Open Mon.-Sat. 8am-8pm, Sun. 8am-1pm.

Red Cross: (tel. 35-80-40) 20 Ote. and 10 Nte. 24-hr. ambulance service.

Pharmacies: Farmacias del Ahorro (tel. 31-33-83), on the corner of Av. 2 Ote. and Calle 2 Nte. Open daily 7am-11pm. **Sanborn's** also has a pharmacy where some English is spoken. Open Mon.-Fri. 7am-11pm, Sat.-Sun. 7am-1pm.

Hospital: Hospital UPAEP, Av. 5 Pte. 715 (tel. 46-60-99 and 32-91-51). **Hospital Universitario** (tel. 43-13-77), Calle 13 Sur at Av. 25 Pte., 10 blocks south and 7 blocks west of the *zócalo.* 24-hr. emergency service. Some English spoken.

Emergency: Dial 06. Also try the **Policía Auxiliar** (tel. 88-18-63). Open 24hr.

Police: Dirección de Policía (tel. 32-22-23 or 32-2-22), 9 Ote. and 16 Sur.

Post Office: (tel. 42-64-48), 16 de Septiembre at Av. 5 Ote. one block south of the cathedral, in the same building as the state tourist office. Open Mon.-Fri. 8am-8pm, Sat. 9am-1pm. Northern office, Av. 2 Ote. 411, on the 2nd floor. Open Mon.-Fri. 8am-7pm, Sat. 9am-noon. The two branches have separate *Lista de Correos,* so make sure you know where your mail awaits. **Postal Code:** 72000.

Telephone code: 22.

ACCOMMODATIONS

Puebla is well stocked with budget hotels. It's a good idea to ask to see your room first; same-priced rooms can vary widely in their size and decor. Hot water availability varies from hotel to hotel.

Hotel Imperial, Av. 4 Ote. 212 (tel. 42-49-80; fax 46-38-25). On the expensive side, but oh, the amenities! Telephone and TV in all rooms, 24-hr. hot water supply, workout area, laundry service, pool table, and a Hershey's kiss on your pillow every night. Breakfast included. A 30% discount for proud *Let's Go* owners makes the Imperial's luxury more affordable. 15% discount for groups with over 10 people. Singles 108 pesos. Doubles 106 pesos.

Hotel Teresita, Av. 3 Pte. 309 (tel. 32-70-72), two blocks west of the Cathedral. Ask for a remodeled room and you'll get carpeting, television, and a refreshingly unlumpy bed. There is 24-hr. hot water in the sleek bathrooms, but not much space in the room to perform a dance celebrating the discovery of this budget pleaser. Singles 50 pesos. Doubles 70 pesos, with all the amenities 85 pesos.

Hotel Victoria, Av. 3 Pte. 306 (tel. 32-89-92), diagonally across from Hotel Teresita. Fluorescent lights illuminate the mismatched furniture in the large rooms. Tile floors and sandwich bags tied to the shower heads lend an institutional feel. After 10pm ring bell to enter. Singles 50 pesos. Doubles 60-70 pesos.

Hotel Cabrera de Puebla, Av. 10 Ote 6 (tel. 42-13-04). The entrance to the hotel is through a glass-enclosed alley between two stores and up a staircase. Green paint and copious plants make you feel like you're on a nature retreat. Rooms all have private baths and 24-hr. hot water, rotary phones that would remind your grandmother of her childhood, and towels folded in contrived, vaguely swan-like shapes on the bed. Singles 100 pesos. Doubles 150 pesos. Add 10 pesos for TV. Cash only.

FOOD

If you're going to splurge in one town, Puebla is the place to do it. Be sure to try the famous *mole poblano*; this heavenly dish is a mainstay on nearly every menu in town. Popular desserts are *yemas reales* (candied egg yolk), *camote poblano* (sweet potato), and a variety of almond-based sweets. Many restaurants line the streets near the *zócalo*; as always, for truly cheap eats the **mercados** are the way to go. A homey meal at the **Mercado San Francisco del Alto Garibaldi,** at Av. 14 Ote, between Calles 12 and 14 Nte., goes for only 5-15 pesos (open daily 7am-3am).

Restaurant El Vegetariano, Av. 3 Pte. 525 (tel. 46-54-62). Popular in a city of carnivores for one very good reason—terrific food. Try the always tasty *comida corrida* (14 pesos), or opt for meatless *antojitos* (10 pesos). Their *energética,* a plateful of tropical fruits topped with yogurt and their very own granola, is an unbridled breakfast joy (11 pesos). Open daily 7:30am-9pm. The same people operate **La Zanahoria,** Av. Juárez 2104, in the Zona Esmeralda.

Puente de Ovando, Av. 3 Ote. 1008 (tel. 46-10-44). Head east from the southeast corner of the *zócalo;* it's just across Blvd. Héroes 5 de Mayo, on the left. The *cafetería* on the first floor serves *poblano* classics in an enchanted garden setting. The sounds of the trickling fountain are almost as sweet as their excellent *mole poblano* (21 pesos). Soups (12-15 pesos) and meat entrees (28-42 pesos) in the pricier restaurant upstairs. Café and bar open daily 8am-11:30pm.

Super Tortas Puebla, Av. 3 Pte. 317. Hordes of Mexicans come here to indulge in the country's favorite lunchtime tradition, the *torta* (6-7 pesos). For a nostalgic dining experience, savor yours in the back room near a pastel-colored shrine to Marilyn Monroe. Open daily 9am-10:30pm.

Restaurant El Cazador, Av. 3 Pte. 147 (tel. 32-76-26), one block west of the *zócalo*'s southwest corner. Meats galore, as the name "The Hunter" suggests: *manitas rebosadas* (muffled pig hands), *sesos empanizadas* (breaded brains), and *riñones a la Mexicana* (Mexican-style kidneys—the organ, not the bean). Five-course *comida corrida* 16 pesos (1-5pm). Open daily 8am-10pm.

SIGHTS

Historic Puebla is a sightseer's paradise—which is, perhaps, the reason why busloads of Mexican students and *norteamericanos* from nearby language schools file into the *zócalo* every weekend, cameras in hand. Most sights are within walking distance of the city center. If you have only a short time in Puebla, the **Museo Amparo, Capilla del Rosario,** and **Casa de Aquiles Serdán** should top your list. Churches close

How to Make a Mesoamerican Quilt

Inside the white-washed **Iglesia del Espíritu Santo,** Camacho at Calle 4 Sur, is the tomb of the princess Mirrah, *la china poblana.* According to legend, this Indian noblewoman was abducted by pirates from China and brought to New Spain, where her captors sold her into servitude in 1620. The princess resigned herself to her fate, adopting Catholicism and a new name—Catarina de San Juan. She never forgot her blue blood, however, and distinguished herself from other *poblanas* by wearing elaborately embroidered dresses. By her death in 1668 at age 80, she had gained the town's appreciation by teaching many women to sew in the unique, multi-hued style that has been characteristic of the state ever since. Today, the *china* stands for *poblana* identity, strength, and beauty—an icon comparable to the Southern Belle.

between 2 and 4pm; shorts are usually acceptable. Museums often give 50% discounts to students with ID.

Near the Zócalo

In Puebla, modernity is tempered by many pre-18th-century architectural elements. The oldest buildings in town date from the 16th century and are notable for their Romanesque porches and smooth columns. While few original 16th-century edifices still stand, some later buildings on the west and north ends of the zócalo consciously attempt to imitate their style.

Puebla boasts over 100 churches. Gothic, classical, and even Baroque, many of them were built during the 17th century using oddly-shaped red bricks and carefully painted *azulejos de talavera* (celebrated *mudéjar*-style Puebla tiles). For a prime example, head to the **Casa de los Muñecos** (House of the Dolls; tel. 46-28-99) at the zócalo's northeast corner at Calle 2 Nte. Named for the *talavera* figures that populate the house, the building is a remarkable example of artistic spite: legend has it that the so-called "dolls" are actually caricatures of the architect's enemies.

The **Catedral Basílica de Puebla,** Av. 3 Ote. 302 at 5 de Mayo, stands adjacent to the zócalo. It was entirely constructed by *indígena* laborers working under Spanish direction between 1575 and 1649. Music sometimes echoes from the cathedral's two organs (one is 400 years old) and from the 19 bells of the bell tower. The interior of the cathedral gets its zing from chandeliers, gold plating, and Pedro Muñoz's fine woodwork on the choir stalls on the pulpit's periphery. At 72m high, the cathedral is the tallest in Mexico (open daily 10am-12:30pm and 4-6pm). From 11am to noon, if the sexton is in the mood, visitors can climb the right tower of the cathedral for a panoramic view of Puebla (5 pesos). Two volcanoes, **Popocatépetl** and **Ixtac-cíhuatl,** are visible to the northwest. To the northeast, you can see **La Malinche,** the volcano named in honor of Cortés's Aztec lover and interpreter. Be sure to start your climb by 11:30am; the lower door is locked at noon.

The art collection of the late textile magnate José Luis Bello is housed in the **Museo Bello,** Av. 3 Pte. at Calle 3 Sur (tel. 32-94-75), one block west of the southeast corner of the zócalo. The museum is crammed with ivory, iron, porcelain, earthenware, and *talavera* artifacts from different places and periods in world history; highlights include a collection of decorative keys and locks, a musical crystal door, and voluminous books of Gregorian chants from the 16th, 17th, and 18th centuries. A knowledgeable tour guide will spit out information about prominent pieces and answer questions in a spooky robot-like voice. Guided tours are offered in Spanish and English. (Open Tues.-Sun. 10am-5pm. Admission until 4:30pm. Admission 5 pesos. Free Tues.)

South of the Zócalo

The **Casa de la Cultura,** Av. 5 Ote. 5 (tel. 46-53-44), one block from the zócalo behind the Cathedral, in the same building as the tourist office, is an appropriate place to begin a visit to Puebla. Foreign students practice their Spanish in the courtyard, while tourists view traveling art exhibits. Folk dances are performed every Saturday and Sunday; movies are shown all week. Check the board on the right as you walk in from the street for the latest schedules. The same building houses the impressive **Biblioteca Palafoxiana** (tel. 46-56-13), a beautiful library holding 43,000 16th-century volumes. Belonging to no specific religious order himself, Don Juan de Palafox was also a vocal critic of the Jesuits, condemning their aspirations to power, land, and money. His 6000-book library, which he donated to the city in 1646, includes a 1493 illuminated copy of the Nuremberg Chronicle (open Tues.-Sun. 10am-5pm; admission 5 pesos).

Around the corner from the *Casa de Cultura* and two blocks away from the zócalo is the **Museo Amparo,** Calle 2 Sur 708 (tel. 46-46-46). Devoted to the history of Mesoamerican art, the exhibit begins with a timeline comparing the development of Mesoamerican art with that of Oceania, Asia, Africa, and Europe from 2400 BCE to 1500 CE. From there, the rooms guide you through the techniques, uses, and trends in the art of dozens of Mesoamerican indigenous groups without losing the global perspective. Objects are presented in their contexts of use, in relation to other cultures, and finally as individual masterpieces. The last rooms of the museum jump to the colonial era, recreating the house as it once looked. As if Mexican pride hadn't been stroked enough, the exhibits open and close with two memorable paintings by Diego Rivera. Explanatory material is in both English and Spanish. Headphones provide visitors with more information on the pieces from the high-tech monitors in each room of the museum; explanations come in 5 languages (open Wed.-Mon. 10am-6pm; admission 10 pesos, students 5 pesos, free Mon. Guided tour Sun. at noon; headphone rental 5 pesos with a 5 peso deposit).

Northeast of the Zócalo

The extravagant, gilded **Iglesia de Santo Domingo** was constructed between 1571 and 1611 on the foundation of a convent, two blocks from the *zócalo's* northwest corner heading away from the Cathedral along 5 de Mayo, between Av. 4 and 6 Pte. Statues of saints and angels adorn the fantastic altar, but the church's real attraction is the exuberant **Capilla del Rosario,** laden with enough 23½-karat gold to make Liberace wince. Masks depicting an *indígena,* a *conquistador* in armor, and a *mestizo* hang above each of the three doors along each side of the chapel. On the ceiling, three statues represent Faith, Hope, and Charity. The 12 pillars represent the 12 apostles; the six on the upper level are each made from a single onyx stone. Since there was no room for a real choir, designers painted a chorus of angels with guitars and woodwinds on the wall above the door (open daily 9:30am-12:15pm and 4-6pm).

Casa de Aquiles Serdán, originally the home of the homonymous printer, patriot, and martyr of the 1910 *Revolución,* serves today as the **Museo Regional de la Revolución Mexicana** at Av. 6 Ote. 206 (tel. 32-10-76). Hundreds of bullet holes, both inside and out, bear witness to the assassination. The museum includes photos of Serdán, the bloody battles of the Revolution, the bedraggled battalions of Reyes and Obregón, and of the dead Zapata and Carranza. One room is dedicated to Carmen Serdán and other female revolutionaries *(las carabineras;* open Tues.-Sun. 10am-4:30pm; admission 4 pesos, children 2 pesos).

When Benito Juárez's Reform Laws went into effect in 1857, they not only weakened the power of the Church but also forced the nuns at the **Convento de Santa Mónica,** on 5 de Mayo and 16 Pte., into hiding. The convent operated in stealth for 77 years before being accidentally discovered. Now an *ex-convento,* the building serves as a museum for religious art (open Tues.-Sun. 10am-5pm; admission 7 pesos, Sun. free). Regional clothing is sold at the tourist-happy **Mercado El Parián,** Av. 4 Ote. and Calle 6 Nte. (open daily 9am-7pm). The **Barrio del Artista,** on Av. 6 Ote. and Calle 6 Nte., is a pedestrian strip where local artists exhibit their work in small cubicles and paint the portraits of passers-by.

The oldest church in Puebla, begun in 1535 and finished in 1575, is the **Templo de San Francisco,** Av. 14 Ote. and Calle 10 Nte. The church's dark bell tower was added in 1672. Near the church is the **Teatro Principal** (tel. 32-60-85), on Av. 8 Ote. at Calle 6 Nte. The *teatro* is a prime example of Puebla's distinctive 16th-century architecture (open daily 10am-5pm except when in use).

In the Outskirts

A short trip from the *centro,* the **Centro Cívico 5 de Mayo** commemorates the Mexican army's victory over the French in the celebrated Puebla battle of 1862. To get there, walk three blocks from the *zócalo* away from Av. 5 de Mayo until you reach Blvd. Héroes del 5 de Mayo, where you can catch a #72 bus or #8 *colectivo* (both 1.50 pesos). They will drop you off by the cement octopus that memorializes Benito Juárez (don't ask). Facing the monument, cross the street to the left and walk uphill. On the road past an information center a large, wavy representation of the Mexican flag marks a fork. To the right is the **Fuerte de Loreto,** which now houses the **Museo de La No Intervención.** The road to the left makes a loop; the first building is the **Museo de Historia Natural,** full of fossils, live snakes, and well-behaved school kids (open Tues.-Sun. 10am-5pm; admission 5 pesos, children 2 pesos, Tues. free). Next to it is the **Recinto Ferial,** an exposition center and fairgrounds; the tourist office distributes a pamphlet listing its monthly activities. The **Parque Rafaela Padilla de Zaragoza** comes next, providing a large, nature-filled oasis. Rambling trails descend to a theater, a playground, a rink ideal for rollerblading, and benches that beckon to picknickers. The administration building near the entrance shows National Geographic style videos (1 peso). The immersion in nature would be complete save for the oversized statues of animals and piped-in radio shows (open daily 9am-10pm). At the tip of the loop, the **Fuerte de Guadalupe** offers a panorama of the city, and is "an altar to the patriotism of the heroes of the Fifth of May," as the signs so delicately put it. The last point of interest is the **Museo Regional de Antropología,** on your right as you leave the fort and head back towards the flag (open Tues.-Sun. 10am-4:30pm; admission 10 pesos, student discounts for Mexican students only, free Sun.).

ENTERTAINMENT

For evening entertainment, take a stroll along the **Zona Esmeralda,** on Av. Juárez, west of Calle 13 Sur. Although the best discos rock in nearby Cholula, this neighborhood has scores of movie theaters, shops, ethnic restaurants, and bars. A youngish Mexican crowd boogies to the beat of salsa and disco at **Pagaia,** Juárez 1906 (tel. 32-46-85), after Calle 19 Sur (cover 12 pesos; open Fri.-Sat. 10:30pm-5am). **Charlie's China Poblana,** two blocks up at Juárez 2118 (tel. 46-31-84), is another hot spot on the emerald strip. The neon-and-glass floor will make you feel like Michael Jackson singing "Billie Jean" (open daily 1pm-midnight).

During the day, the **Plazuela de los Sapos,** on Calle 6 Sur between Av. 5 Ote and Av. 7 Ote., has no toads, per se, but rather furniture and antique shops. After sundown, *mariachis* outside entertain those who arrived too late to squeeze into **Los Alambiques,** Calle 6 Sur 506. Join the college-age crowd bopping to an infectious mix of English and Spanish dance tunes (cover 10 pesos; open Wed.-Sat. 9pm-3am). For those who prefer to hear both sides of the conversation, bookstore/cafe **Teorema** (tel. 42-10-14), Reforma 540 at Calle 7, is a hip hangout; lively conversation pervades this literary lair down to the last shelf (cover 7.50-10 pesos; open 9:30am-2:30pm, 4:30pm-2am; bookstore closes and music starts at 9pm).

To catch a flick, try the centrally located **Cine Continental,** Av. 4 Ote. 210 (tel. 32-19-55), next to the Hotel Imperial (10 pesos), or the brand-new **Multicinemas** on Blvd. Héroes del 5 de Mayo 907, at the corner of Av. 9 Ote. (15 pesos).

▒ Cholula

Legend holds that there are 365 churches in the city of Cholula. A photo mural in a bar near the *zócalo* depicts 128 of them, while the tourist office issues maps pointing out 38. Though the exact number may be in dispute, the prevalence of churches reminds the 100,000 residents of Cholula and the small number of foreign tourists of the city's sacred place in history. Founded in the 5th century BCE, Cholula bills itself as the oldest site of human habitation in Mexico. Seven pre-Hispanic cultures lived in the area which was named Cholula ("water that falls in the place of escape") after the arrival of Toltecs expelled from Tula around 1000 CE. Each successive culture group added a tier to the **Great Pyramid,** strengthening its reputation as a center for worship of the god Quetzalcóatl. When Cortés and his men entered the city in 1519, he decimated the townsfolk as well as the temples. On top of the religious ruins, the Spanish constructed Catholic churches, including the glittering **Santuario de los Remedios,** to outshine the pyramid. Together, the pyramid and its incongruous crown constitute Cholula's main attraction and a tangible symbol of the endurance of indigenous beliefs which underlie the Catholic practices. Not only did the Catholic churches take the locations of pre-Hispanic temples, but they also took their names: San Pedro Mexicaltzingo and Santa Maria Xixitla, for example. While many visitors are drawn to the city by its ancient roots and still vibrant mix of religions, every semester thousands of students from all parts of the world come for a different reason—to study at the modern **Universidad de las Américas (UDLA).**

ORIENTATION

Cholula is on Route 150, 122km east of Mexico City and 8km west of Puebla. To get from the Estrella Roja bus station to the center of town, walk 100m away from the station and turn left on the first street, Av. 5 de Mayo. Walk four blocks toward the large yellow church of San Pedro on the right side of the street. With the Church on the right, you are facing the edge of the *zócalo. Colectivos* to Puebla can be flagged down at a variety of locations in the city center, including the corner of Av. 4 Pte. and Calle 3 Nte., as well as at Morelos and Calle 4 Sur (½hr. to Puebla's CAPU, 2 pesos). After the *colectivos* stop running at 8pm, you'll have to negotiate a price with a local taxi (20 pesos or more).

The numbered streets in Cholula form a grid with the *zócalo* roughly at the center. But beware: the municipality of Cholula encompasses two towns: San Pedro Cholula and San Andrés Cholula. The *zócalo,* tourist office, and majority of the restaurants are located in San Pedro; streets from the Archaeological Zone—where the Pyramid is— moving away from the *zócalo* are in San Andrés. As usual in Mexico, the same street may go by different names along different stretches.

Cholultecos insist that it is safe to walk around at night; crime seems to be directed against business establishments rather than individuals. The walk from San Andrés to Cholula past the pyramid can be uncomfortably lonely, but cabs travel the distance for about seven pesos.

PRACTICAL INFORMATION

Tourist Office: Av. 4 Pte. 103 (tel. 47-33-93). Facing the *zócalo* with the yellow Church of San Pedro on the right, turn right and walk toward the red and yellow arches; the office is inside a white building on the left side of the street right past the public library. Little English spoken, but you can always point your way to the free city map. Open Mon.-Fri. 9am-8pm, Sat.-Sun. 11am-4pm.

Currency Exchange: Casa de Cambio Azteca, Av. Morelos 605 (tel. 47-08-19). Open Mon.-Fri. 9am-7pm, Sat. 9am-2pm. Though they have more limited hours, the banks around the *zócalo* offer comparable rates. **Bancomer,** in the arcade on the side of the *zócalo* near the Church of San Pedro, is open for exchange Mon.-Fri. 9am-2:30pm. **Banamex,** Morelos 8, on the side of the *zócalo* opposite the Church of San Pedro, has an **ATM.** Open Mon.-Fri. 9am-5pm. The **Hotel Calli Quetzal- cóatl** will exchange money after hours at less-than-favorable rates.

Telephones: LADATELs line the west side of the *zócalo,* but don't forget your phone cards. Or try the phone inside the Casa de la Cultura, which takes coins.

Telegrams: Telecomm, Av. 5 Pte. 102A (tel. 47-01-30). Open Mon.-Fri. 9am-3pm.

Fax: In Telecomm office (see above). **Centro de Copiado Cholula,** Morelos 8B (tel. and fax 47-14-72), on the south side of the *zócalo.* Open daily 8am-9pm.

Buses: Estrella Roja, at Av. 12 Ote. To Mexico City (every ½hr. between 5am and 8pm, 2hr., 20 pesos). More destinations through the Puebla bus station.

Market: Cosmo del Razo, Av. Hidalgo and Av. 5 Norte. Cheap prices on meat, fruit, flowers, and clothing. Wed. and Sun. are *días de plaza* when the already crowded market swells with even more merchants.

Laundromat: Lavandería Burbujas (tel. 47-37-66), on Av. 14 Ote. one block from the Hotel Las Américas towards the *zócalo.* 3kg for 10 pesos. Home delivery. Open Mon.-Sat. 8:30am-7pm.

Red Cross: (tel. 47-03-93), Calle 7 Sur at Av. 3 Pte., a bit of a hike from the *centro.* Walk-in service. Open 24hr. No English spoken.

Pharmacy: Farmacia Moderna, Morelos 12 (tel. 47-11-99), on the *zócalo.* Open daily 8am-8pm.

Hospital: Clínica de IMSS (tel. 47-53-14), Calle 4 Nte. and Av. 10 Ote. Open 24hr. **Hospital San Gabriel,** Av. 4 Pte. 503 (tel. 47-00-14).

Police: (tel. 47-05-62), at the Presidencia Municipal, Portal Guerrero 1, in the arcade under the arches on the side of the *zócalo.*

Post Office: At the intersection of Av. 7 and Av. 5 Pte. Open Mon.-Fri. 8am-7pm, Sat. and holidays 8am-noon. **Postal Code:** 72760.
Telephone Code: 22.

ACCOMMODATIONS

Though more expensive hotels have recently set up shop in increasingly touristed Cholula, two budget standouts hold firm.

Hotel Reforma, Calle 4 Sur 101 (tel. 47-01-49). From the *zócalo,* walk two blocks on Morelos towards the Great Pyramid, then turn right. Rooms feature no fewer than four mirrors, full baths with hot water, and photographs of area churches. The real churches with their real bells lie just outside the hot pink-accented courtyard, so alarm clocks are not necessary. The front gate is locked from 10:30pm-8am; ring to enter. Singles 60-70 pesos. Doubles 70 pesos.

Hotel Las Américas, Av. 14 Ote. 6 (tel. 47-09-91), in San Andrés, is well worth the hike. To reach the hotel from the *zócalo* or the *Estrella Roja* bus station, catch the San Andrés *colectivo* in front of the bus station (2 pesos) and ask to be dropped off at Av. 14 Pte.; the hotel is half a block west. Spacious rooms with reliable hot water, TVs, and phones. Singles 50 pesos. Doubles 60 pesos.

FOOD

Opportunities for the budget diner abound in the area around the *zócalo* and on Morelos/Hidalgo. For the cheapest eats in town, check out the food counters at the **mercados** on the north side of the *zócalo* and on Hidalgo and 5 Nte. As always, avoid anything uncooked (including partially cooked meat) and unpurified water.

Los Tulipanes, Portal Guerrero 13, on the side of the *zócalo* near the Church of San Pedro, serves up a great breakfast (starting at 10 pesos) or light meal (*comida corrida* 17 pesos). Taste terrific *tortas* (8-9 pesos) and sip savory soups (5-12 pesos). Open daily 8am-9:30pm.

Restaurant Colonial, Morelos 605 (tel. 47-25-08), across the street from the entrance to the pyramid. Sit in a quiet, secluded courtyard and enjoy regional specialties from quesadillas (18 pesos) to fried chicken (32 pesos). For the carnivore in all of us. Open daily 9am-10pm.

La Lunita (tel. 47-00-11), Av. Morelos at 6 Norte, occupies a graffiti-laden spot next to the railroad tracks and diagonally across from the steps up the pyramid. Serves complete breakfasts in the morning (20 pesos), but only comes alive at night, when there's dancing and a miraculously stocked bar (beer 7 pesos). Open daily 8am-2am or whenever the dancing stops.

SIGHTS

When Cortés destroyed the Toltec temple atop the misshapen hill that dominates Cholula, he was unaware that the hump of earth was actually the **Great Pyramid** of a culture that had dominated the area more than eight centuries before. This ancient civilization mysteriously collapsed in 700 CE, and since then the pyramid's outer layers of adobe brick have disintegrated and sprouted trees. When the Toltec-Chichimec groups settled in Cholula in the 12th century, they named the pyramid Tlachiaualtepetl, or "man-made hill," and are believed to have practiced human sacrifice atop it. Twentieth-century archaeologists tunneled into the "hill," discovering three other pyramids built one on top of the other, the oldest of which dates from roughly 200 CE. Sophisticated drainage systems preserved the structure, which is volumetrically the largest pyramid in the world. Today, the archaeological tunnels and some excavations on the south and west sides of the pyramid are open to visitors. Due to a lack of funds, only 5% of Cholula's ruins have been uncovered. The entrance to the tunnel is on Morelos, at the base of the pyramid. To reach the ruined structure, walk from the *zócalo* on Morelos, away from the red and yellow arches, and cross the railroad tracks; 50m farther on the right is the ticket booth. Avoid the pyramid's tunnels if you're claustrophobic or otherwise opposed to dark, cramped passageways. If you decide to brave it, guides will take you through the bewildering, unmarked excavation tunnels for 30-35 pesos. Look for the section of the main staircase that has been excavated from bottom to top to get an idea of the height of one of the smaller pyramids. Dioramas in illuminated sections of the tunnel demonstrate the evolution of the pyramid across the centuries. (Tunnel and ruins open Tues.-Sun. 10am-5pm. Admission 14 pesos, 25 pesos to use a camcorder. Free for children and seniors, and for everyone on Sunday.)

Just across the street from the tunnel, the **Museo del Sitio** displays a model of the pyramids in their original configuration; it makes the whole complex easier to understand. Fragments of the remarkable frescoes found on the second pyramid are exhibited in the back room. The fresco of the drinkers, as it was found on the pyramid, is 2.5m high and 65m long, making it one of the longest murals of pre-Hispanic Mexico. The museum's **bookstore** specializes in the art and culture of Cholula. (Museum open Tues.-Sun. 10am-5pm. Free admission with pyramid ticket.)

Upon exiting the tunnels, turn right on the path and follow it to the south of the pyramid to the **Patio de los Altares,** a large grassy area with extraordinary acoustics. Clap your hands while standing in the center of the courtyard. Wow. Follow the path as it takes you back to the railroad tracks; make an immediate right outside the fence where it ends, and begin climbing. No ticket is required to reach the **Santuario de Nuestra Señora de los Remedios,** the church built atop the pyramid in 1594 and the highlight of the Zone. Trekking up the pyramid demands as much effort as a Stairmaster workout, but the reward comes with the superb view of Cholula and its many churches. On a clear day, the snow-capped volcanoes **Popocatépetl** and **Ixtaccíhuatl** are visible in the distance. The inside of the church affords a stunning view as well—ornate gold decorations and fresh mums.

The only other churches worth visiting are the **Capilla Real** and the **Convento de San Gabriel,** on the side of the *zócalo* opposite the arches. The churches stand on the side of the **Templo de Quetzalcóatl,** yet another Spanish answer to pre-Hispanic temples. Unadorned but for its 49 domes, the Capilla Real possesses remarkable structural elegance. The steps in front of the entrance to San Gabriel are from the pyramid it replaced. (Open Mon.-Sat. 9am-1pm and 4-7pm, Sun. 9am-7pm.)

Aficionados of religious art and architecture should not miss the world-renowned church in the town of Tonantzintla, only 15 minutes away. Catch the bus marked "Chipilo" at Av. 6 Ote. and Av. 5 de Mayo (1.50 pesos). The bright saffron façade of **Santa María Tonantzintla** covers a startling interior, where over 450 stucco faces stare out from every spare inch of wall and ceiling. Saints, musicians, and chiefs congregate with animals and flowers in an explosion of spooky excess; the handiwork of the same indigenous artisan who executed the plans of European artists in Puebla's Capilla del Rosario (p. 407). Here the artisan reinterprets the colonial style in a sort of indigenous rococo. Only a 15-minute walk (or an even shorter 1-peso minibus ride) away lies the town, and 15th-century church, of **San Francisco Acatapec.**

ENTERTAINMENT

Thanks to its student population, Cholula sprouts distractions left and right. Bulletin boards at the **Casa de la Cultura,** Av. 4 Pte. 103A (tel. 47-19-86), in the same white building as the tourist office, advertise special events, films, local arts programs, new book clubs in the area, and the schedules of local aerobics classes (open Mon.-Sat. 9am-5pm; Spanish bookstore upstairs). For those looking for something on the alcoholic side, Cholula seems to have almost as many bars and discos as it has churches; hordes of weekend warriors drive up from Puebla just to get down. The city's nightlife is at its best Wednesday through Saturday during the school year; things slow down considerably during the student-less summer. Many popular bars and discos line the streets of San Andrés, within a block or two of the Hotel las Américas. **Exótica,** on Av. 14 Ote in San Andrés, is the latest hot spot, open only on weekends.

Diagonally across the street, **Club Keops,** on the corner of Ave. 14 Ote. and 5 de Mayo, caters to gay patrons. **El Wilo** (tel. 47-21-06), diagonally across from Le Chat, is a Mexican fantasia in red, white, and green (open Mon.-Sat. 8pm-3am). Back under the arches on the corner of the *zócalo,* **Bar Enamorada** features music (sometimes live) Thursday through Saturday nights (open daily 10:30am-midnight).

Veracruz

The state of **Veracruz** is a thin strip of land that stretches 300km along the Gulf of Mexico. Unlike most of Mexico, its subsistence does not come from farming. Although many local residents make their living from farming, mainly tobacco or coffee, and small-scale cattle ranching, the state's main income comes from oil and fishing. But the state that works hard, it seems, also parties hard: *veracruzanos,* also known as *jarochos,* are renowned for their delightful sense of humor, their wonderful seafood and coffee, and their Afro-Caribbean inspired music, which relies heavily on the marimba. The Afro-Caribbean influence dates back to the days when Veracruz city was the main slave trading port for the country and pervades not only the state's music but also its cuisine and ethnic makeup.

Much of Veracruz, especially the verdant volcanic hills of La Sierra de los Tuxtlas, remains relatively untouristed. Local color is supplied by the over-hyped but still vital *curandero* culture. *Curanderos* (medicine men), called *brujos* (witches) by locals, practice a mixture of conjuring, devil-invocation, and natural healing. Their rituals combine elements of European, African, and pre-Hispanic traditions. Some incantations are recited in Náhuatl, and the *diablo* they invoke is probably a spiritual descendant of Huichilobos, a Tuxteco god. Locals may visit *curanderos* to heal a snake bite, or to discover if a spouse is being unfaithful. Some *curanderos* head to Catemaco, where they hawk their services to *gringos* in search of spooky thrills.

■ Xalapa (Jalapa)

Perched high upon a mountain slope, Xalapa (pop. 288,000) surprises visitors with its decaying colonial beauty, its lush surroundings, and its subculture of talented artists. While other cities list countless churches as their most salient characteristic, Xalapa is home to a world-class museum, the University of Veracruz, and an emerald necklace of magnificent parks and gardens.

The capital of the state of Veracruz since 1885, Xalapa was first settled by Náhuatl speakers who dubbed the area "spring in the sand." After the Spanish conquest, Xalapa's annual fairs earned the city the economic importance it continues to enjoy today. Downtown Xalapa is the busy, giddy center from which the rest of the city ripples outward, merging gracefully with the raw beauty of the Veracruz landscape. Steep cobblestone streets provide a magnificent view of the verdant peaks surrounding Xalapa at every turn, while the bustling avenues give constant evidence of a city fairly bursting at the seams with artistic energy.

ORIENTATION

Xalapa lies 104km northwest of Veracruz along Route 140 and 302km east of Mexico City. The **train station** is at the extreme northeast edge of the city, a 40-minute walk or 6-peso taxi ride from *el centro*. To get from the **bus station** to the *centro*, catch buses marked "Centro" or "Terminal" (1.50 pesos); a taxi will cost 8 pesos.

Xalapa, like many other hilly towns, can be quite confusing. The **centro**, or downtown area, centers on the **cathedral** and **Palacio de Gobierno.** The street that separates them is **Enríquez,** which runs along **Parque Juárez.** Streets that branch from Enríquez towards the park and the Palacio de Gobierno run downhill; streets that split from Enríquez on the cathedral side run uphill. This uphill/downhill distinction works best for the streets near the center of town. Going away from the park towards the cathedral, Enríquez becomes two streets: **Xalapeños Ilustres** to the left and **Zamora** to the right. From the park, away from the cathedral, Enríquez becomes **Av. Camacho.**

PRACTICAL INFORMATION

Tourist Office: (tel. 18-01-96) A kiosk in the bus station, to the far left as you enter the terminal, is the best source of information. Open daily 8am-10pm.

Currency Exchange: Banamex, at the corner of Xalapeños Ilustres and Zamora (tel. 18-17-13), is open Mon.-Fri. 9am-5pm and has a **24-hr. ATM.** Across the street, **Dollar Fast,** Xalapeños Ilustres 15 (tel. 17-28-91; fax 12-06-60), buys and sells U.S. dollars and travelers' checks. Open Mon.-Fri. 9am-2pm and 4-6pm.

American Express: Carrillo 24 (tel. 17-41-14; fax 12-06-01), three blocks from Parque Juárez past the cathedral off Enríquez. Cashier open Mon.-Fri. 9am-2pm and 4-7pm. **Viajes Xalapa,** a full-service **travel agency,** shares the office.

Telephones: LADATELs outside the Palacio de Gobierno on Enríquez and outside the post office. *Caseta* at Calle Guerro 9, off the southwest corner of the Parque Juárez. Open daily 9am-10pm.

Telegrams and fax: Telecomm, Zamora 70, around the corner from the post office. Open Mon.-Fri. 8am-6pm, Sat. 9am-1pm. Also available at the bus station.

Buses: CAXA, in a state-of-the-art building at 20 de Noviembre 571, east of the city center. The station has long-distance phones, telegraph service, a pharmacy, shopping, food, and drink. **ADO** (tel. 18-99-88) travels first-class to Campeche (8:15pm, 15hr., 214 pesos), Catemaco (8am, 4½hr., 58 pesos), Mérida (8:15pm, 18hr., 251 pesos), Mexico City (23 per day 12:30am-midnight, 5hr., 70 pesos), Papantla (9 per day, 4hr., 54 pesos), Puebla (9 per day, 3hr., 40 pesos), San Andrés Tuxtla (10 per day, 3½hr., 55 pesos), Santiago Tuxtla (2:30pm, 3½hr., 52 pesos), Tuxtepec (6am and 3:30pm, 5½hr., 55 pesos), and Veracruz (43 per day 5:30am-11.00pm, 2hr., 24 pesos). Slightly slower, slightly cheaper second-class service to almost identical destinations provided by **Autobuses Unidos (AU).**

Market: Jaúregui, Lucio at Altamirano, two blocks uphill from the right of the cathedral. Open daily 8am-6pm. **Chedraui** is a supermarket in the Plaza Crystal mall, on the corner of Independencia and Lázaro Cárdenas. Open daily 8am-9pm.

Laundromat: Lavandería Los Lagos, Dique 25 (tel. 17-93-38), right around the corner from Casa de Artesanías. Open Mon.-Sat. 9am-2pm and 4-7pm.

Red Cross: Clavijero 13 (tel. 17-81-58 or 17-34-31), a block uphill from Parque Juárez. 24-hr. ambulance service. English-speaking staff Tues. and Sat. nights.

Pharmacies: Farmacia Benavides (tel. 18-92-01), Enríquez on the corner of Revolución next to the cathedral. Open 24hr.

Hospitals: Hospital Civil, Pedro Rendón 1 (tel. 18-44-00), corner with Bravo. 24-hr. emergency care. **IMSS,** Lomas del Estadio (tel. 18-55-55). No English spoken.

Emergency: Dial 06.

Police: Helpfully sprinkled throughout the city, and at the Cuartel San José, on the corner of Arteaga and Aldama (tel. 18-18-10).

Post Office: In the Palacio Federal, at Zamora and Diego Leño (tel. 17-20-21). Open Mon.-Fri. 8am-5pm, Sat. 8am-1pm. **Postal Code:** 91001.

Telephone Code: 28

ACCOMMODATIONS

And the Lord God, seeing the plight of the weary budget traveler, was moved to take pity upon her, and said, "Let there be Xalapa." The city is full of comfortable, economical, and convenient accommodations, many of them on **Revolución,** close to the *centro,* the market, and the parks. All rooms in the hotels listed have private baths with showers and 24-hour hot water.

Hotel Limón, Revolución 8 (tel. 17-22-04), half a block up Revolución from Enríquez; go up past the left side of cathedral. Medium-sized, spotlessly clean rooms surround a patio with *mudéjar* wall tiles. Try to get a room at the far end of the hotel; rooms facing Revolución are much noisier. Singles 38 pesos. Doubles 45-55 pesos. Triples 68 pesos. Quints 90 pesos.

Hotel Citlalli, Clavijero 43 (tel. 18-34-58). Two blocks up the steep hill from Enríquez, at the edge of Parque Juárez away from the cathedral. Clean white stucco

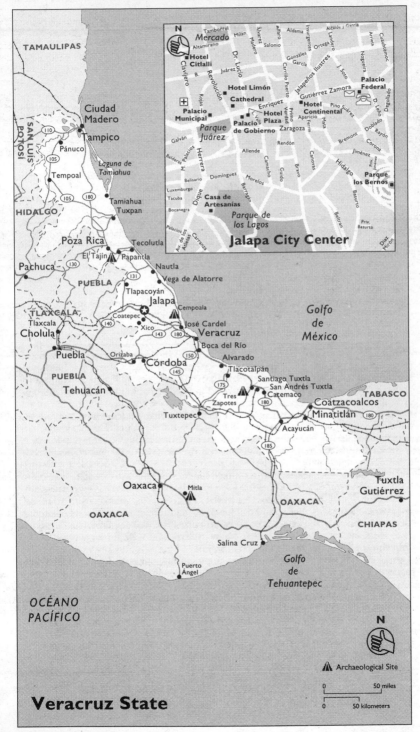

Jalapa City Center

VERACRUZ

Veracruz State

N

▲ Archaeological Site

| 0 | 50 miles |
| 0 | 50 kilometers |

rooms with wood accents, TVs, phones, *agua purificada*, and huge sparkling bathrooms. Singles 65 pesos. Doubles 85 pesos. Additional person 18 pesos.

Hotel Plaza, Enríquez 4 (tel. 17-33-10), next to the Palacio de Gobierno. Two floors of faded but adequate rooms. Most second-floor rooms wrap around an open-air patio and have elegant varnished wooden doors and high ceilings. Singles 35 pesos. Doubles 40-45 pesos. Quads (up to 6 people) 75 pesos.

FOOD

Filled with high-quality cafés and cheap eateries, Xalapa is a true culinary paradise. As always in Mexico, particularly cheap cuisine can be found in the market. There are vegetarian restaurants on **Murillo Vidal,** downhill from the post office.

La Sopa, Callejón del Diamante 3-A (tel. 17-80-69). Two blocks from the park, past the Palacio de Gobierno, on a pedestrian street across Banco Serfín. Another reason to love Xalapa. Inexpensive, delicious food in an irresistibly hip ambience. Advertisements for plays and exhibits cover the front doors. At night, musicians move in and tables move out to make way for dancing. *Comida corrida* 10 pesos. Open Mon.-Sat. 1-5:30pm and 7:30pm-midnight, music starts at 9pm.

Café de la Parroquia, Zaragoza 18 (tel. 17-44-36), one block downhill from the Palacio de Gobierno. Like its famous cousin in Veracruz, the café is always full and lively. Delicious *café lechero* (5 pesos), breakfasts (13-34 pesos), and *antojitos* (13-25 pesos). Open Mon.-Sat. 7:30am-10:30pm, Sun. 8am-11pm. Another location on Camacho on the way to the Teatro del Estado (tel 17-71-57).

Enrico's Restaurant, Enríquez 6 (tel. 17-64-47). Facing the Palacio de Gobierno, next to the Hotel Plaza. Hearty breakfast buffet (15 pesos) attracts a mature crowd and ice-cold beverages (9 pesos). Open Mon.-Sat. 8am-9pm.

SIGHTS

The inscription above the entrance to the galleries of Xalapa's **Museo de Antropología** (Av. Xalapa) admonishes the Mexican visitor to pause, for "this is the root of your history, your crib, and your altar." Below, a massive Olmec head stares grimly out across three millennia. Displayed in spectacular marble galleries and outdoor gardens, the museum's Olmec heads are perhaps the most impressive of its 3,000 items. The heads commemorate leaders of the little-understood Olmecs, who ruled the Gulf Coast of Mexico around 1000 BCE, but were unknown to archaeologists until the 1930s, when remains of them were found in the Veracruz rain forest. A group of Totonac figurines and masks subvert the austerity of the Olmec heads with their merry smiles, while nearby the Huastec deity Tlazoltéotl, associated with procreation, stands sculpted in soft, minimalist relief. The bookstore inside the lobby sells an assortment of anthropology books; there is also a cafeteria. (Open daily 9am-5pm; admission 10 pesos, students 8 pesos; camera 6 pesos, video camera 30 pesos. Tours in English Mon., Wed., and Fri. 11am). To get there, catch a yellow "Tesorería" bus on Enríquez (1.50 pesos); take a taxi (6 pesos); or walk on Enríquez/Camacho away from the cathedral, make a left on Av. Xalapa, and walk on for several blocks until you see the museum on your left (45min.).

Some of Xalapa's most popular sights are its **public parks and gardens,** the hallmarks of a rich and livable city. The **Parque Ecológico Macuitepetl** is primarily a preserve for the flora and fauna indigenous to the Jalapa area, but also serves as one of the city's principal recreational areas. A brick path meanders past smooching lovers to the summit of an extinct volcano 186 meters above the city, where a spiral tower offers a commanding view of the city and mountains. To get there, take a "Mercado-Corona" *colectivo* (1.50 pesos) from Revolución and Altamirano (1.20 pesos), or hail a taxi (6 pesos). Downhill from Parque Juárez on Dique lies the **Paseo de los Lagos,** where a bicycle path traces the perimeter of several urban lakes. On sunny afternoons, the park is dotted with children, chirping birds, panting joggers, and still more amorous young couples. Like any urban park, it can be dangerous at night. At the west end of the park, near Dique, the **Casa de Artesanías** (tel. 17-08-04), a non-profit state-run handicrafts store, features work by Veracruzan artisans. Fine pieces, including meticulously embroidered shirts, are cheaper here than in private shops (open Mon.-Fri. 8am-8pm, Sat.-Sun.10am-1pm).

Through the east entrance of the **Palacio de Gobierno,** off Enríquez on the side opposite Parque Juárez, lies a marble courtyard with a staircase marching upward into the bureaucratic chambers above. The bannister is guarded by bronze *conquistadores*, their swords beaten into lampposts instead of plowshares. The mural on the wall, by Mario Orozco Rivera, depicts a family overcoming ignorance and injustice. Note the gory figure on the left—no smooching here. Nearby, the terraces of **Parque Juárez,** built in 1892, share their view of the city and mountains with a small café. Carefully cut hedges line the walkways and enclose beds of flowers. In order to enjoy the view from the terrace, you may have to dodge the droves of young lovers who congregate here in the evenings and the gay men cruising for dates. One place where you'll be sure to avoid public displays of affection is the 18th century **cathedral** on the corner of Enríquez and Revolución (open daily 9am-1pm and 4-7pm).

The **Museo de Ciencía y Tecnología** (tel. 12-50-88), on Av. Murillo Vidal, is devoted almost exclusively to transportation. Polished examples of planes, trains, and automobiles make for colorful lawn decorations; inside the museum ends up looking like a car dealership. IMAX-theater shows are included with admission, but canceled if fewer than 50 people attend (11am—your best bet—1 and 4pm; open Tues.-Sun. 9am-6pm; admission 20 pesos, students 10 pesos, planetarium 2 pesos). Ironically, it's hard to get to the museum. A taxi from the *centro* will cost 6 pesos; the *microbús* that stops across the street from the museum will take you back to Enríquez (1.50 pesos).

ENTERTAINMENT

Xalapa is bursting with cultural opportunities. Ask at the bus station kiosk, or pick up a copy of a local newspaper for information about concerts, dance, and theater. The **Ágora de la Ciudad** cultural center, located at the bottom of the stairs in the Parque Juárez (tel. 18-57-30), has a screening room, gallery space, and loads of information and schedules about local events. The **Teatro del Estado** (tel. 17-31-10), a 10-minute walk from Parque Juárez on Enríquez/Camacho, at the corner of Ignacio de la Llave, holds enticing performances—the excellent **Orquesta Sinfónica de Jalapa** and the **Ballet Folklórico de la Universidad Veracruzana** appear regularly. A city with more than 6000 students, Xalapa is also one of the major destinations in Mexico for aspiring artists. **La Unidad de Artes,** Belisario Domínguez 25, posts announcements of exhibitions, plays, and recitals by students. For something much more low brow, **Cine Jalapa,** Camacho 8, shows first-run movies from the U.S. The **Festival de las Flores** drowns the town in petals every April.

On weeknights, the cafés along Enríquez and Zaragoza brim with activity. The newly opened **Tierra Luna,** Diego Leño 28 (tel. 12-13-01), brews a great *capuchino* (5 pesos) and has frequent live music (open Tues.-Thurs. 8am-10pm, Fri.-Sat. 8am-11pm, Sun. 10am-6pm). As the weekend approaches, however, people migrate from café tables to bars and dance floors. Near the *centro* is **B42** (tel. 12-08-93), on Camacho just west of Parque Juárez—follow the throngs (open Thurs.-Sun. 9pm-2am, cover 15 pesos, Thurs. is salsa night). **7a Estación,** 20 de Noviembre 57 (tel. 17-31-55), just below the bus station, is another popular disco (cover 10-15 pesos depending on the night, open Thurs.-Sun. 9pm-2am).

Local students say the best place to hang out is the **Plaza Crystal** on Av. Lázaro Cárdenas, a mall featuring several bars, including **Next,** which offers pool, darts, table hockey, and disco. To get to the Plaza Crystal, take a bus marked "Sumidero" or "Circunvalación" from the bus stop on Zaragoza, located down the stairs on the left side of the Parque Juárez. Be prepared to take a cab back (7 pesos).

VERACRUZ

■ Near Jalapa

XICO AND CASCADA DE TEXOLO

It's hard to believe that **Xico** is located a mere 19km from Xalapa—here, there are almost as many mules on the road as there are automobiles. Xico is known for its cuisine (*mole xiqueño* is a specialty) and its nine-day festival dedicated to Mary Magdalene, the town's patron saint. The festival begins on July 22 and includes bullfights and a running of the bulls.

Most tourists go to Xico for the awe-inspiring view of the **Cascada de Texolo** (Texolo Falls), 3km from the town. Immortalized in the film *Romancing the Stone*, the dramatic waterfall crashes into a gorge alive with vivid greenery, the songs of passing birds, and the constant drum of water as it spills into the river below. There is a restaurant and viewing area across from the falls; a bridge leads to the other side of the gorge, where several paths yield stunning views of other waterfalls and dense vegetation.

Getting There: To get to Xico from Xalapa, take the "Terminal" bus from the stop on Enríquez in front of the *3 Hermanos* shoe store, to the right of the cathedral as you face it, to the Excelsior terminal (about 10min., 1.50 pesos). From there, cross the street towards the roundabout where buses are lined up and take a "Xico" bus (45min., 2.50 pesos).

To reach the falls, get off the bus as soon as the blue "Entrada de la Ciudad" sign appears on the right side of the road. Climb straight up the hill; soon the road will split at a restaurant called *Las Artas*. Take the left branch and turn left at the top of the hill, keeping a small vanilla and purple church on the right. Descending the hill, you will reach another fork guarded over by a makeshift shrine to the Virgin. Bear right after paying respects and keep her in mind as you lose hope on the interminable stone road ahead. The road curves to the right and then downhill to the viewing area, *Restaurante El Mirador*. On the other side of the gorge, two gentle waterfalls are visible. The first appears as soon as you step off the bridge. Down a level by the white picket border, another waterfall, elegant and slender, plunges from the electricity plant to the river below. Only after returning across the bridge and turning right towards the white fence of the observation deck, can you see the water whose rumble you had heard so loudly. Unlike the other two, this fall impresses with its brute force and sheer volume.

To return to Xalapa and develop that film, re-trace your steps, but be aware that the walk will take 40 minutes and is not a smooth one. Even with a car, the trip will not be much shorter and certainly not any smoother. As you walk downhill past the Los Artas restaurant, stay on the right side of the street to hail a passing bus marked "Xalapa," which will deposit you back at the Excelsior Terminal.

■ Tuxpan (Tuxpam)

As the sun rises over the Río Tuxpan, boats of fishermen set out for the day. Much like their Olmec, Huastec, and Totonac predecessors, boys standing on the shore fling their nets into the water, draw them back, and fling them out again. The scent of freshly caught *mariscos* pervades Tuxpan's markets, and fruit vendors traverse the streets near the riverfront, selling bananas and mangos by the bag. Tuxpan's active *centro* can sometimes seem overwhelming, but relief is at hand: Playa Azul is just 12km away. On weekends, the beach overflows with families splashing about and digging in the sand.

Orientation Tuxpan is 347km northwest of Veracruz. The city spreads along the northern bank of Río Tuxpan. Activity centers around two park-like plazas: **Parque Rodríguez Cano,** on the waterfront, just south of the busiest part of town, and **Parque Reforma,** between Juárez and Madero. The bridge lies on the eastern edge of town. Streets perpendicular to the bridge and parallel to the water run roughly east-west. To get to the town center from the **ADO bus station,** head left 50m to the water, and then right (west) along Reyes Heroles for three blocks; you will be at Parque Rodríguez Cano. Walk one block north back to Juárez, then left (west) three blocks; Parque Reforma will be on your right. A taxi to Parque Reforma costs 5 pesos. To get to the beach, catch a "Playa" bus from the bench along the boardwalk by the ferry docks (every 10min. 6am-8:30pm, 2.50 pesos).

Practical Information The **tourist office,** Juárez 20 (tel. 4-03-22 or 4-01-77), is in the Palacio Municipal in Parque Rodríguez Cano. Enter on the Juárez side—it's a small, unmarked office across from Hotel Florida. The friendly staff offers no maps but has some brochures (open Mon.-Sat. 8am-3pm and 4-7pm). **Bancomer** (tel. 4-12-58) is on Juárez at Zapata (open Mon.-Fri. 9am-1:30pm). **Banamex** (tel. 4-08-40), just southwest of Parque Reforma, has a 24-hour **ATM.** No **LADATELs** exist, but many stores in the *centro* have long distance *casetas,* including **Papelería La Violeta,** Morelos 21 (tel. 4-38-00; open Mon.-Sat. 9am-2pm and 4-8pm, Sun. 9am-2pm).

Each **bus** line has its own station. **ADO,** Rodríguez 1 (tel. 4-01-02), three blocks east of Parque Cano down Reyes Heroles, has first-class service to Jalapa (7 per day, 6hr., 74 pesos), Mexico City (10 per day, 6hr., 72 pesos), Papantla (6 per day, 2hr., 16 pesos), Tampico (every hr., 3hr., 49 pesos), and Veracruz (8 per day, 6hr., 95 pesos). **Estrella Blanca,** Cuauhtémoc 18 (tel. 4-20-40), two blocks past the bridge, a left on Constitución, and then three blocks west, offers second-class service to Guadalajara (5 per day, 20hr., 145 pesos), Mexico City (9 per day, 9hr., 65 pesos), Monterrey (7 per day, 138 pesos), and nearly all points in between. **Ómnibus de México,** Vicente Guerrero 30 (tel. 4-11-45), at the bridge, has first-class service to Guadalajara (2 per day, 15hr., 181 pesos), Mexico City (5 per day, 6hr., 72 pesos), and Querétaro (2 per day, 8hr., 87 pesos).

Mercado Rodríguez Cano, west of and diagonally across from the ADO station, sells fruits, fish, clothing, and souvenirs (open daily 9am-6pm). **Farmacia Popular,** Independencia 4 (tel. 4-03-11), is on the riverfront side of the market (open 24hr.). The **Red Cross,** Galeana 40 (tel. 4-01-58), is eight blocks west of *el centro* along the river, next to the police station. **Hospital Emilio Alcázar,** Obregón 13 (tel. 4-01-99), is one block west of the bridge, then a block and a half inland and up the inclined driveway on the right. No English is spoken (open 24hr.). In an **emergency,** dial 06. The **police** can be found at Galeana 38 (tel. 4-02-52 or 4-37-23), next door to the Red Cross (open 24hr.). To reach the **post office,** Clavijero 28 (tel. 4-00-88), walk north under the bridge past the vendors. Continue straight ahead, crossing the wide Cuauhtémoc; Clavijero is the small street running northwest (open Mon.-Fri. 8am-6pm, Sat. 8am-1pm). **Postal Code:** 92800. **Telephone Code:** 783.

Accommodations Budget accommodations in Tuxpan cluster around the two central parks, ensuring a reasonable measure of safety into the evening hours. **Hotel Parroquia,** Escuela Militar 4 (tel. 4-16-30), to the left of the cathedral on Parque Rodríguez Cano, offers rooms with spacious bathrooms and balconies overlooking the park and river—all at rock-bottom prices. Full-length mirror, fan, and TV lounge provide those little extras (singles 55 pesos; doubles 69 pesos). **Hotel El Huasteco,** Morelos 41 (tel. 4-18-59), is half a block east from the northeast corner of Parque Reforma. While the small, windowless rooms are not easy on the claustrophobic, impeccable cleanliness and refreshingly cold A/C more than compensate (singles 52 pesos; doubles 68 pesos). **Hotel del Parque,** Humboldt 11 (tel. 4-08-12), on the east side of Parque Reforma, puts you right in the thick of things if you can deal with a little noise—the hotel is right above a gym/Tae Kwon Do studio. Tiled floors lead to drab rooms. Some have a gorgeous view of the plaza, some have seatless toilets, some have both (singles and doubles 60 pesos).

VERACRUZ

Food Balancing traditional Mexican decor (simple, elegant wooden furniture and colorful tiles) with modernity (TVs to track *telenovelas* or *fútbol* matches), **El Meji-cano,** Morelos 49 (tel. 4-89-04), at the corner of Parque Reforma, serves up tasty regional cuisine. Sample *carne a la tampiqueña* (28 pesos) or *antojitos* ranging from *bocoles* (2 pesos) to *tacos de bistec* (16 pesos). The hot chocolate is rich and creamy (6 pesos; open daily 7am-2am). The same owner operates **Cafetería El Mante,** Juárez 8 (tel. 4-57-36), one block west of Rodríguez. Enjoy your hotcakes (12 pesos) while soaking in the warm glow from bright orange tablecloths. Decorated with fish nets and cartoonish sea characters, **Barra de Mariscos del Puerto** (tel. 4-46-01), at Juárez and Humboldt, across from the southeast corner of Parque Reforma, offers *parrillada de mariscos,* a veritable seafood menagerie that can feed two for 35 pesos (open daily 8am-midnight).

Sights and Entertainment *Tuxpeños* are justly proud of their river's relaxed beauty and scenic shores. Palm trees line the boardwalk and goods are sold up and down the river; under the bridge, piles of pineapples, bananas, shrimp, and fish can be had for a bare minimum at the huge open-air market which flows from the indoor market on Calle Rodríguez. Located on the waterfront, **Parque Rodríguez Cano** comes alive every Monday at 5:30pm for the **Ceremonia Cívica,** when government officials make speeches and schoolchildren march in an orderly procession. On the west side of Parque Reforma is the **Museo Arqueológico.** Located inside the Casa de la Cultura, the museum showcases Huastec and Totonac carvings, figurines, and other archaeological remnants. Most of the introductory information is in Spanish (open daily 10am-8pm; free).

Twelve kilometers from the city center, Tuxpan's **beach** can be crowded and slightly dirty, especially during the high season, but the wide expanse of fine sand stretches far enough for you to stake a private claim somewhere down the line. The beach is accessible by the "Playa" bus (every 15min. 6am-10pm, the last bus returns to Tuxpan at 8:30pm, 2.50 pesos).

Though there are a number of **bars** in Tuxpan's *centro,* the best nightlife in town can be found a few blocks down the river after the crowds in Parque Reforma thin out. At **Mantarraya** (tel. 4-22-04), Reyes Heroles at Guerrero, a young crowd grooves to American pop and techno hits (cover 30 pesos, including 2 drinks). Just past Allende on Reyes Heroles, facing the river, **La Puesta del Sol** (tel. 4-73-66) serves food, beer, and mixed drinks to quiet customers enjoying the live salsa and tropical music. A block away is the classy **Charlôt** (tel. 4-40-28), which serves appetizers and drinks both indoors and out (open Tues.-Sun. noon-midnight). Turn right on Pérez to find the glowing neon entrance of **La Bamba** (tel. 4-62-09), a high-tech bar featuring

---

Our Man in Havana

Mexico has a long tradition of close and friendly relations with Cuba. When Fidel Castro fled the island in the late 1950s, it was in Tuxpan that he organized the revolutionary forces that months later led the country in the fight against dicta-tor Batista. The first hopeful years of the Cuban revolution are celebrated in the **Casa de la Amistad México-Cuba.** Photographs of a young, beardless Fidel line the walls, and a colorful mural depicts the valiant leader and his fellow boatsmen disembarking under the watchful gazes of Latin-American heroes Benito Juárez, José Martí, and Simón Bolívar. The final room on the tour displays pictures of doctors and farmers, symbolizing Cuba's social progress, as well as a proud look back through the guestbook and the diverse crop of visitors expressing support for the Cuban Revolution. To get to the museum, take a blue ferry (0.70 pesos) across the river. Walk right (west) along the sidewalk and continue straight up the dirt road, past the overgrowth to the paved sidewalk, turn left, and enter on the side of the two, small white buildings with the boat out front (open daily 9am-2pm and 3-7pm; free, but donations are always welcome).

large-screen music video entertainment and serving cocktails and beers by the bucket to a professional crowd.

■ Papantla

Crawling up the green foothills of the Sierra Madre Oriental, Papantla (pop. 125,000) looks out onto the magnificent plains of Northern Veracruz. The town's hilly topography and *indígena* presence recall the region's pre-Colombian past. Papantla is one of the few remaining centers of Totonac culture, a living testament to a civilization that once dominated the northern half of what is now Veracruz. The Totonacs were conquered by the power-hungry Aztecs around 1450, but the vanquished soon took their revenge, helping Cortés crush the Aztec Empire in the 16th century. Today, ancient Totonac rituals persist in the flight of the *voladores,* a thrilling acrobatic ceremony once laden with religious meaning, now performed for the benefit of delighted tourists. Papantla also makes a terrific base for exploring **El Tajín,** the ruins of the Totonac capital and one of the most impressive archaeological sites in the Republic, 12km south of the city (see p. 425).

Orientation Papantla lies 250km northwest of Veracruz and 21km southeast of Poza Rica along Rte. 180. Downtown hustle and bustle centers around **Parque Téllez,** the white-tiled plaza. The cathedral rises on its southern side while **Enríquez** borders it on the north. Sloping downhill to the north are **Juárez** (on the east side) and **20 de Noviembre** (on the west side), both perpendicular to Enríquez. To get from the **ADO bus station** to *el centro,* turn left onto Juárez out of the station and veer left at the fork. Taxis (4 pesos to the *centro*) pass frequently along Juárez. If you arrive at the **second-class bus station,** turn left outside the station and ascend 20 de Noviembre three blocks to the northwest corner of the plaza.

Practical Information The **Chamber of Commerce,** Ramón Castaneda 100 (tel. 2-00-25), has brochures and maps of El Tajín and Veracruz state. Follow Lázaro Muño (the narrow street running east from the plaza) four blocks downhill and turn right (open Mon.-Fri. 10am-2pm and 4-8pm, Sat. noon-8pm). The staff of the **tourist office** (tel. 2-01-23), on the second floor of the **Palacio Municipal,** on the west side of the plaza, is more elusive (supposedly open Mon.-Fri. 10am-4pm and 6-8pm). **Banamex,** Enríquez 102 (tel. 2-00-01), has a 24-hour **ATM** (open Mon.-Fri. 9am-1:30pm). The pharmacy on the eastern side of the plaza has **LADATEL** phone service (open daily 9am-10pm). Collect calls can be made from **Hotel Tajín,** Núñez y Domínguez 104 (tel. 2-10-62; open 24hr.). The **telegram office** is on Enríquez 404 (tel. 2-05-84), about five blocks east of the *zócalo* (open Mon.-Fri. 9am-8pm, Sat. 9am-noon).

Papantla has two **bus stations.** The first-class **ADO** station, Juárez 207 (tel. 2-02-18), serves Jalapa (7 per day, 4hr., 54 pesos), Mexico City (5 per day, 5hr., 63 pesos), Tuxpan (3 per day, 2hr., 15 pesos), Veracruz (5 per day, 4hr., 55 pesos), and Villahermosa (1 per day, 11hr., 173 pesos). The second-class terminal, commonly called **Transportes Papantla,** 20 de Noviembre 200, offers frequent service to Poza Rica (every 10-15min. 6am-11:30pm, 35min., 4 pesos). Pay after boarding.

Poza Rica (21km northwest of Papantla) is a nearby transportation hub. Their **ADO** station (tel. 2-04-29 or 2-00-85) runs buses to Jalapa (17 per day, 4hr., 58 pesos), Mexico City (21 per day, 5½hr., 59 pesos), Papantla (23 per day, 30min., 5 pesos), Puebla (7 per day, 5hr., 55 pesos), Tampico (32 per day, 4½hr., 63 pesos), Tuxpan (35 per day, 1½hr., 12 pesos), Veracruz (17 per day, 4½hr., 59 pesos), and Villahermosa (8 per day, 12hr., 179 pesos).

The **Red Cross** (tel. 2-01-26) is on Pino Suárez, at Juárez (open 24hr.). **Farmacia Benavides,** Enríquez 101-E (tel. 2-02-68), is at the northern end of the plaza (open daily 7:30am-1am). **Clínica IMSS** (tel. 2-01-94), 20 de Noviembre at Lázaro Cárdenas, provides emergency medical assistance. From the ADO station, take a right and walk two blocks to Cárdenas, then turn left; IMSS is half a block up on your right (open

24hr.). The **police** (tel. 2-00-75 or 2-01-50) are in the Palacio Municipal (open 24hr.). The **post office** is on Azueta 198, 2nd floor (tel. 2-00-73; open Mon.-Fri. 9am-1pm and 4-7pm, Sat. 9am-noon). **Postal Code:** 93400. **Telephone Code:** 784.

Accommodations Few accommodations are available in tiny Papantla. **Hotel Tajín,** Núñez y Domínguez 104 (tel. 2-01-21), half a block to the left as you face the cathedral, displays in its lobby a carved stone wall from El Tajín. Perched on a hill above the city, the balconies afford panoramic views. Amenities include bottled water, black-and-white TVs, and phones (singles 75 pesos, with A/C 107 pesos; doubles 107 pesos, with A/C 138 pesos). Large glass windows and a curious combination of bold colors lends a Brady-esque feel to **Hotel Totanacapán** (tel. 2-12-24 or 2-12-18), 20 de Noviembre at Olivo, four blocks down from the plaza. Hallway murals are quite pleasant, but the ever-vigilant Carol Brady would have replaced some of the furniture by now (singles 95 pesos, with A/C 90 pesos; doubles 90 pesos, with A/C 120 pesos). **Refresquería Papantla** crowns the top of a massive hill just seconds away from the Monument to the Voladores. Don't let the name fool you; this twelve room guesthouse offers monthly lodging with a stunning vista of Papantla and the surrounding valleys for the remarkable cost of 200 pesos per month.

Food Papantla's few restaurants serve regional delicacies to tourists looking for the real thing. Most eateries stick to beef and pork offerings with just a smattering of seafood. **Restaurant Tajín,** Jesús Nuñez y Domínguez 104, half a block east of the cathedral, serves up a homey atmosphere complete with flowers and numerous pictures of El Tajín. Breakfast specials run 12-20 pesos, *comida corrida* 18 pesos (open daily 7am-10pm). Large murals and a view of the plaza enliven **Sorrento,** Enríquez 105 (tel. 2-00-67), a popular breakfast hangout. Meal specials include *camarones fritos* (14 pesos) and steak enchiladas (12 pesos; open daily 7am-10pm).

Sights and Entertainment Papantla's biggest attractions are the relics of its Totonac heritage. South of the plaza is the **Catedral Señora de la Asunción,** remarkable not so much for its interior, which houses four large murals of Christ's life and death, but for the stone mural carved into its northern wall, measuring 50m long and 5m high. Called **Homenaje a la Cultura Totonaca,** the mural was created by Teodoro Cano to honor local Totonac heroes and folklore figures. Its focus is the plumed serpent Quetzalcóatl, whose image runs along the full length of the carving. At the far left of the mural is a representation of the Dios del Trueno (God of Thunder), who announces the coming of the rains. From left to right, the mural follows a rough chronological outline, moving from the mythical first family of the Totonacs to the discovery of corn, which represented an end to the group's nomadic lifestyle. The mural moves on to depict the Pyramid of the Niches, the focal point of El Tajín, flanked by faces with characteristic round cheeks, smallish noses, and smiles, and ballplayers vying for the right to ritualistic death and deification.

North by Northwest

Papantla's *voladores* are renowned for their graceful acrobatics. The performance begins with five elaborately costumed men climbing a stationary pole to a platform about 20m above the ground. Having consumed courage-enhancing fluids, four of the hardy five start to "fly"—hanging by their feet from ropes wound around the pole, spinning through the air and slowly descending to earth. Meanwhile, the fifth man plays a flute and dances on the pole's pin-head. Originally, each of the four fliers corresponded to one of the four cardinal directions; positions assumed during descent were related to requests for specific weather conditions. Lately, however, the performance has lost its meteorological significance and has been subjugated to commercial exigencies like so many other expressions of *indígena* religion. Instead of performing once every 52 years, the *voladores* now fly as often as tourists can afford to feed them pesos.

The cathedral's spacious courtyard commands a view of the *zócalo*. Called the **Plaza de los Voladores,** the courtyard is the site of the ceremony in which *voladores* acrobatically entreat the rain god Tlaloc to water the year's crops. In early June, during the 10-day **Festival of Corpus Christi,** the *voladores* perform as often as thrice a day. During the festival, Papantla comes alive with artistic expositions, fireworks, traditional dances, and cockfights.

Papantla's latest effort to enshrine its *voladores* is the **Monumento al Volador,** a gigantic flute-wielding *indígena* statue erected in 1988 atop a hill and visible from all over town. To get to the monument, where you can read explanatory plaques and see Papantla in its entirety, walk up Reforma along the right side of the cathedral and up the narrow alleyway, following the road as it curves left; then make a sharp left before the road starts to slope down and walk uphill.

A time-worn mural decorates the inside of the *zócalo's* centerpiece, a domed kiosk. Painted by Arturo Cano in the 1960s, the mural represents the Totonac conception of creation. The four cardinal points are personified as warriors, each representing different natural calamities that have befallen Mesoamericans. The *zócalo* is furnished with a set of benches inlaid with mosaics and framing small paintings of the Totonacs rendered in a style typical of northern Veracruz.

The town's two markets are situated next to the central plaza. **Mercado Juárez,** at Reforma and 16 de Septiembre, off the southwest corner of the *zócalo,* specializes in poultry and veggies but is neither particularly colorful nor low-priced. **Mercado Hidalgo,** on 20 de Noviembre, off the *zócalo's* northwest corner, vends more arts and crafts items than can be found at Juárez; look for regional foods as well as traditional handmade clothing, including striking white sailor shirts and intricately embroidered dresses.

■ El Tajín

The impressive ruins of El Tajín only hint at the thriving Totonac civilization that once spread across modern-day northern Veracruz. Named for the Totonac god of thunder, El Tajín served as the political and religious center of the Totonac people. Marked similarities between buildings at this site and those at Teotihuacán reflect the influence of Aztecs and Maya. Just by the entrance stands a large pole, the apparatus of the *voladores.* June through August, the *voladores* perform almost hourly; the rest of the year, they descend through the air only on weekends. The daring acrobats—who typically request a ten-peso donation when they are through—generally perform after a large group has finished touring the ruins. To enter the ruins, one must pass through the **Museo del Sitio del Tajín** (16 pesos), which holds a sampling of Totonac crafts, household items, and remains. All explanatory information is in both Spanish and English. A brochure about El Tajín can be purchased at the information desk for 15 pesos.

From the museum building, a straight path leads to the ruins themselves. Plaques with information in Spanish, English, French, German, and Totonac are scattered throughout the site. The best sources of information are the blue uniformed "rangers" stationed throughout El Tajín. Native Totonacs themselves, the rangers may offer to give you an *ad hoc* tour of a certain area and will eagerly answer any questions you pose, although their English proficiency may be limited.

The **Plaza del Arroyo,** the central rectangular plaza formed by four tiered pyramids, lies just to the left of the gravel road. Each pyramid is pointed toward the northeast at a 20° angle, in a feat of architectural planning maintained in all the early buildings at this site. The heart of El Tajín is just past the pyramids. Two identical, low-lying, slanted constructions to the left of the observation area form a central ballcourt in which the famous one-on-one game called **pok-ta-pok** was played. While the game vaguely resembled soccer, feet weren't allowed to make contact with the ball. Every 52 years, a contest was held between the most valiant ballplayers; the winner won the honor of offering his heart for sacrifice. Another I-shaped court can be seen north of the eastern pyramid.

Across from the plaza is an elevated central altar surrounded by dark, black stone temples; two of these temples can be climbed. Just left of the altar is a split-level temple that displays a statue of Tajín. This area was known as the **Central Zone,** and is unique because the styles and functions of the buildings here vary considerably. To the northwest stands **La Pirámide de los Nichos,** a fascinating structure with seven levels and a total of 365 niches corresponding to the days of the year. Each niche was once painted in red and blue. The Totonacs marked time in 52-year epochs, during which a single flame was kept continuously burning. At the end of each epoch, the carefully nurtured flame was used to ritually torch many of the settlement's buildings. Each new epoch of rebuilding and regeneration was inaugurated by the lighting of a new flame. Today, ritual ceremonies are held annually at the pyramid during the vernal equinox. Farmers place seeds in the pyramid's niches and later retrieve them for planting.

Farther north and atop a hill is **Tajín Chico,** accessible either by a series of large stepping stones or an easy-to-ascend staircase off to the west. Whereas Tajín was a public religious and social center, archaeologists hypothesize that Tajín Chico was where the ruling class and political elite actually lived. Newly uncovered in the Tajín Chico area is **Building I,** where several colored paintings, representing different gods from the Tajín pantheon are visible. While some buildings here are in good condition, most have yet to be excavated and are off-limits to the public. As a result, park officials don't mind if visitors scamper up the higher buildings to get a view of the site and surrounding hills. A good deal north of Tajín Chico is a partially unearthed palace for the god Tajín; its façade displays a Mayan-influenced arch of great interest to scholars retracing patterns of cross-cultural interaction in Mesoamerica. One of the buildings just to the northwest, which may soon be open to visitors, is the **Complex of the Columns,** where an account was found of someone called 13-Rabbit, likely a religious leader. East of Tajín Chico, down the hill and around the curve in the gravel road, is the **Great Xicalcoliuhqui,** a tremendous recreational area still being unearthed (open daily 9am-5pm; admission 16 pesos; free Sun. and holidays).

Getting There: El Tajín is accessible via *pesera* from the bus stop in Papantla on Calle 16 de Septiembre, one block east of the cathedral's southeast corner (3 pesos). Buses run on the half-hour (roughly) and cost 3 pesos. The bus will first pass through El Chote and stop at the entrance to El Tajín, marked by a stone mural. To return to Papantla, walk down the access road to the main highway and cross the road to the bus stop to catch a *pesera* running back to Papantla (3 pesos). Service is also available from the **Transportes Papantla** second-class terminal in Papantla; from here it's necessary to go through El Chote and switch buses before arriving at the site.

■ Veracruz

It used to be that wealthy Mexicans vacationed in Miami, the middle class in Acapulco, and the poor stayed home. With time, however, the rich have switched to Acapulco, the middle class to Veracruz, and the poor still stay put. Tourism hasn't always been kind to the city, as evidenced by the over-grown beach-front hotels and glitzy nightclubs. But it's no mystery why people flock here: *veracruzanos* are charming and delightful; their city, they proudly point out, has grown to half a million without losing its identity or peaceful pace of life.

Founded in 1519 by Hernán Cortés, the Villa Rica de la Vera Cruz (Rich Town of the True Cross), has always been a place where Mexico rubs up against the rest of the world. The city prospered as the only port in New Spain officially permitted to trade with the mother country. In the last two centuries, the city was invaded three times: twice by the U.S., once by France. Today, locals, tourists, and sailors alike meander the streets, sip some of the country's best coffee while they listen to the *marimbas,* and dance all night to music with a strong Afro-Caribbean influence.

Veracruz City Center

Baluarte de San Francisco, 5
Faro Venustiano Carranza, 4
Museo Cultural de la Ciudad, 6
Plaza de la República, 2
Train Station, 1
Zócalo, 3

ORIENTATION

Veracruz lies on the southwestern shore of the Gulf of Mexico, 104km south of Xalapa, 424km west of Mexico City, and 376km north of Oaxaca. To get to the *zócalo* from the **bus station,** take a "Díaz Mirón" bus (1.40 pesos) to Parque Zamora and walk away from the park on Independencia for seven blocks. A taxi will cost you 9 pesos. From the **train station,** turn right at the exit and walk toward the opposite end of the Plaza in front of you. The Plaza ends at Lerdo; take a right and follow it into the *zócalo.*

Downtown Veracruz is laid out grid-style; streets run either parallel or perpendicular to the coast. **Díaz Mirón** runs north-south and converges with **Avenida 20 de Noviembre** at **Parque Zamora,** south of downtown. Here, the two streets become **Independencia,** the main drag. Independencia forms the boundary of the *zócalo* farthest from the water. **Miguel Lerdo,** to your left as you face the Palacio Municipal, has a string of hotels and restaurants. It runs towards the water and the **Plaza de la República,** home of the train station, the post office, and drop-off point for many municipal bus routes. To your right is **Zamora;** across **Zaragoza** towards the Gulf it becomes **Malecón,** the boardwalk. At the edge of the water, Malecón makes a 90° turn to the right and becomes **Ávila Camacho,** which follows the Gulf to **Boca del Río,** a suburb housing some of the posher discos and restaurants.

The *centro* is generally safe, but visitors should be careful. Never give the name of your hotel to somebody you just met—thieves have been known to chum up to tourists in the *zócalo* and then rob them at their hotel. Do not walk far from the downtown area after dark. Women may find themselves the object of more male attention in Veracruz than in smaller towns, typically in the form of invitations from random men. A firm and polite refusal will be grudgingly accepted during the day, but at night it may well be taken as a challenge to overcome. Be firm.

PRACTICAL INFORMATION

Tourist Office: (tel. 32-19-99), in the Palacio Municipal on the right side as you face it in the *zócalo*. Helpful staff speaks some English and hands out maps and brochures. Open Mon.-Sat. 9am-9pm, Sun. 10am-1pm. **Seguridad Para el Turista** (tel. 91-800-90-392) provides medical and legal services for tourists.

U.S. Consulate: Víctimas del 25 de Junio #384 (tel. 31-01-42), at Gómez Farías), several blocks south of the *zócalo*. Open Mon.-Fri. 9am-1:30pm.

Currency Exchange: Banamex (tel. 32-82-70), on Independencia one block from the *zócalo*, has 6 **ATMs**. Open for exchange Mon.-Fri. 9am-5pm. Virtually the only place open for exchange on the weekends is **Mini Súper Pete's,** Aquiles Serdán 797 (tel. 32-09-18), two blocks from the *zócalo* (open daily 9am-5pm).

American Express: Camacho 222 (tel. 31-46-36), inside "Viajes Olymar," across from Villa del Mar beach. "Villa del Mar" bus stops at Serdán and Zaragoza. Won't cash traveler's checks. Open Mon.-Fri. 9am-1pm and 4-6pm, Sat. 9am-noon.

Telephones: LADATELs on the *zócalo*, by the Palacio Municipal and cathedral.

Telegrams and fax: (tel. 32-25-08) on Plaza de la República, next to the post office. Open Mon.-Fri. 9am-5pm, Sat. 9am-noon.

Airport: (tel. 34-00-08), 8km south of downtown Veracruz on Route 150. **Aeroméxico,** (tel. 35-01-42). **Mexicana** (tel. 32-22-42, at airport 38-00-08). Both represented by **Viajes Carmi,** Independencia 837 (tel. 31-27-23), north of the *zócalo*. Open Mon.-Fri. 9am-1:30pm and 3:30-7:30pm, Sat. 9am-1pm.

Buses: Central de Autobuses, on Díaz Mirón 1698. **ADO** (tel. 37-57-88), first-class to Cancún (10:35pm, 21hr., 281 pesos), Catemaco (5 per day, 3hr., 34 pesos), Mexico City (19 per day on the hr., 5½hr., first-class 102 pesos, deluxe 117 pesos, ultradeluxe 149 pesos), and Xalapa (48 per day 1:25am-11pm, 1¾hr., first-class 24 pesos, deluxe 28 pesos). **Cristóbal Colon** (tel. 37-57-88), first-class direct to Oaxaca (11pm, 6½hr., 124 pesos) and Tuxtla Gutierrez (6 and 7pm, 12hr., 1630 pesos). **Cuenca** (tel. 34-54-05), second-class to Oaxaca (7am and 8pm, 6½hr., 65 pesos) and Tuxtepec (every hr. 5am-7pm, 3hr., 28 pesos). **AU** (tel. 37-57-32; buses leave from La Fragua, one block behind ADO station), second-class to Córdoba (3:40, 5, and 6:20pm, 1½hr., 29 pesos), Mexico City (every hr. 6am-1am, 6½hr., 87 pesos), Orizaba (3:40, 5, and 6:20pm, 2½hr., 33 pesos), Puebla (every hr. 6am-7pm, 11pm, and midnight, 4½hr., 67 pesos), and Xalapa (1am and every hr. 6am-4pm, 1hr. 40min., 21 pesos). **Líneas Interunidas** (tel. 37-28-78) operates from the AU terminal to Catemaco (every 30min. 2am-midnight, 3½hr., 28 pesos), San Andrés Tuxtla (every 10min. 2am-midnight, 3hr., 26 pesos), and Santiago Tuxtla (every 10min. 2am-midnight, 2½hr., 24 pesos).

Trains: Ferrocarriles Nacionales de México (tel. 32-33-38), at the far end of Plaza de la República, one block from the *zócalo*. First-class to Mexico City (10pm, 12hr., 50 pesos). Yup, twice as slow as buses. Tickets sold Mon.-Sat. 6-9am, 10-11am and 4-9:30pm, Sun. 6-10am and 7-9:30pm.

Taxis: Taxi Confort (tel. 37-65-85 and 37-67-15) will come pick you up and transport you in air-conditioned cars for about 3 pesos more than unaffiliated taxis. You may save money, though, since many taxis raise their prices for tourists.

Car Rental: Autover, Serdán 14 (tel. 32-40-21 and 31-25-68), between Xicoténcatl and 16 de Septiembre near the Gran Café de la Parroquia. Affiliated with Hertz.

Bookstore: La Literaria, Independencia 1415 (tel. 32-11-15), between the *zócalo* and Parque Zamora, on the right as you walk to the park. English magazines, some books, and a full-service stationery store. Open daily 9am-2pm and 4-8pm.

Cultural Center: Instituto Veracruzano de la Cultura (IVEC; tel. 31-66-45), in a purple building on the corner of Canal and Zaragoza, four blocks from the Palacio Municipal. Sponsors dance classes, music recitals, and international exhibitions with topics like the Afro-Cuban influence in Veracruz. Bulletin boards announce events at other venues. Open Mon.-Sat. 9am-9pm, Sun. 9am-3pm. Free.

Markets: Mercado Hidalgo, on the corner of Cortés and Madero, one block from the Parque Zamora away from the Gulf. Fruit, vegetables, piñatas, seafood, flowers, meat, you name it. Open daily 8am-6pm. **Supermarket: El Alba** (tel 32-24-34), M. Lerdo between Independencia and 5 de Mayo, just one block from the *zócalo*. Open Mon.-Sat. 9am-2:30pm and 5-9pm. **ATM** at Banco Serfín next door helps you fund those purchases.

Laundromat: Lavandería Automática Mar y Sol, Madero 572, near the intersection with Serdán. Same- or next-day service. 3kg washed and dried for 24 pesos. Open Mon.-Fri. 9am-2pm and 4-8pm, Sat. 9am-5pm.

Red Cross: (tel. 37-55-00), on Díaz Mirón between Orizaba and Pérez Abascal, one block south of the Central de Autobuses. No English spoken. 24-hr. emergency service and ambulance on call.

Pharmacy: Farmacia del Ahorro (tel. 37-35-25), Paseo del Malecón on the corner of Gómez Farías, two blocks from the *zócalo*. Open 24hr.

Hospital: IMSS, Díaz Mirón 61 (tel 22-19-20). **Hospital Regional,** 20 de Noviembre 284 (tel 32-36-90).

Police: (tel. 38-05-67 or 38-06-93), in the Palacio Municipal.

Post Office: Plaza de la República 213 (tel. 32-20-38). Open Mon.-Fri. 8am-8pm, Sat. 9am-1pm. **Postal Code:** 91700.

Telephone Code: 29

ACCOMMODATIONS

Veracruz has three peak seasons: *Carnaval* (the weeks before Ash Wednesday), *Semana Santa* (the week before Easter), and summer (July and August). The city is full of hotels, but many fill up well in advance during the first two peak periods, and some raise their rates. At other times, reservations are not necessary. Rooms with ceiling fans or large windows are commonplace and not so pricey, but you'll have to pay more for the luxury of a room with air conditioning, often much needed.

Near the *Centro*

These hotels are either on the *zócalo* or around the corner towards the Plaza de la República, on Morelos. The area, full of revelers all night every night, is fun, loud, and relatively safe. Hotels listed have private bathrooms with 24-hour hot water.

Hotel Concha Dorada, M. Lerdo 77 (tel. 31-29-96), on the *zócalo* to the left of the Palacio Municipal. Despite its premier location, the hotel's entrance is obscured by the labyrinth of café tables under the *zócalo's* arches. Rooms are remarkably insulated from the hubbub outside. Singles 70 pesos, with A/C 85. Doubles 80 pesos, with A/C 97. Each additional person 21 pesos.

Do the Right Thing

Every Mexican president since the 1810 Independence War has eaten at the **Gran Café de la Parroquia,** which has also served lesser politicians, luminaries such as Colombian author Gabriel García Márquez, and each person in the city—judging from the nightly crowds. But a torrid story lays beneath the peaceful appearances. Years ago, the café decided to expand, and opened a smaller branch in addition to the original one a few blocks away on Paseo del Malecón. Eventually, however, the Gran Café lost the lease for its original location. Soon after, the Gran Café de los Portales opened in that very space, veiling itself in la Parroquia's tradition. But **justice** prevailed, and the folks from the original café managed to rent another site in the same building, at the corner closer to the *zócalo* and only a few stores from the original site. *Veracruzanos* remain loyal and still sip their café at la Parroquia, clinking their spoons against their glasses for refills, and not the least confused that there are two Gran Cafés in the same building. Make sure you head to the original (newer looking) café, not its imitator.

Hotel Sevilla, Morelos 359 (tel. 32-42-46), where the *zócalo* meets the Plaza de la República. Uninspiring rooms with TV, fan, and street noise. Singles 60 pesos, peak season 95. Doubles 70 pesos, peak season 115.

Hotel Oriente, M. Lerdo 20 (tel. 31-26-15; fax 31-27-40), behind the Palacio Municipal. Rooms have A/C, color TV, phone, and a view of the plaza. Restaurant and parking. There's very little "oriental" about it—except that it's east of the *zócalo*. Singles 88 pesos, peak season 101. Doubles 110 pesos, peak season 126.

On Díaz Mirón and Near the Bus Station

Not as central, but slightly cheaper and less likely to be full. Hotels close to the bus station tend to be very noisy, for obvious reasons. At night, take a cab back.

Hotel Acapulco, Uribe 1327 (tel. 31-87-27). From the bus station on Díaz Mirón, walk several blocks towards downtown, then make a left on Uribe. Friendly family offers spotless, comfortable rooms with ceiling fans. Very clean bathrooms. Happily free of noisy bus traffic. Singles 52 pesos, peak season 69. Doubles 65 pesos, peak season 87. Triples 78 pesos, peak season 104.

Hotel Central, Díaz Mirón 1612 (tel. 32-22-22), next to the ADO station. When the architects of Tomorrowland were done in Anaheim they designed this modern-looking hotel, complete with faux marble lobby. Rooms have TV, phone, and large bathrooms; some even have balconies. Singles 90 pesos, 100 peak. Doubles 100 pesos, peak season 110. Add 10 pesos for A/C.

Hotel Rosa Mar, La Fragua 1100 (tel. 37-07-47), behind the ADO station. On a forgettable strip of aging storefronts, it valiantly tries to remain a clean, wholesome establishment. Convenient for catching early morning buses. Singles 45 pesos. Doubles 60-70 pesos. Add 15 pesos for A/C, 5 pesos for color TV.

FOOD

Shrimp, octopus, red snapper, and a host of other sea beasts are hauled in daily from the Gulf. The **fish market** on Landero y Coss, between Arista and Zaragoza, lets you enjoy them at incredibly cheap prices. Watch out for *ceviche* (raw seafood marinated in lemon juice): it's delicious, but can make you very, very sick if prepared improperly. Ice cream shops sell delicious flavored ices made with mango, coconut, strawberry, and purified water (4 pesos)—great for fighting the heat. And don't leave without trying what's arguably the best coffee in the country.

Gran Café de la Parroquia, Gómez Farías 34 (tel. 32-35-84), at the corner of the Malecón. One of Veracruz's greatest traditions; the entire town always seems to be here. Sit back to people-watch, eavesdrop, and enjoy their famous *café con leche* (5 pesos; food 11-35 pesos). Open daily 6am-1am.

El Torbellino, Zaragoza 384, at the corner of E. Morales. There's no sign out front, but what they save in advertisement, they invest in well prepared, delicious food. Memorable fish 14-25 pesos. Open Thurs.-Tues. 11am-7pm.

El Cochinito de Oro, Zaragoza 190 (tel. 32-36-77), on the corner of Serdán. Serves not only seafood specials (18-20 pesos), but also *comida corrida* (14 pesos) and *antojitos* (6-12 pesos). Eating at this welcoming, roomy restaurant, you appreciate not only the locals' food but also their friendliness. Open daily 7am-5pm.

Alaska (tel. 31-78-73), in the Parque Zamora. Remember the diner in Happy Days? Alaska's got the jukebox and the soda fountain plus the lackadaisical ice cream licker. Frozen treats 9-12 pesos, *antojitos* 12 pesos; the view of the peachy-keen park is free. Open daily 8am-midnight.

Kabuki, Rayón 500 (tel. 32-70-05), near Parque Zamora. A trickling waterfall and a small wooden bridge at the entrance bring a little piece of Japan to Veracruz. Unfortunately, some of the prices come with it. Sushi 35 pesos, noodle dishes 15-35 pesos. Open Sun.-Thurs. 2-11pm, Fri.-Sat. 2pm-midnight.

SIGHTS AND SAND

In the evening, the hymns of the cathedral spilling out into the *zócalo* yield to the seductive rhythms of *marimba*. Crowds gather on benches and outside bars to drink in music that doesn't relent until daybreak. On Tuesday, Thursday, and Saturday nights around 8pm, *veracruzanos* young and old gather for the slowly swaying *danzón*, an old Veracruz tradition. The band strikes up a tune, and couples—men in white wearing straw hats, women clutching their sandalwood fans—file out onto the makeshift dance floor where they sway to the nightly rhythms.

Museums and Monuments

The **Castillo de San Juan de Ulúa** (tel. 38-51-51), Veracruz's most important historic site, rests on the tip of a finger of land that juts into the harbor. Spaniards first arrived at this point on the saint's day of San Juan; "Ulúa" was the greeting the native Totonacos offered the sailors as they disembarked. Construction, using coral as bricks, began in 1582 as part of the system of fortifications built around the Spanish Caribbean to protect the trade fleet and treasure from pirates. The fort has served many uses since its inception, including a high-security prison much like Alcatraz. Chucho el Roto, Mexico's Robin Hood, was perhaps its most famous prisoner. Enter the site through the arched entrance and head for the last room on the right. As you enter, there are two openings in the wall to the left. The hole closer to the grass leads to some stairs and a dim, dank room that was known as Purgatory. The other room contains Hell, surrounded by walls nine meters thick, where prisoners lost their sense of time and their sanity. To maintain yours, walk towards the row of 14 arches that hold a small museum. Through the arches, you can take in a panoramic view of the city and the hungry angelfish nibbling for crackers. To reach the fort, take a "San Juan de Ulúa" bus (1.40 pesos) in front of the Aduana building in the Plaza de la República (open Tues.-Sun. 9am-4:30pm; admission 14 pesos, videocamera 25 pesos, guides in Spanish 20 pesos, free Sun. and holidays).

The bus from San Juan de Ulúa will drop you off at Plaza de la República. Walk straight one block and turn left on Malecón. Almost at the end of the street, you will see a yellow lighthouse on the right, between Hernández and Xicoténcatl. Outside is a larger than life statue of Carranza—Mexican revolutionary, constitution-drafter, president, and native *veracruzano*—coquettishly dressed with a *guayabera*. Upstairs and to the left is the **Museo Venustiano Carranza** (a.k.a. **Museo de la Revolución),** a four-room tribute displaying some of his belongings. The museum, owned by the Mexican navy, proudly displays a gilded version of Article 32 of the 1917 Constitution. This provision, promulgated by Carranza, nationalized the navy (open Tues.-Sun. 9am-5pm; free).

The **Baluarte de San Francisco,** on Canal between 16 de Septiembre and Gómez Farías, two blocks from the lighthouse on Xicoténcatl, is a 17th-century bulwark that protected inhabitants from swashbuckling pirates like Frances Drake. It is all that remains of the old city wall that once enclosed the area between the train station and Parque Zamora. The museum inside displays a beautiful collection of pre-Hispanic gold ornaments; the roof affords a great view of the city (open Tues.-Sat. 10am-4:30pm; admission 14 pesos; Sun. and holidays free). Farther down Canal away from the water, turn right on Zaragoza to see the **Museo Cultural de la Ciudad,** Zaragoza 397 (tel. 31-84-10). Paintings, models, dioramas, and Spanish explanations tell the history of the city from pre-Hispanic times to the present. The museum's most interesting attraction is a relic from its days as an orphanage. In the back stairwell, a stained-glass window depicts Talinmasca, an orphan whose transgressions, legend has it, brought thunder, lighting, and the fierce autumn winds called *nortes* to the area (open Tue.-Sun. 9am-4pm; admission 3 pesos).

Beaches and Beyond

The beaches in Veracruz are not world-class, but they are a refreshing break from the heat. The harbor is a case study in the toxic impact of big oil in big cities. Locals still swim in the water, but considering the health risk, the short trip south of the city is a better idea. **Playa Villa del Mar** is a fairly pleasant hour-long walk from the *zócalo* along the waterfront; it is also accessible via one of the frequent "Villa del Mar" or "Boca del Río" buses that stop on the corner of Serdán and Zaragoza (1.50 pesos). Villa del Mar attracts sunbathers, baseball players, soccer enthusiasts, and vendors of flavored ices called *glorias* and *raspados*. The **Acuario de Veracruz** (tel. 32-79-84), in Centro Comercial Plaza Acuario near the beach, has Sea World-like glass tunnels through communities of native Gulf Sea life and a display of exotic imports. (Aquarium open Sun.-Thurs. 10am-7pm, Fri.-Sat. 10am-7:30pm, admission 12 pesos, seniors 10 pesos, children 5 pesos. Mall open daily 10am-10pm). Farther on Blvd. Camacho away from downtown Veracruz, luxury homes and pricey resorts hog the waterfront. A peaceful stretch of sand is **Costa de Oro** (Gold Coast), between the orange-pinkish hotels Fiesta Americana and Torremar.

The best beach in the Veracruz area is **Playa Mocambo,** next to the Hotel Torremar, in the neighboring city of Boca del Río. Take a "Boca del Río" bus from Zaragoza and Serdán (25min., 1.50 pesos) and ask to be dropped off at Mocambo. Walk past the air-conditioned Plaza Las America and follow the "Playa" sign across the street and down. At the bottom, veer left to head for the beach, or go straight into the **Balneario Mocambo** (tel. 21-02-88), which has a clean, Olympic-sized public pool surrounded by artificial palm trees, changing rooms, and a pool-side bar-restaurant (open daily 9am-5pm; admission 16 pesos, children 8 pesos). Catch the bus back to Veracruz at the top of the drive.

ENTERTAINMENT AND SEASONAL EVENTS

Neither rain nor darkness will prevent the nightly release of tension on the streets and in the clubs of Veracruz. Apart from the spontaneous singing in the *zócalo,* most action takes place along **Av. Camacho** in Boca del Río. **Café Andrade** (tel. 32-82-24) is on Blvd. Camacho at the corner of Callejón 12 de Octubre, across the street from the Plaza Acuario. Rather than go the way of Starbucks, this chain retains local flavor and popularity. They sell beans from nearby Coatepec for grinding at home, and the pungent smell permeates the place (open daily 8am-midnight). Next along the strip is **Master Club Billar,** Blvd. Camacho 4 (tel.37-67-48), one of the friendlier, safer poolhouses you've ever seen. TV, music, bar, A/C, and tables for dominoes or cards (open daily 1pm-2am, pool 25 pesos per hr.). The evening comes to a sizzle at the **Blue Ocean,** Blvd. Camacho 9 (tel. 22-03-55). Outside, green lasers beckon to dancers; inside, a waterfall and a mix of English and Spanish tunes keep the crowd moving. Its older brother, **Ocean,** Ruíz Cortines 8 (tel. 37-64-80), is just around the corner (cover Fri.-Sat. 30 pesos; both open Thurs.-Sat. 11pm-6am; no jeans, shorts, or tennis shoes). Every weekend, **Carlos 'n Charlie's,** Blvd. Camacho 26 (tel.22-29-09), past Blue Ocean along the water, fills to the point of immobility—but that's okay since everyone sits, drinks, and sings along merrily with the salsa music. Think TGIFriday's run by the Mad Hatter: if you tell the waiter it's your birthday, you'll get a whipped cream pie in the face…how funny (no cover, open daily noon-2am). For a more sedate atmosphere head to **Le Blé,** Hernández y Hernández 391-A (tel. 32-69-32), an elegant air-conditioned café closer to downtown Veracruz. Try their sublime desserts: homemade apple pie, carrot cake, and chocolate torte (8 pesos; live music most nights, jazz on Wed.; open daily 8am-midnight).

If two hours of air-conditioning appeals to you, catch a movie—who cares what's showing? For English-language films, check out **Plaza Cinema,** Arista 708 (tel. 31-37-87) or **Cinema Gemelos Veracruz,** at Díaz Mirón 941 (tel. 32-59-70), between Iturbide and Mina (15 pesos).

Every midnight, December 31, *veracruzano* families dress in their Sunday best and fill Blvd. Camacho, looking east to the Gulf to witness the first sunrise of the year. With that auspicious start, a year of celebrations begins. The climax comes early, in late February or early March, just before Ash Wednesday. **Carnaval** literally invades the *zócalo* and usurps the streets with parades, expositions, dance performances, and music. With the requisite ceremonies and parades, a king and queen are crowned. There's an entire office devoted to organizing the week-and-a-half-long event, the **Consejo Directivo del Carnaval** (tel. 32-31-31 ext. 149-172; fax 32-75-93). If you are able to, by all means come—but make hotel reservations early.

■ Near Veracruz

ZEMPOALA RUINS

The ruins at **Zempoala** (sometimes Cempoala), one of the most impressive archaeological sites in the state, lie 40km north of Veracruz, off Route 180. Zempoala was one of the larger southern Totonac cities, part of a federation that covered much of Veracruz in pre-Hispanic times. In 1469, the Aztecs subdued Zempoala and forced them to join their federation. Cortés arrived in 1519, attracted to the glitter of the seashells in the stucco used to build the structures (thinking, of course, that they were gold). The Totonacs were happy to lend Cortés soldiers for his campaign against Montezuma at Tenochtitlán in 1521.

Once a city of 30,000 people, the site's stone structures surround a grassy field next to present-day Zempoala. A museum, to your left as you enter, displays a small collection of pottery and figurines unearthed here, and sells a much-needed English mini-guide to the ruins (3 pesos). The structure closest to the entrance is the **Temple of Death.** Continuing to the left, you will see **three pyramids.** Climbing the narrow stairs is forbidden, just like in the old days, when only priests and sacrificial victims were allowed in the altars that topped the temples. The pyramid on the left is dedicated to Tlaloc (god of water), the one on the right to the moon, and the one in the center, decorated with circular stone receptacles for the hearts of people sacrificed in religious offerings, to the sun. Turning to the right, you will encounter the largest structure on the site, the **Templo Mayor.** When Cortés arrived, the Spaniards erected an altar to the Virgin on top of the temple, literally imposing Catholicism on the Totonacs. In front of the Templo Mayor is the **throne** where the king sat to observe the sacrifices that took place on the platform next to him. The throne also faces the temple known as **Las Chimeneas.** Moving towards the entrance of the site, you will see a fenced-in structure. For the Totonacs, this piece played a central role in the "New Five Ceremony," a five-day fast that took place when a century of the ritual calendar ended every 52 years. Every spring equinox (March 21), people still come to the circle to expel negative energy and absorb positive energy (open daily 9am-6pm; admission 10 pesos, video camera 25 pesos; free Sun. and holidays).

Getting There: From the second-class bus station on La Fragua, in Veracruz, **Autobuses TRV** sends buses to **Cardel** (every 8min. 5am-9:15pm, 45min., 6 pesos), where you can take a bus to Zempoala (every 30min. 7am-7pm, 15min., 2.5pesos). Ask the driver to let you out at **las ruinas,** at the intersection of Av. Prof. José Ruíz and Av. Fco.

Clueless

Even if he's sitting at the right café, a guy can't claim to really know Veracuz until he's worn the traditional white shirt called *guayabera.* The name comes from the word *guayaba,* Spanish for "guava." Cuban guava collectors got tired of shimmying up and down the tree countless times, so they designed a shirt with four pockets to expedite the task. From there, the *guayabera* shirt passed to Panama and then Mexico, where Carlos Cab Arrazote added the thin pleats that form vertical stripes connecting the pockets. His grandson continues the family business, **Guayaberas Finas,** Zaragoza 233 (tel. 31-84-27, fax 31-33-43), between Arista and Serdán, in Veracruz city. Everyone who's anyone has bought one of their high-quality, hot-weather shirts—check out Dwight Eisenhower's note of appreciation on the store's wall. Fashion tip: shirts are not meant to be tucked in (*guayaberas* 150-1,400 pesos; also sells women's clothing; open Mon.-Fri. 9:30am-8pm, Sat. 9:30am-7pm, and Sun. 10am-4pm).

del Paso y Troncoso Norte. If driving from Veracruz, follow Rte. 180 past Cardel, take the Zempoala city turn-off, and proceed until an obscured "Zona Arqueológica" sign appears on the right (about 1km before town). To get back, stand across the street from where you were dropped off and hail a passing "Cardel" bus (2.5 pesos), where you can catch a bus to Veracruz (every 10min. midnight-8pm and every 15min. 8-10pm, 45min., 6 pesos).

■ Catemaco

Everyone says Catemaco is for tourists. The 26 hotels that occupy nearly every street corner say so. The row of lakeview restaurants say so. The young men who yell *"lancha?"* at every passerby, hoping to find passengers for their tours to a nearby island populated with monkeys, say so. And if you decline, a new proposition will promptly be made. *"Brujo?,"* the men will ask. *Brujería* (witchcraft) is what originally attracted people to Catemaco, the site of annual gatherings of shaman, medicine men, and witches from all over Mexico. As a result, traditional *curandero* culture has become grist for the tourist mill. For disbelievers, the beautiful lake-isles that have been likened to Switzerland are enchanting in their own way.

Orientation and Practical Information Catemaco lies along Rte. 180 and is a frequent stop for both first- and second-class buses. Streets are poorly marked, but the basilica on the *zócalo* is usually visible. From the **Autotransportes Los Tuxtlas** stop, turn right and walk until you come to **Madero,** a large street with a strip of grass in the center. Turn left and walk towards the twin orange spires of the basilica, which awaits at the corner of **Boettinger** and Madero. To the left, **Carranza** runs past the Palacio Municipal. Straight ahead, the road becomes **Aldama.** One block downhill to the right is **Playa** and then **Malecón,** which follows the curves of the beach. The **ADO** station is on Aldama, one block behind the basilica.

Señor Agustín Moreno, owner of **Hotel Las Brisas,** Carranza 3, next to the clock on the Palacio Municipal (tel. 3-00-57), provides **tourist information,** including maps of the region. Since there are no banks to exchange money, have pesos handy or obtain them from **Banamex** in San Andrés Tuxtla. If push comes to shove, **Hotel Los Arcos,** Madero 7 (tel. 3-00-03), on the lakes, will exchange dollars at extremely unfavorable rates. The **telephone** *casetas* in town do not allow international collect calls, so try the **Hotel Catemaco,** to the right of the Palacio Municipal, instead. Find the **telegraph office** (tel. 3-00-52) on Carranza, a short distance southwest of the *zócalo* (open Mon.-Fri. 9am-3pm).

First-class **ADO buses** (tel 3-08-42) leave for Córdoba (9:30pm, 5hr., 65 pesos), Mexico City (9:30 and 10pm, 9hr., 141 pesos), Puebla (10pm, 6hr., 101 pesos), Villahermosa (12:20pm, 5hr., 70 pesos), and Xalapa (5:45am, 1 and 6pm, 3hr., 36 pesos). **AU** (tel. 3-07-77) goes to Mexico City (11:30am and 9pm, 9hr., 132 pesos), San Andrés (11:30am and 9pm, 20min., 2 pesos), and Veracruz (11:30am, 3½hr., 32 pesos). **Autotransportes Los Tuxtlas** goes to San Andrés (every 10min., 20min., 2 pesos) and Santiago (every 10min., 40min., 4 pesos).

The **market** is on Madero before the *zócalo* (open daily 6am-8pm). **Farmacia Nuestra Señora del Carmen** (tel. 3-00-91) is at the corner of Carranza and Boettinger (open daily 7am-9pm). The **Centro de Salud,** on Carranza (tel. 3-02-47), is in a white building with a blue roof, three blocks south of the *zócalo*, on the left. Some English is spoken. Medical services are available 24 hours. The **police** (tel. 3-00-55) are in the Palacio Municipal, on the *zócalo*. The **post office** is on Mantilla, between the lake and Hotel Los Arcos (open Mon.-Fri. 9am-4pm, Sat. 9am-1pm). **Postal Code:** 95870. **Telephone Code:** 294.

Accommodations Most hotels cluster around the *zócalo* and the waterfront. Although they fill up during Christmas and *Semana Santa,* you'll practically have the town to yourself on a weekday during the off-season. It is not safe to camp on the beaches, since crime has recently been a problem in the area (see p. 436 for camping possibilities in the area). The **Hotel Julita,** Playa 10 (tel. 3-00-08), on the waterfront, one block downhill from the *zócalo,* is a very good deal, boasting an unbeatable location and large rooms with springy beds and fans (singles 30 pesos, peak season 40; doubles 60 pesos). **Hotel Acuario** (tel. 3-04-18), next to the Palacio Municipal at Boettinger and Carranza, provides large, relatively clean rooms with 70s curtains, some with balconies (singles 40 pesos; doubles 50 pesos).

Food When choosing a waterfront restaurant, pay attention only to the establishment's view of the lake, since food tastes pretty much the same everywhere. *Mojarra* and *topote* will hop right from the lake onto your plate, but make sure to have them fried, since the waters can be polluted. *Mojarra* is prepared in a variety of ways, while the bite-sized *topote* is fried up whole and heaped with *tamales.* Shrimp, much of it from surrounding rivers, is also a local specialty. **Restaurant La Casona del Recuerdo,** Aldama 6 (tel. 3-05-76), just off the *zócalo,* is a haven from the busy waterfront. The terrace in back overlooks a peaceful wooded garden. *Mojarra* goes for 14 pesos, shrimp 20 pesos (open daily 8am-8pm). On the waterfront, across from the Hotel Julita, **7 Brujas** (tel. 3-01-57) serves the standard seafood dishes (20-35 pesos). Take your very own *bruja* doll home (5 pesos; open daily 8am-10pm). Diagonally across from Hotel Julita, on Malecón, **Restaurant La Ola** (tel. 3-00-10) fries up a mean *mojarra* (17-22 pesos; open daily 8am-10pm).

Sights, Entertainment, and Seasonal Events The rocky beaches of **Laguna Catemaco** don't resemble Cancún, but a dip in the lake can be a refreshing break from the hot Veracruz sun. The water immediately in front of town is not safe for swimming. A hiking path runs along the edge of the lake—walk down from the *zócalo* to the waterfront and turn left. The trail, bordered by trees knotted with character, will guide you the 1.5km to **Playa Expagoya** and then another ½km down the road to the more secluded and sandy **Playa Hermosa,** the first swimmable beach on the trail. The path is not safe at night.

The lake is nearly circular, about 15km across, and several small islands dot its smooth surface. The waterfront is lined with long, flat-bottomed, brightly colored *lanchas* equipped with chairs and canopies. These boats lie ready to take you on an hour-long trip to the best-known island of the lot, **Isla de Changos.** A tribe of semi-wild, red-cheeked *changos* (mandrills, a kind of baboon) was brought from Thailand for a scientific experiment by the University of Veracruz in 1979, who wanted to see if the animals could survive in their new environment. Lo and behold, 17 years later the *changos* are alive and well and posing for snapshots. Knowing that the *lanchistas* bring coconuts and tortillas, the bravest *changos* climb right into the boat to pose for camera shots and collect their reward. En route to the island, you'll pass a cave-shrine that stands on the spot where a woman had a vision of the Virgin Mary over a century ago. Negotiate with the *lancheros* for longer trips, including an exploration of the rivers that feed the lake or a trip to the tropical forests of the nearby national park. The *lanchas* leave from the docking area below the *zócalo* (standard tour of the lake, including the Isla de Changos and the shrine of the Virgin, 150 pesos per boat, 30 pesos per person on a *colectivo;* go in the morning or on the weekend if you want to share the boat to save money).

Catemaco's **bars** and **discos** are the best in the Tuxtlas area. **Chanequa's,** in the Hotel Playa Azul (tel. 3-00-42 or 3-00-01), some distance outside of Catemaco, is said to be the hottest. Walking there at night is difficult and dangerous; a boat will take you for 20 pesos. The road along the beach dominates nightlife in Catemaco. Starting four blocks from the Hotel Julita, one block away from the water on Madero, **Jahac 45** (tel. 3-08-50) is a video bar and disco (cover 12 pesos; open Fri.-Sat. after 9pm). Next on Playa, moving closer to the Hotel Julita, is **Luna 90,** a disco above Restaurant La Luna (cover 15 pesos; open Fri.-Sat. after 9pm). Just past Hotel Julita is the bar portion of the restaurant **7 Brujas** (open daily until 10:30pm). A few doors down from the bar is **Pescado Loco,** which plays a seafood salad of music from salsa and *rancheras* to English pop (cover 15 pesos; open Fri.-Sat. 9pm-3am).

In addition to **Semana Santa** and Christmas festivities, the town goes crazy on July 16, the day of it's patron saint Carmen. May 30 is the Day of the Fisherman.

■ Near Catemaco: The Gulf Coast

Some say that the only reason to go to Catemaco is for its proximity to secluded beaches on the Gulf Coast. Waves, they will tell you, crash more crisply in the absence of Corona bars and souvenir shops. These beaches are not spectacular, but they are secluded—cattle roam the spaces between fishing villages with no telephone lines and only the most basic services. The state of Veracruz wants to pave the road to the coast and to develop the region for tourism. When this will happen is anyone's guess, but the sage traveler will visit the area before it does.

Getting to the Gulf Coast near Catemaco is an adventure. Public transportation to the area is limited to **Transportes Rurales's** small pickup trucks, affectionately dubbed *piratas* by locals. A four-door vehicle with wooden benches built into its caged-in bed, a *pirata* can carry the entire population of a small town. Men are expected to yield indoor seats to children and the elderly. From Catemaco, *piratas* depart from the intersection of two unmarked streets on the eastern edge of town. To get to them follow the lakefront past 7 Brujas for several blocks until you pass the last restaurant before foliage takes over the street; then turn left and walk until the intersection of a paved road. Queues for the *piratas* begin to your left next to the trucks. A man with a clipboard can give you a general idea when your ride will leave. Often you will have to wait until several passengers have congregated to go in your direction. There are two main routes: one that ends at **Montepío** on the Gulf Coast and one that goes to **Coyamé** on the other side of Lake Catemaco. The *piratas* operate daily 6am-6pm.

The Road to Montepío

The first point of interest on the way to Montepío (besides the jaw-dropping views) is **Sontecomapán,** 20km from Catemaco (4 pesos). This is also the end of the paved road. Hold on tight for the points beyond. Sontecomapán is a small town beside an eponymous saltwater lake that empties into the Gulf of Mexico. *Lanchas* are available for excursions on the lake. Sontecomapán is accessible by pickup truck. Farther down the road lies the village of **La Barra,** a small fishing community where Laguna Sontecomapán empties into the Gulf of Mexico. To get there, ride a pickup 8km beyond Sontecomapán until the road forks. Your *pirata* will normally follow the left fork; you can either negotiate with the driver to take the right fork instead, or you can hop off, take a right, and hike the 5 to 6km to La Barra yourself. Once there, locals will show you a modicum of hospitality if you introduce yourself politely; a friendly *viajero* will be allowed to camp near someone's home.

The *pirata* route comes closer to the coast near **Playa Jicacal** and **Playa Escondida;** ask the driver to let you off (50min., 9 pesos). A 30-minute walk through a lush and remote rural area leads to Playa Jicacal, a true gem. The long, slightly stony beach is almost completely empty; the only footprints lead to a few modest fisherman's shacks and—inevitably—a *refresco* stand and snack bar. The beach is said to be safe for camping, and hammock-hanging sites may be available. Safety goes hand and hand with good manners, and campers who wish to crash on the beach would do well to ingratiate themselves with the *jicacaleños.*

Instead of turning right to Playa Jicacal, you can walk uphill to the left for Playa Escondida (Hidden Beach), a beach that lives up to its name. The simple white **Hotel Playa Escondida** (tel. 91-294-2-10-10 in San Andrés) appears like a mirage. In fact, everyone who arrives at the hotel wonders how the other guests heard of it. A night at the hotel provides not only access to the small rocky beach below, but also the chance to explore the surrounding jungle (singles with fans 80 pesos; doubles with fans 90 pesos). The remote hotel has a full-service restaurant perched high over the waves of the Gulf of Mexico. A complete lunch of soup, chicken, tortillas, and drink tastes all the more scrumptious because you had to trek so far to reach it (26 pesos). Swimming is possible at both beaches, but a strong undertow sometimes makes taking a plunge dangerous even for the natatorial expert.

At the end of the *pirata* route is the tiny village of Montepío, 40km (2hr.). The town consists of a handful of buildings, including a little light blue church whose façade is barely big enough to accommodate the door. There are some very modest restaurants, a **pharmacy** (open daily 10am-2pm), and a **health clinic** (open 24hr.) scattered around the church and along the road. Montepío is less spectacular than Playa Escondida, but it does offer a long, narrow beach framed by a tall bluff and volcanic rocks on one end and the green hills of the Sierra on the other. Locals rent horses for 15 pesos per hour. Pick-up trucks (every hr. 6am-6pm), take travelers to a nearby **biological research station,** where young scientists may tell you about the flora and fauna of the area and show you the snakes and monkeys they're studying. The new **Hotel Posada San José** (tel. 91-294-2-10-10) stands on the banks of the small river leading to the beach. The *posada* is pretty clean and features a restaurant serving a 15-peso *comida corrida.* The beach is said to be safe for camping. Day-trippers are beginning to discover Montepío, so if you want the town to yourself, plan on spending the night.

Coyamé

Alternatively, you can take a *pirata* headed for Coyamé, 12km from Catemaco, where you can watch the cool waters that are bottled up from underground springs. Seven kilometers *en route* to Coyamé, the **Proyecto Ecológico Educacional Nanciyaga,** or simply **Nanciyaga** (tel. 3-01-99, 3 pesos in *pirata*), has lured Hollywood producers, beauty queens, and uptight Americans to its cleansing font of pre-Hispanic therapy. From the highway, turn right and walk in front of the "Nanciyaga" sign on a dirt path that leads towards the shore of the lake. All of the vegetation in the area is part of a preserve, a fact that forced the makers of Sean Connery's "Medicine Man" to alter the landscape with styrofoam trees. Remains from the movie shoot as well as a facial mask of local mud and sips of natural spring water are part of the tour of the site (10 pesos; consultation with a real medicine man 40 pesos more). Guests can stay overnight in mosquito-netted bungalows and enjoy the Olmec *temazacal* sweat lodge, full-body mud baths, open air concerts, and boat tours of the lake that sparkles through the trees (130 pesos; day pass 45 pesos; activities like massages and vegetarian meals require advance reservations). *Lanchas* or taxis will also take you to Nanciyaga (20 pesos). To return to Catemaco, walk back to the highway, cross the street, and flag down any *pirata* headed back to town.

■ San Andrés Tuxtla

Lodged between the lush lakeside resorts of Catemaco and the Olmec artifacts of Santiago, San Andrés Tuxtla (usually just San Andrés) is the relatively untouristed anchor of 125,000 inhabitants that keeps the Sierra de los Tuxtlas peacefully down-to-earth. A quiet little town, San Andrés serves mainly as a center for the tobacco and cattle industries of the surrounding countryside, and offers a cache of budget hotels, an entertaining *zócalo,* remarkably friendly people, and some nearby natural attractions. As the transportation hub of the region, San Andrés serves as a good base from which to stage day trips to most locations in Los Dos Tuxtlas.

Orientation and Practical Information Located midway between Catemaco and Santiago Tuxtla on Route 180, San Andrés is built on and around a volcanic range that hugs the Gulf Coast. The downtown area lies in the slightly raised center of a valley. To get there from the bus station, walk down **Juárez,** the city's main street. Branching off Rte. 180, Juárez descends a steep hill, crosses a small

VERACRUZ

stream, and gradually ascends to meet the cathedral, at the north corner of the *zócalo*. Right before reaching the cathedral, Juárez passes by the **Palacio Municipal** on the right and intersects **Constitución** to the left and **Madero** to the right, in front of the Palacio Municipal. Following Constitución to the left, you will come to the intersection of **Pino Suárez**, where some hotels are located. The walk takes 10 minutes from the bus station; a taxi costs 5 pesos.

The often deserted **tourist office** is on the first floor of the Palacio Municipal, right in front of the cathedral (open Mon.-Fri. 9am-1pm and 4-6pm). You're more likely to find somebody at **Protux Viajes**, 16 de Septiembre 6 (tel. 2-21-75), around the corner. They provide pamphlets and information about San Andrés and environs (open Mon.-Sat. 8:30am-2pm and 4:30-8pm). Exchange your money at **Banamex** (tel. 2-03-50), on the south side of the *zócalo* (open for exchange Mon.-Fri. 9am-2:30pm). They have a 24-hour **ATM**. There are no **LADATELs** in San Andrés. Long-distance *casetas* can be found at **Pipisoles**, Madero 6B (open Mon.-Fri. 8am-10pm, Sun. 9am-1pm) and at **Protux Viajes**. Coin-operated phones are available outside the **Telmex** office on Carranza at the corner of Bernardo Peña; to get there take Madero past the Palacio Municipal and turn right on Carranza (open Mon.-Fri. 8am-5pm). The **telegram office** (tel. 2-08-20) is on Constitución 93 at the corner of Pino Suárez (open Mon.-Fri. 8am-6pm, Sat. 9am-noon).

Autotransportes Los Tuxtlas (tel. 2-14-62), on Rte. 180 just beyond the ADO station, sends **buses** to Catemaco (every 10min. 4am-10pm, 15min. 2 pesos), Coatzacoalcos (every 10min. 4am-10pm, 3½hr., 25 pesos), Santiago Tuxtla (every 10min. 4am-10pm, 20min., 2.50 pesos), and Veracruz (every 15min. 2am-10pm, 3½hr., 26 pesos). **ADO** (tel. 2-08-71), at the intersection of Juárez and Route 180 (also called **Blvd. 5 de Febrero**), runs buses to Mexico City (1:30am, 9, 10:30 and 11:10pm, 7½hr., 140 pesos; comfy deluxe service 11pm, 7½hr., 161 pesos), Veracruz (27 per day 5am-10:30pm, 2½hr., 34 pesos), and Villahermosa (13 per day 12:45am-10:45pm, 5hr., 73 pesos). **AU** (tel. 2-09-84) goes to Puebla (9:50pm, 6hr., 94 pesos), Veracruz (noon and 9:50pm, 2½hr., 30 pesos), and Xalapa (noon and 9:50 pm, 4hr., 52 pesos). **Cuenca** covers Tuxtepec (10 per day 4am-6pm, 3hr., 29 pesos).

The **market, Mercado 5 de Febrero**, spills onto the streets several blocks from the *zócalo*. To get there, walk on Madero, turn right on Carranza and walk uphill (open daily 6am-10pm). **Lavandería Tintorería Roxy**, at Agosto 776 (tel. 2-12-94), will wash and dry 3kg of your dirtiest duds for 11 pesos (open Mon.-Sat. 8am-8pm). The **Red Cross** is at Boca Negra 25 (tel. 2-05-00), north of the *zócalo* (open 24hr.). **Farmacia Garysa**, Madero 3, is in the "Canada" building to the left of the Palacio Municipal (open 24hr.). The **Hospital Regional** (tel. 2-31-99), at the edge of town, has an ambulance service. The **police** (tel. 2-14-99) are located on Pasaje Rascón, near the Palacio Municipal (open 24hr.). The **post office** (tel. 2-01-89) is at La Fragua and 20 de Noviembre, one block from the *zócalo* (open Mon.-Fri. 8am-8pm, Sat. 8am-12:30pm). **Postal Code:** 95700. **Telephone Code:** 294.

Accommodations and Food   Although San Andrés remains almost tourist-free, budget accommodations with private bath and hot water are abundant. Two of the best bargains are within spitting distance of each other, just to the left of the cathedral. Follow the street in front of the church to the left and turn right onto Pino Suárez at the orange Fénix supermarket. The **Hotel Colonial,** Pino Suárez 7 (tel. 2-05-52), has a spacious lobby and more modestly-sized rooms cooled vigorously by a ceiling fan. Mural-sized map behind the check-in desk gives a comprehensive overview of the area (singles 30 pesos; doubles 50 pesos). **Hotel Figueroa,** at Pino Suárez 2 (tel. 2-02-57), is across the street. Rooms on the central courtyard look across to the home of the family that runs the place, while others line the arcaded balcony. All have portable fans (singles 30-60 pesos; doubles 45-80 pesos). The most affordable rooms with all-important, life-sustaining air conditioning are in **Hotel Isabel**, Madero 13 (tel. 2-16-17), to the left of the Hotel Parque next to the *zócalo* (singles 70 pesos, with A/C 85 pesos; doubles 90 pesos, with A/C 110 pesos).

Several sidewalk cafés on the *zócalo* serve breakfast and large coffees, and afford a pleasant view of simple small town life. A number of good lunch spots line Madero, while the cheaper sidewalk stands proliferate in and around the market. **Restaurant La Caperucita,** Juárez 108 (tel. 2-05-11), downhill from the cathedral, specializes in large and filling fried *misantleca* (big disk-o-dough stuffed with beans, ham and cheese, 12 pesos). They also serve delicious tacos, fruit shakes, and *refrescos* at mind-bogglingly low prices (open daily 7am-midnight). The older and more affluent huddle at **Restaurant del Parque** (tel. 2-01-98), on the ground floor of the Hotel Parque on the *zócalo*. Food (breakfast 9-12 pesos, *antojitos* 6-10 pesos, *tortas* 9-15 pesos) is secondary to the socializing (open daily 7am-midnight). The friendly folks at **El Pequeño Archie,** on Pino Suárez just downhill from the hotels and across the street from the movies, serve up a delicious *comida corrida* (10 peso) and *antojitos* (6-10 pesos; open Mon.-Sat. 8am-9pm, Sun. 8am-2pm).

Sights, Entertainment, and Seasonal Events Even non-smokers will be impressed by the **Tabacos San Andrés Factory,** where Santa Clara cigars are made. From the *zócalo*, walk up Juárez to the ADO and turn right—it's about 200m down Route 180 (here called Blvd. 5 de Febrero) on the right. An open door and the smell of tobacco leaves invite you in. The amicable staff will gladly walk you through the entire process, from selecting the leaves to rolling the stogies to putting on the company seal. A skilled worker can produce 800 cigars a day. You can purchase some near the entrance: the bottom of the line starts at 100 pesos, while a box of 25 of their finest *puros* goes for 500 pesos (open Mon.-Sat. 7am-7pm; for information on customs regulations limiting the number of cigars you can take back into your country, see p. 11).

The sheer number of video rental stores just about says it all: San Andrés is not exactly a town that parties until dawn. Unless you brought your VCR along, you might be hard up to find nighttime entertainment. Most of the action centers on the *zócalo*, where folks in San Andrés gather to meet, gossip, see, and be seen. On Sunday nights, families bring their children, and the square becomes a little kiddie carnival, with balloons and small electric cars for hire. **Cinemas San Andrés,** on Pino Suárez across from El Pequeño Archie, brings English-language movies to the big screen for 8 pesos. For anything more high-paced than people- and film-watching, catch the bus to **Catemaco,** bursting at the seams with bars and discos.

On Independence Day, September 16, giant balloons of colorful paper are flown over the *zócalo*. The town's patron saint is celebrated on November 30. December

---

Blue Lagoon

La Laguna Encantada is a volcanic lake 2km northeast of the city, surrounded by lush vegetation and known mainly for its queer tendency to rise during the dry season and fall during the rainy season. To get there, walk north on Serapio Rendón (perpendicular to, and a couple of blocks north of, Pino Suárez) until you hit Blvd. 5 de Febrero (Rte. 180); then walk east on 5 de Febrero until a sign for the lake appears on the left (40min.). The trail can be muddy and rocky, so come prepared. Taxis will take you there reluctantly, due to poor road conditions (18 pesos). The lake is very clean for swimming; it may be populated by washerwomen, fishermen, and birds, or even crowds of people, depending on the season, the weather, and the day of the week. As tempting as a solitary day in the woods may sound, for safety reasons it might be best to go with a friend.

On the opposite shore, which is accessible via the trail that circumnavigates the lake, a complicated series of unmarked trails leads to the spring whence the lake's waters flow, and then up a steep hill to **La Coberna del Diablo,** where witches from around Mexico gather on the first Friday in March. The remains of their ceremonial candles spot the rocks on the way up to the . Don't go in: if the devil doesn't get you, the sulfuric gases and tarantulas will.

VERACRUZ

12 is the day of Guadalupe, Mexico's patron virgin. As part of the celebrations, young people playfully hit each other with wooden figures called *majigangas*.

■ Near San Andrés Tuxtla: Salto de Eyipantla

To reach the more accessible **Salto de Eyipantla** waterfall, take a minibus from the market that bears the name of these spectacular falls (35min., 1.80 pesos). The bus will make a U-turn and stop at a small market. Walk straight behind the bus for a few minutes until you encounter a parking lot and children clamoring to give you flowers—beware, the "gifts" will turn into pleas for money. Proceed through a restaurant at the end of the lot. Immediately after the entrance (admission 1 peso), you'll find the 244 steps that descend to the base of the falls. A movie starring Lorenzo Lamas and a deodorant commercial were both filmed in this historic point. Don't expect a solitary communion with nature, though—you'll have to angle your camera shots of the falls so as not to include the kiosks. The bus back to San Andrés stops every 10 minutes at the very stop where it left you.

■ Santiago Tuxtla

Of the three cities that constitute Los Tuxtlas, Santiago (pop. 50,000) has the least to offer visitors in terms of sights and recreational activities. Its attraction stems from its connection to two influential forces in Mexican history: the Olmecs and Hernán Cortés. The colossal stone heads and Catholic ceremonies that each left behind comingle in this community known for its superstition and elaborate festivals.

Orientation and Practical Information The **ADO bus station,** like everything else in Santiago, is just a few blocks from the *zócalo*. To reach the town center, walk downhill from Rte. 180. The first right is **Ayuntamiento,** which leads to the **Palacio Municipal** with its clock tower on the right and the *zócalo* in front of it. From the ADO bus station, walking downhill and then following **Morelos** will bring you to the **Autotransportes Los Tuxtlas** station on the left and **Calle Obregón** on the right.

The **Presidencia Municipal** (tel. 7-02-83), on the second floor of the Palacio Municipal, serves as a **tourist office** when not filing paperwork about cattle (open Mon.-Fri. 9am-5pm). **Currency exchange** is simply not possible in Santiago, so come armed with pesos. The closest bank is in San Andrés. Somebody at the **telephone office,** in the corner of the Palacio Municipal at the intersection with Ayuntamiento, should be able to help with long distance calls.

ADO (tel. 7-04-38) sends buses to Mexico City (9:20, 10:45, and 11:30pm, 7hr., 137 pesos), Veracruz (10 and 11am, 1 and 6:45pm, 2¼hr., 31 pesos), and Xalapa (6:45, 7:50, and 9am, 4½hr., 55 pesos). **Cuenca** sends buses to San Andrés (every hr. 9am-10pm except 4 and 7pm, 20min., 2.50 pesos) and Tuxtepec (every hr. 4:35am-6:35pm, 4hr., 27 pesos). **Autotransportes Los Tuxtlas** buses leave right next to the ADO station for Catemaco (every 10min. 8am-10pm, 40min., 4.50 pesos) and San Andrés (20min., 2 pesos).

The **market, Mercado Municipal Morelos,** begins to the left of the *zócalo* as you face it from the Palacio Municipal and continues one street over to the left (open daily 5am-8pm). The nearest **Red Cross** is in San Andrés; for **24-hour ambulance service** dial 2-05-00. **Farmacia San Felipe**, just off the *zócalo* at Eduardo Murguía 13 (tel. 7-01-36), is open 24 hours. The **Clínica Doctores Castellanos,** across from the Hotel Castellanos (tel. 7-02-60), provides medical assistance day and night. Find the **police** (tel. 7-00-92) downstairs in the Palacio Municipal (open daily 24hr.).

Accommodations The **Hotel Castellanos** (tel. 7-03-00), on the corner of 5 de Mayo and Comonfort at the far corner of the *zócalo*, is not only a place to stay; its also Santiago's most interesting attraction. The rooms fit together like wedges in a Trivial

Pursuit game piece; each offers air conditioning, telephones, color TV, and a balcony with a panoramic view. If you can stop admiring the scenery or the painted ceramic bathroom sinks, there is also a pool and restaurant. Too bad it's so expensive (singles 115 pesos; doubles 138 pesos; triples 161 pesos). Both less stimulating and less expensive, **Casa de Huéspedes Morelos,** Obrégon 15, downhill from the bus stations (tel. 7-04-74), has basic small rooms with fans and bathrooms with hot water (singles 40 pesos; doubles 60 pesos; triples 70 pesos).

Sights and Seasonal Events The largest Olmec head ever discovered (45 tons) sits complacently at the far end of Santiago's *zócalo,* shaded from the sun by a large cupola. The sculpture is immediately recognizable as Olmec because of its distinctive facial features (heavy lips and slanted eyes), ears, and "helmet." The **Museo Regional Tuxteco,** to the left of the head along the *zócalo,* displays terra cotta masks of the Totonacs and another Olmec head, along with other artifacts from around the region (open Mon.-Sat. 9am-5pm; admission 10 pesos). Celebrations for the **fair** in honor of Santiago, the town's patron saint, take place July 20 to 29 and include a choreographed fight between Christians and Moors, a dance contest, and a **torneo de cintas** where men dress in medieval gear and ride horses.

■ Near Santiago Tuxtla

TRES ZAPOTES RUINS

Tres Zapotes, one of the three main Olmec ceremonial centers, reached its peak between 900 and 300 BCE. Today, calling the artifacts on display a museum would be either optimistic or an exaggeration. There are no written explanations to elucidate the small sheltered gathering of carved stones, nor are artifacts even located at their original sites. If you have even a cursory knowledge of Spanish, solicit explanations from the attendant at the ticket booth.

The Olmecs did not construct great cities, but they did fill them with noteworthy art. The most imposing figure at Tres Zapotes is one of the trademark Olmec stone heads that always seems to carry the label "colossal." The monumentality of their sculpture contrasts with the delicate details and precise techniques they used to carve them. Archaeologists believe the heads constitute portraits of actual leaders. The helmet that adorns the head may have been worn during ritual ball games that appeared first in Olmec centers and then spread to Mesoamerica. To the left of the head is the **Stela C,** which, together with its more famous other half (now at the National Anthropology Museum in Mexico City, see p. 103), bears the oldest date in the Americas—31 BCE, inscribed in Olmec glyphs similar to those later used by the Maya. The date is visible on the back of the stela as a bar (representing "5") and two dots, giving a total of 7 on their calendar. **Stela A** lies in the transept to the left. Decorations in the stela include the figure of a man with a jaguar's head lying down on top, a serpent coiling upon itself (on the right side) and a man holding an axe (on the left side). **Stela D,** to the right of the head, again resembles a tablet. Within the mouth of a jaguar are renderings of three people whose relative heights symbolize their power and importance: the war god (on the far right) holds a staff, the woman (in the middle), identifiable by her skirt, is the moon goddess; a character depicting *el pueblo* (on the far left) is kneeling to both deities. Opposite Stela D, a large volcanic rock with a jaguar in the center broods unhappily. On one side of this piece, **Life** is represented by a bloody mouth, while **Death,** on the other side, takes the form of a skeletal face. In the center rests God, the jaguar (museum open daily 9am-5pm; admission 7 pesos, free Sun.).

Getting There: From the Museo Regional Tuxteco in Santiago, walk towards the clock tower and turn right on Zaragoza. Pass through the market and cross the bridge to Morelos, where you can take a *taxi-colectivo* to Tres Zapotes (30min., 7 pesos). You will be let off in the town of Tres Zapotes. From the stop, turn left and walk to the first cross-street. Turn left and walk around the chain-link fence until you see the entrance to the sight, on your right. A taxi will take you to the place where the artifacts were actually found (1km, 6 pesos).

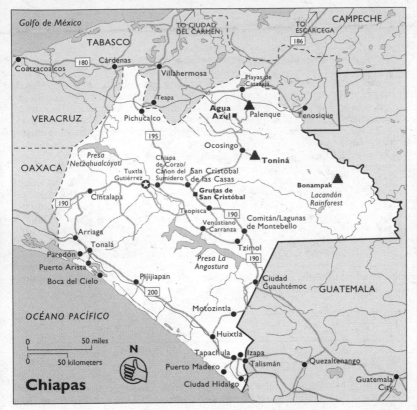

Chiapas and Tabasco

Chiapas is special. Its climate is unique for southern Mexico—the chilly nights and crisp fresh air give the highlands a distinct flavor. Cortés had the Sierra de Chiapas in mind when, to demonstrate what Mexico looked like, he crumpled a piece of parchment and dropped it on the table. In these rugged green mountains, buses careen around hairpin turns above deep valleys before hurtling down into jungles on rutted roads. One of Mexico's most beautiful cities, San Cristóbal de las Casas, rests high amid these peaks.

Throughout the state, you will hear diverse Mayan dialects and find markets and other public places filled with *indígenas*. Indeed, the state is part of the Mayan heartland; the Lacandón Rainforest shields the remote ruins of Bonampak and Yaxchilán and is still home to the Lacandón Indians, the one Maya population to escape the Conquest. Chiapas's *indígenas* remain fiercely traditional—in many communities, schools teach in the local dialect as well as in Spanish, and regional dress, while it varies across communities, is almost always maintained.

Tabasco, perched on the lush Isthmus of Tehuantepec, connects the Yucatán Peninsula to the Gulf coast and the rest of the country. *Tabasqueños* proudly boast that their state is one of the wetter places on earth, second only to the Amazon Basin. Whether this claim is valid or not, or why one would boast about it, is not important. What matters is that Tabasco, dotted by lakes and swamps, criss-crossed by rivers,

The State of Things

Most *chiapanecos* farm for a living, an activity largely regulated by land bosses *(caciques)* who represent well greased cogs in the PRI political machine. Seventy-seven percent of the territory is privately owned by *caciques*, and one in four Mexican land disputes occurs here—although the state contains only 3% of the nation's people. Poor *campesinos* in Chiapas often labor for as little as 10 to 15 pesos per day. When the Zapatista rebels rose up in January of 1994 and took San Cristóbal, their basic demands—land, democratic reforms, health care, and education—reflected years of injustice, struggle, and resentment. The rebels are still hiding in the fringes of the Lacandón Rainforest; their refusal to accept the government's peace plan, paired with the government's inability to achieve democratic reforms, makes a prolonged stalemate seem likely.

The Mexican military has moved into towns and cities throughout the state; Palenque, Ocosingo, San Cristóbal, and Comitán are heavily occupied. Travelers to the region, however, have little to be concerned about. The most military action one is likely to witness is soldiers from all parts of the country calling home from a long-distance *caseta*. Travelers are more likely to experience peaceful peasant protests than armed fighting. It would be wise, however, to keep abreast of political developments before a trip to Chiapas, and talk to tourist officials and travelers who are returning from your intended destinations.

and swathed in dense, humid jungle, does see an awful lot of rainfall. In Tabasco, a traveler without rain gear is a very unhappy traveler indeed.

TABASCO

■ Villahermosa

By 1596, the Spanish colonists were weary enough of defending the coast against British and Dutch pirates that they migrated inland up the Río Grijalva to found Villahermosa. The city was relatively poor and substantially isolated, an agricultural center of minor importance, accessible only by river. All this has changed, however, in the past 50 years. In the 1940s, railroad tracks were laid, connecting Villahermosa to the rest of the Republic. The discovery of oil in the region in 1974 completed the transformation and gave the ailing city a shot in the arm. Rail lines and petro-profits have transformed Villahermosa (pop. 1.6 million) from boondock to boomtown, a dense urban forest of satellite antennae, luxury hotels, and apartment complexes. The city recently underwent a cosmetic make-over to attract tourists, relocating most of the state's archaeological treasures to two museums in the city center—Parque-Museo La Venta and the Museo Regional de Antropología.

ORIENTATION

Tabasco's state capital lies 20km from the border with Chiapas and 298km west of Escárcega, the major crossroads for Yucatán-bound travelers. The spine of the downtown area is **27 de Febrero. Paseo Tabasco** runs north-south and connects the Tabasco 2000 complex to *el centro*, intersecting 27 de Febrero in front of the cathedral. *Saetas* (public buses) and *combis* (each 1.50 pesos) run from 6am to 10:30pm. First- and second-class **buses** depart from the eastern part of town. An **airport** lies northwest of the city, 14km from the downtown area; taxis shuttle between the airport and *el centro* (40 pesos *especial*, 15 pesos *colectivo*).

To reach downtown from the **first-class ADO station,** walk 2½ blocks to the right on Mina to Méndez. From there, take a *combi* labeled "Tierra Colorada Centro-Juárez" and get off a few minutes later at **Parque Juárez.** Most hotels are south of the park on either **Madero** or its parallel cousin **Constitución**. Walking from the station to Parque Juárez takes 15 to 20 minutes; upon exiting the terminal, head right down Mina for eight blocks, then turn left onto 27 de Febrero. Eight more blocks takes you to the intersection with Madero. To get downtown from the **second-class bus terminal**, cross Grijalva on the pedestrian bridge to the left of the station exit, then jump on a bus labeled "Indeco Centro" (1 peso) and disembark at Parque Juárez on Madero. To make the 25-minute walk from the station, cross the bridge and continue south on Mina for three blocks until you reach the ADO station (see above). A cab ride to the center of town costs about 6 pesos.

PRACTICAL INFORMATION

Tourist Offices: Instituto de Turismo, Paseo Tabasco 1504 (tel. 16-10-80), on the first floor of the Tabasco 2000 building. English-speaking staffers are happy to answer questions. Open Mon-Fri. 9am-3pm and 6-9pm, Sat. 9am-1pm. **Tourist Information Booths** at the airport and Museo La Venta. Open daily 7am-4:30pm.

Currency Exchange: Banamex (tel. 12-00-11), Madero at Reforma. Open for exchange Mon.-Fri. 9am-5pm. 24-hr. **ATM. Bancomer** (tel. 14-00-50), Juárez at Zaragoza, a few blocks west of Madero. Open Mon.-Fri. 9am-1:30pm.

American Express: Patriotismo 605 (tel. 91-800-5-00-44). Open Mon.-Sat. 9am-6pm.

Telephones: Long-distance calls are best made from pay phones on the street, since many *casetas* do not allow collect calls. You can make collect calls at **Café La Barra,** Lerdo 608 (tel. 12-20-06). Open Mon.-Sat. 7am-1pm and 3:30-8pm.

Telegrams: Lerdo 601 (tel. 14-28-32 or 14-28-33), at Saenz, around the corner from the post office. Open for telegrams and **fax** Mon.-Fri. 8am-7pm, Sat. 9am-1pm.

Airport: (tel. 56-01-57; fax 56-01-58), on the Villahermosa-Macupana highway. **Aeroméxico,** Via 3 #120 (tel. 16-31-32). **Aviacsa,** Mina #1025 (tel. 14-57-70 or 14-57-80). **Mexicana,** Via 3 #120 (tel. 16-31-31 or 16-31-38).

Buses: The first-class terminal is at Mina 297 at Merino, a couple of blocks east of Juárez. **ADO** (tel. 12-21-42 or 12-14-46) to Campeche (4 per day, 5hr., 95 pesos), Cancún (8 and 10pm, 11hr., 196 pesos), Chetumal (8 and 10pm, 8hr., 119 pesos), Escárcega (5 per day, 6hr., 63 pesos), Jalapa (7:30 and 10pm, 8hr., 136 pesos), Mérida (5 per day, 8hr., 136 pesos), Mexico City (7 per day, 11hr., 214 pesos), Oaxaca (6, 8, and 9:45pm, 11hr., 157 pesos), Palenque (8 per day, 2hr., 32 pesos), Paraíso (4 per day, 45min., 22 pesos), Playa del Carmen (8 and 10pm, 8hr., 182 pesos), Puebla (8:40, 9:45, and 11:15pm, 8hr., 182 pesos), Veracruz (9 per day, 7hr., 70 pesos), Tapachula (6:30am, 6, and 10pm, 12hr., 169 pesos), Teapa (5 per day, 45min., 13 pesos), and Tuxtla (9 per day, 6hr., 63 pesos). **UNO** (tel. 14-58-18) has *servicio de lujo* (luxury); tickets must be purchased 5 days in advance. **Luggage storage** 7am-11pm, 1 peso per piece per hr.

Car Rental: Agrisa (tel. 12-91-84 or 14-29-86) in the Holiday Inn annexed to the Tabasco 2000 shopping mall. Open Mon.-Fri. 8am-8pm, Sun. 9am-2pm.

Radio Taxi: (tel. 15-82-33 or 15-23-39). On call 24hr.

Market: Pino Suárez, encompassed by Pino Suárez, Constitución, Hermanos Zozaya, and Grijalva, in the northeast corner of town. Open daily 6am-6pm.

Supermarket: Bonanza (tel. 14-22-80), Madero at Zaragoza. Open 7am-10pm.

Laundromat: Lavandería Rex, Madero #705, just past Méndez. High per piece rates, but try to swing a per kg deal. Open Mon.-Fri. 9am-6:30pm, Sat. 9am-1pm.

Red Cross: (tel. 15-55-55 or 15-56-00), on General Sandino in Colonia 1 de Mayo. Take the "1 de Mayo" bus from Madero. No English spoken.

Pharmacy: Farmacia Canto, Madero 602 (tel. 12-20-99). Open daily 7am-11pm.

Medical Services: Clínica 39, Zaragoza 1202 (tel. 12-20-49), at Carmen Buen Día. English-speaking staff. Not free. Open daily 7am-8pm.

Emergency: Dial 06.

Police: (tel. 13-21-10), 16 de Septiembre at Periférico. No English. Open 24hr.

Post Office: Saenz 131 (tel. 12-10-40), at Lerdo, three blocks west of Madero. Open Mon.-Fri. 8am-7pm, Sat. 9am-1pm. **Postal Code:** 86000.

Telephone Code: 93.

ACCOMMODATIONS AND CAMPING

Most budget accommodations cluster around the 27 de Febrero and Madero intersection. **Camping** and **trailer parking** are allowed in La Choca Park in Tabasco 2000, but the site lacks facilities.

Hotel Madero, Madero 301 (tel. 12-05-16), near 27 de Febrero. Rooms of wildly varying quality. Shop around. Even the dustiest are clean, ample, and equipped with fans. Singles 40 pesos. Doubles 50 pesos. Triples 80 pesos.

Hotel San Miguel, Lerdo #315 (tel. 12-15-00). Small rooms have soft red beds and ceiling fans. The yellow baths sparkle. Singles 37 pesos. Doubles 47 pesos, with two beds 52. Triples 57 pesos.

Posada Hotel Brondo, Pino Suárez 209 (tel. 12-59-61), near Sánchez Mármol. Light and airy rooms range from comfy to spartan. All doubles have private baths. Communal facilities are pristine. Suites for up to four people come with kitchen and living room. 44-105 pesos.

Casa de Huéspedes Teresita, Constitución 224 (tel. 12-34-53). Snazzy lobby surrounded by small, colorfully tiled rooms. All come with fans. Some have balconies. Singles and doubles 30 pesos. Triples 35 pesos.

FOOD

It's hard to compete in the culinary world when you've got Chiapas to the south and all of Yucatán to the east. So, easy enough, Villahermosa doesn't. The main produce **market** operates off Pino Suárez near Zozaya, a few blocks from Puente Grijalva.

Aquarius, Av. Mina 309 (tel. 14-25-37), a short jaunt from the first-class bus station. Healthy cuisine offers respite from artery-clogging meat and fat. The *comida del día* is a deal: soup, salad, main dish, dessert, and a fruit drink, all for 19 pesos. *Licuados* 2-12 pesos. Open Mon.-Sat. 7:30am-10pm, Sun. 8am-9pm.

El Torito Valenzuela, 27 de Febrero 202 (tel. 14-11-89), at Madero, next to Hotel Madero. After dinner mints from a *taquería?* Yup. And the steaming, veggie-filled tacos are even better. Huge *comida corrida* 20 pesos. Open daily 8am-midnight.

Café Bar Impala, Madero 421 (tel. 12-04-93). A tiny, intimate 1940s joint which serves up superb *tamalitos de chilipín, panuchos* (fried tortilla shell stuffed with meat and beans), and tacos (each a mere 1.50 pesos). Open daily 8am-8pm.

Restaurant Madan, Madero 408 (tel. 2-16-50), a block south of Hotel Madero. Sleek A/C and "good ole days" pictures of Villahermosa. Popular with locals, but a tad more expensive. *Cochinita pibil* tacos 18 pesos. Enchiladas *pobladas* 18 pesos. Open daily 7am-11:30pm.

SIGHTS

While exploring the ruins at La Venta, Tabasco, in the early 1940s, U.S. archaeologist M.W. Sterling discovered six massive sculpted stone heads. Further studies indicated that La Venta was a principal ceremonial center of the **Olmecs.** The Olmecs numbered only 250,000 at the height of their civilization (800-200 BCE), but their distinctive artistic style influenced groups from the Ríos Sinaloa and Panuco in northern Mexico to the Nicoya Peninsula in Costa Rica. They worshiped the jaguar as a divine creator, and sculptors at La Venta produced numerous jade carvings in the animal's image. Some human faces were given a "jaguar mouth" to symbolize the intermingling of the divine and the mortal. The Olmecs' colossal sculptures range from 2 to 10m in height. Each of the spherical heads wears a war helmet, and the faces are characterized by thick eyelids, a wide nose, and prominent lips.

Three of the giant heads, along with 30 other stone pieces, have been moved to the **Parque-Museo La Venta,** an archaeological park in northern Villahermosa. Doubling as archaeological park and zoo, the site is enchanting. La Venta's Olmec sculptures take center stage, displayed along a pathway which winds through a verdant jungle only minutes from the *Zona Remodelada*—only the traffic on Grijalva reminds you that you're actually in a city. Buzzing mosquitoes keep the unprepared tourist cruising along at a slightly-faster-than-these-bloody-insects-can-fly pace. Plaques along the way illuminate the faded Olmec art. While a few creatures, notably the crocodiles, put in cameo appearances along this pathway, most are located at the park's northern edge. Here, birds flit through the aviary, grand felines bask in the sun, and cheeky monkeys toy with those iguanas foolish enough to enter their pit. You can get a good look at the jaguars, which roam around their enclosure in the south of the park, halfway around the archaeological walk, near the gift shop.

To get to the *parque-museo,* take the "Tabasco 2000," "Carrisal," "Petrolera," or "Palacio" **bus** (1.50 pesos) from Madero in the center to the intersection of Tabasco and Ruiz Cortínez. Walk northeast on Cortínez for ten minutes until you reach the "La Venta" entrance (site open daily 9am-4:30pm; admission 15 pesos; 2-hr. tours in Spanish or English about 25-45 pesos for 1-35 people).

Return to Paseo Tabasco through the **Parque Tomás Garrido Canabal,** which lies on the Laguna de las Ilusiones and surrounds the Parque-Museo La Venta. Landscaped alcoves hide benches and fountains. Climb the 40m *mirador* for an excellent view of Villahermosa and look for the manatees that swim in the *laguna* below. The main entrance is at the corner of Tabasco and Grijalva (free).

Northwest on Paseo Tabasco, away from the city center and Río Grijalva, is **Tabasco 2000,** a long strip of sparkling new buildings that includes the city's Palacio Municipal, a convention center, several fountains, a shopping mall, and a **planetarium** (tel. 16-36-41), with Omnimax shows dubbed in Spanish (shows daily at 5:15, 6, 7, and 8pm; admission 10 pesos). Take the "Tabasco 2000" bus from the city center and tell the driver where you want to get off.

The catalyst for the creation of the Parque-Museo La Venta was Carlos Pellicer Cámara, Tabasco's most famous poet. His name graces the **Museo Regional de Antropología Carlos Pellicer Cámara,** the main attraction at Villahermosa's new **Center for the Investigation of Olmec and Mayan Cultures (CICOM).** The first floor focuses on the life, times, and arts of the Olmecs and the Maya, while the top floor includes representative pieces from all of Mexico's indigenous tribes. Guide books (in English or Spanish) are available at the ticket counter. The center also houses a public library, an arts school, and a theater. From the *Zona Remodelada,* the museum is best reached by a 15-minute walk south along the Río Grijalva. The #1 and "CICOM" buses pass often (open daily 9am-7:30pm; admission 5 pesos).

Fourteen kilometers from the hustle and bustle of Villahermosa, elephants and zebras run free at the ecological reserve known as **Yumká** (Elf Who Tends the Jungle). A multitude of animals from around the world roam the three *tabasqueño* ecosystems: jungle, savannah, and wetlands (open daily 9am-5pm; admission 15 pesos, children 10 pesos; ticket counter closes at 4pm). A *colectivo especial* is the only way of getting there (40 pesos).

Rain Man

This guy had *ganas.* He also had beady, comma-shaped eyes, an astonishingly protruding hook nose (it's...it's almost indecent!), and a mouth permanently fixed with a horrid grimace. He was schnaz god and rain god, terrible and necessary, moody and—damnit—hard to please. He was **Chac.** There was no god more pragmatically important to the Maya; because of the complete lack of above-ground water in the Yucatán, they depended on his rains to bring drinking water and corn. Attempting to appease this master of waters, the Maya sacrificed their children (their tears were associated with the rain), revered the frog and the turtle (their cries were thought to provoke downpours), created artificial clouds through badly burning fires, and made Chac the most respected god in the whole Yucatán. Chac responded to all the adulation with cold indifference. He grimaced, mockingly. And in the end, they say it was a severe drought that brought about the fall of the Maya.

ENTERTAINMENT

Villahermosa presents two basic nightlife options: the discos in the luxury hotels and a myriad of cultural activities. The **Instituto de Cultura Tabasco** (tel. 12-90-24), in the Edificio Portal del Agua on Magallanes, publishes a monthly calendar of musical, theatrical, and other cultural events; look for it in museums and major hotels.

The hottest mix of *salsa,* tropical music, and visual stimuli are found at **Video Bar Factory,** on Av. Méndez (open Tues.-Sat. 10pm-3am), **Tequila Rock** (tel. 16-53-63), on the part of Paseo Tabasco that extends into the Holiday Inn (open Wed.-Sat. 10pm-3am), and **Estudio 8** (tel. 14-44-66), in the Hotel Maya on Paseo Tabasco before Tabasco 2000 (open Thurs.-Sun. 9pm-2 or 3am). An older crowd frequents **Disco KU,** on Av. Sandino, and the ambitiously named **Snob,** Juarez 106 in the Hyatt (both open Tues.-Sat. 10pm-3am). Taxi drivers are well-acquainted with disco hot spots and are the only efficient means of reaching them.

For mellower diversion, head to **Galería El Jaguar Despertado,** Sáenz 117 (tel. 14-12-44), near Reforma in the *Zona Remodelada.* The café in the back sometimes features live classical music or jazz, but, even without the tunes, the fountain, the original Mexican art, and the gallery upstairs attracts an interesting mix of intellectuals and romantics (open Tues.-Sat. 3-9pm).

■ Near Villahermosa

COMALCALCO

Whereas La Venta documents Tabasco's Olmec past, Comalcalco demonstrates the Maya's dominance over the area in the later Classic period (200-700 CE). One of the northernmost Mayan settlements, Comalcalco has yielded evidence of contacts with other Yucatecan Mayan settlements, as well as with the Toltecs, Mexica, and Totonacs. The site's most distinctive feature is its architecture: unlike those of other Mayan cities, the pyramids and buildings of Comalcalco were constructed from packed earth and clay and later covered with stuccoed oven-fired bricks. Eroded but still imperial, the ruins contrast dramatically with the jungle behind them. Do not climb the temples—Uzi-toting guards are serious about the *"no subir"* signs.

With 10 levels, the hulking 25m-high **pyramid** to the left of the entrance to the site is Comalcalco's best-known landmark. The north face bears traces of the elaborate stucco carvings that once completely covered the structure's sides. Behind the pyramid lies the north plaza, surrounded by a series of ruined minor temples and mounds. If you look closely at the dilapidated walls, you can see the insides of Comalcalco's brickwork and oyster-shell mortar.

From the plaza, a well-worn path leads up the side of the acropolis area and passes a group of three temples on the way. As with the main pyramid, vestiges of elaborate decorative carvings can be seen on each of these temples. Farther up the acropolis, turn right to reach the **Tomb of the Nine Knights of the Night,** named after the nine bas-relief figures on the walls of the tomb. Visible from the acropolis, three sides of Comalcalco's **ballcourt** (to the left) remain unexcavated and covered with tropical vegetation. Several temples, including one known as **The Palace,** stand in pieces atop the acropolis against a backdrop of tall, square brick columns and several roofless rooms (site open daily 10am-5pm; admission 10 pesos).

Getting There: The site lies 34km northwest of Villahermosa, 2km from the town of Comalcalco, and is accessible by the bus that travels to Paraíso via Comalcalco. Get off at Comalcalco and walk back a block on Méndez to Rte. 187. From this corner catch a *combi* (about 2 pesos) and ask the driver to let you off at the access road to *las ruinas.* From here, the walk to the site is a pleasant 1km. You can also take a taxi *(especial)* directly to the site from the Comalcalco bus station (about 5 pesos).

TABASCO COAST

In terms of natural beauty, the beaches of the Tabasco Coast pale in comparison to those of the Jalisco Coast or Quintana Roo. Nevertheless, Tabasco's beaches are clean and good for swimming, although oil drilling has not had a salutary effect on the coastal ecosystem. Most of the small resort towns offer budget accommodations, and all are adept at preparing delicious seafood. Each about 70km from Villahermosa, the westernmost resorts on the coast, **El Paraíso** and **El Limón,** can be reached by bus. From Villahermosa and El Paraíso, buses run daily to the resort at **Puerto Ceiba,** where you can rent boats to explore its lagoon. From there, you can reach a number of small fishing villages that owe their livelihoods to oysters. Farther to the west and harder to reach, **Pico de Oro** and **Frontera** both bask on the sandy shore and provide possibilities similar to those at the closer El Paraíso and El Limón.

Getting There: To catch a bus after visiting the ruins, wait where the access road intersects Rte. 187 and flag down a blue bus or green-and-white *combi* marked "Paraíso." Many buses leave El Paraíso for Villahermosa. Check the return times at the corresponding Villahermosa bus stations. Buses leave from the *zócalo.*

■ Teapa

An hour's drive south of Villahermosa along roads flanked by banana groves, Teapa's (pop. 35,000) sulfuric spa and splendiferous caverns lure daytrippers from the state capital. The town itself is slow-moving; its dilapidated, leafy *zócalo* and quiet streets make for peaceful strolling.

Orientation and Practical Information The **Transportes Villahermosa-Teapa** bus lets you off at the main bus terminal on Méndez, from which local buses whisk visitors to either the spa or the caves. If you arrive by **Cristóbal Colón,** walk 200m to the left to the main bus terminal, and an additional five minutes to reach the *zócalo.* Teapa's main drag is **Méndez.**

Banamex, Méndez 102 (tel. 2-02-84), offers a 24-hr. **ATM** (open Mon.-Fri. 9am-1:30pm). **Cristóbal Colón** sends **buses** (tel. 2-03-52) to Tuxtla Gutiérrez (8 and 9:30am, 5hr., 48 pesos) and Villahermosa (5pm, 1hr., 9 pesos). Second-class buses run to Villahermosa every hour (station open daily 7am-10pm). You can check your **baggage** out back by the bathrooms. Villahermosa is much more easily reached by hopping into one of the red **taxis** in the center of town. They leave as soon as they have five people (approximately every 20min., 45min., 15 pesos). **Farmacia Espíritu Santo** is on Calle Dr. Ramón Medina 106 (tel. 2-00-93; open daily 7am-10:30pm, but provides 24-hr. service if you ring the bell in the upper-left-hand corner of the doorway). The **police** (tel. 2-01-10) are in the Palacio Municipal on Méndez (open 24hr.). The **post office** is at Calle Manuel Buelta 109, near the *zócalo* (open Mon.-Fri. 9am-3pm). **Postal Code:** 86800. **Telephone Code:** 932.

Accommodations and Food Teapa's accommodations are a scant bunch without a bargain in sight. Your best bet is **Casa de Huéspedes Miye,** Méndez 211 (tel. 2-00-11), in the center of town. Colorful rooms have shiny bathrooms, but no hot water (singles 30 pesos; doubles 40 pesos; add 10 pesos for private bath). Across the park from the church on Av. Plaza de la Independencia, **Hotel Jardín** (tel. 2-00-27) is another possibility. Lime-green rooms have respectable bathrooms and powerful ceiling fans (singles 40 pesos; doubles 50 pesos; triples 60 pesos). For cheap, steaming food, head to **La Bella Sultana,** Av. Carlos Ramos 275, a long walk from the center. From the *zócalo,* head out of town past the clock tower/arch, a dry bridge, and the PEMEX station; then cross the street and head for the airy, corrugated roof. The excellent service whisks out tacos starting at 2 pesos (open daily 6am-1pm and 4pm-12:30am). **Josegay,** Méndez 125, makes a divine *mole de pollo* (15 pesos; open daily 8am-midnight).

■ Near Teapa

LAS GRUTAS COCONÁ

Just a few kilometers from town, **Las Grutas Coconá** were discovered in the late 1800s. A path winds for 500m into the hillside, passing impressive caverns and underground lagoons along the way. Bringing along a flashlight or hiring an eight-year-old guide (a small tip is standard) will make your visit to the caves much more scintillating. One hundred and fifty meters into the cave system, shine your light into the roof of the tunnel on the bend. Sometimes you can catch the tiny bats during their *siesta*. Farther on you'll enter a breathtaking, acoustically funky domed cavern replete with mighty stalactites. Beyond, a wooden walkway leads over a pool into a dripping cave. The final cave is draped in gloom and can only be explored with the help of a flashlight. On the way back, look for a left-hand turnoff where a lone lightbulb has given life to a cluster of ferns. Here you can limbo beneath a one-meter ledge to reach a secluded emerald pool filled with blind fish (*grutas* open daily 9am-6pm; admission 3 pesos).

Getting There: *Combis* for the *grutas* leave from Calle Bastar on the right hand side of the church (every 20min., 1.50 pesos). Taxis charge 10-15 pesos.

EL AZUFRE SPA

El Azufre Spa, 5km west of Teapa, is a classic case of a fine resource which has seen its heyday go by. The site sports three pools, a picnic area, *cabañas,* and a modest restaurant. Unfortunately, the pungent, sulfuric tepid springs are diminished by their dilapidated surroundings. The tiled, shallow swimming pools which collect the spring water are chipped and cracked, and an inch of slimy, green ooze meets your every step. If you can join the Mexican families in ignoring the conditions, you might enjoy the pleasant outdoor setting. Should you become addicted to the waters, huge rustic *cabañas,* featuring three single beds and oodles of hammock hooks, can be rented (singles and doubles 50 pesos; triples and quads 100 pesos; admission to the spa 10 pesos).

Getting There: To reach El Azufre from Teapa, take the **Pichucalco** bus (every hr., 2 pesos) from the bus terminal on Méndez, and ask the driver to let you off at the short access road to the spa. A Pichucalco-bound taxi-*colectivo* will cost you 6 pesos. To return, walk back to the highway and flag down a returning vehicle.

CHIAPAS

■ Tuxtla Gutiérrez

An energetic young city, Tuxtla Gutiérrez (pop. 350,000) is the capital of Chiapas and the focal point of commerce and transportation for much of southern Mexico. The city was named for a progressive *chiapaneco* governor who, rather than succumb to imperialist right-wing forces, wrapped himself in the Mexican flag and dramatically lept to his death from a church spire. While Tuxtla's rapid industrialization has left its grimy mark, the city has recently added some splashes of color to the urban landscape: young couples stroll arm in arm through verdant parks, and flaming red parrots squawk with pleasure in one of the best zoos in Latin America.

ORIENTATION

Tuxtla Gutiérrez lies 85km west of San Cristóbal and 293km south of Villahermosa. *Avenidas* run east-west and *calles* north-south. The central axis of the city, upon which the *zócalo* rests, is formed by **Avenida Central** (sometimes called **Avenida 14 de Septiembre**) and **Calle Central.** Streets are numbered according to their distance from and geographical relation to the central axis. For example, 2 Calle Oriente Sur lies south of Av. Central and two blocks east of Calle Central. Fifteen blocks west of the town center, Calle Central becomes **Blvd. Dr. Belisario Domínguez;** 11 blocks east it is known as **Blvd. Ángel Albino Corzo.**

To get to the *centro* from the **ADO/Cristóbal Colón bus station,** walk left on 2 Nte. Pte. (away from the buses) for two blocks. The *zócalo* is two blocks to your left on Av. Central. The **Autotransportes Tuxtla Gutiérrez station** is in a cul-de-sac near Calles 3 Sur and 7 Ote. From the station, turn right and then right again into the walled-in alley that doubles as a market. Make the first left onto 2 Sur and continue west to Calle Central—the *zócalo* is two blocks to the right. Travelers from Chiapa de Corzo often disembark at a small station on 3 Ote. between 2 and 3 Sur. Facing the street from the bus stop, head left for Av. Central, then left again for the *zócalo.*

Major **bus** lines run west on 2 Sur, east on 1 Sur, north on 11 Ote., and south on 12 Ote (daily 5am-11pm, 1.50 pesos). *Colectivos* run frequently through the city from 6am-10pm (1.50 pesos). As locals often crowd the *colectivos* in the *centro,* it may be more efficient to walk to your destination outside the *centro* and then catch a (less full) *colectivo* running back into town.

PRACTICAL INFORMATION

Tourist Offices: Federal and State Office, Blvd. Dr. Belisario Domínguez 950 (tel./fax 2-45-35), at Edificio Plaza de Las Instituciones. Stupidly located 17 long blocks west of the *zócalo,* just past Bancomer. Excellent maps. Well-informed staff is multilingual. Open Mon.-Fri. 9am-9pm, Sat. 9am-6pm, Sun. 9am-3pm. Free state-wide **tourist information hotline** (tel. 91-800-2-80-35).

Currency Exchange: Banamex, 1 Sur Pte. 141 (tel. 2-87-44), at Calle Central. Credit card cash advances. 24-hr. **ATM.** Open for exchange Mon.-Fri. 9am-1pm. **Bancomer,** Av. Central Pte. 314 (tel. 2-82-51), at 2 Pte. Open for exchange Mon.-Fri. 9am-noon. Some local businesses may also change currency.

American Express: (tel. 2-69-98), Plaza Bonampak, Local 14, on Blvd. Dr. Belisario Domínguez, across from the tourist office. Doubles as a travel agency. English spoken. Open Mon.-Fri. 9am-2pm and 4-6:30pm, Sat. 9am-1pm.

Telephones: Public phones take coins, credit cards, or LADATEL phone cards.

Telegrams: (tel. 3-65-47; fax 2-42-96), 1 Nte. at 2 Ote., next to the post office. Open for telegrams and **fax** Mon.-Fri. 8am-6pm, Sat. 9am-1pm.

Airport: Aeropuerto Francisco Sarabia (tel. 5-01-11), 15km southwest of town. **Aerocaribe,** Av. Central Pte. #206 (tel. 2-0020, at airport tel. 5-15-30). **Aviacsa,** Av. Central Pte. #1144 (tel. 2-80-81) or at the airport (tel. 5-10-11). **Taxtel** (tel. 5-31-95) run to the airport and charge 20 pesos; a cheaper option is to grab a cab off the street (12 pesos).

Buses: Cristóbal Colón, 2 Nte. Pte. 268 (tel. 2-51-22), at 2 Pte. First-class to Chetumal (12:30 and 2:30pm, 13hr., 155 pesos), Campeche (7:30am and 3:30pm, 12hr., 132 pesos), Cancún (12:30 and 2:30pm, 18hr., 238 pesos), Comitán (every hr. 5am-11pm, 3½hr., 33 pesos), Escárcega (12:30pm and 3:30pm, 9½hr., 103 pesos), Mérida (7:30am and 3:30pm, 14hr., 177 pesos), Mexico City (5 per day, 15hr., 253 pesos), Oaxaca (11:30am, 7:15, and 9:30pm, 10hr., 110 pesos), Ocosingo (6 per day, 4hr., 36 pesos), Palenque (6 per day, 6hr., 61 pesos), Playa del Carmen (12:30 and 2:30pm, 17hr., 227 pesos), Puebla (5 per day, 13hr., 218 pesos), San Cristóbal (every hr. 5am-11pm, 2hr., 17 pesos), Tapachula (every hr. 6am-11pm, 6hr., 82 pesos), Tonalá (every hr. 6am-11pm, 3½hr., 36 pesos), Tulum (12:30pm, 16½hr., 208 pesos), Veracruz (7:30 and 8:45pm, 12hr., 151 pesos), and Villahermosa (5 per day, 6hr., 63 pesos). **Autotransportes Tuxtla Gutiérrez,** 3 Sur Pte. #712 (tel. 1-28-51), between 5 and 6 Ote, offers similar service with slightly cheaper fares. *Combis* leave from their stand on 2 Sur Ote., next to Hotel San Antonio, for San Cristóbal (every 20min., 1½hr., 10 pesos). To reach Chiapa de Corzo, hop on a **Transportes Chiapa-Tuxtla** *microbús* at the station at 2 Av. Sur Ote. and 2 Calle Sur. Ote. (every 10min., 25min., 3 pesos). You can also try hailing the bus as it leaves town on Blvd. Corzo.

Car Rental: Budget, Blvd. Dr. Belisario Domínguez 2510 (tel. 5-06-72). From 349 pesos per day. Open daily 9am-7pm.

Laundromat: Lavandería Automática Burbuja (tel. 1-05-95), 1 Nte. Pte. 413A at 3 Nte. Pte. Open Mon.-Sat. 8:30am-8pm, Sun. 9am-1pm.

Red Cross: 5 Nte. Pte. 1480 (tel. 2-04-92), on the west side of town. Open 24hr.

Pharmacy: Farmacia 24 Horas, 1 Sur Pte. 716, between 6 and 7 Pte. Open 24hr. **Farmacia Regina** (tel. 2-14-66), on the southwest corner of the *zócalo*. Open daily 7am-12pm.

Hospital: Hospital Regional Dr. Domingo Chamona, (tel. 2-14-40) 9 Sur Ote., at 1 Ote. 24-hr. emergency service.

Emergency: Dial 08 or call **Policía de Seguridad Pública** (tel. 2-05-30 or 3-78-05).

Police: (tel. 2-11-06), in the Palacio Municipal, at the north end of the *zócalo*. Go left upon entering the building. No English spoken. Open 24hr.

Post Office: (tel. 2-04-16), 1 Nte. at 2 Ote., on the northeast corner of the *zócalo*. Open Mon.-Fri. 9am-7pm, Sat. 9am-1pm. **Postal Code:** 29000.

Telephone Code: 961.

ACCOMMODATIONS AND CAMPING

Hotels cluster around the *zócalo*. Tuxtla also has a stellar youth hostel.

Villas Deportivas Juvenil, Ángel Albino Corzo 1800 (tel. 3-34-05), next to the yellow footbridge. Take a *colectivo* east on Av. Central (1 peso) and tell the driver it's next to the Ángel Corzo statue on Blvd. Corzo. Single-sex 4-person rooms have comfy beds. Communal bathrooms and showers are well maintained. Guests can use the soccer fields and basketball courts, but admission to the pool is restricted. Beds 25 pesos per person. Breakfast 10 pesos, lunch and dinner 12.50 pesos.

Hotel Oasis, 11 Ote. Sur #122 (tel. 3-72-52), off Av. Central. Classy rooms with rosy wood. Bathrooms sparkle. Cable TV and phones. Singles 60 pesos. Doubles 70 pesos. Triples 80 pesos. Quads 100 pesos. Each additional person 10 pesos.

Hotel San Antonio, 2 Av. Sur Ote. 540 (tel. 2-27-13), between 4 and 5 Ote. Cavernous rooms have fans and bathrooms that spout hot water. Singles 40 pesos. 10 pesos per extra person. A/C rooms for 1-2 people 70 pesos, for 3 80 pesos.

Hotel Avenida, Av. Central 244 (tel. 2-08-07), 1½ blocks west of the *zócalo*, between 1 and 2 Pte. Shiny, happy green rooms come with solid wood furniture, large beds, and sweet smelling bathrooms. Ask for a room off the street. Singles 50 pesos. Doubles 65 pesos. Triples 90 pesos. Quads 120 pesos.

FOOD

Culinary miracles don't happen in Tuxtla, but the city is speckled with quality, inexpensive eateries. *Licuados* come in every flavor imaginable, from mango to spinach.

Restaurante Imperial, Calle Central Nte. 263 (tel. 2-06-48), 1 block from the *zócalo*. 14 pesos for a hungry-man sized *comida corrida* with a bottomless basket of tortillas. Not a gringo in sight. Open daily 7am-7pm.

La Antigua Fogata, 4 Ote. Sur #115, just off Av. Central. 22 years of know-how goes into bringing you a succulent ¼ chicken *al carbón* with all the works (6 pesos). Open daily 7:30am-12:30am.

Restaurante Vegetariano Nah-Yaxal, 6 Pte. 124 (tel. 3-96-48), just north of Av. Central. Peruse books on yoga theory and PC parenting as you enjoy your veggie salad with alfalfa germ (10 pesos). Smooth *licuados*. Open Mon.-Sat. 7:30am-9pm.

Las Pichanchas, Av. Central Ote. 837 (tel. 2-53-51), 8 blocks east of the *zócalo*, between 7 and 8 Ote. Look for the giant neon sign. *Tamales* 10-12 pesos. *Chinbos* (bread soaked in sweet wine) 8 pesos. Live marimba band daily 2:30-5:30pm and 8:30-11:30pm, *ballet folklórico* 9-10pm. Open daily 8am-midnight.

SIGHTS

The shady forest foliage of the **Miguel Álvarez del Toro Zoo** offers a refreshing change of scenery from Tuxtla's gritty urban landscape. Renowned throughout Latin America, the zoo houses only animals native to Chiapas, including playful monkeys, stealthy jaguars, bright green parrots, and hairy tarantulas (open Tues.-Sun. 9am-5:30pm; free). To get to the zoo, take the "Cerro Hueco" or "Zoológico" bus, which leaves from 1 Ote. between 6 and 7 Sur (every 30min., 1.50 pesos). The bus traces an indirect and sometimes unbearably slow route to the zoo's front gate. To return to the center, catch the same bus at the zoo's entrance.

The **Conviviencia Infantil** (though many signs still read **"Parque Madero"**) unfurls in the northeast part of town at the intersection of 11 Ote. and 5 Nte. Its focal point is a large and modern theater, the **Teatro de la Ciudad Emilio Rabasa.** Films by Latin American directors and performances of *ballet folklórico* dominate the schedule. Films and art shows are often free; prices for theater performances vary. Monthly schedules for city- and state-wide events are available at the tourist information center. On the pleasant *paseo* east of the theater is a children's amusement park (open Tues.-Sun. 9am-10pm). Past the amusement park is the open-air **Teatro Bonampak,** where free folk dance performances are held (Sun. 5-8pm). The eastern extremity of Parque Madero is demarcated by a light aircraft next to the open-air theater, upon which several eight-year-old fighter-pilots-in-the-making usually clamber. A broad concourse, lined with fountains and bronze busts of famous Mexicans, leads west of the theater past the **Museo Regional de Chiapas,** which displays the region's archaeological finds (open Tues.-Sun. 9am-4pm; admission 14 pesos, free Sun.). Farther down the concourse, at the **Jardín Botánico Dr. Faustino Miranda,** you can amble under towering *ceiba* (silk-cotton trees) and admire the colorful grandeur of Chiapanecan flora (open Tues.-Sun. 9am-6pm). Across the concourse is the **Museo Botánico** (open Mon.-Fri. 9am-3pm, Sat. 9am-1pm). Back in the center, the air-conditioned **Cinema Vistarama Tuxtla** (tel. 2-18-31), at 1 Sur and 5 Ote., shows mostly American films with Spanish subtitles (admission 12 pesos).

If you're interested in the ruins at Bonampak, visit **Hotel Bonampak,** Blvd. Dr. Domínguez 180. Its faithful replica of the human sacrifice mural at Bonampak, the lost Mayan city of the Lacandón jungle, is infinitely clearer and brighter than the original. In fact, many postcard photographs of the mural are actually taken here rather than at the site itself. To get to the hotel, which is always open, walk or take a *colectivo* west on Av. Central until it becomes Blvd. Dr. Domínguez one block before the federal tourist office, and cross the road.

▓ Chiapa de Corzo

Most people look past Chiapa de Corzo's scant attractions and instead to the **Cañón del Sumidero,** an impressive vegetation-clad canyon that stretches 32km to the north of the city. Carved out by the industrious Río Grijalva, the mist-enshrouded slopes of the gorge rise as much as 1200m above the water. According to local lore, nearly 15,000 Chiapan *indígenas* threw themselves into the canyon in 1528 after their chief, Sanguiem, was burned alive by the Spaniards.

Orientation and Practical Information Chiapa de Corzo overlooks the Río Grijalva, 15km east of Tuxtla and 68km west of San Cristóbal. Most sights lie near the *zócalo* **(Plaza Ángel Albino Corzo),** which is bounded on the north by 21 de Octubre (the Tuxtla-San Cristóbal highway), on the east by La Mexicanidad, on the south by Julián Grajales, and on the west by 5 de Febrero. Boats leave for **El Sumidero** from the river bank, two blocks south of the *zócalo* on 5 de Febrero.

Contact the **tourist office** in **Tuxtla** for detailed tourist information. **Bancomer** (tel. 6-03-20) is on the eastern side of the *zócalo* (open Mon.-Fri. 8am-1pm). **Transportes Chiapa-Tuxtla** *microbúses,* heading back to Tuxtla, stop on 21 de Octubre opposite the police station (every 10min., 25min., 3 pesos). **Farmacia Esperanza** (tel. 6-04-54) is on 21 de Octubre, one block east of the *zócalo* (open Mon.-Sat. 7am-11pm., Sun. 7am-2pm). The **police station** (tel. 6-02-26) is in the Palacio Municipal, on the northeast side of the *zócalo* (open 24hr.). The **post office** is on Calle Cenullo Aguilar #244, a block and a half north of the *zócalo* (open Mon.-Fri. 8am-6pm). **Postal Code:** 29160. **Telephone Code:** 968.

Accommodations and Food Most people visit Chiapa de Corzo as a daytrip from Tuxtla. If you spend the night, **Hotel Los Ángeles,** Julián Grajales 2 (tel. 6-00-48), at La Mexicanidad on the southeast corner of the *zócalo,* is the only budget game in town. Huge rooms have stained glass, carved dark wood furniture, and fans, and the cramped bathrooms are respectably clean (singles 60 pesos; doubles 80 pesos; triples 100 pesos; quads 120 pesos). Since you've come to Chiapa to see the river, you may as well head to the waterfront for mid-range, filling food. **Restaurant Comitán,** to the left as you hit the dock, offers a 16.50 pesos breakfast special, occasional live *marimba* performances, and an airy if fly-obscured view of the lush, winding river banks (open daily 7am-7pm). **Restaurant Nancy,** around the corner to the right as you hit the dock, is shorter on atmosphere but longer on selection—come here if you crave a wide variety of seafood goodies (15-25 pesos). When they have *marimba,* they play it loudly (open daily 8am-6pm).

Sights Carved out by the Río Grijalva, the **Cañón del Sumidero** stretches for 32 vegetation-clad kilometers north of Chiapa de Corzo. A two-hour round trip *lancha* journey begins with humble views of cornfields and floating Mexican garbage, but shortly after the Belisario Domínguez bridge, the hills jump to form near-vertical cliffs which rise as much as 1200m above water level. Protected as a natural park, these steep walls are home to troupes of playful monkeys, hummingbirds, and soaring falcons, while the murky waters harbor crocodiles and turtles. Along the meandering river lies a dripping cave and the park's most famous waterfall, the **Árbol de Navidad.** This spectacular *cascada* plummets from the sky, rambling over a series of scalloped rock formations before disintegrating into a fine mist that envelops passing boats. El Sumidero's northernmost extremity is marked by the 200m-high hydroelectric dam **Netzahualcóyotl,** which, with the Río Grijalva's three other dams, provides a quarter of Mexico's electricity.

Boats leave as soon as they're full from Chiapa's *embarcadero* (dock) at the end of 5 de Febrero, two blocks south of the *zócalo* (daily 7am-4:30pm, 50 pesos per person). Boats can also be taken up the canyon from Cahuaré, where the highway to Tuxtla Gutiérrez crosses the river near the Cahuaré Island Resort. The trip down the river is best made during August, at the height of the rainy season, when all four waterfalls gush their hardest.

Most of Chiapa de Corzo's architectural gems date from the city's colonial period. The *zócalo* contains two colonial structures: a small clock tower and a fountain shaped like the crown of Queen Isabel of Spain. Often called **La Pila,** this famous Moorish fountain taps underground waterways 5km long and provided the town with fresh drinking water during a 1562 epidemic. Inside the fountain, tile plaques tell the story of Chiapa de Corzo's colonial-era history. The red-and-white **Catedral de Santo Domingo** is one block south of the *zócalo* near Río Grijalva. The most famous of the four bells dangling in its tower, "Teresa de Jesús," is named after a mystical Spanish saint (open daily 6am-2pm and 4-6:30pm). Alongside the cathedral, a 16th-century ex-convent houses the **Museo de la Laca,** which displays fine examples of Mexican lacquerwork, a handicraft practiced only in Chiapa de Corzo and four other cities (open Mon. 9am-1pm and 4-7pm, Tues.-Sun. 9am-7pm; free). You can also join one of the ongoing lacquering lessons (Mon.-Fri. 4-7pm; free).

During Chiapa's **Fiesta de San Sebastián** (Jan. 16-22), *los parachicos,* men in heavy costumes and stifling masks, dance from dawn to dusk. The fiesta's *gran finale* is the mock **Combate Naval** between *"españoles"* and *"indios."* More a beauty pageant than a battle, the *combate* features elaborately decorated boats, costumed sailors, and fireworks.

■ San Cristóbal de Las Casas

High up in the Meseta Central de Chiapas, San Cristóbal de las Casas derives its immense popularity from its picturesque setting, comfortable climate, and its beautiful colonial architecture. At an altitude of 2100m, the city center nestles in the Valley of Hueyzacatlán, while its outskirts cling to the steeply rising slopes of the surrounding mountains. The city's wonderful major buildings and narrow streets are colonial in style. Buildings not constructed by the Spanish are artful imitations of the tile-roofed structures that the *conquistadores* wove around courtyards and gardens. You'll probably notice the thin air as soon as you start to climb one of the city's delightful cobbled streets near the edge of town. Top off this combination with a spectacular setting (a 360° view of the lush green mountains), and you'll understand why Mexican and foreign tourists alike have flocked here for years.

Though San Cristóbal is an aesthetic wonder, its life has long been animated by the age-old conflict between *mestizos* and *indígenas*. Founded in 1528 by the invading Spaniards and their Aztec allies, San Cristóbal de las Casas was once the colonial capital of the region, a *mestizo* enclave in the midst of Mayan territory. The town was named after the vocal Dominican friar Bartolomé de Las Casas, who spoke out against his countrymen's brutal treatment of indigenous peoples. Over the years, *mestizo* culture has became increasingly dominant in San Cristóbal, and some *indígenas* have adopted Western clothing and manners as their own. For most, however, tense syncretism has been the rule of the day. Catholicism mixes with shamanistic practices, and most women still wear braids with colorful ribbons and wear grand *rebozo* scarves. Moreover, while Spanish is the city's official language, the Mayan tongues of Tzeltal or Tzotzil are spoken in the nearby villages.

On January 1, 1994, the day that NAFTA came into effect, a band of rebels, calling themselves Zapatistas (after the revolutionary leader Emiliano Zapata), rose up against the government in San Cristóbal. Led by a masked figure known as Sub-commander Marcos, the rebels insisted that land be redistributed to the poor, a demand that many San Cristóbal residents supported. The choice of day was appropriate, as the Zapatistas called for Mexico to pull out of NAFTA, which has since caused the price of maize, the area's subsistence crop, to rise dramatically. Deadlocked negotiations have since moved to San Andrés Larraínzar, 26km northwest of the city; for many, they are simply an extension of the historical *chiapaneco* conflict between the colonized and their colonizers. Today, the city is manned rather heavily by military police, although not in numbers to make the situation intimidating; more often than not, the military band is simply arriving to give a boisterous concert in the *zócalo*. The recent conflict is no reason to avoid San Cristóbal, as locals express no hostility towards foreigners. If anything, residents are even more eager to please visitors now that tourism has dropped off.

ORIENTATION

Nestled high in the Altos de Chiapas (2200m above sea level), San Cristóbal lies 83km east of Tuxtla Gutiérrez, 78km northwest of Comitán, and 191km southwest of Palenque. Rte. 190, the Pan American Highway, cuts east from Tuxtla Gutiérrez, touches the southern edge of San Cristóbal, and then heads southeast to Comitán and Ciudad Cuauhtémoc at the Guatemalan border.

First- and second-class **bus stations** are scattered along the Pan American Highway near Av. Insurgentes. From Cristóbal Colón, take a right (north) on Insurgentes and walk seven blocks to the *zócalo*. From the second-class stations, walk east two or three blocks on any cross-street and turn left on Insurgentes. Since San Cristóbal is a popular destination for tourists, most of whom travel by bus, book seats as far in advance as possible during the Christmas season and *Semana Santa*. At other times, reservations made one day in advance will suffice.

Most of San Cristóbal's clearly labeled streets fall into a neat grid. The *zócalo*, also known as **Plaza 31 de Marzo,** is the city center. The four cardinal directions are indicated by prominent landmarks around town: the church and former convent of Santo Domingo are to the north, the blue-trimmed Templo de Guadalupe is on the hill to the east, the Cristóbal Colón first-class bus station lies to the south, and the Templo de San Cristóbal resides on the mountaintop to the west.

Streets change names when crossing imaginary north-south and east-west axes centered at the *zócalo*. **Av. Insurgentes** connects the town center to the Pan American Highway, becoming **Av. Utrilla** past the *zócalo*. Municipal buses and *colectivos* criss-cross town with destinations indicated on the window—just wave to catch one (1.50 pesos). Taxis (tel. 8-03-96) line up along the north side of the *zócalo*. Standard fare within town is 6 pesos, while prices to nearby villages are negotiable.

PRACTICAL INFORMATION

Tourist Office: (tel. 8-06-60, ext. 126), in the northwest corner of the *zócalo*, under the arches of the Palacio Municipal. Helpful staff speaks English and doles out maps. Bulletin boards have info on cheap accommodations, tours, and cultural events. Open Mon.-Sat. 9am-8pm, Sun. 9am-2pm. **Information Booth** at the Cristóbal Colón terminal. Maps and brochures. Some English spoken. Open 24hr.

Travel Agencies: Viajes Pakal, Cuauhtémoc #6-A (tel. 8-42-93; fax 8-28-19), between Insurgentes and Hidalgo, one block south of the *zócalo*. Daytrips to Palenque, Agua Azul, Grutas de San Cristóbal, and nearby villages. Trips to Bonampak, Yaxchilán, and Guatemala by special arrangement. Open Mon.-Fri. 9am-2pm and 4-8pm, Sat. 9am-1pm. **Viajes Lacantún,** Madero 16 (tel. 8-25-88), half a block east of the *zócalo*, for flights within Mexico and abroad. Open Mon.-Fri. 9am-2pm and 4-7pm, Sat. 9am-1pm.

Currency Exchange: Bancomidad (tel. 8-17-77; fax 8-01-99), on the southwest corner of the *zócalo*. 24-hr. **ATM.** Open Mon.-Fri. 9am-2pm.

Telephones: Collect calls can be placed from public pay phones at the Palacio Municipal and throughout the *centro*.

Telegrams: Mazariegos 29 (tel. 8-42-71), 2½ blocks from the *zócalo*. Open for telegrams, **fax,** and **money orders** (tel. 8-06-61). Mon.-Fri. 8am-6pm, Sat. 9am-noon.

Buses: Cristóbal Colón (tel. 8-02-91), Pan American Highway at Insurgentes, 7 blocks south of the *zócalo*. Open daily 6am-10pm. First-class service to Campeche (7:30am, 2:30 and 5:30pm, 10hr., 108 pesos), Cancún (2:30pm, 15hr., 199 pesos), Chetumal (7:30am and 2:30pm, 12hr., 147 pesos), Escárcega (7:30am and 2:30pm, 5:30pm, 7½hr., 85 pesos), Guatemalan border (8 per day, 3hr., 25 pesos), Mérida (5:30pm, 12hr., 158 pesos), Mexico City (3:30 and 5:30pm, 18hr., 266 pesos), Oaxaca (5pm, 12hr., 124 pesos), Palenque (6 per day, 5hr., 39 pesos), Puebla (3:30 and 5:30pm, 16hr., 234 pesos), Puerto Escondido (7:30am and 6:15pm, 12hr., 134 pesos), Tuxtla Gutiérrez (every hr., 2hr., 17 pesos), and Tulum (7:30am and 2:30pm, 13hr., 181 pesos). **Maya de Oro** buses run from the same station to Campeche (9:30am, 10hr., 126 pesos), Cancún (2:35pm, 15hr., 227 pesos), Mérida (9:30am, 12hr., 183 pesos), Mexico City (4:35pm, 18hr., 309 pesos), Oaxaca (7:15pm, 12hr., 147 pesos), Playa del Carmen (2:35pm, 13hr., 216 pesos), and Puebla (4:35pm, 16hr., 258 pesos). **Autotransportes Tuxtla Gutiérrez** (tel. 8-27-28), on Ignacio Allende, half a block north of the highway. Open 5am-11pm. **Luggage storage** 9am-8pm (5 pesos per piece). Express service to Comitán (10:30am and 12:45pm, 1½hr., 17 pesos), Mérida (6:15pm, 12hr., 153 pesos), Mexico City (8 per day, 17hr., 237 pesos), Palenque (7 per day, 4½hr., 41 pesos), and Villahermosa (7 per day, 7hr., 66 pesos).

Car Rental: Budget, Mazariegos 36 (tel. 8-18-71 or 8-31-00), 2 blocks west of the *zócalo*. With prices starting at 253 pesos per day, it's time they changed their name. Open Mon.-Sat. 8am-2pm and 3:30-8pm, Sun. 8am-noon and 5-7pm.

Bike Rental: Bicirent, Belisario Domínguez 5-B (tel. 8-63-68), between Real de Guadalupe and Madero. 23 pesos per 3hr. or 50 pesos per day. Guided tours.

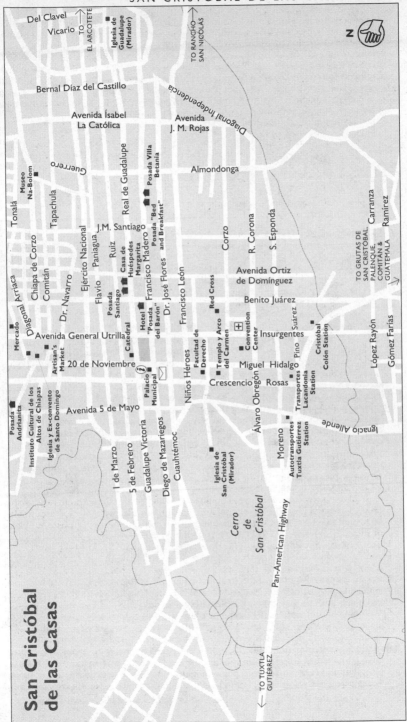

San Cristóbal
de las Casas

Markets: Between Utrilla and Domínguez, 7 blocks north of the *zócalo*. Best selection on Sat. Open daily 6am-2pm. Huge artisan's market forms around the Santo Domingo Church, 5 blocks north of the *zócalo* on Utrilla. Open daily 8am-5pm.

Laundromat: Orve, Domínguez 5 (tel. 8-18-02), between Real de Guadalupe and Madero. 21 pesos for 1-3kg, 7 pesos per additional kg. Open Mon.-Sat. 8am-8pm.

English Bookstore: Librería Soluna, Real de Guadalupe 13-B (tel. 8-68-05), 1 block east of the *zócalo*. Open Mon.-Sat. 9am-8pm, Sun. 11am-6pm.

Red Cross: Ignacio Allende 57 (tel. 8-07-72), 3 blocks south of the Pan American Highway. No English spoken. 24-hr. emergency service.

Pharmacy: Farmacia Regina, Mazariegos at Crescencio Rosas (tel. 8-02-41). No English spoken. Open 24hr.

Hospital: Hospital Regional, Insurgentes 24 (tel. 8-07-70), 4 blocks south of the *zócalo*, across from Santa Lucía, in Parque Fray Bartolomé. Open 24hr.

Police: (tel. 8-05-54), in the Palacio Municipal, on the west side of the *zócalo*.

Post Office: (tel. 8-07-65), Cuauhtémoc at Crescencio Rosas, 1 block southwest of the *zócalo*. Open Mon.-Fri. 8am-7pm, Sat. and holidays 9am-1pm. **MexPost,** in the same office, open Mon.-Fri. 8am-7pm. **Postal Code:** 29200.

Telephone Code: 967.

ACCOMMODATIONS AND CAMPING

Budget travelers say *Amen.* San Cristóbal is teeming with inexpensive hotels. Most lie on **Real de Guadalupe, Madero, Insurgentes,** and **Juárez,** with prices decreasing relative to their distance from the *zócalo*. Camping is only available outside of town (see below). Due to the altitude, the temperature often drops below 10°C (50°F), making hot water and blankets indispensable.

Hotel Jovel, Paniagua 28 (tel. 8-17-34), 2½ blocks east and 2 blocks north of the *zócalo*. Great natural lighting illuminates rooms with wooden floors and colorful bedspreads. The solarium is perfect for an afternoon read. Hot water and medical service 24hr. Staff will watch luggage for a number of days. Singles 40 pesos. Doubles 50 pesos. Triples 60 pesos. Add 10 pesos for private bath.

Posada Villa Betania, Madero 87 (tel. 8-44-67), 4 blocks east of the *zócalo*. The fireplace looks so inviting, you muse. You shroud yourself in a wooly blanket and sip complimentary tea as you watch the sparks fly. You dream of taking a steamy hot shower, and the next morning your prayers are answered. You gently ignore the bubble-gum pink walls. Singles 40 pesos. Doubles 60 pesos. Triples 80 pesos.

Posada Bed and Breakfast, Madero 83 (tel. 8-04-40), 4 blocks east of the *zócalo*, just before the Posada Villa Betania. A little yellow room gets you a whole lot of breakfast. Singles 25 pesos, with bath 30 pesos. Doubles 40 pesos, with bath 45 pesos. Triples 80 pesos. Quads 90 pesos. Bed in a 7-person dormitory 20 pesos.

La Casa de Gladis, Real de Mexicanos 16 (tel. 8-57-75), 6 blocks north and 2 blocks west of the *zócalo*. Tall-ceilinged rooms with thick walls. Quiet courtyard sports brightly painted furniture. Communal bathrooms are exceptional. Hot water daily 8am-8pm. Doubles 50 pesos. Triples 50 pesos. Quads 80 pesos. 15 pesos to camp or sling a hammock. Bed in a 7-person dormitory 20 pesos.

Hotel Posada del Barón, Belisario Domínguez 2 (tel. 8-08-81), 1 block east of the *zócalo*. Gleaming rooms with colorful bedspreads. Modern bathrooms with hot water. Singles 50 pesos. Doubles 60 pesos. Triples 70 pesos.

Casa de Huéspedes Margarita, Real de Guadalupe 34 (tel. 8-09-57), 1½ blocks east of the *zócalo*, just past the Posada Santiago. Cavernous rooms with blue-tiled floors and black ceilings give way to a pleasant courtyard filled with gregarious guests. No rooms with private baths (some lack windows too), but clean communal facilities offer hot water 24hr. Rent a horse in the lobby. Singles 28 pesos. Doubles 35 pesos. Triples 42 pesos. Bed in a 4-person dormitory 15 pesos.

Rancho San Nicolás (tel. 8-00-57), on the extension of Francisco León, 1km east of town. If no one's around, ring the bell for the Hacienda across the road. Rooms, camping, and trailer park in a pastoral setting complete with whispering trees. Never fear—hot water here. During high season (Dec.-Feb.), rooms are often full, so call in advance. RVs 35 pesos. Camping 15 pesos. Rooms 25 pesos. Each additional person 20 pesos. Horse rental 20 pesos per hr., 50 pesos per day.

Na-Bolom, Vicente Guerrero 33 (tel. 8-14-18), at the end of Chiapa de Corzo in the northeast section of town. This museum (see p. 460) doubles as a hotel. 14 fabulously furnished rooms with fireplaces, each decorated in the style of a different *indígena* village. Enormous, ranch-style meals. Singles 185 pesos. Doubles 215 pesos. Triples 240 pesos. Guests get free admission to the museum tour and film. Proceeds support the work of the center.

FOOD

The town should have been called "San Cristóbal de la Comida Bien Rica." Local specialties include *sopa de pan* (a doughy mass floating in vegetable broth), scrumptious *tacos al pastor,* full-bodied *chiles rellenos,* and grainy wheat breads from the Barrio San Ramón. Top it all off with the exquisite *cerveza dulce* or some of Mexico's best coffee.

Cafetería del Centro, Real de Guadalupe 15B (tel. 8-63-68), 2 blocks east of the zócalo. Comida corrida (soup, entree, rice, bread, postre, and coffee 15 pesos) is as good as it gets. Excellent breakfasts 9-13 pesos. Open daily 7am-9pm.

La Casa del Pan Cantante, Navarro #10 (tel. 8-04-68), at Domínguez. Bread overflows from baskets and the aroma of vegetable *hojaldres* (15 pesos) fills the air in this imaginative vegetarian restaurant. Daunting pro-Zapatista mural leaves no doubt as to the establishment's political stance. *Menú del día* 23 pesos. Live Latin American guitar music Fri. and Sat. starting at 8pm. Open Tues.-Sun. 7am-9:30pm, until 11:30pm on music nights.

La Salsa Verde, 20 de Noviembre 7, 1 block north of the *zócalo.* Everything from cactus to cow udder. Tacos 3 pesos each. Open daily 6-10pm.

Centro Cultural El Puente, Real de Guadalupe 55 (tel. 8-22-50), 3 blocks from the *zócalo.* Café, language school, cinema, local art, and silky jazz combine with a distinct leftist flavor. Vegetarians can feast on the cheese, tomato, and avocado omelette (13 pesos). Sandwiches 9-12 pesos. Open Mon.-Sat. 8am-11pm.

El Oasis, 1 de Marzo #6C, 1 block north of the cathedral. Veggie cuisine. 4-course *comida corrida* 20 pesos. Excellent breakfasts. Open Mon.-Sat. 7am-8pm.

Restaurante Madre Tierra, Insurgentes 19 (tel. 8-42-97), opposite the Iglesia de San Francisco, 2½ blocks south of the *zócalo.* Homey, rich interior promises similar food. Muesli, with raisins, almonds, and bananas (13 pesos), makes for a super start to the day. Excellent bakery next door. Open daily 8am-9:30pm.

Emiliano's Mustache, Crecencio Rosas 7, 1 block west and 1 block south of the *zócalo.* Come for the tacos—all the locals do. Tacos 2 pesos each, order of 7 13 pesos. Open daily 8am-1am. Taco stand open daily 6pm-1am.

Café Altura, 1 de Marzo #6D (tel./fax 8-40-38). The best coffee in town. Veggie cuisine isn't bad either. Open daily 7am-9pm.

SIGHTS

Since its construction by the Spanish in the 16th century, San Cristóbal's *zócalo* has been the physical and spiritual center of town. The colonial **Palacio Municipal** and the **cathedral,** with its white Corinthian columns and patterned wooden roof, dominate the heart of the city. Consecrated in 1528, the cathedral pews are filled with a bevy of devout followers, and its rafters with a flock of chirping birds (cathedral open daily 7am-7pm).

North on Utrilla and beyond the **Iglesia de la Caridad** is the **Iglesia y Ex-convento de Santo Domingo.** Santo Domingo's walls are covered in restless gold leaf which slithers in elaborate patterns up walls, around portraits, and over the left nave's exquisite pulpit. Though somewhat weathered, the church's intricate Baroque façade stands out from the exterior; look for the crest of the Spanish empire, comprised of a pair of two-headed eagles (open daily 7am-8pm).

Stashed in Santo Domingo's *ex-convento* is **Sna Jolobil** (tel./fax 8-26-46), which means "House of Weaving" in Tzeltal. It is a cooperative of 1500 weavers from 10 Tzotzil and Tzeltal villages in the *chiapaneco* highlands whose objective is to preserve and revitalize their ancestral weaving techniques. While many of the extremely high quality, intricately embroidered *huipiles* will cost more than your plane ticket home, Sna Jolobil is a great place to window-shop and view the area's traditional garments (open Mon.-Sat. 9am-2pm and 4-6pm). Another cooperative, **J'pas Joloviletic**, is at General Utrilla 43 (tel. 8-28-48), on the opposite side of Santo Domingo from Sna Jolobil (open Mon.-Sat. 9am-2pm and 4-7pm, Sun. 9am-1pm).

Next door to Sna Jolobil, the **Centro Cultural de Los Altos de Chiapas** houses an excellent multi-media exhibit on the history of San Cristóbal and Chiapas. On display are colonial artifacts, photographs, and a collection of Chiapanecan textiles, some of which are many hundreds of years old. During the summer, visitors bring along penknives to leave their mark on the avocado tree in the courtyard (open Tues.-Sun. 10am-5pm; admission 10 pesos, free Sun.; free group tours in Spanish).

San Cristóbal's most famous museum is **Na-Bolom,** Guerrero 33, at the end of Chiapa de Corzo. Located in the northeastern section of the city, Na-Bolom (House of the Jaguar) is a private house which turns into a museum twice daily. For many decades Trudy and Franz Blom worked and studied among the dwindling communities of the Lacandón Rainforest along the Guatemala border. After the death of her husband in 1963, Trudy Blom continued their work, winning acclaim as an ecologist, ethnologist, and photographer before her death in the winter of 1993. Many volunteers live at Na-Bolom, carrying out the jungle reforestation project begun by Ms. Blom and conducting tours of the Fray Bartolomé de Las Casas library, the gardens, and the Bloms' personal museum. The library's manuscripts concentrate on Mayan culture, with numerous periodicals, news clippings, and rare papers dealing with rainforest ecology and the plight of *indígena* refugees (library open Mon.-Fri. 10am-1:30pm). The small, ornate chapel (the building was originally intended as a seminary) now serves as a gallery of colonial *chiapaneco* religious art created by *ladinos* and *indígenas* alike. Other rooms are devoted to archaeological finds from the nearby site of Moxviquil, religious artifacts from the Lacandón Rainforest, and the work of artists in residence (museum open daily by guided tour at 11am and 4:30pm in Spanish and 4:30pm in English, followed by a 15-min. film; admission 15 pesos; museum shop open Tues.-Sun. 9am-1pm and 4-8pm; café open daily 10am-2pm and 4-8pm). You can also stay in one of Na Bolom's 14 fabulously decorated rooms (see p. 459).

It's an arduous climb to the top of the **Iglesia de San Cristóbal de las Casas;** by the grace of God, the ascent has been broken into 285 steps. Behind the church stands a 6m-tall crucifix built of license plates. All that remains of the iron-frame Christ is his left arm, dangling grotesquely by the wrist. The monument dares you to feel any sense of reverence. To reach the stairs, walk three blocks south on Insurgentes and

---

A Stranger Among Us

Chiapas is one of the few regions in the Republic where traditional dress codes are still strictly maintained. Each *indígena* group has distinctive clothing patterns and colors. Outsiders who wear *indígena* clothing may offend natives here, since the patterns and styles of garments are sometimes invested with social meaning. Women should avoid wearing broad, ribboned hats, which are reserved in most villages for men. Revealing clothing is often received coldly. Keep shorts hidden until you feel the ocean spray on your face. Some villagers don't take kindly to gawking foreigners, and they particularly object to being photographed. Visitors to *indígena* communities should not snap photos without explicit permission to do so, since some locals fear cameras might take not only their image but also their spirit. Uncooperative tourists have been jailed for just one shot. And don't even dream of taking pictures (or notes, for that matter) in churches.

turn right on Hnos. Domínguez; the stairs are three blocks ahead. Women traveling alone should avoid the area after dark (open daily dawn-dusk)

The **Facultad de Derecho** (Law School) of the Universidad de Chiapas, the fourth oldest law school in Mexico, is located on the corner of Miguel Hidalgo and Cuauhtémoc and boasts some fanciful murals painted in 1992 by Carlos Jurado. Enter the building, turn around, and you'll be greeted by Bosch-like lions, flying zeppelins, and blue devils (open daily 7am-8pm). A superb collection of **regional clothes** is displayed in **Sergio Castro's** home, Guadalupe Victoria 47 (tel. 8-42-89), west of the *zócalo*. In about an hour, Sergio can show you his collection of sartorial splendor. Call in advance for an informative and friendly tour. There is no charge, but a tip is appropriate (open daily 6pm-8pm).

San Cristóbal's daily morning **market** overflows with fruit, veggies, and an assortment of cheap goods. There aren't really any *artesanías* on sale though—look to the market around Iglesia de Santo Domingo for souvenirs. Try coming on Sunday, when *indígenas* from nearby villages turn out in droves (market open daily 7am-3pm or until the afternoon rain). Utrilla and Real de Guadalupe, the two streets radiating from the northeastern corner of the *zócalo,* are dotted with colorful shops which sell *típico* attire for less than the market stands or neighboring villages. Locals do their shopping on Saturday mornings. Watch, listen, and learn—these experts wrote the book on bargaining.

ENTERTAINMENT AND SEASONAL EVENTS

Locals and tourists enjoy an after-dinner *paseo* (stroll) in the *zócalo*, but by 10 or 11pm the *mariachi* bands are usually left in the dark—most folks in San Cristóbal turn in early. Nonetheless, a few Latin-music clubs stay open late in order to accommodate San Cristóbal's young crowd. **La Galería,** Hidalgo 3 (tel. 8-15-47), is a chic courtyard restaurant with live music nightly until 2am during the high season (cocktails around 10 pesos). **Disco Palace,** Av. Crescendio Rosas 59 (tel. 8-26-00), fills with locals weekends after 10pm. **Disco Pop-Rock** (tel. 8-11-81), in the Hotel Maya Quetzal on the Pan American Highway, 300m west of the Cristóbal Colón bus station, is much less crowded but fun on a Saturday night (open Sat. only after 10pm). Both discos charge a cover of about 15 pesos, depending on the night. For entertainment that's easier on your pulse rate, try **El Puente,** which sponsors movies and lectures (see p. 459). **Cinemas Santa Clara** (tel. 8-23-45), on 16 de Septiembre between Escuadrón and 28 de Agosto, screens U.S. movies.

In San Cristóbal and the nearby villages, hardly a week goes by without some kind of religious festival. The city's *Semana Santa* celebration is rather *tranquila*. Many business establishments close their doors, and the processions and cultural events that take place are decidedly reverent and low-key. On Easter Sunday, however, *Semana Santa* gives way to the week-long **Feria de la Primavera y de la Paz.** Before the riotous revelry really gets going, a local beauty queen is selected to preside over the festivities, which include concerts, dances, bullfights, cock fights, and baseball games. Hotel rooms for either week must be reserved several months in advance. The *fiesta* of the city's patron, San Cristóbal, is celebrated July 18-25 with elaborate religious ceremonies and numerous concerts.

■ Near San Cristóbal

Sunday morning is the best and often the only time to visit the markets of nearby villages. However, because service is always routed through San Cristóbal, visiting more than one village in a single morning is almost impossible. Buses and *combis* leave from the lot one block past the market at Utrilla and Honduras. Destination signs next to the buses are only occasionally accurate; always ask drivers where they're going. Drivers don't leave until the *combi* is completely full, so be prepared to squeeze in.

Another option for transportation and information is the venerable **Mercedes Hernández Gómez.** Something of an expert on local *indígena* culture and a splendid storyteller, Gómez meets interested travelers daily at 9am in the *zócalo,* carrying an umbrella so as to be easily spotted (Monday tours must be arranged by speaking with her in advance on Sunday morning). Tours go to San Juan Chamula and Zinacantán, lasting until about 3pm. The 40-peso fee includes transport, church entrance, and a sip of *posh* inside a Chamula hut. An equally viable option is the intelligent and gregarious **Raúl López** (tel. 8-34-41), who, having lived all of his thirtysomething years in San Cristóbal, happily divulges a wealth of information on everything from local customs to the Zapatista uprising to religion and back again, all with a refreshing frankness. Raúl, who only speaks Spanish (his *compañero* Manuel gives the same tour in English), meets interested travelers outside the cathedral daily at 9:30am (tour covers the same villages; 40 pesos; van returns around 2pm).

SAN JUAN CHAMULA

The community of San Juan Chamula (96 villages, 75,000 inhabitants) is the largest and most touristed of the villages around San Cristóbal. Visitors come to Chamula to check out the spectacular traditional clothing, and witness a civic and religious structure quite unlike any other in Mexico. Older Chamulan men wear traditional black wool *sarapes* tied with thick leather belts, while many of the younger men have switched to blue *sarapes.* Designs on the sleeves of the tunics indicate the wearer's *pueblito* or *colonia.* Village officials (elected by a hand-count) and elders drape ribbons over their large *sombreros.*

Chamulans, who expelled their last Catholic priest in 1867, are famous for their fierce resistance to Mexico's religious and secular authority. Villagers have far more faith in the powers of the village shaman, and Catholic bishops are allowed into the church solely for baptisms. Similarly, the government medical clinic is used only as a last resort, after incantations with eggs, bubbly *refrescos,* and chickens have failed.

Before entering the brightly painted **church** (open 24hr.), you must obtain a permit (3 pesos) from the tourist office on the *zócalo* and show the permit to the guards inside the church. **Under no circumstances should you take pictures**—Chamulans believe that a part of their soul is captured in every snapshot, and they must go through extensive healing ceremonies to regain it. Inside the church, pine needles, candles, and chanting Chamulans fill the pewless hall as they petition Catholic saints on a conversational level. Different colored candles signify different levels of prayer-severity, and other Mayan rituals are aided by the ubiquitous Pepsi bottle. The importance of carbonated beverages cannot be overstated; Chamulans believe that **burping** helps to purify the self by expelling evil spirits. Prior to the discovery of fizzy drinks, locals had to drink gallons of water to achieve the same cathartic effect.

To the left of the church stands a cluster of distinctive, green foliated Mayan crosses. The crosses' origin is in the crucifix-shaped Tree Of Life, featured on the sarcophagus of King Pakal at Palenque. When Fray Bartolomé de Las Casas showed up bearing the Christian cross, he waltzed right into Chamula, whose residents believed he was a messenger from the gods. Chamula's small but diverse artisan's **market** is down a side street on the opposite end of the *zócalo* from the church.

The best time to visit Chamula is during **Carnaval,** which draws 40,000 *indígenas* and countless tourists, one week before Ash Wednesday. While they coincide with Lent, the festivities have their origins in the ancient Mayan ritual concerning the five "lost" days at the end of the 360-day agricultural cycle. Expect to see religious leaders dashing through fire in order to purify themselves, and singing and dancing men decked out in monkey skins. In addition to Chamula's *carnaval* (see Entertainment and Seasonal Events, above) and the assumption of the *cargo* (Dec. 3-Jan. 1), the *fiestas* of San Sebastián (Jan. 20), San Mateo (Sept. 21-22), and San Juan Bautista (June 22-24) warrant a trip to the village.

Getting There: *Combis* to Chamula leave from San Cristóbal, on Utrilla near the market (approx. every 30min. 6am-5pm, 30min., 3 pesos). To reach Chamula by car, drive west from the *zócalo* on Guadalupe Victoria and bear right after crossing the small bridge on Diagonal Ramón Larraínzar. At the fork, bear right for Chamula, which is at the end of an 8km stretch of paved road.

ZINACANTÁN

Just beyond Chamula lies the smaller community of Zinacantán (pop. 35,000), comprised of 36 villages. Here, the men (and even the young boys playing basketball in the *zócalo*) wear beautiful, bright red *sarapes,* decorated with colorful stitched flowers and dangling tassels of deep red and purple. During *fiestas,* residents wear heelguards on their *huaraches* (sandals) in accordance with ancient Mayan custom. Many of the women walk about bare-footed. This is not an indication of poverty but rather a reflection of the Mayan emphasis on the importance of female fertility— they believe that women can draw fertility from the ground. Thus, as girls approach puberty, they begin to go without shoes. The unfortunate few women who are sterile are cast out of the village and must move, usually to San Cristóbal.

Somewhat exceptional for a *chiapaneco* village is the fact that Zinacantán has accepted the Catholic clergy. The village's handsome, whitewashed **church** dates back to the 16th century and features standard Roman columns and Corinthian arches. It is used exclusively for Catholic worship, while the small white convent has been set aside for ritual healing and pre-Conquest forms of worship. But you won't find confessionals in the church—confession here is a public act, directed at the effigies on the altar. The Catholic priest, independent of the village church, merely busies himself with confirmation, baptism, and wedding ceremonies. To enter the church you must pay a 3-peso visitor's fee at the tourist booth in front. Tourists who step inside the convent are expected to drop a small donation into the *limosna* box. As with all traditional communities, Zinacantán does not tolerate picture-taking, note-taking, or hat-wearing.

Of late, the invisible hand has caught Zinacantán in its grip—the village's flower industry has flourished and Zinacantán has gained a considerable economic edge over neighboring San Juan Chamula. Every Friday morning, town residents inaugurate what they hope will be a profitable weekend by marching down Av. Insurgentes in San Cristóbal. Today, Zinacantán is not a poor Mayan settlement. Many houses contain stereos, TVs, and gas stoves, although these serve principally as status symbols and women prefer to cook directly on the ground. The children who bother tourists for pesos are mainly joking and will be severely scolded by their parents if caught. If you wander around town long enough you'll stumble upon a backyard full of women weaving, and may well be invited in to browse the selection of clothes—you won't find souvenirs any more authentic than this.

Zinacantán's festivals include Fiesta de San Sebastián (Jan. 18-20), *Semana Santa,* Fiesta del Patron San Juan (July 24-29), and the Fiesta de San Lorenzo (Aug. 10-20).

Getting There: *Combis* to Zinacantán (3 pesos) leave San Cristóbal from the lot near the market as they fill up (daily 6am-8pm). If driving, follow Guadalupe Victoria west from the *zócalo* and turn right after crossing the small bridge on Diagonal Ramón Larraínzar. At the fork, turn left toward the "Bienvenido a Zinacantán" sign.

SAN ANDRÉS LARRAÍNZAR

Site of the Zapatista negotiations during the summers of 1995 and 1996, San Andrés Larraínzar lies 26km northwest of San Cristóbal and 16km from Chamula. Because there are no convenient tours to the village, its 5000 citizens are better disposed toward the outsiders who do make the trip. Mexicans refer to the village as Larraínzar, but local Tzotziles prefer San Andrés. Since many of the villagers are reluctant to carry their produce all the way to San Cristóbal, the **market** (open Fri.-Sun. until 1pm) is better stocked here than at Chamula or Zinacantán. For a panoramic view of the beautiful green valleys and patches of **corn fields** which surround the city, walk up the hill from the main church to La Iglesia de Guadalupe.

Getting There: Starting at 6am, *combis* (50min., 5 pesos) make several trips to San Andrés from the small terminal behind the San Cristóbal market—continue on the dirt road for about a block and the stop will be on your right. It's best to return before 2pm, soon after the market begins to shut down and before the *combis* stop running. Hitching is conceivable but difficult, and not recommended by *Let's Go* as a safe means of travel. To reach San Andrés by car, take the road northwest from San Cristóbal to Chamula and continue past the village. On a curve some 10km later, a prominent sign announcing "S.A. Larraínzar" points left to a road climbing the steep side of the valley; the village lies approximately 6km beyond the fork.

CHENALHÓ

Chenalhó (pop. 6000) seems even more remote from San Cristóbal than its 32km would suggest. Foreigners are rare birds here. In Chenalhó, typical dress for men varies from white or black ponchos worn over pants and bound with heavy belts, to short, light, white tunics. Women who have not adopted more current fashions dress uniformly in dark blue *nalgas* (skirts) and white *tocas* (shawls) embroidered with bright orange flowers. A small store behind the enclosed market supplies the town with nearly all its clothing. The market spreads out into the plaza in front of the church on Sunday and sells mostly foodstuffs, including *chiche,* a potent drink made from fermented cane. Villagers enthusiastically wave visitors into San Pedro, the church in the town's center, which serves as a secular as well as a religious meeting place. Inside, the main aisle often shimmers with the light from candles riding. Chenalhó residents celebrate the Fiesta de San Sebastián (June 20) and the Fiesta de San Pedro (July 29) in grand style.

Getting There: Autotransportes Fray Bartolomé de Las Casas usually operates buses to Chenalhó and the even more remote town of **Pantelhó.** The San Cristóbal bus leaves from the station on Utrilla north of the market at about 2pm. The bus sometimes does not return until the next day, so make sure you have a ride back to San Cristóbal before you go. Bus trips take two hours. Driving to Chenalhó can cut transit time in half, but the cost to your car's suspension system will be high—a ride on the dirt road northwest of Chamula is guaranteed to chatter some teeth.

HIKING TO EL ARCOTETE

Although a number of trails wind their way through San Cristóbal's countryside, the tourist office recommends that you not hike to or between the outlying villages—assaults (by bandits and poisonous snakes) are not uncommon. If you're desperate for a hike, consider undertaking the three- to four-hour round-trip trek to **El Arcotete,** a natural arch formed where a small river cuts through a spur of rock. Unfortunately, the first half of the hike is alongside the highway, and then past a trash-filled park. Once on the ridge, however, the trail leads through beautiful pine forest with splendid views of the mountains.

Getting There: To reach the arch, head east on Calle Flavio Paniagua, in the northeast section of town. From a plateau level with the Iglesia de Guadalupe to your right, a 15-minute climb takes you steeply up to the *carretera*. Continue to climb along the roadside, as the city begins to spread out below you. A 30-40-minute walk brings you to a yellow "Prohibido Tirar Basura" sign, just as the highway begins to bear left. Leave the highway and continue to the right of the sign, through the forest. You'll eventually come upon a tiny *indígena* village, about 15 minutes from the highway. From here, the trail leads down through pristine pine forest to a gorgeous secluded clearing, 15 minutes from the village. At the bottom of the clearing to the right of an abandoned hut, a narrow trail leads 100m through the woods to a small river; El Arcotete is to your left. The water's not deep enough for swimming, but you can probably wade through the arch to the other side.

GRUTAS DE SAN CRISTÓBAL

The Grutas de San Cristóbal lie just off the Pan-American Highway, 10km southeast of San Cristóbal. From the small entrance at the base of a steep wooded hillside, a tall, narrow fissure, incorporating a chain of countless **caves**, leads almost 3km into the heart of the rock. Because of the caves' unusual shape, the cave floor is not particularly user-friendly for walking. Instead, a modern concrete walkway, at times 10m above the cave floor strewn with boulders, navigates 750m into the system. The dimly-lit caves boast a spectacular array of stalactites and columns. If you're feeling youthful, stamping on the boardwalk at certain points generates a rumbling echo throughout the caves (caves open daily 9am-5pm; admission 2 pesos). Consider soliciting the help of one of the local youths who hang around outside to help uncover the natural light and shadow formations (a small tip is appropriate).

Getting There: Almost any east-bound *microbús* passing across the road from the Iglesia de San Diego passes the *grutas* (15min., 2 pesos). From the highway, a five-minute walk through the park brings you to the entrance.

■ Comitán

Eighty-six kilometers southeast of San Cristóbal, Comitán is the last major town on the Pan American Highway before the Guatemalan border (85km away). While rapid growth has transformed Comitán into a dreary maze of tangled streets, the city can be active and genial, and its verdant multi-terraced *zócalo* breeds raucous *marimba*-inspired fun. Situated at the end of the Palenque-Ocosingo-San Cristóbal-Comitán corridor, which separates the Lacandón rainforest from the rest of Chiapas, this city is the southernmost point with a significant military presence. However, memories of large-scale Zapatista stunts are gradually fading into the past—the chirpy staff of the tourist office will tell you of its ordeal with relish and tourists stop over as frequently as ever, usually on the way to and from Guatemala.

Orientation and Practical Information To reach the *zócalo* from the Cristóbal Colón bus station, cross over the **Pan-American Highway** and turn left. Two hundred meters later, take the first right onto **4ª Calle Sur.** Walk five blocks east, turn left, and walk three blocks north, past the post office, to the *zócalo* on **Av. Central.**

The **tourist office** (tel. 2-40-47 or 2-23-44), on the first floor of the Palacio Municipal, overflows with brochures and maps (open Mon.-Sat. 9am-9pm, Sun. 9am-2pm). Guatemalan visas can be obtained from the **Guatemalan Consulate,** 1ª Sur Pte. (tel. 2-04-91), at 2ª Av. Pte. Sur; look for the blue-and-white flag (open Mon.-Fri. 8am-4:30pm). **Banca Serfin,** at 1ª Av. Sur Pte. 1 (tel. 2-12-96 or 2-15-70), just off the southwest corner of the *zócalo,* changes U.S. dollars only Mon.-Fri. 10am-noon. They also have a 24-hour **ATM** (bank open Mon.-Fri. 9am-1:30pm).

Cristóbal Colón (tel. 2-09-80), on the Pan-American Highway between 4ª and 8ª Calles Sur Pte., runs to Mexico City (2pm, 16hr., 284 pesos), Puebla (2pm, 14hr., 153 pesos), Ocosingo (1:45pm, 4hr., 29 pesos), Palenque (1:45pm, 6hr., 57 pesos), San Cristóbal (12 per day, 1½hr., 12 pesos), Tapachula (7 per day, 6hr., 52 pesos), Tuxtla Gutiérrez (12 per day, 3½hr., 33 pesos), and Villahermosa (1:45pm, 9hr., 79 pesos). **Autotransportes Tuxtla Gutiérrez** (tel. 2-10-44), on the Highway between 1ª and 2ª Calle Sur Pte., has first-class service to San Cristóbal (9 per day, 2hr., 13 pesos), continuing to Tuxtla (3hr., 25 pesos). Nine second-class buses also make the run to San Cristóbal and Tuxtla daily. **Transportes Cuxtepeques,** on the Highway between 1ª and 2ª Calles Nte. Pte., provides the fastest and most direct service to San Cristóbal (every 30min. 4am-6pm, 3hr., 25 pesos). You can shorten the walk to any of these stations by catching a *microbús* on the highway (1 peso). **Taxis** (tel. 2-01-27 or 2-01-05) can be found in the *zócalo.*

Comitán's indoor **market** is on Central Benito Juárez, just before 2 Oriente Sur, one block east of the *zócalo* (open daily dawn-dusk). Pick up groceries at **SúperMas,** 2ª Poniente #8 (tel. 2-17-27), one block south and one block east of the *zócalo* (open daily 8am-9pm). **Farmacia Regina,** 1 Sur Ote. 1 (tel. 2-11-96 or 2-07-54), is on the south side of the *zócalo* (open daily 8am-9pm). The **Red Cross** (tel. 2-18-89) is on 5ª Calle Nte. Pte., 2½ blocks west of the highway. In case of emergency contact the **Hospital Civil,** at 2 Calle Ote. Sur and 9 Sur Ote. #13 (tel. 2-01-35 or 2-20-51). The **police** (tel. 2-00-25) are on the ground floor of the Palacio Municipal. The **post office,** Central Dr. Belisario Domínguez 45 (tel. 2-04-27), is one and a half blocks south of the *zócalo* (open Mon.-Fri. 8am-7pm, Sat. 9am-1pm).

Accommodations and Food Comitán is full of grotty, overpriced "budget" accommodations. A select few places stand out from the dregs, however. All establishments listed are within a few blocks of the *centro*. **Hospedaje Montebello,** 1ª Calle Norte Pte. 10 (tel. 2-35-72), between Av. Central Nte. and 1ª Calle Pte. Nte., one block north of the *zócalo,* is one of the few places in town whose prices fairly reflect the quality of the rooms. Large, clean wood-ceilinged rooms open onto a considerably cheerier courtyard (25 pesos per person with decent communal facilities, 30 pesos with private bath). **Pensión Delfín,** Central Belisario Domínguez 21ª (tel. 2-00-13), on the west side of the *zócalo,* offers authentic wood-paneled rooms with firm beds and clean private baths (singles 55 pesos; 10 pesos per additional person, up to 7-person suites). Several *taquerías* cluster around the northwest corner of the *zócalo* and on Calle Central Nte. selling tacos for a pittance (2 pesos each).

■ Near Comitán

PARQUE NACIONAL LAGUNAS DE MONTEBELLO

A hop, skip, and a 52-km bus ride from Comitán lie the pine-covered hills of the **Parque Nacional Lagunas de Montebello.** Some 68 lakes peacefully await exploration in this scenic playground. Unfortunately, only 16 have trails leading from the main road and some are notorious for bandit attacks. Be sure to inquire ahead at the Comitán tourist office or with guides at the lakes before undertaking any off-the-beaten-path hikes. Buses unload passengers anywhere along the road to **Laguna Bosque Azul** or **Laguna Tziscao.** Camping is available at both of these sites, and Tziscao offers *cabañas* (30 pesos per person).

Getting There: From Comitán, the blue "Montebello" bus leaves the station on 2ª Av. Pte. Sur, between 2ª and 3ª Calles Sur Pte. (every 15min. 5:30am-5pm, 1hr., 8 pesos). The bus swings by the Cristóbal Colón bus station for those who want to head straight to the lakes.

Say Anything

You're cruising down the Spanish superhighway at full speed, not even slowing down for the subjunctive tense. Irregular verbs? Not a problem. You hit the gas and chuckle at all the slow drivers you've left behind in a cloud of dust. Crazy cats couldn't even conjugate *ser* properly. Then bam!—all of a sudden you have no vehicle. In fact, you're not even on the right road. What was that *tope* to end all *topes?,* you ask. That, dear befuddled driver, was Mayan. After all, this is the Yucatán, and though the ancient Maya cities lay in ruins, the language is still very much alive. Drive through the Yucatán and you're certain to encounter Mayan newspapers, Mayan radio, and lots of Mayan conversation. Here are some basics:

Hello	*ache*	Nothing	*mix-ba*
Hasta la vista	*kaka-te*	Shut Up!	*hutz-utz*
What?	*bax-a-walik*	Fuck you	*to-pana*
Hunger	*naha*	Let's fuck	*kooz-itzx*

OTHER SIGHTS

Just 22km south of the city lie the recently unearthed ruins of **Tenam Puente,** including a ballcourt and a handful of smaller pyramids. To reach the site, take the "Francisco Sarabia" bus from the Transportes Comitán-La Trinitaria station on 1ª Calle Sur Pte., between 3ª and 4ª Calles Pte. Sur (Mon.-Fri. 8am and 2pm, 30min., 3 pesos); it will drop you off at the access road, a couple of kilometers from the entrance. Check with drivers for return schedule (site open daily 8am-5pm; free).

32km from the Comitán-Cuauhtémoc (Pan American) highway, on the way to Lagunas Montebello, lies another set of Mayan ruins at **Chinkultic.** Perhaps more interesting than the 7th-century pyramid and ballcourt are the diminutive *cenote* (freshwater sink-hole) and the striking view of the lake region from the hilltop. The "Montebello" bus can drop you off at the access road, an easy 2km from the ruins (site open daily 8am-5pm; free). Hikers can also venture to **Grutas El Paso del Soldado,** 2km east of Laguna Monte Azul (called Laguna Bosque Azul by locals).

Popular with locals but more obscure than Montebello is the **Cascada de Chiflón,** a 250m waterfall 45km west of Comitán. The lake is relatively safe (albeit cold) for swimming, but don't venture too close to the waterfall, or you may take a once-in-a-lifetime plunge. There are some nice places to camp in this area, but no facilities. To get to Chiflón, take a *combi* to La Mesilla from the Tuxtla Gutiérrez bus station on the highway (every 30min. 5:45am-10am, 45min., 7 pesos). The waterfall is a 5km walk from the roadside.

■ Ocosingo

More rural than the bustling *zócalo* first lets on, tourist-free Ocosingo (pop. 24,000) straddles the hilltops of central Chiapas. As the nearest large settlement to the Lacandón rainforest, the fringes of which harbor the majority of Zapatista rebels, the military importance of Ocosingo's location is brutally obvious—and visibly so. Ocosingo's residents still bear painful memories of the January 1994 uprising, when a shoot-out in the market between the army and Zapatista-allied locals claimed dozens of lives. Today, the market bustles like any other in Mexico, and the soldiers are mostly preoccupied with trying to reach family and friends from the *caseta* in town. Nevertheless, armed infantrymen are likely to form the backdrop of any meal on the *zócalo.* Nothing, however, can detract from the city's stunning natural beauty.

Orientation and Practical Information Ocosingo lies 72km northeast of San Cristóbal de las Casas and 119km south of Palenque. To get to the *zócalo* from the **Cristobal Colon bus station,** walk uphill about 200m and take a left at the sign pointing to Ocosingo. Once on the road, take the first right and walk uphill 6 blocks to the *zócalo.* From the **Autotransportes Tuxtla station,** walk uphill two blocks and take a left at the "centro" sign. Three blocks downhill brings you to the *zócalo.* The town is laid out in the customary compass grid, but it's small enough that street names can be ignored almost entirely. From the *zócalo,* cardinal directions are marked by the Hotel Central to the north, the Iglesia de San Jacinto to the east, the Palacio Municipal to the west.

Ocosingo has no **tourist office,** but the staff on the 2nd floor of the Palacio Municipal (tel. 3-00-15) tries hard. They really do. No English is spoken (open Mon.-Fri. 9am-2pm and 6-9pm). **Banamex** (tel. 3-00-34), in the northwest corner of the *zócalo,* does not change U.S. dollars, but a lengthy procedure will get you cash advances on major credit cards (open Mon.-Fri. 9am-1:30pm). *Caseta* (tel. 3-00-54), is on 1 Ote. in an orange building on the left one and a half blocks north of the church (open Mon.-Sat. 9am-9pm).

Autotransportes Tuxtla Gutiérrez (tel. 3-01-39), on the highway, offers first-class service to Campeche (8:50am, 7hr., 100 pesos), Cancún (8:30am, 14hr., 200 pesos), Mérida (8am, 10hr., 136 pesos), Mexico City (12:45pm, 18hr., 248 pesos), Palenque

(12 per day, 2hr., 16 pesos), Puebla (12:45pm, 16hr., 223 pesos), and Villahermosa (4 per day, 5hr., 55 pesos). **Cristóbal Colón** (tel. 3-04-31) runs buses to Escárcega (9:30am, 4:30, and 7:30pm, 6hr., 73 pesos), Mexico City (3:30pm, 18hr., 245 pesos) via Puebla (16hr., 216 pesos), and Tuxtla Gutiérrez (6 per day, 3½hr., 36 pesos). Free **luggage storage.**

The **market** is two blocks south and three blocks east of the *zócalo* (open daily 5am-7pm). Take dirty clothes to **Lavandería Automática "La Espuma,"** just off Calle Central Nte., two blocks north of the Hotel Central and to the left. A **pharmacy, Cruz Blanca,** 1 Ote. and 2 Sur (tel. 3-02-33), is one block south of the church (open daily 7am-9pm). In case of a **medical emergency,** contact **IMSS** (tel. 3-01-51), 1.2km south of the *zócalo* on 1 Ote. Sur (open 24hr.). In case of an **emergency,** contact the staff at the Palacio Municipal (tel. 3-00-15) or the police. The **police** (tel. 3-05-07) are on Calle Central between 1 Pte. and 2 Pte. (open 24hr.). The **post office** is at 2 Sur Ote. 12, one block south of the *zócalo* (open Mon.-Fri. 9am-1pm and 3-6pm, Sat. 9am-1pm). **Postal Code:** 29950. **Telephone code:** 967.

Accommodations and Food Hotel Central, Av. Central 1 (tel. 3-00-24), on the north side of the zócalo, is smartly decorated in shades of aqua, well lit, and spacious. Rooms come with mineral water, cable TV, and fans (singles 60 pesos; doubles 80 pesos; triples 100 pesos). **Hotel Agua Azul,** 1 Ote. #127 (tel. 3-03-02), two blocks south (downhill) of the church, has small dim rooms with squishy beds, slanted ceilings, and uneven floors. The overgrown balcony adds flair. A tame white-tailed stag loves to lick hands (singles 40 pesos; doubles 50 pesos; triples 70 pesos). **Hotel Margarita,** Calle Central Nte. 6 (tel. 3-02-80), half a block north of Hotel Central, has clean and roomy hastily whitewashed rooms (singles 65 pesos; doubles 75 pesos; triples 85 pesos; quads 95 pesos; TV and A/C 15 pesos extra).

Restaurant La Montura, Av. Central 5 (tel. 3-05-50), in the Hotel Central on the north side of the *zócalo,* is somewhat overpriced, but the outdoor tables under the arcade are the most pleasant in town. Entrees are 25-30 pesos, delicious *tortas* stuffed with *frijoles* and avocado go for 10 pesos (open daily 7am-11pm). **Restaurante Las Cazuelas,** 1 Ote. #127, in the Hotel Agua Azul, serves up tasty food in a tiny log cabin with tree-trunk tables. The menu changes at the whim of the chef or the season. All meals cost 13 pesos (open daily 7am-10pm). **Restaurant Los Arcos** (tel. 3-00-65), on Av. Central, on the northwest corner of the *zócalo,* is easy to miss. With food this cheap, you can almost forgive the bare decor. Savor the chicken for 12-14 pesos, or the biggest damn *plátano frito* you've ever seen in your life for 5 pesos (open daily 6am-9pm).

■ Near Ocosingo: Toniná Ruins

While the ruins of Toniná rarely surface on lists of Mexico's can't-miss sights, they're larger and more interesting than over-billed Bonampak and comparable in size, though not in splendor, to Yucatán's Ruta Puuc sites of Kabah, Sayil, and Labná. After a brief conflict-imposed absence, the archaeologists and their builders are back at the site, carefully reconstructing the main pyramid. As these ruins don't have the user-friendly plaques present elsewhere, a guide is more crucial than elsewhere.

The Toniná complex, encompassing 15 acres of ruins, was a religious and administrative capital for the Mayan city-state that flourished from 300 to 1000 CE. Structures at Toniná do not share the orthodox symmetry or precise floorplan of Monte Albán or Chichén Itzá. Many statues have lost heads and feet to decay and neglect, and because the governor of Ocosingo took stones from the site to build roads around the turn of the century, the pyramids will never be fully restored.

The entrance path, which leads across the river east of the ruins and up a small gully, emerges at the **Plaza of War,** the first artificially terraced level of the site. Trees and grass have overgrown a pyramidal mound on the left; nearer the river is the grassy depression of the unexcavated **main ballcourt,** beyond which lies a **sacrificial**

altar. The ruins of a smaller ballcourt lie forgotten at the back of the plaza, next to chunks of statues scattered near the fence. Extensive glyphs on the back of these figures relate to the scenes on the front, often giving the *fechas fatales* (birth and death dates) of prominent characters. Three animals—the snake, the bat, and the jaguar—appear together repeatedly.The three stelae at the foot of the first level commemorate the inauguration of new governments.

Toniná's chief attraction is a massive **pyramid** which towers 60m over the plaza. The pyramid's seven tiers corresponded to the city's various social strata, from the general populace to the high priests, whose temples are perched on the seventh level. Well preserved panels and sculptures survive from almost all of the levels, but most have been moved to the on-site museum or hauled off to Mexico City.

At the center of the pyramid's fifth level gapes a royal grave. Here, archaeologists discovered a stone sarcophagus made of a single piece of limestone, which held a king's body and two unidentified corpses. To the left of the grave on the same level is a shrine to Chac, the Mayan rain god. The stone originally above the figure, carved in 300 CE, is now in the museum. The **Altar de Monstruo de la Tierra** is on the right on the sixth level.

The seventh level of the pyramid was Toniná's religious focal point, and it supports four large pyramids dedicated to a curious mix of cosmic and civic forces. The lowest and least impressive is the **Temple of Agriculture,** on the far right of the terrace. This crumbling pyramidal building contained private rooms for ranking priests and governors. Considerably higher, the **Pyramid of Life and Death** rises to the left of the Temple of Agriculture. Archaeologists believe this mound once housed the king and the royal family. Behind it loom Toniná's two most important temples. The higher **Pyramid of War,** on the right, served as an observatory; from the top of the structure, guards would scan the countryside for foreign heavies. Nearby, the **Pyramid of Finances** is aptly symmetrical. From the peak of either pyramid, you can enjoy a brilliant view and a cool breeze. Below the Pyramid of War is a newly excavated statue of **King Zotz-Choj** (the jaguar-bat king), whose giant headdress is adorned with an eagle, serpents, and symbols for wind, smoke, and fire.

Getting There: The ruins are located 15 bumpy kilometers from **Ocosingo** (a 30-min. drive). By car, follow 1 Ote. south out of town, past the clinic on the right. Bear right past the radio station on the left. Follow the signs for "Toniná ruins" to the Rancho Toniná; the road to the left of the gate leads to ruins and museum. Inquire at the ranch about camping. Travelers without a car can catch a morning *colectivo,* dole out a steep **taxi** fare (80-100 pesos one way), or walk for days. You can catch a *colectivo* pickup truck from the market or go to the *crucero,* a juncture where several buses and trucks go by, some of which may take you near the ruins. To get to this *crucero,* walk 10 minutes to the right on the dirt road behind the market. If you're part of a group, consider chartering a *colectivo "especial"* to take you to the ruins (30 pesos one way). Nearly all *colectivos* stop on the highway just uphill from the "Tuxtla Gutiérrez" station.

■ Palenque

The ruins of Palenque straddle a magnificent 300-meter-high *palenque* (natural palisade) in the foothills of the Altos de Chiapas. Dozens of thundering waterfalls tumble into the yellow-green savannah, and the vast, sweaty, tropical rainforest blankets the region in emerald hue. Visitors are mesmerized even without the aid of the hallucinogenic herbs and fungi that flourish in the moist shadows of the forest.

Eight kilometers from the ruins is the sleepy town of Palenque (pop. 17,000), sometimes called Santo Domingo. While most visitors see the town as little more than a base for exploring nearby ruins and waterfalls, Palenque's hilly streets can be charming. The Chiapas conflict has left hotels emptier than in the past. An occasionally scribbled "CHIAPAZ" (peace in Chiapas) and sincere group conversations in the *parque* regarding the day's *campesino* action are reminders that the conflict is far from resolved.

ORIENTATION

Palenque is in the northeastern corner of Chiapas, 274km from Tuxtla Gutiérrez. Streets running east-west are labeled *avenidas,* while those running north-south are *calles.* **Avenida Juárez** runs west, away from the *parque* (town square) towards the ruins and highway. Parallel to Juárez to the south are Avs. **5 de Mayo** and **20 de Noviembre.** To the north lie **Miguel Hidalgo, Nicolás Bravo, Reforma,** and **Domínguez.** From west to east, the *calles* are **Allende, Aldama, Abasolo, Independencia, Jiménez,** and **Guerrero.** The *parque* is bounded by Hidalgo, 20 de Noviembre, Independencia, and Jiménez. To get to the *parque* from the bus station, walk five blocks uphill (east) on Juárez.

PRACTICAL INFORMATION

Tourist Office: In the **Casa de las Artesanías,** at the corner of Juárez and Abasolo. Very friendly, helpful staff speaks some English and can provide excellent maps of the town and ruins. Open Mon.-Sat. 8am-8:30pm, Sun. 9am-1pm.

Currency Exchange: Bancomer, Juárez 40 (tel. 5-01-98), 2 blocks west of the *parque.* Open for exchange Mon.-Fri. 9am-1:30pm. **Viajes Yax-Ha** (see travel agencies) has a *casa de cambio.*

Telephones: Caseta California, Juárez #4 (tel. 5-11-50 or 5-12-12; fax 5-09-97), half a block from the *parque.* Open daily 8am-3pm and 6-11pm.

Telegrams: (tel. 5-03-68), on Hidalgo, 1½ blocks east of the *parque* in the Chakamax building, next to the post office. Open Mon.-Fri. 9am-3pm, Sat. 9am-1pm.

Travel Agencies: Yax-Ha, Av. Juárez 123 (tel. 5-07-98; fax 5-07-67), next door to Bancomer. Trips to Misol-Ha, Agua Azul, Yaxchilán, and Bonampak. VW rental. Reasonable exchange rate for U.S. dollars. Open daily 8am-9pm, varies on Sun.

Buses: All stations are located 5 blocks west of the *parque* on Juárez. **ADO** runs first-class buses to Campeche (8am, 6hr., 78 pesos), Cancún (8pm, 12hr., 179 pesos), Chetumal (8pm, 7½hr., 102 pesos), Escárcega (8am, 3hr., 45 pesos), Mérida (8am, 8hr., 118 pesos), Mexico City (6pm, 12hr., 245 pesos), Oaxaca (5:30pm, 13hr., 181 pesos), Playa del Carmen (8pm, 11hr., 165 pesos), Puebla (6pm, 10½hr., 213 pesos), and Villahermosa (11 per day, 2hr., 40 pesos). **Cristóbal Colón** sails for Campeche (noon, 6:30, and 10:30pm, 6hr., 76 pesos), Escárcega (noon, 6:30, and 10:30pm, 3hr., 48 pesos), Mérida (noon, 6:30, and 10:30pm, 8hr., 114 pesos), Ocosingo (4 per day, 2hr., 25 pesos), San Cristóbal (4 per day, 4½hr., 39 pesos), and Tuxtla Gutiérrez (4 per day, 6hr., 73 pesos). **Autobuses de Tuxtla Gutiérrez** offers first- and second-class service.

Trains: Past the Cabeza Maya 6km north of town. Morning train runs to Tabasco, Veracruz, Puebla, and Mexico City. Evening train runs to Campeche and Mérida. Taxis to the station charge about 10 pesos.

Taxis: (tel. 5-01-12). 20 pesos to the ruins; 7 pesos in town.

Laundromat: Lavandería "Ela," 5 de Mayo at Allende, opposite the Hotel Kashlan. 20 pesos for 3kg. Same-day service. Open Mon.-Sat. 8am-1pm and 4-7pm.

Pharmacy: Farmacia Central, (tel. 5-03-93), Av. Juárez near Independencia. Changes dollars at slightly unfavorable rates. Open daily 8am-2pm and 4-9pm.

Medical Services: Centro de Salud y Hospital General (tel. 5-00-25), on Juárez near the bus station, at the western end of town. Open 24-hr. No English spoken.

Police: (tel. 5-08-28), in the Palacio Municipal on Calle Independencia. Open 24hr.

Post Office: Independencia at Bravo, north of the *parque.* Open Mon.-Fri. 9am-1pm and 3-6pm, Sat. 9am-1pm. **Postal Code:** 29960.

Telephone Code: 934.

ACCOMMODATIONS

Budget travelers can either stay in town or sack up at one of the hotels along the highway en route to the ruins. Of the two options, the latter tends to be much more

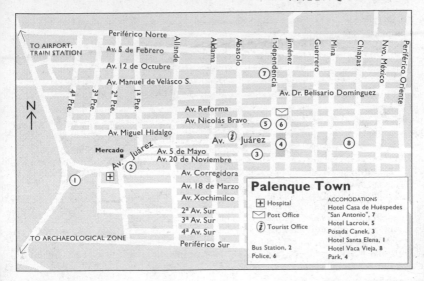

Palenque Town

✚ Hospital
✉ Post Office
ℹ Tourist Office

Bus Station, 2
Police, 6

ACCOMODATIONS
Hotel Casa de Huéspedes
"San Antonio", 7
Hotel Lacroix, 5
Posada Canek, 3
Hotel Santa Elena, 1
Hotel Vaca Vieja, 8
Park, 4

expensive, with the exception of **Mayabell Trailer Park and Camping** (tel. 5-05-97; fax 5-07-67), which allows guests to pitch a tent, string up a hammock, or put down a sleeping bag under a *palapa* for about 15 pesos per person (10 peso deposit, 10 pesos for hammock rental). Electricity, water, and decent sewage facilities are available for trailers (10 pesos per car). The few rooms boast terracotta honey-comb tiles, plaid bedspreads, standing fans, and private bathrooms (singles 70 pesos; doubles 90 pesos; triples 110 pesos; 10 pesos per additional person; 100 peso deposit). There's also a large swimming pool and attached restaurant. Three-hour guided horseback tours of the jungle available (120 pesos). Mayabell, 6km from town and 2km from the ruins, is accessible by *combi* (3 pesos).

All of the hotels listed below are in the town center, within easy walking distance of the *parque* and bus station. Camping outside of a campground might be unsafe. *Let's Go* does not recommend sleeping in tombs.

Posada Canek, 20 de Noviembre 43 (tel. 5-01-50), between Independencia and Abasolo, half a block from the *parque*. Large, clean rooms with wooden beds (the frames, that is) and flowered sheets. The view of the mountains is just smashing. Singles 20 pesos for a bed in a 5-person dormitory or 50 pesos for a room with private bath. Doubles 50 pesos. Triples 70 pesos. 20 pesos per additional person.

Hotel Vaca Vieja, 5 de Mayo 42 (tel. 5-03-77 or -88), 3 blocks east of the *parque* in a quiet part of town. Modern rooms with varnished wooden furniture, firm beds, and dauntless ceiling fans. Singles 50 pesos. Doubles 60 pesos. Triples 70 pesos. Prices rise by 10 pesos during the high season.

Hotel Lacroix, Hidalgo 10 (tel. 5-00-14), just off the *parque* and opposite the church. Popular with generations of archaeologists, Lacroix is the oldest hotel in town. A wild mural, complete with a giant skull and a dancing Mayan, decorates the entrance. Often full. Singles 60 pesos. Doubles 70 pesos. Triples 80 pesos.

Hotel Santa Elena (tel. 5-10-29), on Jorge de la Vega Domínguez, around the corner from the ADO bus station. Plain 'n' clean. Wood-paneled rooms with fans and soapy-green bathrooms. Singles 50 pesos. Doubles 65 pesos. Triples 100 pesos.

Casa de Huéspedes Hotel "San Antonio," Independencia 42 (tel. 5-09-55), 4½ blocks north of the post office. Average rooms. Very *tranquilo*. Singles 30 pesos. Doubles 40 pesos. Triples 55 pesos. Quads 75 pesos. Sextuples 85 pesos.

CHIAPAS & TABASCO

FOOD

Thanks to the strong non-*indígena* presence in Palenque, local menus have taken on a sort of culinary condescension. Fortunately, quality remains high, albeit spiceless, and prices are reasonable. For cheap produce, try the market on Velasco Suárez, four blocks west and four blocks north of the *parque*. If you plan to spend the day at the ruins, you might want to brown-bag it—the sole on-site eatery is a glorified snack bar.

Restaurante Las Tinajas, 20 de Noviembre 41, at Abasolo. Hammock hooks and kids doing homework? That's right, this is a home; be prepared to be fed like it was your own. Excellent veggie selection—try the *tlacoyos* (beans and cheese wrapped in tortillas, 12 pesos) or a *licuado* (5 pesos). Open daily 7am-11pm.

Restaurant Rocamar, 20 de Noviembre at Independencia, near the *parque*. Smartly decorated tables set the stage for a seafood extravaganza. Most entrees 25 pesos. Open daily 8am-8pm.

Restaurant Yunuen, 5 de Mayo 42 (tel. 5-03-88), at Chiapas annexed to the Hotel Vaca Vieja, 3 blocks east of the *parque*. Small, friendly, and very inexpensive. Feast on the *comida del día*—soup, chicken, rice, tortillas, fruit and coffee for a mere 18 pesos. Open daily 7am-11pm.

Restaurant Maya, Independencia at Hidalgo (tel. 5-00-42), right on the *parque*. Filling sandwiches (10-15 pesos), breakfast of granola, juice, toast, and coffee (20 pesos), and standard entrees (20-30 pesos). Open daily 7am-11pm.

SIGHTS

During the Mayan Classic Period (300-900CE), one of Palenque's ancient names meant "Place of the Sun's Daily Death"—the city was obviously of great importance to the Maya. Though impressive, the ruins only hint at the former magnitude of the city, as less than 10% of the pyramids have been shorn of their dense jungle blanket.

Palenque owes much of its finery, including its unparalleled stucco bas-relief sculptures, to an early ruler, the club-footed god-man **King Pakal** (615-683CE). According to inscriptions made at the time of his death, Pakal lived into his fifth *katan* (20-year period) and was then succeeded by his elderly son Chan-Bahlum. Chan-Bahlum celebrated his ascension by building a great pyramid-crypt (Temple of the Inscriptions) for his father. After Chan-Bahlum died, Palenque slipped into oblivion; some archaeologists speculate that the city had "fulfilled its purpose." When Cortés arrived in the 16th century, he marched right past withered Palenque without noting its existence.

Upon entering the site, you pass the tomb of Alberto Ruz, an archaeologist so devoted to restoring Palenque that he insisted on being buried there. To the right rises the steep **Temple of the Inscriptions.** Named for its magnificent tablets, the Temple was the burial place of King Pakal, and was the first substantial burial place discovered in the Americas. After his disappointing discovery of six unimpressive skeletons, Ruz bore into the interior of the crypt; he discovered the perfectly preserved, elaborately carved sarcophagus of the king. Scholars assert that the first bodies Ruz discovered were symbols of the absolute power Pakal had wielded since age 12 and were charged with bearing the king's elaborate personal effects through the underworld. Visitors can scramble down the slippery stone steps to view the royal crypt. The hollow duct, which allowed Pakal's spirit to exit the underworld and communicate with Palenque's priests, is visible on the right after the staircase.

Next to the Temple is a trapezoidal **palace** complex, consisting of four patios and a four-story tower. This immense complex is replete with religious tributes, such as the relief on the north side depicting the nine gods of the underworld. Other carvings laud the godlike priests and royal families that inhabited its many chambers. The palace's T-shaped air tunnels cooled the air and doubled as representations of Ik, the god of the breezes. Clamber down the staircase from the top of the platform to explore the extensive, dimly lit network of underground passageways. Flat-nosed masks of the rain-god Chac, which glare accusingly off to the north end's stuccoed walls,

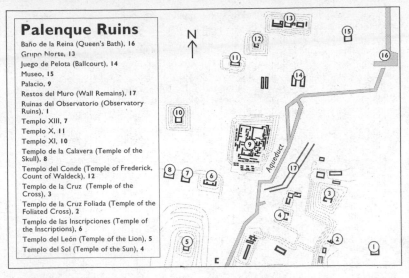

Palenque Ruins

Baño de la Reina (Queen's Bath), 16
Grupo Norte, 13
Juego de Pelota (Ballcourt), 14
Museo, 15
Palacio, 9
Restos del Muro (Wall Remains), 17
Ruinas del Observatorio (Observatory Ruins), 1
Templo XIII, 7
Templo X, 11
Templo XI, 10
Templo de la Calavera (Temple of the Skull), 8
Templo del Conde (Temple of Frederick, Count of Waldeck), 12
Templo de la Cruz (Temple of the Cross), 3
Templo de la Cruz Foliada (Temple of the Foliated Cross), 2
Templo de las Inscripciones (Temple of the Inscriptions), 6
Templo del León (Temple of the Lion), 5
Templo del Sol (Temple of the Sun), 4

reveal the influence of the Olmecs, and suggest a deep-seated societal fear of drought. An exclusively female steam bath and latrines have also been excavated.

A trail leads up the mountainside to the left of the Temple of Inscriptions. About 100m along this trail, on the right, is the **Temple of the Lion.** Descend the pitch-black stairwell inside the structure and you'll come upon the site of the ancient well where a few faint traces of paint are slowly surrendering to the green slime of the jungle. The trail continues up the hill for 7km before reaching the tiny *indígena* village of Naranjo. Guides can be found for this difficult hike through beautiful terrain.

The path between the palace and the Temple of Inscriptions fords the recently reconstructed aqueduct before leading up to the **Sun Plaza,** another landscaped platform comprised of the **Temple of the Sun,** the **Temple of the Cross,** the **Temple of the Foliated Cross,** and the smaller **Temple 14.** The Temple of the Cross was named for a stucco relief of a cross which was found inside and which inspired a flurry of hopeful religious theories among the *conquistadores.* To their dismay, this Maya group is the only one known to have worshipped the cross. For the Maya, the cross represented the tree of life, a snake as its horizontal branch, a bird perched atop it. The outer layer of stucco has worn away, but the inner sanctum protects a large sculpted tablet and reliefs on either side of the doors.

About to be swallowed again by the jealous jungle, the **Temple of the Foliated Cross** lies across the plaza from the Temple of the Sun. Despite the overgrown path, the inner sanctum here contains a surprisingly clear carved tablet. The tablet was carved with an unusual tree (or cross) whose branches are remarkably similar to some of those found in a temple at Angkor-Wat, Cambodia, but nowhere else. To the south, through the wall of trees, several unreconstructed temples surround the uncleared **Plaza Maudslay.** Downhill from Temple 14 and past the palace lie the vestiges of a **ballcourt.** From the absence of stone rings, archaeologists speculate that wooden ones were used instead.

To the left of the ballcourt is the **Temple of Frederick, Count of Waldeck** who lived here for three years while studying the ruins in the 1830s. The four other temples which share the platform with the Temple of the Count comprise the **North Group.** Waterfall enthusiasts may catch a glimpse of the **Queen's Bath** (so named for its exclusively female clientele), a small set of falls just through the trees from the North Group. A second set of falls, **Cascada Montiepa,** is hidden in the jungle, 600m down the road from the ruins. At the right-hand bend follow the path into the woods.

Sadly, overgrown banks and shallow water make swimming impractical. There is also an excellent **museum** 2km before the site near Mayabell. (Archaeological site and museum open daily 8am-4:45pm. Crypt open daily 8am-4pm. Admission 16 pesos, free Sun. Map 3 pesos in Spanish, 4 pesos in other languages.)

Getting There: *Combis* to the site run daily from 6am-6pm (2 pesos); catch them off Juárez on Allende. Visiting the ruins at night is prohibited and extremely unsafe. Do not take shortcuts to the back entrance of the ruins from the campgrounds or the road—it is said that rapes and robberies have occurred on these trails, and the dense jungle leaves you isolated even if there are many other tourists nearby.

■ Near Palenque

CASCADAS DE AGUA AZUL AND MISOL-HA

Both of these large *cascadas* (waterfalls) have overflowed with tourists of late, and for good reason. **Agua Azul**, 62km south of Palenque, is a breathtaking spectacle: the Río Yax jumps down 500 individual falls, then slips into rapids, whirlpools, and calm swimming areas in between. There is a tiny beach and swimming area 20 minutes upstream from the falls—if you swim, stay close to the bank and swim with a friend, as more than 100 people have met their watery end here.

Since the 4km walk from *el crucero* is tiresome, it's best to spend only a day at the falls, returning to Palenque in the afternoon. If need be, campgrounds (tents 10 pesos per person), hammock space (10-15 pesos per person), and *cabañas* (doubles 110 pesos; quadruples 220 pesos) are available on site.

The falls at **Misol-Ha** are 24km from Palenque and only 2km from the highway crossing. There's a large cataract here, and the swimming area is clean and relatively safe. A small restaurant serves up a few good dishes at reasonable prices.

Getting There: The most painless way to visit Agua Azul and Misol-Ha is aboard a **Transportes Chambalu** *combi* (45 pesos roundtrip, admission included). *Combis* leave daily from the Palenque station at Hidalgo and Allende at 10am and noon, and after a 30-minute photo stop at Misol-Ha, proceed to Agua Azul. Passengers are then dropped off right by the falls for a three-hour swimming session. **Buses** between Palenque and Ocosingo or San Cristóbal will also stop at the crossroads for either Agua Azul or Misol-Ha (2 pesos). Since few buses pass after 4pm, leave the falls in the

---

White Men Can't Jump

The great ballcourts found in Chichén Itzá and other Maya cities once witnessed an impressive game called *pok-ta-pok*, in which two contending teams endeavored to keep a heavy rubber ball in constant motion by using only their hips, knees, and elbows. Players scored by knocking the ball through the stone rings placed high on the court's side walls. The elaborate game was so fascinating to the Spanish that in 1528 Cortés took two entire teams back to Europe to perform before the crowned heads. After that, European ball games replaced their unyielding, dead wooden balls with livelier rubber balls.

The ball game was much more than just a cultural pastime for the Maya; it was a contest of **good** versus **evil** linked to a game of the gods. A Maya legend tells that every harvest Hun Hunahpu, god of corn, was decapitated; his head was planted in the ground and became the seed of all corn plants. Every year, the evil gods of the nether-world stole the buried head in an attempt to destroy the Maya. The twins Xbalanque and Hunahpú (the sun and Venus respectively) would then descend to Xilbalba (the netherworld) and challenge the evil gods to an epic game of ball, using the god's head instead of a ball. Invariably, the twins were successful and the seed was recovered. The new crop symbolized the god's resurrection and the Maya's salvation. It is believed that in response to the legend, the captain of the winning team would be decapitated and his head offered to the gods.

early afternoon. Hitchhikers report that steady pick-up truck traffic makes catching a ride fairly easy (admission to each of the falls 2 pesos, 5 pesos per carload). As always, *Let's Go* does not recommend hitchhiking. Never ever.

■ Tonalá

If, while in Chiapas, you're hit by a sudden and irresistible urge to listen to the surf and wriggle your toes in the sand, then head for Tonalá. While the beaches near Tonalá don't compare with Oaxaca's golden stretches of sand, **Puerto Arista** and especially **Boca del Cielo** are pleasant enough spots to spend a few hours. During *Semana Santa*, Christmas, and weekends in July and August, these seaside stretches fill up with Chiapanecan families, but at all other times high noon comes and the tumbleweeds roll through town. Enjoy the sight, but beware the *zancudos blancos,* vicious biting insects that exploit the holey nature of hammocks.

Orientation and Practical Information Tonalá lies 223km northwest of Tapachula and 172km southwest of Tuxtla Gutiérrez. All **bus stations** are on **Avenida Hidalgo,** Tonalá's main street. To get to the *zócalo* from the **Cristóbal Colón** bus station, take a left and head six blocks south. Both the **Autotransportes Tuxtla Gutiérrez** and **Fletes y Pasajes** bus stations are south of the *centro,* so you need to turn right and walk five blocks north. As the coastal highway, Av. Hidalgo runs roughly north-south through town. To the east, **Av. Rayón** parallels Hidalgo, while to the west run **Avenidas Matamoros, Juárez,** and **Allende.** From north to south, **Calles Madero, 16 de Septiembre, 5 de Febrero, Independencia,** and **5 de Mayo** run east-west, completing the grid that makes up the city center.

The **tourist office** (tel. 3-27-87) is at Hidalgo and 5 de Mayo, two blocks south of the bus station, on the 2nd floor of the Esmeralda building (open Mon.-Fri. 9am-3pm and 6-9pm, Sat. 10am-1pm). Many long distance *casetas* line Hidalgo. **Banamex** (tel. 3-00-37 or 3-10-77) is at Hidalgo 137 at 5 de Febrero, half a block south of the *zócalo* (open Mon.-Fri. 9am-1:30pm). Public **telephones** are located throughout the *centro,* but do not accept LADATEL cards.

First-class **buses,** including Maya de Oro (tel. 3-05-40), leave from the **Cristóbal Colón** station, six blocks north of the *zócalo,* for Mexico City (8pm, 13hr., 207 pesos), Oaxaca (10pm, 6½hr., 92 pesos), Puebla (8 and 9pm, 10hr., 183 pesos), Tapachula (every hr. 3am-7pm, 3hr., 48 pesos), Tuxtla Gutiérrez (every hr. 3am-7:30pm, 3hr., 36 pesos), Villahermosa (12:30am, 12hr., 121 pesos). **Autotransportes Tuxtla Gutiérrez,** Hidalgo 56, five blocks south of the *zócalo,* has first-class service to Mexico City (6:30pm, 13hr., 203 pesos) via Puebla (11hr., 178 pesos). **Fletes y Pasajes,** Hidalgo 52 (tel. 3-25-94), 50m south of the bridge and three and a half blocks south of the *zócalo,* sends second-class buses to Mexico City (4 per day, 13hr., 146 pesos), Puebla (4 per day, 11hr., 127 pesos), and Tapachula (6 per day, 3½hr., 36 pesos). From the same building, **TRF** (tel. 3-12-61) has first-class service to Tapachula (1, 3, and 7pm, 3hr., 43 pesos) and Tuxtla (9 per day, 3hr., 34 pesos). **Taxis** (tel. 3-06-20) cruise up and down Hidalgo and hang out in the *zócalo* (40 pesos to Puerto Arista). If you're getting up early, the 24-hour **radio-taxis** (tel. 3-10-00) opposite the Colón bus station will come and rouse you at your hotel.

The **market** is on Matamoros, several blocks southeast of the *zócalo.* Walk south on Hidalgo and right on 5 de Febrero or Independencia to Matamoros (open until 2:30pm, though stalls outside stay open until 6 or 7pm). The **Red Cross** (tel. 3-02-76) is on Av. Joaquín Miguel Gutiérrez (open 24hr.). **Clínica de Especialidades,** Hidalgo 127 (tel. 3-12-90), at Independencia south of the *zócalo,* is a hospital and a pharmacy. One doctor speaks English (open daily 9am-1pm and 5-7pm; open 24hr. for emergency medical service). **Hospital General,** Av. 27 de Septiembre at Mina (tel. 3-06-87), is six blocks south of the *zócalo* and three blocks east before the gas station (open 24hr.). The **police** station (tel. 3-01-03) is two blocks north of Cristóbal Colón and to the right on Calle Libertad. The **post office** is on Zambrano 27 (tel. 3-06-83), two blocks north and half a block east of the *zócalo* (open Mon.-Fri. 8am-7pm, Sat. 9am-1pm). **Postal Code:** 30500. **Telephone Code:** 966.

Accommodations and Food   Hotels in Tonalá are overpriced and under-cleaned. Singles at **Hotel Tonalá** (tel. 3-04-80), a few blocks south of the Cristóbal Colón station are small but drab, and clean (singles 55 pesos; doubles 95 pesos; triples 135 pesos). Cheaper accommodations come at a price at **Hotel Thomás** (tel. 13-00-80), two blocks south of the *zócalo* on Hidalgo before the bridge. Blue cell-like rooms are equipped with pre-historic ceiling fans, and the bathrooms are in dire need of repair (singles 40 pesos; doubles 50 pesos; with A/C 70 pesos).

The pink **Restaurante Nora,** Independencia 10 (tel. 3-02-43), is just east of Hidalgo and a block from the *zócalo*. Nora likes her tablecloths peachy, her aquariums exotic, and her servings of *huevos con chorizo* with tortillas and fried banana (10 pesos), heaping. Three-course *comida corrida* 20 pesos (open Mon.-Sat. 7am-6pm). **Las Fuentes,** Hidalgo 95 (tel. 3-04-03), just past the bridge, has a plain interior and a great four-course *comida corrida* (20 pesos; open Mon.-Sat. 7:30am-9pm).

Sand and Sights   18km southwest of Tonalá, **Puerto Arista** offers 32km of gray sandy beach and the pounding waves of the Pacific. Be especially careful in the late afternoon, when the current tends to flow out to sea. Most beachside restaurants can provide hammocks for the night (about 10 pesos), although they may not even charge you if you enthusiastically patronize their establishment. Obviously, ask before setting up your own hammock or tent on someone else's property.

Hotel Playa Escondida, at the left end of the beach, offers rudimentary singles with fans and patchy paint (singles 50 pesos; doubles 80 pesos; campers can use facilities for 2 pesos). For calmer seas, head to the sheltered saltwater estuary of **Boca del Cielo,** 15km farther down the coast. As the estuary is less than 100m wide, you can wade and then swim across to the beachfront restaurants and open ocean. To get there with your wallet and clothes in a less-than-soaked condition, hop in a *lancha* (25 pesos). There are no hotels in Boca del Cielo, so you'll want to base yourself in Puerto Arista or Tonalá. Every 20 minutes, *colectivos* run to both Puerto Arista (4 pesos) and Boca del Cielo (7 pesos) from their stand on 5 de Mayo, one and a half blocks west of Hidalgo.

■ Tapachula

Must be something about those border towns. Tapachula (pop. 300,000) is loud and dirty, crass and smelly, and let's not forget hot. Only the *zócalo* provides welcome relief from Tapachula's assault on the senses. Topiary trees, their leafy crowns trimmed square and joined to one another, form a green canopy over the *zócalo*'s two square blocks. During the rainy season, hundreds of mostly Guatemalan immigrants crowd under these trees, reading newspapers or socializing. Relaxing outdoor cafés provide sanctuary from the rampant *marimba* music that echoes through the city. For tourists, Tapachula is primarily a point of entry into Guatemala.

ORIENTATION

Tapachula is 18km from Talismán at the Guatemalan border on Rte. 200 and 303km west of Guatemala City. Tonalá lies 220km to the northwest, along the Pacific coast. *Avenidas* run north-south, and *calles* run east-west. *Calles* north of **Calle Central** are odd-numbered, while those to the south are even-numbered. Similarly, *avenidas* east of **Av. Central** are odd-numbered, while those to the west have even numbers. Tapachula's main plaza is at **3 Calle Pte.** between 6 and 8 Av. Nte., northwest of the center. To get to the *zócalo* from the bus station, take an immediate right upon exiting onto 3 Av. Nte. Walk south seven blocks to 3ª Calle Ote. and turn right. The *zócalo* lies five blocks ahead.

PRACTICAL INFORMATION

Tourist Office: (tel. 5-54-09), in the Antiguo Palacio Municipal, south of the Iglesia de San Agustín on the west side of the *zócalo*. Brochures, maps, and enthusiasm. Open Mon.-Fri. 9am-3pm and 6-9pm.

Consulate: Guatemala, 2 Calle Ote. 33 (tel. 6-12-52), between 7 and 9 Av. Sur. U.S. and Canadian citizens need only a passport to acquire a visa. Most European citizens don't need a visa for Guatemala. Go first to **Copias Motta** on Calle Central and 9 Av. Nte. to photocopy the first page of your passport and to obtain a visa application. Visas usually take less than 30min., but arrive early in case of crowds. Open Mon.-Fri. 9am-1:30pm and 3-5pm.

Currency Exchange: Banamex, Av. Central Nte. 9 (tel. 6-29-24). 24-hr. **ATM.** Open Mon.-Fri. 9am-2pm.

Telephones: LADATELs at the Cristóbal Colón bus station or at the Cine Maya on 2 Av. Nte. at 1 Calle Pte.

Airport: On the road to Puerto Madero, about 17km south of town. Served by **Aeroméxico,** 2 Av. Nte. 6 (tel. 6-20-50), **Aviacsa,** Av. Central and Calle 1 Pte. (tel. 6-31-47 or 6-14-39), and **Taesa,** 1 Calle Pte. 11 (tel. 6-37-32; fax 6-37-02).

Buses: Cristóbal Colón, 17 Calle Ote. (tel. 6-28-81), at 3 Av. Nte. Open 24hr. To Brownsville, TX (10pm, 24hr., 467 pesos), Comitán (4 per day, 6hr., 52 pesos), Mexico City (5 per day, 16hr., 282 pesos), Oaxaca (6:30pm, 11hr., 138 pesos), Puebla (4:30, 5:30, and 10:15pm, 14hr., 220 pesos), Puerto Escondido (11pm, 7hr., 144 pesos), San Cristóbal (4 per day, 5hr., 71 pesos), Tampico (10pm, 16hr., 322 pesos), Tonalá (4 per day, 3hr., 48 pesos), Tuxtla Gutiérrez (21 per day, 6hr., 82 pesos), Veracruz (10pm, 12hr., 180 pesos), and Villahermosa (9pm, 12hr., 168 pesos). **Autotransportes Tuxtla Gutiérrez** (tel. 6-95-13), 11ª Calle Ote. #14, between 3ª and 4^a Av. Norte. Open 24hr. Second-class service to Mexico City (12:30 and 7pm, 16hr., 170 pesos) and Tuxtla Gutiérrez (7 per day, 7hr., 52 pesos). **Fletes y Pasajes,** 3^a Av. Norte and 9^a Calle Ote (tel. 6-76-03), has second-class service to Mexico City (1:45pm, 3:30, and 5pm, 17hr., 190 pesos) and Oaxaca (4am, 12:30, and 6:30pm, 13hr., 100 pesos).

Trains: Av. Central Sur 150 (tel. 6-21-76), at the end of the *avenida* behind a miniature plaza. Slow, cheap, unreliable second-class service.

Red Cross: (tel. 6-19-49 or 5-35-06), 9 Av. Nte. at 1 Calle Ote., across from the post office. 24-hr. ambulance service. No English spoken.

Pharmacy: Farmacia 24 Horas, 8 Av. Nte. 27 (tel. 6-24-80), at Calle 7 Pte. No English spoken. Delivery to anywhere within the city available 7am-11pm.

Hospital: (tel. 6-80-80), on the highway to the airport. Open 24hr.

Police: (tel. 5-28-51), Palacio Municipal, at 8 Av. Nte. and 3 Calle Pte. Open 24hr.

Post Office: 1 Calle Ote. 32 (tel. 6-10-28), between 7 and 9 Av. Nte. Open Mon.-Fri. 8am-7pm, Sat. 9am-1pm. **Postal Code:** 30700.

Telephone Code: 962

ACCOMMODATIONS

Due to the huge influx of Guatemalan refugees, budget accommodations are a dime a dozen in Tapachula, especially near the market. Unfortunately, many hotel rooms are as noisy and dirty as the rest of the city. The first two listings provide clean, pleasant accommodations at reasonable prices.

Hotel San Agustín, 12a Av. Nte. #14 (tel. 6-14-53), between 1a and 3a Calles Pte., 2 blocks west of the *zócalo*. Gigantic but stark bare whitewashed 2-room suites that could have been garages at some point. Bathrooms are basic but clean. For more excitement, try out the pool and sundeck. Color TV and sodas for sale in the lobby. One double bed 40 pesos. Two 60 pesos. Three 90 pesos. Four 120 pesos. Squeeze in as many as you like.

Hotel 5 de Mayo, Calle 5a Pte. #22 (tel. 6-39-43), just off Av. 12a Nte., 1½ blocks west of the *zócalo*. Small rooms done in pleasant shades of purple with solid beds and ceiling fans give way to slightly dilapidated bathrooms. Clean communal facili-

CHIAPAS & TABASCO

ties. Singles 25 pesos. Doubles 30 peso, with 2 beds 40 pesos. Triples 45 pesos. Rooms with private bathrooms cost 35, 40, 50, and 60 pesos, respectively.

Hotel Tabasco, Av. Central Nte. 123 (tel. 6-51-33), just north of 17 Calle Ote., very conveniently located 2 blocks west of the Cristóbal Colón bus station. For budget-eers who need a cheap place to crash for the night before an early-morning depar-ture. Street noise free of charge; hot water unavailable at any price. Drab, bare concrete singles are not worth 30 pesos. Each additional person 25 pesos.

FOOD

Food, like all things in Tapachula, comes cheap; too bad the quality is so poor. A **chi-napueblito** is on 1 Calle Pte., one block southeast of the *zócalo,* but portions are often small for the price. For cheap eats, head to the **San Juan food market** on 17ª Calle Pte., north of the *centro* (open daily 5am-5pm). **Mercado Sebastián Escobar,** on 10 Av. Nte. between 5ª and 3ª Calles Pte., sells produce and baked goods.

La Quinta Carmelita, Calle Central Ote. 76 (tel. 5-40-07), about 1½km east of downtown, past the army barracks. Take any eastbound *colectivo* on Calle Central (1 peso). Peaceful. Enjoy the *queso fundido especial* (14 pesos) or a large goblet of cinnamon-chocolate *taxcalate* (8 pesos). Open daily 7am-midnight.

El Charco de las Ranas, 4 Av. Nte. 21, between 1ª and 3ª Calle Pte., next to the Hotel Fénix. Friendly open-air joint. All breakfasts 15 pesos. Open daily 7am-9pm.

La Parrilla, 8 Av. Nte. 20 (tel. 6-40-62), in the southwest corner of the *zócalo.* Cafe-teria style joint where you can watch the morning news or read the paper over a hot breakfast (10-20 pesos). *Tortas* 7-10 pesos. Grilled chicken 20 pesos. Open 7am-12:30am. Dollars and quetzales accepted.

SIGHTS

Tapachula offers a few distractions for those who want to tarry on their way to or from Guatemala. The **Museo Regional del Soconusco** (tel. 6-41-73), in the Antiguo Palacio Municipal on the west side of the *zócalo,* houses a small collection of Olmec/ Mayan ceramic and stone artifacts. Note the mural on the stairway depicting a child sacrifice. Upstairs, a jade-encrusted skull with gold beads for eyeballs grins gro-tesquely (open Tues.-Sun. 10am-5pm; admission 10 pesos, free Sun.). Next door, the second-floor of the **Casa de la Cultura,** 8 Av. Nte. 24 (tel. 6-11-57), hosts occasional and temporary art exhibits (open Mon.-Fri. 9am-1pm and 4-8pm; free). There is an adequate-but-not-spectacular beach at **Puerto Madero,** 27km away, accessible from the second-class bus station Paulino Navarro on Calle 7 Ote. between Av. Central Nte. and Av. 2 Nte. (every 15min., 45min., 3 pesos).

CROSSING THE BORDER TO GUATEMALA

Plan to cross the border early in the day to avoid bureaucratic delay, early and unoffi-cial closings, and wasted time in Talismán. It is also a good idea to buy your **tourist card** (US$5) or obtain a visa from the Guatemalan consulate in Tapachula; the Tal-ismán office has erratic hours.

From Tapachula, **Unión y Progreso buses** leave their station on 5 Calle Pte., a half-block west of 12 Av. Nte., for Talismán (every 5min., 30min., 3.50 pesos). For those who don't want to spend any time in Tapachula, the bus swings by the Cristóbal Colón bus station, on 17 Calle Ote., on its way to the border. Buses from Tapachula drop off passengers at the entrance to the Mexican emigration office. Enter the build-ing and present your **passport** and Mexican **tourist card** to officials behind the desk, then follow the crowd across the bridge, which charges a toll of approximately 3 pesos. Proceed to a small building on the left to have your passport stamped by Gua-temalan authorities; there is a charge of five quetzales. A **taxi** from the *zócalo* to Tal-ismán costs 50 pesos. Those crossing the border **on foot** will be besieged by money changers and self-appointed "guides."

The **money changers** on the Guatemalan side of the border generally give better rates for pesos than those on the Mexican side, but your best bet is to avoid small money changers and head for the **Banco de Quetzal,** on the Guatemalan side.

From Talismán, you can take a **bus** to Guatemala City (4am, about every 2hr. 7am-2pm, and midnight). Don't travel at night, since this route has been recently plagued by assaults. Should you have to spend the night, the **Hotel José Ricardo,** just past the official buildings on the right, offers nice, clean rooms with bathrooms and hot water. They lock the front door, which is reassuring. The various eateries in Talismán can turn seedy when the drunks come out of the woodwork. Women traveling alone should be very careful. The Tapachulan tourist office recommends that tourists do not cross the border at Ciudad Hidalgo, as the bridge there is long and deserted—making travelers particularly vulnerable to assault.

■ Quetzaltenango, Guatemala

Quetzaltenango is full of monuments to what might have been. In 1823, when the Central American Federation broke away from Mexico, Quetzaltenango boldly declared itself the capital of the independent state of Los Altos, which encompassed much of Guatemala's western highlands. Seventeen years later, dreams of independence were smothered by the emergence of Guatemalan dictator Rafael Carrera. With the coffee boom of the 19th century, Quetzaltenango flourished anew, drawing boatloads of German capital and immigrants to its extraordinarily rich land. But alas, Quetzaltenango's aspirations crumbled again in 1902, when a devastating earthquake leveled the city. Somehow still full of ambition, the city leaders rebuilt the city, scattering numerous Neoclassical buildings throughout the small metropolis. By the 1930s, however, Guatemala City had outpaced its rival for the title of national capital. Quetzaltenango remains something of a provincial might-have-been with higher aspirations. City leaders recently constructed the **Pasaje Enrique,** a glass-ceilinged, European-style concourse on the plaza intended to be a sophisticated shopping center. Instead, it sits nearly vacant.

Don't be surprised if you never hear the name "Quetzaltenango" mentioned in town. Locals are more likely to refer to their city as **Xela** (SHEH-lah), an abbreviation of the Quiché name Xelajú, which means "under the ten," a reference to the ten mountain-dwelling gods of the Quiché. Xela has long been a center of Quiché culture; its teeming market and busy Parque Central draw *indígenas* from all over the western highlands. Xela proper won't detain you for more than a day or two; although its markets are among the best in the country, most visitors come to commune with the surrounding countryside and to soak in the hot sulfuric springs in nearby Zunil and Fuentes Georgina.

> Through the spring and summer of 1996, the U.S. State Department warned travelers to exercise extreme caution when traveling in Guatemala. Crime and terrorism in many parts of the country have made inter-city travel hazardous, especially after dark. Several tourists were attacked and even killed as a result of rumors about foreigners abducting Guatemalan children. And though this violence has not occurred in the more heavily touristed parts of the country, U.S citizens are encouraged to register with the U.S. Embassy, and all travelers, especially women, are advised to avoid contact with Guatemalan children. Be sure to call the U.S. State Department's Hotline (tel. (202) 647-5225) to receive the latest warnings.

PASSPORTS, VISAS, CUSTOMS, AND EXCHANGE RATE

All visitors to Guatemala need a valid **passport** and either a **visa** or a **tourist card.** A tourist card can be purchased at the border or at the airport departure gate for US$5, but you can save the fiver by obtaining a free visa at a consulate instead. When your card is issued, Guatemalan officials will decide how long you may stay; authorized stays range from one to three months. An extension on your tourist card can sometimes be obtained at an immigration office. Visas are free at Guatemalan consulates in the U.K., Canada, and the U.S.; citizens of Ireland, South Africa, and New Zealand must pay US$10. Obtain a visa several weeks before leaving home or at consulates in Comitán, Tapachula, or Chetumal. Citizens of most Western European nations need only a valid passport to enter the country. All visitors should carry identification at all times. Visitors departing from the Guatemala City airport must pay an **exit tax.**

Drivers in Guatemala must carry a valid foreign driver's license, a title, and registration. When driving across the border, visitors receive a 30-90 day driving permit. The whole process sounds innocuous enough, but actually amounts to a bureaucratic nightmare. Insurance is not required for driving in Guatemala.

US$1 = 7.56 pesos	**1 peso = US$0.13**
US$1 = 6.09 quetzales	**Q1 = US$0.16**
1 Q = 1.23 pesos	**1 peso= 0.81 Q**

ORIENTATION

Quetzaltenango's *avenidas* run north to south and the *calles* run east to west. *Avenida* numbers increase to the west, *calle* numbers to the south. The **Parque Centroamérica** is at the center of town in Zona 1 and is bordered by 11 Avenida on the east, 12 Avenida on the west, 4 Calle to the north, and 7 Calle to the south. Most services are located in Zona 1. The second-class bus station and the main market are in Zona 3, northwest of the city center. If you arrive at this station, the **Terminal La Minerva,** walk though the market to its south side. Any of the buses going left (east) on 4 Calle or 6 Calle will take you to the Parque (Q0.50). If you arrive on a first-class pullman, you can walk to the park in the time it would take to wait for a bus.

PRACTICAL INFORMATION

Tourist Office: INGUAT, 7 Calle, 12 Av. #11-35 (tel. 761-4931), at the south side of the park. Free city maps. Some English. Open Mon.-Fri. 8am-1pm and 2-5pm.

Currency Exchange: Banco Immobilario, 12 Av., 4 Calle (tel. 761-4161), on the west side of the park. Open Mon.-Sat. 9am-8pm. **Banco Industrial** (tel. 761-2258), on the east side of the park. Home to a 24-hr., Visa-friendly **ATM.** Open Mon.-Fri. 9:30am-7:30pm, Sat. 9:30am-1:30pm.

Telephones: Guatel, 4 Calle, 15 Av. (tel. 761-6200). **Phone, fax,** and **telegram** service. Open daily 7am-10pm.

Buses: Most buses leave from **Terminal La Minerva** at the northwest end of Zona 3. To get to the terminal, take any city bus, since all routes eventually pass through the station; buses on 14 Av. go directly there. The **#6,** from 8 Calle, 12 Av., Zona 1 (Q0.50), is particularly direct. Most buses from La Minerva pass though La Rotonda on Calzada Independencia in Zona 2, which is a 15-min. walk or a Q7 taxi ride away from Zona 1. From Terminal La Minerva, buses leave for Tecún Umán (3½hr., Q11). Buses also run to La Mesilla (8 per day, 6hr., Q12); Guatemala City (every 15min., 5am-5:30pm and at 8pm, 4½hr., Q14); Huehuetenango (every 30min., 5am-5pm, 2hr., Q8); San Andres Xecul (every 30min., 6:30am-6:30pm, 45min., Q2); San Francisco El Alto (6 per day, 1hr., Q2); Momostenango (5 per day, 2hr., Q5); Panajachel (4 per day, 2½hr., Q10); and Chichicastenango (4 per day, 2½hr., Q8). Since direct buses to Panajachel and Chichicastenango run infrequently, it's often easier to take a bus to Los Encuentros in Guatemala City instead; buses to Panajachel and Chichicastenango wait there. Buses to Retalhuleu leave every hr. (7am-5pm, 2hr., Q5). Galgos, Calle Rodolfo Robles 17-43 (tel. 761-2931), runs first-class pullmans to Guatemala City (7 per day, 4½hr., Q18).

Public Transportation: City buses run 6:30am-8pm (Q0.50 per trip).

Taxis: (tel. 761-4085), lined up along the east side of the Park. To Terminal La Minerva Q15, to La Rotonda Q7.

Market: At Terminal La Minerva, Zona 3. Open Mon.-Sat. 6am-6pm. To get there, catch bus #6 from 8 Calle, 12 Av., Zona 1, or any bus to the terminal.

Supermarket: La Selecta, 4 Calle 13-16, Zona 1 (tel. 761-2004). Open Mon.-Sat. 9am-1pm and 3-7pm, Sun. 9am-1pm.

Laundromat: Lavandería Mini-max, 14 Av. C-47, Zona 1 (tel. 761-2952). Wash and dry Q13 per load. Open Mon.-Sat. 7:30am-7:30pm.

Red Cross: (tel. 125), 8 Av. 6-62, Zona 1. Open 24hr.

Pharmacy: Farmacia Nueva, 10 Av., 6 Calle (tel. 761-4531). Open Mon.-Fri. 9am-1pm and 2pm-8pm. There is a rotating schedule for 24-hr. pharmacies; the name of the current *farmacia de turno* should be posted outside every pharmacy.

Medical Services: Hospital San Rafael, 9 Calle 10-41, Zona 1 (tel. 761-4414), is the closest to downtown. English spoken. Open 24hr.

Police: 10 Calle 12-21, Zona 1 (tel. 120). Open 24hr.

Post Office: 4 Calle 15-07, Zona 1 (tel. 761-2671). Open Mon.-Fri. 8am-4:30pm.

ACCOMMODATIONS

Quetzaltenango is sprinkled with bargain hotels and guest houses, most of them within a few blocks of the Parque Centroamérica. The city's high altitude makes it quite cool—the average temperature is 18°C (65°F)—but the air is not exactly clear; most hotels barely fend off the emissions from the armies of smog-spewing, gas-belching, pollution-puking, exhaust-exhaling, fume-farting autos that plague Xela's streets. Bathrooms in all hotels have "hot water," but "hot" sometimes means scalding hot; be sure to check before checking in.

Hotel Horiami, 2 Calle, 12 Av., Zona 1 (tel. 763-0815). The tile floors are well swept and the rooms brightly lit by large windows. The communal bathrooms are irreproachable, and the place takes unusual safety precautions—you have to ring a bell to get in. Well worth the low price. Singles Q18. Doubles Q30.

Casa Kaehler, 13 Av. 3-33, Zona 1 (tel. 761-2091). Most rooms are on the 2nd-floor balcony of this refurbished, colonial-style house with hardwood floors. The 19th-century rockers cozify chilly Xela nights. The front door is locked 24hr.; guests have keys. The communal bathrooms are perfectly adequate, and the management is very friendly. Singles Q42, with bath Q48. Doubles Q48, with bath Q60. All taxes included, so it's not quite as pricey as it sounds.

Pensión Radar 99, 13 Av. 3-27, Zona 1. Next to Casa Kaehler. Rooms are small and dark, but the price is right. Reasonably clean bathrooms. Singles Q18, with bath Q25. Doubles Q24, with bath Q30.

Hotel Río Azul, 2 Calle 12-15, Zona 1 (tel. 763-0654). Large, immaculate rooms have spotless bathrooms and reliable hot water. Communal balconies. Small book exchange. Singles Q65. Doubles Q80.

Pensión Altense, 9 Calle 8-48, Zona 1 (tel. 761-2811). Spacious rooms around a courtyard bursting with geraniums. Large windows with bars for safety look out onto the street or the courtyard. Some rooms and bathrooms are cleaner than others; check first. Q25 per person with bath.

FOOD

If you haven't tried *típico* cuisine, start here. It's affordable, it's delicious, and if your nerve (or stomach) fails, cheap *gringo* food abounds. Many restaurants are within blocks of the Parque Central, particularly on 14 Av.

Ricca Burger, 4a Calle 13-25, Zona 1 (tel. 765-3328). Full-service, plentiful eats in fast-food style cleanliness. Sundry breakfast combinations with coffee Q9. Burgers Q4.25. Full menu meals include *naranjada*, Q9-15. Open daily 7am-10:30pm.

Café Baviera, 5 Calle 12-50, Zona 1. Popular hangout for the Spanish-school crowd, decorated with nostalgic pictures of Xela in the good old days. Pineapple pie (Q6) is superb. Sandwiches Q8 and quiche (not Quiché) Q6. Used books for sale. Open daily 8am-8pm.

La Torre de Pisa, 14 Av. corner of 1 Calle. *Pizza rústica,* chock-full of tomato slices, for just Q1 per slice. Lean in the take-out window to order and eat at the park across the street to avoid the higher prices inside the restaurant. Open daily 7am-10pm.

Restaurante Deli-Crepe, 14 Av. 3-11, Zona 1. A small, tavern-like, crepe-like place, Deli-Crepe is probably the only crepe place in Xela where you'll find crepes; crepes with ham and cheese (Q12.50), or crepes with your choice of dessert topping, including strawberries or more crepes (Q12.50). They also serve other American food like crepes, hamburgers (Q4), and crepes. Open daily 9am-9pm. Crepes!

Restaurant Utz-Hua, (Gesundheit), 12 Av. 3-02, Zona 1. Family-run place which serves mmm-good, mmm-cheap Guatemalan food. Try the *típico* platter with a steak and spicy sausage (Q15) or the *carne asada* in tangy tomato sauce (Q15). *Comida corridente* Q12, fresh fruit Q12. Relax and watch your favorite *tele-novela* on the TV. No crepes whatsoever. Open Mon.-Sat. 7:30am-9:00pm.

Pizza Ricca, 14 Av. 2-42, Zona 1 (tel. 761-8162). Brick-oven pizzas made fresh in a fast-foodish environment. Locals (even *indígenas*) dig into personal pizzas (Q13-22). Spaghetti Q25. Vegetarians' best bet is their tasty cheese pizza. Delivery available. Open daily 11am-10pm.

La Polonesa, 14 Av. "A" 4-45, Zona 1. Small and friendly, serving some of the cheaper meals in town. *Comida económica* Q12. Pancakes Q8. One-quarter chicken with french fries Q12. Half chicken with potatoes, salad, soup, rice, and dessert for Q22. Whole chicken and a Coke Q30. Open Mon.-Sat. 7:30am-8:30pm.

SIGHTS AND ENTERTAINMENT

Xela's biggest attraction is its vibrant produce **market** at Terminal Minerva, which is one of the major commercial centers of the western highlands—you might be the only one there who doesn't speak Quiché. Wooly blankets and hammocks go for about Q60 each. Bargaining is expected—most vendors don't speak English but they know the numbers well from having clashed wills with tourists for generations. Prices can drop 30% in the blink of an eye. Ask before taking any photographs, and beware of pickpockets. To reach the market, take any bus on 14 Av. (Q0.50; open Mon.-Sat. 8am-6pm, Sun. 8am-noon).

Aside from the market, Xela offers few diversions. The **Casa de Cultura,** 7 Calle 11-27, Zona 1 (tel. 761-6427), next to the tourist office on the south side of Parque Centroamérica, presents a swirl of Mayan artifacts, taxidermy, old manuscripts, and local herbology (open Mon.-Fri. 8am-noon and 2-6pm, Sat. 9am-1pm; admission Q6). The Casa de Cultura is also an unparalleled source for information on current cultural events. Nearby is the **Museo de Arte,** corner of 12 Av. and 7 Calle. Traditional scenes alternate with modernist paintings and metallurgical sculpture—don't miss the mechanical Maximón statue (open Mon.-Sat., 8am-1pm, 2pm-8pm; free). On the first Sunday of each month, the Parque Centroamérica hosts an important handicrafts market, accompanied by outdoor concerts and performances of traditional music. The city's main **festival** takes place September 12-18. The **Municipal Theater,** 1 Calle, 14 Av., Zona 1 (tel. 761-2218), houses ballet, *marimba,* orchestra, and theater performances (every other Fri. and Sat., admission Q3-25). **Salón Tecún** (tel. 761-2832), inside Pasaja Enrique by the park, hosts an international backpacking clientele as well as many locals. *Indígena* attire labeled with the village of origin decorates the walls (beers Q5; open 5:30pm-midnight).

■ Near Quetzaltenango

The town of **Zunil,** about 7 km from Xela toward the coast, is home to yet another shrine to the Maya God *Maximón,* also known by his Christian name of **San Simón.** Offerings of any kind may be made to San Simón; the seedier, the better (ask around for directions; admission Q2, or spend the money on good-luck candles for San Simón and entrance is free). A **shaman** also occasionally frequents the shrine. Buses leave

Xela at the corner of 4 Calle and 10 Av. in Zona 1 (via Almolanga) about every 20 minutes (Q1.50). Buses to Zunil also leave from Terminal Minerva.

About 9km from Zunil on a narrow dirt road bubble the hot springs of **Fuentes Georgina.** Set in a forested notch part of the way up a volcano, Fuentes Georgina is a peaceful place to come and purge the cool, wet weather of Quetzaltenango (admission Q5). Cabins with fireplaces for overnight stays are available for Q42 for one person and Q12 for each additional person. There is no bus to Fuentes Georgina, but trucks lined up in front of the church in Zunil will take four to six people there for Q25. Unless you plan to walk back (a manageable 9km downhill) or stay overnight, you'll have to pay the taxi an additional Q40 (Q25 for the trip back and Q15 for the hour the driver waits while you frolic in the springs).

If neither the shaman nor Fuentes Georgina cured your boils and blisters, you could head over to **El Recreo,** just after Almolonga, which is on the way to Zunil. Ask the bus driver to be let off at the hot springs. Other destinations for daytrips include a number of towns specializing in *artesanía.* **Salcajá** (9km from Xela, on the way to Cuatro Caminos) is known for its embroidered textiles and is home to the oldest church in Guatemala (according to some historians). **San Francisco El Alto** (17km from Xela) sits atop a hill overlooking Quetzaltenango. On Fridays, the central plaza bustles with vendors; catch a bird's eye view of this gigantic market from the church roof for Q1. If you decide to spend the night, **Hotel Vista Herma** (tel. 766-1060) has single rooms for Q7, Q6 for each additional person. Some of the rooms have beautiful views of Xela. **Buses** for San Francisco leave from Terminal Minerva about every 30 minutes (Q1.50).

Also quite close to Xela, but placed in wonderful isolation among cornfields, is the *indígena* village of **San Andrés Xecul.** The canary yellow church, with its technicolor cacophony of angels, icons, and adornments, stands in razor-sharp contrast to the town's mud-brick houses. Hike 15 minutes uphill to the chapel for views of the whole town and the farmland beyond. Buses leave from Xela (every 30min., 1hr., Q2); you can also catch them at the Xecul turn-off, about 1km toward Xela from Cuatro Caminos.

Two hours away from Xela, in the heart of Guatemala's wool-growing region, lies **Momostenango.** Here, you'll find popular Wednesday and Sunday markets with produce aplently and (you guessed it) cheap woolen goods (blankets of all sizes, designs and patterns Q70-110, hooded pullovers Q80). Ask for directions to the Mars-like *riscos,* heavily eroded clay formations reminiscent of a Star Trek set—it's only about a 12-minute walk (see Earth Girls Are Easy, p. 22). Another 20-minute walk on the road to the left as you face the church will take you alongside a forested ravine with waterfalls and down a steep-staired path to the **Baños de Payexú,** where water literally bursts out boiling next to the river. Watch respectfully as whole *indígena* families bathe in the steaming water, diluted with cooler river water to avoid poaching the locals like so many eggs. To bathe without the crowds, try coming early in the morning, late in the afternoon, or on a non-market day. Lukewarm water and lukewarm service characterize **Casa Palcom,** a bland, dark, but clean lodge (Q15 per person). **Hospedaje Roxana** is your only other choice; tired beds and questionable linens in tiny, dusty rooms that share a minute but blossom-filled courtyard and a bathroom with cold water only (Q6 per person). The culinary situation is similarly confining; **Cafetería Flipper's** *licuados* are a world full of wonder for parched throats, but otherwise, Momo's a true street-stall and *comedor* town. Given the dearth of comfortable accommodations and eating establishments, it's probably best to view Momo as a daytrip from Xela. **Buses** leave about every 90 minutes from Xela's Terminal Minerva (2hr., Q4). Leaving Momo, hourly buses pass Cuatro Caminos (1hr., Q2.50), regardless of final destination.

The nearby **Volcán Santa María** towers over Xela and is a popular destination for visitors to Quetzaltenango. The tourist office says that there have been no robberies or assaults on the volcano, and INGUAT considers Santa María to be one of the safer climbs in Guatemala. **Buses** to **Llanos de Pinal,** leaving from Terminal Minerva (8am-

5:30pm, Q3), pass near the trailhead for the volcano. Ask the bus driver to let you off at the crossroads near the trailhead (*¿Podría dejarme cerca del camino que sube el volcán?*). Following the road toward the volcano about 200m on the left, you'll pass a plaque dedicated to the Guatemalan Mountaineering Club. From here the road veers to the right, while the trail continues straight. The first section of the trail is wide and strewn with many small boulders. Rising up through a small valley dotted with cornfields, the trail gently curves to the left of the cave (visible if it's not cloudy). Black arrows painted on boulders indicate the appropriate trail.

After an hour's hike, the trail arrives at a flat, grassy area about 50m in length. One trail skirts the edge of the meadow, but the trail up the volcano cuts directly through it. If the weather is clear, the top of the cone can be seen from here. It looks tantalizingly close, but don't be fooled; you're not even a third of the way up. From here, the trail becomes much narrower and steeper, leaving the farmland and proceeding up the mountain surrounded by pine trees and undergrowth. From the meadow, the climb is two to three hours of unspeakable misery. The trail is steep, irregular, and poorly maintained—going down is almost as hard as going up. At this point, the trail is more diligently marked with frequent beer cans, graffiti, and many notches in the trees, but it's still not hard to get lost.

If you're lucky, the view at the summit is spectacular, with the Cuchumantanes to the north and volcanos to the east and west; then again, the view might be nothing at all, as the summit is frequently suffocated by clouds, especially in the afternoon. The best way to catch a view is to head up at dawn; Xela is usually covered by an early morning layer of fog, but the summit is almost always clear. To accomplish this requires that you camp near the summit. There are a number of sites and **camping** is permitted, but only do so if you are adequately prepared with food, water, and especially warm clothing. Otherwise, the climb up Santa María makes a rigorous daytrip. Hikers who attempt this climb should be in good shape and well acclimated to the elevation. The roundtrip takes five to seven hours. If you're hiking during the rainy season (May-Oct.), leave early in the day, as afternoon rains can make the trip down hellish.

▓ Huehuetenango

Huehuetenango has fewer than 40,000 inhabitants, but successfully melds small-town charm and cleanliness with some of the frenzied activity of larger urban centers. As local *indígenas* hustle and bustle in the marketplace, the predominantly *ladino* population scoots about on mopeds and in little cars. The central plaza, replete with a Neoclassical church, manicured gardens, and a *pink* bandstand, brings a mix of serenity and gaudy accoutrements.

Just big enough to supply passers-through with necessities and a little taste of the good life, today's "Huehue" began its life as a suburb of **Zaculeu,** the nearby Maya ruin. Since the Spanish conquest, the area has borne witness to a couple of minor silver rushes and the region-wide coffee boom; the mineral has since petered out, but the beany-brew still runs strong. The Interamerican Highway doesn't go through here, but for a prime pit stop on the way to Mexico or simply an amiable headquarters for exploring nearby ruins, this way (way) cool town should not be overlooked.

ORIENTATION

Huehuetenango lies 226km northwest of the capital and about 90km north of Xela. *Avenidas* run north to south, increasing numerically as you go west. East to west running *calles* increase numerically as you go south. The **main square** is in Zona 1, bounded by 2 Calle and 4 Calle on the north and south, and by 4 Av. and 5 Av. on the east and west, respectively. The main market is just east of the central square.

First- and second-class buses pull into the terminal, which is about 1km west of El Centro. City buses leave for the center about every 15 minutes (Q0.50). Taxis run to the central square for about Q12. The main plaza and surrounding areas provide most practical essentials.

PRACTICAL INFORMATION

Consulate: Get your tourist card at the **Mexican Consulate** inside Farmacia del Cid, on 5 Av., between 4 and 5 Calles. Open Mon.-Fri. 8am-noon and 2-8pm.

Currency Exchange: Bancor, 2 Calle at 3 Av. (tel. 764-2606; fax 764-1487). Gives money, money, money in exchange for traveler's checks. Open Mon.-Fri. 9am-7pm, Sat. 9am-1pm. **Bancafe,** 3 Calle at 6 Av. (tel. 764-1557), also accepts traveler's checks. Open Mon.-Fri 8:30am-8pm, Sat. 10am-2pm.

Telephones: Guatel, 2 Calle, 4/3 Avs., near the square. Open daily 7am-midnight.

Buses: Buses arrive and depart from the orderly terminal just off 6 Calle, about 1km west of the plaza. Most municipal buses pass through the terminal, and there are stops along 5 Calle near the plaza. From the terminal, buses leave for La Mesilla and the Mexican border (every 30min. 4am-7pm, 2hr., Q5); for Quetzaltenango/Xela (every 30-45min. 9am-6pm, 2hr., Q6); and for Guatemala City (every hr., 7am-4pm, 5½hr., Q15). For service to Panajachel or Chichicastenango, it's easiest to take a bus to Guatemala City and then transfer at Los Encuentros. Velasquez runs first-class pullmans from the terminal to Guatemala City (every 2hr. from 7:30am-5:30pm, Q24). To Todos Santos Cuchumatán (4 and 11am, 3hr.).

Public Transportation: Fares within town are Q0.50. Buses to the terminal run along 5 and 6 Calles. Buses to **Zaculeu** leave from 2 Calle and 7 Av. every hr., Q.50; to **Chiantla,** they run every 20min. from 1 Calle and 1 Av., Q1.

Taxis: Line up along 5 Av. in front of the church. To the terminal Q12.

Market: Along 2 Av. between 2 and 3 Calles; sells some food and snappy souvenirs along with loads of practical stuff. Open daily 6am-6pm.

Supermarket: Casa Saenz, 4 Calle and 5 Av. Open Mon.-Sat. 8:30am-12:30pm and 2:30-6:30pm.

Pharmacy: Farmacía Del Cid, 4 Calle and 5 Av. Open daily 8am-12pm and 2-8pm. Near the central square, you're never more than a block from a pharmacy. The rotating schedule of 24-hr. pharmacies is posted in front of every pharmacy.

Medical Services: National Hospital (tel. 764-1414 for **emergencies**), Las Lagunas, Zona 10. Available 24hr. Very little English spoken.

Police: Policía Nacional, 5 Av. between 6 and 7 Calles (emergency tel. 764-1150). Serve and protect 24hr.

Post Office: Mail away at 2 Calle between 4 and 3 Av. Open Mon.-Fri 8am-4:30pm.

ACCOMMODATIONS

Even though Huehuetenango is not a major tourist attraction, cheap (and not coincidentally, shoddy) hotels abound, concentrated mostly to the immediate north and west of the central square. All hotels listed here have hot water.

Hotel Mary, 2 Calle 3-52 (tel. 764-1618), just across the street from the Guatel office. The rooms are narrow and small, but the pink, stuccoed walls and lacquered wooden doors, all centered around a well lit, multi-story atrium, lend an air of sophistication to this inexpensive hotel. The collective baths are clean and odorless. Singles Q25. Doubles Q35, with bath and cable TV Q70. Reservations welcome.

Todos Santos Inn, 2 Calle 6-64 (tel. 764-1241), between 6a and 7a Av. A peek through the whitewashed concrete entrance reveals polished tile floors and rich blue bedspreads, all in color-coordinated rooms. Situated on the quiet end of the square, some rooms have views of the beautiful surrounding countryside. Make friends with Polly the parrot. *Se hable inglés.* Singles Q30, with bath Q45. Doubles Q45, with bath Q70. TV is Q12 extra.

Hotel Viajero, 2 Calle 5-32, Zona 1., one block west of the central square. The ceilings are low, the mattresses stiff, and the single, nude lightbulb a sickly yellow. But the place is generally safe and at Q10 for singles and Q20 for doubles, the prices are hard to beat.

FOOD

Huehue may not be the culinary capital of Guatemala, but the food comes cheap. There are a number of *comedores* just east of the church in and around the marketplace. Most mid-range hotels also have their own (mid-range) restaurants.

Villa Flor, 7 Av. 3-41, Zona 1 (tel./fax 764-2586), located in Hotel Casa Blanca. The hotel devotes its entire Spanish courtyard to the restaurant, a placid oasis from polluted streets. Dine to the gentle gurgling of the fountain while you sip a glass of Guatemalan wine for Q4. Reasonable prices; hamburgers Q9, omelette with ham Q18. Open daily 6am-10pm.

Pizza Hogareña, 2a Calle, just east of the square, across from Guatel. The color-blind may well love the interior; faux gold baroque mirrors, bright green drapes, and tangerine stucco surround the hungry-eña. The food is mega-good, though, and vegetarians will do back flips over the large cheese pizza (Q28). Open Tues.-Sun. 9:30am-9pm.

Jardín Cafe Restaurante, on the corner of 6a Av. and 4a Calle. Feeling Grecian? Come for hanging ferns, industrious ceiling fans, and late-night Mediterranean dinners. Situated on a noisy street corner, the Jardín sports a large menu with both local and American-style food. *Chile relleno con sopa y ensalada* Q20.50, hamburgers Q8. Open daily 2:15pm-10:30pm.

Restaurante Buganvilia, 5 Av., facing the church. This 4-story restaurant, heavily patronized by locals, sticks out like a concrete thumb in this mostly one-story town. On the street level is the kitchen, open to the public, and on the upper three floors are tables with breezy views. The *comida típica* (Q13) changes from day to day, but generally runs heavy on the flesh: *carne asada, chorizo* (sausage), or some sort of chicken. Open daily 7am-10pm.

NEAR HUEHUETENANGO

About 4km west of Huehuetenango lies the ancient Maya site of **Zaculeu,** the former capital and cultural center of the Mam tribe from 600 CE. The Mam reached all the way to Todos Santos, and their language continues in the area today. Ruled by the Quiché until the 15th century, the tribe finally managed to escape oppression by their fellow Indians, but fell right out of the frying pan and into a Spanish fire. When an army led by Gonzalo de Alvarado met the Mam on a battlefield, the Indians took a look at the fearsome Iberians and retreated to their base at Zaculeu. Their home had been built to protect them; the temples, plaza, and ball court that comprise the present site were fortified on three sides. Instead, the Spanish simply waited a few months until hunger set in, and the weakened Mam were forced to surrender.

The United Fruit Company, already notorious for dipping its fingers in places it shouldn't, sponsored an overzealous restoration of Zaculeu earlier this century. Today, Zaculeu is not what you'd expect from ancient ruins—few of the original stones aren't slathered in stucco, no jungly vines envelop the area, and nary a temple is strewn with toppled towers or relics. The site exudes some of the sterility of a mini-golf course, but while perhaps not the best place to explore Maya mysteries, Zaculeu tells us plenty about another odd culture, that of compulsive, overimaginative archaeologists. Bus #2 leaves Huehuetenango from the mini-plaza at 2 Calle and 7 Av. every hour. The walk takes 30 to 45 minutes. Head west on 2 Calle out of town, past the soccer stadium, and from there signs point the way to the ruins; look for the 17m temple (site open daily 8am-4pm; admission Q1).

■ Todos Santos Cuchumatán

If you're lucky enough to get a left side window seat on the bus (or to sit on top), the ride to Todos Santos is one of the more spectacular in Guatemala. Ascending skyward over 1000m from Huehuetenango, the road snakes around sharp ravines; with each turn, the road below looks smaller, narrower—and the low ground much more alluring than before. After a brief passage through a high plateau, the road dives into a valley at dizzying speeds before arriving safely (knock on wood) at Todos Santos. This trip is *not* for those prone to carsickness.

The spectacular, if arduous, three-hour trek is well worth the prize waiting at the end. The small village of Todos Santos Cuchumatán, nestled between two towering bridges, evokes a pre-Columbian lifestyle. In fact, some of the folks here (men decked out in crazy, red-striped, bell-bottom pants and tall cowboy hats, and women dressed in bright red *huipiles* and dark blue *cortes*) might very well have lost track of time as we know it. After all, Todos Santos is one of the few villages left that still uses the 260-day Maya calendar for religious events. Don't worry, though; nobody around here forgets when there's a holiday coming up, especially the **All Saint's Day** celebration from October 31 to November 5. While the core population of Todos Santos is composed of only about a thousand, thousands more depend on the town, particularly farmers who come down from their mountains for trade and services.

There are few services in Todos Santos, and there's no way to get really lost. It might be hard to get directions anywhere, though, since Mam (and not Spanish) is most locals' native tongue. There is a **post office** in the center of town (open Mon.-Fri. 8am-4:30pm). **Buses** back to Huehue leave at 4:30am, 5:30am, and 1:30pm (3hr., Q8). Next to the post office lies a small **museum** where you can ask for directions to the various villages.

Recent spurts of construction have markedly improved local lodgings. **Hospedaje Casa Familiar,** the nicest of the town's three hotels, is just up the street from the museum: signs point the way (singles Q15; doubles Q25). Enjoy views of the mountain from their terraces while you break the fast with oatmeal just like the Mam used to make (Q3.50). Hot water pours from the communal showers. A block before the museum lurks **Hotel Tres Olguitas,** which has divided up a whole floor into a dozen airplane-lavatory-sized but bright rooms (only singles Q10). As a last resort, (without any other element of "resort" attached), there's **Hospedaje La Paz,** also a block before the museum. Rooms are dark, spartan, and have no water—a bit creepy, but super cheapy (singles Q6; doubles Q12). After the bus ride, fill up at **Comedor Katy,** adjacent to Casa Familiar. They serve a fine chicken (Q10), but vegetarians are stuck with eggs and beans (open 7am-9pm).

■ Near Todos Santos

Photographically inclined early risers may want to consider taking the 4:30am bus back to Huehue and asking to be dropped off at **La Ventosa.** The morning light endows this semi-arid hamlet, situated just past the head of Todos Santos' valley, with a gilt lining. Various trails from the main road lead you through stark but captivating countryside, or even to the pine forests and high peaks of the Cuchumatanes. Stick to marked trails and be sure to be back on the road by 3pm when the last buses pass by;

Chariots of Fire

Todos Santos' residents kick off their out-of-control, outrageously fun All Saint's Day revelry with one of the wilder customs around. For the cost of a few quetzales, locals rent horses and enter a no-holds-barred, last-one-standing-wins race through the village. There's no finish line to the course, though its length is finite. Whenever a rider makes it to either of the two ends, he has to take a shot of the specially prepared moonshine; each successful lap incurs another two shots. Thanks to the time-honored tradition of using chickens to whip the horses into gear, the race starts off at break-neck speeds—until riders start to break their own necks, which usually doesn't take very long. Even so, ardent contestants tie themselves onto their horses in order to keep from toppling, and the race's winner is anybody still mounted and conscious at the end. Afterwards, back in town, the marimbas belt out everyone's favorite hits while villagers hold a different "no-bars-barred" competition of a similar sort, *sin* chickens.

otherwise, it's a three-hour walk downhill to Todos Santos. Another six-hour hike from Todos Santos takes you to the beyond-traditional agricultural village of **Tzunul.** Ask locals in Todos Santos for directions. Or, for a less demanding hike, follow the road uphill from Casa Familiar for 20 minutes to the Maya ruins of **Tecun-manchún,** a secluded place to enjoy a picnic or an afternoon nap.

Yucatán Peninsula

The Yucatán's state borders form a "Y" down the center of the peninsula. The eponymous **Yucatán** state sits in the crest of the "Y," **Quintana Roo** sees the Caribbean sun rise on the eastern coast, and **Campeche** faces the Gulf Coast to the west. Hernández de Córdoba mistakenly ran aground here in 1517. When the freshly disembarked sailors asked the locals where they were, the Maya, naturally not understanding Spanish, replied something to the effect of "We haven't a clue what you're talking about." Unfamiliar with the Mayan language, Córdoba only caught the last few syllables of their reply, *"Tectetán,"* and erroneously dubbed the region Yucatán.

The peninsula's geography consists mostly of flat limestone scrubland or rainforest dotted with an occasional *cenote* (freshwater sink-hole). Because of the highly porous limestone subsoil, there are no above-ground rivers in Yucatán. Poor soil and the lack of water make farming difficult, so maize remains the staple crop. The prominence of the rain god Chac at most Mayan ruins testifies to the eternal importance of the seasonal rains, which fall from May to late summer.

Yucatec culture remains essentially Maya and thrives in the peninsula's small towns, where the only evidence of Western influence arrives in the form of the weekly Coca-Cola truck. Mayan is still the first language of most of the inhabitants; *indígena* religions persist (often with a Catholic veneer); fishing, farming, and hammock-making out-produce big industry and commerce; and Yucatec women carry bowls of corn flour on their heads and wear embroidered *huipil* dresses. Burgeoning tourism, however, is threatening the traditional *yucateco* way of life. As *extranjeros* discover the peninsula's fine beaches, beautiful colonial towns, and striking ruins, more workers are drawn by the dubious allure of the tourism industry, flooding the big cities and resorts to work in *gringo*-friendly restaurants, weave hammocks for tourists, or act as multi-lingual guides at archaeological sites.

Since the Maya conquered the peninsula around 500 BCE, the Yucatán has known several masters. Many of the buildings in the Maya's illustrious city of Chichén Itzá are the creations of Toltecs, built after the tribe took the peninsula in the 11th century. Colonialism brought more than just forts and stone cathedrals. Spanish settlers received vast land grants and forced displaced *indígenas* to labor on their estates. Oppressed and humiliated, the *indígenas* rebelled against the white *ladino* overlords repeatedly in the 16th and 17th centuries, and faced even greater exploitation after gaining independence from Spain. In 1847, Maya discontent exploded in a bloody racial struggle, known as the Caste War, which enveloped the peninsula. At the height of the Maya advance, only the cities of Mérida and Campeche remained in *ladino* hands. A rebel Maya community survived as late as 1901, decades after Mexican troops had retaken most of the peninsula. Today, the central conflict is between the region's inhabitants and the throngs of tourists who flood the region; huge cultural, economic, and linguistic rifts have resulted in a relationship that is at its best tangled, at its worst tense.

"The Yucatán" refers to the peninsula, not the state, whereas "Yucatán" without the article can refer to either entity. Yucatán state's rich history draws thousands of visitors each year, who come to scramble up and down the majestic Mayan ruins, marvel at old colonial towns, explore the area's many dark caves, and take a dip in the *cenotes* (freshwater sink holes). Quintana Roo's luscious rain jungle, fantastic coastline, and magnificent Maya ruins were idylls beneath the Caribbean sun until the government transformed the area from tropical paradise to tourist factory. Cancún rapidly became the beachhead for what some wryly call "the Second *Conquista,"* and the nearby beaches and ruins were soon to follow. Although its countryside is dotted with Maya ruins and its coastline is over 200km long, Campeche pulls in fewer visitors than Yucatán to the north or Quintana Roo to the east, perhaps because it lacks a kind of swaggering grandeur—ruins are modest and relatively inaccessible, while the beaches are kept humble by wind and rocks.

CAMPECHE

■ Escárcega

The bus stop—er, town—of Escárcega is a critical transit point at the intersection of Yucatán's Rtes. 261 and 186. The **first-class ADO station** serves gourmet food and Sauvignon Blanc. Just kidding. But it does serve the cities of Campeche (9 per day, 2hr., 33 pesos), Cancún (8:30am, 10:30pm, and midnight, 8hr., 67 pesos), Chetumal (9 per day, 5hr., 57 pesos), Mérida (8:30, 11:30am, and 1pm, 5hr., 73 pesos), Mexico City (2:30, 3:30am, and 4pm, 19hr., 276 pesos), Palenque (1pm, 3½hr., 45 pesos), Playa del Carmen (noon, 8:30, and 10:30pm, 7hr., 120 pesos), Puebla (8:35am and 9:15pm, 17hr., 244 pesos), Veracruz (10:30am and 11pm, 11½hr., 167 pesos), and Villahermosa (noon, 2:30, and 3:15pm, 4hr., 62 pesos), all with a sprig of parsley. One kilometer down Av. Hector Martínez, the **second-class station** runs buses to similar locations and in-between; it sells cheaper wine.

As buses leave around the clock for most destinations, it is unlikely you'll be stranded for very long in Escárcega. However, if you're too tired to continue (wuss), head into town on **Av. Héctor Martínez.** A good many blocks (about 1.5km.), one railway crossing, and two stoplights later, take a right for Escárcega's small *zócalo.* The modern clock tower tells you you've made it. Escárcega and the long road leading to it are not the safest of places after dark, so take a taxi if it's late. For lodging, visit one of the sisters at **Hotel Las Tres Hermanas** (tel. (981) 4-01-10), right on the *zócalo,* which provides comfortable rooms with fans and cable TV (singles 40 pesos; doubles 50 pesos, with two beds 60 pesos; triples 70 pesos). If you think 5 pesos' worth of chiclets (about 4kg) will make your hunger subside on the bus, think again. Better head on over to **Cocina Económica La Tabasqueña,** one block west of the post office on the *zócalo* and across the railroad tracks. Breakfast eggs cost 9 pesos and, if the owner likes you, so does everything else.

■ Campeche

Campeche was once a Mayan settlement called "Ah Kin Pech," or "Place of the Serpents and Ticks." Soon after Francisco Hernández de Córdoba's arrival on the Yucatán Peninsula, the city was renamed and its destiny redirected. By 1540 "Ah Kin Pech" had become "Campeche," and the construction of an important trading port was underway. In the 18th century, as the city awaited stronger defenses against pirates and buccaneers, Ciudad del Carmen, a deep-water departure port in the Bahía de Campeche, surpassed Campeche as the regional trading center. Modern Campeche still plays second fiddle, though now the industry is tourism; the city exerts as much energy attracting *extranjeros* as it once did repelling them. But Campeche has retained its character: sections of the old stone wall still stand, and the *baluartes* (bulwarks) and forts still guard (at least in spirit) the city center.

ORIENTATION

Campeche lies 252km southwest of Mérida and 444km northeast of Villahermosa via Rte. 180. All major routes into the city intersect the peripheral highway that encircles it. A smaller road, **Circuito Baluartes,** circumscribes the old city. All main roads converge on the Circuito in the city center. **Avenida Gobernadores** comes in from the Mérida highway northeast of the city, crosses the peripheral highway, and passes the airport, train station, and bus terminals on its way to the Circuito.

To reach the *zócalo* from the **bus terminals,** catch the "Gobernadores" bus (1 peso) across the street from the station, and ask the driver to let you off at the **Baluarte de San Francisco.** Turn right into the old city and walk four blocks on **Calle 57** to the *zócalo.* If you'd rather walk (15min.), head left on Gobernadores and bear left

Yucatán Peninsula

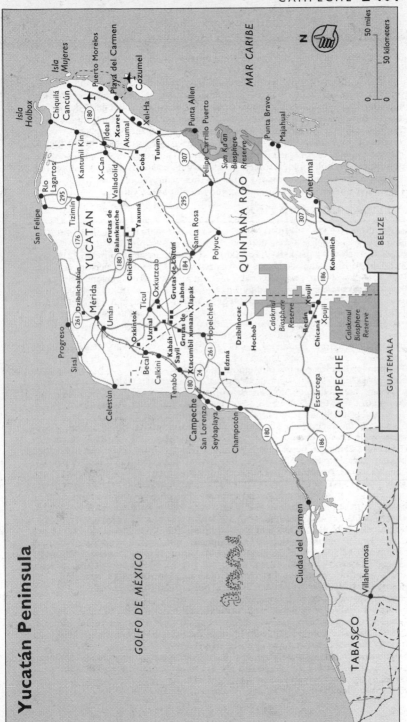

when you reach the Circuito. Three blocks later, turn right on Calle 57 through the stone arch and walk four blocks to the *zócalo*. **Taxis** charge 10 pesos.

The *centro's* east-west streets have odd numbers that increase to the south. **Calle 8** runs north-south between the *zócalo* and the western city wall. Parallel to Calle 8, to the east, lie Calles 10 to 16. The *zócalo* lies near the sea, bordered by Calles 8, 10, 55, and 57. To the west, outside the city wall, **Av. 16 de Septiembre** and **Av. Ruiz Cortínez** also run parallel to Calle 8. North of the *centro*, Calle 8 becomes **Malecón Miguel Alemán**, running past the Iglesia de San Francisco uphill to Fuerte de San José El Alto. **Av. Resugimiento**, the main coastal drag south of the city, runs past the youth hostel and the Fuerte San Miguel on its way to San Lorenzo and Seybaplaya.

A confusing network of **buses** links Campeche's more distant sectors to the old city (1-2 pesos; daily 6am-11pm). The market, where Gobernadores becomes the Circuito, serves as the hub for local routes. Buses have no established stops, but it is possible to flag them down at almost any point on their route. You'll have to get around the city center on foot, since buses only come in as far as the Circuito.

PRACTICAL INFORMATION

Tourist Offices: Calle 12 #153 (tel. 6-67-67; fax 6-60-68), between Calles 53 and 55, next to Iglesia de Jesús. Open Mon.-Fri. 9am-3pm and 6-9pm.

Travel Agencies: Agencia de Viajes Jaina, Av. Ruiz Cartinez #55 (tel. 6-22-23, ext. 352), in the Hotel Ramada. Tours to Edzná (9am, 75 pesos per person) and Ruta Puuc (Sat. 5am-10pm, price negotiable). Open Mon.-Fri. 9am-2pm and 5-8pm, Sat. 9am-1pm. **Prof. Augustín Zavala y Lozano,** at Calle 16 #348 (tel. 6-44-26), gives 4-hr. tours of Edzná (9am and 2pm, 60 pesos). **Destino Maya,** Av. Miguel Alemán 162 (tel. 1-37-26; fax 1-09-34), above Cine Estelar (climb the narrow stairway at the opposite end of the building from the cinema). Organizes all-inclusive group tours. Open Mon.-Fri. 9am-3pm and 6-9pm, Sat. 9am-2pm.

Currency Exchange: Banamex (tel. 6-52-51), at the corner of Calles 53 and 10. Open Mon.-Fri. 9am-5pm. 24-hr. **ATM.**

Telephones: TelMex phones throughout the city.

Telegrams: (tel. 6-43-90), opposite MexPost in the Edificio Federal. Money orders, telegrams, and **fax.** Open Mon.-Fri. 8am-6pm, Sat. 9am-noon.

Airport: (tel. 6-31-09), on Porfirio, 10km from the city center. **Aeroméxico** (tel. 6-58-78 and 6-56-78), at the airport. Taxis to the *centro* cost 25-30 pesos.

Buses: From the **second-class station,** Calle Chile just off Av. Gobernadores, **Camioneros de Campeche** goes to Dzibalchén (6 per day, 2hr., 13 pesos), Escárcega (5 per day, 2½hr., 20 pesos), Holpechén (11 per day, 1½hr., 9 pesos), Iturbide (5 per day, 2hr., 15 pesos), Muna (5 per day, 4½hr., 20 pesos), and Uxmal (5 per day, 4hr., 19 pesos). **Autobuses del Sur** to Mérida (6 per day, 2½hr.), Palenque (11pm, 5½hr., 65 pesos), San Cristóbal (11pm, 12hr., 92 pesos), and Villahermosa (4 per day, 9hr., 76 pesos). The **first-class station** lies on Av. Gobernadores #289, 4 blocks north of Circuito Baluartes at Baluarte San Pedro. **Autotransportes de Oriente (ADO)** to Cancún (10pm, 6hr., 104 pesos), Chetumal (noon and 7pm, 7hr., 90 pesos), Escárcega (9:30am, noon, and 8pm, 2½hr., 34 pesos), Mérida (11 per day, 2½hr., 40 pesos), Mexico City (2:30pm and 7pm, 16hr., 305 pesos), Palenque (10pm and 12:30am, 5hr., 78 pesos), Puebla (7pm, 16hr., 277 pesos), Valladolid (4hr., 77 pesos), Veracruz (10pm, 12hr., 201 pesos), Villahermosa (9:30am, 1:05, and 11pm, 7hr., 95 pesos). **Cristóbal Colón** to San Cristóbal (10pm, 10hr., 108 pesos), Tuxtla Gutiérrez (10pm, 12hr., 132 pesos), and Ocosingo (10pm, 8hr., 105 pesos). **Maya de Oro** offers similar service.

Trains: (tel. 6-51-48 or 6-39-99), 3km northeast of the city center. To Mérida, Mexico City, and anywhere along the way. Second-class daily at 10:30pm, *mixto* Mon.-Sat. at 8am. *Mixtos* include passengers, chickens, and all sorts of weird stuff. Tickets go on sale 1hr. before the train is supposed to arrive.

Taxis: (tel. 6-11-13). 3 stands: Calle 8 at 55, to left of the cathedral; Calle 55 at Circuito, near the market; and Gobernadores at Chile, near the bus terminal. Intra-city travel 7-10 pesos.

Car Rental: Picazh (tel. 6-44-26 or 7-51-42), on Calle 16 #348.

Luggage Storage: 3 pesos per day in the first-class bus station.
Market: On Circuito Baluartes, at Calles 53 and 55. Unexceptional handicrafts and cheap food. Open Mon.-Sat. sunrise-sunset, Sun. until 3pm.
Supermarket: Súper Diez (tel. 6-79-76), in the Pl. Comercial A-Kin-Pech on 16 de Septiembre, across the street from the post office. Open daily 7am-9:30pm.
Laundromat: Lavandería y Tintorería Campeche, Calle 55 #22 (tel. 6-51-42), between Calles 12 and 14. Same-day service. Open Mon.-Sat. 8am-4pm.
Red Cross: (tel. 6-06-66), on Av. Las Palmas at the northwest corner of the city wall. Open 24hr.
Pharmacy: Farmacia Gobernadores, next to the ADO station. Open 24hr.
Medical Services: Seguro Social (tel. 6-52-02), on López Mateos, south of the city. **Hospital General,** Av. Central at Circuito Baluartes (tel. 6-09-20 or 6-42-33).
Police: (tel. 6-21-11), on Calle 12 between Calles 57 and 59. Open 24hr.
Post Office: (tel. 6-21-34), 16 de Septiembre at Calle 53, in the Edificio Federal. Open Mon.-Fri. 8am-8pm, Sat. 8am-1pm. Express mail next door at **MexPost** (tel. 1-17-30). Open Mon.-Fri. 9am-6pm. **Postal Code:** 24000.
Telephone Code: 981

ACCOMMODATIONS

Few budget accommodations have cropped up in Campeche. Several middle-range establishments hover just out of the range of backpackers' pesos, and many of the cheaper places have sunk to unusually low levels of cleanliness and maintenance. The three hotels listed are in the old city, while the youth hostel is farther away, near the coastal highway.

Colonial Hotel, Calle 14 #122 (tel. 6-22-22 or 6-26-30), between Calles 55 and 57, 2½ blocks from the *zócalo*. Pastel-colored rooms. Showers barely have room for both you *and* the water. Singles 61 pesos. Doubles 69 pesos. Triples 86 pesos. 15 pesos per additional person. Add 20 pesos for A/C.
Hotel Regis, Calle 12 #148 (tel. 6-31-75), 1½ blocks from the *zócalo*. Stuccoed walls, high ceilings, and dark designer comforters on large, firm beds. Singles 75 pesos. Doubles 105 pesos. Triples 15 pesos. 30 pesos per additional person.
Hospedaje Teresita, Calle 53 #31 (tel. 6-45-34), between Calles 12 and 14. In a residential part of the old city, 3 blocks northeast of the *zócalo*. The cheapest place in the *centro*, and for good reason. Large, bare, concrete-walled rooms have wobbly fans. Lacks privacy. Communal bathrooms can be malodorous. Rooms 30 pesos. Two rooms have decent private baths, 40 pesos.
Youth Hostel Villa Deportiva Juvenil Campeche (tel. 6-18-02), on Agustín Melgar, several blocks east of the water and the coastal highway. From the eastern section of the Circuito Baluartes, take the "Lerma" bus south along the coastal highway to the intersection with Melgar, then walk half a block toward the ocean. A black iron gate on the left marks the spot. Single-sex college dorm rooms with two bunks and spiffy bathrooms. Table tennis and swimming pool. No hot water. Full July-Aug. and December; call to reserve. Bunk rental 15 pesos plus 20 peso deposit. Breakfast 9 pesos, lunch and dinner 11 pesos.

FOOD

Campechanos will tell you that there are two culinary experiences that visitors should not miss: dinner at San Pancho (see below) and a sampling of *pan de cazón* (stacked tortillas filled with baby shark and refried beans, and covered with an onion, tomato, and chile sauce). Other local specialties include *pámpano en escabeche* (pompano broiled in olive oil and flavored with onion, garlic, chile, peppers, and a dash of orange juice). The dirt-cheap places in the market may serve up just that: dirt, cheap. Except for San Pancho, all listings are near the *zócalo*.

Cenaduría Portales (tel. 1-14-91), better known as **San Pancho** for its proximity to Iglesia de San Francisco. Take any bus headed north on Malecón Miguel Alemán to the church. Cross the plaza east of the church and head left to another smaller square. The restaurant huddles beneath the arches straight ahead. An assembly line of highly-trained sandwich makers jump into action at your order and nearly instantly produce not just a sandwich, but a work of art. Sandwiches 7-10 pesos. Exceptional *horchata* (sweetened rice water, 4 pesos). Open daily 7pm-midnight. This area is not safe after dark—get back on the bus straight away.

Nutrivida (tel. 6-12-21), on Calle 12, between 57 and 59. Serves meatless burgers, delectable home-made yogurt, flaky bread, and fresh juice in a pleasant courtyard. Open Mon.-Fri. 8am-2:30pm and 5:30-9pm, Sat. 8am-2pm.

Restaurant Del Parque, Calle 57 #8 (tel. 6-02-40), at Calle 8. Local fare, including sandwiches (8-10 pesos) and *pan de cazón* (18 pesos). Open daily 7am-midnight.

Restaurant La Parroquia, Calle 55 #9 (tel. 6-80-86), between Calles 10 and 12. TV, locals, and hot hearty food. Seafood starts at 17 pesos. Open 24hr.

SIGHTS AND SAND

The **Fuerte de San Miguel** houses well documented exhibits describing nearby ruins, and displays Mayan jewelry, pottery, and several magnificent jade masks. On the top level, cannons still point out protectively over the sea and Campeche to the north. To reach the fort, take the "Lerma" bus from the eastern end of the Circuito Baluartes, and head south until the bus turns onto the coastal highway near the "Maxi" *tienda*. The road leading up to the fort is about a block ahead on the left (open Tues.-Sun. 8am-8pm; admission 4 pesos, free Sun.).

San Miguel's counterpart to the north, the **Fuerte de San José El Alto**, is a few kilometers from the *centro*. The "Bellavista" or "San José El Alto" bus from the market will drop you halfway up the hill; a five-minute walk will get you to the fort at the top. If you decide to walk, head north on Gobernadores, turn left on Cuauhtémoc, left on Calle 101, and right on Calle 7. Built in 1792, San José was amazingly defensible when in use. The path leading to the portcullis winds deliberately so that battering rams could not be used on the gate. The fort's moat, which encircles the building, supposedly was rife with vicious spikes; the water was obscured with chalk so as to hide them from anyone thinking about jumping in. The view from San José is spectacular; kilometers of green shoreline give way to the urban waterfront (open Tues.-Sun. 8am-8pm; admission 4 pesos, free Sun.).

In the **Baluarte de la Soledad,** across from the *zócalo*, off Calle 8 near Calle 57, the **Museo de Estelas Maya** houses a small collection of well preserved Mayan stelae and reliefs taken from sites in Campeche state, including a phallus the size of a torpedo. Informative texts in Spanish and pictographs elaborate on sculpted figures' occupations. Visitors may also climb the walls of the fort, which is surrounded by a park. A showroom across from the museum occasionally features free exhibitions (museum open Tues.-Sat. 8am-8pm, Sun. 8am-1pm; admission 3 pesos).

In the **Fuerte Santiago**, at the northern corner of the city, the **Jardín Botánico Xmuch'haltún** (tel. 6-68-29), Calles 8 and 51, makes an inviting stop. Over 250 species of plants thrive in an open-air courtyard shaded by trees and marked by walkways, benches, and fountains—walk through the garden, soothe your mind, and refresh your soul (open Mon.-Fri. 8am-3pm and 6-8:30pm, Sat. 9am-1pm and 6-8pm, Sun. 9am-1pm; guided tours Mon.-Fri. from 5-6pm).

Campeche's **cathedral** looms above the *zócalo*. Don Francisco de Montejo first ordered the construction of the cathedral in 1540, but builders did not complete the massive structure until 1705. The cathedral's main attraction is its façade. Inside, you'll find the *Santo Entierro* (Holy Burial), a sculpture of Christ in a carved mahogany sarcophagus with silver trim (open daily 7am-noon and 5-8pm; free).

A little farther from the center of town, the **Iglesia de San Francisco,** Av. Gustavo Díaz, built in 1518, claims to be the oldest church on the American mainland. Inside, yellow Corinthian arches project towards an ornate altar (open daily 8am-noon and 5-8pm). A few blocks south of the *centro*, the **Iglesia de San Román** houses El Cristo

Negro, greatly venerated by *campechanos* and supposedly one of only three black Christs in Mexico (open daily 6am-noon and 4-8pm; free).

Locals head south for **sand** and **sunbathing**. **San Lorenzo** is ideal for swimming, though the beach is pebbly. The closest half-decent stretch of sand is at **Playa Payucán**. The beach is great for snorkeling, but rentals are not available. Buses for **Seybaplaya**, 2km from the beach, leave from behind the market (4 pesos). For those seriously looking for beachy bliss, head for the gorgeous sands of **Sabancuy**, 130km to the south. And please, don't forget the sunscreen.

ENTERTAINMENT AND SEASONAL EVENTS

Campeche sponsors various free outdoor musical events, including the *ballet folklórico* in the *zócalo*. Every Friday night at 8pm, an impressive **light and sound show** at Puerta de Tierra, Calles 59 and 18, recounts in Spanish the dramatic story of residents repulsing pirates. The performers' awful acting is as entertaining as the historical account. Weather permitting, a *ballet folklórico* follows the conclusion of the show (light and sound show 10 pesos, 50% discount with student ID; translated text in three other languages is projected onto the wall). The wildly popular **Noche de Trova,** including music and performances by the *ballet folklórico,* is celebrated in the Parque de Guadalupe on Wednesdays at 8pm and in the *zócalo* on Thursdays at 8pm, but usually only during the high months of July, August, and December. For a complete schedule of events, ask for the *programa de actividades* at the tourist information center. San Román is Campeche's patron, and two weeks of both religious and secular festivities, starting September 15, celebrate his feast.

Atlantis (tel. 6-22-33), at the Ramada Inn on Av. Ruiz Cortínez, lords over Campeche's nightlife (men 65 pesos, women 35 pesos; Thurs. is singles night and free; open Thurs.-Sat. 10pm-3am). **La Cueva de Las Ranas,** near the university on López Mateos, attracts aspiring rock stars and a hip student crowd (open 9pm-3am).

■ Near Campeche

EDZNÁ

If you're already in Campeche, visit the nearby ruins of **Edzná** (House of the Grimaces), where hieroglyphics date back to 652 CE. Despite its lack of elaborately sculpted detail, the **Edificio de Cinco Pisos** (Building of the Five Floors), which towers over the surrounding valley atop the **Gran Acrópolis**, is supremely elegant. Sixty-five stairs, some adorned with hieroglyphics over 1300 years old, lead up to tiers of columns crowned by a magnificent five-room temple. During its Mayan heyday, the perch atop the monument afforded a view of the network of irrigation canals criss-crossing the valley close to the Río Champotón, 20km to the west. The canals were built without the use of wheels, metal tools, or domesticated animals. Nearby, among the many thistle bushes, are the remains of a ballcourt and several other temples of a central plaza which are presently being excavated. Also on display are some

---

Ground Zero

Chances are the dinosaurs didn't die from *chile relleno* indigestion, but their extinction may have more to do with Mexico than you thought. A link has been made between the "dinosaurs became extinct when an enormous meteor struck the earth" theory and why much of the Yucatán lacks above-ground water and topsoil. It turns out the Peninsula may have been ground zero for this catastrophic impact, and whatever soil didn't fly up into space solidified into the porous limestone rock (a nightmare for farmers), which dominates the landscape today. Sure, it's just a theory, but archaeologists *have* identified a large piece of meteor rock that slammed through the roof of the **Grutas de Loltún.** For more theories, see "Earth Girls Are Easy" on p. 22.

YUCATÁN PENINSULA

of the 19 stelae found at Edzná, one crafted as early as 672 CE, others made during the 10th-century evacuation of the ceremonial center.

Mosquitoes at Edzná can be so vicious that you may want to ask Luís at the tourist office what the current state of affairs is before you leave several pints of valuable blood in the jungle. A canteen of water and plenty of repellent are a must (site open daily 8am-5pm; admission 15 pesos, half-price with student ID, free Sun.).

Getting There: One bus makes three roundtrips from the market in Campeche to Alfredo Bonfil (daily starting at 7am, 1½hr., 6 pesos), dropping you off at the Edzná access road. From there, a sign points the way and gives a distance 1500m too long. To avoid being stranded, be sure to ask the driver when he will return. During *Semana Santa,* July, and August, there are cheap guided tours to the ruins every morning at 9am from the Baluarte San Carlos. In the off-season, tours leave on Saturday and Sunday at 9am (ask for details at the tourist office).

DZIBILNOCAC AND HOCHOB

If you want to experience the ruins in solitude, head to Dzibilnocac or Hochob, way, *way* off the beaten path, about 400km from Ticul. Only Indiana Jones wannabes should visit the sites, as they're hard to reach and less impressive than those in Yucatán. **Dzibilnocac** consists of a set of three excavated temples in various states of decay; the highlight is the third temple, a tall, narrow building with rounded corners and a stucco façade—climb to the top for a closer view of a gruesome mask of the rain god Chac. Simple reliefs at the middle levels resemble cave paintings. If you want to explore neighboring farms and cornfields, make sure you wear long pants and thick boots since the area is rife with poisonous snakes. **Hochob's** three temples cluster around a central plaza that swells modestly from the flat rainforest. Deep-relief geometric patterns molded in stucco cover the well preserved temple to the right of the entrance, the front of which once formed an enormous mask of Chac (the door representing his gaping mouth). Climb to the top for a view of the site and the rainforest (both sites open daily 8am-5pm; free).

Getting There: Dzibilnocac lies 61km off Rte. 261, near the small town of **Iturbide.** To reach it by car, exit Rte. 261 at Hopelchén and drive south; you'll see a sign at a fork pointing the way (straight on, *not* to the right) to Iturbide. When you reach the village, bear right at the *zócalo,* and continue out of town (during the rainy season, the road can be treacherous; strongly consider walking). Fifty meters into the forest, the right branch of the fork in the road ends at the ruins. If you don't have a car, get to Iturbide through a **Camioneros de Campeche** bus from Campeche (5 per day, 3hr., 15 pesos) or from Hopelchén (12 per day, 1½hr., 9 pesos).

To reach Hochob, take the road out of **Dzibalchén** (a tiny town between Iturbide and Hopelchén) about 1km toward Campeche, then follow the sign pointing left to **Chencoh,** 9km down a dirt road. In town, make a left at the second intersection of roads lined with stone walls. After passing a concrete platform on the right and a barnyard, turn left again and follow the dirt track 4km into the jungle. Pockmarked with potholes, this road becomes very dangerous in heavy rain. When the road forks, bear left. Park at the *palapa* below Hochob's hilltop site, and continue up the road on foot. The ruins are virtually impossible to reach without a car—there is no public transportation from Dzibalchén (or anywhere else) to Chencoh, and vehicles are rarely sighted;. Those who hitch a ride ask to be let off at the access road to Chencoh, 1km before Dzibalchén. *Let's Go* does not recommend hitchhiking. Stranded travelers can spend the night in Dzibalchén in a tent or on a hammock (there are no hotels); ask at the Palacio Municipal for bathroom facilities or hooks.

GRUTAS DE XTACUMBILXUNAAN

Twenty-seven kilometers from the Yucatán-Campeche border lie the **Grutas de Xtacumbilxunaan** (shta-kum-bill-shoe-NAN, Caves of the Sleeping Girl). A custodian leads a tour past seven deep *cenotes* (natural wells) and points out barely discernible shapes on the cavern's walls and ceilings. These caves are poorly lit, and hardly the high-roofed galleries of Loltún or the clean-cut passageways of Balankanché, but you can still have fun poking around (open daily 9am-6pm; tours in Spanish only; free, but guide expects a tip).

Getting There: The *grutas* lie 1km down the road that crosses Rte. 261 2km south of Bolonchén. Second-class buses drop passengers at the access road.

YUCATÁN

■ La Ruta Puuc (The Mayan Route)

La Ruta Puuc (a.k.a. La Ruta Maya) is a long stretch between Campeche and Mérida that traverses the Puuc Hills. This area was home to about 22,000 people during the Classic period of Mayan civilization (4th to 10th centuries). Decimated by diseases introduced by the Spanish, the Maya slowly surrendered most of their cities and ceremonial centers to the jungle. Beginning in the 18th century, the Mayan population began a slow recovery. While today's Puuc Maya live in towns with paved roads and plumbing, women continue to wear traditional embroidered *huipiles* and Maya remains the dominant language.

The Ruta Puuc refers specifically to the 254km on Rte. 261 between Campeche and Mérida, as well as the Sayil-Oxkutzkub road which branches off just meters after the Campeche-Yucatán border. Taking this turnoff, **Sayil** is the first archaeological site to materialize (5km), followed by **Xlapak** (10km), **Labná** (13km), **Loltún** (25km), **Oxkutzkab** (45km), and **Ticul** (62km). Alternatively, if the turnoff is not taken, the road winds through **Kabah** (right after the border) and the stunning site of **Uxmal** (23km); 16km from Uxmal lies the junction at **Muna.**

The easiest way to see the ruins is by **renting a car.** The drive along the Ruta Puuc is also one of the most liberating and enjoyable "on the road" experiences: smell the air and watch the butterflies fly by. Another option is an **organized tour.** These can be arranged through private companies in either Mérida or Campeche (ask in the tourist office). Public transportation is more difficult. Second-class **buses** traverse Rte. 261 frequently, and will stop when requested, but none travel the Sayil-Oxkutzkub road with the exception of the Autotransportes de Sur "Ruta Puuc" bus that leaves Mérida at 8am and visits Kabah, Sayil, Labná, and Uxmal, returning to Mérida at about 2:30pm. If you don't mind a whirlwind tour through the sites, this bus is an incredible bargain (31 pesos; admission to sites not included). *Combis* are abundant in the morning and make frequent trips between Oxkutzkab, Ticul, Santa Elena, and Muna (it is easiest to get a *combi* to Uxmal from Muna), and they will make any trip if paid enough. Unfortunately, with both *combis* and buses, return trips are not always guaranteed.

The sites along the Ruta Puuc can best be explored using **Ticul** as a base; the town offers cheap accommodations and restaurants. Two to three days should be ample time for exhaustive exploration. Most sites sell *refrescos,* but the only one with accommodations (at ridiculously high prices) is Uxmal. Thank Chac for Ticul.

TICUL

A bustling provincial town off the Campeche-Mérida highway, Ticul (pop. 40,000) is a convenient and inexpensive base from which to explore the nearby Ruta Puuc sites of Uxmal, Kabah, Sayil, Xlapak, and Labná, as well as the Grutas de Loltún. Staying in Ticul is a welcome relief from Mérida—the town's busy residents simply don't have time to heckle tourists. For those with wheels, a number of *cenotes* and colonial buildings await exploration in the nearby towns of Teabo, 30km southeast of Ticul, Mayapán, 45km to the northeast, and Holcá, 105km to the northeast. Maní, 15km east of Ticul, features a colonial monastery; Tekax, 35km to the southeast, a hermitage; and Tipikal, an impressive colonial church.

Orientation and Practical Information Ticul's streets form a grid with the main drag, **Calle 23**, passing east-west through the center. Even-numbered streets run north-south. Most commercial activity transpires between the *zócalo* (Calle 24) and Calle 30, four blocks to the west.

Banco del Atlántico, Calle 23 #195, off the *zócalo,* changes U.S. dollars and traveler's checks (open Mon.-Fri. 9am-2pm). Make cheap **phone calls** from the long-distance *caseta,* Calle 23 #210 (tel. 2-00-00), between Calles 26 and 28 (open 8:30am-10pm). Calls can also be made from the **Hotel Sierra Sosa** (see below; 8 pesos per min. to the U.S.). The **telegram office,** Calle 21 #192-C (tel. 2-01-46), is in the blue and white building behind the post office (open Mon.-Fri. 9am-3pm).

Combis leave from Parque de la Madre, Calle 23 between Calles 28 and 30, for Muna (5 pesos); from Calle 30, between Calles 25 and 25A, for Santa Elena, Uxmal, and Kabah (3 pesos); and from Calle 25, between Calles 26 and 28, for Oxkutzkub (5 pesos). From Muna, 5 **buses** run daily to Campeche (20 pesos) via Uxmal and Kabah. Hourly buses head north to Mérida (7 pesos). The town's pedal-powered **taxis** transport passengers for a couple of pesos.

Farmacia San Jose, Calle 23 #214-J (tel. 2-03-93), is between Calles 28 and 30 (open 8am-1pm and 4-10pm; no English spoken). Dr. Estela Sanabria can be reached at the same number for 24-hour **medical assistance. Police** headquarters (tel. 2-00-10 or 2-02-10) are on the northeast corner of the *zócalo* on Calle 23 (open 24hr.). Ticul's **post office** (tel. 2-00-40) is in the Palacio Municipal on the *zócalo* (open Mon.-Fri. 8am-2:30pm). **Postal Code:** 97860. **Telephone Code:** 997.

Accommodations and Food Ticul has several hotels and good restaurants. **Hotel San Miguel** (tel. 2-63-82), on Calle 28 opposite Parque de la Madre, offers small, clean, battleship-gray rooms with ceiling fans (singles 25 pesos; doubles 32 pesos, with two beds 38 pesos). **Hotel Sierra Sosa** (tel. 2-00-08; fax 2-02-82), on Calle 24, on the northwest corner of the *zócalo,* has rooms with saggy beds, fans, and TVs. Rooms with windows come with street noise. Free coffee and *agua purificada,* but be prepared to be "bugged" all night long (singles 40 pesos; doubles 55 pesos; triples with TV 50 pesos).

Dining in Ticul can be tricky; only one restaurant stays open past 6pm. Luckily, **Los Almendros,** Calle 23 #207 (tel. 2-00-21), between Calles 28 and 30, makes a mean *pollo pibil* (chicken with herbs baked in banana leaves, 21 pesos; open daily 9am-9pm). **Restaurant Los Delfines** (tel. 2-04-01), Calle 27, between Calles 28 and 30, serves shrimp dishes, *chiles rellenos* (21 pesos), and jars of lemonade under a big airy *palapa* (open daily 11am-6pm). Ticul's **market** is just off Calle 23 between Calles 28 and 30 (open daily sunrise-sunset).

Getting to the Ruins Public transportation in Ticul is not geared toward ruin-happy tourists. While Uxmal and Kabah are fairly accessible if you have luck with *combi* transfers, the lack of traffic on the Sayil-Oxkutzcab road will leave the carless traveler frustrated and stranded. In general, you shouldn't rely on direct service, but reconcile yourself to changing buses. To reach the ruins around Uxmal, take a Mérida-bound bus from the Ticul bus station (tel. 2-01-62), on Calle 24 behind the main church, and get off at Muna (every 30min., 3 pesos). *Combis* for Muna leave from Parque de la Madre, Calle 23 between Calles 28 and 30. From Muna, board a southbound bus or *combi* for Uxmal, Kabah, or other sites. You can also reach the ruins by catching a *combi* on Calle 30, between Calles 25 and 25A, to Santa Elena (30min., about 3 pesos). Change *combis* at Santa Elena for Uxmal, 16km from Mérida, or Kabah, south of Campeche. *Combis* are most plentiful in the morning.

To reach the Grutas de Loltún, snag a *combi* to Oxkutzcab at Parque de la Madre; you'll be let off at the intersection of Calles 23 and 26 (15min., about 3 pesos). *Combis* leave for Loltún from the lot across from Oxkutzcab's market "20 de Noviembre." Tell the driver to let you off at the *grutas* (10min., about 3 pesos), as everyone else is probably headed for the agricultural cooperative 3km farther down the road. Because

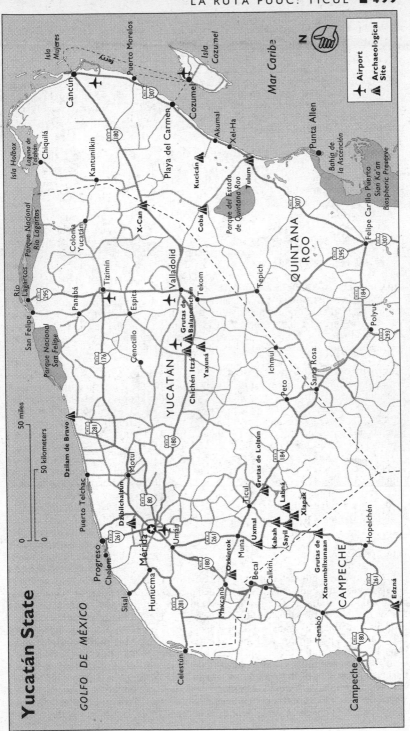

Yucatán State

the road is more crowded with *combis,* it's easier to reach the Grutas than Uxmal or Kabah. Hitchhikers rarely find rides on any of these roads.

UXMAL

Easily the most attractive site along the Ruta Puuc, Uxmal (oosh-MAL) is as wondrous as you've heard. The combination of proud pyramids, finely sculpted reliefs, and immense masks, are simply without peer. And unlike Chichén Itzá, Uxmal is relatively tourist-free. Aided by excellent renovation, it is not hard to envision the teeming capitol of 25,000 that it once was.

Orientation and Practical Information Uxmal is on Rte. 261, the longer highway route *(vía ruinas)* between the state capitals of Mérida (79km north) and Campeche (175km southwest). Kabah, the next Ruta Puuc site, lies 23km to the southeast, and 5km south of Kabah, the Sayil-Oxkutzcab road branches off Rte. 261 and heads east past Sayil, Xlapak and Labná, and the caves at Loltún.

Autotransportes del Sur (ATS) sends six buses a day from Mérida to Uxmal (1½hr., 11 pesos), as well as a "Ruta Puuc" bus which visits Uxmal, Kabah, Sayil, Xlapak, and Labná all in one day for just 31 pesos (see p. 504). From Campeche you'll have to take the **Camioneros de Campeche** bus to Mérida (5 per day, 3hr., 19 pesos). Ask the driver to stop at the access road to the *ruinas*. To return, grab a passing bus at the *crucero* just outside the entrance to the ruins. The last buses to Mérida and Campeche pass at 8pm and 7pm, respectively.

A modern **tourist center** with a small museum, restaurant, gift shop, photographic supply shop, and bathrooms greets you at the entrance to the ruins. The **Kit Bolon Tun auditorium,** also in the tourist center, screens documentaries on the Ruta Puuc and a 15-minute film of the events which take place at Uxmal in celebration of the biannual equinox (3 shows per day in Spanish and 2 in English; free).

Accommodations and Food Room prices being a function of location, Uxmal's accommodations are prohibitively expensive for those on a tight budget. Consider staying 30minutes away in Ticul, where hotel rooms cost half as much. In Uxmal, the cheapest option is **Rancho Uxmal** (tel. 47-80-21), 4km north of the ruins on Rte. 261. From the highway near Uxmal, you can reach Rancho Uxmal by hopping aboard a passing bus or *combi* (about 2 pesos). Thinly carpeted rooms have inviting bedspreads, hand-painted murals, and standard bathrooms. The pool is usually in service during peak season (singles 100 pesos; doubles 150 pesos; triples 170 pesos). Four concrete platforms beneath *palapas* are available for tent-pitching or hammock-slinging (15 pesos per person, including the use of bathroom facilities). The adjacent restaurant of the same name serves a variety of tasty local dishes (20-40 pesos). Diners can use the hotel pool and are entertained Thursday through Saturday at 2pm by Mayan folk dancers (restaurant open daily 7am-9:30pm).

Sights According to the **Chilam Balam,** a Mayan historical account written in phonetic Spanish, Ah Suytok Xiu and his warriors from the Valley of Mexico invaded Yucatán at the end of the 10th century. Xiu and his successors dominated Uxmal until the city's strength was sapped by civil warfare in the 12th century. Because their priests foretold the coming of white, bearded men, the Xiu did not resist when Spanish conquistadors attacked Uxmal. The last Xiu ruler of the city was Ah Suytok Tutul Xiu, whose descendants still live in the Puuc region. Tutul Xiu was baptized as an old man; his godfather was Francisco de Montejo, conqueror of the Yucatán.

The 40m-tall near-pyramid visible upon entering Uxmal is the **Temple of the Magician.** The pyramid, the legend goes, was built by a dwarf-magician who hatched from a witch's egg and grew to maturity in the space of a single year. The legend of the dwarf-magician's birth struck terror into the heart of the governing lord of Uxmal, who, it was prophesied, would be replaced by a man "not born of woman." He challenged the dwarf to a contest of building skills. The dwarf's pyramid, built overnight, easily outclassed the governor's Great Pyramid, still visible to the right of the Governor's Palace. Grasping at straws, the spiteful ruler complained that the base of the dwarf's pyramid was neither square nor rectangular but was actually elliptical. Having undermined the legitimacy of the dwarf-magician's triumph, the governor proposed that he and his adversary compete to see who could break a *cocoyol* (a small, hard-shelled fruit) on their heads. The dwarf-magician, in whose skull a turtle shell had been placed, easily cracked open the *cocoyol*. The governor crushed his unaltered skull trying to match the dwarf fruit for fruit.

The elegant south-facing arch leads to the **ballcourt.** Note the glyphs on the rings through which well padded players tried to knock a hardened rubber ball. Emerging from the ballcourt, head right along a narrow path to the **Cemetery Group,** a small, leafy plaza bounded by a small pyramid to the north and a temple to the west. Stones that once formed platforms bear haunting reliefs of skulls and crossbones. Returning to the ballcourt, head south to the well restored **Great Pyramid,** built by the governor in his contest with the dwarf-magician. The architecture and crude latticework reveal the influences of northern Campeche. To the west, the pyramid looks down on the jagged face of the Palomar, behind which lie the jungle-shrouded remains of the **Chenes Temple.**

The **House of Turtles** and the **Palace of the Governor** top a man-made escarpment east of the Great Pyramid. The two-story House is on the northwest corner of the escarpment and is adorned along its upper frieze with a series of sculpted turtles (turtles symbolized rain and were venerated by the Maya). Over 100m long and built on three landscaped terraces, the palace is typical of Puuc style. The eastern frieze is covered by 20,000 decorations, which together form 103 masks of Chac.

From the Palace of the Governor, try to spot the overgrown, pyramidal **House of the Old Woman,** which lies to the east and can be reached by following the path directly to your left as you emerge from the entrance. About 400m south of the house is the **Temple of the Phalli.** Phallic sculptures hang from the cornices of this ruined building and spurt rain runoff from the roof. Experienced guides are available to give more detailed tours of the site (about 30 pesos per person as part of a group).

KABAH

Once the second largest city in the northern Yucatán, Kabah was built with the blood and sweat of many slaves. The most elaborate of Kabah's structures is the **Codz Pop Temple** (rolled mat in Mayan), immediately to the right of the entrance, which was named for the odd shape of the rain god Chac's nose. The temple's broad façade displays nearly 300 masks of Chac, each comprised of 30 carved pieces. The elaborate Chenes style of the temple is unique to the Codz Pop—its neighbors to the east, **El Palacio** (a 25m pyramid) and **Las Columnas,** were executed in plainer fashion. The site is thought to have served as a court where justices settled disputes with the aid of the gods. Across the highway, a short dirt road leads in three directions. An unrestored group of temples lies to the right, the nearly camouflaged West Group to the left, and a beautifully sculpted arch resides directly ahead. The arch marks the beginning of the ancient *sacbé* (paved, elevated road) which culminated in a twin arch at Uxmal. The perfect alignment of the archway with the north-south line is testimony

Before the Rain

Uxmal's entire nightlife consists of a light-and-sound show celebrating Maya history and culture. The Spanish version (25 pesos) begins at 8pm and ends after the last of the Campeche-bound buses passes. Although it requires language fluency, it is usually more fun than the English version, one hour later (35 pesos). While the lights and the sound remain identical (except for the fact that the text is translated), the crowd in the Spanish show is a spectacle in itself. Don't be shy to join in the clapping and chanting "¡Chaaaac!, ¡Chaaaac!" Guidebooks are available at the bookstore. Bring a raincoat—the chanting might actually work.

to Mayan astronomical understanding (site open daily 8am-5pm; admission 10 pesos, free Sun. and holidays).

Getting There: Bisected by Rte. 261, Kabah lies 23km southeast of its Ruta Puuc cousin, Uxmal. Because of its location on the Campeche-Mérida highway *(vía ruinas)*, it can easily be reached by any second-class bus running between Mérida and Campeche (see p. 503 and p. 490). Buses will stop at Kabah only if a passenger notifies the driver beforehand or if the driver sees a person wildly gesticulating on the shoulder of the highway. Things are easier with the **ATS "Ruta Puuc" bus** (see p. 503). Since almost all the tourists who come to Kabah have cars, many hitchers find rides back to Uxmal or on to the Grutas de Loltún.

SAYIL

The **Palace of Sayil** (The Place of Ants) is an architectural standout among the region's ruins. Between its three terraced levels, the building's 50 rooms exhibit unparalleled ornamental diversity. Walls are carved with rows of slender columns; the second-story frieze depicts the descending serpent-god's body; and elegant second-floor chambers open onto pleasant porticos, each graced by bulging columns. Climb to the top for a gorgeous panoramic view of the rolling, verdant Puuc hills. Behind the palace sits a *chultún* (plastered catch basin) that ancients used to collect rainwater for use during the dry season.

The path continues past the palace to **El Mirador** (the lookout), a lofty temple with grandiose columns. Left of El Mirador, the path leads deeper into the jungle, where the extremely graphic **Estela del Falo** (Stela of the Phallus) will make even the most sexually liberated of visitors blush profusely. A few other temples are barely visible through the dense jungle undergrowth (site open daily 8am-5pm; admission 10 pesos, free Sun. and holidays).

Getting There: Sayil lies 9km past Kabah off Rte. 261 on the Sayil-Oxkutzcab road and 5km past Xlapak. The only public transportation to the site is the **Autotransportes del Sur "Ruta Puuc" bus** (see p. 503). Buses do run, however, from Mérida to Kabah (p. 501), 10km away on the main highway. Some travelers hitch from Kabah to Sayil; *Let's Go* does not recommend hitchhiking as a safe means of travel.

XLAPAK

Nowhere is the fear of drought so apparent as in the ruined palace of Xlapak (shla-PAK), where the rain god Chac still reigns supreme. The western and eastern sides of the buildings are built in contrasting styles, evidence of changing Mayan architectural tastes, but aside from the remarkable crowd of hook-nosed faces peering out from the surface of the partially restored edifice, Xlapak is less interesting than other sights along La Ruta Puuc.

Getting There: Xlapak lies 5km from Sayil and just past Labná on the Ruta Puuc Sayil-Oxkutzcab road. Xlapak can be reached via the **"Ruta Puuc" bus** (see p. 503). Biking from nearby towns is also an option (site open daily 8am-5pm; admission 7 pesos, free Sun.).

LABNÁ

Labná's buildings were constructed towards the end of the late-Classic period (600-900 CE), when the Puuc cities were connected by a *sacbé* (white road). Today, a short reconstructed section of the *sacbé* runs between Labná's two most impressive sights: the palace and the stone arch. When the Yucatán flooded, the raised *sacbé* allowed the Mayans to pass from one city to another. However, more common than floods were droughts. To weather parched conditions, the Maya constructed huge *chultunes* (catch basins), many of which are found at Labná. The *chultunes* collected both water (up to 8000 gallons in each) and the bodies of peasants who couldn't afford to be buried.

Labná's **palace** is on the northern side of the site, to the left as you enter. While the construction of this building occupied the Maya for several centuries, the edifice was never actually completed. Labná's palace is reminiscent of the one at Sayil insofar as both boast an exceptionally ornate second-floor façade. Nearby mosaics depict figures in palm huts, reminding present-day visitors that the stone palaces once housed only the privileged few. Now, they house scores of chipper birds.

Labná is famed for its picturesque **stone arch,** 3m wide and 6m high. Its western façade is intricately decorated in a trellis pattern, while the eastern side remains more bland. Previously thought to have been the entrance to another temple, archaeologists now believe that the arch served as a ceremonial point of entry for victorious warriors returning from the battlefield.

Beyond the arch, on the unrestored base of a pyramid, stands the **observatory,** also known as **El Mirador** (the lookout). Its notable façade rises over the box-like structure and bears sculptures attached by tenons and dowels. The terracing around the temple contained many *chultunes.* The top of the observatory affords a view of the entire site; keep your eyes peeled for falcons' nests (site open daily 8am-5pm; admission 10 pesos, free Sun.).

Getting There: The final destination on the "Ruta Puuc" bus, Labná lies 42km east of Uxmal, 4km beyond Xlapak, and 22km before Las Grutas (see p. 503).

GRUTAS DE LOLTÚN

The Grutas de Loltún are 58km east of Uxmal on the Sayil-Oxkutzcab road. Below a dense jungle of mahogany and *ceiba,* 1.5km of enormous caverns wind through the rock. The ancient Maya first settled this area in order to take advantage of the Grutas' water and clay. Hundreds of years later, Mayan *campesinos* returned to the caves seeking refuge from the Caste War (1847-1848). Important caverns include the **Room of the 37 Inscriptions,** which includes many still-visible markings (i.e., handprints), and the **Na Cab** (House of the Bees), where you can see the *ka'ob* (grindstones) left by the Maya. Ancient inhabitants broke off the stalactite tips in the **Gallery of Fallen Rocks** to use as spears and arrows. In the **Gallery of the Five Chultunes,** a sculpted jaguar head drips water into cisterns while a huge warrior and eagle look on. The **Cathedral** is a palatial room that once hosted Mayan feasts and assemblies. The shadowy silhouette above the entrance is popularly believed to represent the Virgin of Guadalupe. Several caves contain partially hollow stalactites and columns—thump one with the heel of your hand and listen to the soft booming sound *("Loltún...Loltún...")* reverberate throughout the cave system. Archaeologists speculate that the Maya used these formations as a musical means of underground communication.

Entrance to Loltún is only allowed when a guide leads a tour through the caves (9:30, 11am, 12:30, 2, and 3pm). Guides speak Spanish and fluent gibberish with the odd mangled English word thrown in. Bear in mind the exorbitant rates charged by above-ground guides when leaving a tip for the free guide service (admission 22 pesos, 7 pesos Sun.). As you exit the caves (0.5km from the entrance), you'll stumble upon the conveniently located **Restaurant El Huinoc de Loltún,** which serves up a good range of local dishes for about 15-20 pesos.

Getting There: To get to Loltún, catch a bus as far as Muna or Ticul, hop in a *combi* headed for Oxkutzcab, then follow signs to *Centro.* Passing the market on your left, walk two blocks, turn right at the sign for Ruta Puuc, then pray for deliverance—Las Grutas are 7km down the road. A pick-up truck in Oxkutzcab's *zócalo* may be willing to make the trip, though it will cost you at least 20 pesos.

■ Mérida

Built atop the ruins of the Mayan capital of T'ho, modern Mérida is haunted by its pre-Hispanic history—the stones of the city's fortress-like cathedral even bear traces of the Mayan temples from which they were stripped. The Maya called this site "place of the fifth point," to indicate that it was the center of the universe, the spot between the four points of north, south, east, and west. Today, Mérida (pop. 1.5 million) isn't the center of the universe, but it's certainly the center of Yucatán—it's the state's capital and key commercial center. Panama hats, made from the leaves of the *jipijapa* plant and the *guano* palm, come from Becal in the neighboring state of Campeche, hammocks arrive from nearby Tixcocób, and *henequén* is trucked to Mérida from all over Yucatán before being exported as hemp.

Of late, Mérida has become a magnet for immigrants from around the world. *Meri-deños* of recent Lebanese and Syrian descent have made their presence felt in the city, and a small French community is responsible for the Paseo Montejo, Mérida's version of the Champs-Elysées. Mérida is also a big destination for jet-setting tourists who arrive by the plane-load and spend their days shopping and their nights whispering sweet nothings in music-filled parks. Perhaps the tourists are lured by Mérida's anomalous charm—while it is the largest city on the Yucatán Peninsula, it has yet to succumb to big city indifference. Street cleaners struggle to maintain its reputation as "The White City," intimate conversations swirl about the *zócalo,* and every Sunday promenading families come out to enjoy *Mérida en domingo.*

ORIENTATION

Rte. 180 runs from Cancún (322km) and Valladolid (168km) to the east, becoming **Calle 65,** which passes through the busiest part of town, one block south of the *zócalo.* Those approaching on Rte. 180 from Campeche, 153km to the southwest, end up on **Avenida Itzáes** (also called **Avenida de la Paz**), which runs north-south, or on Calle 81, which feeds into the north-south Calle 70. Both intersect Calle 59, the best route to the center of town, running east to a point one block north of the *zócalo.* **Paseo Montejo** begins at Calle 47, running north as Rte. 261. The *zócalo* fills one city block, bordered by Calle 61 to the north, Calle 62 to the west, Calle 63 to the south, and Calle 60 to the east. To reach the *zócalo* from the **second-class bus terminal,** head east to Calle 62, walk three blocks, and turn left (north); the *zócalo* is three blocks ahead. Alternatively, take a taxi (10 pesos). From the **train station,** take a taxi (10 pesos), catch the "Seguro Social" bus, or walk six blocks west on Calle 55 and three blocks south on Calle 60.

Mérida's gridded one-way streets have numbers instead of names. Using the streets which border the *zócalo* as rough directional axes, numbers greater than 60 usually lie west or south, smaller than 60 north or east. Addresses in Mérida are given using an "x" to separate the main street from the cross streets and "y" ("and" in Spanish) to separate the two cross streets if the address falls in the middle of the block. Thus "54 #509 x 61 y 63" reads "Calle 54 #509, between Calles 61 and 63."

Mérida's **municipal buses** (*camiones*) meander along idiosyncratic routes. Precise information is available at the tourist information office, but the city is small enough so that a bus headed in the right direction will usually drop you off within a few blocks of your desired location. Locals and tourists tend to catch buses at their boarding points, usually in the center, a few blocks from the *zócalo.* City buses run daily from 5am-11pm (1.50 pesos). **Taxis** do not roam the streets soliciting riders; it is necessary to phone or to go to one of the *sitios* (stands) along Paseo de Montejo, at the airport, and at the *zócalo.* Expect to pay at least 10-15 pesos for a trip within the *centro.* **Taxi-colectivos,** on the other hand, charge only 1.25 pesos for any destination in the city; dropoffs are on a first-come, first-serve basis.

PRACTICAL INFORMATION

Tourist Information: Central Office, Calle 60 x 57 y 59 (tel. 24-92-90), in the Teatro Peón Contreras. Distributes *Yucatán Today,* a monthly guide listing practical information and local events (free). Additional offices at the airport (tel. 46-13-00) and at the second-class bus station, opposite the ADO information window. All offices open daily 8am-8pm.

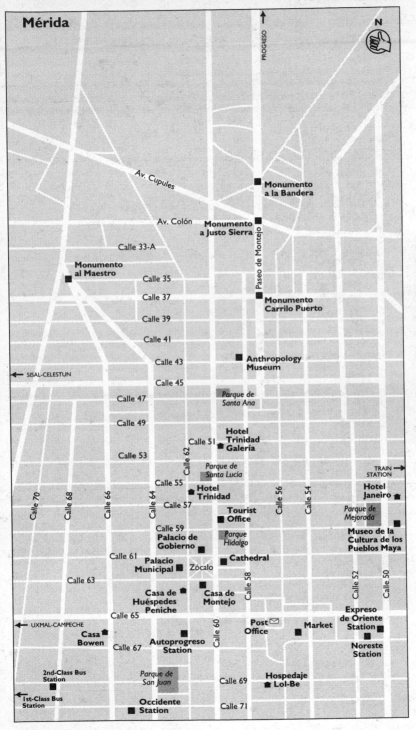

Mérida

PROGRESO

N

Av. Cupules

■ Monumento
a la Bandera

Av. Colón

Monumento ■
a Justo Sierra

Paseo de Montejo

Calle 33-A

Monumento
al Maestro ■

Calle 35

Calle 37

■ Monumento
Carrillo Puerto

Calle 39

Calle 41

Calle 43

Anthropology ■
Museum

Calle 45

◄ SISAL-CELESTUN

Calle 47

Parque de
Santa Ana

Calle 49

Hotel
Trinidad
Galería

Calle 53

Calle 51

Calle 62

TRAIN ►
STATION

Calle 55

Parque de
Santa Lucía

Hotel
Janeiro

Calle 70

Calle 68

Calle 66

Calle 64

Hotel
Trinidad

Calle 56

Calle 54

Parque de
Mejorada

Calle 57

Tourist
Office

Calle 59

Palacio de
Gobierno

Parque
Hidalgo

Museo de la
Cultura de los
Pueblos Maya

Calle 61

Palacio
Municipal

Zócalo

Cathedral

Calle 63

Calle 58

Calle 52

Calle 50

Casa de
Huéspedes
Peniche

Casa de
Montejo

◄ UXMAL-CAMPECHE

Calle 65

Expreso
de Oriente
Station

Casa
Bowen

Post
Office

Market

Calle 60

Calle 67

Autoprogreso
Station

Noreste
Station

2nd-Class Bus
Station

Parque de
San Juan

Calle 69

Hospedaje
Lol-Be

◄ 1st-Class Bus
Station

Occidente
Station

Calle 71

Telephones: LADATELs are the cheapest way to call home; buy a phone card at the stand in the Palacio del Gobierno on the *zócalo*. Otherwise, you'll be left at the *casetas'* mercy.

Telegrams and fax, (tel. 28-23-69; fax 24-26-19), in the same building as the main post office. Entrance around the corner on Calle 56A. Open Mon.- Fri. 8am-7pm.

Travel Agencies: Yucatán Trails, Calle 62 #482 x 57 y 59 (tel. 28-25-82 or 28-59-13, toll-free inside Mexico 91-800-2-02-85; fax 24-19-28). Canadian owner Denis Lafoy is a genial source of information on Mérida and the Yucatán. Arranges cheap all-inclusive daytrips to Ruta Puuc sites (prices vary). Open Mon.-Fri. 8am-2pm and 4-7pm, Sat. 8am-1pm.

Consulates: U.S., Paseo de Montejo 453 (tel. 25-50-11 or 25-55-54), at Av. Colón. Unless you have an emergency, try to go on Thurs. or Fri. Open Mon.-Fri. 7am-1pm. **U.K.,** Calle 58 #498 x 53 (tel. 28-61-52; fax 28-39-62 or 28-61-52). Open Mon.-Fri. 9am-1pm.

Currency Exchange: Banamex (tel. 24-10-11 or 24-11-32), in Casa de Montejo on the *zócalo*. 24-hr. **ATM.** Open Mon.-Fri. 9am-5pm.

American Express, Paseo de Montejo 494 #106 x 43 y 45 (tel. 28-42-22 or 28-43-73; fax 24-42-57). English spoken. Open Mon.-Fri. 9am-2pm and 4-6pm, Sat. 9am-1pm. Money exchange desk closes 1hr. early.

Airport: 7km southwest on Rte. 180. Bus #79, labeled "Airport," runs between the terminals and a midtown stop at the corner of Calles 67 and 60 (every 20min. 5am-9pm, ½-hr., 80 pesos); a taxi charges 30 pesos for that trip. Post office, telegrams, long distance telephone, and car rental. **Aeroméxico,** Paseo Montejo 460 x 35 y 37 (tel. 27-90-00, at airport 46-13-05). **Mexicana,** Calle 58 #500 (tel. 24-66-33, at airport 46-13-32). **Aerocaribe,** Paseo Montejo 500-B x 47 (tel. 23-00-02, at airport 46-13-61). **Aviateca** (tel. 24-43-54, at airport 46-12-96) Calle 58 x 45 y 43. Also at Calle 58 x 49 y 51.

Buses: Only partial listings are given. Most bus lines operate out of the main **second-class** terminal, **Unión de Camioneros,** Calle 69 #544 x 68 y 70, three blocks west and three blocks south of the *zócalo*. **Autotransportes de Oriente (ADO)** (tel. 23-22-87), sends buses to Cancún (every hr. 4:30am-midnight, 6hr., 48 pesos), Chichén Itzá (every hr. 4am-midnight, 2hr., 18 pesos), Chiquilá (12:30am, 6hr., 47 pesos), Playa del Carmen (5 per day, 7hr., 58 pesos), Tizimín (4pm, 3½hr., 25 pesos), and Valladolid (every hr. 4am-midnight, 3hr., 24 pesos). **Autotransportes del Sur (ATS)** goes to Campeche (6 per day, 3hr., 17 pesos), Escárcega (10 per day, 5½hr., 57 pesos), Palenque (6pm and 11:30pm, 14hr., 96 pesos), San Cristóbal de las Casas (6am, 14hr., 124 pesos), and Uxmal (6 per day, 1½hr., 11 pesos). The **first-class** terminal is around the corner, on Calle 70 between 69 and 71. **ATS** provides a special **Ruta Puuc** bus (8am, 31 pesos, admission to sites not included) which visits the archaeological sites of Uxmal, Kabah, Sayil, Xlapak, and Labná, returning around 2:30pm. **Línea Dorada** serves Chetumal (4 per day, 6hr., 79 pesos) and Ticul (7:30am, 1½hr., 17 pesos). **Premier** goes to Tulum (6 per day, 6hr., 57 pesos), Cobá (6 per day, 3hr., 48 pesos), Playa del Carmen (8 per day, 5hr., 70 pesos), Chichén Itzá (8:45 and 9:30am, 2hr., 24 pesos), and Valladolid (5 per day, 2½hr., 32 pesos). **Autobuses de Occidente,** to almost anywhere on the peninsula and Córdoba (3 per day, 17hr., 253 pesos), Mexico City (4 per day, 19hr., 300 pesos), Palenque (8am and 10pm, 8hr., 111pesos), Puebla (9:45pm, 20hr., 296 pesos), Veracruz (9pm, 15hr., 224 pesos), and Villahermosa (9 daily, 9hr., 127 pesos). **Expreso** to Cancún (12 per day, 4hr., 63 pesos) and more. The 7:15pm **Maya de Oro** or the 7:30am **San Cristóbal** bus can take you to Campeche (2½hr., 38 pesos), Palenque (6½hr., 107 pesos), Ocosingo (8½hr., 137 pesos), San Cristóbal de las Casas (12½hr., 149 pesos), and Tuxtla Gutiérrez (16hr., 167 pesos).

Trains: Ferrocarriles Nacionales de México (tel. 23-59-44 or 23-59-66), on Calle 55 x 46 y 48, northeast of the *zócalo*. Cheap and very, very slow. Buy tickets an hour before departure or on board. Or better yet, take the bus.

Taxis: Palacio Municipal, on the northwest corner of the *zócalo* (tel. 28-56-65), **Mercado Municipal** (tel. 23-11-35) at Calles 56 and 65, in **Parque de la Maternidad** (tel. 28-53-22) at Teatro Peón Contreras, and dozens of other *sitios* are on call 24hr. It's much cheaper to use the *camiones* (municipal buses).

Car Rentals: México Rent-a-Car, Calle 60 #495 or Calle 62 #483-A x 57 y 59 (tel. 27-49-16). VW Beetles, including insurance and unlimited *kilometraje*, for 130 pesos a day (5% surcharge with credit card). Open Mon.-Sat. 8am-12:30pm and 6-8pm, Sun. 8am-12:30pm.

Bookstore: Dante (tel. 24-95-22), in Teatro Peón Contreras, Calle 60 at 57. Guidebooks, maps, and magazines in English, French, and Spanish. Open Mon.-Fri. 8am-9:30pm, Sat. 8am-2pm and 5-9pm, Sun. 10am-2pm and 4-8pm.

Laundromat: La Fe, Calle 61 #518 x 62 y 64 (tel. 24-45-31), near the *zócalo*. 13 pesos per 3kg. Open Mon.-Fri. 8am-7pm, Sat. 8am-4pm.

Market: Four square blocks of covered stalls and street vendors extend south of Calle 65 and east of Calle 58. Open dawn-dusk. **Supermarket: San Francisco de Asís,** Calle 65 x 50 y 52 (tel. 24-33-08), across from the market in a huge gray building. Open daily 7am-9pm.

Red Cross: Calle 68 #533 x 65 y 67 (tel. 24-77-74). 24-hr. emergency and ambulance services (tel. 24-67-64). Some English spoken.

Pharmacy: Farmacia Canto, Calle 60 #513 x 63 y 65 (tel. 28-50-27). Open 24hr.

Hospital: Centro Médico de las Américas, Calle 54 #365 (tel. 26-21-11 or 26-26-19), at Calle 33A. 24-hr. service, including ambulance. **Clínica de Mérida** (tel. 25-41-00), on Av. Itzáes x 25 y 27. English spoken in both.

Police: (tel. 25-25-55 or 25-73-98), on Av. Reforma (Calle 72) x 39 y 4, accessible with the "Reforma" bus. Some English spoken.

Post Office: (tel. 24-35-90), on Calle 65 x 56 y 56A, 3 blocks from the *zócalo* in the Palacio Federal. Open Mon.-Fri. 7am-7pm, Sat. 9am-1pm. Branches at Calle 58 x 49 y 51, at the airport, and at the main bus station. **Postal Code:** 97000.

Telephone Code: 99.

ACCOMMODATIONS

Many of Mérida's budget accommodations are set in splendid colonial mansions. Though they may have lost the bustling servants and a coat or two of fresh paint, they nonetheless retain much of the original splendor. It is not every day that a few pesos will garner a room with tall ceilings, sun bleached frescoes, and stained glass.

Casa Bowen, Calle 66 #521-B x 65 y 67 (tel. 24-07-28 or 28-61-09), halfway between the main bus station and the *zócalo*. Feel like an elegant statesperson as you parade, dirty backpack in tow, up the grand staircase to your room overlooking a softly calling garden. Listen to the lilt of international languages from your large room with attractive bedspreads and curtains. Singles 45 pesos. Doubles 50 pesos, with two beds 55 pesos. Rooms with kitchenette and fridge 65 pesos, with A/C 90 pesos. Squeeze in an extra person for 15 pesos.

Hotel Montejo Calle 57 #507 x 62 y 64 (tel. 28-02-77 or 28-03-90), two blocks north and one block east of the *zócalo*. Beautiful colonial mansion with rooms to match. Tall, wood beamed ceilings. Bathrooms in excellent condition. Singles 60 pesos. Doubles 65 pesos. Triples 90 pesos. Add 10 pesos for A/C and 15 pesos for an extra person.

Hotel Macuy Calle 57 #481 x 56 y 58 (tel. 28-51-93; fax 23-78-01). Two blocks north and two blocks east of the *zócalo*. Sky-blue rooms seem to have a bit of sun in every corner. Talk to the parrot, tinker on the piano, or read from a selection of good books. Breakfast of milk, juice, and yogurt included. Singles 60 pesos. Doubles 70 pesos. Triples 80 pesos.

Hotel Trinidad Galería, Calle 60 #456 (tel. 23-24-63; fax 24-23-19), at Calle 51. If you get lost in this sprawling complex, try to make it to the pool; it's sure to calm your spirits. Or try the gallery of local art. Oh yeah, the rooms are sure to be unique and clean. Parking available. Singles 80 peso. Doubles 90 pesos. Larger rooms about 30 pesos more. No A/C. 20% surcharge if you pay by credit card.

Hotel Trinidad Calle 62 #464 x 55 y 57 (tel. 23-20-33). The scattered manifestation of one person's very um, strange taste in, um, art nevertheless adds to the charm of this restored colonial mansion. Guests have access to the pool at the nearby Hotel Trinidad Galería. Singles 45-75 pesos. Doubles 50-80 pesos. Add 10 pesos for private bath. 15 pesos per additional person.

Hotel Janeiro, Calle 57 #435 x 48 y 50 (tel. 23-36-02 or 23-83-73), a hike from the bus station. Though not a mansion, nor charming in the "dahr-ling" sense, it is modern, practical, and very affordable. Peaceful, shallow pool and sun deck. Collection of English paperbacks and guidebooks. Parking available. Singles and doubles with fans 50 pesos. Triples 70 pesos. Add 10 pesos for A/C.

FOOD

Mérida's inventive specialties make good use of the fruits and grains that flourish in Yucatán's hot, humid climate. Try *sopa de lima* (frothy lime soup with chicken and tortilla bits), *pollo pibil* (chicken with herbs baked in banana leaves), *poc-chuc* (pork steak with onions doused in sour orange juice), *papadzules* (chopped hard-boiled eggs wrapped in corn tortillas served with pumpkin sauce), and the dish that raises eyebrows, *huevos motuleños* (refried beans, fried egg, chopped ham, and cheese on a tortilla garnished with tomato sauce, peas, and fried banana). Those who've been burned one too many times by over-seasoned *chiles* can rest assured—in Mérida, the local scorcher, *chile habanero,* does not lurk within dishes but instead waits patiently in a garnish bowl.

The cheapest food in town awaits at the **market,** particularly on the second floor of the restaurant complex on Calle 56 at Calle 67. *Yucateco* dishes go for 5-10 pesos (open Mon.-Sat. 8am-8pm, Sun. 8am-5pm).

Restaurante Amaro, Calle 59 #507 x 60 y 62 (tel. 28-24-51). Excellent meals, both vegetarian and meaty, served in the quiet courtyard of the house where patriot Andrés Quintana Roo grew up. Attentive yet patient service always a plus. Delicate fruit salads 12-14 pesos. Delicious vegetable soup 10 pesos. *Chile relleno* (stuffed green pepper) 27 pesos. Open daily 8am-11pm.

Restaurante y Café Express (tel. 28-16-91), on Calle 60 x 59 y 61, overlooking Parque Hidalgo. Enjoy an open view of the shady park in an atmosphere that exemplifies the sophistication of modern-day Mérida. Well priced breakfast (12 pesos) and *comidas típicas* (23-30 pesos). Open daily 7am-11pm.

El Louvre, Calle 62 #499-D (tel. 25-50-73), on the northwest corner of the *zócalo.* A popular hangout with an unbeatable location, great sandwiches (10-15 pesos), and snappy waiters in bowties. Their name evades us. The menu confidently announces: "Broken English spoken perfectly"—judge for yourself. Open 24hr.

Los Almendros and Los Gran Almendros, Calle 50 #493 x 57 y 59 (tel. 28-54-59), on Parquet Mejorada, and at Calle 57 #468 x 50 y 52 (tel. 23-81-35). Trendy, touristy, but still serving heaping portions of great food. *Pollo pibil* just 21 pesos; *poc-chuc,* the house specialty, 38 pesos. Los Almendros open daily 10am-11pm. Less touristy Gran Almendros open daily 1-5pm.

El Tucho, Calle 60 #482 x 55 y 57 (tel. 24-23-23). A loud and popular restaurant/afternoon cabaret. While performers entertain you, troupes of waiters ferry trays of free *botanas* (hors d'œuvres) between customers. As long as you keep drinking, the food keeps on comin'. Real meals 25 pesos. Open daily 11:30am-9:30pm.

Restaurant Nic-Te-Xa (tel. 23-07-84), Calle 61, on the *zócalo.* Delicious and filling *comida corrida* with *sopa de lima, pollo pibil* with beans and tortillas, and coffee all for just 20 pesos. Open daily 7am-midnight.

SIGHTS

From cathedral towers outlined against a perilously blue sky to couples getting up close and personal in the *confidenciales,* there is always something to see in Mérida's *zócalo.* The *zócalo* is busiest on Sundays, when street vendors cram in dozens of stalls, Yucatecan folk dancers perform in front of the Palacio Municipal, and half the city comes out to people-watch.

While almost all of Mérida's larger historic buildings are within easy walking distance of the *zócalo,* there's no reason to restrict oneself to the downtown area. Verdant parks and fading colonial mansions reward the ambulatory traveler. Public transportation back to *el centro* is easily caught from any main thoroughfare.

The twin towers of the yellow **cathedral** loom over the eastern side of the *zócalo*. The fortress-like presence of the cathedral's Corinthian doors and stark, windowless façade recall the centuries of struggle between Mayans and missionaries. The sturdy stone blocks from which the cathedral was built were stolen from the Mayan temples of T'ho. Built in the austere Herrericano style, the cathedral features rose-colored arched domes and a giant blistering Christ, the second largest crucifix in the world (supposedly open daily 6am-6pm).

On the northern edge of the *zócalo* stands the **Palacio de Gobierno.** Built between 1883 and 1892, it fuses two architectural styles—Tuscan (main floor) and Dorian (upper floor). Inside, wonderful, gigantic murals narrate the strife-filled history of the Yucatán peninsula. The stairway painting illustrates the Mayan belief that humanity comes from maize; an image of the Popol Vuh, the central document of Mayan culture, dominates the next layout (open daily 8am-10pm).

Concerts and classes in *jarana,* the Yucatecan colonial dance, take place under the sheltering balcony of the **Palacio Municipal,** across the *zócalo* from the cathedral. A jail until the 1700s, the building was rebuilt in the colonial style in 1928 (open Mon.-Sat. 8am-8pm).

On the southern side of the *zócalo,* the **Casa de Montejo,** the oldest colonial structure in Mérida, was constructed in 1549 by order of city founder Francisco de Montejo. Built with stones from the Mayan temple T'ho, the carved façade is a boastful depiction of the Spanish conquest. While the expressions on the faces of the soldiers have faded, the anguish of the four Mayan heads on which they stand remains clear. Ironically, the carving follows the Toltec tradition of representing warriors standing on the heads of their conquests. Look for the coats of arms of the King of Spain and of the Montejo family (open Mon.-Fri. 9am-5pm).

Mérida's most impressive museum, the **Museo de Antropología e Historia,** is housed in a magnificent Italian Renaissance-style building on the corner of Paseo Montejo and Calle 43. Archaeological finds on display illustrate the *indígena* history of the Yucatán, and extensive anthropological information on geology, horticulture, linguistic history, demography, religion, and daily life accompanies the artifacts. Grimace at the holes drilled in teeth to be worn as jewelry, stare in awe at the head-flattening devices applied to the craniums of upper-class infants, and envision the quivering heart placed for sacrifice on the *chac mool* (Maya for red fingernails) altar. Mayan murals from minor sites are also housed here, as are prehistoric mammoth tusks and a couple of bones from the caves at Loltún. The shop downstairs sells comprehensive English-language guidebooks for much less than the price charged at the ruins themselves; pick one up here (museum and shop open Mon.-Sat. 8am-8pm, Sun. 8am-2pm; admission 14 pesos, free Sun.).

Celebrating the indigenous crafts and artisans of Mexico, **Museo de la Cultura de los Pueblos Maya** is located six blocks east of the *zócalo* on Calle 59, between Calles 48 and 50, behind the Convento de la Mejorada. The hall upstairs displays a wide array of handiwork, from costumes and masks to pottery, weavings, and *huipile* embroidery. The room of sculpted skeletons offers a taste of the morbid sense of humor that accompanies the festival "Día de los Muertos" (Day of the Dead; open Tues.-Sat. 8am-8pm, Sun. 9am-2pm; free).

On the corner of Calle 59 and Av. Itzáes (Calle 86) lies the **Centenary Park and Zoo.** Any westbound *combí* (1.25 pesos) can drop you off by the PEMEX station on Calle 59, one block east of Itzáes. To reach the zoo, take a five-minute southeasterly stroll through the park and under the snail-paced chairlift. The zoo is home to some truly bored lions, tigers, and bears, as well as preening peacocks, flamingos, antelope, hippos, Aztec dogs, and jaguars. A miniature train full of shrieking schoolchildren whizzes through periodically, but fails to rouse the catatonic creatures. (Park open Tues.-Sun. 6am-6pm. Zoo open Tues.-Sun. 8am-5pm. Admission for both free.)

The **Museo de Historia Natural,** with its main entrance on Calle 59 at Calle 84, one block east of Itzáes, also has a back entrance accessible from the park. Housed in a 19th-century *hacienda*, this small but ambitious collection is concerned with the history of life from the origin of the universe through the emergence of species (open Tues.-Sun. 9am-4pm; admission 10 pesos, free Sun.).

Decaying French-style mansions and local and international boutiques line the **Paseo Montejo;** it would make an elegant Elysian boulevard if the traffic would slow down. Promenades along the Paseo's broad pink sidewalks culminate in the **Monumento a la Patria.** In faux-Mayan style, the stone monument, built in 1956, depicts major figures of Mexican history. For a tantalizing detour from the Paseo, veer left (southwest) onto **Avenida Colón,** a street flanked by closely grouped historic mansions in varying stages of decay; beware the slobbering Rottweilers that guard the houses. A 30-minute walk down Avenida Colón is the **Parque de las Américas,** Calle 20 at Colón, named for its stone monuments to Central and South American states. Leafy topiary sculptures of various animals stand guard.

Mérida takes special pride in the **Teatro Peón Contreras,** on the corner of Calles 60 and 57. The Italian Renaissance-style building is notable for its rococo interior and its history—starting in 1624, it served as a university for nearly two centuries. The **Universidad Autónoma de Yucatán,** on Calle 57 between Calles 60 and 62, is a Hispano-Moorish complex built in 1938. The ground floor of the complex contains a gallery exhibiting works by local artists and a screening room for films by classic directors (*galería* and *videosala* open Mon.-Fri. 9am-1pm and 4-8pm, Sat. 4-9pm, Sun. 10am-2pm; free).

The many churches, statues, and pocket-sized parks scattered throughout Mérida's *centro* also invite exploration. Among the most noteworthy are the Franciscan **Convento de la Mejorada,** on Calle 59, between Calles 48 and 50; the old **Arco** behind the park; the **Iglesia Santiago,** on Calles 59 and 72, one of the oldest churches in Mexico; and the **Iglesia de San Juan de Dios,** located on Calle 64, between Calles 67 and 71, marking the southern limit of the *centro.*

Nowhere else in the Yucatán is there shopping as can be found in Mérida. And nowhere else in Mérida is there shopping to be found as that of the **mercado.** The main market occupies the block southwest of the Palacio Federal, spreading outward from the corner of Calles 65 and 58. Behind the *palacio,* shops, awnings, and tin-roofed shacks ramble for a good many blocks both east and west. The only border is busy Calle 65 to the north, but even there stands spill over onto the other side of the street and around the small square across from the Palacio Federal. The second-floor "artisans' market," part of a modern building behind and to the right of the Palacio Federal, sells mainly regional clothing: white *huipiles* with colorful embroidery skirting the neckline and hem go for 45-60 pesos; *rebozos* (woven shawls) cost 10-15 pesos; and *guayaberas* (Yucatec men's short-sleeve shirts with distinctive vertical columns of double stitching) fall between 50 and 70 pesos. Bargaining is expected, but those who get carried away are looked upon as scornful of the artisans. Cheaper goods such as *huaraches* (hand-made leather sandals) are sold on the first floor of the market. Be sure to give them a try or two for good measure, as the sandals are sometimes hastily made. Although jewelry stores line the streets and glut the market, the best prices are at the smaller *prestas* on the streets, in the market, or at the *zócalo* every Sunday.

ENTERTAINMENT

Mérida's municipal government provides a never-ending series of free musical and dance events: outdoor concerts with traditional Yucatec dancing and dress (Mon. 9pm in front of the Palacio Municipal on the main plaza); 1940s big band music (Tues. 9pm in Santiago Park on the corner of Calles 59 and 72); performances by the university's wonderful **Ballet Folklórico** (Tues. 9pm at the Teatro Peón Contreras, on the corner of Calles 60 and 57, 25 pesos); **"The Serenade,"** which features Yucatec dress, dance and music (Thurs. on the corner of Calles 60 and 55, Fri. at Calles 60 and 57, both 9pm); and **Mérida en Domingo,** when Calle 60 closes to traffic and Hidalgo and Santa Lucía parks, as well as the *zócalo,* become crowded with vendors, food stalls, and live music (all day Sun.).

When in Mérida, do as *merideños* do—keep your eyes peeled for announcements of upcoming events glued to walls all over town. The **Teatro Peón Contreras** (tel. 23 73 54) hosts special events and frequent concerts. Just around the corner on the Parque de la Modernidad, an excellent acoustic guitar trio plays mellow tunes at the **Café Peón Contreras** (every night 8pm-midnight). Avoid the café's expensive food—you can hear the music for free from one of the park benches.

For a less high-brow evening, settle in for a **beer.** Mérida has many good local beers, such as the heavenly **Montejo León**, hard to find in other parts of the country. Denis Lafoy of Yucatán Trails travel agency organizes an informal get-together with beer and free food on the first Friday of every month—inquire for further details (see p. 506). At local establishments, buy a few and you'll get free *botanas* (mini-appetizers). Enjoy comedians and live *marimba* music at **Pancho's** (tel. 23-09-42), Calle 59 x 60 y 62, or **El Tucho** (see p. 508). It is not uncommon for guitar duos to waltz into restaurants near the *zócalo* and play for a nominal fee. Another option is **Tulipanes,** Calle 42 #462-A x 45 y 47; get ready for non-stop music, *yucateco* dance, and a chilling re-enactment of a Mayan sacrifice. For air-conditioned, panchromatic discos, you'll need to stray far from the center and pay 15 pesos for a taxi. **Bim Bom Bao** (tel. 44-42-90), at Calles 4 and 5, is where the rich and the hip hang out. **Kalia,** at calle 22 #282 (tel. 44-42-35) by Calle 37, is where the young and sophisticated dance. The gay bar/disco **Kabuki's** (tel. 23-33-13), on Calle 84, between Calle 61 and 65, rocks into the wee hours Thursday through Saturday.

■ Near Mérida

DZIBILCHALTÚN

Saying the name is half the fun. Situated 20km north of Mérida en route to the Gulf coast, Dzibilchaltún (dzib-ill-shahl-TOON, Place Where There Is Writing on Flat Stones) sprawls over 60 square kilometers of jungle brush. The site flourished as a ceremonial and administrative center from approximately 2000 BCE until the Conquest. While its influence on Mayan culture is of great interest to archaeologists and historians, the excavated site now open to tourists is neither as impressive nor as accessible as the other ruins near Mérida.

The site's **museum**, at the end of the covered walkway, to the left of the entrance just beyond the cactus garden, merits a quick visit. Note the huge, fabulously preserved grimace of Chac (the hook-nosed Maya rain god) brought here from Kabah.

From the museum, follow the path to sacbé No. 1 and turn left. Farther along this road, Dzibilchaltún's showpiece, the fully restored **Temple of the Seven Dolls,** possesses a rare harmony of proportion and style. The seven clay "dolls" discovered here are believed to represent different illnesses or deformities and are now on display in

---

Sleeper

It's hard to leave Mérida without an *hamaca*—hammock vendors are stunningly persistent, their colorful fares beautifully woven. Sure, the hammocks make a nice gift and pack one hell of a nap, but more importantly, *buying a hammock stops those vendors*. Because they know. They can see it in your eyes if you own a hammock. So here's a few tips: (1) a quality hammock is *bien tupida* (tightly woven) so that holes don't readily appear and (2) it is *ancha* (wide), in fact so wide that you can lie across it with room to spare. Good materials include cotton, nylon, or *henequén* (also known as sisal, the port from which it was traditionally shipped), though cotton hammocks tend to be of lesser quality. Expect to pay at least 100 pesos for a medium-sized hammock of good quality. Whatever you end up buying, it would be a good idea to at least see it unfolded and lie in it if at all possible. You can do both of these in peace at **El Aguacate,** Calle 58 #604 (tel. 28-64-29), at Calle 73, where, among their wide selection of colors, sizes, and materials, you are sure to find something to ward off those street vendors.

the museum. The temple also furnishes further proof of the genius of the Maya. Shortly after sunrise, a huge shadow mask of the rain god Chac is said to appear as the sun's rays pierce the temple. The temple is so carefully aligned that it can be used to verify the winter and summer solstices. At 5:30pm on June 21, the sun threads through the tiny space between the door jambs on the north side; at 7:30am on December 21 the phenomenon is repeated on the south side.

The other end of sacbé No. 1 leads to a quadrangle, in the center of which stands a paradigm of 400 years of history: a Mayan temple converted into a chapel. Just beyond the eastern edge of the quadrangle is the **Cenote Xlacah,** reminiscent of Quintana Roo's oval, saltwater *lagunas.* Xlacah served as a sacrificial well similar to those at Chichén Itzá and as a source of water. Divers have recovered ceremonial artifacts and human bones from the depths of the 44m-deep *cenote.* While the *cenote* is not up to the standard set by those in Valladolid, the water invites a non-sacrificial dip among the water lilies and fish. A path to the south leads past a handful of smaller structures to the site's exit. (Site open daily 8am-5pm. Museum open daily 8am-4pm. Admission 22 pesos, free Sun. and for kids under 13. Wheelchair access. Parking 3 pesos.)

Getting There: Getting to the ruins is cake—it's the return trip that might pose problems. Conkal-bound *combis* leave the Parque de San Juan in Mérida approximately every 20 minutes (3 pesos). The *combi* will drop you off at the access road to the ruins, a five-minute walk from the entrance. To get back you'll need to walk back to the Conkal road and pray (like any good Catholic in Mexico) for a *combi* to take you to Rte. 261. Some travelers hitch the 5km to the highway. **Autoprogreso buses** abound on Rte. 261, passing by in both directions every 15 minutes.

CELESTÚN

The idyllic town of Celestún is perfect for a daytrip (or two) from Mérida. The waves are soothing and the breeze refreshing, but the main draw is the **Río Celestún Biosphere Reserve,** home to 230 species of birds. Pelicans, cormorants, and the occasional stork all await the ooohs and aaahs of tourists, but the knockkneed, splendidly pink flamingos hog center-stage.

155km from Mérida, Rte. 281 runs into **Calle 11** in Celestún, on the western shore of the Yucatán. Calle 11 then passes the *zócalo,* **Calle 12** one block later, and hits the shore one block after that (as do all odd number streets). Odd numbers increase to the south, while even numbers decrease moving away from the sand and run parallel to the waves. The *zócalo* is bounded by Calles 11, 13, 10, and 8.

Long distance **phone** calls can be made from **Tlapalería San Luis,** on the Calle 13 side of the *zócalo* or from **Hotel Gutiérrez. Autobuses de Occidente** sends **buses** from a small booth at the corner of calles 8 and 11, at the *zócalo,* to Mérida (14 per day 6am-8pm, 2hr., first-class 14 pesos, second-class 11 pesos). **Farmacia Don San Luis,** Calle 10 #108 (tel. 6-20-02), between Calles 13 and 15 is open daily 8am-11pm. The **health center** (tel. 6-20-46) is on Calle 5, between Calles 8 and 10 (open daily 8am-8pm). The **police** (tel. 6-20-15) stand guard at the Calle 13 side of the *zócalo.* The **post office** is on Calle 11, at the *zócalo,* and shares a building with the **telegram** service (both open Mon.-Fri. 9am-2pm). The **telephone code** is 991.

Accommodations in Celestún are rare but serviceable, and the beach views can't be beaten. All are on **Calle 12. Hotel San Julio,** Calle 12 #93A (tel. in Mérida 23-63-09), offers plain rooms with plainer bathrooms (singles 40 pesos; doubles 50 pesos; triples 60 pesos). **Hotel María del Carmen,** Calle 12 #11 (tel. 6-20-51), has rooms with sea views, balconies, billowing curtains, and immaculate bathrooms (singles 70 pesos; doubles 130 pesos; triples 160 pesos; 10% discount for students). **Hotel Gutiérrez,** Calle 12 #127 (tel. 6-20-41 or 6-20-42), between Calles 13 and 15, has unimaginative blue rooms and matching bathrooms. Not all rooms have a view (all rooms 100 pesos; cram in as many people as you like).

Restaurants line Calle 12, and a few *loncherías* cluster in the *zócalo.* At **Restaurant La Playita,** Calle 12 #99 (tel. 6-20-52), between Calles 9 and 11, pack away a huge steaming plate of sauteed blue crab (*jaiva frita*) with rice and tortillas for just 20 pesos (open daily; schedule changes with the season). The bare interior doesn't take away from the savory seafood at **Flamingo's,** Calle 12, between Calles 9 and 11. A kilo of *pescado frito* goes for 20 pesos (individual orders 10 pesos) and non-alcoholic drinks are a scant 2 pesos (same hours as La Playita). At **Restaurant Celestún,** Calle 12 #101 (tel. 6-20-32), you can dine amid larger (and pinker) than life painted flamingos. Fish fillet costs 25 pesos (open daily 10am-8pm, sometimes 11pm).

The **flamingos** and breathtaking coastline can be viewed in one of two tours offered. The first heads north to **Isla de Pájaros** (Island of Birds), playground for a plethora of winged pals. A stop along the way at a freshwater spring provides welcome relief. The second tour heads south through petrified forests and a tunnel with a watery floor and tree top roof before winding through the abandoned fishing village of **Real de Salinas.** Both tours can be arranged with *lancheros* at the bridge right before the entrance to the town (180 pesos for 1½-2hr.). Depending on the tide, this will accommodate five to eight people. If you want to combine both tours or explore other areas, fishermen can often be coaxed into acting as guides (280 pesos for 3½-4hr.). Hang out on the beach by the *lanchas* to find a ride and a guide.

▨ Progreso

Strategically located on the closest strip of coastline to Mérida, Progreso is a small town in limbo, somewhere between fishing village and commercial center. As the Yucatán's premier commercial fishing port, Progreso has made a small fortune hauling in shrimp, red snapper, octopus, and tuna, and exporting *henequén* (hemp). The town's stunning old mansions attest to the fabulous profits of the lucrative plant. During the summer months, Progreso's proximity to the capital makes it a popular retreat with *merideños,* many of whom make the 33km jaunt northward to enjoy the clean, quiet beaches of the Gulf coast. At other times, the town is remarkably tranquil and tourist-free.

Orientation and Practical Information Calle 19, Progreso's *malecón* (coastal avenue), runs east-west along the beach. Odd-numbered roads run parallel to Malecón, increasing to the south. North-south streets have even numbers and increase to the west. Progreso's *zócalo* is bounded by Calles 78, 80, 31, and 33. To reach the *zócalo* from the **bus station** (tel. 5-30-24), on Calle 29 between Calles 80 and 82, head east on Calle 29 to the end of the block, turn right, and walk two blocks on Calle 80. To reach the beach, follow Calle 80 in the opposite direction.

The often bored, but helpful people in the **tourist office,** Calle 80 #176 (tel. 5-01-04), just past Calle 37, can provide you with a tourist booklet, including a map (open Mon.-Fri. 9am-2pm and 4-7pm, Sat. 9am-noon; some English spoken). **Banamex,** Calle 80 #129 (tel. 5-08-31), is between Calles 27 and 29 (open Mon.-Fri. 9am-1pm). **Long-distance phone calls** can be made from any one of the many TelMex *casetas* found throughout town. The **telegram office** (tel. 5-01-28) is in the same building as the post office (open Mon.-Fri. 8am-6pm, Sat. 9am-noon).

Autoprogreso buses, Calle 62, between Calle 65 and 67, run to Mérida (every 6min. between 5am and 9:45pm, 40min., 4 pesos one-way). *Combis* make the trip in slightly less time for the same price, and leave from Calle 31 on the *zócalo.* **Lavamática Progreso,** Calle 74 #150-A (tel. 5-05-86), between Calles 29 and 31, provides next-day service for 4 pesos per kg (open Mon.-Sat. 8am-1:30pm and 4-7:30pm). The **supermarket San Francisco de Asís** is at Calle 80 #144, between Calles 29 and 31 (open daily 7am-9pm). **Farmacia YZA** is on Calle 78 at Calle 29 (tel. 5-06-84; open 24hr.). 24-hour emergency service is provided by the **Centro Médico Americano** (tel. 5-09-51), at Calles 33 and 82. Some English spoken. The **police station** (tel. 5-00-26) is in the Palacio Municipal on the *zócalo* at Calle 80, between Calles 31 and 33 (supposedly open 24hr.). The **post office** is at Calle 31 #150 (tel. 5-05-65), between Calles 78 and 76, just off the *zócalo* (open Mon.-Fri. 7am-7pm). **Postal Code:** 97320. **Telephone Code:** 993.

Accommodations When not flooded with vacationing city-goers from the south, budget accommodations are as plentiful as shrimp. The **Hotel Progreso,** Calle 78 #142 (tel. 5-00-39), near Calle 29, has colorful rooms with spotless mosaic bathrooms and a breezy feel to boot (singles 60 pesos; doubles 70 pesos; add 30 pesos for A/C, 55 pesos for TV and telephone; 15 pesos per additional person). The **Hotel Miramar,** Calle 27 #124 (tel. 5-05-52), between Calles 72 and 74, offers two options: well kept rooms with bath and skylight or glorified port-a-potties with beds (*sans* the smell). The owner is very amiable (space pod singles 40 pesos; doubles 45 pesos; with two beds 55 pesos; upscale singles 55 pesos; doubles 70 pesos; 15 pesos per extra person; long-term stays cheaper). Clean rooms in ghastly, bright colors are an economical option at the **Posada Juan Carlos,** Calle 74 #148 (tel. 5-10-76), between Calles 29 and 31. Color TV makes up for the cramped bathrooms (singles 40 pesos; doubles 50 pesos; 10 pesos per additional person).

Food Mmmm-mm. Love that fish. And its pretty damn cheap, too. Try the beach end of Calle 80. Fish with a view? Try Avenida Malecón, the main drag along the coast. Unfortunately, some restaurants only open during the summer. **Carabela,** just east of Calle 72 on Av. Malecón, serves up hearty fare and boasts a wide selection of seafood. *Filete empanizado* costs 22 pesos (open daily 7am-midnight). If you like your fish *real* fresh, head to **Pescaría Los Cocos,** on Malecón between Calles 76 and 78, where you can enjoy a freshly caught fish (served whole) for just 12 pesos. At **El Cordobés,** Calle 80 #150 (tel. 5-26-28), you can treat yourself to *pescado en tikinxic,* a slow-cooked fish specialty with *chiles.* Most fish entrees go for 25-30 pesos (open daily 6am-midnight).

Sights Progreso's beaches are decent and fairly clean, but a dip is all you'll get— shallow waters preclude swimming. The beach is packed in July and August, but you'll have the place to yourself the rest of the time. For a more placid spot, head for the beach at **Chelém,** 8km west of town, or the wind-sheltered beach at Yaculpatén, just before Chelém. *Combis* leave for Chelém every 30 minutes from the parking lot outside Supermarket San Francisco on Calle 80 (2 pesos). If he's not too busy, the custodian of **El Faro** (the lighthouse), at Calle 80 near Calle 25, might let you climb the spiral staircase to the top. Step out on the balcony, where you can see the ocean and the kilometers of marshy river that give the city its distinctive briny scent. The 2km *muelle* (pier) clings tenuously to the sandy beach; in the early morning it's a great spot from which to reel in fish.

■ Mérida to Chichén Itzá

The route from Mérida to Chichén Itzá harbors small villages that are quintessential Yucatán. Churches are oversized and blackened by time, *henequén* (hemp) is still harvested, and for many of the inhabitants, Spanish is a second language.

As Rte. 180 heads east from Mérida to Chichén Itzá, it passes the five private *henequén haciendas* of San Pedro, Teya, Ticopó, San Bernardino, and Holactún. Next come the villages of **Tahmek** and **Hoctún** (47km from Mérida). **Izamal** is only 24km northeast of Hoctún, but buses don't make the detour—catch a direct bus from Mérida (see p. 503). This tiny town contains the largest church plaza in Mexico, ringed with rows of yellow arches around the church and convent, and some of the oldest Spanish buildings in the region, dating from 1533 and built from the boulders of the Mayan pyramid that they replaced. Since almost all the buildings in Izamal are yellow, the city is sometimes referred to as *Ciudad Amarilla* (Yellow City). Near Izamal is the weather-worn pyramid of **Kinichkakmó,** Maya for Macaw of Fire, which was plundered by the Spanish for stones to build the church and convent. The ancient *cenote* (freshwater sink-hole) of **Ixcolasc** is only 1km away.

Back on Rte. 180, you will find **Kantunil** (68km from Mérida). **Xocchel** (The Place Where the Chels Read) is an attractive town along Rte. 180 before Kantunil. Next is **Holcá,** and finally, **Libre Unión,** with a sizeable *cenote.* During squabbles between the territories of Yucatán and Quintana Roo, Libre Unión found itself smack on the border. The town voted to stick together and become part of the state of Yucatán— thus earning its name, Free Union.

Some travelers hitch or hop buses from one Mayan village to another along the busy road between Mérida and Chichén Itzá. Those who choose to hitch should bring water—the waits can be long, and shade is sparse. *Let's Go* does not, however, recommend hitchhiking. Second-class bus drivers stop anywhere if requested, but a new fare is charged for each trip, and slow and irregular bus service limits the number of places you can visit in one day. If night begins to fall, be sure to take the next bus to Pisté or Mérida—you don't want to get stranded. If no buses are in sight, there are *palapas* where you can stay in Xocchel and most other towns; ask in the town store in the *zócalo.*

■ Chichén Itzá

Chichén Itzá's reputation as the Yucatán's prize cultural attraction is well deserved. The combination of faultless ancient architecture set to a backdrop of stunning natural beauty provides for an aesthetic experience not easily matched. Yet this alone is not why Chichén Itzá, capital of the Mayan empire at its zenith, continues to fascinate, some 1000 years after its creation. The site's glaring paradoxes are intriguing: a civilization both intellectually advanced and brutally savage; a culture crushed by colonization, yet still thriving in the language, customs, and hearts of many present-day Mayans. You can't claim to have seen Yucatán without a visit to Chichén—don't miss it for the world.

ORIENTATION

The ruins of Chichén Itzá lie 1.5km from **Route 180,** the highway running from Mérida (121km west) through Valladolid (43km east) to Cancún (213km east). As nearly every travel agency in Mexico pushes a Chichén Itzá package, the ruins tend to get overpopulated around noon. In order to avoid the stampede (and hot sun), use nearby **Pisté** (2.5km west of the ruins) as a base and get an early start.

Getting to the ruins is easy. From Pisté, catch a taxi (15 pesos) or flag down any eastbound bus (approximately every ½hr., 2-3 pesos). As with all Mexican buses, a vigorous, supplicatory wave to the driver gets you on the road. To get to Chichén Itzá from other towns, see bus listings for Mérida (p. 503), Cancún (p. 528), and Valladolid (p. 521). To head back to Pisté after a day at the ruins, hang out in the bus parking lot until a taxi or bus swings by. From Pisté you can get to almost any city in the state (see listings below).

PRACTICAL INFORMATION

Services are located in the dominant stone edifice at the site's western entrance. Across from the ticket counter is a small **information booth.** Clear your throat seven times and a Spanish-speaking agent will appear, genie-like, to provide useful information about transportation and lodging. Refer specific questions about the ruins to official guides. The booth often provides free **luggage storage** (open daily 8am-5pm). There are also restrooms, a restaurant, an ice cream parlor, a gift shop (which changes U.S. dollars), a bookstore with guidebooks, an auditorium showing documentaries about the ruins, and a small museum (see p. 516). Parking is available right at the site (daily 8am-10pm, 5 pesos).

Pisté provides a few additional services. Across from the bus station, both **Centro Telefónico** (tel. 1-00-89; fax 1-00-88) and **Teléfonos de México** (tel. 1-00-58, -59, or -60) let you call home (open daily 7am-9pm). The town has no bank; exchange your money at the gift shop at the ruins.

Buses leave from Pisté's bus station (tel. 1-00-52), near the Stardust Inn on the eastern side of town. To Mérida (1st class 3pm, 1½hr., 24 pesos; 2nd class 10 per day, 2hr., 18 pesos), Cancún (1st class 5:30pm, 2½hr., 43 pesos; 2nd class 10 per day, 4hr., 31 pesos), Valladolid (10 per day, 1hr., 7 pesos), and Playa del Carmen (7am, 1 and 3pm, 5hr., 40 pesos). **Farmacia Isis,** Calle 15 #53, lies a short way past the *zócalo* towards the ruins (open daily 7:30am-9:30pm). In case of a medical emergency go to the **Clínica Promesa,** Calle 14 #50 (tel. 6-31-98, ext. 198), in the blue-green building past the *zócalo* and 100m off Rte. 180 (open 24hr). A single **police** officer sits at a desk in the *comisario* on the eastern side of the *zócalo*. The **post office** is in a small gray building near the *zócalo* across from Abarrotes "El Alba" (open Mon.-Fri. 8:30am-3pm). There is a **telephone** (tel. 1-01-24) right around the corner from the ticket counter. The **telephone code** is 985.

ACCOMMODATIONS AND CAMPING

Though a few luxury hotels snuggle right up to the ruins, the more economical options are located in Pisté—either on, or just off Calle 15, the town's main road. You can pitch a tent in the **RV trailer park** right next to the bus station. Spaces have light and power outlets. There are communal bathrooms and a pool. The trailer park is administered by the Stardust Inn (tel. 1-01-22), on the other side of the bus station (25 pesos per person). The tentless can head over to **Posada Olalde,** to the left of Calle 15 (Rte. 180), two blocks down the unmarked dirt road directly across the street from the Carrousel Restaurant. Multi-pastel colored rooms with large, firm beds lead into spotless white bathrooms (singles 80 pesos; doubles 100 pesos; triples 110 pesos). During high season, extra people can string up hammocks for 10 pesos per person. Haggle during the low season. **Posada Carrousel,** (tel. 1-00-78) on Calle 15, is in central Pisté at the large eponymous *palapa* restaurant. Standard pink rooms have fans, hot water, and *agua purificada* (singles 70 pesos; doubles 70 pesos; triples 80 pesos; quads 100 pesos). Ask and ye shall receive a hammock free of charge. Nearby **Hotel El Paso,** Calle 15 #89, offers similar accommodations (singles 70 pesos; doubles 70 pesos; triples 80 pesos; quads 90 pesos). Its restaurant offers a well-priced *menú del día* (25 pesos).

FOOD

For daytrips to Chichén Itzá, packing a lunch means avoiding overpriced cafeteria food. Small grocers line Calle 15 in Pisté. The street is also lined with small restaurants offering cheap and yummy *comida yucateca*. **El Carrousel** (tel. 1-00-78) serves three simple meals a day; try eggs any style (10-12 pesos) or *chilanquiles* (10 pesos; open daily 7am-10:30pm). **Restaurant Sayil,** between El Carrousel and the Stardust Inn, is a peaceful place to savor local dishes like *pollo pibil* (chicken cooked in banana leaf, 12 pesos; open daily 7am-10pm). **Restaurant Poxil** (tel. 1-01-16 or 1-01-23), on the right just past the *zócalo*, serves a filling *comida típica* for just 20 pesos (open daily 8am-11pm).

SIGHTS

As the Mayan name Chichén Itzá (Mouth of the Well) implies, the area's earliest inhabitants were drawn here by the two nearby freshwater *cenotes*. Much of what is known about these sedentary people is based on the pottery shards recovered by archaeologists. Later periods in Chichén Itzá's history are illuminated by the *Chilam Balam*, one of the few pre-Hispanic Mayan texts to survive the early missionaries' book-burnings. The *Chilam Balam* describes the construction of many buildings visible today, focusing on the period between 500 and 800 CE, when construction was purely Mayan.

Chichén was mysteriously abandoned at its height in the 7th century CE, and for the next 300 years it remained a crumbling ghost town. Sometime before 1000 CE, the Toltec tribes of Tula (p. 381) infiltrated the Yucatán and overcame peaceful Mayan settlements, bringing with them the cult of the plumed serpent Quetzalcóatl (Kukulcán). The Toltecs fortified Chichén, which soon became the most important city on the peninsula. Toltec influence is visible in Chichén's buildings, which became more rounded, and in its iconography. Whereas the Mayan depicted only warriors, eagles, and jaguars, the Toltecs brought with them long-nosed representations of Chac (the rain god) and elaborate carvings of lesser gods. They also introduced *chac-mool*, reclining figures representing messengers to the gods that were used as altars for human sacrifice. In 1461, Chichén Itzá was once again abandoned, this time due to war, but religious pilgrims continued to visit the site until well after the Spanish conquest. Today, the relentless flow of tourists ensures that Chichén Itzá will never again stand in solitude.

For a deeper (not to mention air-conditioned) understanding of Chichén and its people, visit the **Centro Cultural Cecijema** (tel. 1-00-04), at Calle 15 #45 in Pisté. The modern gray building houses a small selection of Mayan ceramic replicas as well as attractive rotating exhibits, and the well stocked library offers books both in English and Spanish. A helpful staff gives what amounts to a one-on-one tutor session, or leaves you alone to browse with a cup of coffee. Get your birth date transcribed into the Mayan calendar for a small fee (open daily 8am-5pm; free).

The Ruins

The entire site of Chichén Itzá is open daily from 8am-5pm (admission 30 pesos; free Sun. and for kids under 14). From the main parking lot and visitor's center, the first group of ruins is up the gravel path and to the left. A small **museum** in the **visitor's complex** at the entrance to the site recaps the history of Chichén Itzá and displays some sculptures and objects removed from the sacred *cenote*. Its **auditorium** screens documentaries about the ruins in both Spanish and in English (showtimes vary; both open daily 10am-5pm; free).

If you are mainly interested in the architecture of the ruins, hiring a guide at the entrance is unnecessary. A guidebook (or even just a map) and the multilingual explanatory captions on plaques at each major structure are all you need to appreciate the ruins. Free maps are available around the corner from the ticket counter, at the telephone desk. You'll need a guide to decipher some of the symbolism of the ruins or to follow the enigmatic recurrence of the number seven throughout the structures. Join one of the guided tours which begin at the entrance (Spanish or English, 6-8 people, 1½hr., 40 pesos per person) or get your own group together and hire a private guide (up to 20 people, 2hr., 150 pesos). Ask to see identification, which guarantees certification and foreign language ability.

The first sight to meet your eyes is **El Castillo,** Chichén's hallmark. This pyramid, built in honor of Kukulcán, rises in perfect symmetry from the neatly cropped lawn, culminating in a temple supported by pillars in the form of serpents. El Castillo stands as tangible evidence of the astounding astral understanding of the ancient Maya: the 91 steps on each of the four faces, plus the upper platform, total 365 (the number of days in the non-leap year); the 52 panels on the nine terraced levels equal the number of years in a Mayan calendar cycle; and each face of the nine terraces is divided by a staircase, yielding 18 sections representing the 18 Mayan months. Even more impressive is the precision of El Castillo's axes alignment, which, in coordination with the sun and the moon, produce a bi-annual optical illusion. At sunrise during the spring and fall equinoxes, the rounded terraces cast a serpentine shadow on the side of the northern staircase. The sculpted serpent head at the bottom of the staircase completes the illusion. In March, the serpent appears to be sliding down the stairs precisely in the direction of the Sacred Cenote, while in September the motion is reversed. A light-and-shadow lunar serpent-god, identical to that of the equinoxes, creeps up and down the pyramid at the dawn of the full moon following each of the equinoxes. Twice a year people from all over the world converge on Chichén to see this incredible phenomenon, crowding accommodations with calendrical precision. The exact equinox dates and times vary slightly from year to year, but are always on or around March 21 and September 21.

Nestled within El Castillo is an early Toltec **temple,** the inner chamber of which can be entered through a door at the bottom of the north staircase, behind the serpent's ears. A set of narrow, slippery steps ascends to a ceremonial chamber with a grimacing *chac-mool* sacrificial altar and a rust-red, jaguar-faced throne encrusted with jade stones and flint fangs (open daily 11am-3pm and 4-5pm; free).

West of El Castillo, or to the left of the entrance, lies the **ballcourt.** The enormous "I"-shaped playing field is bounded by two high, parallel walls with a temple at each end. Though this is the largest ballcourt in Mesoamerica, good acoustics make it seem smaller than it is. Voices carry remarkably well along the length of the field and the court produces an amazing side-to-side echo, which repeats seven times. The game played here was called *pok-ta-pok.* Players of the two contending teams endeavored to keep a heavy rubber ball in constant motion by using only their hips, knees, and elbows. They scored by knocking the ball through the stone rings still visible today, high up on the walls in the middle of the I. The elaborate game was so fascinating to the Spanish that in 1528 Cortés took two entire teams back to Europe to perform before the crowned heads. After that, European ball games replaced their unyielding, dead wooden balls with livelier rubber balls.

The ball game was much more than just a cultural pastime for the Maya; it was a contest of **good** versus **evil** linked to a game of the gods. A Mayan legend tells that every harvest Hun Hunahpu, god of corn, was decapitated; his head was planted in the ground and became the seed of all corn plants. Every year, the evil gods of the nether-world stole the buried head in an attempt to destroy the Mayas. The twins Xbalanque and Hunahpú (the sun and Venus respectively) would then descend to Xilbalba (the netherworld) and challenge the evil gods to an epic game of ball, using the god's head instead of a ball. Invariably, the twins were successful and the seed was recovered. The new crop symbolized the god's resurrection and the Mayan's salvation. It is believed that in response to the legend, after a ball game the captain of a victorious team would be decapitated and his head offered to honor the gods.

A short distance from the ballcourt toward the grassy open area is the **Tzompantli,** Aztec for Platform of the Skulls. When the Spaniards conquered the Aztecs, they were shocked to find ritualized human sacrifice and horrified by the racks in Tenochtitlán designed to display the skulls of the sacrificed. Chichén's Toltec-designed structure served a similar macabre purpose. Today, eerie rows of skulls in bas-relief decorate the low platform's walls. Next to the Tzompantli stands the **Platform of Jaguars and Eagles,** named after the military orders who took the names of these ferocious animals and who were charged with obtaining prisoners from other tribes for human sacrifice. To either side of the feathered serpent heads on the balustrades, reliefs of jaguars and eagles clutch human hearts in their claws. East of the platform is the **Temple of Venus,** decorated with a feathered serpent holding a human head in its mouth. The temple's reliefs symbolize many stars and provide information on their motion.

The dirt path leading directly north from El Castillo, over the ancient Mayan roadway, links the ceremonial plaza with Chichén Itzá's most important religious center, the **Sacred Cenote,** 300m away. The roughly circular sink-hole, perhaps 60m across, induced vertigo in the sacrificial victims perched on the platform before their 25m plunge into the murky depths. The rain-god Chac supposedly dwelt beneath the water's surface and needed frequent gifts to grant good rains. Human remains recovered by divers suggest that children and young men were the victims of choice. If they could keep afloat until noon, they were then fished out and forced to tell what they had witnessed during the ordeal.

On the eastern edge of the central plaza, the **Temple of the Warriors** and **Group of the Thousand Columns** present an impressive array of elaborately carved columns which at one time supported a roof of some perishable material. On the temple itself (not open to the public), in front of two great feathered serpents and several sculpted animal gods, reclines one of Chichén's best-preserved *chac-mools*. The ornamentation of this building is largely Toltec; a nearly identical structure stands at Tula, the Toltec capital far to the west. The Temple of the Warriors marks the end of Chichén's restored monuments and the beginning of an overgrown area extending to the southeast of El Castillo. This corner houses the **Palace of the Sculptured Columns,** the back of which hides a couple of beady-eyed masks of Chac. The rest of the quadrangle is comprised of the **Southeastern Colonnade,** the **market** and its courtyard, and the expansive **Western Colonnade.**

A red dirt path on the south side of El Castillo leads to the less photogenic **South Group** of ruins. Beyond the cafeteria and bathrooms, the first pyramid on the right is the **Ossuary,** or **High Priest's Grave,** its distinctive serpent heads mimicking El Castillo. A natural cave extends from within the pyramid 15m down into the earth. The human bones and votive offerings found in this cavern are thought to be those of an ancient high priest. Past the Ossuary, the road forks, presenting two different routes to the second set of ruins in the South Group, often missed by tourists but well worth the visit. The most interesting structure in this group is the **Observatory,** the large circular building on the left-hand side. This ancient planetarium consists of two rectangular platforms with large west-facing staircases and two circular towers. Because of the tower's interior spiral staircase (not open to the public), this structure is often called **El Caracol** (the Great Conch). The slits in the dome of the Observatory could be aligned with the important celestial bodies and cardinal directions. El Caracol was built in several stages by Mayan and Toltec architects. Notice the small red handprints on the wall of the building just as you come up the stairs; these were supposedly the hands of the sun god Itzamná. Walking south from El Caracol, toward the Nunnery at the other end of the clearing, you will pass a tiny, ruined sauna and then the **Temple of the Sculptured Wall Panels** behind it. Though difficult to decipher, the panels on the exterior walls contain emblems of Toltec warriors—jaguars, eagles, and serpents—in three rows.

The largest structure in this part of Chichén is the misnamed **Nunnery,** on the south side of the quadrangle. Although it was probably a Mayan royal palace, its stone rooms reminded Spaniards of a European convent—thus the misnomer. After several superimpositions and some decay, the building is now almost 20m high on a base 65m long and 35m wide. Above the entrance on the eastern side of the building, you can still see Mayan hieroglyphs. Also on the eastern side, a smaller annex built at an angle is visible.

Diagonally across from the nunnery and annex is the religious center, its upper walls encrusted with intricate masks of the hook-nosed Chac. The religious center is remarkable for its fusion of cultural styles: over the doorway are Mayan stone lintels, while the use of wood and inclined edges is evidence of Toltec influence. Above the door are representations of the four *bacabs,* animal deities who hold up the sky.

A poorly maintained path (which is sometimes closed during rainy months) runs about 130m east from the nunnery group, past the chapel to the long **Akab-Dzib.** The oldest parts of this structure are believed to be Chichén's most ancient constructions. The two central rooms were built in the 2nd or 3rd century, while the annexes on either side and to the east were added later. Inside the rooms it is possible to make out the small rose-red hand prints of Itzamná on the ceiling.

The overgrown **Cenote Xtoloc** hides in a dip behind the South Group ticket office. To reach it from the office, take the first left 20m into the site. The *cenote* is in the hollow, beyond the small, ruined temple of Xtolob, the lizard god. There is no path down the steep slope through the undergrowth, and swimming is prohibited because of the dangerous underwater currents. In counterpart to the holy waters of the Sacred Cenote, this pool at one time provided all of Chichén with secular drinking water. Following **sacbé No. 5,** which becomes a narrow, winding trail, takes you to the back of the observatory.

As if Chichén Itzá couldn't muster enough daytime spectacle, those green panels (whose purpose you've been contemplating all day) pop open for the evening **light and sound show.** The buildings are splashed in red, blue, green, and yellow lights while booming voices detail the history of the site (Spanish version daily at 7pm, 12 pesos; English version daily at 9pm, 18 pesos). Avoid the poorly lit and bug infested nighttime walk from Pisté and cab it to and from the show (15 pesos each way).

Chichén Viejo

Beginning about 1km south of the Nunnery, and spreading out southwest of the main site, Chichén Viejo is a collection of unrestored minor ruins scattered throughout the jungle. The **Group of the Initial Series** and the **Phallic Cluster,** the first set of ruins in Chichén Viejo, are easy enough to find on your own. Follow the dirt path (look for the "Chichén Viejo" sign) to the right of the Nunnery past the intersection of other dirt paths to a covered well. Shortly beyond the well, a right at the T-junction brings you to the cluster, set in a clearing. Chichén Viejo carries the only dated inscriptions at Chichén Itzá, one of which can be clearly seen on the one remaining lintel of the Temple of the Initial Series. This block, upheld by two columns, features a hieroglyphic inscription corresponding to July 30, 878 CE. The rest of the temple stands in ruin. The main features of the appropriately named Phallic Cluster jut out proudly from the interior walls of the temple.

The remaining ruins, reached by taking the path to the right of the **House of the Philli,** following the tracks and then cutting through the bushes, are best located with the help of a guide. Though official guides will charge you almost as much as for the main site, you can ask some of the merchants at Chichén if they know of someone who would be willing to serve as guide for a cheaper flat fee. Unlicensed guides can be very knowledgeable, though few speak English. Shrouded by dense jungle, 10 minutes beyond the Phallic Cluster, lie the remains of the **House of the Four Lintels,** carrying another inscription dating to July 13, 881 CE. This **Principal Group of the Southwest,** where hieroglyphs depict the Mayan practice of compressing children's foreheads with stone plates (conical-shaped heads were considered beautiful, as were crossed eyes and precious stones embedded in the flesh of the face) contains a magnificent ruined pyramid, the **Temple of the Three Lintels** (dating to 879 CE), and the **Jaguar Temple,** where a handful of columns salute the ancient military order of the Jaguars.

Turning to the right through the jungle from the Southwest Group, do your best to stumble upon the **Bird Cornice Group,** featuring a strip of carved birds, the **Temple of the Turtle,** where a turtle-shaped stone was found, and the **Temple of the Sculpted Jambs,** whose door jambs are molded into human figures.

■ Near Chichén Itzá

GRUTAS DE BALANCANCHÉN

The inner caves of the **Grutas de Balancanchén** were only re-discovered in 1959 when a local amateur speleologist noticed a passageway blocked up with stones. Further exploration opened 300m of caves filled with stalactites carved to resemble leaves on the ceiling and a huge tree-like column surrounded by dozens of votive vessels with ghoulish masks. Archaeologists have come to believe that the cave was a center for Mayan-Toltec worship of the gods Chac, Tlaloc (the Toltec rain god), and Kukulcán (Quetzalcóatl) during the 10th and 11th centuries. For unknown reasons, subterranean worship in Balancanchén stopped at the end of this period, and the offerings of ceramic vessels and stone sculptures rested undisturbed for eight centuries. The impressive stalactites and a strikingly clear underground river definitely merit a visit, but be prepared for an almost incomprehensible Disney-esque tour which dramatizes the cave's history, keeping up with tour groups via a series of hidden speakers. A guide, available for questions, paces the group through the chambers along the 1km path. Self-guided tours are not permitted. Tours (17 pesos, Sun. and holidays 7 pesos) in Spanish (9am, noon, 2, and 4pm), English (11am, 1, and 3pm), and French (10am).

Getting There: Located 6km east of Chichén Itzá and 2km past the Dolores Alba Hotel, the caves are easily reached by hopping on any bus traveling east on Rte. 180 (3 pesos). When you board, be sure to ask the driver to stop there. To get back, catch any west-bound vehicle, but be prepared to wait.

YAXUNÁ

Yaxuná, 30km southeast of Chichén Itzá, is home to the ruins of yet another ancient Mayan city. The temple was built by the Maya of Cobá, who were planning to make war on the people of Chichén. A 100km *sacbé* (an elevated, wide white stone road), the longest of the area, linked Yaxuná with Cobá. To keep a close eye on their enemy, the Maya of Cobá aligned their temple with El Castillo.

Getting There: There is no public transportation to Yaxuná, but it's possible to hire a truck in Pisté (about 150 pesos roundtrip; arrange for your driver to wait for you and ask to stop at the *cenotes* and caves between Chichén and Yaxuná). Road conditions are incredibly poor: the trip is only possible during the dry season. The easiest route is take Rte. 180 to Libre Unión and then left to Yaxcabah, a small town 17km down the road and 8km from Yaxuná.

■ Valladolid

Valladolid (pop. 100,000) doesn't have the charm of Mérida or the showiness of Cancún. It is a noisy, dirty, crowded city. It sprawls. It screams. Aggressive vendors raise their voices so they can be heard over the din of the frenetic traffic, *indígena* women and children besiege the *zócalo* to sell colorful *huipiles* and chewing gum, and whining mopeds buzz down narrow streets. Aside from a handful of sights—six churches and some *cenotes* (fresh water sink-holes)—this commercial center serves as little more than a stopover for tourists *en camino* to more exotic destinations like Chichén Itzá, Río Lagartos, and Isla Holbox.

Orientation and Practical Information Traversed by Rte. 180, Valladolid lies midway between Mérida and Cancún. Even-numbered streets run north-south, increasing westwards. Odd-numbered streets run east-west, increasing to the south. *El centro* is bordered by Calles 27, 53, 28, and 60. Except for **Cenote X-kekén,** everything lies within comfortable walking distance from the *zócalo* (circumscribed by Calles 39, 40, 41, and 42). To get to the *zócalo* from the bus station, take a taxi (7 pesos) or walk one block south on Calle 54 to Calle 39. Turn left and follow Calle 39 for six blocks.

The *ayuntamiento* (city hall), on the Calle 40 side of the *zócalo,* provides **tourist information** and has a fantastic mural upstairs (open Mon.-Sat. 9am-2pm and 4-7pm). **Bancomer** (tel. 6-21-50), on the Calle 40 side of the *zócalo,* has a 24-hr. **ATM** and the best exchange rates (open for exchange Mon.-Fri. 9am-2pm). There are **LADATELs** on the east side of zócalo. Send **telegrams** (tel. 6-21-70) from Calle 39, two blocks west of the *zócalo* (open Mon.-Fri. 8am-6pm, Sat. 9am-noon).

Buses arrive *de paso:* they'll take you only if they have room. **ADO** (tel. 6-34-49), Calle 37 at Calle 54, sends buses to Cancún (7 per day, 2hr., 32 pesos), Chichén Itzá (8 per day, 1hr., 6 pesos), Mérida (9 per day, 2hr., 32 pesos), Playa del Carmen (noon, 2, and 3pm, 2½hr., 40 pesos), and Tizimín (every hr., 1hr., 8 pesos). To reach Tinum, buy a ticket on a Mérida-bound bus ask the driver to drop you off (½hr., 6 pesos). **Luggage storage** costs 1 peso per piece per day (open 8am-7pm).

Buy the freshest, cheapest fruit at the **market,** bordered by Calles 35, 37, 30, and 32, 5 blocks northeast of the *zócalo* (open daily 5am-2pm). **Lavandería Teresita,** Calle 33 and 42, takes care of your dirty laundry (self-service 7 pesos for 3 kilos, full service 5 pesos per kilo; open daily 7am-7pm). **El Descuento** (tel. 6-26-44), Calle 42 at 39, on the northwest corner of the *zócalo*, is a **24-hour pharmacy.** In a medical emergency look for **Hospital S.S.A.** (tel. 6-28-83), two blocks west of the *zócalo* on Calle 41, then five blocks southwest on Calle 41-A (open 24hr.). The **police** (tel. 6-21-00) are seven blocks east of the *zócalo* on Calle 41. The **post office** (tel. 6-23-26) is on the Calle 40 side of the *zócalo* (open Mon.-Fri. 8am-3pm). **Postal Code:** 97780. **Telephone Code:** 985.

Accommodations The best hotels in town are on the *zócalo*. A handful of unimpressive but cheaper hotels center around the intersection of Calles 39 and 44. **Hotel Zací,** Calle 44 #191 (tel. 6-21-67), between Calles 39 and 37, has fantastically furnished rooms with cable TV, fans, and sparkling bathrooms. A paradise with pool and gardens (singles 70 pesos; doubles 90 pesos; triples 130 pesos; quads 160 pesos, add 15 pesos for A/C). **Hotel María Guadalupe,** Calle 44 #198 (tel. 6-20-78), between Calles 39 and 41, has sterile rooms with dark wood decor and brand new ceiling fans (singles and doubles 50 pesos; triples 70 pesos). **Nuevo Hotel Mendoza,** Calle 39 #204 (tel. 6-20-02), is one and a half blocks west of the *zócalo*. The older rooms with springless mattressed beds and ceiling fans are in fair but used condition (singles 50 pesos; doubles 70 pesos; triples 80 pesos). Newer, larger suites have better baths and come with extra fans, cable TV, and a fridge (singles 80 pesos; doubles 100 pesos; triples 130 pesos).

Food Valladolid's one redeeming grace may be the Yucatec food. Try the *poc-chuc* (thinly sliced grilled pork), the *panuchos* (small tortillas filled with various combinations of chicken, pork, beans, lettuce, tomato, and *chile*), or *escabeche oriental de pavo* (a hearty turkey soup). **El Bazaar,** Calle 39 at 40, is an open-air courtyard with several cafés and juice bars in the heart of the *zócalo*. People-watch as you enjoy tacos (5 pesos) and *yucateco* entrees (12 pesos) from **La Rancherita.** Head to **Sergio's** for a pizza (13 pesos) or *chile relleno* (15 pesos). **Amigo Paisano** specializes in *comida yucatea* and does quite a job of it *(carne molida* 12 pesos; area open daily 6am-midnight). **Restaurante Cenote Zací** (tel. 6-21-07), on Calle 36 between Calles 37 and 39, is a lovely thatched-roof restaurant with elegant decor and background music. The excellent liquor selection includes locally produced Xtabentún, a delectable concoction of rum, anise, and honey (4 pesos). Catch of the day costs 20 pesos (open daily 8am-6pm).

Sights and Entertainment The city's two main *cenotes* (freshwater sinkholes) are its most arresting attractions. **Cenote Zací** (sah-KEY) is only three blocks east of the *zócalo* on Calle 36, between Calles 37 and 39. Well worn stone stairs lead down into a cavernous hollow studded with plunging stalactites. Bats beat their wings as swans and daring locals dive into the murky, jade-colored water. Copious quantities of *chinha* (lake lettuce) pad their landing (admission 4 pesos, children 2 pesos, free view from the *palapa* restaurant at its edge; free parking; open daily 8am-6m). Though farther from the center of town, **Cenote X-kekén** (chay-keh-KEN) is also more striking. Visit before noon, as plunging schoolkids disrupt the deliciously cool, turquoise, glassy surface of the *cenote's* water in the afternoon. At midday, light pours into the cove through the narrow hole in the roof, refracting into the water and reflecting off the jellyfish-like tree-roots to create an eerie glow (open daily 7am-5pm; admission 5 pesos, children 2.50 pesos). To get there by car or bike (20min.) take Calle 39 to the highway, ride toward Mérida. Make a left at the sign for Dzitnup and continue until the damp stairway down to the water's edge. Without your own wheels, take a taxi (15 pesos) or ask the driver of a second-class Mérida bus to drop you off.

The most famous church in town is **San Bernardino de Siena,** affiliated with the **Ex-Convento de Sisal,** Calle 41, four blocks southwest off Calle 46. Built in 1552, these are the oldest ecclesiastical buildings in the Yucatán and possibly all of Mexico. On the altar at the rear of the church is a large image of the Virgin of Guadalupe; original frescoes are visible behind two side altars. Outside, an impressive colonial irrigation system and 17th-century well draw water from an underground *cenote,* over which part of the complex was constructed (open Tues.-Sun. 8am-2:30pm and 5-8pm). The **Catedral de San Gervasio,** with its colonial-style twin towers, stands protectress over the *zócalo* on Calle 41. It would rival San Bernardino de Siena for the title of oldest church in the nation, had residents not violated the sacred right to sanctuary. According to legend, two alleged criminals who took sanctuary in the church were discovered and brutally murdered by an angry mob. When the bishop learned of the mob's sinful actions, he closed up the church and had it destroyed; it was later rebuilt facing another direction (open daily 5am-noon and 3-9pm).

There are two forums of entertainment in Valladolid: people-watching at **El Bazaar** or viewing movies dubbed in Spanish at **Cinema Díaz,** just off the *zócalo,* on Calles 40 and 41 (screenings at 7 and 9 pm).

■ Tizimín

It's one thirty in the afternoon, no clouds, upper nineties. Not a soul within sight of the beautifully manicured *zócalo. It's too hot,* the locals say as they comfortably recline in their hammocks. *Yes, but a good hot,* you reply as you sweat through your last clean shirt. Two-thirty, then three, then four. Clouds have gathered and things have cooled off considerably. It is pleasantly warm. Still no people. The locals lift their heads long enough to comment on the imminence of rain. You simply relax on a nearby bench. It rains. Hard. You get wet. An old man with leathery skin snores in sync with the swinging of the hammock. So goes life in Tizimín, the urban center of a large rural area in the Yucatán.

Orientation and Practical Information Tizimín lies 75km south of Río Lagartos by Rte. 295, and 120km west of Kantunil Kin by Rte. 175. **Bancomer,** on Calle 51 #394 (tel. 3-23-81), exchanges currency on the little square behind the *ex-convento* (open Mon.-Fri. 9am-1:30pm). There are two long distance **telephone** *casetas* near the *zócalo,* but neither makes international collect calls. Buses leave from the terminal at Calles 46 and 47. **ADO** (tel.3-24-24) goes to Cancún (7 and 9am, 3½hr., 30 pesos), Chetumal (5 per day, 5hr., 53 pesos), and Valladolid (13 per day, 1hr., 8 pesos). **Autotransportes del Noreste** (tel. 3-20-37) has first-class service to Río Lagartos (9:15am, 6:45 and 7:45pm, 1hr., 12 pesos) Mérida (7 per day, 2hr., 36 pesos) and Kantunil Kin (10 per day, 1½hr., 12 pesos). **Farmacia Centro de Drogas** (tel. 3-27-26) is on Calle 51 behind the *ex-convento,* next to Bancomer (open Mon.-Sat. 8am-1pm and 5-9pm.) The **Centro Médico de Oriente San Carlos,** Calle 46 #461 (tel. 3-

Sweet Charity

If Chichén Itzá's ruins and Río Lagartos' National Park have failed to make you swoon, Valladolid's **Xtabentún** is sure to do so. As potent as whiskey, this popular yucatec concoction of anise and honey has its origin here. According to legend, Zac-Nicté, a young woman whose beauty had attracted the wicked tribal chief's attention, fell in love with a warrior. Fearing what the chief might do to them, the young lovers sought refuge in the jungle. Coming across a beehive in a *balché* tree, the couple ate their fill of honey and left the rest in a hole in the trunk. The next day they discovered that the honey had magically become Xtabentún. When the chief finally caught up with them, he was so impressed with the drink's taste that he let them go and...they lived happily ever after. You too can sample this and other nectars at the **Sosa factory outlet** (tel. 6-21-42), on Calle 42, between Calles 47 and 49, four blocks south of the *zócalo.* The Sosa family, who have been making the product for over 100 years, sell their entire line here at great discounts (Xtabentún 25 pesos per bottle; open Mon.-Sat. 10am-1pm and 3-6pm).

21-57), has a 24-hour pharmacy and ambulance service. The **post office** is at Calles 48 and 45 (open Mon.- Fri. 9am-1pm and 3-6pm, Sat. 9am-1pm). The **postal code** is 97700. The **telephone code** is 986.

Accommodations and Food Most hotels, restaurants, and services in Tizimín are near the *zócalo*, which residents call *el parque*. To get there on foot from the bus stations (10min.), walk two long blocks down the hill toward the west on Calle 47, passing the market on your left. Turn left on Calle 50 and walk west one block toward the large stone church. **Hotel San Carlos,** Calle #54 #407 (tel. 3-20-94), is the most modern and inviting hotels in Tizimín. From the southwest corner of the *zócalo* (by *Tres Reyes* restaurant) walk west one block and make your first right. The lush garden will lure you into plain, spacious rooms with two beds and private bathrooms (singles 70 pesos; doubles 90 pesos; add 10 and 15 pesos for A/C). **Hotel San Jorge** (tel. 3-20-37), on the southern side of the *zócalo*, provides clean, tall-ceilinged rooms with private bathrooms. *Agua purificada* in the lobby (singles 65 pesos; doubles 75 pesos; add 20 pesos for A/C) **Posada Maria Antonia,** in the *zócalo* on the southern side of the church, has four clean rooms, each equipped with two firm beds, a private hot-water bath, a fan, and TV (singles 63 pesos; doubles 74 pesos; add 15 pesos for A/ C; each additional person 10 pesos).

For the cheapest meal, buy some fruits, vegetables, and bread at the **market** on Calle 47 and picnic in the beautiful *zócalo*. The most popular eatery in Tizimín is the air-conditioned **Restaurante Tres Reyes,** on the *zócalo* (tel. 3-21-06). Meals are hearty and accompanied by flavorful tortillas (*pollo frito con papas* 23 pesos, *camarones al mojo de ajo* 35 pesos; open daily 7am-11pm). **Restaurante Portales** (tel. 3-35-05) provides cheap eats on a pleasant patio on the *zócalo* (huge breakfasts 7 pesos, sandwiches 4 pesos, tacos 6 pesos; open Mon.-Sat. 7am-noon and 5:30-11:30pm, Sun. 5:30-11:30pm). **Restaurante Las Palmas,** Calle 51 #331-A (tel. 3-24-51), between Calles 38 and 40, is a big, comfortable *palapa* that has regional specialties and occasional live music and dancing.

Sights, Entertainment, and Seasonal Events The nearby **archaeological site** of **Kulubá,** although largely unrestored, virtually untouristed, and somewhat hard to reach, is well worth a visit, as much for the beauty of the surrounding countryside as for the well preserved details of the ruins themselves. The ruins date from the Late Classical period (800-1000 AD) and are the easternmost point where influence of the Puuc architectural style has been found. The style here also shows some resemblance to the buildings at Chichén Itzá. The ruins were partially restored in the late 1970s, when the construction of supports for the two main buildings was begun. Although neither building has survived the years intact (parts of both have long since fallen and the stones have become scattered), the details that remain are still impressive. **El Edificio de Las Úes,** a structure about 40m long, 8m high, and 7m wide, is carved with "U"s all along its façade. The original red stucco with which the whole building was once painted can still be seen on the carved portions of the stone. The second partially restored building, the more impressive of the two, features two surprisingly well preserved pairs of masks of the rain god Chac, as well as other carved ornamentation. The building is 50m long, 10m high, and 8m wide, and at one time probably had three pairs of masks of the rain god, all with long curved noses. The ruins are located on a private ranch 33km east of Tizimín. Although the site is not officially open to the public, it can be visited with permission from the ranch's owner— contact Julio César Espinosa, the site's official promoter, at his photography studio, Studio Julio César (tel. 3-40-50), on Calle 50, Bazar Arce, apt. 8. (open Mon.-Sat. 8am-1pm and 5-8:30pm, Sun. 9am-1pm.). To get to the ruins, take the Tixcanal-bound bus a half-block from the *zócalo* and ask the driver to drop you off at Kulubá. **Taxis** from Tizimín charge 100 pesos for roundtrip to the ruins with a wait. Traveling to the site during the rainy season is especially difficult.

Tizimín's *zócalo* features a colonial church and ex-convent. The church, **La Venerada Iglesia de los Tres Santos Reyes,** is named after the patron saints of the town. The **festival** held each year in their honor (Dec. 30-Jan. 12) draws pilgrims from all over the region and provokes processions, dancing, bullfights, and lots of *típico* food. January 6 is the most important day of the festival, when the pilgrims file through the church to touch the patrons with palm branches.

The tiny town of **Kikil,** 5km from Tizimín, has the enormous jungle-encroached remains of a colonial church and ex-convent and the fresh waters of a stunning *cenote*. The church, known to locals simply as **Iglesia Kikil,** is just to the right of the highway as you enter Kikil from Tizimín. The church was burned during the Caste War (1847-48) and has been utterly abandoned to vegetation, but with enormous trees growing atop it, the bulky ruin creates a sublime spectacle. Just inside the gate of the little courtyard to your left as you face the church stands an elaborately carved stone baptismal font which rings like a bell when you strike it with your hand. A beautiful fresh-water *cenote* hides just across the road from the church. Also to be seen in Kikil are traditional Mayan ceremonies, such as the **Ch-Chac,** a rain petition from May through June (taxi to Kikil 12-15 pesos).

■ Río Lagartos

The small fishing village of Río Lagartos (pop. 3,000) is an idyllic, relatively *gringo-free pueblito*. Río's main attraction is the 47,000-hectare **Río Lagartos National Park,** home to some 30,000 pink flamingos, 211 other bird species, spider monkeys, white-tailed deer, and alligators, which gave Río its name. A secluded sugary beach, sumptuous seafood restaurants, and super-hospitable locals often cause travelers to extend their stays.

Orientation and Practical Information Río Lagartos is easily accessed from Tizimín (48 km), Valladolid (104km), and Mérida (156km). There is neither a post office nor a bank in the village; the town's services are practically limited to the long-distance **caseta** in the *zócalo* (tel. 3-26-68 or -65). **Autotransportes de Oriente (ADO)** has frequent buses to Tizmín (6 per day, 1hr., 9 pesos). The cheerful owner of La Cueva de Macumba (see below) can arrange for someone to take you on their boat to **Isla Holbox** (see p. 532), which is infinitely more convenient than traveling by land via Chiquilá, though the total cost of the stunning two-hour journey along the coast will come to at least 400 pesos. **Telephone Code:** 986.

Accommodations There is one. It has four rooms, none of them with locks. **Cabañas Los Dos Hermanos** (tel. 3-26-68 ext. 183) is on the same street as the bus station, three blocks to the east and almost on the beach. Some people may be disquieted by the lack of keys—fret not, the buildings stand in the grounds of the owner's home and nothing has ever been swiped. This apparent security risk is actually an indication of Río's genuine hospitality and the honesty of its inhabitants. As you wander through town you'll notice doors left ajar, bikes leaning against walls, and high-quality fishing nets lying around. As the locals will tell you: ¡*No hay problema!* But as always, use common sense and exercise caution. The sizable *cabañas* each has a double bed with mosquito netting, cable TV, fans, and clean bathrooms with hot water (one room 70 pesos; fit as many people as you like; hammock hooks provided; reservations highly recommended).

Food **Restaurante Isla Contoy** is right on the shore, 3 blocks south and two blocks west of the *zócalo*; from the bus station walk 5 blocks west and a few meters north. Enjoy the beach view and gregarious owner as you sup on delicious *fillete relleno* (breaded fish stuffed with shrimp and salsa, 25 pesos; open daily 6am-11pm). The restaurant also owns four **lanchas** that can be hired for a tour of the park (200-300 pesos, depending on the season). To sample the cooking and decorative tastes of an eclectic native, try **La Cueva de Macumba,** also on the waterfront, two blocks north of the *zócalo* near the lighthouse. The delightfully creative owner has decorated the place with a local economy motif, complete with fishing gear, artfully arranged plumage, and a sea shell chandelier. *Salbutes* (fried tortillas) cost 1.50 pesos apiece. Ask politely and he'll let you climb the ladder to his loft/studio, where you can witness the creative process in action (open daily in the evening).

Sights and Entertainment The only way to see the **Río Lagartos National Park** is by boat; make arrangements with local fishermen or at Restaurante Isla Contoy (200-300 pesos, up to 6 people). The trip starts through the jungly lagoon called **"El Río."** Always be on the lookout for jumping fish and perched birds of prey. Shortly, the lagoon opens up into a shallow bay where you can spot shockingly pink flamingos. Ask to be dropped off at the salt plant if you want to do some exploring of your own. While it's hard to predict when you're likely to see lots of birds (locals searching for conches often scare the flamingos to remote parts), the early morning is your best bet, and December the best flamingo-watching month of the year.

Consistent with the tranquil and laid back attitude with which this fishing town accepts each new day, Río's nightlife does not get much more exciting than a few satisfying beers after dinner. After dark, the lighthouse keeps watch over the *zócalo* with broad, lazy sweeps of its giant beam. Teenagers crowd the foosball tables in the square while screaming kids provide a cacophony of background noise. Every now and then, an energetic game of basketball draws a small crowd. On Saturday nights, **Restaurante Río Lagartos,** 100m south of the two plastic flamingos on Principal (Calle 10) near the bus station, turns into a disco. The brightly painted reefscape walls give way to live music and speakers the size of fridges only once a week; at other times this, too, is a fine seafood joint, where lobster goes for only 55 pesos.

QUINTANA ROO

■ Cancún

Drunk on the success of Puerto Vallarta and Acapulco, Mexican entrepreneurs spent the better part of the 60s searching for the next location to feed their enormous ambitions. Cancún, blessed with kilometers of magnificent white beaches bordering turquoise water, was picked as the site for the new tourist nirvana. This government-backed choice was aesthetically and logistically ideal: connected to the mainland by two bridges, each less than 100 meters, the L-shaped island has 360° water access; it is also conveniently close to the most celebrated Mayan ruins.

Since the first hotel sprung up in 1970, construction has been carefully engineered. The *Zona Hotelera* (Hotel Zone), located almost exclusively on *Isla Cancún,* was built with every conceivable tourist need in mind. There is a water purification system to provide the Hotel Zone with safe tap water, no begging on the streets, and strict zoning laws to prevent a scourge of skyscrapers. Regrettably, the lack of comparable architectural guidelines resulted in a kaleidoscope of disparate styles. Today Cancún (pop. 400,000) is a randomly assembled (albeit modern) jumble, best suited to wealthy vacationers and raucous spring-breakers.

ORIENTATION

On the eastern tip of the Yucatán Peninsula, Cancún twinkles 285km east of Mérida via Rte. 180 and 382km north of Chetumal and the Belizean border via Rte. 307. The resort has two sections: **Ciudad Cancún,** where you'll find most services and shopping, and **Isla Cancún,** home of the *Zona Hotelera* and pure white beaches. The main drag in Ciudad Cancún, **Avenida Tulum,** runs parallel to **Yaxchilán** (Yash-chee-YAN), four blocks over. These two streets roughly form a parallelogram with **Avenidas**

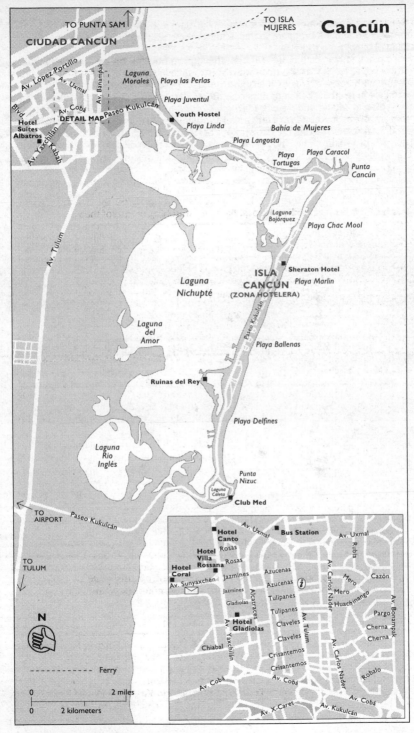

Cancún

TO PUNTA SAM

CIUDAD CANCÚN

TO ISLA MUJERES

Av. López Portillo
Av. Uxmal
Av. Banampak
Av. Cobá
Paseo Kukulcán
Blvd.
Av. Yaxchilán
Kabah
Av. Tulum

DETAIL MAP

Hotel Suites Albatros

Laguna Morales
Playa las Perlas
Playa Juventul
Youth Hostel
Playa Linda
Playa Langosta
Bahía de Mujeres
Playa Tortugas
Playa Caracol
Punta Cancún

Laguna Bojórquez
Playa Chac Mool

Laguna Nichupté

ISLA CANCÚN
(ZONA HOTELERA)

Sheraton Hotel
Playa Marlin

Paseo Kukulcán

Laguna del Amor

Playa Ballenas

Ruinas del Rey

Playa Delfines

Laguna Río Inglés

Punta Nizuc

Laguna Caleta
Club Med

TO AIRPORT
Paseo Kukulcán

TO TULUM

N

- - - - - - Ferry

0   2 miles
0   2 kilometers

DETAIL MAP

Av. Uxmal
Bus Station
Av. Uxmal
Rubia

Hotel Canto
Rosas
Hotel Villa Rossana
Rosas
Hotel Coral
Jazmines
Av. Sunyaxchén
Jazmines
Gladiolas
Alcatraces
Hotel Gladiolas
Chiabal
Av. Yaxchilán
Av. Cobá

Azucenas
Azucenas
Tulipanes
Tulipanes
Claveles
Claveles
Crisantemos
Crisantemos
Av. Cobá

Av. Carlos Nader
Mero
Mero
Huachinango
Av. Tulum
Av. Carlos Nader
Av. X-Caret
Av. Cobá
Av. Kukulcán

Cazón
Pargo
Cherna
Cherna
Robalo
Av. Bonampak

Cobá and **Uxmal.** From the bus station, Av. Tulum and *el centro* stretch to the right of the large white monument in the center of the traffic circle. The *Zona Hotelera's* main drag is **Paseo Kukulcán.**

To reach either section of town from the airport, buy a ticket for a *colectivo*—one of the white jeeps that shuttle new arrivals to their hotels (50 pesos). A private taxi (white with green stripes) will charge around 75 pesos for that trip; at least 30 pesos to take you from the beach to the stores, depending on how far into the *Zona Hotelera* you are; and around 8 pesos for *intra-ciudad.* Always settle the price before getting in. Buses marked *"Hoteles"* travel between Av. Tulum and Paseo Kukulcán around the clock, linking the two sections of town (3 pesos). To get off the bus in the *Zona Hotelera,* don't be shy. Follow the example of the locals by pounding hard on the wall—it's the only way to get the daredevil drivers to slow down enough so that you break only a few bones when jumping off. Many places rent mopeds, useful for exploring the 18 kilometers of beaches which stretch from the Youth Hostel to Punta Nizuc (see p. 529).

PRACTICAL INFORMATION

Tourist Offices: Av. Tulum 22-23 (tel. 84-32-38 or 84-04-37), inside the *Palacio de Gobierno,* or booths all over town. **Cancún Tips,** at Av. Tulum 29 (tel. 84-40-44 or 84-44-43), at Pl. Caracol in the *Zona Hotelera,* and at the airport, is a useful English-language magazine with maps and practical information (US$3). Snag one for free at the airport or from the dispensers; only suckers pay for it.

Consulates: U.S. (tel. 83-02-32), Plaza Caracol, 3rd. floor. Open Mon.-Fri. 9am-1pm and 3-5:30pm. **Canada,** Av. Tulum 200 in Pl. México (tel. 84-37-16). Open Mon.-Fri. 10am-2pm. For emergencies outside of office hours, call the embassy in Mexico City (tel. 91-5-724-7900). **United Kingdom,** in the Hotel Royal Caribbean (tel. 85-11-66, ext. 462). Open Mon.-Fri. 9am-5pm. **France,** Av. Xel-Ha 113 (tel. 87-39-50). Open Mon.-Fri. 11:30am-1pm. **Germany,** Punta Conoco 36, in the *centro* (tel. 84-18-98). Open Mon.-Fri. 9am-1:30pm.

Currency Exchange: Bancomer, Av. Tulum 20 (tel. 84-44-00), has the best rate of all banks on Av. Tulum. Open Mon.-Fri. 9am-1:30pm. Both **Banamex,** Tulum 19 (tel. 84-54-11), and **Banco Serfín,** Av. Tulum at Cobá (tel. 84-14-24), give cash advances on Visa and MC and have Cirrus **ATMs.** Equally competitive but more convenient is **CUNEX Exchange** (tel. 87-09-01), next to Banco Serfín on the corner of Tulum and Cobá. Open daily 8am-11pm.

American Express: Tulum 208 (tel. 84-17-01), three blocks past Cobá away from the city. Open Mon.-Fri. 9am-6pm, Sat. 9am-1pm.

Telephones: LADATELs and a 20- or 50-pesos phone cards make for easy and cheap long-distance calls. The public phone in Pl. Nautilus near the youth hostel is another option, provided you have a big pile of coins. *Casetas* throughout the city tend to charge hefty fees. For local calls, prefix the number you are dialing with "8" (we have already included the magic cipher in our listings).

Telegrams: (tel. 84-15-29), at the post office. Open Mon.-Fri. 9am-8:30pm, Sat. 9am-4:30pm. Allow one day for the message to arrive.

Airport: (tel. 86-00-28), south of the city on Rte. 307. *Colectivos* 50 pesos, taxis 80 pesos (fixed rates to downtown; buy a ticket at the desk). Airlines include **Aerocaribe** (tel. 84-20-00); **Mexicana** (tel. 87-44-44 or 87-27-69); **LACSA** (tel. 87-31-01); **American** (tel. 86-00-55 or 86-00-86); **Continental** (tel. 86-00-06 or 86-01-69); **Northwest** (tel. 86-00-44); **United** (tel. 86-01-58 or 86-00-25).

Buses: (tel. 84-13-78), on Uxmal at Tulum. **ADO** travels to Valladolid (11:30am and 1:30pm, 2hr., 32 pesos); **Premier** to Campeche (11:30am and 1:30pm, 6hr., 98 pesos), Chichén Itzá (8:45am, 2½hr., 47 pesos), Palenque (6pm, 12hr., 155 pesos), and Playa del Carmen (every hr., 45min., 13 pesos). You can save about 25% by hopping on the second-class buses that leave from the curbside and go to Mérida, Tulum, and Chetumal.

Ferries: To Isla Mujeres: take a bus or van marked "Pto. Juárez" to the two ferry depots north of town (Punta Sam for car ferries, Puerto Juárez for passenger ferries). Passenger ferries shuttle across on the half hour 8am-8pm (15 pesos). **To**

Cozumel: from Playa del Carmen, south of Cancún and accessible by bus from the terminal in town (20 or 25 pesos).

Taxis: (tel. 88-69-90). The minimum fare within the *Zona* is 25 pesos; a ride into town can cost as much as 40 pesos. Within the *centro*, a taxi ride should run around 10 pesos. Prices are negotiable; be sure to settle the deal before getting in.

Luggage storage: At the bus station, 5 pesos for 24hr.

Moped Rental: Available from most major hotels; try **Hotel Las Perlas** (tel. 83-20-22), near the CREA youth-hostel (roughly US$60 per day).

English Bookstore: Fama, Tulum 105 (tel. 84-65-86). Newspapers, magazines, guidebooks, maps, and trashy beach books in English. Open daily 8am-10:30pm.

Supermarket: Súper San Francisco (tel. 84-11-55), Av. Tulum next to Banamex. Open Mon.-Sat. 7:30am-10pm, Sun. 7am-9pm. **Súper Deli,** a 24-hr. grocery store, is conveniently located near the youth hostel.

Laundromat: Lavandería Automática "Alborada," Náder 5 (tel. 84-15-84), behind the Ayuntamiento Benito Juárez. Full service 31 pesos, self-service 7 pesos. Self-service hours Mon.-Sat. 8am-6pm.

Red Cross: Av. Yaxchilán 2 (tel. 84-16-16). English spoken. Open 24hr.

Pharmacies: Several along Tulum and Yaxchilán. **Farmacia Paris,** Yaxchilán 32 (tel. 84-01-64), at the intersection with Calle Rosas, is open 24hr.

Medical Assistance: Hospital Americano, Calle Viento 15 (tel. 84-61-33, after hours 84-63-19), five blocks south on Tulum after its intersection with Cobá. **IMSS** (tel. 84-19-19), at Tulum and Cobá. For an ambulance call **Total Assist** (tel. 84-80-92 or 84-81-16), at Claveles 5 near Av. Tulum. English spoken.

Emergency: 06.

Police: (tel. 84-19-13), Av. Tulum next to City Hall.

Post Office: Av. Xel-Ha at Sunyaxchén (tel. 84-15-24). From Tulum, cut through any side street to Yaxchilán and head up Sun Yax Chén. The post office is 4 blocks farther. Open Mon.-Fri. 8am-7pm, Sat. 9am-noon. **Postal Code:** 77500.

Telephone Code: 98.

ACCOMMODATIONS AND CAMPING

The Mexican government may have prevented skyscrapers from going up, but it did not do the same for the prices. If you're not careful, this place will suck money out of you faster than you can sign your next traveler's check. Budget travelers often stay at (or camp in) the **CREA Youth Hostel** and avoid the *Zona Hotelera* altogether. Even in *Ciudad Cancún,* some hotels will charge you upwards of US$20 for a room you wouldn't let your dog sleep in. Some daredevils sleep on the beach in the *Zona;* they should be careful of robbers and the police. With the exception of the CREA, all hotels listed are within a 10- to 15-minute walk from Av. Tulum. During high season, phone reservations are a good idea.

CREA Youth Hostel (HI), Paseo Kukulcán Km. 3 (tel. 83-13-37). From the bus station or anywhere on Av. Tulum, catch the *"Zona Hotelera"* bus (3 pesos) and ask the driver to drop you off at the *"centro juvenil."* 100 single-sex dorm rooms with four bunk beds apiece. Sheets and towels provided. Ceiling fans but no A/C. Use the personal lockers when you leave the room, even to shower. No hot water. Small pool, basketball court, and table-tennis. 85 pesos, plus a 50-peso deposit. 10% discount with HI card. No curfew. Check-out 1pm. Maximum stay 15 days. You can pitch a tent on the front lawn for 40 pesos per person, plus a 50-peso deposit. Locker not included, but place your stuff with hostel security.

Hotel Coral, Sunyaxchén 30 (tel. 84-20-97). Heading west from Av. Yaxchilán, the hotel is two blocks down on the left. Airy and comfortable lobby, friendly staff, and spacious, colorful rooms. *Agua purificada* in the hall. Hot water. Courtyard with pool (usually empty). Check-out 1:30pm. Singles 50 pesos, 25 pesos for each additional person. To make reservations, wire payment 10 days in advance.

Hotel Villa Rossana, Av. Yaxchilán 25 (tel. 84-19-43). On the right, past Sun Yax Chén, as you come down Yaxchilán. Large and well lit rooms with ceiling fans, balconies, and hot water. Pleasant courtyard has a pool. Check-out 1pm. Singles and doubles 75 pesos. Triples 100 pesos. Quads 125 pesos. Add 25 pesos for A/C.

Hotel Canto, Sm. 24, Mza. 22 Retorno 5, Av. Yaxchilán (tel. 84-12-67). As you turn off Av. Uxmal, look for the fading pink building on your right. Clean, plain rooms have A/C, color TV, and phones. Spotless, groovy-blue bathrooms with good showers and hot water. *Agua purificada* in the lobby. Check-out 1pm. Singles and doubles 120 pesos. Triples 130 pesos. Quads 140 pesos.

Suites Albatros, Yaxchilán 154 (tel. 84-22-42), two blocks south of Cobá and across the street from the Red Cross. So nice, it's hard to believe you found it listed in a budget guide. Spotlessly clean, huge rooms with vividly tiled floors, modern art, kitchens, hot water, and A/C. Convenience store and laundromat next door. Upstairs rooms have balconies. Singles 100 pesos. Doubles 140 pesos. 40 pesos for each additional person.

FOOD

American tourists' reluctance to experiment with their taste buds has resulted in an overpriced and underspiced culinary experience. Don't even think of eating in the *Zona Hotelera;* but also avoid eating at the very bottom of the food chain—the roadside booths serving meats of dubious origin. Cholera is not fun, believe us. For good, inexpensive food try the many joints along Avs. Cobá, Tulum and Yaxchilán. **Mercado 28,** behind the post office and circumscribed by Av. Xel-Ha, might be the best option for budget fare. Numerous cafés are located in its western courtyard; a hearty *comida corrida* at **Restaurants Margely, Acapulco,** or **La Chaya** costs only 5-25 pesos! La Chaya offers vegetarian meals (all open daily 8am-6pm). Almost all restaurants listed below are in Ciudad Cancún.

El Tacolote, Av. Cobá 19 (tel. 87-30-45). Look for the sombrero-sporting, taco-gobbling, yellow chicken out front. Prices start at 16 pesos for a large plate of grilled meat and many small tortillas; the *alambre* goes for 25 pesos. Excellent, friendly service. Open daily 5:30pm-2am.

Restaurante Río Nizuc, Paseo Kukulcán, Km. 22. Take the *"Hoteles"* bus (3 pesos) to the last stop near the Hotel Regina (Km. 20), then hail a taxi (15 pesos). A few kilometers west of *Punta Nizuc,* this seafood mecca remains as yet undiscovered by the tourist hordes. Nevertheless, the crowd of locals that gathers to enjoy the secluded sea-level dining attests to the popularity and quality of the food. Enormous servings of freshly fished, deliciously prepared barbecued fish (30 pesos) and *mariscos* (30 pesos). Open daily 11am-6pm.

100% Natural, Sun Yax Chén 6 (tel. 84-36-17), at Yaxchilán; another location in Plaza Caracol. Shaded, leafy porch and lush tropical garden ease over-heated spirits. Delicious food and tropical shakes made from fresh juicy fruit (10-15 pesos) soothe vegetarian stomachs. Open daily 7am-midnight.

SIGHTS

Visitors do not come to Cancún to see Mexico. Most visitors do not even come to Cancún to see Cancún. And even the powdery white sand beaches and glistening blue surf provide only a backdrop for the sight most of the debauched *gringos* have come to see: each other's semi-nude, alcohol-soaked, sunburnt bodies. Cancún's name, meaning "snake nest" in Mayan, has proven to be oddly prophetic. Progress and culture have been summarily executed and buried in a neon tank top. Since fun here requires no more than a credit card and a brainstem, your mind won't be doing much wandering. If it does, however, you run the risk of becoming painfully aware of the reality of poverty and inequality upon which the artifice of Cancún is built.

Even if you stay inland in Ciudad Cancún, you can still take advantage of the well groomed beaches in front of the luxury hotels in the *Zona Hotelera.* Remember, all beaches in Mexico are public property, and travelers often discreetly use hotel restrooms, fresh-water showers, and lounge chairs. If you wisely choose to avoid the resort beach scene, head for the peaceful **Playa Langosta,** west of the CREA, or for the shores south of the **Sheraton Hotel,** some of the safest and the most pleasant in Cancún. The sand is clean, the water transparent, and the waves active. Organized beach activities include volleyball, scuba classes, and Mexican-style painting lessons; become a visitor of the hotel for the day to join in. Boogie boards can be rented at the small marina on the beach (25 pesos for two hours), but Cancún's surf is a whimper to the roar of the rest of the *costa turquesa*. **Playa Chac-Mool,** where waves are about one-meter high, is as exciting as it gets. **Playa Linda,** a 10-minute walk east, provides the closest decent (but shallow) swimming.

Cancún offers watersport adventures of all types for those with hefty bank accounts. **Marina Agua Ray** (tel. 83-17-73), near Pl. Flamingo, provides wave runners, jet skis, and parasailing, scuba diving, snorkeling, water-skiing, and deep-sea fishing equipment—all at obscenely *gringo*-oriented prices. **Scuba Cancún** (tel. 83-10-11), next to Carlos 'n Charlie's, offers various diving lessons and services at comparatively reasonable prices. The dock to the right of the CREA hostel supports a dive shop which offers two hours of snorkeling, equipment included, for US$20.

ENTERTAINMENT

If it is burning greenbacks you have and frenetic, laser-lit partying you lack, you are the reason why Cancún was erected, and your late-night entertainment is ensured. **Discos and bars** are to be found both downtown (south end of Av. Tulum near Cobá) and in the *Zona Hotelera* at Plaza Caracol (km. 9 on Paseo Kukulkán). Most establishments open at 9pm and close when the crowds leave, around 5-6am. Restaurant workers in the *Zona Hotelera* are good at pointing out which spots are hot. Most clubs have a system of cover charges liable to make fellas and feminists fume alike—women get in free just about everywhere.

Near the youth hostel (a 10-minute walk towards the *Zona*), **La Boom** and **Tequila Boom** (tel. 83-11-52), a nightclub and bar under the same roof, provide double opportunity for incessant imbibing and throbbing. Tequila Boom's huge video screens are always accessible free of cover, but the record comes out even due to the pricey beer; it will cost you $US10 to get inside La Boom. The premier attraction on Plaza Caracol is **Dady'O** (tel. 83-33-33), although the cave-like entrance makes you feel like you're heading for fiery hell rather than disco heaven. The cave-scape continues through to the multi-tiered dance floor, above which hangs what appears to be the backside of a failed NASA moon shot. A cafeteria in the club serves snacks (12-25 pesos). Laser show nightly at 11pm (cover US$10; free Tues. and for women on Fri.; open daily 9pm-late). Next door, **Dady Rock** (tel. 83-16-26) has all-you-can-eat/drink deals (US$10-17) several nights a week (open daily 6pm-late). In the vicinity, **Tequila Rock** bludgeons eardrums on several different stage (male eardrums US$15, female eardrums US$5; open bar on Mon.). Closer to Plaza Caracol and a little easier on the ears, **Cat's Reggae Club** provides perhaps the coolest and coziest dance floor. The reggae beat reverberates around colorful walls decorated with portraits of legendary reggae artists (cover 45 pesos, free Mon. or with *Cancún Tips* card). **Christine,** in the Hotel Krystal (tel. 3-11-33), caters to an older, more conservative crowd. Boogeying thirtysomethings look like they've been let loose in an orchestra pit (cover US$10 for men only; no shorts or sandals). In Ciudad Cancún, **Karamba,** a gay disco on Tulipanes just off Tulum, has a spacious multi-level floor, funky pop-art murals, and a colorful variety of dance music (no cover).

Bullfights occur every Wednesday at 3:30pm, in the bullring on Bonampak at Sayil (tel. 84-54-65). Tickets are available at travel agencies on Tulum (210 pesos per person including taxi fare, less if you're in a large group) or at the bullring on a bullfight day. Show includes a cockfight and a performance by the **Ballet Folklórico.** For less brutal entertainment, the right timing could mean enjoying Cancún's celebrated jazz festival (mid- to late-May) or the refreshingly native Caribbean festival (November). Check with the tourist office for info.

■ Isla Holbox and Chiquilá

Isla Holbox (OL-bosh), as in "This is Isla Holbosshhh. Don't tell anyone about it; I want it all to myself." The great thing is, you just about can. Aside from the months of July and December, when Mexican tourists flood the place, this tiny island just off the northeastern tip of the Yucatán Peninsula is home to a handful of *holboxeños* and their fishing. The pace of life here is unbelievably *tranquila,* the beaches and surrounding tiny *islas* inspiring, and the people supremely friendly. If you think you've never seen such a beautiful sunset, stay another night. **Chiquilá** is the unfortunate embarkation point for passengers ferrying to the secluded beaches of Isla Holbox. The small settlement will not delay in-transit tourists, but after the last ferry chugs out to sea, late arrivals usually prefer to head back to civilization for a meal and a bed for two simple reasons: there's no place to stay in Chiquilá, and the mosquitoes suck. Literally.

Orientation and Practical Information Transportation should be planned carefully and in advance, as buses and boats are infrequent, and schedules are hardly permanent. Currently, the easiest way to navigate this chain of variables is to take the 8:30am bus from Cancún (23 pesos), which reaches Chiquilá at 11am, and wait until the 2pm passenger ferry (15 pesos). Impatient travelers can strike up a deal with one of the many fishermen who mull around. The only other passenger ferry leaves at 8am. To catch it, take the 4am Cancún-Valladolid bus, ask the driver (nicely!) to let you off at Ideal, take a taxi from there into Kantunil Kin, and then a local bus to Chiquilá (Chiquilkan, 6 pesos). This ordeal will put you on the beach by 9am. A third option is to take the car ferry, which will transport passengers (departing Chiquilá daily at 10am, returning from Holbox daily at 3pm; cars 300 pesos, humans 5 pesos). The passenger ferry's schedule, however, tends to be somewhat more reliable. Returning from Holbox is much easier, since both Valladolid-bound and Cancún-bound buses meet the early boat. Be ready to leap off when the boat strikes the dock, because the buses wait for no one. If the Cancún bus doesn't show, take the Valladolid-Mérida bus to Kantunil Kin; the Cancún bus swings by here at 6:30am. You can always flag down a Valladolid-Cancún bus at Ideal, though waiting in the sun will be torturous.

Sloshing in an incompletely drained swamp, Chiquilá is neither a pleasant nor an inviting place, and it has neither accommodations nor eateries. If you miss the last ferry to Holbox, try to take a *lancha* (around 100 pesos for up to 5 people); otherwise return to **Kantunil Kin,** a town 43km south of Chiquilá, on the Chiquilá access road. In Kantunil Kin, beds are available at the red-and-white **Casa de Huéspedes "Del Parque"** (tel. 5-00-17), which is on the other side of the basketball court next to the church (singles 55 pesos, doubles 70 pesos, triples 90 pesos).

Holbox's **public telephone** *caseta* is a half-block east of the *zócalo* on Igualdad (open Mon.-Sat. 8am-1pm and 4-8pm; 2-3 pesos). The island's **Centro de Salud,** on the right side of Juárez in the blue-and-white building, houses a doctor who may be awakened in case of a serious emergency. The **police** force lounges in the station at the *zócalo* on the corner of Juárez and Díaz (open daily 9am-2pm and 4-8pm, but don't count on it). There is no bank on the island.

Accommodations and Food Two words: simple and fish. To talk shop with the local hotel mogul, look for Sra. Dinora in **Tienda Dinora** on the southwest side of the *zócalo.* She owns the store and the hotel of the same name, as well as **Posada Los Arcos,** on the southeast side of the *zócalo.* Rooms at both places have tiled floors and bathrooms, hot water, fans, and closets (singles 50 pesos, doubles 70 pesos, triples 80 pesos). Sra. Dinora also rents out similarly prized, crude beachfront *cabañas*— though her hotel rooms are a better value. **Posada D'Ingrid,** one block to the left and two blocks toward the beach from the western corner of the *zócalo,* offers gleaming salmon-colored rooms with hot water, clean bathrooms, ceiling fans, and hooks for two hammocks in addition to the double bed (50 pesos). **Hotel Flamingo** stands close to the dock and features a view of the mainland shaded by coconut palms. Five rooms with flaky paint and clean bathrooms allow space for up to five people (40 pesos); fan and hot water 25 pesos more for one person, 30 pesos for two, 35 pesos for three; 10-20 pesos more during high.

Restaurants in Holbox follow the pace of island life, meandering through time without a fixed schedule. Among them is **Zarabanda,** one block south of the *zócalo* and two blocks east of Juárez (look for the sign on Juárez). The cooks will prepare excellent fish and meat dishes (12 pesos). No menu, no waiters—you just eat what they've got for you (open daily 8am-10pm). **Lonchería El Parque,** off the *zócalo,* two doors down from Dinora's, also serves fresh, cheap seafood. A chicken or beef dish and an ice-cold beer will cost only about 10 pesos (open daily 9am-10pm).

Sights The island's north shore has a pleasant enough beach, but the main draws, aside from sunning and sleeping, are the boat trips provided by local fishermen (4-hr. cruise 150-200 pesos; try to get a group together). East of the island is **Isla de Pájaros,** called **Isla Morena** by locals, home to nearly 40 species of birds, including flamingos and pelicans. Next stop is **Ojo de Agua,** an inlet on the mainland fed by a subterranean freshwater spring. Jump in and splash around in the shallow pools. Finally, you'll head across the lagoon which separates Isla Holbox from the mainland (look out for the many dolphins) to **Isla de la Pasión,** at the western end, so named for the couples of birds and *isleños* that relax there during the off-season. During the high season, this small island caters to day-trippers with its restaurant-bar, live music and volleyball court. To see *holboxeños* at their liveliest, cruise the brightly lit *zócalo* at dusk where old friends and families socialize every night. Be sure to head down to the north shore sometime during the night. There, you can witness *ardentía,* a rare and completely natural phosphorescent phenomenon. Microorganisms respond to movement in the water by turning bright green; just kick the water a bit to see the eery glow. During peak seasons, **Cariocas Restaurant and Disco,** on Igualdad two blocks of the *zócalo,* is *the* place to be.

■ Isla Mujeres

When in 1517 the Spaniard Francisco Hernández de Córdoba blew into this tiny island (7km by 1km, 11km northeast of the coast of Quintana Roo) looking for slaves to work the Cuban mines, he found only women. With the men fishing out at sea, Córdoba saw an island seemingly ruled by the Mayan goddess of fertility, Ixchel. Looking to the deity's numerous female attendants, he dubbed the site "Island of Women." After Córdoba left, the island remained in Spanish hands, existing variously as a private *hacienda,* a haven for pirates, and a home to Caribbean fishermen.

Some present-day inhabitants of the island (pop. 13,500) still fish, but now they also sell goods to the boatloads of daytrippers who arrive each morning from Cancún. However, mind your C's and N's, and don't mistake *la isla* for a smaller version of its across-the-water neighbor. Those who choose to linger on Isla Mujeres will discover beaches of velvety sand, supremely good snorkeling, postcard-perfect azure water, and more breathing room than exists in all of Cancún.

ORIENTATION

Vigorous walkers will have no difficulty getting around the bustling *centro*. The town is laid out in a rough grid. Six major streets run perpendicular to the dock: **Avenidas López Mateos, Matamoros, Abasolo, Madero, Morelos,** and **Nicolás Bravo,** from north to south. **Avenida Rueda Medina** runs the length of the island along the coastline, past **Playas Paraíso, Lancheros, Indios,** and the **Garrafón National Park. Avenidas Juárez, Hidalgo, Guerrero,** and **Carlos Lazo,** in that order, run parallel to R. Medina. Turning left on any of these streets will quickly lead you to **Playa Norte.** Finally, on the southern tip of the island, beyond a disused lighthouse, are the remains of a Mayan temple, **Ix-chel.** A good source of general information is **Islander,** a local publication available at travel agency shops, the ferry dock at Puerto Juárez, and the tourist office in the *zócalo.* Be sure to pick up a map wherever you get *Islander,* as street names have long since faded from most buildings. The best way to explore the island for yourself is by moped—the whole trip won't take more than three hours, even with a few stops for a swim. Public buses go only as far as Playa Lancheros (3 pesos). Taxis, on the other hand, roam the length of Mujeres; you should have no problem catching one unless you're returning from Garrafón long after the park closes.

PRACTICAL INFORMATION

Tourist Office: Hidalgo #7, 2nd. floor at Plaza Isla Mujeres, between Mateos and Matamoros. Most information, including a map of the town, is also available in *Islander, Cancún Tips,* and *Isla Mujeres Tips.* Open Mon.-Fri. 9am-4pm.

Currency Exchange: Banco del Atlántico (tel. 7-00-05), on R. Medina near the ferry dock. Open Mon.-Fri. 9am-2:30pm. Better rates from booths on Av. Hidalgo.

Telephones: Call home from one of the ubiquitous polyphones, or try the long-distance *caseta* in the lobby of **Hotel María Jose** (tel. 7-01-30), on Madero just off R. Medina. Open daily 7am-7pm.

Telegrams: Guerrero 13 (tel. 7-01-13), next to the post office. Open Mon.-Fri. 9am-3pm. They also have a **fax** service.

Ferries: To get to the island, catch a boat from Puerto Juárez, 2km north of Ciudad Cancún and accessible by a "Puerto Juárez" *colectivo* (15min., 3 pesos) or by taxi (25 pesos). Passenger ferries (every hr. 8am-8pm, 45min., 6.5 pesos) and speedier cruisers (every hr. 5:30am-8:30pm, 15min., 15 pesos). Arrive early—ferries are notorious for leaving ahead of schedule if they're full. A car ferry runs to Mujeres from Punta Sam, 5km north of Puerto Juárez (8 and 11am, 2:45, 5:30 and 8:15 pm; 6 pesos per person, 36 pesos per car).

Taxis: (tel. 7-00-66). Lines form near sights and beaches. Rides from town to Playas Paraíso and Lancheros, Garrafón, and the ruins cost 8, 20, and 25 pesos.

Moped Rental: Usually 40 pesos per hr., but shop around. At **El Zorro,** on Guerrero between Abasolo and Matamoros, they go for 100 pesos per day—more time than you'll need to see the entire island. Open daily 9am-5pm.

Markets: Súper Betino, Morelos 3, on the *zócalo.* Non-resort prices. Open daily 7am-11pm. For a better selection of produce, try the **fruit stalls** just outside or the mini-market **Isla Mujeres,** on Hidalgo between Abasolo and Madero.

Laundry Service: Lavandería Tim Phó, Av. Juárez 94 at Abasolo. 4kg for 10 pesos, 2-hr. turnaround. Open Mon.-Sat. 7am-9pm, Sun 8am-2pm.

Red Cross: tel. 7-02-80.

Pharmacy: Farmacia Lily, Madero 18 at Hidalgo (tel. 7-01-64). Two blocks from the dock as the crow flies and one block left. Open daily 8:30am-9:30pm.

Medical Assistance: Centro de Salud, Guerrero 5 at Morelos (tel. 7-01-17). White building at the northwest corner of the *zócalo.* Open 24hr. Some doctors speak English, as does **Dr. Antonio Torres García** (tel. 7-00-21, 7-04-77, or beeper 91-98-88-78–68 code 1465), Matamoros near Guerrero. Will make house calls. Can be reached on VHF *canal* 68. Open 24hr.

Police: Hidalgo at Morelos (tel. 7-00-98), in the Palacio Municipal. Open 24hr.

Post Office: Guerrero and López Mateos (tel. 7-00-85), at the northwest corner of town, around the corner from the Poc-Na Hostel. Open Mon.-Fri. 8am-7pm, Sat. 9am-1pm. **Postal Code:** 70085.

Telephone Code: 987.

ACCOMMODATIONS AND CAMPING

Lacking the flashiness and jaw-dropping prices of Cancún, Isla Mujeres offers a number of opportunities for economical lodging; residents are too busy chasing the waves and enjoying the island breezes to concern themselves with swindling tourists. Prices tend to fluctuate, depending on the season and length of stay; inquire ahead. Camping on the beach is not strictly regulated; most people find **Playa Indios** (½km past Playa Paraíso on R. Medina) the most hospitable and unobtrusive spot to sack out. However, it's always wise to sample local opinion before settling in for the night. All hotels listed below are in town, north of the *zócalo.*

Hotel Marcianito, centrally located at Abasolo 10 (tel. 7-01-11), between Juárez and Hidalgo. All rooms have ceiling fans, hot water, and *agua purificada;* they are tastefully decorated with color pictures of Mayan temples. Check-out noon. Singles 60 pesos. Doubles 70 pesos. Triples 80 pesos. Quads 90 pesos.

Hotel Xul-Ha, Hidalgo 23 (tel. 7-00-75), between Matamoros and López Mateos. White and boxy—very Bauhaus. Clean rooms and bathrooms. Two sets of screened windows provide good ventilation. Lobby with color TV, English paperbacks, and coffee. Quiet location. Check-out noon. Singles and doubles 60 pesos. Triples 80 pesos. 20 pesos more during peak season. Discounts for longer stays.

Poc-Na Youth Hostel, Matamoros 15 (tel. 7-00-59). Revolves around its high-ceilinged *palapa* dining hall, which provides ample opportunities for socializing. So do the dorm-like rooms, each holding 8-14 people (both single-sex and mixed available). Popular among Aussies. Small additional fees for sheets, towels, and lock. Check-out 1pm, 9 pesos more to stay later. 18 pesos per person. Three private rooms available, 40-60 pesos. Cafeteria open 7am-3pm and 6-11pm.

Hotel Carmelina, Guerrero 4 (tel. 7-00-06), at Madero. Small and clean rooms with ample lighting and solid mattresses. All have hot water and fans. Singles 75 pesos. Doubles 105 pesos. Triples 150 pesos. A/C 15 pesos extra.

FOOD

Not surprisingly, seafood is ubiquitous. Try *pulpo* (octopus), delicious and actually not slimy, *caracol* (conch), and the refreshingly tangy *ceviche* (seafood marinated in lime juice, cilantro, and other herbs). For cheap grub, visit the *loncherías* on Guerrero between Matamoros and López Mateos, or look for roaming vendors selling seafood from gigantic pots. Many restaurants close between lunch and dinner.

Café Cito, Matamoros 42 (tel. 7-04-38), at Juárez. Choose anything from crepes (8 pesos) and sandwiches (16 pesos) to the exotic *pez caribeño* (29 pesos). If the meal leaves you yearning to know how a lemonade so divine (5 pesos) could come from a waiter so mortal, spiritual consultations and "emotional release through re-birthing" are available—ask for Sabina. Open Mon.-Wed. and Fri.-Sat. 8am-noon and 6-10pm, Thurs. and Sun. 8am-noon.

La Lomita, two blocks south of Bravo on Juárez. Manages to evade the tourists despite its central location. Feast on the *filete isleño,* the *comida corrida,* or the grilled octopus (20 pesos). Breakfast 10 pesos. Open Sun.-Fri. 9am-11pm.

Chen Huaye ("only here" in Mayan), just off the *zócalo* on Av. Bravo. Ignore the advertisements obnoxiously displayed everywhere: the food is much more personal and infinitely tastier. Try the zesty *pescado a la veracruzana* (24 pesos). Open Thurs.-Tues. 9am-11pm.

El Nopalito, at the corner of Guerrero and Matamoros (tel. 7-05-55), just down the street from Poc Na. Annexed to a Mesoamerican art and curio store, this small and colorful café serves delicately crafted meals on delicate custom-made furniture. *Desayuno tropical* includes yogurt, granola, and fruit salad. Crepes and waffles under 15 pesos. Open Mon.-Sat. 8am-noon and 6-9pm, Sun. 8am-noon.

SIGHTS

In terms of sheer pleasure to the eyes, no human creation on Isla Mujeres could ever compare to the island's natural beauty—the seemingly endless stretches of sand and the abundant marine life. So put on your swimsuit, don some snorkle gear, and go at it. The most popular beach is **Playa Norte. Playas Lanchero** and **Paraíso** (km.3 on R. Martínez) look a lot like it. Snorkeling connoisseurs should head to **Garrafón National Park,** 1km past Lanchero and Paraíso, where the waters feel like blessed champagne and the school of fish recall Harvard—they stick together, there's more than enough, and they know they're what tourists come to see (park open daily 9am-

5pm). **Bahía Dive Shop** (tel./fax 7-03-40), on Rueda Medina across from the car ferry dock, rents quality snorkeling equipment; the staff can direct you to the best spots Or join them year-round for organized reef snorkeling, diving, and fishing trips (US$15, US$40, and US$10; open daily 8:30am-7pm).

La Isleña travel agency (tel. 7-05-78), on Morelos half a block from the dock, organizes trips to nearby **Isla Contoy**, a wildlife sanctuary rife with pelicans, cormorants, and about 5,000 other bird species. The tours include reef snorkeling at **Isla-Che.** (Tour lasts 8:30am-4pm; equipment and two meals included; 175 pesos or US$25; deposit of at least 20 pesos required the previous day; agency open daily 7am-9pm.)

Although not illustrative of how nature currently is, **PESCA**, km 5 on Carretera Sac Bajo, across the Laguna de Makax from the populated northern half of the island, is a heartening example of what it could be. This biological research station is engaged in a breeding program for two (soon to be three) species of sea turtles. Female turtles, captured by PESCA in May, lay their eggs in the safety of the station's beach throughout the summer and are returned to the wild in October. The young are reared for a year before they, too, are released. For 7 pesos, a guide will take you on a stroll through the center to see the turtles and their offspring, at various stages of development depending on the time of year (open daily 9am-5pm).

The remnants of the Mayan temple of **Ix-chel** lay perched on the southern extremity of the island, just past an abandoned lighthouse. Before the eastern and southern walls collapsed into the waves, this temple to the goddess of fertility had slits facing the cardinal directions for astronomical observations. The ruined remains were almost totally wiped out by Hurricane Gilbert in 1988.

ENTERTAINMENT

Isla Mujeres' nightlife is commensurate with its small size and laid-back demeanor. Nevertheless, a handful of locales do what they can to keep peace-loving visitors awake at night. **Restaurant La Peña,** Guerrero 5 at the *zócalo* (tel. 7-03-09), becomes a disco after 11pm. Groovy swings suspended from the ceiling make for great people-watching. **Chimbo's**, on Playa Norte, just about accounts for the rest of Mujeres' nightlife. With a temporary dance floor laid out on the sand and plastic neon palm trees, this place makes up in energetic tackiness for what it lacks in class. At **Pancho Tequila,** on Matamoros between Hidalgo and Guerrero, the small dance floor and lively mix of Mexican and international dance music is as refreshing as the air-conditioning. Things usually start up at the bars after 10pm, but as schedules are erratic, it's best to ask around.

■ Playa del Carmen

Smack dab in the middle of Quintana Roo's proverbial *costa turquesa* (Turquoise Coast), Playa del Carmen (pop. 10,000) is a crossroads for archaeologically inclined travelers en route to inland ruins and those beach hunters heading for Cozumel and

---

Tales from the Crypt

The remnants of the **Hacienda Mundaca,** a 19th-century building, are just before the right-hand turnoff to PESCA, about 3km from town. In the mid-19th century, Fermín Mundaca de Marchaja, a wealthy pirate and slave trader, built these gardens and archways to woo Prisca Gómez, a Spaniard who vacationed on the island. Apparently, he neglected to tell her about his plans, and before the *hacienda* was completed she married another *isleño* (whether he was a gentleman or a fisherman depends on who's telling the story). Mundaca went insane, but not before carving his own gravestone (check the Isla Mujeres cemetery), which reads "As you are, I was; as I am, you will be." Now the site of a re-forestation project, the hacienda's overgrown foundation, a well, and an outhouse are all that remains (grounds open Mon.-Fri. 7am-2:30pm, Sat. 7-10am).

ancún. Though Playa (as locals call it) used to be a fishing village, the vast majority
of its people now earn tourist pesos. As a consequence, it no longer is the budget par-
lise of yesteryear. The town seems to have lost touch with much of its culture and
history, most of which is bundled into one token ruin the size of a beachfront
cabaña. Focusing on the present rather than the past, Playa's *palapas* and moderately priced seafood restaurants look out onto the breezy pedestrian walkway, where
spray-paint artists and hammock vendors hawk their wares.

ORIENTATION

Playa is centered around its main transportation centers, the ferry dock and the bus
stations. The bus drops you off on the main drag, **Avenida Principal** (Juárez), which
runs west from the beach to the Cancún-Chetumal Highway 1.5km away. Most services lie along this road. At the bus station/plaza, perpendicular to Avenida Principal,
runs **Avenida Quinta,** which encompasses most of the *tiendas* and restaurants. East-
west *calles* increase by two in either direction; north-south *avenidas* increase by five.
Playa's *playa* lies one block east of Quinta.

PRACTICAL INFORMATION

Tourist Office: A wooden booth on the northwest corner of the plaza, diagonally
across Av. Quinta from the bus station. Open daily 7am-11pm.
Currency Exchange: Banco del Atlántico (tel. 3-02-72), on the first block west of
the plaza on Av. Principal. Changes U.S. dollars only. Open Mon.-Fri. 8am-1:30pm.
24-hr. **ATM. Bancomer** (tel. 3-04-00), four blocks up the street, offers similar rates
and has another 24-hr. **ATM.** Open Mon.-Fri. 9am-1:30pm.
Telephones: LADATELs dot Quinta. There is a *caseta* inside **Maya Laundry** (tel.
3-02-61; fax 3-02-04), on Quinta one block from the plaza. Open daily 8am-9pm.
Buses: From the corner of Quinta and Principal (tel. 3-01-09), **ADO** runs first-class
buses to Chetumal (6 per day, 4½hr., 64 pesos), Coatzacoalcos (7am and 4:30pm,
12hr., 218 pesos), Córdoba (7am, 22hr., 319 pesos), Escárcega (7am and noon,
6hr., 120 pesos), Mexico (7am, noon, and 7pm, 25hr., 324 pesos), Orizaba (7pm,
14hr., 324 pesos), Puebla (6pm, 23hr., 365 pesos), San Andrés (12:30am, 9½hr.,
254 pesos), Veracruz (3:30pm, 12hr., 287 pesos), and Villahermosa (5 per day,
12hr., 182 pesos). **Cristóbal Colón** goes to Ocosingo (4:30pm, 13hr., 163 pesos),
Palenque (4:45pm, 11hr., 170 pesos), San Cristóbal (4:45pm, 15hr., 189 pesos),
and Tuxtla Gutiérrez (4:45pm, 16hr., 227 pesos). **ATS** has second-class service to
Tulum (11 per day, 1hr., 11 pesos). **Mayab** goes to Mérida (5 per day, 5hr., 69
pesos) via Ticul (3½hr., 56 pesos), making every stop along the way.
Laundromat: Maya Laundry (tel. 3-02-61), on Quinta one block north of the plaza,
on the right. Wash and dry 7.50 pesos per kg. Open daily 8am-8pm.
Supermarket: El Súper del Ahorro (tel. 3-03-06), on Principal 3½ blocks west of
Quinta. Open daily 6:30am-10:30pm.
Pharmacy: Farmacia París (tel. 3-07-44), on Av. Principal opposite the bus station.
Open daily 7am-midnight.
Medical Care: Centro de Salud (tel. 3-03-14), on Av. Principal across from the post
office. Some English spoken. Open 24hr.
Police: (tel. 3-02-21), on Av. Principal two blocks west of the plaza. Open 24hr.
Post Office: (tel. 3-03-00), on Av. Principal 3 blocks from the plaza. Open Mon.-Fri.
8am-6pm, Sat. 9am-1pm. **MexPost** desk has same hours. **Postal Code:** 77710.
Telephone Code: 987.

ACCOMMODATIONS AND CAMPING

As Playa's accommodations begin to test the tempting waters of tourist-gouging
prices, bargains become more and more scarce. Fortunately, as prices rise, so does
quality. Most establishments lie along either Quinta or Principal, close to the beach.

Hotel Lilly (tel. 3-01-16), the flaming pink building on Av. Principal, one block west
of the plaza. Convenient but noisy location near the bus stop. Enormous cushy

beds in meticulously clean rooms. Fans and hot water. Singles 70 pesos. Doub
80 pesos. Triples 100 pesos. If there's no room Dec.-May, the owner will drive y
to **Hotel Los Dos Hermanos,** 3 blocks away.

Posada Las Flores (tel. 3-00-85), on Quinta, 2 blocks north of the plaza. New a
spotless white rooms have firm beds, ceiling fans, and alcove bathrooms. Ha
mock-filled courtyard perfect for taking that afternoon *siesta.* Hot water takes
time coming, but stays. Singles 80 pesos. Doubles 120 pesos. Triples 150 pesos.

CREA Youth Hostel (HI), a 1km trek from the plaza. Walk 4 blocks on Princi
and turn right before Farmacia La Salud (a.k.a. Lupita). Walk another 4 blocks, pa
ing the big concrete IMSS building. The hostel is a block and a half farther on t
left. Deserted during the low season. No hot water. No curfew or maximum s
period. Bring a lock for your locker. Single-sex dorms with quaking bunk beds
pesos with a 25-peso deposit. *Cabañas* with private bathrooms 80 pesos plus
80-peso deposit. 10% discount with HI card.

Campamento La Ruina, on the beach 200m north of the ferry dock. Popular wi
Europeans. Hostel-style, with communal bathrooms and cooking facilities. Ceili
fans. *Cabañas rústicas* with tiny, stiff military-style beds. Singles and doubles
pesos. Triples and quads 70 pesos. Hammock-space under the *palapa* 25 pesc
plus 5 pesos for a hammock rental. Pitch a tent in the sand for 20 pesos, 40 pes
for 2 people, plus 10 pesos for every extra camper. Lockers 5 pesos.

Posada Marinelly (tel. 3-01-40), on Av. Principal, 2½ blocks from the plaza. Conv
niently located. Pleasant, shady courtyard *palapa.* Beds lie on monstrous concre
blocks and are surrounded by similarly stoic furnishings. Singles 70 pesos. Doubl
90 pesos. Triples 100 pesos. Prices rise by 10 pesos during high season.

FOOD

Many snazzy restaurants and aggressive restauranteurs (psst, happy hour!) lin
Quinta. Cheaper fruit and *torta* experiences are to be found along breezy Principal.

Sabor, 1½ blocks north on Quinta. Easily missed if you're scurrying for shade on
hot day; look for the flowery, turquoise *parasoles* next to Pez Vela. Scrumptiou
sandwiches made with whole-wheat bread (10 pesos) and top-notch coffee. Bea
and cheese burritos (11 pesos) fit for Chac. Try the refreshing *agua de chaya* wit
limón and *piña* (4 pesos). Open daily 8am-10pm.

Antojitos El Correo (tel. 3-03-99). Walk up Principal 2 blocks to the clinic, then g
left 1 block. You'll have no trouble finding a feast of warm salvation in the gene
ously seasoned food. Guests have no choice but to try the hearty and ever-changin,
menú del día. For breakfast, try the *huevos a la mexicana* (with tacos, of course
for 10 pesos. Open daily 7am-midnight.

La Lunada (tel. 3-00-56), on Quinta, 3 blocks north of the plaza. Fantastic for break
fast. Homemade yogurt, granola, and a waffle recipe born under the broad skies o
Montana inaugurate the day in style (up to 16 pesos). Ranch-sized plates of egg
with all the trimmings around 15 pesos. Open daily 8am-noon.

Playa Caribe, just north of the bus station on Quinta. Trés chic. Enjoy your soup
fish fillet, and beer (35 pesos) to the sound of happily sunburnt foot traffic. Food
tends to be on the *picante* side. Open daily 6am-11pm.

SIGHTS AND ENTERTAINMENT

Decorated with an occasional palm tree and fringed by the turquoise waters of the
Caribbean, Playa's beach is simply beautiful. Though they are relatively free of sea
weed and coral, the sands remain wrought with scantily clad sunbathing tourists; the
wave that began in Cancún has officially splashed down in Playa. One kilometer
north of town, the beach goes nude. If you want a water-escape, 60-100 pesos
(depending on the place and your bargaining ability) will buy you an hour's worth of
windsurfing. Windsurfers and other gear can be rented from some of the fancier
hotels just south of the pier, or from shacks a few hundred meters north. **Albatros**
offers windsurfing lessons; just look for the pink sign. Although Playa has no snorkel-
ing-friendly reefs nearby, there's a decent reef 200m past the Shangri-La Caribe Hotel.

The high surf often hinders visibility. While the pace of life here is gentle and relaxed, there is one thing the locals do promptly: close shop. Many people move onto **Karen's Grill,** often embellished with popular local bands (happy hr. 7-9pm). If you're looking for a smaller place, hop onto a barside saddle at **La Bamba,** where you can drink and watch music videos until 11pm (or until you fall off the saddle, whichever happens first). Only the **Calypso Bar Caribeño,** with its small dance floor lit an iridescent blue, stays out past midnight, pumping out *salsa* until the first signs of dawn brighten the sea (open daily 10pm-4am).

■ Isla Cozumel

Cozumel (pop. 60,000) originally drew attention to itself as a key trading center for the Maya and later as a pirate refuge for Sir Francis Drake and Jean Lafitte. It took Jacques Cousteau in the 1950s to call worldwide attention to the natural wonders of the nearby Palancar Reef and the sealife it sustains. The reefs were too good to be left to idealistic research, however. Cozumel has been marketed as an "ecological getaway" for tourists wishing to "leave" Cancún's confines and "explore" Mexico (without saying goodbye to luxury, dollars, or sycophantic service). The red-and-white diving banner has become the island's unofficial flag. But not only is the underwater life truly first-rate, it also provides quiet, if bubbly, respite from the boatloads of prepackaged tourists that flood the island.

ORIENTATION

The island of Cozumel lies 18km east of the northern Quintana Roo coast and 85km south of Isla Mujeres. The island is most commonly accessed via ferry from Playa del Carmen (to the west) or Puerto Morelos (to the north). **Ferries** from Puerto Morelos (tel. 2-09-50) transport cars to and from Cozumel twice daily, docking in the island's only town, Cozumel, on the west shore (9am and 1pm, 2½hr., US$30 per car, US$4.50 per person). Tourist vehicles supposedly have priority, but the **car ferry** is inconvenient and unpredictable. The tourist office recommends that you secure a spot in line a full 12 hours in advance. **Water Jet Service** (tel. 2-15-08) sends three boats back and forth between Playa del Carmen and Cozumel. Tickets can be bought at the dock in Cozumel and from the booth on the Playa's plaza (12 trips daily from each shore 4am-8pm, 40min., roundtrip 50 pesos). If you are coming from Cancún, an alternative to the bus-ferry ordeal is the 20-minute **air shuttle** operated by Aerocaribe.

At 53km long and 14km wide, Cozumel is Mexico's largest Caribbean island. Although public transportation is literally nonexistent, downtown streets are clearly labeled and numbered with stubborn logic. If you don't mind occasionally spine-wrenching road conditions, the rest of the island is easily explored by bike or moped. Taxis are everywhere.

As you step off the ferry into Cozumel, **Avenida Juárez,** a pedestrian walkway for the first two blocks, is directly in front of you, running east-west through town. *Calles* run parallel to Juárez and are labeled *Sur* and *Norte* (Nte.) with respect to Juárez. North of Juárez, *calles* increase in even numbers; south of Juárez, they increase in odd numbers. *Avenidas* run north-south, are numbered in multiples of five, and are designated *Norte* or *Sur* with respect to Juárez. **Avenida Adolfo Rosada Salas** is between Calles 1 and 3 Sur. Juárez becomes the **Carretera Transversal** at the eastern edge of town, extending across the island's midsection to the other shore. The road to the airport forms the city's northern boundary. **Avenida Rafael Melgar** runs along the western edge of town next to the sea and leads north to the luxury hotels and the uninhabited northern coast. The national park at **Laguna Chankanaab** and the popular beach at **San Francisco** are south of town on the western shore; off the island's southern tip lie the **Palancar Reefs.** The nearly deserted eastern coast is dotted by Mayan ruins and supports only a few restaurants and camping spots.

PRACTICAL INFORMATION

While there are no consulates on Cozumel, Mr. Bryan Wilson (tel. 2-06-54), who works closely with the Mérida U.S. consulate, provides unofficial, free assistance to English-speaking travelers. In an emergency, knock on the door of the white house at Av. 15 and Calle 13 Sur.

Tourist Office: (tel. 2-01-49 or 2-03-44), on the 2nd floor of "Plaza del Sol," the building to the left of Bancomer. *Cozumel Today* has a decent map. The *Blue Guide to Cozumel* is quite helpful. Supposedly open Mon.-Fri. 8am-2:30pm.

Currency Exchange: BanPaís (tel. 2-16-82), right off the dock, charges a 1% commission for exchanging traveler's checks. Open Mon.-Fri. 9am-12:30pm. **Bancomer** (tel. 2-05-50), on the plaza, has the same rates but charges a flat fee of US50¢ per check. Open Mon.-Fri. 10am-1:30pm. **Banco del Atlántico** (tel. 2-01-42), on the plaza, has a 24-hr. **ATM.** Open Mon.-Fri. 9am-2pm, Sat. 10am-1pm.

Telephones: LADATELs throughout the city. The **Calling Station** (tel. 2-14-17), Av. Melgar between Calles 3 and 5 Sur, allows you to interface with loved ones.

Telegrams: (tel. 2-00-56), next to the post office. From here, you can send telegrams. And yet more telegrams. Open Mon.-Fri. 8am-6pm, Sat. 9am-1pm.

Airport: (tel. 2-04-85), 2km north of town. **Aerocaribe** (2-34-56). **Mexicana** (tel. 2-00-05). **Aerocozumel** (tel. 2-09-28 or 2-05-00). **Continental** (tel. 2-08-47).

Ferries: From the dock at the end of Av. Juárez. Arrive 30min. early as ferries tend to leave before they're supposed to. Schedules change frequently.

Taxis: (tel. 2-02-36). From the plaza, 20 pesos to the airport; 43 pesos to Chankanaab; 70 pesos to Punta Morena. Expect to pay more for more people.

Car Rental: Smart Rent-a-Car (tel. 2-43-81), on Av. 5 between Calle 1 and Salas. VW Beetle US$30 per day, more on peak season. Open daily 7:30am-7:30pm. Will demand a driver's license and major credit card.

Moped Rental: Pretty expensive. Get one outside Hotel Posada Edem (see below) for about 120 pesos. Haggle for all you're worth.

Bike Rental: Rentadora Cozumel (tel. 2-11-20 or 2-15-03), Av. 10 at Calle 1 Sur. 40 pesos per day. Return by 6pm. Deposit required. Open daily 8am-8pm.

Bookstore: Agencia de Publicaciones Gracia (tel. 2-00-31), on the plaza. Last week's *Newsweek* for the price of a meal (25-35 pesos). Open daily 8am-10pm.

Laundromat: Margarita, Av. 20 Sur 285 (tel. 2-28-65), near Calle 3 Sur. Self-service 25 pesos, soap 3 pesos. Open Mon.-Sat. 7am-9pm, Sun. 9am-5pm.

Red Cross: Av. 20 Sur (tel. 2-10-57 or 2-10-58), at Av. Adolfo Salas. Open 24hr.

Pharmacy: Farmacia Kiosco (tel. 2-24-85), on the *zócalo* near Hotel López. Aspirin, band-aids, sunscreen, *agua purificada*, etc. Open daily 8am-10pm.

Medical Services: There are several English-speaking private physicians in Cozumel. **Dr. M. F. Lewis,** (tel. 2-09-12) Av. 50, at Calle 11, for consultations or 24-hr. tourist medical service. **Medical Center (CEM),** Av. 20 Nte. 425 (tel. 2-29-19 or 2-14-19), between Calles 10 and 8 Nte. For an ambulance, call 2-14-19.

Police: (tel. 2-00-92) Calle 11 Sur, near Rafael Melgar, in the Palacio Municipal. For English service, call 2-04-09 and ask for James García or another bilingual officer.

Post Office: (tel. 2-01-06), off Rafael Melgar along the sea, just south of Calle 7 Sur. Open Mon.-Fri. 8am-8pm, Sat. 9am-1pm. **MexPost** (tel. 2-50-91). Express mail service, on Calle 11 Sur between Av. 20 and 25. Open Mon.-Fri. 9am-6pm, Sat. 9am-1pm. **Postal Code:** 77600.

Telephone Code: 987.

ACCOMMODATIONS AND CAMPING

Although hotels in Cozumel are more expensive than in Playa, your extra pesos buy higher quality rooms. Peak-season travelers should expect slightly higher prices and should hunt down a room before noon. Clean, reasonably cheap accommodations lie within blocks of the plaza—resist being roped into a pricey package deal when you step off the ferry. Secluded camping spots are at **Punta Morena** and **Punta Chiqueros,** on the island's Caribbean coast. Short-term campers should encounter no problems with the authorities but, for longer stays, might want to consult the tourist office to find out what the best camping options are.

Hotel Posada Edem, Calle 2 Nte. 12 (tel. 2-11-66), between Calles 10 and 15. Upon docking, go left 1 block, turn right, and walk up 2 blocks. Astoundingly clean rooms with fresh linen, 2 beds, fans, fluffy towels, and hot water. Watch TV in the lobby with the owner and his cute black cat. Up to 3 people 75 pesos, each additional person 10 pesos. Add 65 pesos for A/C and TV.

Hotel Marruang (tel. 2-16-78 or 2-02-08), on Av. Adolfo Salas just past Av. 20. Look for the dentist sign on the big blue building. Brand spankin' new. Spotless, speckled floors lead to comfy beds, ceiling fans, and fantastic bathrooms with hot water. Singles 90 pesos. Doubles 100 pesos. Triples 115 pesos.

Cabañas Punta Morena, Carretera Transversal Km. 17. For those who have their own transportation. Next to a beachfront seafood restaurant, these *cabañas* have a fabulous view of the windy and wavy Eastern seaboard. Accommodations are basic: stone-walled rooms have one double bed and hooks for a hammock. Neat bathrooms lack hot water. Volleyball court on the beach. Surfboards (100 pesos) and boogie-boards (50 pesos) for rent. All rooms 70 pesos. Well-priced restaurant.

Posada Letty (tel. 2-02-57), Calle 1 Sur past Av. 10. Their business card promises "Cleanliness-Order-Morality." We can only vouch for the former. Tidy, pale yellow rooms in a quiet but central location. Hanging rails and ceiling fans. Feels more like a house than a hotel. Singles and doubles 80 pesos. Triples 100 pesos.

Hotel Saolima, Av. Adolfo Salas 268 (tel. 2-08-86), between Av. 10 and 15 Sur. Uninspired rectangular architecture houses a sleepy courtyard and green rooms with soft beds, ceiling fans, and hot water. Singles and doubles 90 pesos. Triples 100 pesos. Add 20 pesos for A/C.

FOOD

Food in Cozumel tends to be expensive, especially if you buy it near the beach or the plaza. Avoiding places that advertise in English will keep pesos in your pockets. There are several moderately priced restaurants a few blocks from the center, as well as some small *típico* cafés hiding on side streets. The **market,** on Av. Adolfo Salas between Av. 20 and 25 Sur, offers the standard items: meat, fish, and fruits. The five small restaurants outside the market offer generous portions of regional dishes. For a quick treat, stop by at the **Panificadora Cozumel,** on Calle 2 Nte. between Quinta and Melgar, where pastries and baked goods can be had for pocket change (open daily 6am-9:30pm).

Cedral Beach Restaurant, opposite the road to the El Cedral ruins on the southwestern tip of the island. A bit far, but worth it. The seafood arrives to shore mere seconds before you do. Accompany Don Carlos, the chef, to choose the very fish you want. Get a few people together and go in for the house specialty, a monstrous red snapper (about 100 pesos—haggle). String up a hammock on the serene public beach for a post-feast *siesta.* Open daily 7am-6pm.

Restaurant El Foco, Av. 5 Sur 13, 2½ blocks from the plaza. Wooden tables and graffiti-adorned walls give it the nonchalance of a well-loved hangout. "Foco special" 18 pesos, *quesadillas* 9 pesos, enchiladas 30 pesos. Open daily 5pm-5am.

El Abuelo Gerardo (tel. 2-10-12), on Av. 10 between Juárez and Calle 2 Nte. A mellow place to grab an ice-cold afternoon beer. *Antojitos* 5-20 pesos. For something more substantial, try a fish filet (22-26 pesos). Open daily 7:30am-10:30pm.

Restaurant Casa Denis (tel. 2-00-67), across from the flea market on the *zócalo.* Ancient sketches and the 116 year-old (and aging!) *mamey* tree glorify this convenient shack. Good view of rip-off restaurants across the plaza. *Comida regional,* including seafood plates, 28-48 pesos. Open daily 7am-10:30pm.

Cocina Económica Mi Chabelita (tel. 2-08-96), on Av. 10 Sur near Adolfo Salas. Great budget dining in a bright, coral-colored garage. Great *comida corrida* (14 pesos). Fried bananas (6 pesos) are simply orgasmic. Open Mon.-Sat. 8am-9pm.

SANDS AND SIGHTS

Most visitors to Cozumel have one sight in mind: the beautiful coral reefs around the island. Mopeds are the best way of getting to your favorite snorkeling spot or finding a new one. Be nice to yourself, and get some wheels. Otherwise, expensive taxis will be your only option. Although hitchhiking is possible, it's uncertain, dehydrating, and not recommended by *Let's Go*.

As you head south out of town on a counter-clockwise circuit of the island, **Hotel La Ceiba** makes a good stop-off point for snorkeling. You could walk through the hotel restaurant sporting a snorkel, fins, and a g-string, and the management still wouldn't care. Even if they did, all beaches in Mexico are public property, so you're just exercising your rights. The hotel has a beach perfect for swimming and a reef and plane wreck offshore waiting to be explored. The **Del Mar Aquatics** dive shop (tel. 2-08-44), at the right-hand end of the beach, rents out snorkeling (US$5 per day) and scuba equipment (US$35 per day; open daily 7:30am-7:30pm).

Chankanaab National Park, a few more kilometers down the coastal highway, is comprised of the *laguna*, a botanical garden, museum, restaurant, snorkel area, and a few gift shops. A stroll through the endemic forest in the botanical garden, past the one-meter beady-eyed sunbathing iguanas, brings you to a few paltry ruins. The perfectly oval natural lagoon, once brimming with reef fish, is now home to the hardy survivors of years of *gringo* sunscreen attrition. Never mind; the real attraction is the abundant tropical fish and corals in the Caribbean a few meters away. The small museum focuses on the park's natural resources and houses some fantastic photographs of the underwater caves in the lagoon (open daily 7am-6pm; admission 35 pesos; for more info, contact the **Fundación de Parques** in town, tel. 2-09-14).

The best underwater sightseeing in Cozumel is likely to be on the offshore reefs, accessible by boat. You can rent snorkeling equipment anywhere on the island, including at Laguna Chankanaab and Playa de San Francisco. The standard rate is US$5-10 per day, plus deposit. Most of the numerous **dive shops** in town are on the waterfront or on Calle 3 Sur between Av. Melgar and Av. 10. Always consider safety before price; look for shops with a **CADO** (Cozumel Association of Dive Operators) insignia on their door. **Blue Bubble Divers** (tel. 2-18-65), Av. 5 and Calle 3 Sur, has a mellow, English-speaking staff and a choice of 20 reefs to visit (3½hr. single tank dive US$50, snorkeling equipment US$6 per day). Another option is **Aqua Safari,** Melgar at Calle 3 Sur (single tank dive US$25, 2-hr. snorkeling boat trip US$15; open daily 7am-1pm and 4-6:30pm).

The route along the eastern coast passes many secluded beaches that would make for good camping spots. Always ask before pitching a tent. While the beaches boast magnificent turquoise waters, the water is turbulent and somewhat dangerous; it should be treated with cautious respect. Midway along the coast, Carretera Transversal branches west and loops back through the jungle to town.

Between beach hops and reef drops, you may want to hunt down one of several small ruins in Cozumel's overgrown interior. You can visit **El Cedral** and the **Tumba de Caracol** ruins on a bumpy trek to the **Celarain Lighthouse** on the island's south-

---

Waterworld

The Palancar Reef of Cozumel, the second-largest in the world, continually draws legions of scuba fanatics eager to explore its dramatic underwater formations. While the aesthetics are unmistakable, few visitors realize the biological importance of those majestic coral pillars. Coral is to a reef as topsoil is to a rainforest—without it, the basis of all life disappears. If the coral is destroyed, the entire reef's ecosystem disintegrates. International law prohibits the harvesting of coral, but it does not forbid the purchase or exportation of coral-derived jewelry and crafts. Several shops in Cozumel sell goods made from black coral, and, by patronizing these establishments, tourists heighten the demand for coral and adversely affect the splendorous reefs they have come to see.

ernmost point. The top of the lighthouse offers a thrilling view of the northern shores of the island. To get to the crumbled stone structures of **San Gervasio,** the only extensively excavated and partially reconstructed ruin on the island, take Juárez out of town. After 8km, a "San Gervasio" sign marks a gravel road branching to the left. The ruins are another 8km down this road (site open daily 8am-4pm; admission 17 pesos).

The small, air-conditioned **Museo de la Isla de Cozumel** (tel. 2-14-75 or -74), on the waterfront between Calles 4 and 6, is filled with photographs and artifacts (open daily 9am-5pm; admission US$3). Check for other cultural events in the **Centro de Convenciones,** between the Plaza del Sol and Bancomer, or in the plaza itself, where locals gather on Sunday nights for family fun.

ENTERTAINMENT

Though not as expensive as Cancún, Cozumel's nightlife is targeted towards the spendthrift *gringos* who jaunt into town from their cruise ships. Cozumel is emptier at night than might be expected for a town of its size, largely because the tour-package herds tend to stay in their hotels after dinner. Obnoxiously boisterous all night long, **Carlos 'n Charlie's** (tel. 2-01-91), on Rafael Melgar just one block north of the dock, entertains *norteamericanos* with crazy drinks, slammer contests, and arm-wrestling matches. Occasional awards free *tequila* to those willing to make fools of themselves (*cerveza* 14 pesos; open daily 10am-1:30am). A mellow, more native crowd enjoys reggae music and relives the swinging 70s at **Joe's Lobster Bar** (tel. 2-32-75), on Av. 10, between Calles 1 and 3 Sur. A live band starts up the action at 10:30pm and the place keeps kicking until 2 or 3am. For the best in live Mexican rock under a hip groovy-colored *palapa,* head to **Raga,** on Salas between Calles 10 and 15. Live music begins and attractive *cozumeleños* converge nightly around 9pm (open daily 5pm-12:30am). **Saramouche** (tel. 2-07-99), a block south of the plaza, is a huge air-conditioned disco where you can salaciously waggle your hips to your heart's content (cover 30 pesos; open nightly 10pm-3am). The only other full-fledged disco is **Neptuno** (tel. 2-15-37), five blocks south of the plaza, where a more Mexican crowd belts out karaoke all night long (open nightly 9pm-early).

For action and romance with happy endings and no alcohol, try **Cinema Cozumel,** on Av. Rafael Melgar between Calles 2 and 4, or **Cine Cecillo Borques,** on Juárez between Av. 30 and 35. Borques is cheaper but more remote.

■ Tulum

On the eastern edge of the age-old Etaib (Black Bees) jungle, halfway down the Caribbean coast of the Yucatán, lies the walled Mayan "City of the Dawn." Although the ruins here are less impressive than those at Uxmal and Chichén Itzá, their backdrop is stunning. Tulum's graying temples and nearly intact watchtowers rise above tall, wind-bent palm trees and white sand pummeled by the steely-blue Caribbean Sea. Tulum brings together two of the best aspects of the Yucatán: archaeological wonders and Caribbean waters. First settled in the 4th century, Tulum was the oldest continuously inhabited city in the New World when the Spanish arrived. Today, sun worshippers of a different kind tramp through the ancient city, complementing their dose of sightseeing with some swimming.

ORIENTATION

Located 42km southeast of Cobá, 63km south of Playa del Carmen, and 127km south of Cancún, Tulum (pop. 12,000) is the southernmost link in the chain of tourist attractions on the Caribbean coast of Quintana Roo and the eastern extreme of the major Mayan archaeological sites. Although few people live here, Tulum sprawls out over three separate areas: *el crucero* (the crossroads), the beach **cabañas,** and **Pueblo Tulum.** Arriving in Tulum from Cancún on Rte. 307, buses first stop at *el crucero,* a few kilometers before town. Here, a couple of restaurants, hotels, and minimarts huddle together 800m west of the ruins. The well paved access road turns south at the ruins, leading to food and lodging at *cabañas* 2km farther down the road. Pueblo Tulum, 4km south of *el crucero,* offers travelers a handful of roadside restaurants, minimarts, and some services.

Second-class **buses** provide cheap transportation from Tulum to nearby cities and to the sights and beaches which lie to the north on Rte. 307. Some travelers hitchhike from sight to sight along the highway. *Let's Go* does not recommend hitchhiking. Taxis congregate at *el crucero* and at the bus stop at Pueblo Tulum.

PRACTICAL INFORMATION

The few services available in Pueblo Tulum are along Rte. 307, which serves as the tiny town's main street. There is no tourist office, though a few stands at the ruins can provide sketchy maps. Those desperate to exchange money can do so at the *crucero* or next to the bus office in Pueblo Tulum.

Telephones: Shiny new public phones line Rte. 307 in Pueblo Tulum. **Caseta de Tulum** (tel./fax 1-20-09) is a block from the bus station. Open daily 7am-9pm.

Buses: A small waiting room sandwiched between two currency exchange booths opposite the Hotel Maya. **ADO** to Coatzacoalcos (8am, 11hr., 207 pesos), Córdoba (8am, 12hr., 307 pesos), Escárcega (8am, 4hr., 109 pesos), Mexico City (8am, 22hr., 384 pesos), San Andrés (4:30pm, 9hr., 243 pesos), Veracruz (4:30pm, 12hr., 275 pesos), and Villahermosa (4:30pm, 9hr., 171 pesos). Various **second-class buses** run to Cancún (14 per day, 2hr., 24 pesos), Chetumal (12 per day, 4hr., 44 pesos), Chichén Itzá (6 per day, 3½hr., 38 pesos), Cobá (7 per day, 30min., 8 pesos), Escárcega (4:30pm, 8hr., 85 pesos), Ocosingo (4:30pm, 15hr., 150 pesos), Mérida (5 per day, 5hr., 49 pesos), Palenque (4:30pm, 14hr., 131 pesos), Playa del Carmen (14 per day, 1hr., 11 pesos), San Cristóbal (4:30pm, 16hr., 168 pesos), and Valladolid (6 per day, 25hr., 27 pesos).

Taxis: Available at *el crucero,* in Pueblo Tulum, along Rte. 307, and at various *cabañas.* From *el crucero* to Pueblo Tulum 10 pesos, to Cabañas Tulum 25 pesos.

Pharmacy: Súper Farmacia, just past the post office. Open daily 8am-9pm. English-speaking Dr. Arturo F. Ventre available Mon.-Sun. 8am-noon and 6-9pm.

Police: (tel. 1-20-55), in the Delegación Municipal, two blocks past the post office.

Post Office: A few hundred meters into town on Rte. 307. Open Mon.-Fri. 9am-1pm and 3-6pm. **Postal Code:** 77780.

Telephone Code: 987.

ACCOMMODATIONS AND CAMPING

Tulum offers two lodging options: hotels at *el crucero* in town, or beachside *cabañas.* If you plan on staying only one night to visit the ruins, the road hotels can't be beat for sheer economy. However, your inner beach-bum will be much happier in the *cabañas.* There you can meet mellow international travelers, perfect your tan on the spectacular beach, and escape the conventional Quintana Roo tourism just a short distance away. Don't be afraid to ask for help with a hammock if it's (blush!) your first time. (Hint: to protect your back sleep across, not lengthwise.) *Let's Go* is not to blame if you end up staying for a month. Or two.

Cabañas Santa Fe, just off the paved road 1km south of the ruins. Follow the signs to Don Armando's and turn left. Several sticks 'n' *palapa* combos to choose from: bare *cabaña* with sand floor and small hammock 40 pesos. One bed *cabaña* with cement floor 70 pesos. Two bed *cabaña* 90 pesos. Hammock rental 10 pesos per night. Mosquito-net rental 5-10 pesos per night. Communal facilities are new, but receive too much attention from guests and not enough from the staff.

Don Armando Cabañas (tel. 45-05-96), on the paved road 1km south of the ruins. A humble paradise with a volleyball court. Don Armando is absolutely delightful, the *cabañas* are solid and safe, and the communal facilities are spotless. *Cabaña* with 1 bed and 1 hammock 65 pesos, with 2 beds 75-85 pesos. Deposit 25 pesos. Camp or hang a hammock for 15 pesos per person.

El Crucero, on Rte. 307 at the turnoff to the ruins. The staff can be hard to find; sometimes they're in the restaurant next door. Small, slightly stuffy rooms with ceiling fans. Windows are small and curtain-less. Check-out 24hr. after you arrive. Singles 50 pesos. Doubles 60 pesos. Triples 70 pesos. Quads 90 pesos.

Hotel Maya, on Rte. 307 away from the bus station in Pueblo Tulum. Displaying amazing architectural skill yet again, the Maya aligned this hotel so that during the vernal equinox, if you stand exactly in the middle of the engulfingly blue rooms with large carved wood beds and spotless blue bathrooms, nothing really cool happens. Singles 65 pesos. Doubles 85 pesos. Triples 100 pesos.

FOOD

Though the points of interest in Tulum tend to be rather spread out, a hearty and inexpensive bite of *típico* food is never too far away. Both the Pueblo and the *crucero* have satisfying and authentic restaurants as well as *mini-súpers;* the former are slightly cheaper and provide filling sustenance for daytrips.

Restaurante El Crucero, in the eponymous hotel. Comfortable and shady interior provides respite from all that Mayan sun. Get intimate with that old standby, *pescado al mojo de ajo* (26 pesos). Breakfast (fruit salad, orange juice, toast, and coffee) 15 pesos. Open daily 7am-9pm.

Restaurante Santa Fe, at the campground on the beach. Mellow reggae tunes and the rumble of surf waft through the newly reconstructed *palapa.* Fresh fish 20 pesos. *Quesadillas* 10 pesos. Restaurant and bar open daily 5am-11pm.

Cocina Económica, a block south of Hotel Maya in Pueblo Tulum. The name almost says it all, but leaves out the crucial "tasty" part. 13 pesos gets you the day's entree with, of course, beans and tortillas. Open daily 7:30am-10:30pm.

SIGHTS

The Ruins

The first thing you see in Tulum will be the still-impressive **dry-laid wall** that surrounded the city center's three landlocked sides. The wall, made of small rocks wedged together, was originally 3.6m thick and 3m high. It shielded the city from the aggression of neighboring Mayan city-states and prevented all but the 150 or so priests and governors of Tulum from entering the city for most of the year. After Tulum's defeat at the hands of the Spanish in 1544, the wall fended off English, Dutch, and French pirates and, in 1847, gave rebel Mayans refuge from government forces during the Caste War. Magnificent representations of a **figure diving into the water** cover the western walls. The images, depicting the Maya sunset god, are illuminated every evening by the rays of the setting sun. Other stone inscriptions (giant phallus, anyone?) show Tulum to have been the center of a religious fertility cult.

Just inside and to the left of the west gate stand the remains of platforms which once supported huts. Behind these platforms are the **House of the Halach Uinik** (the House of the Ruler), characterized by a traditional Mayan four-column entrance; the **Palacio,** the largest residential building in Tulum; and the **Temple of the Paintings,** a stellar example of post-Classical Mayan architecture. Well-preserved 600-year-old murals inside the temple depict deities intertwined with serpents, as well as fruit, flower, and corn offerings. Masks of Itzamná, the Mayan Creator, occupy the northwest and southwest corners of the building.

El Castillo, the most prominent structure in Tulum, looms behind the smaller buildings and over the rocky seaside cliff. Serving as a pyramid and temple, it commands a view of the entire walled city. It also served as a lighthouse, allowing returning fishermen to find the only gap in the barrier reef just offshore. Its walls, like those of many buildings in Tulum, slope outward; meanwhile, the doorposts slope inward. The castle was remodeled and rebuilt many times, hence its architectural and structural eccentricities.

In front of the temple is the sacrificial stone where the Maya held battle ceremonies. Once the stars had been consulted and a propitious day determined, a warrior-prisoner was selected for sacrifice. At the climax of the celebration, attendants painted the warrior's body blue—the sacred color of the Maya—and the chief priest cut his heart out and poured the blood over the idols in the temple. The body was given to the soldiers below, who were thought to acquire the strength to overcome their enemies through cannibalism.

To the right of El Castillo on the same plaza is the **Temple of the Initial Series.** Named after a stela found here, the temple bears a date that corresponded to the beginning of the Mayan religious calendar in the year 761 CE. The **Temple of the Descending God,** with a fading relief of a feathered, armed deity diving from the sky, stands on the other side of El Castillo's plaza. Perched on its own precipice on the other side of the beach, the **Temple of the Winds** was acoustically designed to act as a storm-warning system. Surely enough, before Hurricane Gilbert struck the site in 1988, the temple's airways dutifully whistled their alarm (site open daily 8am-5pm; admission 16 pesos, free Sun.; guided tours about 150 pesos for 1-5 people, 200 pesos for groups up to 25 people).

Getting There: Tulum's ruins lie a brisk eight-minute walk east of Rte. 307 from the *crucero.* For the less mobile (and supremely lazy), a dinky train (7 pesos) covers the distance in a slightly shorter time. Admission tickets are sold at a booth to the left of the parking lot.

The Beach

Hanging out on the beach in *cabañas* is a popular way to end a day at the ruins. Expect the Europeans to turn it into a topless affair, and some to strip to their bare butts. Nude bathing is tolerated, although it usually takes one uninhibited soul to start the ball rolling, so to speak. The ever-vigilant Mexican Navy drops in occasionally to tell everyone to get back in uniform, but once the nudity-patrol is out of sight, the bathing suits make way for the birthday suits once again. *Cabaña* managers complain if you walk through the campgrounds in the buff.

Offshore, you can see the waves mysteriously breaking on Tulum's **barrier reef,** the largest in the Americas; it runs the full length of the Yucatán peninsula, including Belize. Although the water here is not as clear as at Xel-Ha or Akumal (see p. 546), the fish are just as plentiful. To enjoy them, you can rent scuba and snorkeling equipment from the **dive shop** at Cabañas Santa Fe (30 pesos per day; open daily 8am-3:30pm). The shop plans trips to the reef and a nearby *cenote* (US$15, including rental, *antojitos,* and *refrescos*). Get fins if you snorkel; the 500m swim to the reef is often a struggle against a north-south current.

To escape the beaches, waves, and salty water, rent a bike from Cabañas Santa Fe (20 pesos per hr.) and visit one of the *cenotes* in the woods near Pueblo Tulum. Look for a small patch of gravel, large enough for two cars, on the right side of the road as you head toward Chetumal. Follow a rugged path to the serene **Cenote Escondido** or the smaller **Cenote Cristal** 100m farther down the road.

■ Near Tulum

A few kilometers south of Tulum on the coast road lies the 1.5-million acre **Sian Ka'an Biosphere Reserve.** Sanctuary to over 345 species of birds as well as every endangered cat species of southern Mexico, the reserve also guards a wide range of wetland and marine habitats, as well as 27 Mayan sites. Entrance is free but limited, and *lancha* tours are given exclusively by Sian Ka'an biologists. For more info, contact Amigos de Sian Ka'an in Cancún, Av. Cobá 5, (tel. (98) 84-95-83; fax 87-30-80; e-mail: sian@Cancún.rce.com.mx), in Plaza América.

XEL-HA AND AKUMAL

Though swimming is not permitted in the lagoon for which **Xel-Ha** (SHELL-ha) is famous, its natural aquarium, almost 2m deep, is a fun (and expensive) place for snorkeling. You can splash around all you want in the *caleta* (inlet) nearby—check your sunscreen at the front desk. Don't bet on seeing any unusual fish life, though you can find parrot fishes and one-meter-long barracudas towards the rope which marks the open sea. For relative peace during busy times, cross the inlet and explore the underwater caves, where an altar was once discovered. Be careful and don't go duck-diving under overhangs on your own. Note the bizarre incidence of cool seawater with a warm undercurrent of subterranean fresh water. It is the confluence of these water sources—not suntan lotion—that sometimes impairs underwater visibility. The steep 70-peso entrance fee does not include rental of snorkel equipment, which is available near the inlet for 49 more precious pesos (no discounts this time). Visit before noon, when busloads of tourists from the resorts overrun the place. Lockers (7 pesos plus 3-peso deposit) and towels (10 pesos plus 30-peso deposit) are available at the shower area (open daily 8:30am-6pm).

Xel-Ha also maintains a small archaeological site on the highway, 100m south of the entrance to the inlet. **El Templo de Los Pájaros** and **El Palacio**, small Classical and post-Classical ruins, were only recently opened to the public. The former (the ruin farthest into the jungle) overlooks a peaceful, shady *cenote* where swimming is permitted. A strategically hung rope-swing makes the experience all the more Tarzan-esque. The jungle at Xel-Ha is rife with mosquitoes, so bring insect repellent (site open daily 8am-5pm; admission 10 pesos).

A few kilometers north of Xel-Ha towards Playa del Carmen lies the bay of **Akumal**. An older, wealthier crowd is drawn to its underwater attractions. The **Akumal Dive Shop** (tel. (987) 4-12-59) rents **snorkeling equipment** (US$6 per day), organizes snorkeling boat trips (US$20 per person) and scuba trips (US$25 per one-tank dive), and offers cavern-diving courses (US$350; open daily 8am-1pm and 2-5pm).

Getting There: Xel-Ha lies 15km north of Tulum; Akumal is 10km farther north. Get on any northbound **bus** and ask to be let off at the site of your choice (5 pesos). Taxis charge exorbitant rates. Hitchhiking here is tough because the traffic is fast and the wait can be unnerving. *Let's Go* does not recommend hitchhiking. Getting back to Tulum at the end of the day can be especially challenging, as buses begin to come less and less frequently. Vigorously wave down a bus on its way to Tulum or Cancún. Locals will usually be able to tell you when the next one is due to pass.

CENOTE DOS OJOS

Cenote Dos Ojos, 1km south of Xel-Ha, is the second largest underwater cavern in the world, stretching for 33,855m. It was originally a dry cave system with beautiful rock formations in shades of amber as well as massive calcic stalactites, stalagmites, and natural wind-etchings. The whole system was flooded long, long ago, preserving the caves in their new underwater condition. It is now possible to snorkel and dive in the *cenote*, along with tetras, mollies, and swordfish.

The trip begins with a bumpy 20-minute ride in an open truck. Monstrous bugs, fit for any Indiana Jones, movie-drop as you zip through the pristine jungle. A complete underwater circuit of the caves, at a depth of 10m, takes about 45 minutes. Meanwhile, snorkelers can explore the larger of the two (hence, *dos* ojos) cave entrances. For divers and snorkelers alike, this is a unique opportunity to explore a spectacular unspoiled cave system which has only been open to the public since 1993. The dive costs US$50 (plus US$15 equipment rental). Snorkelers pay US$25. Three trips depart daily from Dos Ojos Dive Center (tel. (987) 4-12-71), several hundred meters south of the park entrance, at 10am, noon, and 2pm.

■ Cobá

Deep within the Yucatán jungle, Cobá receives less attention than her big sisters Chichén Itzá and Tulum. The government has poured less money into the site, leaving an estimated 6,500 buildings unexcavated. And for a change, mosquitoes outnumber tourists; Cobá is a site you can truly explore for yourself. In the jungle which surrounds this ancient city (in its heyday, it is estimated, the city spread out over 10 square kilometers), lizards bask on private pyramids, colorful butterflies flit across the paths, and the ever-fierce *yucateca* mosquito is never far away. Early visitors can explore the site to a cacophony of birds, and just might find themselves alone atop a pyramid looking down on one of Cobá's four lakes. The site's isolation only heightens the impressiveness of its towering **Castillo,** which at 42m is the tallest Mayan structure in the northern Yucatán.

Practical Information Expreso de Oriente goes to Cancún (6:30am, 1:30, and 3:30pm, 2½hr., 28 pesos), Chichén Itzá (9:30am and 2pm, 1½hr., 31 pesos), Mérida (9am and 2pm, 2½hr., 53 pesos), Playa del Carmen (4 per day, 1½hr., 16 pesos), Tulum (5 per day, 30min., 8 pesos), and Valladolid (9:30am, 1hr., 24 pesos).

Accommodations and Food Many houses near the ruins rent rooms. The **Hotel Bocadito,** 150m north of the *zócalo's* basketball court, offers budget accommodations with a cheerful red-and-white motif. Rooms around a quiet courtyard, have one or two firm beds and are equipped with ceiling fans and average bathrooms (40-60 pesos). For a comprehensive budget feast, try the hotel restaurant's *menú del día,* which includes soup, nachos, an entree with tacos, bread, dessert, and coffee (28 pesos). Good thing your bed is only a short stagger away (open daily 6:30am-9pm). **Nicté Ha,** on the shore a stone's throw west of the T-junction, is an idyllic spot for breakfast. Mexican crooners pluck out their heartstrings on the radio and early birds (before 8am or so) may catch a glimpse of an alligator paddling about just offshore. The super-friendly owner will let you browse through her Cobá guidebooks on request. Dinner entrees run 30-40 pesos (open daily 6am-9pm). Although the food at the **Hotel Villa Arqueológicas** is a bit expensive, a salad or drink will buy access to their garden-side pool. Restaurant customers can also rent tennis rackets (15 pesos per hr.) and use the pool tables.

The Ruins To get to the ruins, walk south on the main street in town as far as the T-junction at the lake. Here, take a left onto the brilliantly named Av. Voz Suave (Soft Voice); the ruins are a five-minute walk down the road. It's a good idea to find a guide at the entrance, as this will make the visit much more enlightening.

Once through the gate, the site's six attractions are laid out before you in a "Y"-formation, the entrance being at the base of the "Y". Take an immediate right to the **Grupo Cobá.** To the left looms the impressive **Temple of the Churches,** built over seven 52-year periods, each associated with a new chief priest. Only the front face of the temple has been excavated, revealing a corbel-vaulted passageway (to the left) which you can explore. Climb the 24m to the top for the best view the site has to offer: to the northwest lies the town of Cobá, due west is **Laguna Cobá,** and south, **Laguna Macanxoc** (Ma-kan-SHOK). Rising out of the jungle to the northeast are the gray steps of the ancient city's centerpiece, **El Castillo.** In front of the structure is a stone sacrificial table, upon which animal offerings were made to Chac, the rain god. The stela depicts Chac; another nearby features a kneeling Mayan. Follow a second passageway farther south to the **Plaza del Templo,** where assemblies were once held. The red plant dye still visible on the walls of the passageway date from the fifth century CE. A mortar here hints at the staple food of the ancient (and contemporary) Maya—corn. Return to the main path for a look at the **ballcourt.** The only arch which was standing when the site was discovered—it straddled the path—came tumbling down when Hurricane Gilbert struck Cobá in 1988.

A one-km walk up the "trunk" of the "Y" takes you to four other sites. Follow the right branch for another kilometer to reach a collection of eight stelae in the **Grupo Macanxoc.** On the way, you cross over one of the well-engineered Mayan roads called a *sacbé* (white road). This particular road is 20m wide and raised 4m from the jungle floor. The ornate stone slabs of the Grupo Macanxoc were erected as memorials above the tombs of Mayan royals. Especially impressive and well-preserved is the first, the **Retrato del Rey.** The king is shown standing on the heads of two slaves, bow and arrow in hand, wearing a *quetzal*-feather headdress.

Returning to the central part of the "Y" brings you to the **Conjunto de las Pinturas** (Assembly of the Paintings). Like the inscriptions on many of the stelae that hide off the side of the road, the murals lining the edges of the temple atop the pyramid have been badly eroded by heat and humidity, twin avatars of the jungle's destructive power. Nonetheless, the short climb to the top brings you tête-à-tête with an exquisite carved detail of a few fish and Mayan fishermen's faces. Plant dyes were used to create the red, orange, and blue colors. The stone slabs at the base of the pyramid are tombs. The small surface area is explained by the fact that the deceased were buried vertically rather than horizontally.

Continue north to the left-hand branch of the "Y." After 200m, follow an unmarked trail on the right to the three stelae of **Chumuc Múl.** The first stela depicts a kneeling Mayan ballplayer. Sure enough, this is the tomb of a victorious captain. You can make out the *chicle* ball in the upper-left-hand corner. The second stela is of a princess, while the third is of a *sacerdote* (priest). His seal is stamped on top of the slab, along with a jaguar's head, a common Mayan symbol of worship. Two hundred meters farther up this branch of the "Y," you'll run into **sacbé No. 1.** This thoroughfare ran from Chichén Itzá, 101km to the west, all the way to Tulum, 48km to the southeast. Runners were posted every 5km, so messages could be sent between settlements via a series of quick dashes. During the city's height (900-1200 CE), Cobá is believed to have been the major crossroads in a commercial region of 17 cities. Images of the honeybee god around the site are a reminder of this ancient economic hub—the Maya used honey along with coconuts and jade as a medium of exchange.

The tour climaxes with the breathtaking sight of the **Nohoch Múl.** If you believe the legend, which says that each of the nine platforms took 55 years to build, then Mayan slaves labored for almost 500 years (without the wheel, metal tools, or domesticated animals) to complete this *castillo.* Although the view is not as spectacular as that from the Templo de la Iglesia, the 120-step climb *will* make your heart race. The pyramid's nine levels, where Mayan priests once led processions, display carvings of the diving god, a crucial deity in the battle to maintain harmony with the surrounding lakes. Just before the pyramid, Stela No. 20 stands in front of a small ruin. The stela depicts a dignitary of high rank (note the plumed crest and rich clothing) standing on a board supported by two slaves. A deciphered date on the stela reads November 30, 1780.

Regardless of when you arrive at the site, bring a water bottle and wear a hat. And unless you feel like being sacrificed to the mosquito god, bring plenty of repellent as well. During the high season, 11am-2pm are peak tourist hours (ruins open daily 8am-5pm; admission 14 pesos).

▓ Chetumal

Nestled in Quintana Roo's southeastern corner and straddling the border with Belize, Chetumal's (pop. 200,000) one saving grace is that it sits on the Caribbean coast. No beaches, no ruins. But hey—*¡costa turquesa!* Established in 1899 to intercept shipments of arms to Mayan rebels and to prevent illegal timber harvesting, this state capital serves mainly as a stopover for travelers en route to Tikal or Belize.

ORIENTATION

Tucked into the Yucatán's southeastern corner, Chetumal is just north of the Río Hondo, the natural border between Mexico and Belize. There are three principal approaches to the city: Rte. 186 from Escárcega (273km), along the Caribbean coast from Cancún (379km), and from Mérida via Valladolid (458km). The **bus terminal** at Av. de los Insurgentes and Av. Belice is Chetumal's ground transportation hub.

Take a taxi (5 pesos) into town or walk 4km through shadeless streets. Chetumal's thriving shopping district lines **Av. de los Héroes,** starting at Av. Efraín Aguilar at the city's market and extending 1km south to the bay. This compact commercial area encompasses most of Chetumal's hotels and restaurants. At the southern terminus of Héroes lies **Boulevard Bahía,** a wide avenue flanked by statues and small plazas that follows the bay for several kilometers. From here you can see part of Belize, the long spit of land stretching out to the right as you face the sea.

PRACTICAL INFORMATION

Tourist Office: Information booth (tel. 2-36-63), on Héroes at Aguilar. Pick up a map of the city. Open Mon.-Sat. 8:30am-1:30pm and 6-9pm; erratic hours.

Consulates: Belize (tel. 2-01-00), west of Héroes on Obregón, next to Bancomer. To enter Belize for 30 days, all that is needed for U.S., Canadian, and European citizens (except those from Switzerland) is a valid passport and a bus ticket. Open Mon.-Fri. 9am-2pm and 5-8pm. **Guatemala,** Chapultepec 356 (tel. 2-30-45), at Cecilio Chi. For a 30-day free tourist visa, you'll need your passport plus photocopy, and you'll also have to prove you have sufficient funds for your trip. For stays longer than 30 days, you'll have to talk to the kind folk in Guatemala and show, dollar by dollar, how you plan to finance it. Open Mon.-Fri. 10am-5pm.

Currency Exchange: Banamex, Juárez 51 (tel. 2-11-22), at Obregón. Open Mon.-Fri. 9am-2pm. 24-hr. **ATM.** Across the way, **Bancomer** (tel. 2-53-00) has better rates and smaller lines. **ATM.** Open Mon.-Fri. 9am-1:30pm. Erotic hours.

Telephones: Public phones abound and are the cheapest way to call.

Telegrams: (tel. 2-06-51), in the same building as the post office, through the door to the left. Open Mon.-Fri. 8am-6pm, Sat. 9am-1pm.

Airport: (tel. 2-04-65), 5km south of the city on Aguilar. **Aviacsa** (tel. 2-76-76). **Bonanza** (tel. 2-83-06). **Aerocaribe,** Héroes 125 (tel. 2-66-75). Open Mon.-Sat. 8am-1pm and 5-8pm.

Buses: (tel. 2-98-77), at Insurgentes and Belice. **ADO** (tel. 2-51-10) offers first-class service to Campeche (noon, 7hr., 90 pesos), Cancún (4 per day, 5hr., 77 pesos), Escárcega (6 per day, 44hr., 57 pesos), Jalapa (11:30am, 16hr., 254 pesos), Mexico City (4 per day, 22hr., 319 pesos), Palenque (8pm, 8½hr., 102 pesos), Playa del Carmen (4 per day, 4hr., 64 pesos), Veracruz (6:30pm, 15hr., 224 pesos), and Villahermosa (5 per day, 9hr., 119 pesos). **Línea Dorada** goes to Mérida (4 per day, 6hr., 85 pesos). **Cristóbal Colón** trucks to Ocosingo (10pm, 9hr., 125 pesos), San Cristóbal (10pm, 10hr., 147 pesos), and Tuxtla Gutiérrez (10pm, 12hr., 155 pesos). **Batty's Bus** goes south to Belize (11:45am and 3pm, 3hr., 42 pesos). **ATS** goes to Tulum (7 per day, 4hr., 44 pesos). **Lockers** 1 peso per hr.

Market: Corner of Aguilar and Héroes. Vendors peddle everything from a diddle-eyed joe to a damned-if-I-know (see p. 551). Open daily 6am-3pm. **Súper San Francisco de Asis,** next to the bus station.

Red Cross: (tel. 2-05-71), Chapultepec at Independencia, 2 blocks west of Héroes, in the back of Hospital Civil Morelos. Open 24hr.

Pharmacy: Farmacia Canto, Av. Héroes 99 (tel. 2-04-83), conveniently located at the northern end of the market. Open Mon.-Sat. 7am-11pm, Sun. 7am-5pm.

Hospital: Hospital General (tel. 2-19-99), at Quintana Roo and Juan José Sordio.

Police: (tel. 2-15-00), Insurgentes at Belice, next to the bus station. Open 24hr.

Post Office: Plutarco Elías Calles 2A (tel. 2-25-78), one block east of the Mercado. Open Mon.-Fri. 8am-7pm, Sat. 9am-1pm. **Postal Code:** 77000.

Telephone Code: 983.

ACCOMMODATIONS

Chetumal's budget accommodations aren't an extraordinary bunch, but they do score points with location. All are within easy walking distance of the *mercado.* A scenic **trailer park** in Calderitas, 9km northeast of Chetumal, offers electricity, water hookups, and clean bathrooms (vehicles 40 pesos; tent or hammock space 10 pesos per person; big bungalows with kitchen 70 pesos for 1-2 people).

CREA Youth Hostel (HI), (tel. 2-34-65), Heroica Escuela Naval at Calzada Veracruz, at the eastern terminus of Obregón. For once, a youth hostel within manageable walking distance. Clean, modern, single-sex rooms with 2 bunkbeds each. Bed with sheets, towel, and locker 30 pesos. Lawn for camping 6 pesos. 20 peso deposit. Breakfast 11 pesos, lunch and dinner 14 pesos. Front desk open daily 7am-11pm, but you can make arrangements to return later. Bathrooms open 24hr. Fills during July and August, so call to reserve.

Hotel Brasilia, Aguilar 186 (tel. 2-09-64), at Héroes, across from the market. Sparkling white tiles enclose spacious rooms and bathrooms. No one speaks English, but the shower knobs are bilingual: F stands for *fría*, C for cold. Friendly management will store packs. Singles 40 pesos. Doubles 55 pesos. Triples 65 pesos.

Hotel María Dolores, Obregón 206 (tel. 2-05-08), half a block west of Héroes. Look for the chirpy image of Donald Duck at the entrance. Small lime-colored rooms with dark wood decor. Shiny bathrooms. Singles 47 pesos. Doubles 53-60 pesos. Triples 72 pesos. U.S. dollars accepted.

Hotel Doris, Héroes 49, between Obregón and O. Blanco, 5½ blocks south of the market. Musty, uninspired rooms with cement beds offer a smashing view of the rubble garden. Brand new bathrooms are the best part of the deal. Singles 35 pesos. Doubles 40 pesos. 10 pesos per additional person. U.S. dollars are dandy.

FOOD

Aside from a dish or two flavored with coconut (it's the *belizeño* influence), Chetumal offers standard Mexican fare. For cheap eats, try the café/restaurants at the end of Héroes, on 22 de Enero near the bay, or the eateries on Obregón, west of Héroes.

Restaurante Pantoja, M. Gandhi 181 (tel. 2-39-57), past Hotel Ucum, just north of the market. An extremely popular family restaurant, and with good reason: the food is *muy rica* and piping hot. Enchiladas (13 pesos) are *sabrosa*. Gigantic lemonades 2 pesos. Open Mon.-Sat. 7am-9pm.

El Taquito, Plutarco Elías Calles 220, near Juárez, one block west of Héroes. Groove with the locals as you savor *antojito* after *antojito*. Tacos 3 pesos. *Queso fundido* 15 pesos. Open Mon.-Sat. 9am-midnight.

Arcadas Súper and Restaurante, Av. Héroes at Zaragoza (tel. 2-08-84). A neatly packaged open-air café, bar, and supermarket. Aztec soup 8.50 pesos. *Fajitas* and chicken or meat specialties run 26-30 pesos. Open 24hr.

SIGHTS AND SAND

People come to Chetumal to visit **El Mercado.** Period. Oh, it's a sight all right. If you think having your name written on a single grain of rice is a pretty neat idea, welcome to the think tank. If you've been looking for cheap plastics smeared with American iconography, Chetumal's got the goods. Everything from vibrators to packed cheese will make kitsch-fiends squeal with delight. Gaudy? Got it. Cheap? Check. Does a mercado get any more…mercadoish?

Nothing else in town is of much interest to travelers, except the new **Museo de la Cultura Maya,** at Héroes and Mahatma Gandhi, just north of the market. It features replicas of nearby ruins and documents the history of Chetumal (open Tues.-Sun. 9am-7pm; guides available for tours in English or Spanish, and a tip is appreciated; admission 7 pesos).

The nearest beach is the *balneario* at **Calderitas,** a 20-minute bus ride from Chetumal. Buses leave from Av. Colón, between Héroes and Belice (every 30min. 5am-10pm, 1.50 pesos). Although the water is turbid and the shores rocky, the beach looks like a *Where's Waldo* puzzle during summer and school holidays. Much nicer, both for atmosphere and for swimming, are the three watering-holes near the town of **Bacalar,** 38km away. The local bus to Bacalar leaves from Chetumal's bus station (every hr. 5:30am-10:30pm, 5 pesos); *combis* leave from the corner of Hidalgo and Primo de Verdad in front of the public library (every hr., 30min., 5 pesos). The route passes **Laguna Milagros** and **Cenote Azul** before reaching Bacalar. Quieter than the popular Bacalar, especially during the week, both have bathing areas, dressing rooms, and lakeside restaurants. The huge dining room by Cenote Azul, though expensive, is right on the water.

Past the uninteresting Fuerte de San Felipe in Bacalar lie the docks of the **Laguna de Siete Colores,** named for the hues reflected in its depths. The fresh water is warm, perfectly clear, devoid of plant or animal life, and carpeted by powdery limestone, making it excellent for swimming. Nearby are bathrooms, dressing rooms, fruit vendors, expensive dockside restaurants, and a campground.

Much farther afield from Chetumal, the small seaside town of **Xcalac** (200km, 3hr. from Chetumal), the southernmost center of population on the spit of land extending south from the Sian Ka'an reserve, provides super-mellow bungalows, restaurants, snorkeling, and boat rentals. Nearby off the coast lies the enticing **Banco Chinchorro,** the second-largest shipwreck site in the world, making for a funky deep-sea treasure-hunting dive. Buses to Xcalac and the closer, less service-laden **Mahahval** (150km from Chetumal) depart daily at 7am from Av. 16 de Septiembre at M. Gandhi, 20m from the Restaurante Pantoja (18-21 pesos).

Appendices

▪ Glossary

NOTES ABOUT LANGUAGE

Even if you speak no Spanish, a few basics will help you along. Any attempts at Spanish are appreciated and encouraged, and you'll find that many people in larger cites understand some English. You are likely to hear *indígena* languages as well as Spanish. Those who already know Iberic Spanish will find that many common nouns and expressions are different in Mexico.

Pronunciation is straightforward. Vowels are always pronounced the same way: a ("ah" in father); e ("eh" in escapade); i ("ee" in eat); o ("oh" in oat); u ("oo" in boot); y, by itself, is pronounced like i. Most consonants are the same as English. Important exceptions are: j, pronounced like the English "h" in "hello"; ll, pronounced like the English "y" in "yes"; ñ, which is pronounced like the "gn" in "cognac"; rr, the trilled "r"; h is always silent; x has a bewildering variety of pronunciations: sometimes it sounds like the "h" in "hello," sometimes likethe "cz" in "czar." Stress in Spanish words falls on the second to last syllable, except for words ending in "r," "l" and "z," in which it falls on the last syllable. All exceptions to these rules require a written accent on the stressed syllable.

THE BARE MINIMUM

Cheap	Barato
Child	Niño(a)
Church	Iglesia
Closed	Cerrado
Could you speak more slowly, please?	¿Podría hablar más despacio, por favor?
Could you tell me?	¿Podría decirme?
Do you speak English?	¿Habla inglés?
Excuse me	Con permiso
Expensive	Caro
Fat	Gordo(a)
Good morning/afternoon!	¡Buenos días!
Good evening/night!	¡Buenas noches!
Goodbye!	¡Adiós! or ¡Hasta luego!
Ground floor	Planta Baja (PB)
Hello	Hola or Bueno (phone)
How are you?	¿Cómo está?
How do you say...?	¿Cómo se dice...?
I'm fine, thanks	Estoy bien, gracias
I'm sorry	Lo siento
I don't know	No sé
I don't speak Spanish	No hablo español
I don't understand	No entiendo
I would like...	Quisiera...
In Spanish, how do you say...?	¿Cómo se dice... en español?
Man	Hombre
Mr. / Mrs. / Miss	Señor / Señora / Señorita
My name is...	Me llamo...
Neighborhood	Barrio
No	No
No smoking	No fumadores
Open	Abierto

Please	Por favor
Thank you very much!	¡Muchas gracias!
Thin	Flaco(a)
What?	¿Qué?
What did you say?	¿Qué dijo? or ¿Mande?
What is your name?	¿Como se llama?
What time is it?	¿Qué hora es?
When?	¿Cuándo?
When is it open?	¿A qué horas está abierto?
Where is the bathroom?	¿Dónde está el baño?
Woman	Mujer
Yes	Sí
You're welcome!	¡De nada!

CROSSING THE BORDER

Age	Edad
Backpack	Mochila
Baggage	Equipaje
Border	Frontera
Customs	Aduana
Immigration	Migración
Passport	Pasaporte
Suitcase	Maleta
Vaccination Certificate	Certificado de Vacunación

GETTING AROUND

Airplane	Avión
Airport	Aeropuerto
Arrivals & Departures	Llegadas y Salidas
Avenue	Avenida
Bus	Autobús or Camión
Bus depot	Estación de autobuses
Bus stop	Parada
Caution!	¡Atencion! or ¡Cuidado!
Daily	Diario
Danger!	¡Peligro!
Driver	Chofer
East	Este or Oriente (Ote.)
Every half hour	Cada media hora
First class	Primera clase
Freeway	Autopista/Carretera Libre
Highway	Autopista or Carretera
Hitchhike	Pedir aventón or Pedir ride
Map	Mapa
North	Norte
One-way	Ida
On foot	A pie
On the hour	Cada hora
Passenger	Pasajero
Reserved seat	Asiento reservado
Reservation	Reservación
Road	Camino
Round-trip	Ida y vuelta
Second class	Segunda clase
South	Sur
Stop!	¡Alto!

Street	Calle
Subway	Metro
Taxi depot	Sitio
Ticket	Boleto
Ticket window	Taquilla
To get aboard	Subir
To get off	Bajar
Toll	Cuota
Train	Ferrocarr or Tren
Train station	Estación de ferrocarril/de trenes
West	Oeste or Poniente (Pte.)
All the way to the end	Al fondo
How long does it take?	¿Cuánto tarda?
How much is a ticket to...?	¿Cuánto cuesta un boleto a....?
I want a ticket to...	Quiero un boleto a...
I want to get off at...	Me quiero bajar en...
What bus line goes to...?	¿Qué linea tiene servicio a...?
What bus number is it?	¿Cual es el número del autobús?
What time does the bus leave to...?	¿A qué hora sale el camión a...?
I lost my baggage.	Se me perdió mi equipaje.
Will you give me a ride to...?	¿Me da un aventón a...?
Where is ... Street?	¿Dónde está la calle...?
Where is the road to...?	¿Dónde está el camino a...?
How far is...	¿Qué tan lejos está...?
To the left/right	A la izquierda/derecha
Straight ahead	Siempre derecho

ACCOMMODATIONS

Air conditioner	Aire acondicionado
Bar	Bar
Bath or Bathroom	Baño
Bed/Double bed	Cama/Cama matrimonial
Blanket	Cobija
Boarding house	Casa de huéspedes
Cold/Hot water	Agua fría/caliente
Cot	Catre
Dining room	Comedor
Fan	Ventilador
Hotel	Hotel
Inn	Posada
Key	Llave
Manager	Gerente
Motel	Motel
Noise	Ruido
Pillow	Almohada
Room	Cuarto/Recámara
Sheets	Sábanas
Shower	Regadera
Sink	Lavabo
Swimming pool	Alberca or Piscina
Do you have a room for two people?	¿Tiene un cuarto para dos personas?
Do you have any rooms?	¿Tiene cuartos libres?
Do you have ice?	¿Hay hielo?
Please put in a cot.	Por favor ponga un catre
The toilet is clogged up.	El escusado/water está tapado

Do you know of a cheap hotel...?   ¿Sabe de algún hotel barato?

EATING

Apple	Manzana
Beer	Cerveza or Chela or Cheve
Bill	La cuenta
Bakery	Panadería
Bottle	Botella
Bread/Sweet Bread	Pan/Pan Dulce
Breakfast	Desayuno
Cocktail	Coctel
Coconut	Coco
Coffee	Café
Dessert	Postre
Dinner	Cena
Drink	Bebida
Eggs	Huevos
Fixed Menu	Comida corrida
Fish	Pescado
French Fries	Papas Fritas
Fork	Tenedor
Glass	Vaso
Hot Dog	Hot Dog
Ice Cream	Helado
Juice	Jugo
Knife	Cuchillo
Liquor	Licor
Lunch	Comida
Meal	Comida
Meat	Carne
Menu	Menú, carta
Milk	Leche
Napkin	Servilleta
Orange	Naranja
Papa	Potato
Pepper	Pimienta
Pineapple	Piña
Plate	Plato
Porc	Puerco
Purified water	Agua purificada
Restaurant	Restaurante
Rice	Arroz
Salt	Sal
Shellfish	Mariscos
Snack	Antojito or Botana
Soda	Refresco
Spoon	Cuchara
Steak	Bistec
Strawberry	Fresa
Supermarket	Supermercado
Tacos	Tacos
Tea	Té
Tonic	Agua mineral (con gas)
Vegetarian	Vegetariano
Wine	Vino

APPENDIX

I am hungry	Tengo hambre
Waiter/Waitress	Mesero(a)
Waiter!/Waitress!	¡Joven! /¡ Señorita!
Check, please	La cuenta, por favor
I am very drunk.	Estoy bien borracho(a)
Would you like a beer?	¿Quiere una cerveza?

BANK, POST OFFICE, TELEPHONE

Address	Dirección
Airmail	Correo aereo or Por avión
Bank	Banco
Bill	Billete
A call	Una llamada
To call	Llamar
To cash	Cambiar
Certified	Certificado
Change	Cambio
Check	Cheque
Collect	Por cobrar or Cobro revertido
Dollar	Dólar
Envelope	Sobre
Letter	Carta
Long distance	Larga distancia
Mailbox	Buzón
Money	Dinero
Money order	Giro
National currency	Moneda Nacional (M.N.)
Number	Número
Operator	Operador
Package	Paquete
Person to person	Persona a persona
Postcard	Postal or Tarjeta postal
Post office	Correo
Signature	Firma
Standard mail	Correo ordinario
Postcard	Tarjeta
Post office	Correo
Stamp	Estampilla
String	Cuerda
Telephone	Teléfono
Traveler's check	Cheque de viajero
Weight	Peso

Do you accept traveler's checks?	¿Acepta cheques de viajero?
I would like to make a call to the U.S....	Quiero llamar a los Estados Unidos...
The number is...	El número es...

MEDICAL AID AND HEALTH

Allergy	Alergia
Antibiotic	Antibiótico
Aspirin	Aspirina
Bandage	Venda
Birth control pills	Anticonceptivos or Pastillas anticonceptivas
Burn	Quemadura or quemada
Condom	Condón or Preservativo

Cotton	Algodón
Cough	Tos
Dentist	Dentista
Diarrhea	Diarrea
Doctor	Doctor
Drugstore	Farmacia
Fever	Fiebre
Flu	Gripe
Hospital	Hospital
Headache	Dolor de cabeza
Health	Salud
It itches	Me pica
Medicine	Medicina
Pain	Dolor
Pill	Pastilla
Prescription	Receta
Shot	Inyección
Sick	Enfermo/a
Stomach-ache	Dolor de estómago
Sunburn	Quemadura de sol
Toothache	Dolor de muelas
Toothbrush	Cepillo de dientes
Toothpaste	Pasta de dientes or Crema dental
Vitamin	Vitamina

I need aspirin, please.	Necesito aspirina, por favor.
Where is there a doctor?	¿Dónde hay un médico?
I am sick.	Estoy enfermo(a)
I have a stomachache/headache	Me duele el estómago/la cabeza
I have a cough/a cold	Tengo tos/gripe
Help!	¡Ayuda! or ¡Socorro!

CAR TALK

Car	Coche or Carro or Auto or Automóvil
To Drive	Manejar
Driver's license	Licencia de conducir/de manejar
Gasoline	Gasolina
Gas station	Gasolinera
Oil change	Cambio de aceite
Parking lot	Estacionamiento
Repair shop	Taller mecánico
Tire	Llanta
Traffic light	Semáforo

Fill it up please.	Lleno, por favor.
Check the oil, please.	Revise el aceite, por favor.
The tire has a leak.	La llanta está ponchada

SLANG

Asshole	Cabrón(a)
Beat it	Lárgate
Bribe	Mordida
Careful!	¡Aguas!
Drunk	Pedo(a), ebrio(a), cuete
Fool	Baboso(a)
Gringo	Gabacho

Guy/Girl	Chavo(a)
Joint	Churro, Chubi, Chemo
Make Out	Fajar
Marijuana	Mota, Hierba
Money	Lana
Neat	Padre
Oh, wow!	¡Híjole!
Pardon?	¿Mande?
Party	Reventón or Pachanga
Pick someone up, flirt	Ligar ("liga" means "rubber band")
Piss	Agua de riñón
Policeman	Tamarindo, Mordelón (not to their face!)
Right on	Órale
Stingy	Codo
Thief	Caco
To Arrest	Apañar
What's up!	¡Qué onda! or ¡Qué pasó!

ROMANCE

Can I buy you a drink?	¿Te puedo comprar un trago?
How old are you?	¿Cuántos años tienes?
Did you come here alone?	¿Viniste solo(a)?
Where's your boy/girlfriend?	¿Dónde está tu novio(a)?
Where's your husband/wife?	¿Dónde está tu marido/mujer?
What perfume do you wear?	¿Qué perfume usas?
My, what beautiful eyes you have	Que bonitos ojos tienes
I like you	Me gustas
You're *fiiine*	¡Que bueno(a) estás!
Can you do the Macarena?	¿Sabes bailar la Macarena?
Can you teach me?	¿Me enseñas?

CLOTHING

Jacket	Saco
Sweater	Suéter
Shirt	Camisa
Shoes	Zapatos
High heels	Tacones
Tennis shoes	Tenis
Socks	Calcetines
Stockings	Medias
Belt	Cinturón
Pants	Pantalones
Dress	Vestido
(Mini)skirt	(Mini)falda
Bra	Brasier
Garter belt	Liguero
Underwear	Calzones

ANATOMY

Hair	Pelo, Cabello
Face	Cara, Rostro
Head	Cabeza
Eyes	Ojos
Nose	Nariz
Mouth	Boca

Lips	Labios
Tongue	Lengua
Neck	Cuello
Shoulders	Hombros
Breasts	Pechos
Arm	Brazo
Elbow	Codo
Wrist	Muñeca
Hand	Mano
Finger	Dedo
Muscle	Músculo
Belly	Panza
Navel	Ombligo
Hips	Caderas
Ass	Nalgas, culo
Thigh	Muslo
Knee	Rodilla
Calf	Pantorrilla
Ankle	Talón
Foot	Pie
Toes	Dedos del pie
Cigarette	Cigarro

COLORS, DAYS, MONTHS, NUMBERS

black	negro
blue	azul
brown	café
green	verde
pink	rosa
purple	morado
orange	naranja
red	rojo
white	blanco
yellow	amarillo

Day after tomorrow	Pasado mañana
Day before yesterday	Antes de ayer or Antier
Today	Hoy
Tomorrow	Mañana
Yesterday	Ayer

Sunday	Domingo	Thursday	Jueves
Monday	Lunes	Friday	Viernes
Tuesday	Martes	Saturday	Sábado
Wednesday	Miércoles		

0	cero		
1	uno	6	seis
2	dos	7	siete
3	tres	8	ocho
4	cuatro	9	nueve
5	cinco	10	diez
11	once	16	dieciseis
12	doce	17	diecisiete
13	trece	18	dieciocho
14	catorce	19	diecinueve

15	quince	20	veinte
21	veintiuno	101	ciento uno
23	veintitrés	142	ciento cuarenta y dos
30	treinta	200	doscientos
38	treinta y ocho	300)	trescientos
40	cuarenta	400	cuatrocientos
50	cincuenta	500	quinientos
60	sesenta	600	seiscientos
67)	sesenta y siete	700	setecientos
70	setenta	800	ochocientos
80	ochenta	900	novecientos
90	noventa	1000	mil
100	cien	1 million	un millón

■ Weights and Measures

Mexico, like most of the rational world, uses the metric system:

1 ounce = 28.35 grams (g)
1 pound = 0.454 kilograms (kg)
1 inch = 2.54 centimeters (cm)
1 foot = 0.305 meters (m)
1 mile = 1.61 kilometers (km)
1 U.S. gallon = 3.79 liters (L)
°F = 9/5(°C+32)

1 gram (g) = 0.04 ounces
1 kilogram (kg) = 2.21 pounds
1 centimeter (cm) = 0.4 inches
1 meter (m) = 3.29 feet
1 kilometer (km) = 0.612 miles
1 liter (L) = 0.264 U.S. gallons
°C = 5/9(°F-32)

■ Temperature

To convert from °C to °F, multiply by 1.8 and add 32.
To convert from °F to °C, substract 32 and multiply by 0.55.

°C	35	30	25	20	15	10	5	0	-5	-10
°F	95	86	75	68	59	50	41	32	23	14

Temp in °F Rain in	January Temp	Rain	May Temp	Rain	July Temp	Rain	November Temp	Rain
Acapulco	88/72	0.5	90/77	0.0	91/77	8.0	90/75	0.6
Guadalajara	73/45	0.5	88/57	1.0	79/59	7.0	77/50	0.5
La Paz	73/55	0.3	91/63	0.0	97/73	1.0	84/63	0.5
Mérida	82/64	1.0	93/70	3.0	91/73	5.0	84/66	1.0
Mexico City	72/43	0.5	81/55	3.0	75/55	6.0	73/48	0.5
Monterrey	68/48	1.0	88/68	2.0	93/72	3.0	73/54	1.0
Oaxaca	82/46	2.0	90/59	5.0	82/59	8.0	82/50	2.0
San Cristóbal	68/41	2.0	72/48	7.0	72/50	7.0	68/45	3.0
Tijuana	68/43	2.0	73/54	0.2	81/61	0.0	73/50	1.0
Veracruz	77/64	1.0	86/77	4.0	88/75	9.0	82/70	2.0

■ Time Difference

Most of Mexico is six hours behind Greenwich Mean Time, as is U.S. Central Standard Time and Central America. It's always one hour earlier in Baja California Sur, Sinaloa, Sonora, and parts of Nayarit, which are on Mountain Standard Time. And you're yet another hour younger in Baja California Norte, which is always on Pacific Standard Time, like California.

■ Holidays and Fiestas

Granted, every day is a party in Mexico. But some days are better than others.

JANUARY

The 1st is **New Year's Day,** everywhere you go. Have you made your resolutions yet? The 6th is **Three King's Day,** when children awake to find "the Magi" left gifts in their shoes. The 6th is also the day of the **Festival of St. Anthony** in Mexico City and others towns.

FEBRUARY

The 2nd is the **Día de la Candelaria,** and the **Constitution** is commemorated on the 5th. But the real party takes place during the week of the 23rd-27th, when **Pre-Lenten Carnivals** take seaside towns by storm. Veracruz and Mazatlán hold the most famous *carnavales.*

MARCH

Mexico's favorite president ever, **Benito Juárez,** is remembered on the 21st, the day of his birth. The same day, the more pagan **Spring Equinox Festival** starts when the sun draws the shadow of a serpent on the main pyramid of Kukulkán and culminates with light and sound shows, dancers, and music.

APRIL

Semana Santa (Holy Week) makes this one of the more interesting and challenging months to visit Mexico. Celebrations include *ferias,* processions, and re-enactments of Jesus' martyrdom in which lucky young men get to wear crowns of thorns and carry a heavy wooden cross.

MAY

On the 1st, workers celebrate **Labor Day** with parades and speeches. The 5th commemorates the **Battle of Puebla,** when Mexican troops postponed the advances of the invading French army in 1862. For the entire first week of May, the **San Marcos National Fair** brings rodeos, *mariachis,* bullfights, and ranchero music to Aguascalientes. The **Cancún International Jazz Festival** (date varies) brings a touch of class to this party-central of Mexican Beaches, while the **Acapulco Music Festival** (date varies) gathers the best of Mexican pop singers, starlets, and soap-opera actors.

JUNE

On the 10th, the **Feast of Corpus Christi** takes place in Mexico City. *Artesanías* lovers should not miss the **Tlaquepaque Festival,** the 29th in Guadalajara.

JULY

On the third and last Mondays of the month, the **Guelaguetza Festival** in Oaxaca brings together musicians and dancers from every one of the state's regions and ethnic groups.

AUGUST

The **Feast of the Assumption of the Blessed Virgin Mary** rocks Huamantla, Tlaxcala on the 15th. On that day, streets are carpeted with flower petals and colored sawdust. If you're in Mexico City, don't miss the **International Festival,** a performing arts extravaganza featuring first-rate dancing, theater, and music (lasts one-two weeks, dates vary).

SEPTEMBER

On the 15th and 16th, all hell breaks loose for **Independence Day** celebrations. The *fiesta* is particularly crazy in the central *zocalo* in Mexico City. On the 21st, the **Fall Equinox Festival** brings light and sound shows, dancers, and music to Chichén Itzá.

OCTOBER

On the 12th, Columbus's arrival in America is commemorated with the **Día de la Raza** (Race Day). The last two weeks of the month are time for Guanajuato's **Festival Cervantino,** in which human libido runs rampant while the city celebrates the Spanish author with truly quixotic energy. Many of the arts performances are free and open air. The entire month is party-time in Guadalajara. The **Fiestas de Octubre** fill the city with dances, *charreadas* (Mexican rodeos), food, and arts and crafts exhibitions.

NOVEMBER

During **All Saint's Day** and **Day of the Dead,** on the 1st and 2nd of the month, cemeteries are filled with families commemorating dead relatives. Offerings consisting of candles, *copal* (Mexican incense), the dead person's favorite food, and bright orange *zempazúchitl* flowers. Death is not mourned but mocked in a surreal celebration of life: children eat chocolate or sugar skulls with their names written on them and people dressed up as skeletons parade the streets. On a more patriotic note, the **Revolution** (1910-21) is celebrated on the 20th.

DECEMBER

The **Feast of the Virgin of Guadalupe,** held in honor of the country's patron virgin, is celebrated nationally. The most spectacular displays of devotion take place in Mexico City, where pilgrims crawl on their bare knees all the way to the *Basílica de Guadalupe*. During the last two weeks of the month, traditional *posadas* remember the birth of Jesus with songs, *piñatas,* sugar-coated nuts and *ponche,* a delicious fruit-and-rum hot punch. Parties are held every night until Christmas.

APPENDIX

Index

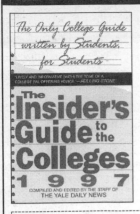

★ Let's Go 1997 Reader Questionnaire ★

Please fill this out and return it to **Let's Go, St. Martin's Press,** 175 5th Ave. NY, NY 10010

Name: _____ **What book did you use?** _____

Address: _____

City: _____ **State:** _____ **Zip Code:** _____

How old are you? under 19   19-24   25-34   35-44   45-54   55 or over

Are you (circle one)   in high school   in college   in grad school
    employed   retired   between jobs

Have you used Let's Go before?   yes   no

Would you use Let's Go again?   yes   no

How did you first hear about Let's Go?   friend   store clerk   CNN
    bookstore display   advertisement/promotion   review   other

Why did you choose Let's Go (circle up to two)?   annual updating
    reputation   budget focus   price   writing style
    other: _____

Which other guides have you used, if any?   Frommer's $-a-day   Fodor's
    Rough Guides   Lonely Planet   Berkeley   Rick Steves
    other: _____

Is Let's Go the best guidebook?   yes   no

If not, which do you prefer? _____

**Which part of Let's Go do you feel needs most to be improved, if any
(circle up to two)?**   packaging/cover   practical information
    accommodations   food   cultural introduction   sights
    practical introduction ("Essentials")   directions   entertainment
    gay/lesbian information   maps   other: _____

How would you like to see these things improved?
_____
_____

How long was your trip?   one week   two weeks   three weeks
    one month   two months or more

Have you traveled extensively before?   yes   no

Do you buy a separate map when you visit a foreign city?   yes   no

Have you seen the Let's Go Map Guides?   yes   no

Have you used a Let's Go Map Guide?   yes   no

If you have, would you recommend them to others?   yes   no

Did you use the internet to plan your trip?   yes   no

Would you buy a Let's Go   phrasebook   adventure/trekking guide
    gay/lesbian guide

**Which of the following destinations do you hope to visit in the next three
to five years (circle one)?**   Australia   China   South America   Russia
    other: _____

Where did you buy your guidebook?   internet   chain bookstore
    independent bookstore   college bookstore   travel store
    other: _____

Mexico City Metro

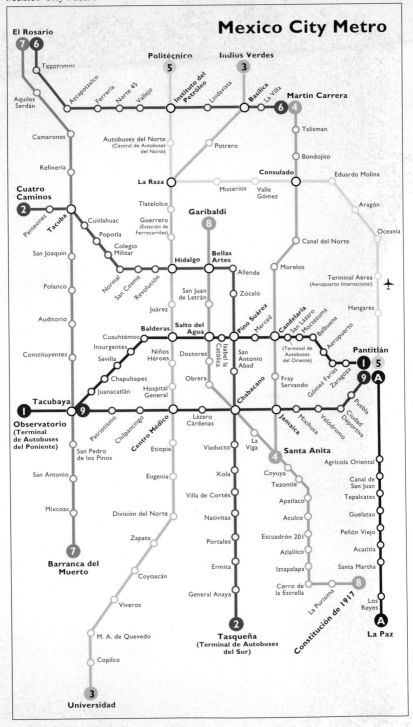

Mexico City Metro

El Rosario 7 6
Tezozomoc
Aquiles Serdán
Azcapotzalco
Ferrería
Norte 45
Vallejo
Instituto del Petróleo
Lindavista
Basílica
La Villa

Politécnico 5
Indios Verdes 3
Martín Carrera 6 4
Talisman
Bondojito
Camarones
Refinería
Autobuses del Norte (Central de Autobuses del Norte)
Potrero
Consulado
Eduardo Molina

Cuatro Caminos 2
Panteones Tacuba
Cuitláhuac
Popotla
Colegio Militar
La Raza
Misterios
Valle Gómez
Aragón
Oceanía

San Joaquín
Tlatelolco
Guerrero (Estación de Ferrocarriles)
Garibaldi 8
Canal del Norte
Polanco
Normal
San Cosme
Revolución
Hidalgo
Bellas Artes
Allende
Morelos
Terminal Aérea (Aeropuerto Internacional)

Auditorio
San Juan de Letrán
Zócalo
Hangares

Constituyentes
Juárez
Balderas
Salto del Agua
Pino Suárez
Merced
Candelaria
San Lázaro
Moctezuma
Balbuena
Aeropuerto
Pantitlán 1 5

Cuauhtémoc
Insurgentes
Sevilla
Niños Héroes
Doctores
Isabel la Católica
San Antonio Abad
(Terminal de Autobuses del Oriente)
Gómez Farías
Zaragoza
9 A

Tacubaya 1 9
Chapultepec
Juanacatlán
Hospital General
Obrera
Chabacano
Fray Servando
Puebla
Ciudad Deportiva

Observatorio (Terminal de Autobuses del Poniente)
Patriotismo
Chilpancingo
Centro Médico
Lázaro Cárdenas
Jamaica
Mixihuca
Velódromo

San Pedro de los Pinos
Etiopía
Viaducto
La Viga
Santa Anita
Agrícola Oriental

San Antonio
Eugenia
Xola
Coyuya
Tezontle
4
Canal de San Juan
Tepalcates

Mixcoac
División del Norte
Villa de Cortés
Apatlaco
Guelatao

Zapata
Nativitas
Aculco
Peñón Viejo

Barranca del Muerto 7
Portales
Escuadrón 201
Acatitla

Coyoacán
Ermita
Atlalilco
Santa Martha

Viveros
General Anaya
Iztapalapa
8
Constitución de 1917

M. A. de Quevedo
Tasqueña (Terminal de Autobuses del Sur) 2
Cerro de la Estrella
La Purísima
Los Reyes

Copilco
A **La Paz**

Universidad 3

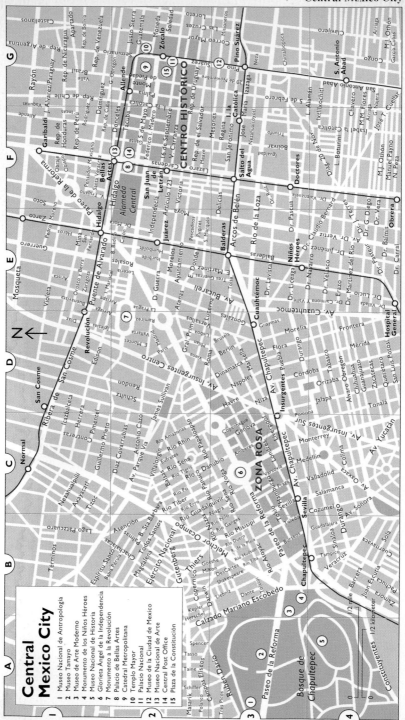

Central Mexico City

1. Museo Nacional de Antropología
2. Museo Tamayo
3. Museo de Arte Moderno
4. Monumento de los Niños Héroes
5. Museo Nacional de Historia
6. Glorieta Ángel de la Independencia
7. Monumento a la Revolución
8. Palacio de Bellas Artes
9. Catedral Metropolitana
10. Templo Mayor
11. Palacio Nacional
12. Museo de la Ciudad de Mexico
13. Museo Nacional de Arte
14. Central Post Office
15. Plaza de la Constitución